CM0074I888

Blackwell Companions to Literature and Culture

This series offers comprehensive, newly written surveys of key periods and movements and certain major authors, in English literary culture and history. Extensive volumes provide new perspectives and positions on contexts and on canonical and post-canonical texts, orientating the beginning student in new fields of study and providing the experienced undergraduate and new graduate with current and new directions, as pioneered and developed by leading scholars in the field.

A COMPANION TO

MEDIEVAL POETRY

EDITED BY **CORINNE SAUNDERS**

A John Wiley & Sons, Ltd., Publication

This edition first published 2010
© 2010 Blackwell Publishing Ltd except for editorial material and organization © 2010 Corinne Saunders

Blackwell Publishing was acquired by John Wiley & Sons in February 2007. Blackwell's publishing programme has been merged with Wiley's global Scientific, Technical, and Medical business to form Wiley-Blackwell.

Registered Office
John Wiley & Sons Ltd, The Atrium, Southern Gate, Chichester, West Sussex, PO19 8SQ, United Kingdom

Editorial Offices
350 Main Street, Malden, MA 02148-5020, USA
9600 Garsington Road, Oxford, OX4 2DQ, UK
The Atrium, Southern Gate, Chichester, West Sussex, PO19 8SQ, UK

For details of our global editorial offices, for customer services, and for information about how to apply for permission to reuse the copyright material in this book please see our website at www.wiley.com/wiley-blackwell.

The right of Corinne Saunders to be identified as the author of the editorial material in this work has been asserted in accordance with the UK Copyright, Designs and Patents Act 1988.

All rights reserved. No part of this publication may be reproduced, stored in a retrieval system, or transmitted, in any form or by any means, electronic, mechanical, photocopying, recording or otherwise, except as permitted by the UK Copyright, Designs and Patents Act 1988, without the prior permission of the publisher.

Wiley also publishes its books in a variety of electronic formats. Some content that appears in print may not be available in electronic books.

Designations used by companies to distinguish their products are often claimed as trademarks. All brand names and product names used in this book are trade names, service marks, trademarks or registered trademarks of their respective owners. The publisher is not associated with any product or vendor mentioned in this book. This publication is designed to provide accurate and authoritative information in regard to the subject matter covered. It is sold on the understanding that the publisher is not engaged in rendering professional services. If professional advice or other expert assistance is required, the services of a competent professional should be sought.

Library of Congress Cataloging-in-Publication Data

A companion to medieval poetry / edited by Corinne Saunders.
      p. cm. – (Blackwell companions to literature and culture)
   Includes bibliographical references and index.
      ISBN 978-1-4051-5963-0 (hardcover : alk. paper)   1. English poetry–Middle English,
1100-1500–History and criticism.   2. Civilization, Medieval, in literature.   I.   Saunders,
Corinne J., 1963–
   PR313.C65 2010
   821′.109–dc22

                                                                                    2009047991

A catalogue record for this book is available from the British Library.

Set in 11/13pt Garamond 3 by Graphicraft Limited, Hong Kong
Printed and bound in Singapore by Fabulous Printers Pte Ltd

1   2010

In Memory of Derek Brewer

Contents

List of Figures

Notes on Contributors

Daniel Anlezark is Senior Lecturer in English at the University of Sydney, where he teaches Old English. He has taught at Trinity College Dublin and Durham University. He has recently edited the Old English dialogues of Solomon and Saturn.

Elizabeth Archibald is Professor of Medieval Literature at the University of Bristol. Her publications include *Apollonius of Tyre: Medieval and Renaissance Themes and Variations* (1991), *A Companion to Malory*, co-edited with A. S. G. Edwards (1996), *Incest and the Medieval Imagination* (2001) and *The Cambridge Companion to the Arthurian Legend*, co-edited with Ad Putter (2009).

David Ashurst is Lecturer in the Department of English Studies at Durham University. He is author of *The Ethics of Empire in the Saga of Alexander the Great* (2009) and co-editor of *The Fantastic in Old Norse/Icelandic Literature* (2006). He is currently preparing a translation of *Alexanders saga* and researching aspects of the nineteenth-century reception of Germanic myth and legend.

Alcuin Blamires is Professor of English at Goldsmiths, University of London. His books have covered medieval debate about gender, illuminated *Roman de la Rose* manuscripts, and most recently *Chaucer, Ethics, and Gender*. He is currently preparing a study of 'shame' in Middle English literature.

Julia Boffey is Professor of Medieval Studies at Queen Mary, University of London. Her research concentrates on late medieval and early sixteenth-century English verse and prose (especially lyrics), with particular interests in textual transmission and reception.

Nancy Mason Bradbury teaches medieval literature in the English department at Smith College in Northampton, Massachusetts. Her work on medieval English romance includes a book, *Writing Aloud* (1998), and a variety of articles. Recent projects include a print symposium on source study in *Studies in the Age of Chaucer* (with

Arlyn Diamond, 2006), an article in *Speculum* on the Medieval Latin *Dialogue of Solomon and Marcolf* (2008) and a guest-edited issue of *Chaucer Review*, 'Time, Measure, Value' (with Carolyn P. Collette, 2009).

Neil Cartlidge is Reader in the Department of English Studies at the University of Durham. He is the author of *Medieval Marriage: Literary Approaches 1100–1300* (1997) and of a critical edition of *The Owl and the Nightingale* (2001). His most recent book is a collection of essays, *Boundaries in Medieval Romance* (2008).

Richard Dance is a Senior Lecturer in the Department of Anglo-Saxon, Norse and Celtic in the University of Cambridge, and a Fellow of St Catharine's College. He is the author of a number of studies of Old and early Middle English language and literature.

Tony Davenport is Emeritus Professor of Medieval Literature in the University of London and Fellow of the English Association. His latest book is *Medieval Narrative: An Introduction* (2004). He has published essays recently on *Pearl*, Middle English romances and the medieval English Tristan.

A. S. G. Edwards is Professor of Textual Studies at De Montfort University, Leicester. Most recently he has edited John Lydgate's *Lives of Saints Edmund and Fremund* (Middle English Texts, 2009, with Anthony Bale) and *Tudor Manuscripts* (British Library, 2009).

Rosalind Field has recently retired as Reader in English at Royal Holloway, University of London. Her publications include 'Romance in England, 1066–1400' in *The Cambridge History of Medieval English Literature*, ed. David Wallace (1999) and 'Romance' in *The Oxford History of Literary Translation in English, Vol. 1*, ed. Roger Ellis (2008). She co-edited *Guy of Warwick: Icon and Ancestor* (2007) and *Christianity and Romance in Medieval England* (2010).

David Fuller is Emeritus Professor of English and former Chairman of the Department of English Studies in the University of Durham, of which he was also Public Orator. He is the author of books on Blake and Joyce, and essays on a range of poetry, drama and novels from Chaucer to T. S. Eliot. He has edited works by Marlowe and Blake, and co-edited (with Patricia Waugh) a collection of essays on critical practice and (with Corinne Saunders) a modernised version of the medieval poem *Pearl*. He trained as a musicologist, and plays the piano and organ. His current research is on Marlowe and Shakespeare in modern performance.

Douglas Gray is the J. R. R. Tolkien Professor of English Emeritus, Oxford, and an Honorary Fellow of Lady Margaret Hall, Oxford. He has written a number of books and articles on medieval English and Scottish literature.

C. Annette Grisé is Associate Professor in the Department of English and Cultural Studies at McMaster University. She studies late-medieval English women's writings, as well as fifteenth-century manuscripts and books written for women. She has special interests in continental holy women and Syon Abbey, and is co-editing a collection on devotional reading.

Ralph Hanna is Professor of Palaeography in the English Faculty, University of Oxford. His most recent protracted studies include *London Literature 1300–1380* (2005) and *Speculum Vitae: A Reading Edition*, EETS 331–32 (2008).

Simon Horobin is a Reader in the Faculty of English and a Fellow of Magdalen College, University of Oxford. He is the author of *An Introduction to Middle English* (2002), *The Language of the Chaucer Tradition* (2003) and *Chaucer's Language* (2006).

Rohini Jayatilaka is based at the Faculty of English Language and Literature, University of Oxford. Her research interests are in Anglo-Saxon history, literature, palaeography and manuscript studies. She is presently Senior Research Fellow investigating the early medieval commentary on Boethius's *Consolation of Philosophy* for the Boethius in Early Medieval Europe Project, funded by the Leverhulme Trust.

Pamela King is Professor of Medieval Studies at University of Bristol. She has published widely on medieval theatre and drama, as well as on late-medieval English literature, funeral art and manuscript studies, and she has a special interest in European civic pageantry.

Hugh Magennis is Professor of Old English Literature at Queen's University Belfast and Director of the University's Institute of Theology. He has published widely on Old English and related literature, with particular reference to hagiography and to the language and imagery of Old English poetry. Recent publications include a critical edition of the Old English *Life of St Mary of Egypt* (2002) and, with Mary Swan, the edited collection *A Companion to Ælfric* (2009). A monograph on translations of *Beowulf* is forthcoming.

Conor McCarthy works in External Relations for the University of Technology, Sydney. His publications include *Seamus Heaney and Medieval Poetry* (2008), *Marriage in Medieval England: Law, Literature and Practice* (2004) and *Love, Sex and Marriage in the Middle Ages: A Sourcebook* (2004).

Andy Orchard is Professor of English and Medieval Studies in the University of Toronto, and Provost and Vice-Chancellor of Trinity College. He has published widely on Anglo-Saxon, Norse and Celtic languages and literatures, as well as on Medieval Latin. He is currently completing a set of translations of the Old Norse Poetic Edda for Penguin Classics, as well as two volumes on *The Anglo-Saxon Riddle Tradition* and *The Poetic Craft of Cynewulf*.

Lucy Perry teaches Old and Middle English Language and Literature at the Universities of Lausanne and Geneva. She has published on Laȝamon's *Brut* and early *Brut* Chronicles as well as Arthurian literature.

Helen Phillips is Professor of English Literature, Cardiff University. Her publications are mostly in the areas of Chaucer, Robin Hood and medievalism Her most recent book is an edited volume of essays on British outlaw traditions, *Bandit Territories* (2008).

Corinne Saunders is Professor in the Department of English Studies at the University of Durham. She specialises in medieval literature and the history of ideas, with a particular emphasis on medicine, gender and the body. She is the author of *The Forest of Medieval Romance* (1993), *Rape and Ravishment in the Literature of Medieval England* (2001) and *Magic and the Supernatural in Medieval English Romance* (2010). She has edited a Blackwell Critical Guide to *Chaucer* (2001), *A Companion to Romance: From Classical to Contemporary* (2004), *Writing War: Medieval Literary Responses* (with Françoise le Saux and Neil Thomas, 2004), *Cultural Encounters in the Romance of Medieval England* (2005), *Madness and Creativity in Literature and Culture* (with Jane Macnaughton, 2005), *Pearl* (with David Fuller, 2005), *A Concise Companion to Chaucer* (2006) and *The Body and the Arts* (with Ulrika Maude and Jane Macnaughton, 2009). She is currently Director of Durham's Centre for Medieval and Renaissance Studies, and is Associate Director of the Centre for Medical Humanities. She is also the English editor of the journal *Medium Ævum*.

John Scattergood is Professor of Medieval and Renaissance English (Emeritus) at Trinity College Dublin and Pro-Chancellor of the university. Among his many books are editions of *The Works of Sir John Clanvowe* (1976) and *John Skelton: The Complete English Poems* (1983), and *The Lost Tradition: Essays on Middle English Alliterative Poetry* (2000). His latest book is *Manuscripts and Ghosts: Essays on the Transmission of Medieval and Early Renaissance Texts* (2006). Another collection of essays, *Occasions for Writing: Essays on Medieval and Renaissance Literature, Politics and Society*, will appear in the autumn of 2009. He is a member of the Royal Irish Academy.

A. V. C. Schmidt is Andrew Bradley-James Maxwell Fellow and Senior English Tutor at Balliol College, Oxford. He has written many books and articles on medieval literature and was a co-editor of *Medium Aevum* 1981–90. He recently completed a two-volume Parallel-Text Edition of *Piers Plowman* (2009) and is currently working on Langland's sacramentality.

Daniel Wakelin is Lecturer in English Literature at the University of Cambridge and a Fellow of Christ's College. He has published *Humanism, Reading and English Literature, 1430–1530* (2007) and is currently researching scribal corrections in Middle English and editing William Worcester's *The Boke of Noblesse*.

Lawrence Warner is Senior Lecturer of Middle English at the University of Sydney. He has published extensively on *Piers Plowman*, including essays in *The Yearbook of Langland Studies* (of which he is also co-editor), *Viator*, *The Journal of the Early Book Society* and *Medium Aevum*, and a forthcoming book. He has also published on Chaucer, Dante, Geoffrey of Monmouth, Shakespeare and Obadiah the Proselyte.

Barry Windeatt is Professor of English in the University of Cambridge, and Fellow and Keeper of Rare Books at Emmanuel College. His research focuses on the imaginative literature, visual culture and contemplative traditions of medieval England in a European context. As part of a current project on text and image in later medieval England he has created the 'Medieval Imaginations' website of images of medieval English visual culture (http://www.english.cam.ac.uk/medieval/) and is also completing a study of the fifteenth-century English poetic.

Matthew Woodcock is Senior Lecturer in Medieval and Renaissance Literature at the University of East Anglia. His publications include *Fairy in the Faerie Queene: Renaissance Elf-Fashioning and Elizabethan Myth-making* (2004) and *Henry V: A Reader's Guide to Essential Criticism* (2008), an essay collection on Fulke Greville (published as *The Sidney Journal* (2001)), and essays on Spenser, Milton, medieval hagiography and entertainments for Elizabeth I. He is currently writing a book on the life and works of sixteenth-century writer and soldier Thomas Churchyard.

R. F. Yeager is Professor of English and Foreign Languages and chair of the department at the University of West Florida. He is President of the International John Gower Society, editor of *JGN: The John Gower Newsletter*, and has published widely on medieval English and European literatures. His special interests are Old English literature and language, the French of England, and the poetry of Chaucer and Gower. He has written and edited more than a dozen books and collections of essays, including *John Gower's Poetic: The Search for a New Arion* (1990), *A Concordance to the French Poetry and Prose of John Gower* (1997), *Who Murdered Chaucer? A Medieval Mystery*, with Terry Jones, Terry Dolan, Alan Fletcher and Juliette Dor (2005), and has edited and translated *John Gower: The Minor Latin Works* (2006) and a companion volume, *John Gower: The French Balades* (forthcoming, spring 2010), and, with Brian W. Gastle, *Approaches to Teaching John Gower's Poetry* (forthcoming 2011), for the Modern Language Association.

Acknowledgements

A volume of this scope and size inevitably owes much to many, and my debts over the several years in which the book has been in the making are numerous. My greatest thanks must go to the authors of these essays for their excellent and original contributions, from which I have learned much, and for their unstinting interest, care, patience and good humour. I am especially grateful to Daniel Anlezark, who more than lived up to the heroic ideals that were his subject by agreeing to write a second essay in a short space of time, and similarly to Andy Orchard. I owe particular debts to all who have generously offered advice on difficult questions of scholarship and reception, especially Tony Edwards and Carl Schmidt. Ian Doyle, Richard Gameson and Julia Boffey offered valuable advice on illustrations. Elizabeth Evershed spent many hours painstakingly formatting the essays to a standard higher than any to which I could aspire. As ever I owe a very great deal to Helen Cooper, friend and mentor over many years, who both advised on matters Chaucerian and generously read my essay with a sharp eye.

I am grateful to my colleagues in the Department of English Studies at the University of Durham for their continued support, especially David Ashurst and Neil Cartlidge, who found the time to contribute to this book, to my successive Heads of Department, Professor Patricia Waugh and Professor Stephen Regan, who warmly encouraged the project, to members of the Centre for Medieval and Renaissance Studies, who have so consistently supported a busy Director, and to my colleagues in the Medical Humanities. I should also like to thank especially Emma Bennett of Blackwell, who persuaded me to edit another Companion, for her unfailing interest and attentiveness, and her patience. The staff of Blackwell, in particular Caroline Clamp and Kathy Auger, have offered much valued assistance and support, as has my copy-editor Neil Dowden.

I am, as always, deeply grateful to my parents and friends for their support and interest, and particularly to David Fuller, who continues to be the most generous and engaged, but also the most acute, of readers, and who has given me much advice and encouragement. This book, and especially its Epilogue, owes much to his wide-ranging and subtle knowledge of poetry. It is a particular sadness that Derek Brewer, whose work was so influential in shaping medieval studies and who was originally to have written the essay on *The Canterbury Tales*, was unable to contribute to or see the volume in which, characteristically, he expressed much interest. This volume is dedicated to his memory, as scholar, mentor and friend.

Corinne Saunders

Introduction

Corinne Saunders

To survey English poetry from its inception in the Anglo-Saxon period through to the fifteenth century is a large aim, and perhaps a surprising one. It is all too common for English 'medieval' writing to be divided firmly into Old English and Middle English, pre- and post-Conquest writing. There are, as this volume shows, many good reasons for such a division: cultural, linguistic and literary. Yet there are also continuities of more and less certain kinds, and a particular aim of this book is to draw attention to such continuities. One of these is the power, flexibility and enduring quality of poetry itself. As the primary literary form in both the Anglo-Saxon and the later medieval period, poetry is a rich and important subject, and one that needs introduction in a world where poetry is too little read. Medieval poetry spanned an enormous range of literary genres from lyric to drama, and whereas we have come to see the novel as the dominant narrative form, in the medieval period narrative too took the form of poetry.

To privilege poetry may seem to be to swim against the tide. The recent drift of medieval studies has been towards the placing of medieval literature within its cultural and literary contexts. Rather than being dominated by Chaucer, Gower and Langland, the 'new map' of medieval literature, as Peter Brown terms it (2007: 3), looks quite different. It emphasises the religious and political attitudes of the period, and their crucial roles in shaping the production and circulation of texts; it stresses too the material culture of manuscripts, book production and dissemination. The literary names of the period are justly celebrated but also seen as 'embedded within a much wider framework of literary and cultural activities than formerly' (Brown 2007: 2). The contextual chapters in this book signal this crucial shift in perspective, and individual contributors draw in differing ways on such contexts. But the aim of the volume is also to return to the stuff of poetry, in order to explore the development and diversity of the medieval poetic tradition. It is intended to fulfil a complementary rather than competitive role in relation to the many excellent *Companion*-style volumes to medieval literature already in print.

The book employs a broadly chronological structure to present the entire range of medieval English poetry from its origins, through its flowering within the great genres of romance, narrative and alliterative poetry and the transformations effected by its great practitioners, to the fifteenth century. Its three parts echo the most common divisions of the medieval period: Old English Poetry, Middle English Poetry, Post-Chaucerian and Fifteenth-Century Poetry. Each section commences with essays on society and culture, language and poetry, and manuscripts and readers; further essays focus on genre and mode, and on individual poets and poems. While the inclusion of three essays on Chaucer reflects his enormous and enduring influence, the rest of the volume provides a much broader medieval context for this. English poetry is placed in terms of Germanic, Continental and Christian traditions, of the social and intellectual developments of the twelfth century onwards, in particular the growth of chivalric and courtly conventions, and of cultural and literary exchange. Emphasis is also placed on the originality of medieval English poetry, and the gradual shaping of unique literary genres. The volume focuses on poetic creativity and tradition, and the fusion of convention and originality, as well as on opening out the medieval thought world more generally. The recurrence and development of topics such as heroism, rule, learning, chivalry, love, gender, faith and, perhaps most of all, poetry across the course of the book is itself an argument for the volume. At the same time, essays (all newly commissioned) draw on current scholarship and debate to demonstrate a variety of approaches to medieval poetry, a subject that can by no means be treated monolithically. Divisions are not intended to be absolute: one emphasis of the volume is the continuity of genres such as lyric, romance, elegy and alliterative poetry. There is also some arbitrariness to chronological and generic categories. For instance, Scots poetry is placed within the final part of the book to reflect the dates of the most celebrated Scots writers, though poetic tradition in Scotland began considerably earlier than the fifteenth century. Drama, despite its ancient origins, is also treated in the third section, since all the surviving evidence is late.

It is not possible to give a date to the earliest English poetry, for the origins of this are lost in the oral tradition of Anglo-Saxon England. In his opening essay, Andy Orchard explores the shifting, multi-cultural quality of Anglo-Saxon England, and the extraordinary adaptability and receptiveness of the Anglo-Saxons to other cultures. Richard Dance continues this discussion in his consideration of the ways that the Old English language developed, and the affiliation between its creative flexibility and the alliterative verse tradition. Rohini Jayatilaka, however, demonstrates how uncertain our knowledge of Old English poetry is: her essay emphasises the marginal nature of the earliest written poetry, the complexity of reconstructing a vernacular tradition that was primarily oral and our inevitably partial knowledge of a poetic tradition when so few examples survive. As Andy Orchard points out in his second essay, Anglo-Saxon poets were deeply influenced by an already highly developed Latin tradition, and while they adopt the forms of Germanic poetry, they also take from Latin writing recurrent patterns and tropes. Orchard emphasises the mixture of conservatism and innovation characteristic of Anglo-Saxon poetry, and the challenge for modern readers of responding to that now unfamiliar balance. As is also the case with Middle English, to some extent the notion of 'Old English poetry' is a modern construct. Yet, as the various essays on heroic and religious poetry in this volume show, there already existed in the Anglo-Saxon period genres and modes which audiences would have recognised. Hugh Magennis explores the legends and heroic ideals inherited from Germanic culture, which shaped Anglo-Saxon notions of the past, and were woven into English verse. Like Jayatilaka, Magennis emphasises the limited nature of our knowledge of the immense body of legend gestured at by surviving poetic texts. Daniel Anlezark demonstrates how Christian poets, probably clerics, adapted Germanic, heroic conventions to very different kinds of subject, often in learned and innovative ways that wove together different cultural traditions and ways of reading, but also engaged with the immediate concerns of the audience. Paradoxically for modern readers, the earliest English poetry is often infused with a keen sense of nostalgia for the past, the loss of great civilisations, the passing of time, and the decline and fall of all things. David Ashurst explores a characteristic response to this powerful elegiac mode: the cultivation of 'wisdom' through an emphasis on proverbial knowledge and truth, and the stability of natural cycles. Change and suffering might be inevitable, but could be met with attitudes of contemplation, resignation and wisdom – and also with intellectual wit, as evinced in the appeal to Anglo-Saxon audiences of riddles, a genre rooted in both classical and biblical traditions. All these strands – heroic, elegiac, didactic – and traditions – classical, Germanic, Christian – are present in the greatest Old English poem, *Beowulf*, the subject again of Daniel Anlezark. *Beowulf*'s epic mode, which resonates with the *Aeneid* and the later *La Chanson de Roland*, stands as evidence that the grandest of poetic traditions flourished in Anglo-Saxon England. Its poet weaves together the story-matter and heroic ideals of the past through the folk motif of the hero's battle against three monstrous enemies, but he also draws on deep classical and Christian learning. The dramatic power and remarkable inventiveness of the poem are partly rooted in the tensions created by its meeting of traditions. At the same time, *Beowulf* engages with immediate anxieties of the Anglo-Saxon present concerning kingship, dynasty, war, reputation and memorialisation. The poet, writes Anlezark, 'asserts the power of well-crafted words to strengthen society within and across time, through the art of collective memory' (p. 159).

Poetry was to remain a living tradition. The Norman Conquest set in train many cultural changes – political, economic, legal, social (discussed in this volume by Conor McCarthy), but English language and literature did not immediately change, as is sometimes assumed. As Simon Horobin shows, the primary effect of the Conquest was to create a trilingual society, but as well, there were many varieties of English, none privileged as correct. The multiplicity of English forms available, and the possibility of drawing on the vocabularies, structures and poetic conventions of French and Latin would underpin the development of a richly varied poetry. Most tantalising is the question of how English poetic tradition was affected immediately following the Conquest. There was no longer a privileged literary language of English, and yet poetic genres were to some extent sustained. This is evident in the long history of lyrics, some of which find their origins in oral composition (as David Fuller shows), and which echo the lyric mode of Old English poems such as *Wulf and Eadwacer* and *The Wife's Lament*. Yet none of these poems would have been termed 'lyrics': as so often, the generic label is a modern one, reflecting similarities of form and a recurrent link with music. Other shared characteristics include a strong tradition of poems spoken in the female voice and about secular love, though this is balanced by and shades into a sacred tradition that reflects the development of popular religion, and responds to the liturgical seasons. What may be in its origins an oral expressive tradition also has the potential to be highly learned, and is consciously taken up by writers such as Chaucer and Lydgate. As Elizabeth Archibald's essay on macaronic poetry shows, lyrics demonstrate the intellectual, sometimes witty, poetic possibilities offered by trilinguality, and reflect a mode of thought that is inherently multilingual. The self-consciousness that begins to be evident in such lyrics is a key quality of much of the most celebrated Middle English poetry.

Self-consciousness is evident too in the emphasis on the historical shaping of English identity found in chronicle and legend. As Lucy Perry shows, while chronicle, though often written in verse, is not an obvious instrument for poetic invention, fiction and history can intersect to produce a powerful literary genre. Among chroniclers, Perry argues, Laȝamon was remarkable in his creative use of native poetic tradition. His *Brut* took up and developed the dramatic potential not only of the Arthurian legend, which would play a crucial role in shaping later Middle English literature, but also the story of King Leir. The *Brut* depicts a new Englishness, rooted in ideas of nobility and 'riht' rule, of which Arthur is the apogee. Laȝamon translates and adapts a French work, Wace's *Roman de Brut*, but to do so adopts both the alliterative form and the values of Anglo-Saxon poetry. The merging of English, Latin and French literary traditions that characterises this early Middle English poetry is also typical of the debate poems discussed by Neil Cartlidge – though, as Cartlidge demonstrates, the genre of debate is also a modern notion. The often-comic subject matter of such poems tends to be drawn from French material, and to belong to a highly learned, Latin clerical tradition. The most famous of these works, *The Owl and the Nightingale*, engages with the courtly matter of love as well as with learned philosophical and theological questions, while its form evinces continuities with Anglo-Saxon poetry and its tone is characteristically, idiosyncratically 'English'. The tradition of dialogue and debate, with its oppositions and dualities, its multiple speakers, and subject matters of love, marriage, women, morality, and the conflict between body and soul, will all recur in later Middle English poetry, as will the self-conscious literariness of the *Owl and the Nightingale*.

The merging of traditions is prominent too within the most influential mode of the later Middle Ages, that of romance – 'the medium for most vernacular storytelling until the fifteenth century', as Nancy Bradbury puts it (p. 289). While earlier analogies may be found – for instance, the Old English prose narrative of *Apollonius*, which is in turn founded on a classical 'novel', medieval romance originates in the twelfth century with the writings of Chrétien de Troyes and Marie de France, who almost certainly lived in Britain. The generic term again indicates the problematic quality of modern labels, for 'romanz' originally signifies writing in the vernacular, but comes to suggest certain kinds of imaginative writing, in particular, secular fictions of love and prowess. Within this mode, there is great diversity, including of verse form, but also a consistent sense of participation in familiar traditions – especially the story matters of Troy, France and Britain. The establishment of a Norman court and nobility brought to England the French romances that in turn inspired the writing first of Anglo-Norman and then English romances. Such works depend on French conventions and are often set within exotic otherworlds, but they are also insular, engaged with English cultural values, and sometimes directly with an English past. The popular and courtly manifestations of Middle English romance are the subjects of Nancy Bradbury and Rosalind Field. Bradbury points to the remarkable flexibility of the narrative verse form, not always thought of by its critics as 'poetry'. Romance may shape meaning not through characterisation and psychological depth so much as through the accruing of action and the patterning of *topoi* and formulae. Field emphasises too the meeting of generic traditions: while Arthurian romance originates with Chrétien, it is also rooted in the chronicles of Geoffrey of Monmouth, Wace and Laȝamon. Courtly romance relies on and gestures to its literary predecessors, sometimes calling them into question, and it exploits sophisticated poetic possibilities. Shaped by the past that is often its subject, the poetry of romance also looks to the present and towards the future in its flexibility and capacity for literary reinvention.

Of special interest is the flourishing in the late medieval period of alliterative verse, used for romance but also for many other types of poetry. John Scattergood surveys the creative force of alliterative poetry in conveying religious and moral subject matter, as well as more radical political and prophetic material. The flowering of alliterative poetry may suggest that there was, at least orally, an unbroken line of development from Anglo-Saxon poetic tradition, focused particularly in the West Midlands and the north-west. The usually non-courtly emphasis of alliterative poetry may reflect its origins in oral tradition – but as many poems, including Langland's *Piers Plowman* and the works of the *Gawain*-poet, demonstrate, this was also a mode that appealed to the learned for its sophisticated creative possibilities as well as its didactic potential, and that moved across the country. While religious and moral alliterative poems are often orthodox, they also test orthodoxies of different kinds. Challenges to orthodoxy are most evident in the alliterative verse that was connected intimately with religious and social politics, especially the Wycliffite movement. Many alliterative poems, as Scattergood writes, are 'intricate, highly-wrought, self-consciously artistic' (p. 347), very far from the alliterative 'rum, ram, ruf' condemned by Chaucer's Parson. Carl Schmidt demonstrates the extraordinary sophistication and technical artistry of *Pearl*, *Patience* and *Cleanness*, while Tony Davenport shows how the same poet also challenges and adapts the conventions of the romance genre in *Sir Gawain and the Green Knight*, to create an effect reminiscent of the French *chanson de geste*. Craft and innovation are at their height in this poetic style of 'lel letteres loken', which revels in its self-conscious ambiguity. Lawrence Warner probes the challenges of interpreting alliterative poetry in his analysis of *Piers Plowman*, which emphasises the range of genres and topics within this extraordinary poem, as well as the balance between Latin and English. Warner argues that whereas modern readings have sought unity, manuscript tradition and early, often political, responses to excerpts of the poem suggest it should be read in undevelopmental terms. The essay is a salutary reminder of the dangers of applying modern literary notions, particularly of closure, to medieval texts.

The possibilities of alliterative poetry are balanced in the development of other modes by John Gower, and, most of all, by his contemporary Geoffrey Chaucer. Gower, as Robert Yeager shows, exemplifies the trilingual capacity of the medieval English poet: Gower was as ready to write in Latin and French as in English. That flexibility is echoed in a willingness to merge genres and traditions. The *Confessio Amantis*, like *The Owl and the Nightingale*, brings together classical, theological and courtly subject matters, here to offer a treatise on love in relation to the seven deadly sins. Yet Gower's learning and intensely literary approach are also directed towards the expression of socio-political ideals and a serious didactic purpose. Chaucer, by contrast, is self-consciously literary: books shape experience and meanings remain ambiguous. Chaucer's poetry too reflects the rich possibilities of the period in its use of English, French and Latin vocabularies and conventions, and its span of modes, genres and subject matters. Chaucer explicitly takes up classical and Continental inheritances, and it is particularly Homer, Virgil, Statius, Ovid and Dante whom he names. Helen Phillips explores Chaucer's reworking of both French courtly poetry and classical texts in his love visions, to achieve 'something rich and strange', a poetic brilliance that looks towards Shakespeare and Keats (Phillips, p. 403). Yet although English influence is unstated, vernacular modes and genres – romance, comedy and lyric – were crucial in shaping Chaucer's writing, which is inevitably embedded too in fourteenth-century culture, values and politics. The 'audacity' of Chaucer's poetry, his ability to weave together traditions, genres and story matters, and seem-ingly to transcend the present, is, as Alcuin Blamires argues, especially evident in the grand project of *Troilus and Criseyde*, with its Italian source, philosophical frame-work, rhyme royal stanza and questioning, dialectal treatment of love. Game-playing is most prominent of all in *The Canterbury Tales* (my own subject in this volume) with its span of narrators and genres, secular and sacred, and its dazzling range of poetic form, convention and diction. The work is the first in English both to use and self-consciously to exploit a generic vocabulary.

With such a literary inheritance, it is not surprising that the fifteenth century produced a wealth of diverse poetic works. Cultural shifts of radical kinds, most of all the civil wars of the 1450s to the 1480s ('Wars of the Roses'), as Matthew

Woodcock shows, also proved to be catalysts for poetic invention, well before this fraught period inspired Shakespeare's English history plays. Tony Edwards illustrates the remarkable possibilities of the highly sophisticated literary language that had emerged in the late fourteenth century, shaped most of all by Chaucer, and inherited and exploited by his followers. The movement between high and low, Latinate and vernacular, could create original and brilliant poetry, exemplified by the works of Dunbar and Skelton. The immediate followers of Chaucer, Lydgate and Hoccleve, as Daniel Wakelin shows, are self-conscious in their writing of English poetry, often referring directly to Chaucer's works. They also bring new intellectual and clerical interests: their poems shift between public and private, between offering advice to princes and reflecting in immediate terms on personal experience. Intimacy, indeed, becomes a poetic effect, underpinned by art and learning. Such flexibility of tone, genre and mode is not only the legacy of Chaucer, but also the culmination of a longstanding tradition.

In this period, English writing was balanced by the poetic tradition developing in Scotland, the subject of Douglas Gray in this volume. Poets such as Henryson and Dunbar found new creative possibilities in their own rich vernacular, and in the Scottish landscape and history. Their often conscious engagement with Chaucer draws both on their classical learning and wide reading, and on their experience of a rapidly changing and often challenging culture. Catherine Grisé explores what the role of women as readers and writers may have been within this diverse world of the fifteenth century, looking at the possibilities of female authorship of lyrics, but also at two works associated with women, *The Flour and the Leaf* and *The Assembly of Ladies*. Both poems reconfigure the conventions of love and chivalry in self-conscious ways that engage with the tradition of writing female experience, particularly in love. The chivalric games depicted vividly evoke the ethos of the fifteenth-century courtly world, the subject of Barry Windeatt. The interweaving of originality and convention is characteristic of late-medieval courtly writing, and strikingly evinced by James I of Scotland's reworking of Chaucerian poetry in *The Kingis Quair*. Most remarkable of all, perhaps, is the poetry of Charles d'Orléans, which spans both French and English, and looks towards the edgy, inventive poems of Wyatt. The adoption by a French poet of the English language and its poetic conventions suggests their unique quality and appeal, and the existence of a highly developed and distinctively English art of poetry in the fifteenth century. As the final essay, that of Pamela King on secular and sacred drama, reminds us, however, more popular vernacular traditions were also sustained. King shows the special power of poetry in shaping affect within religious drama, and the potential within dramatic poetry to range from immediate to grand styles, from affective to comic to political. It would be this genre of poetry, composed for dramatic performance and with its range of popular and courtly possibilities, which would produce some of the greatest works of the Renaissance.

The remarkable range and quality of medieval poetry can tempt the modern reader into an over-determined view of the period. As Ralph Hanna's essay on manuscripts and audience emphasises, there was no fixed canon of medieval poetry in its time, and any listener or reader was likely to have a very partial knowledge. One strikingly original aspect of Chaucer's *Canterbury Tales* is his play with a wide variety of genres which are explicitly named. Yet although familiarity with genre can be assumed, knowledge of specific works cannot. For example, although the works of the *Gawain*-poet are now among the most celebrated of medieval poems, they exist in only one manuscript, and are unlikely to have been known beyond the poet's immediate audience, probably an aristocratic household in the north-west Midlands. In London, the situation was somewhat different: Chaucer refers to Gower and the *General Prologue* suggests that he read Langland; something approaching a circle of readers and writers probably existed in London by the late medieval period. But beyond this all was more fluid. The enormous value of individual books made them rare possessions: households might own just one. Books were therefore likely to be personalised compilations, most often containing a range of genres, both verse and prose. Although the *Canterbury Tales*, the *Confessio Amantis* and *Piers Plowman* did circulate widely, other widely read works are now less familiar. Hanna shows that manuscript compilations were likely to include long verse treatises offering spiritual instruction, such as the didactic *Speculum Vitae* and *The Prick of Conscience*, works that are now almost unknown, along with, perhaps, saints' lives and other devotional or moral works. When romances were included in compilations, they are likely to have been justified by their pious, educative material. The differences between medieval and modern tastes have been formative in shaping a canon of medieval poetry unlike any that might have been shaped in the medieval period. Ralph Hanna and Julia Boffey emphasise too the physical frailty of manuscript books, the complexities of their production, and the vulnerability of the literary text within a world of scribal copying and uncertain transmission. The fifteenth century saw an increase in the supply of and demand for books, the move to make poetic anthologies, and eventually the vast expansion in book production occasioned by the establishment of the first printing press in London. Yet to be an 'author' in an age of patronage was not easy, and Boffey points to the vagaries of transmission of literary works even in the case of those by renowned writers such as Chaucer and Langland. Many questions concerning who and what was read in medieval England remain unanswered; many books and many literary works have been lost. To recognise the limits of our knowledge, as well as the differences between medieval and modern textual culture, is fundamental to an understanding of the poetic traditions of the Middle Ages. But despite those limits, the essays contained in this volume prove beyond any doubt the richness and diversity of medieval poetry, and its shaping influence on later poetic traditions. The Epilogue explores some of the afterlives of medieval poetry, themselves remarkably rich and diverse, and sustained across very different thought worlds. As medieval poetry, now more than ever, continues to inspire new writing and to influence other art forms, there is no doubt of its imaginative appeal.

REFERENCES AND FURTHER READING

Bawcutt, Priscilla and Janet Hadley Williams (eds) (2006). *A Companion to Medieval Scottish Poetry*. Cambridge: D. S. Brewer.

Bolton, W. F. (1986). *The Middle Ages*. Sphere History of Literature 1. London: Sphere.

Brown, Peter (ed.) (2000). *A Companion to Chaucer*. Blackwell Companions to Medieval Literature and Culture. Oxford: Blackwell.

Brown, Peter (ed.) (2007). *A Companion to Medieval English Literature and Culture, c. 1350–c. 1500*. Blackwell Companions to Medieval Literature and Culture. Oxford: Blackwell.

Burrow, J. A. (1971). *Ricardian Poetry: Chaucer, Gower, Langland, and the Gawain Poet*. London: Routledge.

Burrow, J. A. (1982). *Medieval Writers and Their Work: Middle English Literature and its Background 1100–1500*. Oxford: Oxford University Press.

Cannon, Christopher (2008). *Middle English Literature: A Cultural History*. Cambridge: Polity Press.

Green, D. H. (2007). *Women Readers in the Middle Ages*. Cambridge Studies in Medieval Literature 65. Cambridge: Cambridge University Press.

Davenport, Tony (2004). *Medieval Narrative: An Introduction*. Oxford: Oxford University Press.

Ellis, Steve (ed.) (2005). *Chaucer: An Oxford Guide*. Oxford: Oxford University Press.

Fisher, P. J. V. (1973). *The Anglo-Saxon Age, c. 400–1042*. London: Longman.

Fulk, R. D. and Christopher M. Cain (2003). *A History of Old English Literature*. Oxford: Blackwell.

Fulton, Helen (ed.) (2009). *A Companion to Arthurian Literature*. Blackwell Companions to Literature and Culture. Oxford: Blackwell.

Godden, Malcolm, and Michael Lapidge (eds) (1991). *The Cambridge Companion to Old English Literature*. Cambridge: Cambridge University Press.

Gray, Douglas (2008). *Later Medieval English Literature*. Oxford: Oxford University Press.

Green, Richard Firth (1980). *Poets and Prince-Pleasers: Literature and the English Court in the Late Middle Ages*. Toronto: University of Toronto Press.

Greenfield, Stanley B. and Daniel G. Calder (with Michael Lapidge) (1986). *A New Critical History of Old English Literature*. New York: New York University Press.

Griffiths, Ralph (ed.) (2003). *The Fourteenth and Fifteenth Centuries. The Short Oxford History of the British Isles*. Oxford: Oxford University Press.

Hanna, Ralph (2005). *London Literature, 1300–1380*. Cambridge: Cambridge University Press.

Horrox, Rosemary (1994). *Fifteenth-Century Attitudes: Perceptions of Society in Late Medieval England*. Cambridge: Cambridge University Press.

Huizinga, John (1955). *The Waning of the Middle Ages*. Harmondsworth: Pelican. (First pub. 1919.)

Hunter Blair, Peter (1977). *An Introduction to Anglo-Saxon England*. 2nd edn. Cambridge: Cambridge University Press.

Jacob, E. F. (1961). *The Fifteenth Century: 1399–1485*. Oxford History of England 6. Oxford: Oxford University Press.

Lapidge, Michael, John Blair, Simon Keynes and Donald Scragg (eds) (1999). *The Blackwell Encyclopaedia of Anglo-Saxon England*. Oxford: Blackwell.

Lewis, C. S. (1936). *The Allegory of Love: A Study in Medieval Tradition*. Oxford: Clarendon Press.

McKisack, May (1959). *The Fourteenth Century, 1307–1399*. Oxford History of England 5. Oxford: Oxford University Press.

Nicholas, David (1992). *The Evolution of the Medieval World: Society, Government and Thought in Europe, 312–1500*. London: Longman.

North, Richard, and Joe Allard (eds) (2007). *Beowulf and Other Stories: A New Introduction to Old English, Old Icelandic and Anglo-Norman Literatures*. Harlow: Pearson.

Saunders, Corinne (ed.) (2004). *A Companion to Romance: From Classical to Contemporary*. Blackwell Companions to Literature and Culture. Oxford: Blackwell.

Simpson James (2002). *The Oxford English Literary History Volume 2. 1350–1547: Reform and Cultural Revolution*. Oxford: Oxford University Press.

Solopova, Elizabeth and Stuart D. Lee (2007). *Key Concepts in Medieval Literature*. Palgrave Key Concepts. Basingstoke: Palgrave Macmillan.

Southern, R. W. (1953). *The Making of the Middle Ages*. London: Hutchinson.

Stenton, F. M. (1971). *Anglo-Saxon England*. 3rd edn. Oxford: Oxford University Press.

Strohm, Paul (ed.) (2007). *Middle English*. Oxford Twenty-First Century Approaches to Literature. Oxford: Oxford University Press.

Treharne, Elaine and Phillip Pulsiano (eds) (2001). *A Companion to Anglo-Saxon Literature*. Blackwell Companions to Literature and Culture. Oxford: Blackwell.

Turville-Petre, Thorlac (1996). *England the Nation: Language, Literature and National Identity 1290–340*. Oxford: Clarendon Press.

Wakelin, Daniel (2007). *Humanism, Reading, and English Literature 1430–1530*. Oxford: Oxford University Press.

Wallace, David (ed.) (1999). *The Cambridge History of Medieval English Literature*. Cambridge: Cambridge University Press.

Part I
Old English Poetry

Contexts
Genres and Modes

Contexts

1

The World of Anglo-Saxon England

Andy Orchard

The Anglo-Saxon period is often seen as a distinctive phase in the history of these islands (see in general Stenton 1971; Whitelock 1974; Lapidge et al. 1999). But before the Anglo-Saxons came, in the fifth century, the native Britons had already established an enviable culture that, while assuredly Christian, tried hard to ensure that a proud sub-Roman legacy lived on (Collingwood and Myers 1963; Lapidge and Dumville 1984; Todd 1999). Not for nothing did they despise the Germanic invaders who took their lands, illiterate, un-Latinate, and pagan as they proved to be, requiring a second Mission at the end of the sixth century to complete a second Conversion, several centuries after the first had been wholly achieved. For even though they came from the edge of the known world, the Christian learning of certain Britons was legendary right at the heart of the Christian establishment on the Continent: if Jerome (who died in 420), the irascible and in many ways obnoxious translator of the Latin Vulgate Bible, was implacably opposed to what he had condemned as the heresy of the Briton Pelagius (*c.* 354–420/440) with regard to Free Will, he still paid him the unwitting compliment of calling him 'the most Latinate of men' (*homo Latinissimus*), even as Pelagius chose to defend himself in Greek when facing down his opponents in Rome (Rees 1988; Lapidge and Sharpe 1985: 2–20).

Another Briton, Faustus (405 × 410–480 × 490), left his homeland to become bishop of Riez in Southern Gaul, and an implacable opponent of the doctrines of his countryman Pelagius (Lapidge and Sharpe 1985: 21–24). Likewise, Patrick (who likely died in 493), a Briton who went on to evangelise the Irish after being captured by Irish pirates in his teens, bears in his bitter regret for an education cruelly cut short eloquent witness to the standards of British learning in his day (Bieler 1952; Lapidge and Sharpe 1985: 25–26; Dumville 1993; Howlett 1994). More striking still as evidence of the high standards and self-regard of British intellectuals is the highly stylised, deeply learned and pungently affecting (and effective) prose of Gildas (*c.* 516–570), looking back on the mounting waves of Germanic invasions, when the Anglo-Saxons almost swept the British and Celtic indigenous peoples northwards and westwards into the sea, and who saw the whole sorry episode as a punishment from God for his people's louche living and lascivious ways (Winterbottom 1978; Lapidge and Dumville 1984; Lapidge and Sharpe 1985: 27–28).

Indeed, it was the same splenetic reasoning, attributed explicitly to Gildas, that was to be used by two later Anglo-Saxons, namely Alcuin in the late eighth century and Wulfstan in the early eleventh century (Orchard 2000; Bullough 2004), to explain the later waves of Germanic invasions, this time by the Viking Norse, against back-sliding Anglo-Saxons who had forsaken godly ways. And identical logic was used again in hindsight at the end of the eleventh century to explain how a final wave of invaders, namely the Normans, who could trace their own ancestry back to Norseman who settled in Northern France alongside the Bretons of Brittany who had their own ancient affinity with the Britons of Britain, and were there to witness when six centuries of Anglo-Saxon England ended abruptly on the bloody field of Hastings on 14 October 1066.

The notion of Britain as an island subject to continuous waves of foreign raiders, traders and invaders who eventually settled and assimilated is an ancient one, and can be traced early even in Anglo-Saxon sources. So, from the perspective of the Anglo-Saxon Bede (672/3–735), who used Gildas's work in creating his own *Historia ecclesiastica gentis Anglorum* ('Ecclesiastical History of the English People' [*HE*]) in 731, contemporary Britain was a multilingual melting-pot of competing nations, held together by a common (if not exactly identical) Christian faith (*HE* I.1; Colgrave and Mynors 1969):

> Haec in praesenti iuxta numerum librorum quibus lex diuina scripta est, quinque gentium linguis unam eandemque summae ueritatis et uerae sublimitatis scientiam scrutatur et confitetur, Anglorum uidelicet Brettonum Scottorum Pictorum et Latinorum, quae meditatione scripturarum ceteris omnibus est facta communis.

> At present, there are five languages in Britain, after the number of books in which divine law is written, all for considering and setting out one and the same wisdom, which is to say the knowledge of deepest truth and true depth, namely English, British, Irish, Pictish, and Latin, which through the study of scripture has become common to all the others.

It is striking how often this theme recurs in later Anglo-Saxon texts, and indeed in the fifth and final book of the *Historia ecclesiastica*, Bede again returns to the theme of multinational, multilingual Britain, in a series of chapters that implicitly assert the superiority of their Christianity over that of their neighbours, noting how the Anglo-Saxons Aldhelm (*HE* V.18), Ceolfrith (*HE* V.21) and Ecgberht (*HE* V.22) respectively battled against the errors of the British in Wessex, the Picts, and the Irish in Iona (the Latin term *Scotti* refers to both Scots and Irish). In an example of what in Old English poetry is called the envelope pattern, and so signalling the importance of the theme to Bede's entire narrative, he again addresses in turn the current status of each of the constituent nations in the closing chapter of the *Historia ecclesiastica* (*HE* V.23):

> Pictorum quoque natio tempore hoc et foedus pacis cum gente habet Anglorum, et catholicae pacis ac ueritatis cum uniuersali ecclesia particeps existere gaudet. Scotti, qui Brittaniam incolunt, suis contenti finibus nil contra gentem Anglorum insidiarum moliuntur aut fraudium. Brettones, quamuis et maxima ex parte domestico sibi odio gentem Anglorum, et totius catholicae ecclesiae statum pascha minus recto, moribusque inprobis inpugnent; tamen et diuina sibi et humana prorsus resistente uirtute, in neutro cupitum possunt obtinere propositum; quippe qui quamuis ex parte sui sint iuris, nonnulla tamen ex parte Anglorum sunt seruitio mancipati.

> Likewise the race of Picts in this time both has a treaty of peace with the English people and rejoices to be sharing in catholic peace and truth with the universal Church. The Irish, who inhabit Britain, are happy within their borders, and they do not plot any ambushes or attacks against the English people. The Britons, even though with innate hatred they have for the most part opposed the English and the state of the orthodox universal Church of God, both in maintaining their incorrect Easter and in their wrongful practices, are resisted by the power of both God and man, so that they cannot win or succeed in what they want in either respect. And although they have for the most part self-rule, yet in large measure they are governed by and obliged to English rule.

Note the hierarchy here: the Picts get a clean bill of health, the Irish are damned with faint praise for not plotting just at present and the British are roundly castigated for their flaws.

But then the native Britons never seemed to have fared well at the hands of the Anglo-Saxons who supplanted them from vast swathes of what became Anglo-Saxon England, and who were still battling them even at the end of the period. The Modern English term 'Welsh' is itself testimony to the sense of innate ownership felt by this latest wave of settlers, deriving as it does ultimately from an Anglo-Saxon word for 'foreigners' or 'strangers' (*wealas*). History is littered with examples of later invaders displacing, disinheriting and denigrating previous incumbents, but it took the Anglo-Saxons to designate them, formally, as strangers in their own land. It is striking how far the Anglo-Saxons themselves went on to tread the same path as the Britons they supplanted, but never quite replaced: intermarriage, forced or otherwise, and the adoption and adaptation of native patterns of Latin learning that looked back to the glory days of Rome, with a grandeur that still inspired awe centuries later. Indeed, when several different Anglo-Saxon poets describe Roman remains as 'the works of giants' (*enta geweorc*) we can still sense their wonder at what they had inherited (Frankis 1973; Thornbury 2000).

Moreover, if Bede paints a picture of the Britain of his day as linguistically diverse, he is similarly forthright about the fact that the Anglo-Saxons themselves came from disparate parts of the continent, and even if modern scholars have cast great doubt on his easy tripartite division of Jutes (from Jutland) coming into Kent, Saxons (from

Saxony) coming into what became Wessex, Sussex and Essex in the West, South and East respectively, and Angles (from Angeln) coming into East Anglia and what was to become Mercia and Northumbria, the crude division into Saxons in the South and West and Angles in the North and East holds broadly true in both linguistic and cultural terms (*HE* I.15; cf. Sims-Williams 1983; Higham 1994).

Nonetheless, it is clear that throughout the period the Anglo-Saxons themselves recognised regional distinctions at a deeper level than a simple division into Angles and Saxons; well into the tenth and eleventh centuries, and when national concerns are to the fore in a united battle against Viking depredations, it seems that the best way to demonstrate the concerted nature of the resistance is to designate it in terms of a combination of (for example) West-Saxons, Mercians and Northumbrians, together with the men of Essex and Kent. Yet in broad terms a North–South divide is the most evident in educational and political terms, particularly during the seventh, eighth and ninth centuries, and if older histories concentrate on a progressive power-shift southwards from Northumbria to Mercia to Wessex during that period, other factors demonstrate that despite their regional differences, common cultural aspects, particularly (as Bede suggests) in the sphere of Christian Latin learning, combine to present a united front to the outside world (Orchard 2003a).

Like their British predecessors, Anglo-Saxon intellectuals were widely sought abroad for their Christian learning. So, for example, the works of Aldhelm of Malmesbury in Wessex (*c*. 639/40–709/10) were read and imitated (and even perhaps ridiculed) by Irish scholars, and were, like those of Bede of Monkwearmouth-Jarrow in Northumbria, eagerly imported to the Continent by Anglo-Saxon scholars such as Boniface of Hampshire in Wessex (who died in 755) and Alcuin of York in Northumbria (*c*. 735–804), who found themselves living and working abroad. A further feature of the Anglo-Saxon world was the way that foreign learning was keenly welcomed and assimilated, even during Bede's own lifetime. One can only imagine what Theodore (602–690), then a Greek monk of Tarsus of advanced years, felt when he was made Archbishop of Canterbury; in insisting on bringing with him Hadrian (who died in 710), a deeply learned Latin scholar from North Africa, he was able to create a school at Canterbury that was to be the envy of the western world (Lapidge 1986; Lapidge 1995). One of the few alumni of the Canterbury school whose works have survived was Aldhelm of Malmesbury, a scion of the West Saxon royal family who went on to boast that he was the first of the Germanic race to compose significant amounts of Latin verse. Not only were Aldhelm's own works extensively exported both to the Continent and to Ireland, as previously mentioned, but also he influenced directly many subsequent generations of Anglo-Saxon, including Boniface, Apostle to the Germans (and many others in his mission), who was killed in his eighties at Dokkum in 755 by Germanic pirates who foreshadowed the Vikings in their attitude towards Anglo-Saxons in their homeland (Orchard 2001b).

Meanwhile, in the north of England and at about the same time as Theodore was active in the south, Benedict Biscop (*c*. 629–680) brought back vast numbers of books from the Continent and fostered the kind of intellectual environment where Bede could thrive and later Alcuin, who was born around the time that Bede died, could be nurtured. If Bede, like Aldhelm, died in an England they helped to create (although Aldhelm, unlike Bede, did at least leave the country, visiting Rome), it was left to the next generation to take Anglo-Saxon learning back to the Continent. While Boniface was to die in Dokkum, Alcuin, who had left England in 782, died in Tours in 804, a key member of Charlemagne's imported intellectual elite (Orchard 2000; Bullough 2004). Important cultural icons, such as the elaborate and rightly celebrated Lindisfarne Gospels or the mighty Codex Amiatinus, bear eloquent witness to the influence of the Irish on Anglo-Saxon intellectual endeavours, albeit that some Anglo-Saxons (notably Aldhelm, whose early education had a distinctly Irish flavour) seem to have preferred the Mediterranean traditions imported into England at the end of the seventh century by the so-called Canterbury School (Lapidge 2007).

Unfortunately, however, while both Boniface and Alcuin were safely ensconced on the Continent, there were ominous stirrings at home, marked if only in strictly chronological terms by the reign of the mighty Mercian King Offa (757–96). Boniface, with the pope's blessing, felt sufficiently outraged (and sufficiently distant) to lambast Offa's powerful predecessor, King Æthelbald of Mercia (who ruled 716–57), for his voracious and pernicious sexual appetites, which extended even to nuns. It was precisely this kind of moral laxity of the Anglo-Saxons, Alcuin observes with hindsight, and drawing on the parallel deductions of Gildas with regard to the Britons, that made them ripe in God's eyes for retribution in the forms of murderous invaders: for the Britons, Anglo-Saxons; for the Anglo-Saxons, Vikings.

The Anglo-Saxon Chronicle provides a grim catalogue of what was to prove more than two centuries of Viking depredations that culminated in the division of Anglo-Saxon England in King Alfred's time, and its conquest in the time of King Æthelred. But such portentous events begin with a brief and fatal skirmish, perhaps even a trading mission gone wrong, described in the A-text of *The Anglo-Saxon Chronicle* for the year 787, properly 789 (Swanton 1996; Bately 1986):

> Her nom Beorhtric cyning Offan dohtor Eadburge. & on his dagum cuomon ærest III scipu, & þa se gerefa þærto rad & hie wolde drifan to þæs cyninges tune þy he nyste hwæt hie wæron, & hiene mon ofslog. Þæt wæron þa ærestan scipu deniscra monna þe Angelcynnes lond gesohton.

> In this year, King Berhtric married Offa's daughter Eadburg. In his time there first came three ships of Norsemen from Hördaland, and the sea-reeve rode there, and wanted to force them to go to the king's dwelling, since he did not know what they were, and he was killed. And they were the first ships of Danish men who sought out the land of the English people.

Within a few years, the explicitly violent intention of the visitors becomes abundantly clear; the watershed entry for 793 marks the beginning of a litany of disaster, introduced in suitably dramatic terms in the F-text of the *Chronicle* (Swanton 1996; Baker 2000):

Her wæron reðe forebycna cumene on Nordhymbraland, & ðæt folc earmlice drehtan,
ðæt wæran ormete ligræscas, & wæran gesawenæ fyrene dracan on ðan lifte fleogende.
And sona fylygde mycel hunger, & æfter ðan ðes ylcan geares earmlice hæðenra hergung
adyligodan Godes cyrican in Lindisfarenaee, ðurh reaflac & manslyht.

In this year, terrible omens of foreboding appeared over the land of Northumbria, and
miserably terrified the people. There were enormous lightning flashes and fiery dragons
were seen flying in the sky. A great famine immediately followed those signs, and after
that in the same year pillaging by heathen men wretchedly destroyed God's church at
Lindisfarne through plunder and slaughter.

For Alcuin, this was a deadly blow, struck as it was right at the heart of Northumbrian
learning, and one that heralded the slow decline of an early-blooming Anglo-Saxon
intellectual revolution that had flowered both at home and on the Continent; for the
nation as a whole, it marked the beginning of a series of raids of increasing ferocity
and irresistible force that led to ninth-century Anglo-Saxon England being characterised
grimly as 'the crucible of defeat' (Brooks 1979; cf. Keynes 1995; Keynes 1997).

The revival of Anglo-Saxon fortunes occurred primarily in the reign of King Alfred
of Wessex (who ruled 971–99), not for nothing known later as 'the Great' (Keynes
1996; Keynes 2003; Keynes and Lapidge 1983). Alfred's own estimation of the
importance of his achievements can be measured to some extent through the various
versions of *The Anglo-Saxon Chronicle*, the common core of which was compiled during
Alfred's reign, early in the 890s. In attempting an assessment of Alfred's own concerns,
one might compare, for example, two evidently set-piece genealogies of Anglo-Saxon
kings preserved in *The Anglo-Saxon Chronicle*.

One, for the mighty Offa, king of Mercia (757–96), and given in the *Chronicle*'s
account of the first year of his reign (actually under 755, due to a counting error),
recounts sixteen generations, culminating in Woden, the pagan god of battle, magic and
poetry (all aspects of the frenzy with which he is ultimately associated) who gave his
name to the weekday Wednesday. But the genealogy has other highlights that link Offa
of Mercia to other great figures of the past. By this reckoning, Offa is the great-great-
grandson of one Eawa, the bother of the fiercesome pagan King Penda (*c.* 632–55)
who was such an implacable enemy of Christian rulers, including the saintly King
Oswald of Northumbria (who died in battle against him in 642). Offa of Mercia is
also importantly a direct descendant of his legendary namesake, Offa of Angeln, a
mid-fifth-century ruler (given here as the great-grandson of Woden himself) from
precisely the putative time of the great migration to Anglo-Saxon England, and from
precisely the area from which the Mercians derived their roots. A further genealogy, by
far the most spectacular in the entire *Anglo-Saxon Chronicle*, is preserved in two slightly
different versions. The genealogy in question is that of King Æthelwulf of Wessex
(839–58), and, remarkably, it appears neither under the year of his accession, nor of his
death; instead, this extraordinarily lengthy and detailed list is given under the year 855,
exactly a century after that of Offa, and in a year when the most significant events are
given as the first time the Vikings stayed over the winter at Sheppey, and the pious

Æthelwulf both established a tithing system for the church across his whole kingdom and went on a pilgrimage to Rome, returning with a new wife, Judith, the daughter of Charles the Bald of West Francia (ruled 843–77), who later became Holy Roman Emperor (ruled 875–7).

Given the close association of the original core of the *Anglo-Saxon Chronicle*, apparently composed at some point in the 890s, with the court of Æthelwulf's fourth son and eventual successor Alfred (who ruled 871–99), who as a boy had accompanied his father to Rome in 855, it seems appropriate to view Æthelwulf's genealogy as effectively that of Alfred himself (which of course it was). In that light, the genealogy seems an obvious attempt to outdo Offa's, with which it shares a number of features, although it is important to stress that according to these documents Æthelwulf and Offa share only a single named ancestor: the pagan god Woden himself. But while Offa is given as the great-great-grandson of the brother of a notorious pagan who opposed the spread of Christianity at all costs, Æthelwulf appears as the great-great-grandson of the brother of a deeply Christian king of the West Saxons, Ine (who ruled 688–726), who renounced his throne to undertake a pilgrimage to Rome, where he died; while Offa is linked to his continental namesake at the time of the Anglo-Saxon settlements, Æthelwulf's ancestry is traced to Cerdic, whose role in the conquest of the British is documented in the *Anglo-Saxon Chronicle* for the years 495–534, notwithstanding his distinctly non-Germanic name, better understood as a version of the (unattested) British form Caraticos that underlies not only the name of the British ruler Ceredig (perhaps born in the 420s), but also that of the pirate Coroticus to whom St Patrick (who died *c*. 493) directed at a earlier stage of his career some excoriating prose. Like Offa, Æthelwulf can apparently trace his ancestry back to Woden, although unusually, and in a clear spirit of demonstrating that Woden was a man, not a god, Woden's own genealogy is extended backwards, taking in legendary figures who appear (for example) in *Beowulf*, and leading back to an Ark-born son of Noah; the line from Noah back to Adam is biblically sanctioned and presented in the genealogy rather differently from the Germanic style of patronymic ending in -*ing* that precedes it (Sisam 1953; Dumville 1976; Dumville 1986; Anlezark 2002).

From Offa to Woden takes 15 steps; from Alfred to Adam takes three times as long: either 44 or 45 steps, encompassing Woden on the way. Alfred's is in that sense a much more Christian and Judaeo-Christian ancestry than Offa's, but it is particularly interesting that he still does not attempt to side-step Woden, a figure who also features prominently (indeed, as for Offa, ultimately) in the genealogies of the Scandinavian (and specifically Danish) Vikings with whom he was on the one hand brokering a peace, and on the other hand attempting to convert. And that fact alone tells us much about the innate conservatism of the inherited Anglo-Saxon traditions even three centuries after they were supposedly converted. Indeed, it seems striking in this regard that a further genealogy of one of Alfred's West-Saxon royal predecessors (again with a shared ancestry leading back to Woden) should be included in the *Anglo-Saxon Chronicle* juxtaposed with a brief account of the Augustinian mission sanctioned by Pope Gregory the Great (who died in 604); the A-text of *the Anglo-Saxon Chronicle* for the years 595–7 (properly 597–9; Bately 1986) reads as follows:

> 595: Her Gregorius papa sende to Brytene Augustinum. mid wel manegum munecum. þe Godes word Engladeoda godspelledon.
> 597: Her ongon Ceolwulf ricsian on Wesseaxum, & simle he feaht. & won, oþþe wiþ Angelcyn, oþþe uuiþ Walas, oþþe wiþ Peohtas, oþþe wiþ Scottas; Se wæs Cuþaing. Cuþa Cynricing, Cynric Cerdicing, Cerdic Elesing, Elesa Esling, Esla Gewising, Giwis Wiging, Wig Freawining, Freawine Friðugaring, Friðugar Bronding, Brond Bældæging, Bældæg Wodening.

> 595. In this year, Pope Gregory sent Augustine to Britain with very many monks, who preached the word of God to the English people.
> 597. In this year, Ceolwulf began to reign over the West-Saxons; and he constantly fought and struggled against the Angles, or the Welsh, or the Picts, or the Irish. He was the son of Cutha, Cutha of Cynric, Cynric of Cerdic, Cerdic of Elesa, Elesa of Gewis, Gewis of Wig, Wig of Freawine, Freawine of Frithugar, Frithugar of Brand, Brand of Baldæg, and Baldæg of Woden.

What is striking about this genealogy, which directly links King Ceolwulf of the West Saxons both with the Conversion of the Anglo-Saxons (though note that here it is characterised as a mission 'to Britain', as if the already-converted Britons were in need of further correction), and with the pagan figure of Woden, the god from whom so many of the Anglo-Saxon royal lines (as well as that of the Danes) derive, is on the one hand the proud listing of the foes with which he continually strove (Angles, Welsh, Picts, and Irish), and on the other the fact that Ceolwulf's geneaology fits very nearly exactly into the traditional pattern of Anglo-Saxon verse, where two-stress phrases are linked by alliterations between one or both of the stressed syllables in the first half-line and alliterate with the first stressed syllable of the second. In other words, the final stressed syllable of each line does *not* alliterate. One might present Ceolwulf's genealogy as follows, marking stressed syllables with an acute accent, and alliteration in **bold**:

> Céolwulf...Cúþaing.   **C**úþa **C**ýnricing,
> **C**ýnric **C**érdicing,   **C**érdic **É**lesing,
> **É**lesa **É**sling,   **É**sla Gewísing,
> **G**iwís **W**íging,   **W**íg **Fr**éawining,
> **Fr**éawine **Fr**íðugaring,   **Fr**íðugar **Br**ónding,
> **Br**ónd **B**ǽldæging,   **B**ǽldæg **W**ódening.

Granted, the fit is imperfect (there are too many alliterating syllables in the first 'line'), but the format itself, and the fact that certain sections of the genealogies of both Offa and Æthelwulf (for example) can be made to conform to a similar pattern, have suggested to some that such genealogies ultimately derived from traditional and ultimately oral poems, transmitted down family lines, but of an antiquity that is finally unknowable (Moisl 1981).

But if the genealogical information encoded in the Alfredian common core to the *Anglo-Saxon Chronicle* offers one kind of clue to Alfred's perspective, it is also evident that as the fourth of four sons of Æthelwulf to inherit his throne, he could look back on the tumultuous and embattled days of his early life and the early deaths of his brothers from the relative tranquillity of the 990s, and consider himself truly blessed. Nor did he downplay the martial achievements of his father and elder brothers, as is clear from the entry for 851 in the A-version of the *Chronicle* (Bately 1986):

Her Ceorl aldormon gefeaht wiþ hæþene men mid Defenascire æt Wicganbeorge, & þær micel wæl geslogon, & sige namon; & þy ilcan geare Æþelstan cyning, & Ealchere dux micelne here ofslogon æt Sondwic on Cent. & ix scipu gefengun, & þa oþre gefliemdon; & hæþne men ærest ofer winter sæton; & þy ilcan geare cuom feorðe healfhund scipa on Temesemuþan, & bræcon Contwaraburg, & Lundenburg, & gefliemdon Beorhtwulf Miercna cyning mid his fierde, & foron þa suþ ofer Temese on Suþrige, & him gefeaht wiþ Æþelwulf cyning & Æþelbald his sunu æt Aclea mid West Seaxna fierde, & þær þæt mæste wæl geslogon on hæþnum herige þe we secgan hierdon oþ þisne ondweardan dæg, & þær sige namon.

In this year, Ealdorman Ceorl, along with the men of Devonshire, fought against heathen men at Wicganbeorg, and inflicted great slaughter there, and won the victory. And in the same year King Æthelstan and lord Ealchere slew the great army at Sandwich in Kent, and they captured nine ships and put the rest to flight; and the heathen men first stayed over the winter; and in the same year there came 350 ships to the mouth of the Thames, and devastated Canterbury and London, and put to flight Beorhtwulf the king of Mercia with his conscript army, and then went south over the Thames to Surrey, and King Æthelwulf and his son Æthelbald fought against them with the conscript army of the West Saxons at Ockley, and there inflicted the greatest slaughter on a heathen army that we have ever heard of up to the present day, and there won the victory.

Several things are apparent here, not the least of which is that Alfred's father and brother, Æthelwulf and Æthelbald, are credited with the greatest slaughter of heathens to date. Likewise, the sheer geographical sweep of engagements in the space of a single year, from (presumably) Devon in the West to Kent in the East, together with the scale of the threat, given that the 350 ships estimated here come in a sense as reinforcement to a heathen army of unspecified size that 'for the first time' over-wintered in England, is both stark and striking. The putative traders of the first Anglo-Saxon contact with the Norsemen had swiftly evolved into seasonal raiders; but here they are effectively invaders.

Alfred's role, after recovering from a series of setbacks that almost saw him dispossessed, was to rally his troops, fight back (famously rebuilding his naval forces), succeed in battle against heavy odds and eventually secure a settlement that would see the Danes (as the invaders were collectively identified) themselves settled across a great swathe of what had been Anglo-Saxon England, covering much of the east and north of the country, and which came to be known as the Danelaw. That such a grave concession could be rightly seen as a victory for the beleaguered Anglo-Saxons is itself ample testimony to the parlous state of the kingdom Alfred inherited. The settlement brought a period of relative peace, during which Alfred was able to devote himself to rebuilding the shattered remnants of Anglo-Saxon learning, once the envy of Europe, but now decayed almost irretrievably. Alfred has traditionally been seen as the king who began to rebuild Anglo-Saxon England's intellectual reputation, mimicking the methods of Charlemagne, who had brought over foreign scholars to his court, including Alcuin, by relying on a small group of non-West Saxon scholars, including a Frank, an Old Saxon, a Welshman and others from Mercia, where learning had lapsed less severely than in Wessex. If doubts have been rightly expressed recently about how much of the educational programme later attributed to Alfred can really be called his (Stanley 1988; Godden 2007), Alfred's own interests (especially apparently in the traditional vernacular poetry now exemplified for modern readers by *Beowulf*, although there is no evidence that Alfred knew it) must surely have lent considerable impetus to a burgeoning body of texts that took Old English, rather than Latin, as their principal point of focus. From that perspective, let alone his other claims to historical significance, Alfred certainly helped to make England, and English, and English poetry what they were throughout the Middle Ages, and what they remain.

But if Alfred is justly famed for bringing England back from the brink, it was his successors Æthelstan (king of the Anglo-Saxons 924/5–927; king of the English 927–39) and Edgar (king of the Mercians and Northumbrians 957–9; king of the English 959–75) who can more properly be credited with creating a unified kingdom of the English. Æthelstan's interests (and indeed those of his court) were truly international, and he retained the deep interest in learning that characterised his grandfather (Keynes 1985).

The poem celebrating Æthelstan's mighty and defining victory at Brunanburh in 937 (presumably in a traditional heroic style which Alfred would have recognised) likewise takes a truly international perspective, naming (in order) Æthelstan, his brother Edmund and their father Edward briskly in the first seven lines, along with the site of their famous victory. Their enemies, first simply designated thus, are then defined as a mixture of Irish and Vikings, led by Constantine (*Constantinus*, line 38) and Olaf (*Anlaf*, lines 26, 31 and 46), in a carefully choreographed set of verses (lines 10b–12a): 'Hettend crungon / Scotta leode and scipflotan, / fæge feollon' ('the enemies perished, the Irish people, the Viking sailors, the doomed fell'), repeated soon after as a combination of Norse (*guma norðerna*, line 18) and Irish (*Scyttisc*, line 19; cf. *flotena and Scotta*, line 32), faced by the combined forces of West Saxons (*West-Seaxe*, line 20) and Mercians (*Mierce*, line 24); the victorious brothers head back to their 'homeland' (*cyþþe*, line 58), the 'land of the West Saxons' (*West-Seaxna land*, line 59). The final lines of the poem seem to combine both the native and ultimately oral tradition of Old English poetry as well as written history, embodying as they do the so-called 'Beasts of Battle' motif widely attested elsewhere (Griffith 1993), but also gesturing back to a documented past and the view of Anglo-Saxon England first propounded by Bede at the beginning of his *Historia ecclesiastica*, in the passage cited earlier (*Battle of Brunanburh* 60–73):

Letan him behindan   hræw bryttian   60
saluwigpadan,   þone sweartan hræfn,
hyrnednebban,   and þane hasewanpadan,
earn æftan hwit,   æses brucan,
grædigne guðhafoc   and þæt græge deor,
wulf on wealde.   Ne wearð wæl mare   65
on þis eiglande   æfre gieta
folces gefylled   beforan þissum
sweordes ecgum,   þæs þe us secgað bec,
ealde uðwitan,   siþþan eastan hider
Engle and Seaxe   up becoman,   70
ofer brad brimu   Brytene sohtan,
wlance wigsmiþas,   Wealas ofercoman,
eorlas arhwate   eard begeatan.

They let the dark-coloured one break up the carrion, the swarthy raven, with its horned beak, and the dusky-coated one, the eagle white at the rear, enjoy their food, the greedy war-hawk, and the grey beast, the wolf in the wood. There has never been a greater slaughter in this island up till now, of folk felled with the edges of swords before this, according to what books tell us, ancient authorities, since the Angles and Saxons, over the broad seas, proud war-smiths, warriors brisk in glory, to here from the East, came up, sought out the Britons, overcame the Welsh, won a homeland.

These lines also embody elements found earlier in the *Anglo-Saxon Chronicle* (into which *The Battle of Brunanburh* is incorporated), and indeed cited above: the animal imagery, and the view of the Vikings and their allies as simply supplying carrion for the traditional 'beasts of battle', offers a fitting conclusion (for the time being) for Viking incursions first presaged by flying dragons over Northumbria reported for the year 793 (presumably a reference to the infamous dragon-headed longships [*drekkar*] of the Vikings), while the description of the battle as surpassing all other previous slaughters in Britain seems to gesture at the account for the year 851 already cited above, where the mighty victory off Æthelwulf and Æthelbald at Ockley is portrayed as 'the greatest slaughter on a heathen army that we have ever heard of up to the present day' ('þæt mæste wæl geslogon on hæþnum herige þe we secgan hierdon oþ þisne ondweardan dæg'). Note that in *The Battle of Brunanburh*, however, the customary and ultimately oral language of heroic verse ('that we have ever heard of' ['þe we secgan hierdon']) has been replaced by a clear reference to books and book-learning ('þæs þe us secgað bec'). If Æthelstan outdoes his great-grandfather Æthelwulf on the battlefield, he is celebrated for doing so in a manner of which his grandfather Alfred would likely have approved, namely in the mixed medium of written history and heroic verse. The final four lines of the poem make of the battle itself almost a reconquest of Britain, with the Anglo-Saxons, those 'proud war-smiths, warriors brisk in glory' ('Engle and Seaxe…wlance wigsmiþas…eorlas arhwate') occupying the a-lines, their conquered enemies, the Britons and the Welsh occupying the b-lines

('Brytene . . . Wealas'), and a pounding litany of non-alliterating finite verbs describing the successive phases of the Anglo-Saxon victory: 'came up, sought out . . . overcame . . . won' ('becoman . . . sohtan . . . ofercoman . . . begeatan').

But if Æthelstan's victory brought some respite, and the later reign of Edgar (who died in 975) brought enough peace and stability to initiate a further flowering of Anglo-Saxon literature and learning both in Old English and in Latin that was to extend across the millennium, the Danes were far from done, and events came to a head during the lengthy reign of Æthelred, when the first seeds of the Norman Conquest were also sown. It can be a curse to reign for a long time, and certainly the reputation of King Æthelred (who reigned 978–1016, with a period of forced exile in Normandy 1013–14) seems to have declined steadily (Keynes 1978; Keynes 1986); his usual nickname 'the Unready' seems a cruel pun on his name: *æþelræd* means 'noble advice', while *unræd* means 'bad advice'. It is striking that in the entry in the C-version of the *Anglo-Saxon Chronicle* for 991, when what was later clearly seen as a devastating policy was first adopted, the theme of 'advice' is writ large (O'Brien O'Keeffe 2001):

Her wæs Gypeswic gehergod, & æfter þon swiðe raðe wæs Brihtnoð ealdorman ofslegen æt Mældune; & on þam geare man geræedde þæt man geald æerest gafol denescum mannum for ðam miclan brogan þe hi worhton be ðam særiman; þæt wæs æerest X ðusend punda; þæne ræd geræedde æerest Syric arcebisceop.

In this year Ipswich was harried, and very soon after that Ealdorman Byrhtnoth was slain at Maldon, and in that year it was advised that tribute should be paid to the Danes on account of the great terror that they wrought along the coast; first it was £10,000; that advice was first advised by Archbishop Sigeric.

It is hard not to associate the repetition of the element (-)*ræd*(-) here with the name of King Æthelred himself. The litany of payments that begins with this entry shows the utterly disastrous effects of this policy for the coming years: £10,000 in 991, £16,000 in 994, £24,000 in 1002, £36,000 in 1007 and £48,000 in 1012.

Closely connected with this *Chronicle*-entry is the extraordinarily elegiac and retrospective poem *The Battle of Maldon*, which encompasses great swathes of the nation in both geographical and social terms, so transforming a local conflict to a watershed event of national significance. The untimely, brave, noble and (if we are to credit the poem's account) somewhat foolhardy death of Ealdorman Byrhtnoth, who dies fiercely loyal to his king (Æthelred is named three times in the poem, at lines 52, 151 and 203), is matched by the brave, noble and perhaps somewhat foolhardy deaths of many (but not all!) of Byrhtnoth's men. In the poem, the simplest and clearest expression of the heroic creed for which some Anglo-Saxons at least seem to have been prepared to lay down their lives is put in the mouth of the one lowest in social status, as if to indicate that right behaviour is not restricted to rank (*Battle of Maldon* 255–60; Scragg 1981):

Dunnere þa cwæð,   daroð acwehte,   255
unorne ceorl,   ofer eall clypode,
bæd þæt beorna gehwylc   Byrhtnoð wræce:
'Ne mæg na wandian   se þe wrecan þenceð
frean on folce,   ne for feore murnan.'
Þa hi forð eodon,   feores hi ne rohton;   260

Then Dunnere spoke, shook his spear, a simple peasant, he shouted over everything, asked that every warrior should avenge Byrhtnoth: 'In no way can he hesitate, who thinks to avenge his lord among the people, nor care for his life.' Then they went forth, did not pay heed to life.

Here, the poet has carefully emphasised the key notions of vengeance and (not caring about one's own) life through repetition of the key elements (*wræce... wrecan; feore... feores*) in successive lines; in each repetition, one element is given in the voice of the narrator, and one in the voice of Dunnere the peasant.

In this highly choreographed epitaph for Anglo-Saxon valour, Dunnere's shaking of his spear has a significance of its own, matching as it does the actions of his fallen lord, Byrhtnoth, who had likewise waved his spear (and brandished his shield) before uttering his own first words of defiance to the Danish foe (*Battle of Maldon* 42–44: Byrhtnoð maþelode, bord hafenode, / wand wacne æsc, wordum mælde' ['Byrhtnoth made a speech, brandished his shield, waved his slender ash-spear, uttered in words']). As if to emphasise that such defiant (albeit doomed) resistance belongs to an ancient ethic, the poet puts a further (and presumably proverbial) rallying speech into the mouth of the aged Byrhtwold, who brandishes shield and spear in a manner reminiscent of both Dunnere and Byrhtnoth before he speaks (*Battle of Maldon* 312–16; Scragg 1981):

Byrhtwold maþelode   bord hafenode
(se wæs eald geneat),   æsc acwehte;   310
he ful baldlice   beornas lærde:
'Hige sceal þe heardra,   heorte þe cenre,
mod sceal þe mare,   þe ure mægen lytlað.
Her lið ure ealdor   eall forheawen,
god on greote.   A mæg gnornian   315
se ðe nu fram þis wigplegan   wendan þenceð.'

Byrhtwold made a speech, brandished his shield (he was an ancient retainer), shook his ash-spear; he encouraged the warriors very boldly: 'Courage must be the harder, heart the keener, mind must be the greater, as our strength wanes. Here lies our leader, entirely cut to pieces, a good man in the dirt. Ever may he mourn who thinks to turn now from this warplay.'

If the first two lines of Byrhtwold's speech represent heroic generalities of a kind that can be replicated the world over, it is the following lines, with their emphasis on the 'here', and the 'now' and the 'this' that make it plain that he is not simply dealing in Anglo-Saxon platitudes; if the wages of heroism is death, then at Maldon that debt fell due.

The quixotic actions of Byrhtnoth and at least some of his men showed that not all Anglo-Saxons were content to cave in to Danish threats, despite the later and bitter complaints of Archbishop Wulfstan (who died in 1023) in his trenchant 'Sermon of the Wolf to the English' (*Sermo Lupi ad Anglos*), a stock speech, to judge by its survival in full in three different versions in five separate manuscripts and the evident recycling of part of it elsewhere in Wulfstan's work, as was his wont (Orchard 1992; Orchard 2003b; Orchard 2004; Orchard 2007). The *Sermo Lupi* paints a grim picture of cowardly and cowed Anglo-Saxons who repeatedly refuse to stand up to the Viking threats, and in the longest version of the speech that survives, Wulfstan, quoting from a letter of Alcuin's, cites the same reasoning as Gildas (whom he names): just as the Britons received divine retribution for their sinful lives at the hands of the Anglo-Saxons, so too now do the Anglo-Saxons at the hands of the Vikings.

Wulfstan, a wily law-maker and politician, maintained a prominent position not just during Æthelred's reign, but also that of Cnut, the Dane who replaced him; indeed, he wrote law-codes for both. But if the pernicious policy of paying off the Danes (so-called 'Danegeld'), begun in 991, signalled the beginning of the slow decline of Anglo-Saxon moral standards that Wulfstan was to castigate so comprehensively two decades later, still more disastrous was the so-called 'St Brice's Day Massacre', when Æthelred ordered the killing of 'all the Danes who were among the English people' on 13 November, 1002 (*ASC* C: O'Brien O'Keeffe 2001):

> & on þam geare se cyng het ofslean ealle þa deniscan men þe on Angelcynne wæron; ðis wæs gedon on Britius mæssedæig, forðam þam cyninge wæs gecyd þæt hi woldan hine besyrwan æt his life & siððan ealle his witan & habban siþþan þis rice.

> And in that year the king ordered all the Danes who were among the English people to be slain on St Brice's Day, because the king had been told that they planned to kill him treacherously, and then all his councillors, and then take control of his kingdom.

Wulfstan's own role in this extraordinarily provocative pogrom is unclear (Wilcox 2000), although presumably as a senior member of the *witan* (the king's councillors, apparently threatened in the putative Danish plot) he would have played some part. What is certain is that not all the Danes in England were destroyed, though the loss of some very senior figures, most notably the sister of King Svein Forkbeard of Denmark, seems to have led directly to a dramatic increase in Danish attacks, so much so that the C-text of the *Anglo-Saxon Chronicle* for 1011 could make a bold connection with the name of the ill-advised king 'noble-advice' and state baldly that 'all these misfortunes befell us through bad advice' ('Ealle þas ungesælða us gelumpon þuruh unrædas'; O'Brien O'Keeffe 2001).

The writing was on the wall for Æthelred, who saw his kingdom conquered by Svein, who went into exile in Normandy with the ducal family into which he had married through the redoubtable Emma during the years 1013–14, and who was allowed to return to reclaim his kingdom on the sudden death of Svein, 'if he were willing to govern more properly than he had before', according to the C-text of the *Anglo-Saxon Chronicle* ('gif he hi rihtlicor healdan wolde þonne he ær dyde'; O'Brien O'Keeffe 2001). Cnut had other thoughts, however, and returned to England with overwhelming force, taking Æthelred's kingdom, his life and (eventually) his wife. These extraordinary events, told extremely sympathetically from Emma's own point of view, are detailed in a Latin text composed while Emma was still alive, namely the intriguing *Encomium Emmae Reginae*, composed by an anonymous monk of Flanders, which can be closely dated (at least in its final version) to the period 1041–42 (Campbell 1998; Orchard 2001a). Cnut's marriage to Emma (the precise circumstances of which are somewhat sketchy) in 1017, set the seal on the next and final phase of Anglo-Saxon England, as the new (and still) Queen Emma had to come to terms with the fact that her two children by Æthelred, Edward and Alfred, were safe in exile with her family in Normandy. Emma herself, wife of two kings of England (Æthelred and Cnut) and mother to two more (Harthacnut, son of Cnut, and Edward the Confessor, son of Æthelred), embodies the complex and explosive mix of Norman, Norse and Anglo-Saxon interests that was to shatter Anglo-Saxon England in 1066 when King Harold Godwinsson, brother-in-law to Edward the Confessor and son of one of Cnut's most prominent earls (Keynes 1994), had to face in battle first King Harald Hardrada of Norway, who regarded himself as Cnut's heir, at Stamford Bridge, then Duke William of Normandy, Emma's nephew and one who had spent much time with his cousin Edward while the latter was in exile in Normandy (Keynes 1991), at Hastings. In effect Æthelred's marriage to Emma of Normandy marked the beginning of the end for Anglo-Saxon England.

After Cnut's death and a brief shared reign between two of Emma's sons, each the offspring of a different king, it was Edward, Æthelred's son, who gained sole control, following the sudden (and, to some, suspicious) death of Harthacnut in 1042. The twenty-four years of Edward's reign were marked by the king's piety, patience, and prudence, a period of relative stability before Anglo-Saxon England disappeared in the bruising confusion that the quiet and childless Confessor bequeathed to a kingdom that for most of his life he likely never thought he would control. The C-text of the *Anglo-Saxon Chronicle* for the year 1065 inserts a striking poem, again in traditional style, to mark the death of Edward the Confessor (O'Brien O'Keeffe 2001):

And Eadward kingc com to Westmynstre to þam middan wintre, and þæt mynster þar let halgian þe he sylf getimbrode Gode to lofe and Sancte Petre and eallum Godes halgum, and seo circhalgung wæs on Cildamæssedæig, and he forðferde on Twelftan æfen, and hyne man bebyrigde on Twelftan Dæig on þam ylcan mynstre swa hyt heræfter seigð.

> Her Eadward kingc,   Engla hlaford,
> sende soþfæste   sawle to Criste
> on godes wæra,   gast haligne.

He on worulda her   wunode þrage
on kyneþrymme,   cræftig ræda,   5
.XXIIII.,   freolic wealdend,
wintra gerimes,   weolan britnode,
and healfe tid,   hæleða wealdend,
weold wel geþungen   Walum and Scottum
and Bryttum eac,   byre Æðelredes,   10
Englum and Sexum,   oretmægcum,
swa ymbclyppað   cealde brymmas,
þæt eall Eadwarde,   æðelum kinge,
hyrdon holdlice   hagestealde menn.
Wæs a bliðemod   bealuleas kyng,   15
þeah he lange ær,   lande bereafod,
wunode wræclastum   wide geond eorðan,
syððan Cnut ofercom   kynn Æðelredes
and Dena weoldon   deore rice
Engla landes   .XXVIII.   20
wintra gerimes,   welan brytnodon.
Syððan forð becom   freolice in geatwum
kyningc kystum god,   clæne and milde,
Eadward se æðela   eðel bewerode,
land and leode,   oðþæt lungre becom   25
deað se bitera,   and swa deore genam
æþelne of eorðan;   englas feredon
soþfæste sawle   innan swegles leoht.
And se froda swa þeah   befæste þæt rice
heahþungenum menn,   Harolde sylfum,   30
æþelum eorle,   se in ealle tid
hyrde holdlice   hærran sinum
wordum and dædum,   wihte ne agælde
þæs þe þearf wæs   þæs þeodkyninges.

And King Edward came to Westminster towards mid-winter, and had consecrated there the minster which he himself had built in praise of God and Saint Peter and all God's saints; and the consecration of the church was on Holy Innocents' Day; and he passed away on the eve of Twelfth Night, and was buried on Twelfth Night in the same minster, as it says as follows:

In this year King Edward, lord of the English, sent his righteous soul to Christ, his holy spirit into God's keeping. He lived long here in the world in royal power, skilful in counsel, a noble ruler: for a tally of twenty-four and one half years he doled out wealth, ruler of men; Æthelred's son governed gracefully the Welsh and the Scots, the Britons too, the Angles and the Saxons, mighty champions, those the cold seas surround, so that all the young warriors loyally obeyed the noble king. He was ever a kindly and a guileless king, though for long times past deprived of his land he had travelled paths of exile widely throughout the world, once Canute overcame Æthelred's kin, and Danes ruled the dear kingdom of England for a tally of twenty-eight years, doled out wealth. Thereafter there came forth, splendid in array, a king fine in virtues, pure and mild, the noble Edward defended his homeland, country and people, until suddenly there came bitter death, and snatched that noble so dear from the earth; angels carried his righteous soul into the light of heaven. Nonetheless, the wise man entrusted the kingdom to a high-ranking man, Harold himself, the noble earl, who had always obeyed loyally his lord, and in no way held back what was the due of that great king.

The shadow of Æthelred, and the trauma of his later years, lies heavy over these verses. In detailing the peoples over whom Edward ruled, this 'son of Æthelred' (*byre Æðelredes*, line 10) is carefully positioned between 'the Welsh and the Irish and the Britons' ('Walum and Scottum and Bryttum', lines 9–10), on the one hand, and 'the Angles and the Saxons' on the other (line 11); the phrase 'mighty champions' (*oretmægcum*, line 11) could grammatically refer to all five of the peoples Edward ruled, but most easily applies only to the Anglo-Saxons themselves. It is notable that the word 'king', in various manifestations (*kingc*, line 1; *kinge*, line 13; *kyng*, line 15; *kyningc*, line 23; *þeodkyninges*, line 34), refers only to Edward, although Æthelred (lines 10 and 18), Cnut (line 18), and even the hapless Harold (line 30) are all named. Unlike his badly advised father, Edward is designated explicitly as 'skilful in advice' (*cræftig ræda*, line 5), and as if to make amends for the obvious if derogatory pun on Æthelred's name, the poet makes the etymological connection between the second element of Edward's name and the Old English verb *werian* ('to defend'), as well as between the adjective *æðel* ('noble') and the noun *eðel* ('homeland'), in a single line that described how 'the noble Edward defended his homeland' ('Eadward se æðela eðel bewerode', line 24). The nobility of Edward is a constant theme (it appears in lines 6, 14, 24 and 26), and the fact that of the other named characters in the poem only Harold is similarly described as 'the noble earl' ('æþelum eorle', line 31) connects both of them to the 'homeland' (*eðel*, line 24) of Anglo-Saxon England far more closely than either Æthelred or Cnut. That Edward was half-Norman and Harold half-Danish seems to have mattered little to this Anglo-Saxon poet, who finds time to praise them both, at a time when Anglo-Saxon England itself would be dead, politically at least, before a year was out.

In our modern age, when even the term 'Anglo-Saxon' can summon up images of WASP-y, insular, bigoted, aggressive and ignorant types of racist or white supremacist dogma, it is as well to bear in mind that the Anglo-Saxons (as their name suggests, a designation initially bestowed upon them by Continental authors keen to mark a sharp break with their Insular brethren) were themselves a mongrel race of immigrants who assimilated more or less happily, but at least easily, both with those they conquered and with those (notably the Norsemen and the related Normans) who later conquered them. Many kindreds and cultures contributed to the multilingual mixture that Anglo-Saxon England always was, from the earliest periods we can trace; and it is that ability of the Anglo-Saxons to adopt and adapt to other cultures that has ensured that, even now, there is something both strange and familiar about the legacy that they left.

References and Further Reading

Anlezark, D. (2002). Sceaf, Japheth and the origins of the Anglo-Saxons. *Anglo-Saxon England*, 31, 13–46.

Baker, P. S. (ed.) (2000). *The Anglo-Saxon Chronicle: A Collaborative Edition. Vol. 8: MS. F*. Cambridge: D. S. Brewer.

Bately, J. (ed.) (1986). *The Anglo-Saxon Chronicle: A Collaborative Edition. Vol. 3: MS. A*. Cambridge: D. S. Brewer.

Bieler, L. (ed.) (1952). *Libri epistolarum Sancti Patricii Episcopi*. Dublin: Stationery Office.

Brooks, N. P. (1979). England in the ninth century: the crucible of defeat. *Transactions of the Royal Historical Society*, 5th ser. 29, 1–20.

Bullough, D. A. (2004). *Alcuin: Achievement and Reputation*. Leiden: Brill.

Campbell, A. (ed.) (1998). *Encomium Emmae Reginae*. Introduction by S. Keynes. Camden Classic Reprints 4. Cambridge: Cambridge University Press.

Colgrave, B. and R. A. B. Mynors (eds) (1969). *Bede's Ecclesiastical History of the English People*, Oxford Medieval Texts. Rev. edn. Oxford: Clarendon Press.

Collingwood, R. G. and J. N. L. Myres (1963). *Roman Britain and the English Settlements*. 2nd edn. Oxford: Clarendon Press.

Dumville, D. N. (1976). The Anglian collection of royal genealogies and regnal lists. *Anglo-Saxon England*, 5, 23–50.

Dumville, D. N. (1986). The West Saxon genealogical regnal list: manuscripts and texts. *Anglia*, 104, 1–32.

Dumville, D. N. (ed.) (1993). *Saint Patrick, A.D. 493–1993*. Woodbridge: Boydell.

Frankis, P. J. (1973). The thematic significance of *enta geweorc* and related imagery in *The Wanderer*. *Anglo-Saxon England*, 2, 253–69.

Godden, M. R. (2007). Did King Alfred write anything? *Medium Ævum*, 76, 1–23.

Griffith, M. S. (1993). Convention and originality in the Old English 'Beasts of Battle' typescene. *Anglo-Saxon England*, 22, 179–99.

Higham, N. J. (1994). *The English Conquest: Gildas and Britain in the Fifth Century*. Manchester: Manchester University Press.

Howlett, D. R. (ed.) (1994). *Liber epistolarum Sancti Patricii episcopi = The Book of Letters of Saint Patrick the Bishop*. Dublin: Four Courts Press.

Keynes, S. (1978). The declining reputation of King Æthelred the Unready. In D. Hill (ed.). *Ethelred the Unready: Papers from the Millenary Conference*. British Archaeological Reports, British series 59 (pp. 227–53). Oxford: British Archaeological Reports.

Keynes, S. (1985). King Athelstan's books. In M. Lapidge and H. Gneuss (eds). *Learning and Literature in Anglo-Saxon England: Studies Presented to Peter Clemoes on the Occasion of His Sixty-Fifth Birthday* (pp. 143–201). Cambridge: Cambridge University Press.

Keynes, S. (1986). A tale of two kings: Alfred the Great and Æthelred the Unready. *Transactions of the Royal Historical Society*, 5th ser. 36, 195–217.

Keynes, S. (1991). The Æthelings in Normandy. *Anglo-Norman Studies*, 13, 173–205.

Keynes, S. (1994). Cnut's Earls. In A. R. Rumble (ed.). *The Reign of Cnut: King of England, Denmark and Norway* (pp. 43–88). Leicester: Leicester University Press.

Keynes, S. (1995). England, 700–900. In R. McKitterick (ed.). *The New Cambridge Medieval History, II: c. 700–c. 900* (pp. 18–42). Cambridge: Cambridge University Press.

Keynes, S. (1996). On the Authenticity of Asser's *Life of King Alfred*. *Journal of English History*, 47, 529–51.

Keynes, S. (1997). The Vikings in England, c. 790–1016. In P. Sawyer (ed.). *The Oxford Illustrated History of the Vikings* (pp. 48–82). Oxford: Oxford University Press.

Keynes, S. (2003). The power of the written word: Alfredian England 871–899. In T. Reuter (ed.). *Alfred the Great: Papers from the Eleventh-Centenary Conferences* (pp. 175–97). Studies in Early Medieval Britain. Aldershot: Ashgate.

Keynes, S. and M. Lapidge (eds) (1983). *Alfred the Great: Asser's 'Life of King Alfred' and Other Contemporary Sources*. Harmondsworth: Penguin.

Lapidge, M. (1986). The school of Theodore and Hadrian. *Anglo-Saxon England*, 15, 45–72.

Lapidge, M. (ed.) (1995). *Archbishop Theodore: Commemorative Studies on his Life and Influence*. Cambridge: Cambridge University Press.

Lapidge, M. (2007). The career of Aldhelm. *Anglo-Saxon England*, 36, 15–69.

Lapidge, M. and D. N. Dumville (eds) (1984). *Gildas: New Approaches*. Woodbridge: Boydell.

Lapidge, M. and R. Sharpe (1985). *A Bibliography of Celtic–Latin Literature, 400–1200.* Dublin: Royal Irish Academy.

Lapidge, M., J. Blair, S. Keynes and D. Scragg (eds) (1999). *The Blackwell Encyclopedia of Anglo-Saxon England.* Oxford: Blackwell.

Moisl, H. (1981). Anglo-Saxon royal genealogies and Germanic oral tradition. *Journal of Medieval History*, 7, 215–48.

O'Brien O'Keeffe, K. (ed.) (2001). *The Anglo-Saxon Chronicle: A Collaborative Edition. Vol. 5: MS. C.* Cambridge: D. S. Brewer.

Orchard, A. (1992). Crying wolf: oral style and the *Sermones Lupi. Anglo-Saxon England*, 21, 239–64.

Orchard, A. (2000). Wish you were here: Alcuin's courtly verse and the boys back home. In S. Rees Jones, R. Marks and A. J. Minnis (eds). *Courts and Regions in Medieval Europe* (pp. 21–43). Woodbridge: York Medieval Press.

Orchard, A. (2001a). The literary background to the *Encomium Emmae Reginae. Journal of Medieval Latin*, 11, 157–84.

Orchard, A. (2001b). Old sources, new resources: finding the right formula for Boniface. *Anglo-Saxon England*, 30, 15–38.

Orchard, A. (2003a). Latin and the vernacular languages: the creation of a bilingual textual culture. In T. Charles Edwards (ed.). *After Rome: The Short Oxford History of the British Isles*, vol. 1 (pp. 191–219). Oxford: Oxford University Press.

Orchard, A. (2003b). On editing Wulfstan. In Elaine Treharne and Susan Rosser (eds) *Early Medieval Texts and Interpretations: Studies Presented to Donald G. Scragg* (pp. 311–40). Tempe, AZ: MRTS.

Orchard, A. (2004). Re-editing Wulfstan: Where's the point? In Matthew Townend (ed.). *Wulfstan, Archbishop of York: Proceedings of the Second Alcuin*

Conference (pp. 63–91). Studies in the Early Middle Ages. Turnhout: Brepols.

Orchard, A. (2007). Wulfstan as reader, writer, and re-writer. In Aaron J. Kleist (ed.). *Precedent, Practice, and Appropriation: the Old English Homily* (pp. 313–43). Studies in the Early Middle Ages 17. Turnhout: Brepols.

Rees, B. R. (1988). *Pelagius, a Reluctant Heretic.* Woodbridge: Boydell.

Scragg, D. G. (ed.) (1981). *The Battle of Maldon.* Manchester: Manchester University Press.

Sims-Williams, P. (1983). The settlement of England in Bede and the *Chronicle. Anglo-Saxon England*, 12, 1–41.

Sisam, K. (1953). Anglo-Saxon royal genealogies. *Publications of the British Academy*, 39, 287–348.

Stanley, E. G. (1988). King Alfred's prefaces. *Review of English Studies*, n.s. 39, 349–64.

Stenton, F. M. (1971). *Anglo-Saxon England*, 3rd edn. Oxford: Oxford University Press.

Swanton, M. (1996). *The Anglo-Saxon Chronicle.* London: Orion.

Thornbury, E. V. (2000). *Eald enta geweorc* and the relics of empire: revisiting the dragon's lair in *Beowulf. Quaestio*, 1, 82–92.

Todd, M. (1999). *Roman Britain.* 3rd edn. Oxford: Blackwell.

Whitelock, D. (1974). *The Beginnings of English Society.* Rev. edn. Harmondsworth: Penguin.

Wilcox, J. (2000). The St. Brice's Day Massacre and Archbishop Wulfstan. In D. Wolfthal (ed.). *Peace and Negotiation: Strategies for Coexistence in the Middle Ages and the Renaissance* (pp. 79–91). Arizona Studies in the Middle Ages and the Renaissance 4. Turnhout: Brepols.

Winterbottom, M. (ed.) (1978). *The Ruin of Britain: and Other Works.* London: Phillimore.

2

The Old English Language and the Alliterative Tradition

Richard Dance

In most versions of the *Anglo-Saxon Chronicle*, the entry for the year 937 consists of a poem celebrating the victory of Æthelstan and Edmund over a force of Norsemen and Scots. It concludes:

> Letan him behindan   hræw bryttian   60
> saluwigpadan,   þone sweartan hræfn,
> hyrnednebban,   and þane hasewanpadan,
> earn æftan hwit,   æses brucan,
> grædigne guðhafoc   and þæt græge deor,
> wulf on wealde.   Ne wearð wæl mare   65
> on þis eiglande   æfre gieta
> folces gefylled   beforan þissum
> sweordes ecgum,   þæs þe us secgað bec,
> ealde uðwitan,   siþþan eastan hider
> Engle and Seaxe   up becoman,   70
> ofer brad brimu   Brytene sohtan,
> wlance wigsmiþas,   Wealas ofercoman,
> eorlas arhwate,   eard begeatan.
> (*The Battle of Brunanburh* [MS A] 60–73)

They left behind them sharing out the corpses the dark-feathered, black raven, horny-beaked, and the dun-feathered eagle with its white tail enjoying the carrion, the greedy war-hawk, and the grey beast, the wolf of the woods. There has never been greater slaughter in this island before this, of people cut down by the edges of the sword, according to what books tell us, old scholars, since the Angles and Saxons came here from the east, sought Britain over the broad seas, bold war-smiths, overcame the Welsh and, glory-keen warriors, won the land.

This sneeringly jubilant invocation of the coming of the Anglo-Saxon invaders to Britain is presented in the alliterative verse tradition these first English-speaking people brought with them, the form and style of which flourish throughout the Old English period.

Unlike some more recent types of versification, Old English metre is not primarily 'syllable-counting': lines in the above excerpt contain as few as eight syllables (63) and as many as twelve (62). Neither is the rhythm 'fixed', constructed from a series of syllables that regularly alternate with and without emphasis, such as the iambic pentameter of most of Chaucer's *The Canterbury Tales*. The rhythm of a typical pair of lines from *The Battle of Brunanburh* (71–2) may instead be conceived as follows:

$$x\ x\quad /\quad /\ x\quad /\quad x\ x\ /\quad x$$
ofer brad brimu   Brytene sohtan,

$$/\quad x\ /\quad \backslash\ x\quad /\quad x\ x\ x\quad /\quad x$$
wlance wigsmiþas,   Wealas ofercoman,

(Syllables bearing full stress are marked with '/', and those without stress with 'x'; '\' indicates 'secondary stress' (see below).) The crucial syllables are those with full stress ('/'): there are normally four of these per line and, rather than rhyme linking the *ends* of lines, in the Old English tradition it is the first three of these stressed syllables that create the aural connection, by alliteration, *within* each long line (the *b*s and *w*s in bold above). Almost all surviving Old English verse (some 30,000 lines) was composed in a closely similar form of this alliterative metre. It is therefore important to understand the essential properties of the verse-form when one seeks to appreciate the characteristics of the language found in these poems, especially those aspects of usage peculiar to verse. In turn, the linguistic features of this earliest period of English, and its ancestors, can themselves shed light on the mechanisms of the alliterative poetic tradition.

Origins, Forms, Transmission

English belongs to the 'Germanic' branch of the Indo-European language family, closely related to German, Dutch, Frisian and the Scandinavian languages (Bammesberger 1992; Robinson 1992; Nielsen 1998: 19–57). The poetry of the Old English period (*c.* 450–1150) is, moreover, very much akin to the alliterative verse of the other early Germanic languages, including Old Saxon, Old High German and Old Norse, and in order to appreciate the earliest English versification it is helpful to press back as far as we can towards their common beginnings.

Written records of the Germanic languages in the period before the Anglo-Saxon migrations are scarce, and poetry is extremely rare. But the following line of alliterative verse was cut in runes onto a golden drinking horn *c.* 400 AD:

ek hlewagastiz holtijaz horna tawido

This may be translated 'I Hlewagastiz Holtijaz (meaning "of the forest" or "of (the place called) Holt") made the horn'. The horn itself was discovered at Gallehus in northern Schleswig, and hence belongs to the general area from which the Anglo-Saxon migrants set out for Britain (the North Sea coastal regions of what are now the Netherlands, Germany and Denmark), and to the time immediately before they did so (the fifth century). The language of the inscription can for practical purposes be taken to represent the ancestor both of the West Germanic languages (including English) and of Old Norse (Nielsen 1998: 52–5).

It shows several features diagnostic of the Germanic group as a whole. Particularly important are: the sound change known as 'Grimm's Law', which distinguishes Germanic words from their equivalents in all other Indo-European languages by shifting the pronunciation of the consonants they contain (compare, e.g., *horna*, 'horn' acc. sg., with Latin *cornum*; *gastiz*, 'stranger, guest' nom. sg., with Latin *hostis*, 'enemy'); and the 'weak' or 'dental' preterite, a way of forming the past tense of a verb using a *d* that is also unique to the Germanic family (*tawido*, '(I) made', cf. the most common class of past tenses in Modern English, e.g. *loved*, *showed*, etc.) (Bammesberger 1992: 35–40; Robinson 1992: 10–11; Lass 1994: 19–21, 164–6; Nielsen 1998: 46–9). But if the language of this inscription is typically Germanic, it still looks very unlike Old English. If we hypothesise an equivalent piece of writing in the familiar West Saxon of *c*. 900 – *'ic hleogiest hylte horn tawode' – we can immediately see a range of distinctively Old English sound changes which occurred after *c*. 400. Particularly affected are the vowels (the changes known as first fronting, palatal diphthongization and *i*-mutation ('umlaut') are all needed to transform -*gastiz* into -*giest*, for example), and there are markedly fewer unaccented syllables (-*gastiz* > -*giest*, *horna* > *horn*, etc.). (On the major developments in Old English phonology see, e.g., Hogg 1992: 100–22; Robinson 1992: 157–60; Lass 1994: 33–102; Nielsen 1998: 100–6; Mitchell and Robinson 2007: 20–4, 28–9, 38–40).

The steady loss of syllables especially from the ends of words is perhaps the most important effect of another key Germanic innovation: the fixing of word-stress ('accent') to the first syllable of every word's root. In other Indo-European languages, the accent could appear on virtually any syllable (and compare the more mobile accent in word-groups subsequently borrowed into English from Latin, such as *electric*, *electricity*, *electrocution*). In contrast, with the exception of unaccented prefixes (e.g. Old English *ge*-, and usually *a*-, *be*-, *for*-, etc.; Baker 2003: 20–1, Mitchell and Robinson 2007: 13), the main, most emphatic syllable of every Germanic word became the first one, and all subsequent syllables received much less prominence; historically, the result was that these tended to be weakened in pronunciation and eventually disappeared (Bammesberger 1992: 30; Lass 1994: 83–102). The Gallehus inscription shows a variety of Germanic early enough for this process of loss to be relatively little advanced; but nevertheless every word it contains would already have been pronounced with the emphasis firmly on its first syllable. The first syllable of each of the *principal* words would moreover have carried the main stress at the level of the sentence, and of the verse's metre:

$$x \quad / \quad x \backslash \quad x \quad / \quad x\,x \quad / \quad x \quad /\,x\,x$$
ek hlewagastiz holtijaz   horna tawido

The predictable placement of (strong) accent on the first syllable of a word's root, with a concomitant weakening of emphasis on the various other syllables, therefore goes some way towards accounting for the characteristic rhythms of a line of Germanic poetry. This focus on the beginning of words as their prosodic 'business end' is moreover of obvious relevance in understanding the foregrounding of alliteration in the Germanic tradition, rather than some other device like rhyme.

The distribution of the alliteration in the Gallehus inscription is characteristic of all early Germanic poetry. It is an essential rule that the third stressed syllable in each line should alliterate with either or (often, as here) both of the first two; but that the fourth stress should never participate. Any vowel (or diphthong) may alliterate with any other (hence *Brunanburh* 70: 'Engle and Seaxe up becoman'), but (classically at least) the clusters *sc*, *sp* and *st* count as single units and each may only alliterate upon itself (e.g. *Beowulf* 4: 'Oft Scyld Scefing sceaþena þreatum'). (See Baker 2003: 120–2; Mitchell and Robinson 2007: 162–3; and notice that alliteration (and other effects of sound) may be used in much more elaborate patterns for purposes of special ornamentation (Scragg 1991: 62, 67–9; Orchard 1995; Dance 2006).) Incidentally, while this fundamental alliterative emphasis on the first three stresses and the relative lack of attention paid to the fourth may seem rather arbitrary, it echoes the syntax of the Gallehus inscription. The element order of this text is grammatically Subject ('I, Hlewagastiz Holtijaz') followed by direct Object ('horna') followed by Verb ('tawode') (literally 'I, Hlewagastiz Holtijaz, the horn made'). This SOV order is of course no longer one that we would recognise as grammatical in Modern English, which uses SVO (the dominant order in main clauses also in Old English). But SOV appears to have been the natural, 'unmarked' order in early Germanic speech (as it was in Proto-Indo-European; Bammesberger 1992: 60–2; Robinson 1992: 164–7; Lass 1994: 217–24; Nielsen 1998: 128–31), and this original placing of the verb finally, to an extent separated from the noun-based constituents of the clause, may help account for the formalisation of the '3 + 1' pattern in Germanic verse; certainly, it is reflected in the continued 'demotion' of finite verbs in Old English poetry (see below).

These basic patterns of stress and alliteration developed particular forms and rules in the metrical systems of the individual Germanic languages, including Old English, whose poetry is first recorded at the beginning of the eighth century. It is worth pointing out that no contemporary manuals of Old English versification are known to us (as they are for Latin poetry of the same period, or later Icelandic verse). Its principles therefore have to be deduced from the texts that survive, and there is no guarantee that Old English poets would have systematised them in precisely this way. The practice of setting the poetry out on the page in metrically defined units (long lines each divided into two half-lines, or *a*- and *b*-verses) is, moreover, a modern convention; it has no counterpart in manuscript copies of these texts, all of which

are written out continuously, like prose. But let us glance briefly at the most fundamental principles normally understood for Old English 'scansion', i.e. the conventions
for where the main stressed syllables (and the accompanying unstressed ones) may
be positioned in relation to one another in each half-line. Though at first their distribution might appear unruly, there seems to have been a finite number of acceptable
rhythmical 'types'.

The most basic depends upon the 'lift–dip' pattern, i.e. a stressed syllable followed
by one or more unstressed ones. As we have seen, this is the basic word-accent pattern
of the Germanic languages, implying that the scansion of verse was fundamentally
a stylised version of the rhythms of speech (and notice that metrical stress always
coincides with syllables that would be accented in normal spoken usage: emphasis
could not be moved about at will in order to fit the metre). As many as 50 per cent
of all the half-lines in the surviving Old English poetic corpus are constituted of a
controlled version of this essential pattern, i.e. a double 'lift–dip', with a variable
number of unstressed syllables allowable in the first dip. At its most compact, this
'basic' rhythmic structure affords half-lines like

$$/ \quad x \quad / \quad x$$
lað ond longsum   (*Beowulf* 134a)

with which compare more 'stretched' (but still perfectly acceptable) variants
such as

$$/ \quad x \quad x \quad x \quad x \quad / \quad x$$
þegnas sindon geþwære   (*Beowulf* 1230a),

and similar principles apply to the other sorts of half-line to be considered below (all
my examples in this section are taken from *Beowulf*; see Bliss 1962: 30–1).

Most theories of Old English metre categorise the allowable half-line rhythms
according to a finite series of variations upon this basic pattern, known as Type A
(Bliss 1962; Scragg 1991: 58–60; Godden 1992: 492–3; Baker 2003: 122–8; Mitchell
and Robinson 2007: 163–7; though see Bredehoft 2005 for a recent re-envisioning
of the principles). Four further essential patterns are usually recognised:

Type B   which transposes the 'lift–dip' sequences into 'dip–lift', at its simplest giving,
e.g.
$$x \quad / \quad x \quad /$$
ne leof ne lað   (*Beowulf* 511a);

Type C   in which the first 'lift–dip' of Type A is transposed, leading to a 'clashing'
pattern of stress, as e.g.
$$x \quad / \quad / \quad x$$
be sæm tweonum   (*Beowulf* 858b);

Type D   which moves both main stresses to the beginning, e.g.

> / / x \
> har hilderinc   (*Beowulf* 1307a);

Type E   which has a main stress at the beginning and end, e.g.

> / \ x /
> sæbat gesæt   (*Beowulf* 633a).

Notice that the more complex Types D and E have come to require a syllable with 'secondary stress' ('\'), that reduced emphasis which falls most obviously on the second elements of compounds (the stress pattern of OE *sæbat*, 'sea-boat', is analogous to Modern English compounds like *Batman* (/ \) as opposed to *footman* (/ x)). I have skated over a great many complexities in this brief description (and have left out the extra-long, 'hypermetric' verses that sometimes appear in Old English; Scragg 1991: 69–70; Baker 2003: 127–8; Mitchell and Robinson 2007: 166–7). But the practical result is that, especially when all the variants of these basic types are brought in (permitting further unstressed syllables in set positions), a significant (though by no means unlimited) fund of these stylised rhythms was available to the poet (on their combination see, e.g., Scragg 1991: 60–3).

These metrical fundamentals appear to have been highly conventional, and valued by poets throughout the Anglo-Saxon period: clearly early pieces such as *Cædmon's Hymn* (first witnessed in early eighth-century manuscripts) are essentially little different from later poems like *The Battle of Maldon* (not earlier than 991). The undoubted chronological range across which Old English poetry was being composed is nonetheless obscured by the idiosyncrasies of the manuscript record: like most Old English texts, that is, the vast bulk of the poetry is found only in relatively late copies, and in spellings belonging to the South-Western dialect we call 'West Saxon' (the type of Old English presented by student textbooks). West Saxon achieved its status as the pre-eminent dialectal form of written Old English with the late ninth-century literary programme of King Alfred; it enjoyed particular prominence in the tenth and eleventh centuries, and was used in monastic centres well outside Wessex itself, including Canterbury, Worcester and York (Kastovsky 1992: 346–9; Irvine 2006: 49–52). This 'late West Saxon' bias is perhaps especially clear for poetry, the majority of which survives in just four principal manuscripts from around the end of the tenth century. But copies of Old English texts, including a small amount of verse, do survive in other dialects and from other periods. The remaining varieties usually distinguished on geographical grounds are Kentish (or perhaps more accurately 'South-Eastern') and Anglian, the latter sub-divided into Mercian (from the Midlands; all that survives in writing can be better classified as West Mercian) and Northumbrian (our material comes mainly from the North of England, but also some from lowland Scotland, e.g. the Ruthwell Cross inscription) (Kastovsky 1992: 338–51; Nielsen 1998: 75–83, 89–99; Irvine 2006).

For examples of the ways in which Old English might differ across time (diachronically) and across space (dialectally or diatopically), compare the following two versions of the same riddle, ultimately a rendering of a Latin enigma by Aldhelm (the answer is 'Mailcoat'). The first version ('The Leiden Riddle') is recorded in what is probably an eighth-century variety of Northumbrian, preserved in a manuscript copied later on the continent (Leiden, Bibliotheek der Rijksuniversiteit, Vossius Lat. 106); the second, usually known as 'Riddle 35', is in late West Saxon in the Exeter Book (Exeter Cathedral, Dean and Chapter MS 3501), a miscellany produced in the South-West of England in the second half of the tenth century. (Where the two versions differ, I have translated the Exeter text within square brackets below.)

Mec se ueta uong,   uundrum freorig,
ob his innaðae aerest cæn[d]æ.
Ni uaat ic mec biuorthæ uullan fliusum,
herum ðerh hehcraeft, hygiðonc[um min].
Uundnae me ni biað ueflæ, ni ic uarp hafæ,   5
ni ðerih ðreatun giðraec ðret me hlimmith,
ne me hrutendu hrisil scelfath,
ni mec ouana aam sceal cnyssa.
Uyrmas mec ni auefun uyrdi craeftum,
ða ði geolu godueb geatum fraetuath.   10
Uil mec huethrae suae ðeh uidæ ofaer eorðu
hatan mith heliðum hyhtlic giuæde;
ni anoegun ic me aerigfaerae egsan brogum,
ðeh ði n[ume]n siæ niudlicae ob cocrum.
(*The Leiden Riddle*)

Mec se wæta wong,   wundrum freorig,
of his innaþe ærist cende.
Ne wat ic mec beworhtne wulle flysum,
hærum þurh heahcræft, hygeþoncum min.
Wundene me ne beoð wefle, ne ic wearp hafu,   5
ne þurh þreata geþræcu þræd me ne hlimmeð,
ne æt me hrutende hrisil scriþeð,
ne mec ohwonan sceal amas cnyssan.
Wyrmas mec ne awæfan wyrda cræftum,
þa þe geolo godwebb geatwum frætwað.   10
Wile mec mon hwæþre seþeah wide ofer eorþan
hatan for hæleþum hyhtlic gewæde.
Saga soðcwidum, searoþoncum gleaw,
wordum wisfæst, hwæt þis gewædu sy.
(*Exeter Riddle 35*)

The wet ground, incredibly cold, first produced me from its innards. I do not know myself in my mind's considerations to be made with wool from fleeces, from hair through great skill. There are no woofs woven in me, nor do I have warps, nor does thread resound in me through the thrusting[s] of pressers, nor do whizzing shuttles shake in me [nor does whizzing shuttle glide in me], nor must the sley knock me anywhere. Worms did not weave me with the skills of the fates, those which adorn the costly yellow cloth with decorations. But nevertheless, widely across the earth, I am wont to be called desirable clothing amongst heroes. Nor do I dread terror from the peril of a flight of arrows, though it might be taken eagerly from the quivers. [Person clever in your ideas, wise in your words, say in truthful utterance what this clothing might be.]

The differences between these two copies are ample testament to the distances in time and space that separate them. Several are relatively superficial, representing different conventions for the spelling of what was in fact the same sound: e.g. Leiden's typically early <u>, <th> and <b>, frequently appearing for Exeter <w> (the Anglo-Saxon letter 'wynn'), <þ> and <f>. Reflecting a distinct pronunciation are the Leiden forms *ueta* (1), *herum* (4) and *auefun* (9), whose <e> versus Exeter <æ> represents one of the most important dialect divisions between West Saxon and Anglian; similarly significant are the vowels in, e.g., Leiden *heh* (4) rather than *heah*, *uarp* (5) as opposed to *wearp*, *biað* (5) next to *beoð*, and so on. In general, there is a far greater range of unaccented vowels in Leiden, another feature of an early date (before these merged; compare, e.g., *innaðae* (2) with *innaðe*, *hlimmith* (6) with *hlimmeð*); and some important differences in inflexional endings (viz. Leiden's early preterite plural *auefun* (9), Exeter's late *awæfan*).

There are very few similar instances in which an early and a late copy of the same Old English poem are available for comparison (the most important being *Cædmon's Hymn* and *The Dream of the Rood*; see Irvine 2006: 37–40, 42–3). The tenuous, chancy survival of the Leiden Riddle (squashed in at the end of a manuscript of Latin texts copied outside England) should nevertheless caution us against the presumption that there are no other poems which did not have similarly long careers, even if they only come down in single, late copies. The detection of evidence for this is however a complex and often controversial business, and there are several fundamental problems. The first lurks in the nature of the transmission of Old English poetry. Comparison of those few texts extant in multiple versions reveals how liable they were to being altered by successive copyists, leading to suggestions that some scribes took an active, conscious role in effectively 'reperforming' poems on the page (see notably O'Brien O'Keeffe 1990; Orchard 1997: 117–19; and for a contrary view Orton 2000: 200–8). In the case of the Leiden Riddle this is especially obvious at the end (the last two lines are entirely different in the Exeter version), but there are myriad other minor changes to the phrasing, including the substitution of words (*scriþeð* for *scelfath* (7)) and the insertion of new ones (lines 6 and 11), and substantial changes to the syntax (lines 6, 7 and 8). Given this propensity for alteration, some scholars doubt that linguistic features from an earlier version could survive sufficiently distinctly into a later copy to afford proof of a long transmission, which would then inevitably cover its own tracks. As a second and related problem, there are certain linguistic forms (archaic, dialectally marked, or both) that seem to have been regarded as acceptable in the copying of verse, such that their appearance in a poem need not indicate that it was originally produced in the dialect to which said forms properly belong; hence in texts known to be late, Southern compositions like *The Battle of Maldon*, we find 'poetic' spellings such as *baldlice* (*Maldon* 311, cp. WS *beald-*) and *meodo* (*Maldon* 212, cp. WS *medu*). As a result of these difficulties, scholars have sometimes been very wary of attempting to date the original composition of the majority of poems. But dating and localising on the grounds of linguistic evidence (within fairly broad parameters) can nonetheless be defended. Even though there are certain spellings that recur across the Old English poetic corpus, their usage varies significantly from text to text. And a sizeable number of spellings, inflexional forms and even vocabulary do *not* seem to have had a general 'poetic' currency, such that their appearance in a given text can still provide evidence of that piece's transmission from an earlier period and a different dialect; in Riddle 35, for instance, *ærist* (2) and *hafu* (5) point towards a much earlier, Anglian archetype. Certain aspects of metre, especially where this is faulty, can give even stronger indications that a given poem was composed with phonological and inflexional forms other than those with which it is now recorded. On the basis of such deductions, the traditional philological conclusion that some important poems (most famously *Beowulf*, and others including *Genesis A* and *Daniel*) were composed relatively early, and in a non-West Saxon dialect, continues to merit serious attention (on these issues see Godden 1992: 496–8; Irvine 2006: 52–4; and notably Fulk 1992, 2003).

Diction and Expression

I have concentrated so far on the formal characteristics of Old English verse, including its essential prosody and related systems. But as with any variety of language, the production of the earliest English poetry consisted of much more than a mere competence in these structures; to understand its composition, we need to be able to appreciate how poets created meaning *within* the frameworks described above – their 'performance' at the level of stylistic expression. There is not space here to offer anything approaching a thorough account of the stylistic features of Old English verse, and by summarising some of the most important (and recurrent) characteristics of the surviving poems' vocabulary and syntax I do not mean to imply their uniformity; there is a great deal of variety in diction, both between and within poems, something that goes to reinforce the conscious manipulation of traditional devices for effect (see, e.g., Godden 1992: 508–12).

As a starting point, consider the following passage from *The Wanderer*:

> Forðon domgeorne   dreorigne oft
> in hyra breostcofan   bindað fæste;
> swa ic modsefan   minne sceolde,

oft earmcearig,   eðle bidæled,   20
freomægum feor   feterum sælan,
siþþan geara iu   goldwine minne
hrusan heolstre biwrah,   ond ic hean þonan
wod wintercearig   ofer waþema gebind,
sohte seledreorig   sinces bryttan,   25
hwær ic feor oþþe neah   findan meahte
þone þe in meoduhealle   mine wisse,
oþþe mec freondleasne   frefran wolde,
wenian mid wynnum.
(*The Wanderer*, 17–29a)

Therefore those keen on glory often bind their sorrowful mind firmly in their heart (*lit.* breast-chamber); thus I, often wretched and troubled, deprived of my homeland, far from noble kinsmen, have had to tie my spirit in fetters, since very long ago I concealed my lord (*lit.* gold-friend) in the darkness of the earth, and I went from there wretched, winter-troubled over the binding of the waves, sorrowful for lack of a hall (I) sought a distributor of treasure (i.e. a lord), (for) where I could find far or near that one in the mead-hall who might know of my own, or would wish to comfort me, the friendless one, entertain me with joys.

Beginning at the level of vocabulary (or 'lexis'), one of the most notable aspects is the focus on nouns and adjectives. These appear in one of the first three metrically stressed positions of a line (and alliterate) twenty times (*domgeorne*, 'those keen on glory'; *dreorigne*, 'sorrowful (mind)'; *breostcofan*, 'heart', etc.), and only twice occupy the less important fourth stress (*gebind*, 'binding' (24) and the possessive *minne*, 'my' (22)). This reflects the place of nouns and adjectives at the top of a 'hierarchy' of grammatical elements in Old English verse (Godden 1992: 493–4; Lester 1996: 47–8). Other parts of speech are less prominent. At the bottom of the pile are the 'grammatical' words, like prepositions, conjunctions and articles; it is in the interests of the relatively tight rhythm of Old English poetry that fairly few of these should appear in the first place, and they are generally much sparser than in prose. There are only three basic prepositions in the above passage (*in* twice, *ofer* once), and the 'idea' of a preposition is more likely to be expressed by noun inflexions alone, as in *eðle* [dat.] *bidæled* (20), 'deprived of a homeland'. Similarly, notice that articles need to be inferred, hence *domgeorne* and *dreorigne* (17) rather than *þa domgeorne*, *þone dreorigne*, '(the) glory-eager (ones)', '(the) sorrowful (thing, i.e. mind)' (Godden 1992: 504–6; and on such nominalised adjectives, another poetic economy, see Lester 1996: 49). These 'small' words, when they do occur, are almost always strictly positioned, without stress. On the rare occasions when they are 'promoted', this is demonstrably done for a very specific effect: the most famous example is *Beowulf* 196b–7, 'mægenes strengest / on þæm dæge þysses lifes', where the stressing of the demonstratives emphasises the temporally bounded nature of the hero's abilities ('strongest in power on *that* day of *this* life') (Robinson 1985: 54; Lester 1996: 47–8).

Other parts of speech are sometimes fully prominent, sometimes not. Adverbs and conjunctions are quite often stressed, but only sometimes alliterate (here, e.g., *fæste*

(18), but *oft* (20)), and the same is true of non-finite forms of the verb (infinitives and participles; e.g. *bidæled* (20), but *findan* (26)). Perhaps surprising is the comparative lack of weight placed on finite verbs, which are often to be found in subordinate positions (as we noted of the Gallehus inscription above, though this is less the case in Old English prose and may be assumed to reflect less closely the emphases of contemporary speech; Godden 1992: 493–4; Lester 1996: 48–9). In this passage, finite verbs appear in the fourth position without alliteration four times (the relatively 'colourless' *sceolde* ('had to'; 19), *meahte* ('could'; 26), *wisse* ('might know'; 27) and *wolde* ('would wish to'; 28)); they are promoted to a principal stress only three times, and in two cases this may be for a special purpose, the patterned focus on motion in the successive lines beginning with *wod* ('went'; 24) and *sohte* ('sought'; 25).

This onus placed on nouns and adjectives has a series of important effects, and the lexicon of verse needs to be particularly full in this respect (Godden 1992: 498–502; Kastovsky 1992: 352–5; Lester 1996: 50–63; Baker 2003: 130–3). This is of course especially true for those 'heroic' concepts central to the traditional subject matter of Old English poetry, and one of the first things that students notice when translating a poem like *The Battle of Maldon* is the sheer number of different words for man/ warrior, sword, shield, spear, hall, battle and the like. Words for 'spear' in *Maldon*, for instance, include not only the standard prosaic *spere*, but also *gar* (a fairly straight-forward synonym, but found mainly in poetry), and others derived from references to aspects of spears that are distinctively poetic in these special usages: hence *ord*, literally 'point', and *æsc*, 'ash(-wood)', applied by synechdoche/metonymy to the whole object, and used in context as synonyms simply denoting 'spear'. A good example of this 'bleaching' of specific meaning is *franca*, literally '(spear) of Frankish make/style', but whose manufacture has less to do with its mention at *Maldon* 77 and 140 than does the *f*-alliteration of these lines. Very similar things are true of the large number of words for 'man/warrior' in Old English poetry: beside the prosaic *mann*, *wer* or the more specific *cempa* ('soldier'), there is a wide range of (near-)synonyms confined to verse, such as *beorn*, *freca*, *guma*, *hæle(ð)*, *rinc*, *scealc*, *secg*, *wiga*, and the plural-only *firas*, *niþðas*, *ylde* (see, e.g., Baker 2003: 131; Godden 1992: 498–9). Our passage from *The Wanderer* contains several examples from amongst the wide variety of other words regarded as 'poetic' and not occurring in prose, e.g. *hruse* (23), 'earth', *sinc* (25), 'treasure', *brytta* (25), 'distributor' and the rarer *waþm*, 'wave' (24), and others that are recorded in prose but are much more frequent in verse (e.g. *eðel* (20), 'homeland'). Their usefulness in fitting the needs of alliteration is clearly an important motivator in the development of this stock; but their sheer range (and the frequent use of many in non-alliterating positions; Godden 1992: 494, 502) hints also at the delight taken for its own sake in an expressive, colourful diction perceived as proper to verse.

Similar comments may be made regarding compounds, one of the most characteristic features of Old English poetic diction (Robinson 1985: 14–18; Scragg 1991: 65–6; Godden 1992: 499–501; Lester 1996: 51–61; Baker 2003: 131–3). There is nothing inherently 'poetic' about compounding as a process: it was a standard tool of Old English word formation, used to create new items of vocabulary (especially nouns and adjectives), most often in order to specify a type or context for a thing (Kastovsky 1992: 362–76; Lass 1994: 194–8). The first element of a compound typically defines the second in some way, e.g. *sciprap*, 'ship-rope, the sort of rope used on a ship' or *brægdrenc*, 'cough-drink, the sort of drink used to combat a cough, i.e. cough-medicine'; the meaning of such formations is usually transparent, though this does not prevent them being adroitly expressive, even in prose (e.g. *bearhtmhwil*, '(period of) the twinkling of an eye'). For obvious reasons, such creations are especially valuable to the poet: the relatively free addition of a prefixed element allows the construction of a new word alliterating on the sound of one's choice, and affords a large number of total possible permutations. Hence *æscwiga* ('ash (spear)-warrior'), *byrnwiga* ('mailcoat-warrior'), *scyldwiga*, *randwiga*, *lindwiga* (all 'shield-warrior'), *guðwiga* ('battle-warrior') and even *beornwiga* ('warrior-warrior') are all effective synonyms for plain *wiga*, and indeed any other 'man/warrior' word.

There are undeniable instances of the purely utilitarian 'bleaching' of the first elements of compounds, the resultant words entirely synonymous: famously, the Danes in *Beowulf* are at turns referred to as *Norð-Dene*, *Suð-Dene*, *East-Dene* and *West-Dene* with no rationale other than the needs of the alliteration. As is true for non-compound ('simplex') words, however, compounds developed a specific, poetic tradition different from that of prose. They are central to alliterative verse in all the Germanic languages; but there are more, and more varied, instances in Old English verse than anywhere else, indicating the extent to which English poets harnessed their possibilities. Their expressive potential often takes us far beyond the simply or cynically 'mechanical'. Of the nine compounds in our *Wanderer* passage, most occur elsewhere, but only in verse. *Meoduhealle* (27) and *goldwine* (22) are typical in several respects, recorded respectively six and nine further times in the corpus. They are relatively straightforward constructions, constituted of common enough nouns, their first elements in some sense describing their second. But in these cases, of course, the circumstances alluded to by these adjuncts (warriors pledging loyalty to their lord over *mead*, a bond cemented by the giving of *gold*) carry an enormous cultural weight, representing the symbolic cornerstone of heroic social relationships. It is this context that lends these apparently spare combinations of elements their poetic impact (to an important extent their 'meaning'), and indeed that makes sense of the unexpressed relationship between the conjoined words, something that would otherwise not necessarily be easy with a term such as *goldwine* ('gold' plus 'friend', traditionally signifying 'lord').

The 'total' meaning to be ascribed to the elements of a compound when in combination often requires some thought, and this can be still more apparent when the resultant creations are not recurrent and familiar. Note, for instance, *seledreorig* (*Wanderer* 25), certainly not just a synonym of simplex *dreorig* (17), but quite a specific sort of sorrow; its first part *sele*, 'hall', is best interpreted not as the location of the sadness but as the 'object' of sorrowful desire, and the whole therefore as analogous to Modern English *home-sick*. It is recorded only here, and so may have been coined as especially appropriate to the wanderer's anxieties. Similarly complex, and perhaps deliberately polyvalent, is the other unique compound in this passage, *wintercearig* (24): unlike interpretations of the more simply additive *earmcearig* ('wretched and troubled', 20), whose second element it recalls, reactions to *wintercearig* may waver between the superficially satisfying 'troubled because it's winter, wintry-sad' and the speaker describing himself (in an appropriately elemental similitude) as 'winter-sad, troubled like winter itself'. Looking further afield, a comparable, and particularly arch, imaginative challenge is sprung by the *Beowulf*-poet with the words 'Com on wanre niht / scriðan sceadugenga' ('The shadow-goer came creeping in the dark night', *Beowulf* 702b–3a): is Grendel a 'shadow-goer' simply by virtue of going about in, with or through the shadows? or is the relationship between the compound's elements more intimate to his characterization, i.e. 'a goer who *is* a shadow'? The latter is at any rate an interpretation fostered by the collocation with the verb *scriðan*, often used elsewhere in Old English verse of the movement of light or dark, and of literal shadow almost immediately prior to this in *Beowulf* (650).

Some compounds involve a metaphor (or metonymy), and hence a special sort of play with imagery. Take for example *beadoleoma*, literally 'battle-light', whose second element needs to understood as a type of flashing of light obliquely associated with its first part, battle, to arrive at the 'solution', and the actual denotation, 'sword'. This species of 'mini-riddle' is known as a 'kenning' (from a term used by medieval Icelandic poets for the often much more complex counterparts of the device in skaldic verse). Kennings make up a relatively small sub-set of Old English poetic expressions, but there are several recurrent examples, such as *hronrad* ('whale-road, i.e. sea'), *sæmearh*, *merehengest* (both 'sea-horse, i.e. ship') and *wordhord* ('word-hoard, i.e. vocabulary, language'). Phrases consisting of two words, essentially very similarly structured to compounds proper, can also be the vehicle for these picturesque constructs: e.g. *hwæles eþel* ('whale's homeland, i.e. sea'), *yða ful* ('cup of waves, i.e. ocean'), *rodores candel* ('sky's candle, i.e. sun'). This sort of 'noun + noun' phrasal combination, whose first word (in the genitive or dative) defines the second, is very common indeed in Old English verse (viz. *waþema gebind* ('binding of waves', *Wanderer* 24), *sinces bryttan* ('distributor of treasure', 25)); but only when the second component involves a figurative reference is the term 'kenning' usually applied (Scragg 1991: 65–7; Lester 1996: 55–9; O'Brien O'Keeffe 1997: 91–2, 94; Baker 2003: 132).

As these examples indicate, short noun phrases are in many respects equivalent (semantically, and often rhythmically) to compounds, a reminder that 'chunks' of composition at levels beyond the word also play a vital role in the diction of poetry. And if particular words are squarely 'poetic' in their occurrence and function, then so too are certain phrases. When these fit a definable rhythmic sequence (usually a half-line), recurrent phrases are known as 'formulas', and discussion of them has played a major role in the critical analysis of Old English verse. The words 'sinces bryttan' at *The Wanderer* 25b are a case in point: allowing for the inflexion of *brytta*, this phrase occurs as a complete half-line nine further times in Old English poetry (including in *Genesis A*, *Elene* and *Beowulf*). Other formulas in our *Wanderer* passage include 'freomægum feor' (21a; once each in *Genesis A* and *Widsith*), and perhaps 'waþema gebind' (24b; repeated only in *The Wanderer* itself). These instances of phrasal *déjà vu* are far from unusual: it has been calculated that 17 per cent of the half-lines in *Beowulf* are formulas of this sort (O'Brien O'Keeffe 1997: 102).

The existence of such ready-made phrases is obviously beneficial when composing poetry with a conventional rhythmic structure. Since the advent of 'oral-formulaic' theory, it has moreover become clear that the mode of composition using formulas is especially characteristic of poetry that (like the Germanic tradition, or Homeric verse) developed in an oral rather than a written context. Nonetheless, the centrality of formulas to Old English poetry, much of which was demonstrably composed by literate poets, indicates that their presence is best seen as another symptom of the longstanding, traditional style of this verse, rather than telling us anything about how particular surviving poems were produced (Godden 1992: 502–4; Lester 1996: 75–7; Orchard 1997: 103–9; O'Brien O'Keeffe 1997: 98–103; Baker 2003: 136–8; and see further Orchard 2003 on the likelihood that some poems borrowed their formulaic phrasing directly from others in very literary chains of influence). As with other aspects of Old English poetic lexis, moreover, the usefulness of formulas for filling set metrical patterns should not deflect us into thinking of their manipulation as unconscious or artless. Like compounds of the *meoduhealle* type, formulas often carry substantial conventional baggage (*sinces brytta* is another reference to the lynch-pin of the lord–retainer bond), and hence maintaining them has important consequences in itself. Another significant aspect of the longevity of this language is actually its pliability, since 'formulaic' does not have to entail simple verbatim repetition. On the same model as *sinces brytta*, for instance, and filling precisely the same rhythmical structure, notice the extensive range of other 'X brytta' phrases in Old English poetry. More than twenty occurrences of a dozen different variants on this construction are recorded. Some are nearly synonymous, such as *goldes brytta*, 'distributor of gold' (*Genesis A*), and *beaga brytta*, 'distributor of rings' (*Beowulf*). But others are applied to new referents, acquiring their 'meaning' not just from their literal sense but from their provocative resonance with the archetypal version of the formula: thus God, the ultimate, heavenly treasure-giver, is a *lifes brytta*, 'distributor of life' (*Genesis A, Andreas, Christ I*), or a *wuldres brytta*, 'distributor of glory' (*Seasons for Fasting*); and devils and evil-doers are his perverse re-casting, a *morþres brytta*, 'distributor of violence' (*Andreas, Judith*), or a *synna brytta*, 'distributor of sins' (*Elene*). (See Tyler 2006: 77–80, 101–22.)

As a result of the weight accorded to individual lexical elements and the phrases constructed from them, Old English poetic syntax can seem to some modern readers to boil down to a (repetitive) succession of such components bolted together. Needless to say, this is another over-simplification. There is a great variety of ways of linking clauses, with widely contrasting degrees of complexity. And stressing the poetry's tendency towards parataxis (sequences of main clauses), rather than the more explana-tory subordination of most prose, steps over the difficulties faced by modern readers (and editors) in deducing the relationship between many clauses in the first place: multiple interpretations are frequently possible, and arguably deliberate (Robinson 1985: 18–19; Godden 1992: 506–7; Lester 1996: 79–81; Baker 2003: 148–51;

Mitchell and Robinson 2007: 338–41; but see also Fulk 2003: 3–9). But to conclude this survey, I shall glance at perhaps the most characteristic construct of Old English poetic syntax, which does most to enforce its reputation as built from sequences of short phrases: the artful restatement of concepts known as 'variation'.

In Robinson's useful definition (1985: 3), variation (or 'apposition') consists of two or more 'syntactically parallel words or word-groups which share a common referent and which occur within a single clause' (see also Godden 1992: 507–8; Lester 1996: 67–72; O'Brien O'Keeffe 1997: 94–8; Baker 2003: 133–6). A very simple example may already be found in the inscription on the Gallehus horn, where the words 'ek' and 'Hlewagastiz Holtijaz' represent varying ways of expressing the subject of the (same) clause, the maker of the horn, rather than these two pieces of information being expressed in separate, conjoined clauses ('I, Hlewagastiz Holtijaz, made the horn', instead of 'I made the horn, and I am called Hlewagastiz Holtijaz'). The best-known instances of variation in Old English verse are perhaps those in *Cædmon's Hymn*, with its multitude of different phrases meaning 'God'. The last three lines of the poem have three such phrases, all acting in tandem as parallel subjects (in bold), as well as two parallel ways of describing the object of creation, the earth (underlined):

> Þa <u>middangeard</u>   monncynnes **Weard**,
> **ece Drihten**,   æfter teode
> firum <u>foldan</u>,   **Frea ælmihtig**.
> (*Cædmon's Hymn*, WS version, 7–9)

Then **the Guardian of mankind, the eternal Lord, the Lord almighty** afterwards adorned <u>the middle-earth, the world</u> for people.

As the translation demonstrates, this interweaving of phrases doing the same job, distributed across the sentence, is alien to Modern English prosaic syntax, which must put the variants on subject and object together in two sets in order to make clear sense.

As with the choice of vocabulary (and closely related to it), coming back on oneself and reformulating the elements of a sentence in this way can appear to be motivated by a utilitarian hunting for alliteration, the poet delaying the progress of the ideas while he keeps up with the metre. But once again, to understand this device purely as a mechanical consequence of the verse-form would be unjust; even in the relatively straightforward example of *Cædmon's Hymn*, variation allows the central actor in the poem to be lit in his role as Creator from several complementary angles in nine short lines. The following famous passage from *Beowulf* illustrates some other possible (and more complex) effects of the canny application of this mode of expression:

> Dryhtsele dynede;   <u>Denum eallum</u> wearð,
> <u>ceasterbuendum</u>,   <u>cenra gehwylcum</u>,
> <u>eorlum</u> ealuscerwen.   Yrre wæron begen…
> (*Beowulf*, 767–9)

The noble hall resounded; <u>for all the Danes, the city-dwellers, each of the brave ones, the warriors</u>, there was a terrible dispensing of ale. They [Beowulf and Grendel] were both angry . . .

The four parallel terms for the Danes (underlined) put a cumulative, perhaps ironic emphasis on their courtly/heroic attributes at the moment when they are at their most impotent (they play no part in Beowulf's fight with Grendel); and this focus is reinforced by the unusual delaying of the subject of the sentence, the unique *ealuscerwen*, to its very end (this compound is probably best understood as 'a (terrible) dispensing of ale', figuratively meaning 'terror'). (For a similarly dramatic example, see Scragg 1991: 63–4.)

Old English verse thrives on a range of essentially similar types of laconically interlinked, 'lean-to' phrases. Not all of them come under the umbrella of 'variation' as strictly defined, since they can enumerate parallel attributes or actions that do not describe precisely the same thing (for attempts at definitions, see O'Brien O'Keeffe 1997: 96–8). But all contribute to the characteristic impression of this poetry as liking to 'dance round' its ideas, achieving a richness of texture through statement and partial restatement that finds its counterpart in the lexical expressiveness offered by its many available words, compounds and phrases. If we return to where we began, to the end of *The Battle of Brunanburh*, with these structures in mind, we find some other sophisticated examples of this expressive interweaving. In the first sentence cited (lines 60–5a), the three 'beasts of battle' which so often haunt such poetic scenes of slaughter are described in turn: the raven (61–2a), the eagle (62b–4a) and the wolf (64b–5a), all varied with descriptions of their own attributes, are enumerated as parallel objects of the verb *letan* (60a); and each creature is in turn depicted distributing (*bryttian*) corpses and enjoying the carrion in the varied verb phrases interleaved in these lines (60b, 63b). This is an example of Old English poetic diction at its most densely textured, cramming a great deal of imagery into a small (aural and grammatical) space, heavy with compounding and other effects that turn up the stylistic volume of the sentence in a way often to be found in traditional thematic 'hotspots' such as depictions of the beasts of battle (Dance 2006: 307–12).

The final four lines of the poem showcase a different and somewhat more regimented series of parallels. The *b*-verses (70b to 73b) conclude with finite verbs progressively describing the actions of the invading Anglo-Saxons (*becoman*, 'came'; *sohtan*, 'sought'; *ofercoman*, 'overcame'; *begeatan*, 'won'), and different takes on these triumphant incomers, as variations on the composite subject of these verbs, appear in the *a*-verses of lines 70, 72 and 73 (*Engle and Seaxe*, 'Angles and Saxons', who are also *wlance wigsmiþas*, 'bold war-smiths' and *eorlas arhwate*, 'glory-keen warriors'). As an artful expression of the glorious beginnings of English nationhood to which this tenth-century poet looks back, with the Germanic-speaking warriors who came, and sought, and conquered, this passage is suitably successful. And in its form and its stylistic accoutrements it is a highly effective example of something else the Anglo-Saxons brought, the earliest English poetic language.

REFERENCES AND FURTHER READING

Baker, P. S. (2003). *Introduction to Old English*. Oxford: Blackwell.

Bammesberger, A. (1992). The place of English in Germanic and Indo-European. In R. M. Hogg (ed.). *The Cambridge History of the English Language*. Vol. 1: *The Beginnings to 1066* (pp. 26–66). Cambridge: Cambridge University Press.

Bliss, A. (1962). *An Introduction to Old English Metre*. Oxford: Blackwell.

Bredehoft, T. A. (2005). *Early English Metre*. Toronto: University of Toronto Press.

Dance, R. (2006). 'Þær wearð hream ahafen': A note on Old English spelling and the sound of 'The Battle of Maldon'. In H. Magennis and J. Wilcox (eds). *The Power of Words: Anglo-Saxon Studies Presented to Donald G. Scragg on his Seventieth Birthday* (pp. 278–317). Morgantown: West Virginia University Press.

Fulk, R. D. (1992). *A History of Old English Meter*. Philadelphia: University of Pennsylvania Press.

Fulk, R. D. (2003). On argumentation in Old English philology, with particular reference to the editing and dating of 'Beowulf'. *Anglo-Saxon England*, 32, 1–26.

Godden, M. R. (1992). Literary language. In R. M. Hogg (ed.). *The Cambridge History of the English Language*. Vol. 1: *The Beginnings to 1066* (pp. 490–535). Cambridge: Cambridge University Press.

Hogg, R. M. (1992). Phonology and morphology. In R. M. Hogg (ed.). *The Cambridge History of the English Language*. Vol. 1: *The Beginnings to 1066* (pp. 67–167). Cambridge: Cambridge University Press.

Irvine, S. (2006). Beginnings and transitions: Old English. In L. Mugglestone (ed.). *The Oxford History of English* (pp. 32–60). Oxford: Oxford University Press.

Kastovsky, D. (1992). Semantics and vocabulary. In R. M. Hogg (ed.). *The Cambridge History of the English Language*. Vol. 1: *The Beginnings to 1066* (pp. 290–408). Cambridge: Cambridge University Press.

Lass, R. (1994). *Old English: A Historical Linguistic Companion*. Cambridge: Cambridge University Press.

Lester, G. A. (1996). *The Language of Old and Middle English Poetry*. Basingstoke: Macmillan.

Mitchell, B. and F. C. Robinson (2007). *A Guide to Old English*. 7th edn. Oxford: Blackwell.

Nielsen, H. F. (1998). *The Continental Backgrounds of English and its Insular Development until 1154*. Odense: Odense University Press.

O'Brien O'Keeffe, K. (1990). *Visible Song: Transitional Literacy in Old English Verse*. Cambridge: Cambridge University Press.

O'Brien O'Keeffe, K. (1997). Diction, variation, the formula. In R. E. Bjork and J. D. Niles (eds). *A Beowulf Handbook* (pp. 85–104). Exeter: University of Exeter Press.

Orchard, A. (1995). Artful alliteration in Anglo-Saxon song and story. *Anglia*, 113, 429–63.

Orchard, A. (1997). Oral tradition. In K. O'Brien O'Keeffe (ed.). *Reading Old English Texts* (pp. 101–23). Cambridge: Cambridge University Press.

Orchard, A. (2003). Both style and substance: the case for Cynewulf. In C. E. Karkov and G. H. Brown (eds). *Anglo-Saxon Styles* (pp. 271–305). Albany: State University of New York Press.

Orton, P. (2000). *The Transmission of Old English Poetry*. Turnhout: Brepols.

Robinson, F. C. (1985). *'Beowulf' and the Appositive Style*. Knoxville: University of Tennessee Press.

Robinson, O. W. (1992). *Old English and Its Closest Relatives: A Survey of the Earliest Germanic Languages*. London: Routledge.

Scragg, D. G. (1991). The nature of Old English verse. In M. R. Godden and M. Lapidge (eds). *The Cambridge Companion to Old English Literature* (pp. 55–70). Cambridge: Cambridge University Press.

Tyler, E. M. (2006). *Old English Poetics: The Aesthetics of the Familiar in Anglo-Saxon England*. Cambridge: D. S. Brewer.

3

Old English Manuscripts and Readers

Rohini Jayatilaka

When the Anglo-Saxons arrived in Britain from the Continent, in the course of the fifth century, they brought with them a system of writing using the runic alphabet, which had been developed in Northern Europe from the same roots as the Roman alphabet. It seems to have been mainly used, in England at least, for short inscriptions on stone, metal or wood, recording the owner or the maker or serving as memorials, though there may have been some use of runes for messages on wood and perhaps even for records. When Christian missionaries arrived from Rome at the end of the sixth century, they brought with them two new technologies: writing using the Roman alphabet, and book-production using parchment and binding, pen and ink. These quickly became dominant as the medium of texts and records, though runes continued in occasional use throughout the period, both for inscriptions and as an element in texts written mainly in the Roman alphabet in manuscripts (for example, the acrostic signature at the end of Cynewulf's poems, and some of the verse riddles in the Exeter Book). The one poem that is written wholly in runes is the riddling two-line poem inscribed on the whalebone of the Franks Casket (see below).

Both of the new technologies required considerable resources, but especially book-production. Parchment was made from the skins of sheep, goats or calves, which had to be laboriously scraped, washed and trimmed before being cut into uniform sizes to form sheets. After being ruled and framed, usually with a sharp point, these sheets could be gathered into groups or quires, normally of 4 sheets forming 8 leaves or 16 pages. After they were written on, they were then sewn together with thread or cords through the central fold and bound up into a volume, though quires and even volumes could remain loose and unbound for many decades after they were produced, and 'booklets' formed from a single quire or several might circulate on their own before being bound into a larger volume later, which allowed for much rearrangement of contents, both deliberate and accidental.

Bindings might be loosely made from leather or parchment at first, but for permanent use binders employed wooden boards, usually made of oak. The ends of the leather thongs or cords used to assemble the gatherings were secured into the boards by wooden pegs or dowels. The boards were then covered with leather, which might be decorated or covered with rich ornaments for an important manuscript. The production of three lavish copies of the whole Bible, made at Wearmouth and Jarrow in the years 688–716 under abbot Ceolfrith, of which one still survives in Florence (Biblioteca Medicea Laurenziana, MS Amiatino 1, also known as the Codex Amiatinus), required immense expenditure of time and materials. The skins of some 1500 calves would have been needed for these three enormous manuscripts, presumably drawn from the agricultural estates with which the monasteries were endowed. At the other extreme, charters and other legal documents might be written on single leaves or sheets, and then folded and sealed. Ink was usually made from a mixture of oak-gall and carbon or iron extract, and quill pens were generally made from goose feathers. Drafting and informal exercises were largely done on tablets made from wood but covered with a thin layer of wax, and written with a stylus, a pointed implement usually made of hard metal or bone.

The system of writing using the Roman alphabet which the earliest missionaries brought from Rome (at the end of the sixth century) and from Ireland (in the first half of the seventh century) employed a variety of scripts for different purposes, reflecting the status of the particular text that was copied. According to this hierarchy, the 'majuscule' scripts, written between two imaginary lines and generally of uniform height, including Rustic Capitals, Uncial and Half-uncial, were used for writing more formal books; and the 'minuscule' scripts, written between four imaginary lines and using letters with ascenders and descenders, were used for writing documents and less formal books. Rustic capitals were generally used for display purposes in manuscripts; Uncial script, so called because the letters of the script were ideally an inch high, was used for producing high grade, formal books, such as psalters and gospels; and Half-Uncial, a less formal and characteristically Insular script, was used to write various ecclesiastical texts. Insular minuscule scripts (Hybrid, Set, Cursive and Current) also had their own hierarchy, with Hybrid minuscule being the most formal, and Current minuscule being at the lowest end of the scale. By the ninth century, Rustic Capitals, Uncials and Half-Uncials were reserved for rubrics and other display purposes, whilst the Hybrid minuscule was used to write even the most formal books. From the end of the century we begin to see the use of characteristically Anglo-Saxon scripts in English manuscripts: the Anglo-Saxon Pointed minuscule, greatly influenced by Insular Cursive minuscule, was in use by the end of the ninth century; by the tenth century the English Square minuscule was developed in southern England; and by the early eleventh century we see the emergence of a Round minuscule. Caroline minuscule, which had developed in Continental scriptoria, was introduced into English scriptoria in the tenth century. From the middle of the tenth century a distinction developed between Anglo-Saxon minuscule, used for texts in English, and Caroline minuscule, used for Latin texts. Most written texts would have been in Latin in the Anglo-Saxon period, whether they were copies of works written on the Continent and recopied in England, or new texts composed by Anglo-Saxon authors such as Bede and Aldhelm. But from a very early stage it would have been necessary to adapt the Roman alphabet to the English language and find ways of representing sounds not common in Latin. According to Bede, Æthelberht, who was reigning in Kent when Augustine arrived in 597 and presided over the earliest conversions, soon arranged for the laws of his kingdom to be written down, and it is likely that English was also needed for charters and other documents at an early stage. Early writings experimented with 'th' for the sounds of Modern English 'this' and 'thick', and with 'u' for 'w', but eventually scribes and authors settled on the forms 'þ' (adapted from the runic alphabet and called 'thorn') and 'ð' (adapted from an Irish 'd' and named 'eth') for the 'th' sounds, and the form 'wynn', 'ƿ', for 'w' (adapted from the runic alphabet). (The ȝ-shaped letter, later called 'yogh', was initially the standard way of writing the letter 'g' in Latin and English, and it was only in the tenth century that a distinction began to develop between a rounded or 'caroline' g for Latin and a flatter 'g' or 'yogh' for Old English.) But whereas Latin was generally written with the same spellings throughout Britain and the Continent, written Old English varied from region to region and century to century, as it reflected the local variations in speech. As a consequence, Caedmon's Hymn (see below) looks very different in its original Northumbrian form from its later West Saxon form.

If we can trust the reports of the Anglo-Saxons themselves, Old English poetry in the earlier part of the Anglo-Saxon period was recited and heard but not normally set down, circulated or read in written form. Bede in his *Historia Ecclesiastica* (completed in 731) describes the illiterate poet Caedmon reciting, or singing, his vernacular poems based on biblical stories to the monks and nuns of Whitby, to the admiration of his audience, but says nothing of their being written down; nothing in his account suggests that they had anything but an oral existence. Alcuin, writing to an ecclesiastical household perhaps in the bishopric of Leicester around 797, complained of the clerics listening to apparently vernacular poems about old Germanic heroes such as Ingeld, but not of their *reading* such poems. Narrative poems such as *Beowulf* and *Widsith* imagine minstrels singing their poems to the harp in courts and halls, but have nothing to say of writing (which figures in *Beowulf* only as an inscription on a sword recording the fall of the giants). When Old English poems did get written down in the early period, it was in isolation on the fringes of manuscripts devoted to Latin texts. Thus Caedmon's nine-line poem is included, presumably as supporting evidence for the story of his miraculous gift, in the Leningrad manuscript of Bede's *Historia Ecclesiastica* (St Petersburg, Saltykov-Schedrin Public Library, Q.v.i.18) and at the end of the Moore MS (Cambridge, University Library, Kk. 5.16) of Bede's work. Whereas the eighth-century 'Leningrad Bede' is written in double columns, an early Northumbrian text of Caedmon's hymn was added in three continuous long lines, with no punctuation, in the lower margin of the same folio as Bede's Latin paraphrase of the poem (*Historia Ecclesiastica*, iv. 24, f. 107r). The hymn, written in pointed Anglo-Saxon minuscule of the mid-eighth century, appears to have been written by the same scribe who wrote the Latin account of Caedmon, though in a smaller script. In the 'Moore Bede', written in the early eighth century, Caedmon's hymn was added by a contemporary scribe on the last page of the manuscript (f. 128v, 1–3), which was originally blank. Here too the hymn is written in three continuous long lines, with no punctuation.

Similarly, the five-line poem known as *Bede's Death Song*, the only vernacular composition by Bede extant (if it was really composed by him rather than merely recited), was preserved in a Latin letter written by Cuthbert describing the death of Bede. At least forty-five copies of the poem survive, dating from the ninth century onwards, mostly embedded in Cuthbert's letter, but occasionally recorded in the margins of the manuscripts containing the letter. A third example is the fourteen-line poem called *The Leiden Riddle*, an Old English adaptation of one of Aldhelm's Latin verse riddles, which was added, probably early in the ninth century, on the verso of the last leaf (f. 25v) of a ninth-century manuscript (Leiden, Rijksuniversiteit, Vossianus Lat. 4E 106) containing the Latin riddles of Aldhelm and Symphosius.

Poems could also occasionally be set down as inscriptions on stone or ivory. The central part of the poem known as *The Dream of the Rood*, recorded in full only in the Vercelli manuscript (*c.* 1000), was inscribed in runic letters on the borders of a richly carved stone cross, set up at Ruthwell in what is now Scotland in the eighth century. It is inconceivable that anyone could have read the poem with any ease, given the awkward position and ordering of the letters, the use of runes and the height of the cross, so we have to imagine it as having some other function, symbolic or decorative. Also in the eighth century a verse couplet in English was inscribed in runic letters on the borders of one panel of a tiny whalebone casket (known as the Franks Casket, from the name of a modern owner) (see Figure 3.1). Scenes from European history, Germanic legend and Biblical story are carved on all sides of the casket, as are inscriptions sometimes in Latin, sometimes in English prose or verse; sometimes in the Roman alphabet and sometimes in runes. The whole piece seems to have been conceived and designed as a tour de force of Anglo-Saxon multicultural traditions. The verse couplet wittily refers not to the scenes it surrounds, which depict the legend of Weland and the story of the Adoration of the Magi, but to the whalebone of which the casket is made, describing a whale being thrown up on to a beach by the force of the storms; like the other inscriptions, this was presumably composed from the outset for inclusion in its present position on the casket and not for recitation.

The earliest reference to manuscripts devoted to Old English poems is a rather doubtful story told by the Welsh cleric Asser in his *Life of King Alfred*, written in 893. He reports that when Alfred was a child (presumably in the 850s) his mother showed a book of English poetry to him and his brothers, and offered to give it to whichever one of them could learn it most quickly. The book was evidently a somewhat deluxe one, since according to Asser the child Alfred was attracted by the beauty of the initial letter. The story has many doubtful elements (all but one of Alfred's brothers would have been adults when he was a child, and his mother seems to have died or disappeared by the time he was six, when his father remarried) and there may be no truth at all in it, but it perhaps does demonstrate that the idea of a lavish book of Old English poetry existing in the 850s was not inconceivable to Asser. Another

Figure 3.1 The Franks Casket: Reliquary, Northumbria (whalebone), British Museum (left side, Germanic legend of Weland the Smith; right side, Adoration of the Magi).
Photo © Boltin Picture Library/The Bridgeman Art Library.

hint in the same direction is found in the ninth-century Old English translation of Bede's *Historia Ecclesiastica*, which in rendering the story of Caedmon reports that the monks who listened to his poems wrote them down and learned them. There is no particular reason to suppose that the translator had evidence for this, but it does suggest that it was natural for him to suppose that the monks would have done this and that valued English poems would have been recorded in writing. Further evidence for the existence of manuscripts of Old English verse in the ninth century is the case offered by Cynewulf, whose four poems all end with his name in acrostics woven into the fabric of his verse, in a manner which would be very clear to readers but almost impossible for listeners to apprehend. The poems survive only in manuscripts of the late tenth century, but if the scholarly consensus is correct in dating Cynewulf's poems to the ninth century, or even the late eighth, it suggests that a poet at that date – admittedly one of clearly educated and literate background, with good Latin – could count on the written circulation of his poems. And it would perhaps be surprising if learned and bookish religious poems such as *Exodus* and *Guthlac A*, both dated to the eighth century, were not also recorded in writing from the outset.

The earliest surviving *vernacular* manuscript containing poetry is closely associated with King Alfred, but is rather more limited in its verse than the grand collection described by Asser. This is Oxford, Bodleian Library, Hatton 20, a copy of the Old English translation of Gregory the Great's *Pastoral Care* purportedly composed by King Alfred himself, written in prose but with a verse preface of 16 lines and a verse epilogue of 30 lines. The text was composed between 891 and 896 and circulated to the bishops in King Alfred's territories, and this is the copy which was sent to Waerferth, bishop of Worcester, as the inscription 'ÐEOS BOC SCEAL TO WIOGORA CEASTRE' ('This book is to go to Worcester') and the opening words of the prose preface, 'Alfred kyning hateð gretan Wærferð biscep his wordum luflice 7 freondlice' ('King Alfred orders Bishop Waerferth to be greeted with his words in love and friendship'), show. The prose and verse prefaces are written on a separate bifolium (a two-leaf sheet) at the beginning of the manuscript. The prose preface was written by a scribe who evidently did not write anything else in the manuscript. The metrical preface, which is in the voice of the book, not of Alfred himself, opens after the space of a few blank lines with an ornamental zoomorphic initial and appears to have been written by the scribe of the main text. The verse is written in long lines, punctuated by a medial comma-like point, and the end of the preface is marked by a colon and a hook-shaped comma written twice in succession. The metrical epilogue was also written by the main scribe immediately following the text of the *Pastoral Care*. The epilogue begins with a slightly enlarged initial and is written first in five long lines, then eighteen progressively shorter lines, culminating in a punctuation mark made up of two dots above a hook-shaped comma (f. 98r and v).

A similar case from the early decades of the tenth century is the Tanner manuscript of the Old English Bede (Oxford, Bodleian Library, Tanner 10), which incorporates into its prose translation the verse of Caedmon's Hymn. Unlike in the 'Leningrad Bede' and the 'Moore Bede', the hymn is here copied by the main scribe of this manuscript as if it is an integral part of the main text, written in long lines and separated from the main text by a point, the normal punctuation used in the remainder of the text (f. 100r)

But the earliest surviving manuscript containing a substantial body of Old English verse is probably the mid-tenth-century copy of another text linked to King Alfred, the prosimetrical version of Boethius's *De Consolatione Philosophiae* in London, British Library, Cotton Otho A. vi. The Latin text was initially translated, around 900, into Old English prose, but soon afterwards it was revised and rewritten to match the alternation of prose and verse found in the Latin work, by the transformation of the parts of the prose corresponding to verse in the Latin text into quite skilful, if unenterprising, English verse. The resulting text has a verse prologue and 31 further poems, interspersed amongst the prose and written in long lines like the prose. The verse in total runs to some 1750 lines, and makes up about one-fifth of the whole prosimetrical version. The Cotton manuscript is the only surviving copy of this version and appears not to have been quite finished, with the spaces for initials left blank, but the plan seems to have been to mark the alternation between prose and verse with large coloured initials. There is no trace of readers in this copy, but the prosimetrical version seems to have had some circulation since it was apparently used by Nicholas Trevet for his own Latin commentary on the *De Consolatione Philosophiae* around 1300.

A further case of embedding verse in prose texts at this date is the *Parker Chronicle*. The *Anglo-Saxon Chronicle* was written in Old English prose in the 890s, but then continued at various centres of book production thereafter. The Parker copy (Cambridge, Corpus Christi College 173) was originally produced about the year 900 and kept up thereafter at Winchester, and the chronicler who added the annals for 925–55 included two short poems, *The Battle of Brunanburh* celebrating the victory of 937 and *The Capture of the Five Boroughs* celebrating that of 942. Several scribes wrote the entries in the *Parker Chronicle*, but both *The Battle of Brunanburh* (ff. 26r-27r) and *The Capture of the Five Boroughs* (f. 27r) were written by the same scribe. *The Battle of Brunanburh* is the only entry for the year 937, and though *The Capture of the Five Boroughs* begins on the line next to the year 'AN. DCCCCXLI', another scribe added 'AN. DCCCXLII' immediately beneath it. Both poems are in a hand of the mid-tenth century, written in long lines, and punctuated by points. The end of *The Capture of the Five Boroughs*, however, has not been punctuated and the text runs continuously on to the prose text that follows.

A growing interest in combining prose and verse in manuscripts is evidenced too by a strange and battered set of leaves containing two verse dialogues between Solomon and Saturn, running to 506 lines, and bracketing a prose dialogue, in Cambridge, Corpus Christi College 422 (pp. 1–26). The texts were written in Square Anglo-Saxon minuscule around the middle of the tenth century and may have been part of a larger manuscript originally, but these thirteen leaves were subsequently re-used as flyleaves for a liturgical manuscript in the twelfth century. The first six pages contain verse dialogues, the next six prose dialogues, and the final twelve return to the verse text. A leaf was lost (between pp. 12 and 13), and page 14 was used as a palimpsest in the twelfth century. Though a few letters of the verse text of the dialogues on this page are still visible, the text was erased and a Latin excommunication written over it. A leaf was lost after page 18, and again after page 22, and the verse text ends imperfectly at the bottom of page 26. Several pages have been badly damaged by rubbing, as well as by the application of reagents. Page 1, which was an outside page for some time and probably used as a paste-down, is barely legible. The verse dialogues, written in long lines, are not easy to distinguish from the prose lines. Both the verse and the prose are punctuated by medial points, as well as by a triangle of dots followed sometimes by a long comma. In addition to the opening lines of the verse text on page 13, 'Hwæt ic flitan gefrægn' ('Lo I heard contending'), written in majuscule, enlarged initials of varying sizes are used throughout the verse and prose dialogues.

By the last decades of the tenth century vernacular manuscripts in general are becoming much more common in the surviving record, either because more were produced or because a higher proportion have survived, and the key witnesses for the bulk of Old English poetry finally make their appearance. Two of these, the Vercelli Book and the *Beowulf* manuscript, mingle prose and verse like the preceding manuscripts.

The Vercelli Book

Vercelli, Biblioteca Capitolare CXVII, or the Vercelli Book, is a collection of twenty-three Old English prose homilies and saints lives and six Old English poems. It is the work of probably a single scribe, writing Anglo-Saxon square minuscule in the last decades of the tenth century. There are some suggestions that it was produced in south-eastern England, perhaps Canterbury, but by the second half of the eleventh century it seems to have been moved to the Continent, and perhaps it was already at the monastery of Vercelli in northern Italy by then, presented as a gift or abandoned as useless luggage by an Anglo-Saxon traveller en route to Rome. The homilies and poems are interspersed in apparently random fashion. The manuscript begins with five homilies; next come the poems *Andreas* and *The Fates of the Apostles*; then homilies 6–18; then the poems *Soul and Body I*, *Homiletic Fragment I* (with a lost leaf causing the loss of the end of the former and beginning of the latter) and *The Dream of the Rood*; then homilies 19–22; then the poem *Elene*; and finally homily 23. The selection and ordering are hard to explain. Evidently the compiler was interested in religious material only and was apparently unconcerned about the distinction between prose and verse, or between the very mundane quality of some of the homilies and the high rhetoric of *The Dream* or *Elene*. Though he has appropriately linked the account of the apostle St Andrew in *Andreas* with Cynewulf's poem on all the apostles, *The Fates*, some other obvious conjunctions of similar material have been missed, such as that between *The Dream* and *Elene*, with their opening visions of the Cross, or alternatively between *The Dream* and homily I, both on the passion of Christ, or *Soul and Body I* and homily XXII on a similar subject. Linguistic evidence suggests that the scribe or compiler was working from several different earlier collections of texts to produce his own selection, but the principle behind it remains obscure.

The *Beowulf* Manuscript

The manuscript, British Library, Cotton Vitellius A.xv, was badly damaged in the Cotton fire of 1731 and the leaves were mounted separately on paper frames in the nineteenth century. It has two sets of foliation, and there remains some uncertainty concerning the original organisation of it (the foliation referred to here is based on the more recent foliation added to the manuscript). It is a composite manuscript of two parts which were bound up together in the seventeenth century and probably had no connection before then: the first part (fols. 4–93), also known as the Southwick Codex, contains four Anglo-Saxon prose texts written in a mid-twelfth-century hand; and the second part (fols. 94–209) contains three vernacular prose texts, *Beowulf* and a fragment of the Old English poem *Judith*; this second part of the manuscript is also known as the Nowell Codex, after the antiquary Laurence Nowell, who owned the manuscript in the sixteenth century. Some scholars refer to the second part of the Vitellius manuscript as the '*Beowulf* manuscript', whilst others take the term to designate the entire Vitellius manuscript. Views on the precise date of the second part of the manuscript are varied. Neil Ker assigned it to the late tenth or early eleventh century; David Dumville was more specific, dating it to *c*. 997 to 1016; Kevin Kiernan has proposed a date after the accession of King Cnut in 1016; and the most recent edition of the poem by Fulk, Bjork and Niles proposes the manuscript was written *c*. 1000.

In its present arrangement the Nowell Codex opens with an Old English homily on Saint Christopher (ff. 94–98), the beginning of which is lost. This is followed by the Old English prose text known as *The Marvels* (or *Wonders*) *of the East* (ff. 98v–106v), which also occurs in another manuscript in Latin and Old English; it is lavishly illustrated with coloured drawings. Next comes the only surviving copy of the Old English *Letter of Alexander to Aristotle* (ff. 107–31v). The *Beowulf* poem is next (ff. 132–201v), and it is followed by an imperfect copy of the vernacular poem *Judith* (ff. 202–9). A single scribe wrote all three of these prose texts and the *Beowulf* poem as far as the middle of verse 1939b, and a second scribe wrote the rest of *Beowulf* (lines 1940–3182) and *Judith*. Despite the sequence of hands there is some evidence from the manuscript, in the form of wormholes and discolouration, that the collection originally ended with *Beowulf* and that *Judith* may have been placed at the beginning. The battered state of the manuscript is not only the result of the Cotton fire: the beginnings of *St Christopher* and of *Judith* had evidently been lost long before, while the end of *Beowulf* was also damaged earlier. The motive behind the rather odd selection of texts has been much discussed. The compiler was clearly concentrating on vernacular texts but was equally interested in prose and verse and in religious and secular texts. The inclusion of coloured drawings in *The Marvels of the East* suggests a wish to produce a lavish display volume rather than a merely functional collection, but the manuscript as a whole is not particularly handsome and the drawings do not suggest great talent. The most popular explanation has been that the compiler was interested in monsters, which led him to choose *The Marvels* and *The Letter* for their account of fabulous creatures of the east, *St Christopher* for its dog-headed saintly hero, and *Beowulf* for its depictions of Grendel and his mother and perhaps the dragon; *Judith* can only be fitted into the scheme by arguing that the Assyrian general Holofernes, though entirely normal in form, behaves monstrously or that he is decapitated like Grendel (and, one would have to add, many early medieval saints). There is no evidence of subsequent reading or response in the manuscript, and its history is entirely unknown before the sixteenth century.

More striking as evidence of the literary status of Old English poetry by the end of the tenth century are the other two key manuscripts, the Exeter Book and the Junius manuscript, which are both devoted exclusively to verse.

The Exeter Book

Exeter, Cathedral Library MS 3501, also known as the Exeter Book, is a collection of about 132 poems in Old English plus one riddle poem in Latin. It is a rather expansive collection, running to 123 leaves in a large format, some 13 inches high and 9 inches wide, though without any illustrations. The manuscript was produced in the second half of the tenth century, by a single scribe. By about 1050 it was in the possession of Leofric, bishop of Exeter, and one theory suggests it was produced there, but more recent work implies it was written at Canterbury or Glastonbury, and acquired by Leofric as part of his efforts to assemble a library after his appointment to the bishopric, and the removal of the seat from Crediton to Exeter, in 1046. Leofric was probably born in England but was on the Continent during the reign of Cnut and his sons, 1016–42, and returned to work as a cleric in the service of Edward the Confessor. Leofric gave his library to the cathedral of Exeter on his death and the manuscript has remained there ever since, though most of his other books were distributed elsewhere at the Reformation. He was evidently a great collector of books, leaving some 66 volumes to Exeter. Most of them were in Latin, including several books of Latin poetry (the satires of Persius, the *Thebaid* of Statius, the work of Prudentius), but he also collected volumes of Old English prose translation (Boethius, homilies, martyrology) and this single volume of verse.

The contents of the Exeter Book form a very eclectic collection. It starts with a sequence of long religious poems, on Christ, the saints Guthlac and Juliana, Azarias (the Old Testament figure Abednego) and the Phoenix. There is then a sequence of shorter poems beginning with *The Wanderer*, mostly wisdom poetry, poems with a moral or sententious edge but not particularly religious, often offering traditional secular wisdom, but interrupted by the heroic poem *Widsith*. Then there are three linked poems on legendary beasts with Christian allegorical interpretations. Then, after the *Soul and Body* dialogue, two short lyrical poems, *Deor* and *Wulf and Eadwacer*, followed by the first long sequence of verse riddles – ingenious, imaginative explorations of birds, animals, forces of nature, domestic objects, tools and weapons. Then the 'elegy' *The Wife's Lament*, and another sequence of short moral or religious poems, and finally two more short elegies and another set of riddles. There is an evident interest here in poetic artistry and craftsmanship, shown for instance in riddles which use runes, especially runic acrostics and puzzles, or the ingenious *Riming Poem*. And clearly whoever compiled this collection was interested in poetry regardless of its subject: religious, lyric, erotic, sexual and heroic poems are all gathered together.

The manuscript was probably a copy of a collection made at least half a century earlier, and thus reflects early tenth-century taste and interests (though one theory prefers to see the collection as much more recent, generated by the tenth-century monastic reform). But some of the poems in it are clearly much older: *Guthlac A* claims to be composed within the lifetime of the saint, who died in 714, and Cynewulf, who is responsible for two of the poems in the Exeter Book, *Christ II* and *Juliana*, is usually thought to have been writing in the early ninth century or late eighth. Some of the poems are clearly bookish in the sense that they are designed to be read on the page (such as the ones using runes) but others invoke a performance situation as if composed to be sung or recited (*Widsith*, the elegies).

The Junius Manuscript

The Junius manuscript, Oxford, Bodleian Library, Junius 11, was in conception the most ambitious of all the four major manuscripts of Old English poetry, though it contains only four poems and was left a long way from completion. The place of origin and provenance of the Junius manuscript remains open, though Canterbury and Malmesbury have been suggested. The manuscript was owned by James Ussher, Archbishop of Armagh, who gave it to the Anglo-Saxonist and collector Franciscus Junius about 1651; and the Bodleian Library acquired it with Junius's manuscripts in 1678.

Junius 11 was originally designed as a lavishly illustrated copy of three long poems, *Genesis*, *Exodus* and *Daniel*. It is in a large format, some 13 inches by 8. The text of the three main poems was written in Anglo-Saxon square minuscule (*c.* 960–90) by one scribe, who left lots of space for illustrations – both whole pages and parts of pages. When he finished the third poem, *Daniel*, he left more blank leaves at the end, perhaps for adding more poems later. The text which he produced is what might be expected of such a book: very neat script, but full of copying errors, as if the look of the text was more important than accuracy. When the scribe had finished he handed it over to an illustrator, who added drawings to illustrate the text up to p. 68. A second illustrator then took over in a more modern style using more colour, but he stopped work at p. 88, part way through *Genesis*, and left the remaining text, which ends on p. 212, unillustrated – including all of *Exodus* and *Daniel*. Subsequently, several other scribes, probably working several decades later, added a fourth poem at the end, *Christ and Satan*. There is some evidence that this may have originally been a separate booklet, which circulated on its own. These scribes too left blank leaves for subsequent illustrations, but no more illustrations were ever added and the blank leaves were later removed for re-use. The volume was perhaps intended as a gift and overtaken by events. Like the Exeter Book, it is devoted exclusively to Old English poetry and therefore testifies to a cultural sense of English poetry as a distinctive medium and perhaps as an art-form. Its primary purpose can scarcely have been to teach Old Testament history: for that, prose would have been more suitable, and the poems chosen are both selective in their treatment and at times very obscure in their allusiveness. As with the Exeter Book and the Vercelli Book, the poems are probably much older than the manuscript: *Genesis* and *Exodus* are both generally dated to the eighth century. One of the oddities of the illustrations is that they do not relate very closely to the actual poem; that is, they are not placed close to the text that they are supposed to illustrate, and they often depict features of the Genesis story that are not actually in the poem: for example, Enoch listening to an angel, and Noah and his sons ploughing (pp. 60 and 77). It may be that they were taken from a different version of the Genesis story, which emphasised different aspects.

Nothing quite so ambitious and important as these two manuscripts was to appear again, or at least to survive, from the eleventh century, but there is continuing evidence of copying and circulation of manuscript verse. A striking case of the continued practice of combining prose and verse is the Paris Psalter, preserved in Paris, Bibliothèque

Nationale, Lat. 8824. This is an oddly shaped manuscript, some 20 inches high but only 7.5 inches wide, with the narrowness accentuated by a double-column layout. On the left is the Latin text of the *Romanum* Psalter, on the right an Old English version of the Psalms; for the first 50 psalms this is a prose version furnished with short introductions indicating the different levels of meaning of each psalm, but for psalms 51–150 it is a metrical rendering. These texts are followed by Latin hymns, a litany and prayers. The whole is the work of a single scribe, writing in the middle or second half of the eleventh century, possibly at Canterbury. It seems to have been designed not for liturgical use but perhaps for private reading. Stray excerpts in other manuscripts indicate that the metrical psalms were taken from a complete set of all 150 psalms, which suggests that the compiler preferred the prose rendering and used that for preference for as long as it lasted. In contrast to codices like the Junius manuscript and the Exeter Book, we are probably seeing here a functional approach to Old English poetry, the verse used simply as an aid to the understanding of the Latin, though this may well not have been the original intention of the poet.

The earlier practice of embedding verse accounts of kings and battles in the prose of the *Anglo-Saxon Chronicle* continues in eleventh-century copies. In one manuscript containing the Old English version of Orosius's history of the world, scribes added a verse *Menologium* (listing the religious feasts of the year) and a set of verse maxims before returning to the historical theme with a copy of the *Anglo-Saxon Chronicle*. The Old English *Orosius* in London, British Library, Tiberius B. i., ff. 3–111v, is written in four hands of the first half of the eleventh century. The verse *Menologium* (ff. 112r to 114v), the *Maxims* (f. 115rv) and the beginning of the *Anglo-Saxon Chronicle* (ff. 115v to 118v) were added by a hand of the mid-eleventh century; the remaining annals of the *Chronicle* (ff.119r to 164r) were added by a variety of scribes of the eleventh and twelfth centuries. The opening lines of the *Menologium*, 'Crist wæs acennyd cyninga wuldor' ('Christ glory of kings was born'), and the *Maxims* 'Cyning sceal rice healdan' ('A king must guard his kingdom') are written in red majuscules, as is the opening line of the *Chronicle* at the bottom of f. 118v. The opening initial C of the *Menologium* and the opening initial Æ of the *Chronicle* are intricately designed, with animal heads and elaborate knotwork and foliation. The enlarged capitals in the body of the *Menologium* are rubricated, but not in the *Maxims*. Both texts are written in long lines and punctuation is by punctus and punctus versus.

Despite these examples of verse in prose contexts, evidence for a focus on Old English verse and a continuing sense of poetry as a distinct form to be copied separately from prose is provided by the complicated case of Cambridge, Corpus Christi College MS 201. Around the beginning of the eleventh century a scribe, possibly at Winchester, started copying an Old English prose translation of the tenth-century Anglo-Saxon guide for monks and nuns, the *Regularis Concordia*, but abandoned it after a few pages and left the rest of the quire blank. On another quire he copied three Old English religious poems, known as *Judgement Day II, An Exhortation to Christian Living* and *A Summons to Prayer*, and again left the rest of the quire blank. Some 40 or 50 years later a scribe at the New Minster in Winchester evidently discovered both quires and decided to use them as the starting point for further texts. To the one containing the prose version of the *Regularis Concordia* he added, on the remaining leaves and a further set of 11 quires, a long series of prose texts, mainly on religious matters but culminating oddly in the unique copy of the prose romance on Apollonius of Tyre. To the one containing the three poems he added two further poems in the same vein, *The Lord's Prayer* and the *Gloria*. The whole body of material was then bound up together. If the manuscript as a whole indicates that both prose and verse could be written by the same scribes and apparently for the same readers and purposes, there is also evidence of a sense that prose belonged with prose and verse with verse.

The most tantalising cases are the poems that survived by the skin of their teeth, whose manuscript contexts can no longer be known. The only medieval copy of *The Battle of Maldon* was already a fragment when its existence was recorded in Sir Robert Cotton's manuscript, Otho A. xii, and it was completely destroyed in the Cotton fire of 1731, though after a copy had been made and an edition printed. Since Cotton had a penchant for breaking up medieval manuscripts and reassembling their contents in different arrangements, it is now impossible to know in what kind of manuscript the poem originally circulated. The unique copy of an apparently epic poem called the *Fight at Finnsburg* was similarly only a small fragment when Hickes printed it in 1705, and was lost soon after. Hickes reported that he found it in a manuscript of late Old English homilies in the Lambeth Palace Library, which might be the collection now termed Lambeth 487, but there is no way of knowing whether it had been part of that manuscript in Anglo-Saxon times; it seems an unlikely conjunction. Another epic poem, *Waldere*, survives only as two leaves, and parts of two others (Copenhagen, Kongelike Bibliotek, NY Kgl. Sam. 167b (4E)), probably rescued from a post-medieval binding in Copenhagen. The poem is written by a scribe of the late tenth or early eleventh century, and there is no punctuation evident in the surviving leaves, but there is a design of interlacing foliage in the lower margin of folio 1v. Unless other parts of the manuscript turn up in similar ways, we will never know whether it came from a manuscript collection of Old English poetry like the Exeter Book or a miscellaneous collection like the *Beowulf* manuscript, or had a codex to itself. Another such casualty was the poem on the letters of the runic alphabet, explained in imaginative and riddling forms: before it was lost the only copy was apparently a single leaf.

Conclusion

As the last examples show, any account of the manuscript contexts of Old English poetry is handicapped by the limited number of surviving examples and the sufferings of manuscripts in later times. Even for the manuscripts that do survive we have remarkably little evidence of what kind of people produced, read and owned them. Devotional use of Old English poetry by religious houses, as with Cambridge, Corpus Christi College 201, is evident, but the producers and users of the Exeter Book or the *Beowulf* manuscript are unidentifiable, and though we know that Leofric of Exeter owned the Exeter Book we cannot tell whether this was a reflection of his ecclesiastical role or of his more general interests as a reader and bibliophile. Old English poems appear frequently alongside Old English prose texts on roughly similar themes (*Beowulf* manuscript, Vercelli Book, Cambridge, Corpus Christi College 201, Paris Psalter, Chronicle manuscripts, Old English Boethius), but also sometimes only in the company of other poems (Exeter Book, Junius manuscript). Strikingly absent are manuscripts combining Old English and Latin poetry, with the only examples being the addition of one Old English poetic riddle at the end of the Leiden manuscript of the riddles of Aldhelm and Symphosius, and the inclusion of one Latin verse riddle in the Exeter Book.

References and Further Reading

Brown, M. P. (1990). *A Guide to Western Historical Scripts from Antiquity to 1600*. London: British Library. (Repr. 1993.)

Brown, M. P. (1991). *Anglo-Saxon Manuscripts*. London: British Library.

Bullough, D. A. (1993). What has Ingeld to do with Lindisfarne? *Anglo-Saxon England*, 22, 93–125.

Conner, P. W. (1986). The structure of the Exeter Book Codex (Exeter, Cathedral Library, MS. 3501). *Scriptorium*, 40, 233–42. (Repr. in Mary P. Richards (ed.). *Anglo-Saxon Manuscripts: Basic Readings* (pp. 301–15). New York: Routledge, 1994; pbk edn 2001.)

Conner, P. W. (1993). *Anglo-Saxon Exeter: A Tenth-Century Cultural History*. Woodbridge: Boydell and Brewer.

Gameson, R. (1992). The cost of the Codex Amiatinus. *Notes and Queries*, 237, 2–9.

Gameson, R. (1996). The origin of the Exeter Book of Old English poetry. *Anglo-Saxon England*, 25, 135–85.

Gneuss, H. (2001). *Handlist of Anglo-Saxon Manuscripts: A List of Manuscripts and Manuscript Fragments Written or Owned in England up to 1100*. Medieval & Renaissance Texts & Studies Series, 241. Tempe: Arizona Center for Medieval and Renaissance Studies.

Gneuss, H. (2003). Addenda and corrigenda to the 'Handlist of Anglo-Saxon Manuscripts'. *Anglo-Saxon England*, 32, 293–305.

Ker, N. R. (1957). *Catalogue of Manuscripts Containing Anglo-Saxon*. Oxford: Clarendon Press. (Reissued with supplement, 1990.)

Kiernan, K. (ed.) (2004). *Electronic Beowulf* (CD-Rom). London: British Library.

Liuzza, R. (2002). *The Poems of MS Junius 11: Basic Readings*. Basic Readings in Anglo-Saxon England 8. New York and London: Routledge.

Lockett, Leslie (2002). An integrated re-examination of the dating of Oxford, Bodleian Library, Junius 11. *Anglo-Saxon England*, 31, 141–73.

Lucas, P. J. (1980). MS Junius 11 and Malmesbury. *Scriptorium*, 34, 197–220.

Muir, B. J. (ed.) (2004). *A Digital Facsimile of Oxford, Bodleian Library, MS. Junius 11* (CD-Rom). Bodleian Digital Texts 1. Oxford: Bodleian Library.

Muir, B. J. (ed.) (2000). *The Exeter Anthology of Old English Poetry: An Edition of Exeter Dean and Chapter MS 3501*. Exeter: University of Exeter Press.

Muir, B. J. (ed.) (2006). *The Exeter Anthology of Old English Poetry* (DVD). Exeter: University of Exeter Press.

O'Brien O'Keeffe, K. (1990). *Visible Song: Transitional Literacy in Old English Verse*. Cambridge Studies in Anglo-Saxon England 4. Cambridge: Cambridge University Press.

O'Donnell, D. (2005). *Cædmon's Hymn: A Multimedia Study, Archive and Edition*. Society for Early English and Norse Electronic Texts, Series A, 7. Cambridge: D. S. Brewer.

Roberts, J. (2005). *Guide to Scripts used in English Writings up to 1500*. London: British Library.

Robinson, F. C. and E. G. Stanley (eds) (1991). *Old English Verse Texts From Many Sources: A Comprehensive Collection*. Copenhagen: Rosenkilde and Bagger.

Scragg, D. G. (1973). The composition of the Vercelli Book. *Anglo-Saxon England*, 2, 189–207.

4

Old English and Latin Poetic Traditions

Andy Orchard

The traditional date of the arrival of Anglo-Saxons in England is given as 449 in the *Historia ecclesiastica gentis Anglorum* ('Ecclesiastical History of the English People' [*HE*]) written in 731 by Bede (672/3–735), with Christianity and Latin learning arriving together in Anglo-Saxon England a century and a half later in 597 (Colgrave and Mynors 1969: 562). But it is another hundred years before a written Anglo-Saxon culture can be traced, one that was to last unbroken for almost four centuries. Alas, the oldest aspects of Anglo-Saxon poetic tradition, when verse was presumably produced orally, transmitted aurally, and preserved perhaps imperfectly in the minds and memories of successive generations of poets and performers, can therefore only be guessed at now (Orchard 1997; Orchard 2009). The existence of essentially similar alliterative metres and traditional formulas based on paired but distinctive half-lines of two main stresses each across a range of related Germanic languages, notably Old Saxon, Old Norse and Old High German, strongly suggests that Old English poetry is part of a common Germanic poetic heritage, but not until those speakers and singers became scribes and sculptors were their words preserved for us to assess, an event that if it is recorded sporadically in Continental Europe at an earlier period, in Anglo-Saxon England can be dated no earlier than the end of the seventh century, by which time a substantial body of Latin verse composed by Anglo-Saxon authors can also be traced. To the extent, then, that it can be evaluated at all from the extant evidence, it is important to realise that right from the start of the written record the Anglo-Saxon poetic tradition is essentially bilingual, and remained so even after the Norman Conquest.

Indeed, many of the earliest examples of Old English verse that survive seem only to do so because they are attached to individuals known and named in a Latin context. So, for instance, *Cædmon's Hymn* (nine lines long), usually described as the beginning of the Old English Christian poetic tradition, is attributed to an illiterate (which is to say un-Latinate) cowherd from Whitby in the time of Abbess Hild (*c.* 614–80), but is primarily preserved in Latin manuscripts of the *Historia ecclesiatica*, alongside

Bede's Latin version, and in a work which itself contains significant amounts of Latin verse (for example at *HE* I.7, I.10, II.1, IV.20 [18], V.7, V.8 and V.19; see O'Donnell 2005; cf. Cavill 2000). Bede's interest in Old English poetry is confirmed by his disciple Cuthbert, who describes how Bede was 'learned in our songs' ('doctus in nostris carminibus'; cf. Plummer 1896: I, clxi; Smith 1968: 23–5), and his skill and interest in Latin verse is attested by many of his own surviving poems, including one in the *Historia ecclesiastica* itself (Lapidge 1994; cf. Jaager 1935; Lapidge 1975; Lapidge 1989). Unfortunately, such a fondness for verse in both Latin and Old English means that when Cuthbert describes Bede on his deathbed reciting the Old English poem now known as *Bede's Death Song* (five lines long), which Cuthbert himself renders into Latin, it is far from clear whether Bede is remembering verses of his own or those of another poet (Tangl 1916; Bulst 1938; Stanley 1974: 17–19); all we can say for certain is that if *Cædmon's Hymn* and *Bede's Death Song* genuinely predate the texts and manuscripts that contain them, and that if the supposed dates of their composition and recitation are to be believed, then they can be dated within the period *c.* 675–735.

Whereas both *Cædmon's Hymn* and *Bede's Death Song* seem originally to have been composed in Old English and only later rendered into Latin (Conybeare 1826: 3–8; Dumville 1981: 148; Kiernan 1990; Orchard 1996; Isaac 1997; O'Donnell 2005), a third apparently early vernacular poem, *The Leiden Riddle* (fourteen lines long), is assuredly an Old English version of a Latin *Enigma* ('riddle') by the Anglo-Saxon Aldhelm (*c.* 639/10–709/10), who prides himself on being the first person of the Germanic race to compose Latin verse (Ehwald 1919: 202/4–7; Smith 1968; and see Dance and Jayatilaka above). We have more than 4,000 lines of Latin verse composed by Aldhelm (who died in 709 or 710 [Ehwald 1919; Lapidge and Rosier 1985; Orchard 1994]), but only the witness of much later writers, including John of Worcester (who died after 1140) and William of Malmesbury (who died around 1143), that he was an outstanding poet in Old English too, an opinion allegedly endorsed by King Alfred himself (Remley 2005), who may indeed have been a distant relative (Lapidge 2007). Although some have seen the influence of Old English poetic techniques on Aldhelm's Latin verse (Lapidge 1979; Orchard 1994: 43–54 and 119–25), and others have even attempted to align existing anonymous Old English poems with his influence (notably *Genesis A*, *Exodus*, *The Dream of the Rood*, *The Ruin* and even *Beowulf* [Cook 1924; Cook 1925; Braswell 1978; Howlett 1992; Wright 1996; Abram 2000; Remley 2005]), no surviving vernacular verse can be linked directly to Aldhelm's name except for a brief and suitably unusual poem in Latin, Greek and Old English that celebrates his life and work.

Nonetheless, an apparently early rendering of Aldhelm's *Enigma 33* (with the solution *Lorica* ['mailshirt']) survives in both an Old Northumbrian version as *The Leiden Riddle* (which may go back to an eighth-century copy) and in a rather different later West Saxon version as *Riddle 35* in the so-called Exeter Book (written around 1000); the vernacular translations, which differ in significant ways, seem to have been transformed in transmission over perhaps two or even three centuries (see Dance above). It should be remembered both that Aldhelm would have spoken a form of early West Saxon some two hundred years earlier than what is normally designated early West Saxon, and that he sent his *Enigmata* to his kinsman, King Aldfrith of Northumbria, who died 704/5, and who may have been responsible directly or indirectly for the Old Northumbrian rendering; as we shall see below, the relationships between the three versions (two in Old English, one in Latin), as well as between each version and the wider corpora of Old English and Latin verse, demonstrate a pattern of intertextuality and individual composition that can be replicated widely in surviving Anglo-Saxon poetry in both languages.

Cædmon's Hymn, *Bede's Death Song*, and *The Leiden Riddle* are all first attested in Northumbrian versions that, being found in manuscripts of the eighth and ninth centuries, are often held to reflect not only the last remnants of an early flowering of Old English literature, but also the 'earliest English verse' (Stanley 1974). These three poems, with a combined total of 28 lines, represent less than a tenth of 1 per cent of the more than 30,000 lines of extant Old English verse, and their somewhat liminal status (discussed by Jayatilaka above) is further reflected by the fact that all are recorded (in the case of the first two, several times) in the margins or at the end of predominantly Latin manuscripts (most of which also contain Latin verse), as well as in Latin renderings the precise relationships of which to the vernacular versions continue to attract academic attention.

In fact, all three Old English poems point in different ways not only to the vitality and innovation of the Anglo-Saxon poetic tradition, expressing as they do new ways of speaking about and viewing old themes, but also in their modes of expression to its fundamental conservatism. Likewise, perhaps the earliest Old English poem to have survived without a (near-)contemporary Latin reflex, is nonetheless found in a ninth-century manuscript (Vienna, Nationalbibliothek, lat. 751 [Mainz, s. ix^med]; cf. Unterkircher 1971) again containing Latin letters and poems from the late seventh and early eighth centuries and associated with the Bonifatian mission to the Continent (Tangl 1916: 283 [no. 146]; Stanley 1974: 7–9):

> Oft daedlata   domę foręldit,
> sigisitha gahuem,   suuyltit thi ana.

Often a deed-slack man puts off glory, every chance of winning: for that, he dies alone.

While the context, part of an attempt by a member of the Bonifatian mission to persuade a wavering colleague to join the enterprise, is purely Christian, the contents of what is described as a 'Saxon proverb' (*Saxonicum verbum*) seem more secular and heroic, a remembered piece of poetry from an older period; parallel sentiments can be found in *Beowulf* (Orchard 2007a). Given the difficulty of dating proverbial poetry, it is hard to say how long this distich circulated in memory before it was written down; it may even be the earliest Old English poetry extant. Its preservation and transmission in such a distinctly Latin context, in a manuscript that not only contains Latin metrical verse by a range of Anglo-Saxon poets, but also Latin rhythmical verse by several Anglo-Saxon poets that, it has been argued, shares its alliterative patterning with traditional Old English verse (Orchard 1994: 43–54; cf. Orchard 1995; Orchard 2008: 55–58), together testify both to the close relationships between Latin and Old English verse within the Anglo-Saxon poetic tradition, and to the role played by memory within that shared tradition.

We know little of how Old English poetry was taught or formed part of a common educational heritage; but we do have a much clearer grasp of how Latin poetry, both Christian and secular, was taught with great intensity in Anglo-Saxon schools (Lapidge 1982; Lapidge 1993: 1–48; Lapidge 1996: 409–54). Much Old English verse that survives is, in so far as it clearly relies on Latin sources in both prose and verse, the work of evidently literate and Latinate authors who had presumably been through the same system of education, requiring as it did the memorisation of significant amounts of Latin verse, which was then remembered, recycled and recast in original composition. It seems therefore reasonable to suppose that similar techniques and tenets of poetic appropriations may have obtained with regard to the vernacular verse composed by literate Anglo-Saxons too, and that alongside the oral and inherited tradition of verse there might be conscious copying of one poet by another, as indeed has been demonstrated in several cases (Toswell 1993; Powell 2002; Orchard 2005a; Orchard 2005b; Orchard 2007b; Orchard 2008).

In order to assess the validity and implications of these assumptions, one might revisit *The Leiden Riddle*, which survives in both Latin and Old English and in at least three different versions, each of which sheds different light on the Anglo-Saxon poetic tradition. The 'original', Aldhelm's *Enigma 33*, was part of a series composed early on in its author's Latin poetic career (perhaps some time shortly before 690), and demonstrates many of the hallmarks of Aldhelm's poetic style (Ehwald 1919: 111–12):

> Roscida me genuit gelido de uiscere tellus;
> Non sum setigero lanarum uellere facta,
> Licia nulla trahunt nec garrula fila resultant
> Nec crocea seres texunt lanugine uermes
> Nec radiis carpor duro nec pectine pulsor;   5
> Et tamen en uestis uulgi sermone uocabor;
> Spicula non uereor longis exempta faretris.

The dewy ground gave me birth from chilly innards; I was not produced from a shaggy fleece of wool; no yarn draws me, nor sounding threads leap about; nor do Chinese worms weave me from their saffron floss; nor am I drawn from wheels, nor beaten with the harsh comb; yet still will I be called 'clothing' in common speech; I fear no darts drawn forth from lengthy quivers.

The solution, *Lorica* ('mailshirt') explains the apparent contradictions inherent in the use of seven negatives in seven lines (Steen 2008: 91–8). The poem is a reasonable example of Aldhelm's early poetic art, but seems more an exercise in including as many clothing-related terms as possible than an attempt at elegant composition. Nonetheless, as commonly in his verse, Aldhelm here seems to be building his poem on remembered phrases from earlier school-text authors whose works he had acquired and assimilated: so, for example, the sequence *roscida… tellus* (line 1) is also found (as *roscida tellus*) in Dracontius (*De laude Dei* I.65); both *roscida… gelido* (line 1) and *pectine pulsor* (line 5), as *gelidumque… roscida* and *pectine pulsat*, in Vergil (*Aeneid* VII.683 and VI.647); *lanarum uellere* (line 2) as *lanarum uellera* in Cyprianus Gallus (*Genesis* 992), and *nulla trahunt nec… fila* (line 3) as *nulla trahunt… nec fila* in Ovid (*Metamorphoses* XIV.265). All these are authors and texts that Aldhelm can be shown elsewhere to have known (Orchard 1994: 126–238; Lapidge 2006: 178–91; cf. in general Gneuss 2001).

Still more striking is the extent to which Aldhelm recycles his own formulaic phrasing throughout his verse, not only in his *Enigmata*, but also in his *Carmina ecclesiastica* ('Church poems') and *Carmen de uirginitate* ('poem on virginity') as the following parallels from almost every line of the poem indicate (with echoes highlighted by **bold italics**):

<1>	Frigidus ex **gelido** prolatus **uiscere** terrae	*Enigma 27 1*
	Me pater et mater **gelido genuere** rigore,	*Enigma 44 1*
	Florida **me genuit** nigrantem corpore **tellus**	*Enigma 97 1*
<2>	Lurida **setigeris** redundant uiscera **filis**,	*Enigma 12 2*
	Vellera setigero producens corpore fulua;	*Enigma 17 2*
<4>	**Nec** culter malas uestis **lanugine** rasit.	*Carmen ecclesiasticum 4.7 16*
<5>	Et potiora cupit, quam **pulset pectine** chordas,	*Carmen de uirginitate 67*
<6>	Quod dum compertum **uulgi sermone** crebrescit	*Carmen de uirginitate 1808*
<7>	**Spicula** dum patitur **longis exempta faretris**	*Carmen de uirginitate 2276*

One might note how Aldhelm closely echoes the opening line of the *enigma* on *Lorica* in the opening lines of no fewer than three further *enigmata* (on *Coticula* ['whetstone'], *Ignis* ['fire'] and *Nox* ['night'] respectively), even to the extent of retaining the same metrical structure and simply substituting one synonym for another (compare *uiscere tellus* and *uiscere terrae* at the end of the opening lines of *enigmata* 33 and 27). Likewise, Aldhelm's *Enigma* 12 (solution *bombix* ['silkworm']) opens with a pair of lines very similar to what is found in the first four lines here: 'Annua dum redeunt **texendi** tempora **telas**, / Lurida **setigeris redundant viscera filis**'; presumably the fact that Aldhelm's *enigma* on *Lorica* also mentions silkworms has triggered the association.

It is furthermore clear not only that Aldhelm adopted and adapted formulaic phrasing from the works of earlier poets of his acquaintance, as well as repeating formulas apparently of his own devising, but that he was himself imitated by later generations of Anglo-Saxon poets (Orchard 1992). So, for example, Boniface (*c.* 675–755), part of whose *enigma* on *vana gloria* ('vainglory'), lines 20–1 reads as follows (the parallels with Aldhelm's *Enigma 33*, lines 4 and 6 are highlighted in **bold italics**):

'Et gemma et aurum et *uestis, lanugine texunt* / Quam *Seres uermes*, propria ad mea iura recurrunt'. Likewise, Tatwine, archbishop of Canterbury 731–4, seems to echo Aldhelm's *enigmata* (note especially the parallels to the opening line of *Enigma 33* above) in his own *enigmata* on 'spark' ('Iam nasci *gelido* natum *de uiscere* matris' *Enigma 31*, line 2) and 'whetstone' ('Natum *me gelido* terrae *de uiscere* dicunt' *Enigma 39*, line 1).

As elsewhere with Aldhelm's own borrowings from the works of previous poets, it is striking here how Tatwine's lines resemble each other even more closely than they do those of Aldhelm from which they seem to derive. In both cases, as widely with respect to Anglo-Saxon verse composed in both Latin and (as we shall see) Old English, it appears that individual poets, even if they identify themselves as part of a recognisable and distinctive Anglo-Saxon poetic tradition inherited in part from a shared body of formulaic phrasing, were also sensitive to the purple passages and familiar phrases of particular predecessors, some of which they appropriated, and others of which they strove to imitate and assimilate as their own.

Aldhelm's *Enigma* on the *Lorica* was not only echoed by himself and other Anglo-Latin poets, but was also translated rather closely into Old English as *The Leiden Riddle*:

> Mec se ueta uong,   uundrum freorig,
> ob his innaðae   aerest cæn[d]æ.
> Ni uaat ic mec biuorthæ   uullan fliusum,
> herum ðerh hehcraeft,   hygiðonc[um min]
> Uundnae me ni biað ueflæ, ̄ni ic uarp hafæ,   5
> ni ðerih ðreatun giðraec   ðret me hlimmith.
> Ne me hrutendo   hrisil scelfath,
> ne mec ouana   aam sceal cnyssa.
> Uyrmas mec ni auefun   uyrdi craeftum,
> ða ði geolu godueb   geatum fraetuath.   10
> Uil mec huethrae suae   ðeh uidæ ofaer eorðu
> hatan mith heliðum   hyhtlic giuæde.
> Ni anoegun ic me aerigfaerae   egsan brogum,
> ðeh ði n[ume]n siæ   niudlicae ob cocrum.

The wet ground, wondrously chilly, first gave me birth from its innards; I do not know in my thoughts that I was produced from woolly fleeces, or hairs, through lofty skill. There are no twisted wefts for me, nor do I have warps, nor through a threat of violence does a thread resound in me, nor do humming shuttles shake in me, nor a sley beat me about; nor did worms weave me with the skills of fate, those who craftily decorate fine yellow cloth. Nonetheless, I will be called a desirable garment widely over the earth among heroes; nor do I fear the flight of arrows with the terrors of awe, even though it be drawn purposefully from quivers.

The broad strategy here, of translating two long lines of Old English by a single Latin hexameter, is one found elsewhere in Anglo-Saxon translations into vernacular verse (Steen 2008: 35–110), albeit that since lines 7–8 of the Old English coincide with line 5 of the Latin and lines 9–10 of the Old English with line 4 of the Latin, we can perhaps assume that the original Old English translator was working from a manuscript version of Aldhelm's *Enigma 33* where lines 4 and 5 were transposed, a circumstance that while not unknown with regard to others of Aldhelm's *Enigmata* is not in fact attested in any known manuscript version of this one. The deliberation of this translation strategy is emphasised through the capitalisation of the Old English, present in the Leiden manuscript: Aldhelm's seven hexameter lines are marked off by seven capitals in alternate long lines of the vernacular version.

One might expect that such a clear strategy would, given that it inevitably produces more words of Old English than the original Latin (here eighty-nine Old English for forty-six Latin, almost twice the number), perhaps lead to the use of 'filler' or 'formulaic' phrases, and indeed variants on the phrase 'uidæ ofaer eorðu' (line 11: 'widely over the earth') do seem commonplace (note that there is no equivalent in the Latin source). But what is striking is that in fact very little of the diction of *The Leiden Riddle* can be matched elsewhere in the extant Old English poetic corpus, again with one rather compelling exception: the entirety of line 2 ('ob his innaðae aerest cæn[d]æ' ['first gave (me) birth from its innards']) is also found in an updated form in *Paris Psalter 126.4*, line 4 (as 'of innaðe ærest cende'). Given, however, that the phrase from *The Leiden Riddle* clearly derives directly from the opening line of the Latin ('genuit…de uiscere' ['gave (me) birth from…innards']), whereas the Vulgate biblical source for the *Paris Psalter* rendering speaks vaguely only of 'children' (*filii*) at this point, although interestingly it does go on, like the final line(s) of both *The Leiden Riddle* and its Latin source to speak of both 'arrows' (*sagittae*) and (in some versions) 'a quiver' (*faretram*), it is tempting to suggest that the poet of *The Paris Psalter* is deliberately alluding to *The Leiden Riddle* here.

Assuredly, when yet another Anglo-Saxon poet produced the updated version of *The Leiden Riddle* that survives in the Exeter Book as *Riddle 35*, a number of changes to the Northumbrian version were made (see Dance above), of which the most obvious is the substitution of two completely new lines in the Exeter Book text, to replace the final two lines of *The Leiden Riddle* that refer to quivers and arrows; instead, *Riddle 35*, lines 13–14, read:

> Saga soðcwidum, searoþoncum gleaw,
> wordum wisfæst, hwæt þis gewædu sy.

You who are clever in cunning thoughts, securely skilled in words, say in truthful utterance what this garment might be.

The substituted lines comprise a challenge to provide a solution of a type relatively common elsewhere among the Exeter Book *Riddles*, but rare among the Anglo-Latin tradition of *Enigmata* (Orchard 2005a). Indeed, these final lines can be matched closely not only in the Exeter Book *Riddles*, but also elsewhere, in a range of poems including

Andreas, Juliana, Elene, Beowulf and the *Paris Psalter*. A full list of parallels (indicated by *bold italics*) runs as follows:

<13>	*sæde soðcwidum* snotre gastas	*Sat* 469
	secge soðcwidum þy sceolon gelyfan	*And* 733
	searoþancum beseted snaw eorðan band	*And* 1255
	sohton *searoþancum* hwæt sio syn wære	*El* 414
	Simon *searoþoncum* þæt he sacan ongon	*Jul* 298
	searoþoncum slog ic asecgan ne mæg,	*Jul* 494
	searoþoncum besmiþod þær fram sylle abeag	*Beo* 775
	ðurh sefan snyttro *searoðonca* hord	*CPPref* 7
<14>	þæt we *wisfæstra* *wordum* hyran	*And* 1167
	wisfæstne wer *wordes* gleawne	*And* 1648
	weras *wisfæste* *wordes* cræftige	*El* 314
	witgan *wisfæste* *wordum* sægdon	*Christ A* 64
	wisfæstum men *hwæt* seo wiht *sy*	*Rid28* 13
	wisfæstum werum *hwæt* seo wiht *sy*	*Rid41* 9
	wisfæstra hwylc *hwæt* seo wiht *sy*	*Rid67* 16
	wisfæst wordum þæs ðe hire se willa	*Beo* 626
	þæt heo his *wisfæst* *word* wynnum efnan	*PPs102,1* 4
	he him *wisfæstlic* *word* onsende	*PPs106,1* 1
	wordum wisfæstum þæt he wel þunge	*Prec* 3

Such heavily formulaic phrasing contrasts sharply with what was observed with regard to *The Leiden Riddle* earlier, and again underlines the fact that these lines are a later addition. What is particularly striking about these parallels is first the extent to which the final line can be echoed in the final lines of three further Exeter Book *Riddles*, and second the apparent overlap in diction between these verses and poems either signed by the poet Cynewulf (notably *Elene* and *Juliana*) or which (in the case of *Andreas*) can be shown to have themselves been influenced by Cynewulf's verse (Powell 2002; Orchard 2005b; Friesen 2008).

Bede's observation that Cædmon inspired imitators, and that 'others among the English attempted to make religious verse, but no one could equal him' (*HE* IV.24: 'alii post illum in gente Anglorum religiosa poemata facere tentabant, sed nullus eum aequiperare potuit'), gives a sense that even at this earliest stage of extant Old English verse there was a shared impulse towards the kind of religious poetry that Cynewulf later composed, and, if William of Malmesbury is to be believed, Aldhelm (a near-contemporary of Cædmon's) also inserted words of scripture into his own Old English poetry (Remley 2005). Such evidence of 'schools' of Anglo-Saxon poetry, particularly among literate and Latinate Anglo-Saxons (whose works comprise the great bulk of what has survived), with chains of poetic influence linking individual poems and poets, and so providing useful hints of comparative chronology, seems to have been far more widespread than has commonly been accepted (Orchard 2005b; Orchard 2007b; Orchard 2008). Many scholars (especially those unfamiliar with the parallel Latin tradition of Anglo-Saxon poetic composition) prefer instead to describe the clear similarities between individual poems as the by-product of an 'oral-formulaic' tradition of shared expressions, whereby Anglo-Saxon poets borrowed more-or-less randomly from a common stock. In order, however, to emphasise the extent to which there seem to be identifiable schools with separate chains of transmission within both the Old English and Latin strands of the Anglo-Saxon poetic tradition, it may be useful to trace just two: one involving Aldhelm (in Latin) and the other the anonymous Old English poem *Andreas* (cf. Orchard [forthcoming]).

It has long been recognised that Aldhelm's 'Church poems' (*Carmina ecclesiastica*) were, like his *Enigmata*, widely imitated by generations of later poets. So, for example, one might cite the following brief (and, one would think, deeply unmemorable) passage on the birthday of the Virgin Mary (*Carmen ecclesiasticum* 3.59–64 [Ehwald 1919: 17]):

> Istam nempe diem qua templi festa coruscant
> Natiuitate sua sacrauit uirgo Maria   60
> Quam iugiter renouant Augusti tempora mensis
> Diuiditur medio dum torrens Sextilis orbe
> Qui nobis iterum restaurat gaudia mentis
> Dum uicibus redeunt solemnia festa Mariae

Moreover that very day, on which the feasts of the temple shine, the Virgin Mary consecrated with her own birth, [that day on] which continually the days of the month of August renew, when burning Sextilis [= the Roman month on August] is divided in the middle of its rotation, that again restores the joys of the mind to us, when in due course the solemn feasts of Mary return.

It is hard to see the appeal of such a dense and distinctly unpoetic passage, but Aediluulf, an Anglo-Saxon poet composing more than a century after Aldhelm death, evidently echoes it in a passage of his own on the Virgin Mary in his poem *De abbatibus* ('On the abbots'), which is generally dated to the first quarter of the ninth century, and seems to have been composed in the north of England; both Crayke, near York, and Bywell, near Hexham, have been suggested (Campbell 1967; Howlett 1975; Lapidge 1990). The passage reads as follows (*De abbatibus* 465–9 [Campbell 1967: 37–9]; parallels are indicated by ***bold italics***):

> Vel quacumque *die* cum ***templi festa coruscant***   465
> Omnibus his laetus nimium per ***gaudia*** sancta
> Aurea dulcisonae ***restaurat*** munera ***mentis***
> Ac fratres precibus mulcet ***sollemnia festa***
> ad letos caelebrare pie gentricis honores.

Or on whatever day, when the feasts of the temple shine, excessively happy because of all these things, [Abbot Sigbald] restores the golden gifts of a sweet-sounding mind, and gently urges the brothers to celebrate the solemn feasts of the pious mother with joyful honours.

Note that the nine shared words appear in precisely the same order in each text, and that Aediluulf has effectively extracted all the specific information about the festival mentioned by Aldhelm, including the name of the Virgin Mary herself (transformed here into the more generic *pie genetricis* ['kindly mother']) and the two ways of denoting August, and has apparently blended in a phrase from Bede in line 467 (Bede's metrical *Vita Cuthberti* I.628 begins *Aurea dulcisonis*) before introducing a final line (469) which not only summarises the preceding lines, but seems to be entirely original.

In a further set of examples of Aediluulf borrowing specifically from the same poem by Aldhelm, it seems that a depiction of a golden chalice was particularly memorable. The original brief description from Aldhelm runs as follows (*Carmen ecclesiasticum 3* 72–5 [Ehwald 1919: 18]):

> *Aureus* atque *calix gemmis fulgescit opertus*,
> *Vt caelum rutilat stellis* ardentibus *aptum*,
> *Ac lata argento constat fabricata patena*:
> *Quae* diuina gerunt *nostrae medicamina uitae*. 75

And a golden chalice covered with gems gleams, so that it seems to reflect the heavens with their bright stars; and there is a large paten made from silver. These things bear the holy medication for our life.

This rather short passage seems to have been remembered and recycled by Aediluulf no fewer than three times, including two obviously related passages that appear closely together (*De abbatibus* 449–50; 625–7; 649–53 [Campbell 1967: 37, 51, and 53]; parallels are indicated by **bold italics**):

> *Aureus* ille *calix gemmis* splend*escit opertus*,
> *Argenti*que nitens *constat fabricatus* in altis. 450

That golden chalice, which he gave in his piety to the church of the great mother, shines, covered with gems, and stands on high, made from silver.

> *Vt caelum rutilat stellis ful*gentibus omne 625
> Sic tremulas uibrant subter testudine templi
> Ordinibus uariis funalia pendula flammas.

As the whole sky shines with gleaming stars, so beneath the roof of the church hanging torches dangle their tremulous flames in a number of rows.

> *Aureus* ille *calix* tetigi quem carmine dudum
> *Ac lata argento* pulcre *fabricata patena* 650
> *Cael*atas faciem praetendunt *apte* figuras
> Talia dum sanctae cumulant penetralia casae
> Munera *quae nostrae* seruant *medicamina uitae*

That golden chalice, which I mentioned above in my poem, and the broad paten fairly made from silver show surfaces well engraved with figures.

In the second example here, it is notable that in line 626 an earlier line from the same poem by Aldhelm is also echoed (*Carmen ecclesiasticum* 3 53 reads 'Congrua promamus *subter testudine templi*'), perhaps sparked off by the use of Aldhelm in the preceding verse; at all events, the phrase is familiar enough to be re-used by Aediluulf later in his own poem (at line 446). The third example is intriguing, since the context strongly suggests that in his line 651 ('*Cael*atas faciem praetendunt *apte* figuras') Aediluulf is echoing, whether consciously or not, line 73 of Aldhelm's poem ('Vt *cael*um rutilat stellis ardentibus *aptum*'), while in fact he has substituted one etymologically distinct term (*caelatas* ['engraved']) for another (*caelum* ['heaven']) that sounds similar (one might also point to the slight resemblance between the sounds of *praetendunt* in Aediluulf's line and *ardentibus* in Aldhelm's); such imprecise recollections again perhaps suggest memorial transmission.

Precisely similar chains of influence from one specific poet or poem to another can be found in Old English verse too. Perhaps the clearest example is the anonymous poem *Andreas* (Brooks 1961; Boenig 1991), a versification of the life of the Apostle Andrew, which has been shown to share considerable overlaps of diction with several specific texts, notably *Beowulf* and the four signed poems of Cynewulf (Powell 2002; Orchard 2005b; Friesen 2008; Orchard [forthcoming]). A prime example of the *Andreas*-poet drawing on earlier verses known to him is the extent to which he appears to have internalised Cynewulf's grim description of how the wicked Eleusius had Juliana cruelly tortured. The passage by Cynewulf reads as follows (*Juliana* 227b–46):

He bi feaxe het
ahon ond ahebban   on heanne beam,
þær seo sunsciene   slege þrowade,
sace singrimme,   siex tida dæges,   230
ond he ædre het   eft asettan,
laðgeniðla,   ond gelædan bibead
to carcerne.   Hyre wæs Cristes lof
in ferðlocan   fæste biwunden,
milde modsefan,   mægen unbrice.   235
Ða wæs mid clustre   carcernes duru
behliden homra geweorc.   Halig þær inne
wærfæst wunade.   Symle heo wuldorcyning
herede æt heortan,   heofonrices god,
in þam nydclafan,   nergend fira,   240
heolstre bihelmad.   Hyre wæs halig gæst
singal gesið.   Ða cwom semninga
in þæt hlinræced   hæleða gewinna,
yfeles ondwis.   Hæfde engles hiw,
gleaw gyrnstafa   gæstgeniðla,   245
helle hæftling,   to þære halgan spræc.

He ordered her to be hung and hauled up on a high gallows by her hair where she, dazzling as the sun, suffered beating and greatly savage treatment for six hours of the day: and he, the hateful oppressor, straightaway ordered her to be taken down and commanded that she be led to prison. The worship of Christ was firmly enfolded within her breast and in her gentle spirit, an unbreakable strength. Then the prison door, the work of hammers, was fastened with a bar; the holy girl stayed inside, secure in faith. She constantly praised the king of glory in her heart, the God of the heavenly kingdom inside that confined space, the saviour of men, covered in darkness. To her the Holy Spirit was a constant companion. Then suddenly the enemy of men entered into that prison, cunning in wickedness. Skilled in torments, he had an angel's form, the soul's oppressor, prisoner of hell, spoke to the saint.

Michael Lapidge has identified a Latin text remarkably close to what must have been Cynewulf's source, which at this point reads as follows (double-underlined forms can be matched in *Juliana* [Lapidge 2003: 158–9]):

Tunc praefectus iussit eam capillis suspendi. Adpensa uero per sex horas, iussit eam deponi …et sic eam in carcere praecipi…Tunc Belial daemon ueniens in figura angeli.

Then the prefect ordered her to be hung by the hair. When she had been suspended for six hours, he ordered her to be taken down…and so to be cast into prison. Then the demon Belial, coming in the shape of an angel…

While Cynewulf preserves the basic sequence of events in the Latin, it is worth pointing out that he has considerably condensed matters, and (for example) omitted entirely a lengthy speech by Juliana in which she reminds God of the protection he has offered the faithful in the past, by providing a litany of beneficiaries. Cynewulf eschews the list, and instead offers a general description of pious prayer (lines 233b–242a), bracketed off by an envelope pattern (*Hyre was Cristes lof / in ferðlocan…Hyre wæs halig gæst / singal gesið*) that precisely marks off the departure from the Latin source. Such is the originality of Cynewulf, and his awareness of his own role in a developing tradition.

But Cynewulf's passage clearly appealed to the *Andreas*-poet, who appears to have imitated aspects of it on at least four occasions (*Andreas* 51b–58; 1074b–1077; 1341–2; 1462b–1463 [Brooks 1961: 2, 35, 43, and 47]; parallels are indicated by *bold italics*):

> Hwæðre he in breostum þa git
> *herede in heortan heofonrices* weard,
> þeah ðe he atres drync atulne onfenge.
> Eadig ond onmod, he mid elne forð
> *wyrðode wordum* wuldres aldor,
> heofonrices weard, halgan stefne,
> of *carcerne*. Him *wæs Cristes lof*
> on *fyrðlocan fæste bewunden*.   55

And yet even then within his breast he praised in his heart the guardian of the heavenly kingdom, although he accepted the dread drink of poison. Blessed and resolute, with zeal he went on worshipping with words the prince of glory, the guardian of the heavenly kingdom, with a holy voice, from prison. The worship of Christ was firmly enfolded within his breast.

> Him seo wen gelah,
> syððan *mid* corðre   *carcernes duru*   1075
> eorre æscberend   opene fundon,
> on*hliden hamera geweorc*,   hyrdas deade.

This expectation cheated them when in their pomp the angry spear-carriers found the door of the prison open, the work of hammers unlocked, and the guards dead.

> Ongan eft swa ær   eald*geniðla*,
> *helle hæftling*,   hearmleoð galan.

Again as before, the old enemy, hell's captive, began to wail a lament.

> *Þa com* dryhten god
> *in þæt hlinræced,   hæleða* wuldor.

Then the Lord God, Glory of men, came into that locked building.

Only the first two passages have any basis whatsoever in the analogues, although it is notable that in neither case does the translated portion overlap with that borrowed from *Juliana*; it is as if the *Andreas*-poet has chosen to augment his source by recourse to a familiar extract from his own reading. In the first case, the analogue reads as follows (Blatt 1930: 35/6–7): 'Cum autem illum pessimum bibisset potum, nichil eum nocuerat' ('But although he had drunk the very bad drink, it had not harmed him at all'); in the second (Blatt 1930: 75/1): 'Cum autem invenissent eam apertam, et custodes mortuos' ['After they had found [the prison] open, and the guards dead']. Here again the *Andreas*-poet, like Cynewulf, has departed considerably from his Latin source. He has also augmented his Cynewulfian borrowings with recourse to other poems he seems to have known, as well as by the use of such poetic commonplaces for God as 'wuldres aldor', 'heofonrices weard' and 'dryhten god', each of which is widely attested. Others of his augmentations can be more specifically identified. So, for example, in the case of the first passage cited here (*Andreas* 51–8), it seems that the *Andreas*-poet has supplemented the words drawn from *Juliana* with a half-line from *Guthlac A* (*eadig ond onmod*; *Guth A* 745 and *And* 54), a poem with which he seems on other evidence to have been very familiar (Orchard forthcoming); in the case of the second passage cited here (*Andreas* 1074–7), the opening half-line (*him seo wen gelah*) may have been drawn from either *Genesis A* (lines 49 and 1446) or, more likely, *Beowulf* (line 2323), given the clear links that connect *Andreas* and *Beowulf* elsewhere (Powell 2002; Friesen 2008); the third passage (*Andreas* 1341–2) likewise opens with a phrase (*eft swa ær*) that may have been drawn from either *Guthlac A* (390) or *Beowulf* (lines 642 and 1787). But perhaps the key point to make here is to highlight the extent to which all four passages from *Andreas*, despite their evident overlap of diction with the parallel passage from *Juliana*, are also largely comprised of phrases that are found elsewhere in *Andreas*, sometimes uniquely so. A good example is found in line 1076, where the phrase 'eorre æscberend' is unique to *Andreas*, being found only here and at line 42; likewise, if the phrase 'halgan stefne' (line 56) can be matched in *Exodus* 257 (a poem of which there is little evidence of the *Andreas*-poet's direct knowledge), it is clearly one that appealed to the poet, appearing as it does also in *Andreas* 537, 873, 1054, 1399 and 1456. However much he relied on earlier sources, it is evident that the *Andreas*-poet has not only memorised this particular passage from Cynewulf's *Juliana*, but also has adopted and adapted it for his own use.

Even within the constraints of the tradition, there was ample opportunity for individual talent to develop and shine. A final example where aural embellishments seem to have been consciously employed by the *Andreas*-poet will suffice to underline the point that however much Anglo-Saxon poets need to be seen as part of a developing tradition, it is their originality and innovation that marks them out, and perhaps prepares their work to be imitated in turn by other poets working within the same tradition. The passage in question comprises an extraordinary description of how the apostle's companions report that they were lifted bodily into heaven by miraculous eagles (*Andreas*, lines 863–74 [Brooks 1961: 28]):

> Þa comon earnas   ofer yða wylm
> faran on flyhte,   feðerum hremige,
> us ofslæpendum   sawle abrugdon,   865
> mid gefean feredon   flyhte on lyfte,
> brehtmum bliðe,   beorhte ond liðe.
> Lissum lufodon   ond in lofe wunedon,
> þær wæs singal sang   ond swegles gong,
> wlitig weoroda heap   ond wuldres þreat.   870
> Utan ymbe æðelne   englas stodon,
> þegnas ymb þeoden,   þusendmælum,
> heredon on hehðo   halgan stefne
> dryhtna dryhten.   Dream wæs on hyhte.

Then eagles came over the surging of the waves, coming in flight, exulting in their feathers; then they took away our souls as we slept, and with joy bore them through the air in flight, happy in their cries. They showed love in acts of kindness, and dwelt in praise: there was continual singing and the expanse of the sky, a radiant throng of hosts, and a band of glory. Round about the prince stood angels, thegns about their master in their thousands: they praised in the heights with a holy voice the lord of lords; there was rejoicing in hope.

The Phoenix, another Cynewulfian poem with which the *Andreas*-poet seems to have been acquainted (Orchard forthcoming), seems to have supplied the inspiration for lines 866 and 871 (cf. *Phoen* 123 and 340 '*flyhte on lyfte*'; *Phoen* 164 '*utan ymb æpelne*'), while a repeated phrase in *Beowulf* 860 and 1773 ('*under swegles begong*') may have suggested line 869, a phrase that the *Andreas*-poet repeats elsewhere ('*under swegles gang*' in lines 208 and 455); and line 873 includes the phrase 'hlagan stefne' already remarked upon as a particular favourite within *Andreas*, where it appears no fewer than six times. Likewise, the poet has leant not only upon his vernacular predecessors, but also upon a Latin source, the precise details of which remain uncertain. There are two Latin analogues here; the first is the so-called Casanatensis version (Blatt 1930: 65/11–15; <u>double-underlined</u> forms have a parallel in the Old English):

> Et <u>nos</u> translati sumus sompno gravi. <u>Tunc descenderunt aquile</u> et <u>abstulerunt animas nostras,</u> <u>duxerunt</u>que <u>nos</u> in paradisum celestem, et vidimus magna mirabilia. Vidimus <u>dominum</u> iesum christum sedentem in throno glorie sue, et omnes <u>angeli circumstantes,</u> <u>ymnumque dicentes.</u>

> And we were carried off in deep sleep. Then eagles came down and took away our souls, and led us to heavenly paradise, and we saw great wonders. We saw Lord Jesus Christ sitting on the throne of his glory, and all the angels standing around, saying a hymn.

The second derives from the so-called Bonnet Fragment (Blatt 1930: 14/19–26; <u>double-underlined</u> forms have a parallel in the Old English):

> Translati enim sumus in somno graviori, et <u>descenderunt aquile</u> et <u>rapuerunt animas nostras</u> et <u>duxerunt nos</u> in paradysum, quod est in celis, et vidimus <u>dominum</u> nostrum Iesum Christum sedentem in throno gloriae suae, et omnes <u>angeli circumstante[s].</u>

> And we were carried off in rather a deep sleep, and eagles came down and snatched our souls, and led us to paradise, which is in heaven, and we saw our Lord Jesus Christ sitting on the throne of his glory, and all the angels standing around.

It is important to emphasise the extent to which the *Andreas*-poet has massively surpassed both of his putative Latin analogues in purely artistic terms; the accounts given in both the Casanatensis version and the Bonnet Fragment are relatively unadorned (with indeed the likelihood that eye-skip from *vidimus* to *vidimus* may account for the significant difference between the two texts). By contrast, the *Andreas*-poet has divided his passage into three clear units, each marked by the artful use of aural effects. The opening and closing sections (lines 863–7 and 871–4) are the only ones which derive at least part of their sense from the Latin, and both conclude with similar assonance on words with medial -*ht*-/-*hð*- ('flyhte...brehtmum...beorhte' [lines 866–7]; 'hehðo...dryhtna dryhten...hyhte' [lines 873–4]). The middle section (lines 868–70), which has no parallel in the analogues, continues the end-rhyme of line 867 (*bliðe... liðe*) with a series of more-or-less perfect end-rhymes of its own (*lufodon... wunedon*; *sang... gong*; *heap... þreat*), as well as beginning with a pun on the elements *luf-* and *lof-* that is particularly widespread in texts associated with Cynewulf (Orchard 2005b). The *Andreas*-poet's sensitivity to sound-effects is clear, and the originality of his approach within the patterns laid down by his predecessors is plain.

It will be clear from the above examples that the Anglo-Saxon poetic tradition was at once both innately conservative, in preserving phrases and forms from earlier verses learnt or inherited, and innovative, in encouraging individual poets to seek beyond what was handed down, and to discover their own voices, for future generations to appreciate and even imitate. The challenge for modern readers, untrained in such a tradition, and often insensitive to patterns of repetition and allusion, is surely to seek beyond the printed page, to see chains of borrowing that bind lines of individuals within the broader tradition, and to hear the distant echoes of poets long perished, but whose works live on.

References and Further Reading

Abram, C. (2000). In search of lost time: Aldhelm and 'The Ruin'. *Quaestio*, 1, 35–49.

Blatt, F. (ed.) (1930). *Die lateinischen Bearbeitungen der Acta Andreae et Matthiae apud anthropophagos*. Zeitschrift für die neutestamentliche Wissenschaft 12. Giezen: Tüpelmann.

Boenig, R. (ed.) (1991). *The Acts of Andrew in the Country of the Cannibals: Translations from the Greek, Latin, and Old English*. Garland Library of Medieval Literature, ser. B, 70. New York: Garland.

Braswell, B. K. (1978). 'The Dream of the Rood' and Aldhelm on Sacred Prosopopeia. *Mediaeval Studies*, 40, 461–7.

Brooks, K. R. (ed.) (1961). *Andreas and the Fates of the Apostles*. Oxford: Oxford University Press.

Bulst, W. (1938). Bedas Sterbelied. *Zeitschrift für deutsches Altertum*, 75, 111–14.

Campbell, A. (ed.) (1967). *Æthelwulf: De Abbatibus*. Oxford: Clarendon Press.

Cavill, P. (2000). The Manuscripts of 'Cædmon's Hymn.' *Anglia*, 118, 499–530.

Colgrave, B. and R. A. B. Mynors (eds) (1969). *Bede's Ecclesiastical History of the English People*. Oxford Medieval Texts. Rev. edn. Oxford: Clarendon Press.

Conybeare, J. J. (1826). *Illustrations of Anglo-Saxon Poetry*. London: Harding and Lepard.

Cook, A. S. (1924). Aldhelm and the Source of 'Beowulf' 2523. *Modern Language Notes*, 40, 137–42.

Cook, A. S. (1925). 'Beowulf' 1422. *Modern Language Notes*, 39, 77–82.

Dumville, D. N. (1981). 'Beowulf' and the Celtic world: the uses of the evidence. *Traditio*, 37, 109–60.

Ehwald, R. (ed.) (1919). *Aldhelmi Opera*. Monumenta Germaniae Historica. Auctores Antiquissimi 15. Berlin: MGH.

Friesen, B. (2008). Visions and revisions: the sources and analogues of the Old English 'Andreas'. Unpublished PhD dissertation. University of Toronto.

Gneuss, H. (2001). *Handlist of Anglo-Saxon Manuscripts. A List of Manuscripts and Manuscript Fragments Written or Owned in England up to 1100*. Tempe, AZ: MRTS.

Howlett, D. R. (1975). The provenance, date, and structure of *De Abbatibus*. *Archaeologia Aeliana*, 5th ser. 3, 121–30.

Howlett, D. (1992). Inscriptions and design of the Ruthwell Cross. In B. Cassidy (ed.). *The Ruthwell Cross* (pp. 71–93). Princeton, NJ: Princeton University Press.

Isaac, G. R. (1997). The date and origin of 'Cædmon's Hymn'. *Neuphilologische Mitteilungen*, 98, 217–28.

Jaager, W. (ed.) (1935). *Bedas metrische Vita sancti Cuthberti.* Palaestra 198. Leipzig: Mayer & Müller.

Kiernan, K. S. (1990). Reading 'Cædmon's Hymn' with someone else's glosses. *Representations*, 32, 157–74.

Lapidge, M. (1975). Some remnants of Bede's lost 'Liber Epigrammatum'. *English Historical Review*, 90, 798–820.

Lapidge, M. (1979). Aldhelm's Latin poetry and Old English verse. *Comparative Literature*, 31, 209–31.

Lapidge, M. (1982). The study of Latin texts in late Anglo-Saxon England: 1. The evidence of Latin glosses. In N. Brooks (ed.). *Latin and the Vernacular Languages in Early Medieval Britain* (pp. 99–140). Leicester: Leicester University Press.

Lapidge, M. (1989). Bede's Metrical *Vita S. Cuthberti*. In G. Bonner, D. Rollason and C. Stancliffe (eds). *St Cuthbert: His Life, Cult and Community to A.D. 1200* (pp. 77–93). Woodbridge: Boydell.

Lapidge, M. (1990). Aediluulf and the School at York. In A. Lehner and W. Berschin (eds). *Lateinische Kultur im VIII. Jahrhundert. Traube-Gedenkschrift* (pp. 161–78). St Ottilien: EOS Verlag.

Lapidge, M. (1993). *Anglo-Latin Literature, 900–1066.* London: Hambledon.

Lapidge, M. (1994). *Bede the Poet.* The Jarrow Lecture 1993. Jarrow: St Paul's.

Lapidge, M. (1996). *Anglo-Latin Literature, 600–899.* London: Hambledon.

Lapidge, M. (2003). Cynewulf and the *Passio S. Iulianae.* In M. Amodio and K. O'Brien O'Keeffe (eds). *Unlocking the Wordhord: Anglo-Saxon Studies in Memory of Edward B. Irving, Jr* (pp. 147–71). Toronto: University of Toronto Press.

Lapidge, M. (2006). *The Anglo-Saxon Library.* Oxford: Oxford University Press.

Lapidge, M. (2007). The Career of Aldhelm. *Anglo-Saxon England* 36, 15–69.

Lapidge, M. and J. L. Rosier (1985). *Aldhelm: the Poetic Works.* Cambridge: D. S. Brewer.

O'Donnell, D. P. (2005). *'Cædmon's Hymn': A Multimedia Study, Archive and Edition.* Includes CD-ROM. Cambridge: D. S. Brewer.

Orchard, A. (1992). After Aldhelm: the teaching and transmission of the Anglo-Latin hexameter. *Journal of Medieval Latin*, 2, 96–133.

Orchard, A. (1994). *The Poetic Art of Aldhelm.*

Cambridge Studies in Anglo-Saxon England 8. Cambridge: Cambridge University Press.

Orchard, A. (1995). Artful alliteration in Anglo-Saxon song and story. *Anglia*, 113, 429–63.

Orchard, A. (1996). Poetic inspiration and prosaic translation: the making of 'Cædmon's Hymn'. In J. Toswell and E. Tyler (eds). *'Doubt Wisely': a Festschrift for E.G. Stanley* (pp. 402–22). London: Routledge.

Orchard, A. (1997). Oral tradition. In K. O'Brien O'Keeffe (ed.). *Approaches to Reading Old English Texts* (pp. 101–23). Cambridge: Cambridge University Press.

Orchard, A. (2005a). Enigma variations: the Anglo-Saxon riddle-tradition. In K. O'Brien O'Keeffe and A. Orchard (eds). *Latin Learning and English Lore: Studies in Anglo-Saxon Literature for Michael Lapidge.* 2 vols (I, pp. 284–304). Toronto: University of Toronto Press.

Orchard, A. (2005b). Computing Cynewulf: the 'Judith'-connection. In J. Mann and M. Nolan (eds). *The Text in the Community: Essays on Medieval Works, Manuscripts, and Readers* (pp. 75–106). Notre Dame: University of Notre Dame Press.

Orchard, A. (2007a). Monasteries and courts: Alcuin and King Offa. In R. North and J. Allard (eds). *'Beowulf' and Other Stories: A New Introduction to Old English* (pp. 219–45). London: Pearson.

Orchard, A. (2007b). Multiplication, intoxication, and fornication: the burgeoning text of 'Genesis A'. In J. Roberts and A. Minnis (eds). *Text, Image, Interpretation: Studies in Anglo-Saxon Literature in Honour of Éamonn Ó Carragáin* (pp. 333–54). Turnhout: Brepols.

Orchard, A. (2008). Reconstructing 'The Ruin'. In H. Scheck and V. Blanton (eds). *(Inter)Texts: Studies in Early Insular Culture Presented to Paul E. Szarmach* (pp. 47–70). Arizona: MRTS.

Orchard, A. (2009 forthcoming). The word made flesh: Christianity and oral culture in Anglo-Saxon England. *Oral Tradition.*

Orchard, A. (forthcoming). The originality of 'Andreas'. In A. Scheil (ed.). *Studies on 'Andreas'.* Old English Newsletter Subsidia Series.

Plummer, C. (ed.) (1896). *Venerabilis Baedae Opera Historica.* 2 vols. Oxford: The Clarendon Press.

Powell, A. M. (2002). Verbal parallels in 'Andreas' and its relationship to 'Beowulf' and Cynewulf. Unpublished PhD dissertation. University of Cambridge.

Remley, P. G. (2005). Aldhelm as Old English poet: 'Exodus', Asser and the 'Dicta Ælfredi'. In K. O'Brien O'Keeffe and A. Orchard (eds). *Latin Learning and English Lore: Studies in Anglo-Saxon Literature for Michael Lapidge* (pp. 90–108). Toronto: Toronto University Press.

Smith, A. H. (ed.) (1968). *Three Northumbrian Poems*, repr. with corrections. London: Methuen.

Stanley, E. G. (1974). The oldest English poetry now extant. *Poetica* (Tokyo), 2, 1–24.

Steen, J. (2008). *Verse and Virtuosity: The Adaptation of Latin Rhetoric in Old English Poetry*. Toronto: University of Toronto Press.

Tangl, M. (ed.) (1916). *Die Briefe des Heiligen Bonifatius und Lullus*. Monumenta Germaniae Historica. Epistolae selectae 1. Berlin: MGH.

Toswell, M. J. (1993). The metrical psalter and 'The Menologium'. *Neuphilologische Mitteilungen*, 94, 249–57.

Unterkircher, F. (ed.) (1971). *Sancti Bonifacii epistolae: Codex vindobonensis 751 der Österreichischen Nationalbibliothek; Faksimile-Ausgabe der Wiener Handschrift der Briefe des Heiligen Bonifatius*. Graz: Akademische Druck- und Verlagsanstalt.

Wright, C. D. (1996). The blood of Abel and the branches of sin: *Genesis A, Maxims I*, and Aldhelm's *Carmen de uirginitate*. *Anglo-Saxon England*, 25, 7–19.

Genres and Modes

5

Germanic Legend and Old English Heroic Poetry

Hugh Magennis

Widsið maðolade,   wordhord onleac,
se þe monna mæst   mægþa ofer eorþan,
folca geondferde;   oft he on flette geþah
mynelicne maþþum.   Him from Myrgingum
æþele onwocon.   He mid Ealhhilde,
fælre freoþuwebban,   forman siþe
Hreðcyninges   ham gesohte
eastan of Ongle,   Eormanrices,
wraþes wærlogan.   Ongan þa worn sprecan.

Widsith spoke, unlocked his word-hoard, he who among men travelled through most tribes and peoples over the earth; often on the floor of the hall he received a splendid treasure. His family originated from the Myrgings. With Ealhhild, the gracious weaver of peace, he made his way at the start east from Ongel to the home of the king of the glorious Goths, Eormanric, the cruel oath-breaker. He began then to speak a great many things.

These opening lines of *Widsith* (1–9),[1] a poem of 143 lines from the later-tenth-century Exeter Book, provide a useful entry point to the subject of the present chapter. Most of *Widsith* consists of a speech, introduced in this opening passage, that is presented as the personal utterance of a poet from former times, and the first word of the poem is taken by most scholars to be the poet's name, though it could also conceivably, if less satisfactorily, be translated as 'the far-travelled one'. The passage introduces a personal utterance by Widsith, but presents itself as the declaration of an impersonal traditional narrator, who knows about the poet Widsith and about his place in the heroic world. The character Widsith may or may not be the invention of the *Widsith* poet but much of the information this character imparts about himself is clearly fictitious and his name appears to be a characterising epithet. Widsith belongs to the pre-Christian culture of the early Germanic tribes, though (at the end of the poem) the poet attributes to him an anachronistic reference to one God (lines 133–4).

The body of the poem – the *wordhord* that Widsith unlocks – is a kind of catalogue of heroic legend, in which Widsith lists the personages and peoples he has met and heard about, his speech constituting the most extensive repository we have from Anglo-Saxon England of reference to legendary material. The poem has been seen indeed as representing the repertoire of a *scop*, 'poet'. Joyce Hill lists 158 different names from the poem in the glossary of proper names of her edition of *Widsith* and other heroic poems (Hill 2009: 95–131); by way of comparison, *Beowulf* contains just over a hundred proper names.

The opening passage of the poem brings us into the heroic world. We hear about the famous and cruel Gothic king Eormanric, a figure widely referred to elsewhere in Germanic legend. We hear also about a noble lady called Ealhhild, known only from *Widsith*, and are introduced to Widsith himself and to his people, the Myrgings, who have been identified as a tribe living probably in what is now Holstein. The opening section also mentions Ongel, the continental territory of the Angles, ancestors of one of the tribes of English settlers. To a modern readership, such names mean little, as is the case with most of the names mentioned in Widsith's speech. Anglo-Saxons would have recognised more of them than we do but this is still specialised knowledge, preserved and transmitted by poets. And, although the sheer extent of Widsith's lists impresses, it is likely that even for poets many of the people mentioned would have been no more than names (some appear indeed to be inventions) and that current legends would have been associated with only a minority of them.

The opening lines of *Widsith* illustrate aspects of the 'social' world of heroic poetry as well as its *dramatis personae*. There is reference to the custom of a noblewoman being married into a foreign tribe as a 'peace-weaver' and to the giving and receiving of gifts in the definitive context of the Germanic hall, the hall being presented in the poetry as the focus and symbol of cultural life. The hall is the place of feasting and drinking and is where the *scop* performs songs celebrating the exploits of heroes and receives his reward for doing so, as Widsith has on his travels in the past (lines 3–4). The performance of heroic song in the hall provides entertainment, and praise, but at the same time it has a central role in reinforcing in highly traditional terms the values and identity of the community that the *scop* addresses.

A fundamental quality that the opening passage of *Widsith* brings out about heroic poetry is its orality. Within him Widsith has knowledge of heroic stories and mastery of the poetic language, techniques and structures that enable him to bring forth in speech the tales stored in his memory, and enable him also spontaneously to generate new poetic utterances. Widsith's speech itself begins, 'Fela ic monna gefrægn mægþum wealdan' (line 10; 'I have heard of many men ruling tribes'), a statement that launches him into his first list, of rulers and their peoples. In this statement Widsith places himself in oral tradition, in which lore is received through hearing (*gefrægn*, 'I have heard') and exists only in memory and communal performance, not in any codified form.

We can study the surviving poems only as texts but in order to understand them as literature it is essential to do so with awareness of their oral background and poetics. Germanic heroic poetry had its origin and most of its existence in a non-literate world, a world of what has been referred to as one of 'primary orality' (Havelock 1963; Ong 1982). The vast majority of compositions in this tradition would never have been written down and no two performances by a *scop* of the same poem would ever be the same. What has been preserved in writing must be only the tip of the iceberg of a tradition that was pervasive in Anglo-Saxon England, as were related traditions in other parts of the Germanic world. In this oral context it is the resources – metrical, thematic and verbal – that Widsith has internalised as a traditional poet, which along with his own skill facilitate the fluency that oral composition and performance demand.

The fact that the existing poems have been preserved as texts raises the fraught question of whether, although belonging to an oral tradition, these poems are themselves really oral at all in the way that they purport to be. Have our poems been transcribed from oral performance, or are they literate compositions, intended as 'texts'? It is possible that at least one, and perhaps more, of the poems discussed in the following sections was an oral poem frozen into textuality, as it were, by being written down but that others, particularly *Beowulf* in the view of many scholars, were always written poems. *Widsith* may be something of a hybrid, its core composed and transmitted orally from earlier Anglo-Saxon England but its present form the work of a literate poet, who draws upon learned as well as oral traditions.

The Heroic World and Heroic Poetry in Old English

Widsith is one of a small number of surviving Old English poems that scholars have classified as belonging to the category being considered in the present chapter, that of 'heroic poetry'. The term implies poetry that portrays the ethos and culture associated with the age of the pre-Christian Germanic tribes of the late Roman and post-Roman world, as imagined in later centuries. The ethos of heroic poetry is expressed in the words and actions of the characters, and also through the voice of the narrator, who, as in our initial quotation from *Widsith*, adopts a traditional (male) persona, impersonal in his expression and communal in his perspective.

By the Anglo-Saxons and other Germanic peoples this earlier period was conceived of as a larger-than-life age of legends and heroic actions. It mostly predates Anglo-Saxon England and is lacking in Anglo-Saxon *dramatis personae* but was evidently seen by Anglo-Saxons as of foundational significance to their cultural identity. The surviving heroic poetry from Anglo-Saxon England is characteristically set in this heroic age itself and represents figures, peoples and legends of that age, but it is also usual to include in the Old English heroic corpus at least one poem, *The Battle of Maldon*, that deals not with the legendary material of the distant past but with an episode from (late) Anglo-Saxon history, presented in heroic terms. Thereby, *Maldon* claims continuity with venerable poetic tradition and associates its characters and their sentiments with those of great former times.

The Germanic heroic age was a real period in history, stretching roughly from the fourth to the sixth centuries AD. Many of its key personages are known from historical records, not least the formidable Eormanric, who is recorded by the historian Jordanes as having died in 375. The latest datable figure in *Widsith* is Ælfwine, who is Alboin, the Lombard king; he is reported to have been killed in 572. The heroic age was the period of the great expansion and migration of Germanic tribes across western Europe, into the territories of the old Roman Empire, where they grew in wealth, exerted military power and established kingdoms. It was also the period of the rise of the Huns, a powerful non-Germanic tribe with which the Germanic tribes came into conflict. The military successes of the Huns culminated, and ended, in the career of their great fifth-century king Attila, an important figure in Germanic legend, though he is mentioned only twice in surviving Old English heroic texts (*Widsith*, line 18, and *Waldere*, line 6).

In heroic poetry this period gets 'rewritten' in legendary terms, becoming mythologised and idealised, with much conflation and indeed distortion of the historical events and their actors. Looking to a common Germanic past and radically simplifying the complexities of history, the poetry imagines the earlier centuries as an age beyond the limitations of the present and celebrates the deeds of the great figures who lived and died by the code understood to define that age. The poetry constructs a meaningful Germanic narrative, expressive of values of abiding concern to its creators and their audiences.

Widsith, and Anglo-Saxon heroic poetry more generally, shows a particular interest in early Denmark and surrounding areas. *Widsith* alludes to the conflict between Hrothgar and Hrothulf and between both of them and Ingeld, mentioning also the great hall Heorot (lines 45–9), thereby touching on material that is treated more fully in *Beowulf*. *Beowulf* itself deals with Danes and Swedes and Geats, among others. Its Geatish king Hygelac is one of the 'datable' figures in heroic legend known from historical sources, though appearing in *Beowulf* as the lord of a fictitious hero, who may well be the invention of the *Beowulf* poet himself. Hygelac appears, as Chlochilaichus, in Gregory of Tours's *History of the Franks* (written in the late sixth century), where, wrongly depicted as a Danish king, he is described as leading an attack against the Franks *c.* 521 and being killed in the campaign; in his appearance in *Beowulf* we see the fusion of real history and legend writ large. It has been suggested that the interest in Danish and other Scandinavian figures evident in *Beowulf* and elsewhere may have a bearing on the dating of Old English heroic literature, since the Danes would have been seen as enemies for large stretches of the Anglo-Saxon period, but there has been little agreement on what this circumstance might actually tell us about dating the poetry; for *Beowulf* itself, dates from the seventh century to the eleventh have been proposed (Chase 1981).

The ethos that heroic poetry represents is that of the aristocratic warrior elite of a tribal society. At its centre is the 'heroic code', a code of honour, with its ideals of personal glory, courage and loyalty, which find expression in the definitive context of the *comitatus*. The *comitatus* is that close and intensely personal fellowship of the lord and his retainers that acts out its social life in the tribal hall and fulfils its sworn obligations on the field of battle. The heroic code is binary in nature and highlights the shame of failure, cowardice and treachery, making for a black-and-white interpretation of human behaviour but also for a productive tension between the uncompromising demands of the code and the imperfection of many of the people who see themselves as bound by it. The poetry is populated by heroes of startling potency, the most notable being Beowulf, but also by weaker characters, and even the great heroes are fallible. The characteristic subject matter of heroic poetry is conflict, and with individuals and groups so insistently 'on their honour' there is no shortage of occasions for such conflict.

The heroic world is strongly patriarchal. Women have an honoured place within it but their role is seen essentially as being supportive of male endeavours; females serve and advise male warriors, and they incite them to action, but it is not their role to take part in violence themselves. According to the strict gender demarcation of heroic society, women have their 'natural' place in the domestic sphere, as mothers, wives and daughters, always operating in relation to a male reference point; even when queens are described as giving gifts, it is implicitly a male reference point that legitimises their action. Women also function as 'peace-weavers' (as Ealhhild in our passage from *Widsith*), serving through marriage to cement alliances or heal rifts between tribes. Women normally conform to the requirements of their society and accept its values just as much as men do, even though they may become figures of personal grief as a result of male conflict. When they do not conform to their expected role it is a source of great cultural anxiety and threat (Overing 1990; Magennis 2002).

The extant Old English heroic poems, the chance survivals of what must have been a pervasive literary tradition, are:

Widsith, as briefly described above;
a short (42-line) lyrical piece in the Exeter Book, called *Deor*, also grouped by critics with the so-called Old English 'elegies', and presenting itself as the utterance of another *scop* ('Deor') who lives in the heroic age;
the great epic *Beowulf*, preserved uniquely in a manuscript of the early eleventh century, a poem that as well as relating the adventures of its hero alludes to a wealth of other legendary material, with just over a hundred different proper names mentioned in the poem (3182 lines overall);
The Battle of Finnsburh, or *The Fight at Finnsburh* or *The Finnsburh Fragment*, a fragment of 47 lines from a poem dealing with story material also referred to in *Beowulf*, and known to us only from the transcription of it made in 1705 from a now-lost stray manuscript leaf; features of the text of the fragment suggest that the transcription was made from a late Anglo-Saxon manuscript;
Waldere, another fragmentary text, consisting of two 31-line passages from a poem on the legend of the hero Waldere, preserved in a couple of stray manuscript leaves from the end of the tenth or beginning of the eleventh century;

The Battle of Maldon, a longer fragment (325 lines), incomplete at beginning and end, giving an account in heroic terms of an historical battle that took place in 991. *The Battle of Maldon* is another poem extant only in a transcription, made in the early eighteenth century; the original manuscript (in which the poem was already fragmentary) was destroyed by fire in 1731.

As discussed in other chapters of this volume, aspects of the heroic world feature elsewhere in Old English poetry, particularly in wisdom poetry and the 'elegies' but also in religious verse and even riddles. It is also possible that some of the elegies not only draw on heroic ideas but are based on particular stories from heroic legend. In *Wulf and Eadwacer*, for example, the occurrence of the name 'Eadwacer' (if it is a name) has suggested to some that the poem may relate to legends concerning the Germanic hero Odoacer, and striking correspondences to the story of Signy in the Old Norse *Volsunga saga* have also been pointed out. The editor of the standard edition of *Wulf and Eadwacer* probably expresses the majority view when she writes that it is best to regard the figure of Eadwacer in *Wulf and Eadwacer* as 'imaginary' (Klinck 1992: 175), but the claims of legend continue to be pressed.

Far more heroic poems survive from the related tradition of Germanic heroic poetry in Old Norse, but these survivals too are due only to chance. Most of the existing Old Norse poems are preserved in a single key manuscript written *c.* 1270, the Codex Regius, which contains a collection of twenty-one poems, some of which appear to date back as far as the ninth century. Many Old Norse poems that we know about are not extant. The thirteenth-century Icelandic prose saga *Volsunga saga*, for example, is a cycle of heroic legends based on older poetry, most of which has not survived; *Volsunga saga* includes many revealing, and tantalising, quotations from its lost source poems. Evidence concerning lost Old Norse heroic poems about figures from early legend is also abundantly present in the *History of the Danes* written in Latin by the twelfth-century cleric Saxo Grammaticus; in this work Saxo adapts traditional oral material and he includes many translations from Old Norse poetry. From Old High German only one fragmentary piece survives, *Hildebrandslied*, or the *Lay of Hildebrand*, which may have been originally composed in the seventh century.

Whatever the date of the surviving Old English poems, it is clear that heroic poetry and the legends associated with it remained popular throughout Anglo-Saxon history. Heroic poetry was good entertainment but it also embodied a value system that must have continued to have considerable purchase on the minds of the population. Some Christian writers express antipathy towards heroic poetry but the fact that it is known to have been read in some monasteries and was also copied into manuscripts (most copying of manuscripts in Anglo-Saxon England took place in monasteries) shows that not all those in religious life were necessarily so hostile. The heroic tradition was widely taken up, indeed, and adapted by Christian poets, giving them a lively medium for transmitting to vernacular audiences narratives from the Bible and the lives of the saints. In Old English biblical poems and saints' lives there is an attempt to assimilate Germanic-heroic and Christian traditions, resulting in a 'Germanisation' of sacred story, with biblical figures and saints being presented in heroic terms and living in a version of the heroic world. The assimilation of Christian and Germanic in Old English religious narrative verse appears clumsy in some texts but also produces some effective poetry, including such masterpieces of Anglo-Saxon literary culture as *Exodus* and *The Dream of the Rood*.

This tradition of Christian narrative verse persisted into late Anglo-Saxon England, if the generally accepted late dating of the Old Testament poem *Judith* is correct. Evidence for continuing interest in heroic poetry in late Anglo-Saxon England is also to be seen in the copying activity referred to above, in the adoption of the heroic mode apparent in *The Battle of Maldon*, and in the appropriation of some of the language and ideas of the tradition in another battle poem, though one that lacks key features of the traditional poetry, *The Battle of Brunanburh* (the actual battle took place in 937). *Brunanburh* notably lacks the personal dimension characteristic of heroic poetry and portrays no code of loyalty among its warriors; rather than presenting a *comitatus*, it glorifies a king and prince, and does so in nationalistic terms alien to heroic tradition. Nonetheless, the poem draws upon the heroic ethos of glory and shame, and expects its audience to be on the right wavelength to understand its heroic associations and to appreciate its use of heroic diction.

Extant Heroic Poems from Anglo-Saxon England

As we have seen already, *Widsith* is a catalogue poem rather than a narrative one telling a particular story. There is a narrative component to *Widsith*, as Widsith outlines aspects of his own experience, particularly with Ealhhild at the court of Eormanric, but the bulk of his utterance takes the form of lists of names. There are three separate list passages in the poem, each of them connected by linking passages. After an introductory general statement from Widsith (lines 9–17), saying that rulers ought to govern in moral ways (*þeawum*, line 11), the first list (lines 18–49) is one of rulers and their peoples: 'Ætla weold Hunum, Eormanric Gotum' (line 18; 'Attila ruled the Huns, Eormanric the Goths'), etc. Then Widsith mentions his wide travels and his experience as a poet (lines 50–6), before embarking on a second list (lines 56–87), the form of which is illustrated in its opening lines (lines 56–8):

> Ic wæs mid Hunum   ond mid Hreðgotum
> mid Sweom ond mid Geatum   ond mid Suþdenum.
> Mid Wenlum ic wæs ond mid Wærnum   ond mid wicingum.

> I was with the Huns and the glorious Goths, with the Swedes and with the Geats and with the South-Danes. I was with the Wendles and with the Wærns and with the Wicings.

Among the tribes that Widsith has been with are the Greeks and Romans (lines 76, 78) and also the Israelites, Assyrians and other ancient oriental tribes (lines 82–4). This list modulates into a more discursive account of Widsith's time with Eormanric (lines 88–108), by whom he was treated generously, as he was by Queen Ealhhild. The third list (lines 109–130) mentions people he visited on his travels among the Goths and mostly has the form 'Heðcan sohte ic ond Beadecan ond Herelingas' (line 112; 'Hethca I visited and Beadeca and the Herelings'); these names, like many others in the poem, are mostly unknown to us and surely would have been largely so in Anglo-Saxon England. After this, Widsith makes a statement about good lords (lines 131–4), and then there is a closing passage which is usually taken to be in the voice of the impersonal narrator (lines 135–43), referring to the wandering life of *gleomen* and saying that those who reward them gain praise (*lof*, line 142).

Widsith presents a virtuoso display of arcane knowledge and extols the role of the traditional poet, asserting that those who reward the poet themselves deserve and acquire repute. It has been seen as a clever begging poem (Eliason 1966) but makes a serious statement about the value of poetic tradition and about the importance of preserving that tradition. The poem gives a strong impression of the sheer breadth of heroic legend and identifies the poet, personalised in the figure of Widsith, as its custodian and propagator. *Widsith* presents itself, in a sense, as the embodiment of its own message about tradition, in the process bringing us to the heart of the imagined heroic world. The poem also emphasises the responsibility of rulers to govern well (which includes looking after poets properly); it places the theme of good governance, very relevant to Anglo-Saxon audiences, in a heroic context and associates principles of order with the heroic past that the poem celebrates. The heroic past is shown in *Widsith* to have meaning for the present. Going further, John D. Niles, considering *Widsith* in its tenth-century context, suggests that it 'synthesizes historical and geographical knowledge so as to justify an emergent Anglo-Saxon social order, lending that order the patina of antiquity while wrapping its controlling ethos in an aura of rightness or inevitability' (Niles 2007: 84).

Deor is unique among Old English poems in having a fully-developed stanza-like structure with a series of sections (of unequal length) and a refrain at the end of each section. Each of the first five sections alludes to an episode from Germanic legend, the poem's speaker finding consolation in the fact that the misfortune or hardship suffered by the people referred to passed away. He is encouraged to hope that present troubles too will pass away: hence the refrain line: 'Þæs ofereode, þisses swa mæg' ('That passed away, so can this' [more literally, 'It passed away with respect to that, so it can with respect to this']). The sixth and final section presents a general gnomic reflection, observing that the wise Lord brings about change, showing favour to many but a portion of woes to others. In this section the speaker, who now identifies himself as 'Deor', also turns to his own situation: he had been a *scop* of the Heodenings but lost his position to Heorrenda, and he ends his utterance with a final repetition of the refrain line, leaving us uncertain whether he is saying that his troubles too passed away (in which case the phrase 'þisses swa mæg' must be offering consolation for some new misfortune), or whether his reiteration of this statement is an (optimistic? ironic?) expression of hope that things will eventually turn out well for him. An Anglo-Saxon reader or listener might have taken it either way.

Heorrenda is the Old English form of Hôrent, the name of a famous singer in Middle High German tradition, and the Heodenings appear to be a Scandinavian tribe or dynasty whose name derives from Heoden, a figure known from Norse legend. The *scop* Deor is placed in a recognisable legendary context, therefore, and is presented as inhabiting the heroic world with its personal bond between lord and follower – his lord has been loyal (*holdne*, line 39) to him, and is a 'protector of men' (*eorla hleo*, line 41) – but his Christian reference to the wise Lord (*witig dryhten*, line 32) is anachronistic, and his overall message has been seen as having Boethian overtones, suggesting the world of Latin learning. Moreover, his name looks fictitious or, perhaps, cryptic (*deor* literally means 'wild animal'), and why does he say 'Me wæs Deor noma' (line 37; 'My name was Deor'), using the past tense?

A series of personages from Germanic legend are referred to in the opening five sections of *Deor*, who have all undergone or brought about suffering. Welund suffered at the hands of Nithhad but that passed away; we know from other sources that Nithhad had Welund hamstrung, which the latter avenged by killing Nithhad's sons and raping his daughter. The second stanza is linked to the first, for it is about Beadohild, the daughter of Nithhad, who received consolation for being raped; we know that she gave birth to the great hero Widia. Next comes a stanza about someone apparently called Mæthhild; she is not known directly from Germanic legend, though scholars have cited possible analogues. The fourth stanza mentions Theodric (the Ostrogoth) without elaborating on how he is connected with misfortune; he may have been known to the Anglo-Saxons as a tyrant and therefore a perpetrator of suffering. The final figure to be mentioned, in the fifth stanza, is Eormanric, who was of 'wolfish thought' (*wulfenne gehoht*, line 22) and was 'a savage king' (*grim cyning*, line 23), another tyrannical figure. The treatment of all of these figures, as of Heorenda and the Heodenings in the final stanza, is highly allusive, to the extent of tending towards the cryptic. The specifics of the stories are not given and it is not said how they ended. The audience is evidently expected to fill in the details from their own knowledge. Like *Widsith*, *Deor* transports its readers or listeners back to the world of Germanic legend, which is a world of heroic values but also, here, of cruelty and ruthlessness. The reference to the wise Lord is somewhat startling in this fierce context.

Beowulf, the most celebrated Old English poem, is treated separately in Chapter 8: the following discussion concentrates on it specifically as a heroic poem. *Beowulf* is quintessentially heroic in some ways; it relates the great deeds of a hero, guided by the heroic code, against terrible monsters, placing him in the legendary world of early Scandinavia. In significant respects, however, *Beowulf* is also *un*representative. It derives from oral tradition but comes across as the work of a literate culture, showing a considerable amount of Christian learning (Cavill 2004) and being reminiscent of Latin epic in its scale and loftiness rather than resembling other existing poems of Germanic tradition, which are relatively short. There might have been other long poems in Germanic tradition (we cannot tell, for example, the original length of the 'fragments' discussed below) but no other long heroic poem has survived as such.

Beowulf belongs to the oral heroic tradition and, like *Widsith*, itself portrays an oral culture, with the poet adopting the stance of the oral *scop* in his narrative voice. The poem's narrative voice is exclamatory and communal, and the narration and speeches are rich in gnomic and proverbial-sounding lore, the sentential utterances assuming assent from the community for whom and to whom the narrator speaks: 'Swa sceal geong guma gode gewyrcean' (line 20; 'So must a young man bring it about by generosity...').

The poem is *of* the tradition that depicts the heroic age but it is *apart* from that tradition in outlook and understanding. This apartness gives it its tone, which is highly reflective; *Beowulf* is as much an elegiac meditation as a narrative poem. It presents the heroic world with sympathy but, more than any of the other poems discussed here, as remote from present experience, a distant world that the poet can identify himself and his Anglo-Saxon audience with in terms of origins but that is not the world he knows in Christian Anglo-Saxon England. In its treatment of the heroic age *Beowulf*, unusually, attends acutely to the bloody and unhappy consequences of feuding, and the position of women in the heroic world receives notable consideration, with female figures playing a more central role in the narrative than in other poems. And, while scenes of triumph and success are recounted, *Beowulf* ends in sadness and there is a sense throughout of darkness closing in. Mutability, not an obvious concern of other heroic poems, is a key theme.

The protagonist of *Beowulf* is an invented figure, unknown elsewhere in Germanic legend (though some of his exploits are paralleled in later analogues), but the central story of the poem is surrounded by a mass of 'genuine' legendary material, treated allusively. The effect of the more than a hundred proper names in *Beowulf* is to create a rich picture of Scandinavian legendary history and of the relationships between famous tribes. Such material used to be thought of as digressive and distracting from the poem's main concerns but, as well as providing an authenticating setting for the central story, the 'background' legendary material reflects key concerns of the poem overall.

The narrative of the 'Finnsburh episode' plays a particularly significant role in the poem. This episode is treated at some length, though still allusively, in a lay performed by the *scop* at Heorot in celebration of Beowulf's victory over the monster Grendel (lines 1068–1159). It tells of the killing of the Danish hero Hnæf at the hands of the sons of Finn in the Frisian stronghold, of the grief of Hildeburh at the loss of her sons and brothers, of an uneasy peace between the two hostile groups, and of the bloody vengeance on the Frisians finally exacted by the Danes. None of the background of the story is filled in and the identities and relationships of the *dramatis personae* are not explained, the assumption being that the audience will be able to supply this information from prior knowledge. It is assumed that they know that the Danish princess Hildeburh (from a period previous to that of the foreground events of the poem) is married to Finn, king of the Frisians, and that, on a visit to them by Hildeburh's brother Hnæf and his followers, violence breaks out at which Hnæf is killed, as are the sons of Finn and Hildeburh and many others. It is not mentioned whether there had been a history of feud or enmity between Danes and Frisians, though we may suspect this to be the case; an informed audience would know.

The lay in *Beowulf* recounts the aftermath of the initial bloodbath, telling how the uneasy truce is agreed between the remaining Danes, led by Hnæf's retainer Hengest, and the Frisians, according to which the two sides will observe peace over the winter, before the Danes can return to their own land. Hengest, however, confined in the stronghold of the enemy who has killed his lord, broods on revenge all winter, and when spring comes Finn is put to the sword and the hall is 'reddened with the blood of enemy warriors' ('Ða wæs heal roden / feonda feorum', lines 1151–2); afterwards all of Finn's treasure is seized and Hildeburh is brought home across the sea to her people.

The Finnsburh episode exemplifies the kind of legendary amplification ubiquitously found in *Beowulf*. It is also interesting in the present context because its content provides a link with one of the other surviving Old English heroic texts, *The Battle of Finnsburh*. *The Battle of Finnsburh* describes a surprise night attack on a hall at 'Finnsburuh' (line 36) and the courageous defence of those inside. It is clearly from the same story as the *Beowulf* episode but appears to deal with the beginning of the hostilities, a stage of the story not elaborated in *Beowulf*. The fragment begins with the end of a sentence that also seems to be the end of a speech, to which another speech is immediately made in reply by a 'king young in battle' ('heaþogeong cyning', line 2). This figure must be the Danish leader Hnæf, whose name appears towards the end of the existing text. The speech alerts the Danes that they are being attacked and urges them to defend themselves well. In the ensuing battle, which is vividly described, the Danes defend the doors of the hall; several of the warriors, including Hengest, are mentioned by name. The battle lasts for five days and during this time none of the sixty men inside the hall is killed, though they cause much slaughter against the attackers. The Finnsburh episode in *Beowulf* indicates that Hnæf dies in this battle and that after it the two sides agree a truce, but the fragment breaks off while the battle is still continuing.

As in *Beowulf*, the approach to legendary material is allusive, with no explanatory information given about the people mentioned, and as in *Beowulf*, there is a concentration on dramatic moments rather than on clearly-defined narrative sequence. There is nothing of the reflectiveness or thematic complication of *Beowulf*, however, and no sign at all of Christian influence. *Finnsburh* is interested in heroic action and in the sentiments of the warriors in the thick of things, and it presents what is very much an exciting eye-witness account of the battle of the hall. Narration and speeches are exclamatory and abrupt, though stylised rhetoric is also incorporated within this mode, notably in the speech of the king young in battle, which contains a series of mannered images, as the speaker, probably responding to a complementary series of questions in the preceding speech, rhetorically eliminates possibilities about what could be causing the flashing lights that can be seen in the night, and identifies them finally as coming from weapons (lines 3–7):

Ne ðis ne dagað eastan,   ne her draca ne fleogeð,
ne her ðisse healle   hornas ne byrnað.
Ac her forð berað;   fugelas singað,
gylleð græghama,   guðwudu hlynneð,
scyld scefte oncwyð.

This is not day breaking from the east, nor is a dragon flying here, nor are the gables of this hall on fire, but here they are bearing forth [their weapons], the birds [of battle] are singing, the grey-coated one howls, the battle-wood resounds, shield answers shaft.

The half-line images here are extravagant but starkly expressed; there are no adjectives, for example. The passage presents a cumulative contrastive sequence, first saying what is not causing the flashing (three things), then what is (the approaching warriors), and then providing (in an extension of the image of the approaching warriors) an anticipatory description of battle, replete with beasts of battle.

In *Beowulf* the first-person narrator pays attention to the thoughts and intentions of characters and is constantly generalising from the particular; the narration also has a retrospective quality, with the narrator commenting on actions completed: 'þa wæs sund liden' (line 223: 'then had the sea been crossed'), 'Hæfde þa gefælsod' (line 825: 'he had then cleansed [the hall]'), 'Hæfde...gilp gelæsted' (lines 829–30: 'He had fulfilled his vow'). In *Finnsburh* there is an element of the latter, where the poet comments on the exceptional extent of the loyalty of the Danes to their lord (lines 37–40), but the emphasis is very much on immediacy of narration and on the actions and speeches of the story, which to a large extent speak for themselves.

Direct speech figures importantly in the poem, contributing to this sense of immediacy and also serving, economically, to further the narrative. The speech of the *heaþogeong cyning* tells us what is happening in the opening sequence and later we move from the indirect discourse of one of the attackers asking 'hwa ða duru heolde' (line 23: 'who held the door') to the actual words of one of the door-defenders; speeches are part of the action.

The qualities I have highlighted in *The Battle of Finnsburh* lend an archaic feel to the poem. For this reason, it has been suggested that *Finnsburh* must be an early composition and that it was probably a 'lay' of perhaps 200–300 lines, rather than a large-scale work. On the other hand, there are features of the text of the poem, notably the appearance of metrically irregular half-lines, the application of the word *swanas* to noblemen – suggesting Norse influence (if *swanas*, an emendation, is the correct reading) – and the use of unusual words, that have been seen as pointing to composition in later Anglo-Saxon England. In the light of Hnæf's mannered opening speech, it has also been claimed that '[t]he style of the *Fragment* suggests that the original poem was quite long' (Cavill 2002). 'Quite long' is still surely likely to mean hundreds rather than thousands of lines, however.

As I have emphasised, in style and approach *The Battle of Finnsburh* contrasts markedly with *Beowulf*. If it is in fact a composition from later Anglo-Saxon England, *Finnsburh* shows the continuation of traditions from an earlier period. The evidence for late composition is far from conclusive, however, as the most significant 'late' features may reflect the transmission of the poem rather than its origin. Whatever its date, *Finnsburh*, powerful and uncomplicated, perhaps gets us closer to the world of primary orality than any of the other poems discussed here.

Waldere treats its material in a more leisurely fashion and, while sternly heroic in its value-system, is notable for its incorporation of Christian sentiments on the part of its characters. The existing fragments consist almost entirely of carefully developed speeches, each stretching over many lines; we hear little of the direct voice of the narrator. The speeches themselves express the heroic outlook uncompromisingly, finding no conflict between this and a trust in the favour of God. The fragments are from what appears to be a version of a story (not otherwise known from extant Anglo-Saxon writings) that is also treated, among numerous analogues, in a Frankish Latin epic of the ninth or tenth century, *Waltharius*, in which the eponymous hero (Old English Waldere), prince of Aquitaine, along with his betrothed Hiltgunt (Hildegyth) flees from the court of Attila (Ætla), where he has lived as a hostage, taking with him as much treasure as he can manage. On their journey the lovers are attacked by the Frankish king Guntharius (Guthhere) and his warriors, including the great champion Hagen (Hagena). The men are all badly wounded but survive. They call off the fight and the story ends with the marriage of the two lovers and the accession of the hero to the throne of Aquitaine. The Old English fragments appear to be from the part dealing with the fight between Waldere and the Franks. In the first fragment, Hildegyth (in a speech that breaks off before its end) encourages Waldere in the fight, praising his sword Mimming. The second begins with the end of a speech presumably by Guthhere or Hagena which refers to the power of other swords, and then Waldere (in another speech that breaks off) challenges Guthhere to attack him, expressing faith in the favour of God. We cannot tell whether the Old English poem covered the whole story but this seems likely. If so, the complete poem would have been of considerable length, surely larger in scale than *The Battle of Finnsburh*.

The legend as it appears in *Waltharius* combines traditional heroic themes, such as the clash of loyalties and the defence of a narrow place, with an 'ungermanic' tone of amused irony, an interest in love and a concern for Christian morality, and the Latin poem ends with reconciliation and happiness. Such 'ungermanic' features do not come out in the existing text of *Waldere*, which is likely to represent an earlier, unsoftened, version of the story. Hildegyth, for example, appears here as the traditional female inciter rather than a romantic figure. The fragments are made up of fierce dialogue, highly oppositional in style, which expresses heroic values in black-and-white, either-or terms. And *Waldere* also places itself in the world of known heroic legend, with references in the fragments to Weland, Theodric, Widia and Nithhad, as well as to the *dramatis personae* of the immediate story.

Unlike the other works covered in this chapter, the final poem to be discussed, *The Battle of Maldon*, is not about legendary heroes from the heroic past but gives an account of a real battle fought between Anglo-Saxons and Viking invaders on the Essex coast in 991 (as reported in the *Anglo-Saxon Chronicle*). In the poem this battle is essentially conceived in heroic terms, the actions and sentiments of the warriors resembling those of people in *Beowulf* or *The Battle of Finnsburh*. The Anglo-Saxon leader Byrhtnoth and his men are motivated by the heroic imperatives of honour and glory, and after Byrhtnoth has been cut down his followers demonstrate their personal loyalty to him by fighting on to avenge him. As in poetry set in the heroic age, much of the account consists of formal speeches, oppositional in style, and the battle is described as a series of one-to-one encounters; the theme of the beasts of battle is incorporated, as is that of the defence of a narrow place – the Vikings can only come ashore across a narrow causeway – and, reinforcing the bond between warriors, the poem alludes to the hall behaviours of boasting at the feast and gift-giving. There are 'non-heroic' features too, however, indicative of the fact that this late poem is somewhat removed from the inherited tradition. The Anglo-Saxons are presented as fighting for their religion and homeland as well as for 'heroic' reasons, and, untypical of the aristocratic world of heroic poetry, one of the English warriors is said to be a *ceorl*, 'freeman' (line 255); also, the ideal of warriors dying for their lord, highlighted in the poem, is not thought to be an 'authentic' heroic feature (Woolf 1976).

At the beginning of the text as we have it, Byrhtnoth encourages his warriors as they prepare for battle. Then a Viking messenger appears announcing that the seamen are willing to accept tribute instead of battle, a proposal that Byrhtnoth contemptuously refuses: the messenger must report back that the lord and troop facing them will defend their land against the heathen. Things are now at something of a stalemate, however, since the Anglo-Saxons hold the causeway and the Vikings cannot get ashore. But Byrhtnoth, 'for his ofermode' (line 89; 'because of his pride/over-confidence' [?]), allows the enemy to come across the causeway, so that battle can take place. In the ensuing combat Byrhtnoth is killed, commending his soul to God in his dying speech. At this point, three brothers, 'the sons of Odda', flee from the Anglo-Saxon ranks, one of them escaping on Byrhtnoth's own horse. They are followed by many others, who have been deceived into thinking that it was Byrhtnoth who rode away. Byrhtnoth's *heorðgeneatas*, 'hearth-companions', fight on, however, making heroic declarations and falling one after another in the battle. The text breaks off in the course of celebrating their courage. The names of many Anglo-Saxon warriors are included in the poem but the Vikings remain undifferentiated and nameless.

The Battle of Maldon draws upon archetypal heroic ideas and language to show greatness on the part of the warriors at Maldon even in defeat. Scholars still debate whether the *ofermod* of Byrhtnoth is to be seen as a grave sin or a kind of 'admirable' heroic fault but the tone of the poem overall is one of celebration rather than of condemnation of unnecessary loss of life. There is no interest in political or strategic considerations or in the implications of what looks like disastrous defeat.

It is quite possible that the course of the actual battle was similar to that described in the poem but that Byrhtnoth was motivated by tactical rather than heroic considerations. In allowing the Vikings to cross the causeway he was offering battle at a site advantageous to the land army, and to begin with things went well. The turning point was not Byrhtnoth's act of *ofermod* nor even necessarily his death; what gave victory to the invaders, enabling them to inflict slaughter on the remaining Anglo-Saxon warriors, was the confusion following the flight of the sons of Odda, one of whom was mistaken for Byrhtnoth. Whatever the course of the real event, the *Maldon* poet mythologises the battle and its Anglo-Saxon participants. In the poem's ideologically charged depiction of battle, heroism is allied with Christian faith and with attachment to country, to the extent of making Byrhtnoth a saint-like defender of 'Æþelredes eard', 'the land of [king] Æthelred' (line 53). The ideals of heroism, inherited from the distant past and resonating deep in Anglo-Saxon consciousness, are used to give meaning to recent history, providing an affirmation of communal identity in anxious times. As the end of the Anglo-Saxon period approaches, the heroic tradition remains meaningful for the *Maldon* poet and capable of imaginative adaptation.

NOTE

1   All quotations of Old English poetry are from the Anglo-Saxon Poetic Records (ASPR) edition; translations are my own.

REFERENCES AND FURTHER READING

Primary Texts

Bradley, S. A. J. (trans.) (1982). *Anglo-Saxon Poetry*. London: Dent: *The Battle of Finnsburh*, pp. 507–9; *The Battle of Maldon*, pp. 518–28; *Beowulf*, pp. 408–94; *Deor*, pp. 362–5; *Waldere*, pp. 510–12; *Widsith*, pp. 336–40.

Fulk, R. D., Robert E. Bjork and John D. Niles (eds) (2008). *Klaeber's Beowulf and the Fight at Finnsburg, Based on the Third Edition with First and Second Supplements of Beowulf and the Fight at Finnsburg Edited by Fr. Klaeber*. Toronto: University of Toronto Press.

Hill, Joyce (ed.) (2009). *Old English Minor Heroic Poems*. 3rd edn. Durham Medieval and Renaissance Texts, 2. Durham: Centre for Medieval and Renaissance Studies, University of Durham/Toronto: Pontifical Institute of Medieval Studies: *Deor*, pp. 37–8; *The Finnsburh Fragment*, pp. 42–3; *Waldere*, pp. 39–41; *Widsith*, pp. 31–6.

Krapp, George Philip, and Elliott Van Kirk Dobbie (eds) (1931–53). *The Anglo-Saxon Poetic Records*. 5 vols. New York: Columbia University Press: *The Battle of Finnsburh*, VI, *The Anglo-Saxon Minor Poems*, 3–4; *The Battle of Maldon*, VI, *The Anglo-Saxon Minor Poems*, 7–16; *Beowulf*, IV,

Beowulf and Judith, 1–98; *Deor*, III, *The Exeter Book*, 178–9; *Waldere*, VI, *The Anglo-Saxon Minor Poems*, 4–6; *Widsith*, III, *The Exeter Book*, 149–53.

Scragg, D. G. (ed.) (1981). *The Battle of Maldon*. Manchester: Manchester University Press.

Secondary Reading

Cavill, Paul (2002). *The Fight at Finnsburh*. In Robert Clark (ed.). *The Literary Encyclopedia*. www.LitEncyc.com.

Cavill, Paul (2004). Christianity and Theology in *Beowulf*. In Paul Cavill (ed.). *The Christian Tradition in Anglo-Saxon England: Approaches to Current Scholarship and Teaching* (pp. 15–39). Cambridge: D. S. Brewer.

Chase, Colin (ed.) (1981). *The Dating of 'Beowulf'*. Toronto Old English Series, 6. Toronto: University of Toronto Press.

Eliason, Norman E. (1966). Two Old English 'scop' poems. *PMLA*, 81, 185–92.

Frank, Roberta (1991). Germanic legend in Old English literature. In Malcolm Godden and Michael Lapidge (eds). *The Cambridge Companion to Old English Literature* (pp. 88–106). Cambridge: Cambridge University Press.

Havelock, Eric A. (1963). *A Preface to Plato*. Oxford: Blackwell.

Hill, John M. (1995). *The Cultural World in 'Beowulf'*. Toronto: University of Toronto Press.

Hill, John M. (2000). *The Anglo-Saxon Warrior Ethic*. Gainesville, FL: University Press of Florida.

Howe, Nicholas (1985). *The Old English Catalogue Poems*. Anglistika, 23. Copenhagen: Rosenkilde and Bagger.

Hume, Kathryn (1974). The concept of the hall in Old English poetry. *Anglo-Saxon England*, 3, 63–74.

Klinck, Anne L. (1992). *The Old English Elegies: A Critical Edition and Genre Study*. Montreal and Kingston: McGill–Queen's University Press.

Magennis, Hugh (2002). Gender and heroism in the Old English *Judith*. In Elaine Treharne (ed.). *Writing Gender and Genre in Medieval Literature*. Cambridge: D. S. Brewer.

Magennis, Hugh (2003). *Waltharius*. In Robert Clark (ed.). *The Literary Encyclopedia*. www.LitEncyc.com.

Niles, John D. (2007). *Old English Heroic Poems and the Social Life of Texts*. Studies in the Early Middle Ages, 20. Turnhout: Brepols.

O'Keeffe, Katherine O'Brien (1990). *Visible Song: Transitional Literacy in Old English Verse*. England: Cambridge Studies in Anglo-Saxon England, 4. Cambridge: Cambridge University Press.

Ong, Walter J. (1982). *Orality and Literacy: The Technologizing of the Word*. London: Methuen.

Orchard, Andy (1997). Oral tradition. In Katherine O'Brien O'Keeffe (ed.). *Reading Old English Texts* (pp. 101–23). Cambridge: Cambridge University Press.

Overing, Gillian R. (1990). *Language, Sign, and Gender in Beowulf*. Carbondale, IL: Southern Illinois University Press.

Woolf, Rosemary (1976). The ideal of men dying with their lord in the *Germania* and in *The Battle of Maldon*. *Anglo-Saxon England*, 5, 63–81.

6
Old English Biblical and Devotional Poetry

Daniel Anlezark

The story of Old English Christian poetry begins with the cowherd Cædmon in the late seventh century, at the Anglo-Saxon monastery at Whitby, under the Abbess Hild. In his *Ecclesiastical History* (IV: 24) Bede tells of a miraculous vision, as Cædmon, ignorant of song, escapes the harp passed around at a feast:

> He left the place of feasting and went to the cattle byre, as it was his turn to take charge of them that night. In due time he stretched himself out and went to sleep, whereupon he dreamt that someone stood by him, saluted him, and called him by name: 'Cædmon', he said, 'sing me something.' Cædmon answered: 'I cannot sing; that is why I left the feast and came here because I could not sing.' Once again the speaker said: 'Nevertheless you must sing to me.' 'What must I sing?' said Cædmon. 'Sing', he said, 'about the beginning of created things.' Thereupon Cædmon began to sing verses which he had never heard before in praise of God the Creator.
>
> (Colgrave and Mynors 1969: 417)

The Old English text of this song is a regular companion of Bede's Latin version in the margins of the *History*'s early medieval manuscripts:

> Nu scylun hergan   hefaenricaes uard,
> metudæs maecti   end his modgidanc,
> uerc uuldurfadur,   sue he uundra gihuaes,
> eci dryctin,   or astelidæ.
> He aerist scop   aelda barnum
> heben til hrofe,   haleg scepen;
> tha middungeard   moncynnæs uard,
> eci dryctin,   æfter tiadæ
> firum foldu,   frea allmectig.
>
> (Dobbie 1942: 105)

> Now must we praise the Guardian of heaven-kingdom, the Maker's might and his
> purpose, work of the Glory-Father, because he, the eternal Lord, appointed the origin
> of each wonder. He, the holy Creator, in the beginning created heaven as a roof for the
> children of men; then middle-earth, mankind's Guardian, the eternal Lord afterwards
> made the earth for men, the Lord almighty.

The poem delights in the lexical variation enjoyed by Anglo-Saxon poets. God is
variously *hefaenricaes uard, metud, uuldurfadur, eci dryhten, haleg scepen* and *frea allmectig*.
Just as he is 'Guardian of heaven-kingdom' in the opening line which praises him
in his glory and power, he is also 'mankind's Guardian' as the emphasis shifts to
God's creative action and care for humanity. The poem balances God's remoteness
with his closeness to humanity and human creativity through a play on the verb
scepan and its related nouns. The verb means 'to create by giving shape': *scepen* is the
Creator. In Old English, however, the noun *scop* has the technical meaning of 'poet'.
So while God created in the beginning (*he aerist scop*), Cædmon is also God's first
English poet; this poem itself is a divine gift, created by God.

Cædmon reports his vision to his master, who takes him to Abbess Hild. Once it is
decided that the vision is of divine origin, Cædmon becomes a monk and develops
his gift:

> He learned all he could by listening to them and then, memorising it and ruminating
> over it, like some clean animal chewing the cud, he turned it into the most melodious
> verse: and it sounded so sweet as he recited it that his teachers became in turn his
> audience. He sang about the creation of the world, the origin of the human race, and
> the whole history of Genesis, of the departure of Israel from Egypt and the entry into
> the promised land and of many other stories taken from the sacred scriptures: of the
> incarnation, passion, and resurrection of the Lord, of his ascension into heaven, of the
> coming of the holy spirit and the teaching of the apostles. He also made songs about
> the terrors of the future judgement, the horrors of the pains of hell, and the joys of the
> heavenly kingdom.
>
> (Colgrave and Mynors 1969: 419)

Bede's account suggests a corpus of sacred verse in the vernacular circulated in the
early eighth century; Old English sacred verse by others also circulated, Bede tells
us, 'but none could compare with [Cædmon]'. Bede's evaluation suggests a personal
familiarity with this poetry, though we cannot be certain that any of the verse surviving
today was known by Bede or composed by Cædmon. (On the circulation of Old
English verse, see the essay by Rohini Jayatilaka in this volume.)

The largest surviving collection of Old English Christian verse is found in
manuscript Oxford, Bodleian Library Junius 11, from the late tenth century. In the
seventeenth century this came to be known as 'The Cædmon Manuscript', an overly
confident attribution no longer acceptable on a range of philological and stylistic
grounds. Editors recognise at least four poems in this book, with two composite texts.
The first three, based on Old Testament books, form a discrete grouping: *Genesis*

(comprising *Genesis A* and *Genesis B*), *Exodus* and *Daniel*. The fitt sections of these three poems are numbered consecutively, beginning at Fitt I and ending at Fitt LV, for the last section of *Daniel*. Within a few decades, the book was augmented by the addition of *Christ and Satan*, also divided in fitts, beginning again at I. It is not known for whom the book was made, but a wealthy patron is likely (see Karkov 2001).

Genesis is the second longest poem in Old English after *Beowulf*, and shares many of the epic's thematic interests: relationships between men and women; concern for begetting offspring; the dynastic transmission of power; acquisition of wealth; success or failure of alliances; and very specifically God's war with the giants, which has its roots in Cain's murder of Abel, and its climactic conflict in the Flood. Many of these themes are already present in the biblical text, though some are given prominence in the poet's handling of his source. *Genesis A* begins at the beginning:

> Us is riht micel   ðæt we rodera weard,
> wereda wuldorcining,   wordum herigen,
> modum lufien.   He is mægna sped,
> heafod ealra   heahgesceafta,
> frea ælmihtig.   Næs him fruma æfre,
> or geworden,   ne nu ende cymþ
> ecean drihtnes,   ac he bið a rice
> ofer heofenstolas.   Heagum þrymmum
> soðfæst and swiðfeorm   sweglbosmas heold,
> þa wæron gesette   wide and side
> þurh geweald godes   wuldres bearnum,
> gasta weardum.   Hæfdon gleam and dream,
> and heora ordfruman,   engla þreatas,
> beorhte blisse.   Wæs heora blæd micel!
>   (Krapp 1931: 1, lines 1–14)

It is very right for us that we should praise with words the Guardian of the heavens, the Glory-King of hosts, should love him in our hearts. He is powerful of strength, origin of all noble creatures, the Lord almighty. There never was beginning for him, an origin made, nor will an end ever come for the eternal Lord, but he will forever be in power over the thrones of heaven. In high powers, firm in truth and abundant, he hold the vaults of heaven, which were established broad and wide through God's rule for the sons of glory, for the guardians of souls. They had joy and happiness, and their source of being, the troops of angels, bright bliss. Their glory was great!

Resonances of theme and expression with Cædmon's hymn are apparent, and may be more than the result of a coincidence of subject matter. It is possible that the poet here is deliberately echoing the well-known poem, though both also reveal a debt to the opening of the Preface to the Canon of the Mass, the high point of the key ritual of the Christian liturgy: 'Vere dignum et justum est, aequum et salutare, nos tibi semper, et ubique gratias agere: Domine sancte, Pater omnipotens, aeterne Deus…' (It is truly fitting and right, our duty and our salvation, always and everywhere to give thanks to you, Lord, holy Father, almighty and eternal God…) (Michel 1947).

The fall of the angels is not described in the Bible, but *Genesis A* follows a tradition which saw their creation before that of the earth. In the peace following the celestial warfare, Adam and his race are created to occupy the thrones abandoned by Lucifer and his rebels:

> Sceof þa and scyrede   scyppend ure
> oferhidig cyn   engla of heofnum,
> wærleas werod.   Waldend sende
> laðwendne here   on langne sið,
> geomre gastas;   wæs him gylp forod,
> beot forborsten,   and forbiged þrym,
> wlite gewemmed.
> …
> Þa þeahtode   þeoden ure
> modgeþonce,   hu he þa mæran gesceaft,
> eðelstaðolas   eft gesette,
> swegltorhtan seld,   selran werode,
> þa hie gielpsceaþan   ofgifen hæfdon,
> heah on heofenum.   Forþam halig god
> under roderas feng,   ricum mihtum,
> wolde þæt him eorðe   and uproder
> and sid wæter   geseted wurde
> woruldgesceafte   on wraðra gield,
> þara þe forhealdene   of hleo sende.
> (Krapp 1931: 4–5, lines 65–71a, 92–102)

Then our Creator shoved out and cut off that arrogant race of angels from the heavens, the troop without a covenant. The Ruler sent the hostile army on a long journey, the sad spirits; their vaunting was exhausted, the boast utterly broken, their triumph humbled, beauty defiled.…Then our Prince considered in his thought, how he might settle with a better troop the great creations and the native-seats after that, the bright radiant thrones, those which the boastful destroyers had given up, high in the heavens. Therefore holy God took control under the skies, with royal powers, intended that the earth and sky above and the broad water be established for him, a created world in compensation for the hateful ones, those who refused tribute, sent out from his protection.

This conflict that takes place outside biblical history establishes thematic emphases and narrative patterns developed throughout the poem, and indeed across Junius 11. The most important of these focuses on the idea of covenant; the Old English noun *wær* has a range of meanings, including 'covenant', 'fidelity' or 'bond of friendship' (Lucas 1992). In the poem God's creatures are lost when they break the bond uniting them in friendship with their Creator; within this relationship they enjoy God's protection (*hleo*). This vocabulary, employed throughout the poem, overlaps with secular use, and so presents a God familiar in heroic martial terms. Closely related to these themes, and running throughout the poem, is the motif of exile. The fallen angels have no hope of restoring their covenant, and their exile is permanent.

The exile of the human race begins with Adam and Eve's banishment from paradise, and is extended in Cain's exile after Abel's murder. Noah's exile with his family in the ark separates them from the earth as it is washed clean by the Flood (Anlezark 2006). Their return to the land is accompanied by a new bond between Creator and creature:

> 'Weaxað and wridað, wilna brucað,
> ara on eorðan; æðelum fyllað
> eowre fromcynne foldan sceatas,
> teamum and tudre. Ic eow treowa þæs
> mine selle, þæt ic on middangeard
> næfre egorhere eft gelæde,
> wæter ofer widland. Ge on wolcnum þæs
> oft and gelome andgiettacen
> magon sceawigan, þonne ic scurbogan
> minne iewe, þæt ic monnum þas
> wære gelæste, þenden woruld standeð.'
> . . .
> Ða Noe ongan niwan stefne
> mid hleomagum ham staðelian
> and to eorðan him ætes tilian.
> (Krapp 1931: 47–8, lines 1532–42, 1555–7)

'Increase and multiply, enjoy the good things, favours on earth; in your noble lineage fill the plains of the earth with your descendants and offspring. I give you my pledge, that I will never again lead the ocean-army onto middle-earth, the water over the wide land. You will be able often and again to see true sign of this in the clouds – when I show my rainbow – that I will fulfil my covenant with men, while the world stands.' . . . Then Noah began to establish anew a home with his protecting-kinsmen, and cultivate the earth for food.

As in the scriptural text, verbal echoes tie this new beginning to the account of creation, and Noah, like Adam, becomes a father of the human race; however, a new dimension is added to God's relations with humanity in Noah's covenant.

The last twelve-hundred lines of the poem tell the story of Abraham, a wandering exile chosen for an everlasting covenant, with a homeland promised for his descendants. *Genesis A* reveals an awareness of the symbolism of biblical typology, whereby the personalities and events of the Old Testament were interpreted by Christian commentators as figural prophecies of the New; however, these are never laboured in a poem that prefers the literal story and its moral lessons over complex theological

ideas (see Daniélou 1960; de Lubac 1998). This is not to say the poet does not adapt
the material for his Christian audience. One example is his presentation of Abraham's
circumcision. The phrasing of the passage recalls the covenant with Noah:

> 'Ic þa wære forð
> soðe gelæste,   þe ic þe sealde geo
> frofre to wedde,   þæs þin ferhð bemearn.
> Þu scealt halgian   hired þinne.
> Sete sigores tacn   soð on gehwilcne
> wæpnedcynnes,   gif þu wille on me
> hlaford habban   oððe holdne freond
> þinum fromcynne.'
> (Krapp 1931: 69, 2309b–16a)

'Henceforth I will truly fulfil the covenant, which I formerly gave to you, consolation
as a pledge, because your heart mourned. You shall sanctify your household. Set the
sign of victory true on each male, if you wish to have me as a Lord or faithful friend
for your descendants.'

The Anglo-Saxon reader does not need to know details of Jewish practice, and the
poet may well have feared confusion or bewilderment if circumcision were described.
As with other typologically charged episodes, the poem here is informed, rather than
dominated, by the commentary tradition, according to which circumcision prefigured
baptism as a sign of the covenant with God. The poem's interest in genealogy and
emphasis on offspring is also theologically potent in the case of Abraham, the literal
father of the Jewish people, but interpreted by Christians as their spiritual father.

Genesis B (lines 235–851), a translation from Old Saxon, has been interpolated
into the text of *Genesis A*, possibly to make good a gap in the story created by the
loss of manuscript leaves (Doane 1991). The poem begins after the divine injunction
not to eat the forbidden fruit in *Genesis A*. The transition between the poems is
smooth enough, however, especially at the end of *Genesis B*, and it is possible that
the inclusion was the result of design rather than necessity. *Genesis B*, if treated as a
separate poem, presents the interrelated drama of the two falls which introduced
rebellion and sin to heaven and earth. The Anglo-Saxon compiler's choice to include
a retelling of the fall of the angels points to a sensitivity to the Old Saxon poem's
thematic focus on human and demonic psychology. Lucifer's brightness is found not
simply in his light:

> Gesett hæfde he hie swa gesæliglice,   ænne hæfde he swa swiðne geworhtne,
> swa mihtigne on his modgeþohte,   he let hine swa micles wealdan,
> hehstne to him on heofona rice,   hæfde he hine swa hwitne geworhtne,
> swa wynlic wæs his wæstm on heofonum   þæt him com from weroda drihtne,
> gelic wæs he þam leohtum steorrum.
> (Krapp 1931: 10, lines 252–6a)

He had established them so blessedly, one he had made so potent, so mighty in his intellect, so much he let him rule, highest after him in the kingdom of the heavens, he had made him so radiant, so delightful was his stature in the heavens, which came to him from the Lord of hosts, he was like the dazzling stars.

The psychological interest is signalled by the poet's repeated use of compounds containing Old English *mod* ('mind'): the angel of light's great *modgeþoht* ('intellect') leads him to the sin of pride (*ofermod*, lines 262, 272, etc.). After he is thrust into hell, Satan's disguised demonic emissary to Eden attempts to trick Adam, and promises that if he should eat the forbidden fruit, his 'modsefa mara wurde' (mind will become great, line 501). Adam, however, already has a good mind, and is able to reason for himself:

> 'Nat þeah þu mid ligenum fare
> þurh dyrne geþanc   þe þu drihtnes eart
> boda of heofnum.   Hwæt, ic þinra bysna ne mæg,
> worda ne wisna   wuht oncnawan,
> siðes ne sagona.   Ic wat hwæt he me self bebead,
> nergend user,   þa ic hine nehst geseah;
> he het me his word weorðian   and wel healdan,
> læstan his lare.   Þu gelic ne bist
> ænegum his engla   þe ic ær geseah,
> ne þu me oðiewdest   ænig tacen
> þe he me þurh treowe   to onsende,
> min hearra þurh hyldo.'
>   (Krapp 1931: 19–20, lines 531b–42a)

'I do not know, if you are come with lies through hidden thoughts or you are a messenger of the Lord from heaven. Indeed, I cannot at all penetrate your logic, your words nor reasoning, your mission nor sayings. I know what he himself commanded me, our Saviour, when I saw him last; he told me to honour his words and hold them well, to fulfil his teaching. You are not like any of his angels whom I saw before, nor have you revealed to me any sign which he my Commander has sent me as a pledge through his favour.'

Adam is more than simply obedient, and uses his observation and reason to reject the devil's attack. The devil turns to Eve, appealing not to her reason, but her emotions of fear and love. He threatens her with God's wrath at Adam's refusal to eat the fruit, and urges Eve to exploit her husband's trust in her in order to change his mind:

> 'Gif þu þeah minum wilt,
> wif willende,   wordum hyran,
> þu meaht his þonne rume   ræd geþencan.
> Gehyge on þinum breostum   þæt þu inc bam twam meaht
> wite bewarigan,   swa ic þe wisie.
> Æt þisses ofetes!'
>   (Krapp 1931: 20, lines 559b–64a)

'But if you, willing woman, will obey my words, you will broadly be able to think out
a solution. Think in your heart how both of you together can ward off [God's] punishment, as I suggest. Eat of the fruit!'

The intimacy between the man and woman is intensified in Old English by the use
of the dual pronoun *inc* (you two), as the devil manipulates Eve's love of Adam to
get the better of her reason. Eve, the poet observes, doesn't stand a chance because
'hæfde hire wacran hige metod gemearcod' (the Creator had limited her to a weaker
mind, lines 590b–1a). This kind of casual antifeminism is characteristic of much
medieval literature, though here, in a curious twist of the widespread tradition blaming
woman for the fall of man, it is offered as an explanation of Eve's failure. Adam is
not similarly excused.

    Genesis A concludes with the sacrifice of Isaac, as Abraham demonstrates his extreme
faith and obedience, and is rewarded with the promise of a multitude of descendants.
The Old English *Exodus* immediately follows in Junius 11, and traces the flight of
the Hebrews out of Egypt from the time of the plagues to the crossing of the Red
Sea. The work is undoubtedly by a different author, whose style and inventive vocabulary is more complex and allusive than the poet of *Genesis A*, and who is more fully
engaged with the commentary tradition. The hero of the poem is Moses:

> Hwæt! We feor and neah gefrigen habað
> ofer middangeard Moyses domas,
> wræclico wordriht, wera cneorissum,
> in uprodor eadigra gehwam
> æfter bealusiðe bote lifes,
> lifigendra gehwam langsumne ræd,
> hæleðum secgan. Gehyre se ðe wille!
> . . .
> He wæs leof gode, leoda aldor,
> horsc and hreðergleaw, herges wisa,
> freom folctoga. Faraones cyn,
> godes andsacan, gyrdwite band,
> þær him gesealde sigora waldend,
> modgum magoræswan, his maga feorh,
> onwist eðles, Abrahames sunum.
> . . .
>   Ða wæs forma sið
> þæt hine weroda god wordum nægde,
> þær he him gesægde soðwundra fela,
> hu þas woruld worhte witig drihten,
> eorðan ymbhwyrft and uprodor,
> gesette sigerice, and his sylfes naman,
> ðone yldo bearn ær ne cuðon,
> frod fædera cyn, þeah hie fela wiston.
> (Krapp 1931: 91, lines 1–7, 12–18, 22b–9)

Listen! Far and near over middle-earth we have heard tell out about Moses' judgements, extraordinary laws, for the generations of men, the healing of life after the baleful journey, in heaven above for each of the blessed, a lasting counsel for heroes, for each of the living. Let him listen who will!...He was dear to God, the leader of the people, quick-witted and spirit-wise, the army's guide, the noble commander. The nation of Pharaoh, God's enemy, he bound beaten, where the Lord of victories gave him, the courageous people's prince, the life of his kinsmen, habitation of the homeland, to the sons of Abraham.... That was the first time that the God of hosts spoke to him, when he told him of many a true wonder, how the wise Lord made the world, the expanse of the earth and sky above, established with victorious empire, and told him his own name, which the children of men had not known before, the wise nation of patriarchs, though they knew much.

The opening of the poem felicitously follows on from *Genesis* in a number of ways. Moses is a descendant of Abraham, and a great protector of this noble line. Furthermore, *Exodus* emphasises the martial element in the biblical source, an accommodation to Anglo-Saxon taste facilitated by the Old English heroic poetic idiom. Moses is also an author. Medieval tradition understood him as the author of the Pentateuch – it was Moses who first wrote down the stories not only of his ancestor Abraham, but also of the Creation and the Flood. In rendering the sacred text into Old English, the Anglo-Saxon poet is confident that he is interpreting a textual tradition initiated by Moses under divine inspiration.

The poet's heightened awareness of the depth of the scriptures is revealed in his treatment of the crossing of the Red Sea. At the moment the tribes of Israel step into the miraculous path across the sea-bed, the poet digresses to recall their ancestry:

> Him wæs an fæder,
> leof leodfruma, landriht geþah,
> frod on ferhðe, freomagum leof.
> Cende cneowsibbe cenra manna
> heahfædera sum, halige þeode,
> Israela cyn, onriht godes,
> swa þæt orþancum ealde reccað
> þa þe mægburge mæst gefrunon,
> frumcyn feora, fæderæðelo gehwæs.
> Niwe flodas Noe oferlað,
> þrymfæst þeoden, mid his þrim sunum,
> þone deopestan drencefloda
> þara ðe gewurde on woruldrice.
>   (Krapp 1931: 101, lines 353b–65)

For them there was one father, beloved origin of the people, he received the land-right, wise in spirit, dear to noble-kinsmen. A particular one of the patriarchs begot a generation of brave men, a holy people, the nation of Israelites, the upright of God, just as the elders recount skilfully, those who have studied most a distant tribal origin, the noble pedigree, of each great house. Noah journeyed over new floods, the glorious chieftain, with his three sons, the deepest of drowning-floods which ever happened in the worldly-kingdom.

The focus on the descent of the tribes leads into the poet's emphasis on Noah's role in rescuing all earthly life, which he describes with a poetic coinage as 'maðmhorda mæst' (the greatest of treasure-hoards). This may be read literally, but also evokes the commonplace allegorical association between ark and church. The digression develops the theme of descent:

> Swa þæt wise men   wordum secgað
> þæt from Noe   nigoða wære
> fæder Abrahames   on folctale.
> Þæt is se Abraham   se him engla god
> naman niwan asceop;   eac þon neah and feor
> halige heapas   in gehyld bebead,
> werþeoda geweald;   he on wræce lifde.
> (Krapp 1931: 101, lines 377–83)

It is what wise men say in words, that Noah was the ninth father of Abraham in the counting of the people. That is the Abraham for whom the God of angels created a new name; furthermore, far and near holy multitudes were given into his protection, the power of the nations; he lived in exile.

Noah is also an ancestor, but of the whole human race. The genealogical motif is pervasive, but the poet's choice of words is powerfully evocative of the commentary tradition, which understood the world's Christian nations as Abraham's true offspring. The poet focuses on one particular episode of Abraham's life: the sacrifice of Isaac. The angelic intervention that saves Isaac not only promises Abraham a physical line of descent, but also an eternal covenant signalled in his new name:

> 'Ne sleh þu, Abraham,   þin agen bearn,
> sunu mid sweorde!   Soð is gecyðed,
> nu þin cunnode   cyning alwihta,
> þæt þu wið waldend   wære heolde,
> fæste treowe,   seo þe freoðo sceal
> in lifdagum   lengest weorðan,
> awa to aldre   unswiciendo.
>   . . .
> He að swereð,   engla þeoden,
> wyrda waldend   and wereda god,
> soðfæst sigora,   þurh his sylfes lif,
> þæt þines cynnes   and cneowmaga,

randwiggendra,   rim ne cunnon
yldo ofer eorðan,   ealle cræfte
to gesecgenne   soðum wordum'
(Krapp 1931: 103, lines 419–25; 432–8)

'Abraham, do not slaughter your own child, your son with the sword! The truth is
made known, now that the God of all things has tested you, that you keep your covenant
with the Ruler, which will become an enduring peace-pledge for you in your life-days,
unfailingly for ever and ever....He, the Chief of angels, Ruler of fates, and Lord of
hosts, Righteous in victories, swears and oath on his own life, that men across the
earth will not be able with all their skill to count in words your people, generations
of descendants, shield-bearing warriors.'

The poet's sophistication is not laboured; he assumes rather than explains the etymology of 'Abraham': 'father of many nations' (Genesis 17: 5) (see Robinson 1968). The
framing of the digression is carefully balanced and theologically aware: the close
enumeration of the Israelites entering the sea yields to the innumerability of Abraham's spiritual descendants. An allegorical and typological reading of these episodes
is demanded by the way the poet has included them. At the narrative level the shift
from the climactic action of the Red Sea crossing is jarring. However, when read
from a theological point of view, the transition is seamless. Noah, Isaac and Moses
are all typological prefigurations of Christ; Noah, Abraham and Moses represent three
high-points of God's dealing with the human race, and whose great obedience is
rewarded with the three covenants. In Christian understanding these are not offered
just to the Jewish people, but in Christ, the literal descendant of Abraham, are extended to the whole human race through the new covenant of Christ's death and
resurrection, events anticipated in the sacrifice of Isaac. To become a Christian,
one must be baptised; the two great prefigurations of baptism are Noah's Flood and
the passing through the waters of the Red Sea. Baptism incorporates a Christian
into the church, which is prefigured in the communities of the saved elect found
both in the ark and the tribes of Israel. The poet's inspiration for this allegorical shift
was undoubtedly the Easter Vigil, the apex of the Christian liturgical calendar, when
all three stories are read to the Christian faithful and new Christians baptised (Bright
1912). The poem certainly draws moral lessons from the past, as God guides and
protects those who obey him, but the allegorical dimension intimately implicates
Anglo-Saxon Christians in these ancient events by making them spiritual descendants
of the patriarchs.

The themes of land, law and covenant fidelity developed in *Genesis A* and allegorised in *Exodus* are ultimately derived from their scriptural sources, and are also found
in the next poem in Junius 11, *Daniel*, based on the Book of Daniel 1–5. In the
developing narrative of the manuscript, the reader finds the Hebrew people settled
in the land promised to Abraham, but failing in their observance of the Law given
through Moses:

> Gefrægn ic Hebreos   eadge lifgean
> in Hierusalem,   goldhord dælan,
> cyningdom habban,   swa him gecynde wæs,
> siððan þurh metodes mægen   on Moyses hand
> wearð wig gifen,   wigena mænieo,
> and hie of Egyptum   ut aforon,
> mægene micle.   Þæt wæs modig cyn!
> Þenden hie þy rice   rædan moston,
> burgum wealdan,   wæs him beorht wela.
> Þenden þæt folc mid him   hiera fæder wære
> healdan woldon,   wæs him hyrde god,
> heofonrices weard,   halig drihten,
> wuldres waldend.
>
> . . .
>
> Þa hie æcræftas ane   forleton,
> metodes mægenscipe,   swa no man scyle
> his gastes lufan   wið gode dælan.
>   (Krapp 1931: 111, lines 1–13a, 19–21)

I have heard of the Hebrews living blessedly in Jerusalem, sharing the gold-hoard, holding the kingdom, as was natural for them, when through the Creator's power an army of many warriors was given into Moses' hand, and they journeyed from Egypt by a great wonder. That was a brave nation! While they could guide the kingdom, rule the cities, their glory was bright. While that people wished to keep their fathers' covenant with him, God was their protector, the guardian of heaven-kingdom, holy Lord, glory's Ruler.... Then at once they abandoned Law-craft, the Creator's majesty – so no man should separate his spirit's love from God.

This failure, and a refusal to listen to the prophets' warnings, leads to the siege and destruction of the city by the Chaldeans, and a return to exile:

> and gelæddon eac   on langne sið
> Israela cyn,   on eastwegas
> to Babilonia,   beorna unrim,
> under hand hæleð   hæðenum deman.
>   (Krapp 1931: 113, lines 68–71)

and also led the nation of Israel on a long journey, on roads east to Babylon, innumerable sons, heroes to be subjugated to the heathen.

The opposition between the Babylonian king Nebuchadnezzar and the Hebrew captives becomes the thematic focus of the poem: he struggles, as in the biblical text, towards recognition of the true God, while the exiled children of Israel must repent of their sins. The poet sets up a story of two conversions, emphasised through careful alterations to the scriptural story. One example is his comment added to Daniel 1: 4–5:

> Wolde þæt þa cnihtas   cræft leornedon,
> þæt him snytro on sefan   secgan mihte,
> nales ðy þe he þæt moste   oððe gemunan wolde
> þæt he þara gifena   gode þancode
> þe him þær to duguðe   drihten scyrede.
> > (Krapp 1931: 113, lines 83–7)

He desired that the boys learned knowledge, so that he might explain wisdom to them from his mind, not at all because he could or would remember to be grateful to God for the gifts the Lord provided for his benefit.

The Hebrews' conversion must come before the king's. The faith that the Israelites have lost is recovered in the face of martyrdom when Nebuchadnezzar has the youths Annanias, Azarias and Mishael cast into a furnace for refusing to worship his idol. There they sing two canticles; the first articulates a national repentance:

> 'Geoca user georne nu,   gasta scyppend,
> and þurh hyldo help,   halig drihten,
> nu we þec for þreaum   and for ðeonydum
> and for eaðmedum   arna biddað,
> lige belegde.   We ðæs lifgende
> worhton on worulde,   eac ðon wom dyde
> user yldran;   for oferhygdum
> bræcon bebodo   burhsittende,
> had oferhogedon   halgan lifes.'
> > (Krapp 1931: 119, lines 291–9)

'Assist us eagerly now, Creator of spirits, and help us through grace, holy Lord, now that we for our afflictions and necessities and humiliation beg for mercies, surrounded by flame. Living in the world we brought this about, and our elders also committed crimes; in arrogance the citizens broke commandments, despised the calling of holy life.'

Their situation parallels that of Satan lamenting his damnation within the flames in *Genesis B* and *Christ and Satan*, and the *oferhygd* of their fathers echoes the pride of Lucifer before his fall. However, God has made a covenant with his people, and there is hope for the penitent:

> 'Ne forlet þu usic ane,   ece drihten,
> for ðam miltsum   ðe ðec men hligað,
> and for ðam treowum   þe þu, tirum fæst,
> niða nergend,   genumen hæfdest
> to Abrahame   and to Isaace
> and to Iacobe,   gasta scyppend.'
> > (Krapp 1931: 119–20, lines 309–14)

'Do not abandon us altogether, eternal Lord, because of the mercies which are yours,
and because of the promises which you, firm in glories, Saviour from affliction, Creator
of Spirits, promised to Abraham, and Isaac, and Jacob.'

The three are visited by an angel, and sing a second song in praise of the Creator. At the
narrative level, the miracle leads Nebuchadnezzar to reconsider his position as the poet
subtly alters the source (Daniel 4:24–5) to emphasise the king's mental process:

> Geseah ða swiðmod cynig,   ða he his sefan ontreowde,
> wundor on wite agangen;   him þæt wræclic þuhte.
>
> . . .
>
> Đa þæt ehtode   ealdor þeode,
> Nabochodonossor,   wið þam nehstum
> folcgesiðum: 'Þæt eower fela geseah,
> þeode mine,   þæt we þry sendon,
> geboden to bæle   in byrnende
> fyres leoman.   Nu ic þær feower men
> geseo to soðe,   nales me sefa leogeð.'
> (Krapp 1931: 119, 122, lines 268–9, 409–15)

Then the obstinate king saw, when he trusted in his mind, a miracle going on in the
torture; that seemed alien to him.... Then Nebuchadnezzar, the nation's leader, considered
that with his closest advisors: 'That many of you saw, my people, that we sent three
into the burning fire's flames, commanded to the pyre. Now I truly see four men there,
if my mind does not at all lie to me' (emphasis added).

The exploration of the individual conversion emerges from the Israelites' national
return to covenant fidelity, and begins with the proof of God's power this return
represents. The attention to mental process in *Daniel* is comparable to the temptation
scene in *Genesis B*, though here the movement is towards, rather than away from,
God. Nebuchadnezzar's recognition of God's power does not, however, lead immediately
to a clear understanding of his own relationship to God, and despite warnings interpreted
for him by Daniel, the king succumbs to delusions of grandeur:

> wearð ða anhydig   ofer ealle men,
> swiðmod in sefan,   for ðære sundorgife
> þe him god sealde,   gumena rice,
> world to gewealde   in wera life:
> 'Đu eart seo micle   and min seo mære burh
> þe ic geworhte   to wurðmyndum,
> rume rice.   Ic reste on þe,
> eard and eðel,   agan wille.'
> Đa for ðam gylpe   gumena drihten
> forfangen wearð   and on fleam gewat,
> ana on oferhyd   ofer ealle men.
> (Krapp 1931: 128, lines 606–14)

then he became stubborn above all men, obstinate in mind, because of the special grace that God had given him, the empire of men, the world to rule in mortal life: 'You are the great and glorious city of mine, that I made so gloriously, a spacious empire. I exult in you: city and homeland I will possess.' Then for that boast the lord of men was seized with madness and departed in flight, alone in his pride over all men.

Now exiled himself, the king recovers his human mind and reason only at the time decreed by God:

> Seofon winter samod   susl þrowode,
> wildeora westen,   winburge cyning.
> Ða se earfoðmæcg   up locode,
> wilddeora gewita,   þurh wolcna gang.
> Gemunde þa on mode   þæt metod wære,
> heofona heahcyning,   hæleða bearnum
> ana ece gast.   Þa he eft onhwearf
> wodan gewittes,   þær þe he ær wide bær
> herewosan hige,   heortan getenge.
>   (Krapp 1931: 128, lines 620–30)

The king of the wine-city suffered punishment for seven years altogether in the wilderness of wild beasts. Then the wretch looked up, the beast-minded one, through the drifting clouds. He remembered then in his mind that the Creator should be high-king of the heavens, the one eternal Spirit for the children of men. Then after that he returned from his mad mind, where formerly he widely bore a belligerent mind close to his heart.

The poet does not translate the biblical emphasis on the king's physical bestiality, but with a turn to the heavens introduces a familiar metaphor of mental and spiritual transformation. The gesture develops the contrast between the two kings: the 'king of the wine-city' must recognise his dependence on the 'high-king of the heavens'. In the course of time and generations, Nebuchadnezzar dies and is succeeded by Belshazzar. The pattern of events at the poem's end mirrors that of its beginning: the new king turns from God, and in the wake of Daniel's famous reading of the writing on the wall suddenly loses his kingdom to invading Medes. *Daniel* develops a theme running through much of the Old Testament, and found in *Genesis* and *Exodus*: those who wish to enjoy God's favour in this world must adhere to his covenant. This relationship is as true for English Christians as for the ancient chosen people. As a migrant people the Anglo-Saxons believed they had been chosen by God to settle Britain, where he formed a Christian covenant with them and made them a great nation (Howe 1989). At the spiritual level, the true homeland of the Christian is in heaven, but by breaking the covenant both the earthly homeland and the heavenly could be lost. At a more personal level, the poem teaches the spiritual value of suffering, offering hope to the chastised penitent.

Azarias, found in the Exeter Book, and *Judith*, found in the *Beowulf* manuscript, both develop oppositions between God's chosen people and hostile neighbours in more allegorical terms than *Daniel*. *Azarias* is closely related to *Daniel*, and corresponds to lines 279–415 of the longer poem, narrating the episode of the three youths in the furnace. Divorced from its narrative context, and with a radically different conclusion, the episode presents a Nebuchadnezzar utterly inimical to God and his saints, leaving the king frustrated in his impotent fury. The poem *Judith* is based on the biblical book of the same name. Judith's decapitation of the lecherous and quasi-demonic Holofernes has been a popular subject of Western art and literature across the centuries, representing the victory of feminine virtue over the presumptions of male desire (Chance 1986: 31–52). The beginning of *Judith* has been lost, though it is generally agreed that what survives represents the greater part of the original poem. Judith is recast as a radiant virgin, who defends the besieged city of Bethulia against the Assyrian army through her holiness and courage:

> Hie ða on reste gebrohton
> snude ða snoteran idese;   eodon ða stercedferhðe,
> hæleð heora hearran cyðan   þæt wæs seo halige meowle
> gebroht on his burgetelde.   Þa wearð se brema on mode
> bliðe, burga ealdor,   þohte ða beorhtan idese
> mid widle ond mid womme besmitan.
> (Dobbie 1953: 100, lines 54b–9a)

They then quickly brought to the bed the wise lady; then the brave-hearted heroes went to inform their superior that the holy woman had been brought into his pavilion. Then the prince, ruler of cities, was happy in mind, intended to defile the bright lady with filth and sin.

Judith soon beheads the drunken general, and his terrified army is routed. *Judith* is agreed to be relatively late, probably from the tenth century, though its provenance is unknown. The original audience is likely to have been female, and perhaps cloistered, given the emphasis on the spiritual strength derived from virginity, the poem's allegorical shift to spiritual warfare, and the resistance Judith shows to Holofernes' desire to rape her. This shift does not diminish the strength of Judith's characterisation, and the poet's presentation of the heroine wraps her in the heroic language usually reserved for men, juxtaposed with the conventional language of female courtliness:

> Eodon ða gegnum þanonne
> þa idesa ba   ellenþriste,
> oðþæt hie becomon,   collenferhðe,
> eadhreðige mægð,   ut of ðam herige,

þæt hie sweotollice   geseon mihten
þære wlitegan byrig   weallas blican,
Bethuliam.   Hie ða beahhrodene
feðelaste   forð onettan,
oð hie glædmode   gegan hæfdon
to ðam wealgate.
                            (Dobbie 1953: 132b–41)

Then the two ladies went from there bold in courage, until they came, brave in heart, triumphant maidens, away from the army, so that they could see the beautiful city, Bethulia, its walls shining. Then they, ring-adorned, sped forth on the way, until glad of heart they reached the city gate.

The practical heroine is also praised for her wisdom, and recycles the bag in which she has brought provisions, stuffing the general's severed head into it before returning with her attendant to the city.

The final poem in Junius 11 is a later addition to the collection, and presents three separate poems on episodes in Christ's cosmic struggle against Satan. The first is a lament of the fallen angels, a subject addressed in *Genesis B*. In *Christ and Satan* (I) the poet presents hell as a place of utter deprivation, as the devil laments his loss in terms reminiscent of the Old English elegies:

                    Word spearcum fleah
attre gelicost,   þonne he ut þorhdraf:
'Eala drihtenes þrym!   Eala duguða helm!
Eala meotodes miht!   Eala middaneard!
Eala dæg leohta!   Eala dream godes!
Eala engla þreat!   Eala upheofen!'
                    (Krapp 1931: 141, lines 161b–6)

Words flew out in sparks most like poison, when he exploded: 'Alas the Lord's glory! Alas the Protector of hosts! Alas the Creator's might! Alas middle-earth! Alas the daylight! Alas God's joy! Alas the troop of angels! Alas heaven above!'

The subject of the fall of the angels was a popular one in Anglo-Saxon literature, and like other descriptions of hell could be used as a warning to readers against joining the damned spirits (see Anlezark 2003). The second poem in this Satanic anthology tells the story of Christ's visit to Hell in the time between his death and Resurrection. These events are fully narrated in the apocryphal Gospel of Nicodemus, a work with quasi-canonical status in the Middle Ages; another poem on the same subject, *The Descent into Hell*, survives in the Exeter Book. Central to the drama in *Christ and Satan* is the consternation of the devils as the victorious Christ arrives from his crucifixion, ready to liberate the Old Testament saints who have waited faithfully for his coming:

> Þa wæron mid egsan   ealle afyrhte,
> wide geond windsele   wordum mændon:
> 'Þis is stronglic,   nu þes storm becom,
> þegen mid þreate,   þeoden engla.
> Him beforan fereð   fægere leoht
> þonne we æfre ær   eagum gesawon,
> buton þa we mid englum   uppe wæron.'
>   (Krapp 1931: 148, lines 383–9)

Then they were completely terrified with fear, abroad throughout the wind-hall complained in words: 'This is serious, now the storming has come, a Lord with his army, Prince of angels. Before him goes a more beautiful light than we ever saw with our eyes, except when we were with the angels above.'

The final section of *Christ and Satan*, which is badly damaged, is based on the gospel story of Christ's threefold temptation by Satan in the wilderness (Matthew 4:1–11). The only temptation fully preserved is the final one, in which the devil promises Christ earthly dominion (lines 679–88). Satan is rebuked, sent back to the punishments of hell, and commanded to measure its dimensions. The same devil who has promised power to Christ is ultimately mocked by the wretched spirits who have given in to his deceits:

> Locade leas wiht   geond þæt laðe scræf,
> atol mid egum,   oððæt egsan gryre
> deofla mænego   þonne up astag.
> Wordum in witum   ongunnon þa werigan gastas
> reordian and cweðan:
> 'La, þus beo nu on yfele!   Noldæs ær teala!'
>   (Krapp 1931: 158, lines 724–9)

The hideous false creature looked across that hateful cavern with his eyes, until a terrible horror was aroused in the multitude of devils. In the tortures the accursed spirits began to cry out and say in words: 'Hey, so stay in evil now – you wanted no good before!'

This gospel story may seem a strange note to end on, especially as historical order would place it between the lament of the fallen angels and the harrowing. However, the text was set down for the first Sunday in Lent, the season when Christians follow Christ's example and practice penance in the ongoing war against the devil. The seasonal overtones of this final episode of the poem (and the manuscript) return the reader to the struggles of Christian life in the world, with a warning about the price of rendering obedience to the devil.

The liturgy would have been the principal avenue through which most Anglo-Saxons, educated or illiterate, lay or religious, encountered the sacred scriptures, and for most it would have been the main context for the expression of piety and devotion. It is likely that the shape not only of *Exodus*, but of the whole Old Testament narrative of Junius 11, was informed by the liturgical use of the Bible. Not only does the subject matter of the three poems represent pericopes read at the Easter Vigil, but also the two canticles sung by the youths in the furnace were regularly sung in the monastic office (Remley 1996). The liturgy of monastic life centred on the singing of the full Psalter in a weekly cycle, augmented by a number of biblical canticles. This practice is undoubtedly the inspiration behind the Paris Psalter, in which Old English prose versions of the first fifty Psalms are followed by poetic renderings of the remainder. The practice of glossing Latin Psalters in Old English, making them easier to follow for those whose Latin might not have been up to scratch, was widespread in Anglo-Saxon England. The full translation of the Psalms in the generously illustrated Paris Psalter points to lay – perhaps royal – piety. It was probably the desire for a devotional life close to that of the monasteries which led to the translation into verse and prose of other parts of the Benedictine Office in the early eleventh century, a work associated with the great Anglo-Saxon statesman Archbishop Wulfstan of York (Ure 1957). The liturgy of the church in Advent is the inspiration behind the *Advent Lyrics* in the Exeter Book, a group of meditative poems based on the 'O antiphons' sung at Vespers in the week before Christmas (Burlin 1968).

The most famous Old English poem drawing on liturgical inspiration is *The Dream of the Rood*, which tells of a midnight vision of the Cross and the change it has brought about in the visionary's life. The mysterious sight reflects both the historical reality of the crucifixion, and the use of the Cross as a symbol in the liturgy:

> Syllic wæs se sigebeam,   ond ic synnum fah,
> forwunded mid wommum.   Geseah ic wuldres treow,
> wædum geweorðode,   wynnum scinan,
> gegyred mid golde;   gimmas hæfdon
> bewrigene weorðlice   wealdendes treow.
> Hwæðre ic þurh þæt gold   ongytan meahte
> earmra ærgewin,   þæt hit ærest ongan
> swætan on þa swiðran healfe.
>
> (Krapp 1932: 61, lines 13–20a)

Glorious was the victory-tree, and I stained with sin, greatly wounded with woes. I saw the tree of glory, honoured in clothes, shining joyfully, adorned with gold; gems had nobly enclosed the Ruler's tree. However, through that gold I could perceive the ancient strife of outcasts, that it first began to bleed on the right side.

The dreamer's sombre mood and the Cross's history of cruelty are contrasted in the poem to the heroic lightness of Christ's rush towards death:

> Geseah ic þa frean mancynnes
> efstan elne mycle   þæt he me wolde on gestigan.
>
> ...
>
> Ongyrede hine þa geong hæleð,   (þæt wæs god ælmihtig),
> strang ond stiðmod.   Gestah he on gealgan heanne,
> modig on manigra gesyhðe,   þa he wolde mancyn lysan.
> > (Krapp 1932: 62, lines 33b–4, 39–41)

I saw the Lord of mankind hasten with great courage, because he wished to climb up on me....The young hero stripped himself, that was God almighty, strong and resolute. He climbed onto the high gallows, brave in the sight of many, when he wished to free mankind.

The bloodstains of the past give way to the dressing of the Cross – a practice associated with the liturgy of Good Friday – while the precious metals and jewels recall processional crosses, and those worn as pious ornaments (Ó Carragáin 2005). The transformation undergone by the Cross from suffering to glory presents a pattern for the dreamer and those like him who will wear the Cross on Doomsday:

> Ne þearf ðær þonne ænig   anforht wesan
> þe him ær in breostum bereð   beacna selest
> > (Krapp 1932: 64, lines 117–18)

None need be terrified then who bears the best of signs on his breast.

Devotion to the Cross is symbolic of faith in Christ, but with an emphasis on the Christian's willingness to enter into suffering to find redemption.

The Anglo-Saxons enjoyed a range of literature exemplifying the Christian struggle in the world, and four poetic saints' lives present this in different ways: *Andreas*, *Juliana*, *Elene* and *Guthlac*. Such lives were enormously popular across the Middle Ages, and reflect little concern with narrative realism. The reality of the saint's life is the contest between God and the devil, and the soul is its field of battle. In *Andreas*, Andrew is sent to rescue another apostle, Matthew, who has been taken captive by the cannibalistic inhabitants of Mermedonia. After an angel announces his rescue mission to him, a reluctant Andrew is ferried to the city by Christ in disguise. On arrival, Andrew frees Matthew, but then must begin the task of bringing the gospel to a city in the grip of demonic captivity. At the prompting of a devil, the saint is tortured:

> Wæs þæs halgan lic
> sarbennum soden,   swate bestemed,
> banhus abrocen.   Blod yðum weoll,
> hatan heolfre.   Hæfde him on innan

> ellen untweonde,   wæs þæt æðele mod
> asundrad fram synnum,   þeah he sares swa feala
> deopum dolgslegum   dreogan sceolde.
> > (Krapp 1932: 37, lines 1238b–44)

The saint's body was sodden from grievous wounds, drenched with blood, the bone-frame broken. Blood surged in waves, with hot gore. Within himself he had undoubting courage, that noble spirit was devoid of sins, though he had to endure many a sorrow from deep hacking blows.

Andrew's passion has been promised by God, and his suffering patterned in the poem on Christ's; the apostle brings the gospel, but must show both God himself and the pagan cannibals his extreme devotion to the cause. Andrew is ultimately victorious, and a flood deliberately evocative of Noah's washes the city clean before its inhabitants receive baptism. The battle against the devil is taken up in a different way in two poems in the Exeter Book about St Guthlac, a Mercian prince who became a hermit in the fens at Crowland at the beginning of the eighth century. In the tradition of St Anthony of Egypt, Guthlac battles tempting demons in his wilderness retreat (Roberts 1979).

Juliana, also in the Exeter Book, is one of four poems signed by the Anglo-Saxon poet Cynewulf. The poem is set in the great age of Christian martyrdom, when the religion was proscribed throughout the Roman Empire. St Juliana was probably an historical figure, but the account of her passion is the stuff of Christian romance, with little or no historical grounding. The opening locates the action in Nicomedia in the time of Emperor Maximian, under the governor Eleusius. In a pattern of events found in many such lives, the virginal Christian girl is promised in marriage to the pagan governor. Her twofold refusal of her father's choice of husband asserts not only the independence of her Christian conscience from pagan coercion, but also the sexual power of her virginity against a disordered and frustrated male desire:

> Ða for þam folce   frecne mode
> beotwordum spræc,   bealg hine swiþe
> folcagende,   ond þa fæmnan het
> þurh niðwræce   nacode þennan,
> ond mid sweopum swingan   synna lease.
> Ahlog þa se hererinc,   hospwordum spræc:
> 'þis is ealdordom   uncres gewynnes
> on fruman gefongen.   Gen ic feores þe
> unnan wille,   þeah þu ær fela
> unwærlicra   worda gespræce,
> onsoce to swiðe   þæt þu soð godu
> lufian wolde.
> > (Krapp and Dobbie 1936: 118, lines 184–95)

Then before the people he spoke taunts in a savage mind, the overlord enraged himself, and commanded the virgin to be stretched out naked in cruel torture, and the one without sin flogged with whips. The soldier laughed, spoke in mocking words: 'Just so is mastery in our struggle seized from the start. I will still grant you life, even though you earlier spoke many impious words, too eagerly rejected the idea that you might love the true gods.'

The sexual overtones of the conflict between Juliana and her suitor are as obvious today as they would have been to the Anglo-Saxon reader, and Juliana's heroic resistance to the point of martyrdom undoubtedly would have appealed to the readers of *Judith*. Nor is Juliana simply a passive player in the drama of her death: the saint rebukes her torturers and she herself punishes a devil that visits her in prison. Another powerful female saint is described in *Elene*, also by Cynewulf. The poem first tells of a miraculous vision of the Cross by the emperor Constantine, and then the mission of his mother, St Helen, to Jerusalem to find the lost Cross of Christ. Like Judith and Juliana, Helen is a strong woman in God's service, who can use violence against his enemies; all three are models of the new Eve, the Christian woman who can overcome the devil. The antisemitism of *Elene*, which casts Jewish characters in the oppositional role ascribed to devils in other lives, can shock modern audiences. However, for the medieval Christian the final conversion of Jewish characters to Christianity would serve as a happy conclusion to the action. The legend of the finding of the Cross was enormously popular in the Middle Ages as one of the founding events of Christendom, and is referred to in passing in *Dream of the Rood*. Both poems are found in the Vercelli Book, suggesting the compiler had a particular interest in devotion to the Cross and its associated legends.

Dream of the Rood ends with a movement upwards, fusing the moments of Christ's Resurrection, Ascension and final triumph at the Last Judgement in the eschatological return of the poem's young hero to his homeland (lines 147–56). The return of Christ to heaven in the Ascension is the subject of *Christ II* in the Exeter Book, also signed by Cynewulf. Here too the emphasis is on the protection offered by the mysteries of the redemption to the Christian both in the world and at the Judgement:

> Ne þearf him ondrædan   deofla strælas
> ænig on eorðan   ælda cynnes,
> gromra garfare,   gif hine god scildeþ,
> duguða dryhten.   Is þam dome neah
> þæt we gelice sceolon   leanum hleotan,
> swa we widefeorh   weorcum hlodun
> geond sidne grund.
> (Krapp and Dobbie 1936: 24–5, lines 779–85)

No one on earth of the race of men need dread the devils' arrows, the enemies' spear-charge, if God shields him, the Lord of hosts. The Judgement is nigh, when we alike must obtain rewards, as we for a long time have prepared by our works across the broad earth.

Christ II is as much focused on the coming Judgement as it is on the Ascension: the Christ who departed into the clouds will return on them. The theme of Judgement was universally popular among medieval preachers and poets. Three surviving Old English poems specifically about the Last Judgement emphasise both the transience of this world and the permanence of the afterlife (Caie 1976). *Judgement Day II*, a translation of a Latin poem attributed to the Venerable Bede, opens with a vision of earthly beauty:

> Hwæt! Ic ana sæt   innan bearwe,
> mid helme beþeht,   holte tomiddes,
> þær þa wæterburnan   swegdon and urnon
> on middan gehæge,   ealswa ic secge.
>   (Dobbie 1942: 58, lines 1–4)

Listen! I sat alone within a grove, sheltered from above, amidst a forest, where brooks bubbled and ran in the middle of the glade, just as I say.

Cool waters give way to a celestial fire which no overarching tree can ward off. As pleasant as this world can be, it is impermanent:

> Eall eorðe bifað,   eac swa þa duna
> dreosað and hreosað,
> and beorga hliðu   bugað and myltað,
> and se egeslica sweg   ungerydre sæ eall
> manna mod   miclum gedrefeð.
>   (Dobbie 1942: 60, lines 99–103)

The whole earth will shake, so also the mountains will collapse and fall, and the cliffs of the hills bend and melt, and the terrible roar of the raging sea will greatly trouble all people's minds.

Bede's story of Cædmon locates the origins of Old English Christian verse in miraculous inspiration on the one hand, and the classroom on the other. The surviving poetry presents a slightly different picture. Anglo-Saxon biblical poetry is undoubtedly the work of Latinate scholars – or they would not have been able to translate the biblical text. To varying degrees their works reveal the influence of a commentary tradition passed on in the classroom and the shape of the Bible experienced through the liturgy. The fact that these Old English poems were made at all, however, suggests a desire to communicate biblical stories and their Christian meanings to a wider audience. The evidence of Junius 11 suggests that patrons, perhaps among the laity, desired collections of such poems to assist their devotion, a development in late Anglo-Saxon also apparent in the Paris Psalter. The same is true of saints' lives translated from Latin sources, pointing to poets creating works with an appeal to a range of readers, almost certainly including devout women. Old English biblical and devotional verse reflects many of the hopes and anxieties of the Anglo-Saxon Christian – over property, faith and pain – with the promise of final redemption for those who persevere through the devil's temptations, keeping the Christian covenant in expectation of the final disintegration of this world.

REFERENCES AND FURTHER READING

Anlezark, Daniel (2003). The fall of the angels in 'Solomon and Saturn II'. In K. Powell and D. Scragg (eds). *Apocryphal Texts and Traditions in Anglo-Saxon England* (pp. 121–33). Cambridge: D. S. Brewer.

Anlezark, Daniel (2006). *Water and Fire: The Myth of the Flood in Anglo-Saxon England*. Manchester: Manchester University Press.

Bradley, S. A. J. (trans.) (1987). *Anglo-Saxon Poetry*. London: Dent.

Bright, J. W. (1912). The relation of the Cædmonian 'Exodus' to the Liturgy. *Modern Language Notes*, 27, 97–103.

Burlin, R. B. (1968). *The Old English Advent: A Typological Commentary*. New Haven, CT: Yale University Press.

Caie, G. D. (1976). *The Judgment Day Theme in Old English Poetry*. Copenhagen: Nova.

Chance, Jane (1986). *Woman as Hero in Old English Literature*. Syracuse, NY: Syracuse University Press.

Colgrave, B. and R. A. B. Mynors (eds) (1969). *Bede's Ecclesiastical History of the English People*. Oxford: Clarendon Press.

Daniélou, J. (1960). *From Shadows to Reality: Studies in the Biblical Typology of the Fathers*. London: Burns and Oates.

de Lubac, H. (1998). *Medieval Exegesis: The Fours Senses of Scripture*. 2 vols. Grand Rapids, MI: Eerdmans.

Doane, A. N. (ed.) (1991). *The Saxon Genesis: An Edition of the West Saxon Genesis B and the Old Saxon Vatican Genesis*. Madison, WI: University of Wisconsin Press.

Dobbie, E. V. K. and G. P. Krapp (eds) (1931–53). *Anglo-Saxon Poetic Records*. 6 vols. New York and London: Columbia University Press.

Howe, Nicholas (1989). *Migration and Mythmaking in Anglo-Saxon England*. New Haven, CT: Yale University Press.

Karkov, C. E. (2001). *Text and Picture in Anglo-Saxon England: Narrative Strategies in the Junius 11 Manuscript*. Cambridge Studies in Anglo-Saxon England 25. Cambridge: Cambridge University Press.

Lucas, P. J. (1992). Loyalty and obedience in the Old English 'Genesis' and the Interpolation of 'Genesis B' into 'Genesis A'. *Neophilologus*, 76, 121–35.

Marsden, R. (2004). Wrestling with the Bible: textual problems for the scholar and the student. In P. Cavill (ed.). *The Christian Tradition in Anglo-Saxon England: Approaches to Current Scholarship and Teaching* (pp. 69–90). Cambridge: D. S. Brewer.

Michel, L. (1947). 'Genesis A' and the 'Praefatio'. *Modern Language Notes*, 62, 545–50.

Ó Carragáin, É. (2005). *Ritual and the Rood: Liturgical Images and the Old English Poems of the Dream of the Rood Tradition*. London: University of Toronto Press.

Remley, P. G. (1996). *Old English Biblical Verse: Studies in Exodus, Genesis and Daniel*. Cambridge Studies in Anglo-Saxon England 16. Cambridge: Cambridge University Press.

Roberts, Jane (ed.) (1979). *The Guthlac Poems of the Exeter Book*. Oxford: Clarendon Press.

Robinson, F. C. (1968). The significance of names in Old English literature. *Anglia*, 86, 14–58.

Ure, J. M. (ed.) (1957). *The Benedictine Office: An Old English Text*. Edinburgh: Edinburgh University Press.

7
Old English Wisdom Poetry

David Ashurst

Wisdom literature, offering observations and instruction, is a common phenomenon in many cultures and languages. It features prominently in the Old Testament, where it is most notably represented by Proverbs and Ecclesiastes and where it was well known to the Anglo-Saxons. Most central to the corpus of wisdom poems in the form extant in Old English are *Maxims I, Maxims II, The Fortunes of Men, The Gifts of Men, The Rune Poem, Solomon and Saturn II, Precepts* or *A Father's Instructions to His Son*, and *The Wonders of Creation* or *The Order of the World*. See also the *Menologium, Solomon and Saturn I, Bede's Death Song* and *Pharaoh*.

A good text with which to begin an investigation of Old English wisdom poetry is *The Rune Poem* (ed. Dobbie 1942: 28–30), which has come down to us in the printed version by George Hickes (1703–5: I, 134–5) but which survived until the Ashburnham House fire of 1731 in the unique manuscript Cotton Otho B.x, fol. 165r–165v. It exhibits many of the features characteristic of the genre but at the same time is revealingly atypical in certain ways.

The Rune Poem takes the most widely disseminated form of the *futhorc*, the Anglo-Saxon runic alphabet, and for each of its twenty-eight characters, plus one extra, provides a short verse paragraph of explanation and reflection based on the name of the rune. So the lines on *ðorn* ('thorn', lines 8–10), for example, observe in faintly whimsical fashion that a thorn is very sharp, painful to grasp and exceptionally cruel to anyone who lies among such things. More earnestly and with a twist pointed out by Shippey (1976: 135, note 4), the paragraph on *gyfu* ('generosity', lines 19–21) declares that open-handedness is an honourable quality that brings status to those who display it, whilst to the dispossessed it offers property when they have no other means. What puts *The Rune Poem* squarely in the category of Old English wisdom poetry is the character, together with the structure, of such observations, for they conform to the gnomic type of verse, which may be described as follows:

The reader is offered a series of didactic generalizations that may be understood either literally (e.g. 'a blind person must do without his eyes') or metaphorically (e.g. 'a fallen tree grows least'). Typically subject and predicate of a gnome are balanced across the verb *sceal* 'shall, ought to, is accustomed to' or *biþ* 'will be, habitually is'. (Fulk and Cain 2005: 171. Cf. Larrington 1993: 6; Cavill 1999: 45–50)

In fact all but three of *The Rune Poem*'s twenty-nine verse paragraphs begin with a *biþ* gnome, which the succeeding lines then elaborate or modify in various ways, the exceptions being paragraphs 15, 16 and 23.

As regards the character of the gnomes and their literary contexts, the first thing to note is that *The Rune Poem* strikingly displays a frank and simple delight in making statements about the phenomena of nature, and often on how these impinge directly on human life; it is equally striking that it does so without the need to say anything especially clever, perceptive, original or deep. So, for example, it says the following in connection with the name of the eleventh rune:

> (is) byþ oferceald, ungemetum slidor,
> glisnaþ glæshluttur, gimmum gelicust,
> flor forste geworuht, fæger ansyne.
> (lines 29–31)

Ice is excessively cold, immoderately slippery; it gleams, clear as glass, very much like gems; it is a floor made by frost, beautiful to see.

Of the poem's twenty-nine paragraphs, numbers 2, 3, 9, 13, 15, 16, 18, 21, 25 and 26 have this general character. This emphasis stems, of course, from the rune names, which were a given that the poet had to work with. A similar pleasure in such simple statements can be seen, for example, in the remarks in *Maxims II* (ed. Dobbie 1942: 56, lines 26–7 and 29–30), to the effect that a dragon, old and magnificent with treasures, has to be in a barrow, and a bear, ancient and terrifying, has to be on a heath; likewise this tendency is evident in lines 71–2 from *Maxims I* (ed. Krapp and Dobbie 1936: 159), which note laconically that frost must freeze, fire must consume wood and soil must bear growth. Because of the prevalence of statements such as these, Page (1999: 77) judged the author of *The Rune Poem* to be 'literal-minded': this is true enough, but if we disparage the work on that account we will miss what it has to offer and will, in effect, be rejecting a quality that its original audiences would have found not merely acceptable but appealing, for a great deal of Old English poetry, not of the wisdom genre alone, works by way of the commonplace and familiar, as Tyler (2006) has recently discussed.

It is, nevertheless, more typical of Old English wisdom poetry to make a metaphorical use of natural phenomena to illustrate truths about the world and human existence. Hence *Solomon and Saturn II* (ed. Dobbie 1942: 38–48) repeatedly offers statements about nature in this way, for example when Solomon says that fire and the coldness of frost cannot survive together (line 355–6), by which he seeks to demonstrate that the good and the wicked cannot both enter the kingdom of God, or when he comments on the pending destruction of the ungodly by noting that leaves are green only for a short while before they turn brown and fall (lines 314–22). Similarly, but without making the connection explicit, *Maxims I*, lines 25–6, asserts that a tree has to lose its leaves and its boughs have to mourn; here the audience is left to see a correspondence between this remark and the statement, in the preceding lines (23–5), that a man and woman have to bring a child into the world – the inference being that the parents are bound to lose the child in one way or another, though not necessarily through its death.

The prevalence of this kind of expression in Old English wisdom poetry strongly suggests that what we have here is not simply a matter of a poet searching for a metaphor to express an abstract thought, but a fundamental and pervasive belief in real correspondences between the macrocosm of the natural world and the microcosm of a human life, both as observed exclusively from the perspective of this world (so 'leaves drop, children depart or die') and as seen *sub specie aeternitatis* (so 'the saved and the damned are eternally incompatible, like heat and cold'). Alternatively it may be said of Old English wisdom poetry, adopting a remark made specifically about the *Seafarer* (Conner 2001: 266), that 'the poet's world of common sense was shaped by the metaphors of his or her religion' and that 'the world of bare fact reflects rituals of transition and transformation'. Although these statements could be taken to imply that the religious framework of thought had logical and temporal priority over the poems, which is not necessarily the case, it would be correct to say that in the wisdom poetry of the Anglo-Saxons the verbal conceptualisation of the 'bare facts' of the natural world and the metaphors of religion interpenetrate and are mutually dependent. In view of this it is possible, for the most part, to endorse the view expressed by Harbus (2002: 65) that 'the single most prevalent characteristic of the gnomic literature is the valorisation of the mental world', even in connection with the gnomes that appear to celebrate natural objects for their own sake. In addition it can be seen that Harbus's further statement (2002: 81), made in connection with *The Gifts of Men* (ed. Krapp and Dobbie 1936: 137–40), that the poet's premise is that 'the well-informed person is one who knows the true nature of things and is equipped to interpret the world', is in fact valid for Old English wisdom poetry in general.

None of these considerations of meanings and correspondences, however, should be allowed to desensitise us to the sheer delight we are invited to take in simple statements such as that a wild boar must live in a wood, *toðmægenes trum* ('in the power of its tusks'), that a fish must spawn in water, or that a river, *flodgræg* ('water-grey'), must flow downhill (*Maxims II*, lines 19–20, 27–8 and 30–1 respectively). Likewise, in *The Rune Poem* (lines 88–9), we are clearly meant to share the natural satisfaction of the *iar*, whatever kind of river-creature it may be, eel or newt, when the poet tells us that it 'hafaþ fægerne eard, / wætre beworpen, ðær he wynnum leofaþ' ('has a beautiful dwelling place, surrounded by water, where it lives joyfully'). In this respect Old English wisdom verse offers us a gentle pleasure disdained by most other kinds of poetry.

Much the same points can be made in connection with statements that celebrate and comment on human qualities and possessions or social activities and obligations, which in the case of *The Rune Poem* form the substance of paragraphs 4, 5, 6, 7, 8, 10, 14, 19, 23 and 27. These include a whimsical paragraph on *rad* ('riding', lines 13–5), which notes that this activity is much more strenuous when undertaken outside than in the house. Also included are one on the social pleasures of *peorð* (an indoor game of some kind, lines 38–40) and one that celebrates the horse (*eh*, lines 55–8) as a status symbol and talking-point between men, much like an expensive car today. This last paragraph also remarks, with a neat twist, that a horse is always a benefit to the restless (or perhaps, more ominously, 'to the uneasy' – *unstyllum*). Sections on more abstract topics include lines 22–4, on *wenne* ('joy'), which use the technique of stating the obvious by noting that you experience this quality when you have prosperity rather than pain, but which also associate it, unexpectedly, with the abundance that characterises walled towns. Lines 27–8, in contrast, observe that *nyd* ('need, hardship') can constitute a form of help and salvation for those who know when to respond to it. Several more paragraphs (1, 12, 20 and 24) are overtly religious rather than ethical: so lines 32–4 and 74–6, for example, celebrate *ger* ('year', but here used to mean a productive season as in the Old Norse *ár*) and *dæg* ('day') as gifts from the Lord.

All the topics just mentioned are typical of Old English wisdom poetry, as too is the mix of social and spiritual concerns. In *Precepts* (Krapp and Dobbie 1936: 140–3), for example, the wise father giving advice passes to and fro between, on the one hand, social good of a kind that would have been recognisable to any well-intentioned heathen and, on the other, a specifically Christian spiritual righteousness; and he does so without apparent pattern or awareness of any distinctions to be made between the two ethical perspectives, the implication being that such is the nature of the Christian life. The father's first instruction to his son, in fact, neatly illustrates the contiguity, if not continuity, of the social and spiritual modes of ethical motivation (line 4): 'Do a þætte duge, deag þin gewyrhtu'. Following Shippey (1976: 49), one could translate this as 'Always do what would be right, and what you have done will bring you profit', but the semantic possibilities of the verb *dugan* ('to be worth something, to thrive, to be virtuous') render both clauses of the line ambiguous, so several permutations of the sense would be feasible. The first paragraph of *The Rune Poem* displays a somewhat similar fluctuation between the purely social and the religious, as the modern reader is apt to see things. Its opening statement, to the effect that money is a consolation to every man, suggests the kind of hard materialism often encountered in wisdom poetry, for example in *Maxims I* line 143, which states perfunctorily that no one can acquire too much wealth; but *The Rune Poem* passage then goes on to say that everyone should freely share this consolation of money if they wish to gain honour in the sight of the Lord.

Vainglory (Krapp and Dobbie 1936: 147–9) reveals a different aspect of the interface between the two ethical frames of reference by showing a keen sense of a spiritual dimension to social interaction. The behaviour of the obstreperous drunkard at the feast, who also makes an appearance in *The Fortunes of Men* (Krapp and Dobbie 1936: 155, lines 48–57) and elsewhere, is seen as subject to the devil's flying darts (*Vainglory*, lines 26–7). The drunken warrior himself hurls showers of missiles in the form of malicious speeches because of his pride and envy, and he allows treacherous shafts to penetrate the wall of the fortification that God has commanded him to defend (lines 33–9). Here the constant shifting of the focus – now on the warrior in the hall, now on the Christian soul failing to resist the devil – in a text that is now literal, now metaphorical, is impressive. At the same time the relationship between the two frames of reference is sufficiently free for the social actuality never to settle once and for all into a mere symbol for a spiritual predicament. Likewise in *Maxims I* and *II* the relationship between statements concerning the social and the spiritual – and also concerning the world of nature – is fluid and frequently uncertain; in the case of these poems, however, the jamming together of gnomic utterances belonging to different spheres of knowledge has been a problem for many modern readers who have looked for greater consistency and coherence than the works offer.

Structure, or the apparent lack of it, in Old English wisdom poetry has been a major issue in the appreciation of the genre and has attracted much negative criticism. Those works of a catalogue nature, in particular, are likely to be seen as inorganic and badly ordered, as noted by Howe (1985: 12). In the case of poems that primarily offer advice along with apparent facts, the problem of structure may be seen as especially pressing if it is true, as Cavill (1999: 10) says, that the poetry and expressions normally classed as gnomic 'structure reality as perceived by society, and in turn construct the reality that society perceives'. In this respect, however, *The Rune Poem* in particular fares well because it has a ready-made structure and unity imposed on it by the traditional sequence of the runic characters, and although the individual paragraphs are heterogeneous in their topics and do not cohere into any kind of argument, this fact is determined and justified by the heterogeneous nature of the rune names. A definite though limited concern for structure and unity in this poem is indicated, furthermore, by the fact that the poem follows the traditional division of the set of runic characters into groups of eight: the first eight runes are given three long-lines each, whilst thereafter the three-line paragraph remains the most frequent in occurrence and is used to end the second and third groups of eight. The first two paragraphs of the second group of eight each consist of two hypermetric lines, and since the meanings of these paragraphs, the first a nature gnome on 'hail' and the second an ethical reflection on 'hardship', do not suggest any reason for the adoption of hypermetric form, it is possible that the change is meant to signal that from this point the apparently stanzaic form of the poem is to be varied. If this is the case, the alteration succeeds admirably because each pair of hypermetric lines has the same number of accented syllables as a three-line 'stanza' but sounds strikingly different. A concern for variety within uniformity is also indicated by the fact that the almost constant 'x *byþ* y' opening of the paragraphs is followed by sentences of nicely varied syntactic structures. It is also evident that the poet, or possibly a redactor, did not ignore the question of the poem's overall rhetorical effect, for the supplementary rune *iar* (the water creature mentioned above), which would normally be in the twenty-ninth position, has been given the penultimate place so that the twenty-eighth rune, *ear* ('earth', line 90), can be placed last. This seems to have been done so that the work can conclude with a meditation on the grave (Page 1973: 85), construed as the place in which the pallid corpse begins to choose earth as its bedfellow (lines 91–3) and where 'wynna gewitaþ, wera geswicaþ' ('joys pass away, agreements fail', line 94). Thus, with a kind of rhyme, the poem does not merely end but achieves an ending.

Precepts is another wisdom poem that reveals a definite, though much more limited, concern for structure and responds to it by disposing the wise father's instructions into ten utterances, the number, though not the instructions, corresponding to the Decalogue. The precepts themselves, furthermore, appear to have been arranged according to the three ages of life, beginning with youth and ending with old age (Howe 1985: 145–51). The poem can hardly be faulted in this respect although it is difficult to be enthusiastic about it as a whole because the advice given is relatively bland and colourless.

There is nothing colourless, however, about *The Fortunes of Men*, which, after a short preamble stating that loving parents will nurture their children and raise them to maturity, offers two contrasting and unequal catalogues of misfortunes and blessings. There is no doubt that one is meant to enjoy the list of disasters (lines 10–57): the details of the Old English catalogue are piquant, to say the least, and include references to how a raven pecks the eyes from the head of a hanged man, who cannot beat it off with his hands as he dangles amid the vapours of his own corpse (lines 33–42); there is even a sort of grim humour at the expense of a man who falls from a high tree, *fiþerleas* ('wingless') but nevertheless *on flihte* ('in flight', line 22) for a short while. Likewise the list of activities engaged in by those whose lives turn out well is vivid and delightful in the abundant details it gives. These include the techniques used by one man to give a spirited performance on the harp, thus gaining payment from his lord (lines 80–4), and the methods by which another trains a hawk (lines 85–92). The lists themselves have the open-ended quality and heterogeneous nature common to catalogues, but they are unified by the insistent use of anaphora on the word *sum* ('a certain one') – one does this, one does that – which also features prominently in *The Gifts of Men* and lines 80–4 of *The Wanderer* (Krapp and Dobbie 1936: 134–7). Between the two lists in *The Fortunes of Men*, moreover, there is a brief passage (lines 58–63) that may be taken as the crux of the poem, for it says that one person, through the power of God, will use up his misfortunes in youth and live on into a prosperous old age; thus, it continues (lines 64–7), the Lord apportions things to men, giving prosperity to one person but to another a share of hardships. Hence the link to the list of blessings has been forged. However shallow the poet may be in his theology, therefore, he is evidently striving to express a balanced view that makes sense of the world as a unity through a poem that is itself balanced and unified.

The same cannot be said of *Maxims I*, which follows *The Fortunes of Men* in the Exeter Book. This poem, or group of three poems, has defied attempts to produce a satisfactory, integrated reading of it. A drift of ideas may perhaps be discerned in the first two parts but, as Larrington (1993: 129) has observed, 'to pose questions of unity and coherence may be to make the wrong sort of demands' on the work. It nevertheless offers many delights of the kinds mentioned above plus a marvellous unpredictability, and in many parts it possesses an exhilarating rapidity of motion from one idea to the next.

Similar qualities, at first bewildering though exhilarating, can be found in *Maxims II*, though here the work more readily invites appreciation as a unity and appears more manageable if only because it is short. High levels of patterning quickly become apparent in the poem. The first four lines, which are hypermetric, begin with 'Cyning sceal rice healdan' ('A king must hold/rule/preserve a kingdom') and end climactically with 'Þrymmas syndan Cristes myccle' ('The powers of Christ are great'). Line 3 introduces a sequence of superlatives, 'Wind byð on lyfte swiftust' ('Wind is the swiftest in the sky'), which is developed in parallel and varied lines (4–11). Lines 17–39, 43, 45 and 48–9 are constructed in such a way as to ring the changes on the preposition *on* (which has many different meanings including 'on, on to, in, into, to, at, against' etc.), whilst lines 51–54a are structured tightly by placing the preposition *wið* ('against') in the penultimate position in every half-line. Lines 1b–13a are made up of *byð*-gnomes, whilst lines 14–57 concentrate on *sceal*-gnomes and the remaining lines (57b–66) relinquish the *byð-sceal* format in order to meditate on the nature of God as judge. In addition to the usual alliteration, furthermore, there is much use of assonance, both on its own and in conjunction with alliteration: see especially lines 1–3 on *ea* and *eo*, 34–5 on *eo* with the antithesis *on eorþan* ('on earth') and *on heofenum* ('in heaven'), 47–9 again on *eo* with the same antithesis and 51–2 on *ēo*; and see lines 7, 8, 11 and 23 (which includes full rhyme). Note also the repetition of *fyrd* and *lað* in lines 52a and 53a. In this poem, then, we are clearly being invited to enjoy the way in which the poet plays with the sound of words, sometimes in patterns that coincide with meaning, as in the *eorðe-heofon* antithesis, but also purely for its own sake. This love of patternings that are not always meaningful is by no means characteristic of all Old English wisdom poetry – assonance and rhyme, for instance, play only a small part in *The Rune Poem* – but it does occur quite frequently, for example in lines 4–9 and 15–19 of *The Fortunes of Men*, line 33 of *Vainglory*, and several parts of *Maxims I*, such as lines 19, 23, 67, 85–6, 117, 120–1 and 159, the last of which contains an interesting play on words ('Treo sceolon brædan ond treow weaxan', 'A tree must broaden and faith increase').

One older strand of criticism commonly dismissed *Maxims II* for reasons typified by Dobbie's remark (1942: lxvi) that 'it is evident that the poet has no definite idea in mind beyond putting a number of unrelated ideas into alliterative form'. Such a judgement is unfortunate because it neglects the sheer pleasure in words and patterns above and beyond those required by alliterative metre, which, as we have just seen, is a major part of what the poem offers. More recent criticism, furthermore, has emphasised the various kinds of patterning to the point of declaring the work 'inherently structural' (Barley 1977: 245) with its employment of parallelism, antithesis and metaphor to establish relations. And although the poem does not have an argument it can be said to have what Larrington (1993: 130) calls a 'movement' from the earthly to the divine. In the manner that we have seen is typical of much Old English wisdom poetry it tacks to and fro between society and nature, with plunges into the metaphysical workings of God; but further to this one could tentatively characterise the first section of the poem (lines 1–17a) as being generally concerned with power and the things that challenge or reinforce it, whilst the second part (lines 17b–49) dwells on place and belonging, with a passage (lines 42–45a) devoted to beings who by their actions or nature in some way exclude themselves from full enjoyment of human society – the thief who walks in gloomy weather, the monster that lives in the fen and (pointedly or perhaps ironically) the girl who chooses secret means to have a lover rather than to have a marriage negotiated by her people. After this a section on the conflicts of existence (lines 50–55a) leads into a final passage on divine judgement and salvation (lines 55b–66).

In the penultimate section of *Maxims II* the conflicts mentioned are not contingent but essential. They are irreducible polarities and oppositions about which we must be ever mindful: 'God sceal wið yfele, geogoð sceal wið yldo, / lif sceal wið deaþe' ('Good must be against evil, youth against old age, life against death', lines 50–1), and 'A sceal snotor hycgean / ymb þysse worulde gewinn' ('The wise man must always think about the conflict of this world', lines 54b–55a). Thus the poem asserts that the world of humanity is fractured. This is a concept also acknowledged by *Vainglory* (lines 21b–77a), which outlines two irreconcilable types of person, the proud and the humble, and by *Solomon and Saturn II* (lines 353–8), which, as discussed earlier, says that people cannot all enter the kingdom of God any more than fire and frost can exist together in the same place. The fracture is confirmed in the last lines of *Maxims II* and the other main ideas of the poem are subsumed in the concept of the divine judgement, which is the ultimate exercise of power and of division into places of belonging; this is an act of God, we are told, about which we can have faith but not certain knowledge. Overall, in fact, *Maxims II* is open in thought as in structure: it does not have a clear message but it is a satisfying reflection on the ways in which the world, even in theological terms, makes partial sense yet is not completely intelligible. The play of certainty and doubt is summed up in lines 62b–63a, which consider ultimate destiny in relation to each person: 'drihten ana wat, / nergende fæder' ('the Lord alone knows, the redeeming father'). Many things fit, the poem gives us to understand, but others fit by not fitting; and whilst God may somehow makes sense of all this, we ourselves can only trust while acknowledging that we do not know what the future of the redeemed will be like (lines 64–7). Far from being a piece of sloppy thinking or a thoughtless metrical exercise, therefore, *Maxims II*, with its emphasis on pleasurable but sometimes meaningless patterning, emerges as a poem that speaks powerfully to us in our post-modernist, post-structuralist world where faith plays no less divisive a role than at any time in history. Of all the Old English wisdom poems, it is the one that best supports the view of Hansen (1988: 10) that this genre is 'concerned with the nature, function and value of its own discourse'.

A simpler educational purpose than this, of course, lies behind many Old English wisdom poems, as we have already seen in connection with *Precepts* and as is exemplified by a poem such as the *Menologium* (ed. Dobbie 1942: 49–55), which sets forth details of the Christian year and its feasts. This aspect of wisdom poetry, nevertheless, should not be overemphasised, as consideration of *The Rune Poem* indicates. On the most basic level, one purpose of *The Rune Poem* is surely to inculcate a knowledge of the runes by helping to fix their names and hence the phonetic values of the characters themselves in the minds of its audience. Since the verse commentaries on the rune names, however, are far longer than would be necessary for purely mnemonic purposes (Larrington 1993: 134) it is clear that the main focus of interest is the commentaries themselves. Putting this another way, the main pleasure offered by the poem is not truly didactic any more than the statements of the obvious in *Maxims I* and elsewhere, as discussed above, are truly informative.

The way in which the rune names fit with their respective verses in *The Rune Poem*, however, suggests that readers were being invited to play a kind of educational game, for although each name is an essential part of the metrical and alliterative pattern of the line in which it occurs, the evidence of Hickes's printed version indicates that the name was probably not present in the manuscript, where its place would have been taken by only the rune itself. A reader familiar with the rune would automatically supply its name, but others would be prompted to recollect or guess the name with the help of the information and alliteration in the accompanying line. To this extent the poem is akin to a series of riddles, albeit simple ones, and provides something of the pleasure offered by the riddles in the Exeter Book. The passage on the fifteenth rune (lines 77–80), in fact, is especially riddle-like in describing its subject, *ac* ('oak'), as something that on the ground is fodder for an animal of the children of men and that often travels over the gannet's bath. Actual riddles also feature notably in *Solomon and Saturn II*, where one speaker requires the other to solve an enigma in lines 210–11 ('sea'), 230–7 ('books') and 283–91 ('old age'). Beyond these details, however, it may reasonably be said that Old English riddles and wisdom poetry have a natural affinity for one another, 'for it often happens that the pleasure of reading poetry of this kind derives from the shock of recognising the knowledge that one has always had' (Niles 2006: 310; cf. Tigges 1994).

When the relevant knowledge has been gained or recognised, a work like *The Rune Poem* is bound to change in the nature of its appeal. Once committed to heart, or if it was read or recited with the rune names in place, it would have less of a riddling character but would still offer a different pleasure characteristic of wisdom literature, for it would then function as an elaborated list of nouns. The love of lists or catalogues (discussed at length in Howe 1985), together with the related love of names, is perhaps the feature of Old English wisdom poetry that makes it most alien to a modern audience but was a widespread source of delight in the Middle Ages. A very strong interest in lists is apparent in Old Norse wisdom poetry, for example, especially in the *Ljóðatal* section of *Hávamál* (ed. Evans 1986, stanzas 146–63), which lists magic spells without actually disclosing them, and in *Vafþrúðnismál* (ed. Machan

2008) and *Grímnismál* (ed. Neckel 1914: 54–66), which are essentially catalogues of mythological names cast, very effectively, into dialogue form. The extant Old English wisdom poems do not exhibit a similar concern for heathen mythology and its magic, but the love of lists is exemplified in such poems as *The Gifts of Men*, which consists largely of a catalogue of human talents, and *The Fortunes of Men*, which, as discussed earlier, lists misfortunes and blessings, while the *Menologium* is a catalogue of Church feasts. The specific love of proper names can be seen in the list of places mentioned in *Solomon and Saturn II* (lines 186–201). And one could point also to the very large number of names found in *Widsith* (ed. Krapp and Dobbie 1936: 149–53), which is not usually thought of as a wisdom poem but which is not far removed from the wisdom genre since it has the character of a sustained display of knowledge.

The idea that ancient perceptions and judgements are being transmitted in Old English wisdom poetry is invoked explicitly in *Vainglory* (line 1), which uses the phrase *on fyrndagum* ('in days of old') to authenticate the views expressed there, while *Solomon and Saturn II* (line 179) uses the same phrase to contextualise the exchange of wisdom contained within it. The latter poem pits the Judaeo-Christian wisdom of Solomon against the pagan wisdom of the Chaldean nobleman Saturn, in terms that favour Solomon but by no means pour contempt on Saturn, whom Solomon addresses as *broðor* ('brother', line 330) and who is said approvingly to have the keys to certain books (*sumra hæfde* [...] *boca c{.}g{.}*, lines 183–4). In view of this it is fair to ask what the attitude of Old English wisdom poetry is towards its heritage of pre-Christian lore – and here again *The Rune Poems* proves useful for the analysis.

The date of the poem itself is uncertain, but some of the material in it is likely to be old: the case of the second rune, *ur* (line 4), is particularly revealing as the poem takes this as meaning 'aurochs', a wild bovine animal which, as Halsall (1981: 105) points out, was extinct in Anglo-Saxon England although it survived on the Continent. The implication is that the Old English understanding of the rune name had been handed down for several centuries. This is the kind of ancient knowledge that the poet of *The Rune Poem* was willing to transmit. The situation is rather different, however, where rune names that are likely to have been associated with heathen gods are concerned. The nineteenth rune name, *Tir*, is presented as designating a heavenly body (*tacna sum*, line 48) that is beneficial to princes and always runs its course above the mists of night. The corresponding name in the Norwegian and Icelandic rune poems (ed. Halsall 1981: 181–3 and 183–6, lines 23 and 24 respectively) is *Týr*, explicitly identified in both poems as one of the Æsir, the reigning family of gods in Old Norse mythology. It is likely that the Old English rune name originally designated the corresponding god Tīw, whose name early replaced that of Mars (Halsall 1981: 135–7), as in *Tiwesdæg* (*dies Martis*, 'Tuesday'); but in *The Rune Poem*, although there may indeed be some association between the word *Tir* and Mars as a planet, the concept of Tīw as a god is nowhere in evidence. More problematic is the treatment of the fourth rune name, *os*, which seems to be understood as the Latin word for 'mouth', since it is declared to be *ordfruma ælcre spræce* ('the source of every utterance', line 10). The Old English word *ōs* in fact means 'heathen god' and descends from the etymon that also gives rise to the Old Norse *Áss*, the singular of *Æsir*. Since the Icelandic rune poem (line 10) gives the form *óss* and identifies this as a designation of Óðinn, *valhallar vísi* ('chieftain of Valhöll', line 12), it is interesting to note that Óðinn's nature, in Old Norse mythology, as the bestower of eloquence, patron of wisdom (as in *Hávamál*) and god of the warrior class, may be anticipated in *The Rune Poem* not only by the description of *os* as the source of utterances but also as *wisdomes wraþu* ('support of wisdom', line 11) and *eorla gehwam eadnys* ('a joy to every nobleman', line 12). Larrington (1993: 137) judges the connection with Óðinn to be probable even though it is concealed. If the interpretation of *os* as the Latin 'mouth' is accepted as the way in which these lines are most likely to have been understood and as they were probably intended, it can be seen that at some stage a radical step was taken to avoid the heathen connotations of the original rune name and perhaps of some verbal formulae that adhered to it.

On the whole, therefore, it can be seen that *The Rune Poem* neutralises any heathen mythological relics it may have inherited. In this it is in line with the trend of all Old English poetry, but here some vestiges of the lore attendant on the ancient rune names may have been retained, though the fact may not have been apparent to the work's early audiences or to its author. The main point to be made in connection with the preservation of ancient wisdom, however, is that whereas the pagan lore of the ancient Mediterranean world represented by Saturn in *Solomon and Saturn II* was acceptable within certain limits, the heathen lore of the north was not.

Another aspect of wisdom poetry that has not so far been discussed here is the connection to personal knowledge and experience. This is not exhibited by *The Rune Poem* or *Maxims II*, but it is a feature of *Precepts*, where it is emphasised that the speaker is a *frod fæder* who is a *modsnottor mon* ('wise father', 'a man of discerning mind', lines 1–2), and of *Vainglory*, which claims that the wisdom it embodies was acquired from a man who was a *frod wita* ('wise philosopher', line 1). *Maxims I* and *The Order of the World* (ed. Krapp and Dobbie 1936: 163–6), taking a slightly different tack, both begin by putting the speaker of the poem in the position of the wise man, who offers himself for questioning. It is a curious and perhaps significant characteristic of these Old English poems that the wise man is anonymous, for wisdom literature in other contexts or languages shows a strong tendency to attach wise sayings to the names of famously wise persons. Hence the Old Testament has collections of sayings attributed to Solomon; medieval Latin literature includes a widely disseminated collection known as the *Disticha Catonis* 'Distichs of Cato' (ed. Boas and Botschuyver 1952), which exists in an Old English prose translation (ed. Cox 1972); Old Norse gives various names of Óðinn to collections of sayings in *Hávamál* 'The Sayings of Hávi' (ed. Evans 1986) and *Grímnismál* 'The Sayings of Grímnir' (ed. Neckel 1914: 54–66); and Middle English writing offers the so-called *Proverbs of Alfred* (ed. Arngart 1978). In the main corpus of Old English wisdom poetry this tendency is exhibited only by the two *Solomon and Saturn* poems (ed. Dobbie 1942: 31–48), where Solomon, however, is a clearly fictionalised figure who has little to do with the biblical character of that name. The speakers of *Deor* (ed. Krapp and Dobbie 1936: 178–9) and *Widsith* (ed. Krapp and Dobbie 1936: 149–53), if these works may be viewed as outliers of the genre, are the only other named bearers of wisdom, and these shadowy figures are barely more than names. They certainly do not function as authenticating representatives of wisdom as Solomon, Cato or Óðinn do. In the case of *Deor* especially it can be seen, rather, that the knowledge of Germanic legends displayed in the poem partly authenticates itself and is partly authenticated by the role of Deor as a *scop* learned in traditional lore, much as the views expressed in *Vainglory* are authenticated by the role of the anonymous sage as 'beorn boca gleaw' ('a man skilful with books', line 4). At the same time, Deor's existential wisdom, expressed in the refrain 'Þæs ofereode, þisses swa mæg' ('As to that, it passed; as to this, it can do likewise', lines 7, 13, 17, 20, 27 and 42), is both authenticated and questioned by the narrator's briefly sketched personal experience as the one-time *scop* of the Heodeningas, who has now lost both his place and his lord's favour (lines 35–41). This vignette of personal experience is not only offered by the poem for the sake of underpinning the wisdom of the text, however, but as an example of the sort of tribulation that may come upon a man. In this respect *Deor* links with the list of typical tribulations given in *The Fortunes of Men* and with many other vignettes of different kinds found throughout Old English wisdom poetry – the girl seeking a lover in *Maxims II* and the brawling drunkard in *Vainglory* being just two cases in point.

The emphasis on wisdom exemplified in, and to some extent born out of, personal experience that is apparently specific and yet is offered as typical, is attached to a character who is often anonymous but may occasionally be known as no more than a name, is also displayed to an even greater extent in some of the Old English poems that have long been termed elegies – of which *Deor* is commonly classed as one. It is this aspect of the works, in fact, that led Greenfield (1966: 143), in a famous attempt to define the Old English elegy genre, to characterise it as offering 'a contrasting pattern of loss and consolation, ostensibly based on a specific personal experience'. The usefulness of the term 'elegy' has been much debated in recent decades, so that Fulk and Cain (2005: 181), for example, reject it on the grounds that it 'contributes to ahistorical and ethnocentric misconceptions about these poems'. Other scholars, however, continue to defend it as a convenient appellation for poems that concentrate on a complex of themes such as exile, loss of loved ones, scenes of desolation and the transience of worldly joys. Klinck (1992: 11), not surprisingly, defended it thus in her authoritative edition of what she sees as the main examples of the genre, namely *The Wanderer, The Seafarer, The Riming Poem, Deor, Wulf and Eadwacer, The Wife's Lament, Resignation, Riddle 60, The Husband's Message* and *The Ruin*.

In view of this controversy, and given the reliance of the so-called elegies on personal experience, together with the prevalence of gnomic utterance in them, it is perhaps best to see them as extensions of the wisdom-poetry genre. Some of the best known of them, however, are distinct in that they have the quality of a complaint or lament and may bear some relation, as Woolf (1975) pointed out, to the Latin *planctus* genre; *The Seafarer, The Wanderer, The Wife's Lament, Wulf and Eadwacer* and *The Riming Poem* share this characteristic. The lament is not typical of the wisdom literature discussed above, although *Deor* has something of this quality and may be seen as both a wisdom poem and an elegy.

The 'specific personal experience' on which these poems are ostensibly based (to revert to Greenfield's phrase) is by no means always clear. This fact has very probably worked in favour of the poems because it has provoked much controversy and fascination. *Wulf and Eadwacer* (ed. Krapp and Dobbie 1936: 179–80), for example, is 'one of the most of enigmatic of poems and has generated intense but largely unresolved argument about its interpretation' (Marsden 2004: 335). In it the female speaker appears to address two men, but it is not certain what the relationships are or even whether Wulf and Eadwacer are actually personal names, nor what the *hwelp* ('cub') referred to in line 16 may be. In the face of these uncertainties it is difficult to see what lessons can be drawn from the poem, and yet its relation to wisdom poetry is emphasised by the fact that it ends with a gnomic utterance, and a particularly haunting one (lines 18–19): 'Þæt mon eaþe tosliteð þætte næfre gesomnad wæs, / uncer giedd geador' ('That can easily be separated which was never joined – the song of us two together'). If the poem has any relevance at all to human relationships, the point of this final statement is surely to promote a brave and bitter acceptance of desolation when desolation cannot be avoided.

The interpretive problems of *The Wife's Lament* (ed. Krapp and Dobbie 1936: 210–11) are scarcely less acute although recent editors, including Pope and Fulk (2001), have tended to go for the most straightforward interpretation of this work as a woman's acutely emotional lament over her separation from her lover, rather than as some kind of allegory or riddle. In the context of the present discussion of wisdom poetry, however, the most pressing problem, as it will seem to many modern readers, is the fact that after more than forty lines of anguished complaint on the part of the isolated woman, the poem plunges into a gnomic passage (lines 42–50a) that outlines the good qualities every young man should have, before it links up again with the situation of the speaker's beloved, and then rounds off the lament, as in *Wulf and Eadwacer*, with a final gnome: 'Wa bið þam þe sceal / of langoþe leofes abidan', ('Woe it is to the one who has to wait for the beloved in longing', lines 52b–53). After drawing attention to this plunge, Larrington (1993: 187; cf Cavill 1999: 1–2) suggests that what it shows is that the tradition of gnomic reflection in lament had become so conventional that it was felt a moral had to be tacked on somewhere, textual incongruity not withstanding. This may be so, but a more positive view would be that the love of wisdom poetry was so great that no incongruity was perceived; rather, an opportunity for offering delightful platitudes had been seized. One can see a parallel to this more positive attitude, in fact, in the Old Norse context of the poem *Sigrdrífumál* (ed. Neckel 1914: 185–92), where a valkyrie, having just been awakened from a magic sleep by Sigurðr, regales the hero with thirty stanzas of instruction; and far from perceiving this as an absurdity or a blemish in his narrative, the author or redactor of the prose *Völsunga saga* (ed. Finch 1965: 36–40), in telling his version of the story, includes thirteen of these stanzas and offers a page of prose advice in place of the rest. What we should learn in connection with *The Wife's Lament*, therefore, is that we cannot have a proper appreciation of such so-called elegies unless we approach them from the direction of wisdom poetry, having educated ourselves first in the proper love of that genre.

It is with this understanding that one should read *The Seafarer* (ed. Krapp and Dobbie 1936: 143–7). As a poem in which textual problems abound and interpretive difficulties are legion, *The Seafarer* has inspired a vast secondary literature. Whilst its vivid sea imagery and what was once thought to be the pre-Christian ethos of certain parts of the poem have long excited interest, *The Seafarer* as a whole has usually taken second place to *The Wanderer* because the latter has seemed more of a unity. To some extent this perception is due to the fact that wisdom utterances of one kind or another are dispersed throughout *The Wanderer* and are used to bracket the entire piece: see especially lines 1–5, 12–13, 15–16, 29–33, 55–7, 64–74, 80–4, 106–10 and 112–15. In *The Seafarer*, by contrast, the first sixty-four lines offer an extensive set of thoughts and images, apparently personal in nature, on the subject of travel by sea, while the rest of the poem, following a reference to this dead life *læne on londe* 'temporary on land' (line 66), drops the sea imagery in favour of a religious discourse on the transitory nature of the world, and breaks into a series of gnomes (lines 103–16) before ending in homiletic fashion (lines 117–24). The seafaring section of the poem is tied to wisdom literature not so much by the presence of gnomic utterances, which are scarce here (though see lines 39–43 and 47), as by its repeated insistence that the speaker has knowledge and understanding of a kind that a comfortable landlubber must lack (line 12–16, 25–30 and 55–7). This concern for the possibilities and limits of knowledge, united with the idea that there are two kinds of people (in this case the saved and the damned, although the interpretation is uncertain because the text is corrupt), re-emerges at the end of the gnomic section in lines 113–16, which assert that fate and the Lord are mightier than any man's thought. Despite correspondences of this and other kinds, however, and assuming, as most scholars do, that the poem is continuous and not the product of one or more quires falling out of the manuscript, *The Seafarer* presents the modern reader with an aesthetic challenge similar to the one discussed above in connection with *The Wife's Lament*. Attempts to affirm and explain the unity of the poem, such as that by Conner (2001: 266) quoted earlier, are in part a response to this challenge: they have much to recommend them, but it may be said that they betray a certain anxiety that the Anglo-Saxon audiences would probably not have felt. Seen as functioning in the mode of wisdom poetry, as in the case of *Maxims II*, *The Seafarer* is free to be open in thought and structure, reflecting the fact that mankind has no more than an imperfect understanding, an understanding of the world that makes partial sense but does not quite cohere.

In conclusion three matters should be emphasised. First, it will have been noted that one absence from the above discussion is an analysis of terms designating various kinds of sapiential utterance, such as adage, aphorism, apothegm, axiom, dict, dictum, maxim, precept, proverb, saw, saying and *sententia*. For an important treatment of the relevant terms and the uses of the types of utterance they designate, together with the relationships between them, see Cavill (1999: 41–81). The omission of this topic in the present discussion has been dictated partly by considerations of space, but more out of a desire to reflect the fact that although Old English wisdom poetry exhibits a love of naming things and of making lists, it characteristically resists categories, systematisation and exhaustiveness. This resistance, it has been argued above, is one of the strengths of wisdom poetry and in some works is in fact the main point of the writing, though it has often been perceived as a weakness.

Second, Old English wisdom poetry has frequently been referred to above as a genre. This is reasonable since there is a sizable group of poems that are widely accepted as sharing generic characteristics, many of which have been examined here. It must be acknowledged, however, that the sapiential manner is so pervasive in Old English that the wisdom 'genre' can threaten to subsume much else in the poetry, or the integrity of a given poem can be compromised through the recognition of wisdom poetry fragments embedded within it. The term 'wisdom poetry' remains too useful to be given up, but genre considerations modelled on the mathematical theory of sets – in which other genres intersect with the wisdom set or become subsets of it – need to be used with discretion if they are used at all.

Finally, the term 'wisdom poetry' suggests something weighty, revelatory, consequential, definitive. On occasion it can be some, if not all, of these things. Equally often, however, it is likely to be light, and far from being revelatory may be disarmingly obvious or wilfully obscure; it can toy with sounds and patterns for their own sakes, and in tackling the big questions of existence can neutralise definite answers even as it seems to give them. It is hard to imagine, in fact, that anyone ever became well informed through reading Old English wisdom poetry, but easy to see how people were entertained by it. The thoughtful and observant reader, nevertheless, would come away from the best poems with an awareness that many things, including some of the most important, cannot be known – which is indeed the beginning of wisdom.

REFERENCES AND FURTHER READING

Primary Texts

Arngart, Olof Sigfrid (ed.) (1978). *The Proverbs of Alfred: An Emended Text*. Lund: Gleerup.

Boas, Marcus and Hendrik Johan Botschuyver (eds) (1952). *Disticha Catonis*. Amsterdam: North-Holland.

Cox, Robert S., Sr. (ed.) (1972). The Old English 'Dicts of Cato'. *Anglia*, 90: 1–42.

Dobbie, Elliott van Kirk (ed.) (1942). *The Anglo-Saxon Minor Poems*. Anglo-Saxon Poetic Records 6. New York: Columbia University Press. *Bede's Death Song* (pp. 107–8); *Maxims II* (pp. 55–7); *Menologium* (pp. 49–55); *The Rune Poem* (pp. 28–30);

Solomon and Saturn I (pp. 31–8); *Solomon and Saturn II* (pp. 38–48).

Evans, David A. H. (ed.) (1986). *Hávamál*. London: Viking Society for Northern Research.

Finch, Ronald G. (ed.) (1965). *Völsunga saga: The Saga of the Volsungs*. London: Nelson.

Halsall, Maureen (ed.) (1981). *The Old English Rune Poem: A Critical Edition*. Toronto: Toronto University Press.

Hickes, George (ed.) (1703–5). *Linguarum veterum septentrionalium thesaurus grammatico-criticus et archæologicus*. Oxford. 2 vols. Repr. Hildesheim: Olms, 1970.

Klinck, Anne L. (ed.) (1992). *The Old English Elegies: A Critical Edition and Genre Study.* Montreal: McGill–Queen's University Press.

Krapp, George Philip and Elliott van Kirk Dobbie (eds) (1936). *The Exeter Book.* Anglo-Saxon Poetic Records 3. New York: Columbia University Press. *Deor* (pp. 178–9); *The Fortunes of Men* (pp. 154–6); *Maxims I* (pp. 156–63); *The Order of the World* (pp. 163–6); *Pharaoh* (pp. 223); *Precepts* (pp. 140–3); *The Gifts of Men* (pp. 137–40); *The Seafarer* (pp. 143–7); *Vainglory* (pp. 147–9); *The Wanderer* (pp. 134–7); *Widsith* (pp. 149–53); *The Wife's Lament* (pp. 210–1); *Wulf and Eadwacer* (pp. 179–80).

Machan, Tim William (ed.) (2008). *Vafþrúðnismál.* 2nd edn. Durham: Centre for Medieval and Renaissance Studies.

Neckel, Gustav (ed.) (1914). *Edda: Die Lieder des Codex Regius.* Heidelberg: Winter.

Pope, John C. and R. D. Fulk (eds) (2001). *Eight Old English Poems.* 3rd edn. New York: Norton.

Shippey, T. A. (ed. and trans.) (1976). *Poems of Wisdom and Learning in Old English.* Cambridge: D. S. Brewer.

Secondary Reading

Barley, Nigel F. (1977). Structure in the 'Cotton Gnomes'. *Neuphilologische Mitteilungen*, 78, 244–9.

Cavill, Paul (1999). *Maxims in Old English Poetry.* Cambridge: D. S. Brewer.

Conner, Patrick W. (2001). Religious poetry. In Phillip Pulsiano and Elaine Treharne (eds). *A Companion to Anglo-Saxon Literature* (pp. 251–67). Oxford: Blackwell.

Fulk, R. D. and Christopher M. Cain (2005). *A History of Old English Literature.* Oxford: Blackwell. (Originally pub. 2003.)

Greenfield, Stanley B. (1966). The Old English Elegies. In E. G. Stanley (ed.). *Continuations and Beginnings: Studies in Old English Literature* (pp. 142–75). London: Nelson.

Hansen, Elaine Tuttle (1988). *The Solomon Complex.* Toronto: Toronto University Press.

Harbus, Antonina (2002). *The Life of the Mind in Old English Poetry.* Amsterdam: Rodopi.

Howe, Nicholas (1985). *The Old English Catalogue Poems.* Copenhagen: Rosenkilde and Bagger.

Larrington, Carolyne (1993). *A Store of Common Sense: Gnomic Theme and Style in Old Icelandic and Old English Wisdom Poetry.* Oxford: Clarendon Press.

Marsden, Richard (2004). *The Cambridge Old English Reader.* Cambridge: Cambridge University Press.

Niles, John D. (2006). *Old English Enigmatic Poems and the Play of the Texts.* Turnhout: Brepols.

Page, R. I. (1999). *An Introduction to English Runes.* 2nd edn. Woodbridge: Boydell.

Schneider, Karl (1959). *Die Germanischen Runennamen.* Meisenheim: Hain.

Tigges, Wim (1994). Snakes and ladders: ambiguity and coherence in the Exeter Book riddles and maxims. In Henk Aertsen and Rolf H. Bremmer (eds). *Companion to Old English Poetry* (pp. 95–118). Amsterdam: VU University Press.

Tyler, Elizabeth M. (2006). *Old English Poetics: The Aesthetics of the Familiar in Anglo-Saxon England.* York: York Medieval Press.

Woolf, Rosemary (1975). 'The Wanderer', 'The Seafarer', and the genre of Planctus. In Lewis E. Nicholson and Dolores Warwick Frese (eds). *Anglo-Saxon Poetry: Essays in Appreciation for John C. McGalliard* (pp. 192–207). Notre Dame, IN: Notre Dame University Press.

8

Old English Epic Poetry: *Beowulf*

Daniel Anlezark

At the end of the Old English epic poem *Beowulf*, a cavalcade of princes circles the dead king's newly erected tomb, singing his praises:

> cwædon þæt he wære   wyruldcyninga
> manna mildust   ond monðwærust,
> leodum liðost   ond lofgeornost.
> (Klaeber 1950: lines 3180–2)

They said that he was of all the world's kings, the mildest of men and the most gentle, the kindest to his people and the most eager for praise.

Some have found in this last word of the poem, *lofgeornost*, a sting in the tail, a definitive moral judgement passed by the poet on the emptiness of the heroic life of the pagan past, a mournful condemnation of a whole system in the imperfection of one extraordinary man (Stanley 1963). The dead king Beowulf, whose youthful adventures are traced for us before the account of his defeat by a dragon in old age, may embody other virtues, but his eagerness for praise might seem from a retrospective Christian moral viewpoint to equate to vaunting pride. The contest with the dragon, in which the beast is killed by Beowulf's young companion Wiglaf, delivers to his people a useless treasure, bereft as they are of a leader and a royal hall in which the dragon's wealth might be shared out. In the world of *Beowulf*, heroes are brave and die, but others are prudent and live; great kings preside over the ceremonial life of the hall, sharing out treasures, while failed rulers become misers and slaughter their people; great heirlooms are passed from one generation to the next, just as the feuds and unsettled debts of blood are passed from the old to the young. This idealising portrait of the 'real' life of the Germanic peoples of a former age, however, overlaps with the world of shadows and monsters of the night – Grendel, his mother and the dragon – three creatures whose combats with the hero provide the tripartite structure of the poem. Doubtless the monsters serve a metaphoric purpose, providing moral mirrors for the poem's human characters, and especially in their encounters with Beowulf point the audience towards an interrogation of the hero's psychology.

Beowulf survives uniquely in the British Library manuscript Cotton Vitellius A xv, written around the year 1000 (Dumville 1998). There is no doubt that the poem was composed well before this copy, though there is considerable debate as to how long before. It also appears that *Beowulf* may have gone through some revisions in the process of transmission, leaving us with evidence variously dating the poem anywhere between 700 and 950, though a few estimations fall outside these parameters (Chase 1981). There is no doubt that both the poet and audience were Christians; whenever it was first composed, *Beowulf* represented a former age of pagan Germanic heroes. Early scholars of the poem tended to dismiss certain Christian references as interpolations, caveats inserted into an ancient poem by a moralising monk (Irving 1997: 178). The most famous of these comes early in the poem, when the poet turns from the unfolding action of the poem, and reflects on the fate of idolators:

> Hwilum hie geheton   æt hærgtrafum
> wigweorþunga,   wordum bædon
> þæt him gastbona   geoce gefremede
> wið þeodþreaum.   Swylc wæs þeaw hyra,
> hæþenra hyht;   helle gemundon
> in modsefan,   Metod hie ne cuþon,
> dæda demend,   ne wiston hie drihten God,
> ne hie huru heofena Helm   herian ne cuþon,
> wuldres waldend.   Wa bið þæm ðe sceal
> þurh sliðne nið   sawle bescufan
> in fyres fæþm,   frofre ne wenan,
> wihte gewendan
>   (Klaeber 1950: lines 175–86a)

At times they offered to idols at pagan altars, prayed in words that the soul slayer might provide comfort before the national disasters. Such was their custom, the hope of the heathen – they recalled hell in their minds, they did not know the Creator, the Judge of deeds, nor knew they the Lord God, nor indeed how to worship the Protector of the heavens, Wielder of glory. Woe to him who must with cruel hatred thrust his soul in the fire's embrace, await no comfort, no change at all!

The passage strikes an emphatic note not found elsewhere in *Beowulf*, which on the whole avoids the theological, as opposed to ethical, implications of the life of the ancient pagans. While this passage may be the product of a later revision, there is no doubt that the poem thoroughly integrates Christian perspectives on its action. References to the Creation, Cain and the Flood, as well as to the pervasive power of God, are a part of the fabric of the poem, threads impossible to remove without undoing its entire fabric (Osborn 1978). The references to Cain, though brief, might be comprehensible to one unfamiliar with the Book of Genesis; the oblique references to the Flood, however, imply on the part of poet and listener a shared knowledge not only of Genesis, but also of a range of legends that had accreted to the biblical narrative.

The poem's original audience was undoubtedly aristocratic. *Beowulf*'s primary interest is in this social group, and the way it used, passed on, and lost power. The poet lingers over descriptions of court ceremony, comments on the manners and conduct of his characters, and takes delight in describing precious objects distributed as gifts. This does not mean that the poem is superficial; rather, its surface texture dazzles the listener and reader, inviting them into a pagan world in which such things provided a measure of moral worth in a system of reciprocal gift-giving and reward. The poem's characters value ceremony and wealth, but do so because these support a fragile social order, which in *Beowulf* is constantly on the brink of chaos.

It is in the midst of this chaos that the poem opens and closes. A weeping woman stands by Beowulf's funeral pyre, lamenting the uncertain fate of the Geatish people, now that their king is dead, with no obvious successor:

> swylce giomorgyd Geatisc meowle
> æfter Biowulfe bundenheorde
> song sorgcearig sæde geneahhe
> þæt hio hyre hearmdagas hearde ondrede,
> wælfylla worn, werudes egesan,
> hynðo ond hæftnyd.
> (Klaeber 1950: lines 3150–5a; 1998: Mitchell and Robinson 1998: 160)

> also a Geatish woman, sorrowful, sang a song of mourning, with hair tied up, for Beowulf, said readily that she dreaded the hard harmful days, many a bloody battle, the host's terror, slight and slavery.

At the beginning of the poem, another nation, Denmark, is discovered in a similar plight; comfort is sent them by God himself, in the person of the sea-borne waif, Scyld Scefing. This framing of the narrative between two moments of chaos is characteristic of the poet's rhetorical style, whereby important narrative events, small and large, are given structural emphasis. Scyld's reign is narrated in the space of a few lines, as he conquers neighbouring tribes, forcing them to yield tribute. Crucial to the alleviation of the Danes' misery is the birth of an heir, who will provide ongoing stability for the people:

> Ðæm eafera wæs æfter cenned,
> geong in geardum, þone god sende
> folce to frofre; fyrenðearfe ongeat,
> þe hie ær drugon aldorlease
> lange hwile.
> (Klaeber 1950: lines 12–16a)

A boy was born to him afterwards, young in the courts, whom God sent as a comfort
to the people; he perceived their desperation, that they had endured, lordless, for such
a long time.

At the end of the poem, the dying Beowulf regrets that he has not produced a
similar heir for his own people (lines 2729–32a). Scyld founds a dynasty, leaving his
name to the royal house and nation: the Scyldings. With the rapid passing of generations Hrothgar comes to the Danish throne, succeeding his brother Heorogar in
circumstances not described. Nevertheless, the inevitable ensuing problem is alluded
to later in the poem, in the tension arising from the presence of Hrothulf, Heorogar's
son, in the royal hall beside Hrothgar's own young sons (lines 180b–91). After establishing his power, Hrothgar builds himself Heorot, a hall famous across the nations
(lines 67b–82a).

The Danes were known to the Anglo-Saxons as a great nation – certainly more
famous than Beowulf's Geats – but the poem's attitude to the Danes is difficult to
pin down. In an influential study, Dorothy Whitelock suggested that the poem's
positive presentation of the Danes meant the poem must date from before the onset
of the Viking attacks on England in the 790s (Whitelock 1951). This position has
proved to be too simplistic – not only were Anglo-Saxon attitudes to the Vikings
various and complex, but we must also ask how sympathetic the presentation of the
Danes in *Beowulf* actually is. Furthermore, are the Danes simply to be read as Danes,
or as representative of any great kingdom? By the time Beowulf comes across the sea
from what is now southern Sweden (the poem's presentation of the geography involved
is accurate), Grendel has been attacking the Danish hall for twelve years. These attacks
have led the Danes to worship at heathen shrines, and are felt as a particular grief
by the aged king Hrothgar, who cannot defend his people:

> Swa ða mælceare   maga Healfdenes
> singala seað;   ne mihte snotor hæleð
> wean onwendan;   wæs þæt gewin to swyð,
> laþ ond longsum,   þe on ða leode becom,
> nydwracu niþgrim,   nihtbealwa mæst.
>   (Klaeber 1950: lines 189–93)

With the cares of the time Healfdene's son seethed obsessively; nor could the wise hero
avert the grief; the strife was too great, loathsome and long, which befell the people,
oppressive and spiteful, greatest of night evils.

Heorot stands empty by night, and the nation is deprived of its seat of government,
which Grendel holds in contempt: he does not approach the throne; he will not
pay compensation for those he has killed (lines 154b–69). Not only does Grendel
stand outside the lawful order, but also he renders Hrothgar powerless to rule. Many
Danes have made ceremonial boasts that they will defeat the monster, but all have

failed, demonstrating the limits not only of the legal order, but the heroic system as well.

News of this devastation travels far, much as the fame of Heorot itself had travelled, reaching the land of the Geats. Beowulf, the young Geatish prince, sets out for Denmark, apparently on an impulse, with fourteen companions and the intention of defeating Grendel. The group's journey is a classic set piece exemplifying the oral formulaic tradition in which the poem is composed (Foley 1976):

> Gewat þa ofer wægholm   winde gefysed,
> flota famiheals   fugle gelicost,
> oðþæt ymb antid   oþres dogores
> wundenstefna   gewaden hæfde
> þæt ða liðende   land gesawon,
> brimclifu blican,   beorgas steape,
> side sænæssas;   þa wæs sund liden,
> eoletes æt ende.   Þanon up hraðe
> Wedera leode   on wang stigon,
> sæwudu sældon, –   syrcan hrysedon,
> guðgewædo;   Gode þancedon
> þæs þe him yþlade   eaðe wurdon.
>   (Klaeber 1950: lines 217–28)

Then went across the waves' surge, hastened by the wind, the foamy-necked floater most like a bird, until on time on the second day the bow-bowed ship had travelled so far that the seafarers saw land, shining ocean-cliffs, steep hills, broad headlands; then was the sea crossed, the voyage at an end. From there quickly the people of the Weders climbed up onto the plain, moored their ship, shook out their mail-shirts, their battle clothes; they thanked God that the wave-paths had been easy for them.

The passage is rich in the compound nouns cultivated in the Anglo-Saxon poet's art, woven effortlessly into the description of the sea journey that itself requires no exertion from the travellers. The metaphor of the flying bird is extended to the warriors themselves, who shake their chain mail-shirts like wet feathers. Equally formulaic is the response of the coast watcher, who probes the intention of the young troop:

> Gewat him þa to waroðe   wicge ridan
> þegn Hroðgares,   þrymmum cwehte
> mægenwudu mundum,   meþelwordum frægn:
> 'Hwæt syndon ge   searohæbbendra,
> byrnum werede,   þe þus brontne ceol
> ofer lagustræte   lædan cwomon,
> hider ofer holmas?   Hwæt ic hwile wæs
> endesæta,   ægwearde heold,
> þe on land Dena   laðra nænig

> mid scipherge   sceðþan ne meahte.'
> (Klaeber 1950: lines 234–43)

Hrothgar's thane rode his horse down to the shore, and forcefully shook his mighty
spear in his hand, interrogated them formally: 'What are you, armoured warriors,
protected by mail coats, who have come sailing in this way over the sea-street in a tall
ship, here over the waves? Indeed for a time I have been a coastguard, and kept sea-watch
so that no hostile forces with a ship-army should ever attack the land of the Danes.'

The guard fulfils his role with fine words – his is the first of many formal speeches
in the poem – and his audience must be impressed by his eloquence. The performance
is far from wooden, and the formulaic utterance from which the poem is constructed
is given complex undertones by the poet. While the coastguard is charged with
national defence, in the context of the action presented so far we are entitled to ask
what it is he is defending. The coastguard performs his role nobly, but his words
ring empty given that Denmark's real threat is to be found within its borders, not
without. Indeed, Grendel himself is a border dweller, an enemy without weapons,
whom fine words will not hold back. The coastguard's promise that his young companions will watch over the Geats' boat – reminding the foreigners even as they
arrive that they must later depart (lines 296–8) – suggests an undercurrent of tension
in the encounter. The arrival of the young man who has 'counsel' for the 'wise old
king' in his 'shame' (lines 277–9) represents a degree of humiliation for any Danish
warrior, especially one who boasts of his role as the kingdom's defender.

The arrival of the Geatish troop at Heorot is similarly splendid and charged, with
their boar-crested helmets shining as they march (lines 303b–6a), and their welcome
qualified. The poet has not yet announced Beowulf's name, which is reserved for the
appropriate moment. The Geats are greeted by Hrothgar's steward, Wulfgar:

> 'Hwanon ferigeað ge   fætte scyldas,
> græge syrcan   ond grimhelmas,
> heresceafta heap?   Ic eom Hroðgares
> ar ond ombiht.   Ne seah ic elþeodige
> þus manige men   modiglicran.
> Wen' ic þæt ge for wlenco,   nalles for wræcsiðum,
> ac for higeþrymmum   Hroðgar sohton.'
> (Klaeber 1950: lines 333–9)

'Where do you bring those shields from, grey mail-coats and grim helmets, a collection
of spears? I am Hrothgar's herald and servant: I have never seen so many courageous
foreign men. For your pride, I suppose, not because of exile, and for valiance you have
sought Hrothgar.'

Wulfgar again draws attention to the question of the hero's motivation. The Geats
are not allowed to carry their weapons into the hall – this is normal protocol, but

again is a paradoxical gesture given Grendel's nocturnal raids. He bears no weapons, but enters the hall unannounced, simply forcing the doors open with his touch (lines 721a–2). The tension implicit in Beowulf's exchange with the coastguard continues in his arrival at Heorot. Wulfgar, who knows noble custom (lines 369b), informs the king of the young man's name. Hrothgar knows him:

> Hroðgar maþelode,   helm Scyldinga:
> 'Ic hine cuðe   cnihtwesende.;
> wæs his ealdfæder   Ecgþeo haten,
> ðæm to ham forgeaf   Hreþel Geata
> angan dohtor;   is his eafora nu
> heard her cumen,   sohte holdne wine.
> Ðonne sægdon þæt   sæliþende,
> þa ðe gifsceattas   Geata fyredon
> þyder to þance,   þæt he þritiges
> manna mægencræft   on his mundgripe
> heaþorof hæbbe.   Hine halig God
> for arstafum   us onsende,
> to West-Denum,   þæs ic wen hæbbe,
> wið Grendles gryre.   Ic þæm godan sceal
> for his modþræce   madmas beodan.'
>   (Klaeber 1950: lines 371–85)

Hrothgar spoke, protector of the Scyldings: 'I knew him when he was a boy—his old father was called Ecgtheow, to whom Hrethel of the Geats gave his only daughter in marriage; now his hardy heir has come here, sought a faithful friend. Seafarers have said, those who carried precious gifts to the Geats as thanks, that he has the strength of thirty men, strong in battle, in his handgrip. Holy God in his grace has sent him to us, to the West-Danes, so I have hope, against Grendel's terror. To this good man I shall offer treasures for his reckless courage.'

Hrothgar's recognition might seem to be no more than an old man's fond recollection of a friend's son, but immediately he emerges as master of the situation; a wise king questions travellers, maintains good relations with neighbouring tribes, knows who marries whom, and keeps an eye open for promising warriors. Protecting the Scyldings involves more than success in battle.

The following exchange between the king and the young prince reveals the king's subtlety. Once ushered into the hall, the hero bluntly declares the purpose of his visit:

> 'Wæs þu, Hroðgar, hal!   Ic eom Higelaces
> mæg ond magoðegn;   hæbbe ic mærða fela
> ongunnen on geogoþe.   Me wearð Grendles þing
> on minre eþeltyrf   undyrne cuð;
> secgað sæliðend   þæt þæs sele stande,
> reced selesta   rinca gehwylcum

idel ond unnyt,   siððan æfenleoht
under heofenes hador   beholen weorþeð.
...
              ac ic mid grape sceal
fon wið feonde   ond ymb feorh sacan,
lað wið laþum;   ðær gelyfan sceal
Dryhtnes dome   se þe hine dead nimeð.
Wen' ic þæt he wille,   gif he wealdan mot,
in þæm guðsele   Geotena leode
etan unforhte,   swa he oft dyde,
mægen Hreðmanna.'
              (Klaeber 1950: lines 407–14, 438b–45a)

'Be hale, Hrothgar! I am Hygelac's relative and retainer; in my youth I have done many a famous deed; this problem with Grendel was revealed to me on my native soil; seafarers say that this hall stands, most excellent of buildings, idle and useless to every warrior, after evening's light is hidden under heaven's gleaming vault....but I shall come to grips with the fiend and wrestle for life, foe against foe; let him trust in the Lord's judgment, he whom death takes! I suppose that, if he can win, he will eat of the Geats, the virtue of the Hrethmen, unintimidated in that war-hall, as he has often done.'

Remarkably, Beowulf offers no reason for his quest other than that his own people advised him to the venture, 'because they knew the might of my strength' (line 418), and asks as a favour (line 428) that he be allowed to fight Grendel. The young man has come to test his strength, the dead Hrethmen (another name for the Danes) are incidental. The boasting words reiterate the humiliation of the Danes casually offered to the coastguard. Hrothgar, however, is not to be humiliated, and reveals his command of diplomacy and courtly protocol. Beowulf has presented himself as the generous, and almost disinterested, saviour of Hrothgar's people, but the king outlines his own interpretation of events:

'For gewyrhtum þu,   wine min Beowulf,
ond for arstafum   usic sohtest.
Gesloh þin fæder   fæhðe mæste;
wearþ he Heaþolafe   to handbonan
mid Wilfingum;   ða hine Wedera cyn
for herebrogan   habban ne mihte.
Þanon he gesohte   Suð-Dena folc
ofer yða gewealc,   Arscyldinga.
...
Siððan þa fæhðe   feo þingode;
sende ic Wylfingum   ofer wæteres hrycg
ealde madmas;   he me aþas swor.'
              (Klaeber 1950: lines 457–64, 470–2)

'For past favours, Beowulf my friend, and for done deeds, you have sought us out. Your father struck up the greatest of feuds; by his own hand he became the killer of Heatholaf among the Wylfings; then the nation of the Weders would not keep him for fear of war. From there he sought the folk of the South-Danes over the surge of waves, the Honor-Scyldings...Later I settled that feud with compensation; I sent ancient treasures to the Wylfings over the water's crest; he swore oaths to me.'

The king of the 'Honour-Scyldings' does more than save face, and we see a difference between his public and private interpretations of events. Privately he sees God's hand at work in the brave young man; publicly he locates the youthful gesture within the system of reciprocity which binds heroic society together. The old king imposes order on the young man's impulsiveness in two significant ways: by interpreting his good deed as directed by God; and by incorporating the son's promised act into a system of social obligation that extends across the generations to his father's oath of gratitude. However much the hero thinks he can act as an independent agent, his freedom is bound by society's conventions, and far from creating an indebtedness on the part of the Danes should he succeed, Hrothgar thanks him for coming to repay his father's debt. The king's diplomatic skill, found both in the present situation and in his former resolution of Ecgtheow's feud, develops the notion that there is more to good kingship than the application of force and violence, as suggested in the poem's earlier brief account of Scyld. By contrast, the catastrophic diplomacy of the Geats later in the poem, involving themselves in the internal struggles of their neighbours, provides the background to the desperate situation of the nation after Beowulf's death. Hrothgar's skill and good judgement are, however, balanced by affection. He develops a strong emotional attachment to the young man he knew as a child, and who has returned to rescue his nation's honour, and the old king's tears at their final parting are as moving as they are genuine (lines 1870–80a).

That Beowulf also poses a threat is underlined when the resentment only hinted at in the coastguard's reception bursts out of Unferth, Hrothgar's *thyle* (line 1165, 'spokesman'). Beowulf's boasting of his credentials proves too much for this retainer to bear:

> Unferð maþelode, Ecglafes bearn,
> þe æt fotum sæt frean Scyldinga,
> onband beadurune – wæs him Beowulfes sið,
> modges merefaran, micel æfþunca,
> forþon þe he ne uþe, þæt ænig oðer man
> æfre mærða þon ma middangeardes
> gehede under heofenum þonne he sylfa –:
> 'Eart þu se Beowulf, se þe wið Brecan wunne,
> on sidne sæ ymb sund flite,
> ðær git for wlence wada cunnedon
> ond for dolgilpe on deop wæter
> aldrum neþdon?'
> (Klaeber 1950: lines 499–510a)

Unferth spoke, son of Ecglaf, who sat at the feet of the lord of the Scyldings, let loose his secret hostility – for him Beowulf's journey, that brave seafarer, was a great insult, because he would not allow that any other man on middle-earth should care more for glory under the heavens, than he himself: 'Are you that Beowulf who contended with Breca in a swimming contest on the sea, where in your pride you two probed the waves and for a foolish boast risked your lives in the deep water?'

The rebuke cuts to the core of Beowulf's motivation in the present venture: does he seek glory for its own sake? The reproof is answered in detail by Beowulf, who adds some harsh words for Unferth:

> Beowulf maþelode, bearn Ecgþeowes:
> 'Hwæt, þu worn fela, wine min Unferð,
> beore druncen ymb Brecan spræce,
> sægdest from his siðe!
> ...
> Wit þæt gecwædon cnihtwesende
> ond gebeotedon – wæron begen þa git
> on geogoðfeore – þæt wit on garsecg ut
> aldrum neðdon, ond þæt geæfndon swa.
> ...
> þeah ðu þinum broðrum to banan wurde,
> heafodmægum; þæs þu in helle scealt
> werhðo dreogan, þeah þin wit duge.
> Secge ic þe to soðe, sunu Ecglafes,
> þæt næfre Grendel swa fela gryra gefremede,
> atol æglæca ealdre þinum,
> hynðo on Heorote, gif þin hige wære,
> sefa swa searogrim, swa þu self talast;
> ac he hafað onfunden, þæt he þa fæhðe ne þearf,
> atole ecgþræce eower leode
> swiðe onsittan, Sige-Scyldinga'
>   (Klaeber 1950: lines 529–32a, 535–8, 587–97)

Beowulf spoke, the son of Ecgtheow: 'Indeed, Unferth my friend, drunk with beer, you have said very many things concerning Breca, explained his adventures!...Being boys, we two talked and boasted – we were both still in our youth – that out on the ocean we would risk our lives, and we did so....though you became your brothers' killer, of your closest kin; for that you will suffer torment in hell, though your wit is sharp. I tell you truly, son of Ecglaf, that Grendel never would have worked such terror, that terrible monster, against your lord, or shame in Heorot, if your courage and your mind were as aggressive as you yourself reckon; but he has found out that he need fear no feud, no cruel sword attack from your nation, from the Victory-Scyldings'

Hrothgar is pleased with the sharp response, which, in addition to proving Beowulf's determination, dismisses boyish folly as past, and indicates acceptance that this present undertaking is a service to Hrothgar. Unferth is more than a narrative foil to the hero, and their dealings continue across the battles with Grendel and his mother. Before Beowulf descends into the mere to fight Grendel's mother, Unferth offers him his precious sword, Hrunting. This gesture comes as a surprise, though the poet points out that Unferth's earlier hostility was the result of his drunkenness (lines 1465–72); however, like its owner, the sword fails at the moment of greatest need (lines 1522b–8).

The developing interaction between the two does not so much reveal the nature of the drunken Unferth as point to Beowulf's maturing character: he moves from an initial sharpness towards the weaker man to magnanimity when returning to him his useless sword:

> Heht þa se hearda   Hrunting beran
> sunu Ecglafes,   heht his sweord niman,
> leoflic iren;   sægde him þæs leanes þanc,
> cwæð, he þone guðwine   godne tealde,
> wigcræftigne,   nales wordum log
> meces ecge;   þæt wæs modig secg.
>   (Klaeber 1950: lines 1807–12)

The tough one ordered Hrunting to be borne to Ecglaf's son, he bid him take his sword, the lovely iron; he said thanks to him for the loan, and said that he reckoned it was a good friend, skilful in battle, and he did not in any way talk down the sword's edges; he was a noble man.

Beowulf emerges from the poem as a complex character rather than a simple hero type. At times we are told what the narrator thinks of him, elsewhere the opinion of other characters; sometimes the difference between the two viewpoints is unclear. The best example of this is in the final assessment of the dead king's worth, delivered from the point of view of those he has left behind. One of the most surprising assessments of Beowulf's character is offered on his return home from Denmark:

> Swa bealdode   bearn Ecgðeowes,
> guma guðum cuð,   godum dædum,
> dreah æfter dome,   nealles druncne slog
> heorðgeneatas;   næs him hreoh sefa,
> ac he mancynnes   mæste cræfte
> ginfæstan gife,   þe him God sealde,
> heold hildedeor.   Hean wæs lange,
> swa hyne Geata bearn   godne ne tealdon,
> ne hyne on medobence   micles wyrðne
> drihten Wedera   gedon wolde;
> swyðe wendon,   þæt he sleac wære,
> æðeling unfrom.   Edwenden cwom
> tireadigum menn   torna gehwylces.
>   (Klaeber 1950: lines 2177–89)

So the son of Ecgtheow showed his courage, known to men in battle, for good deeds, he struggled for esteem, in no way slew, drunken, his hearth-companions; his heart was not savage, but he kept the great gift, the greatest strength of all mankind, which God had given him, brave in battle. For a long time he had been despised, as the sons of the Geats reckoned him no good, nor did the lord of the Weders wish to do him much honour on the mead-benches; because they thought that he was slack, a weak prince. Reversal came to the victorious man for all his anxieties.

The poet's choice to delay this assessment is striking, and is in opposition to his narrative technique of anticipating the outcome of events such as battles, even before they take place: for example, we know before Grendel arrives at Heorot that Beowulf will defeat him (lines 696b–702a), and before the two meet that the dragon will kill and be killed (lines 2419b–24). The focus of narrative tension, it would seem, is on the quality of Beowulf's character. Coming where it does, the previous negative assessment places the entire action of the earlier part of the poem in a new perspective, and suggests that the Danish reactions on his arrival are in harmony with the estimations of Beowulf's own people. Beowulf clearly becomes a new man, and Hrothgar's confidence in him, and the nurturing of the young prince revealed in his 'sermon' on the hero's return from the mere, are placed in a new light (lines 1700–84). Hrothgar's evocation of the negative example of Heremod, a failed Danish king who turned in on himself and destroyed his companions, certainly offers wisdom for any warrior. But this advice now can be seen to address the young Beowulf's dangerous leanings, and is more pointedly directed towards his maturing character, warning him that God's blessings should not be taken for granted (lines 1722b–7).

Beowulf is still young, and his parting promise to Hrothgar of a forest of a thousand spears to support Danish allies in time of need suggests the impetuousness of youth (lines 1824–35). Hygelac seems unlikely to honour such a pledge (cf. lines 1996–7a), and it becomes clear that in the Geats' later troubles the Danes have felt no reciprocal obligation. Beowulf's apparent naïveté is belied by his careful analysis of the Danes' own precarious relations with the Heathobards. His account of the coming diplomatic marriage of Hrothgar's daughter Freawaru constitutes another surprise for the reader:

> Hwilum for duguðe   dohtor Hroðgares
> eorlum on ende   ealuwæge bær;
> þa ic Freaware   fletsittende
> nemnan hyrde,   þær hio nægled sinc
> hæleðum sealde.   Sio gehaten is,
> geong, goldhroden,   gladum suna Frodan;
> hafað þæs geworden   wine Scyldinga,
> rices hyrde,   ond þæt ræd talað,
> þæt he mid ðy wife   wælfæhða dæl,
> sæcca gesette.
>   (Klaeber 1950: lines 2020–9a)

'At times Hrothgar's daughter bore the ale-cup to the hall-thanes, to the earls up the back; I heard the men in the hall call her Freawaru, when she gave the studded chalice to the men. She is promised, young, gold-adorned, to the gracious son of Froda; the friend of the Scyldings has arranged this, the kingdom's shepherd, and accepts the counsel that he should settle his share of feud and slaughter by means of a wife.'

The young princess is to be sent as a 'peace-weaver', to be the bride of Ingeld, a legendary hero so famous the poet feels no need to mention him by name. The reference to this marriage reveals both the shared knowledge the poet expects of his audience, and the demands he makes on their attention to his narrative. The forthcoming marriage has been mentioned in passing (nearly two thousand lines earlier) when describing the building of Heorot, with a pessimistic and oblique reference to the future strife between Hrothgar and Ingeld, which will see its destruction:

> Sele hlifade,
> heah ond horngeap;   heaðowylma bad,
> laðan liges;   ne wæs hit lenge þa gen,
> þæt se ecghete   aþumsweorum,
> æfter wælniðe   wæcnan scolde.
> (Klaeber 1950: lines 81b–5)

The hall towered, high and horn-gabled – it awaited battle-fires, the flame of hatred; the time was not yet near that the sword-hate among sworn in-laws should reawaken after cruel violence.

Beowulf's astute pessimism about the prospects of this marriage for settling the ongoing dispute between Dane and Heathobard, are rooted in his own belief in the overriding demands of the heroic code. The old warrior will goad the young to revenge, even at the wedding feast, on seeing Danish guests wearing Heathobard heirlooms:

> 'Meaht ðu, min wine,   mece gecnawan,
> þone þin fæder   to gefeohte bær
> under heregriman   hindeman siðe,
> dyre iren,   þær hyne Dene slogon,
> weoldon wælstowe,   syððan Wiðergyld læg,
> æfter hæleþa hryre,   hwate Scyldungas?'
> (Klaeber 1950: lines 2047–52)

'Might you, my friend, recognize that sword, which your father bore into battle on his final journey under the helmet, the dear iron, where the Danes struck him, the brave Scyldings, controlled the field of slaughter after the rout of heroes, when Withergild lay dead?'

Beowulf asserts that the desire for revenge, the emotions generated by the humiliation endured at the feast and the fondness for 'dear iron' will cause the marriage treaty to fail.

Beowulf's gloomy predictions about Freawaru's marriage present only one of many instances where the poet reveals an interest in the place of women in aristocratic society. The description of Beowulf's arrival home from Denmark is interrupted by another 'digression', first into an account of Hygd, his uncle Hygelac's queen, and then within this digression, into the stormy character of the legendary Thryth, whose deadly jealousy was finally brought under control after her marriage to the Offa, king of Angeln. Beowulf's account of the coming marriage follows soon after, introducing the Danish princess in her ceremonial role of serving the cup in Heorot, ideally symbolising and strengthening the peaceful cohesion of warrior society. Earlier, our attention in Heorot had been directed to Hrothgar's queen Wealhtheow (lines 1169–92). With Beowulf's account of the marriage, the poem's technique of retrospectivity again comes into play. The great feast in which Beowulf's victory over Grendel was celebrated saw the singing of the Lay of Hildeburh (lines 1063–158), a Danish princess married to the Frisian king Finn. During a visit from her brother Hnæf, the guests are betrayed. In the ensuing battle both Hnæf and his nephew – the son of Hildeburh and Finn – are killed:

> 'Het ða Hildeburh   æt Hnæfes ade
> hire selfre sunu   sweoloðe befæstan,
> banfatu bærnan,   ond on bæl don
> eame on eaxle.   Ides gnornode,
> geomrode giddum.'
>   (Klaeber 1950: lines 1114–18a)

'Then Hildeburh ordered that her own son be given for burning on Hnæf's pyre, burn the body, and placed on the pyre at the uncle's shoulder. The lady mourned, wailed a lament.'

Like the Geatish woman's at the poem's end, Hildeburh's situation is desperate, but the poet emphasises not so much her passive acquiescence with her lot, as the impossibility of succeeding in her peace-weaving role in the face of male violence. A stalemate forces the survivors of both sides to put aside their differences, and they live together through the winter (lines 1080b–107). The coming of spring, which elsewhere the poet associates symbolically with the renewal wrought by Beowulf's destruction of the Grendel-kin (lines 1605b–11), here leads to the renewal of violence by Hengest:

> Đa wæs winter scacen,
> fæger foldan bearm;   fundode wrecca,
> gist of geardum;   he to gyrnwræce
> swiðor þohte   þonne to sælade,

> gif he torngemot þurhteon mihte,
> þæt he Eotena bearn irne gemunde.
> Swa he ne forwyrnde woroldrædenne,
> þonne him Hunlafing hildeleoman,
> billa selest on bearm dyde,
> þæs wæron mid Eotenum ecge cuðe.
> (Klaeber 1950: lines 1136b–45; Mitchell and Robinson 1998: 86)

'Then winter was gone, and earth's bosom was fair; the exile desired to leave, the guest from the courts; even more than sea-voyages, he pondered a vengeance for grief, whether he might bring about a hostile meeting, remind the sons of the Jutes of iron. So he did not refuse the custom of this world when Hunlafing placed a battle-blade, the best of swords upon his lap; its edge was known among the Jutes.'

As in Beowulf's predictions concerning Freawaru's marriage, in the story of Hildeburh the hero is incited to violence by the sight of family heirlooms, which provoke the enraged shame of those whose feuds are unsettled (lines 1142–5). Hengest kills Finn, and his people are destroyed by their 'guests', much as the 'guest' Grendel destroys the Danes, and Beowulf is a fatal 'guest' (line 1522b) for Grendel's mother. The lay of Hildeburh is sung on the eve of Grendel's mother's own revenge visit to Heorot, and in immediate context reveals her refusal to accept the relegation of women to a passive role in the face of male violence. In the wider context Hildeburh's fate hints menacingly at the outcome of Freawaru's marriage (with its own unwelcome guests), even as this second Danish princess moved silently, and to the reader invisibly, through the hall as the song about the ancient battle was sung.

The lay of Hildeburh is framed by the two monstrous attacks on Heorot by Grendel and his mother, and through this framing we can begin to interrogate what *Beowulf*'s monsters are about. We should not doubt that to the Anglo-Saxon, the existence of spectral creatures like Grendel and his mother, and the dragon, was entirely plausible. The poet, however, is not so much interested in these creatures as examples of monstrosity, but rather in their metaphoric potential, though their terror undoubtedly enhances the poem's emotional impact. Yet it would be absurd to reduce Grendel to a one-dimensional metaphoric function, as both his characterisation and his role in the poem suggest a complexity not easily defined. When Grendel is first introduced his character is given a social, historical and moral dimension:

> Ða se ellengæst earfoðlice
> þrage geþolode, se þe in þystrum bad,
> þæt he dogora gehwam dream gehyrde
> hludne in healle; þær wæs hearpan sweg,
> swutol sang scopes.
> . . .
> Wæs se grimma gæst Grendel haten,

> mære mearcstapa, se þe moras heold,
> fen ond fæsten; fifelcynnes eard
> wonsæli wer weardode hwile,
> siþðan him scyppend forscrifen hæfde
> in Caines cynne. Þone cwealm gewræc
> ece drihten, þæs þe he Abel slog;
>   (Klaeber 1950: lines 86–90a, 102–8)

Then the alien spirit, he who dwelled in darkness, wretchedly suffered for the while, because each day he heard the rejoicing loud in the hall; there was the harp's sound, the clear song of the scop.... The grim ghost was called Grendel, a mighty prowler of the borderlands, who held the moors, fens and firm ground; this unhappy man dwelled all the while in the domain of giants, since the Creator had cursed him among Cain's race. The eternal Lord avenged that death, when he killed Abel.

Grendel is more than a relic of the primeval time, physically distorted like all of Cain's descendants, and like them akin to demons – his opposition to the social happiness in Heorot aligns him with Cain's rejection of fraternal happiness with Abel. But as we have seen, other troubles in Heorot are more mundane: war with the Heathobards, Hrothgar's possibly disputed succession, Unferth's own fratricide. Grendel's attacks begin as soon as Heorot is built – the building represents the culmination of Hrothgar's reign, his rule over the Scyldings, and success in war. Grendel confronts the king with the limits of his power, and no amount of wisdom, heroic boasting, or military prowess can halt the attacks. Grendel controls the hall by night, feasting on the warriors in their place of feasting, halting the ceremony of gift-giving, and paralysing national life in Hrothgar's declining years. In addition, the arrival of Beowulf presents us with parallels between the young hero and Grendel: for example, Beowulf, like Grendel, is inordinately strong. Beowulf has the strength of thirty men in his grip, while Grendel devours thirty men in the hall. Beowulf's grip proves to be the stronger, as Grendel leaves his arm behind in Heorot. In a more subtle way the two are paralleled in their immaturity. Grendel has failed to make the fundamental transition into adult male life; he is a warrior who lives alone with his mother, rejecting the company in the hall. Beowulf, unlike Grendel, submits to Hrothgar's throne, and accepts the terms of his service. While he is clearly different from other men, and his monster-slaying feats separate him from them, he is engaged in a complex quest for maturity. His contest with Breca demonstrated his physical strength, but also a dangerous potential within a fragile political system, in which a strong young aristocrat with a group of friends might seize power from a king as inept as Hygelac appears to be. However, Beowulf returns to Geatland with no intention of seizing his uncle's hall in the way Grendel has occupied Heorot. Indeed, in the wake of Hygelac's disastrous last raid, Beowulf refuses the offer of power made to him by the royal widow Hygd, who does not trust that her son can hold 'the ancestral seat' (lines 2367–72). Eventually the kingdom does pass to Beowulf, and his fifty-year reign is largely untroubled (lines 2200–10a; 2729–39a). But when Beowulf in his turn has ruled into old age, the dragon comes.

The dragon is an ancient creature, occupying a barrow hiding the wealth of long-dead men, the cursed treasure of a failed nation (lines 2231b–77). The manuscript page describing the disturbance of the dragon is badly damaged (fol. 179r). A cup is stolen to placate a fugitive servant's lord, and the dragon is enraged by the theft. The cup – a symbol of social cohesion – is useless to the solitary dragon. But the dragon, like the failed king Heremod, loves wealth for its own sake, confounding the very idea of its value by removing it from the economy of heroic life. The dragon's night-time attack ravages the kingdom, and focuses on Beowulf's royal seat:

> Þa wæs Biowulfe   broga gecyðed
> snude to soðe,   þæt his sylfes ham,
> bolda selest,   brynewylmum mealt,
> gifstol Geata.
> (Klaeber 1950: lines 2324–7a)

Then that disaster was quickly and truly made known to Beowulf, that his own homestead, best of buildings, had disintegrated in waves of fire, the gift-throne of the Geats.

The giving of treasure in the lost hall forms a focus in recrimination directed by Wiglaf towards those warriors who have failed in their duty to the dead king:

> 'þæt, la, mæg secgan   se ðe wyle soð specan,
> þæt se mondryhten,   se eow ða maðmas geaf,
> eoredgeatwe,   þe ge þær on standað, –
> þonne he on ealubence   oft gesealde
> healsittendum   helm ond byrnan,
> þeoden his þegnum,   swylce he þrydlicost
> ower feor oððe neah   findan meahte,
> þæt he genunga   guðgewædu
> wraðe forwurpe,   ða hyne wig beget.'
> (Klaeber 1950: lines 2864–72)

'Oh, he can say that, he who would tell the truth, that the liege-lord who gave you those treasures, the equipment that you stand in there – when on the ale-benches he often handed out helmets and byrnies to those sitting in the hall, a prince to his noblemen, the finest such that he could find anywhere, far or near – that all that battle-dress he utterly and entirely threw away, when war overtook him.'

Wiglaf loots the dragon's hoard, wealth for his people which Beowulf wants to gaze on before he dies (lines 2743b–82). The episode makes demands on the audience's powers of recollection; almost two thousand lines earlier a Danish poet had celebrated Beowulf's victory over Grendel with a song about Sigemund, in this poem the slayer of the dragon Fafnir, without the aid of his nephew Fitela (lines 874b–97; Orchard

2003:108–10). This foreshadowing of the diminution of Beowulf's powers, insufficient
for a similar task, has taken a long time to be fulfilled.

  The treasure is also useless to the Geats, without a hall to share it in, or a king
to share it out. Wiglaf's words make apparent the fact that even while the king was
alive, before the dragon was roused, the ceremonial gift-giving in his hall was already
a gesture devoid of meaning. The failure was hardly Beowulf's, as the king kept his
side of the social contract. But with the king dead, it is only appropriate that the
plundered wealth is committed with him to the earth:

> Hi on beorg dydon   beg ond siglu,
> eall swylce hyrsta,   swylce on horde ær
> niðhedige men   genumen hæfdon,
> forleton eorla gestreon   eorðan healdan,
> gold on greote,   þær hit nu gen lifað
> eldum swa unnyt,   swa hit æror wæs.
>   (Klaeber 1950: lines 3163–8)

In the barrow they placed rings and jewels, all such trappings that those inconsiderate
men had seized earlier from the hoard, abandoned the treasures of men for the earth to
keep, gold in the dirt, where it still remains, as useless to men as it ever was.

Beowulf is a poem about the glorious potential of society – the beauty of precious
objects, the wealth of song in the hall, the joy of conviviality; but it is also about
the limits of human beings to maintain happiness, limitations explored in relation
to the disastrous potential of individual failings in society's rulers. This tension between
communal well-being and individual discontent is expressed in the poem through a
complex story about the pre-Christian past. In this former age the pattern of society
was much as it was in the poet's own time: kings fought, ruled and died; queens
married, provided heirs and struggled to maintain peace. Ambitious young warriors
performed courageous deeds in the hope of great rewards, and in the communal life
of the hall drank together and heard songs about great heroes. But some kings fail,
and some young warriors go wrong. When the desire for violence and wealth are
divorced from the desire for social well-being, the idealised life of the hall is destroyed.
Grendel loves violence for its own sake, and is not interested in the rewards and
prestige brought by animosity directed against a nation's enemies; instead, he literally relishes the taste of blood. His mother has no desire to settle her dispute with
the Danes peacefully, and she is so far removed from the peace-weaving role that she,
like the young Thryth, spreads death. The dragon, like Heremod, sits on his wealth,
removed from society and gift-giving, and similarly leaves it in chaos. Within this
web of social convention, tales of past heroes and fantastic monsters, the poet weaves
the character of Beowulf, an unpromising young warrior who proves to be a great
king. The hero is strong, and dangerous, but ultimately such a young man, with the
right advice and the blessings of God, can provide great benefit to his people. The

mournful note on which the poem ends does not suggest the failure of these ideals. Rather, it laments the impossibility of enduring happiness in a world where a ruler's heroic desire for prestige, essential to maintaining power, is rarely accompanied by an eagerness for social happiness – expressed in mildness, gentleness and kindness to his people.

Beowulf is not simply a poem about a lost age, nor just an invitation to a latter-day Anglo-Saxon audience to imitate ancient Germanic virtue. An important theme running through the poem is found in the focus on the binding of the present to the past – in the dynastic passing on of power, through unresolved ancient feuds, in the continued use of ancient objects and in the transmission of heroic memories through song. In his attention to the art of singing, the poet asserts the power of well-crafted words to strengthen society within and across time, through the art of collective memory. The life of Beowulf is framed by the murky anarchy which is the product of forgetting social obligations and noble traditions. The words of the epic created by the poet discover order in the midst of this ancient chaos, an order echoing across the tradition that the poet evokes through singers within his song, a living tradition into which he invites his own noble audience.

REFERENCES AND FURTHER READING

Anlezark, Daniel (2006). *Water and Fire: The Myth of the Flood in Anglo-Saxon England.* Manchester: Manchester University Press.

Bartlett, Adeline Courtney (1935). *The Larger Rhetorical Patterns in Anglo-Saxon Poetry.* New York: Columbia University Press. (Repr. New York: AMS Press, 1966.)

Bjork, Robert E. and John D. Niles (eds) (1997). *A 'Beowulf' Handbook.* Lincoln, NE: University of Nebraska Press. (Repr. Exeter: University of Exeter Press, 1998.)

Bonjour, Adrien (1950). *The Digressions in 'Beowulf'. Medium Ævum* Monographs 5. Oxford: Blackwell.

Chance, Jane (1986). *Woman as Hero in Old English Literature.* Syracuse, NY: Syracuse University Press. (Repr. Eugene, OR: Wipf and Stock, 2005.)

Chase, Colin (ed.) (1981). *The Dating of 'Beowulf'.* Toronto: Old English Series 6. Toronto: Centre for Medieval Studies, University of Toronto: University of Toronto Press. (Pbk 1997.)

Damico, Helen, and Alexandra Hennessy Olsen (eds) (1990). *New Readings on Women in Old English Literature.* Bloomington, IN: Indiana University Press.

Dumville, D. N. (1998). The *Beowulf* manuscript and how not to date it. *Medieval English Studies Newsletter,* 39, 21–27.

Fell, Christine, Cecily Clark and Elizabeth Williams (1984). *Women in Anglo-Saxon England: And the Impact of 1066.* Oxford: Blackwell.

Foley, John Miles (1976). Formula and theme in Old English poetry. In Benjamin A. Stolz and Richard S. Shannon (eds). *Oral Literature and the Formula* (pp. 207–32). Ann Arbor, MI: Centre for the Coördination of Ancient and Modern Studies, University of Michigan.

Fulk, R. D., Robert E. Bjork and John D. Niles (eds) (2008). *Klaeber's 'Beowulf and the Fight at Finnsburg'.* 4th edn. Toronto: University of Toronto Press.

Irving, Edward B., Jr. (1997). Christian and Pagan Elements. In Robert E. Bjork and John D. Niles (eds). *A 'Beowulf' Handbook* (pp. 175–92). Lincoln, NE.

Klaeber, F. (ed.) (1950). *Beowulf and the Fight at Finnsburg.* 3rd edn. Lexington, KY: Heath.

Liuzza, R. M. (trans.) (2000). *Beowulf: A New Verse Translation.* Peterborough, ON: Broadview.

Mitchell, Bruce and Fred C. Robinson (eds) (1998). *Beowulf: An Edition with Relevant Shorter Texts.* Oxford: Blackwell.

Orchard, Andy (1995). *Pride and Prodigies: The Monsters of the Beowulf Manuscript*. Cambridge: D. S. Brewer. (Repr. Toronto: University of Toronto Press, 2003.)

Orchard, Andy (2003). *A Critical Companion to 'Beowulf'*. Cambridge: D. S. Brewer.

Osborn, Marijane (1978). The great feud: scriptural history and strife in 'Beowulf'. *PMLA*, 93, 973–81.

Stanley, E. G. (1963). 'Hæthenra hyht' in 'Beowulf'. In Stanley B. Greenfield (ed.). *Studies in Old English Literature in Honor of Arthur G. Bordeur* (pp. 136–51). Eugene, OR: University of Oregon Books. (Repr. New York: Russell and Russell, 1973.)

Whitelock, Dorothy (1951). *The Audience of 'Beowulf'*. Oxford: Clarendon Press.

Part II
Middle English Poetry

Contexts
Genres and Modes
Poets and Poems

Contexts

Contexts

9

The World of Medieval England: From the Norman Conquest to the Fourteenth Century

Conor McCarthy

English Identities and the Idea of the Nation

To write about 'medieval England' is not a straightforward matter. The creation of a single English political community took place in the tenth century, through the unification of the Anglo-Saxon kingdoms under the rulership of the West Saxon kings Æthelstan and subsequently Edgar. The concept of an English nation, however, seems to predate this political unity by some centuries, going back at least to the Venerable Bede's eighth-century literary construction of an English people (*gens Anglorum*) as a single Christian community, a construction that endures into King Alfred's ninth-century use of the term *Angelcynn* to encompass a single people with a common faith, culture and language (Foot 2002).

If the tenth century saw the creation of a united English kingdom, however, the Norman conquest of 1066 saw that kingdom absorbed into a larger political unit centred on northern France, and political involvement in France remained constant through the rest of the period. The division of England and Normandy between the two elder sons of William I in 1087 suggested that perhaps the Anglo-Norman realm might not endure, but William I's youngest son, Henry, reunited England and Normandy under his rule in 1100. The succession to the English throne in 1154 of Henry II, son and heir of the count of Anjou, and his marriage to Eleanor of Aquitaine, saw the creation of an 'Angevin Empire' encompassing England, Normandy, Anjou and Aquitaine. This empire collapsed between 1200 and 1204 when the Capetian kings of France seized King John's lands in France, including Normandy, and even, in 1216–17, invaded England in support of rebellious barons. Although the territorial losses were not conceded until the Treaty of Paris in 1259, this defeat marked the end of the Angevin empire (Bartlett 2000: 11–28).

In the two centuries after 1204, while the kings and nobility of England continued to act politically and militarily in France, England became their centre of gravity in a way that was not true of the period 1066–1204. Despite the loss of Normandy,

English monarchs retained their jurisdiction over the duchy of Gascony in south-western France, and disputes over the status of the English king's lands in France were the source of intermittent diplomacy and warfare. In 1337, Edward III's claim to the French throne itself (via his mother Isabella, daughter of Philip IV of France) initiated what would become the Hundred Years' War. The English achieved early military success, particularly at Crécy (1346) and Poitiers (1356), where the French king was captured, but military success was followed by diplomatic failure. English attempts to reach a favourable peace settlement alternated with overseas interventions designed to outmanoeuvre the French. All failed, and a truce in 1396 saw Richard II married to Isabella, the six-year-old daughter of the French king, without resolving the issues in dispute (Prestwich 2005: 292–327; Harriss 2005: 411–34).

The near total replacement of the Anglo-Saxon ruling class by a Norman nobility following the invasion of 1066 meant that the English nobility was, through much of the early part of this period, both ethnically and linguistically French, and French endured as the language of the king's court and the nobility throughout. Linguistically, therefore, medieval England was trilingual, with Latin, French and English all in regular use to different ends (Clanchy 1993: 197–223). Admittedly, French as spoken in England showed signs from an early date of being an acquired language, a supplement to English: in the late twelfth century, Walter Map refers disparagingly to *Gallicum Merleburge* ('Marlborough French'); at the end of the fourteenth, Chaucer's prioress speaks French 'after the scole of Stratford atte Bowe' (Bartlett 2000: 486–90). The Norman nobility themselves moved to adopt an English cultural identity (albeit a hybrid one), listening to French romances of Anglo-Saxon heroes identified as 'nos auncestres' and venerating Anglo-Saxon saints. But native English hostility to a ruling class identified as Norman rather than English is visible, unexpectedly, in some late thirteenth-century texts by Robert of Gloucester and Robert Mannyng (Turville-Petre 1996: 7, 94–97).

The boundaries of England itself were far from fixed in the eleventh century. Offa's Dyke was recognised as a boundary of sorts between England and Wales, but there was an extensive borderland known as the Welsh March (from Old English *mearc*), where Domesday book describes a militarised landscape of wastelands and castles (Bartlett 2000: 69–71), and the Normans began to push out of England and into southern and eastern Wales in the late eleventh century. There was a similar lack of definition on the Scottish border, where Northumbria, Cumbria and Lothian formed a liminal zone at the beginning of the period, and the border was not decisively fixed until the treaty of York in 1237 (Rothwell 1975: 354–55).

English overlordship over Wales, Scotland and Ireland ebbed and flowed throughout the period: England's dominance over its immediate neighbours reached a peak in 1175, when Henry II received a delegation of Welsh leaders at Gloucester, and imposed the treaty of Falaise on the king of Scotland, and the Treaty of Windsor on the representatives of the Irish high-king; it reached another following Edward I's conquest of Wales in 1282–83 and political ascendancy over the Scots in the 1290s (Davies 2000: 4–10, 14, 22–29, 83–87). English claims to overlordship over its Celtic neighbours, while based firmly on military and political power, were in part underpinned by literary ideology. The idea of a unified Britain was a powerful one in the period (for both the English and the Welsh, to different ends), particularly following the appearance of Geoffrey of Monmouth's *History of the Kings of Britain* in the 1130s, a work used for political ends when Edward I adopted its materials in justification of his claim to rule Scotland (Davies 2000: 31–53; Turville-Petre 1996: 81). Substantial English colonisation of Wales, Scotland and Ireland in this period again led to hybridity, which attempts at cultural demarcation and legislation against 'degeneracy' sought, unsuccessfully, to contain, and it is possible to read the monstrous human–animal hybrids inscribed in the narratives of Gerald of Wales, for example, as representative of the hybrid identities exemplified by Gerald himself (Cohen 2000).

All of this makes 'medieval England' a difficult place to locate or define. The geographical boundaries of England, themselves not entirely fixed in the eleventh and twelfth centuries, were narrower than the political and legal influence of a developing English state the reach of which extended politically and militarily into Wales, Scotland, Ireland and France. Nor was the identity of people of English descent equivalent to the political community of the state, for the ruling class of medieval England in this period was of primarily Norman descent, and could be identified as such (albeit in polemical terms) as late as the end of the thirteenth century. Additionally, substantial English colonial populations existed outside of England itself, in Wales, Scotland and Ireland. Medieval English identities, then, political, cultural, ethnic and linguistic, could be complex, multifaceted and sometimes hybrid.

Demographics

Evidence for the population of medieval England comes from two sets of sources from either end of this period: the Domesday survey of 1086, and the poll tax records from the end of the fourteenth century (1377, 1379 and 1380–81). None of these records attempt a full census of population, and so, of necessity, population estimates are an extrapolation from the numbers recorded. Domesday lists 268, 863 tenants – heads of households who are landholders. It omits the northern counties and the cities of London and Winchester, visibly underreports ecclesiastical numbers, and excludes sub-tenants and the landless entirely. On the basis of these figures, and estimates of household size and likely exclusions, historians estimate a total population in 1086 of at least one million and at the very most just over two million, with a likely figure being somewhere in between (Goldberg 2004: 72; Bartlett 2000: 290–92).

The 1377 poll tax records were compiled for tax purposes, and aimed to record all adults over the age of fourteen, excluding the very poor, the tinners of Cornwall, and those living in the counties of Durham and Cheshire, all of whom were tax exempt. The recorded lay population of 1,355, 201 persons (clergy were recorded separately) suggests a total population of at least two million (Myers 1969: 995–97;

Goldberg 2004: 72–73). While it is an increase on the 1086 estimate, this figure disguises the events of intervening years. Historians agree that the 'long thirteenth century' to around 1315 saw a significant expansion in the English population, with an estimated peak of four to six million (Harriss 2005: 214; Hatcher and Bailey 2001: 30–31), before an initial setback caused by devastating weather and consequent agricultural crisis and famine in 1315–17, and the death of perhaps half the country's population with the arrival of the Black Death in 1348. The mid-century plague outbreak was followed by another, the 'Grey Death', of 1361–62, with subsequent epidemics in 1369, 1375 and 1391, and localised outbreaks in the fifteenth century (Goldberg 2004: 165). While the Black Death has conventionally been identified with bubonic plague, scientists and historians have now cast doubt on this verdict (Prestwich 2005: 538–42). Whatever the nature of the disease, its devastating effect on the population would keep numbers depressed for the remainder of the fourteenth and fifteenth centuries.

Monarchy, Government and Law

Kingship in medieval England had both secular and sacred elements. The king fulfilled many roles: political and judicial, as head of state and protector of peace, order and justice; military, as defender of the realm and leader in war; economic, as greatest and wealthiest of English lords, dispenser of patronage, and authority for both coinage and taxation; and sacral, as God's anointed and protector of the Church. Kingship was conferred through coronation at Westminster Abbey, where the king took the coronation oath, was acclaimed by the people, and anointed and enthroned. Kingship was hereditary: the kings of England were descended from William the Conqueror, and, through Henry I's marriage to Matilda of Scotland, from the Anglo-Saxon kings of Wessex. It was also, at times, contested. The 1066 invasion itself was the result of a succession crisis in the English monarchy, and the eleventh and twelfth centuries saw repeated conflicts over the throne between members of the royal family: hence Gerald of Wales' description of the Norman and Angevin kings as princes who succeeded one another 'by killing and slaughtering their own' (cited in Bartlett 2000: 7).

While kings had always sought the counsel and consent of the leading lords of the realm in political matters, the idea of parliament, a body representative of a broader political community, was an innovation of the thirteenth century. An initial impetus may perhaps be seen in the writs of King John, issued at moments of crisis in 1212 and 1213, summoning representatives from each county to join him at a specified location. The word 'parliament' itself was first used to describe a representative assembly in 1237. Parliaments were attended by the great lords, sacred and secular, each of whom received an individual summons to attend, and by the representatives of the commons, elected for each county and borough. Parliament's business was in three areas: war, and business related to the king and the royal family; the common business of the realm such as judgments and legislation; and the private petitions of members, relating either to individual or collective grievances. The most usual business of parliament came to be assent to taxation, increasingly important in state finance during the fourteenth century. In times of difficulty, however, parliament also came to be a focal point for tensions between the monarch and the political community, and parliament played a significant role in the depositions of both Edward II and Richard II (Davies and Denton 1981).

Legal and governmental structures, and the written documentation that accompanied them, underwent significant expansion during the later Middle Ages. What we now call the common law developed in the twelfth century through the expansion of institutions previously in existence. It did not have a monopoly on legal authority, but sat alongside a number of other jurisdictions: primarily those of the ecclesiastical courts and the private jurisdictions of manorial lords, but also the separate law that applied in areas such as the king's forest and the border areas of the march, among others. The common law operated through a number of different tribunals. The court of common pleas operated at a fixed location, while the court of the king's bench was intended to follow the king around the country. In addition to the county courts presided over by the sheriff in each of England's thirty-nine counties, royal justice was also administered at a local level by itinerant justices 'in eyre' sent into the counties. This system of general enquiry was replaced in the late thirteenth century by assize justices and commissions of oyer and terminer (to 'hear' and 'determine') that held inquiries into specific incidents. Following the condemnation of ordeals by hot iron or cold water by the Church in 1215 (the option of trial by battle endured), the later Middle Ages saw the growth of the jury trial; the period also witnessed the growth of a secular professional legal class (Baker 2002: 12–22, 71–76, 155–59).

The primary legal jurisdictions other than the king's were those of the Church and the manorial lords. The Church's jurisdiction was based on the canon law that operated throughout Christendom, codified in the *Corpus Iuris Canonici*. The ecclesiastical courts claimed jurisdiction over all clergy (who claimed immunity from the criminal law), but also over the laity in relation to specific matters deemed spiritual: the creation of the marriage bond, sexual offences, the making of wills, the taking (and breaking) of oaths and defamation (Baker 2002: 126–30). The private jurisdiction that lords exercised over the tenants through the manorial court was not arbitrary, but based on local custom, which might differ from the common law in matters of detail. For unfree tenants, excluded from access to the king's courts, the manorial court was the primary source of legal redress.

Problems of lawlessness and violence seem prominent in the later medieval period. In the early fourteenth century, the commissions of Trailbaston targeting armed gangs suggest problems of social order – the commissions address crimes of violence, but also suggest difficulties in addressing these crimes through the usual legal processes because of bribery and intimidation of juries (Rothwell 1975: 519–22, 612–21). Warfare, social unrest and economic issues may all have contributed to increases in crime at specific periods, and there was certainly a contemporary sense of crisis at specific moments, such as in the early fourteenth century. Violent criminals in fourteenth-century England were by no means exclusively to be found among the socially vulnerable or marginal: the gentry tended to use force in disputes for land or political gain, and criminal gangs might be made up of gentry or even clergy; the Folville gang, which comprised members of a Leicestershire gentry family who committed murder, rape, kidnap and robbery, was a prominent example (Prestwich 2005: 507–11; Harriss 2005: 197–201).

Legal scenarios and legal language are prominent in medieval English poetry, but literary texts do not always accord with legal perspectives. Two poems from MS Harley 2253 illustrate the point: in the Anglo-Norman 'Outlaw's Song of Trailbaston', the narrator vigorously protests his own innocence, and asserts the corruption of accusers, jurors and justices, all from the safety of the woods where he hides as an outlaw (Rothwell 1975: 919–20). Another Harley poem is a Middle English satire on the ecclesiastical court: the poem's narrator rails against the court, which imposes public penance upon him for fornication and seeks to force him to marry his mistress (McCarthy 2004: 210–13).

Rebellion and Revolution

Notwithstanding their oaths of loyalty to the king, the medieval nobility was accustomed to the resolution of disputes through force of arms, and noble rebellion was a recurrent feature of medieval English politics. Rebellion might be motivated by personal grievance, by participation in a dispute within the royal family itself, or by a desire for political reform. Rebellion was sufficiently acceptable as a form of political protest that defeated noble rebels were rarely subjected to severe punishments of mutilation, dispossession, or death in the period prior to the fourteenth century (Bartlett 2000: 51–67). Several times during this period, however, the country descended into a state of civil war: in 1088 when Norman magnates rebelled against William Rufus; in the rebellion in 1173–74 of Henry II's son, Henry 'the young King'; in 1215–17, when the barons sought to impose the *Magna Carta* reforms upon King John; in 1264–65 when Simon de Montfort led reform-minded barons against Henry III; and at either end of the fourteenth century, when conflict led to the deposition and murder of both Edward II and Richard II.

While most acts of rebellion in medieval England were initiated and prosecuted by members of the nobility, the rising of 1381 was a prominent exception. Large numbers of the population, initially in Essex and Kent but subsequently elsewhere through the country, attacked royal officials and destroyed administrative documents. Proceeding from the countryside to London, the rebellion plunged the government into an unprecedented crisis for a four-day period in mid-June: rebels burned John of Gaunt's palace at the Savoy, plundered the Temple, surrounded the King at the Tower of London, and executed the chancellor and treasurer (among others) as traitors. The rebel demands, as articulated in the inevitably hostile chronicle accounts that are our sources, include the end of villeinage, fixed rents, the disendowment of the church, the abolition of lordship except that of the king, the abolition of outlawry, the reduction of the ecclesiastical hierarchy and (cryptically) that there should be no law except the law of Winchester. In negotiation with the rebels, Richard II made a number of concessions, including the issue of charters (subsequently revoked) abolishing villeinage and the sacrifice of a number of his supporters: actions that succeeded in persuading the Essex rebels to return home. The subsequent actions of the Mayor of London led to the fatal wounding of the rebel leader Wat Tyler, and allowed an opportunity for the London citizenry to surround the Kentish rebels and escort them from the city (Myers 1969: 127–40).

Identifying the identity and motivations of the rebels is difficult. Chronicle accounts identify them pejoratively as *rustici*, 'peasants,' but there is evidence that the rising had a much broader social basis: the *Anonimalle* chronicle quotes the rebels (in English) identifying themselves with 'the trew communes'. The outrage of the chroniclers gives us a sense of the strength of the social divisions being transgressed: the spectacle of the rebel leader Wat Tyler shaking King Richard by the hand, and addressing him as '*frer*', 'brother', is recounted by the horrified *Anonimalle* chronicler (Strohm 1992: 33–56; Myers 1969: 127–40). The immediate provocation for the rebellion may have been an understandable sense of injustice associated with the imposition of the third poll tax in 1381 (Goldberg 2004: 183–84), but the demands reportedly articulated by the rebels also suggest the pressures for change in later fourteenth-century England: in particular the extreme pressure that altered social circumstances imposed on relations between landlords and unfree peasants, the broad sense of outrage at clerical wealth and corruption, and the anger concerning the maladministration evident in royal justice and government. Most intriguing as evidence of rebel intent for readers of medieval literature are the half-dozen Middle English texts ascribed to the authorship of rebel leaders, short letters or 'broadsides' intended for a popular audience, which contain a number of explicit references to William Langland's *Piers Plowman* (Justice 1994).

Medieval English Society

Medieval authors often treat society as being composed of three 'estates', *oratores*, *bellatores* and *laboratores* – those who pray, those who fight and those who work. The reality of medieval English society, especially in the later period, was somewhat more complex. The three estates model does not take account of the rise of business and law as means of social advancement, in addition to the traditional sources of wealth via landholding and military success: this rise is evident in the poll tax rates for 1379 where a sergeant at law pays 40 shillings, the same as a baron or a knight, and a great merchant pays 20 shillings, the same as a bachelor or a squire (Douglas 1969: 125–26). The three estates model ignores the growth of the towns: the pre-plague population of London may have reached 100,000, and four other towns, York, Norwich, Winchester and Bristol, had populations of 10,000 or more (Harriss 2005: 271–73).

The model may also obscure other social distinctions, such as gender, apparent to contemporaries: women were often thought of as a 'fourth estate' (Mann 1973: 121). It may also be the case that the crucial distinction within medieval English society was not that between the knighthood, the religious and those who worked the land, but between those who were free and those who were not: despite the abolition of slavery in the eleventh century, unfree status endured until the end of the period, when it began to dissolve under social and economic pressures. The three estates model is nonetheless a useful one – it is noticeable that Chaucer's *General Prologue* to *The Canterbury Tales* seems to include an idealised representative of each of these three estates among its portraits, in the figures of the Knight, the Ploughman and the Parson (Mann 1973: 55).

Those Who Fight – the Nobility

The nobility were the secular elite of medieval English society, an elite that was small in number. For the period to 1337, when Edward III instigated the title of duke for his eldest son, earl (Latin *comes*) was the only formal honorific title in use in England, and the number of earls remained few – seven or so at any one time in the eleventh century, nine in 1300, and never more than twenty (Given-Wilson 1996: 7–8, 29–30; Bartlett 2000: 208–12; Prestwich 2005: 354–61). The upper nobility also included up to two hundred barons, the great lords who held land directly from the king; towards the end of the fourteenth century, this upper stratum of the nobility had become more clearly defined as those seventy or so families who received an individual summons to parliament. Beneath the higher nobility was the knighthood, numbering perhaps five thousand in the eleventh and twelfth centuries, but declining to perhaps 1,500 knights, supplemented by an equivalent number of esquires who had not formally assumed knighthood, at the beginning of the fourteenth (Given-Wilson 1996: 14–16, 65; Bartlett 2000: 216–18; Prestwich 2005: 389–413). As a wealthy elite, the nobility maintained households and retinues that were both substantial and expensive: in 1384 the retainers of Edward Courtenay, earl of Devon, included seven knights, forty esquires, fifty-two valets, four minstrels, eight chaplains, three ladies-in-waiting, six pages and fourteen lawyers, of whom a majority might have been household members. At the other end of the spectrum, an esquire might have maintained a household of between ten and twenty persons (Given-Wilson 1996: 88–89).

The military function of the nobility was a defining aspect of their identity, although in fact military service was a wider obligation: every English male between the age of fifteen and sixty was legally required to possess weapons and to know how to use them. The Statute of Winchester (1285) outlined the arms which men of each social class should possess: from those at the top of the social scale required to have a hauberk, an iron helmet, a sword, a knife and a horse, to those at the bottom, required to possess bows and arrows (Rothwell 1975: 461–62). Medieval armies were not entirely composed of levies of knights and infantry, but were supplemented by hired soldiers, and for the most part warfare consisted of skirmishes and sieges rather than large-scale pitched battles. Castles were an innovation brought by the Normans to England, and perhaps one thousand castles were constructed in England between the mid-eleventh and early thirteenth centuries: initially motte-and-bailey castles where a wooden structure was surrounded by earthworks, but from the twelfth century onwards more permanent structures built in stone (Bartlett 2000: 269–86).

The military ethos of the nobility was codified in a series of chivalric values considered appropriate to their estate. Ideas of chivalry have a number of potential sources: the notion of dubbing to knighthood bears some resemblance to earlier ideas of the conferring of arms by a lord as a mark of majority or honour, and in that sense chivalric ideologies look as if they evolve from within the military class itself. The effort of the Church to modify and control aristocratic violence through the Truce of God and Peace of God movements of the tenth century, followed by the articulation of a positive model of Christian knighthood through the launching of the Crusades in the late eleventh century, provided ecclesiastical endorsement for a model of chivalry in the service of Christ. Finally, chivalric values were given prominent literary articulation within medieval romance, which not only provided positive archetypes of chivalric behaviour, but also a chivalric mythology through its narratives of great heroes from the days of Charlemagne, Arthur and the Trojan war (Keen 1984).

In addition to their military function, the nobility occupied simultaneous roles as landholders and administrative officials. For the most part, knights were bound by military tenures that required them to provide military service in exchange for landholding. The land they held in this way provided them with their primary source of income, for the peasants who held the land from them did so in exchange for labour on the lord's own demesne land or for money rent. Additionally, the nobility acted as agents of government: administrative and judicial offices throughout the country were held by members of the nobility, appointed by the king.

Those Who Pray – the Clergy

Medieval England was part of the world of medieval Christendom, a world of belief with its earthly focus on Rome and on Jerusalem, as exemplified in the Hereford *mappamundi*, where England sits at the edge of the world in the lower left corner of a map centred on Jerusalem, with the earthly paradise located at the very top. With the exception of the small Jewish community that migrated from Rouen in the immediate aftermath of the Conquest, which was expelled from England in 1290, everyone in the country was regarded as a member of the Catholic faith.

The institutional Church contained a wide variety of personnel. The secular clergy were associated with some nine thousand parishes, as well as cathedral chapters, private households and colleges. They were presided over by the Archbishops of Canterbury and York, and the bishops of fifteen other English dioceses. In the mid-thirteenth century, monks and nuns made up some 550 male and 150 female religious communities. Those withdrawing from the world for religious purposes included anchorites and anchoresses, who lived in tiny cells attached to churches. From the early thirteenth century, the growing interest of the Church in the spiritual lives of the laity (and a substantial increase in lay piety) was reflected in the evangelising mission of the friars, mostly in urban contexts.

Church and state were heavily implicated in each other's workings, a relationship which led to tensions between them. Issues at stake in Church–state frictions included the right of the king to appoint bishops, a widespread source of conflict between a newly assertive papacy following the eleventh-century papal reform, and European rulers whose use of bishops as senior officers of government gave them a pressing need to determine appointments. There was also conflict concerning whether the tenure of ecclesiastical property differed from secular property and was immune from the king's recovery, a matter of anxiety given the enormous landed wealth of the church, which made leading bishops the equivalents of the great secular barons. A further cause of difficulty was the practice of clerics serving as judges in the king's courts, a necessity in the early days of judicial expansion. Tensions could lead to open conflict, as in the case of Henry II and Thomas Becket, where dispute led to Becket's exile, return and subsequent murder in Canterbury Cathedral in December 1170 (Bartlett 2000: 402–09).

The medieval religious worldview included a focus not just on this world, but on the next: on the soul's journey after death to Heaven, Hell or Purgatory. The idea of Purgatory as an actual location, an intermediate place between Heaven and Hell for the purgation of worldly misdeeds, is a medieval innovation. This notion of a third place was indebted both to the thinking of earlier Christian writers, especially Augustine, and to early medieval visions of the otherworld, but the doctrine of Purgatory, and the word itself, is a creation of the late twelfth century, and was officially adopted at the Second Council of Lyons in 1274. While the idea of Purgatory receives its greatest expression in Dante's *Commedia*, it is a creation at least partly indebted to literary texts composed in England, and in particular a medieval Latin text, the *Tractatus de Purgatorio Sancti Patricii*, written in the 1180s by the English Cistercian H. de Saltrey (Le Goff 1984). The *Tractatus* tells a story of a knight named Owein who journeys to Purgatory through an entrance to the otherworld located in Ireland, at Lough Derg. The story was an enormously influential one, translated into French as Marie de France's *Espurgatoire S. Patrice*, and into Middle English in the *South English Legendary* and in two verse translations, both called *Owayne Miles*.

The question of what could be done in this world to ensure salvation in the next loomed large for medieval Christians, and the idea of Purgatory is an appropriate innovation for an era where sin and repentance were central to religious thought. The Church preached the avoidance of sin – particularly the seven deadly sins of lust, gluttony, greed, sloth, wrath, envy and pride – and provided the opportunity for redemption of sins through the sacrament of confession and the performance of penance. God's grace could also be conferred through the sacraments, five of which were required for all Christians – baptism, confirmation, the eucharist, confession and extreme unction (matrimony and religious orders were optional). But even with the benefits of the sacraments, prayer and good works, Christians could not merit salvation without God's grace, and the question of the role that individual action could play in contributing towards salvation is a central one, for example, in Langland's *Piers Plowman*.

The medieval Church was the keeper of literate culture in medieval England: in the medieval mind, the pairs 'cleric' and 'lay', 'literate' and 'illiterate', were equivalent, although in reality these distinctions broke down with the expansion of lay literacy in the twelfth and thirteenth centuries (Clanchy 1993: 224–52). The clergy were the providers of education: at parish level, children might learn the rudiments of reading from a local priest; at the other end of the educational spectrum, the Church provided higher education via the cathedral schools, or, from the thirteenth century, at the Universities of Oxford and Cambridge. The university curriculum in arts, the basic degree, covered the seven liberal arts: grammar, rhetoric and logic (the trivium), arithmetic, music, geometry and astronomy (the quadrivium); higher degrees were awarded in law, medicine and theology (Harriss 2005: 344–51). This was an era of substantial intellectual endeavour following the expansion in European intellectual horizons across multiple disciplines with the 'twelfth century renaissance', the rediscovery of ancient Greek scientific and philosophical works (especially those of Aristotle) and the rise of scholasticism (Swanson 1999). The medieval English Church produced a number of leading intellectuals during the period, including Anselm of Canterbury, John of Salisbury, Robert Grosseteste, Roger Bacon, John Duns Scotus, William of Ockham and Robert Holcot.

In addition to being the source of higher learning, however, in the later fourteenth century the University of Oxford also became a source of heresy – contributing to the spread of beliefs contrary to those accepted as Christian doctrine by the Church. The thinking and preaching of an Oxford intellectual, John Wyclif, and his attacks upon the inadequacy of the earthly Church, influenced the rise of a popular heretical movement, Lollardy, whose translation of the Bible into English and attacks on Church authority resonated with tendencies in contemporary culture towards vernacularity, lay piety and anticlericalism. Contemporaries felt Wyclif's teaching influenced the revolt of 1381; Lollardy persisted after Wyclif's death, and the early fifteenth century saw both persecution and revolt (Lambert 2002: 247–305; Myers 1969: 837–64; Harriss 2005: 376–86). The poetry inspired by Lollardy is discussed by John Scattergood in this volume.

Those Who Work – the Peasantry

The economy of medieval England was overwhelmingly one of small-scale peasant farming, with the vast majority of the population devoted to working the land, predominantly in arable cultivation of cereal crops. Field systems varied by region, but midland England was characterised by small villages centred around a church and a manor house and surrounded by large open fields, with villagers farming individual strips of land within the larger fields. Usually one in two or one in three of these arable fields were left fallow each year for animals to graze on, with animal manure providing fertiliser to replenish the soil. In contrast to the open-field system of midland England, other parts of the country had smaller clusters of houses or individual farms surrounded by smaller field enclosures (Hanawalt 1986: 19–21).

Peasant holdings were small: in theory, the standard holding was a virgate or yardland of some 30 acres, but in practice, many tenants had much smaller holdings, and there were substantial differences in prosperity and standards of living within the medieval English peasantry (Hanawalt 1986: 6). Yields from farming were low: perhaps a quarter of a ton of wheat per acre, whereas modern farming yields three tons per acre or more (Bartlett 2000: 305). Oxen or horses were used for ploughing; livestock were predominantly cattle, pigs and especially sheep, with a substantial export trade in wool during the period. The warmer climate in what has been hypothesised as a 'medieval warm period' meant that it was possible to cultivate grapes for wine in the south of the country at the beginning of this period, although changes in climate were to bring difficulties later (Bartlett 2000: 288–89; Prestwich 2005: 3–9). Many smallholders may have held additional employment as farm labourers, bakers, butchers, cooks, brewers, millers, smiths, carpenters, thatchers, shoemakers, tailors, weavers, dyers and so on; regional industrial specialisations included cloth production, metalworking, lead-mining and iron-mining (Hatcher and Bailey 2001: 49–51, 135–37).

Peasant families lived in timber-framed houses, with walls filled in with turf, cob (a mixture of mud, straw and chalk), clay or, most commonly, wattle and daub (woven branches caked in mud and limewashed). Houses were thatched, and chimneyless – smoke escaped through a hole in the roof. Floors were made from clay and covered with straw, and windows had shutters rather than glass. Houses varied in size – a cottage might be a one- or two-room house, about twelve feet wide and around sixteen feet in length for a one-room house and up to twice that for two rooms. The typical peasant dwelling, a long-house, could include a byre in the same building as the living space, and be upwards of forty-nine feet in length. More prosperous peasants had houses with separate buildings for animals, perhaps centred on a courtyard. Medieval peasant houses were impermanent, normally lasting only a single generation, and movable (Hanawalt 1986: 31–44; Bartlett 2000: 301).

Peasants, free and unfree, held their land from the lord of the manor in return for service or money rent. The distinction between free and unfree status (villeinage) was a crucial one in law, for as the common law developed during the twelfth century, it denied villeins access to the king's courts. Villein status was inherited and often contested, and it came to be associated with three tests: the payment of *merchet* (for permission to give a daughter in marriage), the payment of *tallage* (arbitrary levies demanded by the lord), and the provision of regular and undefined labour services (Bartlett 2000: 321–25). Other levies included *heriot*, paid whenever a servile tenant gave up his holding, *chevage*, paid to gain the lord's consent to reside outside the manor, and *leyrwite* and *childwite* paid in compensation for illicit intercourse and the birth of illegitimate children. Not all peasants were unfree: estimates suggest that less than 60 per cent of rural tenants (and so less than half of households overall) in later thirteenth century England were unfree, and that these tenants held around 30 per cent of the land (Hatcher and Bailey 2001: 99).

Substantial changes to the medieval English rural economy occurred during this time, with the period up to the early fourteenth century witnessing the growth of the overall population, the land under cultivation and the intensity of farming, as well as towns, trade, markets and industrial activity. In the fourteenth and fifteenth centuries, by contrast, population fell by over a half, rural and urban settlement, trade and economic activity all contracted. Social conditions also changed substantially as lords abandoned direct farming in favour of rental income and villeinage disappeared (Hatcher and Bailey 2001: 3). The years 1315–17 represented a crucial moment in this transformation of the medieval English economy, when dreadful weather and animal disease caused famine, and hardship was compounded by war with Scotland; demographic and economic stagnation followed (Prestwich 2005: 527–38). Another crucial moment was represented by the plague of 1348: the enormous death toll was followed by a steep rise in real wages for the rural workers who survived, and, despite government attempts to contain wage rises through measures such as the Statute of Labourers (Myers 1969: 993–94), peasant living-standards rose and villeinage gradually disappeared. Historians continue to debate whether the devastating effects of famine and plague were themselves the primary cause of the radical social and economic changes seen in fourteenth-century England, or whether they simply exacerbated changes that would have come to the fore in any case, whether because of population pressure leading to demographic crisis, class tension pitting tenants against oppressive landlords, or an increase in commercialisation, urbanisation and trade that changed the nature of the medieval English economy (Hatcher and Bailey 2001).

The Fourth Estate

Women were often thought to constitute a 'fourth estate' within medieval society, and the representation of women in the estates satire of Chaucer's *General Prologue* conveys a sense of the predominant options available for adult women within medieval society: marriage or entry into religion. Research suggests that the percentage of women who married was high (Hanawalt 1986: 142). Much of the work performed by medieval peasant women was directly focused on the household: cooking, baking, brewing, butter and cheese production, caring for children and animals, spinning wool and the manufacture of cloth, as well as some agricultural work, including reaping and gleaning (Hanawalt 1986: 141–55). Work for women outside the household was often closely related to domestic and family roles, in professions such as brewing, clothmaking, wetnursing and midwifery, as well as retailing or service.

Women's work in higher social classes was similarly focused on the running of the household, but on a much larger scale, extending to estate management in the absence of a husband on business. Married women suffered substantial legal disadvantages: under the common law (sometimes modified by local custom), all authority over property was vested in the husband during marriage, although a wife could recover any of her landed property alienated by her husband without her consent after his death.

There is a substantial volume of writing on the subject of women across a range of medieval genres and texts. The predominantly clerical authorship of these texts, however, means that they are for the most part written by authors who are male, celibate and suspicious of women. As a consequence, anti-feminism is a prominent feature of writing on women across the Middle Ages. The indebtedness of medieval writing to ideas of authority means that antifeminist texts draw on the authorities of Scripture, classical writing and the Church Fathers, all of which provide substantial precedent for medieval anti-feminist attitudes. Positive models of women are available in medieval Christian thought: predominantly in relation to the three grades of chastity, in particular holy widowhood and virginity, and in historical examples of Old Testament heroines, Christian martyrs and the idealised figure of the Virgin Mary. Proto-feminist responses to anti-feminist writing are also to be found, and works such as debate poems may present arguments from both sides. All in all, however, the volume of anti-feminist writing in the Middle Ages far outweighs such efforts at balance (Blamires 1992).

The Ties of Affection: Love, Marriage and Sexuality

Love, marriage and sexuality are the subjects of much discussion and debate in medieval poetry, from *The Owl and the Nightingale* to the 'marriage debate' of *The Canterbury Tales*, but also in other texts, including legal, medical and theological writings. Love can be described in medieval writing as something akin to friendship, or as an obsessive psychological illness akin to melancholy; it can be rational, or it can be the opposite; it can be a fleeting passion, or the emotional basis for a lifetime of marriage; it can be motivated by sexual lust or by religious fervour. Some medieval texts reflect a broad perspective: Saint Augustine in the *City of God* offers a nuanced discussion distinguishing between a number of different emotions, alike but not interchangeable, which can be described as love (McCarthy 2004: 36–38).

People in medieval England were free to marry by consent alone: according to ecclesiastical law, the bond of marriage was one formed by mutual consent, and forced marriages could be annulled by the Church courts, which had jurisdiction over marriage as a spiritual matter. While the Church sought to regulate the behaviour of those to be married, its consensual model meant that it also reluctantly recognised 'clandestine' marriages, where consent was exchanged outside the prescribed ecclesiastical context. The problem of people agreeing to marriage in unorthodox settings was one that Church legislation complained against throughout the thirteenth and fourteenth centuries (McCarthy 2004: 72–82). Marriages were also occasions on which property transfers took place within and between families; what this meant in practice was that it was difficult to get married without access to sufficient property to establish an economically viable family unit (McCarthy 2004: 112–21). Medieval English people usually married in their early to mid-twenties, with spouses generally being close in age (literary portraits of couples substantially mismatched in age are not representative of actual practice) and the Church encouraged *maritalis affectio*, love between spouses.

Much of our evidence for medieval sexual behaviour comes from an ecclesiastical establishment uneasy about all forms of sexual activity, and obsessively keen to regulate it. Ecclesiastical views on sexuality are set within a model of three grades of chastity (virginity, widowhood and marriage, in that order of merit), a model present, either manifestly or latently, in much medieval writing about marriage. Throughout the medieval period, men and women could publicly vow themselves to virginity (conventionally in the context of entering religious life, or less usually while remaining in the world), or to chastity in widowhood after the death of their spouse. The difficulty for ecclesiastical writers was in reconciling the merits of marriage with suspicion concerning sexual behaviour, and ecclesiastical anxiety about marital sex endures throughout the period. The medieval Church condemned all sexual behaviour outside of a marital context, heterosexual or otherwise, as sinful, and sought to police sexual activity through the ecclesiastical courts. The direct mapping of contemporary categories of sexual identity onto medieval categories of sexual identity seems anachronistic, but it is clear that sexual identities were as complex and varied in the Middle Ages as they are today: witness, for example, the case of John/Eleanor Rykener, a transsexual prostitute brought before a London court in 1394 (McCarthy 2004: 126–28).

Conclusion

The world of medieval England, then, is not reducible to a single world-view. The model of the three estates might attempt a social overview, but its view of medieval society is static, unable to take account of the realities of social change. This certainly tells us something about mindsets: medieval society is conservative and hierarchical, oriented towards and validated by the past, a society that draws on (or invents) worlds gone by: not for nothing do English kings adopt Arthurian legend to their own ends, and London describe itself as a New Troy. But medieval England is also a complex society undergoing substantial changes. It is possible to identify opposing world-views between landlords and villeins, justices and outlaws, bishops and Lollards, and the period sees challenges to some of society's most authoritative institutions: monarchy, lordship and the Church. The realities of the society with which medieval English poetry engages, then, are as complex, vibrant and nuanced as that poetry itself.

REFERENCES AND FURTHER READING

Baker, J. H. (2002). *An Introduction to English Legal History*. London: Butterworths.

Bartlett, Robert (2000). *England Under the Norman and Angevin Kings 1075–1225*. Oxford: Oxford University Press.

Blamires, Alcuin, with Marx, C. W., and Pratt, Karen (eds) (1992). *Woman Defamed and Woman Defended: An Anthology of Medieval Texts*. Oxford: Oxford University Press.

Clanchy, M. T. (1993). *From Memory to Written Record: England 1066–1307*. Oxford: Blackwell.

Cohen, Jeffrey Jerome (2000). Hybrids, monsters, borderlands: the bodies of Gerald of Wales. In Jeffrey Jerome Cohen (ed.). *The Postcolonial Middle Ages* (pp. 85–104). New York: St. Martin's.

Davies, R. G., and Denton, J. H. (eds) (1981). *The English Parliament in the Middle Ages*. Manchester: Manchester University Press.

Davies, R. R. (2000). *The First English Empire: Power and Identities in the British Isles 1093–1343*. Oxford: Oxford University Press.

Douglas, David C., and Greenaway, George W. (eds) (1953). *English Historical Documents 1042–1189*. London: Eyre and Spottiswoode.

Foot, Sarah (2002). The making of 'Angelcynn': English identity before the Norman conquest. In R. M. Liuzza (ed.). *Old English Literature: Critical Essays* (pp. 51–78). New Haven, CT: Yale University Press.

Given-Wilson, Chris (1996). *The English Nobility in the Late Middle Ages: The Fourteenth-Century Political Community*. London: Routledge.

Goldberg, P. J. P. (2004). *Medieval England: A Social History, 1250–1550*. London: Arnold.

Hanawalt, Barbara A. (1986). *The Ties that Bound: Peasant Families in Medieval England*. Oxford: Oxford University Press.

Harriss, Gerald (2005). *Shaping the Nation: England 1360–1461*. Oxford: Oxford University Press.

Hatcher, John, and Bailey, Mark (2001). *Modelling the Middle Ages: The History and Theory of England's Economic Development*. Oxford: Oxford University Press.

Justice, Steven (1994). *Writing and Rebellion: England in 1381*. Berkeley: University of California Press.

Keen, Maurice (1984). *Chivalry*. New Haven: Yale University Press.

Lambert, Malcolm (2002). *Medieval Heresy: Popular Movements from the Gregorian Reform to the Reformation*. Oxford: Blackwell.

Le Goff, Jacques (1984). *The Birth of Purgatory*. Trans. Arthur Goldhammer. Chicago: University of Chicago Press. (Original work pub. 1981.)

Mann, Jill (1973). *Chaucer and Medieval Estates Satire: The Literature of Social Classes and the General Prologue to the Canterbury Tales*. Cambridge: Cambridge University Press.

McCarthy, Conor (2004). *Love, Sex and Marriage in the Middle Ages: A Sourcebook*. London: Routledge.

Myers, A. R. (ed.) (1969). *English Historical Documents 1327–1485*. London: Eyre and Spottiswoode.

Prestwich, Michael (2005). *Plantagenet England 1225–1360*. Oxford: Oxford University Press.

Rothwell, Harry (ed.) (1975). *English Historical Documents 1189–1327*. London: Eyre and Spottiswoode.

Strohm, Paul (1992). *Hochon's Arrow: The Social Imagination of Fourteenth-Century Texts*. Princeton, NJ: Princeton University Press.

Swanson, R. N. (1999). *The Twelfth-Century Renaissance*. Manchester: Manchester University Press.

Turville-Petre, Thorlac (1996). *England the Nation: Language, Literature, and National Identity, 1290–1340*. Oxford: Oxford University Press.

10
Middle English Language and Poetry

Simon Horobin

Middle English is a term employed to describe the English language used between 1100 and 1500, distinguishing it from Old English, or Anglo-Saxon, which preceded it, and Modern English which followed it. It is important to emphasise at the outset of this discussion that this term is really a scholarly convenience to refer to a period in the history of English that witnessed considerable linguistic variation and change. The start date of 1100 is of course related to the Norman Conquest of 1066 which led to the replacement of English by Norman French as the primary written language of England. During the Anglo-Saxon period Old English was used for a range of different functions, including historical writing, religious writing, legal documents and literature. By the end of the period a single variety of Old English, known to scholars as late West-Saxon, had been selected for use over a wide geographical area, functioning as a kind of standard language. But the Norman Conquest led to the appointment of Normans to the major administrative posts, while the nobility read literature in Norman French. English did continue to be used, primarily as a spoken vernacular by those who were illiterate. Where it was written down it was largely intended for a local audience, and as a consequence the spelling conventions were adjusted to reflect a local pronunciation. The result of this was that, unlike Present-day English (PDE) which comprises numerous spoken dialects but one single written standard, Middle English was made up of numerous different written varieties reflecting its many different spoken varieties. The dominance of French and Latin as the languages of the written record in the early Middle English period means that we have comparatively little English poetry that survives from between 1100 and 1350.

During the fourteenth century, however, the status of English began to change due to a combination of social and political factors (discussed more extensively in the previous chapter). The status of French in England had begun to wane throughout the thirteenth century, partly the result of the loss of Normandy to the French crown in 1204. The loss of Normandy led to a greater separation between England and France so that French noblemen with lands in England gave up their French lands and began to assimilate to English culture. The French language used in England during this period, known as Anglo-Norman, began to lose its status, coming to be seen as a bureaucratic language used by clerks and no longer fashionable amongst the nobility. By contrast with the fashionable Parisian French, the Anglo-Norman pronunciation was ridiculed as provincial. The chronicler Walter Map spoke scornfully of insular French as 'Marlborough French', while Chaucer's Prioress speaks French 'after the scole of Stratford atte Bowe', in the manner of the London suburbs rather than the royal court. The Hundred Years' War (1337–1453) served to fuel anti-French feeling, and English began to be taken up as part of the nationalistic agenda (Turville-Petre 1996).

While the fourteenth century witnessed a decline in the fortunes of French in England, English saw a corresponding increase in status. Improved labour conditions following the outbreaks of Black Death meant that the peasant class was able to better its social and economic position. As a result a middle class emerged, comprising literate English speakers eager to enjoy the same cultural pursuits as their Norman predecessors. This created a market for literary composition in the vernacular which led to the decision of major poets such as Chaucer, Gower, Langland and the *Gawain*-poet to write in English rather than French. John Gower did write one poem in Anglo-Norman, *Mirour de l'omme*, but the fact that this work survives in just one manuscript suggests that it failed to find an audience.

Despite the re-emergence of English as a national vernacular in the fourteenth century, a standard variety was much slower to emerge and it was not until the fifteenth century that such a standard became established. The standard that emerged was based upon the London dialect, a natural choice given that London was the location of the court, parliament and the law courts, and the centre for book production. The use of English in documents issued by the Chancery, Signet and Privy Seal offices from the 1420s onwards led to the establishment of a written variety that was circulated widely and adopted by writers across the country (Samuels 1963, 1989; Benskin 2004). This written variety received special endorsement when it was adopted by William Caxton as the variety used in the books that issued from the printing press established by him in Westminster in the 1470s (Fisher 1996). It is the emergence of this standard variety, its adoption by prestigious institutions and its dissemination throughout the country that mark the end of the Middle English period in 1500.

From our modern perspective, which takes the existence of a standard language based upon a southern dialect for granted, it is easy to forget that this situation did not apply in the Middle English period. Poets like Chaucer, Gower, Langland and the *Gawain*-poet wrote in their own dialects rather than in a single national standard, with the result that many Middle English texts vary considerably in spelling, grammar and vocabulary. Students who are familiar with the works of Chaucer, for instance, are often shocked by how different the language of the *Gawain*-poet is, considering that the two writers were contemporaries. As an example let us compare the following extract from *Patience* with the language of Chaucer:

Pacience is a <u>poynt</u>, þaʒ hit displese ofte	*virtue; though*
When heuy herttes ben hurt wyth <u>heþyng</u> <u>oþer</u> elles,	*scorn; or*
Suffraunce may aswagen hem and þe <u>swelme</u> <u>leþe</u>,	*heat; ease*
For <u>ho</u> quelles <u>vche</u> a <u>qued</u> and quenches malyce;	*she; each; evil*
For <u>quoso</u> suffer cowþe syt, <u>sele</u> wolde folʒe,	*whoso; happiness*
And quo for <u>þro</u> may noʒt <u>þole</u>, þe þikker he sufferes.	*anger; endure*
Þen is better to abyde þe <u>bur</u> <u>vmbestoundes</u>	*onslaught; from time to time*
Þen ay þrow forth my þro, þaʒ <u>me</u> <u>þynk</u> ylle.	*it seems to me*
I herde on a halyday, at a hyʒe masse,	
How Mathew <u>melede</u> þat his Mayster His <u>meyny</u> con teche.	*said; disciples*
<u>Aʒt</u> <u>happes</u> He hem hyʒt and vcheon a <u>mede</u>,	*eight; beatitudes; reward*
<u>Sunderlupes</u>, for hit dissert, vpon <u>a ser wyse</u>:	*severally; various ways*
Thay arn <u>happen</u> þat han in hert pouerté,	*blessed*
For <u>hores</u> is þe heuen-ryche to holde for euer;	*theirs*

(*Patience*, lines 1–14)

Perhaps the most obvious difference concerns the use of the letters <þ> 'thorn' and <ʒ> 'yogh' in the extract from *Patience*, where Chaucer's text would use <th> and <gh>. This is really an editorial difference; many Chaucerian manuscripts use <þ> and <ʒ> but editors of Chaucer traditionally modernise these features. So while *noʒt* and *noght*, *þe* and *the*, may appear significant differences, they are in fact merely the result of editorial preference. Other differences in spelling conventions are indicative of dialect distinctions, such as the use of <qu> where Chaucer's dialect has <wh>; compare *quo* with Chaucerian *who*. It is often difficult to establish whether differences in spelling conventions signal differences in pronunciations, although the spelling of *vche*, 'each', seems to imply a different pronunciation from the Chaucerian *eche*. This passage also reveals differences in pronouns; the third person singular feminine pronoun in *Patience* is *ho*, a western form derived from OE *heo*, whereas Chaucer uses the eastern form *she*, derived from *heo* by a different development. The neuter possessive pronoun *hit*, 'its', is also western; Chaucer uses the form *his* which appears elsewhere in this text. There are also differences in morphology in that the third person singular present indicative ending in *Patience* is the predominantly northern ending -es, *quelles*, *quenches*, *sufferes*, whereas Chaucer's equivalent is the southern ending -eth. Finally there are differences in vocabulary which relate to the different dialects of their authors. As a more northerly text *Patience* includes a greater proportion of words derived from Old Norse. Some of these are open-class words, such as *heþyng* (ON *hæþing*), where Chaucer would use *scorn*, or *ylle* (ON *illr*), where Chaucer's equivalent would be *evil*. In Chaucer's works these words appear only in the northern dialect speech in the *Reeve's Tale*, demonstrating that Chaucer considered them to be northernisms. Borrowing from Old Norse was not limited to open-class words like these but also included pronouns, adverbs and parts of the verb 'to be', as shown by the following examples in the above passage: *ser* 'various' (ON *sér*), *arn* (ON *eru*). The third person plural pronoun *thay* is also of Old Norse origin, but this form is paralleled in Chaucer's dialect; neither Chaucer nor the *Gawain*-poet has adopted the forms *their*, *them* (see below).

Present-day attitudes to dialect use often stigmatise non-standard varieties in some way; it is important to realise that these social stereotypes are comparatively recent developments and that such attitudes to regional variation are not found in Middle English (Machan 2003). The *Gawain*-poet may have written in a north-western dialect, but his works are no less sophisticated than those of London poets such as Gower and Chaucer. Middle English writers were aware of dialect differences, though comparatively few make overt reference to them. Those writers who do refer to their dialect, such as the Canterbury monk Dan Michel who described his work *Ayenbite of Inwyt* (1340) as written in the 'Engliss of Kent', or the fifteenth-century friar Osbern Bokenham who wrote in 'Suffolk speche', make no apology for using dialect. The best-known evidence for awareness of dialect distinctions in this period is Chaucer's depiction of Northern dialect in the speech of the two Cambridge students in the *Reeve's Tale*, John and Aleyn, a dialect that reflects their origins 'fer in the North' (Tolkien 1934). It is easy for modern readers to assume that Chaucer's use of the northern dialect was intended to portray the students as uncouth and ignorant, but this assumption is based on modern dialect stereotypes and overlooks the fact that they are clearly intended to be of a higher social class and intellect than the miller, and that it is the students who outwit the miller in the tale's conclusion. It is important also to recognise that this imitation of northern dialect is not entirely consistent, but is limited to a number of salient features which give a flavour of the dialect (Horobin 2001). Here is an extract of a speech by one of the students, John, addressed to the miller Symkyn:

> 'Symond,' quod John, 'by God, nede has na peer.
> <u>Hym boes</u> serve hymself that has na <u>swayn</u>,   *he must; servant*
> Or elles he is a fool, as clerkes sayn.
> Oure manciple, I <u>hope</u> he wil be deed,   *think*
> Swa werkes ay the <u>wanges</u> in his heed;   *back teeth*
> And <u>forthy</u> is I come, and <u>eek</u> Alayn,   *therefore, also*
> To grynde oure corn and carie it <u>ham</u> agayn;   *home*
> I pray yow spede us <u>heythen</u> that ye may.'   *hence]*
> (A 4026–4033)

This short extract contains a number of the dialect features used by Chaucer to signal the differences between the southern and northern varieties. First we see the use of the long *a* sound in words like *na, swa, ham* where the southern dialect would have a long *o* sound, eg *no, so, home*. The construction 'I is', rather than 'I am', is a feature of northern grammar in this period, and the <-es> endings of the singular and plural forms of the present tense are also northern features. There are also a number of words of Old Norse derivation, like *swayn*, meaning 'servant', and *heythen*, meaning 'hence'. Another northern dialect word is the verb *warkes*, meaning 'aches', a usage which survives into the modern northern dialect. The use of the verb *hope* to mean 'think' rather than 'wish' in this context: i.e. 'I think our Manciple will die', rather than 'I wish him dead', is another northernism which produces a rather subtle joke.

I have said that Chaucer wrote in the London dialect of Middle English but even this is misleading in implying a single, coherent linguistic variety. The late Middle English period was a time of considerable social and geographical mobility and the fourteenth century witnessed large-scale immigration from the provinces into London. As a result London became a centre of considerable dialectal diversity, with Londoners adopting many linguistic features employed by immigrant speakers (Burnley 1983; Horobin 2003). A comparison of some of the features employed by Chaucer as northernisms in the Reeve's Tale with later varieties of London English makes clear these changes. Following the influx of northern speakers into London in the late fourteenth century, the London dialect adopted a number of northern dialect features. For instance, the third person plural pronouns *they*, *their*, *them*, derived from Old Norse, first appeared in Middle English circa 1200 in the East Midlands as a result of contact with Norse-speaking settlers. By the mid-fourteenth century the nominative pronoun *they* had been adopted in London where it was used alongside the OE derived forms *her* and *hem*. So Chaucer used *they*, *her*, *hem*, only using *their* and *them* in his portrayal of northern dialect. But fifteenth-century manuscripts of Chaucer's poetry frequently employ *their* and *them* throughout, showing how these two forms were gradually integrated into London English so that a previously northern feature came to be accepted in the south. Changes like this do not occur overnight and there must have been a considerable period during which both forms, *her/their* and *hem/them*, were simply acceptable alternatives (Horobin 2003). This kind of variation is particularly useful for a poet in that it allows considerable flexibility. Poets like Chaucer were able to draw on variants like these to enable them to find rhyming alternatives. A good example of this is found in Chaucer's use of the third person singular present indicative ending -es. Chaucer's usual ending for this part of the verb is -eth, the typical southern form; that the -es ending was generally considered a northern form is shown by his use of this ending in the speech of the northern students in the *Reeve's Tale*. But Chaucer did also draw on this variant to provide himself with an alternative form of the verb in rhyme, as the following example from the *Book of the Duchess* shows:

> That never was founde, as it telles,
> Bord ne man, ne nothing elles.
> (*Book of the Duchess*, lines 73–4)

As well as grammatical variants such as those discussed above, London English also contained words derived from the northern dialects whose meanings overlapped with those used in southern varieties, providing further alternatives. A good example is the verb *callen* 'call' which is of Old Norse origin (ON *kalla*) and which is recorded earliest in Middle English in northern and eastern texts. The southern equivalent is the verb *clepen*, derived from OE *cleopian*, and this is the word that appears most commonly in Chaucer's works. Chaucer did know the verb *calle* but mostly used it in rhyme, typically with *alle*; the only instances of its use outside rhyme are in the northern dialect in the *Reeve's Tale*: 'For by that lord that called is Seint Jame' (A 4264). This distribution demonstrates that Chaucer considered *callen* a northern word but one which he was willing to draw on in certain rhyming contexts.

If we compare these restrictions in the use of Old Norse derived words like *them*, *their* and *callen* and the northern third person singular present indicative ending -es with the works of the *Gawain*-poet then we find some interesting differences. The *Gawain*-poet uses both *clepe* and *calle*, although *calle* is much the commoner of the two; while the -es ending is his regular form. But his usual forms of the oblique third person plural pronouns are *hem/hom* and *her/hor*. Like Chaucer he clearly knew the Old Norse derived pronouns and used *þayr* twice and *þayres* once in *Sir Gawain and the Green Knight*, although in his usage they are not dialectally marked. Just as the diversity of London English enabled Chaucer to draw upon variants in his poetry, so the *Gawain*-poet exploited variation available to him in his local dialect. For instance, his usual form of the feminine third person pronoun is *ho*, although on five occasions in *Sir Gawain* he used the more northerly form *scho*. Different forms of words with identical meanings were a useful resource for poets writing in the alliterative metre which demanded a large number of synonyms with different initial sounds. So the *Gawain*-poet drew upon both the Norse-derived verb *gyue* and the Old English-derived *yeue* in particular alliterative contexts. Where alliteration on the hard *g* sound (as in the PDE pronunciation of this word) was required the Norse forms were used, as in the use of *gif* in the following line: 'I schal gif hym of my gyft þys giserne ryche' (*Sir Gawain*, line 288). In the following example alliteration is on the *y* sound (as in PDE *yellow*) and so the Old English-derived form *ȝef* is selected: 'I ȝef yow me for on of yourez, if yowreself lykez' (*Sir Gawain*, line 1964).

As well as being able to draw upon different forms of words with similar meanings, the *Gawain*-poet also employed different pronunciations of the same word in certain rhyming contexts. A major north–south dialect distinction in Middle English was the pronunciation of the reflex of Old English long *a* sound in words like *home*, *stone* (OE *hām*, *stān*). In the southern dialects of Middle English this vowel was rounded and pronounced with the long *o* sound found in the Present Day English pronunciation of these words, whereas the northern dialects preserved an unrounded long *a* pronunciation. The *Gawain*-poet generally employs the southern pronunciation, as in the following example of *homes*: 'Langaberde in Lumbardie lyftes vp homes' (*Sir Gawain*, line 12). But the position of the poet's dialect, close to the border where the two pronunciations met, meant that he was able to draw upon the northern pronunciation as well. This was obviously less useful when writing alliterative metre, but of considerable value when the poet was composing rhyming verse, as in the bob and wheel of *Sir Gawain*. In the following example we see the poet drawing upon the northern pronunciation of *home* to enable a rhyme with *shame* and *game*:

> For schame!
> I com hider <u>sengel</u>, and sitte   *alone*
> To <u>lerne at</u> yow sum game;   *learn from*
> Dos, techez me of your wytte,
> Whil my lorde is fro hame.
>   (*Sir Gawain*, lines 1530–4)

Not all differences between the language of the *Gawain*-poet and Chaucer can be attributed to their different dialects. Another obvious difference between the works of these two contemporary poets concerns the metre in which they wrote. *Sir Gawain* is written in an alliterative metre which employed a distinctive lexicon upon which its practitioners drew. This specialised lexicon comprised numerous synonyms for certain key concepts, enabling the poet to employ a rich and varied lexis. Another important function of these synonyms was to allow a poet to draw upon synonymous words with different initial sounds, an important resource for a poet writing in a metre dependent upon alliteration. Examples of this rich store of synonyms include terms for 'man', which comprised words like *mon, kniȝt, noble, prince, burn, freke, gome, hathel, lede, renk, schalk, segge, wyȝe*. While such words were not regional but rather belonged to a particular stylistic register, the primarily western and northern distribution of alliterative verse meant that many of these specialised words would have been unfamiliar to southern and eastern audiences. It is presumably in recognition of this fact that William Langland made very little use of this vocabulary for his alliterative poem *Piers Plowman*, despite his own western origins (Turville-Petre 1977). While Langland's poem opens with the dreamer wandering over the Malvern Hills of Worcestershire, it shows considerable awareness of London life and its institutions. It is thought that Langland himself was resident in London while he worked on the B and C revisions, as is implied in passus V of the C version (Samuels 1985). The large number of surviving manuscripts of the poem, copied in a range of different dialects, demonstrates its widespread appeal and implies that Langland's decision to avoid specialised alliterative lexis was a sensible one. By contrast *Sir Gawain and the Green Knight*, *Winner and Waster*, *The Parliament of the Three Ages*, *The Alliterative Morte Arthure* and several other alliterative works survive in single copies, perhaps, though not necessarily, indicative of a more restricted audience. Further evidence of the perceived difficulties of alliterative vocabulary is found in the way that some scribes replaced such words when copying texts for a different audience. The London scribe Richard Frampton made numerous such replacements when he copied the alliterative *Siege of Jerusalem* into a manuscript intended for a London readership (Turville-Petre 1997).

The rhyming verse of London poets like Chaucer and Gower does not draw upon a specialised vocabulary such as that found in alliterative verse, but there is evidence of fine-grained stylistic connotations attached to some words that are particular to courtly verse of this kind. Donaldson has noted that the word *hende*, meaning 'noble', carried lowly connotations for Chaucer and is only applied to clerks and other characters of dubious moral or social standing (Donaldson 1970). But the *Gawain*-poet appears to have no such misgivings about this word, which he used as a noun to refer to both Gawain and the Pearl maiden (*Sir Gawain*, line 827; *Pearl* line 909). Another interesting example of a word that is stylistically marked in Chaucer's poetry is the word *lemman* 'lover', as is made clear by the narrator in the *Manciple's Tale*. In this tale the narrator refers to Phebus' wife's lover as her *lemman*, but then immediately retracts the word with the following elaborate apology:

> And so bifel, whan Phebus was absent,
> His wyf anon hath for hir lemman sent.
> Hir lemman? Certes, this is a <u>knavyssh</u> speche!   *churlish*
> <u>Foryeveth</u> it me, and that I yow biseche.   *forgive*
> The wise Plato seith, as ye may rede,
> The word moot nede accorde with the dede.
> If men shal telle proprely a thyng.
> The word moot cosyn be to the werkyng.
> I am a <u>boystous</u> man, right thus seye I: *plain*
> Ther nys no difference, trewely,
> Bitwixe a wyf that is of heigh degree,
> If of hir body dishonest she bee,
> And a povre wenche, oother than this-
> If it so be they werke bothe amys-
> But that the <u>gentile</u>, in <u>estaat</u> above,   *noble; rank*
> She shal be <u>cleped</u> his lady, as in love;   *called*
> And for that oother is a povre womman,
> She shal be cleped his wenche or his lemman.
>   (H 203–20)

Here the narrator is making the point that, while *lemman* and *lady* may have the same referent, there is a major difference in their connotations. The word *lady* is used to signal a woman of high social class, while *lemman* is suitable for a lover of low social standing. It is therefore inappropriate to use the words *lemman* or *wenche* to refer to a noble woman, who must be referred to using a more elevated term such as *lady*. This usage is reinforced by the appearances of these words elsewhere in Chaucer's works. The word *lemman* is used by the miller's daughter in the *Reeve's Tale*, by the parson to describe the concubines of lecherous priests, by the steward who threatens to rape Constance, and to refer to extra-marital lovers in the *Summoner's Tale*. The *Gawain*-poet by contrast appears not to have considered the word to have been marked in such a way, and even uses it to refer to Christ:

> If þou wyl <u>knaw</u> what kyn he be,   *know*
> My Lombe, my Lorde, my dere <u>juelle</u>,   *jewel*
> My <u>ioy</u>, my blys, my lemman fre,   *joy*
>   (*Pearl*, lines 794–6)

The art of correct speech, which included the appropriate use of vocabulary, was of great importance during the Middle Ages and this is reflected in the language of its poetry (Burnley 1998). Speech was considered to be an outward reflection of inner personality, so that someone of noble breeding would use more elevated diction than a peasant. The correct observance of the codes of polite speech was therefore an important way of signalling a sound moral character, as is indicated by the narrator's statement about the purity of the Knight's speech in the *General Prologue*: 'He nevere yet no vileynye ne sayde' (A 70). This comment rests on the assumption that the purity of the knight's speech is a reflection of his moral purity. A similar assumption lies behind the identification of the dreamer in the *Romaunt of the Rose* as a member of the gentle class on the basis of the courtliness of his diction:

> I love thee bothe and preise,
> Sen that thyn aunswar doth me ease,   *since*
> For thou answerid so curteisly.
> For now I wot wel uttirly   *know*
> That thou art gentyll by thi speche.
> For though a man fer wolde seche,   *far; seek*
> He shulde not fynden, in certeyn,
> No sich answer of no vileyn;   *such; peasant*
> For sich a word ne myghte nought
> Isse out of a vilayns thought.   *issue from*
> (*Romaunt of the Rose*, lines 1983–92)

These conventions of courtly speech were part of a social register rather than a regional one, so that we find similar attitudes in the works of the *Gawain*-poet; perhaps most apparent from the association of Gawain's reputation with the arts of noble speech. On his arrival at Bertilak's court the noble men and women are excited by the prospect of witnessing first-hand Gawain's legendary eloquence:

> Now schal we semlych se sleʒtez of þewez   *demonstrations, courteous manners*
> And þe teccheles termes of talkyng noble. *spotless*
> (*Sir Gawain*, lines 916–17)

Thus, despite his regional origins, the *Gawain*-poet was equally conscious of the importance of using the socially appropriate terms when referring to elevated concerns such as the arts of love, chivalry, hunting and so on. An important aspect of this noble speech is the use of correct terminology, or, to use the Middle English word, *termes* (Burnley 1977). The importance of correct terminology as an index of social sophistication is apparent from the highly technical description of the arming of Gawain:

> Þe stif mon steppez þeron, and þe stel hondelez,   *armour*
> Dubbed in a dublet of a dere tars,   *dressed; jacket; rich fabric*
> And syþen a crafty capados, closed aloft,   *afterwards; skilfully made hood*

Þat wyth a bryȝt <u>blaunner</u> was bounden withinne.   *fur*
Þenne set þay þe <u>sabatounz</u> vpon þe <u>segge</u> fotez,   *steel shoes; knight*
His legez lapped in stel with luflych <u>greuez</u>,   *shin armour*
With <u>polaynez</u> piched þerto, policed ful clene,   *knee armour*
Aboute his knez <u>knaged</u> wyth knotez of golde;   *fastened*
Queme <u>quyssewes</u> þen, þat coyntlych closed   *fine thigh pieces*
His thik <u>brawen</u> þyȝez, with <u>þwonges</u> to tachched;   *muscular; laces*
And syþen þe <u>brawden bryné</u> of bryȝt stel ryngez   *embroidered mail coat*
<u>Vmbeweued</u> þat <u>wyȝ</u> vpon <u>wlonk</u> stuffe,   *enveloped; knight, splendid*
And wel <u>bornyst</u> <u>brace</u> vpon his boþe armes,   *burnished; arm pieces*
With gode <u>cowters</u> and gay, and glouez of plate,   *elbow pieces*
And alle þe godlych gere þat hym gayn schulde
þat tyde;

(Sir Gawain, lines 570–585)

The majority of the specialised terms employed in this description is of French origin; in the above extract we find *dublet* 'jacket', *capados* 'hood', *blaunner* 'fur', *sabatounz* 'steel shoes', *polaynez* 'armour for knees', *quyssewes* 'thigh pieces', *brace* 'pair of arm pieces', *cowters* 'elbow pieces'. The use of correct jargon to recount aristocratic pursuits is also found in descriptions of feasting, greeting, hunting and love-making in the poem. Even the 'breaking', or cutting open, of the deer was carried out 'derely [...] as þe dede askez', gracefully, in the appropriate manner, further demonstrating the poet's obsession with correct procedure. The close association between the deed and its related vocabulary is shown by the density of specialised French-derived lexis used to describe the disembowelment: *gargulun* 'throat', *avanters* 'part of the numbles', *haunche* 'haunch', *noumbles* 'offal' (*Sir Gawain*, lines 1325–1352). The large number of French-derived words in these passages reveals the extent to which Middle English was indebted to the French language. The height of this process of lexical borrowing was the mid to late fourteenth century, the period in which the major Middle English poets were all active. It is therefore not surprising that each of these poets used considerable numbers of words of French origin. But more interesting than the sheer number of French words is the kind of words and how they are used. French culture was particularly admired for aristocratic pursuits such as hunting, music, fashion, cooking, dance, love-making and science, and it is in these areas that the largest number of borrowings occurred. We have seen how the *Gawain*-poet drew upon specialised terms borrowed from French for descriptions of courtly pursuits in *Sir Gawain*. Chaucer refers to terms belonging to a range of other fields: the terms of love, philosophy, astrology, law, alchemy, the church and medicine. These specialised registers drew heavily upon French vocabulary, as is apparent from the alchemical terms used by the Canon's Yeoman, *orpyment*, *squames*, *curcurbites*, *alambikes*, or the Franklin's alchemical terms, *tables Tolletanes* and *proporcioneles convenientz*.

Noble speech was not simply a matter of using the correct jargon. How a person spoke, and how he or she addressed another person, were often perceived as being as important as what was said. Once again the model is French practice and French influenced the pragmatic structure of Middle English as well as its lexicon. This is particularly apparent in a change that took place in the functions of the second person pronouns: *thou* and *ye*. In Old English the distinction between these two was solely one of number: OE *þū* (ME *thou*) was the singular form and *gē* (ME *ye*) was the plural form. French differs from this practice in maintaining a pragmatic distinction in the use of the singular and plural pronouns when used to address an individual. In Modern French the plural *vous* is used to indicate respect and formality, while the singular form, *tu*, is reserved to signal familiarity, equality or a lack of respect. The same situation obtained in the Middle Ages, and the influence of French upon polite usage in Middle English led to the adoption of this practice. As a result many Middle English writers employed *ye* as a polite form and *thou* as a form encoding intimacy or lack of respect. Such usage is particularly associated with romances where it became conventional for noble men and women to address each other using the plural pronoun, even in contexts where the power in the relationship was extremely one-sided. When the marquis Walter sets out the terms of the agreement by which he is willing to marry the humble Griselda in an extremely unromantic marriage proposal in Chaucer's *Clerk's Tale*, he addresses her using the polite form:

> I seye this: be ye redy with good herte
> To al my <u>lust</u>, and that I frely may,   *desire*
> As me best thynketh, do yow laughe or <u>smerte</u>,   *suffer*
> And nevere ye to <u>grucche</u> it, nyght ne day?   *complain*
> And <u>eek</u> whan I sey 'ye,' ne sey nat 'nay,'   *also*
> Neither by word ne frownyng contenance?
> Swere this, and heere I swere oure alliance.
>
> (E 351–7)

This polite usage may be contrasted with the same speaker's direct and disrespectful manner of addressing Griselda's father Janicula, where Walter's social superiority is clearly marked:

> Janicula, I neither may ne kan
> Lenger the <u>plesance</u> of myn herte hyde.   *pleasure*
> If that thou <u>vouche sauf</u>, what so bityde,   *agree*
> Thy doghter wol I take, <u>er</u> that I wende,   *before*
> As for my wyf, unto hir lyves ende.
>
> (E 304–8)

Where two lovers were of an equal social status the plural form was generally employed, as is true of the two lovers throughout Chaucer's *Troilus and Criseyde*. The switch from *ye* to *thou* could, however, be used as a means of signalling moments of particular intimacy, as in the sole use of the singular form by Troilus when pledging his commitment to his lady: 'For I am thyn, by God and by my trouthe!' (3.1512). As well as using the correct pronoun of address, polite usage was characterised by the use of elevated forms of address. In his advice to Troilus when writing his first letter to Criseyde Pandarus emphasises the importance of addressing his lover in suitably elevated forms of address. The narrator's summary of the letter's content that follows lists a number of lover's terms used by Troilus to address Criseyde:

> First he gan hire his righte lady calle,
> His hertes lif, his <u>lust</u>, his sorwes <u>leche</u>,   *desire; physician*
> His blisse, and <u>ek</u> thise other termes alle   *also*
> That in <u>swich</u> cas thise loveres alle seche;   *such*
>   (2.1065–8)

A further feature of polite usage is concerned with how the message itself is conveyed, and with the avoidance of direct statement or coercion. Just as polite address must include appropriately elevated forms of address and correct vocabulary, it should also avoid placing obligations upon the addressee. A good example of this is found in *The Canterbury Tales* where the host, Harry Bailly, calls upon the prioress to tell her tale as part of the storytelling competition. Even though she is bound by the agreement established in the General Prologue, the host is extremely careful not to place the prioress under any obligation. Rather than simply asking her directly: 'Will you tell the next tale?', he employs an elaborate and highly decorous circumlocution. In order to avoid any direct confrontation in which the prioress might feel constrained to agree, the host couches his request in a series of conditional and subjunctive clauses so as not to offend her by making a demand that is against her will: 'by youre leve', 'if so were that ye wolde'. The actual request is postponed until the very end, and when it comes it is made in formal and elevated language, using French vocabulary, *vouche sauf*, and suitably respectful forms of address, *ye, my lady deere*: 'Now wol ye vouche sauf, my lady deere?'. By showing considerable concern for the prioress's wishes, Harry Bailly avoids any attempt to coerce her or place a demand upon her, despite the fact that she is bound by the terms of the contest to tell a total of four tales over the course of the journey:

> 'My lady Prioresse, by youre leve,
> So that I <u>wiste</u> I sholde yow nat greve,   *knew*
> I wolde <u>demen</u> that ye tellen sholde   *judge*
> A tale next, if so were that ye wolde.
> Now wol ye <u>vouche sauf</u>, my lady deere?'   *agree*
>   (B2 1637–41)

The same principles of noble speech that we have observed here are also observed by Gawain, highlighting once again the two poets' shared understanding of the rules of courtly speech despite their differing dialectal backgrounds. The most famous example of Gawain's exploitation of these linguistic devices is found in the speech in which he takes over the beheading game from Arthur (Spearing 1964). This is an extremely delicate speech; Gawain wants to relieve Arthur of the Green Knight's challenge, but at the same time must avoid implying that he is not up to the job, or that he himself would be a better choice. To achieve this delicate balance Gawain begins by arguing that the challenge is foolish and beneath Arthur. By contrast with the worthy king Gawain is the lowliest of the knights, and his death would cause the least loss. But just as important as what he says is the manner in which he speaks. Just as Harry Bailly avoids placing the prioress under any direct obligation, so Gawain must be careful to appear to be acting according to the king's wishes and under his command. So he begins not by asking permission to get up, but by begging Arthur to command him to get up. He also asks the Queen's permission and hopes that it will not actively cause her displeasure if he does so. As with Harry Bailly's speech, the actual request is delayed by the intrusion of subordinate clauses claiming that the challenge is too foolish for Arthur, and that, since he asked first, Gawain should take it on: 'syþen þis note is so nys þat noʒt hit yow falles'/'I haue frayned hit at yow fyrst'. He further delays the request by heaping on more qualifications and conditions concerning the acceptance of his request, 'if I carp not comlyly', 'I hope', 'I wot'. The avoidance of direct statement is also apparent in this elaborate request, which employs conditionals and subjunctives such as 'Wolde ye', 'I wolde com', 'me þink hit':

'Wolde ʒe, <u>worþilych</u> lorde,' quoþ Wawan to þe kyng,	*worthy*
'Bid me <u>boʒe</u> fro þis benche, and stonde by yow þere,	*leave*
Þat I wythoute <u>vylanye</u> myʒt voyde þis table,	*discourtesy*
And þat my <u>legge</u> lady lyked not ille,	*liege*
I wolde com to your counseyl bifore your cort <u>ryche</u>.	*noble*
For me þink hit not <u>semly</u>, as hit is soþ knawen,	*appropriate*
Þer such an <u>askyng</u> is <u>heuened</u> so hyʒe in your sale,	*request, raised*
Þaʒ ʒe ʒourself be <u>talenttyf</u>, to take hit to yourseluen,	*desirous*
Whil mony so bolde yow aboute vpon bench sytten,	
Þat vnder heuen I <u>hope</u> non <u>haʒerer</u> of wylle,	*think; higher*
Ne better bodyes on <u>bent</u> þer <u>baret</u> is rered.	*field; fighting*
I am þe wakkest, I wot, and of wyt feblest,	
And lest <u>lur</u> of my lyf, <u>quo laytes þe soþe</u> –	*loss; who wants to*
	know the truth
Bot for as much as ʒe ar myn <u>em</u> I am only to prayse,	*uncle*
No <u>bounté</u> bot your blod I in my bodé knowe;	*worth*
And syþen þis <u>note</u> is so <u>nys</u> þat noʒt hit yow falles,	*business; foolish*
And I haue <u>frayned</u> hit at yow fyrst, foldez hit to me;	*requested*
And if I <u>carp</u> not <u>comlyly</u>, let alle þis cort rych	*speak; appropriately*
<u>bout</u> blame.'	*without*

(*Sir Gawain*, lines 343–361)

We get a good sense of the various features that make up this elaborate and decorous style by contrasting it with the speech of the Green Knight. Where Gawain's speech employs subordination to avoid speaking directly, the Green Knight's speeches employ coordination to achieve a deliberate directness and bluntness. Where Gawain's speech is characterised by its use of conditionals and verbs in the subjunctive mood, indicating uncertainty and hesitancy, the Green Knight employs the indicative and imperative moods, commanding Gawain to fulfil his obligation to seek out the Green Chapel to receive the return blow:

Loke, Gawan, þou be <u>grayþe</u> to go as þou <u>hettez</u>,	*ready; promise*
And <u>layte</u> as <u>lelly</u> til þou me, <u>lude</u>, fynde,	*seek; loyally; knight*
As þou hatz hette in þis halle, <u>herande</u> þise knyȝtes;	*hearing*
To þe grene chapel þou chose, I charge þe, to <u>fotte</u>	*receive*
Such a <u>dunt</u> as þou hatz dalt – disserued þou habbez	*blow*
To be <u>ȝederly</u> ȝolden on Nw ȝeres morn.	*promptly*

(*Sir Gawain*, lines 448–453)

There are also important distinctions in the forms of address used in this speech and that of Gawain. Where Gawain consistently addressed Arthur using the respectful plural pronoun, *ȝe, yow*, the Green Knight employs the familiar and disrespectful singular pronoun *þou, þe*. Gawain avoids directly addressing the king and queen by name, preferring respectful and honourable titles: 'worþilych lorde', 'my legge lady'. By contrast the Green Knight addresses Gawain directly by his name, 'Gawan', and then simply as *lude*; he makes no attempt to soften these abrupt and insolent forms of address by couching them with personal pronouns or adjectives, such as 'my worthy Gawain'.

Such examples serve to show how an understanding of the pragmatic conventions that underlie Middle English literary writing is essential to a full appreciation of its nuances of meaning. As we have seen, Middle English was characterised by considerable variation, in spelling, pronunciation, grammar, lexis and pragmatics, all of which could be exploited in a range of different ways, metrical, rhythmical, dialectal, stylistic. It is only by understanding the ways in which the language varied during this period, and the literary and sociolinguistic implications of this variation, that we can fully appreciate the ways in which the language and its rich resources were exploited by Middle English literary writers.

References and Further Reading

Benskin, M. (2004). Chancery standard. In C. J. Kay, C. Hough and I. Wotherspoon (eds). *New Perspectives on English Historical Linguistics: Selected Papers from 12 ICEHL. Volume II: Lexis and Transmission* (pp. 1–40) Amsterdam: Benjamins.

Blake, N. F. (ed.) (1992). *The Cambridge History of the English Language. Volume II 1066–1476*. Cambridge: Cambridge University Press.

Burnley, J. D. (1977). Chaucer's termes. *Yearbook of English Studies*, 7, 53–67.

Burnley, J. D. (1979). *Chaucer's Language and the Philosophers' Tradition*. Cambridge: D. S. Brewer.

Burnley, J. D. (1983). *A Guide to Chaucer's Language*. Basingstoke: Macmillan. (Repr. (1988). *The Language of Chaucer*. Basingstoke: Macmillan.)

Burnley, J. D. (1998). *Courtliness and Literature in Medieval England*. Harlow: Longman.

Donaldson, E. T. (1970). Idiom of popular poetry in 'The Miller's Tale'. In *Speaking of Chaucer* (pp. 13–29). London: Athlone.

Fisher, J. H. (1996). *The Emergence of Standard English*. Lexington: University of Kentucky Press.

Horobin, S. (2001). J. R. R. Tolkien as a philologist: a reconsideration of the northernisms in Chaucer's 'Reeve's Tale'. *English Studies*, 82, 97–105.

Horobin, S. (2003). *The Language of the Chaucer Tradition*. Cambridge: D. S. Brewer.

Horobin, S. (2006). *Chaucer's Language*. Basingstoke: Palgrave Macmillan.

Horobin, S. and J. J. Smith (2002). *An Introduction to Middle English*. Edinburgh: Edinburgh University Press.

Machan, T. W. (2003). *English in the Middle Ages*. Oxford: Oxford University Press.

Rothwell, W. (1994). The trilingual England of Geoffrey Chaucer. *Studies in the Age of Chaucer*, 16, 45–67.

Samuels, M. L. (1963). Some applications of Middle English dialectology. *English Studies*, 44, 81–94. Repr. in M. Laing (ed.) (1989). *Middle English Dialectology: Essays on some Principles and Problems* (pp. 64–80). Aberdeen: Aberdeen University Press.

Samuels, M. L. (1985). Langland's dialect. *Medium Ævum*, 54, 232–47. (Reprinted in J. J. Smith (ed.) (1988). *The English of Chaucer and his Contemporaries* (pp. 70–85). Aberdeen: Aberdeen University Press.)

Smith, J. J. (1996). *An Historical Study of English: Function, Form and Change*. London: Routledge.

Spearing, A. C. (1964). *Criticism and Medieval Poetry*. London: Edward Arnold.

Tolkien, J. R. R. (1934). Chaucer as a philologist: The Reeve's Tale. *Transactions of the Philological Society*, 1–70.

Trotter, D. A. (ed.) (2000). *Multilingualism in Later Medieval Britain*. Cambridge: D. S. Brewer.

Turville-Petre, T. (1977). *The Alliterative Revival*. Cambridge: D. S. Brewer.

Turville-Petre, T. (1996). *England the Nation: Language, Literature, and National Identity, 1290–1340*. Oxford: Clarendon Press.

Turville-Petre, T. (1997). The 'Pearl'-poet in his 'fayre regioun'. In J. Burrow, A. Minnis, C. C. Morse and T. Turville-Petre (eds). *Essays on Ricardian Literature in Honour of J. A. Burrow* (pp. 276–294). Oxford: Clarendon Press.

11

Middle English Manuscripts and Readers

Ralph Hanna

Nearly all medieval texts – and Middle English verse is no exception – come down to us solely through the manuscript record. Middle English poems were originally disseminated through individually produced handwritten copies, most usually made on animal skin rather than paper (although use of the latter material became common in the fifteenth century). This procedure for circulating and consuming literary materials implies various forms of 'textual culture' quite foreign to our modern behaviours. The modes by which texts were produced, communicated and used by their original audiences thus contrast strikingly with modern practices. This essay will develop some of these contrasts, always proposing problems, rather than offering a definitive guide for engaging with the very different textual practices that mark medieval poems and their original use.[1]

To understand what medieval textual culture was like, one must forget a number of assumptions we make, often unconsciously, about the business of 'reading literature'. Today, we assume that, when we read poetry, we are all reading the same text, often in a prescribed version, the recommended 'set' texts of university curricula or the 'standard editions' produced for scholarly consumption. This set or standard text has been fixed by being set in print-type, and it has been quite extensively mediated to facilitate modern use. The text comes with capitalisation and punctuation and, usually, if it is a medieval text, is accompanied by extensive lexical glosses and annotation provided by a scholarly editor. This annotation includes notes explaining references most readers are not supposed to know for themselves – for example, who is the 'Gaufred, deere maister soverayn' addressed in Chaucer's *Nun's Priest's Tale*, line 3548?

In reading texts like these, we further implicitly assume that what we read has transhistorical value. In spite of trenchant criticisms of such a notion, university syllabi are still established to present 'great books' or 'central/important texts' or 'texts of outstanding interest'. And in the early twenty-first century, when publishers' commitment to medieval topics has declined, those texts given 'standard' forms and made the subject of most critical discussions equally must be those of wide appeal. Generally speaking, today we read from a canon of great poets and/or great literary works.

Moreover, the modern print circulation of medieval poetry is as a sequence of discrete texts. For 'major authors' or 'major works', we turn to single text volumes: *The Riverside Chaucer*, Tolkien and Gordon's *Sir Gawain and the Green Knight*, editions of *Piers Plowman* by Pearsall or Schmidt, for example. Alternatively, we have recourse to anthologies, collected volumes that implicitly promise that we are receiving a carefully selected 'best of', whether it is the best of a specific genre (Thorlac Turville-Petre's *Alliterative Poetry*) or the best illustrations of some poetic continuity (Derek Pearsall's *Chaucer to Spenser*). Only occasionally and often accidentally do the presentations to which we are accustomed overlap with something resembling the original circulation of medieval poems. One good example – all the texts of a single medieval book presented in their sequence – might be the useful alternative to the Tolkien–Gordon *Gawain*, Malcolm Andrew and Ronald Waldron's *Poems of the Pearl Manuscript*. But this edition is scarcely so different from *The Riverside Chaucer* as it might appear, since the editors might well have called the book *Poems of the Pearl* [or *Gawain*] *Poet*.

These literary behaviours, which we take so much for granted, have been constructed by print itself, and by the modern institution of Studying Literature, which seeks to accommodate or assimilate medieval poetry to the forms of more recent culture. Chaucer, for example, should, as a great English poet, look as if he could sit on a shelf cheek by jowl (or cover by cover) with other Greats, Shakespeare or Milton or Wordsworth, for example. But the medieval situation in which Chaucer wrote and in which his works circulated was quite different. Rather than being machine-produced, each of his poems, like all other medieval texts, circulated in an individually made, hand-produced book.

Perhaps the easiest way to start understanding such a hand-made book is to look at a facsimile, a photographic (or now digitised) image of a single manuscript page. For these purposes, I will refer to Figure 11.1.[2] First, this book is hand-written (as were all English books until Caxton brought the printing press to England about 1475). This example has been written quite professionally, in a relatively formal and readily legible set hand (although many individuals who were not professional writers made books for their private use, sometimes with varying degrees of legibility).

But, however clear the script, certain aspects of the presentation will probably be confusing. First of all, the text far from always conforms to our modern habits of word-division. The scribe writes 'whatsoever' as if it is three spaced words in line 14; on the other hand, he twice writes our 'or to' as if a single word (lines 21, 22), and twice fuses the article 'a' with the following adjective ('aparfite', lines 25, 29–30). More disquietingly, his alphabet includes letter-forms we no longer use, ones often silently 'normalised' to modern equivalents in print editions. He routinely uses the letter þ 'thorn', where we would write 'th' ('þe preyer' in line 1 or 'þee' [thee] in line 5). Another obsolete letter, shaped like the numeral 3, also appears for our 'y' ('3ift' [gift] line 7, '3it' [yet] line 20).[3] Further, as is noticeable from some of the examples I have cited, the scribe frequently refuses to write words in full, but has recourse to

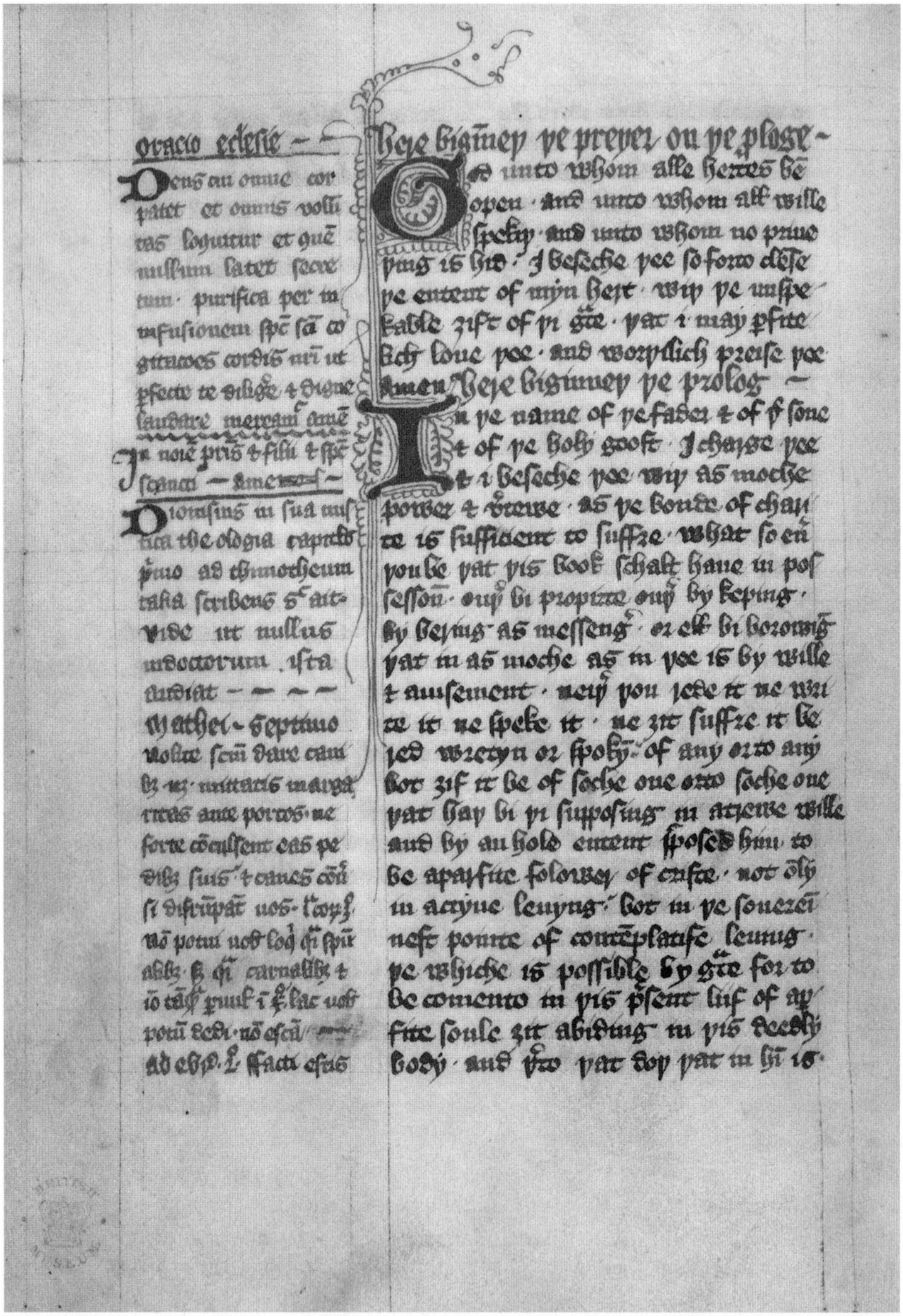

Figure 11.1 *The Cloud of Unknowing*, with continuous marginal gloss in Latin, s.xv[1]. British Library, MS Harley 674, fol. 17v.
© British Library.

abbreviations. For instance, the raised hook at the end of 'whatsoever' in line 14 means 'supply an "er" here', and the cross-stroke on the foot of the 'p' of 'a parfite' in line 29 indicates 'give me an "er" or an "ar" here'.[4]

But details like this represent only the beginning of our possible estrangement from a text in manuscript. Unlike modern English, Middle English has no standard spelling system, and scribes often provide, for no apparently good reason, more than one spelling for the same word. In the rubrics (headings written in red) here, for example, the scribe has both 'prologe' and 'prolog'. Moreover, spelling is not just individually idiosyncratic; acceptable spellings vary by location, and familiar words will frequently appear in forms not immediately recognisable. Northerners might employ 'swilk' or 'slike', for example,[5] while Chaucer generally uses the slightly more transparent 'swiche' – all to represent modern 'such'. And while the scribe will have done the best he could to reproduce whatever copy he had, transmitted medieval texts often vary from each other and frequently include sporadic unintelligible bits that rebuff even experienced scholars.

Figure 11.2 shows another manuscript of Middle English verse, a copy of Chaucer's *Troilus and Criseyde*. This will reveal other commonplace features of texts circulating in manuscript. One immediately evident absence is that of punctuation.[6] It appears minimally here, and then in but a single form, the solidus or virgula '/' at the middle of many lines (for example, lines 2, 12, 13, 16, 17). This mark, which is usually of about the same force as a modern comma, appears in circumstances where we might find a comma not emphatic enough, and its force is less grammatical (as our punctuation is) than metrical; it typically marks a caesura or major pause within a verse line.[7] Unlike the example with which I began, with its explanatory Latin, the verse text is provided with minimal explanation. Here, two later hands have offered marginal marking to set off Troilus's famous first song; otherwise about all one can expect are rare interlinear glosses (frequently in Latin) to clarify spellings otherwise ambiguous.[8]

Such direction as one gets is, like the punctuation, mainly metrical. Like many later Middle English copyists, this one emphatically ensures that the reader responds to the form of Chaucer's elegant rime royale stanza. He sets each example off with a blank line (a serious addition to the cost of the book, since these lines eventually add up to extra leaves, about three pages simply in Book I of *Troilus*, for example). Further, stanzas are not just separated but have additional double marking – alternating red and blue paragraph signs (here not just at the head of the first line, as is more usual, but ornamentally extended for the full duration of each stanza) and joining braces on each side of the writing area. (Another, more fastidious scribe might have arranged red lines on the right side of the text-column to bracket Chaucer's repeated rhymes and thereby elucidate the complex structure of the rime royal stanza.)[9]

Finally, to return momentarily to the example with which I began, individual texts or their parts may be introduced by headings (often in red, hence 'rubrics', from the Latin word 'ruber'). This is the only thing in a medieval manuscript that even approximates our modern title-page. But these headings may provide only generic designations of subjects ('A noble song of X', for example), rather than what we would consider a

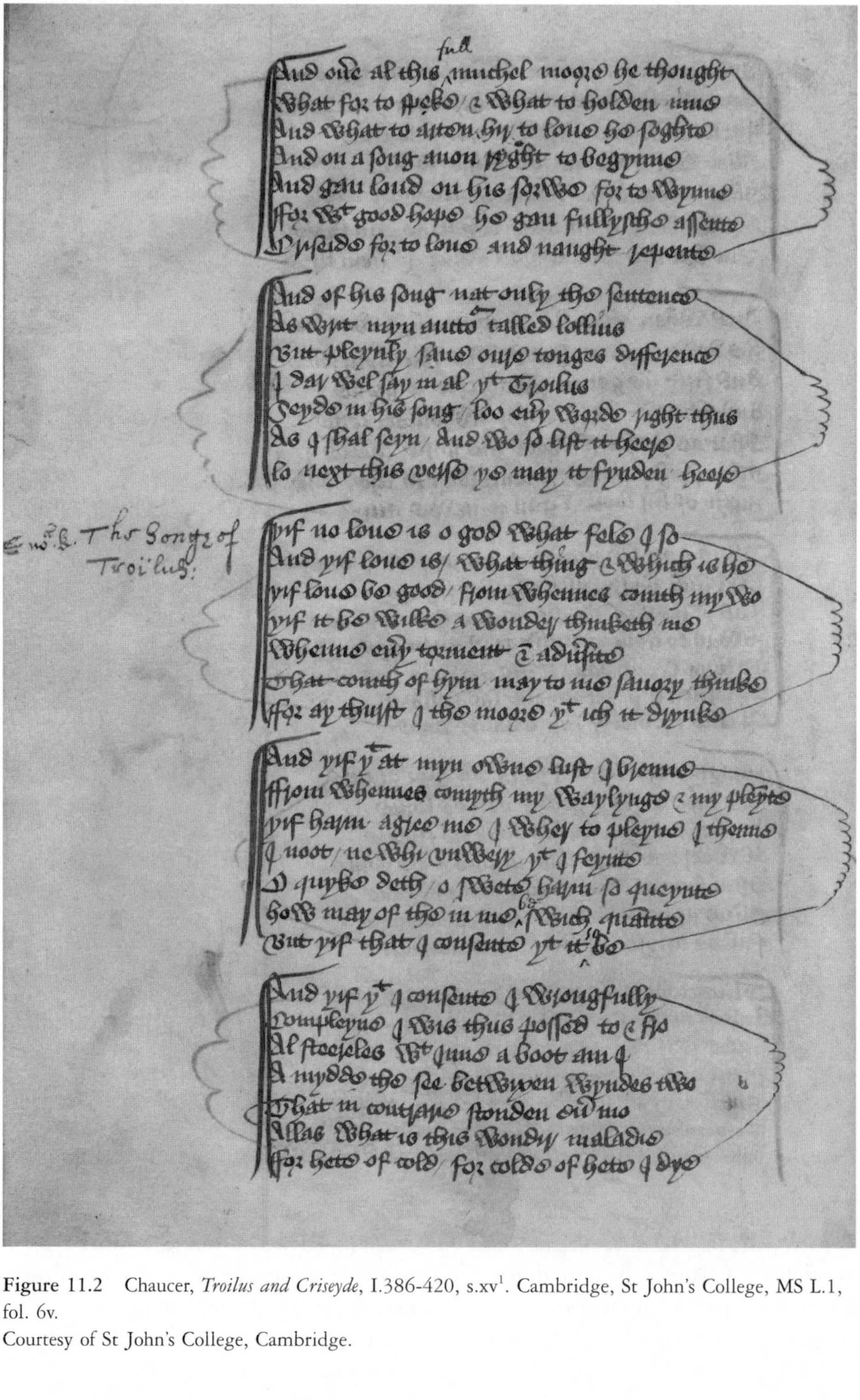

Figure 11.2   Chaucer, *Troilus and Criseyde*, I.386-420, s.xv¹. Cambridge, St John's College, MS L.1, fol. 6v.

Courtesy of St John's College, Cambridge.

proper title. In manuscript rubrics, the author is frequently unmentioned, and even when ascriptions to an author occur, their value may be dubious. Northern scribes, for example, are particularly fond of telling readers that virtually any devotional text, whether in prose or verse, was written by the local hermit/sage Richard Rolle.

Further, although the book-producers responsible for copying Chaucer (or any other medieval author) certainly had to obtain a pre-existing copy of his works to reproduce, and although some of them certainly knew other persons engaged in precisely the same procedures, each volume remained unique. Unlike modern booksellers with their standing stock of volumes for sale, a possibility foreign to manuscript culture until just before the era of print, medieval handwritten books were customarily 'bespoke'.[10] As a luxury item requiring some substantial expenditure, each book formed a separate 'special order'.

In such a situation, every book was the product of precise and specific negotiations between the book-producers and their client. These would have extended so far as to stipulate the extent of decoration or whether the book was supposed to be provided with a binding. Each choice would potentially add to the cost of the finished item, and, given that different portions of book-production might rely on a different range of specialist crafts, would increase the number of labouring hands involved in the work.[11]

Quite in contrast to the modern assumption of a general community of readers, all treated to the same text, every manuscript volume reflects an individual situation. Its production was inspired by the tastes and desires of a single reader, the person who commissioned the book; these individual choices have become instantiated through this individual's temporary employment of or partnership with a potentially diverse array of book artisans. Thus, the expectation that 'Chaucer' could always mean the same thing or appear in the same way (the assumption one makes in taking up *The Riverside Chaucer*) did not obtain in the Middle Ages.

Moreover, 'bespoke' books may potentially present even a single page of a medieval poet in a manner thoroughly unique. We assume that when we read a printed text, we are reading the same words as everyone else. No medieval reader could have assumed so (and indeed, may not even have wished to do so). First of all, print culture has increasingly enforced quite a stringent sense of accuracy in reproducing texts, thoroughly foreign to the Middle Ages. In the manuscript period, scribes do not usually seem to have adhered to any similar view. Thus, when faced with the need to write an article or demonstrative, for example, they often seem to have provided 'the', 'this', or 'that' (maybe even 'thilke') according to taste, rather than according to what their copy read. Similarly, since the scribe was being paid to copy (and paid because he was a professional at it),[12] when confronted by a blotch in his copy, or by a reading he found difficult or did not understand, evidence frequently implies that he would improvise. And beyond such forms of possibly motivated inaccuracy, hand-copying is a tedious and repeated muscular act that produces a good deal of inadvertent misrepresentation of intention, no matter how carefully one goes about it: repeated or omitted words, dropped lines, the same word opening wrongly repeated at the head of the following word, and so on.

As a result, no two manuscript copies of 'the same work' ever have exactly the same text, even when one of the books has certainly been copied from the other or from exactly the same materials.[13] Medieval books rebuff the modern notion that we all read the same text, and their variation is persistent. In their great edition of *The Canterbury Tales*, John M. Manly and Edith Rickert required only two volumes to present the text they thought Chaucer had written, but four volumes to present the manifold variant readings recorded in the surviving manuscripts.[14]

This situation should put a substantial query next to any published poetic text. The medieval versions of the text will have been irremediably plural, but a modern copy of the poem will be like everyone else's and will have achieved that status only through non- indeed anti-medieval procedures. All modern reading versions of medieval poems must face, in one way or another, the variation of the surviving medieval copies; that is the only evidence for what the author wrote. But modern presentation relies on scholarly techniques, in the main developed during the Renaissance to deal with the variation in classical texts. These seek to reduce variation and to construct a 'synthetic text', a single reading version deemed superior to any single manuscript because relying on the readings of all or several of them. This constructed text, whilst a convenient source of reference, thus can never correspond in all its detail to any single medieval manuscript witness. It is a hypothetical construction of modern scholars following modern scientist methods, and its construction does not reproduce any recorded medieval attitude to this text or to texts in general, just as it does not reproduce any single manuscript or medieval reading experience.[15]

Most textual variation in Middle English poetry probably represents some combination of inadvertence, confusion and adherence to a non-modern conception of accuracy. But study of a great many poems will throw up more pregnant examples of the influence of medieval 'bespoke' book-production on transmitted texts. Since books represented sizeable investments, and since purchasers probably knew the texts in some detail before they would consider the expense involved in ordering a personal copy of them, they might request a new book with the text in some individualised form. Rather than what the poet had written, they may have preferred to read a version loosely based on it, perhaps, but with different details or presentation. A quite substantial number of manuscripts present poems that have been tailored in some respect to meet specific audience expectations or desires.

I cite simply one well-known example, the excellent brief romance *Sir Orfeo*, a comic retelling of the sad Ovidian story of Orpheus and Eurydice (see also Nancy Bradbury's essay in this volume). In two of its manuscripts, the text forms a narrative triptych. Orpheus first loses his wife to the faery king; he then resigns his kingdom to his steward, lives as a wild man in the woods, and regains his wife. In the third narrative movement of the romance, he covertly returns to his court (as a shaggy wild man, he needs no disguise) and tests his steward's loyalty before revealing himself in a happy ending.

Or so runs the story in two of the manuscripts. But in the third, British Library, MS Harley 3810, the text appears severely truncated. In contrast to the roughly six hundred lines of the other copies, the Harley version runs just over five hundred. About half the omitted material occurs in the concluding 50–60 lines of the poem, which in the other versions recount Orfeo's testing of his steward. Plainly, the patron of Harley 3810 (who may have been the scribe, copying this small booklet for his own amusement) was vastly more interested in love beset, lost and regained, than he was in the restoration of Orfeo's kingdom. And he set out to re-craft the poem in order to insist upon amatory themes, rather than on the exile-return pattern frequent in insular romance, or the marvel of finding a conscientious royal servant (frequently villainous characters in poems of this genre).[16]

Self-tailored poetic renditions of this sort interface with a further, apparently commonplace, form of medieval 'readership' and book-use. People, whether literate or not, were accustomed (and expected) to engage with texts orally, through the ear, as part of a performative presentation. A well-known example appears in Chaucer's *Troilus and Criseyde*, when Pandarus finds Criseyde among a company of women *hearing* a romance of Thebes read aloud by one of their number.[17] Plainly, Chaucer here describes intelligent and 'well-read' people, and they are capable of making literate critical judgements about a text orally communicated. But the romance of Thebes here is conveyed as some form of oral 'performance'. Any work on this subject would probably be very long, and the audience may have wished to hear only a single episode of the text. Alternatively, they might have participated in the full text over several (or a good many) meetings, each the social occasion for reading an episode or narrative unit. And some poems presented in this way may never have been considered wholes, but only consumed in excerpts or selected episodes. Such apparently commonplace behaviours indicate that tailored texts in manuscript may provide the only reflection visible today of a considerably more fluid form of textual consumption than we, committed to the author's full text as Literary Monument, would be willing to countenance.

'Bespoke' book-production has a further effect on textual consumption and on a medieval reader's, or listener's, sense of how a text might mean. Modern study prioritises 'major works', ambitious, large and self-substantial texts. Although there are many of these current in the Middle Ages, and although a number of them conventionally appear in forms consonant with our text editions, as large single-volume renditions, this is not the most usual form poetic manuscripts assume. Most typically, book-owners commissioned (or prepared for their private use) miscellaneous volumes, frequently mixtures of verse and prose. They grouped together sequences of texts that interested them, often irrespective of such modern considerations as authorship, literary history, or anything resembling a modern sense of genre.

Most Middle English poems thus do not appear as discrete texts to be consumed in isolation but as single items in much more extensive personalised anthologies. Their meaning for medieval readers would appear to be contextualised, involved with and influenced by the meanings of those texts with which the individual poem has been presented. These possible contextualisations are notoriously diverse; often the same text might for different readers imply differing meanings and ones that might

challenge modern categorisations. Most particularly, manuscript collocations imply
that medieval book-producers and readers were more apt to respond to texts in terms
of their thematic content than we are today.

The alliterative poem *The Siege of Jerusalem* provides an apt example. This briefish
(about 1350 lines) treatment of the destruction of the Jewish Second Temple in 70
A.D. never appears outside an anthology-volume. In such books, *The Siege* is presented
in a variety of contexts. In British Library, MS Cotton Caligula A.ii, it appears along
with more than twenty-five other texts, nearly all in verse and in the main 'romances'
(and with one other alliterative poem, 'Susannah'). But several scribes respond to the
poem's insistence that the destruction of the Temple constitutes an appropriate revenge
for Jewish complicity in the crucifixion and thus offer the text as if it were an apocryphal pendant to the gospels. Thus, in Princeton University Library, MS Taylor 11,
the work follows a series of English prose meditations on the Passion (translated from
a Bonaventuran text). Only once (in Cambridge University Library, MS Mm.v.14)
does the poem occur in a context consonant with modern readings as a learned history
in alliterative verse – and on that occasion in the company of prose historical texts
in Latin, not other Middle English poetry at all.[18]

This is not to say that work- or author-based presentations of poetry are foreign to
the medieval period. But such efforts frequently are rather qualified; for example, although
there are many single manuscripts totally devoted to *The Canterbury Tales*, the surviving
evidence for Chaucer's canon is dispersed. In the Middle Ages, one could not have a
Riverside Chaucer; the evidence of the surviving manuscripts implies that readers who
wanted 'Chaucer's Works' would probably have had to acquire them piecemeal, perhaps
in three (or more) separate – and separately negotiated – volumes (Seymour 1995–97).

Only one medieval manuscript in any way approximates a treatment of Chaucer
resembling the modern *Riverside* edition. This book, Cambridge University Library,
MS Gg.iv.27, forms a very large anthology; it is not, like those manuscripts followed
most closely in making modern editions, a book produced in London but in East
Anglia.[19] As a one-volume introduction to the poet, its contents are extensive; clearly,
a single provincial patron wanted continuous access to many of Chaucer's works.
And he was able to obtain what he sought: the manuscript contains a full *Canterbury
Tales* (with illustrations of some pilgrims) and a *Troilus and Criseyde*, along with
two of Chaucer's dream poems (*The Parliament of Fowls* and *Legend of Good Women*),
as well as a selection of lyrics. Not only might one notice the uneven coverage of
Chaucer's shorter works here, but also a tendency to include materials only 'Chaucerian',
rather than authored by the poet. Thus, the volume contains a couple of imitative
lyrics and John Lydgate's dream vision, 'The Complaint of the Black Knight'. The
only comparable volume, a very long way short of the inclusiveness of Gg.iv.27's
presentation, is another provincial book, British Library, MS Harley 1239. This includes
the *Troilus*, with an extensive (and unusual) selection of 'major Canterbury tales'
(including, for example, those of the Knight, Wife of Bath and Franklin).

Elsewhere, the majority of copies of *The Canterbury Tales* provides full texts of the
poem, but rarely anything further of Chaucer's. Yet even then *The Tales*, as these

books present them, provide surprises to a reader coming to them from Benson's edition. In many copies, links between the individual tales are not those familiar from modern reading texts; moreover, very few copies present the poem in the order customarily read today.[20] And the very notion of a full and continuous poem, although confirmed by the majority of the evidence, would be challenged by a quite substantial number of copies like Harley 1239 that consider Chaucer's lengthy work as material for excerption. Something like a quarter of the surviving copies presents only selections from the whole – and then scarcely items that would accord with modern anthologising tastes. The tales of 'moral Chaucer', the prose *Melibee*, *The Prioress's Tale* and *The Clerk's Tale*, are far more apt to be singled out for inclusion in anthologies than our favourites such as those of the Wife of Bath and Pardoner (and Chaucer's *fabliaux* never occur so) (Silvia 1974 and Owen 1991: passim).

Most usually, a medieval reader who wanted both Chaucer's *Troilus* and his *Tales* had to arrange for the production of two separate volumes. Indeed, virtually all the sixteen more or less complete copies of the *Troilus* were originally produced as single-text volumes containing this poem alone. But the two thoroughly exceptional copies, as well as the binding of the text in Bodleian Library, MS Digby 181 with an originally separate volume,[21] show interesting efforts to anthologise the poem with other Chaucerian works.

Like the added portions of the Digby MS, in these books Chaucer's great amatory romance is joined with similarly amatory works, his dream visions and lyrics. Durham University Library, MS Cosin V.ii.13 has but a single extra text, which is in fact not Chaucer's but 'Chaucerian', Thomas Hoccleve's 'Letter of Cupid'. Its anthologisation is minimal in comparison with the extensive materials of the second MS bound in Digby 181, or with Bodleian Library, MS Arch. Selden B.24, produced for the Scottish Sinclair family. These books include extensive mixtures of Chaucer with variously imitative fifteenth-century vision poetry (in Selden a great deal of it distinctly Scots and unparalleled elsewhere, for example, the unique copy of James I's *Kingis Quair*). Such volumes, rather than being overtly author-concerned, may qualify notions of 'Chaucer' since their clearly thematic arrangement suggests he is of interest as an English love-poet (and perhaps not as a unique, but only the most outstanding example).

Books like the Digby and Selden manuscripts are engaged in fusing *Troilus* with a third and usually discrete strand of Chaucer transmission. On the basis of the surviving manuscripts, a medieval reader would generally have sought minor oddments of Chaucer, the dream-visions and lyrics (not to mention the prose) in locales apart from either of the poet's major works. There is a healthy number of books seeking to present the dream materials and sometimes the lyrics, but again within the anthologising, and thematically focussed tendencies I have already described.[22] And Chaucer's prose seems never to have appealed to the audiences who read his poetry, but to specialised scientific (*The Treatise on the Astrolabe*) and Latin-learned audiences (*Boece*, the translation of Boethius's *Consolation of Philosophy*).

As the Chaucerian example suggests, medieval books are idiosyncratically individual, and their potential appeal diverse. This follows from their bespoke production. But manuscript circulation also indicates a significant gap between medieval and modern literary tastes. Since books were commissioned by readers for their personal (or household) use, works that show today extensive patterns of circulation, that is extensive remains in manuscript, are more likely to have appealed to a wide range of readers than not.

Yet simultaneously, the 'Gawain-manuscript' offers an interesting counter- example to our sense that the 'literarily good' is somehow widely recognised (and thus universally available). The circulation of *Sir Gawain and the Green Knight* (and the other poems in the same volume) was minimal, although generally typical of alliterative poems, which infrequently survive in multiple copies. Had the single manuscript, British Library, MS Cotton Nero A.x, been lost, we would not know at all of a poet certainly Chaucer's rival in sophistication. Like most alliterative poets, it would appear, this author, although probably familiar with London and its institutions, wrote in 'provincial' circumstances, for a local lordly court somewhere in Northern England.[23] His works were restricted in circulation, and he may not have been known as a poet at all anywhere but in his 'home country'. Similarly, various parts of Britain may have had distinctly regional senses of what constituted 'English poetry', perhaps the finest examples being works composed in late fifteenth- and early sixteenth-century Scots, the poems of Robert Henryson, William Dunbar and Gavin Douglas – as well as works in the vibrant late alliterative tradition.

But the obverse of near non-survival is abundant evidence for the popularity in verse of forms we today find frankly rebarbative. While there are considerable difficulties in understanding what the survival rates of medieval manuscripts might mean, and the variety of situations they might reflect, if one looks at the apparent medieval version of the 'weekly hit parade', certain shocks occur. Poems we would consider important literary monuments are indeed prominent among surviving manuscripts: Chaucer's *Canterbury Tales*, for example, is the second most widely attested Middle English poem in manuscript (about ninety copies, with the provisos above). And other works we recognise as central portions of the medieval poetic tradition show similar signs of wide circulation (and knowledge among a variously dispersed readership). *Piers Plowman*, Gower's *Confessio Amantis* and Hoccleve's *Regiment of Princes* all survive in something between forty and sixty copies each.[24]

But other examples of poetic works apparently popular on the basis of extensive manuscript survivals are generally today not even read by specialists. The all-time winner in the medieval popular verse sweepstakes is a mid-fourteenth-century North Yorkshire poem of spiritual instruction, *The Prick of Conscience*. This work provides a morbid consideration of 'The Four Last Things' (death, judgement, heaven and hell). Its poet claims that he writes for local laymen who cannot deal with or gain access to the Latin clerical handbooks on which he profusely and overtly draws. But in spite of its origins in a peripheral area of the country, the work 'had legs', escaped its regional culture quite completely, was revised and promulgated in new forms (including, bizarrely enough, a translation into Latin prose), and eventually reached every corner of England.[25]

Teaching people the requirement and methods of 'dying well' (essentially holding the world in contempt while alive in it) was clearly good poetic business in the fifteenth century. But *The Prick* had more to offer to medieval taste: it was lucidly written in octosyllabic couplets and contained a number of useful mnemonic tags in Latin. It could apparently be read as a compendium of devotional information so far afield from its original Northern audience as Devonshire. One surviving copy, Oxford, St John's College, MS 57, was included in the repertoire of the first English commercial scriptorium, in London in the 1450s (see Mooney and Matheson), perhaps the most impressive sign that the poem was perceived as an important cultural monument.

Far from so popular, but still at the foot of the 'top ten', is a similar North York-shire production from *c.* 1350–70. This poem, *Speculum Vitae*, is a huge compendium of basic Christian lore, centred about definitions of the vices and virtues. At 16,100 lines, it is nearly twice as long as *The Prick* – and, although widely known, with perhaps forty-five surviving copies, whole and fragmentary, it never circulated south of the Wash. At this size, it is not likely that any medieval reader ever consumed the poem in its entirety, but rather that it was consulted selectively and topically for instruction in religious basics; the manuscripts encourage such spot consultation through an elaborate apparatus, designed to locate discussions quickly. There is at least one good reason why these two poems are little read or known: *The Prick* has been edited only once, in 1863; and only 370 lines of *Speculum* had appeared in print before 2008.[26]

Poems like these raise in a very serious way the spectre that medieval conceptions of poetry and poetic value differ markedly from modern ones. On the basis of wide dissemination of poets such as *The Prick* and *Speculum*, for medieval readers poetry did not have to offer amusement, but might more importantly be useful for edification. Nor did poetry necessarily exist to offer glorious language, but rather a plain style that might convey information clearly. And most of the remaining 'top ten' Middle English verse hits reinforce this view emphatically. They include, for example, several of the English verse mnemonics inserted into a Latin book for priests, *Speculum Christiani*.[27] These rather brief snatches offer authoritative information about various basic topics of Christian instruction. They challenge not only our sense of what poetry is good for, but equally our sense that poetic importance and readability are at least partly a function of scope/size.

The remainder of the 'top hits' prove similarly instructive in this regard. One of the most widely disseminated Middle English poems comes from the oeuvre of the extraordinarily prolific (and until recent years, extraordinarily despised) fifteenth-century poet John Lydgate, monk of Bury St Edmunds (*c.* 1370–1450). Modern interest has centred in Lydgate's historical and courtly writing, often extensive in its scope: *The Fall of Princes*, Chaucer's *Monk's Tale* writ very large – it is supposedly the longest poem in English – survives in nearly as many copies as *Speculum Vitae* (see Nolan 2005). But more popular in the medieval period were Lydgate's small portable compendia of knowledge – the short poems known as 'The Dietary' (rules for keeping healthy) and 'The Kings of England', a handy verse historical mnemonic.

The most popular larger Lydgate poem again comes from outside the range of 'Lydgate as read', his lengthy work of Marian devotion *The Life of Our Lady*.[28]

Plainly, there are ways in which our refined literary senses do not coincide with medieval conceptions of 'the good of literature'. The differences are perhaps most starkly expressed in the prologues to a range of thirteenth- and fourteenth-century poems, both Middle English and Anglo-Norman.[29] Their authors, who all intend to provide sober basic religious instruction, distinguish two ways one might go about the production and use of verse. They contrast two poetics. That of 'romance', stories of famous knights, kings and conquerors, they condemn as 'vanity', a foolish waste of time and intellectual abilities. In its place, they claim to offer a 'true' poetry, founded in biblicism, intellectual in its appeal and directed to the salvation of the soul.

Only one poet likely to be read in a twenty-first century medieval literature course actually takes such views seriously. This is, of course, Langland, the opening to whose poem *Piers Plowman* (and the persistent interest in time-wasting in it) makes a colourful allusion to such discussions. But one major lesson to draw from any survey of Middle English poetry in manuscript is the relative isolation in the period of those poetic objects that appeal most strongly to modern aesthetic sensibilities. For a great many medieval writers and readers, such works would have represented vain and frivolous recreation, not the activities of a serious individual.[30]

This may raise a further caveat about medieval reading practices and their fundamental differences from modern ones. English Studies are now the province of university departments and, following the construction of such modern institutions, which are driven by the much more extensive post-1500 canon, are emphatically monolingual. But this could never have been the situation in the Middle English period. During this time, England, at any serious intellectual level, was a trilingual society, and many of its most inventive minds did not write in the native tongue at all.[31] Moreover, given the trilingual proficiency of all serious persons, 'literature' was never just insular but might regularly engage readers with texts produced on the Continent as well. Chaucer, heralded during his lifetime by Eustache Deschamps as 'grant translateur', learned to be a poet by reading personal copies of Dante and Boccaccio, which he had probably obtained during his two Italian diplomatic missions of the 1370s. But he was scarcely unique in having Continental tastes, and many surviving royal and aristocratic library lists indicate individuals prepared for a steady diet of Continental French literary works.

Although everyone had spoken English as a birth tongue since at least 1175, to be 'literate' originally meant to have Latin proficiency. From just the time when English became everyone's birth-tongue, the late twelfth century, Latin language instruction in grammar schools had come frequently to be delivered through the language of the Conquest, Anglo-Norman. This state seems to have continued widely until at least the mid-fourteenth century; as a result, the truly 'literate' had competencies in multiple languages. And they might feel inclined to seek out texts, regardless of their origins, in any one of these. Thus, Middle English verse represents but a small part of a literate person's literary experience. This might extend from contact with utterly ubiquitous Latin liturgical books, Statius's verse (his *Achilleid* was one of the texts routinely used in a grammar school), or Ranulf Higden's universal history *Polycronicon*, to French romances, some of them Continental. Although medieval English poets, Chaucer especially, stand at the head of our literary tradition, one always needs to recall that, in the situation in which these figures composed, they represented a distinctly minority interest.

A final consideration, worth at least broaching even though definitive answers elude us, may be framed through a pair of questions: who read Middle English verse? How did they analyse, understand or use their verse texts? Neither question admits of any very satisfactory answer. As regards potential readers, one can assemble a long list of individuals (including women) who have left their signatures in surviving books, and a considerably more limited list of individuals known, primarily through wills and book lists, to have owned books, some of these surviving copies.

Such information is promising. But ownership does not tell anything about how a book was used (indeed, if it was read at all). Moreover, only a small percentage of those names that do occur in surviving books are at all identifiable with any particular individual; many of the names are about as distinctive as 'John Doe', and relatively few are accompanied by any indication of the locale where the individual was prominent. Very few such signatures are dated, and the majority, on the basis of their script, appear to be those of second- and third-generation users of the volumes, not those of the persons who may have arranged for the book's production.[32]

Readers thus can generally be identified only in a broad and generic manner, largely predicated on the historical probabilities outlined in those studies of lay literacy cited in n. 12. Readers of Middle English poetry are likely to have been of middle-class status. Surviving evidence from higher social ranks implies that greater magnates and royalty were, even in the later fifteenth century, more apt to read materials, often imported, in languages other than English.[33] But even purchasing a second-hand book would have been a significant financial investment, and the opportunity to use such a volume would have required some significant leisure space and a level of educated awareness. On this basis, one might expect the readers of English verse to be drawn from groups like prosperous urban merchants and tradesmen or their rural equivalent. This latter group would have been formed from substantial gentry property-holders and minor magnates, members of the baronial class, important persons in their home locales who swelled out the number of 'lords' attending Parliament.[34]

Very little survives to indicate how such individuals might have responded to their texts. Plenty of verse manuscripts include medieval annotations, but these marginal additions can scarcely be described as revelatory: most frequently they comprise the instruction 'Nota (bene)' (pay [close] attention to this) or, more enigmatically, a pointing hand. Nor, most usually, are such materials accompanied by any indication of what in the text one is to respond to – not even to which lines the signs refer. Perhaps the one conclusion one can draw from such marks of interest is that readers were drawn to pithy and sententious statements on a variety of topics, not necessarily limited to those a modern reader would highlight as central to a medieval poet's work.

A bit more information on reading strategies may be forthcoming from later writers' comments on their predecessors, in this case primarily Chaucer. One continuous thread of such commentary concerns diction, for example Dunbar's applause for Chaucer's 'fresch anamalit termes celicall' ('The Golden Targe' 257). The earlier poet, from this perspective, is rhetorically valuable, a font of colourful words (which may imply admiration of Chaucer's use of figurative language), implicitly literary terms derived from Romance languages, perhaps especially high-style Latinate usage ('celicall' echoing Latin 'celicalis', not English 'heavenly'). On the other hand, Hoccleve praises Chaucer's learning, his capacity to instruct as 'vniuersel fader in science' or as un-matched 'in philosophye . . . in our tonge' (*Regiment* 1964, 2087–8). (His views might remind one of those marginal fingers pointing at a particularly sententious bit of poetry.) But whether such opinions might be generalised to all poets or simply reflect Chaucer's impact remains doubtful.

The single capacity we might associate with all readers, however, suggests an approach to verse resembling Dunbar's. Because all sophisticated literates were apt to be trilingual, they would have undergone some form of grammatical training. This introductory discipline conventionally proceeded by teaching the skills of 'commentary'. Students were routinely sensitised to the power of the apt word (the single productive form from a range of synonyms), to the evocative quality of rhetorical figures (why one might use a simile), to the importance of non-natural word order to poetic statement, and to the building up of an argument, a complicated textual statement, from short constituent passages.[35] Numerous manuscripts and early printed books communicate such teaching materials and provide some indication of how students were informed about the capacities of (Latin) verse. Commentary techniques are, of course, the pro-genitors of modern literary criticism, largely grammatical and rhetorical in its aims. It is perhaps fitting to conclude at a juncture where medieval and modern textual cultures, so often disparate, might be perceived as approaching one another.

NOTES

1   The archive of surviving Middle English verse texts, generally accurate for major works, was first laid out in Brown and Robbins (1943). This volume, based upon the manuscripts, has received several supplements, identifying more recent discoveries (but never re-examining Brown and Robbins's original archive), most recently Boffey and Edwards (2005). The unrivalled survey of Middle English manuscript culture remains Griffiths and Pearsall (1989).

2   There is also a black and white image and discussion in Roberts (2005) at 204–6. For the 'modern' equivalent of the text here, see *The Cloud*, 1/1–2/5.

3   And the scribe might also have used the letter 'yogh' in the middle of a word like 'niȝt' to indicate our modern 'gh'. (The letter's name indicates that it customarily represents 'y' at the head of a word and 'gh' everywhere else.)

4   A glance at the Latin notes down the left side of the page will show a great deal more of this behaviour, including things that Latin readers have to learn the way interested moderns acquire the 'thousand basic characters' of Chinese: could one guess that 'spc sci' in line 7 of the Latin meant 'spiritus sancti' [of the Holy Spirit]?

5 As does the Northumberland student Aleyn four times in Chaucer's *Reeve's Tale*, at lines 4130, 4170, 4171, 4173.

6 Even our assumption that verse texts should be presented in poetic lines is not a given of medieval texts in manuscript. In Old English, verse is conventionally recorded as continuous prose (see Roberts (2005), plate 11, p. 61), sometimes (as here) inconsistently punctuated to indicate line boundaries. This convention is gradually, but never totally, abandoned in Middle English and still can be found in fifteenth-century handwritten books. See, for example the piece printed as prose, following the manuscript presentation, at *Yorkshire Writers* (1895–96) 1: 110–12.

7 Compare the pointing of Figure 11.1 discussed above, a good deal heavier but never in any close correspondence with modern practice.

8 For example, at *Piers Plowman* B 10.366 'And our *bakkes* that moth-eeten be', one scribe, concerned lest his readers construe 'bakkes' as the word 'backs', offers above the line the accurate gloss 'id est panni' ('that is, clothes'). Similarly a number of scribes explain the difficult word in Chaucer's *Knight's Tale* 1985 'And therout came a rage and swich a *veze*' by inserting the Latin 'id est impetus' ('that is, rush') above the line.

9 One last thing to notice about the *Troilus* plate: the text has been corrected. On three occasions, alternative readings are provided between the lines (at lines 1, 27 and 28). The corrections are not medieval, but of about 1600 or shortly thereafter. The moral is not entirely that the scribe was careless, but that medieval books, to an extent impossible in modern print mass-production, are marked by individual histories of ownership and use.

10 Mooney and Matheson (2003) describe the first evidence for apparent repeated copying of a text for 'standing bookseller's stock'.

11 For brief introductions to the techniques used to produce a medieval book, one can recommend de Hamel (1992), Ivy (1958) and Shailor (1991). On the cost of books, see Bell (1936). For a rare example of a surviving contract to produce a book (a Latin Psalter in 1346), see *The Fabric Rolls*, 165–66. For a provocative analogy, the formal contracts between painters and patrons, see Baxandall's (1986) discussion, 3–23. For the most elaborate decoration of medieval volumes, painterly illustration of texts, infrequent in Middle English poetic manuscripts, see Scott (1996).

12 Medieval views of literacy emphasised the ability to read (and to comprehend) a text, not the ability to copy one out. This was a manual craft and one in London, for example, governed by membership in a craft guild. One can learn a great deal about medieval conceptions of literacy from Clanchy (1993), Aston (1984) and Parkes, 'The Literacy of the Laity' (Parkes 1991: 275–97).

13 Compare the discussion at *Piers Plowman*, ed. Kane and Donaldson (1975: 35–37, 40–42. Two of the manuscripts the editors here puzzle over, British Library, MS Additional 10574, and Bodleian Library, MS Bodley 814, were certainly copied either one from the other or both from the same copy of the poem. Although rare, the situation is not unique, and there are several other well-known examples (for instance, British Library, MSS Harley 4196 and Cotton Galba E.ix of *The Prick of Conscience*).

14 See *The Text*, vols 3–4 with Chaucer's text; vols 5–8 with 'collations', records of the unprinted – and thus erroneous – readings of all the manuscripts.

15 For an amusing and informative history of scholarly procedures for dealing with manuscript books, here centring on Old French texts, see Cerquiligni (1999). One could, however, draw conclusions from Cerquiglini's demonstration different from his gamesome praise of variation as The Medieval Form of textuality. Texts do need to be 'made new' to ensure their continuing appeal to modern audiences, and the (unobvious) procedures for doing this require thought.

16 For a graphic demonstration of this redactor at work, see *Sir Orfeo*, ed. Bliss (1966), which prints all three texts in parallel, esp. 46–51 (from about line 538 of the Auchinleck version on).

17 At 2: 78–108, an experience replicated in the portrait of Chaucer himself reading to a courtly garden party at the head of the most expensively produced copy of this poem, Cambridge, Corpus Christi College, MS 61. For the most recent reproduction, see *The Cambridge Illuminations*, 275.

18   Identifying and exploring such juxtapositions in any detail requires seeking out the catalogues
     describing the holdings of individual libraries. In a few lucky cases, there exist catalogues centred
     around Middle English materials, for example Guddat-Figge (1976). On such 'miscellanies',
     see Boffey and Thompson (1989), Boffey and Meale (1991) and the series of important studies in
     Yearbook of English Studies 33 (2003), a volume edited by Phillipa Hardman.
19   There is a very useful full facsimile, *The Works*. On the importance of the 'early London booktrade'
     to Chaucer and Gower, see the indispensible essay by Doyle and Parkes (1978).
20   Perhaps the best introductions to the problem of tale-order are Owen (1982) and Benson (1981).
21   The current binding is that affixed by Sir Kenelm Digby in the second quarter of the seventeenth
     century. While he may have joined two originally separate volumes, he equally may simply have
     rebound an already composite medieval book.
22   Prominent examples of such volumes could include Cambridge University Library, MS Ff.i.6;
     Cambridge, Magdalene College, MS Pepys 2006; Cambridge, Trinity College, MS R.3.19; Bodleian
     Library, MSS Bodley 638, Fairfax 16, and Tanner 346; Longleat House, Marques of Bath, MS 258.
     The majority of these, as also Selden B.24, have appeared in full facsimiles; see for example, *MS
     Fairfax 16* (1979).
23   The great study outlining the cosmopolitan sophistication of such an author is Salter (1983), esp.
     52–116. On the manuscripts communicating alliterative poems, see Doyle (1982).
24   The only comprehensive survey of *Piers* manuscripts appears at the openings of the relevant volumes
     of the Athlone edition of G. Kane, gen. ed., *The A Version* 1–18 (a little skimpy); *The B Version*
     1–15; *The C Version* 1–18. See further Doyle (1986) and Benson and Blanchfield (1997). A full
     survey of Gower manuscripts will appear in a forthcoming catalogue edited by D. Pearsall and
     K. Harris. Seymour (1974) describes manuscripts of Hoccleve's *Regiment.*
25   For a demonstration of this prolific circulation, about 125 copies in all, see Lewis and McIntosh
     (1982).
26   See *The Pricke* and Ullman (1884) 468–72. For the elaborate aids for readers that typify the
     manuscripts of *Speculum Vitae*, see Gillespie (1989: 318, 332–35). This forms an outstanding
     vernacular example of what Parkes calls 'ordinatio'; see 'The Influence'.
27   For an edition, see *Speculum Christiani* (1933: 16–37, 58–61, 124–31; and 331–6, 160–9 and
     336–40). These poems often circulated independently of the Latin prose into which they are
     inserted here, as well as independently of one another (a further example of an excerptable text).
28   On Lydgate's manuscript circulation, see Pearsall (1997). For editions of the brief 'Dietary' and
     'Kings', see *Secular Lyrics* (1955: 73–76) and *Historical Poems* (1959: 3–6), respectively.
29   The best-known (and widely cited) example appears at the opening of the early Northern poem
     of Bible history, *Cursor Mundi*, composed *c.* 1300; it is conveniently printed at Bennett and
     Smithers (1966 et seq.: 184–89).
30   Particularly, were one to consider the massive remains in Middle English prose; two texts, the
     Wycliffite biblical translation and the prose *Brut*, the standard 'history of England', survive in far
     greater numbers than any poetic text.
31   For information about the vaster circumambient literature written by Englishmen in other languages,
     see the informative bibliographies, in the main predicated upon the manuscript record, Sharpe
     (1997) and Dean (1999).
32   For an exemplary discussion of an unusually well-documented case, see Keiser's two studies of
     the important Yorkshire copyist, Robert Thornton (Keiser 1979; Keiser 1983).
33   Thus, for example, the historical core of the British Library's Royal collection consists of Burgundian
     books, in French or Latin, produced for Edward IV during his periods of continental exile.
34   See, for example, the booklist printed and discussed by Hamel (1990).
35   Commentary also contributes to sophisticated medieval literary theory, typically learned and Latinate;
     see the collection *Medieval Literary Theory* (1991).

REFERENCES AND FURTHER READING

Alliterative Poetry of the Later Middle Ages: An Anthology (1989). Ed. T. Turville-Petre. London: Routledge.

Aston, M. (1984). *Lollards and Reformers: Images and Literacy in Late Medieval Religion*. London: Hambledon Press.

Baxandall, M. (1988). *Painting and Experience in Fifteenth-Century Italy*. 2nd edn. Oxford: Oxford University Press.

Bell, H. E. (1936). The price of books in medieval England. *The Library*, 4th ser. 17, 312–32.

Bennett, J. A. W. and G. V. Smithers (eds) (1966 et seq.). *Early Middle English Verse and Prose*. Oxford: Clarendon Press.

Benson, C. D. and L. S. Blanchfield (1997). *The Manuscripts of* Piers Plowman*: The B-version*. Cambridge: D. S. Brewer.

Benson, L. A., Jr (1981). The order of the 'Canterbury Tales'. *Studies in the Age of Chaucer*, 3, 77–120.

Boffey, J. and A. S. G. Edwards (2005). *A New Index of Middle English Verse*. London: British Library.

Boffey, J. and C. Meale (1991). Selecting the text: Rawlinson C.86 and some other books for London readers. In F. Riddy (ed.). *Regionalism in Late Medieval Manuscripts and Texts* (pp. 143–69). York Manuscripts Conferences: Proceedings Series 2. Cambridge: D. S. Brewer.

Boffey, J. and J. J. Thompson (1989). Anthologies and miscellanies: production and choice of texts. In J. Griffiths and D. Pearsall (eds). *Book Production and Publishing in Britain 1375–1475* (pp. 279–315). Cambridge: Cambridge University Press.

Brown, C. and R. H. Robbins (1943). *Index of Middle English Verse*. New York: Columbia University Press.

The Cambridge Illuminations (1981). Ed. P. Binsky and S. Panayotova. London: Harvey Miller.

Cerquiglini, B. (1999). *In Praise of the Variant: A Critical History of Philology*. Trans. B. Wing. Baltimore: Johns Hopkins University Press.

Chaucer to Spenser: An Anthology of Writings in English, 1375–1575 (1999). Ed. D. Pearsall. Oxford: Blackwell.

Clanchy, M. T. (1993). *From Memory to Written Record: England 1066–1307*. 2nd edn. Oxford: Blackwell.

The Cloud of Unknowing (1944, 1958). Ed. P. Hodgson. Early English Text Society 218. London: Oxford University Press.

Dean, R. J. (1999). *Anglo-Norman Literature: A Guide to Texts and Manuscripts*. Anglo-Norman Text Society occasional publications 3. London: Anglo-Norman Text Society.

de Hamel, C. F. (1992). *Scribes and Illuminators*. Medieval Craftsmen series. London: British Library.

Doyle, A. I. (1982). The manuscripts. In D. A. Lawton (ed.). *Middle English Alliterative Poetry and its Literary Background: Seven Essays* (pp. 88–100, 142–47). Cambridge: D. S. Brewer.

Doyle, A. I. (1986). Remarks on surviving manuscripts of *Piers Plowman*. In G. Kratzmann and J. Simpson (eds). *Medieval English Religious and Ethical Literature: Essays in Honour of G. H. Russell* (35–48). Cambridge: D. S. Brewer.

Doyle, A. I. and M. B. Parkes (1978). The production of copies of the 'Canterbury Tales' and the 'Confessio Amantis' in the early fifteenth century. In M. B. Parkes and A. G. Watson (eds). *Medieval Scribes, Manuscripts and Libraries: Essays Presented to N. R. Ker* (pp. 163–203). London: Scolar.

The Fabric Rolls of York Minster (1859). J. Raine Jr (ed.). Surtees Society 35. Durham: George Andrews.

Gillespie, V. (1989). Vernacular books of religion. In J. Griffiths and D. Pearsall (eds). *Book Production and Publishing in Britain 1375–1475* (pp. 317–44). Cambridge: Cambridge University Press.

Griffiths, J. and D. Pearsall (eds) (1989). *Book Production and Publishing in Britain 1375–1475*. Cambridge: Cambridge University Press.

Guddat-Figge, G. (1976). *Catalogue of Manuscripts Containing Middle English Romances*. Texte und Untersuchungen zur englischen Philologie 4. Munich: W. Fink.

Hamel, M. (1990). Arthurian romance in fifteenth-century Lindsey: the books of the Lords Welles. *Modern Language Quarterly* 51, 341–61.

Hardman, Phillipa (ed.) (2003). Medieval and early modern literary miscellanies. *Yearbook of English Studies*, Special Number 33.

Historical Poems of the XIVth and XVth Centuries (1959). Ed. R. H. Robbins. New York: Columbia University Press.

Ivy, G. S. (1958). The bibliography of the manuscript book. In F. Wormald and C. E. Wright (eds). *The English Library before 1700* (pp. 32–65). London: Athlone Press.

John Lydgate: Poetry, Culture, and Lancastrian England (2006). Ed. L. Scanlon and J. Simpson. Notre Dame: University of Notre Dame Press.

Keiser, G. R. (1979). Lincoln Cathedral Library MS. 91: life and milieu of the scribe. *Studies in Bibliography*, 32, 158–79.

Keiser, G. R. (1983). More light on the life and milieu of Robert Thornton. *Studies in Bibliography*, 36, 111–19.

Lewis, R. E. and A. McIntosh (1982). *A Descriptive Guide to the Manuscripts of the* Prick of Conscience. Medium Ævum Monographs n.s. 12. Oxford: Society for the Study of Mediæval Languages and Literature.

Medieval Literary Theory and Criticism, c. 1100–c. 1375: The Commentary Tradition (1991). Ed. A. J. Minnis and A. B. Scott. 2nd edn. Oxford: Clarendon Press.

Mooney, L. R. and L. M. Matheson (2003). The Beryn scribe and his texts: evidence for multiple-copy production of manuscripts in fifteenth-century England. *The Library*, 7th series, 4, 347–70.

MS Fairfax 16, Bodleian Library (1979). Introd. J. Norton-Smith. London: Scolar.

Nolan, M. (2005). *John Lydgate and the Making of Public Culture*. Cambridge Studies in Medieval Literature 58. Cambridge: Cambridge University Press.

Owen, C. A., Jr (1982). The alternative reading of the 'Canterbury Tales': Chaucer's text and the early manuscripts'. *PMLA*, 97, 237–50.

Owen, C. A., Jr (1991). *The Manuscripts of the Canterbury Tales*. Cambridge: D. S. Brewer.

Parkes, M. B. (1991).'The influence of the concepts of *Ordinatio* and *Compilatio* on the development of the book'. In *Scribes, Scripts and Readers: Studies in the Communication, Presentation and Communication of Medieval Texts* (pp. 35–70). London: Hambledon Press.

Parkes, M. B. (1991). The literacy of the laity. In *Scribes, Scripts and Readers: Studies in the Communication, Presentation and Communication of Medieval Texts* (pp. 275–97). London: Hambledon Press.

Pearsall, D. (1997). *John Lydgate (1371–1449): A Bio-bibliography*. English Literary Studies Monograph Series 71. Victoria, BC: University of Victoria.

Piers Plowman: A New Annotated Edition of the C-Text (2008). Ed. D. Pearsall. Exeter: University of Exeter Press.

Piers Plowman: The B Version (1975). Ed. G. Kane and E. T. Donaldson. London: Athlone Press. (*The A Version*, ed. G. Kane, appeared in 1960; and *The C Version*, ed. G. Russell and G. Kane, in 1997, from the same publisher.)

The Poems of the Pearl Manuscript (1978 et seq.). Ed. M. Andrew and R. Waldron. York Medieval Texts second series. London: Arnold.

The Pricke of Conscience (Stimulus Conscientiae): A Northumbrian Poem (1863). Ed. R. Morris. Berlin: Ascher.

The Riverside Chaucer (1987). L. D. Benson et al. (eds). 3rd edn. Boston: Houghton Mifflin.

Roberts, J. (2005). *A Guide to Scripts Used in English Writings up to 1500*. London: British Library.

Salter, E. (1983). *Fourteenth-Century English Poetry: Contexts and Readings*. Oxford: Clarendon Press.

Scott, K. L. (1996). *Later Gothic Manuscripts 1390–1490. A Survey of Manuscripts Illuminated in the British Isles*, vol. 6, 2 vols. London: Harvey Miller.

Secular Lyrics of the XIVth and XVth Centuries (1955). Ed. R. H. Robbins. 2nd edn. Oxford: Clarendon Press.

Seymour, M. C. (1974). The manuscripts of Hoccleve's 'Regiment of Princes'. *Transactions of the Edinburgh Bibliographical Society* 4, 255–97.

Seymour, M. C. (1995–97). *A Catalogue of Chaucer Manuscripts*. 2 vols. Aldershot: Scolar.

Shailor, B. A. (1991). *The Medieval Book, Illustrated from the Beinecke Rare Book and Manuscript Library*. Medieval Academy Reprints for Teaching Series. Toronto: University of Toronto Press.

Sharpe, R. (1997). *A Handlist of the Latin Writers of Great Britain and Ireland before 1540*. Publications of the Journal of Medieval Latin 1. Turnhout: Brepols.

Silvia, D. S. (1974). Some fifteenth-century manuscripts of the 'Canterbury Tales'. In B. Rowland (ed.). *Chaucer and Middle English Studies in*

Honour of Rossell Hope Robbins (pp. 153–63). London: George Allen and Unwin.

Sir Gawain and the Green Knight (1968). Ed. J. R. R. Tolkien and E. V. Gordon. Rev. N. Davis. 2nd edn. Oxford: Clarendon Press.

Sir Orfeo (1966). Ed. A. J. Bliss. 2nd edn. Oxford: Clarendon Press.

Speculum Christiani (1933). Ed. G. Holmstedt. Early English Text Society 182. London: Oxford University Press.

Speculum Vitae: A Reading Edition (2008). Ed. R. Hanna using materials assembled by V. Somerset. 2 vols. Early English Text Society 331–32. Oxford: Oxford University Press.

The Text of the Canterbury Tales (1940). Ed. J. M. Manly and E. Rickert. 8 vols (1940). Chicago: University of Chicago Press.

Ullman, J. (1884). Studien zu Richard Rolle de Hampole. *Englische Studien*, 7, 415–72.

The Vision of Piers Plowman: A Critical Edition of the B-Text (1995). Ed. A. V. C. Schmidt. 2nd edn. London: J. M. Dent.

The Works of Geoffrey Chaucer: A Facsimile of Cambridge University Library, MS. Gg.4.27 (1979–80). Introd. M. B. Parkes and R. Beadle. 3 vols. Cambridge: D. S. Brewer.

Yorkshire Writers (1895–96). Ed. C. Horstman. 2 vols. London: Swan Sonnenschein.

Genres and Modes

12

Legendary History and Chronicle: Laȝamon's *Brut* and the Chronicle Tradition

Lucy Perry

When we apply the adjective 'legendary' to 'history', we are speaking from our modern appreciation of what 'history' is, that is, accounts of past events and circumstances which can be confirmed from documentary evidence. Legendary history is on the contrary unhistorical. Moreover, modern readers associate writings of history with prose rather than verse. They have an assumption that a poet's engagement with the truth or historical accuracy is subordinate to the seeking of poetic effect. Medieval chroniclers were no less concerned by truth and accuracy and would authenticate their work with chronological and genealogical details, names and dates. Yet, a belief in the didactic significance of history required that '"universal truths" to be deduced from any specific episode were just as important as the need to provide an incontestably factual account of that episode' (Given-Wilson 2004: 2). The medieval vision of history was informed by the Christian view of the history of man's salvation and historiographers interpreted events as the workings of Providence. In the twelfth century, a period during which Anglo-Latin historiography flourished through the pens of writers such as William of Malmesbury and Henry of Huntingdon, 'the providential view of history was subtly modified to allow a larger role for purely human causation, and to reflect a lively interest in psychological motivation' (Hanning 1966: 126). At the same time, with the dissemination of vernacular literatures of entertainment such as *chansons de gestes* and romances, and the inevitable cross-fertilisation between genres, this secularisation creates a potential for romancing the past, and we see increasing transmission of legendary, pre-historical matter alongside accounts of later, documented, historical events.

Historiography about England in English has a long history beginning with the ninth-century translation of Bede's *Historia ecclesiastica gentis Anglorum, The Ecclesiastical History of the English People* (completed around 731). This century saw too the original compilation of *The Anglo-Saxon Chronicle*, like the translation of Bede, part of the programme of education and the rebuilding of a patriotic identity instigated by King Alfred (871–99). *The Anglo-Saxon Chronicle* continued to be compiled beyond the end of the Anglo-Saxon period, notably in the version now known as *The Peterborough Chronicle*, well into the reign of the Norman kings, concluding with events of 1154. Prose is the dominant form of *The Anglo-Saxon Chronicle*, although verse is incorporated into later annals in some manuscripts, in the form of the epigrammatic (as in the annal of 1075), of memorials (such as those that record the coronation of Edgar in 973 and his death in 975), of the panegyric, (such as *The Battle of Brunanburh* in the annal of 937), and of some verse narrative accounts (for example, the death of the *atheling* Alfred in 1036) (Swanton 2000). Historical verse in Old English is also found in the fragmentary *Battle of Maldon*, in which poetic imagination is brought to bear on an historical event of 991 to celebrate the heroic spirit of the English leader Byrhtnoth and his comrades as the Anglo-Saxons face defeat against marauding Vikings.

Bede himself was highly regarded by twelfth-century historians both as an authority and as someone to be emulated in his professionalism. *The Ecclesiastical History* and *The Anglo-Saxon Chronicle* made available to later historiographers materials for the Anglo-Saxon period. The history of earlier inhabitants of the land, obscured by time and lack of information, was the subject of legend. A Britonnic account, Gildas's *The Ruin of Britain*, written around 540 and a source for Bede's own history, gives some insight into that period between the end of the Roman occupation and the settlement of Germanic tribes. It is not, however, chronicle, but more a tirade: 'a fierce denunciation of the rulers and churchmen of his day, prefaced by a brief explanation of how these evils came to be' (Winterbottom 1978: 1). The *Historia Brittonum*, a collection of prose writings from the ninth century formerly attributed to Nennius, is where we first find the name of the Romano-British war lord who is to become, in legend and romance, King Arthur.

Geoffrey of Monmouth, a contemporary of Henry of Huntingdon and William of Malmesbury, furnishes Arthur with a pedigree and a complete biography in the context of a coherent, if imaginative, account of British kings. In the *Historia Regum Britanniae* (*The History of the Kings of Britain*), Geoffrey provides a foundation myth which stretches back to Troy and 'which enter[s] the collective historical memory of the English people in the mid-twelfth century, there to remain for the rest of the middle ages' (Given-Wilson 2004: 5). Brutus, Aeneas's great-grandson, liberates the Trojans from servitude in Greece and leads them to Albion, the land that will become known as Britain, reputedly named after its founder. The capital is built and named New Troy and thereafter king succeeds king. After the lengthy section relating the deeds of Arthur, the narrative turns to the reigns of the last kings of the Britons, the division of the land between the Angles and the Britons, the conversion of the Germanic tribes by Augustine and finally the supremacy of the Angles and Saxons. The last king of the Britons, Cadwalader, goes on pilgrimage to Rome, where he receives the sacrament of confession and dies, and the Britons retreat into Wales. All this, Geoffrey explains, he has translated from a 'very old book in the British tongue' (Reeve 2007: 4; see also Wright 1988). Geoffrey's *Historia* became a popular and widely disseminated work, today extant in some 219 manuscripts (Reeve 2007:

xxxi–li). It initiated what was to become one of the most popular groups of texts in the medieval period, the *Brut* chronicles, and it also provided the seeds of Arthurian romance. Two hundred and fifty years after Geoffrey wrote the *Historia*, the opening stanza of *Sir Gawain and the Green Knight* gives a succinct summary of the ups and downs of British history after the arrival of Brutus, providing an historical context for tales of the knights of King Arthur:

> On mony bonkkes ful brode Bretayn he settez
> with wynne,
> Where werre and wrake and wonder
> Bi syþez hatz wont þerinne,
> And oft boþe blysse and blunder
> Ful skete hatz skyfted synne.
> (*Sir Gawain and the Green Knight*, ll. 14–19)

The *Historia* was translated into several vernacular languages (French, English, Welsh and Old Norse), into prose and into verse. A major difference between responses to Geoffrey of Monmouth's *Historia* and to the works of his translators is that we attribute to Geoffrey a consciousness of his 'fictionality', as a romancer, imitator, or parodist. Yet, a serious intent is deemed to lie behind his work, which serves as a commentary on the political and social climate of his own times through the representation of the remote past (see Brooke 1986; Flint 1979; Gillingham 2000). There was some scepticism among medieval historians concerning Geoffrey's *Historia*, his most vehement critic being William of Newburgh who, writing at the end of the twelfth century, deems Geoffrey's work to be *fabula* rather than *historia* (Walsh and Kennedy 1988: 28–37). Yet, Geoffrey's translators engage with their material as authoritative history. The first known translator of the *Historia* into a vernacular was Wace, a Jersey-born Norman clerk associated with the court of Henry II and Eleanor of Aquitaine, who completed his *Roman de Brut* in 1155 (Weiss 2002). He turned Geoffrey's concise prose into the octosyllabic lines of French verse. Laȝamon, translating the *Roman de Brut* in the early thirteenth century, composed the earliest English *Brut* chronicle. An increasing demand for verse *Brut* Chronicles in the early fourteenth century spawned *The Metrical Chronicle of Robert of Gloucester* (c. 1300), *Castleford's Chronicle* (completed after 1327) and Robert Mannyng's *Chronicle* (completed 1338). The writer of *Castleford's Chronicle* brings additional legendary material to his prologue, giving an account of Albina and her sisters, whose progeny are the giants that Corineus and his fellow Trojans must slay. By this time, it was the practice for chroniclers to take their histories beyond 689 and continue the accounts of kings up to their own times. In this way, the matter of Britain was appropriated as part of the history of the English nation.

In the early fourteenth century, choosing to write an historical text in English that looked to the remote past of England was a political choice. Our chroniclers of the early fourteenth century are polemical in their descriptions of the relations between the languages of England and in their discussion of the plight of the English under the Norman yoke (Turville-Petre 1988; Mitchell 1999). Far from the French-speaking, aristocratic milieu for which Wace wrote when he translated the *Historia* into the chivalric world of the *chansons de gestes*, Mannyng's verse was written for his 'fellows' of the Gilbertine order. It is not intended, the author tells us, for performers, whether reciters, minstrels or harpers, but for 'symple men', common men, who do not know 'strange Inglis' (Part I, l. 78). He opts to write in a simple language, complaining that many before him have used an English so intricate that no-one can read it. We can only speculate about Laȝamon's intended audience but by means of his prologue he aligns his work to serious and professional history. In addition, the poet constructs his identity innovatively, in a way that anticipates Chaucer's engagement with his material (Brewer 1994: 191). Laȝamon's prologue, scholastic in form, names the author, describes source materials and their arrangement, and lays out the aim of the writer and the purpose of the work (Allen 1992: 411 n. 1). Laȝamon names three sources: Bede, a book written by Albin and Austin (Augustine), and Wace. Laȝamon follows the method of the professional historian in finding in Bede's writing textual authority for his own work. Of the source materials Laȝamon mentions, however, the last-named, the book by Wace, is the only one that can be assuredly identified as a source, and the book written by Albin and Austin remains unidentifiable.[1]

Our fourteenth-century chroniclers, while choosing to write in English, adopted imported prosodic practices, as in the rhyming tetrameters of Castleford's *Chronicle* which reflect the Continental verse form of the octosyllabic rhyming couplets. Mannyng self-consciously imitates the form and style of his French sources (Johnson 1991: 134–135). In Part I his verse reflects the French octosyllabic couplets of the *Roman de Brut*, while in Part II he takes on a longer line suggested by Langtoft's alexandrines (Sullens 1996: 61–62). The verse form of Robert of Gloucester's *Chronicle* referred to by Wright (1887: I, xxxix) in the nineteenth century as 'doggerel' ballad metre, might be more correctly defined as a loose metre of rhyming couplets, lines approaching alexandrines.

Three generations earlier Laȝamon was using a diction and an alliterative form which gives the impression of an inherited, thoroughly native mode. His style is marked by compound lexical forms, formulaic phrases ('burnen to-breken꞉ blod ut ȝeoten. / ueldes falewe wurðen꞉ feollen here-mærken', C. 13709–10), and formulaic themes, such as the messenger or the feast. However, it is not to late Old English poetry but to late Old English prose and other West Midland prose texts contemporary to Laȝamon's *Brut*, such as *Ancrene Wisse*, that we should turn for comparative alliterative forms (Blake 1969–70: 122). Rosamund Allen offers another solution to the problems of defining Laȝamon's verse form: its loose metre with ornamentation comprising alliteration, rhyme, consonance and assonance suggests a metrical system based on a variety of 'sound echoes' for a 'listening audience'; 'a subtle and highly inventive blend of sound effects, far from "classical alliterative verse", not exactly rhymed verse [...] not "rhythmic prose" either' (Allen 2002: 252, 271–72, 279).

Laȝamon's *Brut*, containing as it does elements of Continental or Anglo-Norman romance within a native idiom, demonstrates the eclectic nature of literature in thirteenth-century England. Courtly tropes that were to become increasingly influential are evident: for example, scenes of the reception of lovers' messages and episodes of disguise and recognition, picked up from Wace's *Roman de Brut*, find enhanced expression in Laȝamon's *Brut*. The English word *hende*, so associated with romance that Chaucer is able to call it up playfully when portraying Nicholas and Alison in the *fabliau* context of the *Miller's Tale*, already has courtly connotations. The superlative is applied to Igerne, as Uther observes and flirts with her. One king, Merian, is a 'swiðe hende mon' (C. 3476), a phrase that translates 'ki mult fu bels' ('who was very handsome', *RdeB.* l. 3673, p. 93). Where Wace points to Merian's knowledge of dogs, birds and hunting skills (p. 93), emphasising his technical achievement and expertise, Laȝamon places his emphasis on possessions and sport in terms of entertainment: 'hundes and haukes: he hæuede vnimete. / þat æuere-elche dæi: he pleuwede mid his deoren' ('he had numerous hounds and hawks so that everyday he amused himself with his deer', C. 3477–78). Moreover, Laȝamon fleshes out his *Brut* considerably, adding direct speech that enhances the communication between characters. By giving space to gestures and elaborating upon physical and emotional responses, he endows his characters, men and women, with a sensibility in line with the growth of the individual in literature and with developments of romance.

Laȝamon's *Brut*: The Earliest English *Brut* Chronicle

While the text of Wace's *Roman de Brut* is extant in nineteen complete manuscripts and in some dozen or so fragments, Laȝamon's *Brut* survives in just two manuscripts: London, British Library, Cotton MS Caligula A. ix (hereafter Caligula [C.], *c.* 1275 (*MED*)) and London, British Library Cotton MS Otho C. xiii (hereafter Otho [O.], dated 1300 (*MED*)) (see Brook and Leslie 1963–78).[2] The Otho manuscript, which provides a redaction of a text similar to that found in the Caligula manuscript, has been badly damaged by fire. Otho is often regarded as a *modernised* version, rewriting what we might consider some of the more difficult or outmoded vocabulary. However, as both manuscripts date from the second half of the thirteenth century, an audience evidently existed for both versions at a time when the language and literature of England were responding to diverse cultural and social phenomena.

Laȝamon promises in the prologue:

> þet he wolde of Engle: þa æðelæn tellen.
> wat heo ihoten weoren:] wonene heo comen.
> þa Englene londe: ærest ahten.
>
> (C. 7–9)

that he would tell about the noble people of England – what they were called and whence they came – those who first possessed England.

The reiterated use of *aðel- forms* in Caligula brings to Laȝamon's *Brut* an argument distinct from the *Roman de Brut*: '*æðel* [is] a favourite word, symptomatic of Laȝamon's enthusiastic, generous, and idealizing turn of style' (Brewer 1994: 190). The redactor of Otho, however, avoids these groups of words, sometimes to significant effect. The adjective when used of people carries connotations of 'noble birth, noble; excellent, famous', and when used of things may be translated as 'excellent, splendid, fine' (*MED* s.v. *athel*). The abstract noun *aðel(e* means 'nobility or lordship and its appurtenances, such as hereditary estates, power, honor, fame', and the verb *aðelen* 'to provide (with possessions); be generous or kind to (sb.)' (*MED*, svv). In Caligula, the physical attributes that define Wace's Britons are combined with an innate quality that is connoted by *aðel-* forms. Attributes of physical strength and power in Wace are transmuted into wider abstractions, the extrinsic and the intrinsic reflected in the idea of one of noble bearing. Ebrauc, who 'was an extraordinarily powerful man, very large and very strong' (*RdeB*. p. 39; 'Cist fud de merveillus esforz / E mult fud gros e mult fu forz', ll. 1495–96), becomes in the *Brut* 'æðelest alre kingen, / þe æuer sculde halden lond: oþer bi-witen leode' ('noblest of all kings that ever ruled over land or governed a nation', C. 1306–07). Similarly, Gloigin, one of Ebrauc's daughters, is 'æðeleste' (C. 1361; Otho: 'wisest to neode'), rather than 'plus fu granze e plus senee' ('the tallest and the wisest', *RdeB* l. 1570, p. 41). Again, Custance, a Roman senator, later to become king through marriage to Coel's daughter Helena, is 'æðelest alre cnihten' (C. 5461; Otho: 'cniht mid þan beste'), conflating Wace's information that 'no-one knew his equal for bravery and strength' and that he, conquerer of Spain, was 'greatly esteemed' (*RdeB*. p. 143).

Paradigms of Kingship

While many elements of medieval kingship are clearly presented in the *Brut* chronicles through the line of hereditary kings, the concept of kingship is paradigmatically played out in Laȝamon's *Brut*, as his poetic and formulaic mode allows for repetition and variation that explore with depth, and prompt an audience's reflection upon, this theme. Nobility is an essential quality of the medieval ruler and is one of three aspects that Jacques Le Goff identifies as the essence of medieval kingship: a king is noble (i.e. of high birth), he is the monarch (i.e. the sole head of state), he is Christian (Le Goff 1993: 2). The first two aspects, nobility and sole sovereignty, become apparent almost from the beginning of the line of British kings – shared sovereignty when it occurs rarely promotes stability – and the third aspect will come with the conversion of the Britons to Christianity. However, Laȝamon, in his vision of the ruler, emphasises nobility as an aspect not just of high birth, as one idea of medieval kingship would hold, but as belonging to the innate qualities that are part of the wider ideal of nobility.

Laȝamon articulates the king-making process early on. After the defeat of the Greeks under Brutus' leadership, Membricius proposes that his fellow Trojans demand ships and provisions from the Greeks, in order to leave for a new home in a distant land. Furthermore, Brutus should be given Ignogen, the Greek king's daughter, as his wife. Membricius states that they will travel far until they arrive at the land where they will 'fondia þeo leoden. / wer us beo iqueme' ('establish the nation where it pleases us', C. 479–80), which Brutus will rule. Only when they have established their people in their new land, then they will elect their king. While for Laȝamon territory, nation and kingship are inextricably bound, Mannyng has Membricius preemptively refer to Brutus as king, before he has secured his realm (l. 1223). With Brutus already in the position of lordship, the hereditary kingship will be secured by his aristocratic lineage and by the royal blood of his queen. From this moment the line of kings should be dictated by birth.

In founding the city of New Troy, which he entrusts to his people, Brutus marks his dominion over the island of Britain, establishing 'good laws' by which the citizens may live in peace:

> He hehte þat luue scolde꞉ liðen heom bi-tweonen.
> ælc halden oðren riht. ba bi daie ꞉ bi nith.
> ꞉ wea-swa nolde꞉ he sculde beon iwite.
> ꞉ swa vfele he mihte don꞉ þat he sculde beon ihon.
> For swulchen eiȝe gode꞉ heo hefden muchele drede.
> ꞉ bi-comen riht-wise men꞉꞉ rædes heo luueden.
>
> (C. 1041–46)

He commanded that love should exist between them, that each uphold the rights of others, and whoever would not should be punished, and he might behave so evilly that he should be hanged. Because of such good laws they had much fear and became righteous men who respected counsel.

In this short passage key words that will recur set the tone for Laȝamon's vision of the kingdom of Britain: a land where peace brings its own rewards and wrong-doing is punished; a land where justice (*riht*) is upheld; a land where counsel (*ræd*) is respected. All these benefits are aspects associated more generally with lordship. Put another way, lordship and kingship are dual aspects of sovereignty:

> Kingship was an exalted lordship [...]. The taking and giving of counsel was essential to the stability and hence the strength of a great lordship. [...] It was the duty of a good lord to 'do right' in matters such as claims to inheritance, the proper provision for wives and widows, the administration of fiefs in wardship, the exaction of obligations and the punishment of defaulters and faith-breakers. (Warren 1987: 10, 14)

Laws, which guide men to righteousness and punish those who are cruel and errant, become the cornerstone of this British kingdom. As Christopher Cannon has argued 'Laȝamon makes [law] a general principle of governance, adding it to numerous passages where Wace's text does not have it' (Cannon 2000: 339). Several kings are remarkable for establishing peace after periods of disorder, and for re-establishing law, among them Ruhhudibras (C. 1403–5), Dunwale (C. 2123–24). Laws alone, however, are insufficient to maintain stability, for it takes a good king to ensure that laws remain a part of the fabric of society. Laȝamon's vision of a king as responsible for upholding the law is not unique in historical narrative. *The Peterborough Chronicle* illustrates this social expectation of kingship, as can be seen in the negative example of King Stephen in the entry for the year 1137:

> Then when the traitors realised that Stephen was a mild man, gentle and good, and imposed no penalty, they committed every enormity. They had done him homage and sworn oaths, but they held to no pledge.
>
> (Swanton 2000: 263).

Laȝamon's interest in exploring the essence of kingship is displayed by his placing a greater emphasis than does Wace on the misdeeds of kings. A king's selfish ambition or indulgence will bring discord and divide a kingdom. Malevolent ambition can set one brother against another: Membriz kills his brother, and rules wickedly. His treacherous treatment of his subjects is compounded by homosexual excess. His violent death proves fitting. Separated from his retainers as they pursue a female deer in the hunt (a significant change from the French where the animal hunted is a 'cerf', a male deer), Membriz is set upon by wolves and torn limb from limb, symbolic of the hanging, drawing and quartering that 'good laws' would have prescribed for him. With the death of Membriz, whereas Wace remains focussed on the king's demise, 'Thus Menbriz was torn limb from limb, destroyed and devoured' (*RdeB.*, p. 39), Laȝamon reminds us of Membriz's betrayal of his brother Malin (C. 1304), suggesting a causal relationship between earlier sins and a nasty end.

Treachery is for Laȝamon the most heinous of crimes. A religious man, his training as a priest must have shaped his moral view of the world. Yet his definition of good kingship is pragmatic: if a king maintains the laws, supports his people and protects his kingdom (C. 9916–17), he will then be respected and loved by his people, as Arthur is (C. 9960). Likewise, Cassibellaune, whose laws are just, is a good king loved by his subjects (C. 3569): until treachery strikes from within, Cassibellaune is able to protect his land from the campaigning forces of Julius Caesar. In their aristocratic lineage and their nobility of character, kings are distinct from warriors and war-leaders, a differentiation that for Le Goff (1993: 6) recalls Tacitus' observation: warriors and war-leaders are distinguished by strength and courage, a king by high birth. But the best of kings in Laȝamon's *Brut* distinguish themselves both as leaders in war and as warriors of note, in addition to their kingly qualities. Cassibelaune is a good warrior, 'god cniht', as well as a very good king, 'swiðe god king' (C. 3571). Constantin too balances good kingship (C. 5553) with a good warrior (C. 5557), and becomes emperor of Rome. Guencelin, a king of whom Laȝamon has little to say, is not only a good king but also a 'clæne mon' (C. 3135), translating 'Guincelins fu de bone vie ('Guencelin led a good life', *RdeB*. l. 3335, p. 85). 'Clæne' ('morally clean', 'righteous' 'pure', *MED s.v.* clene 2a) provides an additional quality to his good kingship. To be wanting in sexual morality, however, need not be a hindrance to good kingship. As for many chroniclers of his day, for Laȝamon the proof of a good king lies in his ability to maintain peace in his own land and in his success in warfare. Thus Laȝamon, surprising as it may seem for a medieval cleric, is able to pronounce that the king Malgus, despite the culture of homosexuality he promotes in his court, is a good king, gaining territory and showing generosity to his subjects, while his courtiers display worthiness. Robert Mannyng and the writer of *Castleford's Chronicle* are not so content to brush over such moral failings. Both separate Malgus's moral failing from his kingly successes. After a splendid beginning, marked by his exemplary knightship, generosity and suzereinity over other kings, Malgus's reign takes, in its third year, a bad and rather undignified turn:

> he ȝede to synne sodomyke;
> at Wynchestre at his bathing,
> sodanly mad he ending.
> (Robert Mannyng, I, ll. 13824–26)

By having Malgus die whilst bathing, Mannyng suggests a luxurious rather than heroic end to the reign. There is yet greater emphasis in *Castleford's Chronicle* on the perversion and foulness of the sin of sodomy (ll. 24135–41) (Eckhardt 1996). These contrast strikingly with Laȝamon's last words on Malgus, that he was a good king, 'buten of þere sunne˸ þat ich iseid habbe' ('except for that sin that I have mentioned', C. 14399).

Just as a king, physically strong in his youth, weakens with age, so his mind may become enfeebled and his rule ineffective. Leil, despite his laws, is unable to sustain peace in his kingdom. His earls and barons fight amongst themselves and have only scorn for their king, who dies of a broken heart (ll. 1390–95). Such brief accounts of the early kings of Britain establish a paradigm that is explored more fully in the extensive accounts of some later kings.

Extending the Paradigm – King Leir and His Daughters

In the Leir episode, a story familiar from Shakespeare's *King Lear*, the kingship paradigm comes under close scrutiny vis à vis old age, and abdication is explored as an alternative to enfeebled rule. Leir, having ruled for sixty years, decides to divide his realm among his daughters, Gornoille, Regau and Cordoille, but first asks them to declare publicly their love for him. The use of direct speech, a prominent narrative device in Laȝamon's work and a means by which he often elaborates upon Wace's narrative, is here used not only to bring out dramatic tensions but also to further the overall argument. Words are explored for their worth, and utterances are proven true or untrue, wise or foolish, by the actions that ensue. In the opening scene, narrative commentary shapes our response to Leir's words, which are evil ('vuel', C. 1470, 1537), foolish council ('vnra[d]', C. 1517), folly ('sothscipe', C. 1510). Although almost half of the narrative is composed of direct speech, what we learn in the Leir episode is rather the accuracy of the age-old maxim that actions speak louder than words.

A thematic strand running throughout the Leir episode in Caligula is idealised nobility, with clusters of words built on the root *aðel*. The use of this group of words is no mere formulaic reflex but rather is thematically consistent, and often reinforced poetically by alliteration within the line, for example with 'alde' (C. 1478), old, or 'ældede', aged (C. 1467). The adjective is used in the Leir episode in points of contrast, emphasising an ironic distinction between past and present, appearance and actuality, or intrinsic attributes and external worth. After a brief summary of Leir's sixty-year reign, we move to an account of his old age and a lengthy narrative of his abdication and its consequences. Leir is described as 'wakede an aðelan' (C. 1467), 'weakened in his nobility/power'. The noun is tinged with irony as 'þe alde king' sits in state, 'on æðelen', in majesty (C. 1478). His diminished dignities suggest ill judgement in the disposal of his kingdom and an ironic opposition is established between the aged king and his youngest daughter when Cordoille, sent away by her father without dowry or possession other than her clothes, is also described as 'æðele' (C. 1610). The introduction of such epithets and tag phrases by Laʒamon is to some extent called for by the long line of his verse, where the second half-line is often given over to ornamentation, but the clustering and patterning in this episode brings out a particular theme. Laʒamon's repeated use of *aþel-* forms carries forward the question of nobility's dependence on exterior signs. The Otho redactor's substitution of this group of words suspends this enquiry.

Filial love provides a means to explore the equation further. Gornoille despises the lordship or, as Allen (1992) puts it, 'honoured state' of her father (C. 1639). In the tempering role that Laʒamon gives to Meglaunus, Gornoille's husband, he speaks 'mid aðelere spiche' ('with noble/sincere words', C. 1661). By providing dialogue consisting of Gornoille's complaining (C. 1640) and the noble words of her husband, Laʒamon places the weight of responsibility on the malicious daughters, deaf to their husbands' more moderate advice. It is on Cordoille's actions and her understanding of what it is to be noble that the debate turns. In the competition between the daughters at the start of the episode, moves in the language games of Gornoille and Regau proceed through comparison: 'þeou ært leouere þene mi life' ('you are dearer than my life', C. 1487), 'Al þat is on liue nis [me] swa dure / swa me is þin an lime forðe min ahʒene lif' ('No-one living is as dear to me as is one of your limbs, which is more to me than my own life', C. 1503–04). Cordoille declares her love straightforwardly: 'Ich habbe to þe sohfaste loue: for we buoð swiþe isibbe' ('I have for you true love, for we are very closely related', C. 1523). Her love for her father is defined neither by superlatives nor by comparatives, but by absolutes. However, in her folly she does not recognise the dangers when words carry all power. Leir regards himself to have been dishonoured ('unaðelede' [Madden 1847: III, p. 459, note to v. 3174] MS: unæleledæ) by her words (C. 1585). His humiliation must be complete before he sees the wisdom in her warning, that men love him only for what he has, and that the honour Leir will receive will be no more and no less than his possessions (C. 1525–27). When Leir is informed of Cordoille's promise to restore him to his former honourable state, 'Sone werð þe alde king: wunliche iæðeled' ('immediately the old king is joyfully comforted', C. 1800). While the *MED* suggests that 'werð iæðeled' should here be translated 'was relieved or comforted', the word's etymological root (cf. Old English *geæþelian* 'to ennoble, make excellent') releases connotations that reinforce the argument of the episode. Cordoille learns to display greater reserve, deferring to the primacy of masculine rule. Exercising her power as queen and as king's daughter, she returns to Leir the outward trappings of nobility, so that he may meet the king of France with dignity. Thus, Cordoille is an agent allowing men to communicate. She is one of several women in *Brut* chronicles who act as intermediaries, enabling kingship as queens and queen-mothers; yet when their sons or their husbands threaten the basis of good kingship, they will act more directly, as do Tonwenne and Guendoline. Other women such as Ronwenne and Guinevere are, like Gornoille and Regau, destroyers of kingship, through murder, betrayal, or humiliation. In these chronicles, women have their roles to play, but remain in the background, only to be brought forward at times of crisis. Yet Laȝamon provides greater space for female identity or agency, be it in giving a name to Brian's sister, Galarne, or providing Ronwenne with a dramatic scene during which she herself, rather than a servant, adds poison to Vortimer's wine cup. It is in line with this exploration of women's roles that, with the death of Leir, Laȝamon states that Cordoille's nephews would not tolerate that a queen be king in this land (C. 1871).

The Apogee – Arthur

Laȝamon's manifesto for kingship is given yet more definition in the Arthurian section, where, as Rosamund Allen noted, 'no less than four definitions of the ideal ruler' are given (Allen 2001: 8). While other kings, namely Ebrauc (C. 1306), Argal (C. 3374) and Arthur's uncle Aurelien (C. 8367, 8835, 8945, 9049), are awarded the epithet *æðelest alre kingen*, or some variation thereof, Arthur qualifies emphatically as 'aðelest kingen', noblest of kings (Noble 2002). Arthur's nobility is drummed home not only by the repetition of this tag in the b-verse of the long line, but by the length and breadth afforded the story of Arthur through the expansive poetic description, the detail of his combative skills and conquests, the marvellous landscapes through which he moves, and the mysterious supernatural associations of his conception and death.

In Laȝamon's *Brut* Arthur's reign provides a model of kingship not only for the Britons or their descendants, the Welsh, but also for the English. While the Britons await Arthur's return from Avalon where he still is believed to live, Laȝamon explains that all we can know of the truth is the prophecy of Merlin: 'þat an Arður sculde ȝete: cum Anglen to fulste' (C. 14297). That *one like* Arthur should come to support the *English* is in line with Laȝamon's argument initiated in the Prologue, that the ancestors of the Britons endow the land of England and thereby the English with an innate nobility. Robert of Gloucester's *Metrical Chronicle* asserts Arthur's death, stating that the Welsh (*Brutons*) and the Cornish believe him still to be alive. Robert takes authority from the discovery of bones identified as those of Arthur and Guinevere. These bones found in a Glastonbury grave during the reign of Henry II were transferred to a dedicated tomb in 1278 in the presence of Edward I. The late-fourteenth-century English romance the Alliterative *Morte Arthure*, which has the chronicle tradition as background, locates Avalon in Glastonbury and gives Arthur a Christian burial. Mannyng, being faithful to Wace's translation, adds his own clearly sceptical commentary on Arthur's death: Arthur was so badly wounded he had to die (I, l. 13724), and such a tone recurs in Part II as Mannyng draws to a close celebrating Edward I (1272–1307) as one of a line of feared and famous kings, with the reminder that all, even those of great courage, are finally defeated by death (II, 1.8314).

The permeable boundary between fiction and historical truth, between romance and history (Field 2008: 296), is demonstrated clearly in Laȝamon's use of circumstantial detail in an action-filled narrative and his dwelling on the marvellous, as for example in his invention of the boat steered by two elfin women. One of these women is Argante, who is untainted by her notorious romance *alter ego*, the sorceress Morgan le Faye. Such a boat, occupied by ladies, ferries Arthur to Avalon in the mid-fourteenth century romance the Stanzaic *Morte Arthur*, which is indebted to French romance, principally the prose *Mort Artu*. A further significant addition by Laȝamon is the ominous dream that signals the approaching death of King Arthur. It is filled with striking images: Arthur astride the roof of his hall as if he were riding, Mordred hacking at its supporting posts with a war-axe, Guenevere tearing the roof apart with her bare hands, Walwain's plunge to the ground, a broken man, the fall of the hall, Arthur lopping off Mordred's head, cutting Guenevere into pieces and throwing her in a deep pit, and the flight of his followers. A contrasting section of the dream, filled with religious symbolism, places Arthur alone on high moors where he sees griffins and frightful birds (C. 14006), and from which he is carried by a lioness into the sea.[3] All assert the marvellous nature of Arthur's kingship, and change the pace of the account of the lineage of British kings. While this dream is unique to Laȝamon's *Brut*, the Alliterative *Morte Arthure* includes a prophetic dream, similarly positioned prior to the revelation by messenger of Mordred's treachery, and the poet names as his source here 'cronicles' (l. 3218). In this dream Arthur escapes from a wasteland occupied by savage animals to a *locus amoenus* where he meets Dame Fortune, whose wheel as it turns finally drags Arthur under and crushes him.

Chroniclers are arbiters of truth. Arthur's Round Table, mention of which is first found in Wace's *Roman de Brut*, provides the opportunity for Wace and those chroniclers who follow him to reflect upon the Round Table as inspiration for fictional tales of Arthur. Laȝamon's poetic imagination finds full expression in a figurative exploration of the art of the poets and storytellers who feed off Arthur (C. 11454–99). The magical table becomes transfigured as the breast of Arthur; the knights become the poets who feast and take their fill around it. The audience, as Elizabeth Bryan has remarked, is asked 'to see Arthur simultaneously as one of those seated at the Round Table and as the table itself, nourishing storytellers who sit at it' (Bryan 1992: 34). In this image analogous to that of the Pelican in its Piety from *The Bestiary* and calling to mind the sacrament of the Eucharist, the narrative hints at parallels between Arthur and Christ.

The Arthurian episodes of the Laȝamon's *Brut* abound with such complex figurative manoeuvres, which further demonstrate the author's poetic skill. The Saxon wars, in which Arthur must prove his kingly qualities, are filled with animal imagery in both short and extended, or epic, similes: Arthur rushes into battle like a grey wolf coming out of a snowy wood intent upon his prey (C. 10041–43), he is enraged like a wild boar when he comes across swine (C. 10609–10), he leaps like a lion across the River Avon (C. 10613), he courses into battle as quickly as a bird flies (C. 10656). The heroic images of lion, wolf, and bird in flight are set against an image of the floundering Saxons in the River Douglas, who are compared to a wild crane separated from its flock, pursued by hawks and hounds and about to meet its death (C. 10061–67). In the battle of Bath, Arthur likens his opponent Colgrim to a goat fighting with its horns on a hill while Arthur is the wolf triumphant against 500 goats (C. 10629–36). An elaborate metaphor follows this image as Arthur observes the Saxon Baldulf:

> Nu he stant on hulleː] Auene bi-haldeð.
> hu ligeð i þan stræmeː stelene fisces.
> mid sweorde bi-georedeː heore sund is awemmed.
> heore scalen wleoteð: swulc gold-faȝe sceldes.
> þer fleoteð heore spitenː swulc hit spæren weoren.
> Þis beoð seolcuðe þingː isiȝen to þissen londe.
> swulche deor an hulleː swulche fisces in wælle.
>
> (C. 10639–45)

Now he stands on the hill and sees in the Avon how steel fish lie in the river, armed with swords; their swimming is impaired. Their scales float like gilded shields. There their fins drift as if they were spears. This is an amazing thing to see in this land, such beasts on the hill, such fish in the water.

This is by any account a strange and strangely elaborated conceit. The metaphoric fish, mailed soldiers in the water, are endowed by means of simile with scales like shields and severed fins adrift like spears. Vehicle and tenor, figurative and actual, seem not so much confused as inverted. The disturbance nevertheless is resolved in the wonderment of the final two lines in a reprisal of the epic simile, now as metaphor (such beasts on the hill), providing an expansive landscape, a magnificent figure of the shattering, disorienting effects of battle.

The Saxon war, occurring early in his reign, provides an arena in which Arthur may prove his leadership qualities. One epic simile occurs when Arthur delights in the defeat of Childric, whom Arthur declares to be like the once bold and proud fox,

now despised, as it is dug out of its hole (C. 10398–413). Arthur agrees to let the
Saxons return to their land, seduced by the idea that fame of his mercy and his
generosity will spread (C. 10422–27). For Laȝamon the motive for Arthur's
agreement lies in inexperience and youthful vanity. At this moment of bad judgment,
he describes Arthur as 'aðelen bidæled' (deprived of nobility or dignity, C. 10428):
he lets the fox go. Mannyng neither builds Arthur up with such epic hyperbole, nor
does he shame him so severely. On the contrary, he remarks that granting the Saxons
their lives was a 'grete curtesi' (I, 9827) though it provides them with the opportunity to turn and attack in the south–west. Arthur's mercy is better placed when
he responds to the pleas of clerics and Scottish women to treat kindly the Scots who
were allied with the Saxons. Arthur must now prove his difference from the blood-
thirsty heathens and in Laȝamon's *Brut* he is provided with the chance to display his
Christian compassion: 'þa toc he to ræde. and reosede on heorte' ('then he gave it
some thought and was moved to pity in his heart', C. 10944). These two half-lines
structured on double alliteration and assonance in a chiastic pattern ('he to ræde' –
'reosede on heort') emphasise the process of internal reflection. The phrase 'reosede
on heorte' is used of Arthur in other places, when he learns of the death of Uther,
his father (C. 9925), and when he learns of the plight of the Scandinavian kings Loth,
Angel and Vrien (C. 11065). The verb *reusen* is associated with the Christian virtue
of compassion, pity and repentance (*MED*, s.v. (1)). Moreover, the only other person
to whom this emotion is attributed is Pope Gregory in his response to the English
slaves in Rome (C. 14711). Arthur in his crusade against the Saxons is marked
emphatically as a Christian king.

Conclusion: British History for the English

The meeting of Gregory and the slaves is a providential moment which in Bede's
Ecclesiastical History helps justify the passing of dominion over the island of Britain
to the Anglo-Saxons. Neither Wace nor Geoffrey of Monmouth tells the story of
Gregory and the English slaves: their chronicles are after all about the Britons, and
Gregory's encounter with English slaves in a Roman market place is part of the
conversion story of the Anglo-Saxons. With the appropriation of the matter of
Britain into English history, however, this anecdote again becomes relevant.

Unlike Wace, whose brief prologue names no sources but simply explains the
subject matter, naming himself as the translator, Laȝamon firmly locates himself in
the territory of his historical matter, among the books and in the land where the
history takes place, in Areley Kings, in the Welsh Marches. We are also able to locate
the chronicles of the fourteenth century, in Lincolnshire (Robert Mannyng's *Chronicle*),
in the South West Midlands (*The Metrical Chronicle of Robert of Gloucester*) and in
Yorkshire (*Castleford's Chronicle*). These English chroniclers are appropriating the deeds
of British kings for the land and the people of England, but in addition a localised
polemic can be identified in their arguments (Turville-Petre (1988)). In a tone different

to that of Wace and Geoffrey of Monmouth, Laȝamon shows a respect for the descendants of the Britons, the Welsh. Even as dominion passes from British to Saxon kings, the Britons, settled in Wales, live according to their own laws and their customs (C. 16089). This endorsement is notably different from Wace's view (inherited from Geoffrey of Monmouth) that 'the Welsh have quite altered and quite changed, they are quite different and have quite degenerated from the nobility, the honour, the customs and the life of their ancestors' (*RdeB*. p. 373). Laȝamon, on the contrary, from his vantage point by his church high on the hill in the Welsh Marches, states that in the land of Wales they continued to live according to their laws and customs, laws and customs that were the cornerstone of the nation and, when upheld, made a king a good king.

Clinging to Dame Fortune's wheel in the Alliterative *Morte* are eight of the Nine Worthies. The philosopher who interprets the dream explains that Arthur completes the number, and states that he will be the subject for both 'romaunce' and 'cronicle':

> This shall in romaunce be redde with real knightes
> Reckoned and renownd　with riotous kinges,
> And deemed on Doomesday　for deedes of armes,
> For the doughtiest that ever　was dwelland in erthe;
> So many clerkes and kinges　shall carp of your deedes
> And keep your conquestes　in cronicle for ever.
> 　　(Alliterative *Morte Arthure*, in Benson (1986), ll. 3440–45)

This metatextual discourse maintains a distinction between chronicle and romance. In romance, Arthur's deeds are accounted ('reckoned') and celebrated ('renowned') while chronicle provides a record of deeds and conquests. This may to some extent reflect the debate about the appropriate form for chronicle in which some French and English writers participated. Verse marks the literature of entertainment while prose is more serious. John Trevisa's patron, when given the choice, asked for the translation of the *Polychronicon* to be in prose for reasons of clarity (Given-Wilson 2004: 144). Given the similarities of position and content of Arthur's dream, it is possible that the poet of the Alliterative *Morte Arthure* knew Laȝamon's *Brut*. Nevertheless, one might think that our poet has in the mind here the prose *Bruts*, given the wide popularity of these texts by the time the Alliterative *Morte* was composed.

The Anglo-Norman prose *Brut* was transmitted in short and long versions during the fourteenth century and translated into Latin and English. From the late fourteenth century the Middle English prose *Bruts* were widely disseminated, extant in 181 manuscripts and thirteen early printed editions (Summerfield with Allen 2008: 349). *The Anonymous Short English Metrical Chronicle*, which is extant in seven versions dating between *c*. 1300 and *c*. 1432, shares some details with the prose *Bruts* (Summerfield with Allen 2008: 344). This proliferation of the prose *Bruts* against the apparently narrower transmission of the verse *Bruts* seems to suggest that, like modern readers, medieval readers came to prefer their history in prose. Yet, while Mannyng carefully sets out his rationale for his choice of language and style as clarity of expression and ease of understanding, prose does not come into the discussion. Even though his work is not intended for harpers or performers, it is poetic composition that inspires him: 'Mannyng's very attentiveness to the stylistic quality of the French writers whose work he follows, or has read, confirms his own ambitions as a self-conscious stylist' (Johnson 1991: 135). His sources though were not confined to the verse chronicles of Pierre de Langtoft and Wace: he produces 'an encyclopaedic compilation which draws on a wide range of vernacular and Latin resources', including Geoffrey of Monmouth's work and Bede's *Historia* (Johnson 1991: 135–36). And it is largely his relationship to his historical matter and his polemical treatment of the materials that proves of interest as we attempt to trace a national consciousness in vernacular writings of the period. Yet there is still much we do not fully understand about how Mannyng positions himself and about the terminology that he uses in his discourse on the writing of verse and verse production of the period. Laʒamon's *Brut* sets up both similar and different problems in determining its place in literary history in terms of Laʒamon's language and verse style. Yet, in its variety, from apparently mundane lists of short-lived kings or uneventful reigns to extravagant, epic descriptions or profound explorations of a theme, this earliest English legendary chronicle invites, indeed depends upon, an engagement with its poetic language and style.

NOTES

1 For a convincing appraisal of Laʒamon's naming of his sources, see Johnson (1994: 148–49). See Galloway (2006) for a further exploration of Laʒamon's Prologue.
2 All quotations are taken from this edition. For an edition with glossary, see Madden (1847). Useful editions and translations: Barron and Weinberg (1995) and Allen (1992).
3 For an explanation of the symbolism in this dream, see Mercatanti (2002: 245–48).

REFERENCES AND FURTHER READING

Allen, Rosamund (1991). Female perspectives in romance and history. In M. Mills, Jennifer Fellows and Carol M. Meale (eds). *Romance in Medieval England* (pp. 133–147). Cambridge: D. S. Brewer.

Allen, Rosamund (trans.) (1992). *Lawman: 'Brut'*. London: Dent; Rutland, VT: Charles E. Tuttle.

Allen, Rosamund (1998). Eorles and beornes: contextualising Lawman's 'Brut'. *Arthuriana*, 8 (3), 4–22.

Allen, Rosamund (2001). 'Where are you, my brave knights!': authority and allegiance in Laʒamon's *Brut*. In Christian J. Kay and Louise M. Sylvester (eds). *Lexis and Texts in Early English: Studies Presented to Jane Roberts* (pp. 1–12). Amsterdam: Rodopi.

Allen, Rosamund (2002). 'Nv seið mid loftsonge': a re-appraisal of Lawman's verse form. In Rosamund Allen, Lucy Perry and Jane Roberts (eds). *Laʒamon: Contexts, Language, and Interpretation* (pp. 251–82). King's College London Medieval Studies, 19. London: King's College London Centre for Late Antique and Medieval Studies.

Allen, Rosamund, Lucy Perry and Jane Roberts (eds) (2002). *Laʒamon: Contexts, Language, and Interpretation*. King's College London Medieval Studies, 19. London: King's College London Centre for Late Antique and Medieval Studies.

Barron, W. R. J. and S. C. Weinberg (eds and trans) (1995). *Laʒamon: Brut or Hystoria Brutonum*. Harlow: Longman.

Benson, Larry D. (ed.) (1986). *King Arthur's Death: The Middle English Stanzaic 'Morte Arthur' and Alliterative 'Morte Arthure'*. Exeter: Exeter University Press.

Blake, N. F. (1969–70). Rhythmical alliteration. *Modern Philology*, 67, 118–124.

Brewer, Derek (1994). The Paradox of the archaic and the modern in Layamon's *Brut*. In Malcolm Godden, Douglas Gray and Terry F. Hoad (eds). *From Anglo-Saxon to Early Middle English: Studies Presented to E. G. Stanley* (pp. 188–205). Oxford: Clarendon Press.

Brook, G. L. and R. F. Leslie (eds) (1963–78). *Laȝamon: Brut. Edited from British Museum MS Cotton Caligula A ix and British Museum MS Cotton Otho C xiii*. 2 vols. London: Oxford University Press.

Brooke, Christopher N. (1986). Geoffrey of Monmouth as historian. In D. N. Dumville and C. N. Brooke (eds). *The Church and the Welsh Border in the Central Middle Ages* (pp. 95–106). Rev. version. Woodbridge: Boydell Press. (First pub. 1976 in C. N. L. Brooke, David Luscombe, Geoffrey Martin and Dorothy Owen (eds). *Church and Government in the Middle Ages: Essays Presented to C. R. Cheney* (pp. 77–91). Cambridge: Cambridge University Press.)

Bryan, Elizabeth J. (1992). Truth and the Round Table in Lawman's 'Brut'. *Quondam et Futurus*, 2, 27–35.

Cannon, Christopher (2000). Laȝamon and the laws of men. *ELH*, 67, 337–63.

Coleman, Joyce (2003). Strange rhyme: prosody and nationhood in Robert Mannyng's Story of England. *Speculum*, 78, 1214–38.

Donoghue, Daniel (1990). Laȝamon's ambivalence. *Speculum*, 65, 537–63.

Eckhardt, Caroline D. (ed.) (1996). *Castleford's Chronicle or the Boke of Brut*. 2 vols. Early English Text Society, o.s. 305 and 306. Oxford: Oxford University Press.

Field, Rosalind (2008). Romance. In Roger Ellis (ed.). *The Oxford History of Literary Translation in English: Volume I to 1550* (pp. 296–331). Oxford: Oxford University Press.

Flint, Valerie I. J. (1979). 'The Historia Regum Britanniae' of Geoffrey of Monmouth: parody and its purpose: a suggestion. *Speculum*, 54, 447–468.

Galloway, Andrew (2006). Laȝamon's gift. *PMLA*, 121, 717–34.

Gillingham, John (2000). The context and purposes of Geoffrey of Monmouth's 'History of the Kings of Britain'. In *The English in the Twelfth Century: Imperialism, National Identity and Political Values* (pp. 19–39). Woodbridge: Boydell Press. (Originally pub. in John Gillingham (1991). *Anglo-Norman Studies*, 13, 99–118.)

Given-Wilson, Chris (2004). *Chronicles: The Writing of History in Medieval England*. London: Hambledon Continuum.

Hanning, Robert W. (1966). *The Vision of History in Early Britain from Gildas to Geoffrey of Monmouth*. New York: Columbia University Press.

Johnson, Lesley (1991). Robert Mannyng's history of Arthurian literature. In Ian Wood and G. A. Loud (eds). *Church and Chronicle in the Middle Ages: Essays Presented to John Taylor* (pp. 129–147). London: Hambledon Press.

Johnson, Lesley (1994). Reading the past in Laȝamon's *Brut*. In Françoise Le Saux (ed.). *The Text and Tradition of Laȝamon's* Brut (pp. 141–160). Cambridge: D. S. Brewer.

Knight, Rhonda (2002). Stealing Stonehenge: translation, appropriation, and cultural identity in Robert Mannyng of Brunne's *Chronicle*. *Journal of Medieval and Early Modern Studies*, 32, 41–58.

Le Goff, Jacques (1993). Le Roi dans l'Occident médiéval: caractères originaux. In Anne J. Duggan (ed.). *Kings and Kingship in Medieval Europe* (pp. 1–40). London: King's College London Centre for Late Antique and Medieval Studies.

Le Saux, Françoise H. M. (1989). *Laȝamon's Brut: The Poem and its Sources*. Cambridge: D. S. Brewer.

Le Saux, Françoise H. M. (ed.) (1994). *The Text and Tradition of Laȝamon's Brut*. Cambridge: D. S. Brewer.

Madden, Frederic (ed.) (1847). *Laȝamon's Brut or Chronicle of Britain: A Poetical Semi-Saxon Paraphrase of The Brut of Wace*. 3 vols. London: Society of Antiquaries of London. (Repr. New York: AMS Press, 1970.)

Mercatanti, Gloria (2002). Some rhetorical devices of the Latin tradition in Laȝamon's 'Brut'. In Rosamund Allen, Lucy Perry and Jane Roberts (eds). *Laȝamon: Contexts, Language, and Interpretation* (pp. 241–49). King's College London Medieval Studies, 19. London: King's College London Centre for Late Antique and Medieval Studies.

Mitchell, Sarah L. (1999). 'We Englisse men': construction and advocacy of an English cause in the chronicle of Robert of Gloucester. In Erik Kooper (ed.). *The Medieval Chronicle* (pp. 191–201). Amsterdam: Rodopi.

Noble, James (2002), Laȝamon's Arthur: aðelest kingen. In Rosamund Allen, Lucy Perry and Jane Roberts (eds). *Laȝamon: Contexts, Language, and Interpretation* (pp. 285–97). King's College London Medieval Studies, 19. London: King's College London Centre for Late Antique and Medieval Studies.

Reeve, Michael D. (ed.) (2007). *Geoffrey of Monmouth. The History of the Kings of Britain: an edition and translation of the De Gestis Britonum {Historia Regum Britanniae}*. Trans. Neil Wright. Woodbridge: Boydell Press.

Sullens, Idelle (ed.) (1996). *Robert Mannyng, The Chronicle*. Binghamton, NY: Medieval & Renaissance Texts and Studies, Binghamton University.

Summerfield, Thea (1998). *The Matter of Kings' Lives: The Design of Past and Present in the Early Fourteenth-Century Verse Chronicles by Pierre de Langtoft and Robert Mannyng*. Costerus New Series 113. Amsterdam: Rodopi.

Summerfield, Thea and Rosamund Allen. (2008). Chronicles and historical narratives. In Roger Ellis (ed.). *Oxford History of Literary Translation in English: Volume 1 to 1550* (pp. 332–363). Oxford: Oxford University Press.

Swanton, Michael (ed. and trans.) (2000). *The Anglo-Saxon Chronicles*. New edn. London: Phoenix Press.

Tolkien, J. R. R. and E. V. Gordon (eds) (1967). *Sir Gawain and the Green Knight*. 2nd edn. Rev. Norman Davis. Oxford: Clarendon Press.

Turville-Petre, Thorlac (1988). Politics and poetry in the early fourteenth century: the case of Robert Manning's Chronicle. *Review of English Studies*, 39, 1–28.

Walsh, P. G. and M. J. Kennedy (eds and trans) (1988). *William of Newburgh: The History of English Affairs*. Warminster: Aris & Phillips.

Warren, W. L. (1987). *The Governance of Norman and Angevin England 1086–1272*. London: Edward Arnold.

Weinberg, Carole (1995). By a noble church on the bank of the Severn: a regional view of Laȝamon's 'Brut'. *Leeds Studies in English*, n.s. 26, 49–62.

Weinberg, Carole (2000). Victor and victim: a view of the Anglo-Saxon past in Laȝamon's 'Brut'. In Donald Scragg and Carole Weinberg (eds). *Literary Appropriations of the Anglo-Saxons from the Thirteenth to the Twentieth Century* (pp. 22–38). Cambridge: Cambridge University Press.

Weiss, Judith (ed. and trans.) (2002). *Wace's 'Roman de Brut': A History of the British*. Rev. edn. Exeter: University of Exeter Press.

Winterbottom, Michael (ed. and trans.) (1978). *'Gildas': The Ruin of Britain and Other Works*. London: Phillimore.

Wright, Neil (ed.) (1988). *Geoffrey of Monmouth. The Historia Regum Britannie of Geoffrey of Monmouth. 2, The First Variant Version. A Critical Edition*. Cambridge: D. S. Brewer.

Wright, William Aldis (ed.) (1887). *The Metrical Chronicle of Robert of Gloucester*. 2 vols. London: Eyre and Spottiswoode for Her Majesty's Stationery Office.

13

Medieval Debate-Poetry and
The Owl and the Nightingale

Neil Cartlidge

Debate-Poetry as Genre

If 'debate-poems' can reasonably be defined as poems 'in which two or three persons, personified things or abstractions, deliver speeches in a dispute, either in order to compare the merits and qualities of the speakers themselves or to determine some extraneous problem' – as Hans Walther long ago suggested in his seminal study of medieval Latin debate-poetry (Walther 1920) – then there is no question that *The Owl and the Nightingale* (ed. Cartlidge 2001) is, in these terms, a Middle English debate-poem. Its 1,794 lines are entirely devoted to reporting an imagined dispute between the two birds of the title – a dispute in which the 'merits and qualities' of the speakers are certainly discussed at some length, along with a wide range of more 'extraneous' issues, including the validity of astrological prognostications, the barbarism of northern peoples and the nature of women's experience of marriage. But what are the implications of this categorisation of *The Owl and the Nightingale* as a debate-poem? Should we imagine that this poem was originally conceived as a contribution to an established tradition of texts fitting Walther's definition? Would its author have regarded the 'debate-poem' as an autonomous literary genre in anything like the same way that a modern novelist, say, would regard the novel as a self-sufficient and, to some extent, self-evident category? Can it be shown that *The Owl and the Nightingale* has any direct genetic links with any other debate-poems – and, if so, how important are these other poems to any interpretation of *The Owl and the Nightingale* itself? Or is the very notion of debate-poetry simply a distraction – a case of literary criticism finding more significance in a particular poetic shape than medieval poets would themselves have recognised?

These questions have become difficult to discuss in part because of the rather undiscriminating way in which Walther's study has been used. Its chief claim to importance is as a 'pioneering' work (cf. Schmidt's preface to Walther 1920) – a first attempt at surveying what was, and to some extent still is (even over eighty years

later), relatively intractable literary-historical terrain. Walther was at considerable
pains to emphasise the practical difficulties of his task; his conclusions were often
quite tentative; and he made no claim to provide any account of the influence that
Latin debate-poems might have exerted on vernacular literary texts. He certainly
identified a number of medieval Latin poems to which his own definition of debate-
poetry applies – but not nearly so many as is sometimes assumed. Indeed, a significant
proportion of the texts that he discusses are not debate-poems at all – by any standard,
including his own. This was a consequence of his deliberate policy of adducing a
wide range of different kinds of text for the sake of 'elucidation and analogy' (Walther
1920: 3); but, in practice, this simply means that he gives a rather misleading
impression of the scale, currency and homogeneity of debate-poetry as a literary-
historical phenomenon. It is perhaps the sheer breadth of Walther's approach that
has fostered the apparent assumption that debate-poems were so numerous in
medieval Latin that the precise nature of their mutual interrelationships, or of their
relationships with other texts, is hardly worth thinking about, let alone examining
in any detail (e.g. Pearsall 1977: 91; Lerer 1999: 27).

For example, it is still sometimes asserted (with or without direct reference to
Walther) that there was an extensive tradition of medieval Latin debate-poems
dramatising the confrontation between Winter and Summer, or between Winter and
Spring. In fact, apart from the eighth-century debate often ascribed to Alcuin (ed.
Godman 1985: 144–49), which seems to have been very widely circulated, Walther
could only identify five other medieval Latin seasonal debates – and each of these is
extant only in a single copy (which makes it extremely unlikely that any of these
five had any influence on each other, or indeed much influence more generally). One
of them is a rather self-consciously learned, but by no means intellectually sophisticated, debate-poem preserved only in a thirteenth-century manuscript now in
Göttingen (ed. Walther 1920: 191–203). Two others – closely related, and to some
extent overlapping in content – survive together in a thirteenth-century manuscript
now in Paris (ed. Walther 1920: 203–209). Both of them seem to refer pointedly
to another medieval debate-poem, the 'Altercation between Ganymede and Helen'
(ed. Lenzen 1972; trans. Boswell 1981: 381–98), with which they share not only
their opening half-line, but also a conspicuous interest in the theme of homosexuality.
The other two texts listed by Walther are extant only in unique copies, one in
Cambridge (ed. Walther 1920: 209–11; see also Rigg 1968: 68), and the other in
Vienna (Walther 1920: 45). These four texts can be supplemented by two other
seasonal debates of which Walther was not aware, but they too are very rare texts
(Schmidt, supplementary notes to Walther 1920: 259–60). Eight poems on the same
theme may seem like quite enough to constitute a 'tradition', but what this brief
census surely demonstrates is that the only medieval Latin debate between the seasons
that is at all likely to have had any significant circulation or influence is the
Carolingian one associated with Alcuin, and that all of the other treatments of the
theme should probably be seen as testimony to the influence exerted by this one,
very well-known, debate-poem.

Similarly, it is often assumed that debates between personifications of the Body and the Soul were numerous in medieval Latin literature (and that Walther proves this), but in fact Walther lists just four of them – to which two more unknown to him might also be added. Of these six texts, four apparently survive only in single copies (see respectively Wilmart 1939: 193, n. 1; Walther 1920: 215–16; Heningham 1937; and Dreves and Blume 1886–1922: vol. 21, 115–16); and another in just two (ed. Wilmart 1939). This leaves just the so-called 'Vision of Philibert' (Wright 1841: 95–106) – a 300-line poem which survived into the twentieth century in at least 170 medieval copies (Cartlidge 2006). Walther rightly emphasises that 'almost all treatments of this material after the thirteenth century stand more or less under the influence' of the 'Vision of Philibert' (Walther 1920: 66). In other words, if the occurrence of Body-and-Soul debates in a strikingly wide range of vernacular literatures (from Icelandic to Greek, and from Hungarian to Spanish) owes anything at all to the precedent provided by Latin literature, then the form that this precedent took was almost certainly this single, very widely circulated text – and not a 'tradition' of medieval Latin debate-poems on this theme. The real story here is perhaps not that of debate-*poetry*, but of a relatively small number of particularly influential debate-*poems*.

Middle English Debate-Poetry

Attempting to transfer Walther's definition of debate-poetry to 'Middle English debate-poetry' brings with it some special problems of its own. Thomas L. Reed's lengthy study of Middle English debate-poetry begins with a reference to Francis Lee Utley's survey of 'Dialogues, Debates, and Catechisms' in *A Manual of the Writings in Middle English*, which he claims is 'indispensable for this or any other study of Middle English debate poetry' (Reed 1990: 1; Utley 1975). Yet Utley was not particularly concerned with delineating 'debate-poetry' as such; and his chapter can hardly be taken to demonstrate the existence of any very substantial tradition of debate-poetry in Middle English literature. Of the 76 items he lists under 'Dialogues, Debates, and Catechisms', only a very small number – apart from *The Owl and the Nightingale* itself – can easily be accommodated under Walther's definition of debate-poetry. In several of the texts that Utley includes, dialogue is wholly subordinated to didacticism – as in the case of question-and-answer texts like *Ypotis* (item 71) or *Sidrac and Boccus* (item 75). In others, dialogue is not the only structural principle, or even the most prominent one. For example, *Vices and Virtues* (item 26) is primarily an analysis of sins and their remedies; while *Dives and Pauper* (item 36) is a prose treatise on the Ten Commandments. Many other texts cited by the *Manual* can be placed in much more appropriate generic categories. For example, *The Mumming of the Seven Philosophers* (item 42) is a drama; while *De Amico ad Amicam* and the *Responcio* to it (item 58) are fictive letters. A large number of the items listed in the *Manual* actually refer to motifs taken from the repertoire of the Middle English lyric – Christ rebuking humanity; Annunciation-scenes; conversations between lovers; Holly-and-Ivy carols; and so on. Other items are either very short or fragmentary – such as the single stanza containing a dialogue between two demons (item 15); or the three couplets cited from the Book of John Grimestone (item 37). Still others are extracts – such as the tale taken from Caesarius of Heisterbach (item 13); the conversation between the emperor Antiochenus and his dead father 'imbedded in a narrative ascribed to Vincent of Beauvais' (item 25); or the exchange between a Monk, a Nun and a Brother Superior that serves as prologue to 'a prose version of selected parts of the New Testament' (item 39). And there are also several translations – such as Seneca's 'Old Age' and 'Friendship' (item 44); and Trevisa's version of the 'Dialogus inter militem et clericum' (item 40). In the end, what is most striking about the 76 items gathered under this heading in the *Manual* is just how disparate they are – how little they have in common *apart* from the fact that each of them depicts at least two speakers.

Utley himself seems to recognise that, even within the larger category of 'debates, dialogues and catechisms', there is a hard core of texts that are fundamentally shaped and characterised by debate in a way that others are not. These he tends to refer to as 'true debates' – as, for example, in his discussion of the Holly-and-Ivy carols, where he picks out one particular specimen as 'the one true debate in the lot' (Utley 1975: 725). Yet, in practice, he often makes no distinction between these 'true debates' and other texts that are thematically related to them, but that are not, in themselves, debates. For example, while Utley lists no fewer than 13 treatments of the Body-and-Soul theme (item 18), most of these are not, strictly speaking, debate-poems. In eight of them the confrontation extends no further than the Soul's reproaches to the Body. The Body does not reply, so no debate actually occurs. These texts are better classified as 'Soul's Addresses', rather than as 'Body-and-Soul debates'; and, as such, they scarcely even belong to Utley's broader category of 'debates, dialogues and catechisms', let alone to 'debate-poetry' as Walther defines it. What unites such poems as a group is that the Soul reproaches the Body – whether or not the Body replies seems to be incidental. From this point of view, the theme is clearly a much more important common denominator than the form in which it is treated. Of the remaining five Body-and-Soul texts listed by Utley, one is in prose; and another exists only in a printing of 1613. That leaves just three 'true debates' within the group. All three of them reveal the influence of the 'Vision of Philibert' – and so testify to the prominence of that poem in medieval culture generally, and not necessarily to any independent Middle English tradition of Body-and-Soul debate-poetry.

The Owl and the Nightingale is one of five Middle English 'bird-debates' cited by Utley (items 45–49). The others are 'The Thrush and the Nightingale' (from the thirteenth century; ed. Conlee 1991: 237–48); 'The Cuckoo and the Nightingale' (or 'Book of Cupid') by Chaucer's contemporary, Sir John Clanvowe, who died in 1391 (ed. Conlee 1991: 249–65; Scattergood 1975); and two fragmentary fifteenth-century poems – both called 'The Clerk and the Nightingale' and possibly representing two parts of the same poem (ed. Conlee 1991: 266–77). To these five items might be added a sixth – William Dunbar's 'The Merle and the Nightingale' (ed. Conlee 1991: 278–85) – a sixteenth-century text to which Utley briefly refers (Utley 1975: 723). On the face of it, these poems have too much in common with each other not to be closely related. For example, each of them contains at least some discussion of the dignity and morality of women (or of the love of women); and each of them features a nightingale as one of the antagonists. There are also sometimes quite detailed correspondences linking individual poems. So, for example, in 'The Thrush and the Nightingale', the Thrush's boast to 'have leave' ('habbe leue') to sing in orchards and arbours where ladies are to be found ('Thrush', ll. 97–102) recalls two different claims made by the Nightingale in *The Owl and the Nightingale* – to have royal permission to sing wherever she wants to ('war ich wulle': *Owl*, l. 1109) and to sing 'wherever there are ladies and pretty girls' ('Þar lauedies beoþ & faire maide': *Owl*, l. 1338). Both poems employ the topos of the wild becoming tame ('Thrush', l. 174; *Owl*, l. 1444); both emphasise the anger of the disputants ('Thrush', l. 49; *Owl*, ll. 933, 1043); and both depict the birds attempting to define the moral significance of their songs – using rather similar language in order to do so:

> [Nightingale:] Also ich sugge one mi song...
> ('Thrush', l. 122)

Thus I say in my song...

> [Nightingale:] Ich teache heom bi mine songe...
> (*Owl*, l. 1449)

I teach them by my song...

Similarly, 'The Clerk and the Nightingale' echoes 'The Thrush and the Nightingale' in its reference to Adam (as a victim of feminine treachery). Just as the Thrush declares 'I take witnesse of Adam, / Þat wes oure furste man' ('Thrush', ll. 70–71), so the Nightingale in 'The Clerk and the Nightingale' declares 'Wyttenesse Adam, þe formast man' ('Clerk' I, l. 43). Meanwhile, 'The Cuckoo and the Nightingale' resembles *The Owl and the Nightingale* in the way that the Cuckoo, like the Owl, characterises the Nightingale's song as a trivial, weedy sound:

> [Cuckoo:] ffor my song is boþ trwe & plein,
> And þouȝ I cannot crakil so in vayne,
> As þou dost in þi þrote...
> ('Cuckoo', l. 118–20)

For my song is both clear and in tune, even though I can't twitter pointlessly like you do in your throat...

> [Owl:] ...ich singe efne,
> Mid fulle dreme & lude stefne....
> Mi stefne is bold & noʒt unorne:
> Ho is ilich one grete horne –
> & þin is ilich one pipe
> Of one smale wode unripe.
>   (*Owl*, ll. 313–14, 317–20)

I sing smoothly, with a rich timbre and resonant voice [...] My voice is strong and by
no means feeble. It sounds like a great horn, while yours is like a whistle made out of
a little, unripe weed.

Such correspondences seem far too specific to be entirely coincidental, but at
least some of them can be explained by the influence of Old French literature, in
which there was an extensive tradition of poems featuring birds as advocates
or champions in debates about love. They include: the 'Fablel dou Dieu d'Amours'
(ed. Lecompte 1910–11; Oulmont 1911: 197–216; trans. Windeatt 1982: 85–91);
'Florance et Blancheflor' (ed. Oulmont 1911: 122–42; trans. Windeatt 1982: 92–95);
'Hueline et Aiglantine' (ed. Oulmont 1911: 157–67); 'Blancheflour et Florence'
(Oulmont 1911: 167–83; Windeatt 1982: 96–99); and 'Melior et Ydoine' (Oulmont
1911: 183–96; Windeatt 1982: 100–3). These texts offer parallels with the
English ones, not just in the general conception of birds as antagonists, but
also in various points of detail. So, for example, just as both the Thrush
(in the 'Thrush and the Nightingale') and the Nightingale (in *The Owl and
the Nightingale*) claim to frequent the places where ladies are to be found, so
in 'Melior et Ydoine' the speakers justify their choice of champions in terms of
their familiarity with what are clearly supposed to be distinctively feminine
environments:

> Fet Ydoigne: 'Jeo veille aver
> Le malvys qe chaunt si cler,
> K'est en la chaumbre nurrie
> E siet d'amur, jeo vous affy.'
> Feies Meillur: 'Vous dites bien;
> Ore jeo choiserai le mien.
> Jeo voile aver la russinole
> Qe est nurri de haut escole
> Sovent en chaumbre de curtine;
> La nature siet d'amur fine.'

Ydoine said, 'I wish to have the thrush, which sings so clear and which is brought
up in the chamber and knows about love, I assure you.' Melior said, 'You speak well.
Now I will choose mine. I wish to have the nightingale, which is brought up in a
lofty school, often in a curtained chamber, and of its nature knows about pure love.'
(Windeatt 1982: 102)

Similarly, the claim made by the Nightingale in 'Florance et Blancheflor' that 'Love has made me counsellor and judge in the royal court' ('Amors m'ont fet lor conseillier / En cort roial os bien jugier', lines 329–330) is analogous to the Wren's characterisation in *The Owl and the Nightingale*:

> Þe Wranne was wel wis iholde
> Vor, þeg heo uere ibred a wolde,
> Ho was itoȝen among mankunne
> An hire wisdom brohte þenne.
> Heo miȝte speke hwar heo walde,
> Touore þe king þah heo scholde.
> (*Owl*, ll. 1723–28)

The Wren was thought to be very wise, for even though she'd been bred in the forest, she'd been brought up among mankind and that was the source of her wisdom. She was allowed to speak wherever she liked – and even before the King if she chose.

Yet there is one important respect in which the Old French bird-poems do not resemble their Middle English counterparts – and that is that they can scarcely be described as debate-poems at all. The French bird-poems do contain a certain amount of verbal confrontation, but only a limited amount of it, and certainly no sustained debate comparable with what is to be found in *The Owl and the Nightingale* – or even in 'The Thrush and the Nightingale'. The ultimate medium for the resolution of the birds' differences in the French poems is not verbal competition at all, but physical combat. In 'Melior et Ydoine', for example, the Thrush and the Nightingale (each of them incongruously armed in flowers) joust together; and the Nightingale achieves victory only by driving his lance through the body of the Thrush. In sum, what unites all these bird-poems (whether French or English) is their use of birds as participants in quarrels about women, about love and/or about class – but not necessarily any extended commitment to debate itself, whether as an idea or as a structural principle. Thus, the increased emphasis on verbal disputation that tends to distinguish the English bird-poems from their French counterparts is precisely what literary tradition does *not* explain. Even if the English bird-poems were indeed generically dependent on the French ones (as seems very likely), then their concentration on *debate* is not an aspect of their dependency on their models, but a significant departure from them. This is a perspective that lends a certain edge to the possibility frequently hinted at in *The Owl and the Nightingale*, but ultimately never realised – the possibility that the poem's protagonists might abandon their debate in favour of some more violent means of resolution. So, for example, the narrator's observation that the Nightingale was so offended by the Owl's words that she would have been prepared to fight 'Mid sworde an mid speres orde, / ȝif ho mon were' (*Owl*, ll. 1068–69) seems much less hypothetical (if no less incongruous) in the light of the fact that several of the French poems do actually depict birds fighting judicial duels against each other. What all of this illustrates is that, even as 'debate-poetry' starts to look less and less cohesive as a generic category, and thus less and less reliable as a means of defining the rules by which the *Owl*-poet worked, so it becomes more and more apparent just how freely and inventively he manipulated his literary inheritances.

The Owl and the Nightingale as a Debate-Poem

It might seem from everything I have said so far that I have been intent on destabilising the very notion of debate-poetry as a distinct literary genre – and it is certainly true that I think describing *The Owl and the Nightingale* as a debate-poem begs more questions than it answers. That is not to say that debate-poetry seems to me to have no significance or urgency as a topic for critical and historical discussion – indeed, quite the reverse. The various ways in which medieval culture depended on patterns and practices of opposition or contrariety have recently been recognised in a number of studies (e.g. Brown 1998; Kay 2001; Bouchard 2003). What I want to emphasise, however, is that medieval debate-poetry is a very complex phenomenon, so complex that it is hazardous to generalise either about the circulation and origins of individual debate-poems, or about the contexts and purposes for which they were designed – despite the fact that there is a very long tradition in literary history of doing exactly that. It might ultimately be much more useful to analyse medieval debate-poetry, not as if it were a single literary tradition, but as a set of related traditions – not as genre, in other words, but as a nexus of genres (each with their own governing assumptions and their own socio-cultural affiliations). From this perspective, labelling *The Owl and the Nightingale* as a debate-poem certainly provides no short-cut to defining its author's ambitions or assumptions.

Nevertheless, there is a sense in which *The Owl and the Nightingale* itself might be said to tie together the various disparate strands of medieval debate-poetry in such a way as to justify the impression that debate-poetry did indeed constitute a distinct genre in medieval literature – and to do so much more deliberately and more self-consciously than any other medieval text. Even if the apparent coherence of medieval debate-poetry is no more than a kind of literary-historical illusion – even if the re-semblances between, say, the Winter-and-Spring/Summer debates, the Body-and-Soul debates and the bird-debates turn out to be merely superficial, with no consequence at all for our understanding of their implied purposes or their implied audiences – then there is still some justification, I would suggest, for reading *The Owl and the Nightingale* as if it were complicit in the creation of that illusion. To put it another way: even if the genre of medieval debate-poetry never existed, the *Owl*-poet seems to have found it necessary to invent it – or at least to pretend that it did exist. This odd effect can be explained by the fact that *The Owl and the Nightingale* is much longer than medieval debate-poems tend to be, so that it is effectively as an exercise in artful amplification – and the raw material for that amplification is often found in other debate-poems. In order to sustain the disagreement between the two birds for nearly 1800 lines, the poet plunders a wide range of literary sources; but, since he is always looking for material that expresses, or supports, antithesis, he naturally turns most readily to the themes and motifs that tend to appear in debates. The poet might even be said to have made a virtue out of a necessity, in the sense that the poem's very indebtedness contributes to its veneer of deliberate allusiveness. This veneer serves, in turn, to provide a kind of justification for the claim implicitly made by both of its protagonists, that they are, as it were, connoisseurs of debate-culture. Indeed, just as the two birds constantly attempt to outdo each other, so too does it often seem that the poet is deliberately attempting to outdo his sources. In that respect, *The Owl and the Nightingale* could reasonably be described both as a self-conscious summation, and a self-conscious surpassing, of received literary possibilities.

When the Nightingale attempts to answer the Owl's claims to piety with the allegation that she is guilty of spiritual pride, it is surely no coincidence that she chooses to do so precisely in terms of the motivating antagonism of the 'Vision of Philibert' – the confrontation between the Body and the Soul:

> Sei me soþ, ȝef þu hit wost,
> Hweþer deþ wurse: flesch þe gost?
> Þu miȝt segge, ȝef þu wult,
> Þat lasse is þe flesches gult...
> (*Owl*, ll. 1407–1410)

Tell me, if you know the answer, who does worse: the flesh or the spirit? You'd possibly want to admit that the flesh is less guilty...

The Body in the 'Vision of Philibert' makes no suggestion that the Soul is guilty of pride, but it does insist that the Soul's responsibility for sin is relatively much greater than its own:

> Tunc, si velle spiritus in opere ducatur
> per carnem pedissequam suam, quid culpatur?
> culpa tangit animam, quæ præmeditatur
> quicquid caro fragilis vivens operatur.
> Peccasti tu gravius, dico, mihi crede,
> carnis sequens libitum fragilis et fœdæ...
> ('Vision of Philibert', ll. 130–35)

Moreover, if the soul was seduced by the flesh, its handmaid, into assenting to the deed, how is the flesh to blame? The fault is the soul's, who devises whatever deeds are committed by the body (susceptible as it is) in life. Believe me, I think you've sinned much more gravely than me, in bowing to the wishes of your feeble and filthy body...

This emphasis on the question of relative culpability also appears in some of the vernacular Body-and-Soul debates, as, for instance, in the Middle English poem that begins 'Als I lay' (ed. Conlee 1991: 18–49):

> Soule, ȝif þou it me wilt atwite
> Þat we schul be boþe y-spilt,
> ȝif þou hast schame & gret despite,
> Al it is þine owhen gilt.
> Y þe say at wordes lite,
> Wiþ riȝt resoun, ȝif þatow wilt:
> Þou berst þe blame & y go quite,
> Þou scholdest fram schame ous haue yschilt.
>
> ('Als I lay', ll. 177–84)

Soul, if you want to reproach me for the fact that we shall both be destroyed, and if you've incurred shame and great scorn, then the guilt is entirely yours. If you like, I'll explain it very briefly to you in just and reasonable words: you shoulder the blame and I'm acquitted – you should have protected us from shame.

When the Nightingale abruptly gives up on this particular line of argument, as she does just a few lines later, she then introduces a contrast that provides matter for debate in various medieval texts – the contrast between maidens and wives:

> ȝet ȝif ich schulde a luue bringe
> Wif oþer maide, hwanne ich singe,
> Ich wolde wiþ þe maide holde,
> ȝif þu const ariht atholde.
> Lust nu, ich segge þe hwareuore
> Vp to þe toppe from þe more...
>
> (*Owl*, ll. 1417–22)

But if, in singing I had to bring either a married woman or a maiden towards love, my choice would be the maiden, as long as you understand me correctly. Just listen and I'll tell you my reasoning from top to bottom...

Several medieval texts compare the relative attractions of maidens and wives as potential lovers in a fashion that is implicitly masculine, cynical and to some extent self-consciously Ovidian (Cartlidge 2001: 90, n. to ll. 1515–18) and there are also a few texts that deploy the distinction between maidens and wives as a means of comparing different kinds of female experience (see e.g. Revard 1982; Revard 2004). In other words, when this contrast between wives and maidens gives rise to debate, it usually implies either a self-consciously masculine perspective from which women are talked about, or a self-consciously feminine perspective from which women talk about themselves. *The Owl and the Nightingale* contrives to find a new perspective of its own. Even though neither of its avian protagonists has any direct experience of the injustices suffered by women, they are still female – and so naturally keen to express solidarity with their human 'sisters'. Yet it is hardly inevitable that a disagreement between an owl and a nightingale should come to devolve on a debate about whether or not the pre-marital sexual relationships of maidens are more excusable than the extra-marital sexual relationships of wives – no matter how convincingly the poet depicts the birds' eager partisanship. In the immediate context of the debate, the Nightingale raises these issues principally as a tactical means of refuting, or at least evading, the allegation that she condones adultery, but this is hardly the most obvious or logical means of doing so. The Owl, meanwhile, is apparently so keen to pursue the debate about marriage that she is even prepared, not just to stop attacking the Nightingale's record on adultery, but even to risk condoning adultery herself (as she does explicitly at ll. 1539–44). The explanation for the birds' willingness to translate their animosity so arbitrarily into a debate about marital status is surely that the contrast between maidens and wives was already an established literary topos.

Elsewhere in the poem, the contest between the Owl and the Nightingale is clearly shaped by reference to the opposition between winter and summer. This first emerges as one of the poem's implied sub-themes when the Nightingale attempts to reinforce her emphasis on the intrinsic gloominess of the Owl's song, by exploiting the natural fact that owls (unlike nightingales) are sometimes heard singing in the middle of an English winter:

> A wintere þu singest wroþe & ӡomere:
> An eure þu art dumb a sumere.
> (*Owl*, ll. 414–16)

> In winter you sing grimly and dolefully,
> but in the summer you're completely dumb.

According to the Nightingale, this preference for singing in winter demonstrates that the Owl is so deeply envious of other people's misfortunes that she is incapable of celebrating with them when they are happy, but is more than willing to do so when times are hard:

> Hit is for þine fule niþe
> Þat þu ne miӡt mid us bo bliþe,
> Vor þu forbernest wel-neӡ for onde
> Wane ure blisse cumeþ to londe.
> Þu farest so doþ þe ille:
> Evrich blisse him is unwille.
> (*Owl*, ll. 417–22)

> It's because of your vile malice that you can't share in our happiness; for you're nearly burnt-up with envy when there's happiness on earth. You're like a mean fellow who doesn't like any kind of fun.

The particular logic of this passage recalls the Carolingian debate between Spring and Winter, in which Winter is characterised as a bad-tempered miser:

Haec inimica mihi sunt, quae tibi laeta videntur,
Sed placet optatas gazas numerare per arcas...
('Spring and Winter', ll. 31–32)

The things I hate are those which seem delightful to you.
I like to count my coveted treasures in their chests...

This suggestion is also developed in some of the vernacular seasonal debates. For example, in Nicole Bozon's 'De l'Yver et de l'Esté' (ed. Bossy 1987: 2–15), Summer complains:

Tant estes de grant demesure
Qe de belté n'avez cure,
A vostre vueil. [...]
Vus n'avez cure d'autre vie,
Fors fere mal e freyterye
A tote gent.
('De l'Yver et de l'Esté', ll. 43–45, 52–54)

You are of such arrogance
That you take no heed of beauty,
Such is your ill will.
The only occupation you care for
Is harming and chilling
All people.

Bozon's poem, like *The Owl and the Nightingale*, also implies a world that is distinctively agricultural. Just as the envious man described by the Nightingale finds matter for *Schadenfreude* in the confusion of flocks (ll. 427–28), so Winter, in the French poem, takes malicious pleasure is disrupting the work of ploughmen. Yet what is striking here is not so much that correspondences between *The Owl and the Nightingale* and these seasonal debates exist, as the extent to which they have been absorbed into the very structure of the English poem. The Nightingale moves so rapidly from attempting to identify the Owl with winter to accusing her of malice and jealousy, that her line of thought seems quite arbitrary, even elliptical; and again the explanation for that is surely that she is building on associations already established in other texts. The Owl's counter-argument – in effect a defence of Winter – also has literary precedents. For example, her description of midwinter festivities looks like an elaboration of one of Winter's arguments in the Carolingian debate:

Sunt mihi divitiae, sunt et convivia laeta,
Est requies dulcis, calidus est ignis in aede.
('Spring and Winter', ll. 25–26)

I have wealth, I have joyous banquets,
I have sweet rest and a hot fire at home.

Hit is gode monne iwone,
An was from þe worlde frome,
Þat ech god man his frond icnowe;
An blisse mid hom sume þrowe,
In his huse, at his borde,
Mid faire speche & faire worde –
& hure & hure to Cristesmasse…
                    (*Owl*, 475–83)

It's customary with worthy people (and has been since the beginning of the world), that every good man acknowledges his friends; and on some occasion celebrates with them, in his home and at his table, with pleasant conversation and talk – and, in particular, at Christmas…

These lines, in turn, probably reflect the influence of Virgil's poetry – this time, not his *Eclogues*, but his *Georgics* (ed. Mynors 1985; trans. Lewis 1983):

hiems ignaua colono:
frigoribus parto agricolae plerumque fruuntur
mutuaque inter se laeti conuiuia curant.
inuitat genialis hiems curasque resoluit…
                    (Virgil, *Georgics*, I. 299–301)

Winter's an off-time
For farmers: then they mostly enjoy their gains, hold jolly
suppers amongst themselves.
Genial winter invites them and they forget their worries […]

Correspondingly, when the Nightingale boasts of her own joyful association with summer, she speaks in such a way as to sound as if she is not just exploiting that association, but actually usurping the role established for Summer in the debates between seasons:

Ac ich alle blisse mid me bringe:
Ech wiȝt is glad for mine þinge,
& blisseþ hit wanne ich cume,
& hiȝteþ aȝen mine kume.
Þe blostme ginneþ springe & sprede,
Boþe ine tro & ek on mede.
                    (*Owl*, ll. 433–438)

But I bring joy entirely when I arrive. Every creature is glad because of me. They rejoice about it when I turn up and they look forward to my coming. The blossoms are then sprouting and growing, both on the trees and in the meadows.

This might be compared with the claims made by Spring, in the Carolingian debate, on behalf of the cuckoo:

Opto meus veniat cuculus, carissimus ales!
Omnibus iste solet fieri gratissimus hospes
In tectis modulans rutilo bona carmina rostro.
                ('Spring and Winter', ll. 10–12)

I hope that my cuckoo will come, dearest of birds!
He is always everyone's favourite visitor,
as he sings good songs with his shining beak on the roofs.

Nicole Bozon's Summer also argues that he brings joy to the world; and he chooses the nightingale as his ambassador:

Ju su de paraïs transmys
Pur vus remuer del pays
            E gent amender.
Je faz russinole chaunter,
Arbres floryr, fruit porter,
            Sauntz contredit.
Je faz floryr le verger,
Fueil e flur novel porter,
            A grant delit.
('De l'Yver et de l'Esté', ll. 239–47)

From heaven I am sent
To expel you from this land
And improve the people.
I make the nightingale sing,
Trees flower and bear fruits –
None will gainsay it.
I make orchards flower
And bear fresh leaves and flowers,
For great delight.

Many more such comparisons between *The Owl and the Nightingale* and other debate-poems could be made – and probably more than enough to justify the suggestion that the Middle English poem was designed to serve as a kind of summation or celebration of the imaginative possibilities implicit in the various medieval traditions of debate-poetry. Yet I also suggested earlier that *The Owl and the Nightingale* presents itself not just as a response to such traditions, but also, to some extent, as a deliberate outdoing of them. So, for example, while it is by no means unusual for debate-poems to emphasise the anger of one or other of their protagonists (and indeed I have already cited this topos as one that *The Owl and the Nightingale* shares with 'The Thrush and the Nightingale'), only *The Owl and the Nightingale* goes so far as to provide a diagnosis of its physiological effects:

...wraþþe meinþ þe horte blod
Þat hit floweþ so wilde flod
An al þe heorte ouergeþ
Þat heo naueþ noþing bute breþ;
An so forleost al hire liht
Þat heo ne siþ soð ne riht.
(Owl, ll. 947–52)

For wrath so whips up the blood that it rushes like a fierce torrent, completely overwhelming the heart so that it contains nothing but vapour and is so deprived of all its
lucidity that it recognises neither right nor truth.

In the context of the birds' petty quarrel, such anatomical pedantry appears not just
incongruous, but downright extravagant. Similarly, while it is hardly surprising that the
antagonists in debate-poems are occasionally motivated by 'spite and vexation' – as, for
example, in the case of Pseustis in the 'Eclogue of Theodulus', who is 'motus felle
doloris' (l. 14) – both the Owl and the Nightingale carry the expression of malice to a high
art. Their mutual vindictiveness is emphasised even in the first few lines of the poem:

An aiþer aȝen oþer sval,
& let þat vole mod ut al;
& eiþer saide of oþeres custe
Þat alre worste þat hi wuste...
(Owl, ll. 7–10)

And each of them swelled up against the other and vented all her malicious feelings,
saying the very worst thing they could think of about their antagonist's character...

And it is amply illustrated thereafter. Here, for example, is the Nightingale gleefully
celebrating the death of her opponent at the hands of a violent mob – deliberately
adding insult to injury by suggesting that it is only then that the Owl does anybody
any good:

...children, gromes, heme & hine,
Hi þencheþ alle of þire pine.
ȝif hi muȝe iso þe sitte,
Stones hi doþ in hore slitte
An þe totorued & toheneþ,
An þine fule bon tosheneþ.
ȝif þu art iworpe oþer ishote,
Þanne þu miȝt erest to note:
Vor me þe hoþ in one rodde
An þu mid þine fule codde,
An mid þine ateliche swore,
Biwerest manne corn urom dore.
(Owl, ll. 1115–1126)

For children and menials, peasants and farm-hands, are all intent on doing you harm. If they can catch sight of you sitting there, they put stones in their pockets, and they pelt you and smash you to pieces and shatter all your bones. Once they've stoned you or shot you, that's the first time you've ever been useful for anything: for they hang you on a stick and then with your rotten corpse and your horrible neck you keep the animals off mankind's corn.

Or again, while several seasonal debates insist on the association between summer and love – as, for example, in the case of Nicole Bozon's 'De l'Yver et de l'Esté', where according to Winter, Summer's followers 'call themselves fine lovers' ('se fount coyntes d'amours', l. 188) – only in _The Owl and the Nightingale_ is this developed into an extended image of madness and chaos:

> Vor sumeres tide is al to wlonc
> An doþ misreken monnes þonk –
> Vor he ne recþ noȝt of clennesse:
> Al his þoȝt is of golnesse.
> Vor none dor no leng nabideþ,
> Ac eurich upon oþer rideþ.
> Þe sulue stottes ine þe stode
> Bot boþe wilde & mere-wode.
> [...]
> A sumere chorles awedeþ,
> & uorcrempeþ & uorbredeþ
> Hit nis for luue noþeles,
> Ac is þe chorles wode res...
>
> (_Owl_, ll. 489–96, 509–512)

For summer-time is far too splendid, and it disturbs a man's mind – for he doesn't think about clean living: he sets his mind on lechery. Indeed, there's not an animal able to wait, but each of them climbs upon the next; and even the draught-horses in the paddock go wild in their madness for mares! [...] In summer the yokels are driven wild, contorting and deforming themselves. However, this is not out of love, but because of the yokel's mad fury...

In short, what distinguishes _The Owl and the Nightingale_ from other medieval debate-poems is not so much the nature of its subject-matter, as the energy and extravagance with which that subject-matter is developed. Even if many of the moves that it makes are recognisably those of other debate-poems, the sheer copiousness and self-confidence with which it appropriates them makes the poem seem like a virtuoso performance.

The Owl and the Nightingale and the _Petit Plet_

One of the more unfortunate consequences of the tendency to assume that _The Owl and the Nightingale_ depends, for its structure and many of its ideas, on 'medieval debate-poetry' in general, is that its relationships with individual debate-poems have not been investigated nearly as rigorously as they might have been. Of all such poems the one that most insistently begs comparison with *The Owl and the Nightingale* is the *Petit Plet* (ed. Merrilees 1970), an Anglo-Norman poem of nearly 1800 lines, which can be found in both of the extant manuscripts of the English poem (Cartlidge 1997: 253–56). The protagonists in the *Petit Plet* are not birds, nor are they female – they are an Old Man ('Le Veillard') and a Young Man ('L'Enfant') – but their attitudes sometimes correspond very closely with those of the Owl and the Night-ingale. So, for example, the question central to the *Petit Plet* is whether it is better to serve God with a cheerful heart or to concentrate on the sombre inevitability of death. The Old Man accuses the Young Man of being foolish ('poi...senez') for taking pleasure in things that are transient ('Ki mult vus endurra petit', l. 104), whereas the Young Man sees no reason for being any more morose than he needs to be ('De trop duleir n'i vei resun', l. 137). This is an issue that the birds discuss in very similar terms (ll. 713–50, 849–932) – with the Owl taking what is essentially the Old Man's position, the Nightingale the Young Man's:

> [Owl:] Ich rede þi þat men bo ȝare,
> An more wepe þane singe,
> Þat fundeþ to þan houen-kinge,
> Vor nis no man witute sunne.
> Vorþi he mot, are he wende honne,
> Mid teres an mid wope bete...
> (*Owl*, ll. 860–66)

So I advise that anyone seeking the King of Heaven must be in readiness, crying rather than singing, for there's no one without sin. That's why, before leaving this world, everyone should make amends with weeping and with tears...

> [Nightingale:] Ich warni men to here gode,
> Þat hi bon bliþe on hore mode;
> An bidde þat hi moten iseche
> Þan ilke song þat euer is eche.
> (*Owl*, ll. 739–42)

I remind people of what is good for them, and that they should be cheerful in spirit; and I urge them that they should be seeking that song that is perpetual.

Like the Owl and the Nightingale, the Old Man and the Young Man also debate the value of marriage, but this is an issue where the nature of the protagonists makes a difference to the direction of the debate. Whereas the English poem's comparison of maidens and wives ultimately hinges on a comparison of the complaints that women might make against two different kinds of masculine misbehaviour – that of the cynical seducer (ll. 1423–41) and that of the jealous or violent husband (ll. 1521–64)

– the French's poem discussion of marriage amounts to a debate about the probity of women. Yet one of the arguments adduced by the Young Man against women is that 'they gather together to discuss their complaints' ('Enz en chapitres moevent lur plet', l. 1396) – very much as the birds do in *The Owl and the Nightingale*. In effect, the two poems illustrate each other – with the birds competing to criticise men in just the way that the Young Man fears women naturally do, and the Young Man exemplifying precisely the cynicism that the birds think typical of men's attitudes towards women. Even when the two poems' protagonists bring different perspectives to bear, they still seem to inhabit social worlds that are imagined in very similar ways.

Moreover, the two poems have much in common stylistically, despite the fact that they are written in different languages. Both of them self-consciously cultivate pro-verbial wisdom – as expressed, for example, in *The Owl* by the birds' deference to the sayings that they ascribe to King Alfred, and, in the *Petit Plet*, by the narrator's claim that his poem contains many pertinent proverbs ('verraiz respiz', l. 15). Many of these proverbs imply contexts that very similar – in some cases strikingly similar. Just as the Nightingale tells her story about the Owlet's intrusion in the Hawk's nest in order to illustrate the principle (which she defines in proverbial terms) that a bad apple always reveals himself ('Þeʒ appel trendli fron þon trowe.../ He cuþ wel whonene he is icume', ll. 135, 138), so the Young Man alludes to the same principle by quoting the proverb that 'you'll never make a good hawk out of a kite or a buzzard' ('Car de escufle u de busard/ Bon ostur averez vus mult tart', ll. 837–38). Straight after this, he goes on to cite another proverb for which there is also a direct parallel in *The Owl and the Nightingale* (and again it involves a reference to the hawk):

> En pes serra vostre curage
> En cumpaignie de home sage;
> E si les fous vulez crere,
> Ja en averez vus pes en terre.
> (*Petit Plet*, ll. 841–44)

As long as you're in the company of a wise person, your heart will be in peace, but if you want to trust the fools, you'll never have any peace on earth.

> 'Loke þat þu ne bo þare,
> Þar chauling boþ, & cheste ʒare!
> Lat sottes chide & uorþ þu go!'
> [...]
> Wenestu þat haueck bo þe worse
> þoʒ crowe bigrede him bi þe merse,
> & goþ to him mid hore chirme,
> Riʒt so hi wille wit him schirme?
> Þe hauec folʒeþ gode rede:
> & fliʒt his wei & lat hi grede.
> (*The Owl and the Nightingale*, ll. 295–97, 303–308)

'Watch that you aren't around where there's babbling and brawling at hand! Let fools bicker and you walk away!' [...] Do you think that the hawk is any the worse for the fact that the crows cry out against him along the field-edges, pursuing him with their racket, just as if they wanted to fight him? The hawk has a good policy: he flies on his way and lets them all shout.

There are a number of other points at which the *Petit Plet*'s turns of phrase also closely resemble those of *The Owl and the Nightingale*. The Young Man's suggestion that his opponent's tongue is 'lavish with precepts as a priest's on Sunday' ('Tant avez la lange pleine/ Des diz le prestre al dimeine', ll. 185–86) recalls the Owl's suggestion that her opponent chatters like an Irish priest ('Þu chaterest so doþ an Irish prost', l. 322). Similarly, the Old Man's acknowledgment that in youth 'the blood is warm and the heart light' comes close – both in sentiment and in imagery – to the Nightingale's suggestion that a maiden is led amiss only by her 'ȝunge blod' (l. 1434).

The divergences between the two poems are ultimately most apparent in terms of what they conceive the rules of debate-poetry to be. That is, while it makes good sense to describe both *The Owl and the Nightingale* and the *Petit Plet* as debate-poems, what emerges from this is not so much a basis for comparison, as an illustration that – even in the case of poems that otherwise have so much in common – debate-poetry can still function in radically different ways. So, for example, whereas the dispute between the Owl and the Nightingale generally develops in ways that are arbitrary and unpredictable enough to convey at least the illusion of spontaneity, the *Petit Plet* appears much more programmatic. Far from developing organically (as in *The Owl and the Nightingale*), the debate in the *Petit Plet* follows quite a strict agenda, with the Old Man citing a series of misfortunes that have befallen him and inviting the Young Man to offer consolation for each in turn. This agenda is clearly based on a particular source – a collection of Stoical dicta known as *De remediis fortuitorum* ('On the remedies for misfortunes', ed. in Palmer), and often ascribed to Seneca. Although the *Petit Plet* expands this source in various ways, it retains much of its essential dogmatism. Indeed, it could even be argued that the *Petit Plet* is hardly a 'true debate' at all in the sense that it is ultimately less concerned with competition than with consolation. The Old Man's misfortunes are presented as a challenge to the philosophical ingenuity of the Young Man, but it is always implicit that this a challenge that he is capable of meeting – and to that extent the *Petit Plet* is (like its source) really only a pretext for rehearsing a particular kind of sententious discourse. The question is never 'which figure will win the debate?', but only 'how will the Young Man go about winning the debate?' Even so, the *Petit Plet* is in some ways a more troubling and disorientating poem than the *The Owl and the Nightingale*, precisely because of the way in which the rigidity of its structural assumptions often conflicts with the actual effect of the antagonists' words. Even though it is the Young Man's 'wisdom' that the poem pretends to celebrate, much of what he says is conspicuously illogical or unsympathetic – to the point, at times, of remarkable ineptness. So, for example, the Old Man is hardly likely to be consoled for the death of his children by the curious argument that it is much worse for a king to lose a child than for a beggar to do so (*Petit Plet*, ll. 1123–1130). Similarly, when the Young Man attempts to console the Old Man for the loss of his wife with the misogynistic commonplace that women can never be trusted anyway, his argument is not just inappropriate (since, as the Old Man makes clear, his wife deserved no such reproach) – but so breathtakingly insensitive as to seem incompatible with 'wisdom' of any kind. When the Old Man goes on to praise his wife in movingly insistent terms, the Young Man chooses to interpret this – even more crassly – only as an illustration of the tactical effectiveness of praise when training dogs, horses or women (*Petit Plet*, ll. 1280–81). Implicitly reducing women to the level of animals as it does, this comparison is offensive not just to women, but also to the Old Man – whose powerful testimony to his wife's virtues hardly invites so perversely inhumane a response.

Like *The Owl and the Nightingale* then, the *Petit Plet* tends to mix moments of seriousness and apparent conviction with argumentative manoeuvres that are blatantly spurious or absurd: but what makes the *Petit Plet* so particularly disconcerting is the way in which this mixture is distributed among the speakers. Whereas *The Owl and the Nightingale* makes no clear suggestion that either of its protagonists has any more authority than the other, the *Petit Plet* clearly insists on the intellectual superiority of the Young Man – but then makes him a much less appealing speaker than his opponent. It could be argued that the *Petit Plet* is ultimately a much more provocative poem than *The Owl and the Nightingale*, precisely because it creates an expectation of ordered authority, which it then subverts. What the comparison between these two poems illustrates is that even where there is so much in common (in terms of context, scale, style and detail), the creative possibilities of debate-poetry could still be realised in strikingly different ways.

References and Further Reading

Bossy, Michel-André (ed. and trans.) (1987). *Medieval Debate Poetry: Vernacular Works*. New York: Garland.

Boswell, John (1981). *Christianity, Social Tolerance, and Homosexuality: Gay People in Western Europe from the Beginning of the Christian Era to the Fourteenth Century*. Chicago: University of Chicago Press.

Bouchard, Constance B. (2003). *'Every Valley Shall be Exalted': The Discourse of Opposites in Twelfth-Century Thought*. Ithaca, NY: Cornell University Press.

Brown, Catherine (1998). *Contrary Things: Exegesis, Dialectic, and the Poetics of Didacticism*. Stanford, CA: Stanford University Press.

Cartlidge, Neil (1997). The composition and social context of Oxford, Jesus College, MS 29 (II) and London, British Library, MS Cotton Caligula A.ix. *Medium Ævum*, 66, 250–69.

Cartlidge, Neil (ed.) (2001). *The Owl and the Nightingale: Text and Translation*. Exeter: University of Exeter Press. (Repr. 2003.)

Cartlidge, Neil (2006). In the silence of a midwinter night: a re-evaluation of the 'Visio Philiberti'. *Medium Ævum*, 75, 24–45.

Conlee, John W. (ed.) (1991). *Middle English Debate Poetry: A Critical Anthology*. East Lansing: Colleagues Press.

Dreves, Guido Maria, and Clemens Blume (eds) (1886–1922). *Analecta hymnica medii aevi*. 55 vols. Leipzig. (Repr. Frankfurt am Main: Minerva, 1961.)

Godman, Peter (ed.) (1985). *Poetry of the Carolingian Renaissance*. London: Duckworth.

Heningham, Eleanor Kellogg (ed.) (1937). An early Latin Debate of the body and the soul, preserved in MS Royal 7 A VII in the British Museum. Doctoral dissertation. New York University.

Kay, Sarah (2001). *Courtly Contradictions: The Emergence of the Literary Object in the Twelfth Century*. Stanford, CA: Stanford University Press.

Lecompte, I. C. (ed.) (1910–11). 'Le Fablel dou Dieu d'Amors'. *Modern Philology*, 8, 63–68.

Lenzen, R. W. (ed.) (1972). Altercacio Ganimedis et Helene: Kritische edition mit Kommentar. *Mittellateinisches Jahrbuch*, 7, 161–86.

Lerer, Seth (1999). Old English and its afterlife. In David Wallace (ed.). *The Cambridge History of Medieval English Literature* (7–34). Cambridge: Cambridge University Press.

Lewis, C. Day (trans.) (1983). *Virgil: The Eclogues: The Georgics*. Oxford: Oxford University Press.

Merrilees, Brian S. (ed.) (1970). *Chardri: Le Petit Plet*. Anglo-Norman Text Society 20. London: ANTS.

Mynors, R. A. B. (ed.) (1985). *P. Vergili Maronis: Opera*. Oxford: Oxford University Press.

Oulmont, Charles (ed.) (1911). *Les débats du clerc et du chevalier dans la littérature poétique du moyen-âge*. Paris: Champion.

Palmer, R. G. (1953). *'De remediis fortuitorum' and the Elizabethans*. Chicago: Institute of Elizabethan Studies.

Pearsall, Derek (1977). *Old English and Middle English Poetry*. London, Henley and Boston: Routledge & Kegan Paul.

Reed, Thomas L., Jr. (1990). *Middle English Debate Poetry and the Aesthetics of Irresolution*. Columbia: University of Missouri Press.

Revard, Carter (1982). 'Gilote et Johane': an interlude in MS Harley 2253. *Studies in Philology*. 79, 122–46.

Revard, Carter (2004). The Wife of Bath's grandmother: or, how Gilote showed her friend Johane that the wages of sin is worldly pleasure, and how both then preached this gospel throughout England and Ireland. *Chaucer Review*, 39, 117–36.

Rigg, A. G. (ed.) (1968). *A Glastonbury Miscellany of the Fifteenth Century: A Descriptive Index of Trinity College, Cambridge, MS 0.9.38*. London: Oxford University Press.

Scattergood, V. J. (ed.) (1975). *The Works of Sir John Clanvowe*. Cambridge: D. S. Brewer.

Utley, Francis Lee (1975). Dialogues, debates and catechisms. In J. Burke Severs and Albert Hartung (eds). *A Manual of Writings in Middle English* (669–745 and 829–902). Vol. 3. New Haven: Connecticut Academy of Arts and Sciences.

Walther, Hans (1920). *Das Streitgedicht in der lateinischen Literatur des Mittelalters*. Ed. Paul Gerhard Schmidt. Munich: Beck. (Repr. Hildesheim: Olms, 1984.)

Wilmart, A. (ed.) (1939). Un grand débat de l'âme et du corps en vers élégiaques. *Studi Medievali*. NS 12, 192–209.

Windeatt, B. A. (trans.) (1982). *Chaucer's Dream-Poetry: Sources and Analogues*. Cambridge: D. S. Brewer.

Wright, Thomas (ed.) (1841). *The Latin Poems Commonly Attributed to Walter Mapes*. London: Camden Society. (Repr. Hildesheim: Olms, 1968.)

14

Lyrics, Sacred and Secular

David Fuller

Those who composed, wrote down, sang, danced, or read short stanzaic poems between the twelfth and the fifteenth centuries would not have thought of them as lyrics – a term first used in the late sixteenth century.[1] To their first performers or readers these poems often served a practical rather than the expressive function we associate with lyric from Wyatt to Heaney – a practical function, from helping the company at a feast to make merry to prompting a sinner to repent. Stanzaic poems were not 'lyrics'. Nor were secular and sacred sharply separate. Feasts often celebrated a religious festival; a sinner might sin in love. And, more generally, the world was God's creation; there was no entirely secular realm: celebration of earthly pleasure or lamentation of earthly suffering both commonly incorporated in their joy or sorrow at the conditions of life some religious aspect. Religious feeling was often touched with feeling that might now be regarded as secular, and vice-versa: love had a religious aspect, because human and divine love were seen as ultimately having some relationship (whether of continuity or contradiction), or because certain sorts of love, or love in certain contexts, were sinful. The obvious modern categories for these poems can, then, be misleading.

But not entirely. 'Lyric' (adapted to the lyre; intended to be sung; characteristic of song) points to an important association with music – with song and with dance. Even the poems not written (as many were) to be sung exploit the music of words in patterns of rhyme, assonance, and alliteration. In a context of conventions of subject, feeling and expression, the verbal music of a poem may often be the aspect of composition that gave the poet most freedom for creativity or craft, and so a significant source of pleasure for the reader; and the association with dance – and through music and dance with one of the roots of poetry: rhythm – often means that formal and metrical patterns have significant expressive value, or are simply in themselves beautiful. Equally, though powerful conventions of feeling in love and religion mean that Jesus may be addressed, like a lover, as 'my sweet leman [beloved]', and devotion to the beloved may be expressed with a quasi-religious fervour, poems addressed to Christ or to the Virgin, and poems of a love that is 'soft, sweet, and lecher [lecherous]', form distinct groups. Some qualifications must be recognised; but the modern categories – lyric, sacred, secular – also point to real qualities.

Medieval lyrics are preserved in sources of very different kinds. Some are in elaborate collections, of which the grandest is the late fourteenth-century illuminated Vernon manuscript, and the most important for its love lyrics, the early fourteenth-century Harley manuscript. A few collections are by known compilers, some of whom were also writers and translators.[2] Most poems are anonymous. Some are in anthologies apparently made for private reading, occasionally with musical notation, sometimes in miscellanies of other kinds of writing, such as sermons, but many are simply written in the margins or interstices of manuscripts of diverse kinds (Figure 14.1). These contexts of preservation usually tell little or nothing about the contexts of composition and use – the author, original audience, or circumstances in and for which a poem was written, though the commonly Franciscan context of religious lyrics has been taken to indicate a connection with preaching. Otherwise it is difficult to draw conclusions from sources in themselves so heterogeneous, particularly when the evidence they offer is so partial; and especially with the secular poetry, a great deal, probably much the greater part, must have been lost. What is clear from the sources is that lyrics served a range of functions, from private devotion and public religious teaching to performance heightening occasions of entertainment and revelry. And while poems scribbled in a margin imply simple spontaneous pleasure, the grand manuscript collections indicate cultivated aristocratic cultures in which poetry – especially religious poetry – was highly and deliberately valued. That is, lyrics were for every kind of poetic taste and every order of society: the range was from Bob Dylan to Geoffrey Hill, and from the most ephemeral CD insert to the most exclusive limited edition.

Some lyrics that were straightforward for contemporary readers or those who heard them read or sung remain simple for modern readers. Many do not. One of the pleasures of the lyrics is their use of language that was marked (whether aureate or colloquial) in the dialects in which they were composed or written down; but often their language has elements that have not passed into modern English, and so what was once vigorously colloquial has become abstruse – its sense, and still more its flavour, difficult to grasp. As with reading poetry in a foreign language, the reader who can feel the movement of the syntax and hear the structural relationships of words will grasp a good deal. In reading poetry it is a fundamental error to think of everything about meaning as dependent on semantic content, and by concentrating on that miss the meanings inherent in structuration. (This is, of course, a two-way process: grasping structure often depends on some understanding of semantic content.)

The opening of a Harley lyric, the prayer of an aged penitent, shows some typical difficulties.[3]

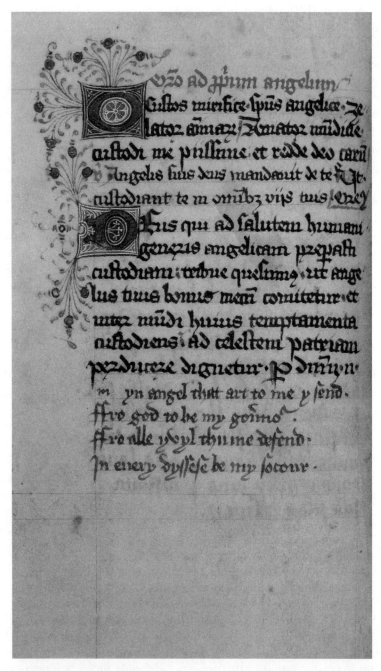

Figure 14.1   Durham Cathedral Library MS A.IV.25, f.9v, from a fifteenth-century manuscript book of prayers and devotions. The original text on this folio records Latin prayers to a guardian angel, to which is added, in a fifteenth-century hand: 'Myn angel that art to me ysend. / ffro god to be my gouernor. / ffro alle yvyl [evil] thu me defend. / In euery dyssese [distress, trouble] be my socour.' By permission of Durham Cathedral.

Heȝe louerd, þou here my bone,
þat madest middelert & mone
   ant mon of murþes munne.
trusti kyng ant trewe in trone,
þat þou be wiþ me sahte sone,
   asoyle me of sunne.
Fol ich wes in folies fayn,
In luthere lastes y am layn,
   þat makeþ myn þryftes þunne,
þat semly sawes wes woned to seyn.
Nou is marred al my meyn,
   away is al my wunne.

vnwunne haueþ myn wonges wet,
   þat makeþ me rouþes rede;
Ne semy nout þer y am set,
þer me calleþ me fulle-flet,
   ant waynoun wayteglede.

A twelve-line stanza rhyming *aabaabccbccb*, in which the *a*- and *c*-lines have four beats and the *b*-lines three, is followed by a five-line stanza rhyming *abaab* with the same alternation, *a*-lines with four beats, *b*-lines with three. It is a beautifully symmetrical music, which brings out the syntactic groupings. The poem co-operates throughout with the form set up by these opening stanzas: hearing the verbal music is a guide to construing the syntax. Some of the words have not passed into any form of modern English and have simply to be glossed: 'luthere lastes': 'base vices'. But many of the unfamiliar words or forms can be construed in terms of more or less evident modern equivalents: mone / moon; sunne / sin; thunne / thin (meagre); thryftes / thrifts (gains). Bone / boon, asoyle (assoil) / absolve, though archaic, only became so much later, so any reader of medieval lyrics is likely to recognise them in the same way. There are genuine difficulties, epitomised by the end of the short stanza – 'fulle-flet /…waynoun wayteglede' – but these were unusual words for contemporary readers. The speaker reports colourful abuse: as it were, bone-idle bum, work-shy Weary Willie. The flavour, based on alliteration, rhythmic emphasis, colloquialism and the combination of unusual elements is, as much as the precise content, what gives meaning: 'fulle-flet', 'filling-the-floor' ('waste of space'); 'waynoun wayteglede', Old French abuse ('dog') plus Old English-based invention, 'one-who-sits-gazing-at-the-fire' – likewise 'waste-of-space', with a heightened tone of colourful vituperation. What is needed is not a glossary that gives plain sense 'equivalents' (wastrel, sluggard) but a feeling for linguistic background (etymology) and tonal register that can only come from wide reading in the contributory languages or from a historical dictionary. The reader should not get lost in the glossary, and must recognise when something more than simple equivalence is required to give the full linguistic flavour.

Then the sense and flavour of individual words has always to be complemented by a feeling for verbal music. Like Hopkins or Dylan Thomas, medieval lyric poets often choose words for sound as much as, or even more than, for sense, using terms that are unlikely to have been usual elements of their non-poetic diction in order to create beautiful or expressive aural effects. In 'Lenten ys come with loue to toune' the twelve-line stanzas are built from triolets, a couplet plus a third line which rhymes with the other last lines of each group: *aax bbx ccx ddx*. This rhyme scheme is complemented by an alliterative pattern joining the two halves of each line, and linking the second line of each triolet with the third (the line to which it is not linked by rhyme):

Lenten ys come with *l*oue to toune,	a	*Spring; among us*
with *b*losmen ant with *b*riddës roune,	a	*song*
that al this *b*lissë *b*ryngeth.	x	
Dayëseyës in this *d*alës,	b	
*n*otës suete of *n*yhtegalës –	b	
uch foul *s*ong *s*ingeth.	x	*each bird*
The *th*restelcoc him *th*reteth oo:	c	*song-thrush; wrangles*
a*w*ay is huerë *w*ynter *w*o	c	*their*
when *w*odërovë springeth.	x	*woodruff*
This *f*oulës singeth *f*erly *f*ele,	d	*wonderfully much*
ant *w*lyteth on huerë *w*inë *w*ele,	d	*chirp; abundant delight*
that al the *w*odë ryngeth.	x	
(Brook 1968: 43–44, with alliterative patterns brought out by italic.)		

The pattern is intensified towards the end of the stanza because the final triolets share the same linking alliterative sound (w). In the second stanza the rhyme scheme and alliterative pattern within the line are repeated, though the alliterative linking is abandoned; but in the final stanza the last three triolets are linked by having each just one alliterative consonant, so that the poem ends in a riot of chiming sounds:

The *m*onë *m*andeth hirë lyht;	*sends forth*
so doth the *s*emly *s*onnë bryht,	*fair*
when *b*riddës singeth *b*remë.	*loudly*
Deawës *d*onketh the *d*ounës,	*moisten*
*d*eorës with huerë *d*ernë rounës,	*animals; unintelligible cries*
*d*omës fortë *d*emë;	*tell their tales*
*w*ormës *w*oweth under cloude,	*make love {woo}; ground*
*w*ymmen *w*axeth *w*ounder proude,	
so *w*el it *w*ol hem semë.	
Yef me shall *w*ontë *w*ille of on	*lack; pleasure; one*
this *w*unnë *w*eole y *w*ole forgon	*abundance of joy; forgo*
and *w*yht in *w*ode be flemë.	*quickly; fugitive*

A riot of chiming sounds, which is all part of the exuberance of excess; but sound should not deflect from sense. Not all is well in this celebration of spring, new life, and love. Worms may get on with some humorously humanised mating ('woweth'), but in the real human world their model is not followed: women think it proper to be stand-offish. The speaker fears he may be left out.

This is an aureate, late (fourteenth-century) example of art that revels in its artfulness. But from the beginning the best of these lyrics often show a similar if more muted art of musical structuration. Among the earliest recorded is this prayer of St Godric of Finchale, County Durham (*c.* 1170).

Saintë Marië viergenë,	
moder Jesu Cristës Nazarenë,	*mother*
onfo, schild, help thin Godrich,	*receive; shield*
onfangë, bring heylichë with thee in Godës richë.	*received; {him} honourably; kingdom*
Saintë Marië, Cristës bur,	*bed-chamber*
maidenës clenhad, moderës flur,	*virgin of virgins; flower*
dilië min sinnë, rix in min mood,	*blot out; reign; heart*
bring me to winnë with the selfë God.	*bliss; with that self-same God*

(Dobson 1979: 103, 228; the two stanzas are not set to the same melody.)

Two broadly symmetrical stanzas, each beginning in parallel with an address to the Virgin, each with further subsidiary patterns between and within them (lines 3 and 4: 'onfo...onfangë'; lines 4 and 8: 'bring...bring'; lines 6 and 7, each in two symmetrical halves – 'maidenës...moderës', 'dilië min...rix in min'); the rhymes, including in the second stanza internal rhyme ('sinnë' / 'winnë'); the plainly stated traditional paradox of Mary as supreme example of both virginity and motherhood; the play on the writer's name ('Godrich...Godës richë'). Unlike 'Lenten is come' no attention is drawn to this art. It is art in the service of prayer. But it is art not prayer that makes the poem – the first song in English to be written down with its own music.

All the elements of St Godric's prayer are present in the words, their meanings and structures; but it is also typical of these lyrics to engage the reader in what is left in part an open imaginative space in which the fancy is invited to play.

Fowelës in the frith,	*birds; wood*
The fissës in the flod,	*fish; river*
And i mon waxë wod.	*must go mad*
Mulch sorw I walkë with	*sorrow*
for beste of bon and blod.	*creature*

(Brown 1932: 14. Dobson 1979: 246.)

Like 'Lenten ys come' and St Godric's prayer, this combines the two great formal features of medieval poetry, alliteration (which points the rhythms) and rhyme (which ties together the two statements of feeling); but the poem's imaginative force comes not only from this dynamic contrast of shapely form expressing chaotic feeling but also from engaging the reader to supply connections. The inner world is turbulent; the natural world is as it always is; the birds and fish are just there – but the reader may reflect that they are likely to be coupling without complication; and perhaps that the speaker is amazed to find no response in nature to his or her extreme state of feeling, that the natural world goes about its normal business indifferent to human affairs. The juxtaposition has some such meaning, but the poem does not exactly say this: inexplicitness invites the reader to fill in connections.

Some lyrics are open in a different way, combining sacred and secular language or frames of reference.

> Mirie it is, while sumer ilast   *lasts*
>   with fughelës song,   *birds'*
> oc nu necheth windës blast,   *nears*
>   and weder strong.   *severe weather*
> Ej! ej! what this nicht is long,
> and ich wid wel michel wrong,
> soregh and murne and fast.
> (Brown 1932: 14. Dobson 1979: 241.)

This may be purely secular, but it may be religious. The natural fact of summer giving way to winter can be felt as imaging another natural fact, the approach in old age to the longest night of all, death – the night in which no man can work (John, 9.4). 'Wid wel michel wrong' may mean 'entirely unjustly': no context is given, but the speaker can be thought of as a betrayed husband, wife, or lover; anyone looking back on happiness from which they are separated by some resented change of circumstance. But the phrase may also mean great wrongs done not *to* but *by* the speaker, who not only sorrows but fasts – implying penitence, sorrow for sin. It is typical of the openness of some Medieval lyrics that feeling is conveyed in a way stimulating to the imagination precisely because vivid particulars are not translated into limiting frames of reference, as in the 'Corpus Christi Carol'. This wonderfully mysterious poem of wounded knight and weeping maiden may remind one of Wallace Stevens' warnings to those who cannot take poetry without prose: 'Poetry must resist the intelligence almost successfully'; 'A poem need not have a meaning and like most things in nature often does not have'.[4] The reader's first and last activity is to dwell in this poem's evocative images. If translation into other terms is required the poem can be read as about Christ and the Virgin or as about the legend of the Holy Grail, and was perhaps adapted in a late version to refer to the displacement of Catherine of Aragon by Anne Boleyn (Greene 1962: 128–30, 230–31).

Even more poised between sacred and secular is the mysteriously suggestive 'Maiden in the mor lay'.[5]

Maiden in the mor lay –
  in the mor lay –
seuenyst fulle, seuenist fulle.
Maiden in the mor lay –
  in the mor lay –
seuenistes fulle ant a day.

Welle was hire met.
wat was hire mete?
  the primerole ant the –   *primrose*
    the primerole ant the –
Welle was hire mete.
Wat was hire mete?
  the primerole ant the violet.

Welle was hire dryng.
wat was hire dryng?
  the chelde water of the –
    the chelde water of the –
Welle was hire dryng.
Wat was hire dryng?
  the chelde water of the welle-spring.

Welle was hire bour.
wat was hire bour?
  the rede rose an te –
    the rede rose an te –
Welle was hire bour.
Wat was hire bour?
  the rede rose an te lilie flour.

This has been read as a poem about the Virgin mother of Christ, with whom the rose and the lily are traditionally associated; but this reading has been criticised as a desperate attempt to understand symbolism by means of a kind of allegorical translation that scarcely fits this suggestive writing. The repeated structural formula of question, half-answer, question, full answer may seem reminiscent of a spell. (The differently structured first stanza has the same elements of incantatory repetition and delayed full information.) Seven is conventional in many areas, but here the main point seems rather a conventional expectation weirdly exceeded: 'seuenistes fulle ant a day'. If, in this context of quasi-spell and inscrutable action mysteriously over-gone, feeding on primrose and violet adds to the suggestion of non-human being, then the well may suggest a water-spirit. Beyond this, meaning is likely to depend on a sense of cultural placing not supplied by the poem in itself. Context, with a poem such as this, cannot depend solely on what can be derived directly from the words: it must depend on acculturated intuition dwelling imaginatively on all the evidence we have of a lost world. John Speirs plausibly suggests a context of the kind of festival in-corporated into Christian practice but pre-Christian in origin. Peter Dronke invokes a more definite context of European folk-lore, and invents a dance-drama action which fits with and fills out the sense of the words.[6] Any satisfying critical account must register meanings that incorporate eerily mysterious beauty and formulaic incantation.

No more than with the poetry of Herbert or Hopkins do more straightforwardly sacred medieval lyrics require that readers share their religious beliefs, but they do require that readers understand the religion on which they draw, that is, be able to enter imaginatively into the world in which such beliefs were universally entertained, and the ecclesiastical practices based on them were widely understood. Medieval Catholic Christianity could take simple forms for uneducated people, but it was also hugely sophisticated, in theology, in its use of the Bible and conventions of its interpretation, in the elaborate and subtle drama of its liturgies, and in its structur-ing of the year into liturgical seasons (Advent, Christmas, Lent, Easter, Whitsun, Ascensiontide), each with its own forms of observance – the twelve days of Christmas leading to Epiphany (the presentation of gifts by the Magi), or the forty days leading to Candlemas (the purification of the Virgin and presentation of Christ in the temple), with similar structures for the other seasons.[7] Modern readers do not always need to draw on knowledge of this beyond what is implied within the poems themselves, and in any case should always give full attention to the beauty of what can be appreciated without information. But modern readers do often need information that those who composed or wrote down these poems could assume. The test of information is that it should lead to knowledge of the poetry as poetry, that it should not load on to poems exposition that poetic pleasure does not require. Deciding what the limits of such knowledge may be, and how it may resonate, is not simple: debates between scholars and critics about the proper needs and scope of information in interpretation have a permanent life in informed reading.[8]

For modern readers difficulties dependent on information may be most acute with religious lyrics in relation to the Virgin. Though Mary has a small role in the biblical accounts of the life of Christ, and a limited role in most contemporary Christianity, in the medieval Church she became a central figure – the most important purely human figure in history; the one human being whose co-operation with the divine plan was essential to redeeming mankind from the sin of Adam. The moment of assent to that co-operation – the Annunciation – was especially celebrated. It is a major subject in medieval visual art – as are the Virgin's seven (or five) sorrows, her seven (or five) joys (particularly her Assumption and Coronation), and her assumed present state as intercessor for humankind. Mary was a model for all Christians – male and female – in her ideal and heroic co-operation with the divine will. She is a central figure in medieval religious lyrics.

'Marye, maydë mylde and fre' (Brown 1957: 46–49) illustrates the difficulties. The poem is an address to the Virgin partly in terms of Old Testament types – as the poem puts it, 'by ryghte toknynge'; that is, understanding a range of Old Testament incidents related to salvation as prefiguring Mary. This was a standard way of relating the Old Testament to the New, understood as based on Christ's exposition of scripture to his disciples.[9] The elaboration in this lyric reads like a compendium of possibilities. Mary is the dove of Noah (Genesis 8.11), a sign of peace between God and mankind; the burning bush (Exodus 3.2), in which God reveals himself to Moses; the true Sarah (Genesis 16), the wife of Abraham through whom the people of God are brought into being; the sling of David (Jesus is the stone), used to kill Goliath (1 Samuel 17.40–54) – as it were, to defeat the Devil: a narrative of salvation brought about by individual heroic action. She is the rod of Aaron (Numbers 17.8), which God causes to blossom miraculously; the temple of Solomon (1 Kings 6; Malachi 3.1), a place of religious purity in which God dwells on earth; and the fleece of Gideon (Judges 6.36–40), which God uses to send a sign of salvation (following Isaiah 45.8, the dew on the fleece was taken to signify Christ). She is Judith and Esther – both heroines of biblical salvation-narratives; the gate seen by Ezekiel (44.2) through which God enters, and which is therefore kept closed (and so a type of her virginal conception). She is Rachel (Genesis 29.15–30), mother of Joseph, the principal slavific figure of the final part of Genesis; the mountain of Daniel (2.31–45), which in the dream of Nebuchadnezzar Daniel interprets as initiating a kingdom that will never be destroyed – in Christian tradition the kingdom of Christ; and (finally in New Testament prophecy) she is the Woman clothed with the sun and the moon of Revelation (12), who brings forth a male child that is attacked by the Devil and will rule all nations. All of these analogues of the Virgin are more or less standard, and can be paralleled from ecclesiastical and theological sources, but clearly they presuppose a detailed knowledge of the Bible and conventions of its interpretation. The poem is addressed to a learned, even specifically a clerical readership. The question for modern readers seeking not sound doctrine but poetic pleasure is how far these sometimes bizarre analogues are made imaginatively interesting. As with passing reference in Dante or Milton, Pound or Eliot, the words of the poem must give some immediate feeling of their own; and imaginative resonance does not come simply from information: if the reader does not draw on real knowledge of the substance of an allusion (his or her own reading of whatever the source may be) there can be no reverberation. But even without this, the reader may find something compelling about the very strangeness of this heterogeneous collection of biblical allusions, and its combination with completely other registers – legendary and scientific (the penitent sinner as tamed unicorn; virginal conception as glass through which sunlight passes without breach). The contexts of utterance – the speaker's profession of personally unworthiness, plea for personal aid, and sense of community with all sinners whom the Virgin might pity – provide points of connection for any reader with his learned awe of the 'quene of paradys, / of heuene, of erthe, of al that hys'. But 'Marye, maydë mylde and fre' is not now, and never was, a poem in which the words work of themselves.

Poems to or about the Virgin can wear their learning more lightly. In its combination of biblical, liturgical and natural imagery 'I syng of a myden' (Brown 1939: 119) allows different levels of appeal to clerical and non-clerical readers.

I syng of a myden	that is makëles,	
kyng of allë kyngës	to here sone che ches.	*she chose*
he cam also stylle	ther his moder was	*silently, gently*
as dew in aprylle,	that fallyt on the gras.	
he cam also stylle	to his moderës bowr	
as dew in aprille,	that fallyt on the flour.	
he cam also stylle	ther his moder lay	
as dew in aprille,	that fallyt on the spray.	*leafy, blossoming shoot*
moder & mayden	was never non but che –	
well may swych a lady	godës moder be.	

Mary is 'makëless' in a double sense: she is without an equal (matchless, supreme); she is without a mate (betrothed to Joseph but not married to him: this sense stresses the importance of her virginity). The two meanings are complementary: Mary is without equal because she is a virgin mother. 'Che ches' stresses her willing assent. That she becomes mother of the Saviour is not simply by God's fiat: her willing response is vital – a model for the reader. 'He cam': following Luke (1.35), 'he' in the Annunciation is usually thought of as the third aspect of the divine Trinity, the Holy Spirit. But the three aspects of the Trinity (Father, Son, Spirit) constitute a mysterious unity, so the Christ aspect can be stressed here: 'he cam...his moder'. The three-fold formula of repetition – he came 'ther his moder was...to his moderës bowr...ther his moder lay' – suggests stages of increasing intimacy. But there are also constant elements: 'also stylle...as dew in aprille'. April: spring, renewal. 'Stylle': unlike the usual mode of human conception; unlike any manifestation of sexual passion. 'Stylle' also makes Christ's conception analogous to his ethically indicative mode of appearance on earth – born among the poor quietly, in a stable: precisely the opposite, in its humility, of what was expected of a Messiah and King of kings. 'Stylle' is appropriate to Christ's earthly identity as well as to this miraculous mode of conception. 'As dew' has biblical resonances – for example (there are many possibilities), of Judges 6.37–38: dew on (or not on) the fleece of Gideon, a sign from God of his special favour; or Psalms 109 [110] v. 3 ('Dixit Dominus' – a Christological text: 'ante luciferum, tamquam rorem, genui te' [Vulgate]: before the day star, as the dew, I begot you); or Proverbs 3.20 ('by the wisdam of [the Lord]...the clowdis bi dew togidere waxen' [Wycliffe]). But 'as dew' can also function purely as a natural image. Like April, water is associated with renewal, with making the barren fecund; but, unlike rain, dew does not fall: it condenses, so appears more mysteriously. 'Dew' regularly has the figurative sense of a refreshing power that appears in a gentle manner (*OED sb* 2: the first example of this sense is *c.* 1200). Biblical resonance is seconded by a famous passage of (appropriately) Advent liturgy, the Advent prose (based on Isaiah 45.8), 'Rorate coeli de super' (drop down ye heavens from above; 'rorare', to drop or distil as dew). So the poem may make use of the reader's knowledge of the Bible and the liturgy, but it does not rely on that. The normal associations of 'dew', and a common figurative extension of these, give the necessary general sense, which the biblical and liturgical associations reinforce, but which is present without them.

Poems concerned with Christ often draw on a similar combination of the biblical and liturgical, though the greater proportion of biblical materials may make these easier for the modern reader to understand. A favourite subject is Christ on the Cross, sometimes in dialogue with the reader, addressed as crucifying him afresh by his or her sins, sometimes in dialogue with his mother (as in 'Stond wel, moder, under roode': Brown 1932: 87–91; Dobson 1979: 254–55). Designed to prompt the medieval listener or reader to dwell imaginatively on the sufferings of Christ and so gain a deeper sense of the evil of sin and the necessity of repentance, these poems served a function similar to the rood screen of the medieval church, on which the crucified Christ, with vividly depicted wounds, was central, and to the many paint-ings and carvings of the crucifixion that were made for use in private devotion. A scribal annotation of one such poem indicates the seriousness with which the medi-eval reader was ideally to respond: 'In seiynge of this orisoun [prayer] stynteth & bydeth at euery cros & thyketh whate ye haue seide' (Brown 1957: 114). 'At euery cros' here means at a sequence of marks in the manuscript (+), but it might as easily refer to stages in the fourteen 'Stations of the Cross' (scenes showing the Crucifixion of Christ from his condemnation by the Sanhedrin to his entombment) with which the walls of medieval churches were regularly decorated. The liturgical background of these poems in the Good Friday Reproaches (*Improperia*), based on Micah 6.3, is clear in poems such as William Herebert's 'My folk what habbe y do to the' (a trans-lation of the Reproaches) or 'Mi folk, nou answere me' (Brown 1957: 17–28, 88–89). Christ reminds his people of his care of them as shown in the salvation narrative of Exodus and contrasts this with their treatment of him in the crucifixion, understood not as an historic event of which the Jews of first-century Palestine are guilty but as a continuously occurring event in which the individual sinner repeats the historic inflictions.

The other great preoccupations of the religious lyrics are Death and Judgement. That no sin is forgotten by the recording angel, that good deeds are an investment, that riches cannot be taken out of this world and one will be called to account for their use: death is a subject about which a vivid sense of reality was readily eschewed in favour of moral and theological commonplaces. The threat of judgement deployed to prompt penitence; the comfort of resurrection deployed to mitigate the sorrows of bereavement: these are strategies in which a predominance of sound doctrine is almost a guarantee of dull poetry. Of lyrics in this moral vein, the most widely circulated, found in some forty versions, more or less elaborate, is 'Erth upon erth', based on a text from the Ash Wednesday liturgy, 'memento homo quid cinis est et in cinerem reverteris' (remember, man, that you are dust, and that you shall return to dust), which, like much of the liturgy, is biblical in origin (here from Genesis 2.7). The poem plays

on different meanings of its central term connected with mortality: earth as the soil
in which one is buried; as the body (Adam, made by God out of the *adamah*, the
clay); as material wealth seen from an eternal perspective (muck, dross); and as the
world, in which one may be lured to seek temporary benefits at an eternal cost (Gray
1975: 91–92 prints two versions, one early and brief, one late and elaborate). One
of the best poems in this death-and-judgement vein, which again the number of
surviving versions (including mural and tombstone inscriptions) shows circulated
widely, is 'If man him bithocte' (Brown 1932: 19–20). Its verbal chain embodies the
threatened sinner's stages of descent: from deathbed, to floor (to be wound in a
shroud), to grave, and – completing the descending pattern because conceived as at
earth's centre – to hell.

If man him bithocte	*considered*
indelike & ofte	*inwardly*
hu arde is te fore	*the going*
fro beddë te flore,	*to*
hu reuful is te flitte	*sorrowful; the flight*
fro flore te pitte,	*(the grave)*
fro pitte te pine	*torment*
that neurë sal fine,	*end*
i wenë non sinne	
sulde his hertë winne.	

While the poetic pleasures of theologically sound sacred song may be modest, it
appears that, at least in some instances, the Church associated the pleasures of secular
song with Riot. Gerald of Wales (*c.* 1146–*c.* 1223) narrates an incident in which a
priest, kept awake all night by singing in his churchyard, began his morning service
not with the expected 'Dominus vobiscum' (the Lord be with you) but with the
refrain of a love-song that had kept him awake. The scandal caused his bishop to
anathematise the song in his diocese.[10] A thirteenth-century sermon takes as its text
a fragment from a song about meeting a lover at a wrestling match and losing him at
a stone-casting said to have been typical of lyrics sung and danced by 'wilde wimmen
& golme' in the preacher's district. A story told by Robert Mannyng of Brunne in
his *Handlyng Synne* about singing and dancing in a churchyard, though it originates
from eleventh-century Saxony, is clearly told as relating to sins needing to be discour-
aged in fourteenth-century England. No extant lyrics have the riotously secular tone
suggested by this evidence of what has been lost, but it nevertheless provides a
context that is suggestive about the flavour of lyrics in which love is treated as frankly
sexual, at least from the viewpoint of the Church – poems which are mildly indecent,
such as 'I haue a gentil cook [cock]' (Robbins 1955: 41–42), or which treat religion
irreverently, such as 'As I went on Yol day' (Robbins 1955: 21–22), spoken by a
woman who wittily tells how the priest by whom she is pregnant appealed to her
by the ways he read and sang the office. The fourteenth-century 'Red Book of Ossory'
('red' because of its binding), a collection of Latin hymns composed to secular melodies

by Bishop Richard Ledrede precisely to displace love songs with songs of holiness, is suggestive about the attitude of the Church to secular poetry of any kind, the main subject of which is the theologically dangerous one of love.

The secular lyrics are among the first love poems in English. It is open to question whether they reflect to any considerable degree special modes of feeling developed in the eleventh and twelfth centuries in the courts of Provence, expressed variously in the lyrics of the troubadours, and known as 'courtly love' or '*fin' amor*' – the woman idealised and distant; the lover ennobled by his love, which inspires every form of admired behaviour from courtesy to courage; love conceived as an unqualified and quasi-religious dedication, usually concealed, and, as well as a source of exalted feeling, full of pain because of apparently insuperable obstacles to fulfilment.[11] Certainly there is a considerable measure of convention about these poems – common attitudes (the lover and the beloved appear with repeated formulaic characteristics) which may issue in (alliterative) formulae repeated from poem to poem. And some of the pleasure for a reader is noticing how inventively a poet varies these conventions of feeling and expression. But while, as in 'Bytuene Mersh and Aueril' or 'Mosti ryden by Ryb-besdale' (Brook 1968: 33–34, 37–39), the woman may be an exemplum of beauty and the lover suffering and unrequited, even this can be varied with clearly non-conventional specific details (as in the East Midland locations of 'When the nyhtegale singes': Brook 1968: 63), and quite other formulae are common. The *chanson d'aventure* and the *pastourelle* are both ways of staging an incident or dialogue of love-encounter variously conducted and resolved, sometimes with the man's sexual attentions accepted ('In a fryht as y con farë fremedë': Brooke (1968) 39–40), sometimes with some lively expression from the woman, who is anything but aristocratically distant ('Nou sprinkës the sprai': Greene 1962: 101–2). And far from all secular poems are directly concerned with love – though they often arrive at love and sex at last. The *reverdie* (spring song) is popular, including one of the most famous of all medieval lyrics, 'Svmer is icumen in' (Brown 1932: 13; and see above, 'Lenten ys come'). And there are one-offs, such as 'Mon in the mone stond ant strit' (Brook 1968: 69–70), an enigmatic poem about the misdoings of a peasant hedge-maker; or 'Swarte smekyd smethes, smateryd with smoke' (Robbins 1955: 106–7), a noisily alliterative and expletively colloquial expression of rage at industrial noise.

For the lyrics that were actually sung, relatively little music survives. As written down the settings are mostly monophonic (for a single unaccompanied voice) – though this may often mean only that the accompaniment to be supplied would have been obvious to anybody likely to use the notation. Even more than in the editing of texts (which can be highly problematic) transcription of the music is an act of interpretation: widely differing 'realisations' for performance can be equally plausible, especially given that songs would have been realised in many different ways by their first performers. The most common of all extant forms of medieval lyric, the carol – a dance-song with a uniform stanza pattern and a chorus repeated after each stanza – must particularly have been performed in ways adapted to the occasion.[12] If the verses were sung by a soloist, and the refrain by the whole group, perhaps (as some manuscript illuminations suggest) dancing with joined hands in a line or circle, the singing-dancers would certainly want whatever rhythmical accompaniment was available – plucked strings, strident winds, varied percussion, if they could get it.

While the melodic line of extant monodies rarely seems adjusted to suit verbal rhythms or to point specific senses, it usually reflects the general character of a poem and may point stages of its development. There is a general appropriateness in the austere monody of St Godric as in the lilting rhythms of 'Gabriel fram heven-king' (Dobson 1979: 261–68). The pathos of 'Stond wel, moder, under rode' (Dobson 1979: 254–55) is intensified by the higher pitch of more desperate utterances ('Moder, merci, let me deye') and modulated towards reconciliation in the lower pitch of the final prayer to the Virgin. But music is not always helpful: 'Edi be thu, heven-queene' (Dobson 1979: 258), though its source is a manuscript that belonged to a religious house, is not alone in having music which, if not at downright variance with the poem, at least suggests a less serious reading of its forms of address and petition than the words alone imply. Where music exists for these lyrics it is usually worth consulting: it may not invariably embody a fully satisfying characterisation.

While their original music may not always help, medieval lyrics have been brought to new audiences by creative and instructive interaction with modern composers. Settings regularly performed include Arnold Bax's 'This worldës joie', Peter Warlock's 'Adam lay ybounden' and 'I saw a fair maiden', John Joubert's 'There is no rose' and 'O Lorde, the Maker of Al Thing', and settings of 'I sing of a maiden' by Bax and Lennox Berkeley. But the most prominent and copious composer to set medieval lyrics has been Benjamin Britten, in a sequence of works from early and late in his life: 'A Hymn to the Virgin' ('Of one that is so fair and bright', 1931), *A Boy was Born* (1933, including the 'Corpus Christi Carol'), *A Ceremony of Carols* (1942, including 'There is no rose', 'I sing of a maiden', and 'Adam lay i-bounden'), *Spring Symphony* (1949, including 'Sumer is icumen in'), and *Sacred and Profane* (1975, eight medieval lyrics, including Saint Godric's 'Sainte Marye', 'Foweles in the frith', 'Lenten is come with love to toune' and 'Maiden in the mor lay'). These highly characterful, and (particularly in *Sacred and Profane*) sometimes surprising settings have returned medieval lyric poetry to a more diverse audience through music that explores and intensifies its expressivity.

Though this poetry comes from a world in which finally everything has its meaning in relation to religion, we should not think of the people who composed or enjoyed it as freed by their religious framework from existential insecurities. The conditions of Christian belief were quite different from those of the modern world – a Universal Church within which conflict of opinion was limited, a similarly limited knowledge of the diversity of belief systems throughout history, and a sense of history and the universe utterly different from a modern sense of geological time and cosmic space. This poetry comes from what was intellectually a comfortingly coherent world. But in other ways the people who composed and enjoyed this poetry endured far more alarming conditions of life than those of any likely reader of this book – in terms of the instability of social order, a limited understanding of disease and medicine, and so much greater vulnerability to accidents of circumstance and subjection to natural conditions. This poetry came into existence within material and intellectual conditions vastly different from those of the modern West. But the insecurities that for its present readers may arise from greater diversity of belief and scepticism, and the knowledge that the whole of human existence is the merest eye-blink when viewed in relation to cosmic time and our planet infinitesimally small when viewed in relation to cosmic space, are mitigated by a greater stability of social order and protection from insecurities of food supply, provision of shelter, seasonal variation, and natural disaster, that, in the West at least, we now enjoy. Taken all together the conditions of life – intellectual and material – were perhaps not so different. A simpler intellectual coherence has to be off-set against greater radical instability of other kinds. When, as they frequently do, these poems ask in some form the question 'ubi sunt qui ante nos fuerunt?' ('Where beth they biforen vs weren?', Brown 1932: 85–87), the answer is not characteristically a simply comforting one. That this should be so is not incompatible with Christian texts (certain of the Psalms, most of Job, Ecclesiastes, Lamentations) or with Christian doctrine: the world is fallen; sin and Satan, though they will ultimately be defeated, often temporarily triumph. But while there is no shortage in these lyrics of versified doctrine, in the best of them the stress does not fall only on Christian consolation, hope, and celebration. Insofar as there are resolutions to the enigmas of suffering and transience in a world thought of as governed by beneficent omnipotence, the main stress in these poems still often lies on the recognition that, as the psalmist has it, 'Homo vanitati similes factus est; / Dies eius sicut umbra praetereunt' (Psalm 143 [144], v. 4, Vulgate); 'A man to vanyte is maad lijc: his daiys as shadewe passen' (Wycliffe). Taken altogether these conditions of existence and these frameworks of belief gave to the best of these lyrics, whether of devotion, lament, or celebration, an edge of urgent intensity.

NOTES

1   Sir Philip Sidney, *An Apology for Poetry* (*c.* 1586), describing the poems of Henry Howard, Earl of Surrey (1516/17–1547).
2   These include William of Shoreham (early fourteenth century), the Franciscans William Herebert (fl. 1290s–1333), John Grimestone (*c.* 1375) and James Ryman (late fourteenth century), the Augustinian friar John Awdelay (fl. 1417–26) and the London grocer Richard Hill (fl. 1503–36). For an account of how the authorship of a small body of lyrics can be assigned to women see Sarah McNamer (2003).
3   The text here is not in modernised orthography and glossed, but, so as to give the full impact of its linguistic difficulty, as printed in the more purist version of Brown 1957: 3–4. Elsewhere quotations are glossed and in partially modernised orthography, using *th* for thorn and eth, *y* or *gh* for yogh, *w* for wynn. The texts are presented broadly on the assumptions about metrics and editorial practice described in Duncan 2005: 19–38, marking 'e' (ë) where this was probably pronounced but would be silent in modern English.
4   'Adagia', *Opus Posthumus*, ed. Samuel French Morse, New York: Knopf, 1957, 171, 177.
5   Robbins 1955: 12–13. Written in abbreviated prose in the unique manuscript source, the precise construction of this poem is contested. See Duncan 2005: 32–35.

6   For Speirs and Dronke, allegory (D. W. Robertson) and a critique of allegorisation (E. Talbot Donaldson), see Luria and Hoffman 1974: 321–5. Wenzel (1974) offers contemporary manuscript evidence reinforcing Dronke's conjecture that the poem was a secular dance song and that its central figure is from folklore.

7   The full Christmas season is deployed in a simple and exemplary way in 'Make we myrth / For Crytes byrth', Greene 1962: 56–57.

8   See, for example, the comments of the scholar Richard Leighton Greene on the criticism of Leo Spitzer ('ponderous to the point of hilarity' – but on another view imaginatively engaged by detail): Greene 1962: 219. Cf. the debate about interpretation of Herbert between the scholar Rosemond Tuve ('On Herbert's "Sacrifice"', *Kenyon Review*, 12 (1950), 51–75) and the critic William Empson (*Argufying: Essays on Literature and Culture*, ed. John Haffenden, London: Chatto, 1987, 250–55). Fundamentally Empson objects that scholars only allow 'the surface meaning of the poem, the part that was meant to be quite obvious' (*William Empson: Selected Letters*, ed. John Haffenden, Oxford: Oxford University Press, 2006: 192). Greene makes fair points against Spitzer's scholarship; whether these seriously impugn Spitzer's criticism is open to question.

9   Luke, 24.44–45. Cf. the Old Testament story of Jonah in the belly of the whale related to the death and resurrection of Christ in Matthew, 12.38–42, 16.1–4 and Luke, 11.29–32. Similarly cf. John, 3.14, on the serpent raised on a pole by Moses, the sight of which saved life (Numbers, 21.9), as prefiguring the crucified Christ.

10 For this and the following references see Brook 1968: 4–5.

11 The classic account of 'courtly love' by C. S. Lewis (1936, Chapter 1) has been variously challenged, as by Donaldson (1970). Reiss (1979) surveys the history of the term most used and the difficulty of deducing for it any consistent meanings in a range of European cultures, including English.

12 The medieval carol has no necessary connection with Christmas, or with religious content of any kind – though there is often a connection with celebration and feasting.

References and Further Reading

Editions and Selections

Brook, G. L. (ed.) (1968). *The Harley Lyrics: The Middle English Lyrics of MS Harley 2253*. 4th edn. Manchester: Manchester University Press. (1st edn 1948.)

Brown, Carleton (ed.) (1932). *English Lyrics of the XIIIth Century*. Oxford: Clarendon Press.

Brown, Carleton (ed.) (1939). *Religious Lyrics of the XVth Century*. Oxford: Clarendon Press.

Brown, Carleton (ed.) (1957). *Religious Lyrics of the XIVth Century*. 2nd edn, rev. G. V. Smithers. Oxford: Clarendon Press. (First edn 1924.)

Davies, R. T. (1962). *Medieval English Lyrics: A Critical Anthology*. London: Faber.

Duncan, Thomas G. (ed.) (1995). *Medieval English Lyrics 1200–1400*. Harmondsworth: Penguin.

Duncan, Thomas G. (ed.) (2000). *Late Medieval English Lyrics and Carols 1400–1530*. Harmondsworth: Penguin.

Gray, Douglas (ed.) (1975). *A Selection of Religious Lyrics*. Oxford: Clarendon Press. (Repr. as *English Medieval Religious Lyrics*. Exeter: University of Exeter Press, 1992.)

Greene, Richard Leighton (ed.) (1962). *A Selection of English Carols*. Oxford: Clarendon Press.

Greene, Richard Leighton (ed.) (1977). *The Early English Carols*. Oxford: Clarendon Press, 1935. (2nd edn, rev. and enlarged.)

Hirsh, John C. (2005). *Medieval Lyric: Middle English Lyrics, Ballads, and Carols*. Oxford: Blackwell.

Luria, Maxwell S. and Richard L. Hoffman (1974). *Middle English Lyrics*. New York: W. W. Norton.

Robbins, Rossell Hope (ed.) (1955). *Secular Lyrics of the XIVth and XVth Century*. Corrected edn. Oxford: Clarendon Press. (1st edn 1952.)

Silverstein, Theodore (ed.) (1971). *Medieval English Lyrics*. London: Arnold.

Stevick, Robert D. (ed.) (1994). *One Hundred Middle English Lyrics*. 2nd revised edn. Urbana: University of Illinois Press. (1st edn Indianapolis, IN: Bobbs-Merrill, 1964.)

Music

Dobson, E. J. and F. Ll. Harrison (1979). *Medieval English Songs*. London: Faber.

Stevens, John (1952). *Medieval carols*. Musica Britannica 4. London: Stainer and Bell.

Stevens, John (1982). Medieval lyrics and music. In Boris Ford (ed.). *The New Pelican Guide to English Literature, vol. I, part 1, Medieval Literature: Chaucer and the Alliterative Tradition*. Harmondsworth: Penguin.

Manuscript Facsimiles

Facsimile of British Museum MS. Harley 2253. Intro. N. R. Ker (1965). Early English Text Society 255. London: Oxford University Press.

Facsimile of Oxford, Bodleian Library, MS Digby 86. Intro. Judith Tschann and M. B. Parkes (1996). Early English Text Society, s.s. 16. Oxford: Oxford University Press.

The Vernon Manuscript: A Facsimile of Bodleian Library Oxford, Ms. Eng. Poet. A.1. Intro. A. I. Doyle (1987). Cambridge: D. S. Brewer.

Scholarship and Criticism

Boklund-Lagopoulou, Karin (2002). *'I have a yong suster': Popular Song and the Middle English Lyric*. Dublin: Four Courts.

Burrow, J. A. (1984). Poems without contexts: the Rawlinson lyrics. In *Essays on Medieval Literature*. Oxford: Clarendon Press.

Chambers, E. K. (1945). The carol and fifteenth-century lyric. In *English Literature at the Close of the Middle Ages*. Oxford: Clarendon Press.

Donaldson, E. Talbot (1970). The myth of courtly love. In *Speaking of Chaucer*. London: Athlone.

Dronke, Peter (1968). *The Medieval Lyric*. London: Hutchinson.

Duncan, Thomas G. (ed.) (2005). *A Companion to the Middle English Lyric*. Cambridge: D. S. Brewer.

Gray, Douglas (1972). *Themes and Images in the Medieval English Religious Lyric*. London: Routledge.

Gray, Douglas (1983). Songs and lyrics. In Piero Boitani and Anna Torti (eds). *Literature in Fourteenth-Century England: the J. A. W. Bennett Memorial Lectures, Perugia 1981–1982*. Cambridge: D. S. Brewer.

Gray, Douglas (ed. and completed) (1986). Lyrics. In J. A. W. Bennett, *Middle English Literature*. Oxford: Clarendon Press.

Greentree, Rosemary (2001). *The Middle English Lyric and Short Poem*. Annotated Bibliographies of Old and Middle English Literature. Vol. 7. Cambridge: D. S. Brewer.

Howell, Andrew J. (1980). Reading the Harley lyrics: a master poet and the language of conventions. *ELH*, 47, 619–45.

Kane, George (1951). The Middle English religious lyrics. In *Middle English Literature: a Critical Study of the Romances, Religious Lyrics, 'Piers Plowman'*. London: Methuen.

Lewis, C. S. (1936). *The Allegory of Love: A Study in Medieval Tradition*. London: Oxford University Press.

Manning, Stephen (1962). *Wisdom and Number: Toward a Critical Appraisal of the Middle English Religious Lyric*. Lincoln: University of Nebraska Press.

McNamer, Sarah (2003). Lyrics and romances. In Carolyn Dinshaw and David Wallace (eds). *The Cambridge Companion to Medieval Women's Writing*. Cambridge: Cambridge University Press.

Moore, Arthur K. (1951). *The Secular Lyric in Middle English*. Lexington: University of Kentucky Press.

Oliver, Raymond (1970). *Poems without Names: The English Lyric, 1200–1500*. Berkeley, CA: University of California Press.

Ransom, Daniel J. (1985). *Poets at Play: Irony and Parody in the Harley Lyrics*. Norman, OK: Pilgrim Books.

Reiss, Edmund (1972). *The Art of the Middle English Lyric: Essays in Criticism*. Athens, GA: University of Georgia Press.

Reiss, Edmund (1979). *Fin'Amors*: its history and meaning in medieval literature. *Journal of Medieval and Renaissance Studies*, 8, 74–99.

Spearing, A. C. (2005). *Textual Subjectivity: The Encoding of Subjectivity in Medieval Narratives and Lyrics*. Oxford: Oxford University Press.

Speirs, John (1957). Carols and other songs and lyrics. In *Medieval English Poetry: the non-Chaucerian Tradition*. London: Faber.

Spitzer, Leo (1962). Explication de texte applied to three great Middle English poems. In Spitzer, ed. Anna Hatcher. *Essays on English and American Literature*. Princeton, NJ: Princeton University Press.

Stevick, R. D. (1966). The criticism of Middle English lyrics. *Modern Philology*, 64, 103–17.

Weber, Sarah Appleton (1969). *Theology and Poetry in the Middle English Lyric: A Study of Sacred History and Aesthetic Form*. Columbus, OH: Ohio State University Press.

Wenzel, Siegfried (1974). The Moor Maiden – a contemporary view. *Speculum*, 49, 67–74.

Wenzel, Siegfried (1986). *Preachers, Poets, and the Early English Lyric*. Princeton, NJ: Princeton University Press.

Woolf, Rosemary (1968). *The English Religious Lyric in the Middle Ages*. Oxford: Clarendon Press.

Websites

http://www.luminarium.org/medlit/lyrics.htm
Contains texts, performances, and links to other online resources.

The complete Harley lyrics can be found at:

http://etext.lib.virginia.edu/toc/modeng/public/AnoHarl.html

The Vernon Manuscript Project, the aims of which include creating a digital edition of the manuscript to be published on DVD in the series Bodleian Digital Texts:

http://www.medievalenglish.bham.ac.uk/vernon/

Recordings

English Medieval Songs (2000). Russell Oberlin, countertenor; Seymour Barab, viol. Lyrichord (recorded 1958).

Fleagle, John (2004). *Worlds Bliss: Medieval Songs of Love and Death*. Magnatune. (Medieval lyrics set to melodies composed and accompanied in a modern version of broadly 'medieval' style.)

Now make we merthe (1994). Boston: Skyline Records. (Compiled from recordings originally issued in 1965 and 1966 in the British Council series 'The English Poets: from Chaucer to Yeats'.)

'Sumer is icumen in': Medieval English Songs (2002). The Hilliard Ensemble. Harmonia Mundi. (Recorded 1985; largely Latin texts, but some vernacular settings.)

The Medieval Lyric (2001). A project supported by the National Endowment for the Humanities and Mount Holyoke College. Director, Margaret Switten. Anthology III, CD 5: Medieval English Lyric (sung monodies and readings).

http://www.mtholyoke.edu/acad/medst/medieval_lyric (largely focussed on continental lyric).

Selected Middle English Lyrics (1990). Directed by Tom Burton; read by Basil Cottle and Rosamund Allen. Adelaide: Chaucer Studio. (Re-issued on CD; Provo, Utah: Chaucer Studio, 2008.)

15

Macaronic Poetry

Elizabeth Archibald

The term 'macaronic' is used by literary critics to describe two forms of bilingualism found in Middle English poetry (and elsewhere in Europe too). In the stricter sense it describes the addition of Latin endings to vernacular words to create an effect like schoolboy dog Latin or the modern Franglais; in the looser sense it describes any mixing of words in different languages. 'Macaronic' seems to have been used first in the stricter sense in Italy in the late fifteenth century, and this usage was encouraged by the sixteenth-century Italian writer Teofilo Folengo in his long macaronic poem *Baldus*, where his explanation of the term is not complimentary:

> This poetic art is called 'macaronic' from *macarones*, which are a certain dough made up of flour, cheese, and butter, thick, coarse, and rustic. Thus, macaronic poems must have nothing but fat, coarseness, and gross words in them.
>
> (Wenzel 1994: 3)

In the fifteenth-century morality play *Mankind*, for instance, the vice Nought deploys macaronics in this sense to mock the pious use of formal Latinate speech and biblical quotations:

> Mankind: Davide seyeth, '*Nec in hasta, nec in gladio, salvat Dominus*'.
> (David says, 'The Lord saves neither with the spear nor with the sword')

> Nought: No, mary, I beschrew yow, it is *in spadibus*!   *curse*
>   Therfor Cristys curse cum on yowr *hedibus*!   *heads*
> (Mankind 397–400; Bevington 1975: 917)

The immediate effect here is comic, but the underlying intention is serious. Though the vices are amusing, they seek to corrupt Mankind and send him to hell; he will be saved by Mercy, whose speech is formal and highly Latinate. Folengo says that macaronic verses must cause laughter, and this is a common critical assumption: according to Cuddon's *Dictionary of Literary Terms*, 'the intention in macaronics is nearly always comical and/or nonsensical', and 'many writers of light verse have diverted themselves by composing macaronics' (Cudden 1998). For the Middle Ages this may be true of hybrid words with Latin endings, but comedy is by no means always the dominant tone of medieval macaronic writing in the second and less strict sense of the term, the juxtaposing of two or more languages.

This kind of macaronic writing is much commoner in Middle English poetry (and also prose) than the hybrid formations, and can take many forms. The second (and sometimes third) language may appear as a word or phrase, a refrain, an occasional sentence, an alternating half or whole line, or even a block of lines. Some macaronic writers use a regular format; others introduce a second language at unpredictable intervals. English can be juxtaposed with Latin or with French, or both; it may be used just for a brief aside, a translation or paraphrase of an authoritative source, or a proverb or song title; or it may be the dominant language, with brief quotations or refrains in Latin or French. Diller claims that 'fully symmetrical bilingualism is extremely rare' in medieval writing, but in fact there are numerous examples of poems in which there is a regular alternation between languages, by half-line, whole line, or stanza, so that considerable knowledge of all the languages concerned is needed for comprehension (Diller 1997–8: 519).[1] Macaronic writing can be used for many purposes (religious, political, polemical, amorous, satirical, comic) and in many genres (lyric, drama, sermon, complaint).

Macaronic poetry has not attracted much attention until recently from Anglophone medievalists, though French critics have showed more interest in it. But in the last decade the broader topic of multilingualism has become increasingly popular, and modern sociolinguistic approaches to bilingualism and code-switching are being applied to medieval texts. (The essays by Richard Dance, Simon Horobin and A. S. G. Edwards in this volume discuss further the subject of language.) It should not surprise us that there is so much macaronic literature: post-Conquest England was a trilingual society (Latin, Anglo-Norman and English – and in Wales some people were quadri-lingual). As Turville-Petre puts it, 'Three languages existed in harmony, not just side by side but in symbiotic relationship, interpenetrating and drawing strength from one another; not three cultures but one culture in three voices' (Turville-Petre 1996: 191). This does not mean that a large proportion of the population in the period was functionally trilingual, but multilingualism was certainly not restricted to a highly educated élite. In the courts of law, as Clanchy points out, some officials would have had to be multilingual: questions were written in Latin or French but the jurors spoke English, so the chief clerk and the foreman of the jury had to be able to read French and sometimes Latin, and to translate accurately – the penalty for any oral variation from the written text was imprisonment. Clanchy remarks of the foreman that 'The linguistic ability he required was of a high standard', and goes on to comment more generally on 'the multilingual competence of English administrators' under Henry III in the mid-thirteenth century (Clanchy 1993: 207 and 222).

Further evidence of this multilingualism is the extent of macaronic usage found in English business and legal records, both in the strict sense of hybrid words and in the looser sense of bilingual juxtaposition, which has been discussed extensively by William Rothwell and Laura Wright; indeed, Wright has commented that 'it is easier to find macaronic documents for the late medieval period in the Record Office than it is to find monolingual ones' (Wright in Rothwell 1994: 50).[2] Rothwell notes that hybrid forms such as *apud garderobam Londonie* and *warantizabimus* are presumably what was meant by 'Latyn corrupt', a phrase used in Chaucer's 'Man of Law's Tale' to describe the speech of the Roman princess Custance when she is shipwrecked in Northumberland (Chaucer 1987: *Canterbury Tales* II.519). There are so many examples of such 'Latyn corrupt' that Rothwell concludes:

> In view of the mass of documentary evidence of macaronic Latin being used for trade and business in general, both national and international, it would appear not unreasonable to conclude that the same macaronic Latin would have been spoken as well as written in western Europe and that, as a lingua franca, it would have been understood in the regions to the north of Britain...
>
> (Rothwell 1994: 53)

Such comments should make us reconsider the macaronic poetry (and prose) of medieval England. It has been claimed that a student audience would have been required to appreciate the dog Latin in *Mankind*, but in view of the discoveries of Wright and Rothwell, both *Mankind*'s macaronic jokes and the bi- and trilingual lyrics may have seemed less unusual and more comprehensible to wider audiences than critics have previously supposed.

Another important form of evidence for multilingualism in medieval England is the existence of manuscripts containing texts in different languages, often copied by the same scribe, such as the famous anthologies, or miscellanies, Oxford, Bodleian Library Digby 86 (late thirteenth-century) and London, British Library Harley 2253 (early fourteenth-century). Some members of the family for whom the Harley manuscript was produced in the West Midlands (possibly the Talbots) must have been trilingual: the manuscript includes complete texts in Latin, French and English, and also three macaronic pieces.[3] In 'Against the King's Taxes' each line begins in French and continues in Latin. 'Mayden moder milde' praises the Virgin in alternating lines of English and French:

> Mayden moder milde,
>   Oieȝ cel oreysoun;
> From shome þou me shilde
>   E de ly mal feloun;
> For loue of þine childe
>   Me meneȝ de tresoun;
> Ich wes wod ant wilde,
>   Ore su en prisoun.
>
> (1–8)

Gentle maiden-mother, / Hear this prayer; / Protect me from shame / And from the evil one; / For love of your child / Deliver me from wickedness; / I who was mad and wild / Am now in prison.

Turville-Petre comments that it 'alternates English and French lines to heighten the tone of the lyric, so that the heartfelt simplicity of the English combines with the gracious euphony of the French', but this seems to imply an unequal balance (Turville-Petre 1996: 202–3). Is the English alliteration in lines 1, 3 and 7 not euphonious, and does the French not express heartfelt simplicity too? The placing of the main verb is distributed fairly equally: in lines 2, 6 and 8 it is in French, but in lines 3 and 7 it is in English. The use of the two languages seems to me balanced and equal. Certainly it would not be possible to follow the sense of the poem without understanding both English and French. The third macaronic piece in this manuscript, 'Dum ludis floribus', alternates French and Latin, mostly in half lines, until the very end, where English is introduced for the first time:

> Scripsi hec carmina in tabulis;
> Mon ostel est en mi la vile de Paris;
> May y sugge namore, so wel me is;
> Ʒef hi deʒe for loue of hire, duel hit ys.
>   (17–20)

I have written this song on my tablets; / My lodging is in the middle of the city of Paris; / I can say no more, so good it is for me; / If I die for love of her it'll be a sad thing.

The writer may have been an English clerk studying in Paris.

Two trilingual poems are among a group of love lyrics included, surprisingly, in the middle of the Armburgh Papers, a recently discovered fifteenth-century roll otherwise entirely devoted to letters concerning a protracted family lawsuit.[4] Both poems are in the order French (Anglo-Norman)/English/Latin; the French and English lines rhyme together, as do the shorter Latin lines. The first lyric is known from several other manuscripts, though the Armburgh version (set out below on the left) is slightly different (and does not include the lady's response found elsewhere); critics often refer to it under the title 'De Amico ad amicam' (from a [male] lover to his [female] beloved).[5]

A celuy que pluys ayme de mounde	A celuy que plus eyme en mounde,
Of all that I have founde	*Of alle tho that I have found*
Carissima	**Carissima,**
Salutez ad verray amour	Saluz ottrey e amour,
With grace joie and honour	*With grace and joye and alle honour,*
Dulcissima.	**Dulcissima.**
...	...
Dishore serray joious *and fayne*	Tost serroy joyous et seyn,

<table>
<tr><td>

Yf ge will me in certaigne
Amare
Assech serra iououz *and lele*
Ther were nothing that myght me
Grauare.
(Armburgh, lines 1–6, 13–18)

</td><td>

Yif thou woldest me serteyn
Amare;
Et tost serroy joious et lé,
There nys no thyng that shal me
Gravare.
(*LMELC* 12, lines 1–6, 49–54)

</td></tr>
<tr><td>

To her whom I love most
in the world, of all [those]
that I have found, most dear,
greetings to very love [I send
greetings and love], with
grace, joy, and [all] honour,
most sweet...

</td><td>

I would be entirely joyful
and well if you will [would]
indeed love me; I will [would]
be [entirely] joyful enough and
loyal [happy], there would be
[is] nothing that might [shall]
oppress me.

</td></tr>
</table>

According to Wehrle this construction, vernacular lines with four (or sometimes three) main stresses followed by Latin lines with only one stress, is unique. Wehrle comments: 'Nowhere in the poems is the thought interrupted due to the commingling of the languages, for the poet has so cleverly strung them together that the thought runs on as though the poem were written in one language only' (Wehrle 1933: 121). This is more noticeable in some stanzas than in others: in the first stanza quoted above, *carissima* and *dulcissima* are not grammatically necessary and could be read as grace-notes, but in the second stanza quoted, the Latin verbs *amare* and *gravare* are indispensable to the sense of the stanza. In other versions of the poem the alternation of vernaculars is absolutely regular, but the Armburgh scribe includes some English synonyms in the French lines (for instance lines 13 and 16) so that the thought really does run on between languages. Some critics argue that the three languages have distinct roles. This may be true at some points in the poem, but does not seem to me plausible overall, especially in view of the variations in the Armburgh version, where the English often continues both the content and the syntax of the French. In my view the uses of the three languages are not so easily distinguished; critical attempts to do so may well derive from an attitude to the hierarchy of language in medieval Britain that is now being questioned by current research on multilingualism.

Trilingual poetry is a form of showing off, so it is not surprising to find it used for satire and complaint as well as love. A poem about the dreadful state of the world found in several manuscripts, beginning 'Quant houme deit parleir' (also known as 'Proverbia trifaria'), mixes Latin, French and English throughout in a random order, usually by half lines:[6]

> Fals mon freynt covenaunt; quamvis tibi dicat 'habebis',
> Vix dabitur un veu gaunt; leve lefmon postea flebis.
> Myn ant þyn duo sunt, qui frangunt plebis amorem,
> Ce deus pur nus sunt facientia sepe dolorem.
>
> (R 19–22)

A false man breaks his promise; although he may say to you 'you shall have it', he will hardly give an old glove; believe it, dear one, afterwards you will weep. Mine and thine are twain which break the people's heart; for us these two are often causing sorrow.

Aspin comments that rhyme between languages is rare here, and that it always occurs in internal rhymes. On the metre she notes: 'If intended as hexameters, the poem is a *tour de force*; but it reads much more smoothly if treated according to the English system of stresses' (Aspin 1953: 160). A less complicated and more regular structure is found in another Anglo-Norman poem about Magna Carta (*c.* 1308), this time in two languages only, alternating every two lines:

> La purveance est de cyre,
> Jo l'enteng e byn le say,
> And is yholde to neȝ the fyre
> And is molten al away.
> Jeo ne say mes ke dyre,
> Mes tot y va tribolay
> Curt and laghe, hundred a[nd] syre;
> Al it god a duvele way.
> (VI, lines 17–24; *A-NPS* 1953: 56–66)

The provision is made of wax, I understand it and know it well, and it has been held too near the fire and has all melted away. I no longer know what to say, but all goes out of joint, court and law, hundred and shire, it all goes the way of the devil.

Here the two languages are equally balanced.

Complaints about the state of the nation are common in Middle English poetry. Some of the passages in 'On the Times' are very reminiscent of *Piers Plowman*, which is macaronic in the sense that it includes many quotations in Latin from the Bible and other theological writings, and occasional Latin words such as *contra* (see Alford 1992). The opposite format also occurs: English proverbs and snatches of verse are sometimes included in Latin sermons (Fletcher 1998). The use of Latin refrains such as *Deo gracias* in lyrics and carols occasions one of the most prominent forms of macaronic writing. A number of late medieval poets, including John Lydgate in East Anglia and William Dunbar in Scotland, made striking use of a line from the Office of the Dead, *Timor mortis conturbat me* (the fear of death troubles me greatly), in reflections on mortality.[7] Lydgate's poem is not personal, but in 'I that in heill wes and gladnes' (sometimes called 'Lament for the Makars'), Dunbar presents himself as Death's next victim after a long line of distinguished poets, both English and Scots, starting with Chaucer and ending with his Scottish contemporary Walter Kennedy:

> Gud Maister Walter Kennedy
> In poynt of dede lyis veraly –
> Gret reuth it wer that so suld be:
> *Timor mortis conturbat me.*

Sen he has all my brether tane
He will naught lat me lif alane;
On forse I man his nyxt pray be:
Timor mortis conturbat me.

(89–96)

Good Master Walter Kennedy / Lies at the point of death, truly; / It would be a great
pity that this should be so: / *The fear of death troubles me greatly.*
Since he has taken all my brothers / He will not let me alone live; / Of necessity I must
be his next prey: / *The fear of death troubles me greatly.*

This powerful poem has been much discussed as a very early instance of a subjective
sense of a poetic tradition and avocation: Dunbar's listing of previous poets, leading
up to his own awareness of imminent death, can be read as presenting a sort of
apostolic succession.

A variation on the same theme and refrain appears in a more complex anonymous
poem, 'Illa iuventus that is so nyse', a lament for a sinful life in alternating half-lines
of Latin and English; the refrain is bilingual, unusually, and rhymes across the languages (*LMECL* no. 88, trans. Duncan):

> *Alas, my hart will brek in thre;*
> *Terribilis mors conturbat me.*
>
> Illa iuventus that is so nyse   *that time of youth; foolish*
> Me deduxit into vayn devise;   *led me; idle pleasure*
> Infirmus sum, I may not rise –   *infirm I am*
>   Terribilis mors conturbat me.
>   *Alas, my hart etc.*
>
> Dum iuvenis fui, lytill I dred,   *while I was young little did I fear*
> Set semper in sinne I ete my bred;   *but always*
> Iam ductus sum into my bed –   *now I am led*
>   Terribilis mors conturbat me.
>   *Alas, my hart etc.*

(1–12)

Here both languages are crucial to the sense, and are effectively integrated in a
regular structure in which each line begins in Latin and ends in English, though the
number of syllables allotted to each language does vary. In the penultimate stanza,
even Christ is made to speak macaronically:

> Christus se ipsum, whan he shuld dye,   *Christ Himself*
> Patri suo his manhode did crye: *to his father*
> 'Respice me, Pater, that is so hye,   *look upon me, Father*
>   Terribilis mors conturbat me'.

(18–21)

The Latin is not particularly difficult, but understanding this poem would require more than an aural familiarity with the liturgy.

Refrains in macaronic poems are not always in Latin, or from ecclesiastical sources. Latin refrains can also be irreverent, of course, as in two lyrics about lecherous ecclesiastics. In 'Ther was a frier of order gray', the refrain is an inversion of a phrase from the Paternoster: without the negative in 'lead us not into temptation', the line 'inducas in temptacionibus' becomes an invitation to pleasure, and the grey monk succeeds in seducing the nun he is pursuing (*LMELC* no. 142). In 'As I went on Yol Day' the female narrator describes her seduction by 'jolly Jankin' the clerk; the spelling of the refrain, 'Kyrieleyson', suggests a pun on the name Alison, and the structure of the poem wittily reflects the structure of the Mass (*MEL* no. 129). Dunbar also plays with liturgical structure and language in his elaborate and witty 'Dregy' (from the Latin *Dirige*, part of the Office of the Dead), 'We that ar heir in hevynnis glorie', addressed to James IV (Dunbar 1998: no. 84). The king used to spend Lent with the Franciscans in Stirling; Dunbar's poem urges him to stop meditating on the next world and return to the pleasures of Edinburgh, where the food and drink are much better than in Stirling. Most of the poem is in Scots, but it ends with an ingenious adaptation of the Paternoster, subverting the meaning of the familiar phrases:

> *Et ne nos inducas in temptationem de Strivilling*
> *Sed libera nos a malo illius.*
>
> (Lines 97–8)

> And do not lead us into the temptation of Stirling, but free us from its evil.

There is an even more unexpected twist in the final lines of the version in the Bannatyne manuscript:

> *Libera famulos tuos apud villam de Stirling versantes*
> *A penis et tristitiis eiusdem,*
> *Et ad Edinburgi gaudia eos perducas*
> *Ut requiescat Strivilling. Amen.*
>
> (Lines 108–111)

> Free your servants living in the town of Stirling from its torments and woes, and lead them to the joys of Edinburgh, that Stirling may be at rest. Amen.

There is an implied criticism here; it is not only the king who is to benefit from the move from Stirling to Edinburgh.

This poem indicates that the royal court offered an alert bilingual audience, and this is even more true of Dunbar's macaronic masterpiece 'The Testament of Mr. Andro Kennedy', where he alternates Latin and Scots (not entirely regularly or predictably) in a mock testament (Dunbar 1998: no. 19).

I, Maister Andro Kennedy,
   Curro quando sum vocatus,   *run when I am called*
Gottin with sum incuby,   *begotten by some incubus*
   Or with sum freir *infatuatus*;   *infatuated*
In faith I can nought tell redly,
   Unde aut ubi fui natus,   *whence or where I was born*
Bot in treuth I trow trewly
   Quod sum dyabolus incarnatus.   *that I am the devil incarnate*
   …
A barell bung ay at my bosum,
   Of warldis gud I bad na mair.   *worldly good; desire no more*
Corpus meum ebriosum   *my drunken corpse*
   I leif on to the toune of Air,
In a draf myddyng for evir and ay,   *rubbish heap*
   Ut ibi sepeliri queam.   *that I may be buried there*
Quhar drink and draff may ilka day   *dregs; every day*
   Be cassyne *super faciem meam.*   *thrown over my face*
               (Lines 1–8, 33–40)

Nothing is predictable here: although the poem begins with a fairly regular alternation of Latin and Scots, even in the first stanza there is a half line of Latin where we expect a whole line. As the poem continues we never know which language will start each stanza, and whether the lines will alternate regularly or not. This energetic poem belongs to a very old tradition of mock testaments; some of the Latin suggests the legal texts being parodied. But the lexical range is very wide, with borrowings from the Bible and the liturgy as well as legal formulas, and pure invention too; as Bawcutt notes, the vernacular may undercut the Latin, or *vice versa*, and 'the two languages are in witty equilibrium' (Bawcutt 1992: 352). This poem requires a sophisticated audience.

Latin may have been the language of formality and learning, but it could also be used colloquially and humorously; in late fifteenth-century Scotland Dunbar expects his audience to be attuned to idiosyncratic bilingual writing drawing on a range of sources and registers. This is even more true of the writing of John Skelton (*c.* 1460–1529), honoured with the title of 'laureate' by both Oxford and Cambridge, praised by Erasmus, tutor to the future Henry VIII, and in later life rector of the rural parish of Diss in Norfolk. (On Dunbar and Skelton, see further the essays by A. S. G. Edwards and Douglas Gray in this volume.) Many forms of macaronic writing are represented in Skelton's work (Skelton 1983).[8] Some of his poems are entirely in Latin, others begin and end with formal Latin verse; *Speke, Parott*, a satire on court politics, is sprinkled with words and phrases in many languages, including French, Spanish, German, Latin and Greek. He often used Latin macaronics in both the strict and loose sense for polemical and/or comic purposes. In *Collyn Clout* he attacks ignorant, lecherous, drunken priests (Skelton 1983: no. XIX):

> Some are *insufficientes*,
> Some *parum sapientes*,
> Some *nichil intelligentes*,
> Some *valde negligentes*,
> Some *nullum sensum habentes*,
> Some bestyall and untaught...
> (Lines 223–8)

Some are inadequate, some not wise enough, some not at all intelligent,
Some greatly negligent, some with no sense at all...

In spite of their ignorance, they use their positions to pursue women:

> *Cum ipsis vel illis*   *With these or those*
> *Qui manent in villis*   *who stay in towns*
> *Est uxor vel ancilla.*   *there is a wife or maidservant*
> 'Welcom Jacke and Gylla!'
> 'My prety Petronylla,
> And you will be stylla,   *if*
> You shall have your wylla!'
> Of such paternoster pekes   *dolts*
> All the worlde spekes.
>   (Lines 255–61)

In 'Phyllyp Sparowe' (Skelton 1983: no. VII), a mock dirge for a little girl's dead bird, Skelton borrows from the liturgy in the same spirit as Dunbar, subverting the words and the standard context, and he also does this in 'Ware the Hauk' (Skelton 1983: no. VI), a polemic against a hawking parson who had invaded Skelton's church:

> *Fratres, orate*   *Brothers pray*
> For this knavate...   *Knave*
>   (Lines 64–5)

In Skelton's writing Latin and English flow together very naturally, suggesting that he himself thought and perhaps even sometimes spoke macaronically.

Macaronic writing flourished in medieval England from the twelfth to the sixteenth century (there was also some in the Anglo-Saxon period). It offers splendid opportunities for showing off poetic skill, for emphasising passion (amorous or irate), for inveighing and for entertaining. The strict form of macaronics, Latin endings on English words, does invite an amused response, though the context may be serious, as in the morality play *Mankind*. In the looser sense, however, the mingling of two or more languages could be comical, but could also be put to serious use, in hymns and prayers, in love poems, and in social and political commentary. Clanchy comments that 'Often perhaps it was the most sophisticated and not the most primitive authors who experimented with vernaculars' (Clanchy 1993: 215). In the light of recent research, we should read macaronic poetry not as an occasional *jeu d'esprit*, but rather as a reflection of the multilingual society of England in the later Middle Ages.

NOTES

1   The best survey of Middle English macaronic poetry is still Wehrle (1933), which is more wide-ranging than the title suggests.
2   Similar evidence is provided by medical texts: see Hunt (2000).
3   Texts and translations are taken from Turville-Petre (1996).
4   *The Armburgh Papers: The Brokholes Inheritance in Warwickshire, Hertfordshire and Essex c. 1417–c.1453, Chetham's Manuscript Mun.E.6.10 (4)* ed. Christine Carpenter (Woodbridge: Boydell Press, 1998), pp. 58–9 and 155–68; I am grateful to Professor Helen Cooper for bringing these poems to my attention.
5   *Armburgh Papers*, ed. Carpenter, pp. 155–6. The more usual version is printed in *Late Medieval English Lyrics and Carols 1400–1530*, ed. Thomas G. Duncan (London: Penguin, 2000), pp. 13–15 (abbreviated hereafter as *LMELC*; lyrics will be cited by number in this edition). The companion volume *Medieval English Lyrics 1200–1400*, ed. Thomas G. Duncan (Harmondsworth: Penguin, 1995), will be abbreviated as *MEL*.
6   It is printed in three versions as 'On the Times' in *Anglo-Norman Political Songs*, no. XV, ed. and trans. Isabel Aspin, Anglo-Norman Texts XI (Oxford: Blackwell for the Anglo-Norman Text Society, 1953), pp. 157–68 (cited hereafter as *A-NPS*).
7   John Lydgate, 'So as I lay this othir nyght', in *Minor Poems*, ed. H. N. McCracken, 2 vols, EETS, ES 107 and OS 192 (London: Oxford University Press, 1910–34), II, no. 73; William Dunbar, *Poems of William Dunbar*, no. 21, ed. Priscilla Bawcutt, 2 vols (Glasgow: Association for Scottish Literature, 1998), I, 94–7. All references to Dunbar will be to this edition.
8   Translations are taken from this edition, though I have sometimes expanded them.

REFERENCES AND FURTHER READING

Alford, John (1992). *Piers Plowman: A Guide to the Quotations*. Medieval and Renaissance Texts and Studies 77. Binghamton, NY: Medieval and Renaissance Texts and Studies.

Archibald, Elizabeth (1992). Tradition and innovation in the macaronic poetry of Dunbar and Skelton. *Modern Language Quarterly*, 53, 126–49.

Baswell, Christopher (2007). Multilingualism on the page. In Paul Strohm (ed.). *Middle English* (pp. 38–50). Oxford Twenty-First Century Approaches to Literature. Oxford: Oxford University Press.

Bawcutt, Priscilla (1992). *Dunbar the Makar*. Oxford: Clarendon Press.

Bevington, David (ed.) (1975). *Mankind*. In *Medieval Drama* (pp. 903–38). Boston: Houghton Mifflin.

Bullock-Davies, Constance (1966). *Professional Interpreters and the Matter of Britain*. Cardiff: University of Wales Press.

Chaucer, Geoffrey (1987). *The Riverside Chaucer*. Ed. L. D. Benson et al. Oxford: Oxford University Press.

Clanchy, Michael T. (1993). *From Memory to Written Record, England 1066–1307*. 2nd edn. Oxford: Blackwell.

Cuddon, J. A. (1998). *A Dictionary of Literary Terms*. 4th edn. Rev. C. E. Preston. Oxford: Blackwell.

Diller, Hans-Jürgen (1997–8). Code-switching in medieval English drama. *Comparative Drama*, 31(4), 506–537.

Dunbar, William (1998). *Poems of William Dunbar*. Ed. Priscilla Bawcutt. 2 vols. Glasgow: Association for Scottish Literature.

Duncan, Thomas G. (ed.) (2005). *A Companion to the Middle English Lyric*. Cambridge: D. S. Brewer.

Fein, Susanna (ed.) (2000). *Studies in the Harley Manuscript: The Scribes, Contents and Social Contexts of British Library MS Harley 2253*. TEAMS. Kalamazoo, MI: Medieval Institute Publications.

Fletcher, Alan J. (1998). *Preaching, Politics and Poetry in Late-Medieval England*. Dublin: Four Courts Press.

Greene, Richard L. (ed.) (1977). *The Early English Carols*. 2nd edn. Oxford: Clarendon Press.

Harvey, Carol (1978). Macaronic techniques in Anglo-Norman verse. *L'Esprit Créateur*, 18(1): 70–81.

Hunt, Tony (2000). Code-switching in medical texts. In D. A. Trotter (ed.). *Multilingualism in Later Medieval Britain* (pp. 131–47). Cambridge: D. S. Brewer.

Lusignan, Serge (1986). *Parler vulgairement: Les intellectuels et la langue française aux XIIIe et XIVe siècles*. Paris: Vrin.

Lusignan, Serge (2004). *La Langue des rois au Moyen Age: Le français en France et en Angleterre*. Le Noeud gordien. Paris: Presses Universitaires de France.

Lydgate, John (1910–34). *Minor Poems*. Ed. H. N. McCracken. 2 vols. Early English Text Society, e.s. 107 and o.s. 192. London: Oxford University Press.

Putter, Ad (2009). The art of multilingualism: two trilingual lyrics in context. In Jocelyn Wogan-Browne et al. (eds). *Language and Culture in Medieval Britain: The French of England c. 1100–c. 1500* (pp. 397–406). Cambridge: D. S. Brewer.

Rothwell, William (1994). The trilingual England of Geoffrey Chaucer. *Studies in the Age of Chaucer*, 16: 45–67.

Skelton, John (1983). *The Complete English Poems*. Ed. John Scattergood. Harmondsworth: Penguin.

Stein, Robert. M. (2007). Multilingualism. In P. Strohm (ed.). *Middle English* (pp. 23–37). Oxford Twenty-First Century Approaches to Literature. Oxford: Oxford University Press.

Trotter, D. A. (ed.) (2000). *Multilingualism in Later Medieval Britain*. Cambridge: D. S. Brewer.

Turville-Petre, Thorlac (1996). *England the Nation: Language, Literature, and National Identity, 1290–1340*. Oxford: Clarendon Press.

Wehrle, W. O. (1933). *The Macaronic Hymn Tradition in Medieval English Literature*. Washington, DC: Catholic University Press.

Wenzel, Siegfried (1986). *Preachers, Poets, and the Early English Lyric*. Princeton, NJ: Princeton University Press.

Wenzel, Siegfried (1994). *Macaronic Sermons: Bilingualism and Preaching in Late Medieval England*. Ann Arbor: University of Michigan Press.

Zumthor, Paul (1960). Un Problème d'esthétique médiévale: l'utilisation poétique du bilinguisme. *Moyen Age*, 66: 301–36 and 561–94.

16

Popular Romance

Nancy Mason Bradbury

Verse romance was an expressive form of widespread influence in Western Europe between the twelfth and the fifteenth centuries. Retold in long prose versions in the fifteenth and early sixteenth centuries, medieval romances helped to pioneer some of the most important features of the modern novel, including a sustained interest in the inner life and moral development of a fictional protagonist. A key work in the history of the novel, Cervantes' *Don Quixote*, ridicules but also sustains an ongoing dialogue with chivalric romance. The traditional ballad and the fairy tale, much imitated by later poets and fiction writers, also number medieval romance among their most important ancestors. Romance settings, plots and characters influence today's popular culture in the United Kingdom and the United States: witness the current fascination with knights, wizards, dragons and magical objects in popular fiction and visual media.

Medieval romances allow modern readers to test for themselves familiar but dubious generalisations about medieval literature, including the unsustainable assertions that erotic love is always adulterous, that women are wooed and never wooers, that medieval authors either ignore or vilify non-Christian cultures, or that French romances appealed to elite sensibilities while those in English addressed a bourgeois or lower class audience. Indeed, medieval romances appear to have played a similar demystifying or debunking role in the societies that originally produced them. They often test accepted beliefs about heroism, chivalry and love, and they delight in heightening the tensions or exposing the outright gap between chivalric ideals and the realities of medieval life.[1]

Middle English romance merits two chapters in a companion to medieval English poetry because verse was the medium for most vernacular storytelling until the fifteenth century. The surviving verse narratives span a wide spectrum, from easily memorised, ballad-like rhymes that are stylistically simple but often quite powerful and allusive (*King Horn*, *Havelok*, *Athelston*) to more densely textured and bookish romances, including those of Geoffrey Chaucer, John Gower and the author of *Sir Gawain and the Green Knight*. This chapter treats those anonymous metrical tales commonly assigned to the popular end of this spectrum (more soon about the nebulous term *popular*); in the one that follows, Rosalind Field takes up Arthurian and other romances associated with medieval elites on the basis of such features as more densely and complexly crafted syntax, overt canonical aspirations, bookish allusions and special familiarity with court culture.

Until quite recently, with a few notable exceptions, literary scholars rarely thought of verse romances as instances of poetry.[2] Especially under the pervasive influence of New Criticism in the middle decades of the last century, most scholars followed Chaucer in dismissing their diffuse, repetitive, highly formulaic verse as mere doggerel. To the aspersions cast by *Sir Thopas*, Chaucer's brilliantly derisive parody of English romance, mid-century critics added a new stigma of their own, branding romance authors 'commercial hacks', though in fact we know very little about the identities or circumstances of these authors. In subsequent decades, however, scholars have become more sceptical about adopting Chaucer's devastating parody as a reliable guide to the value of English romance. Chaucer's works clearly reveal aspiration to high poetic status that extended beyond England, and thus his assessment of the native English romances was hardly that of a neutral observer; in the words of Ralph Hanna, it was 'very likely constructed precisely to displace his predecessors and to define a canon in which they would have no part' (Hanna 2005: 108). Not only does *Sir Thopas* reveal a deep familiarity with the idiom of metrical romance, but it also mocks distinctive stylistic features found in Chaucer's own verse (Burrow 1971: 2–21; Gaylord 1982: 311–29; Bradbury 1998: 176–89). The 'commercial hackwork' thesis that flourished in the mid-twentieth century has since diminished in importance amid the variety of literary and performance contexts currently put forward for the genesis and dissemination of verse romance in England.[3]

After a brief look at some salient features of English verse romance followed by an equally abbreviated discussion of what it might mean to call them 'popular' in the period roughly 1300–1500, this chapter undertakes the once-novel activity of reading popular verse romances as significant instances of medieval English poetry. The poetic qualities of these texts need not be exaggerated: their most apparent strengths are narrative and very often their verse serves as a workaday medium for getting a character from here to there. Yet even the most apparently simple verbal structures in these texts possess surprisingly powerful meanings and resonances if they are given the right kinds of readings, readings that get under their conventional surfaces, hear the undertones and overtones activated by their formulaic diction, attend to the organising powers of their striking symbolic objects, and recognise the creativity involved in recombining familiar structural elements.

What is a Romance?

The Old French word *romanz* was first used in a literary sense to identify works in French, as opposed to Latin, which was once the norm for European literature and scholarship. Writing in the mid-twelfth century, Robert Wace sets his *Brut*, a legendary history of Britain, against its Latin model with these words: 'Del livre oez la verité / Qui en romanze est translaté' ('Hear the truth of the book, which is translated into *romanze*', 7–8). Similarly, the original meaning of *romance* in English seems to have been 'a work in French'. The version of *Beves of Hampton* found in the Auchinleck Manuscript (*c.* 1330) refers to its French model as 'the Frensch' or 'the romance' (1782, 1537) in ways that suggest that these terms were interchangeable.[4] In both French and English, however, the word *romance* quickly attached itself to a particular type of vernacular narrative: secular fictions that recount a series of martial and / or amorous adventures. In addition to their interest in love and adventure, many romances share other features in common: love of the marvellous, representation of ancient or foreign cultures in the garb of medieval European feudal culture, and a happy ending marked by the hero's successful completion of his adventures, often followed by his marriage. Medieval sources almost always refer to romances by the names of their heroes or (much less frequently) heroines, suggesting that the presence of a particular type of protagonist was a defining trait of romance for its original audiences.

Their characteristic language and narrative techniques are easier to understand if we bear in mind that medieval romances circulated in many different ways. The role of oral reading and recitation in their transmission has been obscured by a series of misconceptions passed down from eighteenth- and nineteenth-century antiquarians: the term *minstrel* in the later Middle Ages almost always refers to a musician, not a reciter of narratives; the long narrow manuscripts once called holster books were rarely if ever intended to slip conveniently into an entertainer's saddlebag; the references romances make to performance before listening audiences are a feature of their storytelling style, not necessary indicators of oral delivery. Nevertheless, we have evidence, unsurprisingly scanty, but still clear, that romances were indeed performed orally, whether read from the page or recited as memorised 'rimes'. The external evidence for recitation of romances before a present audience comes largely from contemporary writers who took pains to distance themselves from such a practice, including Robert Mannyng, who announces early in his chronicle history of England:

> I *mad* noght for no *disours*,   *composed; reciters,*
> Ne for no *seggers*; no *harpours*.   *tellers; harp-players*
> (Robert Mannyng, *Chronicle*, Part I, ed. Furnivall, ll. 75–76)

Mannyng complains later in the same work that his favourite metrical romance, *Sir Tristrem*, would be the best of stories if men kept to the wording as 'Thomas' composed it, but instead, incompetent reciters spoil the tale:

> But I here it no man so say,
> That of som *copple* som is away;   *couplet*
> So thare fayre saying here beforn
> Is *thare trauayle nere forlorn*.   *their work is almost wasted*
>   (*Chronicle*, Part I, ll. 101–14)

Other evidence that romances passed through memories as well as written texts includes the testimony of many modern editors who report variations in romance texts that do not resemble the relatively small-scale changes familiar from scribal copying.[5] Research into the effects of memory on the transmission of texts helps to confirm the judgments of these editors: compared to scribal variation, memory tends to produce changes of a different nature and scale. Certain romances show, for example, conflation of passages at a considerable remove from one another, a common trick of the memory, but a source of variation unlikely to occur when a scribe is copying a page at a time (Putter and Gilbert 2000: 9).

The four tales deplored in the quotation below from the *Speculum Vitae*, a didactic work of the 1360s or 1370s, number among the best-known English metrical romances, and again the clerical speaker dissociates himself from those who recite romances aloud ('gestours / That make spekyng in many a place'):

> I warne yow ferst at the begynning,
> I wil make no veyn spekyng
> Of dedes of armes ne of amours,
> Os don mynstreles and other *gestours*,   *As do; storytellers*
> That make spekyng in many a place
> Of Octouian and Isanbrace
> And of many other gestes,—
> And namely whan they come to festes,
> Ne of Beus of Hamptoun,
> That was a knyght of gret renoun,
> Ne of sir Gy of Warewyk
> *Al thow it mowe som men like ...*   *Although some men might like it*
> For I holde that nowht bot vanyte.
>   (*Speculum Vitae* 35–48)[6]

Later in the fourteenth century, Chaucer uses *Sir Thopas* to dissociate his own work from 'romances' about Horn, Beves, Guy, and other heroes (ed. Benson, *CT* VII.897–900). We have no way of knowing the degree to which the tales mentioned by these fourteenth-century authors resemble the surviving written texts, but such references combine with the internal evidence briefly summarised above to show us that romances did not circulate by scribal copying alone, a point to which we shall return in seeking to understand their verbal art.

The evidence is of course much more concrete and plentiful for the circulation of romances in writing, both in short, individual pamphlets and in large collections that also contained sermons, saints' legends, chronicle histories, and other materials devotional and didactic (Guggat-Figge 1976; Meale 1989). In some cases the soft cover pamphlets or booklets that preserved individual romances were themselves eventually bound up into larger collections, where their soiled and heavily worn first and last pages still testify to their earlier independent circulation. Romance texts were copied under a variety of circumstances. A given tale might be copied by a professional scribe, either to fill a standing order from a buyer, or with a buyer found subsequently. A version of a tale could be authored, copied and presented to a patron who did not pay directly for the individual work, but helped to support its author by retaining him as a contributing member of a large, wealthy household or a court. Private individuals copied romances into personal, household collections. Several important manuscript collections that include romances are available in facsimile editions, and a modern reader unfamiliar with English romances can learn a great deal about their transmission and social location by comparing what appear to be professionally executed scribal copies like those in the famous Auchinleck Manuscript (National Library of Scotland MS Adv. 19.2.1) with a 'homemade' miscellany such as that transcribed by Robert Thornton (MS Lincoln Cathedral 91), and with a genteel commonplace book such as the Findern Anthology (Cambridge University Library MS Ff.1.6), whose copyists are believed to include the members of a gentry household as well as those neighbouring gentlewomen whose names appear in the manuscript.[7]

What is a 'Popular' Romance?

If we begin with a simple definition of *popular*, 'in wide circulation', 'available even to those without considerable wealth or special training', then romances were clearly all too popular in the estimation of the medieval clerics who denounced them as 'veyn speking' and 'nowht bot vanyte', as did the author of the *Speculum Vitae*. In chronicling the history of England, Robert Mannyng laments the absence of reliable written sources in French or Latin for the kingship of the early romance hero Havelok; all he can discover is what 'thise lowed ['uneducated'] men upon Inglish tellis'.[8] In the mouths of these 'uneducated' tellers, however, Mannyng finds that the tale of Havelok was common enough. But even the earnest cleric Mannyng was a fan of *Sir Tristrem*, as we have seen, evidence that English metrical romances were not entertainments only for the uneducated. Rather than positing a stable, class-based opposition between high and low culture in premodern Europe, the social historian Peter Burke argues that the upper classes participated actively in late medieval and early modern popular culture: 'In 1500 [...] what we now call popular culture was everyone's culture; a second culture for the educated, and the only culture for everyone else' (Burke 1978: 270).

One of the most easily recognisable features of the shared or 'popular' culture was its reliance on a common stock of tough yet flexible verbal and narrative units. In Burke's words, 'folksongs and folktales, popular plays and popular prints all need to be seen as combinations of elementary forms, permutations of elements which are more or less ready-made' (Burke 1978: 124). Across the spectrum, from popular (everyone's culture) to elite (a more exclusive culture for the privileged), Middle English romances all make use of a common stock of pre-existing units, but their presence tends to be more conspicuous at the popular end, where the texts are most likely to pass in and out of oral circulation. While highly literate modern writers are taught to think of ready-made phrases as aesthetic failings, the challenge to the composers of romance was to make apt use of existing verbal formulas that brought with them a fund of meanings and associations built up by prior application in similar contexts. A tale's larger units, or episodes, were often as ready-made as its language. Later novelistic fictions seek to disguise the gaps between episodes, but romances frequently herald them loudly: 'now we leave x and return to y'. As with its formulaic language, we tend to think of the episodic quality of romance primarily as an aid to its creators, allowing them to string together ready-made episodes like beads on a string. Episodic construction is also important to an audience, however: its manageable and well-marked units allow readers and hearers to grasp more easily the story's emphases, which are often signalled by large-scale structural repetitions and parallels. Like formulas, these traditional episodes can also carry resonances from their use in earlier contexts (Foley 1995). An important study by Helen Cooper (2004) analyses many of these tough and amazingly enduring narrative elements in English romance.

Thus many Middle English metrical romances fit nicely into Burke's vision of popular entertainments that make use of ready-made elements and circulate widely as part of a shared culture. Most medieval households allowed for little segregation by class, and a romance read or recited aloud could reach a variety of listeners. Despite their casts of royal and aristocratic characters, popular romances develop universal human themes: leaving home, selecting a life partner, or establishing adult identity in a wider social world. The degree to which universal themes shape a tale, in place of more particularised plights relevant only to the ruling classes, offers one index to the scope of a tale's intended audiences. The physical and social settings that draw from the poet the most detailed and sympathetic representations also serve as a gauge of a romance's breadth of imagination and social vision. The surviving version of *Havelok* offers beautifully realised scenes of everyday life among the tradespeople of Lincoln and Grimsby, and the hero of *Sir Isumbras* spends an interestingly detailed interlude labouring as an ironworker. The voices of the socially marginalised cannot be heard directly anywhere in Middle English romance, but when their lives and concerns are not just sympathetically presented, but artistically *represented* in full and rich detail, again we might locate such texts toward the popular end of the spectrum of surviving romances.

A further complication, however, is that the protean nature of romance – its ability to adapt to different social, historical, and material conditions – means that even versions of a single tale can register at quite distant points on a spectrum from popular to elite productions. An interesting example is the *Seege of Troye*, a relatively short narrative that shares its style and narrative technique with the simplest of verse romances and its distinguished subject matter with some of the most prestigious literary works of the Middle Ages.[9] Like other romances that survive in more than one copy, the *Seege* defies recension back to an 'original' or 'authorial' text; instead its editor prints four different and irreconcilable manuscript versions (one of them in fifteenth-century prose). Read aloud, read privately, or recited from memory (a feat made easier by its wealth of structural parallels and verbatim repetitions), the verse versions of the *Seege* are sufficiently entertaining and self-explanatory to reach audiences with a minimum of prior literary experience. The *Seege* introduces even the best-known figures from classical literature and identifies them as Greeks or Trojans throughout. Learned treatments of the Troy legend stress the transitory nature of human glory in the light of cosmic forces, but, almost alone among late medieval Troy stories, the *Seege* puts no emphasis on the role of Fortune in the fall of a once-proud civilisation, and instead takes a stand on an issue of widespread and demonstrable interest to fourteenth-century English audiences, both popular and elite: the meaning, boundaries and implications of treason, understood as a violation of the complex social and personal virtue known as *trouthe* (Green 1999).

Two of the *Seege*'s manuscript settings, Egerton 2862 and Lincoln's Inn 150, are consistent with the internal evidence for its deliberate accessibility to wide audiences; both are ordinary, minimally ornamented books containing mostly English metrical romances. MS Arundel 22, however, is a much more handsomely executed book in which the *Seege* serves as the first part of a continuous legendary history of the British monarchy in English, parts two and three being translations first from Geoffrey of Monmouth's *Historia Regum Britannia* and then from Wace's *Brut*. Where Wace had omitted from his *Brut* some esoteric statements called the 'Prophecies of Merlin' that are present in Geoffrey's *Historia*, the Arundel copyist supplies them, awkwardly integrated and still in Latin, but apparently of interest to the book's imagined or commissioning readers. Thus while the un- or minimally lettered may represent part of the *Seege*'s contemporary audience, its treatment in Arundel 22 suggests that its audience also extended to those of some substantial means and education who happened to have a use or a desire for an account of the Trojan War in English. In a more dramatic instance, the rowdy, anti-authoritarian *Tale of Gamelyn* (mid to late fourteenth century), a ballad-like work in the Robin Hood tradition, might not survive in writing at all if Chaucer's scribes had not found a use for it in a highly prestigious literary setting: it fills what they saw as a gap in *The Canterbury Tales* left by the apparently fragmentary state of the *Cook's Tale* (ed. Skeat 1884).

The *Seege of Troye* and other romances that survive in multiple copies suggest that the more we happen to know about a tale's circulation, the less confidently we can assign it to one or the other end of a spectrum from popular ('widely shared') to elite ('exclusive') productions. The cultural historian Roger Chartier argues that such will always be the case: 'it is pointless to try to identify popular culture by some supposedly specific distribution of cultural objects or models. Their distribution is always more complex than it might seem at first glance, as are their uses by groups or individuals.' Therefore, Chartier argues, we can never finally pin down the 'always illusory correspondence between a series of cultural artifacts and a specific socio-cultural level' (1995: 88–89). Support for his point comes from a striking exception to the assumption that, because Norman French was the language of the post-Conquest upper classes and English the language of ordinary people, Anglo-French romances were more refined and courtly, their English counterparts more 'popular'. While this generalisation about the 'correspondence between a series of cultural artifacts and a specific socio-cultural level' holds true in some cases, recent scholarship demonstrates that the qualities long said to make the English *Guy of Warwick* the quintessential popular romance were already present in its model, the Anglo-French *Gui de Warwic*. *Gui* and *Guy* share, for example, a male-Cinderella figure as hero; an accumulation of sensational, often violent, episodes; and a 'recycling of conventional motifs' (Field 2007: 46–8). The unexpected 'popular' qualities of *Gui* bear out Carol Meale's manuscript-based observation, 'There is no necessary reason to assume that those for whom works in English were intended were of a different class or were any less sophisticated in their literary tastes than those who either read, or listened to, Anglo-Norman' (Meale 1994: 211). Instead of seeking a one-to-one correspondence between a cultural object and a specific socio-cultural level, Chartier recommends that we think instead in terms of appropriation in both directions: apparently elite works can function in what seem to be popular contexts and apparently popular works crop up in relatively exclusive ones. Just as intellectuals, medieval or modern, draw freely upon expressive forms accessible to very wide audiences, so popular culture regularly appropriates the most exclusive cultural materials imaginable, if it happens to have a use for them.

The Poetry of Popular Romance

In 1965, Derek Pearsall published a pioneering and still very useful account of the development of romance verse forms, from the earliest surviving texts to *c*. 1400.[10] He divides the corpus of about fifty metrical romances into two broad categories: those in four-stress rhyming couplets (19 tales) and those in tail-rhyme stanzas (25 tales, plus 6 that are closely related as predecessors or successors to tail rhyme). The couplet form is thought to descend from the twelfth- and thirteenth-century French octosyllabic couplets employed in a wide variety of narratives, including the epic *chansons de geste*. In English, this short couplet often served as the medium for tales 'more prosaic, realistic, historical and martial' than those in the other major form, tail-rhyme stanzas, the medium of choice for tales that are 'more emotive, more concerned with love, faith, constancy and the marvellous' (Pearsall in Brewer 1988: 16). *King Horn, Havelok, Richard Coeur de Lion* and *Beves of Hamptoun* exemplify early couplet romance; *Havelok* in particular derives an air of historicity from its recognisable English settings and detailed scenes from ordinary life. Susan Crane (1986) has shown how these early insular romances engage with important contemporary issues such as just rule and rightful inheritance of title and property. Interestingly, the version of *Guy of Warwick* in the Auchinleck Manuscript begins as a characteristic 'epic romance' in rhymed couplets, but when the hero's adventures become less martial and more emotionally and spiritually charged in its second half, the composer (whether the same or a different one) adopts tail-rhyme stanzas. Romances from a third group, made up of some lyrical French love-romances and the so-called Breton lays, 'cut across the broad formal distinction between "epic" and "lyric" romance' as drawn by

Pearsall: works in this category are composed in rhymed couplets like 'epic' romance, but are often magical, lyrical and affective in ways more characteristic of the tail-rhyme stanza (in Brewer 1988: 22).

Readers in search of a survey of the whole corpus of romance (including alliterative tales as well as metrical), with summaries of each tale, should consult Severs 1967, and, for more up-to-date scholarship, the cogent historical survey by Field 1999 and the medieval chapters in Saunders 2004. Rather than aiming for a comprehensive overview, I devote the rest of this chapter to a closer look at a few representative texts from each of Pearsall's three types with attention to their familiar, conventional and often highly effective ways of meaning.

The poetic qualities of couplet romance are well displayed in *King Horn*, the earliest of English romances (ed. Fellows 1993). Its verse form is less regular than later romances in couplets – it consists of short lines of varied syllabic number and rhythm, often bearing three rather than four stresses – but, as Pearsall points out, it contains in embryo much of the future language and technique of couplet romance. An earlier version of Horn's story exists in Anglo-French, but a number of factors, including specifically English puns on the word *horn*, suggest that the tale was already circulating in English when the French version was composed. Although its air of historicity earns for it a place among 'epic' romances, the English tale's narrative and poetic art is very much of a type we now recognise from later ballads, folk tales and fairy tales. Its hero possesses a numinous beauty that carries all before it. When it comes time to sum up the tale in two lines, the poet singles out this central fact:

> Her endeth the tale of Horn
> That fair was and noght *unorn*   *plain, unattractive*
> (1527–28)

The poet uses repetition and simple comparisons to convey the fact and the intensity of Horn's fairness but never details a single individual characteristic:

> Fairer ne miste non beo born,
> Ne no rain *upon birine*,   *rain down upon*
> Ne sunne upon bishine.
> Fairer nis non thane he was:
> He was bright so the glas;
> He was whit so the flur;
> Rose red was his colur.
> (10–16)

Horn's fairy-tale beauty is radiant, clear, and highly contrastive ('whit' and 'rose-red'). It sparkles like glass, a simile particularly appropriate to this kind of art, which itself strives toward 'the clear, the unambiguous, the extreme, and the distinct' (Lüthi 1987:15). The hero's beauty is one with his Christianity: 'Muchel was his fairhede / For Jhesu Christ him makede' (83–4). It has the power to transfix others, an effect that German folk-tale scholars call *Schönheitsschock* or 'beauty-shock'. When pagans invade Horn's homeland, kill his father and seize him, his beauty alone causes the pagans to spare the youths: 'Yef his fairnesse nere / The children alle aslaghe were' (87–88). To avoid future revenge for the death of Horn's father, the pagan invaders set the rightful heir and his young companions adrift in a rudderless boat. The youths wash ashore in the land of Westernesse, where the king too is dazzled by their fairness, especially that of Horn, whom he readily adopts. Others in the tale also yield to the shock of Horn's beauty, but none so powerfully as the king's daughter, Rymenhild, who is driven to near-frenzy by passion for this youth whose fairness illuminates her whole chamber:

> Of his feire sighte
> All the *bur* gan lighte.   *bower*
> (385–86)

The central quality of Horn's existence is a shining beauty that signifies at once his Christianity, his noble birth, his moral worthiness and above all his special quality as *hero*; his fairness is as transparent as glass in its meaning.

In its effects, Horn's beauty borders on the magical, and other important elements of the tale possess the same quality. Although it is presumably guided to safety by divine Providence, the boat in which the hero and his companions are set adrift seems itself to belong to the natural world, until Horn addresses it from the shore of Westernesse. He asks that, if it returns to his homeland, it carry to his mother the reassurance that he is safe and, to the pagans who exiled him, the promise that he will seek revenge. Horn's words to the boat can of course be taken figuratively as an apostrophe, but the tale's spare abstraction confers on each of its small number of material objects potential magical powers, as well as potential symbolic meaning. Horn's eponymous musical instrument is another such object, as is a ring that Rymenhild gives him, which will protect him if he thinks of her. She tells him of a dream about fishing in the sea and catching a fish so large it rips her net, which prevents her from catching the fish she wanted (658–64), a dream whose symbolism not only expresses her erotic longings for Horn, but also foretells her repeated near-marriages to the wrong suitors as she awaits his return. The boat, the horn, the ring, the fish and net – all of these symbolic objects signify powerfully because the rest of the tale is so spare: they loom so large because, unlike a realistic fiction full of authenticating detail, *King Horn* has so few concrete particulars.

Although it is a point that pertains to all three formal types of romance, not just those in couplets, it is worth noting before we leave *King Horn* that it illustrates beautifully the characteristic use of prefabricated materials in popular art forms. Exposure in a rudderless boat, for example, is a widespread romance motif, particularly useful because it allows the villains to dispense with the threat to their conquest that a legitimate heir poses, but without transgressing against the hero's youth, beauty and vulnerability by shedding his blood. So persistent is this motif or type-scene that it carries with it a near-verbatim verbal formula as it moves from tale to tale: Horn is set adrift in a vessel 'Withute sail and rother' (192), a version of a formulaic expression that accompanies this motif for many centuries across the languages of Europe (Cooper 2004: 105–36). Like its individual episodes, the tale's overall story pattern – exile and return – is equally prefabricated and governs a wide variety of traditional narratives. The pattern tends to throw particular emphasis on another highly conventional narrative element, a recognition scene staged late in the tale, when the hero returns in disguise or transformed by suffering. The return of Odysseus and the non-naturalistically protracted process by which Penelope gradually recognises him is a famous instance. Near the end of *King Horn*, Rymenhild responds with great interest to the arrival of an unknown pilgrim, but here too it takes a series of tokens and very broad clues to lead her to recognise this stranger as her beloved. At every level, the story of Horn is fashioned out of ready-made units: small-scale verbal formulas like 'withute sail and rother', individual episodes such as casting innocents to sea in a boat, and the over-arching exile and return story pattern that shapes the whole tale. Because an audience familiar with the tradition has encountered these formulas, type scenes and story patterns before, their recurrence draws upon a freight of associations and resonances from a reader's or hearer's prior literary experiences. Foley (1995) uses the term 'traditional referentiality' to describe this special evocative power that formulas, type scenes, and story patterns build up over time and many uses. Its force is metonymic: each recurrence offers a small part of a traditional field of reference as a representative of the whole field.

The tail-rhyme stanza, the second form in Pearsall's tripartite division, is also used for medieval lyric poetry; it lends itself to emotive tales that incline toward tests of faith and constancy. Named for the shorter rhyming lines (the 'tails') embedded among the longer lines of each stanza, tail-rhyme stanzas come in a variety of forms, the most common of which is a twelve-line stanza with the rhyme scheme aab ccb ddb eeb, where the b rhyme lines (the 'tails') have only three accented syllables, while the other lines have four. Compared to the Romance languages in which such complex stanza forms first flourished, English is notoriously rhyme-poor, and tail rhyme put considerable strain on the composers of long narratives, who had to provide as many as four rhyming words per stanza on a single sound to fill the b position. A skilled user of the form such as the *Athelston*-poet sometimes repeats one of the rhyme words in the b position, as with 'telle' in the stanza quoted below, an effect that is rarely obtrusive and often appears deliberate. Less talented tellers use a wealth of prefabricated expressions in the tail lines, some of them emphatic but nearly empty of content, such as 'forsooth as I you say'.

The tail-rhyme stanza below from the well-wrought story of *Athelston* shows the suitability of the form to imitating in verse the redundancies and commonplaces characteristic of ordinary speech, as well as expressing the oaths, vows, and asseverations central to the plots and themes of romance. The stanza begins with King Athelston's response to one of his sworn brothers, a lying traitor, who has just made the false accusation that someone is plotting to kill the king. The king asks the identity of the alleged plotter, and the traitorous baron demands that the king first swear never to reveal the source of his information:

> Thenne said the King, 'So moot thou thee,
> Knowe I that man and I him see?
>   His name thou me telle.'
> 'Nay,' says that traitour, 'that wole I nought
> For all the gold that evere was wrought,
>   Be masse-book and belle,
> But-yif thou me thy trouthe will plight
> That thou shalt nevere *bewreye* the knight   *betray*
>   That thee the tale shall telle.'
> Thanne the King his hand up *raughte*,   *reached*
> That false man *his trouthe betaughte* –   [*To*] *that false man pledged his word*
>   He was a devil of helle!
> (*Athelston*, ed. Trounce, 1951; lines 145–56 [spelling modernised])

The stanza is a miniature guide to the language and gesture of oath swearing, and it also illustrates the tale's ironic play with the keywords of oath-based relationships: the king pledges his *trouthe* not to betray a *traitour*. Its last line illustrates the effective use of a tail-line for summary comment, here a spirited condemnation of the villain.

As an illustration of the heightened lyrical and affective qualities of tail-rhyme romance, we may look at the early fourteenth-century *Sir Isumbras*, another relatively short, highly readable tale in many ways characteristic of popular romance. It appears to have been well known in its day because its protagonist is twice named in catalogues of typical romance heroes, in both the *Cursor Mundi* (*c.* 1320) and the *Speculum Vitae* (*c.* 1370). Because its plot structures and its narrative techniques overlap with those of the saint's life, its status as a romance is sometimes questioned. But one can just as easily take this overlap as a reminder that generic identity is a fluid matter of shared conventions and audience expectation, not a life membership in a single fixed category. Exemplary and hagiographical elements are by no means rare in metrical romance, and *Isumbras* incorporates them in highly characteristic form. The version of the tale preserved in MS Cotton Caligula A.ii (ed. Mills 1973) exemplifies the pressure exerted by the tail-rhyme stanza on a poet's rhyming skills: its tail-lines make occasional use of the form's established line-fillers: 'The sothe as I telle yow' (33), 'In story as we rede' (510). Pre-modern audiences did not share the New Critical horror of 'hackneyed' phrases, however, and they are much less obtrusive in verse read or recited aloud. As formulaic language becomes less of a barrier to literary criticism, new and more sympathetic readings of popular romances become possible. Thus a recent critic writes of *Isumbras*, 'its careful composition repays close reading for both structure and poetic idiom' (Fowler 2000: 98; and see also Mills 1994: 1–24).

Sir Isumbras is another of the exile and return stories so characteristic of medieval romance, and its carefully patterned structure is indeed effective: in the first half of the tale, the hero undergoes loss after loss, and in the second half, what he has lost gradually returns to him, giving the tale a satisfying symmetry of form. The opening stanzas report that Isumbras possesses all the requisite chivalric virtues: he is *doughty* in battle, *curteys*, *fre* (generous) and *gentil*; he is king of *curteyse* and his *gentylnesse* has no limits. In this 'exemplary' or 'hagiographical' romance, however, chivalric virtues alone will not suffice. Isumbras has succumbed to worldly pride, lost sight of what is due to God, and thus earned the rebuke of a bird bearing God's message, 'Thow haste foryete what thou was' (50). The hero is stripped of everything he values in a way that recalls the sufferings of Job. In the dramatic manner of its presentation, the tale also anticipates the later morality play *Everyman*, in which every worldly connection abandons the hero in its turn. Isumbras's horse dies under him, his hawks and hounds break for the woods, the buildings of his manor catch fire, his wife is soon taken from him by a heathen king, and his children are carried off by exotic beasts. Near the middle of the tale, Isumbras turns to God, acknowledging that he has gone 'all amysse' (384) and asking to be shown the way. After a period of humble manual labour, he is forgiven, and his many gifts begin to come back to him, including his wife and children. Husband and wife take arms against an enormous host of Saracens and, joined by their three sons, they win a symbolic Christian battle. Isumbras's earlier *curteyse* thus gives way to a truer and more complete form of chivalry, one in which humility, self-abnegation and fighting for the faith complement his original virtues.

As we have seen, the tail-rhyme stanza lends itself well to representing speech, with its tail-lines that pause to repeat, asseverate, dilate, intensify, or comment. Its characteristic idiom is also well adapted to representing oaths, rituals and vows – language that is formulaic in life as well as literature. *Isumbras* is strong in the language of avowal, as we can see in this early stanza, in which the hero resolves that his family, not yet lost to him, will go on pilgrimage:

> He toke his mantell of ryche pall
> And ovur his wyfe he lette hit fall
>   With a drewrye mode.
> His ryche *sirkote* then toke he   *surcoat*
> To his pore chyldren thre
>   That naked byfore hym stode.
> 'Do ye schull aftur my *rede*,   *counsel*
> To seke God wher he was quykke and dede,
>   That for us shedde his blode.
> For Jesu Criste that is so fre,
> Hym to seche wher it be:
>   He sende us our lyves fode.'
>   (127–38)

As this stanza also demonstrates, clothing and nakedness signify powerfully in this romance, as they do in many others, including *Havelok* and Chaucer's *Clerk's Tale*;

Elizabeth Fowler aptly describes *Isumbras* as a tale of 'divestment and investiture' (2000: 100–6). In the first half of the stanza, Isumbras takes off the trappings of his noble station, his 'mantell of ryche pall' and his 'ryche sirkote'. When he was still a generous and wealthy lord, 'in world was none so fre' (30), he gave away rich robes (26), apparently with little thought. But in his new afflicted state, when he takes off his only remaining garments to cover his wife and children, he exhibits a more meaningful form of *fredom* than in his earlier worldly largesse. With its sacramental references to Christ's yielding up his own body and blood, the second half of the stanza re-values the chivalric virtue of generosity by setting a new standard of what it means to be *fre*. In keeping with Christ's higher and more visceral standard of self-sacrifice, Isumbras marks himself with the sign of the cross, not emblazoned on *mantel*, *ryche sirkote*, or shield, but cut with a knife into his shoulder (139–40). Effects such as these rely on what Foley (1995) calls traditional referentiality: as a result of prior experience of the same words or phrases in the same contexts, an audience recognises *fredom* as central to the values of chivalry. Only then can it grasp the import of its spiritual revaluing in a tale such as *Isumbras*, which uses its audience's knowledge of the fictions of feudalism to lead towards ideals of a different sort.

With its air of historicity and its brisk narrative movement, *King Horn* has served here as an early example of couplet or 'epic' romance; and *Sir Isumbras* represents romance in tail- rhyme stanzas, with its extended capacity for exploration of emotional response, gradual spiritual development and other forms of lyric dilation. Pearsall's third grouping consists of the tales called Breton lays and some early French-derived love-romances that cut across the distinction between couplet and tail-rhyme romance: their form is the couplet but they share the affective and lyrical qualities of tail rhyme. So named because they purport to derive from the Celtic oral traditions of Brittany and Wales, the Middle English Breton lays include *Sir Orfeo*, *Sir Degare* and *Lai Le Freine*. *Freine* first appears among the twelfth-century *lais* of Marie de France, who also attributes their origins to Breton singers or storytellers. *Florys and Blauncheflour* (ed. Fellows) makes no claim to be a Breton lay, but falls into this third category by virtue of its tender love story, in which song-like repetition at times functions almost as musical expression, rather than forwarding the narrative. Raised as siblings, the title characters are to be separated for the first time so that the boy can go to school, and the boy responds to this unwelcome news:

> Florys answerd with wepyng,
> As he stood byfore the kyng:
> Al wepyng seide he,
> 'Ne shal not Blancheflour lerne with me?
> Ne can y noght to scole goon
> Without Blaunchefloure,' he saide than,
> 'Ne can y in no scole syng ne rede
> Without Blancheflour,' he seide.
>
> (15–22)

Those familiar with the ballad technique of 'incremental repetition' will recognise its precursor here: the verse gives a little information, then repeats that information with a little more detail added, often for the purpose of enhancing an emotional effect. Late in the fourteenth century, a new cluster of tales suggests a revival or continuation of interest in lyrical couplet romance: *Emare*, the *Erl of Tolous* and *Sir Launfal* (another tale also told by Marie) all claim Breton origin, as does Chaucer's *Franklin's Tale*, a positive transformation of the romance genre that tempers the ridicule offered by *Sir Thopas*.

The Breton lay *Sir Orfeo* (ed. Shepherd 1995) has long been heralded as one of Middle English romance's jewels, and it will serve here to illustrate the art of lyrical couplet romance. This version of the classical legend of Orpheus brings the story home to England by transforming the Greek city of Thrace into the English royal capital of Winchester. It combines classical and Celtic mythology to an effect both brilliant and haunting. *Sir Orfeo* can be termed *popular* only under such a definition as is adopted here: it rewards the attention of readers or listeners with and without formal education or experience of court life. Its very up-to-date knowledge of French ecclesiastical architecture indicates that its audience extends to elites: the fairy king's underground castle boasts flying buttresses and arch-stones painted in bright, contrasting colours (Lerer 1985: 92–109, esp. 98–101). Yet the festive atmosphere of oral performance characteristic of the most popular Middle English romances is not only adeptly managed, but thematised in the tale itself: *Orfeo* can be read as an enchanting Breton lay, but also as an insightful work *about* the art and performance of the Breton lay. By the fourteenth century, Orpheus already had a long history of representing the poet, artist and musician, and in *Sir Orfeo*, recurrent references to the power of Orfeo's performances, his 'melody' and 'minstrelsy', apply to the teller of this lyrical tale as well. The poem's intriguing symbolic objects include Orfeo's harp and the 'fair ympe-tree', or grafted fruit tree, under which Queen Heurodis is marked for abduction by the king of fairies. The tale also employs the verbal repetition and larger-scale patterning native to English metrical romance, often to an especially memorable effect.

Just as medieval romances are themselves retellings of traditional stories, a miniaturised, internal form of retelling is one of their central narrative and poetic techniques. Often an event is first directly presented by the tale's narrating voice, then recounted in the speech of one of the characters, and sometimes told yet again from the point of view of a different character. In oral storytelling, such a device may function on the most basic level to ensure that a listening audience follows the complexities of the plot, but it can function in more subtle ways as well. The passages from *Orfeo* that follow illustrate how effectively this technique can carry over into written texts. The queen has had what she believes to be a dream, the contents of which have not yet been disclosed. The narrator describes the terror this encounter inspires in her:

Sche crid and *lothli bere* gan make;	*horrifying sound*
Sche *froted* hir honden and hir fet,	*rubbed*

> And *crached hir visage*—it bled wete;   *scratched her face*
> Hir riche robe hye *al to-ritt*   *ripped to pieces*
> And was *reveyd* out of hir witt.   *driven*
>
>   (78–82)

The narrator's description is powerful enough, but its emotional impact is even stronger when the effects of the dream on Heurodis are retold from the point of view of her appalled husband:

> O lef liif! what is te
> That ever yete hast ben so stille,
> And now gredest wonder schille?
> Thi bodi that was *so white y-core*,   *of so choice a whiteness*
> With thine nailes is al to-tore.
> Allas! thi *rode* that was so red   *complexion*
> Is al wan, as thou were ded;
> And also thine fingers smale
> Beth al blodi and al pale.
> Allas! thi lovesom *eyghen* to   *eyes*
> Loketh so man doth on his fo!
>
>   (102–12)

Orfeo's version includes most of the same details, but it registers each as a shocking change from her customary appearance: the snow white skin and rosy cheeks central to beauty in these tales is here recast as deathly pale skin reddened by freshly drawn blood. The repetition of 'Allas' at the head of the line, the many pronouns of familiar direct address – *thi, thine, thou* – and the more intimate view of her body make her husband's account more personal and affecting, especially the final contrast, which could only come from Orfeo's point of view: the eyes in which he was accustomed to see love now look at him as though he were an enemy. The tale has captured our full attention when the queen herself begins yet another retelling, this time spoken by the only one who can tell us firsthand what happened under the tree to frighten her so badly (98–140). Retelling is obviously a narrative technique, but also a matter of verbal patterning and thus an important poetic device as well.

A final example of this poem's accomplished verbal art is its description of the fairy otherworld into which Orfeo follows Heurodis. It combines the underworld of classical mythology, inhabited by shades of the dead, with a Celtic fairy kingdom whose inhabitants are, like Heurodis, living beings magically enthralled:

> Sum stode withouten hade,
> And sum *non armes nade*,   *had no arms*
> And sum thurth the bodi hadde wounde,
> And sum lay *wode y-bounde*.   *mad and restrained*
> And sum armed on hors sete,
> And sum a-strangled as thai ete,

And sum were in water *a-dreynt*,	*drowned*
And sum with fire al *for-schreynt*;	*shrunken; maimed*
Wives ther lay on child-bedde,	
Sum ded and sum *a-wedde*,	*crazed*
And wonder *fele* ther lay bisides,	*many*
Right as thai slepe *her under-tides*.	*their late mornings away*

(391–402)

This technique – overlaying a very rigid verbal structure ('And sum…' 'And sum…') on a chaotic vision of horror and misery – anticipates Chaucer's memorable description of the murals that ornament the temple of Mars in the *Knight's Tale*.

Even the other manuscript versions of *Orfeo* blunt some of the delicate effects in Auchinleck, however, and it is important to recognise that the accomplishments of the Auchinleck *Orfeo* represent, not a different verbal art, but a particularly skilled application of the same techniques found in other popular romances, including repetition with variation, symbols that signify with great interpretive clarity, and effective use of traditional referentiality, by which prior encounters with the same materials (formulas, type scenes, or story patterns) provide rich contexts and resonances, especially for those contemporary readers and listeners, elite and ordinary, who knew the traditional romance idiom well.

Popular romances can indeed be poetic, then, and not just in the technical sense that they are rendered in verse. These familiar yet evocative tales ask audiences to look beyond appearance and beneath the surface: the unpromising boy might be an exemplary prince, the ugly old woman a shape-shifting fairy, an apparently helpless innocent may wield extraordinary power, an ordinary object may become charged with transcendent significance. They use fantasy settings and situations to explore realms of experience very real but largely off limits to clerical literature, such as feminine desire, transgression of gender norms, or doubts about the benevolence of the cosmos toward mortals. By providing glimpses into other worlds, in which other rules apply, romances call into question the often harsh and limiting boundaries of their historical present. They allow their audiences to imagine other worlds and other ways of being, but most medieval English romances begin in and quickly return to the historical and political realities of their own world. Their poetry is the poetry of everyday life, ordinary speech, widely shared wishes and the most universal of human relationships, couched in an idiom as sturdy and traditional as the best of the genre's heroes and heroines.

NOTES

1　For a spirited account of the continued relevance of medieval romance to modern readers, see the 'polemical introduction' to McDonald 2004.
2　Among early close readings of metrical romance are Mehl 1969, Burrow 1971 and Ganim 1983.
3　For overviews with references, see Field 1999 and Putter and Gilbert 2000:1–38.

4   *The Romance of Beues of Hamtoun*, ed. Eugen Kölbing, Early English Text Society e.s. 46, 48, 65 (London: Oxford University Press, 1885, 1886, 1894).

5   Putter and Gilbert list 14 romances as examples in n. 22 (2000: 33).

6   Cited by Baugh (1967: 10).

7   Meale 1989: 217 and n. 94. The three facsimile editions are *The Auchinleck Manuscript: National Library of Scotland, Advocates' MS 19.2.1*, ed. Derek Pearsall and I. C. Cunningham (London: Scolar Press, 1977); *The Findern Manuscript (Cambridge University Library MS Ff.1.6)*, ed. Richard Beadle and A.E.B. Owen (London: Scolar Press, 1977); and *The Thornton Manuscript (Lincoln Cathedral MS 91)*, ed. Derek Brewer and A. E. B. Owen (London: Scholar Press, 1975).

8   [*The Chronicle of Robert Mannyng of Brunne*, Part 2] *Peter Langtoft's Chronicle*. 2 vols, ed. Thomas Hearne (Oxford, 1725), text cited by page number. See Bradbury 1998: 68–70 for discussion of this passage.

9   *The Seege or Batayle of Troye*, ed. Mary Elizabeth Barnicle, Early English Text Society o.s. 172 (London: Oxford University Press, 1927). For critical readings of this text, see Bradbury 1998: 99–132 and McDonald 2000: 181–99.

10 Reprinted in Brewer (1988), from which my citations are drawn.

REFERENCES AND FURTHER READING

Baugh, Albert C. (1967). 'The Middle English romance: some questions of creation, presentation, and preservation'. *Speculum*, 42, 1–31.

Benson, Larry D. et al. (1987). *The Riverside Chaucer*. Boston: Houghton, Mifflin.

Bradbury, Nancy Mason (1998). *Writing Aloud: Storytelling in Fourteenth Century England*. Urbana: University of Illinois Press.

Brewer, Derek (1988). *Studies in Medieval English Romances*. Cambridge: D. S. Brewer.

Brewer, Derek (2004). The popular English metrical romance. In Corinne Saunders (ed.). *A Companion to Romance* (pp. 45–64). Oxford: Blackwell.

Burke, Peter (1978). *Popular Culture in Early Modern Europe*. London: Temple Smith.

Burrow, J. A. (1971). *Ricardian Poetry*. London: Routledge.

Chartier, Roger (1995). *Forms and Meanings: Texts, Performances, and Audiences from Codex to Computer*. Philadelphia: University of Pennsylvania Press.

Cooper, Helen (2004). *The English Romance in Time: Transforming Motifs from Geoffrey of Monmouth to the Death of Shakespeare*. Oxford: Oxford University Press.

Crane, Susan (1986). *Insular Romance: Politics, Faith, and Culture in Anglo-Norman and Middle English Literature*. Berkeley: University of California Press.

Fellows, Jennifer (ed.) (1993). *Of Love and Chivalry: An Anthology of Middle English Romance*. London: Dent Everyman.

Field, Rosalind (1999). Romance in English, 1066–1400. In David Wallace (ed.). *The Cambridge History of Medieval English Literature* (pp. 152–176). Cambridge: Cambridge University Press.

Field, Rosalind (2007). From *Gui* to *Guy*: the fashioning of a popular romance. In Alison Wiggins and Rosalind Field (eds). *Guy of Warwick: Icon and Ancestor* (pp. 44–60). Cambridge: D. S. Brewer.

Foley, John Miles (1995). *The Singer of Tales in Performance*. Bloomington: Indiana University Press.

Fowler, Elizabeth (2000). The romance hypothetical: lordship and the saracens in *Sir Isumbras*. In Putter and Gilbert (eds). *The Spirit of Medieval English Popular Romance* (pp. 97–121). Harlow: Longman.

Furnivall, F. J., ed. (1887). Robert Mannyng. *The Story of England* [*The Chronicle of Robert Mannyng of Brunne* Part I]. 2 vols. Rolls Series 87. London: Longman.

Ganim, John M. (1983). *Style and Consciousness in Middle English Narrative*. Princeton, NJ: Princeton University Press.

Gaylord, Alan T. (1982). The moment of 'Sir Thopas': towards a new look at Chaucer's language. *Chaucer Review*, 16, 311–29.

Green, Richard F. (1999). *A Crisis of Truth: Literature and Law in Ricardian England*. Philadelphia: University of Pennsylvania Press.

Guddat-Figge, G. (1976). *Catalogue of Manuscripts Containing Middle English Romances*. Munich: Wilhelm Fink.

Hanna, Ralph (2005). *London Literature, 1300–1380*. Cambridge: Cambridge University Press.

Lerer, Seth (1985). Artifice and artistry in 'Sir Orfeo'. *Speculum*, 60, 92–109.

Lüthi, Max (1987). *The Fairy Tale as Art Form and Portrait of Man*. Trans. Jon Erickson. Bloomington and Indianapolis: Indiana University Press. (Original German publication, 1975).

McDonald, Nicola (2000). 'The Seege of Troye: 'ffor wham was wakened all this wo'?' In Ad Putter and Jane Gilbert (eds). *The Spirit of Medieval English Popular Romance* (pp. 181–99). Harlow: Longman.

McDonald, Nicola (ed.) (2004). *Pulp Fictions of Medieval England: Essays in Popular Romance*. Manchester: Manchester University Press.

Meale, Carol M. (1989). Patrons, buyers and owners: book production and social status. In Jeremy Griffiths and Derek Pearsall (eds). *Book Production and Publishing in Britain, 1375–1475*. Cambridge: Cambridge University Press.

Meale, Carol M. (1994). 'Gode men / Wiues maydnes and alle men': romance and its audiences. In *Readings in Medieval English Romance* (pp. 209–25). Cambridge: D. S. Brewer.

Mehl, Dieter (1969). *The Middle English Romances of the Thirteenth and Fourteenth Centuries*. London: Routledge.

Mills, Maldwyn (ed.) (1973). *Six Middle English Romances*. London: Dent-Everyman.

Mills, Maldwyn (1994). 'Sir Isumbras' and the styles of the tail-rhyme romance. In Carol M. Meale (ed.). *Readings in Medieval English Romance* (pp. 1–24). Cambridge: D. S. Brewer.

Pearsall, Derek (1965). 'The development of Middle English romance'. *Mediaeval Studies*, 27, 91–116. (Reprinted in Derek Brewer (1988). *Studies in Medieval English Romances*. Cambridge: D. S. Brewer, pp. 11–35.)

Putter, Ad and Jane Gilbert (eds) (2000). *The Spirit of Medieval English Popular Romance*. Harlow: Longman.

Saunders, Corinne (ed.) (2004). *A Companion to Romance*. Oxford: Blackwell.

Severs, J. Burke (ed.) (1967). *A Manual of the Writings in Middle English*. Vol. 1: *Romances 1050–1500*. New Haven: Connecticut Academy of Arts and Sciences.

Shepherd, Stephen H. A. (ed.) (1995). *Middle English Romances*. New York: W. W. Norton.

The Tale of Gamelyn (1884). Ed. W. W. Skeat. Oxford: Clarendon Press.

Trounce, A. McI. (ed.) (1951). *Athelston*. Early English Text Society o.s. 224. London: Oxford University Press.

17

Arthurian and Courtly Romance

Rosalind Field

An examination of courtly and Arthurian vernacular narrative in post-Conquest England can start with the *Roman de Brut* of Wace. There is courtliness in historical narrative before Wace – in Geoffrey of Monmouth's *Historia Regum Britanniae* and in Gaimar's English history – but it is in Wace's translation of Geoffrey that the reign of Arthur becomes accessible to a later generation of romance writers (Weiss 1999). The influence of Wace on Chrétien and thence on French romance is well-charted, and the presence of the *Brut* in both the vernaculars of England is ubiquitous throughout the medieval period.

But Wace is not only a starting point and influence on courtly Arthurian writing, he is also a courtly poet of considerable achievement and one who exemplifies many of the traits characteristic of courtly writing. He is a clerical writer, he is writing for a known courtly environment, he is a stylistic innovator with a strong authorial presence. And he creates a strong sense of the courtly, as is evident in three passages that we will examine here:

> Les tecches Arthur vus dirrai,[1]
> Neient ne vus en mentirai;
> Chevaliers fu mult vertuus,
> Mult fu preisanz, mult glorius;
> Cuntre orguillus fu orguillus
> E cuntre humles dulz e pitus;
> Forz e hardiz e conqueranz,
> Large dunere e despendanz;
> E se busuinnus le requist,
> S'aider li pout, ne l'escundist.
> Mult ama preis, mult ama gloire,
> Mult volt ses fai metre en memoire,
> Servir se fist curteisement
> Se se cuntint mult noblement.

Tant cum il vesqui e regna
Tuz altres princes surmunta
De curteisie e de noblesce
E de vertu e de largesce.
            (Lines 9015–32; Weiss 1999)

I will tell you what Arthur was like and not lie to you. He was a most mighty knight, admirable and renowned, proud to the haughty and gentle and compassionate to the humble. He was strong, bold and invincible, a generous giver and spender, and if he could help someone in need, he would not refuse him. He greatly loved renown and glory, he greatly wished his deeds to be remembered. He behaved most nobly and saw to it that he was served with courtesy. For as long as he lived and reigned, he surpassed all other monarchs in courtesy and nobility, generosity and power.

            (Trans. Weiss)

This passage serves to demonstrate why our discussion of courtly narrative in English begins with the other vernacular of medieval England. The passage is full of courtly terminology that has made its way into English, and without which English poets cannot express the ethical and social concepts of courtliness: chevalier, virtuous, glorious, piteous, hardy, praise, glory, memory, courteously, nobly, prince, courtesy, noblesse, virtue, largesse. We cannot translate these words into English, and certainly not into fourteenth-century English; they become English. The ethical portrait of the fifteen-year-old Arthur is also a significant mixture of the glorious, somewhat vainglorious, ruler and the humane protector of his people. This is the fullest and most positive portrait of Arthur before Tennyson; a standard for future writers and one few manage to subscribe to fully.

The great set-piece of Arthur's coronation was established in Geoffrey's Latin, but expanded in terms of courtly detail and tone in Wace's translation (lines 10337–588). The courtly inspiration of female attention and beauty is recognised in Geoffrey, but the detail of dress, music and courtly entertainment is further elaborated by Wace. The effect of this, perhaps surprisingly, is not so much idealistic as realistic. Like Chaucer in *The Knight's Tale*, Wace is aware of the behind-the-scenes bustle of preparation (10337–59) with servants arranging lodgings, sinking tethering posts, fetching oats and straw while others shake the dust from long-stored mantles. An evening of drunken gambling is another of Wace's additions, and while this may have literary antecedents (Weiss 1999: 267) its effect is to suggest a courtly reality which is less glamorous and dignified than the scenes of coronation ritual. Wace's court is crowded, noisy, chaotic – the court of Henry II as described by other clerics of the court, notably Walter Map. We need to notice this clerkly humour at the expense of courtly dignity – it is a note we will meet frequently and it indicates that courtly literature is not always deferential. Courtly realism is the product of the insider who presents the court, warts and all, to an audience appreciative of the accuracy of his portrait.

However, a serious ideal finds expression in Wace in another addition to *Historia Regum Britanniae*. After the challenge from Rome, Geoffrey gives Cador of Cornwall a speech welcoming the prospect of a war that will rouse the Britons from sloth, exemplified in women and dice. Wace counters this with a speech from Gawain praising peace – 'Peace is good after war and the land is the better and lovelier for it. Jokes are excellent and so are love affairs. It's for love and their beloved that knights do knightly deeds' (10767–72).[2] The move from the epic values of Geoffrey's chronicle of British history to the romance values of chivalry and courtesy is unmistakable. Wace thus provides models for later literature in courtly diction and ethic, in the idealised courtly portrait, in detailed and humorous courtly realism. He also versifies his prose source, thus setting the pattern for English Arthurian fiction until Malory.

Wace inspires important translations of Arthurian material into Middle English – by Laȝamon a generation later, and, in a much freer treatment, by the Alliterative *Morte Arthure* at the turn of the fourteenth century. These authors are not only operating in a different language from Wace but in a different cultural situation. Laȝamon (considered in Lucy Perry's essay in this volume) is not a courtly author, although his importance as the first English-language author to deal with Arthur is considerable. The *Morte Arthure* author may be writing from within the world of the court and he is certainly more urbane and travelled than Laȝamon, but that world and its wars has become darker and more problematic (Hamel 1984: 62).

The issues raised by this extraordinary poem are complex and so pertinent to modern readers as well as medieval that discussion has recently focused on the ideas in the poem. However, these ideas are conveyed dramatically and poetically; action and speech and the tone of the poetry carry the complex problems. In this poem, as in the romances of Chaucer, we see that poetry delivers another generic component of courtly romance, that of provoking debate.

The *Morte Arthure*'s concept of Arthur is based on the chronicle tradition – it is about battles and kingship, not individual adventure, and it does not include the Lancelot–Guinevere relationship; the intense relationships are those between Arthur and his followers, most notably his eldest nephew, Gawain (Riddy 2000: 245–8). But any assumption that this indicates a simpler telling of the Arthurian legend than that provided by the romance tradition is soon dispelled as the poem engages directly with problems other versions avoid. The opening scene depicts one of the most splendid feasts in Arthurian literature. The full weight of alliterative poetics swings into operation with a description that is luxuriant and ostentatious, with a sub-text of national pride as Arthur feasts the Roman envoys who have arrived with a demand for tribute:

Pacockes and plovers in platters of gold	*lapwings*
Pigges of pork despine that pastured never;	*piglets; porcupine*
Sithen herons in hedoyne heled full fair,	*hidden in sauce*
Grete swannes full swithe in silveren chargeours,	
Tartes of Turky, taste whom them likes;	*Turkish*
Gumbaldes graithly, full gracious to taste;	*delicacies?*

Connies in cretoyne coloured full fair,	*spiced milk*
Fesauntes enflourished in flamand silver,	
With darielles endorded and dainties ynow;	*custard tarts*
Then Claret and Crete clergially rennen	*sweet wine*
With condethes full curious all of clene silver,	

And the conquerour himselven, so clenly arrayed,	
In colours of clene gold cledde, with his knightes,	
Dressed with his diadem on his dese rich,	*dais*
For he was deemed the doughtiest that dwelled in erthe.	
Then the conquerour kindly carped to those lordes,	*spoke*
Reheted the Romans with real speche:	
'Sirs, bes knightly of countenaunce and comfortes yourselven;	
We know nought in this countree of curious metes;	*exotic meats*
In these barrain landes breedes none other;	*exists*
Forthy, withouten feining, enforce you the more	
To feed you with such feeble as ye before find.'	*inferior food*
'Sir,' says the senatour, 'so Crist mot me help,	
There regned never such realtee within Rome walles!	
There ne is prelate ne pope ne prince in this erthe	
That he ne might be well payed of these pris metes!'	*pleased; excellent foods*

(Lines 182–7, 197–201, 216–230; Benson 1994)

Hamel has shown that the details here portray courtly feasting of the time and include rare and exotic terms such as 'tartes of turky' and 'gumbaldes'. The humorous deprecation with which Arthur offers apologies to his guests is met with a satisfactorily abject response that confirms the supremacy of Arthurian Britain. But this is more subtle than a display of ostentatious barbaric splendour or indeed of late medieval magnificence. It is comparable with *Sir Gawain and the Green Knight* in its exploitation of the traditional opening scene of Arthurian romance, with the challenge to the display of complacent power. Here, though, the narrative sequence is reversed; the challengers from Rome have already arrived and are seated as the chief guests at the feast, which now becomes not an unselfconscious revelry but a pointed political statement. Arthur's status and ambitions are enlarged as Rome becomes not only the seat of ancient power and pagan otherness, but simultaneously the contemporary seat of the papacy, its power expressed through senator and pope. The poet's audience could not be unaware of the Gaufredian narrative in which the challenge from Rome initiates the final stages of Arthur's reign. It is at one and the same time a magnificent statement of the Arthurian myth of British imperial destiny and a prophecy of its downfall. It also lays down an ambitious marker for the poem that follows, superlative in its poetic technique and universal in its application.

    The lengthy scenes of conflict that follow provide an informed and vivid picture of contemporary warfare with an interest in strategy and military technology and an enthusiasm for physical action, grim battlefield humour and the triumphs of victory;

this is far from being a straightforward anti-war poem and it exploits to the full the inherent suitability of alliterative verse for handling violence. But even moments of unmarked detail can deliver a punch of clashing register – as in the line 'Chopped through chevalers on chalk-white steedes' (2116), where the glamorising formulae of chivalric splendour are brutally undermined by collocation with the onomatopoeic 'chop'. This verbal uneasiness is matched on the narrative level by the descriptions of Arthur's progress through Europe, culminating in the description of the siege of Metz:

Ministeres and masondewes they mall to the erthe,	*monasteries hospitals*
Churches and chapels chalk-white blaunched,	*white-washed*
Stone steeples full stiff in the street ligges,	
. . .	
The pine of the pople was pitee for to here!	*pain*
(3038–40, 43)	

It can be argued that Arthur's behaviour here, like that of contemporary English kings, is allowed by the narrow interpretation of the rules of war (Porter 1984; Warm 1997). But the poetry still disturbs with its focus on destruction and victims; a documentary device familiar in modern reportage. This moral questioning is intensified by the vision of Fortune that interrupts Arthur's victorious progress through Italy – the most dramatic and detailed account of that figure in English poetry (3230–392).

The culmination of the poem's critique of war and its effects is found in its handling of the death of Gawain. In chronicle tradition Gawain had always been the foremost of Arthur's knights, as in the later northern Middle English romances. His death and burial at Dover were attested by chronicle and relic. But for this poem he is destroyed before his death in a description of battle madness that is unequalled elsewhere:

But all unwise, wodewise, he went at the gainest,	*madly*
Woundes of those widerwinnes with wrakful dintes;	*enemies; wrathful*
All welles full of blood there he away passes;	
. . .	
There might no renk him arrest; his resoun was passed!	
He fell in a frensy for fersness of herte;	*fit of madness*
. . . .	
Als he that wolde wilfully wasten himselven,	*purposely; destroy*
And for wondsome and will all his wit failed,	*ferocity; wilfulness*
That wode als a wild beste he went at the gainest;	*maddened*
(3818–19, 3825–26, 3835–37)	

Authorial comment is unnecessary as the alliteration emphasises Gawain's loss of reason and suicidal madness. The chivalric knight, model of courtesy, has become a blood-soaked, irrational, berserker. As we see below, at least one medieval reader could relate this poem to *Sir Gawain*, and there may well have been a northern audience for both poems, able to measure the contrast between the youthful Gawain of the one and the suicidal warrior of the other.

The final battle against Mordred and the death of Arthur also receive original treatment, with Mordred himself allowed a moment of insight and regret (3886–94). In another original addition, he is wielding Arthur's sword of state – Clarente – against his father's Caliburne, the two swords depicting the ceremonial and military powers of the throne. Arthur's failure is marked by the turning against each other of these two symbols; Mordred is killed by Caliburne, but Arthur by Clarente. The nature of warfare, of royal power and of kinship are all scrutinised in an ending that offers no supernatural comfort.

This poem provokes complex questions which it does not answer and to expect it to do so is to misunderstand the genre. Unlike religious literature, which forms the staple diet of medieval writing, romance is not in the business of providing answers (Klaeper 2000: 99). The displacement of late-fourteenth-century anxieties – about the moral basis of warfare against fellow Christians, the wisdom of European campaigning, the fear of civil war, and the morality of regal splendour – onto the distant British past provokes debate and re-evaluation. The reader is free to conclude that the Arthurian splendour is worthwhile, despite its tragic ending, but no longer able to believe that such splendour does not come at a cost. Or the reader may feel convinced by the poem that war and ambition are tigers that destroy those who ride them; but will still be moved by the splendour and the pity of war.

Morte Arthure receives emphasis in this chapter as one of the two greatest achievements of English Arthurian poetry and also because it exposes the problem of anonymity in the courtly poetry of the Middle English period. Hamel's portrait of the author and his reading is persuasive – worldly, travelled, multi-lingual and aware of contemporary events. The writer is widely read in romance and history in French and English, and knows Boethius and Dante. Employment in a magnatial household is the clearest context for such a career and access to such a library. Hamel's speculation that he '*might*' (1984: 61; her emphasis) have been attached to the household of John of Gaunt, Henry Bolingbroke or Thomas Mowbray cannot be proved but is a useful corrective to the accidental anonymity of one of the period's major poets.

This literary development of chronicle responds to the positioning of Arthurian legend in a British history that commanded respect. The romance version of Arthur's reign as it developed in France is very different, and it is a version of the French *Mort* that provides the source for the Middle English *Le Morte Arthur*, a poem now overshadowed by Malory's classic Englishing of the French romance of Arthur, to which it made important contributions (Benson 1994). But when *Le Morte Arthur* was written in the fourteenth century, it was the first appearance in English of the story of Arthur's fall told in terms of the fatal love between Lancelot and Guinevere, and the author handles this theme with skill, turning the prose of his source into a narrative poem in an unusual eight-line stanza. Launcelot is the main focus of this version, a flawed hero who demonstrates the contradictions inherent in courtesy. Morality and justice are hopelessly compromised, love and marriage pull in opposite directions, and religion provides a retreat for the penitential individual, not the reassurance of divine providence. Only the intrusive episode of Elaine of Astolat allows another world with different values briefly to challenge those of Camelot.

Every reader and audience knows that Arthurian Britain is doomed, not because it answers a deep folkloric pattern, but because it is familiar history. So readers are not kept in suspense, but rather analyse every scene for signs of inevitable disaster. And this author can manipulate the stanza form accordingly, as when Launcelot makes his fateful visit to Guinevere's chamber on the night of Arthur's absence from court:

> For-why he wend have comen soon,
> For to dwell had he not thought,
> None armour he did him upon   *put on*
> But a robe all single wrought;   *uniquely made*
> In his hand a sword he fone,   *grasped*
> Of tresoun dredde he him right nought;
> There was no man under the moon
> He wend with harm durst him have sought.

> When he come to the lady sheen
> He kist and clipped that sweete wight;   *kissed; embraced*
> For sooth, they never wolde ween
> That any tresoun was there dight;
> So mikel love was them between
> That they not departe might;
> To bed he goeth with the queen,
> And there he thought to dwell all night.
>   (1792–1800)

It is not action that is important here – although this poem's account of the action is more direct than Malory's famous prevarications.[3] It is the fatal delusion of safety, the self-deception emphasised by the echoic repetition with variation in 'For to dwell had he not thought' and 'there he thought to dwell all night', that conveys huge implications about passion and its ability to blind reason, while never undermining the quality of the love between Lancelot and Guinevere. Few, if any, of the later versions have held with such fine economy the balance between the celebration of one of the great loves of western literature and the depiction of its fatal flaw.

Adulterous deception and disloyalty is complicated by the addition of the homosocial intensity of the relationship between Arthur and Lancelot. This is handled with effective simplicity and subtlety, as in the scene at the siege of Joyous Gard where Arthur, unhorsed, is at the mercy of Lancelot:

> 'Alas,' quod Launcelot, 'Wo is me,
> > That ever sholde I see with sight
> Before me him unhorsed be,
> > The noble king that made me knight!'
> He was then so courtais and free
> > That down of his steed he light;
> The king there-on then horses he,
> > And bade him flee, yif that he might.
>
> When the king was horsed there,
> > Launcelot lookes he upon,
> How courtaisy was in him more
> > Than ever was in any man.
> He thought on thinges that had been ere;
> > The teres from his eyen ran;
> He said, 'Alas,' with sighing sore,
> 'That ever yet this war began!'
> > > (2190–2205)

The poetry surpasses the prosaic scene of the French source.[4] Lancelot dismounts to give the king his own horse, rather than simply rehorsing him, and Arthur's response is not a public statement, but a recognition of the emotional power of their mutual past. It is an intensely private moment in a public battle. And it is this version of the scene which is taken up by Malory – and then to the Dyce frescoes of the Palace of Westminster, as it becomes an iconic demonstration of chivalric virtue.

The passing of Arthur is a scene so familiar to modern readers that it is only too easy to overlook this poet's contribution to its development. The battle itself, short as it is, is marked by the heavy alliteration that indicates an English poet writing seriously on the subject of war:

> Many a brand was bowed and bent,
> > And many a knightes helm they brake;
> Riche helmes they rove and rente;   *cut; tore*
> > The riche routes gan togeder raike   *companies; rushed*
> > > (3370–73)

The bleak scene of Bedivere's vigil by the dying Arthur provides the triple attempt to dispose of Excalibur; his report of no event 'but watres deep and wawes wan' is to be repeated verbatim by Malory. When Bedivere finally throws the sword into the water, the quintessential scene of Arthurian magic finds its expression in English:

> Then came an hand withouten rest,
> > Out of the water, and fair it hent,   *seized*
> And braundished as it sholde brast,   *brandished; break*
> > And sithe, as glem, away it glent.   *like a gleam; glided*
> > > (3490–93)[5]

The contrast with the ending of the Alliterative *Morte* demonstrates the range of Middle English poetic responses to the legend of Arthur. It is the stanzaic poem that finds the elegiac note that is to become characteristic of English Arthurian poetry to Tennyson and beyond.

The Arthurian quest: *Ywain and Gawain*

Another late-fourteenth-century poem from the north, *Ywain and Gawain* (Braswell 1995), is of considerable interest as the only (extant) Middle English translation of one of Chrétien's romances. Its English title links it with the Gawain-romances widespread in later Middle English narrative (Hahn 2000). It is a sustained, lengthy and consistent rendering of its famous original, well-handled in the octosyllabic couplet of the French, and lightly modernised and made more pertinent to an insular audience (Mills and Allen 1999). It has been persuasively argued that *Ywain and Gawain* should be viewed not as a simplified translation but as an appropriation of Chrétien's twelfth-century French romance for a different century and a different country (Matthews 1992). Change is not necessarily a sign of inadequacy on the part of the translator, his poetic or his audience; it can be a sign of cultural difference. Moving beyond the narrow consideration of *Ywain and Gawain* as an attempt to translate *Yvain* encourages comparison with other contemporary works, most obviously *Sir Gawain.* The circular structure of the quest, the over-confident hero who grows into humility and self-knowledge, the negotiation of relationships with women, the pervasive sense of serious comedy and, above all, the fourteenth-century preoccupation with 'trawth' are evident in both poems. That the author of *Ywain* is not the *Gawain*-poet's equal, any more than he is Chrétien's, is an obvious point but not the most interesting to come from such a comparison.

The short couplets of *Ywain and Gawain* are suited to the quick-moving action and dialogue of the romance, absorbing courtly French vocabulary into English verse, so that the French, 'il est de haut parage/ Est il de si grant vassalage/ e tant a corteisie et san' (2122–4), gains a touch of alliteration:

> He es cumen of hegh parage   *a noble family*
> And wonder doghty of vassalage.   *courage*
> War and wyse and ful curtayse   *prudent; courteous*
>   (1239–41)

The shift away from the twelfth-century Ovidian love debate with its modish soliloquies and sparkling dialogue towards an emphasis on the problems attendant on action in an increasingly threatening world directs attention to the violence that accompanies this particular quest. From the opening encounter with the churl at the fountain and the killing of Salados to the series of violent combats by which Ywain establishes his knightly identity there is an exploration of chivalry as a means of controlling the armed warrior. But this control seems put at risk by the final combat between the two eponymous heroes. For a fourteenth-century audience, the scene is shadowed by the problems of violence explored in the wider Arthurian narrative, in particular the final clash between Gawain and Lancelot.

Unlike the historical legend incorporated into the *Mortes*, Arthurian chivalric romance can provide suspense. In this romance in particular, the pressure of time and of conflicting priorities is keenly felt. The audience does not know how Ywain will extract himself from the trap in the castle, nor does it know whether he will kill the demon brothers in time to ride off and rescue Lunete from the flames. The suspense is increased by a more leisurely treatment which gives space to a lengthy conversation with the imprisoned Lunete (2100–2200), and later to the damsel's search as Ywain himself becomes the object of the narrative quest (2800–2900). The lion, key to the hero's new identity, also receives generously full treatment, accompanying the human protagonists to the very end (unlike Chrétien's lion, but very like Bevis of Hampton's horse):

> Thus the Knyght with the Liown
> Es turned now to Syr Ywayn
> And has his lordship al ogayn:
> And so Sir Ywain and his wive
> In joy and blis thai led thaire live.
> So did Lunet and the liown
> Until that ded haves dreven them down.   *Until they died*
> (4020–26)

Allusive intertextuality is another feature of courtly narrative, as is evident in the tension between the reputation and the character of the *Gawain*-poet's version of 'Gawain'. The short later romance *The Awntyrs of Arthure* quotes from and alludes to both *Sir Gawain* and the *Morte Arthure*, indicating a later reader who is responding to the provocative relationship between these two northern Arthurian narratives. *Awntyrs* (Hahn 1995), which survives in four very different manuscript versions, combines an ambitious verse form with a revisionist handling of received Arthurian tradition (Allen 1999: 150–5). A poem in two parts, it has been read simply as the work of two authors or, more subtly, as a diptych structure. The first section opens with Guinevere and Gawain lost in the forest around Tern Wathylyng in a storm that accompanies the visitation of a hideous spectre, the ghost of Guinevere's mother prophesying the doom of the Arthurian realm. Her appeal for a trental of masses to redeem her from purgatory points to a source in the Gregory-legend material. But the precisely targeted warning uttered by the ghost in response to Gawain's questions picks up directly on the alliterative *Morte*:

> 'How shal we fare,' quod the freke, 'that fonden to fight,   *warrior; undertake*
> And thus defoulen the folke on fele kinges londes,   *put down; diverse*
> And riches over reymes withouten eny right,   *enter; realms; any*

Wynnen worshipp in werre thorgh wightnesse of hondes?'   *renown in warfare;*
                                                              prowess of arms

'Your King is to covetous, I warne the sir knight.
May no man stry him with strenght while his whele   *No man may overthrow*
stondes.   *him by force while*
                                                             Fortune holds him high
                                                             on her wheel

Whan he is in his magesté, moost in his might,   *{Just at the point} when*
He shal light ful lowe on the sesondes.   *fall full low; seashore*
And this chivalrous Kinge chef shall a chaunce: *shall receive his fate*
Falsely Fortune in fight,
That wonderfull wheelwryght,
Shall make lordes to light –
Take witnesse by Fraunce.   *to fall*

Hit shal in Tuskan be tolde of the treson,
And ye shullen turne ayen for the tydynge.
Ther shal the Rounde Table lese the renoune: *lose its renown*
Beside Ramsey ful rad at a riding   *sudden; battle*
In Dorsetshire shal dy the doughtest of alle.   *die; boldest*
Gete the, Sir Gawayn,   *Take heed*
The boldest of Bretayne;
In a slake thou shal be slayne,   *valley*
Sich ferlyes shull falle.   *Such wonders; occur*

                        (260–73; 291–99)

This relies for its powerful effect on audience recognition of the references to the
narrative of Arthur's last wars as given in the *Morte Arthure*, its very allusiveness
witnessing to the range of that poem's influence. The passage also provides a valuable
piece of evidence in the debate over the culpability of Arthur; for this reader Arthur's
fall is quite clearly a punishment for sin (not that this interpretation should necessarily be privileged over others).

    The storm of the poem's opening owes much to the descriptive poetry of *Sir Gawain*
– 'the sneterand snawe snartly hem snelles' (82) – but *Awntyrs* also brings that poem
into its judgemental reading of Arthurian chivalry: Arthur holds a court echoing that
in the earlier poem, with Gawain wounded in the neck and the emotionally loaded
killing of Gawain's horse drawing on the traditional presence of Gringolet in Gawain
romances in general and *Sir Gawain* in particular.

Courtly Romance: Non-Arthurian

The romances considered in this chapter fall into two overlapping groups, one defined
by subject matter – Arthurian – and one by social and cultural status – courtly. When
we come to consider non-Arthurian, but courtly, romance in Middle English the problematic nature of this classification becomes evident. The courtly romance of the

twelfth century has always been admired and in recent years popular romance has been persuasively rescued and rehabilitated (see further Nancy Mason Bradbury's essay in this volume). But if courtly romance is the 'other' of popular romance, then significant works in the Middle English corpus remain unclassified; narratives that form a large part of the Middle English corpus fall into a limbo – neither of the folk nor of the court (Liu 2006). The nature of the court is largely undefined; the term can be applied not only to royal households but to those of major lords, and to large households that have power but perhaps less cultural sophistication. Further confusion in the assessment of romances is the unspoken but stubborn assumption that lords and ladies have literary tastes superior to country gentry or to the clerics who mediate written culture.

This section will consider representative examples of the longer, ambitious, carefully structured and literary poems that are to be found in some quantity in late Middle English narrative: whether this means they are 'courtly' depends on how we define this term meaningfully for the later English medieval literary world. They are leisurely and imply leisure on the part of their audience and this is one of the signs of the courtly. But such an audience need not be courtly to be able to give quite a lot of time to literary entertainment within the large households that are increasingly seen as the source of literary manuscripts.

An important distinguishing characteristic of these romances is ambition in terms of scope and length and indeed one cause of their neglect is that lengthiness is often a disadvantage in modern terms, being seen as less accessible to modern readers and less useful to modern anthologies. Such romances demand skills from the reader similar to those required for a leisurely nineteenth-century novel: a willingness to be patient, to enjoy the display of the moment without chafing for narrative action, to consider complex scenes in which little apparently happens – all very different from the experience of reading a short popular romance.

Another feature differentiating these works from popular romance is an element of clerical bookishness, most markedly in the English versions of large-scale works on classical subjects often produced for the country courts or households of the gentry or lesser nobility. By contrast with popular romances they are derived from literary predecessors, not traditional story patterns (although their inherited material may well carry these).

We will consider three examples in chronological order across the fourteenth century, each representing a different poetic form and a different relationship to the courtly/ popular dichotomy of modern scholarship.

Kyng Alisaunder

Kyng Alisaunder (Smithers 1957) is a text that immediately raises the question of the usefulness of courtliness as a definition. A romance as bookish, lengthy and demanding as this does not easily fit our concept of popular but is seen as too 'lacking in psycho-logical subtlety and strong in military activity' to be considered courtly (Burnley

1998: 137). It survives in four manuscript copies, and extends to some 8000 lines where it is complete. The earliest version is a fragment of 410 lines in the Auchinleck Manuscript and the suggestion that the same author was responsible for two other texts in that manuscript, *Arthour and Merlin* and *King Richard*, although unproven, is still current. Whatever the case for authorship, these three romances represent an ambitious programme in the reworking of the histories of Britain, Rome and England; such a programme is essentially bookish and clerical. In the case of *Kyng Alisaunder*, competent translation of the Anglo-Norman *Roman de Toute Chevalerie* of Thomas of Kent is made more authoritative by additional material from 'the latin', the *Alexandreis* of Walter of Chatillon.

The biography of Alexander supplies enough fantastic material to capture an audience's interest. Not only is Alexander another Worthy to put alongside the British Arthur, but also his career begins with the occult seduction of his mother, moves through set-piece battles to take in the Wonders of the East and the courtly dalliance with Candace, before the hero dies at the height of his imperial power. But Alexander is not entirely a courtly figure; his splendour is archaic and his wars, which are as pitiless as Arthur's, do not raise the same moral questions. He can show chivalric mercy, but more as a reward for his enemy's fidelity than as a rejection of violence. His values are challenged not by any moral code familiar to a medieval audience, but by the Brahmins.

The author renders the alexandrine *laisses* of his source into his own English couplet form with very little reduction and some additions, including the famous seasonal headpieces that divide his lengthy text into manageable portions and reveal a famil-iarity with Old French *chansons de geste*. The couplet form does not perhaps do justice to the magnificence of Alexander's career as well as the Anglo-Norman *laisses* or the alliteration of *The Wars of Alexander*, but his work shows consideration of the workings and processes of poetry and he is rhetorically trained, and a competent linguist in both French and Latin. Readers have long been impressed by his explicit knowledge of the 'colours' of rhetoric:

> þis bataile distincted is
> Jn þe Freinsshe, wel jwys;
> þerefore [J] habbe [hit] to coloure   *embellish*
> Borrowed of Latyn a nature   *a manner of representation*
>   (2195–98)

The comparison is often made with Chaucer, although perhaps would be better made with Chaucer's Franklin. The sensational creatures of the East are described with relish but a typically bookish precision:

> þe gode clerk men cleped Solim
> Haþ ywriten in his Latin
> þat ypotame a wonder beest is,   *hippopotamus*

More þan an olifaunt, jwis.	*larger*
Toppe and rugge and croupe and cors	*head; back; rump; body*
Js semblabel to an hors;	
A short beek and a croked tayl	
He haþ, and bores tussh, saunz fayl.	*tusks*
Blak is his heued as pycche –	
Jt is a beeste ferliche!	
Jt wil al fruyt ete,	
Applen, noten, reisyns, and whete,	
Ac mannes flesshe and mannes bon	
Jt louþe best of euerychon.	

(5173–86)

The tone becomes more courtly when Canace 'captures' Alexander (disguised as Antygon). As Smithers indicates, this is a scene that looks towards the bedroom games Bertilak's wife plays with Gawain:

And þou art fallen in hondes myne,	
þee to solas and to no pyne,	
For here, vnder þis couertoure,	
Ich wil haue þine amoure,	
To my baundon, leue sire!	*at my disposal*
Longe it haþ ben my desire,	
Ne shaltou haue oþer skape,	
Bot me to baundon late and rape.	*early*
þoo Alisaunder gan ysee	
Pat it most so nedes be,	
He dude al þe ledyes wille	
Vnder couertoure stille.	
Many niȝth and many day	
þus hij duden her play –	
Jn halle at table he sat hire by,	
Jn chaumbre gest, in bed amy.	*lover*
Antygon he hiȝth in halle,	*was called*
And Alisaunder vnder palle.	

(7710–27)

Throughout the poem there is a serious and quite consistent portrayal of Alexander as one of the pagan worthies: whereas the *Morte Arthure* attributes Arthur's fall to the actions of a Christianised Fortune, Alexander's fate is in the hands of the classical sisters, 'Cloto, Lachesis, and Antropo' (6959) – another flourish that does not seem aimed at a popular audience. The final moral, however, reaches beyond the fall of an ancient empire, to a political metaphor all too familiar amid the violent history of fourteenth- and fifteenth-century England: 'When þe heued is yfalle/ Acumbred ben þe members alle' (8018–19).

Mehl's classification of 'Novels in Verse' solves many of the problems in placing a work like this and it is perhaps unfortunate that it has not been widely taken up (Mehl 1968). The definitions of romance, with the underlying expectations of popularity or courtliness, raise the wrong expectations; the novel does provide a more capacious definition making room for this kind of informative and lengthy narrative, wide-ranging historically and geographically.

William of Palerne

William of Palerne (Bunt 1985), an alliterative romance of the mid-fourteenth century, shows the strain of maintaining the distinction between courtly and popular in Middle English romance. It is distinguished from the majority of popular romances in that it not only has a named author – William – but also one who describes the patronage responsible for his poem. It is a translation commissioned by Humphrey de Bohun, duke of Hereford, for the 'ese' of his English-speaking household. As a translation it is remarkable in being the only non-Arthurian Middle English romance translated from a source which apparently has no available insular copy (Field 2008). But this is not enough to ensure its status; otherwise sensible and broad-minded scholars adopt the tones of an Edwardian dowager intent on scenting out social arrivisme. So the audience, 'those who know no French', are interpreted as the menial members ('the kitchen staff' (Pearsall 1977: 157) or the solidly rural ('the rough diamonds of Gloucestershire' (Turville-Petre 1974). As the work is dated by reference to Duke Humphrey (d. 1361), it is a generation earlier than the major alliterative poems, but is contemporary with, or later than, the Auchinleck Manuscript.

So, despite the fact it is over five thousand lines long, alliterative, derived from a continental source and commissioned by the higher aristocracy (and extant in a single MS: Kings College, Cambridge, 13), *William of Palerne* finds its most persuasive defence in a volume devoted to popular romance (Diamond 2000). One passage that has been widely read as proving the uncourtliness of the poem is the advice given by the cowherd to the foster-child he hands over to the Emperor. As David Burnley argues it is advice fitting to the servitor rather than the noble courtier:

> 'bere þe boxumly and bonure, þat ich burn þe love;   *meekly; obediently*
> be meke and mesurabul, nouȝt of many wordes;
> be no tellere of talis, but trewe to þi lord...'
>
> (332–4)

But the poem itself recognises this in the Emperor's amused response. Rather than articulating the poem's values, the cowherd's Polonius-like admonition is firmly dramatic and indeed works ironically within the familiar theme of the *Bel Inconnu*; William, by virtue of his royal birth, rises effortlessly above such concerns.

If ethical discourse does not identify the poem's lack of courtliness, then perhaps its treatment of its source does. The closest discussion of this by Barron concludes that it is a simplified version of the French, as might be expected of an English translation, but has to admit the awkward exception of its lengthy treatment of the pains and pleasures of love-sickness (and to this could be added its non-judgemental depiction of pre-marital lovemaking) (Barron 1982). Alliterative verse may not be the best medium for lightly erotic courtly narrative, but the author does not censor or disapprove of his material.

Alliterative verse, indeed, proves remarkably effective throughout this poem, despite its secular sentimentalism and its absence of violent action. The pastoral scenes with the cowherd are lightly emotional and the account of William as foster-child provides him with a charisma comparable to the young Havelok's but expressed in more courtly terms. The court is lively and familial and its women are active and gossipy. The young lovers are caught up in the trammels of a love that is conventionally courtly in that it is powerful, overwhelming and physical. The novelty of a plot involving a helpful werewolf and the disguising of the lovers as bears and deer provides livelier entertainment than many more polished texts.

Putter's observation that the poem is considered courtly by those who like it, and popular by those who do not, is useful in its emphasis on the subjectivity of such judgments (Putter and Gilbert 2000: 27). Part of the problem is that courtly is too often seen as a marker of quality, rather than a literary mode; it is quite possible to have a mediocre courtly poem, as indeed plenty of lyrics demonstrate. *William of Palerne* is an entertaining, unusual and finished poem with a named author, a known patron and a sense of audience. It provides a measure of the expectations of a mid-fourteenth-century audience for alliterative verse. It is less searching, disturbing and experimental than the alliterative poetry later in the century, instead offering a comforting acquiescence in a world of hierarchy and good humour.

Ipomadon

Of non-Arthurian texts, it is the Middle English *Ipomadon* (Purdie 2001) that reinvents courtliness for its own age: the tail-rhyme version, discussed here, is seen as the most courtly of the three versions, but it is the prose version – perhaps because prose became fashionable – that was owned by Richard III. The tail-rhyme version does not reduce the length significantly (although the other two versions do) so that 10,500 lines of the Anglo-Norman original give nearly 9,000 in Middle English.

If the Arthurian romances we have considered show Middle English authors dealing with the public romance, the courtly tragedy and the quest romance, then *Ipomadon* is something quite different: a romance concerned closely with the self-dramatisation that the romance mode encourages, romance for its own sake, constructing a web of obstacles that love needs to traverse to reach the point at which it more or less began. In other words, it is frivolous, superfluous, humorous and entertaining. It has no claims to historical truth, to exemplary importance, to public concern. This is not entirely the case with the Anglo-Norman original, the *Ipomedon* of Hue de Roteland, which spices its highly entertaining subversion of fashionable chivalric romance with satire, contemporary political comment, even an underlying didacticism concerning good rule and responsibility. But the Middle English version tends to delete this, perhaps because it was so contemporaneous as to be old-fashioned by the fourteenth century (Purdie 2001: lxi–xxxi). What remains is the protracted account of the love between The Fere, a heroine whose pride will not allow her to accept a lover other than the best knight in the world, and Ipomadon, that best knight, who will not reveal himself to be anything other than a fool and a braggart. In Hue's version the reader is encouraged to want to knock heads together when observing the behaviour of these two; in the Middle English they seem to be taken seriously. Both these are courtly responses.

Ipomadon is a romance of the court. It is courtly in the way it depicts the life of the court: the chamberlain with news, the gossip, the ladies, the council. It is not concerned with the world outside the court, with forests, towns or foreign voyages. The action follows the hero from his natal court of Apulia, to The Fere's court in neighbouring Calabria and to her uncle's court of Sicily. As he moves from one to another so he negotiates afresh his identity, as heir to the throne (and then king), to courtly coward and finally down to court fool. Only at the end, in the climactic duel outside the walls of Calabria is the action external to the court, and at that point the hero's identity is merged with that of the only villainous figure in the romance, Lyolyne. If courtly romance is fundamentally concerned with the construction of courtly identity and the individual, then the story of Ipomadon is one constructed to examine that theme in unrelenting detail. It is part of this courtliness that the resulting narrative is both very long and very comic. There is a lot of laughter in this romance; sympathetic, communal, misguided, or cruel, it is the default response of the characters when faced with unfamiliar situations or encounters.

Attitudes to women provide another indication of its courtliness as the Middle English translator consistently contradicts the misogyny of his original, even to the extent of adding passages in praise of women. The three courts are largely defined by, or experienced through, their queens. Ipomadon's mother gradually emerges as the key to the important sub-plot, the mother of an abandoned and lost brother, eventually revealed to be Cabanus; her secret is the unspoken heart of the Apulian court. The Fere dominates the court of Calabria as well as the narrative action, her eponymous self-regard finally tamed by love in a demonstration less of the failings of pride than of the power of passion, a power comically exemplified in the amorous Imayne. And the court of Sicily is a place of teasing, almost decadent, flirtation, centred in the game of the Drew-le-rayne (the queen's darling), something unequalled anywhere else in Middle English. While the activity of Ipomadon himself is the central concern of the narrative, few English romances provide such a rich variety of opportunities for female agency.

The scene that initiates Ipomadon's career at The Fere's court is a clear pointer to the poem's concerns with courtesy. Invited by The Fere to serve the wine, Ipomadon appears to be guilty of a *faux pas* discernible to those with courtly sensitivities:

Right in his mantell as he stode,
Wyth the botteler forthe he youde,
  The cupe on hande he bare:
Al that lovyd that child beforne
For that dede loughe hym to skorne,
  Both the lesse and the more.
'Yif that he shuld serue one,
It were semande,' they sayd ilkone,   *appropriate*
  'Away his mantel were.'
But littill knewe they his entente;
To the buttery dore he went
  And offe he caste hit yare.   *quickly*
    (455–66)

[he makes a gift of his rich mantle to the butler]

'For this vii yere, by my thryfte,
Was not gevyne me suche a gyfte!'
  The mantyll he toke hym tille.
All them that thowght skorne before
Thought themselves folys therefore;
  They satt and held them stille,
And sayden, 'It ws a gentill dede;
There may no man, so God vs spede,
  Otherwyse say be skylle.'
All they spake in prevyte:
'A hundryd men may a man se
  Yet wott not one his wille.'
    (479–90)

At first reading this may impress somewhat negatively with the preciousness of courtly etiquette: does it really matter if a chivalric hero takes off his mantle at the correct moment? But the scene is a complex and exemplary demonstration of courtliness that provides a microcosm of the larger themes of the whole romance. Ipomadon is genuinely courtly in terms of the virtue of largesse or generosity; those who laugh at him are the 'scorners' who are quickly subdued and taught a lesson. And the lesson is not just one of etiquette but more significantly of judging by appearances, a theme vital for the unfolding of the narrative. Those who now consider themselves fools (another central theme) are first silenced and then respond with a murmur of court gossip. Reputation is everything, but it can be constructed and deconstructed. The Middle English author takes no chances with this scene; lines 461–3 are inserted into his close rendering of his original to ensure the significance of the mantle is understood, a courtesy which modern as well as medieval readers can appreciate.

  The tail-rhyme is used here with considerable discipline; no word is superfluous and the tail rhymes themselves are essential to the meaning (Purdie 2008). *Ipomadon* is noteworthy in its readiness to take on the display rhetoric of the love-lament and the soliloquy from its source. Throughout this lengthy romance the author, who is no simple translator, reshapes his source to provide a quintessential romance for his time: he 'must have been conscious of offering a new and updated version of *Ipomedon*' (Purdie 2001: lxxx). And on occasion he strikes the precise note that will carry romance forward for centuries: 'He hovis before that feyre castell; / The wynd wavyd his whyght pensell...' (3089–90).

Conclusion

The romances considered here all operate within the context established by French language romance, insular and continental. But whereas that romance is predominantly written in the octosyllabic couplet and by the thirteenth century often abandons poetry in favour of prose, the English responses and rewritings come in a variety of poetic forms: tail-rhyme and other stanza forms, couplet, alliterative verse. The use of prose for secular narratives is extremely rare before the fifteenth century.

These romances do not form a group – they differ in verse form, in relationship to their originals, in date, geography, provenance and subject matter. What they share is ambition of scope, literary ambition, derivation from books not popular culture. The collection of texts into the Auchinleck MS gives some context to a fragment of *Kyng Alisaunder*, but otherwise these appear to us in our present state of knowledge to be isolated. But they represent the response of Middle English poets to the dominant courtly culture in French-language texts, a willingness to experiment with verse form, to adapt narrative to the different tastes of a later generation and to find the language with which to recast their originals. They bear witness to a willingness to devote material resources, time and attention to a widening of the English romance corpus for a new audience.

Only two of the romances considered here exist in more than one manuscript; that works of the stature of *Morte Arthure* and *Ipomadon*, as well as *Sir Gawain*, only survive by chance or the interest of a collector like Robert Thornton is a reminder of how much must be lost, of how fragmentary our knowledge of the context of these works is. It is also, by a rough estimate, a measure of the lack of 'popularity' of these romances – they are not widely copied or circulated. The two romances that do exist in multiple copies, four each of *Auntyrs* and *Kyng Alisaunder*, have such complex textual profiles as to demonstrate that these are, in effect, numerous versions rather than copies of an original.

Their handling of the subject matter of romance is also varied. There is 'courtly' love in its various guises: adulterous passion in *Le Morte Arthur*; courtship in *Ipomadon*, marriage under strain in *Ywain*, emperilled young love in *William of Palerne*. It is something of a truism to remark that English romance writers do not equal the enthusiasm of their French models for the examination of emotion, but in the majority of the romances considered here, love rather than battle still dominates the narrative and focuses the thematic weight of the romance.

The issues explored reveal the interests and anxieties of those dealing with the world of late medieval England – truth and falsehood, law and violence, marriage and good rule. Poetry provides the medium through which authors and their audiences reach into the romance past and express new meaning for their own present.

NOTES

1 Cf. *Historia Regum Britanniae*: ch. 9: 1: Arthur was then fifteen years old, but a youth of such unparalleled courage and generosity, joined with that sweetness of temper and innate goodness, as gained him universal love.

2 'Bone est la pais emprés la guerre, / Plus bele e mieldre en est la terre; / Mult sunt bones les gaberies / E bones sunt les drueries. / Pur amistié e pur amies / Funt chevaliers chevaleries.'

3 'And whether they were abed other at other maner of disportis, me lyste nat thereof make no mencion, for love that tyme was nat as love ys nowadays.' *Morte Darthur*, ed. Vinaver, XX.3.

4 Cf. *Morte*: Lancelot rescued King Arthur from death, for Hector would have killed him. When Lancelot himself had put King Arthur back on his horse, they left the battle. The king returned to his army and said... 'Did you see what Lancelot did for me today? He was in a position to kill me but refused to touch me. In faith, today he has surpassed in goodness and courtesy all the knights I have ever seen; now I wish this war had never been begun...(p. 145) [Cable trans of Frappier edn of *Mort*: Avez veü que Lancelos a fet hui por moi, qui estoit au desuz de moi ocirre et ne volt pas metre main en moi? Par foi, ore a il passez de bonté et de cortoisie touz les chevaliers que ge onques veïsse; or voudroie ge que ete guerre n'eüst onques esté commenciee' (p. 152: section 116)].

5 Cf. *Mort Artu*: 'he saw a hand come out of the lake which revealed itself up to the elbow, but he saw nothing of the body to which it belonged. The hand seized the sword by the hilt and brandished it in the air three or four times' (Cable: pp. 223–4)....il vit une main qui issi del lac et aparoit jusqu'au coute, mes del cors dont la mein estoit ne vit il point; et la mein prist l'espee parmi le heut et la commença a branler trois foiz ou quatre contremont (section 192, p. 249).

REFERENCES AND FURTHER READING

Primary Texts

Benson, Larry (ed.) (1994). *King Arthur's Death: The Middle English Stanzaic Morte Arthur and Alliterative Morte Arthure*. Kalamazoo, MI: Medieval Institute Publications.

Braswell, Mary Flowers (ed.) (1995). *Sir Perceval of Galles and Ywain and Gawain*. Kalamazoo, MI: Medieval Institute Publications.

Bunt, G. H. (ed.) (1985). *William of Palerne*. Gronigen: Bouma.

Cable, James (trans.) (1971). *The Death of King Arthur*. Harmondsworth: Penguin.

Frappier, Jean (ed.) (1964). *La Mort le roi Artu: Roman du XIIIe siecle*. Geneva: Droz.

Griscom, A. (ed.) (1929). Geoffrey of Monmouth. *Historia Regum Britanniae*. London: Longmans.

Hahn, Thomas (ed.) (1995). *The Awyntrs off Arthur*. In *Sir Gawain: Eleven Romances and Tales*. Kalamazoo, MI: Medieval Institute Publications.

Hamel, Mary (ed.) (1984). *Morte Arthure*. Garland Medieval Texts 9. New York: Garland.

Purdie, Rhiannon (ed.) (2001). *Ipomadon*. London: Early English Text Society, o.s. 316.

Smithers, G. V. (ed.) (1952–57). *Kyng Alisaunder*. 2 vols. London: Early English Text Society, o.s. 227, 237.

Thorpe, L. (trans.) (1966). Geoffrey of Monmouth. *The History of the Kings of Britain*. Harmondsworth: Penguin.

Weiss, Judith (ed.) (1999). *Wace's Roman de Brut, A History of the British: Text and Translation*. Exeter Medieval Texts and Studies. Exeter: University of Exeter Press.

Secondary Reading

Barron, W. R. J. (ed.) (1999). *The Arthur of the English*. Cardiff: University of Wales Press.

Barron, W. R. J. (1982). Alliterative romance and the French Tradition. In David Lawton (ed.). *Middle English Alliterative Poetry and its Literary Background* (pp. 70–87). Cambridge: D. S. Brewer.

Burnley, D. (1998). *Courtliness and Literature in Medieval England*. Harlow: Longman.

Dean, R. and M. B. M. Boulton (1999). *Anglo-Norman Literature: A Guide to Texts and Manuscripts*. London: Anglo-Norman Text Society.

Diamond, A. (2000). Loving beasts: the romance of 'William of Palerne'. In Ad Putter (ed.). *The Spirit of Medieval English Popular Romance* (pp. 142–56). Harlow: Longman.

Field, R. (2008). Romance. In Roger Ellis (ed.). *History of English Literary Translation* (pp. 296–331). Oxford. Oxford University Press.

Hahn, T. (2000). Gawain and Popular Chivalric Romance in Britain. In R. L. Krueger (ed.). *The Cambridge Companion to Medieval Romance* (pp. 218–34). Cambridge: Cambridge University Press.

Johnson, L. (1993). Arthur at the Crossroads. In E.ni Cuillenain and J. D. Pheifer (eds). *Noble and Joyous Histories: English Romance 1375–1650* (pp. 87–111). Dublin: Irish Academic Press.

Krueger, R. L. (ed.) (2000). *The Cambridge Companion to Medieval Romance*. Cambridge: Cambridge University Press.

Liu, Y. (2006). Middle English romance as prototype genre. *Chaucer Review*, 40, 335–53.

Matthews, D. (1992). Translation and ideology: the case of *Ywain and Gawain*. *Neophilologus*, 76, 452–63.

Mehl, D. (1968). *The Middle English Romance of the Thirteenth and Fourteenth Centuries*. London: Routledge.

Mills, M. and R. Allen (1999). Chivalric Romance. In W. R. G. Barron (ed.). *The Arthur of the English* (pp. 111–64). Cardiff: University of Wales Press.

Patterson, L. (1987). *Negotiating the Past*. Madison, WI: University of Wisconsin Press.

Pearsall, D. (1977). *Old English and Middle English Poetry*. London: Routledge.

Porter, E. (1983). Chaucer's Knight, the alliterative *Morte Arthure*, and the medieval laws of war: a reconsideration. *Nottingham Medieval Studies*, 27, 56–78.

Purdie, R. (2008). *Anglicising Romance: Tail-Rhyme and Genre in Medieval English Literature*. Cambridge: D. S. Brewer.

Putter A. and J. Gilbert (eds) (2000). *The Spirit of Medieval English Popular Romance*. Harlow: Longman.

Riddy, F. (2000). Middle English romance: family, marriage, intimacy. In R. L. Krueger (ed.). *The Cambridge Companion to Medieval Romance* (pp. 235–52). Cambridge: Cambridge University Press.

Rushton, C. and R. Radelescu (eds) (2009). *Companion to Popular Romance*. Cambridge: D. S. Brewer.

Turville-Petre, T. (1974). Humphrey de Bohun and *William of Palerne*. *Neuphilologische Mitteilungen*, 75, 250–2.

Vale, J. (1979). Law and diplomacy in the alliterative *Morte Arthure*. *Nottingham Medieval Studies*, 23, 31–46.

Warm, R. (1997). Arthur and the giant of Mont St. Michel: the politics of empire building in the later Middle Ages. *Nottingham Medieval Studies*, 41, 59–71.

18

Alliterative Poetry: Religion and Morality

John Scattergood

I

> But trusteth wel, I am a southren man;
> I kan nat geeste 'rum, ram, ruf', by lettre,   *tell a story in verse*
> Ne, God woot, rym holde I but litel bettre...
>   (*CT*, X [I], 42–4)

The Parson's parodic disclaimer of any talent in alliterative verse and his hints at its provinciality are misleading in all sorts of ways. It is true that much alliterative poetry was written in the north and the west of England, but some poems in this metre demonstrably come from London. Again, he implies that alliterative poetry is metrically all of a piece. The three alliterating stressed syllables of his parody are characteristic of the unrhymed long-line 'classical' measure, but alliteration was used in a much wider variety of contexts: sometimes a leash of alliterating long-lines is closed off by a rhymed 'bob-and-wheel'; sometimes alliteration will coexist through-out a poem with rhyme in formal stanzaic patterns. So the opposition between alliteration and rhyme which the Parson sets up does not accurately reflect poetic practice either. And sometimes alliteration will be used for particular effect in what is otherwise a rhymed, syllabic poem. Recently Ralph Hanna has spoken of alliterative poetry as consisting of 'a variety of forms not simply unrhymed long-lines' (Hanna 1994: 44) and the poems treated in this essay reflect this more capacious sense of alliterative writing. It recognises that, in their forms and genres, alliterative poems can be very varied.

With a few exceptions such as William Langland, son of Stacy de Rokayle of Shipton-under-Wychwood (Oxfordshire) (Kane 1965) and John Clerk of Whalley (Lancashire) (Turville-Petre 1988), the names of the authors of alliterative poetry have not come down to us – and little is known of these two authors except what Langland chooses to tell us about himself and his life in the course of his poem. He was a cleric, as was John Clerk if his surname is indicative. Richard Spaldyng (for whom see below) was a Carmelite friar from Stamford. And there may have been others. *The Blacksmiths* is a brief but memorable poem which exploits, more than any other, the onomatopoeic possibilities of alliterative verse in a complaint about a night-working factory which disturbs the poet's sleep. It is wonderfully precise in its description of the equipment and processes involved in metalworking:

> Of a bole hide ben here barm-felles,
> Here schankes ben schakeled for the fere-flunderes.
> Hevy hamerys they han that hard ben handled,
> Stark strokes they stryken on a stelyd stocke.
> 'Lus, bus, las, das', rowtyn be rowe.
> Swiche dolful a dreme the Devyl it todryve.
>
> (11–16)

Their leather aprons are of bull's hide; their lower legs are protected against the fiery sparks. They have heavy hammers which are wielded strongly; they strike heavy blows on the steel anvil. 'Lus, bus, las, das', they beat in turn. May the Devil destroy such a miserable noise!

The last line is important because it suggests that the poet sees something diabolic in the blacksmiths' shop with its fire, smoke, noise and hard tools, as if the smiths themselves were devilish torturers of the kind sometimes found in medieval depictions of hell. The poem is preserved in a unique copy in British Library MS Arundel 292, 'a miscellany of monastic provenance' from Norwich Cathedral Library, where it is preceded by the complaint of a monk, so its author may have been a cleric (Salter 1979). Also deriving from a clerical context is the opening 41 lines of unrhymed alliterative verse of 'A Bird in Bishopswood', in which an unnamed narrator wanders out in 'þe myry monþ of May' and sees 'þe fairest fowyl of fethyrs þat I had say beforne' which he wants to catch 'to kepyn in my cage'. This fragment is found in London, Guildhall Library MS 25125/32, a rental account relating to St Paul's Cathedral for 1395/6 (Kennedy 1987).

But other alliterative poems clearly derive from baronial or gentry contexts. *William of Palerne* was translated from French at the request of Humphrey de Bohun, earl of Hereford and Essex between 1336 and 1361, by a poet whose name was also William. This appears to be a Gloucestershire poem and may have been translated 'for hem þat knowe no Frensche', to provide entertainment for the members of one of Humphrey's manors there (5532–33). It is likely that the poet was one of the earl's retainers. The work is discussed further by Rosalind Field in this volume. From a similar context comes *The Lament for Sir John Berkeley*, preserved on a blank sheet in Nottingham University Library MS Mi 01, a commission of sewers for the wapentakes of Brigham and Newark in Nottinghamshire for 1394–95 (Turville-Petre 1982). This 91-line poem, which uses end-rhyme as well as heavy alliteration, praises its subject for his probity, his hospitality, his prowess on the hunting field and the culture of his household. It records that he died on a military expedition to Brittany in the service of his king in July 1375, not in battle but of a sudden illness: 'a sselly shoite' ('a wondrous shooting-pain') (76) in his side. When he realised that he was dying Sir John dispatched the poet, whose name may have been 'Turnour', to go home to his wife and get her to say mass and matins for him (88–91). The poet was clearly a member of Sir John's retinue. And again from a provincial gentry background comes *Scotish Ffeilde*, a late alliterative poem dating from after 22 March 1515 since it mentions the death of James Stanley, bishop of Ely (Oakden 1935). The poem, which is very accomplished, offers a conspectus of English history from the landing of Henry VII at Milford Haven in 1485 to the defeat and death of James IV of Scotland at the Battle of Flodden in 1513, stressing the part played by the Stanley family and the men of Lancashire and Cheshire in these events (Scattergood 2000: 226–44). The poet adopts a particularly critical attitude towards the Howards, a powerful Yorkshire family, and seeks to defend the men of Cheshire, who had retreated before the Scots at Flodden, by arguing that it would not have happened if they had been under commanders from the Stanley family:

> For they were wont att all warr to wayte upon the Stanleys;
> Muche worshipp they woone whan they that way serued.
>
> (264–68)

This is clearly part of a struggle for power and influence between two eminent northern English families, and the author is open about his partisanship: he describes himself as a 'gentleman' belonging to the Legh family living in Baguley in Cheshire (416–19), which still owns the Lyme MS, one of the two surviving manuscripts of the poem.

It is likely, therefore, that writers of alliterative poetry came from a variety of places and from different backgrounds, yet, as Geoffrey Shepherd recognised, 'alliterative poems present a remarkably steady view of the poet and his activities' (Shepherd 1990: 180). The poets tend to present themselves as mature and experienced, rather backward looking with a highly developed sense of history, men of independence and strict personal integrity, who see it as their role to cast a cold eye on contemporary life and its mores, and to make recommendations for moral and social improvement. These are personae, of course, but the poems themselves often present admiring views of men of wisdom, and there is more than a little likelihood that the poets saw themselves in this way. In one poet's view, there used to be 'makers of myrthes þat matirs couthe fynde', serious original poets, but now:

> ...a childe appon chere withowtten chyn-wedys,
> Þat neuer wroghte thurgh witt thre wordys togedire,
> Fro he can jangle als a jaye and japes telle
> He schall be leuede and louede and lett of a while
> Wele more þan þe man that made it hymseluen.
>
> (*Wynnere and Wastoure*, 24–28)

...a youth without a beard on his face, who never through skill put three words together, if he can chatter like a jay and recite comic stories he will be believed and loved and appreciated for a time, a lot more than the man who composed the poem himself.

In other poems wisdom is delivered by the old: in one the figure of authority is represented by an 'olde auncyen man of a hundrid wintre', with eyes that are 'al ernest', a beard and white hair but a little bald, 'sad of his semblant, softe of his speche' (*Mum and the Sothsegger*, 956–63), a bee-keeper who preaches a political sermon on the proper organisation of society, taking the bee-hive as his analogy. Moreover, these are men not only of experience but also of authority, particularly the authority which comes from books. One carries with him a bag full of neglected books, 'that was not y-openyd this other half wintre', 'where many a pryue poyse is preyntid withynne' which will help him give counsel to the king (*Mum and the Sothsegger*, 1343–47) – moral and political tracts 'of vice and of vertu'. But although these poets comment sharply on contemporary issues, they sometimes see themselves as memorialists. Like Chaucer, they know that old books are 'of remembraunce the keye' (*LGW*, F Prol. 25–26) and, as Chaucer recommends, they honour these books. Like him, they also know that time can 'frete and bite' at these stories (he is thinking of the destruction of manuscripts by worms and mice) so that they are devoured and lost to 'memorie' (*Anelida and Arcite*, 10–14). Typical of this attitude is the long prefatory lament by the author of *The 'Gest Hystoriale' of the Destruction of Troy* because so many true old stories have slipped out of men's minds and taken with them the memory of important people:

> Soothe stories ben stoken vp, & straught out of mind,   *closed; departed*
> And swolowet into swym by swiftenes of yeres...   *oblivion*
>   (11–12)

It is his task, as he sees it, to recover these 'olde stories' and, based on reliable sources, retell them so that they may be 'solas to sum' (21–22) who had no knowledge of them. He sees himself as a custodian of the past whose poetic skill and integrity preserve in contemporary memory something which is valuable in exemplary ways.

These poets see themselves as special, marked out by their gifts and their calling, and so they are essentially isolated figures, wandering through a world with which they are often out of sympathy. One begins his story with

> ...I schall tell yow a tale þat me bytyde ones,
> Als I went in the west wandrynge myn one.
>   (*Wynnere and Wastoure*, 31–32)

Disappointed at his conversations with representatives of the four principal orders of friars, another poet says, 'Thanne turned y me forthe and talked to my-selue', and it is as he 'wente by the waie wepynge for sorowe' that he meets the Lollard ploughman who offers to teach him his creed (*Pierce the Ploughman's Crede*, 418–421). And it is out of meetings such as this, meetings with equally individual figures critical of contemporary society, that truth – or at least truth for the poet – comes. Sometimes the figures are supernatural. In one Queen Guenevere and Sir Gawain, sheltering from a storm while out hunting, are confronted by a terrifying figure of a woman 'Al biclagged in clay, uncomly cladde' (*Awynters of Arthoure* 106) who emerges from a hellish lake, the ghost of Guenevere's mother who offers a devastating critique of the courtly and militaristic high-life. Wisdom may come, say the poets, from serendipitous encounters, particularly when the context is leisured enjoyment. Or wisdom may come, more ambiguously, from dreams. Langland had, famously, questioned the ways in which dreams signified:

> Many tyme this metels hath maked me to studie   *dream*
> Of that I seigh slepynge – if it so be myghte...
> (*PPl*, B.VII. 144–45)

And he sets text against text in order to come to some sort of conclusion to the question of what sort of wisdom one can trust. Despite this, alliterative poets are sometimes prepared to dream themselves into truth. Despite his loneliness, despite the often strange and esoteric nature of his perceptions, no alliterative poet saw himself as 'the idle singer of an empty day', nor yet as someone who sang to charm his own solitude. These poets feel they have something to say, something important, and they slip easily from truth to moralisation – they think they know what their poems mean – and, as will be seen, from moralisation into prophecy. However shaky the foundations of their knowledge, alliterative poets always seem to be able to speak with authority and to occupy the moral high ground.

From the so-called *First Worcester Fragment* (Worcester Cathedral MS F. 174), rescued in the nineteenth century from its use as stiffening for the cover of another book put together about 1250, comes an admiring account of some saintly pre-Conquest English ecclesiastics and teachers and a lament for the disruption of that tradition of learning:

> Þeos lærden ure leodan on Englisc.
> Næs deorc heore liht, ac it fæire glod.
> Nu is þeo leore forleten, and þat folc is forloren.
> Nu beoþ oþre leoden þeo læreþ ure folc,
> And feole of þen lorþeines losiæþ and þat folc forþ mid.
> (15–19)

These taught our people in English. Their light was not dim but shone brightly. Now that teaching is abandoned and the folk are deprived. Now there are other people who teach our folk, and many of the teachers are damned and the folk with them.

This is certainly a post-Conquest text, and has been dated variously between *c.* 1100 and *c.* 1170. But whether the disruption of learning it refers to was caused by the Norman invasion, which is the traditional view, or whether, as has recently been proposed, it is to be attributed to the earlier incursions of the Vikings (Cannon 2004: 34–41), is difficult to decide. Whatever the answer, however, it is perhaps significant that what may be the earliest surviving post-Conquest alliterative poem should speak of a past full of learned men – ecclesiastics and moralists – for this is very much the temper of later alliterative poetry, whose characteristic subjects are the serious ones of religion, morality and politics, though these issues are often not entirely separable from each other.

II

Texts that may be described as narrowly religious include three remarkable hymns to saints dating from the late-fourteenth and early fifteenth centuries: one addresses Katherine of Alexandria, a second treats John the Evangelist and a third is on John the Baptist. All three have a north-eastern provenance in Yorkshire and Lincolnshire. Each is written in an elaborate fourteen-line stanza rhyming ABABABAB CCDCCD: the octet is written in alliterative long lines, the sestet in short lines with generally two alliterating syllables. Concatenation links the octet and sestet, and sometimes the stanzas are linked using the same device. Each poem is written in the laudatory rhapsodic style one associates with hymns, but each also has a powerful narrative element as the biography of the saint, the sufferings and the miracles, are set out, and this is not surprising since the sources used include the Bible, the *Legenda Aurea* and numerous more local accounts of the saints. Whether or not the similarities of conduct and stanza form are sufficient to justify one in talking about a local 'tradition' of writing is debatable, but there does appear to have been among these authors an agreed way of addressing religious subjects in a highly decorative verbal and metrical manner.

Yet each poem has its own distinctiveness. *The Alliterative Katherine Hymn* is almost certainly the work of Richard Spaldyng, a Carmelite friar in the Stamford convent in South Lincolnshire: he works the name of the saint and his own name into acrostics in lines 225–62. It is the view of Ruth Kennedy that the poem may have been written for some occasion relating to the Stamford Guild of St Katherine (see line 268), perhaps around 1399 (Kennedy 2003: lxiv–lviii). Katherine is praised initially as a protectoress for 'kepyng kaytefs fro kare' (2) and as a guide, a 'lanterne to teche hem below' 93), but subsequently, as the biography develops, for her intelligence: she was a young but highly educated Christian, abducted by the Emperor Maxentius, who tries to destroy her faith. But she argues so convincingly for her beliefs that she converts fifty pagan philosophers (*retorikes*, 21), the Emperor's queen Faustina, and his principal officer Porphyrius – all of whom are prepared to suffer death rather than revert to paganism. Maxentius decides, since he cannot break her will, that she should be killed and much of the poem deals with the way she withstands her scourging, her torture on the wheel and her beheading. Some of the most striking writing appears here:

> Þus was þe cors knytt of a kaytyf vnknyit   *wretch*
> Qwen sche was woundid vnworthi, as woful and wik.
> And as fresch fesaunt to hire fere þan sche flyit,
> Qwen fayntly sche foundyed as a flayn flik…   *stumbled*
> (187–90)

Doctrine is set out here in a memorable and graphic fashion but in easily recognisable terms. The idea that murder unmakes what God has made is conveyed in the wordplay on 'knytt' and 'vnknyit' through the image of the unravelling of a knitted garment, and the belief that at the same instant that the dead body falls to the earth the soul flies up to God the bridegroom is suggested in the contrast between the side of a skinned meat in the larder (*flayn flik*) and a live (*fresch*) female pheasant taking off to join her mate. There is little of this imaginative inventiveness in the other two poems but they have their own resourcefulness.

The *Alliterative John Evangelist Hymn* begins in allusive fashion with comparisons between the saint and jewels (15–17), suggested by the description of the heavenly Jerusalem in Revelations 21: 18–21, but as the poem develops it generally stresses John's purity (*verray virgyn*, 70), his sacrifice on leaving an opulent lifestyle for the simple existence as of one of Christ's disciples (43–45), and his closeness to Christ: 'Thow was sybbe oure saueoure, hir syster sone' (71). It is this relationship which comes to the fore when the poet speaks of John's presence at the crucifixion with Mary, drawing no doubt on artistic representations of Calvary and the many lyrics produced on this theme:

> Free fro thralle vs to brynge   *servitude*
> Heghe one rude walde He hynge,   *cross*
> So lawe wald He lende;
> And þou, His derlyng,
> His modir in kepyng
> To þe He bekende.   *commended, delivered*
> (93–98)

But John is celebrated mainly as a privileged transmitter of Christ's teaching, an authority on the authenticity of his most inward thoughts, 'þe poyntis of His preuate' (86). When John was exiled (*flemede*, 130) to Patmos, no doubt to work in the salt-mines of the Roman penal colony there, he wrote, and is frequently depicted in manuscript illuminations seated with a pen and a small scroll in a rocky island landscape (Scattergood 2006: 73–75) – something the poet may be recalling here, as he describes the saint writing 'with a pen free' (132). Perhaps this poet saw a little reflected glory for himself as someone who was privileged to honour an important saint and, in his own way, act as a transmitter of Christian teaching.

The briefer *Alliterative John the Baptist Hymn* addresses its subject in terms of his birth 'of a byrde baran' (2), as a 'forgoher of Crist' (31), as 'to many folk a frende' (71), and as someone who 'stode stedefastly and thoght not to sese' (118) in the face of persecution. None of this is particularly exceptional. But the writing lifts when his lifestyle is described:

> Blissed be thow, Baptist, so ware and so wys;
> In wode and in wildirnesse was þi wonyng;   *dwelling*
> Neythir purpil ne palle, ne pelle of price   *rich cloth; expensive fur*
> But of camel skyn þow toke þi clothyng.
> Hawes þow hent and rotes of þe ryse,   *Hawthorn berries*
> With borionand bere in the blomyng;   *sprouting barley*
> Hony-comes for ryche mete – wanted þe þis.
>   (85–91)

What is evoked here is an ascetic alternative to the courtly high-life, using ideas from descriptions of the 'golden age' and the literature of withdrawal such as one gets in *Sir Orfeo* or in lyrics such as 'I must go walke þe woed so wyld...' These writers may be operating within (probably) self-defined literary constraints in terms of subject matter and form. But their imaginations are capable of taking in and using some of the possibilities of the broader tradition.

A Pistel of Susan or *Susannah* is also written in an elaborate alliterative stanza, in this case an octet of alternately rhyming long-lines followed by a five-line bob and wheel of shorter lines. It follows closely its source in the Vulgate Daniel 13. Set in the period of the Babylonian captivity, it tells how Susannah, a beautiful and educated Jewess, the wife of Joakim, a rich Jew, is falsely accused of adultery by two elders because she will not commit adultery with them, how she is condemned to death according to Mosaic law (Leviticus 20:10; Deuteronomy 22:22), but rescued by the intervention of the young prophet Daniel who exposes the lies and inconsistencies in the elders' version of events.

Though the poet gives full weight to its Jewish origins and setting, he amplifies the spare biblical narrative, medievalises it, and invests it with his own emphases and meanings. Joakim's household garden (*pomarium*) becomes something like a fourteenth-century moated estate: 'His innes and his orchardes were with a dep dich' (5). Susannah is approached in the garden by the elders as she is about to bathe 'Bi midday or none' (130) – a traditionally dangerous time in both romances and religious texts because of the operations of the 'noonday devil' (*demonio meridiano*) of Psalm 91:6. And Daniel is given an age, 'ȝit failed him of fourten fullich a ȝere' (281), which in medieval terms means that he had not yet finished his first cycle of education and was, therefore, prematurely wise (Burrow 1988: 95–102). None of these details appears in the Vulgate account. But the most important piece of amplification concerns the elaborated description of the garden (66–117), which becomes something of both the Garden of Eden and the *hortus conclusus* of medieval courtly literature. Commentators have compared Susannah 'so semeliche of hewe' (172, 185) to Eve and the elders to the serpent, or seen similarities to Chaucer's tale of May's adulterous assignation with Damyan in her husband's pleasure garden (Kellogg 1960). But Susannah's predicament is more like that of Chaucer's Dorigen as she faces the prospect of being coerced into unwelcome adultery and articulates the harsh choice she has to make:

'I am with serwe biset on eueriche syde.	
ȝif I assent to þis sin þat þis segges haue souȝt,	*men*
I be bretenet and brent in baret to byde;	*destroyed; burnt; wretchedness*
And ȝif I nikke hem with nai hit helpeþ me nouȝt –	*say no to them*
Such torfer and teone takeþ me þis tyde!	*difficulty; suffering*
Are I þat worthliche wrethe, þat al þis world wrouȝt,	*Before; anger*
Betere is wemles weende of þis world wyde.'	*spotless*

(145–51)

The implication of her determination to be without sin (*wemles*) is condemnation to death as a result of the perjured evidence of the 'domesmen' (judges), as the Middle English poet habitually calls the elders, and salvation comes, not as it does for Dorigen through the operations of patience and awakening moral decency, but through the forensic skills of Daniel, which lead to the condemnation and death, according to Mosaic law (Deuteronomy 19: 16–21), of those who had tried to pervert the law by bearing false witness. So justice, both poetic and actual, is meted out. But this may not be the main point of the poem. A powerful subtext in the Middle English version of the story contrasts age, which is associated with voyeurism, lechery and calculated corruptness, with youth, with its associations of purity, simplicity and vitality. Even in the perjured imaginations of the elders this contrast appears as they describe the entirely fictitious man with whom Susannah is supposed to have made love:

He was borlich and bigge, bolde as a bare,	*sturdy*
More miȝti mon þen we his maistris to make.	*strength*
To the ȝate ȝaply þei ȝeoden ful ȝare,	*nimbly; went; quickly*
And he lift vp þe lach and leop ouer þe lake,	*moat*
Þat ȝouthe.	

(226–30)

The poem is, at this level, about the dangers and vulnerabilities of beauty, innocence and trust, but also triumphantly about their survival against the odds.

St Erkenwald is a much more ambitious performance. It may be a north-western poem: London, British Library MS Harley 2250, in which it is uniquely preserved, has Cheshire connections, and the opening line 'At London in Englond noȝt full long sythen...' (1) may suggest that the author thought of himself as an inhabitant of Cheshire which sometimes regarded itself as 'distinct and separable from the crown of England' (Burrow 1993). The poem has recently been tentatively attributed to the Gawain-poet (see A. V. C. Schmidt's essay in this volume). It is a work based on history and centrally concerns London, St Paul's Cathedral, and a bishop of London, St Erkenwald (Turville-Petre 2005).

It is a conversion narrative set in a long perspective of English history, a poem of transformations. The poem opens with an account of things becoming something else, the pagan becoming Christian, old buildings dedicated to heathen gods being renamed and rededicated to Christian worship when the teachings of St Augustine

> ...conuertyd alle þe communnates to Cristendame newe,
> He turnyd temples þat tyme þat temyd to þe deuell,   *adhered, belonged*
> And clansyd hom in Cristes nome and kyrkes hom callid.
> (14–16)

What was 'peruertyd' (10) becomes 'conuertyd', and this leads indirectly, but logically, into the subject of the poem, which is the issue of the salvation of the righteous heathen, another shift from paganism to Christianity – this time generated by the discovery, by workmen digging new foundations at St Paul's, of the well-preserved body of a pagan judge and his miraculous conversion and salvation through the agency of St Erkenwald. The poem works in a binary way and it may be that textually it was meant to fall into a diptych pattern. In the manuscript it has two large capitals, one at the beginning and one at line 177, the arithmetical beginning of the second part of a 352-line poem. The first half of the poem deals with the intellectual and social confusion generated by the finding of the body, the second with the elucidation and the insight produced by St Erkenwald's intervention. Line 177 reads 'Þen he turnes to þe toumbe and talkes to þe corce' which, in the word 'turnes', recognises the shift in the direction of the poem as the transformation of the virtuous pagan into a Christian candidate for salvation begins.

The central concern of *St Erkenwald* was evidently of some contemporary interest: it had been addressed in *Piers Plowman* and it may be that this poem, in some sense, is an answer to Langland. The Emperor Trajan, the archetypal example of the pagan who was saved (Whatley 1984), bursts into Langland's poem in the middle of an argument about the efficacy of the sacraments in ensuring salvation, arguing that it was good deeds, in the form of true judgments, which were crucial in his case:

> ...al the clergye vnder Cryste ne miȝte me cache fro helle,
> Bot onliche loue and leute and my lawful domes   *uprightness*
> (*PPl*, B.XI.139–40)

This secularising, humanist, liberal interpretation of the story, a rather peremptory argument for salvation through good works as it is stated here, effectively diminishes the role of the clergy and the sacraments. Perhaps in response to this, the poet of *St Erkenwald*, as he tells an analogous story, mounts an admiring defence of the importance of the clergy in understanding and interpreting the past, intervening in the present and helping in the achievement of salvation – in which he believes the sacrament of baptism is crucial (Scattergood 2000: 179–99).

The poem opens with mysteries. When the splendid coffin is discovered the border of the lid is 'enbelicit with bryȝt golde lettres' but they are 'roynyshe' (51–52), meaning 'mysterious', perhaps 'runic', and cannot be interpreted. When the uncorrupted body is disclosed with its costly, fresh clothes the assumption is that it is that of an important person, perhaps a king (98), who has recently died. But there is no story about him that is known, no object or inscription by means of which he can be identified (100–104), no mention in a burial register or a chronicle even though the library has been thoroughly searched (154–56): he has 'malte so out of memorie' (158). The populace is confused by the 'meruaile' (65) and disturbed by it until St Erkenwald intervenes, who realises that what he has to deal with can only be elucidated by God:

'Hit is meruaile to men þat mountis to litell
Toward þe prouidens of þe prince þat paradis weldes'.
                    (160–62)

But God's elucidation is mediated through a cleric: St Erkenwald prays to God for assistance (116–21), and prepares himself in his full canonicals to confront the corpse (138–41). And God responds by having the pagan give an account of himself through 'sum lant goste of lyfe of hym that lyfe redes' (192) ('some breath of life borrowed from God who controls life'). The dead pagan explains that he was a judge who lived virtuously and gave true verdicts, who was honoured in his life and given a splendid burial, but, because he was a pagan, was confined to limbo after his death, 'exiled' from the place where 'richely hit arne refretyd þat after right hungride' (303–4). Moved by the story St Erkenwald weeps, and his tears falling on the body are effectively a kind of baptism:

'For þe wordes þat þou werpe and þe water þat þou sheddes,	*utter*
Þe bryȝt bourne of þin eghen, my bapteme is worthyn.	*stream; become*
Þe fyrst slent þat on me slode slekkyd al my tene;	*splash; fell; alleviated; grief*
Ryȝt now to soper my soule is sette at þe table…'	

                    (329–32)

The pagan from limbo is enabled, through the water of baptism, to come to supper with God: the wonderful image of washing before a meal gives an elegant social equivalence to the spiritual transformation and the exile's acceptance into the community of the saved. It is significant that the judge, when he speaks of his salvation, does not, like Langland's Trajan, dwell on his good works, but attributes it to God's grace through the mediation of St Erkenwald:

'I heere þerof my hegh God and also þe, bysshop,	*praise*
Fro bale has broȝt vs to blis, blessid þou worth!'	

                    (339–40)

Here the alliteration again emphasises the binary nature of the poem and its concern with transformation: 'bale' becomes 'blis'. The poem mounts a powerful argument for the importance of the clergy, the efficacy of the sacraments and salvation through grace. It ends on a note of social cohesion, a procession through the streets of London led by the clergy 'and alle þe pepull folowid' (251) – a triumphalist conclusion, though in terms of late fourteenth-century realities a somewhat wishful one.

III

Moral behaviour, transience and the possibilities of damnation or salvation are issues in the last poem considered, though its intellectual centre is elsewhere, but these issues are foregrounded and pondered in other alliterative texts. These issues are often treated in traditional terms but with a bright vitality and inventiveness, which give them a contemporary relevance.

The poet of *Somer Soneday*, in a holiday mood, rises early and follows a deer hunt, the favourite sport of the medieval aristocracy, which he evokes with all its movement, noise and formalised purposefulness:

> Denede dale and downe for dryft of þe deer in drede,
> For meche murþe of mouþ þe murie moeth made.
>
> (14–15)

Valley and hill resounded because of the driving of the fearful deer, for the pleasant blast of the hunting horn made many joyous utterances.

But he is delayed because of the need to cross 'a water wilde' (21), loses contact with the main body of the hunt and finds himself completely alone, cut off from the social activity he was enjoying. 'Þanne les I my layk' (32), he says, which means both 'Then I lost my quarry' and 'Then I lost my joy', and what he sees in the woodland clearing is a reminder of the fragility and transience of high-life prosperity in the form of the goddess Fortune, 'a wifman with a wonder whel weue with þe wynde' (34). He describes the traditional ambiguous attractiveness of Fortune, at times with some wit: 'So ferly fair of face tofore hire I fond' (56), where 'tofore' means 'in front', the better side of the goddess who is notoriously two-faced. He is quite properly afraid of her, especially of writing about her, but decides to go ahead 'redely to roune' (53). What he describes is not particularly original. On the wheel he sees the four stages of rule and power – the aspirant king climbing up, the seated king in place on the top of the wheel, the falling king and the king without authority crushed beneath the wheel. But this is combined with a fourfold scheme of 'the ages of man' – youth, middle age, old age followed by decrepitude and death. The poem is written in a linked sequence of thirteen-line stanzas of the sort already described, but when the kings speak to articulate their situations the poet gives them an extra *versus* of alliterating short lines, which is used to stunning effect in the staccato complaint of the grey-haired falling king:

'Becomen a caytif acast,   *wretch*
Kynges king couþe me calle,
Fram frendes falle,
Lond, luþe, litel, lo! Last.   *people*
Last litel lordene lif,
Fikel is Fortune, nou fer fro,
Her wel, here wo,
Here knyth, her kyng, her caytif.'
                    (121–28)

The alternation of 'wel' and 'wo' and the three stages of rule and life are brought together in a single present – 'her', a poetic equivalent to the sort of artistic illustrations of Fortune's wheel in which the stages are all visible at once. The fourth stage is left incomplete. The poet describes

A bare body in a bed, a bere ibrouth him by,
A duk drawe to þe deþ wiþ drouping and dare.   *grief, fear*
                    (132–33)

But the poem breaks off and the end is lost: the single surviving copy of it occupies what is now the final page (fol. 237) of Oxford, Bodleian Library MS Laud Misc. 108, and at least one and perhaps more folios have become detached. This is a pity because the reader is deprived of the final king's *versus* and the poet's reaction, if any, to what he has seen (Smallwood 1973). However, the trajectory of the poem and its moral message are clear enough, that even what seems to be the most secure kind of prosperity is likely to be undermined by chance and the passing of time.

The Three Dead Kings deals with many of these same issues but, perhaps because it is complete its proposals for moral reformation are more explicit. It is again written in a thirteen-line stanza and is preserved in Oxford, Bodleian Library MS Douce 302, a collection of the poems of John Audelay, a blind Shropshire priest in the service of Lord Strange of Knokin. The poem may not be Audelay's, however, because its dialect is somewhat more northern than his. The story of 'the three living and the three dead' was a popular one in European art and literature, but this is the only literary example of it in English. The poem opens with a graphic account of a boar hunt attended by 'barownce' and 'þre kyngys' (16–18) who owned the woodlands and waste places where it took place and 'lakyd no lorchip in lare' (25). This is not a celebratory poem, however, but one written for those who 'wold lestyn and lere' (26), particularly, one suspects, for those similar to the protagonists.

The poem deals, in an unremitting and calculated way, with the gradual moral awakening of the three kings and, at the same time, dismantles the easy assumptions of the high life. In part this is done through number: the three living speak in turn, as do the three dead, and each speech, though different, addresses similar concerns. Formality and iteration are part of the poet's strategy. But before the three kings encounter the ghosts their moral readjustment begins: the weather deteriorates, wind,

rain and 'myst' separate them from 'al here men and here mete' (30), and they have
to face what is to occur without the supports their social status would normally afford
them. One sees their predicament as a punishment because of their lifestyles:

> 'Al our awnters', quod one, 'þat we ar now inne,   *uncertainties, dangers*
> I hope fore honor of erþ þat anguis be ous an.   *expect*
> Þaʒ we be kyngis ful clene and comen of ryche kyn,
> Moche care vs is caʒt fore kraft þat I can.'
>
> (31–34)

For him, social status and the lifestyle it presupposes carry a burden of guilt. He
puts his trust in Christ and says, 'Our Lord may delyuer vs with lyst' (38). But the
rescue is ambiguous: the weather clears and they find themselves in 'feldus ful fayre
and fogus ful fow' (41), but are confronted by three skeletal ghosts who turn out to
be their fathers. The three kings see these apparitions as agents of moral instruction
and their guilt about their high-life activities reasserts itself and has to be faced. But
when the ghosts speak the moral strictures become more precise and coercive. The
first speaks of the wrongful acquisition of territory, 'fro Loren into Londen' (95),
through force, and warns of retribution:

> 'Þose þat bene not at ʒour bone ʒe beton and byndon,
> Bot ʒef ʒe betun þat burst in bale be ʒe bondon'.
>
> (96–97)

The puns on 'beton' and 'betun' meaning 'beat' and 'atone for' and the play on 'byndon'
and 'bondon' suggest that the punishment fits the crime in a kind of linguistic *contra-
passo*. The second ghost similarly uses puns to make an argument against fleshly lust:

> 'And ʒef ʒe leuyn vpon Crist and on his lore lere
> Leuys lykyng of flesche and leue not þat lare'.
>
> (111–12)

Here the puns are on *leuyn* and *leue*, which both mean 'believe', and *Leuys* which
means 'desist from', and on *lore* which means 'teaching' and *lare* which means 'filth'.
The third, who invites his audience to make 'ʒour merour be me', exposes most
explicitly the social dimension of the poem when he admits to having treated his
tenants and servants badly (120–22). And the poet emphasises this latent egalitarian
aspect of his thinking by having this king say that 'Now nis þer knaue vnder Crist
to me wil enclyne' (125). The three kings take the moral points that are made and
translate them into action: they build a church and the poem becomes an inscription
on the wall (141). The poem closes like an intricate trap: there are numerous paintings
of 'the three living and the three dead' on the walls of late medieval churches which
would validate visually the message of the poem for anyone who had read or heard
it (Tristram 1976: 162–5).

The Parlement of the Thre Ages again treats some of these subjects – transience, the aging process, death, the proper conduct of life – but in a more considered and expansive manner. It is discursively written in alliterative long lines, which gives it latitude for description and speculation. Again, the revelation of wisdom comes by way of a hunt, but this time a hunt of an unofficial sort because the narrator is a poacher who, 'in the monethe of Maye' (1), with cross-bow and dog, stalks and kills a fine stag. The magnificence of the animal and the brutal fact of its death are insisted on:

> ...he was crepyde into a krage and crouschede to þe erthe.   *pressed down*
> Dede als a dore-nayle doun was he fallen...
>
> (64–65)

After this it is just a carcass under the poacher's brittling knife. The splendour of living and its precariousness because of the possibility of unexpected death are themes that run through the poem, and the poacher himself is not immune – in part because he is a criminal. He hides the carcass and waits for nightfall so that he can take his booty home, but falls asleep in the warm sun and dreams 'in that dowte a full dreghe sweuynn' (102) – his fear (*dowte*) contributing significantly to the troubling nature (*dreghe*) of his dream (Peck 1972).

What he sees is a taxonomy of human existence structured according to the idea of the 'three ages of man'. Youthe, Medill Elde and Elde are first described and then debate about lifestyles and moral attitudes. Again, as in some of the poems previously discussed, the formality of the poem's procedure contributes to its meaning. As well as by age and physical appearance each of the protagonists is differentiated in terms of the colour of his clothes, his posture and the objects he has with him. Youthe is 'gerede alle in grene, alle with golde byweuede' (122), Medill Elde with 'rosette' and 'graye' (137–38) and Elde with 'blake' (153) – which have seasonal associations as the growth of spring moves into the decay of winter, and reflect the tendency of human life to move towards death. In terms of posture Youthe is described as a 'bolde beryn one a blonke' (110), Medill Elde 'in his sete satte at his ese' (136) and Elde is 'lenyde one his syde' (152) on a 'couche' (136) – again a progression towards the earth and death. But it is those things that the figures have with them which are the most indicative of their lifestyles and preferences. Youthe has a 'hauke one his fiste' (170) and this, his tall horse and his splendid garments mark him out as a courtier enjoying the high life which he evokes, when he speaks, in all its detail and splendour – outdoor sports like jousting and hawking, and, when he goes back to court, dancing, reading romances, partying, playing chess and so on (249–56). As he sits Medill Elde holds money bags in his lap and thinks 'one his golde and his gude' (139–40). He is a substantial landowner who concerns himself with the good order and profitability of his estates: 'alle his witt in this werlde was one his wele one' (149). He accuses Youthe of living beyond his means, of prodigality (183–93) to which Youthe replies with hints that Medill Elde is guilty of the sin of avarice (195–96, 257–60) and it seems briefly as if the poem may develop into an argument about the proper and improper uses of wealth, about 'winning' and 'wasting' – a subject treated elsewhere in alliterative verse of this period. But the intervention of Elde, who holds beads – a rosary – in his hands, takes the poem in a wholly different direction. It becomes a profound meditation on the inevitability but unpredictability of death, and how one should conduct one's life in relation to this situation in order to earn salvation (Scattergood 2000: 86–99).

Elde's intervention is designed to make the debate redundant. He calls Youthe and Medill Elde 'sottes' but does not say he will refute them, only that he will 'stynte your stryffe and stillen ʒour threpe' (268). He does this by setting the debate in a broader perspective in the manner of a master in a medieval university engaged in a *quodlibet* (scholastic disputation): he listens to the *disputatio* (debate), the improvised exchange between the students, and then delivers a *determinatio* (judgment), which summarises the arguments, comments on them and then draws them to an end in a wider context. In Elde's case this is done by setting the three ages in a linear temporal relation to each other in two ways. First, offering himself as an example (269), he shows that he incorporates all that Youthe and Medill Elde have been – something which was implicit in the ages attributed to the characters: at 100 years Elde is more than the sum of Youthe (30) and Medill Elde (60). And formally his speech includes ideas and phraseology that has been used by or about the previous speakers: 'I was ʒonge in my ʒouthe and ʒape of my dedys' (270, compare 134); '…purcheste me ploughe-londes and pastures full noble' (280, compare 145–46). He even quotes from his own description in regard to his physical appearance (284–87, compare 154–56). Second, he establishes a familial relation between the three ages, 'for Elde es sire of Midill Elde and Midill Elde of ʒouthe' (652). Elde shows that Youthe and Medill Elde were mistaken in assuming their positions were unalterable and arguing for the pre-eminence of their lifestyles: they are subject to time and change and they should logically come to terms with the fact of death in all its paradoxical certainty and uncertainty:

> '…noghte es sekire to ʒoure-selfe in certayne bot dethe,
> And he es so vncertayne that sodaynly he comes'.
>
> (635–36)

Any feelings of security in the present that one might have, he says, are seriously misplaced. Furthermore, Elde generalises his argument by using historical examples to sustain it: the careers of the Nine Worthies are summarised to establish that bravery and military achievement quail before death (582–83), as are the stories of wise men (611) and lovers (612). In his magisterial way he concludes:

> 'Sythen doughtynes when dede comes ne dare noghte habyde,   *bravery, prowess*
> Ne dethe wondes for no witt to wende where hym likes,   *hesitates*
> And therto paramours and pride puttes he full lowe…
> Me thynke þe wele of this werlde worthes to noghte.'
>
> (631–37)

What these exempla demonstrate is not simply that death is common to all, but that what may seem to be of value – bravery, wisdom, love – is destroyed by death, and therefore assumptions of achievement like those of security are vain and not lasting. The anticipated moral follows, sustained by the famous text from Ecclesiastes 1:2 and 12:8 that 'alle es vayne and vanytes and vanyte is alle' (640). From this the conclusion is drawn that men should amend their 'mysse' and think about the health of their souls with particular reference to the sacrament of penance: 'to schryue ȝow full schirle and schewe ȝow to prestis' (644). The argument closes predictably on a moral and religious as well as a grammatical imperative.

The ending of the poem is laconic and understated. As often in alliterative poems the end recalls the beginning: the poacher is awakened by 'a bogle on a bonke [...] blowen full lowde' (652) and finds himself where he was 'in the monethe of May' (656). But time has elapsed since he fell asleep and the sun is setting – suggesting another traditional comparison, of human life to the passing of a day: 'This word ys but a daye'. This adds further meaning to the poem and stresses the precariousness of the poacher's situation: the 'bogle' he hears may not simply be the horn of a forester but death's trumpet. There is no moralisation to the poem because all that needs to be said has been said and the poacher does all that he can do: he throws off his somnolence and renews his activity. Though death may be ultimately unavoidable it is as well to try to avoid it for as long as possible: 'I founded vpon fote', he says, 'and ferkede towarde townn' (659), putting distance between himself and a site of danger.

It is only in a seventeenth-century copy, in the Percy Folio manuscript, that *Death and Liffe* survives, and because it is such a late copy it is difficult to be certain about its date and provenance. But it appears to have been written in the North Midlands in the latter part of the fourteenth or the early fifteenth century, since it has many similarities with *Piers Plowman* and other alliterative poems of that period. Elde's sentiments in the *Parlement* concerning the destruction by death of the bravery, wisdom and joy of love find an echo in this poet's opening prayer:

> For boldnesse of body not blytheness of hart,
> Coninge of clearkes ne cost vpon earth,   *Intelligence*
> But all wasteth away & worthes to nought,
> When Death driueth att the doore with his darts keene.
>
> (7–10)

This poet, like the previous one, addresses the question of salvation and damnation for good or evil deeds (13–14) and prays to God, but he is much more affirmative: 'bringe vs into blisse, that brought vs out of ball' (21). And this affirmation of God's redemption of mankind ushers in a debate in which it is a central feature.

This poem breaks no new ground but deploys the conventions of the tradition with great dexterity and verve (Tristram 1976: 106–7). As in many another alliterative poem, this narrator wanders through a beautiful landscape and 'lying edgelong on the ground' (37) dreams himself first into puzzlement and then into enlightenment.

He finds himself in a strange wood (39) high above a plain where he sees the world, both natural and man-made, laid out attractively before him:

> Both of woods & wasts & walled townes,
> Comelye castles & cleare with caruen towers,
> Parkes & pallaces & pastures ffull manye...
>   (42–44)

This world, populated with all classes of people, is the domain of the beautiful Lady Liffe, 'brighter of her blee then was the bright sonn' (65). Dressed in green (84) – she owes more than a little to Alanus de Insulis's *Natura* – Lady Liffe is the invigorating principle in all things and worshipped by all. The domain over which she and her household preside is full of 'minstrelsye' (110), 'rydinge and reuell that ronge in the bankes' (138) – the activities and joys of the high life. But this well-being lasts only until 'neere noone & one hower after', and all changes between this time and '2 of the clocke', when the poet, using the idea of 'life as a day', announces the coming of Death with a raucous 'horne' (136–47). When Lady Death is described she is in part like a cadaver and in part like the 'loathly lady' of romances:

> Her cheekes were leane, with lipps full side,   *long*
> With a maruelous mouth full of long tushes,   *tusks, teeth*
> & a nebb of her nose to her navel hanged,
> & her lere lyke the lead that latelye was beaten...   *complexion*
>   (167–70)

She destroys the beautiful landscape wherever she passes, the birds and the fishes (191–98), and with her darts she lays low 1500 people, of all classes – suggesting the poet had in mind the conventions of the *danse macabre* (201–9). But at this point comes an intervention which shows that the power of Death is limited and which anticipates the conclusion to the confrontation with Liffe. God sends Countenance (Continuity) who 'ran out of the rainebow through the ragged clowds' (218) and ordered her to stop killing, at once an allusion to the rainbow that was, in Greek mythology, a means by which celestial messengers reach the earth and a reminder of the promise of Genesis 9:13–15 that the living things of the earth will not be destroyed entirely. In the debate that follows Liffe asks why Death kills the body 'that neuer care rought' (239), and is answered in the traditional way that the original transgression of Adam and Eve brought Death into the world and that she is entitled to her 'rent' (260). Life counters that her activities destroy everything that is good – the 'ioy & gentlenesse' of family life, 'ffayth & ffellowship', 'loue & charitye' (292–95). But Death presses on inexorably with the assertion of her power: 'I fayled neuer in fight but I the ffeild wan' (319). She lists among her conquests biblical figures, some of the Nine Worthies and knights of the Round Table (326–43), and ends with:

> 'Haue I not iusted gentlye with Ihesu of heauen?   *nobly*
> He was frayd of my fface in ffreshest of time.
> Yet I knocked him on the crosse & carued through his hart.'
>
> (345–7)

But in debating terms to claim this is a mistake. These are, as Liffe points out, 'wittles words' (362) because they destroy Death's case that her power is absolute. Liffe gives an account of Christ's crucifixion and death, but then goes on to the Resurrection, the harrowing of Hell, and the release of the patriarchs and prophets from bondage, and concludes:

> 'Death was damned that day, daring ffull still.   *cowering*
> She hath no might, nay no maine, to meddle with yonder ost,
> Against euerlasting Liffe that Lady soe true.'
>
> (442–5)

The example of Christ's overcoming of death and the concept of everlasting life effectively win the argument. Those whom Death had slaughtered earlier in the poem are raised with the sign of the cross, 'fairer by 2 fold then they before were' (450), and the awakened poet closes his poem with a prayer, secure in the conventional teaching and the comforts of the faith which his vision has confirmed for him.

The figures in these intricate, highly wrought, self-consciously artistic works play out dramas, different in their details, but identical in their trajectory. Orthodox faith and a moral view of existence are everywhere tested – by physical threats leading sometimes to martyrdom or the possibility of legal punishments, by intellectual confusion as to the meaning of ostensibly marvellous occurrences, by the social allure of the high life of leisure and enjoyment, by the depressing inevitability of the transience of worldly pleasures and achievement. Almost all these poems, however, end by endorsing the moral and religious norms of their society, by conformity to an overwhelmingly comforting spiritual and moral orthodoxy. Though none of them is about courtly love, they briefly test the received values of their society in something of the same way that courtly love did, and C. S. Lewis's famous words on its comparative failure to impinge are apposite in this context: 'we hear the bell clang; and the children, suddenly hushed and grave, and a little frightened, troop back to their master' (Lewis 1936: 43). All except the outsider, that is – the canny, criminal, laconic poacher, who, because he has more contingent priorities in his darkening world, simply gets on with his risky life and by his exception, in a way, inadvertently proves the rule.

References and Further Reading

Primary Texts

Barr, Helen (ed.) (1993). *The Piers Plowman Tradition*. London: J. M. Dent.

Hanford, J. H. and J. M. Steadman (eds) (1918). 'Death and Liffe'. *Studies in Philology*, 15, 221–94.

Hanna, Ralph III (ed.) (1974). *The Awntyrs off Arthure at the Terne Wathelyn*. Manchester: Manchester University Press.

Kennedy, R. (1987). 'A Bird in Bishopswood': Some newly-discovered lines of alliterative verse from the late fourteenth century. In M. Stokes and T. L. Burton (eds). *Medieval Literature and Antiquities: Studies in Honour of Basil Cottle* (pp. 71–87). Cambridge: D. S. Brewer.

Miskimin, Alice (ed.) (1969). *Susannah: An Alliterative Poem of the Fourteenth Century*. New Haven, CT: Yale University Press.

Oakden, J. P. (ed.) (1935). *Scotish Ffeilde*. Manchester: Manchester University Press.

Offord, M. Y. (ed.) (1959). *The Parlement of the Thre Ages*. Early English Text Society, o.s. 246. London: Oxford University Press.

Turville-Petre, T. (1982). The lament for Sir John Berkeley. *Speculum*, 57(ii), 332–9.

Turville-Petre, T. (1989). *Alliterative Poetry of the Later Middle Ages*. London: Routledge.

Secondary Reading

Burrow, J. A. (1988). *The Ages of Man: A Study in Medieval Writing and Thought*. Oxford: Clarendon Press.

Burrow, J. A. (1993). 'Saint Erkenwald' Line 1: 'At London in Englond'. *Notes and Queries*, 238, 22–3.

Cannon, C. (2004). *The Grounds of English Literature*. Oxford: Oxford University Press.

Hanna III, R. (1995). Defining Middle English alliterative poetry. In M. T. Tavormina and R. F. Yeager (eds). *The Endless Knot: Essays in Honor of Marie Borroff* (pp. 43–64). Cambridge: D. S. Brewer.

Kane, G. (1965). *Piers Plowman: The Evidence for Authorship*. London: Athlone.

Kellogg, A. L. (1960). Susannah and the 'Merchant's Tale'. *Speculum*, 35, 275–9.

Kennedy, R. (ed.) (2003). *Three Alliterative Saints' Hymns: Late Middle English Stanzaic Poems*. Early English Text Society, o.s. 321.

Lawton, D. A. (ed.) (1982). *Middle English Alliterative Poetry and its Literary Background: Seven Essays*. Cambridge: D. S. Brewer.

Lewis, C. S. (1936). *The Allegory of Love: A Study in Medieval Tradition*. Oxford: Oxford University Press.

Peck, R. A. (1972). The careful hunter in 'The Parlement of the Thre Ages'. *English Literary History*, 39, 333–41.

Salter, E. (1979). A complaint against blacksmiths. *Literature and History*, 5(ii), 194–215.

Scattergood, J. (2000). *The Lost Tradition: Essays on Middle English Alliterative Poetry*. Dublin: Four Courts Press.

Scattergood, J. (2006). *Manuscripts and Ghosts: Essays on the Transmission of Medieval and Early Renaissance Literature*. Dublin: Four Courts Press.

Shepherd, G. T. (1990). *Poets and Prophets: Essays in Medieval Studies*. Ed. T. A. Shippey and J. Pickles. Cambridge: D. S. Brewer.

Smallwood, T. W. (1973). The interpretation of 'Somer Soneday'. *Medium Ævum*, 42, 238–43.

Tristram, P. (1976). *Figures of Life and Death in Medieval English Literature*. London: Elek.

Turville-Petre, T. (1977). *The Alliterative Revival*. Cambridge: D. S. Brewer.

Turville-Petre, T. (1988). The author of 'The Destruction of Troy'. *Medium Ævum*, 57, 264–9.

Turville-Petre, T. (2005). 'St Erkenwald' and the Crafty Chronicles. In A. M. D'Arcy and A. J. Fletcher (eds). *Studies in late Medieval and Early Renaissance Texts in Honour of John Scattergood: 'The Key of All Good Remembrance'* (pp. 362–74). Dublin: Four Courts Press.

Whatley, G. (1984). The uses of hagiography: the legend of Pope Gregory and the Emperor Trajan in the Middle Ages. *Viator*, 15, 25–63.

19

Alliterative Poetry and Politics

John Scattergood

I

In medieval political writing, whether it is about general issues or particular events, the political is rarely separated from the religious and the moral, and political issues and events are regularly considered from religious and moral angles. They are also frequently treated in a very indirect way because there were serious constraints, both ecclesiastical and secular, on writings that addressed contemporary politics, particularly if reference was made to the king or members of the royal family or magnates. Edward III's Statute of Treasons (1352) defined it as treasonous 'if a man compasses or imagines (*compasser ou ymaginer*) the death of our lord the king, or our lady his consort, or their son and heir'. Action was not necessary: the proscription covered words (and even thoughts, it seems). Richard II revived and revised the 1275 act against the crime of speaking untruths about great men (*scandalum magnatum*) in 1378–79 (Simpson 1990). A number of people were prosecuted under both acts (Scattergood 1971: 21–2). And Henry IV, in 1402, passed an act against the composition and dissemination of political prophecies. Yet political verse continued to be written, including prophecies: the narrator of *Mum and the Sothsegger* had a copy of 'the meruailles that Merlyn dide devyse' (1724) in his bag of books.

And prophecies, of course, had been written earlier. This type of verse is deliberately indirect and mysterious, but the poems are designed to be 'solved', though their meanings may differ from reader to reader (Coote 2000). One of the most enigmatic is generated, according to its heading in the unique copy of it in British Library, MS Harley 2253, by a question put by the Countess of Dunbar to Thomas of Erceldoune, a noted Scottish prophet, as to when the war with England might end. He answers with a series of conditional statements beginning 'When...'. Most of these are *impossibilia* – some natural like 'When hares kindles o þe herston' (4), some moral like 'When ryþt ant wrong assenteþ togedere' (14), some cultural like 'When Loudyon ys forest ant forest ys felde' (3). The statements do not operate in any logical or reasoned way but suggest that before the war ends the world will need to change radically. Despite the generality of the sentiments, however, a number of Scottish place-names appear. One line reads 'When Bambourne ys donged wyþ dede men' (9) and this may refer to the aftermath of the Battle of Bannockburn of 1314. The poem ends with a kind of riddling answer to the original question and seeks ostensibly to summarise the preceding conditional statements:

> Whenne shal þis be? Nouþer in þine tyme ne in myne,
> Ah comen ant gon wiþinne twenty winter ant on.
>
> (17–18)

If 'twenty one' is to be taken literally, and if Bannockburn is the latest reference in the poem, the date suggested might be 1335, roughly the date of the latest political verses in the manuscript. But whatever its date, this is a despairing poem written out of weariness of a situation in which border warfare was endemic (Scattergood 2000a: 177–8).

Political prophecies are usually attributed to notable figures in order to give them status, without much regard to history or plausibility. Thus the northern alliterative *Thomas a Becket's Prophecies*, which are fathered on the Archbishop of Canterbury murdered in his church in 1170, actually deal with the mid-fourteenth-century conflicts between England, France and Scotland (Coote 2000: 130–3). This poem exists in two fragmentary versions. In the longer of these, preserved in Cambridge University Library MS Kk.1.5, Becket, in Poitou, asks about a half-built tower and is told that its construction was interrupted when men working on it 'fand a letter on a stone fast' which bore a message:

> It sayd, 'Masterles men, yhe this tour make;
> A bayre wall come out of Bertane wytht so brode tuskis,   *boar*
> He sall trauyll up yhour towre, and your toune þer after,   *harass*
> And dycht his den in þe derrest place þat euer aucht kynge Charles'.   *prepare, make*
>
> (49–52)

The king, vexed at the implications of this, ordered that the message-bearing stone should be cast into deep water and that the masons should discontinue their work. The citizens, Becket is told, live in fear of the 'bayre' (51) because this is a 'ferly' they cannot explain. Becket prays for illumination and the Virgin Mary brings a 'buke' as a 'gyft' for him (64–65), which explains the cryptic words on the stone with another clearer, but still heavily encoded, account. The 'boar' from England, says the book, will begin unpromisingly but have a glorious career. He will 'tumble up' the land of France, destroying many cities – Abbeville, Montjoy, Caen, Calais and others (103–33). A king will invade England from the north but will be overcome and captured (137–151). After this the boar will resume his European conquests, winning a battle at Boulogne and taking and ruling Paris (156–74). Then he will move to Italy, conquering Lombardy and taking Milan, before going to the Holy Land 'to convert the cateffes that noghtt on crystis lewys' (209) – where he is perhaps to suffer a crusader's death since there is no mention of his return. The poem ends with predictions of doom for England unless the people know Christ (229–39). Then the book is taken back to heaven 'And Beket to Burgone buskes hum full evine' (257) – without further explanation. As often in alliterative poetry, knowledge comes from books, though in this case not one that can be consulted again.

But perhaps none is needed, because to unwrap the encoded 'explanation' is not difficult: in prophecies of this date the 'boar', following the standard interpretation of the 'six kings to follow John' prophecy, is to be identified with Edward III. In the shorter version of this poem in Oxford, Bodleian Library MS Hatton 36, there are two boars, presumably Edward III and the Black Prince. 'Kynge Charles' is Charles V, king of France between 1364 and 1380. The poem is clearly written in the light of English military successes at Crécy in 1346 and Poitiers in 1356. The prophecy is the usual mix of what has already taken place, what may realistically happen, the wishful and the implausible. It hints at conquests to come in Normandy, which was plausible, and in Northern Italy and the Holy Land, which was inconceivable. But what is particularly interesting about it is the way in which English nationalistic aspirations and sentiments are subjected to a clerical agenda. The political self-congratulation and wishfulness are mediated and interpreted by a saint, by means of a miraculous book provided by the Virgin Mary. And the poem ends with threatening statements enjoining Christian obedience and morality.

And this note resonates in other alliterative verse. Confronted by the terrifying authoritative presence of the ghost of Guenevere's mother in *The Awynters of Arthure at the Terne Wathelyne*, and having already heard her account of how persons of wealth and influence fare in the afterlife, Gawain asks her about the fate of warriors:

'How shal we fare,' quod the freke, 'that fonden to fight	*knight*
And thus defoulen the folke of fele kinges londes,	*oppress; many*
And riches over reymes withouten eny right	*travels*
Wynnen worshipp in werre thorgh wightnesse of hondes?'	*strength*
(261–64)	

The answer is in part political and in part moral: 'Your King is to covetous, I warne the, sir knight' (265). She proceeds to caution him against trusting to the stability of worldly prosperity and gives him an instance: 'Take witnesse by Fraunce' (273). She goes on: 'Fraunce haf ye freely with your fight wonnen' and speaks of British hegemony over Brittany, Burgundy and Acquitaine (274–79). This is all stated within the parameters of romance in terms of Arthur's conquests over 'Freol' [Frollo], but no reader or hearer of this poem in late medieval England could have failed to notice the parallels to their own situation, particularly after the conquests of Henry V's reign, nor the moral criticism of the aggressive militaristic ethos that underpinned those conquests. Routes to political statement could be various and are sometimes unexpected.

Wynnere and Wastoure finds its way by a variety of indirections – prophecy, dream and inconclusive debate (Bestoul 1974). It begins by looking back to the legendary foundation of Britain by 'Bruyttus' and says that though many 'selcouthes' [marvels] have happened since then there have never been 'so many as nowe by the nynedele' (1–4). The times are disturbed, he says, and quotes a prophecy 'of Solomon the wyse' about the break-up of traditional social structures, such that one might assume that 'dredfull domesdaye' was approaching (12–18). Two of his lines echo those of Thomas of Erceldoune, but this poet is more confident that he can observe 'sadly' [seriously] and 'the sothe telle' (17) – like other alliterative poets he claims to be a truth-teller. He dreams he sees two armies with banners displayed 'bown for to mete' (52) because this was a sign that they meant to give battle. They are persuaded against fighting by the intervention of the king, pretty clearly Edward III, who sends a messenger, identifiable as Sir John Wingfield by his armorials (117–18) (Salter 1978). The messenger points out that to ride with a banner displayed is the prerogative of the king and that those who transgress against this are guilty of treason, which might mean that 'he shall losse the londe and his lyfe aftir' (130–33). This poem is written in the immediate aftermath of the Statute of Treasons: twice the words about 'les destourbers de la Pees & meintenours des quereles & des riotes', used by Chief Justice Sir William Shareshull as he opened the parliament of 1352, are echoed and once he is mentioned by name (317). But warfare within the realm is not the main subject of the poem.

Fighting is avoided and the issues that divide the armies are made the subject of a debate which the king offers to judge (220). It concerns wealth and its proper uses: on the one side are those who acquire money – the papacy, merchants, lawyers, friars, an unofficial taxonomy of the satirical discontent expressed by late medieval poets about those who exploit their positions or callings to enrich themselves; on the other are the gentry and their dependents, 'sadde men of armes, / bolde sqwyeres of blode, bowmen many' (193–94). The likely political context of the poem is the problem of war-taxation in 1352–53 (Scattergood 2000b: 69–99). Wynnere, who opens the debate, characterises their differences sharply:

> 'Alle þat I wynn thurgh witt, he wastes thurgh pryde;
> I gedir, I glene, and he lattys goo sone,
> I pryke and I pryne, and he the purse opynes.'
>
> (230–32)

Significant here is the image of the purse that Wynnere sews and stitches up, and Wastoure opens, and significant too is the use of the word 'pride', suggesting a moral as well as a financial agenda, which is continued when Wastoure speaks because his main criticism of his opponent is that he is avaricious. But the debate is not formal or particularly structured. It proceeds by means of mutual accusation and critical description of incompatible lifestyles. Wynnere characterises Wastoure as an impoverished landowner, unable to come to terms with the post-plague desolation of the English countryside and its concomitant economic realities:

Why hase this cayteffe no care how men corne sellen?   *wretch*
His londes liggen alle ley, his lomes aren solde...   *lie completely fallow; lambs*

(233–34)

As the debate develops he accuses him further of extravagance in giving livery to his followers (270–72) which is beyond his income, spending nights at 'the taverne byfore þe toune-hede' (277) which he cannot pay for, feasts (330–69) which cost 'a rawnson of siluer', selling or mortgaging his lands 'ʒoure wyfes to paye' (408) and spending the money on costly fashionable clothes. When Wastoure replies he describes Wynnere as an avaricious merchant, constantly worried about his possessions, a hoarder who is no use to society:

What scholde worthe of that wele if no waste come?   *become*
Some rote, some ruste, some ratons fede.   *rats*
Let be thy cramynge of thi kystes, for Cristis lufe of heuen!
Late the peple and the pore hafe parte of thi siluere...

(253–56)

Later come predictions that Wynnere's son and executors will quarrel over his wealth, or friars will acquire it 'to payntten with thaire pelers or pergett with thaire walles' (301), or that he will hang himself because he has lost money speculating about the price of corn (374), and that he will be damned after his death for his covetousness (444).

Both debaters are better at making accusations than at answering them, though Wastoure does argue that his feasts benefit the poor because the uneaten food goes to them (295), and that there is nothing wrong in a man seeking to provide attractive clothes for his 'leman', 'aftir hir faire chere to forthir hir herte' (429), so that she will love him and inspire him to bold deeds – an argument based on the conventions of *fin' amor*. This is a 'horizontal' inconclusive debate, though it would have been possible to resolve it. The poet might have invoked the Aristotelian mean of virtue in relation to the two vices being described – liberality as a mean between prodigality, the excess, and avarice, the deficiency of the central virtue – and might have attempted to distinguish between the relative sinfulness of the two faults, preferring prodigality because it at least benefits others and because it is curable if one runs out of money (Jacobs 1985). This reasoning may be implicit in some parts of the poem but it does not form part of the king's judgment. He recognises that both Wynnere and Wastoure are servants of his household (212) to whom he gives liveries (205), and resolves the debate simply by keeping the two apart, and sending them to where they are best loved – Wynnere to the papal curia (460–65), and Wastoure to Cheapside in London 'þer moste waste es of wele' (473–74). He reserves the right to call Wynnere back when he needs him (466–67), but at this point Wastoure will have to 'cayre vttire' (467). The king contains the situation but does not resolve it or alter it, and the poem appears to propose that the well-balanced economy needs both the accumulation of capital and the free circulation of wealth: as the king puts it, 'þe more þou wastis

þi wele, þe better þe Wynner lykes' (495). This recognises the interdependence of
the two tendencies at a practical level. Some lines – but probably not very many –
are lost from the end of the poem, and it may be that in them the poet elicited more
general moral and philosophical conclusions. But, given the conduct of the debate
and the form of the judgment, that is not likely. The poem does not define a policy,
but raises questions, warns and admonishes. In the characteristic way of medieval
political verse, this poem purports to offer disinterested advice to the king.

II

Poems such as those already discussed may have fed into Langland's work and his
poem, widely known in all its versions, exerted an enormous influence on alliterative
poems of a political temper which followed. *Richard the Redeles*, preserved in a single
copy in Cambridge University Library MS Ll.iv.14 which also contains a copy of *Piers
Plowman*, appears to have been written in 1400, shortly after the accession of Henry
IV though the poet appears not to know of Richard II's death. The poet begins by
saying that he has heard 'selcouthe thingis' and a 'grett wondir' that astonish him,
and these turn out to be arguments about the deposition of Richard II by Henry IV:
'sore were the sawis on bothe two sidis' (I.8). But though he expresses 'pete' for
Richard II and affirms that he was his loyal servant 'while he in helthe regnid'
(I.23–26), he is clearly a Lancastrian. His book is designed to move Richard II from
'mysserewle' should he ever recover the throne, but he asks those who read his advice
to 'amende that ys amysse' (I.59–63) and particularly asks for mercy from his
sovereign if anything should be found offensive so as to make him 'wrothe' (I.76).
These elaborate preliminary manoeuvrings signal that the poet is conscious that by
writing about politics, particularly about kings, he is doing something dangerous,
but believes that it is also his right and duty to do this.

When criticism of Richard II comes in *Richard the Redeles* it takes a variety of
literary shapes. Much of that in Passus I appears to be based on the *gravamina*, the
thirty-two charges of misconduct levelled against Richard II at his deposition. These
were entered in the parliamentary rolls, preceded by a copy of his coronation oath
– presumably as a demonstration of how far he had deviated from it. The poet alludes
to this material and shapes his criticism in terms of it. 'Couetise hath crasid youre
croune for euere' (I. 95), he says, and proceeds to elaborate:

> Of alegeaunce now lerneth a lesson other tweyne,
> Wher-by it standith and stablithe moste –
> By drede, or be dyntis or domes vntrewe,   *blows; judgements*
> Or by creaunce of coyne for castes of gile,   *credit; subterfuges*
> By pillynge of youre peple youre prynces to plese,   *plundering*
> Or that youre wylle were wroughte though wisdom it nolde;
> Or be tallage of youre townnes without ony werre...   *taxation*
>
> (I. 96–102)

The enforcing of unjust judgments through fear or blows (98) alludes to the first of the deposition articles which accused Richard II of intimidating the justices of England into declaring illegal the acts of the Merciless Parliament of 1388. Getting money on credit through trickery (99) refers to the fourteenth article which accused him of raising loans he never intended to repay. The robbery of his people to please his friends (100) is mentioned in the first article and his wilfulness (101) is mentioned in several, particularly the seventh and sixteenth. The criticism in line 102 refers to the fifteenth article which made the point that the king should live off his own revenues unless the country was at war. And the 'lesson' continues in this vein. But in Passus II and III the strategy of the poem alters and it takes on the appearance of a series of political beast-fables. There are two sets of natural images from which the poet extrapolates, each depending on cognisances, badges and armorials used by those involved in the events of 1399–1400, and puns on their names and titles. The poet says that all this is 'derklich endited' (I. 107), obscurely written, in the manner of political prophecies, but the poet's ulterior meaning is not difficult to work out – nor is it meant to be. One set of images relates to Richard II's badge of the white hart worn by his 'large leuerey' (II. 2), retainers who, it is alleged, used their positions to bully the House of Commons (II. 29) and the people: 'They bare hem the bolder for her gay broches' (II. 38). Developing the image, the poet says that these 'harts' have acted against their nature in attacking other animals, and he refers to animals in the cognisances of Richard FitzAlan, earl of Arundel, Thomas of Woodstock, duke of Gloucester and Thomas Beauchamp, earl of Warwick against whom Richard II had moved in 1397. Henry IV, however, whose badge was the eagle, acted according to 'kynde' by using his power to protect his relatives and to prey on things inimical to them (though here the allegory is stretched beyond anything an eagle might actually do):

> Thus baterid this bred on busshes aboughte,
> And gaderid gomes on grene ther as they walkyd   *men*
> That all the schroff and the schroup sondrid from other.   *refuse; rubbish*
> He mellid so the matall with the hand-molde   *pounded, beat; ?hand-mill*
> That they lost lemes the leuest that they had.   *limbs*
>
> (II.152–56)

The references here, through puns on their names, are to Sir John Bushy, Sir Henry Grene and Sir William Scrope, three of Richard II's principal supporters, who were executed at Bristol in 1399. More plausibly, the eagle also chases off the scavenging kites and magpies, who perhaps represent Richard II's less important supporters. In another analogy, again based on bestiary lore, Richard II is represented as a partridge, who appropriates the nest and eggs of another, and Henry IV as the true mother to whom the chicks return when they are fledged and strong (III. 37–61): they act according to 'kynde' and reject the interloper (Barr 1992).

The mode of the poem shifts again in Passus IV, which essentially deals with the packing of the Shrewsbury Parliament of 27–31 January 1398 to serve the king's will and to improve his finances: a 'preuy parlement for profit of hem-self' (IV. 25) is how the poet describes it. Lack of moral courage, intimidation and bribery, self-seeking and self-interest have reduced parliament, more generally, to a body unfit for serious political debate, he says:

Some helde with the mo how it euere wente,	*majority*
And somme dede rith so and wolld go no forther.	
Some parled as perte as prouyd well after,	*spoke; openly*
And clappid more for the coyne that the kyng owed hem	*clamoured*
Thane for comfforte of the comyne that her cost paied,	
And were be-hote hansell if they helpe wolde	*promised reward*
To be seruyd sekirly of the same siluere.	
And some dradde dukis and Do-well for soke...	

(IV. 86–93)

The poem breaks off at this point and one can only speculate how it might have developed. But this lack of a serious examination of royal policy in the premier debating and legislative assembly of the state was clearly a reason for this poet to feel that he was justified in raising political issues publicly in his verse (Scattergood 2000b: 216–17).

Exactly what the relationship is between this poem and *Mum and the Sothsegger*, preserved in a fragmentary copy in British Library MS Additional 41666, has never been firmly established. The fragments may be part of the same poem, or from disparate poems by the same author, or have nothing to do with each other (Barr 1990). They certainly have a similar agenda, and if they are related it would seem that *Mum and the Sothsegger* is the later: there are allusions to the hanging of some friars in 1402 for spreading treasonous rumours that Richard II was still alive (417–421); the 1405 parliament is referred to in lines 120 and 1672; and there is perhaps a reference to Arundel's exemption in 1409 of friars from his constitutions forbidding preaching to those without a licence (408–414). All this places the poem centrally in the reign of Henry IV and it is very much, like the previous poem, a Lancastrian production.

The opening is lost, but what there is begins with what seems to be a review of Henry IV's household, which the poet, in general, finds 'holsumly y-made' and full of 'meritable' retainers (106–7), and there is an admiring portrait of the king who is 'witti and wise, worthy of deedes' (213), endowed, that is, with *fortitudo* and *sapientia*, the traditional moral attributes of the ideal king. The poet is disturbed, however, by his feeling that the king has about him men who, for one reason or another, do not tell him the truth, and that he is badly in need of a 'sothe sigger' close to him who will 'telle hym the tixte, and touche not the glose' (141), with a pun on glossing a text and obscuring a statement or flattering – one of the many uses of Lollard discourse in the poem (Wawn 1983). He points out that 'whenne oure comely king came furst to londe' – an allusion to Henry IV's invasion of England in 1399 – people were confident about voicing their political dissatisfactions: 'Tho was eche burne bolde to bable what hym aylid' (143–44). But now, says the poet, deliberately recalling his earlier words, if 'a burne bolde hym to bable the sothe' he may be destroyed through loss of life, imprisonment or other sorts of punishment: 'Thus is trouthe doune y-troode and tenyd ful ofte' (165–71). It is here that the main issue of the poem becomes apparent and this is foregrounded when the figure of 'Mum' appears – the embodiment of self-interested complaisance and strategic silence, the archetypal flattering yes-man, who contrasts himself with those who are truth-tellers and are always liable to punishment:

> 'Thus leede I my life in luste of my herte,
> And for my wisedame and witte wone I with the beste;   *dwell*
> While sergeantz the sechith to saise by the lappe   *arrest*
> For thy wilde wordes that maken wretthe ofte.'   *anger*
>
> (248–51)

Because he will never 'withseye' what his superiors propose he is routinely admitted to the councils of rulers, but, in contrast, 'the sothe-sigger' poet's words often lead him to endure the anger of the law – an allusion, perhaps, to the legal constraints on political comment, particularly political writing. The poet accuses Mum of allowing the lord whom he serves to 'shame hymself' through ill-advised actions, but Mum counters cynically with 'colorable wordes' and a precept from the schoolbook *Disticha Catonis*: 'of "bable" cometh blame and "be stille" neuer' (289–91). Confused and angry, the poet seeks for views throughout society on the contrasting practices of 'silence' and 'truth-telling', and ends up disillusioned by the responses he gets, particularly from those in the universities and from the friars who conclude, for reasons of self-interest, 'to yeue Mvm the maistrie withoute mo wordes' (400). Like other alliterative writers, this poet abandons society for the countryside, rests on an unploughed strip of land (lynche, 857), sleeps and dreams himself into knowledge and consolation.

The *oraculum* he dreams involves an old country *vavasour*, a bee-keeper, who explains to the poet, in the traditional terms of the beehive, how society works, because the bee of alle bestz best is y-gouuerned' (997). The ideal society he describes is a monarchy but not an absolutist one, and is predicated on the interdependence of the classes each of which has its particular function in the context of labour – except for the 'dranes', the non-productive members of the community, who should be 'quicly' killed (1086). The poet is encouraged by what he hears, and asks the beekeeper about the respective merits of 'Mvm or the sothe-sigger' (1101–2); he is told that an unwillingness to speak out is the cause of 'al the mischief and mysse-reule that in the royaulme groweth' (1115–16). The health of the body politic depends on institutions such as the law-courts and parliament, where truth can be established. But these are deficient, he maintains, and the poet is encouraged to write: 'make vp thy matiere, thou mays do no better' (1278). Again, poetry is proposed as something that can provide a forum for the sort of political debate which does not exist elsewhere, and to counsel the king

the poet opens his bag of political tracts (1343), which provide an index to popular
discontent. But while they are being summarised the poem breaks off.

The Crowned King, preserved in a single copy in Bodleian MS Douce 95, a mid-
fifteenth century miscellany of Latin and English prose and verse, is written in the
context of Henry V's renewal of the war with France in 1414–15. Though it is a
loyal Lancastrian production, the poet, no doubt because he is dealing with royal
matters, seeks to put some distance between himself and what the poem proposes.
On Corpus Christi eve 'six other vij myle oute of Suthampton' (19–20), from which
port Henry V and his armies embarked for France in August 1415, the poet fell into
a company of revellers and went to bed as dawn was breaking. This self-confessed
flawed narrator has a troublesome morning dream, which he, nevertheless, regards as
one of the 'sondry signes' that are sent by God, 'of care and of comfort that coming
is here-after' (8) – an authoritative dream whose interpretation he turns over, in
Langlandian fashion, to his readers: 'deme as you likes' (16).

Like Langland again, he dreams he is 'high on an hill' looking down into a 'dale
deppest of othere' where he sees 'a selcouthe people', but what he sees is not a 'fair
feeld full of folk' labouring at their everyday tasks but 'a crouned kyng of his co-
mounes axe / A soleyn subsidie to susteyne his werres' (31–36) – the large grant of
two tenths and two fifteenths made at the parliament of 19 November 1414 to finance
the invasion of France. But this is as far as the poet will go in his own voice – even
in a dream – and the narrative is taken over by an unnamed 'clerk' for the rest of
the poem, who asks the king's permission before he offers his advice. What he says
is fairly conventional, deriving from the 'mirrors for princes' tradition, but in the
context of the unprecedented (*soleyn*) subsidy, it is shaped and pointed. He begins by
acknowledging the king's power: 'thiself hast lyfe, lyme and lawes for to keep' (52),
but implicit in 'keep' is a sense of obligation and, as the speech develops, this comes
to the fore: the king has to 'iustifie the trouthe', 'rule the be reson', and look outside
himself towards 'the loue of thi ligemen' and the 'grete' grace that God has sent him
(61–76). But the clerk's agenda is only partly clerical. There is much traditional
advice, including strictures aimed at the appointment of appropriate officers of his
household, particularly those who are truthful, and the avoidance of flatterers and
yes-men: 'kepe the fro glosyng of gylers mowthes' (86). But the king's responsibility
to look after his people, in this poem, is largely predicated on money, and derives,
in part, from arguments attendant on granting the subsidy. The 'clerk' reiterates the
traditional attitude to the 'spoils of war' – the financial advantages accruing from
plunder and ransoms – which was an issue raised in parliament:

> Cherissh thy champyons and chief men of armes;
> And suche as presoners mowe pike with poyntes of werre,   *despoil according to the laws of war*
>
> Lete hem welde that they wynne and worthyly hem thonke;
> And suche as castels mowe cacche, or eny clos tounes,   *capture; walled towns*
> Geve hem as gladly – than shalt thou gete hertes.
>
> (94–98)

More generally, the 'clerk' argues that because the king's wealth and his opulent lifestyle are made possible by the labours of his subjects, he has an obligation to 'gouerne hem euen' (73). Here 'euen' is a resonant word because it goes beyond equity and justice and suggests the reciprocity between king and subjects which is implicit in the sort of constitutional monarchic system which was taking shape at this time. But the 'clerk' also adverts to the idea that the earthly king should imitate a divine example: 'taketh a siker ensample that Crist hym-self sheweth' (137). He ends the poem with the wish that Christ should grant us 'prosperite and pees', and adds 'pursue we thereafter' (144). A contemporary proverbial apothegm bearing on this ran as follows:

> Pees maketh plente,
> Plente makith pride,
> Pride makith plee,   *conflict*
> Plee makith povert,
> Povert makith pees.

If the poet of *The Crowned King* has this set of ideas in mind, he is not only adverting in the last line of his poem to the claims of Christian pacifism but also looking in a practical way at the relationship between militaristic wishes for conquest and money, and reminding Henry V of his more mundane obligations to look after his people's financial well-being. In the context of the high expectations of nationalistic expansionism in 1414–15 this conventional but guarded, insistent, prosaic voice was certainly a counterweight to the prevailing conventional wisdom, and it may well have sounded more independent and braver than subsequent readers have thought.

III

Heresy – and in particular, Lollardy – in the later Middle Ages in England was both a religious and a political problem. John Wyclif (1329–84), on the basis of whose work many of its doctrines were defined, was for much of his career a fairly orthodox Oxford philosopher, but in the late 1370s he began to question, with an acerbity that increased as he got older, some of the doctrine and much of the political structure of the medieval church. As one of his fifteenth-century opponents put it:

> Wiþ men in his begynnynge liht lemed he by cunnynge,   *he shed light by his learning*
> But aftir, with wrong wrytyng, he wrouȝte mykil care,
> And, presumynge perilously, foul fel from þe chirche,
> Misauerynge of þe sacrament, infectynge many oþer.   *misinterpreting*
>   (*Friar Daw's Reply*, 151–54)

The final line alludes to Wyclif's most controversial doctrine: he could not accept, on the basis of his 'realist' philosophy of matter, the doctrine of the real presence of

Christ at the Eucharist. But he also questioned papal and priestly authority, and the necessity for church endowment. He questioned the use of auricular confession and could not accept that a priest was capable of absolving a penitent from sin. He questioned the veneration of images and the use of pilgrimages and indulgences as ways to procuring salvation. Instead, he put his reliance on study of the Bible – which he thought should be available in English – and the conscience of the right-thinking individual. Wyclif's ideas had originally been disseminated in academic Oxford and his earliest followers were clerics. But he had some support amongst the gentry, who protected Lollard priests in livings under their control, and amongst independent urban artisans and tradesmen. Once Lollardy extended beyond its original university context, however, it lost precise definition: it became, in J. A. F. Thomson's words rather 'a set of more or less consistent attitudes than [...] a set of carefully worked out doctrines' (Thomson 1965: 244). The term 'Lollard' came to be used as a smear word for anyone remotely unorthodox. Margery Kempe, a mystic from King's Lynn, certainly behaved oddly and certainly discussed religious matters in an open and forthright way, but was no Lollard – though it was a term applied to her by those she had in some way outraged. On one occasion, she recounts in her *Book*, at Hessle in Yorkshire, 'men callyd hir loller, & women cam rennyng out of her howsys with her rokkys, crying to þe pepill, "Brenneth þis fals heretyk"' (129). How widespread the support for Lollardy was is hard to determine, but the authorities took it seriously. Wyclif's ideas were formally examined and condemned, and in 1401 the draconian statute of the burning of heretics (*de haeretico comburendo*) was promulgated at the instigation of Archbishop Thomas Arundel. There were suggestions that Lollard ideas had contributed to the social discontents which resulted in the rising of 1381, but this is hard to prove. An armed rising by the Lollard Sir John Oldcastle in 1414 was certainly a threat to Henry V, though it was poorly supported and easily quelled. But Lollards were pursued throughout the fifteenth century by the authorities and Lollardy was a factor in the religious and political life of the state (Strohm 1998: 32–62, 65–86, 128–52).

Pierce the Ploughman's Crede is a late-fourteenth-century poem preserved in four manuscripts. One is fragmentary and dates from around 1460–70. The other three are all sixteenth-century copies, perhaps indicative of its continuing relevance as reformist religion began to take hold in England. In two of these the poem is appended to texts of *Piers Plowman*, from which it draws inspiration and which it echoes in places (Lawton 1981; von Nolcken 1988). Its narrator is a right-thinking, serious Christian who is worried because he is only partially conversant with the rudiments of his faith: he knows the *paternoster* and most of the *ave*, but needs to be instructed in the *credo* lest the parish priest give him a penance if he does not know it by Easter (9–10). But he is poor and cannot pay for instruction: if somebody teaches him it will have to be 'for Cristes loue' (37). The poem relates his search for basic Christian knowledge and, like many alliterative poems, involves encounters with figures of some authority, but an agenda is gradually disclosed which embodies trenchant criticism of the friars, in part because they have persecuted Wyclif (528–32) and

Walter Brute, the Herefordshire Lollard (657–62), and offers an admiring endorsement of a particular strand of Lollardy.

Because friars have told him that 'alle the frute of the faith was in here foure ordres' (29) the narrator approaches them, each order in turn, but what emerges from these encounters is that the major orders are mutually antagonistic towards each other and mutually disparaging (Lampe 1981). The author of the Wycliffite *Tractatus de Pseudo-Freris* had said: 'yif men askeden of thise foure sectis whether alle thise ordris ben euene goode, thei wolen seye anon, "nay, but oon is betere then an other"' – meaning their own order – and the author of the poem has the friars bear this out. From what the friars say about each other and from what Pierce, the Lollard ploughman, later says emerges a litany of anti-fraternal jibes, some of which go back as far as William of St Amour and many of which appear in Wycliffite polemics. Friars are agents of the devil (460), 'of the kyndrede of Caym' (486), hypocritical Pharisees (487). They are like false apostles (87–93, 708–12), or like false prophets (457–59) who usurp the functions of the secular clergy and sell the sacraments (468–69, 702–18). They are lecherous (44, 59, 83–85), gluttonous (760–65) and slothful. They have fallen away from the ideals of their founders (464–66, 775–78) and have acquired opulent lifestyles. The narrator describes a Dominican priory, perhaps the London Blackfriars (Doyle 1959), emphasising its architectural detail (154–215), suggesting it would have cost 'the tax of ten yer…trewly ygadered' (189), and depicting a well-dressed and overfed member of the order in the refectory:

> A greet cherl and a grym, growen as a tonne,
> With a face as fat as a full bledder
> Blowen bretfull of breth and as a bagge honged   *brimful*
> On bothen his chekes, and his chyn with a chol lollede,   *jowl*
> As greet as a gos eye growen all of grece…
>   (221–25)

Here the comparisons carry the satire – the wine of beer cask (*tonne*), the pig's or sheep's bladder and the goose egg all connote food. The orders are not only greedy but also ungenerous and nobody will teach the narrator his creed unless he becomes a benefactor of the order in some way or pays: as a Carmelite puts it, 'oure power lasteth nought so feer but we some peny fongen' (407). All this contrasts with the poverty of the narrator and, when he appears, the ill-clad Pierce who, with his equally poorly dressed wife and his four thin and 'feble' oxen works the wet and icy fields 'al beslombred in fen as he the plow folwede' (427), while his hungry children cry 'at the londes ende'. Yet it is not from the friars but from this Lollard representative of the agrarian poor that the narrator receives generous friendship, an offer of food and intellectual and religious enlightenment.

There recurs, however, through the poem a subtext which addresses, sporadically and unsystematically, the question of how enlightenment is to be acquired. Lollards valued literacy and books and it is unsurprising that the poem begins with reference to a text and the religious knowledge that may be acquired from it:

> A.   and all myn A.b.c after haue y lerned,
> And patred in my pater-noster iche point after other,   *recited (the Lord's Prayer)*
> And after all myn Aue-marie almost to the ende;
> But all my kare is to comen for y can nohght my Crede...
>   (5–8)

He describes the beginning of the primer, the book of devotions which also served as an elementary schoolbook for the laity and which taught both literacy and the elements of the faith (Scattergood: 2000b: 160–78). The narrator's education has stopped at the creed, but by the end of the poem, thanks to the Lollard ploughman, it has been recited to him and explained (793–821): he has advanced in knowledge one small but important step. So the poem is framed by a specific teaching book and by a precisely ordered process of learning. But as it proceeds, other ways of enlightenment and other texts are mentioned and considered, although most of them are set aside. Images and pictures, which were traditionally used as aids for instructing the unlettered, are here rejected as likely to 'with-drawen his deuocion and dusken his herte' (563) (Aston 1984: 135–72). Nor would moral exempla from stories like the 'gestes of Rome' (43–46) serve. Nor should one give any credence to lullabies purportedly sung by the Virgin Mary to Christ, nor to 'miracles' relating to her life (77–79), nor to miracle plays in general (107). The Bible could obviously be trusted, but not the glosses that traditionally accompanied it, nor the glossators themselves, particularly when they happened to be learned friars:

> Swiche a gome Godes wordes grysliche gloseth;   *man; wickedly*
> Y trowe, he toucheth noght the text but taketh it for a tale.   *believe*
>   (585–86)

The biblical narrative (*tale*), in its literal sense, is ignored and disparaged in favour of the glossator's explanation which is likely to be misleading because 'gloss' has a pejorative association with deceit. The learned, so goes the argument, 'folwen nought fully the feith as fele as the lewede' (826–27), and the ideal preacher and teacher is not necessarily a learned man but rather a man of 'parfite lijf' who is just as likely to be a poor man:

> It mot ben a man of also mek an herte,
> That myghte with his good lijf that Holly Gost fongen;   *receive*
> And thane nedeth him nought neuer for to studyen,
> Ne mighte no maistre ben kald...
>   (830–35)

In the light of this sort of attitude, which sets aside theological and philosophical speculation and relies entirely on the inspiration of the Holy Ghost, all difficulties tend to disappear, even in relation to something as contentious and contested as the Eucharist:

> Therefore studye thou nought theron, ne stere thi wittes,
> It is his blissed body, so bad he vs beleuen.
>
> (824–25)

Because Christ said 'Hoc est corpus meum' (Luke 22:19) everything to the ploughman is clear, though what he asserts is a grotesque oversimplification of what was a complex and dangerous doctrinal issue. But this, in many ways, is typical of the stance the poem endorses. This is not just a polemical Lollard text, but one written from the anti-intellectual, *sola scriptura* side of the movement.

Similarly involving a confrontation between fraternal concerns and Lollards is the sequence generated by the *Jack Upland* polemic – in which, again, an attack on the friars is attributed to a generic, Lollard-orientated countryman. It is not clear whether *Jack Upland* is written in loose alliterative verse or alliterating prose – most recent editors favour the latter – but it is an important text because its provocativeness generated a controversy which produced responses and rejoinders, two of which are in alliterative verse.

Though it attributes itself to a narrator whose name connotes a lack of sophistication and posits an authority based on right-thinking simplicity and directness, *Jack Upland* is cast in an ambitious form. In its opening it sets out the traditional tripartite division of society into 'lordis', 'preestis' and the 'comouns' – a division equated with and sanctioned by the three persons of the Trinity – and seeks to demonstrate how each area has fallen away from its traditional ideals. So the treatise invests itself with a moral and social urgency in terms of contemporary abuses that need to be addressed. But this is simply the preamble to an attack on the friars 'þe fellist folk þat euer Anticrist foond' (JU 69). The narrator's criticisms are in large measure the predictable ones – that the friars were 'laste brouȝt in to þe chirche' (69–70), that there are too many of them amounting to 'greet cumbraunce of þe puple' (357–8), and that their direct relationship with the pope through their provincials means that they are 'not obediente to bisshopis ne lege men to kyngis' (72–73). What is more they pay no 'taligis to oure kyng in help of the rewme & supportynge of pore men' (184–5). Predictably also the wealth of the friars and its contrast with the imitation of apostolic poverty which friars claimed for themselves generates a number of points, and there is a graphic passage on their 'curious & costelew houses & fine & precious cloþinge, delicious and lusti fedynge' which surpasses that of 'lordis & oþere worldly men' (368–71). Their methods of raising money, particularly what Jack Upland sees as their selling of the sacraments, also come in for criticism, particularly the alleged easy penances they give to the rich for sins such as 'pilinge of her tenauntis & lyuinge in leccherie & glotony & oþere heed synnes' (380–81). Nor is he impressed by their learning and disparages, in conventional Lollard fashion, the 'fals fablis...& feined myraclys' of their sermons. He accuses friars of trying to take over some of the functions of the secular clergy and, more than that, of charging 'trewe preestis of erisie & letten þe sowynge of Goddis word' (377–78). He even accuses friars themselves of heresy in their beliefs about the eucharist: 'ȝe seien þat it is an accident wiþouten subject and not Goddis bodi' (393), though this is a charge usually levelled against the Lollards. Though the purpose of the treatise is to attack the friars, the criticisms are framed as questions, often beginning 'whi', and at the end of the text he asks any friar to 'ʒeue Iacke an answere' (409).

This treatise, which appears to date from the last decade of the fourteenth century, is not particularly well organised, not very original and somewhat repetitious. Nevertheless, it had an impact on both reformers and friars. It survives in two late medieval manuscripts and was printed by John Gough in 1536, so it retained some relevance outside its original contemporary context (Heyworth 1967a). It was translated into Latin and influenced the fifteenth-century Wycliffite sermon *Vae Octuplex*, based on the eightfold woes of Matthew 23. It was answered twice, once by the Franciscan John Woodford in a work dated around 1400, and once in alliterative verse by Daw Topias, a fictional friar but one who engages with the Lollard text on a point by point basis.

Friar Daw's Reply, preserved uniquely in Oxford, Bodleian Library MS Digby 41, is odd in the way that its narrator presents himself. His name associates him on the one hand with a jackdaw, a chatterer, and on the other with Chaucer's inconsequential knight Sir Thopas – neither of which is particularly flattering, and both of which may be designed to fashion a narrator, like Jack Upland, who is unsophisticated, so that the reply can appear to be made in kind. But the colophon mentions John Walsingham, so far unidentified, and the author, though in one place he refers to himself as 'lewid as a leke' (45), in another admits to having 'lernede Latyn bi roote of clerkes' while he was a steward at 'Mertoun Halle' (725–26). He exploits his ambiguous position, systematically disparaging Jack Upland's intelligence: he quotes the Bible, sometimes in Latin and sometimes uses the standard gloss as well (425–30); sometimes, as in a passage on the eucharist, he takes ideas from Aquinas (855–62). And it is through his skill in deploying his learning that he seeks to refute Jack Upland, as in his rebuttal of the Wycliffite notion that in begging friars do not imitate Christ because 'he had no need þerto' (JU 273–74) since he was lord of all. First, he distinguishes between Christ in his divinity where he 'is lord of all þingis' and Christ in his human form where 'he was nedi & pore' (701–4), and then supports this by texts such as Matthew 7:20: 'the foxes have holes and the birds of the air have nests; but the son of man hath not where to lay his head'. To this he adds texts referring to beggars (Matthew 20:30, Luke 16:20, Acts 3:12) who all received divine aid (713–39). This again is supported by texts, quoted in Latin, from Jerome and St Bernard (718–22). But Friar Daw's treatise is not wholly defensive and he makes his own points against the Lollards. Wyclif had been condemned as a heretic (71–74), he says, and his followers are also guilty of creating 'divisioun' in the church (649–53). Since the main support for Lollardy comes from among urban artisans (865–67), he argues, there can be little hope that they will be able to understand anything as difficult as the intricacies of the Eucharistic controversy. But the main point, made indirectly, is that Lollards are deceitful in enticing people into the sect: they are wolves in sheep's clothing (383–85); they are ready to 'snarre simple soules' (188–89); they poison the people with 'honyed venym' (127–28); they are like undetected carriers of the plague (416). This is skilful propaganda. He seeks to make Lollards pariahs in a society in which they at once tried to hide and tried to make converts. He seeks to isolate them from the sources of their strength.

This reply ends with a challenge to Jack Upland: if everything has not been sufficiently answered he should say, so that it could be 'amendid' (925–6), and this is taken up, in the margin of MS Digby 41, by a third contributor to this debate. There is doubt about when this text, which is usually entitled *Jack Upland's Rejoinder*, was written, but P. L. Heyworth thinks it is the author's holograph and would date it around 1450 (Heyworth 1967b). Though the author calls himself Jack Upland he is not identical with the initiator of this sequence: he is much more intellectually sophisticated and is not to be fooled by the friar's 'gildyn glose' as 'symple hertes' are (71–72). He has the learning to compete with Friar Daw on his own terms, as when he responds to the friar's defence of the splendour of their buildings by reference to Solomon's temple (I Kings 6) with his own references to the fathers:

> Daw, þou leggist Salomon for ȝour hie houses   *refer to*
> Bot olde holy doctoures ben aȝen þee here,
> And specialy Ierom, þat saiþ in þe lawe:
> Who wil allege þe temple for glorie of our chirche,   *cite*
> Forsake he to be christen & he be newe a Iewe.
>   12a q 2a Gloria episcopi.
> For siþ þe pore lorde, he saiþ, hallowed his pore chirche,
> Take we Cristis crosse, he saiþ, & counte we delices claye.
>   (63–70)

The last two lines translate the appropriate decree from Gratian's authoritative book on canon law. And there follows argument after argument, rebuttal after rebuttal, but nothing significant that is new. Nor is there very much to take matters on in the contribution of another Lollard supporter who adds three groups of lines in spaces left vacant in the margin of the manuscript: some lines condemn Friar Daw's tendentious and opportunistic use of Biblical texts; some deal with the alleged preference of friars for their own prayers instead of the Lord's Prayer; some deal not very skilfully or very satisfactorily with the doctrine of the Eucharist. Predictably, there are plenty of insults for Friar Daw, who is described as a 'jangelyng jay' and 'on of þe falsest þat euer j saw write'.

But by this time the pressure has gone out of the debate and much of the elegance has disappeared from the writing, which takes the form of a severely etiolated version of the alliterative long-line. So it is perhaps appropriate that this poem should end up in the margin.

References and Further Reading

Primary Texts

Barr, Helen (ed.) (1993). *The Piers Plowman Tradition.* London: J. M. Dent.

Dean, James (ed.) (1991). *Six Ecclesiastical Satires.* Kalamazoo, MI: TEAMS Medieval Institute Publications.

Hanna, Ralph III. (ed.) (1974). *The Awntyrs off Arthure at the Terne Wathelyn.* Manchester: Manchester University Press.

Heyworth, P. L. (ed.) (1968). *Jack Upland, Friar Daw's Reply, and Upland's Rejoinder.* Oxford: Oxford University Press.

Lumby, J. R. (ed.) (1870). *Bernardus De Cura Rei Familiaris.* Early English Text Society, o.s. 42. Oxford: Oxford University Press.

Trigg, Stephanie (ed.) (1990). *Wynnere and Wastoure.* Early English Text Society, o.s. 297. Oxford: Oxford University Press.

Turville-Petre, Thorlac (ed.) (1989). *Alliterative Poetry of the Later Middle Ages.* London: Routledge.

Secondary Reading

Aston, M. (1984). *Lollards and Reformers; Images and Literacy in late Medieval Religion.* London: Hambledon Press.

Barr, H. (1990). The relationship of 'Richard the Redeles' and 'Mum and the Sothsegger'. *Yearbook of Langland Studies,* 4, 105–33.

Barr, H. (1992). The treatment of natural law in 'Richard the Redeles' and 'Mum and the Sothsegger'. *Leeds Studies in English,* 23, 49–80.

Bestoul, T. (1974). *Satire and Allegory in Wynnere and Wastoure.* Lincoln: University of Nebraska Press.

Cannon, C. (2008). *Middle English Literature: A Cultural History.* Cambridge: Polity Press.

Coleman, J. (1981). *Medieval Readers and Writers 1350–1400.* New York: Columbia University Press.

Coote, L. A. (2000). *Prophecy and Public Affairs in Later Medieval England.* Woodbridge: York Medieval Press.

Doyle, A. I. (1959). An unrecognised piece of 'Pierce the Ploughman's Crede' and other work by its scribe. *Speculum,* 34, 1959, 428–36.

Ferster, J. (1996). *The Literature and Politics of Counsel in Late Medieval England.* Philadelphia: University of Pennsylvania Press.

Heyworth, P. L. (1967a). The earliest black-letter editions of 'Jack Upland'. *Huntington Library Quarterly,* 30, 307–14.

Heyworth, P. L. (1967b). 'Jack Upland's Rejoinder', a Lollard Interpolator and 'Piers Plowman' B. X. 249 ff. *Medium Ævum,* 36, 242–8.

Hudson, A. (1988). *The Premature Reformation: Wycliffite Texts and Lollard History.* Oxford: Clarendon Press.

Jacobs, N. (1985). The typology of debate and the interpretation of 'Wynnere and Wastoure'. *Review of English Studies,* n.s. 36, 481–500.

Lampe, D. (1981). The satiric strategy of 'Pierce the Ploughman's Crede'. In B. S. Levy and P. S. Szarmach (eds). *The Alliterative Tradition in the Fourteenth Century* (pp. 69–80). Kent, OH: Kent State University Press.

Lawton, D. (1981). Lollardy and the 'Piers Plowman' tradition. *Modern Language Review,* 76, 780–93.

Salter, E. (1978). The timeliness of 'Wynnere and Wastoure'. *Medium Ævum,* 47, 40–65.

Scattergood, J. (1971). *Politics and Poetry in the Fifteenth Century.* London: Blandford.

Scattergood, J. (2000a). Authority and resistance: The political verse. In S. Fein (ed.). *Studies in the Harley Manuscript: The Scribes, Contents, and Social Contexts of British Library MS Harley 2253.* Kalamazoo, MI: Western Michigan University.

Scattergood, J. (2000b). *The Lost Tradition: Essays on Middle English Alliterative Poetry.* Dublin: Four Courts Press.

Simpson, J. (1990). The constraints of satire in 'Piers Plowman' and 'Mum and the Sothsegger'. In H. Phillips (ed.). *Langland, the Mystics and the Medieval English Religious Tradition: Essays in Honour of S.S. Hussey* (pp. 11–30). Cambridge: D. S. Brewer.

Strohm, P. (1998). *England's Empty Throne: Usurpation and the Language of Legitimation 1399–1422.* New Haven and London: Yale University Press.

Thomson, J. A. F. *The Later Lollards 1414–1520.* Oxford: Oxford University Press.

Von Nolcken, C. (1988). 'Piers Plowman', the Wycliffites and 'Pierce the Ploughman's Crede'. *Yearbook of Langland Studies,* 2, 72–102.

Wawn, A. (1983). Truth-telling and tradition in 'Mum and the Sothsegger'. *Yearbook of English Studies,* 13, 270–87.

Poets and Poems

20

The Poet of *Pearl, Cleanness* and *Patience*

A. V. C. Schmidt

I

Standing beside Chaucer, Langland and Gower, the named major poets of the age of Richard II (1377–99), is the anonymous author of *Pearl, Cleanness, Patience* and *Sir Gawain and the Green Knight*. These four masterpieces of the Alliterative Revival are preserved in a unique vellum codex, London, British Library manuscript Cotton Nero A. x. It belongs to the last quarter of the fourteenth century (Doyle in Lawton 1982: 92), and its dozen coloured illustrations to the same date or to 1400–10 (compare Reichardt 1997 with Edwards 1997). *Sir Gawain* was edited for the Bannatyne Club by Sir Frederic Madden (1839), and the other three poems by Richard Morris for the Early English Text Society (1864). The standard study text of all four is by Andrew and Waldron (1978, 4th edn 2002) from which all citations are given here, with occasional reference to the scholarly editions of *Pearl* (Gordon), *Patience* (Anderson) and *Cleanness* (Menner). Gollancz's EETS facsimile (1923), still invaluable for editors since the original manuscript has faded somewhat, reproduces the illustrations in half-tone, as do Edwards and (in part) Reichardt.

The manuscript belonged to Henry Savile of Banke, Yorkshire, in the early seventeenth century and passed from him to Sir Robert Cotton, whose library was left to the nation and housed in the British Museum in 1752. It may have belonged to, or even been made for, the Stanleys of Staffordshire and Cheshire (Wilson 1979), one of the knightly families in whose manor houses, it has been speculated, 'the masters of alliterative verse pursued their calling' (Bennett in Brewer and Gibson 1997: 78). Most scholars ascribe all four pieces to one poet, though neither their consistent North West Midland dialect nor their 'contiguity' suffices to establish '[a] presumption of shared authorship' (Andrew in Brewer and Gibson 1997: 23; Borroff 2006: 42). Both dialect and contiguity have only negative value, even the second only removing possible objections based on *difference* of dialect; so without external evidence, the 'presumption' rests on the works' content, structure, theme and style 'in the fullest sense of that word'.[1] However, since Spearing 1970 there has been near-consensus on the poems' common authorship (Davenport 1978: 1–2; Prior 1996: 4), and their complex numerical or 'tectonic' patterns (Crawford 1993; Condren 2002) reveal a structural 'unity' that renders scepticism hard to sustain.

Still debatable is whether the Cotton Nero poet composed *St Erkenwald*, an alliterative saint's legend in the same East Cheshire/North Staffordshire dialect preserved in BL Harley 2250 (date 1477). Benson's case (1965) against its stylistic affinity with the other four is accepted by Andrew (1997) but has been challenged by Borroff (2006). *Erkenwald* certainly has a 'less exuberant, sparer and more concise' manner (Burrow and Turville-Petre 1992: 198), but this need not tell against its ascription to the *Pearl*-poet; it is a manner well suited to handling such problems as whether righteous pagans are saved, and lines 267–76 even recall the discussion of this topic in *Piers Plowman* (B version, Passus XII 280–90).[2] At the 'tectonic' level, the poem's division into two equal halves of 176 long-lines (perhaps to be arranged in 44 four-line stanzas) recalls *Pearl* (see section II); and if *St Erkenwald* is authentic, its absence from Cotton Nero could be due to its composition for the occasion of the elevation of Erkenwald's feast to first-class status in 1386 (Borroff speculatively locates it between the pairs *Cleanness-Patience* and *Pearl-Gawain*). Finally, in respect of theme, while one Cotton Nero narrative treats the sixth and another the first of the 'Beatitudes' of Mt 5:3–11 ('Blessed are the clean of heart' [*Cleanness* 24]; 'Blessed are the poor in spirit' [*Patience* 11]), *Erkenwald*'s implicit theme is arguably the *fourth*, 'Blessed are they that hunger and thirst after justice'. This Beatitude may be what is alluded to by the revived corpse of the pre-Christian judge whose tomb is discovered in St Paul's Cathedral:

> I hent harmes ful ofte to holde hom to riȝt,
> Bot for wothe ne wele, ne wrathe ne drede
> Ne for maystrie ne for mede, ne for no monnes aghe
> I remewit neuer fro þe riȝt by reson myn awen.
>
> (232–5)

I very often suffered to keep (the people) in the way of justice, but never myself – for harm, benefit, anger, fear, influence or financial advantage – departed deliberately from justice.[3]

Limitations of space prevent further discussion of this work (see John Scattergood's chapter on Alliterative Poetry: Religion and Morality), but recent scholarship seems to be favouring the *Pearl*-poet's authorship of *Erkenwald*.[4]

The Cotton Nero pieces are written by one hand; but textual errors in each poem establish that the scribe was not the author, his Cheshire dialect being slightly more northerly than the poet's Staffordshire (Duggan 1997). An inscription, in the main hand, of the Garter motto *Honi soyt qui mal pence* (fol. 124v) establishes 1348, the year in which Edward III founded the Order, as a downward limit for the copying of the poems. To place their composition between 1350 and 1400 would fit with the known history of Middle English alliterative poetry, as would the descriptions of armour and supposed parallels with historical personages and events in *Gawain*. These have led Cooke and Boulton (1999) to favour the earlier part of this half-century, and they even propose as 'the patron of the *Gawain*-poet' Henry of Grosmont, Earl of Lancaster (author of the *Livre des Seyntz Medicines* and a founder member of the Garter), the father of Chaucer's original 'White' in *The Book of the Duchess*. Most scholars, however, recognise in the bedroom-scenes in Fitt Three of *Gawain*, for example, a tonal sophistication equal to that of the bedroom-scene in Book Three of Chaucer's *Troilus and Criseyde*, the 'courtly' masterpiece of the 'Ricardian Age';[5] and since 'stylistically *Pearl* would not be out of place in the international gothic culture associated with the court of Richard II from the mid-1380s', a more plausible 'patron' might be one of those 'expatriate' Cheshire gentry who 'broadened and strengthened local links with great magnates and the court' (Bennett 1997: 84).[6]

The grounds for preferring a later date are not wholly speculative; but the chronology of fourteenth-century alliterative works remains uncertain. *Winner and Waster*'s topical references suggest 1352–3; *William of Palerne* was written (according to its author 'William') at the behest of Humphrey de Bohun, Earl of Hereford (d. 1361); and the Z and A texts of *Piers Plowman* belong on internal grounds respectively after 1362 and before 1370, B to 1378–9, and C to 1386–8. In attempts at dating, two *Piers Plowman* passages have been claimed to show our poet's influence on Langland. In the B-text, the treatment of 'patient poverty' (e.g. in B XIV 218–20) has been compared to the presentation of the virtue of patience as an efficacious means to master all the vices in *Patience* 1–4. And the close verbal parallel between *Cleanness* 1638 'And þe byȝe of bryȝt golde abowte þyn nekke' and *Piers Plowman* C Pr 178 'Bere beyus of bryghte gold al aboute here nekkes' has long been noticed (Menner 1920, supported by Anderson 1969: 21–2). But this seems unlikely; for whereas *Piers Plowman* was a well-known London poem, the Cotton Nero pieces enjoyed very limited circulation (though *Gawain* is echoed in the early fifteenth-century Northern poem *The Awntyrs of Arthur*) and their dialect would have been found difficult by readers in the capital like Chaucer and Gower. More probably, *Patience* reflects Langland's treatment of this virtue; and there are suggestive similarities between the contrast of *cortesye* and *couenaund* in *Pearl* 481, 563 and *Piers Plowman* C XIV 214–15.

It hardly strains belief that an anonymous North-West Midlands writer should have read the best known of all Ricardian alliterative poems. Reminiscences in *Pearl* of the *Olympia* (*c.* 1360), a Latin Eclogue by Boccaccio on his dead daughter Violante, could be coincidental (Gollancz 1921: 244); but if genuine, they would accord with placing *Pearl* in the 1370s. So would the poem's apparent echoes of *The Divine Comedy* (Kean 1967), a work Chaucer might have brought back from his first Italian journey (1373). Contact with Chaucer's circle would not have been difficult if our poet worked as a clerk for a Cheshire gentleman of the King's household during the 1380s and 1390s; and without assuming 'influence', we may detect a shared 'courtly' suppleness of tone in Lady Bertilak's conversations with Gawain and Troilus's with Criseyde:

'I schall happe yow here þat oþer half als
And syþen carp with my kny3t þat I *ca3t* haue'
(*Sir Gawain* III 1224–5)

'Now be ye *kaught*; now is there but we tweyne!
Now yeldeth yow, for othere bote is non!'
(*Troilus* III 1207–8)

Pearl's use of the twelve-line 'extended ballade' stanza leads Fein (1997) to propose a date after 1380, when the famous 'Vernon' Lyrics were written in this form, while its cultural sophistication suggests to Bowers (2001) a social and political context that supports the 1390s. Unfortunately, the exact place of the four poems in fourteenth century literary history cannot be established without knowledge of the author's name. Attempts have been made to identify him, most ingeniously by Kooper (1982), who finds the name John Massey concealed in stanza five of *Sir Gawain* in a cryptogram, a signature and an acrostic. But while such attempts have not satisfied strict criteria for recognising authorial encipherment in literary texts, further scrutiny of these works, which reveal fascination with the properties and relationships of numbers, may yet uncover convincing clues to their author's identity (adding *Erkenwald* to the canon would not supply a name, since it too is anonymous).[7]

Cleanness and *Patience*, which the manuscript places second and third in order, are sometimes considered earlier works because of their relative formal simplicity and dependence on Old Testament books for narrative material (though the former opens with the Parable of the Wedding Feast [Mt 22:1–14; Lk 14:16–24] to illustrate the meaning of 'cleanness'). Both poems draw their homiletic 'theme', however, from the New Testament (Matthew 5:3–10 is cited at *Cleanness* 23–8 and *Patience* 9–28). *Patience* identifies 'patience' as the moral virtue signified by Matthew's first and eighth Beatitudes, which call blessed those who 'han in hert pouerté' (i.e. the poor in spirit) and those who 'con her hert stere' (interpreting 'suffer persecution for justice' sake' as 'exercise self-control in adversity' [*Patience* 13, 27]). *Cleanness* focuses on the sixth beatitude, 'Blessed are the pure in heart'. Even if its illustrative use of three 'exemplary sequences' (as opposed to *Patience*'s one) need not imply later composition (cf. Andrew and Waldron 1978), their explicit use of the same Gospel passage may argue for placing *both* before *Pearl*. Yet the latter could be claimed to exemplify implicitly the Third Beatitude (Mt 5:5): 'Blessed are they that mourn; for they shall be comforted', translated in *Patience* as 'Thay ar happen also þat for her harme wepes, / For þay schal comfort encroche in kythes ful mony' [17–18]). And though *Pearl*'s Gospel source in fitts IX–X is the Vineyard Parable (Mt 20:1–16), in citing this 'theme-text' in its *liturgical* context:

As Mathew melez in your messe   *speaks; mass*
In sothful gospel of God almy3t
(*Pearl* 497–8)

it recalls closely the lines in *Patience* (9–10)

> I herde on a halyday at a *hyȝe masse,*
> How *Mathew melede* þat his Mayster His meyny con teche.   *followers*

Such verbal affinities closely connect the three religious poems; yet though the pearl image, central to *Pearl* and used metaphorically at *Cleanness* 1113–32 in a passage on shrift, is found in *Sir Gawain* (in a related but different figurative use) at 2364–5, it is absent from *Patience*. And while recurrent motifs, sources and images support common authorship of all four pieces, they make it no easier to determine the chronology of the homiletic narratives relative to the dream vision than that of *Pearl* to the chivalric romance *Sir Gawain*. Similarly, the poems' remarkable 'tectonic' patterning, which authenticates their manuscript sequence, indicates only that they are to be *read* in succession (Condren 2002), not that they were composed in that order. An especially close link between *Pearl* and *Gawain* may be suggested by both poems' use of 101 stanzas and a complex verse-form; but *Pearl* outdoes *Gawain* in its demanding rhyme scheme and concatenation of stanzas and stanza-groups.

II

Although the poems have few textual errors, two need discussion before a detailed examination of the poet's structural aesthetic. *Pearl* 472 must be scribally lost, and probably had a sense like Gollancz's conjectured 'Me þynk þou spekeȝ now ful wronge.' *Patience*'s lines from 'Bitwene þe stele...' to 'lost be þerfor' that appear after 'Þat on hande...hyȝe worlde' may have been cancelled but mistakenly copied by the scribe (Anderson 1969, after Gollancz); re-positioning them after 509 (Andrew and Waldron 1978, following another suggestion of Gollancz) improves the flow of sense without perceptible disturbance (unless the lines are printed in quatrains). It may even be that both position-shift and quatrain-format are correct, if the poet *intentionally* omitted a line after 512 (= Anderson 1969: 515) in order to make *Patience*'s line-total echo *Gawain*'s. Counting *Pearl* 472 and *Gawain*'s motto, the line-totals are: *Pearl* 1212; *Cleanness* 1812; *Patience* 531; *Gawain* 2531. The 'outer' poems composed in stanzas and rhyme add up to 3743 lines, the 'inner' poems in unrhymed quatrains to 2343, giving 6086 lines altogether. Now the ratio of this line-total (6086) to the sum of the outer pair (3743) is 1.625, which almost equals that of the outer to the inner pair (3743 : 2343 = 1.597). Both ratios closely approach the proportion known as 'division into mean and extreme ratio', whereby, of three ascending magnitudes *a*, *b* and *c*, the ratio of *a* to *b* is the same as that of the sum of *a* and *b* to *c*, or $a:b = (a+b):c$. This proportion was called in the Middle Ages the 'Divine Proportion', on account of its mathematically unique property as 'a continuous ratio that leads toward...the infinitely large or the infinitely small...[d]epending on whether one proceeds from the largest to the smallest magnitude, or from the smallest to the largest' (Condren 2002: 14, 15–16).[8] Within *Cleanness*, too, sectional divisions highlighted by large and small capitals indicate the operation of the same Golden Ratio, validating these markings as more than non-significant features of scribal layout (Crawford 1993). Finally, *Patience*'s five-fold division by initial manuscript capitals has also generated intriguing (if complicated) 'tectonic' analyses of the work's 'poetic mathematics' (Gilligan 1989).[9] Taken as a single unified sequence, the four poems have been convincingly argued by Condren to represent the Cosmos as conceived by medieval man.[10]

Though such analyses of the poet's 'fayre formez' (*Cleanness* 3) are arrestingly precise, it is left to the reader's alertness to recognise, for example, that the product of 12×12 in *Pearl*'s line-total is the numerologically significant 144 (see below), or that the pentangle's 'five fives' (*Gawain* 640–65) are recalled in the 2525 obtained by taking this poem's last long-line (which echoes its first) as its 'notional final line'. *Gawain*'s 101 stanzas are not grouped into sections, but *Pearl*'s fall into 20 fitts, all but one containing five stanzas. *Pearl*'s total of 101 stanzas (indirectly confirmed as correct by *Gawain*) makes it unlikely that fitt XV's sixth stanza (lines 901–12) is otiose (Gordon and Gordon 1953: 88), since it clearly contributes to the meaning. Indeed, in choosing 101 the poet may have aimed to *avoid* the 'perfect' number 100 (the *Divine Comedy*'s total of cantos), so as to reflect 'structurally' St Gregory's teaching that perfection is found through acknowledging imperfection: 'The more imperfect a man sees himself to be, the more perfectly may he rise from there to the height of humility' (*Moralia in Job* 5.4.5, cited in Straw 1988:188).[11] *Pearl*'s 101 stanzas are, of course, 'numerically' necessary to yield a line-total the product of whose digit-pairs 1212 is 144. And 12 certainly proves to be important in *Pearl*: it is the number of the Heavenly Jerusalem's foundations and coursings (991–2), precious stones (994) and gates (1034–5); multiplied by 1000 it yields the city's area of 12,000 square furlongs; and its square 144 represents the city-wall's height in cubits.[12] As the 'number of the Blessed' (Rev 21:16–17; *Pearl* 869–70), its square multiplied by a thousand (= 144,000) both discloses the functional significance of the 'numerical' product 144 and intimates a mystical congruence between city and inhabitants that is already implicit in Revelation's vision of 'New Jerusalem' as a 'spatial' symbol of spiritual beatitude. But in addition to arithmetical patterning, *Pearl* uses *geometric* patterning: line 1 ('Perle plesaunte to prynces paye') is echoed in line 1212 ('And precious perlez vnto His pay'), this circularity imaging the form of a pearl. Somewhat less obviously, 'squareness' also plays a part in the design. Construction *ad quadratum* 'on the basis of the square' was favoured by Gothic cathedral architects, in part because the square's arithmetical equivalent (four) was associated with the Four Elements of the material world (in contrast to the spiritual world figured by the circle). The poem's 'macrostructure' is reflected in its 'microstructure' in that the Extended Ballade Stanza resembles a 'double square' of eight lines joined to a 'single square' of four lines by the b-rhyme, which creates a 'bridge' couplet at lines 8–9.[13] Finally, analysis of the stanza's 'quadrate' tectonics reveals a remarkable result: that the ratio of its *mean* (8) to its *whole* (12) is 2:3, or approximately 0.6, which is the reciprocal of the Divine Proportion *phi*.

At each level of 'tectonic' structuring, the *Pearl*-poet arouses admiration for the skill with which (in Chaucer's words) he sends

> his hertes line out from withinne
> Aldirfirst his purpose for to wynne   *From the start*
> (*Troilus and Criseyde*, I 1067–9).[14]

And close study of his *ad quadratum* ground-plan further reveals how it was by adding a sixth stanza to fitt XV that he made it possible for stanza 51 (= lines 601–12) to stand *exactly* at the poem's 'sovereign mid-point' (Spearing 1985: 126–30; Fein 1999b: 30), acting as a 'hinge' between the 50 stanzas that flank it like the left and right hand panels of a diptych.[15] A similar 'diptychal' pattern on a smaller scale occurs within the second half (the 'right-hand panel' of the 'diptych'), where the aforementioned extra stanza in XV occupies a *secondary* 'mid-point' position between the two fitt-sequences that run from XI to XV:5 and from XVI to XX:5. This stanza, no. 76 (lines 901–912), significantly echoes the theme of the 'sovereign' central stanza (with 'more and lasse' 601 compare 'Neuer þe les' 901). In this way, against the heavenly 'sympelnesse' of the Pearl Maiden, for whom 'þe grace of God is gret inoghe' (612), the poet 'wins his purpose' of counterpoising the Dreamer's earthly 'bone', which is provoked by his sense of the uncertainty ('joparde' 602) of divine justice.

The challenge of tectonic geometry would have been relatively straightforward compared with that of attaining 'divinely proportioned' arithmetical line-ratios; for without decimals, the poet was obliged to multiply compound fractions, achieving only approximate results. But his computational skill, his commitment (as firm as that of Boethius or Dante) to the philosophical and artistic significance of 'measure' and his conviction that cosmic 'purpos' is discernible in (and expressible through) mathematical ratios all suggest that he was a learned cleric trained in the *Quadrivium* (the second part of the university Arts course, consisting of Arithmetic, Geometry, Music and Astronomy). Like similar inferences about the education of Langland, who used a distinctive formal syllogism at B VIII 20–6 (Schmidt 1995: 438), this conclusion is probably more solid than the 'biographical' assumption that the *Pearl*-poet was a married clerk in minor orders who lost an infant daughter.[16] The manuscript sequence (as said above) need not be that of the poems' composition; but the formal complexity, tonal sophistication and inventive originality of the two 'outer' poems' suggest that they were the later, their proportions being expertly adapted to those of the two 'inner' poems. What is certain is that the writer's 'poetic mathematics' evokes in the outer poems an unchanging spiritual 'order' against which he sets the emotional tumult of human beings before the reality of death. The two homiletic narratives, for their part, make clear that his deepest interest as a moralist lay in *breaches* of that order. For while the poems' preoccupation with integrity and obedience suggests the spiritual harmony possible if man obeyed God's ordinances, they also depict (with a power unparalleled before Milton) the macrocosmic disruption caused by sin.

The art of the Cotton Nero poems is manifested not only in their architectonic beauty but also in the concrete force of their diction and the athletic vigour of their alliterative verse, which stretches the traditional medium to its limits. If *Pearl* enables us to *see* 'another world', *Cleanness* makes us *feel* with equal immediacy the remarkable things of 'this world'. To take one example, in lines 1445–1500, between 'bracketing' references to Baltazar's service of Satanas 'wyth bost and wyth pryde' and his transformation into 'a boster on benche…dronkken as þe deuel', the poet gives us an extraordinarily vivid description of the Temple 'gere' designed by Solomon 'Wyth alle þe syence þat hym sende þe souerayn Lorde' (1454). The great candelabrum's 'wyly' carving is endowed with a sensuous plasticity like that of the contemporary arcade in Ely Cathedral's Lady Chapel (Clifton-Taylor 1967: 184):

> þe boȝes bryȝt þerabof, brayden of golde,
> Braunches bredande þeron, and bryddes þer seten
> Of many koynt kyndes, of fele kyn hues,
> As þay with wynge vpon wynde hade waged her fyþeres
> (1481–4)

As striking here as the fantastic imagery is the wittily foregrounded 'union of opposites' from which medieval aesthetics taught that beauty arises – stillness and motion, immobility and vitality, solidity and lightness. 'Bryȝt', 'koynt' and 'fele kyn' all testify to the poet's passion for the luminous, the ingenious, the aboundingly various. But whereas his contemporary Langland marvels at God's 'kynde craft' displayed in nature's beauty –

> I seiȝ floures in þe fryth and hir faire colours
> And how amonge þe grene gras grewe so manye hewes
> (B XI 364–5)

the *Cleanness*-poet lauds man's 'curious crafte', which honours the Creator by applying 'syence' to 'compas and kest' his 'clene' poems (1452–5). For it is surely hard not to detect here the master wordsmith's pleasure in the goldsmith's art as tacitly celebrating the poetic 'syence' shown in making *fyþeres* assonate with *wynge* and *wynde* while relinquishing their alliterating consonant. Just as the poet's larger structural forms exemplify a Boethian–Augustinian 'aesthetic of proportion', his delight in colour pays homage to the complementary 'aesthetic of light' that derives from 'Dionysius the Pseudo-Areopagite', the sixth-century Christian Neoplatonist author of a number of theological works that deeply influenced medieval ideas about the nature of beauty (Von Simson 1956; Bruyne 1998 [1946]).

III

Cleanness illustrates the evil of sexual impurity (and the value of purity) through three 'negative exempla' of grave breaches of Natural Law (the Folk before the Flood; the

Cities of the Plain; Baltazar's Feast), all of which are ferociously punished. This Law (263) is not a thing of ascetic rigour, for it is said to find proper expression in physical love between spouses, which the poet celebrates with 'courtly' delicacy as a privileged residue of the prelapsarian state (*Cl* 697–710).[17] But precisely because he regards such a *craft* as *kynde* (697), he sees the Sodomites' *asyse* or 'custom' (844) as a wilful rejection of God's *skyl* or 'rational plan' and their perversion as arising (like Baltazar's) from a *heþyng* or 'contempt' of God (Lecklider 1997: 89) that is also *heþyng of seluen* 'contempt for oneself' (710, 579): 'scorning nature' (709), they scorn Nature's God. However, while very severe against *all* 'fylþe of þe flesch' that 'bysulpez [defiles] mannez saule' (547, 575), *Cleanness*, strikingly, emphasises sodomy rather than fornication as the *chief* sin against natural law. Divine punishment is therefore 'condign', befitting the sin (as specified in Wisdom 11:17): 'wode stremez' (364) and 'felle [...] fyr' (954) fall from above and rise from below to symbolise at once God's anger and nature's indignation at the *heþyng* both the Antediluvians and the Sodomites show towards their spiritual and bodily *kynde*.[18]

Against the arrogant lawlessness of the sinners the first and second exempla set the reason-guided righteousness of Noah (328) and the courteous humility of Abraham and Lot, who both wash the feet of their divine guests (617–18, 802). The 'cleanness' of these *positive* exemplars is described as earning the blessing of a long and prosperous life. In the third exemplum, it may not be immediately obvious how Baltazar's 'boba-unce and blasfamye' (1712) differs from Nabugodenozar's (1661), until Daniel points out that he has 'His vessayles avyled in vanyte vnclene' (1713). For just as the 'vessel' of the human body is seen to be defiled by wrong intercourse, so the cup consecrated for use in the Jewish Holy of Holies (a 'type' of the Eucharistic chalice [Lecklider 1997: 191]) stands as a metonym for the king's body. When Baltazar drinks from it to his 'wenches', he too displays *heþyng* towards both himself and 'Hym þat alle goudes giues' (1528): in shocking contrast to Abraham's moderate (but not meagre) hospitality (620–46), his banquet's flaunted excesses defy the God who, as a key biblical text of the Middle Ages has it, 'ordered all things in measure, and number, and weight' (Wisd 11:21). In all three exempla, divine punishment purges sin (by water, fire or blood) and solemnly warns the world of judgement if 'God þay forȝeten' (1528).

Only a third as long as the poem on purity, *Patience*'s engagingly lively re-telling of the Book of Jonah 'negatively exemplifies' the virtue that it understands essentially as acceptance of one's 'destyne' without 'grychchyng' or complaint (49, 51). When commanded by God to preach repentance to the sinful Ninevites, Jonah, fearing what they may do to him, takes ship to escape; but as in *Cleanness*, the sea obediently performs God's bidding, so that when the sailors seek relief from its turbulence by throwing the prophet overboard, he ends in the jaws of a whale 'beten fro þe abyme' (247–8). Tactile alliterative sound-groups brilliantly mimic Jonah's horrible experience as 'He glydez in by þe giles þurȝ glaym ande glette [slime and filth]' (269); and the description of his diminutive figure entering 'As mote in at a munster dor, so mukel wern his chawlez' exploits 'Miltonically' antithetical magnitudes to image the beast's interior as a grotesque 'cathedral' where man can humbly discover his infinitesimal littleness. Jonah's ordeal teaches him to respect God's omnipresent power and to ask forgiveness for his insubordination. Though not a model character like that 'cleaner' seafarer Noah, he is allowed to fore-glimpse Hell in the whale's 'stomak þat stank as þe deuel' (274–5) so that he might be spared the reality; for Jonah's change of heart is the precondition of bringing the Ninevites to repent and receive forgiveness of their 'malys' (70).

It is here that the terse yet tonally varied *Patience* exhibits an engagingly sardonic humour absent from the longer but more monotone *Cleanness*. For neither God's 'patience' (long-suffering) towards both prophet and Ninevites nor three days spent in 'a bouel of þat best' brooding on 'His myȝt and His merci, His mesure [moderation] þenne' (293–5) serve to quench *his* resentment. Jonah may not have come to grief, but as he wonders why God threatens those he means to forgive anyway, he grows vexed that his warning has been proved 'false' (by being heeded!) The irony climaxes when the 'janglande' prophet (433) sees his beloved woodbine shelter destroyed by a diminutive 'worme' (as effective an agent of omnipotence as the 'wylde walterande whal') and, when asked by God why he is enraged 'for so lytel', promptly raps out the droll rejoinder 'Hit is not lyttel [...] but lykker to ryȝt ('much more a question of what is just')' (493).

Jonah's woodbine may indeed be a 'little' *cumfort* (485) to lose compared with a beloved child carried off by death; but his protest comically foreshadows the *Pearl*-Dreamer's more serious 'temptyng' of divine 'wyt' (903). Similarly, God's justification of his mercy to mankind anticipates the Maiden's in the Parable of the Vineyard. Lines 501–23 reveal a Creator motivated by pity more than anger, seeking to forgive rather than punish, and 521–3 show how *divine* 'patience' towards human ill-doing teaches by example how human beings should treat each other:

> Couþe I not þole bot as þou, þer þryued ful fewe.   *endure*
> I may not be so malicious and mylde be halden,   *stern*
> For malice is noȝt to mayntyne boute mercy withinne.   *without*

And here, it is because *Patience*'s all-powerful God uses humble 'New Testament' accents that guilty Nineveh is not 'swolȝed swyftly with þe swart erþe' (363). Finally, the poem's unconventional exploration of 'suffraunce' (529) as entailing both strictness towards oneself and mildness to others anticipates *Pearl*'s great central stanza, with its unexpected insistence that God is 'large' ('generous') 'Queþersoeuer He dele nesch oþer harde' (gently or sternly). The lesson for Prophet and Dreamer is that *everything* God sends, pain or pleasure, must be accepted as a 'gift' – quite the hardest lesson for mankind to learn.

IV

If *Pearl* is not to be thought of as 'a continuous allegory, in which the primary elements of the literal narrative yield other, more or less concealed meanings' (Cherniss 1987:

167), then its many symbols require to be interpreted in relation to their immediate context. The 'makellez perle' of Matthew's miniature parable (Mt 13:45–6), for instance, is an analogy for 'þe reme of heuenesse clere' (733–5), while the priceless pearl placed at the centre of the Maiden's breast 'in token of pes' (742), possesses, like a priest's mass-vestments, a spiritual signification that *follows* upon its literal function (see 220–7). *Pearl*, like the other Cotton Nero poems, 'continually force[s] readers to confront the very concept of infinity' (Condren 2002: 41); but this does not necessitate denying (as Condren thinks) 'the felt life it portrays' and 'the human dilemmas it features'. *Pearl* especially *could* not enforce such a 'confrontation' unless it treated those things with real seriousness. Written in the first-person in a demanding lyric stanza that provides an ordering framework for intense emotion, *Pearl* is a measured transformation of human *desolatio* into religious *consolatio*, a disciplining of the feelings it enacts. But the 'coumforde' (369) its distraught protagonist initially seeks is nothing less than the restoration of a cherished person snatched from him by death. And if (as the Middle Ages recognised) human beings set supreme store by love, then their greatest pain is the beloved's death, which ends what is 'felt' as having greatest value in life. This 'human dilemma', accordingly, is what the poem aims to address.

The Dreamer articulates the dilemma in his protest (331–2) at Pearl's dismissal of his 'madde' expectation that he can join her in 'blys' across 'þys water fre' (290–300):

> What seruez tresor bot garez men grete,   *make; weep*
> When he hit schal efte with tenez tyne?   *anguish; lose*

These lines echo Boethius's assertion that 'in alle adversites of fortune the most unzeely [wretched] kynde of contrarious fortune is to han ben weleful [happy]' (Chaucer's *Boece*, II Pr 47–9).[19] But though the Maiden resembles Lady Philosophy, her answer to the Dreamer's cry that losing her again would be *durande doel* ('perpetual torment') (336), namely to bid him 'loue ay God, in wele and wo' (342), is nearer to Job than to Boethius (cf. Job 1:21–2). For the hope she offers in his 'doel-dystresse' (337) is not the consolation of philosophy but the 'comforte' of the all-powerful Lamb who 'may þy langour lyþe [assuage your anguish]' (357) and who chastises the Dreamer only by denying access to 'mo of His mysterys'. This *hope* is founded on *faith* in God's power to rescue man from the 'dilemma' of loving and of losing a supremely valued love through death (both God's power and his love were seen as exemplified in Christ's Raising of Lazarus [Jn 11:1–44]). The faith that the Maiden seeks to strengthen the Dreamer in is thus faith in a God 'Þat lelly hyȝte your lyf to rayse, / Þaȝ Fortune dyd your flesch to dyȝe', who acts *through* his power but *out of* his *caritas* 'love' (305–6).

Now *caritas* ('love') as described in I Jn 4:8–10 aims at another's good, not one's own, implying that love that seeks the happiness the loved one can give is only a higher form of 'self-love'. But as the order of nature necessarily precedes the order of grace, *caritas* begins from – though it does not begin as – *cupiditas* or 'desire'; human beings, before they can love undesiringly as God loves them, must love desiringly, because love is first love of what they come to know through the senses. When discussing 'love' in *Pearl*, it might be preferable to employ a dichotomy that is not strictly an antithesis, and to speak not of 'cupidity' as *replaced by* 'charity' but of 'carnal love' as *fulfilled in* 'spiritual love'. For the Christian doctrine of Resurrection sees the carnal less as the 'bodily' than as the 'limited', the spiritual less as the 'bodiless' than as the 'unlimited': not the *opposite* of the physical but rather its *meaning*. 'Carnal love' so defined has potential to become spiritual love by advancing from temporal existence, through death, to everlasting life in a transfigured (yet ultimately *bodily*) condition. *Pearl* may in this way be seen to propose not the extinction but the purification of carnal love, giving *through* the protagonist a teaching that is essentially *for* the reader whose perplexities he voices. The *Pearl*-Dreamer, being no more allegorical than the Pearl Maiden, is a concrete individual encountering in a 'gostly drem' (790) a particular woman in the blessed state granted her after death through the grace of God; which, as she says five times in fitt XI (in the central stanza), 'is gret innoghe'.

Presented though a structure both dauntingly complex and compellingly lucid, the 'story' of *Pearl* is essentially a simple one. The Dreamer falls asleep in a garden where someone he loves deeply (his 'pearl') lies buried, overpowered by a grief that even the incarnate Christ cannot relieve (fitt I); on awaking there he willingly consigns his Pearl to God, receiving in return the comfort of the risen Christ offered daily in the Mass (fitt XX). His inner transformation results from both seeing and conversing with Pearl's glorified spirit; so that during his 'auenture' (64), his feelings for her develop from a carnal into a spiritual love; instead of desiring her alive again, he undesiringly *wills* her true good, life in heaven with her 'spouse' Christ. The poem's 'core' is the debate in fitts V–XVI, and the 'nucleus' of this core is stanza 51. This stanza's first and last lines (ll. 601, 612) embed the word *God* (the 'Alpha and the Omega' of Rev 1:8) in phrases referring first to his kingdom, then to his grace, concepts that fitt VIII understands as interchangeable. Of its seven quantity terms, four compose two anti-thetical pairs (*more: less; much: lyttel*); two are near-synonyms (*large: gret*); one (*innoghe*) mediates between the first two pairs to furnish the 'true' sense of the third (its sense in the proverb 'Enough is as good as a feast'). Enclosing the dialogic 'core' are two descriptive sections, fitts II–IV (the Earthly Paradise) and XVII–XIX (the Heavenly Jerusalem); these are flanked by two fitts set in the 'worlde wete' (761), the transience and pain of which acquire new meaning from the Lamb's 'wounde weete' (1135) (White 1987). The moral or tropological meaning of this great Icon of 'perfection in imper-fection' is that God has known human dilemmas, has experienced life and death, and has found a means to turn earthly 'doel' into heavenly 'delyt'. Its anagogical meaning is that what Christ underwent for man 'as lombe þat clypper in hande nem [took]' (802) will be made sacramentally present in the 'bred and wyn / Þe preste vus schewez vch a daye' (1209–10), which anticipates the banquet of heaven.

However, though *Pearl*'s main concern may be to 'purify' love and re-form its protagonist in 'faith and feeling', inasmuch as he represents mankind, a transvaluation of his ideas is required (Horgan 1981) whereby the *reader* may accept the poem's more general claim that God's righteousness is grounded in his goodness and cease regarding justice as an arithmetical apportionment of divine reward to human merit. Through the Dreamer, the poet accordingly voices any 'worldly' reader's probable inference from the Vineyard Parable's moral that 'þe lasse in werke to take more able, / And euer þe lenger þe lasse þe more' ('the longer you do less, the more you will get paid') (599–600). The Maiden's defence of God's *fraunchyse* (609) in the 'sovereign' stanza is accordingly needed to confute this conclusion, if the 'claim' mentioned above is to hold. Her case is that in heaven *everyone*, through God's grace, will receive 'enough', whether they die young or live long in a world 'wet' with growth and grief. For there is no injustice where all have 'innoghe', no resentment in a 'court' where (unlike earthly courts) each wishes others' happiness to be greater, not less (Prior 1996: 176). This 'counter-intuitive' teaching recalls Virgil's instruction to Dante in *Purgatorio* XV 46–75, which may be the poet's source. The Maiden's challenging lesson cannot win assent without prior faith that God's *caritas* wills only man's good; and because beatitude consists of participation in the divine nature, it must remain finally beyond the comprehension of an earthly 'mynde' driven to 'maddyng' by desire to possess it (1154). But the Maiden has also declared that this heavenly 'participation' is experienced in 'the communion of saints' (445–67), and this should caution against over-emphasising the 'exclusivity' of the Lamb's love (Prior 1996: 58): for *all* the blessed are his 'brides'. Moreover, mystic participation in this 'communion' is *now* granted 'þe god Krystyin' through its earthly 'type', the Eucharist. For the Eucharist, notwithstanding Prior's denial (1996:66) that it 'deals with present reality', is to be understood *both* as 'present reality' and 'pledge of future glory'. If, to return to *Cleanness*, Baltazar's chaotic feast emblematised sin's dark disorder, *Pearl*'s heavenly banquet represents a bright harmony restored through Christ's sacrificial death in 'þe olde Jerusalem' (941). The source of the all-pervading luminosity in 'þe nwe' (943) is thus fittingly 'Þat glorious gyltlez þat mon con quelle' (799), the Lamb whose 'glentez glorious glade' (1144) reveal the *dele* of the *rode* transfigured into the *delyt* of the *mes* (a word meaning both 'meal' and 'mass').

Pearl's Dreamer awakens in the August garden fully conscious of what he implicitly knew before sleeping: how without the 'crokez kene' (40) that cut the grain 'No whete were ellez to wonez wonne' (32). The poem's essential 'wheat' is the 'comfort' of the *kynde of Kryst* (55) obtained by the Maiden for her father through a 'syʒt' of heaven by Christ's special 'fauor' (967–8). The fruit of this 'fauor' is the 're-formed' love called *caritas*. For as 'Charity revealed', Pearl offers to the Dreamer (as Beatrice does to Dante) the available face of God, for a particular individual, but one who also represents suffering mankind. His privileged 'syʒt' teaches unambiguously that re-birth through death is the precondition for possessing 'This makellez perle, þat boʒt is dere' (733). But it also, we may assert, validates a carnal love that has been transformed into spiritual love through humble acceptance of the necessity of his own as well as his daughter's death (320–21):

> Þy corse in clot mot calder keue   *sink*
> For hit was forgarte at paradys greue   *lost*

This process reaches completion when the Dreamer hands over his *perle* to her Creator in the final stanza, an act not of loss but of gain. In simultaneously handing over his *Pearl* (and reversion to the neuter pronoun *hit* at 1207 strongly hints at this meaning), the *poem's* creator once more loses nothing (Prior 1996: 162). Because art, like heaven, 'Hatz a property in hitself beyng' (446), growing in value the more that it is shared, the final beneficiaries of the poet's 'charity' are his readers.

NOTES

1   That is 'as the distinctive power acquired by language in the hands of a gifted poet...' where 'items in a shared vocabulary and phraseology become charged with expressive force as devices contributing to the portrayal of human experience' (Borroff 2006: 46).

2   The *Piers Plowman* echoes include 16a (= *PP* B XX 387), 59b (= C Pr 222), 199 (= C 3.318 / B IX 111), 234 (= B IV 135), 237 (= C II 52). A distinctively Langlandian metrical variant occurs at 221 and 300. *Piers Plowman* is cited from my Parallel-Text edition (1995).

3   As well as the fourth, the related eighth beatitude is thematically relevant to *Erkenwald*: 'Blessed are they that suffer persecution for justice' sake; for theirs is the kingdom of heaven' (Mt 5:10), as noted by Baldwin (1988:126), who also sees *Pearl* as illustrating the *third* beatitude, 'Blessed are they that mourn' (Mt 5:5). *St Erkenwald* is cited from Burrow and Turville-Petre (1992).

4   Borroff (2006: 48–52) adduces as new evidence recurrent verb-phrases for 'sitting' and 'lying', and noun-phrase periphrases for 'God'. For 'tectonic' evidence of *Erkenwald*'s possible connection with the Cotton Nero group see n. 10 below.

5   The name applied to this period by Burrow (1971).

6   This court may be 'ideally' represented in the sumptuous early fifteenth-century frontispiece to Corpus Christi Cambridge MS 61 of *Troilus* (Salter, 'The Troilus Frontispiece' [1978]). Its artistic quality, not far below the 'January' and 'May' illustrations in Jean de Berry's *Très Riches Heures* of the same period, is of a different order to that of Cotton Nero A. x; but the latter may possibly be a copy of a superior original now lost.

7   Only *The Destruction of Troy* has a known author, John Clerk of Whalley, who encoded his name in the text (Turville-Petre 1988).

8   Later called the Golden Section, it is today the ratio *phi*, which has the decimal value 1.61803, with 0.61803 for its 'reciprocal' (a reciprocal is one of two numbers whose product is 1). If we proceed from the smallest magnitude to the largest, the reciprocal ratio resulting is 0.615 / 0.625.

9   *Patience*'s initial capitals occur at lines 1, 61, 245, 305 and 409. *Cleanness* has three sections marked by 8-line ornamental capitals at lines 1, 557 and 1157. In section one, 3-line capitals occur at lines 125, 193, 249, 345 and 485; in section two, at 601, 689, 781 and 893; and in section three at 1357. Andrew and Waldron's (1978) five-part structure (p. 25) shows only *one* of the manuscript's thirteen divisions (that at 601) coinciding with any of the fourteen they discern on the basis of the disposition of thematic material (though they recognise that ll. 557–600 'function as a transitional passage between the [...] Flood and [...] Abraham' [p. 135]). Menner (1920) adds three editorial sub-divisions in sub-section XIII (= ll. 1357–1812) and two in sub-sections XI (893–1156) and XII (1157–1357).

10 While we would not expect a work uniquely attested in another manuscript source to participate in Cotton Nero's 'tectonic' relationships, *St Erkenwald*'s line-total (352) accords intriguingly with that of the shortest piece *Patience* (531) in that the ratio of 352:531 (= 0.662), approaching the 'reciprocal' of *phi* (0.618), displays the Divine Proportion that determines the canonical four.

11 One textual exemplification of Gregory's maxim is the 'missing' line that leaves *Patience*'s line-total as 531. Another is *Gawain*'s terminal 'bob', 'wheel' and Garter motto; for these, by producing 2531,

purposefully mar the 'perfect' 2525 which, when divided by 25 (the square of the poem's key symbolic number 5), yields the required 'imperfect' stanza-total of 101 (this notwithstanding that *Gawain*'s stanzas have *irregular* line-lengths).

12 In medieval numerology the noughts in 144,000/12,000 may be ignored as representing 'nothing'.

13 Exactly these proportions occur in the nave and crossing of an 'ideal' Cistercian church sketched in the *Album* (p. 28b) of the thirteenth-century French architect Villard de Honnecourt (Bruyne 1998 [1946]: 23).

14 Chaucer's source is Geoffrey of Vinsauf's *Poetria Nova* 43–5: *intrinseca linea cordis / praemetitur opus*, where the sense of *praemetitur* ('measures out in advance') is architectonic and *linea* denotes the master-mason's plumb-line used to ensure straight elevations.

15 Harwood 1991 compares *Pearl* with the devotional diptych to bring out a 'chiastic' pattern of thematic oppositions between its first ten and last ten fitts. The importance of the sovereign mid-point in the thirteenth-century *Loue Ron* (which the *Pearl*-poet may have known) is brought out by Susanna Fein (1999a). See also her observations on the use of first-and-last line circularity and a sovereign centre line in the fourteenth-century *Quatrefoil of Love* (Fein 1999b).

16 The poet's status as a cleric attached to a secular cathedral is maintained by Lecklider (1997).

17 See the *Sarum Missal*'s Order of Matrimony cited in Lecklider (1997: 132).

18 This account of the poet's view of sexuality, based on Schmidt (1987), is challenged by Keiser (1997: 240–1).

19 The passage is used by both Dante and Chaucer (*Inferno* V 121–3; *Troilus and Criseyde* III 1625–8).

References and Further Reading

Primary Texts

Anderson, J. J. (ed.) (1969). *Patience*. Manchester: Manchester University Press.

Andrew, M. and R. Waldron (eds) (1978). *The Poems of the Pearl Manuscript*. London: Arnold. (Rev. repr. Exeter: Exeter University Press, 2002.)

Burrow. J. A. and T. Turville-Petre (1992). *A Book of Middle English*. Oxford: Blackwell.

Gollancz, I. (ed.) (1921). *Pearl*. London: Chatto & Windus.

Gordon, E. V. (ed.) (1953). *Pearl*. Oxford: Clarendon Press.

Madden, F. (ed.) (1839). *Syre Gawayne: A Collection of Ancient Romance-Poems*. London: Bannatyne Club.

Menner, R. J. (1920). *Purity*. New Haven: Yale University Press.

Morris, R. (ed.) (1864). *Early English Alliterative Poems in the West-Midland Dialect of the Fourteenth Century*. Early English Text Society, o.s. 1. (2nd edn London, 1965.)

Schmidt, A. V. C. (1995a). *The Vision of 'Piers Plowman'*. London: Dent.

Schmidt, A. V. C. (1995b). *Piers Plowman: A Parallel-Text Edition of the A, B, C and Z Versions*. Vol. I: Text. London: Longman.

Secondary Reading

Andrew, M. (1997). Theories of authorship. In Brewer and Gibson (eds). *A Companion to the Gawain-Poet* (pp. 23–33). Cambridge: D. S. Brewer.

Baldwin, A. P. (1988). Sacramental perfection in *Pearl, Patience* and *Cleanness*. In P. Boitani and A. Torti (eds). *Genres, Themes, and Images in English Literature* (pp. 125–40). Tübingen: Gunter Narr.

Bennett, M. J. (1983). *Community, Class, and Careerism: Cheshire and Lancashire Society in the Age of* Sir Gawain and the Green Knight. Cambridge: Cambridge University Press.

Bennett, M. J. (1997). The historical background. In D. Brewer and J. Gibson (eds). *A Companion to the Gawain-Poet* (pp. 71–90). Cambridge: D. S. Brewer.

Benson, L. D. (1965). The authorship of 'St Erkenwald'. *Journal of English and Germanic Philology*, 64, 393–405.

Boitani, P. and A. Torti (eds) (1988). *Genres, Themes, and Images in English Literature*. Tübingen: Gunter Narr.

Borroff, M. (2006). Narrative artistry in 'St. Erkenwald' and the 'Gawain'-Group: the case for common authorship reconsidered. *Studies in the Age of Chaucer*, 28, 41–76.

Bowers, J. M. (2001). *The Politics of Pearl: Court Poetry in the Age of Richard II*. Cambridge: D. S. Brewer.

Brewer, D. and J. Gibson (eds) (1997). *A Companion to the Gawain-Poet*. Cambridge: D. S. Brewer.

Bruyne, E. de (1998 [1946]). *Etudes d'Esthétique Médiévale*. 2 vols. Paris: Albin Michel.

Burrow, J. A. (1971). *Ricardian Poetry*. London: Routledge & Kegan Paul.

Cherniss, M. D. (1987). *Boethian Apocalypse: Studies in Middle English Vision Poetry*. Norman, OK: Pilgrim Books.

Clifton-Taylor. A. (1967). *The Cathedrals of England*. London: Thames & Hudson.

Condren, E. (2002). *The Numerical Universe of the Gawain-Pearl Poet: Beyond Phi*. Gainesville: University Press of Florida.

Cooke, W. G. and D'A. Boulton (1999). 'SGGK': a poem for Henry of Grosmont? *Medium Ævum*, 68, 41–54.

Crawford, D. (1993). The architectonics of 'Cleanness'. *Studies in Philology*, 90, 29–45.

Davenport, W. A. (1978). *The Art of the Gawain-Poet*. London: Athlone Press.

Doyle, A. I. (1982). The manuscripts. In D. A. Lawton (ed.). *Middle English Alliterative Poetry and its Literary Background* (pp. 88–100). Cambridge: D. S. Brewer.

Duggan, H. N. (1997). Meter, stanza, vocabulary, dialect. In D. Brewer and J. Gibson (eds). *A Companion to the Gawain-Poet* (pp. 221–43). Cambridge: D. S. Brewer.

Edwards, A. S. G. (1997). The manuscript: British Library MS Cotton Nero A. x. In D. Brewer and J. Gibson (eds). *A Companion to the Gawain-Poet* (pp. 197–219). Cambridge: D. S. Brewer.

Fein, S. G. (1997). Twelve-line stanza forms in Middle English and the date of *Pearl*. *Speculum*, 72, 367–98.

Fein, S. G. (1999a). Roll or codex? The diptych layout of Thomas of Hales's 'Love Rune'. *Trivium*, 31, 13–23.

Fein, S. G. (1999b). Quatrefoil and Quatrefolia: the devotional layout of an alliterative poem. *Journal of the Early Book Society*, 2, 26–45.

Gilligan, J. (1989) Numerical composition in the Middle English *Patience*. *Studia Neophilologica*, 61, 7–11.

Harwood, B. J. (1991). 'Pearl' as diptych. In R. J. Blanch, J. N. Wasserman and M. Troy (eds).

Text and Matter: New Critical Perspectives of the Pearl-Poet (pp. 61–78). New York: Whitson.

Horgan, A. D. (1981). Justice in 'The Pearl'. *Review of English Studies*, 33, 173–80.

Kean, P. M. (1967). *'The Pearl': An Interpretation*. London: Routledge & Kegan Paul.

Keiser, E. (1997). *Courtly Desire and Medieval Homophobia: the Legitimation of Sexual Pleasure in Cleanness and its Contexts*. New Haven: Yale University Press.

Kooper, E. (1982). The case of the encoded author: John Massey in 'Sir Gawain and the Green Knight'. *Neuphilologische Mitteilungen*, 83, 158–68.

Lawton, D. (ed.) (1982). *Middle English Alliterative Poetry and its Literary Background*. Cambridge: D. S. Brewer.

Lecklider, J. K. (1997). *'Cleanness': Structure and Meaning*. Cambridge: D. S. Brewer.

Peck, R. (1973). Number structure in 'St Erkenwald'. *Annuale Medievale*, 14, 9–21.

Prior, S. P. (1996). *The Fayre Formez of the Pearl Poet*. East Lansing: Michigan State University Press.

Reichardt, Paul F. (1997). 'Several illuminations, coarsely executed': the illustrations of the *Pearl* manuscript. *Studies in Iconography*, 18, 119–142.

Salter, E. (1988 [1978]). The Troilus frontispiece. In D. Pearsall and N. Zeeman (eds). *English and International: Studies in the Literature, Art and Patronage of Medieval England* (pp. 267–71). Cambridge: Cambridge University Press.

Schmidt, A. V. C. (1988). *Kynde craft and the play of paramorez*: natural and unnatural love in 'Purity'. In P. Boitani and A. Torti (eds). *Genres, Themes, and Images in English Literature* (pp. 105–24). Tübingen: Gunter Narr.

Spearing, A. C. (1970). *The Gawain-Poet: A Critical Study*. Cambridge: Cambridge University Press.

Spearing, A. C. (1985). *Medieval to Renaissance in English Poetry*. Cambridge: Cambridge University Press.

Turville-Petre, T. (1988). The author of 'The Destruction of Troy'. *Medium Ævum*, 57, 264–9.

Von Simson, O. (1956). *The Gothic Cathedral*. London: Routledge.

White, H. (1987). Blood in 'Pearl'. *Review of English Studies*, 38, 1–13.

Wilson, E. (1979). 'SGGK' and the Stanley family of Stanley, Storeton and Hooton. *Review of English Studies*, 30, 308–16.

21

Sir Gawain and the Green Knight

Tony Davenport

I

Although *Sir Gawain and the Green Knight* is often referred to as the best of Middle English romances, it is not a typical example of the kind. Metrical romances mostly delineate whole-life experiences, in a story of a prince or knight from birth to the achievement of position, bride and a secure future (*Havelok the Dane, King Horn, Bevis of Hampton*), or the testing of a heroine or hero (*Emaré, Le Bone Florence of Rome, Sir Eglamour of Artois*), or the break-up and subsequent reuniting of a family (*Octavian, Chevalere Assigne, Sir Isumbras*). The world of romance is one of virtuous characters subjected to temporal tribulation and preserved by a benevolent providence from ultimate harm. *Sir Gawain* stems from the epic/chronicle material of Arthurian history and, though Arthurian stories share a landscape of court, castle and forest with romance narratives of triumph over circumstance, they have at their back a sense of the rise and fall of a dynasty and the knowledge that Arthur and his court are an instance of the transitoriness of power. *Sir Gawain* tells of only an episode in its hero's life and he is a hero who has a history outside this poem; he has both a past which other characters in the poem are shown to know about and with which the poet assumes his audience is familiar, and a known future which, at the end of the poem, is still to be enacted. Camelot too is presumed to be familiar and the reader is asked to imagine the court before the Grail quest has cast its shadow, before Guenevere is suspected of adultery, before the threat of civil war, while the king is young and eager to learn of chivalrous deeds and while the court is capable of absorbing the lessons of experience.

The form in which experience comes is the startling arrival of the gigantic Green Knight whose challenge to the court's pride is the extreme Christmas sport of mutual beheading. Though Arthur's nobles are cautious enough to protect Arthur from the adventure and allow Gawain to take it on, Arthur himself is guilty of lack of fore-thought in presuming that, if Gawain strikes cleanly and strongly with the huge green axe, that will be the end of the matter: by the time the headless, bleeding knight has bent down and rescued his rolling head from the courtiers' feet, Gawain has promised to find an unknown Green Chapel, there to submit to his own beheading in a year's time. This first section of the poem, a brilliant dramatic scene, presents the reader with an intriguing combination of historical characters, accompanied by heroic and courtly setting and attitudes, and bizarre fantasy. Arthur and Gawain behave according to the rules and expectations of society and nature, but it appears these rules do not keep out the impossible. What then does the honour system of chivalry do when faced with the unknown? First it arms itself, and so when Michaelmas comes and the hero has to leave the court and undertake a winter journey towards probable death, he is clad in the protection both of literal armour and of metaphorical virtue, as represented by the pentangle upon his shield. After that Gawain is on his own; with the courtiers lamenting his departure, he leaves, perhaps never to return, to traverse England and Wales and sleep outdoors with icicles above his head. But, though Gawain's ride is cold, lonely and testing, on Christmas Eve his situation improves to the extent of finding a castle where he is immediately disarmed and made welcome by its lord, his court, and the lord's young wife, who is accompanied by a particularly ugly old lady. There, when the Christmas festivities are over, he is reassured that the Green Chapel is near at hand and persuaded to remain as a guest for the three days remaining before New Year. Heroic and super-natural expectations seem oddly to have turned domestic, even more so when his host proposes that in that time Gawain stay at home to recover from his journey, while he goes hunting, but that they shall have a game of mutual exchange of each day's gains. What Gawain gains unexpectedly in three teasing visits to his bedroom by the alluring lady of the castle are kisses, one, then two, then three in succession on the three days, and these he returns to the lady's husband in joking exchange for the products of the hunt. On the third day, however, the lady, giving up her attempts to persuade Gawain to display his skill as a lover, homes in on a weak link in his armour of moral steadfastness, and inveigles him into accepting her green belt as a keepsake by convincing him that it will protect him from being killed; this he agrees to conceal. The final part of the poem is devoted mainly to the second meeting between Gawain and the Green Knight, though the hero has first to resist the tempting opportunity to run away offered to him by his guide. The confrontation is again unexpected: once Gawain has found the courage passively to kneel ready for the blow of the axe, he has to suffer only a slight wound, but, before his euphoria has chance to blossom, he finds himself at the receiving end of a moral lesson. His retention of the belt was the breaking of a promise: his chivalrous performance was flawed. The challenge that he has faced was a plot against Camelot by Morgan le Fay, the ugly old woman, who is also his aunt. Gawain is full of self-reproach and he returns to Camelot downcast, but there is greeted with relief and joy, and the green belt, which he has worn as a sign of shame, is adopted as a token of honour. The story is a clever combination of a series of surprising situations, with a central mystery not revealed until the end.

Closest to *Sir Gawain* as a type of narrative is a group of late romances which share its hero: *The Awntyrs of Arthur*, *The Wedding of Sir Gawain and Dame Ragnel*, *Golagros and Gawain* and several others (Hahn 1995), which seem to demonstrate something of an English fashion for poems about Gawain, a fashion which *Sir Gawain* may have begun, since it was written almost certainly before the end of the four-teenth century and perhaps as early as 1350–70, whereas the other Gawain-poems are probably all fifteenth-century works. One of them, *The Greene Knight*, a rehash of the plot-material of *Sir Gawain*, would seem to be directly derived from the earlier poem. What this English fashion consists of is placing a leading Arthurian knight, King Arthur's eldest nephew and his presumptive heir, who nevertheless appears often as a secondary or subsidiary figure in earlier French romance, at the centre of a series of moral conundrums. Several of these poems envisage a challenge to Camelot by an outsider (sometimes a bizarre or monstrous one) who is overcome but who is, in some sense, assimilated into the Arthurian ethos. In the light of the earlier and later treatments of the figure of Gawain, and of the contradictions between epic narratives and romance, one must recognise in *Sir Gawain* a meeting-place of literary traditions.

One such tradition is that of medieval French courtly romance beginning in the late twelfth century with Chrétien de Troyes, who recognised in the chronicle material of Geoffrey of Monmouth and Wace the opportunity for narrative about chivalrous ethics, treating the adventures of individual knights of the Round Table. In *Erec et Enide* Chrétien examines the conflicting demands of married love and the public duty of knighthood; in *Cligés* the contest between adulterous love and moral virtue; in *Lancelot* the strains put upon the knight's honour by the demands of love; and in *Yvain*, one of the romances in which Gawain appears, again Chrétien explores the tensions between the hero's love for his wife and the call of knight-errantry, for which Gawain is the spokesman. It was Chrétien who established the pattern of Arthurian narrative in which Arthur, though the figurehead in whom authority is vested, remains at home while knights go out to experience adventure, which they report on their return to court. This pattern survives in *Sir Gawain*, although in Chrétien's romances Arthur's inactivity presumes that he is past his period of youthful exploits – indeed he is an old man in *Yvain* – which does not fit the *Gawain*-poet's description of the king as 'so joly of his joyfnes' (Tolkien 1967: l.86). For Chrétien Gawain too is a secondary figure (though he is praised as a model of prowess, com-passion, sense and courtesy in *Yvain* and given a major role in *Perceval*, Chrétien's Grail romance). It is perhaps for this reason that Gawain does not appear as a primary hero in subsequent French Arthurian narratives and gradually suffers denigration in comparison to Lancelot and others. Between Chrétien and the composition of *Sir Gawain* lies a complex mass of French Arthurian writing in verse and prose in some of which, the *Prose Tristan* for instance, Gawain appears as an unworthy knight, guilty of some villainous acts; he can behave as an impulsive libertine, so that the idea of Gawain as a model of courtesy has some opposition to overcome (Whiting 1947; Schmolke-Hasselmann 1980/1998).

If, looking from one direction, one can see *Sir Gawain* as a French courtly narrative (Putter 1995), from another it is part of the fourteenth-century growth of English alliterative poetry (Turville-Petre 1977). Unlike Chaucer's Parson, whose literary talents are pretty limited, the *Gawain*-poet *can* 'geeste "rum, ram, ruf" by lettre' and in so doing proclaims himself a northern man and embraces the writing of verse which renders actions, sights and sounds with particular clarity and force, and tends towards a seriousness of mind contrary to courtly flippancy. Alliterative poets did make direct adaptations of French romance (*William of Palerne*, translated 1350–60 at the behest of Humphrey de Bohun, Earl of Hereford, and *Chevalere Assigne*, a late fourteenth-century abbreviation of part of the *chanson de geste* concerning Godfrey of Bouillon), but *Sir Gawain* shows a more complex mixing of motifs, suggesting kinship rather with alliterative poems which combine courtly scenes and moral allegory, such as *The Parliament of the Three Ages* and *The Awntyrs of Arthur*. Comparison with the major alliterative treatment of Arthurian material, the alliterative *Morte Arthur*, which is roughly contemporaneous with *Sir Gawain*, makes clear the *Gawain*-poet's mixed purposes. At the beginning of *Sir Gawain* we are promised a 'stori stif and stronge', which could be taken to introduce a narrative of Arthur's major battles or at least of a hero fighting 'In bataille or in tourneyment', as Chaucer put it in *Sir Thopas* (716). The story does not fulfil such expectations: much of it takes place indoors with the focus on courtly conduct; the outdoor scenes are about winter, hunting and the hero's loneliness as much as deeds of heroism. In the final scene between Gawain and the Green Knight there is little physical conflict: it is more a contest of words than of blows. Despite the poet's use of heroic vocabulary, this is no historical battle poem. What it is essentially is an 'invented' fiction. I place the word *invented* in inverted commas because in one sense the narrative is completely second-hand: the plot-elements, the Green Knight's beheading challenge to Camelot, the lord of Hautdesert's exchange bargain with Gawain, the tempting visits of the lady of Hautdesert to Gawain's bedroom, are all found separately elsewhere in French and Irish texts (Brewer 1973/1992) and the composition of the poem may be described as an ingenious and elegant compilation forming a kind of Chinese box – the beheading game begins and ends the poem but its outcome is decided by the hero's conduct in the exchange of winnings which in turn is the product of the temptation scenes. Yet in another sense the narrative is invented, in that the poet has combined the historical characters (Arthur, Gawain, Guenevere, Morgan – one could debate in what sense they are historical, but their names are familiar) with the non-historical figures of the Green Knight/Bertilak and the anonymous Lady of Hautdesert, and used these figures to cast a new light on the characters that we may have thought we knew. The result is a re-defining, of Gawain in particular.

The idea of the defining of the hero is very clear in the different parts of the story, since Gawain is given a characterising passage at each stage. On his first appearance, when he volunteers to take on the Green Knight's absurd challenge in an exaggeratedly modest speech, he portrays himself as the least worthy member of the Arthurian court, to be valued only because of his connection to Arthur:

'I am þe wakkest, I wot, and of wyt feblest,
And lest lur of my lyf, quo laytes þe soþe –   *loss; seeks*
Bot for as much as ȝe ar myn em I am only to prayse,   *uncle*
No bounté bot your blod I in my body knowe;
And syþen þis note is so nys þat noȝt hit yow falles,   *foolish*
And I haue frayned hit at yow fyrst, foldez hit to me...'   *asked; assign*

(354–9)

One perceives this as an act of courtesy, an example of fitting and conforming conduct, appropriate to the king's nephew and to a young knight anxious to demonstrate his loyalty to king and court. In contrast to this self-definition is the public face of Gawain's knighthood for which the poet conspicuously uses his own narrating voice when the hero is to leave Camelot on his uncertain quest. Here Gawain is given an identity both heraldic and schematic through the device on his shield, in a protracted analysis of its meaning:

And quy þe pentangel apendez to þat prynce noble   *appertains*
I am in tent yow to telle, þof tary hyt me schulde;
Hit is a sygne þat Salomon set sumquyle*sign*
In bytoknyng of trawþe, bi tytle þat hit habbez,   *right*
For hit is a figure þat haldez fyue poyntez,
And vche lyne vmbelappez and loukez in oþer,
And ayquere hit is endelez...

(623–9)

The poet's description of the intricate symbol and his meticulous explanation of the five ways in which Gawain fulfils the ideal of truth, and exemplifies virtue and complete absence of 'vche vylany', uses a range of vocabulary that is extraordinary for a romance narrative: not only the word *pentangel* (which apparently does not occur again in English until 1646, when Sir Thomas Browne explains Solomon's sign in *Pseudodoxica Epidemica*) but also the language of geometry and textual exegesis with a touch of the law (*tytle*) too. By means of this impressive passage the poet makes it clear that Gawain sets forth on his adventure not merely as the representative of Camelot and chivalry but also of Christian virtue. It is thus particularly striking that despite this fanfare of spectacular symbolism, the poet quickly undercuts the whole adventure by allowing the sorrowing bystanders to voice the thought that a worthy knight is being wasted on an exercise in pointless bravado:

'Who knew euer any kyng such counsel to take
As knyȝtez in cauelaciounz on Crystemasse gomnez?'   *trifling arguments*

(682–3)

By encouraging an element of scepticism in his audience the poet perhaps prepares us not to swallow whole the third of these definitions of Gawain's identity, when the tactful questions of the courtiers at Hautdesert elicit the information that he is a great prince from a great court:

> Vch segge ful softly sayde to his fere:
> 'Now schal we semlych se sle3tez of þewez   *skilled demonstration of manners*
> And þe teccheles termes of talkyng noble,   *faultless*
> Wich spede is in speche vnspurd may we lerne,   *success; without asking*
> Syn we haf fonged þat fyne fader of nurture ...'   *received*
>   (916–19)

Although there is no flat contradiction between this perception of Gawain as a royal prince 'Þat alle prys and prowes and pured þewes / Apendes to hys persoun and praysed is euer' (912–13) and the earlier description of him as 'tulk of tale most trwe / And gentylest kny3t of lote' (638–9), beneath the superlative praise is a contrast between a fully armed hero, gleaming in resplendent gold, ready for robust adventure and the disarmed dinner-companion whispered about as a model of polite behaviour, whose manners and language are to be watched and copied. In this contrast the pattern of the rest of the narrative is conveyed. Gawain is not to face battle with a dragon or an armed opponent but to be watched in his social conduct and judged for his truth in that. It is significant that Gawain's main challenges occur when he is either lying down in his bed or kneeling down waiting for the axe to descend. That is, his heroism is both passive and, in some respects, comic (Mann 1994). Unexpectedly Gawain is a romance hero who is to be embarrassed, first by the bold Lady's visits to his bedroom, where he first pretends to be asleep and then has to rally his courtly wits to fend her off while remaining a perfectly behaved guest, then by having to return her kisses to his hearty host, and finally by being caught out in a piece of dishonesty.

In tune with this exposure of the hero to comic situations is the frequency of laughter in the poem. There are nearly as many references to laughter in this work of 2530 lines as in the 32,000 lines of Gower's *Confessio Amantis*, and that is merely in terms of the recurrence of the word *laugh* in its various grammatical forms and variant spellings; there are actually fewer *occasions* of laughter in Gower's poem. *Sir Gawain* surpasses *Troilus and Criseyde* in references to laughter, despite the joking of Pandarus, and even the whole of *The Canterbury Tales* finds Chaucer needing laughter on only about thirty occasions in comparison to the twenty in *Sir Gawain*. There are three kinds of laughter in the opening scene at Camelot: the mirth of the court (69), the Green Knight's scorn at the dazed lack of response to his challenge (316) and the relieved laughter of Arthur and Gawain when the Green Knight has departed (464, 472). There is some suggestion in the comments of the courtiers at Gawain's departure that this latter mirth was out of place, to be associated with folly and failure to see the serious consequences of rash response to a foolish game, but the courtiers themselves show the propriety of social laughter in hiding their anxiety about Gawain's fate. After Gawain's mirthless journey the arrival at the Castle of

Hautdesert is full of amused pleasure: the Lord's laughter (909, 1068) carries a hidden warning but we do not know that at the time and it seems natural that Gawain's relieved laughter at learning that the Green Chapel is near at hand, and that his quest can be achieved (1079), should join in with his host's as they agree to exchange their gains (1113). The Lady of Hautdesert is a laughing temptress, 'wyth lyppez smal laȝande' (1207) and, whatever the tension in the courtly bedroom duologues, on the surface the mood is lighthearted, both speakers on the first day punctuating their words with appropriate laughter (Gawain at 1217, the lady at 1290). The meeting with the Lord at the end of his hunt and the exchange of winnings occur in a mood of carefree cheer (1398). The second day follows the pattern set by the first, the Lady ready with early laughter (1479) before she mobilises her forces, the pair sharing mirth (1554) and the Lord returning with his quarry ready to laugh with his guest (1623). On the third day the Lady catches Gawain unawares in a deeply troubled sleep but as soon as he recovers his wits she is leaning over him, 'laȝande swete' (1757), in order to kiss him. Although this is the crucial encounter and the moral issues between the two are more explicitly identified, as Gawain in his own thoughts articulates the danger of the situation, he manages appropriate diverting laughter as a piece of strategy (1777) and when the Lady openly challenges him to justify his failure to engage in the game of love in the form of a prior commitment to another woman, his social aplomb is equal to it:

> Þe knyȝt sayde, 'Be sayn Jon,'
> And smeþely con he smyle,   *gently*
> 'In fayth I welde riȝt non,
> Ne non wil welde þe quile.'
> (1787–91)

In this third section of the poem laughter becomes more and more double-edged, and the poet leaves it to us to judge the effect of Gawain's extreme mirth (1885–92) and the joy of the whole company (1952–6) at the end of the third day's manoeuvrings. Mirth is suspended as Gawain makes his anxious way to the Green Chapel for his second meeting with the Green Knight, but it is with good humour that the hero's adversary re-assumes his other identity, discloses his name and Morgan's instigation of the plot, and invites Gawain back to the castle (2389). Despite the hero's own self-reproaches, laughter is the note that the poet chooses to give to Arthur and the courtiers at Camelot as their reaction to Gawain's story:

> Þe kyng comfortez þe knyȝt, and alle þe court als
> Laȝen loude þerat…
> (2513–14)

So the poem ends in restoration and cheerful acceptance. Gawain's symbol of shame becomes the court's badge of identity and, if one takes notice of the motto of the

Order of the Garter written in the manuscript after the last line of the poem, a point of historical placing: Edward III founded the order in 1348/9 which, if the poem is read as a celebration of a chivalric brotherhood based on courageous humility, suggests a much earlier date for *Sir Gawain* than the reign of Richard II (Ingledew 2006). The comic element in *Sir Gawain* is something that many commentators seem ill at ease with; religious interpreters want the poem to be unremittingly moral and seem to think that comedy is trivialising rather than entertaining the idea that it may be a more mature form of art than tragedy. Romances with happy endings are always comic in the sense of resolving disruptions to social life (Simpson 2002). One of the reasons for the Arthurian episode, which avoids the parts of the history that lead to disaster and death, is to assimilate the material to the pattern of romance.

II

To consider *Sir Gawain and the Green Knight* as an example of Middle English poetry is to be struck immediately by the range and the professionalism of poetic craft in the work. To begin with, the poet shows a strong sense of form. The closing lines of the poem echo the opening, as is the case in *Pearl* and in *Patience* and one of the reasons for thinking that one poet may have composed all three works. In *Sir Gawain* the repetition is a reminder of the literary and historical traditions to which the material of the poem belongs, as well as associating the story with 'þe best boke of romaunce'. There is an overall awareness of structure in the division of the poem into four fitts (that is, sections of appropriate length to be read at one sitting), marked by extra-large capitals in the manuscript and signalled to the reader at appropriate points. The last four lines of the first fitt (487–90) round off the opening scene and look forward, making one aware of a narrator's voice directing the action. Similarly the last four lines of fitt III (1994–7) close off the scenes at Hautdesert and lead into the final section. Though there is not such a marked division at the end of fitt II, the opening of fitt III ('Ful erly byfore þe day þe folk vprisen') indicates the shift from Christmas enjoyment to the significant three-day action that follows. The structure of fitt III itself is the most symmetrically organised piece of narrative in Middle English: three days of simultaneous action in hunting-field and bedroom in an a-b-a pattern (opening of hunt, bedroom conversation, completion of hunt), followed on each day by a meeting in the hall. The pattern encourages readers to observe the subtleties of variation, the similarities and differences in the large-scale deer-drive, the fierce challenge of a boar-hunt, the dogged pursuit of a scent in a fox-hunt, the ambiguities and rhetorical shadow-play in the conversations between Gawain and the Lady, the gradations of *bonhomie* in the exchanges of winnings between Gawain and his host. Symmetry governs the poem overall: the hero returns to Camelot at the end of his adventure, the Green Knight disappears when the beheading game is complete just as he had appeared from nowhere at the start, the action has moved through marked stages, the challenge, the journey, the testing, the judgment and return.

From the beginning there is an air of purposeful direction. The first two stanzas form a prologue, neatly identifying historical context and subject-matter, whetting the audience's appetite with promise of 'an outtrage awenture of Arthurez wonderez' and identifying the alliterative poetic style in which the narrative is to be conveyed, 'With lel letteres loken' as tradition requires. When he has to bridge the gap between New Year and Gawain's setting out to seek the Green Chapel, the poet supplies the appropriate rhetorical topos of the passage of the seasons with its poignant sense of transience and uses the opportunity to register the uncertainties of the adventure. When the hero prepares for his quest, the poet not only fulfils epic expectation with the hero's arming but also adds a rhetorical flourish by matching lines with content for the description of the five ways in which Gawain satisfies the symbolism of the pentangle (twenty-five long lines plus the five short lines of the bob and wheel [640–69]). When two new characters (the ladies at Hautdesert) appear, the poet offers another rhetorical display by describing them in tandem as an antithesis of youth and age. Throughout the poem there is an interplay of indoor and outdoor scenes: Camelot at Christmas, Gawain's lonely winter journey, the alternation of hunting field and bedroom, the warmth and comfort of Hautdesert followed by Gawain's chilly early waking and his ride by rushing mountain streams to the Green Chapel. These contrasts are conveyed by apt linguistic shifts, most marked in the differences between quick-moving lines of outdoor action ('And þay chastysed and charred on chasyng þat went' [1143]), and the tortuous sentences of the dialogues about love between Gawain and the Lady:

> 'Madame,' quoþ þe myry mon. 'Mary yow ȝelde,
> For I haf founden, in god fayth, yowre fraunchis nobele,   *generosity*
> And oþer ful much of oþer folk fongen bi hor dedez,
> Bot þe daynté þat þay delen, for my disert nys euen,   *courtesy; distribute; does not*
>   *match what I deserve*
> Hit is þe worchyp of yourself, þat noȝt bot wel connez.   *your own sense of honour*
>   (1263–7)

The active verbs in one sort of line set off the subjunctives, past participles and vague expressions of nebulous values in the other. The command of courtly vocabulary, the intellectual strain in the choice of words at times, alongside the vigour of the onomatopoeic rendering of craggy landscape and vigorous movement, communicate great verbal awareness in the creation of a world for the narrative to inhabit.

Unusual in the technique of the poet is the verse-form he uses. Unlike the Alliterative *Morte Arthure* which is entirely in unrhymed alliterative long lines, *Sir Gawain* is one of the Middle English alliterative poems which combine long lines with shorter rhyming ones to form stanzas. However, stanzas are normally regular, as in the thirteen-line stanza used in *The Awntyrs of Arthur* (nine long lines plus four shorter ones) or in *Susannah* (eight long lines plus the five-line 'bob and wheel') (Turville-Petre 1974, 1977). The interest of the verse-form used in *Sir Gawain* is that, though each stanza ends with a bob and wheel, the stanza length is unfixed: the shortest stanza has only twelve long lines plus bob and wheel, the longest thirty-seven long lines, so that even the shortest (and there is only one) has a total of seventeen lines. Of the hundred and one stanzas, only seven are shorter than twenty lines, including the first two stanzas; only fifteen are of thirty or more lines and no such stanza occurs in the first fitt of the poem and only one in the final fitt, which is a simple indicator of the priority of the narrative situation over form. The dramatic situations of the opening scene at Camelot and the closing confrontation between Gawain and the Green Knight prove less apt to give rise to extended stanzas than the descriptive scenes of Gawain's journey, of new places and characters and of the hunts and conversations of fitt III. Can this varying stanza be regarded as working in the same way as stanzas of fixed length and pattern? The *Gawain* stanza has been described in various terms, for example as a 'strophe' (Duggan 1997) or a 'paragraph' (Burrow 2001). The terms seem to recognise the hybrid nature of the stanza: it has the formal qualities of the thirteen-line stanza with bob and wheel, or one of its variants, but the stanzas work like the verse paragraphs of poems in the long line, such as the Alliterative *Morte Arthure*. In this *Sir Gawain* shares characteristics with the divisions used in French *chansons de geste*, which are known as *laisses*.

The *laisse* is a section or group of lines of no specific length; it is sometimes defined as a strophe, but strictly speaking this is not the case: a strophe ought to be part of a repeated pattern of matched strophe and antistrophe, as in the complaint in Chaucer's *Anelida and Arcite*. In the *Chanson de Roland* the *laisses* vary between 5 and 34 lines and the length of each depends on how much emphasis the poet wishes to give to the subject. Here and in a number of other *chansons de geste* each line in the *laisse* is linked to the others by terminal assonance; in some later examples of the genre assonance is superseded by monorhyme and *laisses* may be of much greater length. Alliteration might be seen to provide a comparable oral effect in Middle English. Among the features of the *laisse* identified by Rychner in his standard work on the genre (Rychner 1955) useful touchstones are the characterisations of opening and closing lines. The opening line frequently names the hero; the hero is not usually named again in the same stanza, as if the opening line defines a topic and the rest of the *laisse* details the acts and words which embody it. Closing lines may sum up or define an attitude, though another type may anticipate what comes next, but they often have some ring of finality, even with an effect of refrain. Among the most interesting effects are the links between *laisses*: Rychner labels as *enchaînement* the effect of overlapping, where the beginning of a *laisse* repeats material or a phrase from the end of the preceding one. The often commented-on use of *laisses similaires*, where the same event (the death of Roland is the most famous example) is reported in two or more successive *laisses* with changing assonance is an extended form of such overlapping. In the *Chanson de Roland* most of the *laisses* deal with one motif or narrative episode and so have the characteristics of a good paragraph: the opening line sets a topic, sometimes summing up what has preceded, and the rest of the section develops it, while the concluding line rounds it off (van Emden 1995).

Chanson de geste and romance used to be thought of as successive historical stages of medieval French narrative, but the *chanson de geste* went on flourishing into the thirteenth century and the two genres exchange effects with one another (Kay 1995). They are sometimes preserved together in the same miscellanies and seem likely to have been intended for similar courtly audiences. Since *Sir Gawain* draws on French courtly romance for some of its plot material, ideas of the Arthurian court, social attitudes and trappings, it is not unlikely that the poet absorbed some of the *chanson de geste*/romance interchanges and, even if indirectly, some idea of the modes of the earlier narrative type. Direct knowledge by an English alliterative poet of French epic historical writing in *laisses* is indicated by *Chevalere Assigne*; this has lost the paragraph divisions of its source material but preserves, in its abbreviated form of the story, something of the staccato narrative manner that division into *laisses* encourages. For the *Gawain*-poet perhaps the connection is a more diffused one, but the resemblance between the *Gawain* stanza and the *laisse* is, nevertheless, suggestive. Although romance develops stories which illustrate aspects of courtesy rather than dramatising acts of military heroism, it retains the themes of honour and challenge, and alternates scenes of royal ceremony with displays of courage. This is particularly the case in fitt 1 of *Sir Gawain*, where the situation (the arrival of a hostile challenger at Camelot and the response of king and hero) comes closest to the material of *chanson de geste*. Gawain's initial speech, though a model of courtesy and deference, where the poet employs complex syntax to convey the layers of self-abnegation on the hero's part, nevertheless takes colour from echoes of the sort of heroic pride that Roland expresses in accepting the unwelcome task, wished on him by Ganelon, of holding the rearguard as Charlemagne's army withdraws from Spain. The translator, Dorothy Sayers, has imitated in English the assonances at the ends of the lines:

> When Roland hears what he's appointed to,
> He makes reply as knighthood bids him do:
> 'My noble stepsire, I owe you gratitude
> That I'm assigned the rearguard at your suit.
> Charles, king of France, the loss shall never rue
> Of steed or palfrey thereby, I warrant you,
> No saddle-beast, nor hinny neither mule,
> Pack-horse nor sumpter thereby he shall not lose,
> Save first the sword have paid the reckoning due.'
> Quoth Ganelon: 'I know it; you speak truth.'
> (*The Song of Roland*, Laisse 59)

Formality of expression disguises but does not conceal the tensions between public and private feeling; the meticulous listing of horses articulates both proud determination not to be found at fault and bitter resentment at the humiliation of the commission. The *Gawain*-poet uses his stanza with similar double-edged feeling, placing his hero centre stage by naming him in the opening line and then using the speech to draw in the hearers, king, queen and courtiers, and set up the antithesis between 'vylanye' and what is 'semly':

> 'Wolde ʒe, worþilych lorde,' quoþ Wawan to þe kyng,
> 'Bid me boʒe fro þis benche, and stonde by yow þere, *come*
> Þat I wythoute vylanye myʒt voyde þis table,
> And þat my legge lady lyked not ille,
> I wolde com to your counseyl bifore your cort ryche,
> For me þink hit not semly, as hit is soþ knawen, *seems to me*
> Þer such an askyng is heuened so hyʒe in your sale, *raised*
> Þaʒ ʒe yourself be talenttyf, to take hit to yourselven, *eager*
> Whil mony so bolde yow aboute vpon bench sytten,
> Þat vnder heuen I hope non haʒerer of wylle, *better*
> Ne better bodyes on bent þer baret is rered.' *field; battle*
>
>   (343–53)

Having shown deference to the court, Gawain then turns to himself in abject modesty, in the passage quoted earlier. The wheel at the end of the stanza shifts from Gawain's voice as the courtiers agree that he should be the one to take on the Green Knight's challenge:

> Ryche togeder con roun, *Nobles; whispered*
> And syþen þay redden alle same *advised; with one accord*
> To ryd þe kyng wyth croun,
> And gif Gawan þe game.
>   (362–5)

The stanza functions not merely as the next stage in the story but as a scene in itself, introduced at the end of the previous stanza and then composed as dramatic performance, leading to a coda in the wheel where the result of the speech is decided. The name of Gawain in the last line echoes the opening of the stanza and thereby defines it as a unit.

Other *laisse*-like features in *Sir Gawain* are stanzas that begin with a definition of the situation and close with the reaching of a point of decision, as with 250–78 (moving from 'Þenn Arþour bifore þe hiʒ dece þat auenture byholdez' to Arthur's response to the challenge 'Here faylez þou not to fyʒt'); stanzas which repeat a word or phrase from the previous stanza – Rychner's *enchaînement* – as with 107ff. (where 'Thus þer stondez in stale þe stif kyng hisseluen' overlaps with 'He stiʒtlez stif in stalle' from the preceding wheel); a clustering of stanzas, particularly descriptive ones, where continuity of subject-matter is enhanced by recurrent words and phrases (as with the three stanzas devoted to describing the Green Knight where *grene* keeps echoing, three times linked with *gome*); and ending stanzas with lines which sum up or express an attitude with epigrammatic finality (as with several stanzas in fitt IV, such as 'Drede dotz me no lote' [2211], 'Of steuen mon may þe trowe' [2238]).

The relationship between late medieval courtly tales of adventure and chivalrous conduct and earlier heroic stories of battle and conquest may be nostalgic, ironic or downright bathetic, and fourteenth- and fifteenth-century Arthurian narratives are particularly apt to seem to be performing a balancing act between past celebration of heroes and present questioning of heroic values. Part of the language in which *Sir Gawain* articulates its version of such questioning comes from the echoes evoked by its verse-form, together with heroic vocabulary and trappings, and the reference to the adventures which Gawain has on his journey away from and back to Camelot but which the poet chooses not 'at þis tyme in tale to remene' (2483). The poetry displays a number of stylistic currents running side-by-side or sometimes in antithesis: the verse-unit which the poet has invented proves adaptable to the varying circum- stances of the tale. The declamatory style with a large element of direct speech modulates in fitt II where passages of description accumulate details in turn of seasonal change, of armour, of geography and landscape, of weather and nature and then of architecture when Gawain finds the castle which is to be his harbour. The scenes at Hautdesert are crammed with evocative particulars of courtly entertainment, of physical appearances, of the activities and trappings of the hunt. Cross-threading with these are the displays of courtly conversation between Gawain and the Lady: cleverly using Gawain's reputation against him, the poet's style is literary and allusive. The Lady knows how romance heroes ought to behave and forces on him an interpretation of knightly conduct entirely in terms of boudoir devotion and chivalrous action in the service of love:

'...of alle cheualry to chose, þe chef þyng alosed	*praised*
Is þe lel layk of luf, þe lettrure of armes;	*sport; lore*
For to telle of þis teuelyng of þis trwe knyʒtez,	*endeavour*
Hit is þe tytelet token and tyxt of her werkkez,	*inscribed* [like a motto]; *text*
How ledes for her lele luf hor lyuez han auntered,	
Endured for her drury dulful stoundez,	*love-making; times*
And after wenged with her walour and voyded her care,	*won retribution*
And broʒt blysse into boure with bountees hor awen...'	*merits*

(1512–19)

The bookish flavour of this (*lettrure, tyxt* and *werkkez* [in the sense of literary works, that is, romances]) confirms the reader's sense of *Sir Gawain* as a sophisticated, literary poem which is presenting behaviour as double-layered: we know that the Lady is teasing the hero by suggesting that he should love by the book and that these dialogues are an elaborate game, reminiscent of the ironic conversations of Andreas Capellanus, in which Gawain learns to kiss on command and to match the Lady in polite verbal fencing.

III

The Gawain who returns chastened to Camelot is no longer quite the traditional hero, 'Gawain the good', who appeared at the beginning: shamed by being exposed in the lie of retaining and concealing the green belt out of fear of the Green Knight's axe, and thus breaking the terms of his exchange bargain with Bertilak, he is not consoled by his adversary's forgiving praise, though Camelot's happiness at his safe return would seem to endorse the verdict that, even though he 'lakked a lyttel',

> 'As perle bi þe quite pese is of prys more,   *pea*
> So is Gawayn, in god fayth, bi oþer gay knyʒtez.'
>   (2364–5)

Compared to other Middle English romances *Sir Gawain* comes closest to being a portrait of its hero, who is allowed a far wider range of thought and feeling than figures such as Havelok or Guy of Warwick: he is lonely and cold, embarrassed and afraid, has bad dreams, has to control erotic and nervous thoughts, and has even to quell the instinct of self-preservation. His return to Camelot, ashamed at being 'tane in tech of a faute' (2488), is in tune with earlier self-criticism, as when he realises that his courtesy towards the Lady may rebound and expose him to misjudgement:

> Such semblaunt to þat segge semly ho made   *demonstration of regard*
> Wyth stille stollen countenaunce, þat stalworth to plese,   *secret looks of favour*
> Þat al forwondered watz þe wyʒe, and wroth with hymseluen,   *astonished*
> Bot he nolde not for his nurture nurne hir aʒaynez,   *publicly differ from her*
> Bot dalt with hir al in daynté, how-se-euer þe dede turned   *politely*
>   Towrast.   *awry*
>   (1658–63)

The poet is exploring the idea of the hero, using several images of his character and placing him between two courts, a known picture of Camelot in its early years of power and optimism and the invented provincial court of Hautdesert. This is a vivid creation of a model social unit, praised for its hospitality and the care with which Gawain himself, his horse and his armour are looked after, portrayed in action in the hunts, where the observation of the close season, the smooth organisation of a deer drive, the expert breaking up of the carcases of the quarry, the physical strength and courage of the Lord's killing of the boar and the careful persistence of the pursuit of the fox all characterise an ideal of estate management. But this apparently safe environment conceals its hazards.

Balancing the character of Gawain as he is tested and tempted is the enigmatic figure of the Green Knight/Bertilak, who shifts through several phases of appearance and nature. He begins as a grotesque, if oddly elegant, phantom, exaggeratedly super-human and unnatural in size, colour and invulnerability. He reappears as a stereotype of the bluff and cheerful host, but emerges as Gawain's rival, both in being the husband of the tempting Lady and in his bold leading of the hunts, the boar-hunt in particular. At the climax of the narrative he is a powerful master-figure, modulating and losing his supernatural qualities to become a judge and explicator and finally a knight with a name, who has been merely lent supernatural power and whose name carries a hint of allegorical meaning. At the end he is a green knight in no more than the temporary sense of knights who change the colour of their armour – like the hero of *Ipomadon* who fights in a three-day tournament successively in the disguises of white knight, red knight and black knight. The poet has constructed a cryptic diagram from the contrast between his two knights. Gawain is a known hero who moves in the course of the action from an apparently stable identity towards insecurity and self-questioning. The Green Knight is an anonymous and disguised figure who admits a named identity at the very close of the action, though he remains inexplicable in rational terms.

This is but one of the uncertainties about the poem which have made it one of the most discussed of medieval texts. Are we meant to disapprove of Camelot? Is the final laughter at Gawain's shame a sign of the court's superficiality in comparison to the hero's self-blame? Can we accept the idea that Bertilak has the moral authority to act as Gawain's judge when he was only an instrument of Morgan's malice against Guenevere and Camelot? Is Gawain's anti-feminist outburst (2414–28) simply an apt psychological touch of sulky irritation at being found out or a declaration of one of the poem's themes – that, left to themselves, men are decent and truthful, if stupid at times, while women are more intelligent but deceptive? Is masculinity on trial or chivalry or Frenchified court manners? One could find justification for all these and more in the cultural history of the late fourteenth century in Britain. Chaucer raises some of the same questions in his treatment of related material in *The Wife of Bath's Tale*: another ugly old woman and a knight (an undeserving one in this case) caught in a bed where he has to learn a lesson. The problem in *Sir Gawain*, or rather the merit, is that the poet is subtle and does not punctuate his narrative with explanations: the only place where he does attribute specific meaning is the explication of the pentangle, but by the end of the poem that emblem of Gawain's physical and moral qualities seems to have been replaced by the green 'bende of þis blame' (2506). Elsewhere the poet animates his narrative with imaginative language but works by hints not by labels. So, for example, some interpreters have taken the parallel between the hunts and the bedroom scenes as a symbolic representation of Gawain's position (he is a hunted victim, or he is like a deer, like a boar, like a fox), but others have rejected that sort of crude signposting and seen more in the ironic contrast between the two actions and in the indirect expression of Bertilak's role in the main plot. What the poet does is set the scenes vividly before the reader with hints of the Lady's double-dealing, producing dramatic irony that the reader appreciates only with hindsight. One of the pleasures of the poem is the element of mystery – a concealed plot which may mean that there is, as is often the case in detective stories, some sense of the author's misleading the reader – which leaves matter to chew over when the poem ends.

References and Further Reading

Anderson, J. J. (2005). *Language and Imagination in the Gawain Poems*. Manchester: Manchester University Press.

Brewer, Derek and Jonathan Gibson (eds) (1997). *A Companion to the Gawain-Poet*. Cambridge: D. S. Brewer.

Brewer, Elisabeth (1992). *Sir Gawain and the Green Knight: Sources and Analogues*. Cambridge: D. S. Brewer. (Originally pub. 1973.)

Burrow, J. A. (2001). *The Gawain-Poet*. Tavistock: Northcote House.

Davenport, Tony (2004). *Medieval Narrative*. Oxford: Oxford University Press.

Duggan, H. N. (1997). Meter, stanza, vocabulary, dialect. In D. Brewer and J. Gibson (eds). *A Companion to the Gawain-Poet*. (pp. 221–42) Cambridge: D. S. Brewer.

Hahn, Thomas (ed.) (1995). *Sir Gawain: Eleven Romances and Tales*. Kalamazoo, MI: Medieval Institute Publications.

Ingledew, Francis (2006). *Sir Gawain and the Green Knight and the Order of the Garter*. Notre Dame, IN: University of Notre Dame Press.

Kay, Sarah (1995). *The Chansons de Geste in the Age of Romance*. Oxford: Oxford University Press.

Mann, Jill (1994). Sir Gawain and the romance hero. In Leo Carruthers (ed.). *Heroes and Heroines in Medieval English Literature* (pp.104–17). Cambridge: D. S. Brewer.

Putter, Ad (1995). *Sir Gawain and the Green Knight and French Arthurian Romance*. Oxford: Clarendon Press.

Rychner, Jean (1955). *La Chanson de Geste: Essai sur l'art epique des jongleurs*, Geneva: Droz; Lille: Giard.

Schmolke-Hasselmann, Beate (1998). *The Evolution of Arthurian Romance*. M. and R. Middleton (trans). Cambridge: Cambridge University Press. (German original pub. 1980.)

Simpson, James (2002). The comic. *Reform and Cultural Revolution* (pp. 255–321). Oxford: Oxford University Press.

The Song of Roland. (1937). Trans. Dorothy L. Sayers. Harmondsworth: Penguin Books.

Tolkien, J. R. R., Gordon, E. V. and N. Davis (eds) (1967). *Sir Gawain and the Green Knight*. 2nd edn. Oxford: Clarendon Press.

Turville-Petre, Thorlac (1974). Three poems in the thirteen-line stanza. *Review of English Studies*, 25, 140–47.

Turville-Petre, Thorlac (1977). *The Alliterative Revival*. Cambridge: D. S. Brewer.

Van Emden, Wolfgang (1995). *La Chanson de Roland*. London: Grant and Cutler.

Whiting, B. J. (1947). Gawain: his reputation, his courtesy and his appearance in Chaucer's 'Squire's Tale'. *Mediaeval Studies*, 9, 189–234. (Repr. in Raymond H. Thompson and Keith Busby (eds). (2006). *Gawain: A Casebook* (pp. 45–94). New York: Routledge.)

22

William Langland: *Piers Plowman*

Lawrence Warner

Piers Plowman generated as tumultuous a public life and complex a production history as any other work of its era or perhaps of any other. It might thus better be studied as an event comprising the actions of an author, audiences, scribes and editors than as just the work of a single poet. Whether because of its public reception or his mono-maniacal vision, its author, now called William Langland more out of convenience than any firm knowledge of his identity, spent some three or four decades, from the 1360s until about 1390, writing and revising his great poem (see Kane 2004). The results are three authorial forms, now called the A, B and C versions, and a substantial handful of conflations of these versions compiled by enterprising scribes and readers. What did they encounter in the poem? It is fair to say that they did not turn to it for its plot. While all three versions do have certain governing principles and thematic developments, often, especially in the 7000-plus lines of its two longer versions, B and C, those are subsumed under the treatment of a particular idea that bears little relation to the action. But a general sense of the poem's overall structure, or its plot, such as it is, at the least helps ground readers' appreciation of any given topic, even if it need not govern their responses.

An interesting and previously unknown summary that a mid-nineteenth-century anonymous reader inscribed into his or her copy of a sixteenth-century edition of the B version shows the degree to which any reading of the poem is necessarily shaped by both the particular interests of the reader and the material circumstances of the encounter:

> In the Introduction Simony, and the connivance of the Civil Law, are reproved. The first part of the Vision opens with the Castle of Care, and Holy Church, complaining of the general absence of charity amongst the people, and the celibate members of the church. Canto 2. States the origin of Mede, or the Church Property, her endowment by Favell and union with Falsehood, which last is declared void by the King (Nation) though formed by Simony, and Civil Law. Canto the 3rd. Mede brought before the King,

to whom, and his nobles, she gives precious gifts; but is drawn aside by the clergy, who promise her the indulgence of her amours with the great and rich. Canto the 4th. The King sends Conscience to fetch Reason to Mede. Peace complains that Wrong has taken his wife, (or his rights and property) from him. Mede offers Peace a bribe, which he accepts; but the King insists that Wrong shall not go unpunished. The King compels Reason to abide with him. Canto 5th. Reason describes the causes of public trouble; Lechery, Envy, Wrath, (in nunneries), Covetousness (admirably described) Gluttony, Drunkenness (a spirited scene) Sooth, with ignorance in the Clergy. Repentance advised. Canto 6th. Part lost. The duties of the people. The poet disclaims against the general taste for idleness and mendicity, as well as waste; points out that mendicants should be made to work. He warns, that if these vices be not cured, want will ensue. Canto 7th. Advice as to honesty and industry. Honesty the surest road to welfare. Popes' pardons will not avail at the day of judgment. Canto 8th. Speaks of good works under the titles of Do-well, Do-better, & Do-best. Canto 9th. Dowell dwelleth in man. Tithes should be given to relieve the poor. Praises marriage. Canto the 10th. Riches now preferred to wisdom. Foretells at the latter part, that, for the luxury and wealth of the clergy, a King shall arise, who shall put them to penance, and purify nuns and monks, and barons shall claim their property. The penitent and poor are sooner saved than the rich; and the learned sooner fall from faith than the people of low state. Canto 11th. The poet tells that wealth causes concupiscence – that priests seek out the dying for their goods – that the soul may be saved without masses, that the clergy should not say masses for money – Celibacy indirectly blamed, by the statement, that nature points out the union of the sexes. Canto 12th. States that the discharge of the moral duties in life, is of more avail than pilgrimages.– On baptism. Canto 13 – Speaks of the clergy, and their excesses –their Idolls, the sciences; which are not equal to love and faith. The value of labour &c scarcity when Chichester was Mayor (of London) in April 1350. General praise of labour. Canto 14. Deprecates avarice – praises patience, and the clergy who embrace poverty for the love of religion. The nine advantages of Poverty. Canto 15. Praises Charity, and censures covetousness. The Covetousness of the priesthood reproved. The nobles blamed for leaving their estates from their heirs to the church. The poet recommends for the health of the church, that the nobles should take the lands of the church, and that the clergy should live upon the tithes. Canto 16. Describes Christian charity, and shews how the soul of man whilst bringing forth the fruits of ye spirit, must be supported by the Father, Son, and Holy Ghost; – otherwise the boughs, with the fruit, will be borne to the earth and perish. The mystical union of the Trinity described. Canto 17. Faith and Hope praised, but stated to be nothing worth, even with penance, without the atonement of Christ. The Trinity compared to a hand in different states. A good man compared to a torch. The three things which drive a man from his house – a scolding wife – a roof untiled, and smoke. Canto 18th. Justice and Mercy reconciled, and Satan overpowered, by the death of Christ. Canto 19. Christ's history – the foundation of the true church. Pride introduces corruptions. Pierce laments that Cardinals ever came into England, wishes the Pope would stay at Avignon, or Rome, with his relics, instead of robbing the church. The King, or the law of Justice, demands that right government should be given in return for revenue. Canto 20. Pronounces the Pope to be Antichrist, and tells of the Infidelity which shall follow. The rest of the copy is torn out; but would appear by the Summary to censure the corruption of the clergy and monks, and the neglect of Patrons and Bishops.

(Anonymous post-1841)

In many ways this is a very idiosyncratic summary. The poem itself refers to each division not as a 'canto' but as a 'passus', Latin for 'step' (perhaps the reader had recently been working through Dante). Nor does it have much to repay the reader's obvious interest in clerical celibacy. And while this summary makes clear that the poem is an allegory (e.g. the king represents 'Nation'), a number of the topics or structures that have occupied much of modern criticism, such as the poem's relationships to the Wycliffite heresy or to the role of the friars, or even any sense that it relates a series of dreams by a figure called 'Will', are wholly absent.

Where this nineteenth-century reader, for instance, identifies 'Dowell dwelleth in man' as an episode worth relating, he does not find it worthwhile to point out that Will spends the bulk of the poem searching out Dowel, Dobet and Dobest. Different figures give him different answers: during a waking episode a friar says that Dowel dwells amongst the friars (B.8.18); a few lines later, when Will is again asleep, Thought defines the three *Do*'s as being true in speech and work, patient preaching, and serving as bishop, respectively; in the next passus Wit identifies Dowel with marriage, going on to expound the ethics of sexuality; and so forth. None of these definitions seems to be wholly authoritative: Wit himself is upbraided by his wife Study in passus 10 for his intellectual presumption, for instance. Derek Pearsall has aptly observed that 'The explanations are successively richer and more comprehensive, but cumulative rather than dialectical in their function; what successive speakers say is appropriate to the stage of development for which they speak, not "wrong"' (Pearsall 2008: 40). A number of interpretive questions arise from this aspect of the poem: first, whether the manuscript rubrics that divide the poem into four parts – the *Visio* (Prologue through passus 7 of B) and then the successive *Vitae* of the three *Do*'s – go back to the author or are instead scribal; second, what it would mean for an author or reader to identify a portion of the Dreamer's experiences with one of the *Do*'s; and third, whether we are thus to read the poem as a teleological journey, as an account of spiritual and intellectual progression. Even if earlier accounts of the *Do*'s are not 'wrong', the idea that they correlate to stages of the Dreamer's development does suggest that they correlate as well to stages of the *poem*'s development.

There is no question that the poem moves from the more social concerns of the *Visio*, such as the proper functioning of the king, or each person's responsibilities to the community according to his or her station in life, to more individual and personal concerns in *Dobet* in particular. Will's encounters with Thought, Wit, Study and all the rest of the allegorical abstractions culminate in a magnificent discourse by Imaginatyf ('the power of making pictures, ideas and abstractions from the data of experience, and the power, therefore, by which intellectual truth was gained through sensible objects' [Pearsall 2008: 238]), in which many pressing theological problems, such as the need for justice on the one hand (shouldn't only the good be saved?) and grace on the other (salvation is God's gift to everybody), are rendered comprehensible to the Dreamer. This 'inner journey', in which the dreamer seeks a more mystical meaning than the one he originally hopes Holy Church will explicate, can make for difficult reading, but has in many ways been at the heart of modern criticism of the poem (e.g. Zeeman 2006). No doubt our own advances in the realms of psychology have rendered this one of the richest and most palatable sections of *Piers Plowman*, whereas our distance from the pseudo-feudal world imagined in other parts of the poem makes them seem much more 'medieval'.

All of these approaches are productive and valuable, but just as no one definition of 'Dowel' will suffice for the poem, neither will any one mode of interpretation, or even summary, of *Piers Plowman* account for all of its meanings. This remarkably wide-ranging, rich and often difficult poem ensures that even the most basic plot summary, such as that by the nineteenth-century reader above, will be idiosyncratic and is bound to get some details wrong. This is simply because the poem covers such a wide range of topics via so many genres (dream vision, satire, biblical narrative, confessional manual, and so on; see Justice 1988). Thus such critical responses in effect turn into a new work itself in need of decoding – become, that is, part of the event rather than an external commentary upon it. At the least, this anonymous response shows that *Piers Plowman* holds the interest of readers from cultures quite far removed from that in which Langland was first working. It also shows the extent to which responses cannot help but be governed by the material forms in which audiences encounter it. This reader confronted a copy in which the opening of passus 6 and the conclusion of the poem were missing; in the latter situation he relied upon the summary of main points that Robert Crowley had included in the opening of this edition (his third) and upon his own sense of what would happen. And while today we are quick to categorize any given copy of the poem by its postulated authorial version, medieval audiences, even if aware of different states of the poem, did not approach it in this manner.

It is in large part to Robert Crowley's efforts of 1550, when he produced three printed editions of the poem, that those modern approaches to *Piers Plowman* owe their assumptions. The text he printed became the foundation for modern readers and editions, and it is very common to find that surviving copies of that text contain annotations such as the one cited above. In earlier centuries the poem (in all three versions) was by far the most popular specimen of its form of alliterative long lines, which relies not upon rhyme but rather upon the interplay between stressed and unstressed, and alliterating and non-alliterating, syllables within each individual line. In general, each line has four major stresses or 'lifts', the first three of which usually alliterate, and a medial caesura between the second and third lifts (on alliterative verse see further the essays of John Scattergood, Carl Schmidt and Tony Davenport in this volume). In the line '"I haue *lyued* in *londe*", quod I, / "my name is *longe wille*"' (B.15.152; quotations are from Kane and Donaldson's edition), the words in italics are the lifts, the '/' represents the caesura, the alliteration is on 'l' and there are three unstressed syllables ('my name is') before the third lift. (This line happens to provide an acrostic of the poet's pen name, if the early reference to one 'William de Longlond who made the poem called Piers Plowman' is accurate [see Kane 2004].)

What attracted Langland to this form? As Stephen Barney has observed, the alliterative long line has particular effects that make it apt for satire: 'The rhythmic imbalance at the end of the alliterative line typically lets the sense too seem imbalanced, as if more were needed to bring stability; it releases energy, potentiates, drives forward', as in 'Sholde I neuere ferþer a foot for no freres prechyng' (B.5.633) (Barney 2001: 109). Usually, of course, the alliteration signals the line's emphasis, but this scheme is flexible enough to enable other modes of meaning to establish themselves as well. The line 'That óon *d*ooþ álle *d*ooþ and éch *d*ooþ bi his óne' (B.16.183), for instance, features standard alliteration on *d* as well as the additional, unstressed collocations, marked here by an accent, on the terms 'one', 'all' and 'each' (see Smith 2008: 62). *Piers Plowman* is extant in over fifty surviving witnesses, ranging from brief excerpts to a conflation of all three authorial versions, from the fourteenth through the sixteenth centuries. Other poems in this form rarely survive in more than a single copy, and it seems clear that Langland played a major role in establishing the long-line alliterative verse form as the one in which poets concerned with the topic of *penance*, such as the authors of *Sir Gawain and the Green Knight* and the alliterative *Morte Arthure*, would compose in the latter half of the fourteenth century and into the fifteenth (Lawton 1983).

Piers Plowman's use of this form also makes it one of a group of poems that treat major theological issues in a manner accessible to the laity and to readers of the vernacular. Some recent critics have thus placed the poem within a movement expounding a 'vernacular theology' (Watson 1997), but it equally draws upon Latin registers and traditions. For among the most startling things about the poem in all its forms, especially the longer, B and C versions, is its insistent use of Latin tags and lines, usually set off in the manuscripts by being boxed or even written in red. At certain moments the effect of these Latin lines might seem to substitute for the sense of closure achieved by the Chaucerian iambic couplet. The peaceful end of the debate of the Four Daughters of God, after which Will awakens and urges his wife and daughter to reverence the cross at church on Easter morning, for instance, cites the Psalms as well as a liturgical hymn:

> 'Thow seist sooþ', seyde Rightwisnesse, and reuerentliche hire kiste:
> Pees, and pees hire, *per secula seculorum*:
> *Misericordia & veritas obuiauerunt sibi; Iusticia & pax osculate sunt.*
> Truþe trumpede þo and song *Te deum laudamus*,
> And þanne lutede loue in a loud note:
> *Ecce quam bonum & quam iocundum &c.*
>
> (B.18.420–23*a*)

In this passage, as in many others, the scriptural quotations 'do not merely bolster [Langland's] line of thought, but help to produce it', comments Fiona Somerset in the most comprehensive survey of Langland's Latin (Somerset 2005: 111). Righteousness's verse from Psalm 84, 'Mercy and truth have met each other: justice and peace have kissed' (v. 11; trans. Schmidt 1995), has generated the drama in which the abstractions of that verse, incarnated as 'the Four Daughters of God', embrace each other.

Yet Latin is not merely a monolithic authoritarian mode of discourse that serves to authorize the poet's theology. 'Even when we are reading Middle English, and especially when we are reading Middle English as perfused with Latin as that of *Piers Plowman*', Somerset observes, 'variations within Latinity provide a whole realm of reference, shared between writers and to a more limited extent their readers, in which style, genre, and register can become figures for institutionally specific kinds of knowledge, authority, and power' (Somerset 2005: 115–16). The exchange among the 'lunatik', the 'Aungel of heuene' who '[l]owed to speke in latyn', and the commoners who began to 'crye in vers of latyn' is an especially charged example of the variety of poetic modes manifested in Langland's verse forms (B.Prol.123, 128–29, 143; see Somerset 2005: 117–26). What Chaucer achieves via his storytellers, it would be fair to say, Langland does via the interplay between the English alliterative long line and the Latin that sometimes balances and sometimes disrupts that main form of versification.

The prominence of Latin is also a clue both to Langland's processes of composition and to his poem's creation of meaning. John A. Alford points out that Langland offers his readers some practical advice in how to read this intermixture of Latin and English. The context is Conscience's rebuke of Meed's reading practices:

> 'I leue wel, lady,' quod Conscience, 'þat þi latyne be trewe.
> Ac þow art lik a lady þat radde a lessoun ones
> Was *omnia probate*, and þat plesed hire herte
> For þat lyne was no lenger at þe leues ende.
> Hadde she loked þat left half and þe leef torned
> She sholde haue founden felle wordes folwynge þerafter:
> *Quod bonum est tenete*; truþe þat text made.'
>
> (B.3.337–43)

The lady in question had been attracted by the text 'test all things', but missed the rest of the sentence: 'hold that which is good' (1 Thess. 5:21). *Piers Plowman* is full of quotations that in effect occur at leaf's end, as does the scriptural text that Meed reads: over and over they end with 'etc.', and, as Alford suggests, 'the whole point of some quotations resides in the "etc."' (Alford 1977: 82). The vision we should have of Langland is 'that of a man eking out his poem slowly, even tediously, while poring over a variety of commentaries and preachers' aids' (Alford 1977: 99), structuring his poem as preachers did their sermons, with the authorities from scripture and the commentary tradition providing the substance of the poem, a verbal concordance that he adapted to his poetry, which he both worked out from and moved toward.

Knowledge of this reliance upon verbal concordances enables a more historically responsible contextualization of the most famous response to *Piers Plowman*, one that almost surely lay behind Langland's subsequent revisions and that has served as a touchstone for modern attempts to understand the poem's role in fourteenth-century political and religious controversies. The event was the Rising of 1381, in which the Archbishop of Canterbury was beheaded, the king of England sought refuge in the Tower of London, and the palace of the king's uncle, the most powerful man in the realm, was ransacked. In the letters that he wrote to rally support for the cause, one John Ball urged 'Piers the Plowman' to go to his work – a remarkable situation unprecedented in medieval poetry. What prompted Ball, the poem's earliest identifiable audience, to refer to our poem's titular character? Which version did he know? What does this tell us about the public life of the poem?

Ball must either have had access to a manuscript of *Piers Plowman* or encountered excerpts of it, perhaps in oral form. It seems clear that his primary interest, whatever version he knew, was in the figure of Piers the Plowman himself. Could this be some ancient folk hero to whom Langland and Ball both independently refer? That seems unlikely, for 'there is no literary precedent for Langland's bold move' of establishing a plowman as positive hero; before *Piers Plowman*, '[l]aborers are associated with Cain, priests with Abel' (Kirk 1988: 11, 9). The closest model for Piers's central role lies in the tradition of the 'plowshare of the tongue' (Barney 1973), which depicts preachers as sowers of the word. But it is Langland's re-contextualization of that tradition, especially his invocation of the figure in such realistic (if also allegorical) contexts, that is so striking.

The context of Piers's appearance, in all versions of the poem, is the dreamer's second vision. Some pilgrims are looking for a guide, and along comes a plowman, Piers, who knows the way and offers his services. But first, he says, he has a half-acre that needs plowing: once the pilgrims help him, he will show them the way. It is all rather odd, and it is to John Burrow's classic 1965 essay that we owe the happy situation of the episode making sense. Burrow shows that this scene dramatises a fourfold process of atonement. The sinners in the poem have heard a *sermon*, which moves them to repent their sins by means of *confession*. To achieve this they must pay their debt of temporal punishment, most of which is to be accomplished here via *pilgrimage*. Most, but not all, is thus accomplished: for the remainder they need a *pardon*, by whose power they are finally free of the consequences of their sins.

This is not quite what happens in *Piers Plowman*. Langland instead allegorises the schema via a series of substitutions. In place of individual sinners are allegorical abstractions of the sins, and in place of a preacher is the figure Repentance. That is straightforward enough. But pilgrimage presented particular problems, Burrow notes, since it is clear throughout *Piers Plowman* that its poet put little stock in pilgrimage as a means of effecting atonement. What mattered instead to him were individual works. Hence the third substitution: St Truth rather than, say, the pilgrimage site of St James, is to be the object of the pilgrimage. This leads to the final, and decisive, substitution: the plowing of the half-acre, that is, the faithful fulfilment of the vocation of one's life for pilgrimage. Piers tells knights to defend the realm, labourers to work the fields, women to make clothing, and so forth: this is the 'plowing' in which sinners should engage. Upon repenting, it is the act of 'winning' rather than wasting via empty pilgrimage that will bring the sinner into union with God.

In its context this seems theologically unexceptionable, nothing that any figures of authority would worry much about. Anti-pilgrimage sentiments were not particularly threatening, and were often shared by clerics. But the series of substitutions enacted here all but invites the reader or listener to continue the process. As depicted within this episode, Piers the Plowman might not come across as a revolutionary leader, but Ball seems to have been responding to the rhetorical power of Langland's elevation of a labourer to heroic stature. It seems fair to imagine that to Ball this was the most explosive substitution effected by *Piers Plowman*. From this perspective, it would be entirely beside the point to read the episode of the plowing of the half-acre on its own terms and according to its own penitential logic: it is substitution, opening the door to revolution, that is really at issue here.

What I am proposing is that Ball was not concerned with the entirety of the poem at all. In fact he might never have seen a manuscript of it, or heard any more than some catchphrases that already synecdochically substituted the revolutionary 'Piers the Plowman' for the spiritual guide of Langland's poem. One of the reasons it is worth spending time sorting out the parameters of the poem's influence upon Ball is that this local issue has far-reaching implications upon our sense of how the poem was produced, disseminated, and revised – upon our sense, that is, of its meaning and very being. A growing scholarly consensus has it not only that in 1380 John Ball knew the entire B version, but also that the A version, while already composed, had not even entered circulation by this point. George Kane, for instance, points to parallels between Ball's couplet 'And do wel and better, and fleth synne / And sekeþ pees, and hold ȝou þerinne' and this passage, close to the end of the B version:

> Quod Consience to alle cristene þo, 'my conseil is to wende
> Hastiliche into vnitee and holde we vs þere.
> Praye we þat a pees weere in Piers berne þe Plowman.'
> (B.19.355–57; see Kane 2004)

That *Piers Plowman* is a poem about 'doing well and better' makes the parallel between Ball's and Langland's directives to seek peace and remain therein all the more striking. But such imagery pervades biblical and moralistic writings of the era: Psalm 33:15 alone, 'Turn away from evil and *do good*: *seek after peace* and pursue it', should dispense with the assumption that Ball here necessarily has *Piers Plowman* in mind. It instead seems probable that both Langland and Ball (himself a preacher) are here doing the same thing – relying on a verbal concordance of the sort that, as Alford shows, preachers and Langland exploited – rather than that Ball is responding to *Piers Plowman*. On the one hand readers attempting to place the poem in its historical milieu encounter the ubiquity of such biblically inflected materials in medieval vernacular poetry, Latin commentaries, sermons and indeed nearly all discourse. On the other they quickly realize the difficulty of defining the versions of *Piers Plowman* and the dates of their production and circulation. Together, these difficulties present great challenges to any attempt to gauge precisely where Langland fits on the political landscape of later medieval England. Much more work remains to be done in this area.

For the belief that John Ball knew *Piers Plowman* B has relied upon the understandable, but mistaken, notion that modern editions of the poem simply represent a historically transparent textual situation. In fact, though, those editions, while triumphant interpretations of the surviving records, are by no means 'authoritative'. Since Crowley's editions of 1550, 'the B version' has been by far the most thoroughly studied version. It ends, though the reader whose summary we read above did not know it, with the allegorical personification Conscience abandoning the Holy Church Unity into which he had urged Christians to take refuge and establish themselves, instead setting out to seek Piers Plowman: a radically open-ended conclusion for a poem that has continually refused to come to rest, each of Will's visions ending in frustration and further questing. Yet this version, at least as printed by Crowley and read today, quite probably did not exist until 1390 or later, a decade after John Ball alluded to Piers the Plowman. For the nearly identical appearance of the final two passus in the B and C versions is the result not of authorial satisfaction or death, but instead the desire of scribes to complete their copies – thus the B version, which in the author's now-lost version ended at passus 18, where the dreamer calls his wife and daughter to go to church on Easter morning, incorporates the final two passus of the C version, the building and destruction of Holy Church Unity (Warner 2007a).

The approach to *Piers Plowman* that emphasises its plot above all else, if assumed to be the normative one (as is the case for much modern criticism), thus both fails to account for responses such as that of Ball and assumes a correlation between the surviving shapes of the manuscripts and what Langland originally wrote, despite the chronological lateness of all manuscripts and our knowledge that early readers were happy to conflate what we now take to be separate authorial versions in their quest for a 'complete' copy. Moreover, while some readers sought completeness, others went in the opposite direction, responding to *Piers Plowman* not as a sequential depiction of the dreamer's quest, but instead as a series of set-pieces, or even simply as a repository of particular modes of rhetoric, such as anti-ecclesiastical satire or prophecy. While the manuscripts contain almost no records of attention to spiritual or narrative development, they are full of 'nota' marks, drawings of pointing hands in the margins, and simple crosses next to individual lines: signs of intermittent and local interest. Early scribes, like the anonymous annotator cited above, paid particular attention to passus 5's lively portraits of the personified sins: twelve of the fifteen B-version manuscripts surveyed by David Benson offer some sort of annotation to those portraits, amounting to 117 annotations in total (over half of which occur in three manuscripts). In passus 16, by contrast, only two of these fifteen scribes annotated a mere four passages (Benson and Blanchfield 1997: 238f.).

In the sixteenth century, *Piers Plowman* seems primarily to have been valued as a site of obscure brief political prophecies of a sort that almost never feature in modern criticism even if they are no less part of the text than are the more widely studied passages. Davy the Diker shall die of hunger when you see the sun amiss and two monks' heads, says the narrator in B.6's closing lines (325f). One sixteenth-century manuscript, which titles the poem 'The Prophecies of Piers Plowman', highlights this and four other such 'prophecies'; a mid-century pamphleteer published 'Davy Diker's Dream'; two readers excerpted these lines into their own commonplace books; and two others inscribed them into manuscripts presenting different versions which were deemed incomplete without these lines. So pervasive was this interest that Crowley drew attention to these lines in his address to the reader of his 1550 edition, his aim the denial that they belonged in the poem at all: they were beyond his or anyone's control, leading him to distance them from either himself or Langland, but powerful enough that he felt compelled to print them (Crowley 1550: *iiv).

Today Langland's prophetic streak receives attention insofar as it applies to particular historical circumstances, such as the heated topic of ecclesiastical ownership: 'Ac þer shal come a kyng and confesse yow Religiouses, / And bete yow, as þe bible telleþ, for brekynge of youre rule' (B.10.322–23). The post-1841 summary quoted above draws attention to these lines, and Crowley, too, was happier with this mode of rhetoric (though he denied it was prophetic: it was instead, he said, a prognostication) than with the sort about celestial portents and monks' heads (Crowley 1550: *ii^v). But despite the seeming proto-Protestant character of these lines, or their affinity with the Wycliffite heretical movement of the 1380s, it seems that fifteenth- and sixteenth-century readers did not interpret such 'prophecy' as being particularly reformist in character. In fact one copy of the Davy Diker lines cited above was probably inscribed by a monk-turned-friar who, despite his impeccable Catholic and recusant beliefs, still seems to have preached a sermon based on this latter prophecy about a king who would come to correct the religious. It did not occur to him to connect this passage with Henry VIII's dissolution of the monasteries (Warner 2007b). This *Piers Plowman* – generator of prophecies to be excerpted and circulated, probably orally as well as in script, with no regard to their context in the longer poem – is a phenomenon entirely distinct from, if no less authentic than, the one telling of a dreamer's progression, or at least movement, from Do-well through Do-best that has dominated modern critical discussions.

Readers who have approached *Piers Plowman* in such a piecemeal fashion are not violating its medieval spirit. For one, even the poem's most fundamental themes continually present themselves to the Dreamer and to its audiences as transparent truths, not subject to refinement upon the poem's future revelations. In a pair of major essays, Traugott Lawler has drawn attention to the poem's continual emphases upon, first, the notion that 'to do evil but repent is to do well' (Lawler 2000), and second, the corruption (especially by friars) of the system of absolution via acceptance of payment from sinners without requiring their restitution, which he calls 'miswinning' (Lawler 2006). In doing so Lawler shows that Langland intends the poem to be recursive rather than developmental. Many of these episodes appear initially in the C version, and it is worth noting that they could have been originally transcribed onto single sheets or gatherings, which could easily have circulated independently prior to, or at least as well as, their inclusion in the poem as a whole. In the middle of the lively episode of Meed appears, out of the blue, this warning to mayors to prevent false traders from becoming citizens (one of the treatments of 'miswinning' discussed by Lawler):

> And thenne falleth ther fuyr on fals men houses
> And goode mennes for here gultes gloweth on fuyr aftur.
> Al this haue we seyn, þat som tyme thorw a breware
> Many burgages ybrent and bodies þerynne
> And thorw a candle clemynge in a cursed place
> Ful adoun and forbrent forth alle þe rewe.
> Forthy mayres þat maketh fre men, me thynketh þat ʒe ouhten
> For to spyre and to aspye, for eny speche of suluer,
> What maner muster oþer marchandise he vsed
> Ar he were vnderfonge fre and felawe in ʒoure rolles.
> Hit is nat seemely, forsothe, in Citee ne in borw toun
> That vsurers oþer regraters for eny skynes ʒeftes
> Be yfranchised for a fre man and haue a fals name.
>   (Russell and Kane (1997): C.3.102–14)

In its dramatic context, this passage seems so out of place that J. A. W. Bennett believed it 'to represent an officious scribe's intrusion or a fragment of a larger episodic discourse that was missing from, or never completed in, the Ur-text' (Bennett 1972: 136). The final two passus, too, could easily have served as a pamphlet, just as the individual *Canterbury Tales* most likely found audiences quite apart from that work as a whole during Chaucer's own lifetime. This possibility is not just speculation: Wendy Scase has found powerful evidence that early drafts of some of the new C material indeed circulated independently of the poem as a whole (Scase 1987). What appear to be digressions from the poem's themes might better be taken as evidence that *Piers Plowman* comprises not only an account of a dreamer's quest, but also both a recursive meditation upon major social and spiritual problems and a collection of disparate ruminations loosely connected by the dream-vision frame.

Recognition of this characteristic of *Piers Plowman* enables a much more accurate survey of the history of the poem's production and reception, which themselves were intimately interconnected in its earliest years, than does a sole emphasis upon the Dreamer's journey or the poem's thematic development. If critics rely too heavily upon editions, they might well overlook the ample evidence of early audiences' interest in excerpts, prophecies and stand-alone passages, or upon the manuscript evidence for the poem's non-developmental character. This should also be a relief to modern readers in the sense that *Piers Plowman*, whatever the version, is almost impossible to read cover to cover. It is a poem for dipping into and meditating upon. Too much is going on for it all to remain in any reader's head: hence the inevitable idiosyncrasy of any summary. We today are not so different from many, perhaps a great majority, of its earliest readers or from Langland himself. Finally, this recognition frees up much more of the poem for incorporation into the classroom than might have been the case, and suggests that those who have already been focusing upon particular episodes are following the example of their forebears.

The existence of so many excerpts of a six-line 'prophecy' should even encourage us to let go of the idea of studying the episode per se as the only alternative to reading the poem as a whole. We should feel free to attend to the brief excerpt, even the line, more so perhaps than has been the case in general modern criticism. *Piers Plowman* contains worlds: Will, and a host of critical articles and books, have explored many of these, but others, some only a few lines or even syllables long, await the kind of attention that early audiences, from John Ball forward, long paid them.

References and Further Reading

Editions and Primary Documents

Anon. (post-1841). Annotations in Duke University, shelfmark D-9 L282V c.1. (Robert Crowley's third edition of *The Vision of Pierce Plowman* [STC 19907].)

Bennett, J. A. W. (ed.) (1972). *Piers Plowman: The Prologue and Passus I–VII of the B-text.* Oxford: Clarendon Press.

The Holy Bible (1899). Douay-Rheims version. Rev. Bishop Challoner. Baltimore, John Murphy Company.

Kane, George and E. Talbot Donaldson (eds) (1988). *Piers Plowman: The B Version.* London: Athlone; Berkeley: University of California Press.

Pearsall, Derek (ed.) (2008). *Piers Plowman: A New Annotated Edition of the C-text.* Exeter: University of Exeter Press.

Russell, George and George Kane (eds) (1997). *Piers Plowman: The C Version.* London: Athlone; Berkeley: University of California Press.

Schmidt, A. V. C. (ed.) (1995). *The Vision of Piers Plowman: A Critical Edition of the B-text based on Trinity College Cambridge MS B.15.17.* 2nd edn. London: J. M. Dent; Rutland, VT: C. E. Tuttle.

Secondary Reading

Alford, John A. (1977). The role of the quotations in 'Piers Plowman'. *Speculum*, 52, 80–99.

Barney, Stephen A. (1973). The plowshare of the tongue: the progress of a symbol from the Bible to 'Piers Plowman'. *Mediæval Studies*, 35, 261–93.

Barney, Stephen A. (2001). Langland's mighty line. In Kathleen Hewett-Smith (ed.). *William Langland's 'Piers Plowman': A Book of Essays* (pp. 103–17). New York: Routledge.

Benson, C. David and Lynne Blanchfield (1997). *The Manuscripts of 'Piers Plowman': The B Version.* Cambridge: Boydell and Brewer.

Burrow, J. A. (1965). The action of Langland's second vision. *Essays in Criticism*, 15, 247–68.

Crowley, Robert (ed.) (1550). *The Vision of Pierce the Plowman, now fyrste imprynted by Roberte Crowley, dwellyng in Ely rentes in Holburne.* London. Lehigh University Library, shelfmark 821.1 L265p 1550. (Crowley's first edition, STC 19906.) Available from http://digital.lib.lehigh.edu/bookshelf (accessed 9 January 2009).

Gwynn, Aubrey (1943). The date of the B-Text of 'Piers Plowman.' *Review of English Studies*, 19, 1–24.

Justice, Steven (1988). The genres of 'Piers Plowman'. *Viator*, 19, 291–306.

Kane, George (2004). Langland, William (*c.* 1325–*c.* 1390). In H. C. G. Matthew and Brian Harrison (eds). *Oxford Dictionary of National Biography*. Oxford: Oxford University Press. http://www.oxforddnb.com/view/article/16021 (accessed November 4, 2008).

Kirk, Elizabeth D. (1988). Langland's Plowman and the recreation of fourteenth-century religious metaphor. *Yearbook of Langland Studies*, 2, 1–21.

Lawler, Traugott (2000). The pardon formula in 'Piers Plowman': its ubiquity, its binary shape, its silent middle term. *Yearbook of Langland Studies*, 14, 117–152.

Lawler, Traugott (2006). Harlots' holiness: the system of absolution for miswinning in the C Version of 'Piers Plowman'. *Yearbook of Langland Studies*, 20, 141–89.

Lawton, David A. (1983). The unity of Middle English alliterative poetry. *Speculum*, 58, 72–94.

Scase, Wendy (1987). Two 'Piers Plowman' C-Text interpolations: evidence for a second textual tradition. *Notes and Queries*, n.s. 34, 456–63.

Smith, Macklin (2008). Langland's unruly caesura. *Yearbook of Langland Studies*, 22, 57–101.

Somerset, Fiona (2005). 'Al þe comonys with o voys atonys': multilingual Latin and vernacular voice in 'Piers Plowman.' *Yearbook of Langland Studies*, 19, 107–36.

Warner, Lawrence (2007a). The ending, and end, of 'Piers Plowman' B: the C-version origins of the final two passus. *Medium Ævum*, 76, 225–50.

Warner, Lawrence (2007b). An overlooked 'Piers Plowman' excerpt and the oral circulation of non-reformist prophecy, *c.* 1520–55. *Yearbook of Langland Studies*, 21, 119–42.

Watson, Nicholas (1997). Visions of inclusion: universal salvation and vernacular theology in Pre-Reformation England. *Journal of Medieval and Early Modern Studies*, 27, 145–87.

Zeeman, Nicolette (2006). *'Piers Plowman' and the Medieval Discourse of Desire*. Cambridge: Cambridge University Press.

23
Chaucer's Love Visions

Helen Phillips

Dates for Chaucer's four dream poems are conjectural. The *Book of the Duchess* was written probably between 1368 and the mid-1370s, the *House of Fame* between about 1378 and the mid 1380s, the *Parliament of Fowls* perhaps in the early 1380s, and the *Legend of Good Women* begun in the late 1380s, with Chaucer continuing to work on it during the 1390s. The *Duchess* seems to have been written as a commemoration of Blanche Duchess of Lancaster (d. 1368), John of Gaunt's first wife. Its four-stress rhyming couplets, a common English form for romances, seem also Chaucer's English equivalent to the octosyllabic couplets regularly used in medieval French dream narratives and romances, and its structure and content draw inspiration from several near-contemporary dream poems by French poets (see Phillips and Havely 1994: 29–49, for sources and influences). The *House of Fame*, using the same couplets, draws on the biblical, classical and medieval vision narratives in which mortals are carried to the next world. It is also Chaucer's highly individual creation in the new genre of poems about fame, a fashion which would burgeon in the fifteenth century, whose greatest exponent in Chaucer's time had been Petrarch in his *Triumph of Fame* (between 1356 and 1374). Chaucer's idiosyncratic response to Italian influence appears also in his introduction of a comic eagle, inspired undoubtedly by the eagle as a symbol of St John, the author of the Book of Revelation, itself a vision of the next world, but also by eagles in Dante's *Purgatorio* (Book 9) and *Paradiso* (Books 18–20). The *Parliament of Fowls* starts with a summary of another other-world vision, Cicero's *Somnium Scipionis*, known to medieval writers from Macrobius' fifth-century *Commentary on the Dream of Scipio*. The *Parliament* is also one of the first writings celebrating the courtly cult of St Valentine. Its 'rime royal' seven-line pentameter stanza (ababbcc) is Chaucer's invention, representing his participation in the fourteenth-century interest in vernacular stanzaic experimentation, exemplified both in contemporary French poets' developments in various *formes fixes* lyric structures such as ballades, and by the Italian eight-line *rima ottava* stanza which Boccaccio had popularised as a narrative stanza. That contemporary interest appears also in the ballade inserted into the *Legend of Good*

Women and the roundel in the *Parliament of Fowls*. The *Legend* is in couplets of iambic pentameter, another verse form invented by Chaucer, which will predominate in the *Canterbury Tales*. A collection of tales within a frame story (like the *Tales*), its most obvious inspirations are Ovid's *Heroides*, a series of letters purporting to come from tragic lovers of classical mythology, and the medieval genre of the 'legend', a collection of saints lives, typically including many of the Christian martyrs who died for their faith. Chaucer's heroines are faithful martyrs of passion: either facing death as a result of their own unhappy love or suffering rape. The *Legend of Good Women*, the title commonly used since the sixteenth century, by foregrounding 'good women', has struck many readers as impossible to take literally or seriously and it has often been read as an antifeminist parody disguised as praise of women (see Phillips and Havely 1994: 350–1). Yet, apart from other reasons to find such readings reductive, manuscripts provide several titles and call it variously 'a glorious legende of goode wymmen', 'the Seintes Legende of Cupide' and 'book of the xxv Ladies'. That variety epitomises in a small way the many and complex parameters within which this rich and puzzling text can be read. All Chaucer's dream poems are works of profundity, of multiple layers and discourses, manifestly designed for courtly audiences who might be expected to appreciate writing which combines intellectual challenges with humour and the discourses of courtly love, and which create for English readers works of a calibre and adventurousness to match the best that fourteenth-century French and Italian vernacular culture was offering its readers, not least in the dream genre.

Yet Chaucer is clearly also writing for a greater audience and one beyond his own time, placing his own writings within the great tradition of the past, of classical poetry, and creating new poetry in English, and new kinds of poetry in English, to live for the future. In his legend of Dido (924–9) he talks of following in Virgil and Ovid's footsteps, while producing a piece quite independent, in tone and the moral dignity he gives the heroine, from those predecessors. In the *House of Fame* he contemplates the mighty succession of ancient writers, including Virgil and Ovid, and includes a bold question to his own alter ego, the dreamer, 'Artow come hider to han fame?' (1872) The self-deprecating answer, and the humorous tone generally in which Chaucer presents his own role and art throughout these poems, do not veil either the evidence they give of his interest with his own place among great poets of the ancient and modern world or the original, even revolutionary, ways in which he remakes inherited genres and styles into new forms of his own. Indeed, the strategy of not following the inspiration of predecessors – whether Ovid or Dante – with pompous solemnity is itself a way of striking out upon an individual creative path and marking an insistence on artistic freedom unrestrained by the reins of homage. Another sign of Chaucer's artistic ambition is the appearance in the *House of Fame* of invocations by the poet to the Muses (their first appearance in English poetry) and to Apollo, as the god of poetry. Though he talks with ostensible modesty of hoping the god will help make his 'lyght and lewed' rhymes 'somwhat agreable' (1096–7), rather than proposing a display of 'art poetical', what Chaucer forges in the dream poems is a light but infinitely flexible English style (and 'lewed' meant writing accessible to laypeople, without the necessity for clerical, Latin, education; while 'agreable' presents his ambitions courteously as those of the court servant) which can sing lyrically of love, express tragedy and pathos, and socially and emotionally expressive dialogue, and most originally of all, can explore daring intellectual ideas within and through poetic writing with a complex brilliance that is equalled elsewhere in English poetic history only by Keats and Shakespeare.

The Dream Genre

Guillaume de Lorris's mid thirteenth-century *Roman de la Rose* established dream poetry as a form for presenting the desires and, particularly, the pains and dilemmas of *gentil* lovers. Its handling of those subjects is made more complex and provocative by dream literature's centuries-old association with serious religious and philosophical revelations, and by the frequent inclusion of didactic forms like debate and allegory. Treating passion and desire in a genre with so learned a heritage was itself innovative but the love vision also later became a vehicle for examining passion directly in relation to intellectual ideas, a venture exemplified not least in the continuation of the *Roman de la Rose* by Jean de Meun (*c.* 1374).

Some critics, including Minnis et al. (2000: 161–347) and Lynch (2000), have explored the intellectual contexts of Chaucer's love visions. Lynch, indeed, designates them 'philosophical visions', arguing for the clear presence of contemporary intellectual issues: Ockhamist epistemology, for instance, in the *Book of the Duchess*. This chapter sees them as more polysemic and dialectic in their aesthetics, but the seriousness with which these critics point to philosophical currents in Chaucer's quartet matches their probing, intellectually adventurous mode better than the view common until the 1970s that these were decorative, derivative works concerned with love – essentially gendered feminine – produced before Chaucer's fully 'virile' (Kittredge 1915: 76) *Canterbury Tales*.

Besides *reflecting* contemporary thought, their writing explores deeply and creatively problems that are fundamentally philosophical or political but by venturing beyond the parameters of established conceptualisations, producing provocative instabilities and contradictions in the paradigms and styles they employ. These embedded philosophical issues include the ontological status of subjective emotional experience and the relationship of passion to the religious parameters whose discourses Chaucer's dream poetry often teasingly invokes, while the political topics include tyranny and rule, the idea of the *gentil* man and the oppression of women.

The dream form's openness to controversial topics, contradictory currents and disparate registers is most obvious in the turbulent writing and imagery of the *House of Fame* and *Legend* prologues – texts, interestingly, where Chaucer's own role as writer encounters authority of different kinds. It perhaps also affected Chaucer's endings – incomplete, open-ended or intellectually elusive.

Poet and Prince, Writing and Experience, Signs and Truth

Employing both dream frames and other framing fictions like gardens and temples, Chaucer's narratives belong to the tradition established by the *Rose* and to a creative burst of framed *dits amoureux* produced for French and English courts in the mid- and late fourteenth century by Guillaume de Machaut (1300–1377) and his followers, including Froissart and Oton de Grandson, who also directly influenced Chaucer. These *dits* demonstrate superlative subtlety, poignancy and beauty (Machaut himself was a great composer), avant-garde experimentation with narrative structures, and tensions between diverse world-views and discourses: Christian and pagan, clerkly and courtly, passionate and philosophical. Political engagement is often present: celebration of royal events, oblique allusions to political issues, the contribution of such texts to aristocratic self-presentation and the dissemination of that chivalric myth which is both a validation and aesthetic display of aristocratic power.

This is poetry that combines the expressive resources of lyric and narrative. Characterised by segmentation, parallels and inset lyrics and stories, its structures often bring classical mythology into the design, exemplifying the court artist's role in presenting modern princes in relation to learning and history, and also as the descendants in power, honour and cultural grandeur of antiquity – a parallelism between modern and classical *auctoritas* and authority presented even more directly in medieval romances on classical themes. *Dits* also frequently experiment with the construction of a first-person voice, and relationships between narrator and protagonist: typically a clerkly poet and noble lover. Brownlee (1984) sees the intricacies of that relationship summed up by differences and similarities between *auteur* and *acteur*. Chaucer endlessly explores tensions between protagonist and writer, in the form of relationships between agency and passivity, between the subject of an experience and its receptor (observer, hearer or scribe), or between actuality and books. The dream functions as a medium that can represent either element in these polarities. The dreamer's progress through the narrative also takes on characteristics of both the writer's and the reader's experience.

Knight and cleric/clerk traditionally represented authority in alternative areas of power, culture and literature. Dream poetry, uniting the discourses of both learning and the court, proves apt for interrogating and blurring such oppositions. The *Roman de la Rose* narrator was himself 'l'Amant' but fourteenth-century dream narrators are often detached spectators, watching, hearing and sympathising with the love sorrows of nobles and subsequently writing them. Chaucer's narrators' non-participation in love embodies less some bookish shyness, in the style of consistent character creation perfected by Victorian novelists, than this narratological and ideological interface between agency and reception, action and observation, and also between roles usually attributed to writer and reader. It becomes an interface between experience and the written record. Chaucer at times represents his subject-matter as issuing from others, his superiors, the writing as his own. The social boundaries men like Chaucer, Machaut and Froissart cross, as royal servants, learned poets and non-*gentil* courtiers (and also men in clerkly roles within a secular, lay, environment) perhaps influenced the parallel and interchanging roles between *gentil* protagonists and deferential observers so evident in their love visions.

To those blurred boundaries and exchanges can be added crossed gender boundaries (as when Chaucer's Alcyone prefigures the Black Knight) and fragmented and re-attributed experience, as when the *Duchess* narrator's undefined melancholy seems a preliminary expression of the Knight's loss. Hansen (1992: 63–8, 98–107, 132–40) proposes further analogies: between narrators and female characters, and in an erasure of the female correlated with feminisation of males (see also Margherita on 'paternalising' tendencies in the interpretation of women in the *Book of the Duchess* and its criticism, 1993: 82–99). Chaucer's narrator's typical modes of speaking – unassertive, sympathetic with misery, easy in addressing a fictional female audience – align him sometimes with female experience, a Tiresias of the imagination, and his dream poems touch on both literally abandoned women and the silencing of the female subject by masculine literary culture.

Books, Experience and New Writing

Interplay between experience and *auctoritas* pervades these poems. The *Legend* starts by discussing the validity of experience ('preve', 28, 84) versus books ('autoritees', 83) as bases for knowledge, and specifically for faith.[1] Faith – here in the particular form of female fidelity – becomes the *Legend*'s main subject, with, as in the *Wife of Bath's Prologue*, misogyny itself the site of conflicting witness from experience and 'autoritee' (specifically in male- and cleric-authored books). As some men betray women, male-authored writing betrays the truth of past experience, including that of virtuous and faithful women. This experience/book dichotomy is problematised by the device Chaucer apparently invented of prefacing dreams with allusions to books: Ovid's *Metamorphoses* in the *Duchess*; the *Aeneid* in the *House of Fame*; *Somnium Scipionis* in the *Parliament*; and in the *Legend* books that allegedly defame women (including Chaucer's own *Romaunt of the Rose* and *Troilus*). The books represent old 'autoritee'; the dreams fictionally represent new raw data, experience yet to be recorded in new writing – the very book we are reading. The preliminary book raises, most obviously in *Fame*, an implicit question of how new writing fits into past literary classics – a topical question in a century which saw vernacular poets like Dante ambitious to equal the achievements of Latin literature, and the individual poet beginning to free his identity, fame and creativity from mere service to a patron. Though the *Legend*'s Alceste and Love behave like patrons, Chaucer's list of his writings, like a curriculum vitae (*Legend* G 402–20), asserts that new, late-medieval claim for the artist's ownership of his art and of the oeuvre that embodies his independent identity and career as an artist.

Chaucer's invocations of 'autoritee' are, in practice, not deferential: his preliminary 'olde bokes' (*Legend* 25) provide no clear, unequivocal guidance for interpreting what follows. The didactic dream guides who regularly provide teaching or judgement in other dream poems are replaced by a lost puppy, a comic eagle (comic despite his Dantean ancestry), Africanus who does not compère or explain the *Parliament* dream, and finally two celestial beings (Love and Alceste) who offer instructions yet are themselves in a pupil–teacher relationship. The dreamer's own advice in the *Duchess* has its authority undermined, because of his social deference and his blatant misconceptions about the recipient's situation.

These poems' designs are offered to Chaucer's audience for their own judgement and interpretation. In the *Duchess*, section follows section yet analogies between the shapes of successive sections invite us to read ideas from one onto others. The section describing Alcyone's grief and the advice given there, '[t]o lytel while oure blysse lasteth', (211) can be interpreted as appropriate also for the Knight, as may the hunt's concluding statement 'al was doon...the hert huntyng' (1312–13). The sequences of passages that constitute the prologues of the *House of Fame* and *Legend* offer in extreme form this elusive style of presenting sequences of material for readers' interpretation. Both texts cease just before providing 'gret autoritee' and 'conclusioun'. In the G prologue of the *Legend* Chaucer is, moreover, echoing terminology associated with Wycliffite questioning of interpretative authority, and debates about how texts might be interpreted – and translated – to convey 'naked' meaning (Phillips 2002). His uncertain dreamers, unauthoritative observers or translators, whose unassertiveness about dictating instruction directly may in part reflect Chaucer's own background of princely employment, yet become something more over the course of his dream quartet: unconventional instruments for entering into discussions about women, desire, power and class, but also about exegesis, textual authority and meaning – all problems exercising contemporary thinkers.

Vernacular achievements in their own right, Chaucer's love visions forge English equivalents to courtly styles created by Machaut and Froissart in the lucid, light-flowing and often humorous narrative style of the *Duchess* and its three successors (*Fame* and the *Parliament* include some equally characteristic Chaucerian writing based on Italian inspiration). Courtly English literature was bilingual, both in the ease with which many writers and readers moved between English and French, and in this shared culture at French and English courts. Typifying contemporary boldness in using classical inspiration, Chaucer, like Froissart, invents Ovidian-style mythology, most obviously his complex myth of Alceste's crown and the creation of the daisy (Phillips and Havely 1994: 335–6). Like other *dits* employing fashionable motifs such as the daisy or the God of Love, the *Legend* illustrates the genre's independence in mixing diverse influences – for example, the *Roman de la Rose*, classical mythology, history, Christian symbolism and courtly cults – to create fresh vocabularies for compliment or topical comment.

Intertextuality does not preclude originality: Froissart, Deschamps, Chaucer, Usk and the *Pearl* poet all use the daisy/pearl symbol differently. Whereas Deschamps' daisy ('marguerite') specifically honours Margaret of Boulogne, Chaucer's *Legend* and the anonymous poem *Pearl* make it a multivalent, even elusive, symbol (Phillips and

Havely 1994: 302–3). In both English poems the daisy/pearl symbolises a woman simultaneously in life and death, exploiting its dual symbolic identity as living flower and time-immune jewel. Even when close to sources, Chaucer's effects are original. Thus the *Duchess*'s description of White, constructed largely out of passages from Machaut, emphasises more the young noblewoman's social gifts. And the portrait's overt textuality, with resonances of pre-existing writing and symbolism (Christian as well as courtly), together with its location within Chaucer's design, creates new import: it now becomes the centrepiece of a concentric structure, celebrating the lady at the centre, amidst writing expressing mourning for her. Its verbal stasis and stylistic decoration and allusiveness form a verbal effigy to commemorate a Duchess of Lancaster, like her 1376 tomb in St Paul's (though Chaucer's textual monument lacks any direct Christian reference). White, like the *Legend*'s daisy, illustrates the literary dream's capacity for taking readers into aesthetic states that transcend mortality.

Their intertextuality is no blanket invitation to import meanings from past sources and impose these on Chaucer's texts. That procedure has led at times to interpretations condemning heroines like Cleopatra in accordance with earlier writers' condemnations (Heinrichs 1990: 211–60) or to Christian, allegorised readings of Alcyone (see Phillips and Havely 1994: 35, 47n.). The *Duchess*'s opening illustrates Chaucer's inventiveness within intertextuality: adapted from Froissart's *Paradys d'Amours* it replaces Froissart's statement that love causes his melancholy with an air of mystery – giving the mood general applicability and prefiguring later motifs, like Nature's opposition to excessive grief. Chaucer frequently disregards his inter-texts' hegemonic meanings, whether Christian, philosophical or courtly.

The relationships of books to experience will dominate the *Wife of Bath's Prologue*, which sets female 'experience' against the 'auctoritee' (III. 1) of both clerical power and misogynist attempts to define and contain women. Like his love visions, this witnesses to an increasingly literate laity. Chaucer, the lay bureaucrat and learned non-clerical poet, clearly envisages a lay audience able to appreciate writing that uses classical allusion and philosophical issues. The dream proves a genre that can build structures of profound and searching secular poetry.

The relationship of books to experience shades into questions about how writing and signs relate to truth. The signs, aural and visual, verbal and non-verbal, that constitute human communication are major themes in *Fame*, 'Thisbe' and 'Philomela'. The *Legend* prologues consider evidence for belief that something is true – whether the evidence of books, found through reading, exegesis or translation (topical subjects in the age of Wyclif); of experience (9, 28); or of politics – for instance, the warning for princes about flatterers' misrepresentations (345–61). Chaucer's phrase 'naked text' (G 86), for the writing freed of bias he aims to create to vindicate women, belongs to Wycliffite debate about clerical exegesis: a naked text of scripture would be one without distortion in translation or exegesis. The *Legend*'s concern with written records of the past also recalls questions contemporary historiography was asking about what constituted trustworthy evidence for chronicles (Given-Wilson 2004: 19). *Fame* conveys anxiety about how human records preserve, lose or distort past experience. It moves from dignified pillars of ancient 'storye', history (1419–1512), to less reassuring depictions of fame's chaotic competitiveness, with winners and losers, triviality and seriousness jumbled together, and true and false records issuing simultaneously from one event (2088–2109). Authoritative writers disagree about facts (1465–80) and Fame, whose senses include historiography, seems a capricious, unregulated recorder, her mansions and operations uncertain, fragile and full of gaps, her trumpeter at times deceptive and obscene (1624–56). Here is none of the grand certainty of Dante's sense of the relationship of present writing to a glorious past.

Chaucer's juxtapositions of books with dreams can generate intense critical disagreement. What *is* the bearing of *Somnium Scipionis*, a text virtually devoid of references to love, upon the *Parliament*'s later scenes? Does it dictate correct judgements for interpreting Venus and the love casuistry of aristocrats? Or does this Roman vision of how service to the republic serves celestial purposes pose irreconcilable contradictions when placed within a text that presents conflicting medieval ideas about the nature of love: ideas based on the model of God's rational order for reproduction versus ideas based on princely culture? How the books listed in the *Legend*'s G prologue (273–307) are identified has been a key factor in negative readings of the poem: as a parody of feminist argument or a blasphemous but covertly ironic representation of lust-driven worldlings as saints? If certain items in this list ('Valerye', 'Jerome', especially) denote anti-feminist writings, then for Chaucer's God of Love to recommend these as defending women must be devastatingly ironic, wrecking from within the stated project of defending women. Alternative identifications, however (Phillips 2002: 114–15), vindicate the list as a genuine roll-call of authors praising women, removing crucial ammunition from negative readings of this poem.

Chaucer handles first-person narrative with virtuosity and a teasing relationship to authorial control. Performance, evoking oral delivery, often marks the narrative voice: for example, the *Legend* narrator's roguish self-promotion to a female audience, and derisive catcalls against Jason (232–40, 2560). The narrator is also identified as a translator – another passive self-presentation, evading direct authorial responsibility. Yet Chaucer, like Machaut, gives his narrator his own name (*Fame* 729) and writings (*Legend* 415–30). *Fame* depicts him serving Jove and his nephew Cupid respectfully ('trewely', 'ententyfly', 615, 616), from a marginal position in relation to fully participating members (= lovers) of their court, perhaps suggesting the role of a diligent servant of Richard II or John of Gaunt.

Dreams and Waking

How do Chaucer's dream poems manage fictional dreaming and waking and how do they engage with extra-textual reality?

Each ends differently. The *Duchess* ends *technically*: with a tour-de-force of narrative closure(s), exiting through concentric frames to emerge into statements of death, sorrow, compassion and of moving on – all presented as facts beyond verbal elaboration.

This structure, having celebrated the past, now leaves it. It also represents a princely mourner emerging from inward subjectivity back into the world of his social rank: castle, kingship and emblematic naming of real-life royal titles (Knight 1986: 16–23). Back also to time: its advance, its constraints and its marking of terminations – a bell striking twelve and the hunt's end. That bell is typical of the physical shocks, like a noise, touch or movement, with which many dream poems shift back to waking experience. Moving into an emblematically social, hierarchical and time-marked environment, Chaucer's Knight leaves the time-defying stasis of the central description of White as when alive, a section which represented him temporarily humbled – by love, by sorrow and by those 'Events' that exceed even statesmen's control, and which were summed up in the medieval period by 'Fortune'. Time reminders and the word 'castel' perhaps hint at a second dynastic marriage (possibly already real) between John of Gaunt and Constance of Castile. *Le Songe vert*, a French poem probably written in England, indicates a second marriage for a mourner, perhaps Richard II: its dream ends with his waking as he falls from a tree, contemplating an emblematic fleur-de-lys, to find his black garb turned green. For Chaucer's narrator awakening is also emergence into the role of writer, writer of a new book.

The *Parliament* ends harmoniously – which can only be provisional in so inharmonious a design. Like many love visions (for example, Machaut's *Fonteinne amoureuse* or the *Songe vert*) its end also looks forward to future events beyond the text. And it points back again to books. The dreams in the *Duchess* and the *Parliament*, preceded and followed by reference to books, dramatise dream poetry's tendency to stand poised between past and future textuality.

Such denial of closure increases with endings in the later poems. *Fame*, unfinished, ends paradoxically: announcing an intellectual conclusion, the entrance of *auctoritas*. The *Legend* contains sequential endings and it problematises closure in several ways. Like Machaut's *Jugement du Roy de Navarre*, it reopens topics from previous books (here *Troilus* and the *Roman de la Rose*). Like *Fame*, it ends unfinished upon a promise of conclusion. As in the *Duchess* and *Fame*, the dreamer turns into writer: here at the first ending, after the prologue, when his commissioned legends commence. To end his individual legends Chaucer often uses two motifs: allusions to Ovid's *Heroides* or other ancient intertexts, and his narrator's address to an audience. Both motifs (the old books and new narration) evoke textual representation of women's experiences by past and present male writers.

In his last seven legends – those of bad men – that second motif, whether the narrator addresses a fictional female audience, comments on gender issues in his tale or voices sympathy with women and anger against men, conveys acute awareness – simultaneously playful and provocative – of a male narrator's ambiguous positioning on the gender divide, in his mediation of men's mistreatment of women to a female audience. Frequent directions to 'rede Ovyde' (e.g. 1367) for fuller documentation strike modern readers as dismissive but such brief citation was a scholarly mannerism and used by contemporary chroniclers to validate their accounts (Given-Wilson 1987: 69–72). Concern with historiographic evidence appears too with the assurance that

'Cleopatra' is 'storyal soth' (702). Historical documentation supports a feminist purpose, validating positive beliefs about women, and relates to questions of how writings can represent past experience: as true *keys to remembrance* and reliably *naked texts* (G 26, 86).

Links between dream poetry and contemporary events appear clearest in the connection between the *Duchess* and Blanche of Lancaster's death (see below for possible Lancastrian connections also with 'Cleopatra'). Here encounters across a class divide are respectful: 'Loo, how goodely spak this knyght' (529). *Gentil* ability to master emotion and make courteous conversation is respectfully admired, and details convey a princely ambiance: a servant fetches a book; *Metamorphoses* becomes a book about kings and queens (58). The *Parliament* conveys less complacency about hierarchies. Beginning with a book that teaches links between personal self-control and good order in the state and cosmos, its love debate seems designed to mimic the division between aristocrats and Commons in Parliament. Perhaps relevantly, Parliament, created earlier in the century, was changing. In the early 1380s the Commons could still be assumed to support royal policy, against the magnates. But their late-1380s stand against Richard II, and the complex conflicts and alliances of the 1390s, were hardening the Commons into a distinctive oppositional force. This contemporary double perception of the Commons, from deferential and co-operative to oppositional, matches the *Parliament*'s uneven presentation of order: its mix of harmonious and subversive currents, and its celebration of hierarchy combined with images of freedom from restraint, such as the depiction of Venus, extreme courtly passion, and the churlish disputants. Louise Fradenburg (1984) demonstrates the subversive elements in Chaucer's presentation of the lower birds. The poem, despite promoting notions of social order as divine, disrupts the courtly dream poem's 'image of genealogically transmitted authority' (Hawes 1989) with moments of uncertainty about what authority is being offered (the opening stanzas, the gate's double inscription, and the final stanza), ensuring that aristocratic concepts of what creates social or aesthetic harmony cannot be absolutely hegemonic in this text.

Aesthetic multiplicity and multivalence, tendencies encouraged by dream poetry's structures, thus become in the *Parliament* also political. Its bird assembly satirises various classes but from shifting perspectives, unlike the single-perspective criticism of estates satires. Chaucer's narratives, their structure and writing, often undermine or problematise their conservative promotion of order. Here social voices, class identities, images of rank and 'degree', and aesthetic and moral principles all remain in irreconcilably dialogic encounters.

Fame reflects changing images of the writer: first the retainer of a feudal-style patron, employed to produce *gentil* lovers' poetry (615–40), later an individual artist contemplating the series of great predecessors. *Fame* leaves open whether only princes and dynasties or poets too are candidates for Fame. Knight (1986: 15–23) links *Fame*'s later scenes to Chaucer's changed employment from courtiership in palaces to the Thames-side customs at the heart of mercantile London, presaging his switch from court poetry to the socially more open and bourgeois canvas of *The Canterbury Tales*.

Knight reads *Fame*'s two mansions as feudal versus mercantile economic worlds: a princely fortress with petitioners and a more chaotic, open, and multiple arena, opportunistic and individualistic, corresponding to commercial London, a socio-economic force destined to destroy feudal structures.

Fame raises questions, far ahead of Chaucer's time, about communication, its media and its political importance. *Fame* shifts from writings commanding high cultural dignity, upholding dynastic glory and the aristocratic art of courtly love, towards subjects more like the stuff of newspapers or the characteristic types of news regularly reported by medieval annals: the list in 1960–76 includes tempests, pestilences, political changes, plenty, famine, commerce, economic scarcity, fires, accidents and 'good or mys government' (1975) – miscellaneous but serious events of practical consequences not just for aristocracy but wider classes, whole populations. Such a humdrum, miscellaneous, and less selective (more democratic?) presentation of material claiming a place in history and record supports Delany's characterisation of the second house as 'populated with crowds whose exclusive concern is the present... actively engaged in the business of life or talking about it and their interests include whatever is temporal and temporary' (Delany 1972: 106). Repetition of 'tydynges', especially in conversation with an anonymous everyman bystander (1868–1915), suggests that Chaucer, with his extraordinary sociological prescience, essays here the idea of writings that record ephemera and popularly shared experience of the present: a development that will require printing and modern news media to blossom properly (satisfying what Copeland, an early printer, sees as his public's avidity for 'Newes, newes, have you any newes?'). *Fame*'s theme, communication in many senses, already includes the quotidian and politically potent one of news: Chaucer places couriers and royal messengers – the fastest contemporary news media – among Fame's servants.

The *Legend*'s G prologue includes wording linking it to political concerns of the mid to late 1390s, especially anxiety about royal tyranny and Wyclif-inspired questions about translation and exegesis (Phillips 2002). A celestial Alceste was perhaps the *Legend*'s planned climax, like Mary and Beatrice for Dante. Yet Chaucer's Alceste has multiple identities: faithful wife, paragon of 'fyn lovynge', queen (with the typically fourteenth-century queenly attribute of mercy), heavenly being, wise teacher of kingship, and also the daisy: symbol of much else, including the poet's inspiration. Political symbolism, however, seems clear. Omitting her husband Admetus, Chaucer makes Alceste – though with the ambiguity marking his whole construction – appear virtually Love's consort: an allegory of love but probably also of Queen Anne and Richard II. That receives support from the daisy's habit of turning towards the sun – if Love represents Richard II, whose sunburst badge possibly inspired Chaucer to associate him with the awesome Phoebus of Ovid's *Metamorphoses* VI (64–5, 110–14, 213, 230–3). There the supreme god (= patron?) of poetry is also an awesome, even tyrannical ruler. Ovid's *roi soleil* is a possible, though neglected, source for the complex elements in Chaucer's poem's presentation of the God of Love (already a fearsome overlord in the *Roman de la Rose*).

Love and the *Gentil* Man: Celebrating or Questioning?

The *Legend* takes one feature of the fourteenth-century love vision, its frequent use as a frame for inset tales (often classical) or love complaints, and employs it to interrogate another: its perennial subject-matter of male desire and its association with knightly identity. The cultural myth that upper-class men are abjectly intense lovers as well as great warriors is peculiarly medieval. Aristocrats are Love's servants, whom the poet serves (*Fame* 620–40; *Legend* G 247; see also *Troilus* III. 39–42). The *Legend* prologues associate this idea further with the trope of divine kingship: Richard II as a god, the court poet's service as providing hymns for Love's 'halydayes' (*Legend* F 424, G 410). Chaucer's conceit of pagan heroines as saints of love may, among its multiple cultural affinities, reflect divine imagery associated with Richard (as in Richard of Maidstone's *Concordia* or the Wilton diptych), adding new political implications to old courtly discourse of love as a religion. We should not assess the tone and implications of the saints of Cupid in isolation from the poem's imagery of a god-king nor from that courtly tradition, and certainly not too simply or exclusively as the blasphemy it initially appears to modern readers. Chaucer's god-king fuses cultural images of the prince as aristocratic lover (here as Love incarnate), as lord of poetry and terrifying potentate, with his patronage a sort of divine office, even subject to very topical accusations of heresy (320–40).

Already Chaucer's dream poems had both celebrated love and aristocracy and subjected them to question. The *Parliament* questions the nature of love, through its series of puzzling contrasts, its juxtaposed Venus and Nature, and its birds' debate. The *Legend* radically extends that question, asserting the dignity of sexual love and going beyond either ecclesiastical or patriarchal, or courtly, conceptualisations of good women. It praises as quasi-saints heroines who are neither virgin martyrs nor warrior queens (like women praised in Boccaccio's *De claris mulieribus*, Christian legendaries or Jerome's *Against Jovinian*) but women of sexual experience and, often, powerful passion.[2] Yet all have social consequence and dignity: they are mostly wives and queens in their own right or royal heiresses. This is a mould-breaking validation of marriage and secular, lay lifestyles, and also – existentially – of emotional individual experience.

In the *Duchess*, which fuses love vision and elegy, desire had become a confrontation with loss, mutability. The genre provides an ideal frame for expression of desire but here moving from dream to waking also shows mutability the victor. Intense prostration by love and grief, that sign of the *gentil* man's innate sensitivity, shown in romance heroes from Chrétien's Perceval and Lancelot to Chaucer's Troilus, is here respectfully rendered, though Chaucer's structure surrounds it by passages suggesting brisker attitudes to both desire and loss. Although Chaucer eschews explicitly Christian parameters for considering mutability, those brisker attitudes towards death are susceptible of implicit Christian–Boethian readings, but also fit with princely, dynastic, pressures towards re-marriage.

And dynastic marriage, a matter of supreme importance for the high-born women in Chaucer's audience, seems to underlie the recurrent images of perilous unions with strangers by high-born women in the *Legend*'s legends. They recount ten heroines' tragedies, all caused by sexual desire, their own or other people's. This poem's focus on *female* desire and upon the effects of masculine desire, as culturally constructed (presented here as exploitative oppression), upon women produces gradual questioning of patriarchy as well as the claims of the *gentil* man to his status. Cleopatra and Thisbe find union with loving men and die in a *Liebestod*. Dido, Medea, Phyllis, Ariadne and Hypsipyle love stranger princes who desert them, their tales ending with their committing suicide or facing seemingly certain death. Lucrece and Philomela are rape victims but Chaucer's versions depart from the patriarchally focused approaches of earlier treatments. The last, Hypermnestra, is the victim of callous, dual male exploitation, paternal and marital, while remaining herself courageously true to her duties. Her patriarchal duties to father and husband conflict – tragically for her – with each other and with her own conceptualisation of morality befitting a woman. She acts finally in accordance with a deeper human principle of compassion. 'Thisbe' raises the question of whether ideals are identical for men and women, showing both sexes capable of courage and fidelity; later legends expose more cruelly traditional double standards. These legends are a culmination of the adventurous thinking of Chaucer's dream poetry, stepping outside many established assumptions about love. Above all they subject '*gentil*' men and their desires to scrutiny.

Towards New Writing

The *Legend* develops Chaucer's dream-poem template: it moves between old books, dream and new narrative. It demonstrates how to move from dream poetry into narrative, a new kind of narrative about desire and aristocracy, bringing into full focus disquieting questions often hinted earlier in his dream quartet, including affinities between desire and death, and the tendency of masculine culture and writing to contain or extinguish female agency and experience. Abandonment of the female, whether by male desire or by masculine literary discourses, is no new subject. In the desired but dead White; in the inability of the noble eagles' protestations of their own, male, desire to engage with its female object – the tercel – whose will and selfhood their rhetoric disregards; in *Fame*'s abandoned Dido; and Alceste's self-immolation, transformed into a flower, a jewelled crown and constellation; and finally in the exploited, raped or literally abandoned women in these legends, Chaucer's writing about desire exposes how culture and literature inscribe it as masculine experience, and demonstrates the insecure ontological status of its female object. Whereas courtly writing usually displays only masculine desire, Chaucer's dream poetry gives some space to its objects, often revealed as deprived of life, freedom of action, or reified (Hansen 1992: 58–86; Gilbert 2002). The legends' abandoned women, left alone on bare sea-shores or in bleak and emptied beds, facing extinction, represent the failure of the solipsistic masculine desire presented in courtly love tradition, to encompass union. Courtly rhetoric of desire revels in metaphorical pain, subjugation and death – for men.

Chaucer shows it producing literal 'oppressyoun', 'tyranny' and destruction for women. Paradoxically his heroines, amidst their abjection, also display agency: in love, morality and courage, and in exercising queenly generosity and courage. And – as in another complex male-authored text, Ovid's *Heroides* – in speaking of themselves. These representations, rather than traditional medieval modes of attacking misogyny, like praise of chastity, are Chaucer's novel re-inscription of women against the powers – powers within courtly love literature as well as more obviously within misogynistic culture – that misrepresent or eclipse women's experience.

Cleopatra and 'Wyfhod' in the *Legend*

Cleopatra has first position by express command (566). Cleopatra's literary representation before Chaucer was negative: an Eastern leader defying Rome, a woman seducing great warriors from duty, sensuality over-ruling rationality, a female assuming rule, the epitome of lust and luxury. Chaucer creates a new Cleopatra: the devoted and obedient wife in a perfect royal marriage. He reduces the tradition's negative elements and reverses the accusation that Cleopatra initiated the flight from Actium. His Cleopatra, far from embodying worldly pleasure, epitomises 'contemptus mundi': her body cast naked into 'the pit' (most basic and evocative Middle English word for a tomb), with 'serpents' and 'nadderes'. Embraced with 'ful good herte' and 'good chere', this combines *Liebestod* and *memento mori* (694–701). Yet as model royal wife she builds a magnificent monument for the warrior. The contrast recalls the Black Prince's Canterbury tomb, his proud effigy as a warrior lying above an inscription describing his wretched body brought low in death. It perhaps reflects the 'transi' tombs, just appearing, first in France and later England, showing the dead in earthly pomp above but as corpses, decaying and eaten by vermin below (Kolve 1981).

Chaucer rewrites Cleopatra, I suggest, in part for the world and the personal self-images, male and female, of a late-fourteenth-century English princely household. Antony, a devoted husband with every chivalric virtue (608–12), fights to defend her rights (603–6); Cleopatra has medieval romance prettiness (613); her devotion to her marriage vows is stressed (681–95). The space given to warfare at sea and some details like the 'pesen' (actually 'metal missiles' – *not* 'peas'), 648 are often misinterpreted as absurd (see even the usually sympathetic Frank 1972: 37). But I suggest 'Cleopatra', among other meanings, compliments Constance of Castile, Gaunt's second duchess, and their joint expedition in the late 1380s to Castile to try to recover her father's kingdom. The historical Gaunt, like Antony (and also some of the romance heroes in which medieval noblemen saw their own ideal image of service), fights for his lady's rights. Cleopatra may honour Constance alliteratively as Alceste does Queen Anne. The detailed sea-battle description would have attracted contemporaries: upper-class audiences relished military descriptions, and sea warfare attracted particular patriotic interest after notable naval successes (including Sluys 1340; Winchelsea 1349; and Cadzand 1387), and dramatic fears of French invasion in the late 1380s.

Chaucer makes all his *Legend* heroines wives or as close as possible. 'Thisbe' includes troth-plighting, the essential element in medieval marriage (778). Chaucer's heroines, like Alceste, combine *fin amors* and 'wyfhod' (554–5): an innovative conjunction linking courtly love glamour to the traditionally more sober medieval concept of marriage. Late-medieval defenders of woman, including Philippe de Mézières, had begun to elevate the dignity of marriage – significantly a lay experience and traditionally a target of clerical misogyny – and after Chaucer several feminist works, including the *Chevalier des Dames*, *Champion des Dames* and Christine de Pizan's *Epître au dieu d'amour*, will harness courtly love motifs to that purpose, promoting the idea of fidelity and the defence of women as characteristics of the true gentleman. Like Alexander and Hector, avatars for medieval princes, Chaucer's classical heroines combine courageous, sensational life-stories with virtue, providing glamorous antique *alter egos* for high-born ladies – for whom marriage, dynastic marriage (and often to a foreign prince) was a political destiny: marriage was their political importance. They may also reflect contemporary interest in both the imagery of the Nine Worthy Women and the Ladies of the Garter (McDonald 2000), energetically developed by Richard II.

Dido and Revaluing Male Desire and Female Passion

'Thisbe' declares a man can be 'trewe and kynde' (921); for both sexes this tale opposes a double standard: women can do warlike, courageous acts, men show tenderness and fidelity. But Piramus is Chaucer's *Legend*'s last 'good man'. 'Dido' is the first legend revealing 'bad men'; transferring shame in sexual matters from women to men; exposing masculine deceptive and coercive rhetoric; and – boldest of all – treating intense love in women as an experience meriting moral celebration.

Chaucer's poem shows mistreatment of innocent women increasingly as the dirty secret within that aristocratic masculine ethos and the celebration of masculine desire that dream poetry normally promotes. Chaucer exposes masculine exploitation of women in 'Medea' within a text whose language simultaneously celebrates Jason's chivalric renown, the 'famous knight of gentilesse / Of freedom, and of strengthe and lustynesse' (1403–4). He employs the language of violence for both: this famed and fearsome warrior is also a destroyer of women – their 'devourer and confusion', (1369), 'of love devourer and dragoun' (1581). The ravening predator here is not the mythic dragon.

Aeneas is one of many men who have 'piled' women (1262). Jason also robs women: he 'wedded was / Unto the queen and tok of hir substaunce / What so hym leste unto his purveyaunce' (1559–61) – all in one sentence. His pursuit of the golden fleece looks like commercial enterprise with exploitation of women one of his business skills. Their practice of plundering women without observing bonds of duty aligns these ancient heroes – avatars of European knighthood – with the proto-capitalist individualistic spirit of profiteering that Chaucer treats with moral horror in his *Friar's Tale* (though with witty curiosity in the *Shipman's Tale*, Shipman's and Merchant's portraits, and *Wife of Bath's Prologue*). We could contrast Chaucer's delicate erasure from his earlier literary representation of aristocratic wooing in the *Duchess* (805–1297) of any hint at the colossal advantages marriage to such an heiress could bring. Again Chaucer's dream poetry (like his *Man of Law's Tale*) touches on issues pertinent to aristocratic ladies whose destiny was dynastic marriages. The *Parliament* formel's reluctance to wed figures aristocratic daughters' dilemma facing dynastic and patriarchal pressures. Nature's calm certainty that in time union will follow illustrates the degree to which the philosophy of Nature is employed here to naturalise aristocratic coercions upon women. The *Parliament* is a poem like the *Knight's Tale* about order in love as well as power, yet containing, like the *Knight's Tale*, disquieting challenges to social order.

The *Legend*'s exploitative, princes denature and declass themselves: Chaucer uses 'this gentil man' satirically of Aeneas' (1066, 1074, 1264); Jason, Theseus and Demophon are thieves, foxes plundering a farmyard (1383–95, 2445–51); Tarquin, 'a kynges sone', lowers himself to 'vileyn' (1789, 1819, 1824). In contrast with the magnanimous royal heiresses and queens, consistently described as *gentil* and noble, who manifest true princely virtues, giving assistance and money without calculation, these princes appear not just adventurers but merchant adventurers. This provocative handling of masculine *gentillesse* (also present, diluted by a tolerantly humorous mode, in the *Parliament*) reflects late-medieval debates on true *gentillesse* as virtue, and possibly the effects of declining numbers of literal knights and the entry of 'new men' into land-owning classes, which, historians argue, increased emphasis on *gentillesse* as a code of behaviour, not just lineage or knighthood (Given-Wilson 1987: 69–72). Now Chaucer extends *gentillesse* to cover knights' treatment of *gentil* women.

The dream poems show also Chaucer's changing attitudes towards women's own experience of passion. Earlier poems adopt conventional discourses, whether of courtly love or moral judgements, though Chaucer vacillates in how completely his writing endorses these. One tradition judged passion, especially in women, as 'foolish love', against the Christian duty of rational restraint on sensuality, and the *Duchess* had castigated Dido accordingly, with Medea, Phyllis and Echo, for being driven to extremes by love (724–36). *Fame* is divided about Dido's folly versus Aeneas' guilt. The *Parliament* lists lovers, including Dido, in Venus' temple (281–94) yet diverges significantly from both Chaucer's sources, Dante, whose list was of those damned for lust, and Boccaccio, whose list demonstrates Venus' power. Instead now Chaucer presents the lovers as exempla of *affect*: 'al here love and in what plyt they dyde' (294). Finally, intense emotion, together with the queenly virtues that make them brave, generous, loyal and free of guile, appear to be precisely what validates his *Legend* women as quasi-saints. The dream quartet shows a complete revolution on this subject. The *Legend* shows a radical, new, existential value placed on the intense experience of emotion; absolute fidelity validates these women as exemplary but so, it seems, does the absolute degree of their experience, leading frequently to death.

Chaucer's obvious reason for prefacing *Fame* with Dido is Virgil's famous description of monstrous rumour: it grows from Dido's sexual shame, her 'fault' in the cave with Aeneas, which Virgil judges a pretended marriage (*Aeneid* 4. 321–3; *Fame*, 345–57).

Fame invokes conventional wisdom and the double standard over masculine infidelity: passion is a matter where the woman must avoid folly lest she 'doth amys', where incautious love ('nyce lest', foolish desire), especially if followed by abandonment, brings shame upon her (269–92, 352–60). *Fame* only abruptly and disconnectedly voices criticism of Aeneas but does briefly condemn the deceptive rhetoric with which male desire traditionally cloaks its exploitative approach (278, 330–1). That condemnation becomes harsher in 'Medea and Hypsipyle' and 'Ariadne': the phrase 'of love al the art and craft' (1607), used of Jason's wooing, subsumes the positive and elegant 'art of love' in the artifice and craftiness of tricking women. More condemnation of that masculine rhetoric of desire will appear in fifteenth-century texts, including Chartier's *La Belle Dame sans Merci*. The *Parliament* suggest doubts: its lower birds' ridicule of tropes like dying for love; its revelation of the essentially competitive nature of the male eagles' bids for the female; and the disjunction between their aggressive desire and her own wish. That disjunction recalls what Gilbert (1994: 114–15) calls White's loss of autonomous status, even as she becomes elevated into a Lancastrian 'tutelary spirit'. Hansen (1992: 73–4) sees it as the silencing – killing – of female experience by masculine rhetoric, prefiguring the probing of how masculine writing has betrayed female experience and virtue in the *Legend* prologues. *Fame*'s 'Dido', as prologue to a study of fame, seems also to prefigure the *Legend* prologues' topic of how history records experience – especially female.

Yet 'art and craft' – male wooers' rhetoric and performance – are disconcertingly akin to the writer's own craft, a parallel Chaucer plays with in the *Parliament*'s first lines. Emotion and writing are interwoven in the *Duchess*, and *Fame* represents its narrator as a writer producing love poetry. Though *Fame* and the *Legend* condemn men's false performances to win women, some of Chaucer's legends dramatise his narrator addressing a female audience in a spirit both of performance and flirtation.

The Dido of Chaucer's *Legend* commands more respect than the Dido of his *Fame* or either of his sources: Virgil, for whom ultimately she is a temptation his hero must renounce, or Ovid who, while engaging flamboyantly with her emotions, presents her essentially as that – emotional – and weak. This Dido is impressive. Having built Carthage, she 'regnyth [there] in so gret honour / That sche was holde of alle queenys flour, / Of gentillesse, of freedom, of beaute' (1008–10). Chaucer emphasises that most of his good women are queens, often in their own right, or royal heirs, and constantly calls Dido queen and uses the vocabulary of regality and nobility (e.g. 'of the cete queene, [she] stod in the temple in hire estat ryal / So rychely', 1035–7). Aeneas attracts the vocabulary of nobility but Chaucer qualifies this with hints of mere *seeming*: typical is 1046–8, Dido 'saw the man, that he was lyk a knight…And lyk to been a verray gentil man'. *Fame* treated Dido's trust in Aeneas and their sexual encounter in the cave in an equivocal tone, half pitying and half contemptuous. Now Chaucer is respectful of her passion. His wording equates the cave encounter with marriage (1225–39).

The queens and heroines of Chaucer's *Legend* exemplify the virtues, nobility and magnificence typifying the medieval ideal of a good *king*: rulers in their own right, not merely consorts; commanding large resources; frequently designated as 'noble'; displaying kingly attributes of largesse and 'trouthe'. And also the specifically queenly qualities of mercy and of counsel: Medea and Ariadne impart invaluable knowledge enabling male adventurers to win otherwise unobtainable goals. Chaucer's 'Ariadne' ironically foregrounds a rhetorical metaphor of courtly love, a man's pose as servant of a woman, exposing its ironic relationship to the literal service that Ariadne, like Chaucer's other heroines, gives to an ungrateful man.

Theseus, blatantly a knave here, reappears, apparently an admired ruler acting in harmony with the gods' will, in the *Knight's Tale*. The contrast lies in two moral evaluations of power: 'Ariadne' makes overt the oppression at the heart of rule. Chaucer is not painting a personality with contradictory or changing impulses. Rather, his developing exploration of power and the *gentil* in his dream poetry and his short narratives of tragic women makes possible an acknowledgement of oppression within power that his romance cannot reveal so unambiguously. Here it is princely oppression not of lower-class men but other nobles – women. As in *Anelida* the shorter poetic form allows for displacement of the inherently masculine narrative of the romance with its battles, quests, victories and advantageous marriage. Dream poetry's traditional focus on unhappy love, developing into Chaucer's exposure of ignoble princes, incipiently in *Fame* and overtly in the *Legend*, furnishes a vehicle for deconstructing power. Lee Patterson (1991: 86–7) calls 'Ariadne' Chaucer's 'commentary on the assumptions that make the *Knight's Tale* possible but which it cannot itself make visible' (though see also Knight 1986: 86–7). Whereas the *Duchess* prettily recognised the hurdle of female consent, and the *Parliament* leaves it unresolved, now non-consent is equated in 'Lucrece' and 'Philomela' with 'oppressyoun' and 'tyranny' – rulers' offences, as well as sexual offences.

Writing Patriarchy

Starting with the *Duchess*'s reshaping of Ovid's *Metamorphoses* tale to concentrate on Alcyone not Ceyx, Chaucer's dream poetry refutes the notion of immutably reliable written authority and explores, alongside that, evolving conceptualisations of gender and power. The *Duchess* and *Parliament* move interrogatively between books and experience. *Fame* generates its innovative exploration of communication, history's record, and the poet's relationship to power, out of Dido's sexual tragedy. But 'Philomela', showing another un-*gentil* prince abusing power in his treatment of women, marks the apogee of Chaucer's interest in links between gender and writing, and the relationship of signs – language – to truth and experience. Its physically silenced victim exposes her oppression through the archetypically feminine language of textiles.

Unlike Ovid, Chrétien de Troyes and Gower, Chaucer departs from treating Philomela's rape as a patriarchal matter of family honour and masculine ownership of female honour, with corresponding shame for the woman (even as arousing jealousy in the rapist's wife). *Fame* had attached shame, conventionally, to Dido for extra-marital sex, but 'Philomela' presents what patriarchal tradition constructed as female shame, the experience of rape, powerfully as male violence – Tereus' cruelty pervades the text's wording – and also as masculine shame.

'Phyllis' and Hypermnestra show patriarchy as unsafe for women. 'Phyllis' verbalises bluntly links between marriage and plunder: within one couplet Demophon swears marriage vows to Phyllis and 'piked hire of al the good he myghte' (2466–7). Chaucer shows women faithful but not within safely traditional, male-controlled structures – unlike Jerome's *Against Jovinian*, which sticks to the paradigms of virgin martyrdoms, self-sacrificing chastity or extreme fidelity to father or husband. The perils faced by Chaucer's women instead disprove the patriarchal claim that men protect women within the states of virginity or marriage. Chaucer's writings do not romanticise marriage: its coercive side emerges in romances (the *Man of Law's* and *Clerk's Tales*) as much as its fallible side emerges in fabliaux. Marriage is not a safe state: Dido, Hypsipyle, Medea, Ariadne and Phyllis discover this; Hypermnestra is a self-sacrificing bride; Philomela and Lucrece victims of men who assault the sacred bonds of marriage as well as the bodies of women. His heroines' safest relationships are usually with sisters, not fathers or husbands, though their creator, seemingly in acknowledgement of the threats surrounding women, pleads with his female audience to trust only *him*.

'Hypermnestra' reveals a courageous, virtuous woman caught impossibly between patriarchal duty to father and husband. Death hangs over the narrative. Her father's protestations of his love to her are simultaneously a threat of death. The knife becomes a central motif, symbol of her task but also of her impossible, destructive, dilemma: she must kill yet must not; it is her duty to kill, as a woman owing obedience, yet also impossible because of the nature of her sex. That phallic knife destroys her being, her identity, even her capacity to do her daughterly duty. Chaucer's text spends time initially depicting her as caught between planetary powers and fate, and destined for prison but actually the forces that destroy and imprison her are the jaws of patriarchy's double oppression of women as daughters and wives. De-emphasising his fifty daughters, Chaucer's writing makes her seem her father's favourite daughter and heiress, yet her special value to the father does not save her from his conscienceless exploitation. Like the attractiveness of the *Legend*'s previous rich and beautiful queens to self-seeking males' desires, her value to her father is no protection from the readiness within such cultures for women to be destroyed.

The Duchess started Chaucer's dream poetry quartet with undefined, life-destroying melancholy. 'Hypermnestra' ends thus with a girl awaiting destruction, by conflicting loving duties and patriarchal exploitation. In between, Chaucer's dream poems have frequently centred on pain as the concomitant of love. 'I am sorwe and sorwe is I', says a lover in the *Duchess*; the gate over the garden of love in the *Parliament* promises misery and barrenness together with fruitful happiness; Venus' temple shows love twinned with misery and death (294), with a whole stanza picturing Cupid's elaborate sharpening of his weapons (211–17). The cause of lovers' misery in the *Duchess* is mutability. In the *Parliament* it is perhaps infringement – through devotion to passion – of the godly purpose given to sexual desire in Alain de Lille's vision of Nature, as a force of reproduction in accordance with divine harmony. But the *Legend* appears to celebrate intense feeling itself, in association with other noble virtues: the medieval cultural value placed on martyrdom makes its sexual tragedies documents of heroic virtues.

Chaucer's dream poetry's preoccupation with suffering, found also in *Troilus* and the *Knight's Tale*, extends beyond traditional *topoi* of male desire as pain, wounds and death. It has a narratological parallel in Chaucer's passive, receptive narrators. And his narratives' readiness to depict female experience within a culture that valorises masculine desire. At moments, from Alcyone to Hypermnestra, Chaucer's imagination faces death with, or lies in bed with, lone women in intense emotional experience. Besides these affective, empathetic achievements, his love visions we have seen cumulatively problematise *gentil* male identity. They expose the extinctions (conceptual and bodily) threatened for women by conventional cultural modes for conceptualising desire and marriage; and the oppression of women threatened by structures of power and order. Overwhelmingly secular, these poems show intense moral intelligence and energy, probing what often prove to be contradictory forces and imperatives, without invoking established Christian answers to problems and tragedy. Chaucer's dream poetry offers a sequence of individually profound works and a gradually unfolding body of thoughtful, original and provocative writing.

NOTES

1   Unless otherwise indicated, quotations from the *Legend* prologue are from the F version. All quotations from Phillips and Havely (1994).
2   See Wallace's comment (1997: 341) on Boccaccio's safely conservative approach to praise of women.

REFERENCES AND FURTHER READING

Anon. (1904). *Le Songe vert*. In L. Constans (ed.). *Romania* 33, 642–4.

Brownlee, Kevin (1984). *Poetic Identity in Guillaume de Machaut*. Madison: University of Wisconsin Press.

Copeland, William (1530). Preface to *Parliament of Fowles*. (Printed by Wynkyn de Worde, STC 5092.)

Delany, Sheila (1972). *Chaucer's 'House of Fame': The Poetics of Skeptical Fideism*. Chicago: University of Chicago Press.

Fradenburg, Louise (1984). Spectacular fictions: the body politic in Chaucer and Dunbar. *Poetics Today*, 5, 493–517.

Frank, Robert W., Jr. (1972). *Chaucer and the 'Legend of Good Women'*. Cambridge, MA: Harvard University Press.

Gilbert, Jane (2002). Becoming a woman in Chaucer: 'One ne naît pas femme, on le meurt'. In Nicola F. McDonald and W. M. Ormrod (eds). *Rites of Passage* (pp. 109–29). Cambridge: D. S. Brewer.

Given-Wilson, Chris (1987). *The English Nobility in the Late Middle Ages: The Fourteenth-Century Political Community*. London: Routledge.

Given-Wilson, Chris (2004). *Chronicles: The Writing of History in Medieval England*. London: Hambledon.

Hansen, Elaine Tuttle (1992). *Chaucer and the Fictions of Gender*. Berkeley: University of California Press.

Hawes, Clement (1989). 'More stars, God knows, than a pair': social class and the Common Good in Chaucer's 'Parliament of Fowls'. *Publications of the Arkansas Philological Association*, 15, 12–25.

Heinrichs, Kathryn (1990). *The Myths of Love: Classical Lovers in Medieval Literature*. University Park: Pennsylvania State University Press.

Kittredge, George L. (1915). *Chaucer and his Poetry*. Cambridge, MA: Harvard University Press.

Knight, Stephen (1986). *Geoffrey Chaucer*. Oxford: Basil Blackwell.

Kolve, V. A. (1981). From Cleopatra to Alceste: an iconographic study of the *Legend of Good Women*'. In. J. P. Hermann and J. J. Burke (eds). *Signs and Symbols in Chaucer's Poetry* (pp. 130–78). Tuscaloosa, AL: University of Alabama Press.

Kruger, Steven F. (1992). *Dreaming in the Middle Ages*. Cambridge: Cambridge University Press.

Lynch, Kathryn L. (2000). *Chaucer's Philosophical Visions*. Chaucer Studies 26. Cambridge: D. S. Brewer.

McDonald, Nicola F. (2000). Chaucer's 'Legend of Good Women': ladies at court and the female audience. *Chaucer Review*, 35(1), 22–42.

Margherita, Gayle (1993). Originary fantasies and Chaucer's 'Book of the Duchess'. In Linda Lomperis and Sarah Stanbury (eds). *Feminist Approaches to the Body in Medieval Literature* (pp. 153–61). Philadelphia: University of Pennsylvania Press.

Minnis, A. J., V. J. Scattergood and J. J. Smith (2000). *Oxford Guides to Chaucer: The Shorter Poems*. Oxford: Clarendon Press.

Patterson, Lee (1991). *Chaucer and the Subject of History*. Madison: University of Wisconsin Press.

Phillips, Helen (1995). Chaucer and Jean Le Fèvre. *Archiv*, 232, 23–36.

Phillips, Helen (2002). Register, politics and the 'Legend of Good Women'. *Chaucer Review*, 37(2), 101–29.

Phillips, Helen and Nick Havely (eds) (1994). *Chaucer's Dream Poetry*. Burnt Mill: Longman.

Wallace, David (1997). *Chaucerian Polity: Absolutist Lineages and Associational Forms in England and Italy*. Stanford, CA: Stanford University Press.

24
Chaucer's *Troilus and Criseyde*

Alcuin Blamires

Chaucer's *Troilus and Criseyde* is his longest finished poem and dates from around the mid-1380s. It is a rich and audacious work about love which largely eludes historicising inquiry. Its audacity lies most conspicuously in the vertigo of its unpredictable movements between grandeur and wit, between solemnity and conspiratorial mockery. One moment the narrative rides high in epic rhetoric as (for example) Troilus, awestruck at the prospect of a momentous meeting with Crisedye, invokes a raft of classical gods to assist him in his hour of 'nede' (III. 712–35). The next, we are treated to comic deflation; Troilus's friend Pandarus hurries him impatiently toward Criseyde's room, with 'Artow agast so that she wol the bite?' (III. 737). Readers find themselves caught up in a creative interplay between idealising and pragmatic tonalities which is peculiarly characteristic of the poem. The soaring idealisation seems sometimes coloured with hints of mischievous parody; the humorous pragmatism, on the other hand, can look quite hollow in its insensitivity to those profounder impulses which drive so much of the poem's exploration of love.

In this shimmering configuration of antithetical qualities, *Troilus and Criseyde* recalls Chaucer's *Parliament of Fowls*, composed in the same seven-line 'Rhyme Royal' stanza. The *Parliament* is a short ambitious poem exploring the 'miraculous' power of love through classical, religious, courtly and streetwise perspectives; these converge upon a dispute over whether it is sensible or pointless to persevere in unrequited love. In a way, *Troilus* is a tremendous expansion of that subject, but is built differently – it is like a grand narrative arch raised above the sensual and sentimental romance that the earlier fourteenth-century Italian writer Giovanni Boccaccio had extracted from medieval accounts of the military and sexual adventures involved in the fate of Troy.

Moreover, just as the *Parliament* may be said to exceed its generic category of 'dream-vision', *Troilus* exceeds the generic label of *tragedye* (in the medieval sense of 'conspicuous fall from a high point of fortune') which Chaucer finally applies to it (V. 1786). This is a work that is stunningly compendious in its generic affiliations; it demonstrates no less than the *Canterbury Tales* the urge to accommodate and juxtapose diverse modes. It breathes the ambition and the apparatus of epic (invocations to the pantheon, extended similes, periphrastic statements of date and time), though not the full 'public' ethos of that genre. It constructs the ill-fated love of its central couple into what has been called a 'high romance' (though without incorporating that genre's chivalric quest or optimistic ending: Saunders 2006:138; Windeatt 1983). It incorporates comedic scheming worthy of fabliau (its hero is thrown into the heroine's bed) yet manages to transcend salacious humour. Then again its narrative keeps devolving into the mould of debate, as its protagonists argue elaborately about choices of action. Finally it is ostentatiously studded with incidental generic variegations: dawn-song; lyric – including the first known translation into English of a Petrarchan sonnet; letters, and even philosophical analysis in verse.

Chaucer knew all about planning a substantial work, about the need as the rhetoricians said to survey in advance like an architect ('sende his hertes line out fro withinne', I. 1068) – a prescription which he amusingly applies *within* the poem to the work of wooing). There is no doubt that he planned *Troilus* to be something special. The ambition is there from the outset in wittily designating himself the Pope of love-poetry, servant of the servants of the God of Love (I. 15), and it is there in his closing confidence (as we shall see later) that the poem may take its place in the canon of great literature.

More open to question is whether he knew *exactly* what he wanted to do, by injecting material from Boethius's *Consolation of Philosophy*, on which he had recently worked, and even material from Dante into his main source for the Troilus story, Boccaccio's *Il Filostrato*. Chaucer's poem certainly has a formally satisfying, robust external shape as it traces the pangs of courtship through two books, to the apex of consummation in the midst of Book III, then the separation and subsequent erosion of hope in the last two books. In terms of the poem's local development, however, it is possible to detect signs of 'improvisation' betraying 'gradually changing purposes' as Chaucer seeks to expand the valuation of human love which he finds in Boccaccio (Salter 1991: 95–8). The impression is of a surge of creative energy driving, but complicating, the articulation of love in *Troilus*. Before investigating that, however, we must reckon with the relation of Chaucer's ambition here to heroic or epic literature on Troy.

The underlying plot of *Troilus* is simple: Criseyde is a widow left alone in the besieged city of Troy after her father, Calkas, defects to the Greeks; Troilus falls in love with her, but awe and innocence inhibit his ability to woo her. His friend Pandarus, who is also Criseyde's uncle, acts as match-maker, parries some of her scruples and stage-manages opportunities for the two to meet. Their love is fulfilled, only to be thwarted by Criseyde's transfer to the Greek camp as part of a hostage deal. The couple can find no means of preventing this without provoking a scandal; worse, once in the Greek camp, Criseyde realises the enormity of the promise she has rashly made to get back to Troy, and resigns herself instead to the new attentions of Diomede. Subsequently Troilus, in despair, is killed in battle.

Troy narratives were popular for furnishing foundational myths for medieval European states, including King Arthur's Britain, as at the start of *Sir Gawain and the*

Green Knight. In Chaucer's lifetime there was even a fashion for calling London 'Troynovant' or New Troy (Windeatt 1992: 7–8). Among the late antique and early medieval sources underlying this preoccupation, most were preoccupied with the battles and hand-to-hand combat associated with the remorseless siege of Troy (Benson 1980). The twelfth-century *Roman de Troie* by Benoît de Sainte-Maure even assigned each battle a number, as if in an inventory. But Chaucer declares that to supply an account of Troy's history would amount to a 'digression' from his subject, which is expressly the Double Sorrow of Troilus in Loving (I. 141–4, I. 1–3).

We need to sense the shock-value of demoting the master narrative of Troy's 'destruccion' to the status of *digression* from something more important. Chaucer airily implies that if he had wanted 'to write / The armes' of this worthy man – to write a *Troileid*, so to speak – he could have done so (V. 1765–7).[1] However, the truth is that Chaucer wants to avoid the potentially repetitive conventions of battle-narrative (I. 134–8), whose limitations lay exposed in the vernacular English verse romances circulating in his day. Among other signs of what must have seemed to him the attractive 'modernity' in Boccaccio's *Il Filostrato* ('The One Prostrated by Love') was the Italian poet's unashamed prioritisation of the love affair between Troilo and Criseida over the deeds of prowess otherwise associated with Troy material. Chaucer's work is certainly more self-consciously epic in manner and scope than Boccaccio's, yet it remains an epic wrought from 'private' lives.[2]

Indeed, spurred by Boccaccio's precedent, Chaucer emphatically turns the siege of Troy inside-out (Lynch 2006). His is a citizen's-eye-view of the siege, typified in the description of Troilus returning from combat along the street. This is a markedly muted, indirect vision of military action (II. 610–51). True, the hero's dented armour – his shield pierced by arrowheads which here stand in for the figurative arrows of love – forms part of a package of masculinity which has a striking impact on Criseyde as she catches sight of him from her house. Yet it is his delicate bashfulness at the applause of the crowd that most enthrals her:

> For which he wex a litel reed for shame
> When he the peple upon hym herde cryen,
> That to byholde it was a noble game
> How sobrelich he caste down his yën.
> Criseÿda gan al his chere aspien,
> And leet it so softe in hire herte synke,
> That to hireself she seyde, 'Who yaf me drynke?'
> (II. 645–51)

We should pause to observe the supple easy command of the *ababbcc* rhyme royal stanza. Here (as often) it divides into two: a four-line unit which leads up to a pause, before the *bcc* lines move the stanza to a close. The rhymes are unobtrusive; a gentle framework seeming to facilitate, not strain, the sense; here they are reassuringly allied with the syntactical units 'For which...', 'When...', 'That...', 'How...'. Chaucer is also adept at using either the last couplet or the last line of the stanza to wrap up or crown what goes before. Here the last line is one of the most famous in the poem; but many such lines of epigrammatic force hang in the memory:

> But God and Pandare wist al what this mente.
> (II. 1561)

> 'We usen here no wommen for to selle.'
> (IV. 182)

> Men seyn – I not – that she yaf hym hire herte.
> (V. 1050)

> 'This Diomede is inne, and thow art oute.'
> (V. 1519)

Readers need to know that Chaucer's mastery of this complex stanza, unfamiliar in English at this date, was innovatory: predecessors had mainly used couplets, or the jog-trot octosyllabic 'tail-rhyme'. While there is no way of knowing when Chaucer first used rhyme royal, or whether he developed it from Boccaccio's eight-line stanza of eleven-syllable lines rhyming abababcc (Wallace 2003: 43), it is clear that he already wields it in *Troilus* as a medium capable of every kind of effect. We have just seen it express the subtle emotional trajectory whereby Troilus's demeanour is beheld and allowed by Criseyde to 'sink' into her heart. It can equally express a jaunty changing-room camaraderie afterwards, when Troilus's friend obliges us to reckon with the combat-worn hero's body odour:

> This Pandarus com lepyng in atones,
> And seyde thus: 'Who hath ben wel ibete
> To-day with swerdes and with slynge-stones,
> But Troilus, that hath caught hym an hete?'
> And gan to jape, and seyde, 'Lord, so ye swete!'
> (II. 939–43)

Characteristically, Chaucer's accommodation of speech idiom to the formality of the lines conceals its own art so utterly that it is easily underestimated.[3]

Evidently the heroic business of the siege and defence is being trifled with in Chaucer's poem. We even see amorous intrigue blithely *usurp* the discourse of military strategy and state politics. Thus, when Troilus needs to prod unwanted relatives out of his room to facilitate his first private encounter with Criseyde, he gives them a war document to take away and read. It is a letter from Hector consulting whether some man or other (a suspected traitor perhaps?) 'was worthi to ben ded' (II. 1699– 1700). This is a grim analogy for the chief topic of the poem in Books I and II; that is, whether Troilus himself is 'worthy to be dead' (since he insists that he *will* die) if Criseyde does not show responsiveness to his love. In an analogous usurpation of military matters, the courtship of Criseyde is likened to 'mining' defensive walls (II. 676–9, III. 766–7).

Troy's political needs eventually bite back at the lovers in *Troilus and Criseyde*, not only because their tragedy hinges on the hostage deal that consigns Criseyde to the Greek camp (a 'given' in the received story), but because political responsibilities impinge on any prospect that Troilus, a member of the royal family of Troy, might avert his separation from Criseyde by running off with her. This would be to repeat the public crime of 'ravysshyng of wommen' (abduction) perpetrated in the abduction of Helen by Troilus's brother Paris which – Chaucer's poem cumulatively emphasises – has fuelled the whole Greek attack on Troy. Troilus is acutely aware that he will not be 'suffred [...] to erre' in the same way (IV. 547–50). He is almost prepared to risk such infamy; the poem underlines how close the love-affair gets to becoming, like that of Paris and Helen, a matter of state, without crossing the thin line that would make it so.

Chaucer elaborates the lean Boccaccian narrative he works with partly by multiplying the wooing stratagems wrought by Pandarus, but above all by producing extended dialogues and monologues in which its key characters debate with each other or with themselves concerning how to proceed (Stokes 1983: 18). Debating skills are explicitly acknowledged when Troilus refers, albeit exasperatedly, to how 'wel and formely' Pandarus can 'arguwe' (IV. 497).[4] Medieval English poetry offered precedents for 'formal' debate, most conspicuously in the thirteenth-century *Owl and the Nightingale*. In *Troilus* the result is a poem alive with direct speech, insistently drawing the reader's attention to the differing perspectives of its protagonists. (To that extent it also anticipates the antithetical attitudes that were to be exploited from tale to tale in *The Canterbury Tales*.) Moreover, the clashes of those differing perspectives create a whole that is more complex than the sum of the individual debates. *Troilus and Criseyde* thereby becomes the greatest poetic debate on love in English literature.

The poem's representations of what love is stretch from the sublime to the mildly risible. Modern readers often recoil from the extreme emotional subservience which characterises Troilus's role in courting Criseyde. It has even been disparaged as a form of infantilism (Aers 1988). Yet Chaucer has set a trap here, for he is giving a twist of semi-humorous exaggeration to the medieval cultural conventions of what this poem terms 'love paramours',[5] conventions which demand the solemn deference of the male to the female in formal courtship as if to a feudal overlord or goddess.

However, even the fundamental element of sexual desire takes a variety of forms. It is partly imagined as capitulation to a peremptory god of love, partly as intuitive compliance with the law of nature or 'Kynde' – an all-powerful force respected also by Chaucer's contemporary Gower, which, we are told, should not be resisted since it is a catalyst of worthy behaviour throughout the world (I. 236–8, 253–5). At the same time the poem frankly invokes a familiar colloquial idiom when it understands sexual desire as a condition of 'being hot' for the love-object. Criseyde's niece Antigone scorns those who call it love 'if oon be hoot' (II. 892). Yet this element is never denied in Troilus's love. After his first night with Criseyde, he confesses to Pandarus that his desire is such that 'I hadde it nevere half so hote as now' (III. 1650).

Troilus quickly rephrases this, claiming to detect an indefinable 'newe qualitee' (1654) in his love.[6] For the reader, the most awe-inspiring and simultaneously disconcerting aspect of that quality is its sublimation through language associating it with divine love. At the summit of his period of happiness with Criseyde, Chaucer allows Troilus to offer up a song, adapted from the *Consolation of Philosophy* by Boethius, magnificently celebrating the power of love, ordained by God as author of creation to hold individuals and peoples in amity in the world. The song's first stanza displays the poem's grand manner at its best. With solemn use of reversed initial stress, it hammers out a fourfold incantation, repeating a suspended syntactical structure ('Love' plus relative clause) that impels us right through six lines until the sentence is completed in the seventh:

> 'Love, that of erthe and se hath governaunce,
> Love, that his hestes hath in hevene hye,
> Love, that with an holsom alliaunce
> Halt peples joyned, as hym lest hem gye,
> Love, that knetteth lawe of compaignie,
> And couples doth in vertu for to dwelle,
> Bynd this accord, that I have told and telle.'
>
> (III. 1744–50)

The intuitive human 'accord' achieved between Troilus and Criseyde ('It semed hire he wiste what she thoughte / Withouten word' [III. 465–6]) is one thing. This philosophical appeal to a heaven-ordained love-force claimed to activate all forms of connection is quite another, though splendidly hypnotic in its sheer confidence. But the poem has gone even further than this in a bravura prologue to Book III where the speaker offers a tribute to the planet-goddess Venus as wellspring of a sort of glorious continuum of diverse forms of 'love', from animal instinct to Jupiter's sexual rapacity to human couples who are ethically improved by their amours, to political harmony; all under the assurance that 'God loveth' and that no-one's life has value without love (III. 1–42).

Some readers have been uncomfortable with this bold and seemingly 'un-medieval' synthesis. They note that the speaker declares himself to be Venus's clerk (41), and they resolve that such sentiments are not to be trusted from this enthusiast, any more than from an infatuated Troilus. This speaker, indeed, is often referred to as the poem's Unreliable Narrator, and discussed as though he were a separate character in the story, foolishly committed to its emotions. For all the apparent sophistication of this now entrenched line of response, it has been grossly overplayed in *Troilus* criticism, for it too artificially solidifies a narrator-persona out of the enjoyably supple tonalities of voice which actually constitute the poem's 'textual subjectivity' (Spearing 2005: 68–100). In any case, and not surprisingly given the poem's wobbly representation of a pagan culture, the collage of categories of love is endemic amongst the poem's characters. Pandarus, achieving a successful first meeting between the lovers, hails 'Immortal god', and then goes on 'Cupide, I mene' (III. 185–6). It is a reminder of just how often we are left to make up our own minds about a key strand of diction: which 'god' is meant at various moments in the poem.

Nevertheless, instead of applying medieval preacherly criteria to the poem's colourful enhancement of human love through religious vocabulary, we should probably accept that Chaucer appropriated the register of exalted religious language because there was no other vocabulary available to express the soaring potential of heterosexual bliss that he wanted for this poem: 'the only medieval writings on love which rival the grace and intensity of Chaucer's language in Book III of *Troilus* are religious treatises, and Chaucer had to win the release of his full imaginative powers for this difficult subject by religious means' (Salter 1966: 103). We shall have to return to the challenge this posed near the end of this chapter. Meanwhile we need now to consider other cross-lights on that phenomenon of extreme dedication to love which is the foundation of the poem.

In the numerical centre of the poem Troilus, beginning to delight in his 'heaven' of touching Criseyde's body, lauds Love and Charity, rejoices in being 'bistowed in so heigh a place / That thilke boundes may no blisse pace', addresses Criseyde as his guide appointed by god (which one?), and swears on his life that never will he transgress her will (III. 1254–1302). This ceremonious utterance of elation, reverence and dedication stretches over nearly fifty lines in seven stanzas. In response Criseyde projects a contrasting incisiveness. Thanking him as the trusted 'ground' of her 'ese', she goes on:

> 'But lat us falle away fro this matere,
> For it suffiseth, this that seyd is heere,
> And at o word, withouten repentaunce,
> Welcome, my knyght, my pees, my suffisaunce!'
> (III. 1306–9)

It is a brilliantly poised response. Her sense of how much Troilus means to her shines through the series of epithets in the glowing line of 'welcome'. At the same time her proposal that Troilus and she now 'falle away' from further romantic effusion suggests that Criseyde cannot altogether share his pitch of exalted lyricism (who could?) and is beginning to wonder whether they are ever to make love. It is a significant hint of a temperamental difference between them even on the very brink of consummation. Actually she is voicing the reader's own impression that Troilian reverence needs to be brought down to earth: we really need to 'falle away fro this matere' to restore normality and narrative momentum.

Part of Chaucer's playful audacity in the poem, indeed, is to present a Troilus who keeps being swamped by lyrical or melancholic reveries which threaten to stall the narrative, amidst what has been seen as a kind of 'contemplative' stasis (Saunders

2006: 142). It is not that the soulful profundity of Troilus's love for Criseyde is in question. 'Heightened emotionalism', it has been pointed out, 'is a common feature of late-medieval poetry' (Spearing 2005: 99). But an element of playful mischievousness in representing it is not in question either; it manifests Chaucer's impulse to entertain in his poetry, a levity which is engaging and risky by turns. The levity may be visible in *de*flating remarks made by the poem's speaker or by Pandarus; or it may appear as a wicked tinge of *in*flation that intermittently haunts the characters' lofty utterances. And, to a degree not often acknowledged, Chaucer discloses an almost compulsive tendency to imbue his narrative with knowing exaggeration.

For example, following Troilus's vigil on the city walls waiting in vain for Criseyde to come back from the Greek camp as promised, he declines into desolate misery, physically drained and unable to eat anything. According to Boccaccio, 'there was scarcely enough vitality in his limbs to sustain him' (*Fil.* 7. 20). Chaucer outdoes Boccaccio: 'So was he lene, and therto pale and wan, / And feble, that he walketh by potente' (V. 1221–2). Troilus is reduced to walking *with a crutch*. It is a deliciously over-wrought idea. We register the wackiness of taking to such a literal extreme the conventional malaise of the medieval literary lover who is pining in the deprivation of love.[7] The image audaciously caps the metaphor of love-longing as a 'sickness', which Chaucer has played with throughout Troilus's courtship of Criseyde.

Nevertheless the arias and introspections of Troilus's style of loving, from which radical interventions by Pandarus rescue him into action, are afforded a deeply sympathetic perspective in the poem. We can understand this better if we grasp the role of *compassion* in the poem. Chaucer proposes that his poem will promote 'compassioun' for all those who suffer in love (I. 47–51). From the Latin root, Middle English *compassioun* often signified a now obsolete sense, 'suffering together with another', as well as the now dominant meaning 'sympathy for another's distress that inclines a person to alleviate it'. In both senses, compassion is the presiding emotion of *Troilus and Criseyde*. The poem exists to *share* the sufferings of Troilus and Criseyde out of fellow-feeling (like a brother, says the narrative voice at I. 51) *and* to create an ethos of pitying solicitude for those sufferings. Compassion involves entering companionately into another's suffering, but it need not exclude detachment in the person volunteering it.

Compassion is crucial *within* the love affair, too. What Troilus yearns for, and fears to jeopardise, is compassion or pity in Criseyde. *Troilus and Criseyde* is a poem of conspicuous pathos partly because it is so preoccupied with these emotive determinants of love paramours: with fear (*drede*), supplication (*compleynte*), the spectre of the woman's *wrath* forestalling her pity and compassion. Troilus, momentarily elated by his first sight of Criseyde, is then *unnerved* by the process of falling for her: 'sodeynly hym thoughte he felte dyen, / Right with hire look, the spirit in his herte' (I. 306–7).[8] So, while Criseyde's fears in the narrative are self-evident and have often been noted, arguably it is Troilus's fear that is the more emphatic. Above all he fears angering her: 'lest she be wroth – this drede I moost, ywys' (I. 1019). He is in 'drede' when he first struggles to speak his love to her (III. 92) and hyperbolically proposes to kill himself if that would appease any wrath that his pleas arouse in her (III. 107–10).[9] She in turn solemnly reserves the right to display wrath towards him should he attempt to exercise authority over her in their relationship (III. 173–4).

All this provides some justification for the famously bizarre moment in the poem when Troilus faints right at Criseyde's bedside when she reproaches him for alleged jealousy. The imputed jealousy is Pandarus's brainwave, to persuade her to allow Troilus into her bedchamber at his house; but the consequence is that Troilus suddenly finds that 'wroth was she that sholde his sorwes lighte' (III. 1082), though it is a wrath he does not deserve. Rather, as in the temptation scenes in *Sir Gawain and the Green Knight*, the hero is confronted with an accusatory misconstruction of himself. Troilus keels over and faints (Mann 1980). Chaucer expresses Criseyde's emotional insight in this crisis in her use of the key word to reassure her unconscious lover; ' "Iwys, my deere herte, I am nought wroth" ' (III. 1110).

Troilus is the first hypersensitive hero in English poetry and the first one to be so introspectively anxious. His introspection makes him a proto-Hamlet in whom we recognise that the native hue of resolution is prone to be sicklied over with the pale cast of thought. At the same time his bashfulness and his insistence on deferring to Criseyde's wishes have prompted some critics to think of him as 'feminised' hero, or as a hero who signals a new ideal of masculinity accommodating certain traits previously stereotyped as feminine (Hansen 1992; Mann 2002).

Pandarus, besides being always ready to measure his friend against more conventionally assertive criteria of masculinity, blows fresh air upon Troilus's fraught meditations, and brings an antithetical opportunism and a different register of language into the text. His action of unclothing Troilus and casting him into Criseyde's bed ('for this or that'! III. 1097) to overcome the crisis of the faint is a superb example of the work Chaucer makes Pandarus perform in the poem. It epitomises Pandarus's audacious spontaneous instinct for escalating any 'move' in the 'game' of love; for trying always to catapult the participants ahead of the position they might currently consider it decorous to occupy. It demonstrates, too, his dynamic *involvement* in the love affair. He even makes himself grammatically complicit in it. Thus when news of Criseyde's impending departure breaks, Pandarus exclaims to Troilus: who would have thought that 'in so litel a throwe' Fortune *'oure* joie wold han overthrowe?' (IV. 384–5).

The reason why Troilus can be so completely invested with the idealised role of soulful dedication to love is that Chaucer has hugely enlarged Pandarus's role as 'fabricator' of the actual affair (Fyler 1980). In that role, Pandarus is always impatient to overcome the diffidence of Troilus or the scruples of Criseyde, and to contrive opportunity or to run with it. He is ever on hand to give orders, or supply proverbs, against reverie or melancholy: 'relieve the other's sufferings; get up; don't expire like a gnat; find out what she thinks; write a letter; *do something*'. Nothing could be more humorously or more brusquely opposed to Troilian introspection. Pandarus's motto is to jump on the wheel of Fortune; or, when good luck ('aventure') presents itself – as he impresses upon Criseyde is the case with Troilus's interest in her – 'Cache it anon, lest aventure slake [slacken]!' (II. 291).

One consequence of Pandarus's commitment to 'aventure' is that he embodies a clear-eyed perception of the unreliability, as well as the excitement, of fortune in life. His surprise at the impending loss of Criseyde is not, we notice, that Fortune is overthrowing happiness but only that the downturn has occurred so fast. And, being committed to engaging actively with 'aventure' in order to get results for oneself, he is capable of blurting out shockingly pragmatic consolations to his friend in adverse circumstances, such as 'Artow for hire and for noon other born?' (IV. 1095). To the reader, this is disturbing evidence of Pandarus's slippery openness to the ebb and flow of 'aventure'. By contrast Troilus himself can only intone his all-enduring love:

> 'She that I serve, iwis, what so thow seye,
> To whom myn herte enhabit [devoted] is by right,
> Shal han me holly hires til that I deye.'
>
> (IV. 442–4)

So far we have considered a polarisation in the poetry of *Troilus and Criseyde* between idealistic and pragmatic perspectives on love. However, Chaucer creates in Criseyde's role a more nuanced and enigmatic reading of love – indeed a more nuanced response to life generally. The moment she is introduced, Chaucer is already variegating Boccaccio's representation of a haughty *donna* to achieve a greater complexity. Self-possession has to co-exist in Criseyde with the diffident modesty implicit in her standing inconspicuously at the back of the temple crowd 'ay undre shames drede' (I. 180–2, 290–2). To recall a central motif of our discussion, Chaucer is clearly absorbed by the possibilities inherent in constructing a *compassionate* rendering of Criseyde.

True, the 'given' of her eventual lapse in fidelity is not negotiable, and is even forecast in numerous touches of dramatic irony. For instance, in the case of Troilus's alleged jealousy at Pandarus's house she declares, God knows 'untrewe / To Troilus was nevere *yet* Criseyde' (III. 1053–4). But this very scene, a narrative addition by Chaucer which shows his formal skill in this poem in contriving doublings and anticipations, is raising in advance the spectre of unfaithfulness in Criseyde only for it to be indignantly repudiated. She is hurt that her lover could conceive of her being 'lightly fals' (III. 802–4, 983–4). Her plangent sense of the harm done when people rush into erroneous judgment constitutes a warning to readers to bring mature (and compassionate) understanding to the circumstances under which Criseyde actually will prove 'fals'.

In the meantime it is Criseyde who voices a key sentiment of the poem, under stress of the false allegation. She detects in the report of Troilus's alleged jealousy evidence of the vulnerable and temporary nature of worldly happiness, which clerks call 'fals felicitee'; for either one's happiness is spoilt by anxiety, or one is in a fool's paradise of ignorant bliss. In sum, 'Ther is no verray weele in this world heere' (III. 836). Of course, such moments of philosophical scepticism do not prevent Criseyde from wanting and sensing extreme happiness for herself and her lover in their relationship. She sometimes matches Troilus in expressing the ineffable durability of her love (e.g. III. 1498–1502). Yet, in the famous conversations with Pandarus and the monologue in Book II in which we access her thoughts, we observe a sceptical and astute personality. Her uncle's mind-games find in her a wary antagonist as she moves to 'felen what he meneth' (II. 387; Stokes 1983: 24–6). She sees through his rhetoric and pays back rhetoric of her own, reproaching him vociferously for coming to her with proposals on Troilus's behalf. She is aware of a need 'ful sleighly for to pleie' in order to neutralise Pandarus's threats of suicide (III. 462).

The process, therefore, by which Criseyde is brought to love is more wary than is the case with Troilus. The excitement she signals in that mental exclamation '"Who yaf me drynke?"' (III. 651) merely 'inclines' Criseyde to love, we are told, opening her mind to absorbing self-examination; 'And, Lord! So she gan in hire thought argue' debating with herself 'what to doone best were, and what eschue' (II. 694–6). She worries whether love, with its roller-coaster of emotion, its potential exposure of the self to scandalmongers, its vulnerability to male fickleness, will pointlessly threaten her liberty and self-possession. Since it 'torneth' (an echo of Fortune's wheel) so easily into nothing, she cannot see 'To what fyn' (to what end) is such love (II. 794). But on the other side are Troilus's royal status and his worthiness, now fortuitously in her hands, combined with her own unmarried status that leaves her free to do as her heart wishes: 'To what fyn lyve I thus? / Shal I nat love, in cas if that me leste?' (II. 757–8).

Two things are noteworthy about the poetry here. One is that Chaucer creates through self-debate the viewpoint of a woman who is deeply aware of the risks of what we would call 'commitment'; psychological and emotional risks that are the more onerous for women, she believes, because if things go wrong women have few outlets except to 'wepe and sitte and thinke' (II. 783).[10] Second, her repeated concern for the *fyn* or purpose of her current single life and for the purpose of love that is so often short-lived makes her a key voice in the poem's philosophical questioning about ultimate purposes in life. Critics pursuing dogmatic readings of the poem tend to focus on only one part of her double perplexity. 'The irony', declares Ida Gordon, 'is that Criseyde herself, whose love turned into nothing, is the one to see that this is the nature of this kind of love: her question, "To what fyn is swich love?" is one that is central to the poem's morality' (1970: 102–3). True, but the other half of Criseyde's perplexity is to question what purpose her life will have – given that she wants no husband and that she is not vowed to religion – if she does *not* allow herself to love.

Affected, then, by conflicting impulses and willing to compromise amidst the pressures upon her, Criseyde is represented as allowing herself to be nudged further and further into love. The sophisticated interchanges between Uncle Pandarus and herself project a remarkable game of wits through which she is manoeuvred, some-times unwittingly, sometimes wittingly ('as his nece, obeyed as hire oughte', III. 581) towards consummation with Troilus. She responds particularly to Troilus's discretion and self-restraint, which shield her love from scandal; his ability, as she later puts it, to transcend vulgar desire (III. 477–80, IV. 1677). But these are virtues that can become handicaps when action is required; moreover, we remain residually aware that whereas her relation to him concedes potential imperfection and fragility in human love, his for her is more governed by notions of eternal worship. One critic quotes from *The Great Gatsby* to offer an inspired analogy: 'Troilus has "wed his unutterable visions to her perishable breath"' (Wetherbee 1980: 301).

The downward spiral of the poem's emotional trajectory after the parliamentary Trojan agreement to include Criseyde in the hostage exchange follows through the logic of all this. It is partly structured around extended plangent laments by both Troilus and Criseyde, a poetry of agonising deprivation that perhaps reaches its apogee in *Troilus*. The lovers complement each other at first in their grief-stricken thoughts of becoming martyrs to love and in imagining an afterlife where their souls – in parallel innovatory diction – will 'un-nest' or 'un-sheathe' from their bodies to seek out the other (IV. 305, 776). Yet differences of outlook soon surface, which extend the poem's formal preoccupation with debate.

First there is another debate between Pandarus and Troilus. Pandarus urges the claims of self-interested 'manly' assertiveness, championing resistance to the exchange, if necessary by resort to armed force and blood in the streets if that is the way for Troilus to withhold Criseyde. Troilus objects that he feels trapped by the imperatives of love paramours: discretion, and protection of Criseyde's honour. This debate is complemented by a tense culminating dialogue between the lovers themselves. Criseyde shows her immersion in patriarchal ideology when she assumes that Troilus cannot prevent the exchange by carrying her off since it would be appalling for him to compromise his Trojan duty 'for any womman' (IV. 1557: see Aers 1979). Troilus for his part is full of misgivings about her alternative strategy of finding means to return from the Greek camp. Her clinching arguments concern the claims of reputation, both his and hers. *Name* is not, finally, to be jeopardised:

> 'What trowe ye the peple ek al aboute
> Wolde of it seye? It is ful light t'arede.
> They wolden seye, and swere it out of doute,
> That love ne drof yow naught to don this dede,
> But lust voluptuous, and coward drede.
> Thus were al lost, ywys, myn herte deere,
> Your honour, which that now shyneth so clere.'
> (IV. 1569–75)

Her rhetoric, for all its conversational manner, exemplifies the poem's skills in persuasive oratory. She frames a question ending at the caesura in line 1570; claims the answer is obvious; then supplies it in a way that tactically eliminates innocent objection, as against the uncompromising verdict she predicts if they elope; finally she subsides into the firm but tender concern of the last couplet. As for her own as yet unspotted reputation, she goes on, it would be destroyed: 'My name sholde I nevere ayeynward wynne' (IV. 1581).

'Name' or public reputation is always reckoned precious in medieval courtly poetry. But in Criseyde's case, as she finds herself isolated in the Greek encampment, this prioritisation of her name – of her reputation for sexual propriety – rebounds on her with bitter irony. Pursued by Diomede, a man who combines the opportunistic skill of a Pandarus with a practised and predatory rhetoric of courtship, she gives in, though this is a process which Chaucer surrounds with considerable circumstantial mitigation. In doing so she foresees, and the narrating voice foresees, that her 'name of trouthe in love' will be lost; in fact her name will be 'rolled' on many a tongue and in many a book (V. 1054–61; also 1095–6). (There is here a complex poetic reflexivity. The very book in which we are reading of her 'name' quotes her anticipation of a less compassionate 'name' than that which is inscribed in this poem.) Meanwhile she takes refuge in equivocal responses to Troilus's desperate letters, and, more devastatingly, in the distressing second-best of a mental resolution to be true, at least, to Diomede (V. 1071).

Troilus is among other things a poem of considerable erudition, and Criseyde derives from her fate an erudite lesson which seems to absorb her into a medieval gender stereotype. Looking back, she wishes that when the crunch came she had had sufficient foresight – the third category of prudence, as she properly calls it – to have braved the idea of elopement with Troilus as he suggested (V. 736–49). Chaucer has characteristically sharpened a simpler regret about poor judgment that he found expressed by Boccaccio's Criseida (*Fil.* 6. 5–6) into a precise and learned point concerning *prudentia*. Earlier, Criseyde's schemes at the crisis are pointedly associated with a 'womanly' talent for quick decision-making (IV. 936, 'short avysement'; and IV. 1261–2, 'a womman [...] avysed sodeynly'). More precisely than the modern reader might think, she therefore judges herself according to a gendering that ascribes resilient short-range thinking to women but a longer-range prudential vision to men (Blamires 2006: 70–3).[11]

Book V registers the excruciating cost of 'short avysement' in this instance. There is little in English poetry to match the Poetry of Suffering, as it has been called (Chickering 2000) expressing the remorseless extinction of hope in Troilus as he waits in vain for Criseyde to come back. The grim irony in what transpires is that Diomede woos her in the Greek camp out of mere self-regarding opportunism. He can tell that her heart is elsewhere but reflects, ' "he that naught n'asaieth naught n'acheveth" ' (V. 784). Earlier it was Pandarus especially, and Criseyde under his influence, who shared that approach to life – they were prepared to have a go with Fortune. Criseyde experiences her own misery at letting Troilus down; but she proves temperamentally better equipped than he to accommodate change into her life – as our period might put it, better equipped to 'move on'.

By contrast, Troilus's most characteristic perception of Fortune is not as a wave he might ride but as a malicious deity whom he has uselessly tried to appease (IV. 260–87). He remains the vessel of fidelity or 'trouthe' in the poem, undeviating in dedication and, even knowing that she is definitely lost to him, still protesting his unstoppable love (V. 1695–8). This immovable mentality is rewarded with an unexpected metaphysical experience after he is killed by Achilles. His soul rises up to the outer 'fixed' sphere of the universe, whence he can contrast the flawed, blind, lust-driven business of the world with the absolute 'felicitee' of heaven. The poem then lets rip with resounding closing rhetoric against terrestrial appetites:

> 'Swich fyn [end] his lust, swich fyn hath his noblesse!
> Swych fyn hath false worldes brotelnesse!'   *fragility*
>
> (V. 1831–2)

But this ending has troubled many readers. How consistent is downgrading the claims of human love and asserting instead the primacy of the love of the Christian God with the thrust of the narrative we have experienced?

This is where the poem's prior adoption of religious diction becomes crucial. For some readers the characters' numerous usurpations of religious concepts to express heterosexual love, plus Troilus's paradoxical total self-dedication to a transient human being, and the prominent role of Fortune in the poem, lead logically to such an ending. We should have seen it coming, considering the rash exaltation of erotic ecstasy that has made the narrating voice exclaim enviously at the lovers' first night of union; 'Why nad I swich oon with my soule ybought?' (III. 1319).

On the other hand, the poem has invested so deeply in the couple's love, has so magnificently allied their love with harmonising, unifying principles in the cosmos, and has so inextricably intertwined the concept of amorous with divine Love, that the ending strikes some as an unwarranted narrowing of perspective, an *imposed* resolution, as though a religious fundamentalist had been let loose to trash what has gone before. Did Chaucer, as he worked on Boccaccio's version, become so imaginatively involved in expressing the high reach (the 'newe qualitee') of romantic union, or put another way did he champion their union with so much imaginative *compassioun*, that he outran himself and found that he needed to retrench, as it were, in rounding off the poem?

Whichever interpretative option readers incline to, as they finish the poem they will be hugely conscious of the poetic ambition of its author. The outstanding rhetorical agility and power of *Troilus and Criseyde* is enriched by subtle patterns of imagery (some of which we have noted: but see especially Barney 1972) and by discreet literary allusions. A famous example of the latter comes as an embellishment to the dawning of the day when Pandarus is to commence his campaign to obtain Criseyde's love for Troilus; the dawn song of the swallow 'Progne' (II. 64–70) is a reminder of the story of Tereus, who rapes Procne's sister in Ovid's *Metamorphoses*. It is a poetic cross-reference which disconcertingly acknowledges that there is a kind of masculine 'oppression' of Criseyde – a betrayal of her – in the narrative, which is open to ethical debate.[12]

A second example returns us to the audacity which is such a hallmark of the poem. It is a meta-literary allusion, in the sense that Pandarus refers to a 'letter' that Ovid had imagined (in Book 5 of his *Heroides*), as if the letter were to hand in Troy. It is a letter of forlorn reproach sent by Oenone to her lover Paris after he deserted her for Helen. But in Trojan history, Paris is Troilus's brother. Suddenly Chaucer flings the letter into the social scene of his Troy: 'Yee say [saw] the letter that she wrot, I gesse?', Pandarus asks Troilus (I. 656), referring to Oenone. It is a little masterstroke, and one incidentally that anticipates a stanza near the ending of the poem in nudging the reader against a prejudicial gendering of treachery (V. 1779–85). Troilus's betrayal by a woman is a narrative whose implicit reverse is a woman's betrayal (as in Oenone's or indeed Procne's case) by a man.

Drawing so adeptly on Ovid and other antecedent poets, Chaucer finally writes that he would not have his work presume to shoulder aside other *makyngs* (poems, probably meaning vernacular English ones). Rather, it should humble itself to *poesye*, to the classics:

> But subgit be to alle poesye;
> And kis the steppes where as thow seest pace
> Virgile, Ovide, Omer, Lucan and Stace.
>
> (V. 1790–2)

It was probably the first time any English writer had expressed – with confident modesty – such emulation of the poets of antiquity (Wallace 2003: 48; Spearing 2005: 78–9). In *The Divine Comedy* Dante had imagined himself being received as the 'sixth' among five poetic luminaries (the same ones as here, except that Chaucer's Statius stands for Dante's Horace). Chaucer surely knew that in *Troilus and Criseyde* he had written a poem of enduring power and distinction which could make him, as Dante had aspired to be, 'the sixth among those high intelligences'.[13]

To an extent, Chaucer suffers from being an innovator bringing into English a consummate stylistic ambition, some of whose features have since dulled through frequent recycling in English poetry. His contemporary Thomas Usk already saw the fresh quality of *Troilus*. Usk makes a personification called Love declare that in intelligence and in mature good sense ('in witte and in good reson of sentence') Chaucer 'passeth al other makers' in this poem. He is hailed as the 'noble philosophical poete in Englissh' (Windeatt 1988: 145). To which, in the present discussion, we have sought to add that the achievement of *Troilus* includes the easy mastery of an art that is distinctively audacious as it develops its compassionate, engaging and expansively dialectical response to the emotions of love.

NOTES

1 In the *House of Fame*, Chaucer's imitation of the opening of Virgil's *Aeneid* runs 'I wol now singen, yif I can, / The armes, and also the man...' (143–4). All quotations are from *The Riverside Chaucer* (1988).

2 *Il Filostrato* can be read in Italian alongside *Troilus* in Windeatt (1984); or in an English translation, in Barney (2006).

3 In line 943, the stress in the fourth iambic is attracted towards 'Lord', but can fall equally on 'so', as if Pandarus were holding his nose.

4 Windeatt's indispensable guide to *Troilus* emphasises its generic inclusiveness but makes no connection with debate, assigning its 'dialogic quality' to the influence of Roman drama (1992: 138–79, esp. 161–3); even in pp. 215–28 entitled 'A Debate about Love' (215–28) he does not actually address the prevalence of debate *within* the poem.

5 See V. 330–2 where Pandarus challenges Troilus whether 'any wight / Hath loved paramours as wel as thow?'; or V. 157–8, Diomede's declaration, 'I loved never womman here-biforn / As paramours'.

6 In *Fil.* 3. 62, Troilo says his 'new fire' is 'of another quality than the one before' (Barney 2006: 208). Chaucer more suggestively separates the 'new quality' from the 'heat'.

7 By contrast, a supposition by Troilus that his emotions have taken a physical toll is dismissed as a figment of his imagination (V. 617–23).

8 For a fine account of the poetics of the first impact of Criseyde on Troilus see Stanbury (1992).

9 Conventional worry about prompting 'wrath' in the beloved is insincerely echoed by Diomede (V. 145–7).

10 This idea that women must bottle up emotions because they cannot release them in the many public pursuits open to men goes back to Ovid's *Remedia amoris*, but is repeated near the end of Boccaccio's Preface to his *Decameron*. It is therefore one symptom of Troilus's 'feminisation' that he is so often found sitting and thinking and weeping.

11 For a contrary view see McAlpine (2003).

12 A point unwittingly reinforced by Pandarus at II. 1418–19.

13 *Inferno* IV. 102. At the same time Chaucer is actually echoing Statius, who consigned his epic *Thebaid* to follow in the footprints of the *Aeneid* (Windeatt 1992: 141).

References and Further Reading

Aers, David (1979). Criseyde: woman in medieval society. *Chaucer Review*, 13, 177–200. (Repr. in C. David Benson (ed.). *Critical Essays on Chaucer's Troilus and Criseyde and his Major Early Poems* (128–48). Milton Keynes: Open University Press.)

Aers, David (1988). *Community, Gender and Individual Identity: English Writing 1360–1430*. London: Routledge.

Barney, Stephen A. (1972). Troilus bound. *Speculum*, 47, 445–58.

Barney, Stephen A. (ed.) (1980). *Chaucer's Troilus: Essays in Criticism*. Hamden, CT: Archon.

Barney, Stephen A. (ed.) (2006). *Troilus and Criseyde*. New York: Norton.

Benson, C. David (1980). *The History of Troy in Middle English Literature*. Cambridge: D. S. Brewer.

Benson, C. David (ed.) (1991). *Critical Essays on Chaucer's Troilus and Criseyde and his Major Early Poems*. Milton Keynes: Open University Press.

Benson, Larry D. (ed.) (1988). *The Riverside Chaucer*. 3rd edn. Oxford: Oxford University Press. (Originally pub. 1987.)

Blamires, Alcuin (2006). *Chaucer, Ethics, and Gender*. Oxford: Oxford University Press.

Chickering, Howell (2000). The poetry of suffering in Book V of 'Troilus'. *Chaucer Review*, 34, 243–68.

Fyler, John (1980). The fabrications of Pandarus. *Modern Language Quarterly*, 41, 115–30. (Repr. in R. A. Shoaf and Catherine S. Cox (eds) (1992). *Chaucer's Troilus and Criseyde, 'Subgit to alle Poesye': Essays in Criticism* (pp. 107–19). Binghamton, NY: Medieval and Renaissance Texts and Studies.)

Gordon, Ida (1970). *The Double Sorrow of Troilus: A Study of Ambiguities in Troilus and Criseyde*. Oxford: Oxford University Press.

Hansen, Elaine Tuttle (1992). *Chaucer and the Fictions of Gender*. Berkeley: University of California Press.

Lynch, Andrew (2006). Love in wartime. In Corinne Saunders (ed.). *A Concise Companion to Chaucer* (pp. 113–33). Oxford: Blackwell.

Mann, Jill (1980). Troilus' swoon. *Chaucer Review*, 14, 319–35. (Repr. in C. David Benson (ed.) (1991). *Critical Essays on Chaucer's Troilus and*

Criseyde and his Major Early Poems (pp. 149–63.) Milton Keynes: Open University Press.)

Mann, Jill (2002). *Feminizing Chaucer*. Cambridge: D. S. Brewer.

McAlpine, Monica (2003). 'Criseyde's Prudence'. *Studies in the Age of Chaucer*, 25, 199–224.

Morgan, Gerald (2005). *The Tragic Argument of 'Troilus and Criseyde'*. 2 vols. Lampeter: Edwin Mellen Press.

Muscatine, Charles (1957). *Chaucer and the French Tradition*. Berkeley: University of California Press.

Salter, Elizabeth (1966). 'Troilus and Criseyde': a reconsideration. In John Lawlor (ed.). *Patterns of Love and Courtesy*. London: Arnold. (Repr. in C. David Benson (ed.). *Critical Essays on Chaucer's Troilus and Criseyde and his Major Early Poems* (pp. 92–109). Milton Keynes: Open University Press.)

Saunders, Corinne (2006). *A Concise Companion to Chaucer*. Oxford: Blackwell.

Shoaf, R. A., and Catherine S. Cox (eds) (1992). *Chaucer's 'Troilus and Criseyde', 'Subgit to alle Poesye': Essays in Criticism*. Binghamton, NY: Medieval and Renaissance Texts and Studies.

Spearing, A. C. (2005). *Textual Subjectivity: The Encoding of Subjectivity in Medieval Narratives and Lyrics*. Oxford: Oxford University Press.

Stanbury, Sarah (1992). The lover's gaze in 'Troilus and Criseyde'. In R. A. Shoaf and Catherine S.

Cox (eds). *Chaucer's Troilus and Criseyde, 'Subgit to alle Poesye': Essays in Criticism* (pp. 224–38). Binghamton, NY: Medieval and Renaissance Texts and Studies.

Stokes, Myra (1983). Wordes white: disingenuity in 'Troilus and Criseyde'. *English Studies*, 64, 18–29.

Taylor, Davis (1976). The terms of love: a study of Troilus's style. *Speculum*, 51, 69–90. (Repr. in Stephen A. Barney (2006). *Troilus and Criseyde* (pp. 503–22). New York: Norton.)

Wallace, David (2003). Chaucer's Italian inheritance. In Piero Boitani and Jill Mann (eds). *The Cambridge Companion to Chaucer* (pp. 36–57). 2nd edn. Cambridge: Cambridge University Press.

Wetherbee, Winthrop (1980). The descent from bliss: 'Troilus' III. 1310–1582. In Stephen A. Barney (ed.) (1980). *Chaucer's Troilus: Essays in Criticism* (pp. 297–317). Hamden, CT: Archon.

Windeatt, B. A. (ed.) (1984). *Troilus and Criseyde: A New Edition of the Book of Troilus*. London: Longman.

Windeatt, B. A. (1988). *Troilus* and the disenchantment of romance. In Derek Brewer (ed.) *Studies in Medieval English Romance: Some New Approaches*. Cambridge: D. S. Brewer.

Windeatt, Barry (1992). *Oxford Guides to Chaucer: Troilus and Criseyde*. Oxford: Oxford University Press.

25

Chaucer's *The Canterbury Tales*

Corinne Saunders

> ...whoso list it nat yheere,
> Turne over the leef and chese another tale;
> For he shal fynde ynowe, grete and smale,
> Of storial thyng that toucheth gentillesse,
> And eek moralitee and hoolynesse.
> Blameth nat me if that ye chese amys.
> The Millere is a cherl; ye knowe wel this.
> So was the Reve eek and othere mo,
> And harlotrie they tolden bothe two.
> Avyseth yow, and put me out of blame;
> And eek men shal nat maken ernest of game.
>
> (I. 3176–86)[1]

The Canterbury Tales was Chaucer's most ambitious writing project and the epitome of his literary experimentation. Probably begun in the late 1380s and unfinished at Chaucer's death in 1400, the work is characterised by game and play of different kinds: the tale-telling competition and dramatic rivalry of the tellers, the comedy and 'harlotrie' of certain tales, the game played with the reader invited to 'turne over the leef', and the presentation of Chaucer the pilgrim as a poor storyteller. The greatest play of all, perhaps, is that of genre. The *Canterbury Tales* is the first work to deploy a generic vocabulary in English, and the first so self-consciously to exploit such a vocabulary. Again and again, tales rely on yet subvert the conventions of different literary genres – conventions of language, style, tone, theme and character. Across different genres, the perspectives of experience and authority interweave, playfully, but also in relation to subjects of great 'earnest': gender, love and marriage, sin and virtue, truth and illusion. It is not for nothing that the Canterbury pilgrims, whether for motives sacred or profane, are on their way to the shrine of 'the hooly blisful martir' (I. 17). This is a project framed by the grand design of life, death and judgement, an examination of fallen man and of ideal virtue. The setting of spring, 'Aprille with his shoures soote' (I. 1), is associated with both secular desire and spiritual regeneration.

Whereas the focus of Chaucer's early poetry and *Troilus and Criseyde* is largely courtly, perhaps reflecting their first audiences, *The Canterbury Tales* engages with the entire span of medieval society, a shift that may indicate the increasing variety of Chaucer's audience. His immediate circle probably comprised the knights and clerics attached to royal households in administrative roles; its inclusion of a number of Lollard knights is interestingly suggestive of Chaucer's contact with radical religious thought. The wider audience for Chaucer's works, however, is likely to have been made up of several different groups: aristocratic, courtly, clerical, intellectual and mercantile – and to have included women (see Strohm 1989; Pearsall 1992; Brewer 1998). The large number of manuscripts of *The Canterbury Tales* seems to reflect the growing interest of the middle classes in vernacular literature (on production and circulation of Chaucer's works, see Griffiths and Pearsall 1989; Hanna 1996; and Hanna's essay in this volume), and, as Boffey and Edwards remark, there is little evidence for ownership of manuscripts of *The Canterbury Tales* by the aristocracy (Saunders 2006: 34–50). The *General Prologue* rewrites the genre of estates satire (Mann 1973), which depicts the traditional vices and virtues of members of the three conventional estates (nobility, clerisy and peasantry). Chaucer depicts his figures in unique, idiosyncratic ways, but also includes the new middle classes: the Shipman, with his expert knowledge of the sea, the Reeve, who manages a Norfolk estate, and the Miller, affluent through his dishonest sale of corn. The Merchant, the Wife of Bath with her own cloth-making business and the innkeeper Harry Bailly, as well as five Guildsmen, represent the flourishing urban classes. Members of the professional classes are present – the Physician, Man of Law and Manciple (an agent of an inn of court) – as well as labouring-class city dwellers, though none but the Cook narrates a tale. The multiplicity of voices and persons is unrivalled even by Chaucer's riotous parliament of birds or cacophony of plaintiffs at the court of Fame. Perhaps the closest equivalent is Langland's 'fair field full of folk' whose voices debate, disturb and instruct across Will's sequence of dream visions.

The notion of the story-telling competition is unique, though it engages with an established literary convention, that of the story collection (see Cooper 1983: 8–55). Chaucer would have been familiar with collections of legends, saints' lives, fables, myths and biblical stories, but would have found in none of these a frame narrative comparable to the Canterbury pilgrimage or the use of individualised narrators and generic range. A number of the tales, however, find analogues in Boccaccio's *Decameron* (1340s), which recent evidence suggests Chaucer may well have known from his travels in Italy, and may have been his direct inspiration (see Cooper in Correale and Hamel 2002: 7–18). Boccaccio presents his collection of stories as told by a group of Italian nobles to pass the time during their exile from plague-ridden Florence, although he does not develop the drama of tellers or the possibilities of literary variation. 'Diverse folk diversely they seyde' (I. 3857); the fiction allows Chaucer to evade responsibility for his immoral tales; it also allows for a remarkable play of voices (see David's treatment of the interrelation of morality and poetics, 'sentence and solaas', 1976: 75–76). The links between tales develop the relations that are hinted at in the *General Prologue*, in particular the rivalry between the Miller and Reeve, Friar and Summoner, and Wife of Bath and Clerk.

The project is – not surprisingly – unfinished: Harry Bailly in the *General Prologue* stipulates that two tales be told by each pilgrim, one on the journey to Canterbury, one on the way back (though a later reference in the *Parson's Prologue* [X. 16] implies that each pilgrim will only tell one tale). Twenty-four tales survive, not all complete, two told by Chaucer the pilgrim, one by the Canon's Yeoman who joins the pilgrimage later. While the order of the first fragment (which commences with the *General Prologue* and may have been written late on) and the place of the *Parson's Tale* at the end are clear, the rest is less certain. There is some evidence that Chaucer was still experimenting with links between tellers and tales, as well as, probably, with order. In the fifty-five extant manuscripts of *The Canterbury Tales*, ten fairly consistent groups of tales or 'fragments' may be distinguished, the internal order of which is relatively stable, but which are placed in differing orders in different manuscripts, including in the two oldest and most important extant manuscripts of *The Canterbury Tales*, Ellesmere and Hengwrt.[2] Tales also circulated separately and in smaller groups (there are twenty-eight copies of parts of the work). Chaucer's role in the circulation of his works is uncertain. His witty caution to a friend against marriage, 'Lenvoy de Chaucer a Bukton', urges, 'The Wyf of Bathe I pray yow that ye rede' (29), and thus suggests that Chaucer could expect Bukton to have access to a copy. The ending of *Troilus and Criseyde*, however, draws attention to the instability of manuscript culture with the prayer that none 'mysmetre' (V. 1796) the poem. Chaucer's brief address to 'Adam, his owne scriveyn' vividly evokes the vulnerability of the hand-copied text in its reference to Chaucer's need to 'correcte and eke to rubbe and scrape' (6) Adam's work. The Ellesmere and Hengwrt manuscripts of *The Canterbury Tales* both appear to be in the hand of the same scribe and may have been written in Chaucer's lifetime, perhaps by the professional London scribe Adam Pynkhurst, whom it is tempting to identify with 'Adam scriveyn', but this is by no means certain.[3] Like so many aspects of manuscript culture, Chaucer's role in the production of the poem, and hence questions concerning order and authoritative readings, remain unanswered (see further Boffey and Edwards in Saunders 2006: 36–42). As Ralph Hanna argues in this volume, modern editions of *The Canterbury Tales* present us with a far more fixed poem than that found in its medieval copies.

Perhaps in part because of its instabilities and experimental quality, *The Canterbury Tales* has proven chameleon-like, responsive to a multiplicity of critical approaches (summarised at the end of this essay and in Saunders 2001a).[4] In particular, it seems, Chaucer's writing is congruent with ideas of the post-modern. In the meta-narrative of the Canterbury pilgrimage, tales exist in dialogue with their sources and analogues, with each other, and in (often ironic) relation to their own and other tellers. A more political Chaucer can readily be found. The longstanding notions of game and contest (see Owen 1977) are deployed in Knapp's notion of a 'social contest' (1990) and the

Bakhtinian concept of carnival illuminates *The Canterbury Tales* (Ganim 1990; see also Kendrick's more anthropological study of Chaucerian play [1988]). As well as relations between tellers, those between tellers and tales have been the subject of much scrutiny. C. David Benson revises the traditional dramatic theory to argue that 'the extraordinary variety [of the tales] ought not to be attributed to the psyches of the pilgrims but to the different styles of the poems' (1986: 20): the work is 'an encyclopaedia of kinds' (Cooper 1983: 72–90). Unity has been a key critical issue (see Jordan 1967; Howard 1976), and has repeatedly been found through the idea of Gothic structure, characterised by the variety within the work's overarching design, and its play of light and dark, beauty and grotesque (Ruggiers 1965; and see also Payne 1973; David 1976; Fichte 1980; Lawler 1980; Sklute 1984).

The Canterbury Tales exemplifies and draws attention to all medieval genres – romance, fabliau, beast-fable, saint's life, miracle story, sermon, moral treatise. The links between tales, in particular, signal genre, though not always in modern terms (the *Knight's Tale* is a 'noble storie', an epic or high romance; the fabliaux are 'ribaudye'). The Host's repeated requests for 'myrie' tales elicits many different responses ranging from comic to tragic. Kinds of tales are repeatedly linked to class and profession: the *Knight's Tale* is especially praised by the 'gentils' (I. 3113), the fabliaux are designated 'cherle[s] tales' (I. 3169), the *Man of Law's Tale* is a 'thrifty tale' (II. 1165) told long ago by a merchant, and the *Clerk's Tale* is learned from 'a worthy clerk' (IV. 41) of Padua, Petrarch himself. Such taxonomic naming in part functions to educate the audience in genre, making explicit the differences between familiar forms of vernacular writing. At the same time Chaucer frequently presses genre to its limits, subverting or refashioning literary tradition (see Davenport 1988, and, for Chaucer's various sources, Correale and Hamel 2002, 2005). The two prose tales, the *Tale of Melibee* and the *Parson's Tale*, moral treatises on the virtue of prudence and on the seven deadly sins and their remedies, are not considered here. These works carry the most explicit ethical weight in *The Canterbury Tales* in part because prose functions to detach them from the world of fictional play and game. Within that world, poetry fulfils a dazzling range of functions, from high seriousness to low comedy, from deep pathos to witty discourse, from colloquial dialogue to philosophical disquisition. What follows explores some highlights of Chaucerian play with genre.

Romance, Love and Chivalry

Chaucer's tale of *Sir Thopas* parodies the conventions of metrical romance, its tail-rhyme descending into comic doggerel and its courtly similes reduced to bland or debased clichés. A sequence of familiar romance episodes is gestured at but undercut: the tale, identified as a rhyme learned long ago (VII. 709) and hence as popular romance, is set not in an exotic courtly world but in Flanders; the hero is distinguished by wrestling at a country fair; he only dreams of an elf-queen; and his battle with a giant is postponed because Thopas has left his armour at home. The abortive tale is soon cut off by the Host, 'Namoore of this.../ Thy drasty rymyng is nat worth a toord!' (VII. 919–30). Among all the genres treated in *The Canterbury Tales*, the popular romance is otherwise conspicuous by its absence. Yet although Chaucer satirises the native story-telling tradition, the genre of romance, with its folkloric building blocks and motifs (described by Nancy Bradbury in this volume), is crucial and formative in his poetry. According to a broad definition of romance as courtly narrative (see also Rosalind Field's discussion in this volume), the Knight's, Squire's, Franklin's, and Wife of Bath's tales can be classified as romance, while romance infuses the Man of Law's and Clerk's tales, and the *Merchant's Tale* is a parody of romance. Chaucer both revels in the artistry of romance and interrogates, though in more veiled and subtle form than in *Sir Thopas*, its ready acceptance of ideals.

This is nowhere more striking than in the *Knight's Tale*, probably written as a separate work (it is mentioned in the *Prologue to the Legend of Good Women*, *c*.1386; its source, Boccaccio's *Teseida*, was perhaps obtained by Chaucer in Italy). The tale's courtly and elevated status, fitting to the Knight and to the opening of *The Canterbury Tales*, is made explicit: it is 'a noble storie / And worthy for to drawen to memorie' (I. 3111–12). This is affirmed by the epic setting of Thebes and the epigraph from Statius. Chaucer pares down and adapts Boccaccio's work by intensifying the emphasis on love, adding the details of amphitheatre, temples and tournament, and shaping a complex philosophical perspective indebted to Boethius' *Consolation of Philosophy*. Extraordinary craftsmanship is evident in the tale's symmetry: the two halves are linked by a complex set of parallels, with three temples and three prayers offered up by the three protagonists at the tale's textual and thematic centre. Craft is evident too in the high-flown rhetoric of the work, from the refined discourse of love to the encyclopaedic grandeur of the tournament to the lofty tragedy of the ending.

Yet through this ordered narrative of high chivalry runs a subtext of love and violence. The tale exquisitely fulfils the conventions of courtly romance: Emilye, the pattern of the archetypal romance heroine, is placed in the archetypal romance landscape, the *locus amoenus* employed in so many dream visions from the *Romance of the Rose* onwards. Yet the experience of *fin'amor* becomes more than conventional lovesickness. The two spaces, the Maytime garden and the tower where Palamon and Arcite are imprisoned, reflect the tale's dualistic treatment of love (Kolve 1984; Woods 2008: 15–36), as do the walls of the temple of Venus with their depictions of tragic lovers and 'the firy strokes of the desirynge' (I. 1922). Love causes actual war between the blood brothers, yet Emilye, the 'sweete foo' (I. 2780), is loved and fought over without being known or (exceptional in romance) knowing of their love. Her later prayer that she be allowed to remain a virgin rather than marry suggests the predicament of the woman objectified within the male structures of battle and love (see Crane 1994: 169–85; Saunders 2001b: 287–90). Chaucer uses the imagery of wild beasts in the forest to depict the complete abandonment of the lovers to their destructive passions (I. 1655–60).

The *Knight's Tale* suggests the troubling existential problems of predestination and free will, suffering and providence. Palamon and Arcite echo Boethius' questions:

'"What governance is in this prescience / That giltelees tormenteth innocence?"' (I. 1313–14). Theseus is presented as a figure of the ideal ruler, characterised by reason and pity: by building the amphitheatre he constructs order out of chaos. Chaucer may play on philosophical interpretations of the forest as representative of primordial matter, which is capable of being transformed and civilised (Saunders 1993). The final part of the work celebrates this transformation in its depiction of the glittering world of chivalry: the array of knights, the crowds and festivities, the heraldry and customs of the lists. When the fury sent by Saturn causes the victor, Arcite, to fall, mortally wounded, however, Theseus' order is overturned. The prayers of both Palamon and Arcite are answered, but in a deceptive and cruel manner that calls into question the meaning of existence. Theseus' father, Egeus, offers a stoical response that recalls the context of the tale, 'This world nys but a thurghfare ful of wo, / And we been pilgrymes, passynge to and fro' (I. 2847–48), whereas Theseus' final, Boethian speech stresses the need to make a virtue of necessity while suggesting obliquely the possibility of merciful providence. Yet the weight of the tale is pitched towards the negative, the failure of romance in a world ruled by capricious gods and bereft of free will.

In different ways, though sometimes much more light-heartedly, Chaucer's romances remain troubled and troubling. The unfinished tale told by the Squire counters his father's epic narrative with the more frivolous subject matter of magical gifts and talking birds, but also ironises the romance genre. The setting of the court of Cambyuskan (Ghengis Khan) places the *Squire's Tale* as a romance of the east, in which exotic marvels and strange adventures are to be expected. The tale weaves together traditional romance motifs: the great feast complete with 'strange' foods (V. 67); references to Gawain and Launcelot; the sudden entrance of a knight who presents three magical gifts. Yet the Squire's self-conscious rhetoric creates unease, as does the inclusion of jarring details such as the 'jangl[ing]' of 'lewed peple' (V. 220–21). Chaucer deconstructs the idea of magic by describing the debate of the courtiers over the gifts: they may be illusions, or shaped by natural science rather than 'fairye' (V. 201). The second part of the tale shifts startlingly, however, into a world much closer to that of the *Parliament of Fowls*, as the magical ring enables the heroine Canacee to hear the speech of the birds. The pathos of the female falcon's lament is an unexpected and dramatic response to the Host's request for 'somwhat of love' (V. 2). Her speech exemplifies elegantly the genre of female complaint, while providing a critical commentary in its depiction of male 'newefangelnesse' (V. 610) and betrayal. In its interlaced sequences and use of inset narratives, the *Squire's Tale* seems to have the potential for infinite expansion (Cooper 1991: 223), while it engages too with the unwritten (the incest story inappropriate for the Squire to tell but evoked by the name Canacee); with voices that, like the falcon's without Canacee's magical ring, are silenced, oppressed or repressed.

By contrast to the Squire's sprawling, interlaced romance and the Knight's epic romance, the *Franklin's Tale* that follows is as neatly contained as the garden in which it occurs, despite the Franklin's claim to know no colours of rhetoric. Its magic is humanly contrived and deceptive, and its emphasis is not on action and adventure but high-flown philosophy and idealism. The tale is also generically fixed, identified at the start of the *Franklin's Prologue* as a Breton lay (a sub-genre discussed by Bradbury in this volume). While the story's basic premise, a knight's attempt to win his beloved, is conventional, its enactment is not, and again the romance form is pressed to its limits. The tale sets up at the start an ideal of marriage rooted in *trouthe* and mutuality, and pits against this the idea of enforced love. Aurelius' conventional vocabulary of *fin'amor* is out of place, for consent would render Dorigen an 'untrewe wyf' (V. 984), and the emphasis on misuse of words is sustained when Dorigen is betrayed by her promise made 'in pley', that she will not love Aurelius until the 'grisly rokkes blake' (V. 859) disappear. The story centres on the possibility of false perception, as that which has seemed eternal, a symbol of the possibility of death, becomes transient through the magician's illusion. What will effectively be Dorigen's rape is thus authorised, and her long lament, reminiscent of the complaints in the *Legend of Good Women* and the *Squire's Tale*, underscores her powerlessness by evoking a series of past female victims, each more distant than the one before. As Arveragus' non-coercive generosity inspires forgiveness in both Aurelius and the clerk, the tale seems to uphold mutual *trouthe* over a more traditional romance ideal in which the woman is an object to be fought over and won. Yet it is also profoundly uncomfortable in the sequence of unnatural actions that arise from the unjust placing of twisted words above the marriage vow. Despite the view so emphasised by the Franklin, 'Wommen, of kynde, desiren libertee, / And nat to be constreyned as a thral' (V. 768–69), Dorigen's name is not a possible answer to the Franklin's question 'Which was the mooste fre?' (V. 1622). Like the *Knight's Tale*, the story is also about the gap between real and ideal, and the constraints of a morality at odds with human nature.

The *Wife of Bath's Tale*, as befits its teller, provides the most provocative comment of *The Canterbury Tales* on the themes of freedom and *maistrye*. The conventions of romance, explicitly evoked by the Arthurian context, are repeatedly overturned. The knight-protagonist is distinguished not by deeds of prowess but by rape (a detail not present in the story's several analogues, which include Gower's tale of Florent in the *Confessio Amantis*). Women are given the decisive vote in the knight's trial, and the pattern of the quest is subverted, its object the answer to the riddle 'What thyng is it that wommen moost desiren?' (III. 905). The journey takes the unheroic quester through towns and past houses rather than into the wild forests of romance, as he questions one female figure after another. The tale seems to return to romance with the dance 'under a forest syde' of 'ladyes foure and twenty, and yet mo' (III. 990, 992), but the apparently faery vision is undercut when in their place appears an old hag, 'a fouler wight ther may no man devise' (III. 999). By offering the response that women desire 'sovereynetee' (III. 1048), the hag overturns traditional male assumptions concerning the sensual and material nature of woman. Her demand that the knight marry her seems both to fulfil the ideal of female *maistrye* and to reverse the rape. The rapist becomes the bound husband, his partner not an unwilling virgin but a loathly hag, and his actions not those of desire and pursuit but of revulsion and flight, the source of considerable comedy. The hag becomes a voice of moral authority, expounding upon the true nature of *gentillesse* in a carefully constructed argument that refutes clerical notions of the irrationality of women. The plastic nature of romance seems to authorise her transformation into a beautiful young woman. Yet, troublingly, the victim is forgotten, and the tale ends with a statement of the wife's obedience. The question of whether the conclusion offers a vision of mutuality or silences women has triggered much critical debate (see Dinshaw 1989 and Mann 1991, versus Hansen 1992), but like its narrator, the tale remains ambiguous, affirming as well as questioning the traditional patriarchal structures of romance. Chaucer does not reject the romance genre any more than he rejects gender stereotypes, but his narratives ask crucial questions concerning the nature and constraints of romance ideals, and the possibilities for rewriting them from a female perspective.

Saints' Lives and Virtuous Women

Romance is complemented by and blurs into hagiography, a genre that allows Chaucer to probe further the subject of female virtue. Saintly women stand as counterparts to courtly heroines, their virtue proven by their patient suffering and their chastity. They find a parallel in the child saint of the *Prioress' Tale*. With the exception of the *Physician's Tale*, this group of tales is written in rhyme royal, a stanza form that (as in *Troilus and Criseyde*) allows Chaucer to exploit the affective and rhetorical power of narrative (see Ellis 1986; Bishop 1988; Hill 1991). The *Second Nun's Tale*, 'the lyf of Seinte Cecile', placed as following the 'legende in translacioun' (VIII. 25), is Chaucer's most straightforward in its fidelity to genre and source (probably Jacobus de Voragine's popular collection of saints' lives, *The Golden Legend*), but it is also highly artistic in its play of imagery and meaning, which colours and shapes the depiction of Cecilia's spiritual power. Transformation and the physical manifestation of the celestial are central to the narrative: Cecilia's conversion of the Roman Valerian to Christianity transforms secular marriage to spiritual, 'clene love' (VIII. 159), and the virgin's power is materially visible in the angel who stands over her with fiery sword. Cecilia takes on the male role of preaching and teaching, explicating the Trinity in the rhetorical terms of patristic writers to open the spiritual eyes first of Valerian and then of his brother. Her superior power of argument is most strikingly evident in her interchange with the prefect Almachius: 'Ye han bigonne youre questioun folily'; 'ye axed lewedly'; 'every mortal mannes power nys / But lyk a bladdre ful of wynd, ywys' (VIII. 428, 430, 438–39). Cecilia dies not at Almachius' will but her own, only after enduring the bath of flames unharmed and surviving three days to preach with her throat cut. Whereas the lives of virgin martyrs typically focus on endurance of physical torture, the example of Cecilia is unusual in its emphasis on active intellectual discourse, a quality reflected in the artistry of the narrative. The etymologies of Cecilia's name given in the prologue correspond to the events of the tale, while a series of triads reflects the theological significance of the number three: the three-part prologue; the three conversions; the explication of the Trinity; the three strokes of the executioner; and the three days the saint survives. Cecilia's life is interwoven with the stories of three male martyrs. Structural patterning is enhanced by the red and white imagery throughout, and by the recurrent motifs of blindness and vision. Like the angel at the start, the miracles surrounding Cecilia's death make material the promise of spiritual sight, and pain, blood and violence become mere props in a symbolic pageant of divine *trouthe*. That we learn nothing of the Second Nun renders the tale more transparent: the veil over the spiritual is lifted.

The Prioress's 'miracle' (VII. 691) uses many of the same conventions: at its core is the wounded yet transfigured body of the saint, which recalls Christ's Passion. By contrast to the *Second Nun's Tale*, this narrative works through pathos to depict the natural spiritual power of the innocent child. The *Prioress's Prologue* compares her unlearned style to the lyric voice of an infant, the subject matter of the story. The dramatic account of the child martyr, who sings his *Alma redemptoris mater* (Gracious mother of the redeemer) even while his throat is cut, seems fitting to the Prioress' sentimentality, and the emphasis is not on intellect but melodrama. In this anti-Semitic story, the Jews enact the will of the devil, lured on by 'oure firste foo' (VII. 558) to become the active embodiment of evil (see Rubin 1999). Yet the tale surpasses conventionality in its powerfully dramatic and affective moments: the simplicity of the child who prefers the hymn to Mary he hears sung to the words of his primer, the contrasting deceit of the Jews and their violent assault on the boy, and the wondrous ringing out of the martyr's song. The miracle is shadowed by the piteous anxiety of the boy's mother, her desperate search and her grief over his body.

Chaucer employs the hagiographic structures of innocent chastity and martyrdom to very different effect in his *Physician's Tale* of Virginia, a virgin without access to Christianity. This 'ensample' (VI. 103) presents a stark picture of classical society as a mechanistic world, where the only choice is between death and shame. The tale addresses the problem of achieving a 'remedye' in a world where authority has been corrupted and the formal system of complaint and defence misappropriated. The failure of justice is reflected in Virginius' murder of his own daughter to avoid rape: here there is no miraculous preservation of the virgin as in saints' lives. Virginius uses the conventional terms of hagiography, referring to Virginia as the 'gemme of chastity' (VI. 223), but the genres of classical *exemplum* and saint's life clash uneasily. Death is not Virginia's choice but her father's, and her response is not pious but pathetic:

> 'O mercy, deere fader!' quod this mayde,
> And with that word she bothe hir armes layde
> Aboute his nekke, as she was wont to do.
> The teeris bruste out of hire eyen two,
> And seyde, 'Goode Fader, shal I dye?
> Is ther no grace, is ther no remedye?'
> (VI. 231–36)

Although natural justice is finally restored when the people rise up against Apius, the absence of Virginia in the moral concerning the wages of sin sustains her silencing within the tale. This narrative seems a dark rewriting of the *Franklin's Tale* in its exploration of virtue within a graceless world: it gestures towards the gap between pagan and Christian worlds, and the optimism of the Christian notion of divine providence.

The interplay of romance and hagiography in the *Man of Law's Tale* points up this optimism. Here, as in the Second Nun's and Prioress's tales, the central drama is that of Christian against pagan, but the narrative also uses the folkloric romance motif of the evil mother-in-law: Custance is cast out to sea 'in a ship al steerelees' (II. 439), betrayed first by the mother of the Sultan whom she is to marry, then by the mother of her husband, King Alla. The laments of the narrator and Custance as she sets out on her journey to an unknown husband in a strange land hint at the dark side of the ethic of *fin'amor*, the suffering of women in arranged marriages (Mann 1991: 128). Marriage, the traditional romance ideal, here is the catalyst for Custance's repeated exiles on the sea, and the tale replicates hagiographic structures in its foregrounding of the threat of unruly desire. Custance seems a saint caught within the structures of a romance, an emphasis pointed up by the extended parallels between her sufferings and those of Biblical figures such as Jonah, and by her miraculous preservation. Throughout, however, miracle is accompanied, as in the life of Cecilia, by an emphasis on Custance's active interventions, from her power to convert to her resistance of a would-be-rapist. She is individualised too by affective moments of pathos, perhaps most memorably the depiction of her expression as she is led out to judgement, 'Have ye nat seyn somtyme a pale face, / Among a prees, of hym that hath be lad / Toward his deeth, wher as hym gat no grace...?' (II. 645–47). By contrast to the tale of Virginia, this narrative merges the structures of saint's life and romance to end in restoration and happiness. The virgin martyr is rewritten as the chaste wife.

This mixed generic pattern also distinguishes the *Clerk's Tale*, but here folkloric motifs unsettle the moral impact of a 'legende' described by the Host as 'gentil' (IV. 1212d, e). In Griselda, the peasant girl of 'vertuous beautee' (IV. 211) who inspires the love of a marquis and is rewarded with the outward trappings of nobility, Chaucer makes a radical statement echoing the Wife of Bath's disquisition on *gentillesse* as unrelated to class. As with Custance, Chaucer emphasises Griselda's sexual purity, but here the drama is situated in Walter's inexplicable testing of his wife rather than in the conflict of Christian and pagan, licit and illicit desire. The focus is Griselda's perfect embodiment of the quality of *suffrance*, the Boethian virtue emphasised in the *Franklin's Tale*, but hagiography sits uneasily with romance. The Clerk's final explanation, that the story exemplifies not wifely humility but 'that every wight, in his degree, / Sholde be constant in adversitee / As was Grisilde' (IV. 1145–47), seems deeply unsatisfying. To read Walter as God raises difficult questions concerning divine cruelty and the purpose of suffering, of the kind asked in the book of Job. The ending ignores too the individualised flesh-and-blood quality of the figures within the tale. The narrative suggests the difficulty of reconciling fiction with allegory, human nature with theological doctrine.

Once again the pathos of the individual voice is set against generalising structures and terms. This group of tales is distinguished by memorably poignant, affective gestures and words: Custance looking back to the land and saying simply 'Farewel, housbonde routhelees!' and her prayer for her innocent child, 'What is thy gilt, / That nevere wroghtest synne as yet' (II. 855–56); Griselda's plea for her child, 'Burieth this litel body in som place / That beestes ne no briddes it torace' and her request that Walter treat his second wife 'moore tendrely' (IV. 571–72, 1041). The voices of these women, like Virginia's, speak the unfair, arbitrary nature of suffering, the lack of choice in worlds ordered by men, and the constraint of social and moral structures. Their power to act is circumscribed, yet the pathos and tragedy of their voices endure.

Fabliau and Comedy

Romance and hagiography are complicated too by the comedy that runs subversively through *The Canterbury Tales*, from the Miller's response to the *Knight's Tale* onwards. With the unfinished *Cook's Tale*, the Miller's and Reeve's tales respond in progressively more debased ways to the Knight's elevated romance, each story multiplying characters and copulations, and moving from respectable trade to theft to prostitution, from 'harlotrie' and 'game' to 'jape of malice' to 'litel jape' (I. 3184, 3186, 4338, 4343) – and from Oxford to Cambridge to London. At the same time, these 'cherles' tales provide brilliant instances of comic narrative, dialogue and timing that far exceed the supposed abilities of their tellers (see Craik 1964; Richardson 1970; Jost 1994). There are analogues to both the Miller's and Reeve's tales, but no direct sources. Chaucer made the English comic tale his own, drawing on the widely known Continental, particularly French, form of the fabliau (see Brewer 1996; Hines 1993). Generic play is evident from the start in the Miller's promise of 'a legende and a lyf' (I. 3141), terms suggesting a saint's life rather than a low-life story of the cuckolding of a carpenter by an Oxford clerk, and the revenge taken by his rival.

Chaucer's care in structuring the fragment is reflected in the comic craft of individual plots, perhaps most of all the combination of the adultery plot with the misdirected kiss and the prediction of the Second Flood in the *Miller's Tale*. Vibrant detail fills out these interwoven strands: John's superstitious oaths, Nicholas' music-making, Absolon's fastidious squeamishness, Alisoun's laughter when he has kissed her 'naked ers', '"Teehee!" quod she, and clapte the wyndow to' (I. 3734, 3740). The use of dialogue and swift action within one line are typical, and rhymes frequently function for comic effect: 'kiss/piss' (I. 3797–98; cf. 3345–56, 3377–78, 3425–26, 3803–4). The high romance of the *Knight's Tale* is subversively rewritten in the narrative of the two clerks vying in lust for Alisoun, Nicholas' false astrology, the mocking evocation of divine providence and the comic tragedy of John's fall. Particularly striking is the interweaving and juxtaposition of registers of language. Alisoun is depicted not through courtly metaphors but vibrant natural images: she is 'a prymerole, a piggesnye, / For any lord to leggen in his bedde' (I. 3268–69). The seducer Nicholas sings the hymn of the Annunciation to the Virgin, '*Angelus ad virginem*' (I. 3216); Absolon's love-song evokes and comically rewrites the Song of Songs: his love-longing is like that of the turtle dove but he mourns 'as dooth a lamb after the tete' (I. 3704). The 'melodye' (I. 3652) of Nicholas and Alisoun in bed ends with the ringing of church bells.

Though less rich in rhetoric, the *Reeve's Tale* is similarly sophisticated in comic timing and the understated, satirical craft of its plot, calculated to avenge the Miller's insult to the Reeve's profession. Essential traits are established at the start, in particular, the pride of the dishonest miller and his wife, who is the illegitimate daughter of a parson, and their ambition for their daughter. Malyn's grey eyes and fair hair, conventional courtly attributes, are offset by her 'thikke' body, 'kamus [pug] nose' and 'buttokes brode' (I. 3973–75). Chaucer not only makes the clerks natives of the northern town of Strother, but also represents their northern accents – the first comic use of dialect in English fiction (a feature not included in northern copies of the *Reeve's Tale*). The 'nycetee' (I. 4044, naïveté) of the clerks encourages Simkin to steal their corn, his cunning set against the 'sleighte' of their 'philosophye' (I. 4050), but the balance tips as the 'melodye' (I. 4168) of snores of the drunken miller and his wife incite Aleyn to the still crasser melody of copulation as 'esement' (I. 4186) of his loss. John's subsequent 'swyving' of the wife is marked not by the conventional courtly song of the nightingale but by the 'sing[ing]' of the cock (I. 4233). In typical Chaucerian fashion, the detail of the miller's baldness proves crucial to the denouement, when the wife, mistaking Simkin's head for Aleyn's nightgown, 'smoot the millere on the pyled skulle' (I. 4306). The sexual farce of the obscure and cramped bedchamber, the misplaced furniture and mistaken identities, brilliantly responds, but in a darker key, to the *Miller's Tale*.

The *Reeve's Tale* narrows down comedy; the *Merchant's Tale*, like the Miller's, expands the fabliau form, filling out its basic plot of lust and deceit with clerical, romance and classical material to effect a debased parody of *fin'amor*. In this tale metaphor becomes actuality: youth and age are embodied in January and May, and sight and blindness are made literal. The narrative spans a striking range of discourses: the (retrospectively mock) sermon with its extended biblical examples in praise of marriage; the clerical anti-feminism articulated by January's brothers; the conventions and vocabulary of *fin'amor*, in particular, January's Maytime garden with its referent of the archetypal *locus amoenus* of the *Romance of the Rose*; the parody of the Song of Songs, used by January not to convey sublime and mystical love, but to urge his conniving wife 'to pleye / In his gardyn' (IV. 2134–35); the learned medical detail from classical texts offered in relation to January's preparations for love-making; and the high-flown lament over Fortune's cruelty in blinding him. A comic version of the myth of Pluto and Proserpina, presenting them as the king and queen of 'Fairye' (IV. 2234), plays on the romance motif of the otherworld. Throughout, romance ideals are subverted, and May and Damian are far from the classical lovers, Piramus and Thisbe, to whom they are compared (IV. 2128). May reads Damian's letter in a privy, and love is reduced to sex in a pear tree: 'sodeynly anon this Damyan / Gan pullen up the smok, and in he throng' (IV. 2352–53). The sophistication of the *Merchant's Tale* is rooted in its generic juxtapositions.

The fabliaux contribute in varying ways to the debate on women and marriage ongoing across *The Canterbury Tales*. By contrast to the idealised gender patterns of romance, in these low-life stories of sex and comedy women are active, lustful, adulterous; men are deceivers, seducers, boasters. The satisfaction of desire can be both celebratory and commodifying. In the *Miller's Tale* natural sexual instincts are set against courtly restraint: when 'hende Nicholas' takes hold of Alisoun, 'prively...by the queynte', her threat to crie, '"out, harrow" and "allas"' is short-lived (I. 3272, 3276, 3286). In the *Shipman's Tale*, the Merchant's wife sells her favours to the Monk Don John for a hundred franks, conveniently borrowed from her husband, and flanks are equated with franks: 'I am youre wyf; score it upon my taille' (VII. 416), she says. In the *Reeve's Tale*, sex is similarly an economic transaction. Comedy in the fabliaux can interweave with anti-feminism, empowering in more and less positive ways women who are far from virginal. The gloomy views of January's brothers on wives reflect the Merchant's own experience (I. 1213–14); Pluto cites 'ten hondred thousand' tales of frail and fickle women; and Prosperpina's scolding, 'I am a womman, nedes moot I speke', places her as the archetypal shrew (I. 2240, 2305). Anti-feminist authorities, the tale suggests, are proven correct: May is deceitful and adulterous, the embodiment of female lust; Pluto is the real victim in the ravishment of Proserpina.

Yet like the *Knight's Tale*, the Miller's and Merchant's tales are complicated by their use of the *malmariée* motif and their shifting perspectives. The abundant, vibrant sexuality of Alisoun is 'heeld...narwe in cage' (I. 3224) by her jealous husband; May is bought as an investment by January, 'Oold fissh and yong flessh' (IV. 1418), and the graphic detail of the wedding night approaches a description of rape. In May's acceptance of Damian, there is a sense that January, though he becomes pitiable, gets his come-uppance; reduced to sexual commodity, the woman commodifies herself for a better bargain. The *Reeve's Tale* shifts from its graphic depiction of what is effectively rape to a surprisingly affectionate farewell between Malyn and Aleyn, whose language becomes courtly: 'Fare weel, Malyne, sweete wight!... / I is thyn awen clerk!'; the image of the girl left close to tears creates an unexpected effect of pathos (I. 4236–40). Most troubling perhaps is the *Manciple's Tale*. In part a beast-fable, it is aligned with the fabliaux in its subject matter of adultery and the faithlessness of women. Yet the crow kept luxuriously in its cage but wishing for liberty recalls the falcon in the *Squire's Tale*, and signals Phebus' jealous treatment of his wife. Betrayal is disturbingly emblematised in Phebus' turning of the crow's feathers from pure white to black in anger at the bird's revelation of his wife's adultery. The long moral disquisitions on female vice and the dangers of speaking freely are refracted by the lingering image of the trapped, blackened crow.

The game and play of fabliau, then, though it foregrounds the uncourtly and uninhibited, can be highly sophisticated, interweaving and adapting familiar generic motifs and conventions. The ambiguous treatment of women is mirrored in the *Wife of Bath's Prologue*. The Wife makes explicit the celebratory possibilities of non-clerical writing:

> ...trusteth wel, it is an impossible
> That any clerk wol speke good of wyves,
> But if it be of hooly seintes lyves,
> Ne of noon oother womman never the mo.
> Who peyntede the leon, tel me who?
> By God, if wommen hadde writen stories,
> As clerkes han withinne hire oratories
> They wolde han writen of men moore wikkednesse
> Than al the mark of Adam may redresse.
>   (III. 688–96)

Setting up her own 'experience' against the 'auctorite' of clerks, the Wife confronts the polarisation of the female sex into the types of madonna and whore, defending earthly marriage and sexuality, and enumerating the misogynist stereotypes and legendary examples common to patristic writing. The Prologue equates to the Wife's tearing out of the leaves of Jankyn's book of wicked wives, as she employs the Bible and other clerical authorities subversively and selectively to defend sex and marriage. She, not the Church Fathers, 'glose[s]' (III. 119) the texts. If the Wife's prologue inverts clerical teaching, however, Chaucer at the same time exploits such teaching. The Wife only too obviously fulfils the misogynistic expectations of Jerome, and of 'Valerie and Theofraste' (III. 671): lustful, revelling in sex, gossipping, shrewish, deceitful, admiring Jankin's legs while pretending to weep for the death of her fourth husband, and now on the lookout for the sixth. Chaucer's fiction of the Wife, more than any other, has elicited a varied and conflicted critical response, in that she both steps beyond and is placed within the bounds of female stereotypes, and in that her voice so persistently and persuasively takes on a life of its own (a phenomenon resisted directly, for instance, by H. Marshall Leicester [1984], 'there is no Wife of Bath', and more generally in Leicester 1990). The Wife, loudest of all Chaucer's female personae, speaks for the woman's experiential voice, for the voice of the lion as well as the man to tell its story. It is in keeping with the duality of the Wife that her prologue can most readily be aligned with the fabliaux, while her tale employs the structures of romance to present a considerably more refined version of female desire.

Perhaps the most dazzling generic play of all occurs in the *Nun's Priest's Tale*, which transforms the simple genre of the moral beast-fable into a high-flown, creatively comic narrative. The tale is carefully shaped as a response to the Monk's interminable list of 'tragedies', 'ensamples trewe and olde' (VII. 1998) of those who once 'stood in greet prosperitee' but fell 'of heigh degree / Into myserie' (VII. 1971, 1975–77). The *Monk's Prologue* signals the variety of forms such tales might take – hexameter, prose and 'meetre' (rhyme; VII. 1981) – and the range of classical and

Continental examples is remarkable, including stories probably heard by Chaucer in Italy, for example, that of Bernabò Visconti (see Cooper 1991: 328, and further Wallace 1997). Like the subject matter, the Monk's eight-line rhyming stanza form is highly complex, but the style of the encyclopaedic list militates against thematic development or distinctions between stories. This tale fails to address the Boethian issues of providence and grace. Yet even here there are memorable moments, most notably in the story of Ugolino, where the simple pathos of the starving children's voices (VII. 2433–35) recalls the lamenting female voices of other tales and contrasts with the pious voice of the child in the *Prioress's Tale*. It is left for the Nun's Priest to develop further – and subversively – the themes associated with tragedy: fortune and providence, fate and free will, virtue and vice, and the role of women.

From a particularly popular example of the beast-fable (found in Latin, French and English), Chaucer shapes a comic miniature collection of discourses, genres and themes. The question of the interpretation of dreams, a subject familiar from the early poems, is extensively probed, and Chaucer draws on works of natural philosophy for both Pertelote's dismissive response to Chauntecleer's dream of a terrible beast and her recommendation of natural remedies, 'For Goddes love, as taak som laxatyf' (VII. 2943). Classical dream theory underpins Chauntecleer's lengthy defence of the dream's significance, with its elaborated examples and survey of prophetic dreams ranging from biblical instances to Cicero's dream of Scipio to the legend of St Kenelm. This display of erudition is brilliantly juxtaposed with the images of Chaunticleer clucking after corn and feathering Pertelote twenty times, and the animal features of Chauntecleer and his hens merge comically with the vocabulary and rituals of chivalry and *fin'amor*. Chauntecleer roams proudly in the yard, a prince in his court of hens, his story compared to that of the greatest romance hero, Launcelot de Lake (VII. 3212), but his desire frustrated at night by the narrowness of his perch. Clerical anti-feminism undercuts courtliness as the proverbial definition of women quoted by Chantecleer, '*In principio, / Mulier est hominis confusio*' (In the beginning, woman is man's ruin), and mistranslated as 'Womman is mannes joye and al his blis' (VII. 3163–66), proves true: in yielding to Pertelote's blandishments Chantecleer dismisses the genuine warning of his dream. The 'tragedy' unfolds with a series of rhetorical flourishes: the fox is compared to a sequence of celebrated traitors – Judas, Ganelon, Synon – and Chauntecleer's fall into the fox's jaws is aligned with the betrayals of Christ, Roland and Troy. The tale gestures to the great theological topics of the Fall, fate, fortune and predestination, with references to Augustine, Boethius and 'Bisshop Bradwardyn' (VII. 3242), while the fox's flattery refers to Boethius' treatise on music. The seizing of Chauntecleer leads to a great epic lament, 'O destinee' (VII. 3338ff), which evokes a whole sequence of past tragedies, from the death of Richard I to the fall of Troy and the burning of Rome. The tale also contains a rare reference to contemporary politics: the noise of the chase recalls that of 'Jakke Straw and his meynee' during the English Rising, the 'Peasants' Revolt' of 1381 (VII. 3394). While the moral offered at the end is to 'Taketh the fruyt, and lat the chaf be stille' (VII. 3443), it is precisely the elaboration of the tale that renders it scintillating – its generic parody and play, its juxtaposition of styles, its combination of naturalistic, expressive narrative with high rhetoric, and its extraordinary verbal facility. The simplicity of the life of the 'povre wydwe' in her 'narwe cotage' (VII. 1–2) is opened out to a comedy of epic proportions, which engages with the themes that recur across *The Canterbury Tales*: the truth of books, the opposition of authority and experience, the relation between fortune and free will, the debate over women and the nature of story-telling itself.

Morality, Sin and Damnation

The *Nun's Priest's Tale* offers a comic and redemptive narrative of the Fall. Other tales of sin are bleaker, their comedic 'game', as it is repeatedly termed, troublingly reliant on demonic temptation, their movement infernal. Here the devil is actively abroad, preying on the souls of the sinful, and misplaced *trouthe* opens the way to hell. Both tellers and tales illustrate the corruption of figures who should function as spiritual guides, a motif already evident in Chaucer's decision to make the seducer of the *Shipman's Tale* not a soldier (as in his sources) but a monk, and in the ecclesiastical satire of the *General Prologue*. In the darkly comic tales of the Friar and Summoner, and the proto-confessions of the Canon's Yeoman and Pardoner, play is taken into a new realm of self-seeking vice that directly opposes the ardent, transformative faith represented in the *Second Nun's Tale*. Chilling moral exemplum reaches its height in the Pardoner's corrosive tale of death. These works looks towards the Parson's treatise on the seven deadly sins and recall the spiritual purpose of the pilgrimage, as laughter is countered by the menace of demonic temptation and game proves treacherous.

Misinterpretation of words and misplaced *trouthe* characterise the blindness of sin in the *Friar's Tale*, emphasised by its teller as 'game' (VI. 1275, 1289). Here the devil waits to ensnare the corrupt summoner in the guise of 'a gay yeman, under a forest syde' (III. 1480). The landscape conventionally associated with adventure and the faery in romance here opens the way to hell. The tale depends on such double meanings, as in the yeoman's answer in 'softe speche' when the summoner asks his dwelling place: 'Brother,...fer in the north contree, / Whereas I hope som tyme I shal thee see' (III. 1412–14); the seemingly harmless words play on the traditional associations of the devil with the north. In true Doctor Faustus mode the summoner is promised 'gold and silver' and his every desire, if he will swear 'trouthe' with the 'feend' (III. 1400, 1404, 1448). The working out of the story depends upon a second misleading oath, the old widow's curse committing the summoner to the devil. Chaucer also engages chillingly with the power of demons to take physical shape, offering a description of how they may 'swiche formes make / As moost able is oure preyes for to take' (III. 1471–72), both by effecting new bodies and by taking on the bodies of the dead. The wiles of the devil and the fatal, glamorous allure of sin are consistently presented as real possibilities despite the comic structure of the tale.

These themes are taken into the nether regions of hell in the Summoner's bawdy Prologue and Tale, told to 'quite' the Friar. The Prologue offers a debased miniature of Dante's *Inferno*, a friar's dream vision of a hell where the friars are mysteriously missing, but are revealed by the angels to be in their many millions in the devil's arse. The vision finds its earthly and earthy parallel in the tale, the account of how a fart is divided among a whole convent of friars. This tale too functions through the misdirection of *trouthe*, as the corrupt Friar John demands of his lay brother Thomas the gift of all he has, and swears to divide it between his brethren equally. The tale exploits the reductive effects of vice: words and rude noises become almost interchangeable. Yet the parodic inversions of the tale are also intellectually inventive. The ravished soul of the friar at the start journeys in the opposite direction to the soul of the mystic ravished by God. As well as gesturing to Dante, Chaucer may be parodying the iconographic tradition of Mary's cloak shielding the Cistercians. The narrative meshes with serious theological discourse, particularly in the rhetoric of Friar John, who draws on a variety of clerical authorities, as well as (for his three exempla) on Seneca's treatise on anger. His appropriation of theology, 'Glosyng is a glorious thing', is exclusively to material ends; his teaching, like his amorous treatment of Thomas' wife, inverts religious ideals, and fear of divine judgement and hope for salvation are absent. The summoner in the *Friar's Tale* is literally damned, whereas damnation in the *Summoner's Tale* is rewritten as the stench of hot air (Cooper 1991: 181).

The stench of the devil's breath is more prominent still in the tale of the Canon's Yeoman, who seems to ride straight out of hell on his sweating horse to interrupt the pilgrimage. He and his master, who rides away condemned by the yeoman to the 'foule feend' (VIII. 705), have substituted gold – or their desire for gold – for God. The tale that the Canon's Yeoman tells also interrupts the story-telling competition in its form as a confession of their vicious practices, followed by an account of a second false canon. The story's emptiness of invention reflects the empty promises of alchemy, though Chaucer's interest in occult sciences is also evident in his vivid description of alchemical experiments, and play on the strange, proto-religious, cryptic language of the alchemists. The practices of alchemy within the tale, however, are exposed as a sham: the 'elvysshe craft' is 'madnesse and folye', a 'slidynge science' that has impoverished the yeoman, and led others into poverty (VIII. 751, 742, 732). The 'sleightes and...infinite falsnesse' (VIII. 976) of the second canon rival only those of the fiend himself, and both are depicted in demonic terms. As the experiments of the Canon and his yeoman fail, the pot explodes and the metals pierce the walls, it seems the devil is actually present. As in the preceding tale of St Cecilia, the motifs of blindness and illusion are central: the yeoman has damaged his sight through alchemical experiments, while he and the Canon are metaphorically blind, as are the false canon's victims; all end in literal and metaphorical poverty. The Canon's yeoman concludes, 'God sende every trewe man boote of his bale!' (VIII. 1481), but the message of this tale, like the Friar's and Summoner's, is that there is only the expectation of damnation for the spiritually blind who pursue such false *trouthe*. The story finds its antidote in the immediately preceding Second Nun's tale of true alchemy, where red and white (the alchemical colours) are the colours of divine fire and purity, passion and perfection. The alchemists too attempt transformation of substance in alembics, baths of flame, but their experiments end in corruption and the production of base metals, whereas Cecilia is spiritually transcendent, purified into eternal being.

Chaucer's engagement with the power of evil is most strikingly and disturbingly present in the *Pardoner's Tale*. Like the *Canon's Yeoman's Tale*, this is a narrative out of balance, a 'moral thyng' (VI. 325) preceded by the Pardoner's proto-confession of his corrupt practices, and interrupted by his lengthy homiletic discourse on the evils of drunkenness, gaming and swearing, complete with celebrated examples. The physical emphasis is strangely reductive: the Fall is interpreted as the result of gluttony, and cooks 'turnen substaunce into accident' (VI. 539), the inverse of Transubstantiation. The tale exemplifies spiritual blindness in terms of destructive materialism to prove the Pardoner's central precept, '*Radix malorum est Cupiditas*' (Greed is the root of [all] evils [1 Tim 6.10], VI. 426). The story is understated by contrast to the elevated rhetoric of the preceding homily: apart from the reference to Flanders, the setting is abstract and symbolic – the tavern, the crooked way, the tree where the gold is found. The reductiveness of the rioters' arrogant, ignorant pursuit of this 'privee theef men clepeth Deeth' (VI. 675), the only individual named, is affirmed when they find the treasure: their individual impulses are only towards possession and hence murder. The absolute quality of their materialism finds its natural end in the physical enactment of death. The rioters discover what they are seeking: their own reductionism has reduced them to nothing.

The story's impact is effected by its stark absolutes, the understated inevitability of its narration, and the sinister *danse macabre* of the plot, but most of all perhaps by its peculiar unease. The old man, seeking death but never dying, with his eerie, cryptic direction, 'Now sires...if that yow be so leef / To fynde Deeth, turne up this croked wey' (VI. 760–61), merges the folk-tale figure wearied by eternal life and the devil luring sinners to hell. The Pardoner too elides types and categories: irredeemably corrupt, even when he has confessed his abuses he cannot resist the temptation to sell his wares to the pilgrims; presented as a womaniser with a wench in every town, he is also feminised by his long fair hair, small, goat-like voice and Chaucer's comment, 'I trowe he were a geldyng or a mare' (I. 691). Carolyn Dinshaw (1989: 156–84) argues for the Pardoner as other, occupying, like women, a marginal space in being either literally or figuratively a eunuch. Threatened with castration by Harry Bailly, 'Lat kutte hem of' (VI. 954), the Pardoner is also cut off from the signification of language and its wholeness. Meaning for the Pardoner, as for the Canon and his Yeoman, is situated in the greed he can never satisfy, in the objects that surround him but that he knows to be false: 'substaunce' is indeed reduced to 'accident'. Troublingly, the Pardoner's narrative is also 'cut off' from his persona to fulfil the didactic purpose requested by his listeners. It takes on a moral substance of its own that clashes uneasily with his corrupt practices: 'though myself be a ful vicious man, / A moral tale yet I yow telle kan' (VI. 459–60). The *Pardoner's Prologue* and *Tale* depict a demonic figure who furthers the work of Satan within the world by manipulating fiction, but also, like many of the other tales, they suggest the independent power of words and the multiple possibilities of interpretation.

The conclusion of the *Canterbury Tales* returns to the notion of fiction as dangerous. As the sun goes down and the pilgrims draw nearer to Canterbury, the mood shifts to focus on the celestial city of Jerusalem. The Parson in his prologue opposes story-telling to 'moralitee and vertuous mateere': 'Thou getest fable noon ytoold for me' (X. 38, 31). This opposition is reiterated in the Parson's rejection of poetry, which he depicts in terms of the alliterative tradition of the North ('rum, ram, ruf', X. 43). Poetry is replaced by 'a myrie tale in prose' (X. 46); fiction by penitential treatise. This is the ethos too of the 'retracciouns' immediately following the *Parson's Tale*, which revoke 'the tales of Caunterbury, thilke that sownen into synne' (X. 1084–85). As the end of *Troilus and Criseyde* also does, this final part of the work counters the secular and imaginative with a more sober perspective, which is not necessarily to be read as ironic. It is, however, a perspective that rejects the multiplicity and poly-valence of fiction. Across the *Canterbury Tales*, Chaucer's play with genre has celebrated such qualities, illuminating the rich possibilities of poetry, its delights and dangers, its ability to span secular and sacred, high and low narrative. As Harry Bailly remarks, 'A man may seye ful sooth in game and pley' (I. 4354). The work as a whole voices the power of words to shape and reshape such truth, but also the power of the listener or reader to discern and interpret. It is, finally, left to Chaucer's audience to choose not only tale but meaning, to 'maken ernest of game' – whether that is the game of love, marriage, desire, virtue, sin, corruption or story-telling itself.

Notes

1   All quotations are from *The Riverside Chaucer* (1988), and cited by Fragment and line number.
2   The order of Fragments I and II; VI and VII; and IX and X is stable. Other Fragments are more mobile: the tales of Fragments IV and V, the Clerk's, Merchant's, Squire's and Franklin's tales, are frequently separated. The two recurrent orders for the *Canterbury Tales* differ in the situation of Fragment VIII, the Second Nun's and Canon's Yeoman's tales, sometimes placed before Fragment VI. See further Cooper (1983, in particular 56–71). Modern editions of the *Canterbury Tales* are based on Ellesmere (Huntington Library, San Marino, California, MS Ellesmere 26.C.9) and Hengwrt (National Library of Wales, MS Peniarth 392) manuscripts, both apparently by the same 'Scribe B' (see below). Hengwrt seems to offer the text closest to Chaucer's original, but is somewhat disjointed and not in good condition; it also lacks some sections, in particular the *Merchant's Prologue* and the *Canon's Yeoman's Prologue* and *Tale*. Ellesmere, a much more beautiful manuscript, has occupied pride of place precisely because of its aesthetic appeal, though not all its readings are superior. Its order is that adopted by *The Riverside Chaucer* (and previously Robinson [1933, 1957]). Hengwrt, however, has continued to receive considerable editorial attention since the publication of the eight-volume edition of Manly and Rickert (1940), and is the basis for the ongoing *Variorum Edition* (1979–). A digital facsimile of Hengwrt on CD-ROM was issued in 2002. The electronic age has seen many advances in the editing of Chaucer: particularly prominent are the digital editions published by the *Canterbury Tales Project* led by Peter Robinson. On earlier editions of Chaucer see esp. Ruggiers (1984); on more recent developments see Pearsall 2000, and the resources listed below.

3 On the vexed question of 'Scribe B' and Adam Pynkhurst, see further A. I. Doyle and M. B. Parkes, 'The production of copies of the *Canterbury Tales* and the *Confession Amantis* in the early fifteenth century' in *Medieval Scribes, Manuscripts and Libraries: Essays Presented to N. R. Ker*, ed. M. B. Parkes and A. G. Watson (London: Scolar Press, 1977), pp. 163–210; Linne R. Mooney, 'Chaucer's scribe.' *Speculum*, 81, (2006), 97–138; and Alan J. Fletcher, 'The criteria for scribal attribution: Dublin, Trinity College, MS 244, some early copies of the works of Geoffrey Chaucer, and the Canon of Adam Pynkhurst Manuscripts', *Review of English Studies*, n.s. 58 (2007), 597–621, 624–632. Further articles for and against the identification are forthcoming by Simon Horobin and Jane Roberts respectively.

4 Early twentieth-century criticism emphasised Chaucer's genially realist observation of human nature, most famously in G. L. Kittredge's notion of *The Canterbury Tales* as a 'roadside drama' enacting a benign 'Human Comedy' (Kittredge 1915; see also Manly 1926 and Lowes 1934). Subsequent critical approaches to Chaucer reflect more general critical shifts. Positivist historicism (e.g. Bowden 1967) was countered both by a New Critical interest in language, ambiguity and irony (e.g. Empson 1951; Dempster 1959), and by the exegetical criticism of D. W. Robertson and his followers (see especially Huppé 1967). Chaucer's poetics were more persuasively contextualised in terms of medieval literary and aesthetic assumptions by Robert Jordan (1967). From the 1970s onwards, the 'new historicism' inspired a plethora of studies placing Chaucer's writing in the context both of medieval literature more generally and of other medieval discourses; theories of rhetoric and poetics, for instance, are treated by Burlin (1977), Fichte (1980) and Birney (1985). Traditional biography and source studies were replaced by more ideologically engaged contextual studies (Howard 1987; Pearsall 1992; Brewer 1998) and by wide-ranging works on intertextuality, both literary and intellectual (e.g. Miller 1977). The Marxist and sociological approaches of the 1980s yielded new interpretations (Jones 1982; Aers 1988; Strohm 1989; Patterson 1991; Rigby 1996), including of Chaucer's use of rhetoric and poetics (Koff 1988; Copeland 1991). Wallace (1997) treats mercantile and artistic exchange, and relations between country and city, England and the Continent; Brown and Butcher (1991) argue for the 'reintegration' of Chaucer's work with its socio-political contexts. Feminism and queer theory provided the impetus for other kinds of revisionist readings (see especially Diamond and Edwards 1977; Dinshaw 1989; Martin 1990; Mann 1991; Hansen 1992; Laskaya 1995; Weisl 1995; Burger 2003). Blamires (2006) brings together medieval moral discourses and gender theory to probe Chaucer's ethics. Psychoanalysis and particularly deconstruction have suggested interpretations of Chaucer far distant from those offered by his early critics (e.g. Ferster 1985; Leicester 1990; Shoaf 2001; Fradenburg 2002). A fuller discussion of Chaucer criticism is offered in Saunders (2001a); for a range of critical readings see also Allen and Axiotis (1997) and Ellis (2005). Valuable overviews of different approaches and key issues (textual, cultural and literary) in Chaucer are offered by Brown (2000), Ellis (2005) and, specifically in relation to the *Canterbury Tales*, Cooper (1989), Phillips (2000) and Hirsh (2003). On the reception of Chaucer from medieval to postmodern, see Trigg (2002). On reading Chaucer aloud, including full details of the audio recordings available, see Fuller in Saunders (2006: 263–84).

REFERENCES AND FURTHER READING

Editions

Benson, Larry D. (ed.) (1988). *The Riverside Chaucer*. 3rd edn. Oxford: Oxford University Press. (Originally pub. 1987.)

Kolve, V. A. and Glending Olson (eds) (1989). *'The Canterbury Tales': Nine Tales and the 'General Prologue'*. A Norton Critical Edition. New York: W. W. Norton.

Manly, John M. and Edith Rickert (eds) (1940).

The Text of the 'Canterbury Tales'. 8 vols. Chicago: University of Chicago Press.

Robinson, F. N. (ed.) (1957). *The Works of Geoffrey Chaucer*. 2nd edn. Boston: Houghton Mifflin-Riverside Press; Oxford: Oxford University Press. (Originally pub. 1933.)

Ruggiers, Paul G. (ed.) (1979–). *A Variorum Edition of the Works of Geoffrey Chaucer*. Norman, OK: University of Oklahoma Press.

Secondary Reading

Aers, David (1988). *Community, Gender and Individual Identity: English Writing 1360–1430*. London: Routledge.

Allen, Valerie and Ares Axiotis (ed.) (1997). *Chaucer*. New Casebooks Series. Basingstoke: Macmillan.

Allen, Judson Boyce and Theresa Anne Moritz (1981). *A Distinction of Stories: The Medieval Unity of Chaucer's Fair Chain of Narratives for Canterbury*. Columbus: Ohio State University Press.

Anderson, J. J. (ed.) (1974). *Chaucer: 'The Canterbury Tales'. A Casebook*. London: Macmillan.

Andrew, Malcolm (ed.) (1991). *Critical Essays on Chaucer's 'Canterbury Tales'*. Milton Keynes: Open University Press.

Baldwin, Ralph (1955). *The Unity of the 'Canterbury Tales'*. Anglistica 5. Copenhagen: Rosenkilde and Bagger.

Benson, C. David (1986). *Chaucer's Drama of Style: Poetic Variety and Contrast in the 'Canterbury Tales'*. Chapel Hill: University of North Carolina Press.

Benson, C. David and Elizabeth Robertson (1990). *Chaucer's Religious Tales*. Chaucer Studies 15. Cambridge: D. S. Brewer.

Birney, Earle (1985). *Essays on Chaucerian Irony*. Ed. Bery Rowland. Toronto: University of Toronto Press.

Burlin, Robert B. (1977). *Chaucerian Fiction*. Princeton, NJ: Princeton University Press.

Bishop, Ian (1988). *The Narrative Art of the 'Canterbury Tales': A Critical Study of the Major Poems*. Everyman's University Library. London: Dent.

Blamires, Alcuin (1987). *'The Canterbury Tales'. The Critics Debate*. Basingstoke: Macmillan.

Blamires, Alcuin (2006). *Chaucer, Ethics and Gender*. Oxford: Oxford University Press.

Boitani, Piero and Jill Mann (eds) (2003). *The Cambridge Chaucer Companion*. 2nd edn. Cambridge: Cambridge University Press.

Bowden, Muriel (1967). *A Commentary on the 'General Prologue' to the 'Canterbury Tales'*. 2nd edn. London: Collier Macmillan.

Brewer, Derek (ed.) (1996). *Medieval Comic Tales*. 2nd edn. Cambridge: D. S. Brewer. (Originally pub. 1973.)

Brewer, Derek (1998). *A New Introduction to Chaucer*. 2nd edn. Longman Medieval and Renaissance Library. London: Longman.

Brown, Peter (1994). *Chaucer at Work: The Making of the 'Canterbury Tales'*. London: Longman.

Brown, Peter (2000). *A Companion to Chaucer*. Blackwell Companions to Literature and Culture. Oxford: Blackwell.

Brown, Peter and Andrew Butcher (1991). *The Age of Saturn: Literature and History in the 'Canterbury Tales'*. Oxford: Blackwell.

Burger, Glenn (2003). *Chaucer's Queer Nation*. Medieval Cultures 24. Minneapolis: University of Minnesota Press.

Condren, Edward I. (1999). *Chaucer and the Energy of Creation: The Design and the Organization of the 'Canterbury Tales'*. Gainesville: University Press of Florida.

Cooper, Helen (1983). *The Structure of the Canterbury Tales*. London: Duckworth.

Cooper, Helen (1989). *The Canterbury Tales*. Oxford Guides to Chaucer. Oxford: Oxford University Press.

Copeland, Rita (1991). *Rhetoric, Hermeneutics and Translation in the Middle Ages: Academic Traditions and Vernacular Texts*. Cambridge Studies in Medieval Literature 11. Cambridge: Cambridge University Press.

Correale, Robert M. and Mary Hamel (eds) (2002, 2005). *Sources and Analogues of Chaucer's 'Canterbury Tales'*. Chaucer Studies 28 and 35. 2 vols. Cambridge: D. S. Brewer.

Craik, T. W. (1964). *The Comic Tales of Chaucer*. London: Methuen.

Crane, Susan (1994). *Gender and Romance in Chaucer's 'Canterbury Tales'*. Princeton, NJ: Princeton University Press.

Davenport, W. A. (1988). *Chaucer and His English Contemporaries: Prologue and Tale in the 'Canterbury Tales'*. Basingstoke: Macmillan.

David, Alfred (1976). *The Strumpet Muse: Art and Morals in Chaucer's Poetry*. Bloomington: Indiana University Press.

Dempster, Germaine (1959). *Dramatic Irony in Chaucer*. New York: Humanities Press.

Diamond, Arlyn and Lee R. Edwards (1977). *The Authority of Experience: Essays in Feminist Criticism*. Amherst: University of Massachusetts Press.

Dinshaw, Carolyn (1989). *Chaucer's Sexual Poetics*. Madison: University of Wisconsin Press.

Ellis, Roger (1986). *Patterns of Religious Narrative in the 'Canterbury Tales'*. London: Croom Helm.

Ellis, Steve (ed.) (2005). *Chaucer: An Oxford Guide*. Oxford: Oxford University Press.

Empson, William (1951). *The Structure of Complex Words*. London: Chatto and Windus.

Fein, Susanna Greer, David Raybin and Peter C. Braeger (1991). *Rebels and Rivals: The Contestive Spirit in the 'Canterbury Tales'*. SMC 29. Kalamazoo: Medieval Institute Publications, Western Michigan University.

Ferster, Judith (1985). *Chaucer on Interpretation*. Cambridge: Cambridge University Press.

Fichte. Joerg O. (1980). *Chaucer's 'Art Poetical': A Study in Chaucerian Poetics*. Studies and Texts in English. Tübingen: Gunter Narr.

Fradenburg, L. O. Aranye (2002). *Sacrifice Your Love: Psychoanalysis, Historicism, Chaucer*. Medieval Cultures 31. Minneapolis: University of Minnesota Press.

Ganim, John M. (1990). *Chaucerian Theatricality*. Princeton: Princeton University Press.

Gittes, Katharine S. (1991). *Framing the 'Canterbury Tales': Chaucer and the Medieval Frame Narrative Tradition*. Contributions to the Study of World Literature 41. Westport, CT: Greenwood Press.

Griffiths, Jeremy and Derek Pearsall (eds) (1989). *Book Production and Publishing in Britain, 1375–1475*. Cambridge: Cambridge University Press.

Hanna, Ralph (1996). *Pursuing History: Middle English Manuscripts and their Texts*. Stanford, CA: Stanford University Press.

Hansen, Elaine Tuttle (1992). *Chaucer and the Fictions of Gender*. Berkeley: University of California.

Hill, John M. (1991). *Chaucerian Belief: The Poetics of Reverence and Delight*. New Haven: Yale University Press.

Hines, John (1993). *The Fabliau in English*. Longman Medieval and Renaissance Library. London: Longman.

Hirsh, John (2003). *Chaucer and the 'Canterbury Tales': A Short Introduction*. Blackwell Introductions to Literature. Oxford: Blackwell.

Howard, Donald R. (1976). *The Idea of the 'Canterbury Tales'*. Berkeley: University of California Press.

Howard, Donald R. (1987). *Chaucer and the Medieval World*. London: Weidenfeld and Nicholson.

Huppé, Bernard F. (1967). *A Reading of the 'Canterbury Tales'*. Albany: State University of New York. (Originally pub. 1964.)

Jones, Terry (1982). *Chaucer's Knight: The Portrait of a Medieval Mercenary*. London: Methuen. (Originally pub. 1980.)

Jordan, Robert M. (1967). *Chaucer and the Shape of Creation: The Aesthetic Possibilities of Inorganic Structure*. Cambridge, MA: Harvard University Press.

Jordan, Robert M. (1987). *Chaucer's Poetics and the Modern Reader*. Berkeley: University of California Press.

Jost, Jean E. (ed.) (1994). *Chaucer's Humor: Critical Essays*. Garland Studies in Humor 5. Garland Reference Library of the Humanities 1504. New York: Garland.

Kendrick, Laura (1988). *Chaucerian Play: Comedy and Control in the' Canterbury Tales'*. Berkeley: University of California.

Kittredge, George Lyman (1970 [1915]). *Chaucer and His Poetry*. Cambridge, MA: Harvard University Press.

Koff, Leonard Michael (1988). *Chaucer and the Art of Storytelling*. Berkeley: University of California Press.

Knapp, Peggy (1990). *Chaucer and the Social Contest*. New York: Routledge.

Knight. Stephen (1986). *Geoffrey Chaucer*. Oxford: Basil Blackwell.

Kolve, V. A. (1984). *Chaucer and the Imagery of Narrative: The First Five 'Canterbury Tales'*. London: Edward Arnold.

Laskaya, Anna (1995). *Chaucer's Approach to Gender in the 'Canterbury Tales'*. Chaucer Studies 23. Cambridge: D. S. Brewer.

Lawler, Traugott (1980). *The One and the Many in the 'Canterbury Tales'*. Hamden, CT: Archon.

Lawton, David (1985). *Chaucer's Narrators*. Chaucer Studies 12. Cambridge: D. S. Brewer.

Leicester, H. Marshall (1984). 'Of a fire in the dark: public and private feminism in the Wife of Bath's Tale'. *Women's Studies*, 11, 157–78.

Leicester, H. Marshall, Jr. (1990). *The Disenchanted Self: Representing the Subject in the 'Canterbury Tales'*. Berkeley: University of California Press.

Lindahl, Carl (1987). *Earnest Games: Folkloric Patterns in the 'Canterbury Tales'*. Bloomington: Indiana University Press.

Lumiansky, R. M. (1955). *Of Sondry Folk: The Dramatic Principle in the 'Canterbury Tales'*. Austin: University of Texas Press.

Mandel, Jerome (1992). *Building the Fragments of the 'Canterbury Tales'*. Rutherford, NJ: Fairleigh Dickinson University Press; London: Associated University Presses.

Lowes, John Livingston (1934). *Geoffrey Chaucer and the Development of His Genius: Lectures Delivered in 1932 in the William J. Cooper Foundation in Swarthmore College*. Boston: Houghton Mifflin; Oxford: Clarendon Press.

Manly, John Matthews (1926). *Some New Light on Chaucer: Lectures Delivered at the Lowell Institute*. London: G. Bell.

Mann, Jill (1973). *Chaucer and Medieval Estates Satire: The Literature of Social Classes and the 'General Prologue' to the 'Canterbury Tales'*. London: Cambridge University Press.

Mann Jill (1991). *Geoffrey Chaucer*. Feminist Readings. New York: Harvester Wheatsheaf.

Martin, Priscilla (1990). *Chaucer's Women: Nuns, Wives and Amazons*. Iowa City: University of Iowa Press.

Mehl, Dieter (1973). *Geoffrey Chaucer: An Introduction to his Narrative Poetry*. Cambridge: Cambridge University Press.

Miller, Robert P. (1977). *Chaucer: Sources and Backgrounds*. New York: Oxford University Press.

Olson, Paul A. (1986). *'The Canterbury Tales' and the Good Society*. Princeton, NJ: Princeton University Press.

Owen, Charles A., Jr. (1977). *Pilgrimage and Storytelling in the 'Canterbury Tales': The Dialectic of 'Ernest' and 'Game'*. Norman: University of Oklahoma Press.

Patterson, Lee (1991). *Chaucer and the Subject of History*. London: Routledge.

Payne, Robert O. (1973). *The Key of Remembrance: A Study of Chaucer's Poetics*. 1963. Westport, CT: Greenwood Press, for the University of Cincinnati.

Pearsall, Derek (1985). *'The Canterbury Tales'*. Unwin Critical Library. London: George Allen and Unwin.

Pearsall, Derek (1992). *The Life of Geoffrey Chaucer: A Critical Biography*. Blackwell Critical Biographies. Oxford: Blackwell.

Pearsall, Derek (ed.) (2000). *New Directions in Later Medieval Manuscript Studies: Essays from the 1998 Harvard Conference*. Cambridge: D. S. Brewer.

Phillips, Helen (2000). *An Introduction to the 'Canterbury Tales': Reading, Fiction, Context*. Basingstoke: Macmillan; New York: St. Martin's Press.

Richardson, Janette (1970). *Blameth Nat Me: A Study of Imagery in Chaucer's Fabliaux*. Studies in English Literature 58. The Hague: Mouton.

Rigby, S. H. (1996). *Chaucer in Context: Society, Allegory and Gender*. Manchester Medieval Studies. Manchester: Manchester University Press.

Rubin, Miri (1999). *Gentile Tales: The Narrative Assault on Late Medieval Jews*. New Haven, CT: Yale University Press.

Ruggiers, Paul G. (1965). *The Art of the 'Canterbury Tales'*. Madison: University of Wisconsin Press.

Ruggiers, Paul G. (ed.) (1984). *Editing Chaucer: The Great Tradition*. Norman, OK: Pilgrim Books.

Saunders, Corinne (1993). *The Forest of Medieval Romance: Avernus, Broceliande, Arden*. Cambridge: D. S. Brewer.

Saunders, Corinne (ed.) (2001a). *Chaucer*. Blackwell Guides to Criticism. Oxford: Blackwell.

Saunders, Corinne (2001b). *Rape and Ravishment in the Literature of Medieval England*. Cambridge: D. S. Brewer.

Saunders, Corinne (ed.) (2006). *A Concise Companion to Chaucer*. Oxford: Blackwell.

Shoaf, R. A. (2001). *Chaucer's Body: The Anxiety of Circulation in 'The Canterbury Tales.'* Gainesville: University Press of Florida.

Sklute, Larry (1984). *Virtue of Necessity: Inconclusiveness and Narrative Form in Chaucer's Poetry*. Columbus: Ohio State University Press.

Strohm, Paul (1989). *Social Chaucer*. Cambridge, MA: Harvard University Press.

Trigg, Stephanie (2002). *Congenial Souls: Reading Chaucer from Medieval to Postmodern*. Medieval Cultures 30. Minneapolis: University of Minnesota Press.

Wallace, David (1997). *Chaucerian Polity: Absolutist Lineages and Associational Forms in England and Italy*. Figurae: Reading Medieval Culture. Stanford: Stanford University Press.

Weisl, Angela Jane (1995). *Conquering the Reign of Femeny: Gender and Genre in Chaucer's Romance*. Chaucer Studies 22. Cambridge: D. S. Brewer.

Woods, William F. (2008). *Chaucerian Spaces: Spatial Poetics in Chaucer's Opening Tales*. Albany, NY: State University of New York Press.

Websites and CD-ROMs

Chaucer: Life and Times CD-ROM (1995). Reading: Primary Source Media.

Chaucer: 'The General Prologue' on CD-ROM (2000). Ed. Elizabeth Solopova. Cambridge: Cambridge University Press on CD-ROM.

Chaucer: 'The Wife of Bath's Prologue' on CD-ROM. Ed. Peter Robinson. Cambridge: Cambridge University Press on CD-ROM,

The Hengwrt Chaucer Digital Facsimile CD-ROM (2000). Ed. Estelle Stubbs. Leicester: Scholarly Digital Editions.

http://colfa.utsa.edu/chaucer/ (*The Essential Chaucer (Annotated Bibliography of Chaucer Studies 1900–1984)*)

www.luminarium.org/medlit/chaucer.htm (beginner's guide to Chaucer)

http://icg.fas.harvard.edu/~chaucer (beginner's guide to Chaucer)

http://etext.lib.virginia.edu/ mideng.browse.html (complete original text of *Canterbury Tales*)

http://academic.brooklyn.cuny.edu/webcore/murphy/canterbury/ (text of *Canterbury Tales* put into modern spelling and glossed by Michael Murphy)

http://www.canterburytales.org (ELF Edition of *Canterbury Tales*: original text and modern rhymed translation)

http://www.cta.dmu.ac.uk/projects/ctp/ (*Canterbury Tales* Project: transcriptions of all manuscripts and early printed versions into computer-readable form)

http://icg.fas.harvard.edu/~chaucer/vowels.html (guide to Chaucer's pronunciation with audio illustrations)

www.vmi.edu/english/audio/audio_index.html (guide to Chaucer's pronunciation with audio extracts)

http://cwolf.uaa.alaska.edu/~afdtk/ECT_Main.htm (The Electronic *Canterbury Tales* with extensive links to other sites)

Audio and Video Recordings

Chaucer, Geoffrey. 'The Canterbury Tales': 'The Prologue'. The English Poets from Chaucer to Yeats. The British Council and Oxford University Press. Argo Record Company RG 401.

Chaucer, Geoffrey. 'The Canterbury Tales': 'The Nun's Priest's Tale'. The English Poets from Chaucer to Yeats. The British Council and Oxford University Press. Argo Record Company RG 466.

Chaucer, Geoffrey. *Troilus and Criseyde* (extracts). The English Poets from Chaucer to Yeats. The British Council and Oxford University Press. Argo Record Company ZPL 1003–4.

Chaucer, Geoffrey. *The Canterbury Tales*. Read by Trevor Eaton. Wadhurst: Pavilion Records, 1986–93.

The Miller's Tale (1986) THE 595.

The General Prologue, The Reeve's Tale (1988) THE 606.

The General Prologue, The Pardoner's Prologue and Tale (1988) THE 607.

The Wife of Bath's Prologue and Tale (1989) THE 612.

The Franklin's Prologue and Tale (1989) THE 616.

The Merchant's Prologue and Tale (1990) THE 618.

The Nun's Priest's Tale, The Shipman's Tale, The Prioress's Prologue and Tale (1990) THE 619.

The Friar's Prologue and Tale, The Summoner's Prologue and Tale, The Tale of Sir Thopas (1991) THE 620.

The Clerk's Tale, The Physician's Tale (1991) THE 621.

The Knight's Tale (1992) THES 625 (2 cassettes).

The Man of Law's Tale, The Cook's Tale, The Manciple's Tale (1992) THE 626.

The Second Nun's Prologue and Tale, The Canon's Yeoman's Prologue and Tale (1992) THE 629.

The Squire's Tale, The Monk's Tale (1993) THE 630.

The Tale of Melibee (1993) THE 632.

The Parson's Tale (1993) THE 633.

The Chaucer Studio, an organisation assisted by the English departments of the University of Adelaide and Brigham Young University, in conjunction with the New Chaucer Society, has recorded an almost complete *Canterbury Tales*. For full details, see http://humanities.byu.edu/chaucer/about.htm

Chaucer, Geoffrey. *The Animated Epics: The Canterbury Tales*. 3 videos. Wetherby: BBC Educational Publishing. 474157; 474165; 542047.

26

The Poetry of John Gower

R. F. Yeager

Depending upon what perspective one adopts – and without taking anything substantial away from his friend Geoffrey Chaucer – it is quite possible to argue that John Gower (d. 1408) was the foremost English poet of his age. Consider these facts: an *oeuvre* amounting to nearly 90,000 lines of verse, in three languages and in a variety of forms and styles; sharply pointed, economically limned stories; a moral sensibility and a citizen's commitment to the commonweal that in his every literary endeavour dictated precisely that 'high seriousness' Matthew Arnold chided Chaucer for lacking; a range of source texts, the fruit of years of careful reading, demonstrably larger than any of his great English contemporaries; a thoughtful willingness to experiment with language at a formative time for English; an 'Augustan', even skaldic, capacity for dry wit and ironic understatement. And if we add that Gower, unique among his English contemporaries as far as we know, had a concern for and a control over the copying of his work, such that (unlike, say, Chaucer's) the many manuscripts of Gower's poems show strikingly little verbal variation each to each, we have a portrait of an individual talent most remarkable. Yet while it has ever been possible to praise Gower for any of these qualities – as over the years many have found occasion to do, including Chaucer himself, Hoccleve, Lydgate, Spenser, Ben Jonson, and more recent readers such as C. S. Lewis and Christopher Ricks – it has not always been the fashion to do so. Indeed, Gower, precisely because of the poetic choices he made, all so thoroughly medieval, and supportable in the context of his time and place, has only in the last twenty-five years or so emerged again among critics and scholars from what might be described as a defensive crouch.

Thus the time now seems right to take stock, in a fresh way, of just what sort of a poet John Gower was. Above all else, perhaps, he was ambitious, and self-consciously so. His standing in the eyes of posterity appears to have been seldom from his mind. In this he differs from his peers in England, even at the end of the fourteenth century when the concept of achieving lasting fame as an 'auctor' loomed for some on the horizon of possibility. Chaucer also imagined his own legacy to future generations, and sought to construct it, as we infer from hints such as the poem to Adam his 'scriveyn' (scribe), demanding better copying of his manuscripts so that readers-to-come might not miss his meaning; and, less obliquely, from the closing stanzas of *Troilus and Criseyde*, when the poet prays for his 'litel bok' to 'kis the steppes where as thow seest pace / Virgile, Ovide, Omer, Lucan, and Stace.'[1] Gower, like Chaucer (or even, perhaps, *because of* Chaucer), recognised that making the 'A-Team' meant inclusion amongst 'l'altissimi poeti', as Dante had it when he subtly edged himself into the group of Homer, Horace, Ovid, Lucan and Virgil (*Inferno* I.79–102, the source for Chaucer's list in *Troilus*, discussed further in this volume by Alcuin Blamires). Yet compared to Chaucer's, Gower's authorial self-assertion is bolder, and multifaceted too. Indeed, if Chaucer emulated Dante, Gower more resembles Petrarch, who unabashedly engineered his own laureation in the Roman Forum in 1341 (on Easter Day!), and left a renowned 'Letter to Posterity' describing his career.[2] Gower makes clear claims with the striking tomb he designed for himself in the church of St Mary Magdalen (now St Saviour's, the Cathedral of Southwark), where his effigy in painted alabaster rests its head on volumes of his three major poems, their titles rendered, visible and unambiguous, as *mementi* for every passer-by. His works urge the same: indirectly, as when, again and again in the *Mirour de l'Omme*, *Vox Clamantis*, *Cronica Tripertita* and *Confessio Amantis*, he finds occasion to address his readers in a fictive but nonetheless first-person voice, or elsewhere, with a scantily veiled straightforwardness. Of this latter, the best example is a short poem in Latin entitled 'Eneidos, Bucolis'. Because a prose preface in many manuscripts attributes it to the hand of 'a certain Philosopher' ('quidam Philosophus . . . composuit') and not explicitly to Gower, this brief poem has not always been recognised for what it probably is: Gower's own, not-so-subtle staking of his claim to be Virgil's equal, at the very least, if not his better. Gower, says the poem, wrote Christian truths in three languages, while Virgil, a mere enlightened pagan, used only one to convey much less (Yeager 2005: 84–85).

If 'Eneidos, Bucolis' is Gower's work, its composition in the first decade of the fifteenth century commands attention for an audacity we have grown comfortable attributing to Milton. Indeed, even if the poem is not Gower's, there is no escaping the fact that Gower himself, and his contemporaries as well, apparently accepted his aspiration, and esteemed his writing in three languages as a major achievement. So, after a desire for lasting authorial fame, this trilingual *oeuvre* is the second poetic characteristic of Gower's we ought to recognise, not simply for the learning and labour that went into its production, but also for its uniqueness. No other English writer, post-Roman to post-modern, has left such a body of work to posterity in three languages – nor, perhaps in consequence, can any of his contemporaries, for that fact alone, be seen as quite so quintessentially medieval – or (paradoxically) quite so contemporarily English. Literacy in the England Gower shared with Chaucer, Langland, the *Gawain*-poet, Hoccleve and Lydgate meant a proficiency in two, if not always three, languages; 'vernacularity' almost until Gower's death in 1408 retained a significant Francophone component (Machan 2003: 71–110). That of all Middle English poets, so far as we know, Gower alone elected to capitalise upon the full range of linguistic

strengths thus demands recognition – both for what it says about the English readers
for whom he wrote, and about the poet Gower himself. Trilinguality is the obvious
centre both of his writerly ambition and of his poetic enterprise. The place of Gower's
work in the canon of English poetry cannot be understood properly without acknowledging what he accomplished in French and Latin.

Gower's extant poetry in French – dubbed Anglo-Norman by some, Anglo-French
by others – consists of the *Mirour de l'Omme* ('Mirror of Mankind') and two collections
of balades, the so-called *Cinkante Balades* ('Fifty Balades') and the *Traitié pour essampler
les amantz marietz* ('Model Treatise for Married People').[3] The *Mirour* is one of the
three great tomes pillowing Gower's effigy in Southwark Cathedral, although for that
appearance he coined for it a new Latin title (*Speculum Meditantis*), the better, presumably, to parallel stylistically the titles of the other two books, *Vox Clamantis* and
Confessio Amantis, as they appear on the tomb. That Gower sought such permanent
attention for the *Mirour* is evidence of his esteem for a poem which has survived in
only one manuscript.[4] Unfortunately this sole source, Cambridge University Library
Additional MS 3055, is defective. Four leaves are missing at the beginning and an
unknown number at the end.[5] Even in this damaged state, however, the *Mirour* is a
formidable poem of 29,945 lines arranged in twelve-line stanzas that rhyme ABAABB-
BABBA. The stanza is worth noting for what it suggests about Gower's poetics. His
choice seems to be unique in England, no other English example having been found.
Its first use is attributed to Hélinant (1160?–1230?), a monk of Froidmont abbey,
in his *Vers de la Mort* (ca. 1193–97); subsequent examples occur exclusively in France,
in some sixty morally admonitory poems derived from Hélinant, almost all from the
thirteenth century (Fouillade 1995: 440). That Hélinant himself and not one of his
emulators was Gower's source for the stanza pattern we can be sure, because both the
Vers de la Mort and its author are named in the *Mirour*, and Gower even quotes directly
from the *Vers* (*MO*, 11404–09, adapting *Vers*, XV.10–12).

Although it is impossible to be certain when Gower began or finished the *Mirour*,
most agree that the bulk of it is early work. (On its date and composition see Yeager
2006.) Thus it is informative to discover poetic practices present here turning up
again and again in the later poems, with notable regularity and similarity of purpose.
Indeed, such similarities of style, structure and content (along with Gower's re-titling
of the *Mirour* on his tomb) have led some scholars to argue that Gower conceived his
three longest poems as parts of a single whole (Fisher 1964: 135). While this is
unlikely, the carry-over of characters, minor plots and social concerns from poem to
poem nevertheless offers significant insight into Gower's approach to crafting poetry.
His uses of Hélinant present a case in point. Examined side by side, the *Mirour* and
the *Vers de la Mort* have little in common beyond their over-arching, generic didacticism,
a few lines borrowed verbatim and a rhyming pattern that, precisely on account of
its familiarity in fourteenth-century France and England, would inevitably have been
pegged to its antiquated source by Gower's readers, who then would have expected
from the *Mirour* what the 'gentils' call for from the Pardoner – 'som moral thyng'
(*Canterbury Tales* VI (C) 323–5).

Or perhaps we should say, 'the readers Gower expected' would have made that connection and drawn that conclusion. The *Mirour*, as Gower must have realised and intended, was (like Phoebe's beauty in *As You Like It*) 'not for all markets' (III.v.60). Gower probably had a limited but important readership in mind when he began the *Mirour* – in the court of Edward III, the circle once including the king himself and Henry of Grosmont, first duke of Lancaster and author of the *Livre de Seyntz Medicines* (1354) – and made his stylistic choices accordingly.[6] For this readership both the French language and the recognisably antique *moralistik* implicit in Hélinant's stanza would have held interest, not only because of a peculiar pietism then evident in Edward's inner circle, but also because, in the 1360s when Gower probably wrote most of the *Mirour*, the English dream of a single, insular-continental monarchy still retained its power.[7] That the common language of this empire would have been Anglo-French cannot be seriously questioned.

Gower's French work thus helps us take his measure as a poet in a number of additional ways. Clearly, even from his earliest writings, he aimed to be a public figure of a poet. To set beside a compelling didacticism he had both an eye for centres of power and something of a marketer's understanding of how to shape the product to influence not only the readers of future generations but also the powerful in his own. The *Mirour* provides one example; we see more in his two sequences of balades. Like the *Mirour*, *Cinkante Balades* exists in only a single copy, British Library Additional MS 59495. While an unknown number more must have been made (BL Add. 59495 is not a holograph, and has several scribal blunders uncharacteristic of manuscripts the production of which we suspect Gower oversaw), we are especially fortunate in our possession of this one.[8] It has much to tell us. Although BL Add. 59495 seems too plain to have been a presentation gift from Gower to Henry IV, as opined by Sir Thomas Fairfax, who owned the manuscript in the seventeenth century, its contents nevertheless appear thoughtfully assembled with the king's pleasure – and other purposes – in mind. The first two balades dedicate the collection to Henry; present also are Latin poems written by Gower to celebrate Henry's accession, and 'To King Henry IV In Praise of Peace', Gower's only known poem in English besides the *Confessio Amantis*. His other balade sequence, the *Traitié pour essampler les amantz marietz*, is included as well.[9]

Evidence of several kinds illustrative of Gower's poetic may be gleaned from this mélange. There is the quintessentially political (Gower the Lancastrian partisan); there is the self-conscious trilinguality; and there is the ambitiousness, here pointedly apparent in its style. Broadly speaking, the vogue for writing balades in the late fourteenth century can be traced to the two French masters of the form, Guillaume de Machaut and Eustace Deschamps, sometime pupil of Machaut who perhaps knew Chaucer. (On Machaut and Deschamps in England see Wimsatt 1991; Butterfield 2002.) Machauldian and Deschampian balades are distinctive in several ways, the former being, among other things, more sequentially narrative and lacking an envoy, the latter more often occasional, and completed nearly always with an envoy stanza. (See Sinnreich-Levi 1994; Laidlaw 1999.) Was it thus a competitive and aspiring

Gower, evidently aware of trends across the channel, who took aim at both Frenchmen
by producing in their language his own balade sequences, one each in the signature
styles of Machaut and Deschamps? That the question can be asked at all (and if so,
necessarily answered in the affirmative) further defines the Poet Gower. Bundled in a
single manuscript with material selected for Henry IV – whether or not the king received
or read them – the *Cinkante Balades* and the *Traitié* widen doors to view a Gowerian
macro- and micro-poetics suggested by the *Mirour*. BL Add. 59495 demonstrates a
shrewd artistic self-consciousness extending outward to calculations of a broad politics,
both loyally partisan and proudly nationalistic, from engagements of a finer kind with
over-the-channel contemporaries, conveyed by stanza patterns and verbal echoes.[10]

Because Gower's poetic practices carry over from one language to another, before
looking at his work in Latin and English it is helpful to pause over the French writing,
as it exhibits many of his strategies clearly. In the passage quoted earlier from the
Mirour de l'Omme, we should note that Gower not only identifies Hélinant's *Vers de
la Mort* as his source, but also excerpts and incorporates lines directly from it as well.
Similarly, in many of Gower's balades, lines were borrowed wholesale from his contemporaries on the continent. A single example – *CB* XLIII – must serve here as a case
in point. Its opening, 'Plus tricherous qe Jason a Medée', apparently recalls 'Ho!
Doulce Yseult, qui fus a la fontaine / Avec Tristan, Jason et Medea' from a famous
balade by Oton de Granson, a poet Gower may in fact have known, since he, like
Gower and Chaucer, had ties to the family of John of Gaunt.[11] And its refrain (l. 8),
'C'est ma dolour, qe fuist ainçois ma joie,' matches even more closely 'C'est ma dolour
et la fin de ma joie', a line from a balade of Machaut's (Yeager 1990: 45–113). For
certain readers in the past, such discoveries smacked of plagiarism, but this is to
misapprehend Gower's purposes. What he makes explicit in the *Mirour*, when he
quotes from and names Hélinant, in *CB* XLIII and elsewhere he practises implicitly
– but with the same expectation that his reference would be recognised, at least by
the cognoscenti, for whom Gower always wrote. Importing lines of others into his
own poetry served several purposes for Gower. On one hand, it asserted Gower's claim
to authorial parity – at least! – with the author of the borrowed line (a subtler gesture
of inclusion than when Dante surrounds his Pilgrim-placeholder in the exalted scrum
of 'l'atissimi', but crafted toward the same end); and, on the other hand, it directs the
reader's attention back to the originary context. The move thus facilitates a comparison
of specific poems, the effect of which is to deepen and broaden the resonant field of
Gower's poem, and to underscore the superior moral position of Gower's poem by
setting it against the source. Again, it is a technique familiar from Dante's practice,
who 'quotes' in much the same manner, both from the writings of others and sometimes even from his own, penned (his self-quotation would have us think) at a less
enlightened time in his life.

A poetics of this kind takes for granted an audience of a certain type. At the
outset of his career especially, Gower's ideal reader was himself well read, and in the
loving/painstaking manner very near to parsing that must have characterised how
one made one's way through books in the Middle Ages. ('Skimming', in the period,

is difficult to imagine.) Obviously, too, such readers were an elite subset of a skilled number only slightly larger (Janet Coleman 1981; Joyce Coleman 1996). Imagining Gower imagining them, it is entirely consistent with his ambitious goals to think of him taking pleasure in a poetry so subtly allusive, and of how its subtlety would winnow his audience accordingly. 'Fit audience though few', then, reflects Gower's aspiration as truly as it did Milton's. With one or two outstanding exceptions, he was never, by hope or design, a poet for the general populace.

Nevertheless, paradoxically, this is not to say that the populace was far from Gower's mind on most occasions when he took quill or stylus in hand. Excluding the *Cinkante Balades* and a handful of brief Latin pieces, all Gower's literary energy went toward furthering a poetic discourse about public issues in a voice he clearly laboured to make an instrument of the common good. Pointed social critique and scathing satire are hallmarks that much of Gower's poetry shares with Langland's: ones especially worthy of note since often these aspects of Gower's poetry are overshadowed in modern estimation by the elitism of his solutions (Middleton 1978). Both are visible in the *Mirour*, certainly. In so far as its major subject is the enumeration and remediation of social afflictions, the *Mirour* vehemently catalogues Gower's public concerns; in passage after passage, such as his portrayal of the character Triche (Fraud) busy at work fleecing the innocent in the London streets (*MO* 25501–26437), Gower's bitingly satiric tone and the pungent hurly-burly of the scenes cede little to Langland's.

It is, however, in his Latin poems that Gower's socio-political jeremiad finds its fullest measure. For whatever reason (perhaps because he felt the language limited his audience to cognoscenti; perhaps because, in his own mind, poetry was a quintessentially classicising art, as the book titles on his tomb suggest), Gower seems far more emotionally ready to 'swing for the fences' in Latin than in either French or English. Little in his expansive *oeuvre* can stand beside the vitriol and unvarnished naming of names of the *Cronica Tripertita*, his denunciation of the last years of Richard II; little replicates, either in his own work or in the verse of any of his English contemporaries, the emotional bone-shaking of the 'Visio' (or Book I) from the *Vox Clamantis*; nor does Gower ever come closer to speaking his heart's truth frankly than in several of his brief, occasional Latin poems. Few modern readers hold Latin in the same esteem as Gower, however. A closer look at selected examples is thus helpful for what they reveal of Gower's range, as poet and as man:

> Grene, Scrop, Bussy, cordis sine lumine fusci,
> Omne nephas querunt, quo ledere plus potuerunt:
> Rex fuit instructus per eos, et ad omnia ductus
> Que mala post gessit, quibus Anglia tota pauescit.

Green, Scrope and Bushy, shadowy men without light in their hearts, planned every crime in order to do the most damage: the King was tutored by them, and led to all the evils he committed later, at which all England trembled.

> Nouit enim mundus, Ricardus quando secundus
> Iustos deleuit proceres, quos Anglia fleuit,
> Ipse superbie sic spirat et alcius ire,
> Quod dedignatur proprium regnumque minatur:
> Amplius ex more solito latitante furore
> Seuit, et oppressit populum cui parcere nescit.

Indeed the world knew, when Richard II put down the just nobles, for whom England wept, that he wished thus to strut and swagger higher, because he disdained and diminished his own kingdom: with greater than his usually hidden rage, he vented his fury and oppressed his people, to whom he did not know how to be merciful.[12]

These two passages let us see Gower the public man with his partisan fists balled and blood in his eye. Historians and literary critics alike often choose examples like these from the *Cronica* to support arguments about Gower's fierce loyalty to Henry IV and his hatred of Richard II. Clearly they are not wrong: in 1400 Gower's feelings were high, the lines were written, and they endure as indelible elements of his poetic enterprise. Determining for how long Gower continued to feel as he expresses himself here (and there is indication that dissatisfaction with Henry's government began to creep in not long after the *Cronica* was finished) is beyond our scope, which is rather to note the range of uses Gower believed poetry could effect, in Latin particularly, since nothing so bluntly *ad hominem* or so politically fiery remains in his works in other languages.

Royalty was not Gower's only target, of course, and the historians and critics who cite the *Cronica* frequently scour the *Vox Clamantis* for evidence of public opinion about other social classes, peasants especially, at the outset of Richard's reign. To some degree Gower's longer poetry lends itself to such interpretation because his custom, in all three languages, is to disavow his own agency and address his readers in the persona of popular opinion, as for instance in the *Vox*, ll. 75–80 (see Stockton 1962: 98). Conventional dream visions – the structural starting-point for the *Vox*, the *Confessio Amantis* and (one could argue) the *Miroir* as well – of course establish the dreamer-poet as a reporter, not an *auctor*, but, like the image of John the Baptist 'crying in the wilderness' ('vox clamantis in deserto') he invokes in his title, Gower's description of himself as a *nuncius* ('messenger') pointedly adapts the conventional to suit a politics only apocalyptic language can express.[13] Langland and Gower are again fellow travellers here. Like Langland, Gower grapples openly with social issues in his verse, and for both poets the failure of human institutions initiates and drives their writing toward biblical comparisons. *Piers Plowman* thus has much in common tonally and imaginatively with the *Vox*, where Gower brings his intense outrage at conditions in the commonwealth forward via an allegory intended but lightly to obscure:

> Copia dum tanta monstrorum more ferarum
> Extitit vnita, sicut arena maris,
> Graculus vnus erat edoctus in arte loquendi,
> Quem retinere domi nulla catasta potest.

Hic, licet indignus, cunctis cernentibus, alis
Expansis, primum clamat habere statum.
Prepositus baratri velut est demon legioni,
Sic malus in vulgoprefuit iste malo.

When this great multitude of monsters like wild beasts stood united, a multitude like the sands of the sea, there appeared a Jackdaw, well instructed in the art of speaking, which no cage could keep at home. While all were looking on, this bird spread his wings and claimed to have top rank, although he was unworthy. Just as the Devil was placed in command over the army of the lower world, so this scoundrel was in charge of the wicked mob.

(Stockton 1962: 65)

The lines are taken from the so-called 'Visio', or Book I, of the *Vox*. The immediate scene is the Rising of 1381: the *graculus* is the peasant leader Wat Tyler ('wat' was a general term in England for a jackdaw, or jay) and the 'monsters' the rebels, seemingly plucked from a horror movie of the future (oxen breathe fire [*VC* I.260], foxes bite through iron traps [*VC* I.470] and even flies have fangs [*VC* I.635]); the governing image, however, is the coming of Antichrist and the chaos heralding Doomsday, no less than when Fraud ('frere Flaterere', *PP* CXXIII.313–79) commandeers Piers' storehouse – or when Richard II, overthrowing law itself, deliberately drags his kingdom down to darkness. The irony, bitter and frightening, would scarcely have eluded either Langland or Gower.

If, then, the structure and imagery of the *Vox Clamantis* have much to tell us about Gower's larger poetic strategies, we can find examples in it equally well suited to illustrate the sensitive mechanics that propel his work on a smaller scale. Recent interest in Gower's Latin has drawn constructive attention to his skills as a poet steeped in antique versification and casting himself thoughtfully in the classical mode (Coleman 2002; Echard 2003, 2004b; Carlson 2007). As a result, the informed care with which he assembled his Latin poetry is becoming clear, in detail greater than can be replicated here, where a brief look at a single practice – cento ('patchwork': an amalgam of phrases from another author) – must serve as an example. In the following pairs of lines (*VC* I.1501–07), the first is Gower's, the second appears as in its source in one or another of Ovid's poems. The sample is representative, *mutatis mutandis*, of Gower's handling of the *Vox*:

Qui prius attulerat *verum michi semper amorem*
nam cum praesitieris *verum mihi semper amorem* (*Ex Ponto* IV.6.23)
Tunc *tamen aduerso tempore* cessat *amor*:
hic *tamen adverso tempore* crevit *amor* (*Ex Ponto* IV.6.24)
Querebam fratres tunc fidos, non tamen ipsos
quaerebam fratres, exceptis scilicet illis (*Tristia* III.1.65)
Quos suus optaret non genuisse pater.
quos suus optaret non genuisse pater (*Tristia* III.1.66)

> Memet in insidiis semper locuturus habebam,
> *Verbaque sum spectans pauca locutus humum*:
> *verbaque sum spectans pauca locutus humum* (*Fasti* I.148)

What at one time was seen as Gower's 'schoolboy plagiarism' has since been identified for what it is – his conscious emulation of the difficult cut-and-paste style of certain late Latin poets, most prominently Anicia Faltonia Proba, who reconfigured lines of Virgil's to render the life of Christ (Yeager 1989: 113–32). Far from the lethargy that plagiarism suggests, Gower's cento underscores instead poetic characteristics quite opposite: ambition to join exalted ranks, wide and deep reading of Ovid and a dozen or more others whose works he samples; but most of all perhaps a remarkable eye – and especially a *memory* – for the right line to fit the right new place, and the fine-tuned ear to meld metrics seamlessly. While the *Vox* is the most centonic of Gower's poems, recognising this here has farther-reaching value. We find him applying the same principles elsewhere, in French (in the *Mirour*, as exemplified by the snippet of Hélinant cited earlier, although this is not, strictly speaking, true cento) and in English, as we shall see. In a sense, cento, with its appropriative imperative linking Gower the Poet over space and time to ancient others of his tribe, emblematises his learning, his subtlety and the detailed formalism not simply of his verse in Latin, but comprehensively, of all his art.

Gower's longer Latin work thus can serve as an approximate gauge of his technique and poetic power, and of the general sweep of his civic and moral concerns. Exceptionally in the shorter poems, however, we encounter that *rara avis* – a rounded sense of his heart. Before turning, then, to the English poetry of this most English of trilingual poets, let us consider a few of the short Latin poems, beginning with 'Whatever a Man Writes' ('Quicquid homo scribat'):

> To whatever a man writes, Nature applies a limit
>   Which flees like a shadow, nor returns having fled;
> She has placed a limit on me, so that I am unable
>   To write any longer, because I am blind.
> Although my will remains, my ability passes;
>   It declines to write any more.
> When I was able, I wrote many poems with zeal;
>   One part deals with the world, the other with God.
> But I have left to the world its vanities still to be written,
>   And in a poem of my imagination I write the words concerning God.
> Although the act of writing externally now fails me,
>   Still my mind writes within me and adorns the work.
> Thus because I can write nothing further with my hands,
>   I will write with my prayers what my hands cannot.
> This is what I, a blind man, pray for in these present days,
>   That You make our kingdoms prosperous in the future, O God,
> And grant that I receive your holy light.[14]

It is a critical commonplace to deny medieval poetry a personal voice in favour of one or another literary convention when describing sentiment that, were it from a more recent age, would find acceptance as honestly confessional. Perhaps in most cases there is good reason for this: Gower's balades, to cite a relevant example, are a great deal more about the competitive making of art among poets – about the moving around of the approved building-blocks of poems for coterie applause – than they are about any wooing Gower practised in his youth, as some readers once believed. Yet in the poem above it is difficult not to 'hear' John Gower the man unburdening himself of a sorrow and a resignation uniquely his – no less truly than we claim for Milton in his famous sonnets on his blindness. Nor is the point an unimportant one in any evaluation of Gower's poetic achievement. In Gower's case there is an irony, no doubt, in what remains our contemporary willingness on the one hand to trust as credible emotion, say, his unctuous praise for the usurpers Henry IV and Thomas Arundel, Archbishop of Canterbury (even knowing as we do the immense danger that *failure* to praise these two brought after 1399), while on the other hand relegating to the slag heap of impersonal convention apparent emotion of every softer kind.[15]

'Quicquid homo scribat' offers a place to begin, because most accept Gower's blindness (as they do Milton's) as autobiographical, and hence his statements of sorrow at the loss of his eyes as straightforward and legitimate too. A more difficult problem is raised by two poems on the subject of love: 'Est amor' ('Love Is') and 'Ecce, patet tensus' ('Lo, the Taut Bow'). Gower begins the first with what seems to be a conventional list of Love's contradictions:

> Est amor in glosa pax bellica, lis pietosa,
> Accio famosa, vaga sors, vis imperiosa,
> Pugna quietosa, victoria perniciosa...

In the glossaries love is a warlike peace, a loving litigation, / Infamous lawsuit, wavering fate, unforceful force, / A peaceful fight, a ruinous victory...

(Yeager 2005: 32, 33)

Lines 16–20, however, are wholly original, and in a different metre:

> Magnus in exiguis variatus u test tibi clamor,
>   Fixus in ambiguis motibus errat amor.
> Instruat audia tibi leccio sic repetita:
>   Mors amor et vita participantur ita.

Just as a great public outcry can be divided into small words, / So Love wanders in ambiguous movements but on a fixed course. / Thus a lecture heard repeatedly may instruct you: / In this manner death, love and life have their shares.

The 'lecture repeatedly heard' seems a reference back, to the conventional oxymoronics of Love; but when he speaks of Love's 'ambiguous...but...fixed' wanderings, is

Gower describing his own bewildered erotic experience? Conventional wisdom frowns on biographical reading; yet consider the final lines (Yeager 2005: add ref.). Gower married one Agnes Groundolf in 1398, in a union often described as a *mariage de convenance* – he too infirm by then to care for himself, and she his much-needed nurse (Fisher 1964: 65). But if that scenario accounts for Gower's inclusion of himself in 'Est amor' as a bridegroom, ought we find the oxymorons that open the poem in some sense autobiographical as well as conventional? And how should we accommodate the hardly concealed eroticism of the poem's final lines?

Such questions are framed anew by another short poem, 'Ecce, patet tensus', which in its opening lines depicts Cupid at work (Yeager 2010). Again, the details are conventional, snatches (like 'amor vincit omnia') borrowed, seemingly, from the commonest locations. Still, especially against the backdrop of Gower's life, there may be glints of something more personal. The multiple references to blindness in a poem written when Gower was himself losing his sight and marrying are interesting – as is the recurrent figure of Love's directionless ambience familiar from 'Est amor'. In that context, the apostrophes to a painfully split, tortured human nature with which 'Ecce, patet tensus' concludes are also notable (Yeager 2010). Was marriage to Agnes the 'cure' that grace provided Gower? That there is reason to think so suffices, since the present purpose is to illustrate the challenges alongside the accomplishments that Gower's verse presents. Such leads are useful, along with previous observations of Gower's formal habits and political and social concerns, as we turn to scrutinise his more familiar English poetry.

Gower has left us two known works in English: 'To King Henry IV In Praise of Peace', a poem of 385 lines arranged in fifty-five rime royal stanzas (ABABBCC), preceded by a dedication in Latin to Henry IV, rhyming AAAABBB; and the *Confessio Amantis*. The latter, nearly 30,000 lines long, primarily in octosyllabic couplets, is Gower's best-known work, and – although it was not his final effort – we have good reason to believe that he saw it as his *chef-d'oeuvre*, the crowning achievement of his long authorial career.

Chronologically 'In Praise of Peace' post-dates the *Confessio Amantis* by a number of years, but because the relationship on several levels is close between the two poems, the shorter 'In Praise of Peace' serves as a helpful introduction to many of Gower's concerns, poetic and political, presented more elaborately in the *Confessio*. We should, for example, observe that the ideal reader of both poems is bilingual. English assuredly predominates in each, so that we refer to them as 'the English works', but Gower has limited their full accessibility to those also skilled in Latin. Thus 'In Praise of Peace' opens with the dedicatory address to Henry in Latin, and the *Confessio* prefaces major sections with Latin verses and, either interlineally or in the margin, depending upon the manuscript, includes commentary throughout in Latin prose, generally accepted to be authorial. To charges of furthering an elitist poetics, Gower might suggest we consider – along with noting, perhaps, the amount of Latin Langland required of his readership to understanding *Piers Plowman* – that he wrote for a royal audience: 'In Praise of Peace' for Henry IV, the *Confessio* first for Richard, then later revised with Henry again in mind.[16] Both poems are indeed *specula principium*, 'mirrors for princes', mirroring each other in purpose while differing in kind from broader critiques offered in the *Vox Clamantis* and the *Mirour de l'Omme* of every social rank and class. Noteworthy too is the new poetic vantage Gower adopts: the 'English' poems address their subject with an insider's intimacy. No longer the *vox populi* nor the voice of the solitary Baptist crying from the wilderness, in the *Confessio* and 'In Praise of Peace' Gower 'speaks to power' openly, writing his own name directly into the verse: 'I, Gower, which am al thi liege man, / This lettre unto thin excellence Y sende' (*IPP*, 372–75). Whatever Gower's actual proximity to the persons of Richard and Henry – and certainly there is suggestion enough of his closeness to both – the multivalent resonance of his 'personal' entry into these poems should not be overlooked. Dismissed as self-serving, even sycophancy by some, it is surely a move more valuably understood for what it suggests about the important role played by poetry, and by Gower himself as poet, in the extensive national and regal self-fashioning initiated by Richard II and continued through the Tudors. And it should remind us that even when harnessed for service most public, poetry was, for Gower, a living means of self-expression as well.

Not that he always accomplishes either service or self-expression in obvious ways. Often, as we have seen in his French and Latin work, Gower speaks his mind through his choice of form. A thoughtful juxtaposition of 'In Praise of Peace' and the *Confessio Amantis* provides an instructive example. One clear difference between the two poems is their predominant rhymes: octosyllabic couplets in the *Confessio*, pentameter rime royal stanzas in 'In Praise of Peace'. Again, however, 'predominant' is a key word. On just one occasion Gower forsakes couplets in the *Confessio* – and that moment, both for Amans and for English poetry, is extraordinary. In Book VIII (2217–2300) Amans offers a supplicative prayer to Venus that results, not as he wishes, in the satisfaction of his desires, but rather the opposite: handed a mirror by the Goddess of Love, Amans confronts his advanced age and consequent unsuitability as a lover. Self-recognition transforms a heretofore fictive 'Amans' into a 'John Gower' (VIII.2321) who receives, in his own name, a 'peire of bedes' from Venus (VIII.2908). Instructing him to 'preie hiereafter for the peace', she dismisses 'John Gower' from the dream garden where Amans' shrift has been heard, back to active service in the world of men, of readers royal and common.

Amans/Gower's prayer to Venus is cast in rime royal stanza. That 'In Praise of Peace', the only other poem of Gower's in English, is also crafted in rime royal ought therefore to attract our attention. His earlier mastery of the complex stanza of the *Mirour*, and the various balade styles in the *Cinkante Balades* and *Traitié*, implies that among a variety of choices Gower was purposeful in selecting rime royal for use when and where he did. Comparison of the two instances suggests what that purpose might be. In the *Confessio*, Amans' supplication to Venus returns a fictional character to his 'real' name and function as poet and royal advisor in the historical present of breathing kings and dynastic wars. Pointedly acting in his own name, Gower writes and presents 'In Praise of Peace' to Henry IV. The incidents are self-sustaining and independent

– but for Gower's closer readers, those for whom he wrote 'Eneidos bucolis' and designed his tomb, the identity of rhyme selection implies a level of creative inter-dependence and self-consciousness between works unique among Middle English poets. 'In Praise of Peace', its rime royal stanza reminds us, fulfils Venus's demand of 'John Gower' for eirenic prayer in the world beyond the garden. Characteristically, Gower's poetic practice elides form into statement, statement into form.

And what statements are 'In Praise of Peace' and the *Confessio Amantis* intended to convey? Like all of Gower's works, they address 'discord' – his generic term for the root of human problems, societal and personal. A thoughtful Christian of the Middle Ages, essentially a pacifist, Gower adhered to the Augustinian monad: God the One, centre and circumference of all things, whose singular unity established the model for universal order, macrocosmic and microcosmic. 'Divisioun,' which Gower identifies in the Prologue to the *Confessio* as the cause of ill in England (Pro. 849–55), is, when expanded on a world scale, what sparks his argument to Henry to make peace, not war, both in France and, in particular, in 1402–1404 when 'In Praise of Peace' must have been written, at home against his own now fractured and rebellious countrymen. It is the king's duty, as God's earthly vicar, to reunite them according to God's plan:

> If eny man be now or ever was
> Agein the pes thi preve counseillour,
> Lete God ben of thi counseil in this cas,
> And putte awei the cruel werreiour.
> For God, which is of man the creatour,
> He wolde noght men slowe His creature
> Withoute cause of dedly forfeture.
>
> (IPP.127–33)

The emphasis on counsel in these lines not only bespeaks Gower's notion of the poet's social role, but also lays heavy stress upon the king as properly a rational ser-vant of a rational deity, responsible, thus, for carefully weighing advice:

> Aboute a kyng good counseil is to preise
> Above alle othre thinges most vailable;
> Bot yit a kyng withinne himself schal peise,
> And se the thinges that ben reasonable,
> And theruppon he schal his wittes stable
> Among the men to sette pes in evene,
> For love of Him which is the Kyng of Hevene.
>
> (IPP.141–47)

Choosing the right from among myriad attractive wrongs may be difficult, but nevertheless in Gower's view it is the king's job and the challenge in every individual life. Thus in the *Confessio* his tactics may be new and different, but his strategy remains unchanged. Like a king over his nation, each of us on a lesser level must rule and bring unity and peace to our individual 'little world.' In essence Gower follows Boethius's lead in locating the source of his protagonist Amans's trouble in a misunderstanding of the nature of love, which results in inner discord and a heart, like the surrounding nation, divided against itself 'thurgh lacke of love' (Pro. 892). Genius, however, is a priest of Venus and no Lady Philosophy; nor is the love-besotted and illogical Amans a Boethian impersonator. As the poem's title indicates, the resultant dialogue between these two delivers Amans's confession of how well or badly his love has been pursued (usually the latter), broadly following the familiar sacramental format established by the Church. Hence the *Confessio Amantis* contains, in addition to a substantial Prologue reminiscent of both the *Mirour* and the *Vox* in its concern for the world's shortcomings, and an Epilogue calling for the king's attention and the advent of a new Arion (an eirenic figure of the harper-poet), eight Books, seven devoted to the cardinal sins: Pride (Book I), Envy (II), Wrath (III), Sloth (IV), Avarice (V), Gluttony (VI) and Lust/Incest (VIII). In the remaining Book, VII, Genius breaks the pattern in order to respond to Amans's request to hear what manner of 'philosophie' Aristotle taught Alexander. The result – a 5438-line 'sketch' of humane learning heavily reliant upon Brunetto Latini's *Tresor* – was often decried by early critics of the poem as a digression, and as evidence against Gower's possessing either an architectonic sense, or structural self-control.

More recent scholarly attempts to interpret the *Confessio* as a unified whole have been kinder to Gower, albeit approaches in general have broken into two camps. Not surprisingly, those who see the poem primarily as a political statement focus on the Prologue and Epilogue; for them, Book VII is comfortably absorbed as hermeneutic, in that it contributes to the *Confessio*'s larger purpose by offering a ruler the learned advice of a philosopher (or a poet). (See Coffman 1945 and 1954; Peck 1978; and Ferster 1996: 108–36.) A second group has read the *Confessio* narratologically, skipping about among Genius's many exempla to piece together a moralist / Christian – even apocalyptic – vision for the poem (Cherniss 1987). More recent still are endeavours to triangulate Gower the aspiring and ambitious *auctor* with his two elder avatars in French and Latin – Political and Polemical Gower – by foregrounding as a third strand his debts to (if not his self-conscious competition with) the writing of his own time. Particularly valuable have been comparative studies of the *Confessio* alongside Machaut's *dits*, and against the backdrop of late medieval chroniclers of Ricardian / Henrican historiography (Nicholson 2005).

Taken individually, each of these approaches falls short. What is perhaps most important to notice about the *Confessio* is how *inclusive* Gower seems to have been in its design and crafting, as only a poet can be who comes to his subject at the apex of his powers, and with a substantial career behind him. At the centre of Gower's worldview as poet, believer and moralist is the notion that all things interconnect: indeed, they replicate each other, as elements of a divine plan, differing less in substance than in scale. The *Confessio Amantis* stands as his most complete attempt to articulate this *visio vitae* for the edification and improvement of others. Undoubtedly he intended the point to apply both personally to his readers for the amelioration of their own lives and socially, for the common profit. In this regard Amans is an Everyman, despite the care Gower has taken to portray him as a character whose idiosyncrasies – sometimes funny, sometimes poignant – are distinct, and credibly his own. For without a credible Amans the *Confessio* loses its narrative frame and its collection of tales splinters incoherently. Paradoxically, as Gower knew, Amans must achieve an autonomous existence before he can qualify as one of us, or edify us.

The *Confessio Amantis* is Gower's greatest achievement as a poet because only here does he fully commit to the poet's task of fashioning fiction. In his other major works there are splendid moments: in the *Mirour de l'Omme*, the paean to wool (*MO* 25369–429), the machinations of Triche and the magnificent closing prayer to the Virgin (*MO* 29845–942) in particular stand apart; in the *Vox Clamantis*, the lurid, dark and terrifying allegories of the *Visio* and the savage sketches of a lupine clergy are memorable (*VC* II.1311–2049); even in the *Cinkante Balades* there is genius in the subtle, accretive revelation of the personae of the anonymous lover and his lady, and of their affair. Yet ultimately the *raisons d'être* of these poems are not their fictions, but their polemics and the dance of style. The *Confessio Amantis* alone proposes seamlessness of form and function toward a larger meaning, where polysemy had served before.

Just what set Gower off in this new direction cannot be known. In the earlier of two versions of the *Confessio*'s Prologue he claims as inspiration a command of Richard II, issued during a chance meeting with the king while boating on the Thames, to write 'somwhat of love' (*CA* Pro. 35*–60*). Whether historical or fictional, the moment in a stroke conjoins the great medieval literary genres – the *speculum regis*, which Gower had already mastered, and the allegory of love, with its roots in the *Roman de la Rose*. The challenge for one driven by auctorial ambition is unmistakable, as is likely to have been the appeal – specified, perhaps, by Richard – to compose the work in English, the native tongue in which, as yet, Gower seems to have undertaken nothing. He has clearly been listening to his countrymen's speech with the ear of a poet, nonetheless. The 'Augustan' plain style he hit on for the *Confessio*'s octosyllabic couplets is distinctly un-Chaucerian, but no less sophisticated or effective. (On Gower's 'Augustan' style see Lewis 1936: 201; Davie 1967: 31–33.) When Amans, for example, describes for Genius how he felt when once allowed to touch his lady's hand, 'The Ro, which renneth on the Mor, / Is thanne noght so lyht as I' (IV.2786–87), or in a line such as 'In Temse whan it was flowende' (Pro. 39), Gower confronts us with a unity of music, simile and sense not easily matched in late medieval English verse. The same understated control is registered in the dialogue of which – although it is seldom remarked upon – most of the *Confessio* is composed. Indeed, in many ways the poem is a chorus of English voices, the major ones – Amans, Genius, Venus – kept distinct through no small measure of dramatic talent thoughtfully applied. The tone moves from Genius's sonorous prolixity to Amans's frequent naiveté (here berating himself for standing tongue-tied before his lady):

Bot after, whanne I understonde,
And am in other place al one,
I make many a wofull mone
Unto myself, and speke so:
'Ha fol, wher was thin herte tho,
Whan thou thi worthy ladi syhe?
Were thou afered of hire yhe?
For of hire hand ther is no drede:
So wel I knowe hir wommanhede,
That in hire is nomore oultrage
Than in a child of thre yeer age.
(IV.594–604)

to Venus's dismissive colloquial pungency:

Thou wost wel that I am Venus,
Which al only my lustes seche;
And wel I wot, thogh thou beseche
Mi love, lustes ben ther none,
Whiche I mai take in thi persone;
For loves lust and lockes hore
In chamber acorden neveremore,
And thogh thou feigne a yong corage,
It scheweth wel be the visage
That olde grisel is no fole.
(VIII.2398–2407)

Gower's ear for the English vocal range is ever on display in the *Confessio*, as effective and discernible in the stories as in the frame.

And many of the stories are among the best we have from the period, however much they have suffered in the past from unreflective comparison with Chaucer's. While it seems unlikely that Gower would have shrunk from the encounter (indeed, we have some suggestion of a friendly rivalry written into Venus's demand that Chaucer 'Do make his testament of love' [VIII.*2955] found in the first version of the Epilogue), such competition as perhaps existed between the two friends and foremost London poets can only have been waged on a level more ambitious than a simple juxtaposition of different renderings of the same narrative. The *Confessio*, Gower *may* have thought, could 'quite' *The Canterbury Tales*, but neither he nor Chaucer would have seen – for example – the 'Tale of Florent' (*CA* I.1407–1861) or that of Custance (*CA* II.587–1612) as 'better' or a 'worse' version of the tales of, respectively, the Wife of Bath and the Man of Law. All are parts contributing to greater wholes, their length, development and detail determined by the particular needs of two entirely different poems.

It is worthwhile considering briefly what some of those needs are. Apparently high on Chaucer's list of interests when he was writing what he called, in his Retraction, 'the tales of Caunterbury' (*CT* X.1085) was finding a good story and telling it well. If this seems obvious, it is largely because for the most part Chaucer succeeded – he tells very good stories very well indeed, so well that we go to *The Canterbury Tales* specifically to enjoy them, and almost all of them can stand recitation alone. Gower, in contrast, does not name his English work 'the tales of Genius' or even 'stories from the Confessional'. *Confessio Amantis* means 'Confession of a Lover' and since Gower would have been confident that all his readers participated in the ritual regularly, he could count on them to know what a confession sounded like, and that stories told in confession were didactically, not narratively, driven. Another way to see this is to note that while Chaucer's framing fiction of the tale-telling contest has his Pilgrims (much like himself) consciously striving to make their stories win, the Confession of Gower's Lover is all about probing his main character's motives and teaching Amans a transformative lesson. As a narrator, Genius is not trying to win a contest, but rather persuade a soul to good. And since Gower hopes to do the same, through Amans, for his readers at various levels, his primary criterion for choosing and building narratives is their potential effectiveness in the larger, developing meta-narrative that is the *Confessio Amantis*.

In terms of any critical approach to be taken to Gower's poem, then, this structuring principle must have major implications. One frequent complaint, in particular, that few of his stories are rich enough in detail and plot complexity – the stories of Florent, Custance and Apollonius being the commonest exceptions – to succeed simply as stories, free of their context, seems, in view of Gower's true expectations for the *Confessio*, to be especially unenlightened if not misleading altogether. As tales such as that of Florent show well, Gower could indeed produce stand-alone narratives if he wished; that he included them only occasionally in the *Confessio* suggests the need for direct, close, thoughtful reading to discover his reason for their particular placing. A corollary to this may underlie another common observation, that Gower's English verse is comparatively plain, especially when set beside Chaucer's. Yet as the higher diction and rime royal stanzas of Amans's supplication to Venus show, Gower could also empurple his lines situationally, as he chose. That he did not often do so perhaps has more to say about how he conceived his characters dramatically than about poetic dullness or inability. What voices would be appropriate to Amans and Genius, were they real beings? Or – how true to confessional language would (say) Harry Bailey's bombast be?

Perhaps Gower simply hoped that, by casting the *Confessio Amantis* relatively simply in the simpler of the common vernaculars he spoke, he could get his truths across more effectively to his countrymen. In this wish at least Gower's great English poem takes its appropriate place with the *Speculum Meditantis* (*Mirour de l'Omme*) and the *Vox Clamantis* beneath his alabaster head on his tomb. For in the end, what ought to distinguish Gower the Poet, with his fluency in three languages, Italianate ambition and, as his output suggests, indefatigable energy, is his repeated insistence in work after work that poetry should serve society. Poetry should make things better. If a poet fulfilled his role well – and readers read with care – then poetry probably did.

Notes

1 References to Chaucer are from *The Riverside Chaucer*, ed. Larry D. Benson (Boston: Houghton Mifflin, 1987); for the quotation above see *Troilus and Criseyde*, V.1786; 1791–92. See also 'Chaucers Wordes unto Adam, His Owne Scriveyn', 650.

2 See Morris Bishop, *Letters from Petrarch*, Bloomington, IN: Indiana University Press, 1966, 5–12.

3 In the debate over whether to classify Gower's dialect as Anglo-Norman or Anglo-French recent trends favour Anglo-Norman; e.g. the *Anglo-Norman Dictionary*, second edition, ed. William Rothwell, Stewart Gregory and David Trotter (London: Manley Publishing for the Modern Humanities Research Association, 2005–), accepts Gower among its authors for citation, whereas the first edition (London: 1977–92) did not. Similarly Ruth Dean, in *Anglo-Norman Literature: A Guide to Texts and Manuscripts* (London: Anglo-Norman Text Society, 1999), includes discussion of Gower's works. But the matter remains cloudy. Brian Merrilees argues in a forthcoming study that, regardless of what Gower's spoken dialect may have been, his written record shows strong influence of Continental regionalisms. For present purposes 'French', used generically, will suffice.

4 For general discussions of the *Mirour* and its composition see Fisher 1964: 95, and Yeager in Echard 2004a: 139–45.

5 For discussions of the manuscript see Fisher 1964: 91, and Macaulay 1899–1902: I.lxviii–lxxi. All quotations from Gower are from Macaulay's edition.

6 On *Le Livre* as Gower's inspiration for the *Mirour* see Yeager 2006.

7 The standard date of composition of the *Mirour* is 1376–78; see Fisher 1964: 95. An argument for an earlier beginning date and later completion is made in Yeager 2006.

8 Despite the title, *CB* in BL Add. 59495 actually contains fifty-two: two different balades are numbered 'IIII', and there is a final unnumbered balade.

9 On BL Add. 59495 and Gower's manuscripts generally see Fisher 1964: 303–9, and Pearsall in Echard 2004a: 73–97.

10 Gower's unusual preference in his balades for *fin' amour* – common in Provençal – rather than *amour courtois* as a descriptor, and the number of lines there echoing troubadour poems, has raised speculation about his familiarity with Occitán writers: see Fisher 1964: 76, who would like to tie Gower to a late-blooming London *pui*. By the latter fourteenth century, however, 'troubadour' phrasing was commonplace, and no evidence of a *pui* after 1320 in London has been found. For discussion see Yeager 1990: 66–68.

11 On Gower's proximity to Gaunt see Yeager 2004. Chaucer's wife Philippa was sister to Gaunt's mistress and eventually third wife.

12 *Cronica Tripertita* II.320–23; III.11–16. Macaulay 1899–1902: IV, 328 and 330; translation mine.

13 'The voice of one crying in the wilderness' describing the Baptist is common to all the gospels (Matt. 3:3, Mark 1:3, Luke 3:4 and John 1:23) as well as to Isaiah (40:3). On the title see Wickert 1953.

14 'Quicquid homo scribat finem natura ministrat, / Que velud umbra fugit, nec fugiendo redit; / Illa michi finem posuit, quo scribere quicquam / Ulterius nequio, sum quia cecus ego. / Posse meum transit, quamuis michi velle remansit; / Amplius ut scribat hoc michi posse negat. / Carmina dum potui, studiosus plurima scripsi; / Pars tenet hec mundum, pars tenet illa Deum. / Vana tamen mundi mundo scribenda reliqui, / Scriboque mentali carmine verba Dei. / Quamuis exterius scribendi deficit actus,/ Mens tamen interius scribit et ornat opus. / Sic quia de minibus nichil amodo scribo valoris, / Scribam de precibus que nequit illa manus. / Hoc ego, vir cecus, presentibus oro diebus, / Prospera quod statuas regna futura, Deus, / Daque michi sanctum lumen habere tuum.' Text is from Oxford, All Souls College MS 98; translation mine.

15 Indeed, not pleasing Arundel and Henry may have cost Chaucer his life: see Jones et al. 2003.

16 Surviving manuscripts of the *Confessio Amantis* exhibit three prominent variations which Macaulay described as 'recensions', reflecting his belief that the versions revealed definable stages in Gower's composition process. While in general this is true the chronology of versions and manuscripts is more complicated. See Nicholson 1984 and 1988.

References and Further Reading

Editions

Macaulay, G. C. (ed.) (1899–1902). *The Complete Works of John Gower*. Early English Text Society, e.s. 81. 4 vols. Oxford: Clarendon Press.

Peck, Russell A. (ed.) (1980). *Confessio Amantis*. Toronto, Buffalo: University of Toronto Press in association with the Medieval Academy of America.

Stockton, E. W. (trans.) (1962). *The Major Latin Works of John Gower*. Seattle: University of Washington Press.

Yeager, R. F. (ed. and trans.) (2005). *John Gower: The Minor Latin Works*. Kalamazoo, MI: Medieval Institute Press.

Secondary Reading

Buschinger, D. (ed.) (1998). *Autour d'Eustace Deschamps: Actes du Colloque du Centre d'Études Médiévales de l'Université de Picardie-Jules Verne*. Amiens: Amiens University Press.

Butterfield, A. (2002). *Poetry and Music in Medieval France: From Jean Renart to Guillaume de Machaut*. Cambridge: Cambridge University Press.

Carlson, D. R. (2007). A rhyme distribution chronology of John Gower's Latin poetry. *Studies in Philology*, 104, 15–55.

Cherniss, Michael D. (1987). *Boethian Apocalypse: Studies in Middle English Vision Poetry*. Norman, OK: University of Oklahoma Press.

Coffman, G. R. (1945). John Gower in his most significant role. In *Elizabethan Studies and Other Essays in Honor of George F. Reynolds* (pp. 52–61). Boulder: University of Colorado Press.

Coffman, G. R. (1954). John Gower, mentor for royalty: Richard II. *PMLA* 69, 953–64.

Coleman, Janet. (1981). *English Literature in History 1350–1400: Medieval Readers and Writers*. London: Hutchinson.

Coleman, Joyce. (1996). *Public Reading and the Reading Public in Late Medieval England*. Cambridge: Cambridge University Press.

Coleman, Joyce. (2002). Lay readers and hard Latin: how Gower may have intended the *Confessio Amantis* to be read. *Studies in the Age of Chaucer*, 24, 209–34.

Davie, D. (1967). *Purity of Diction in English Verse (Reissued with Post-Script)*. London: Routledge & Kegan Paul.

Echard, S. (2003). Gower's books of Latin: language, politics and poetry. *Studies in the Age of Chaucer*, 25, 123–56.

Echard, S. (ed.) (2004a). *A Companion to Gower*. Cambridge: D. S. Brewer.

Echard, S. (2004b). Last words: Latin at the end of the *Confessio Amantis*. In R. F. Green and L. Mooney (eds). *Interstices, Interstices: Studies in Anglo-Latin and Middle English Texts in Honour of A.G. Rigg*, 99–121. Toronto: University of Toronto Press.

Ferster, J. (1996). *Fictions of Advice: The Literature and Politics of Counsel in Late Medieval England*. Philadelphia: University of Pennsylvania Press.

Fisher, J. H. (1964). *John Gower: Moral Philosopher and Friend of Chaucer*. New York: New York UP.

Fouillade, Claude J. (1995). In William W. Kibler and Grover A. Zinn (eds). *Medieval France: An Encyclopedia*. New York: Garland.

Green, R. F. and L. Mooney (eds) (2004). *Interstices: Studies in Anglo-Latin and Middle English Texts in Honour of A.G. Rigg*. Toronto: University of Toronto Press.

Hélinand of Foidmont. (1905). *Les Vers de la Mort, par Hélinant, Moine de Froidmont*. Ed. F. Wulff and E. Walberg. Paris: Société d'Anciens Textes Français.

Jones, T., R. F. Yeager, T. Dolan, A. Fletcher and J. Dor (2003). *Who Murdered Chaucer? A Medieval Mystery*. London: Methuen.

Laidlaw, J. (1999). L'Innovation métrique chez Deschamps. In D. Buschinger (ed.). *Autour d'Eustace Deschamps: Actes du Colloque du Centre d'Études Médiévales de l'Université de Picardie-Jules Verne* (pp. 127–40). Amiens: Amiens University Press.

Lewis, C. S. (1936). *The Allegory of Love: A Study in Medieval Tradition*. London: Oxford University Press.

Machan, T. W. (2003). *English in the Middle Ages*. Oxford: Oxford University Press.

Middleton, A. (1978). The idea of public poetry in the reign of Richard II. *Speculum*, 53, 94–114.

Nicholson, P. (1984). John Gower's revisions in the 'Confessio Amantis'. *Chaucer Review*, 19, 123–43.

Nicholson, P. (1988). The dedications of John Gower's 'Confessio Amantis'. *Mediaevalia*, 10, 159–80.

Nicholson, P. (2005). *Love and Ethics in Gower's Confessio Amantis*. Ann Arbor: University of Michigan Press.

Pearsall, D. A. (2004). The manuscripts and illustrations of Gower's works. In S. Echard (ed.). *A Companion to Gower* (pp. 73–97). Cambridge: D. S. Brewer.

Peck, R. A. (1978). *Kingship and Common Profit in Gower's Confessio Amantis*. Carbondale, IL: University of Southern Illinois Press.

Sinnreich-Levy, B., ed. (1994). *Eustache Deschamps: L'Art de dictier*. Cambridge: Boydell & Brewer.

Wickert, M. (1953). *Studien zu John Gower*. Trans. R. J. Meindl (1982) as *Studies in John Gower*. Washington, DC: University Press of America.

Wimsatt, J. I. (1991). *Chaucer and His French Contemporaries: Natural Music in the Fourteenth Century*. Toronto: University of Toronto Press.

Yeager, I. A. (2010). Did John Gower love his wife – and what has it to do with the poetry? *Poetica* (Tokyo), forthcoming.

Yeager, R. F. (ed.) (1989). *John Gower: Recent Readings*. Kalamazoo, MI: Medieval Institute Press.

Yeager, R. F. (1990). *John Gower's Poetic: The Search for a New Arion*. Cambridge: D. S. Brewer.

Yeager, R. F. (2004). Gower's Lancastrian affinity: the Iberian connection. *Viator*, 35, 482–515.

Yeager, R. F. (2006). Gower's French audience: the *Mirour de l'Omme*. *Chaucer Review*, 41, 111–37.

Part III

Post-Chaucerian and Fifteenth-Century Poetry

Contexts
Poets and Poems

Contexts

27

England in the Long Fifteenth Century

Matthew Woodcock

It seems customary to preface any survey of the fifteenth century and its literature with exculpatory caveats, qualifications and definitions of terms. Although historians have long since dispatched the Whiggish notion that the century witnessed the wholesale 'waning' of the medieval period (Lander 1969: 11–18; Du Boulay 1970: 11–16), many questions remain about the remit and methodology of fifteenth-century studies. The concept of a 'long' fifteenth century itself, for example, may puzzle those unfamiliar with literary scholarship on the period, where it functions as an expedient shorthand means of sidestepping the awkward issue of distinguishing the late medieval from the early Renaissance. As Douglas Gray and the contributors to his appropriately titled *festschrift* have shown (Gray 1988; Cooper and Mapstone 1997), continuity in the form, tone and themes of late medieval literature can be traced into the first twenty or thirty years of the sixteenth century. One occasionally finds historical accounts of a short fifteenth century that terminates in 1485 with Henry VII's accession, suggesting that this date marks the end of the late Middle Ages (Jacob 1961; Rubin 2005). However, stretching the 'fifteenth century' from 1399 to 1509 – as is done in this essay – allows one to encompass both the deposition of Richard II, which had such enormous ramifications for decades to follow, and the reign of Henry VII.

Having confronted the vexed issue of periodisation, literary scholars approaching the fifteenth century must still negotiate a number of potentially distracting misconceptions. The first of these is the pervasive influence of Shakespeare's history plays, which provide an engaging, though perforce reductive outline of what has almost become the received view of the fifteenth century: a period of incessant war and rebellion in which few could have had time to concentrate on literary production and appreciation. As we shall see, Shakespeare inherits a tradition of propagandist historical writing that attempted to fashion successive monarchs into heroes and villains, and constructed the Tudor accession as a restorative to the century's chaos and disorder. Another misconception is the perceived 'inbetweeness' of the fifteenth century within English literary history: that it constitutes a dilatory phase between the better-known Ricardian poets and the works of Wyatt and Surrey. With the exception of Gray's *Oxford Book of Late Medieval Verse and Prose*, medieval literature anthologies – until very recently – perpetuated this view, implying there were few recognisable literary landmarks with which to navigate the period. Even now, author-based designations for different phases of the fifteenth century have failed to catch on; rarely do we encounter references to an 'Age' of Lydgate, Malory or Skelton akin to those of Chaucer and Shakespeare.

This essay does not pretend to provide a comprehensive overview of the period's political, social or economic history, for which one is served amply elsewhere (Keen 1990; Pollard 2000; Harriss 2005; Rubin 2005), but introduces key events, concepts and areas of debate relating to English history between 1399 and 1509 that inform the authors, works and forms discussed in the essays following this one. The emphasis here is on information and sources relevant to students of late medieval literature.

Lancastrian Legitimation

The fifteenth century began – ominously enough – with an attempt to kill a king and the successful murder of another. But to understand fully the context and significance of these events we have to look back to the final months of Richard II's reign. Following accusations of treason against Thomas Mowbray, Duke of Norfolk, and an abortive trial by combat in September 1398, Henry Bolingbroke, Earl of Derby, was exiled to France and within five months disinherited of the vast estate of his late father, the most powerful magnate in the land, John of Gaunt, Duke of Lancaster. Richard used the Lancaster windfall to fund (and lead) an Irish military expedition campaign in May 1399. Many of the English nobility feared that if Richard could appropriate the inheritance of one such as John of Gaunt he could easily confiscate their own possessions. They consequently supported Bolingbroke when he returned to England maintaining that he had come to regain what was rightly his. Bolingbroke's greater ambitions soon became clear when he headed for London to claim the crown itself. On his arrival from Ireland, Richard was tricked into surrendering to Henry and, now a prisoner, coerced into abdicating on 29 September 1399. Bolingbroke duly claimed the throne the following day and was crowned Henry IV on 13 October. As Paul Strohm has shown, in order to obfuscate any suggestion of usurpation, Henry conducted a concerted textual campaign that fabricated his descent from Henry III, maintained that he had acted through God's grace and confirmed that Richard had misgoverned the realm thus necessitating deposition (Strohm 1992: 75–94). Poets who had long lamented the failings of Richard's rule, and his abuse of nobles and commoners alike, now endorsed the new king. In 'To His Purse', Chaucer addressed Henry: 'O conquerour of Brutes Albyon / Which that by lyne and free eleccion / Been verray kyng' and Gower's *Chronica Tripertita* offered a similar legitimisation of Henry's divinely ordained title (Chaucer 1987: 656; Gower 1962: 311–26). Works such as the anonymous *Richard the Redeless* (*c.*1399) and its sequel *Mum and the Sothsegger* (*c.* 1409) used critique of Richard's government to proffer advice to Henry about good counsel and the political pitfalls to avoid. Not everyone was as convinced of Henry's legitimacy as Lancastrian propaganda averred and a group of Richard's supporters who had been pardoned at the accession plotted to kill the royal family at Windsor in January 1400. The conspirators were executed but the plot exposed the potential fragility of Henry's power and probably precipitated Richard's murder at Pontefract castle soon after. Richard was interred at King's Langley, Hertfordshire, without any form of state funeral.

Henry soon faced a series of rebellions by Scotland, Wales and the English nobility, particularly Henry Percy, Earl of Northumberland, and his son (also named Henry, though known as Hotspur). The Percys defeated the Scots at Homildon hill in 1402 but proceeded openly to oppose the king; Henry had set a tempting precedent for obtaining the crown through rebellion and usurpation. The Percy rebellions were put down at the Battle of Shrewsbury in 1403 and at Shipton Moor in 1405. The king's eldest son, Henry, was tasked meanwhile with subduing Owain Glyndwr's revolt in Wales. The prince proved more than capable of restoring order, and of acting in his father's stead after the king first became ill in 1406. By 1411 his rule (through the royal council) epitomised the kind of good government idealised by earlier critics of Ricardian politics and celebrated in Thomas Hoccleve's *Regiment of Princes*, written for the prince at this time. Absent from contemporary accounts of young Henry's formative years is any suggestion of the kind of riotous youth evoked on the sixteenth-century stage. Shakespeare presented Henry IV's reign as an anxious, insecure period beset by perpetual unrest and Lancastrian court culture was indeed especially sensitive to dissent and threats of usurpation that were galvanised periodically by rumours that Richard was still alive (Rubin 2005: 173–4).

Following the king's death in 1413, one of Henry V's first deeds was the ceremonial reburial of Richard at Westminster Abbey, simultaneously a penitential gesture and a signal that the former king was truly dead, a further example of what Strohm identifies as the 'symbolic enactment' of Lancastrian legitimacy (Strohm 1998: 2). Early biographies such as the *Gesta Henrici Quinti* (1417) and Thomas Elmham's *Liber Metricus* (1418) nevertheless stressed the sincerity of Henry's piety together with his conviction in his divinely confirmed right to rule. Henry was equally convinced of his right to assert a legitimate ancestral claim to the French throne based on the treaty of Brétigny (1360) that gave his great-grandfather Edward III sovereignty over Calais, Normandy and Aquitaine. Henry's French campaign of 1415 culminated in the celebrated victory at Agincourt and appeared to confirm for contemporaries the justice of the king's cause. He returned to France in 1417 with a committed intention to establish English garrisons and control; by 1419 he had conquered Normandy. In 1420 Henry established diplomatic accord with France and Burgundy through the treaty of Troyes by which he would marry Catherine (daughter of the French King Charles VI), and become regent during Charles' lifetime and heir to the French throne. Henry and Catherine's heir would then be king of England and France. Parliament objected to English monies being used to maintain what were perceived as essentially

French dynastic interests and Adam Usk's chronicle (*c*.1421) recorded scornfully the apparent 'extortion' of the English people to pay for the wars (Usk 1997: 270–71). However, unlike previous French campaigns, which had been little more than extended raids, Henry now sought to colonise Normandy and offered English knights the chance to acquire land and status overseas. Henry spent the remaining two years of his reign overseas fighting pockets of French resistance until shortly after capturing Meaux he died of dysentery on 31 August 1422. Henry's only heir, Henry VI, was less than a year old when he acceded to the throne under the protectorate of his uncle Humphrey, Duke of Gloucester. Henry VI's reign saw repeated challenges to his authority and title as king that culminated in the series of dynastic clashes now commonly known as the Wars of the Roses.

The End of the Hundred Years War and the Wars of the Roses

It is almost impossible to separate the mid-fifteenth-century dynastic conflict in England from the loss of English territory in France. Following several years of English military setbacks and French counter-attacks during the late 1420s the conquest of Normandy began to falter, and emboldened by Joan of Arc's relief of Orleans in May 1429, Charles VI's son, the Dauphin, was crowned Charles VII of France in Rheims in July the same year. Not for the last time was there a rival claimant for Henry VI's throne. Henry was himself crowned in England in November 1429 and in Paris in December 1431. The king's claim to the dual monarchy severely limited the ability to compromise or offer concessions of territory when negotiating with France and Burgundy during the 1430s, an all-or-nothing situation that reached its worst in 1435 when Burgundy allied with France, rejecting the Troyes treaty and Henry's authority. There was a measure of renewed hope in 1437 when Henry came of age and a number of texts soon appeared, including Lydgate's *Fall of Princes* and Tito Livio's *Life of Henry V* (both commissioned by Duke Humphrey), that attempted to shape the king into the mould of his father. Henry might have benefited more from returning to the lessons of Lydgate's earlier works of 1420–23, the *Troy Book* and *Siege of Thebes*, for as James Simpson suggests, the stories of two fallen cities both 'trace a history of chivalric and bureaucratic disaster that stands urgently in need of prudential wisdom devoted to purely secular ends' and anticipate the growing threat of contention between nobles surrounding the king (Simpson 2002: 56). Even with Henry now nominally in power, factionalism became entrenched and the political model for the reign was now firmly established: powerful, aspiring magnates surrounding a passive, pliable and inexperienced king, essentially a power vacuum.

Lack of sustained political and financial support saw the English continue to lose control of Normandy during the early 1440s. In May 1444 they were eventually compelled to agree to the truce of Tours, brokered by the Earl of Suffolk, whereby Henry was betrothed to Margaret of Anjou in exchange for ceding Anjou and Maine. The remaining English territory in France was left fatally exposed and within four years Charles VII's armies flexed their muscles and launched an attack on Normandy. The English were routed in less than a year and several thousand settlers who had obtained territory under Henry V were dispossessed and forced to return to England in a form of postcolonial diaspora. Suffolk was widely blamed for the losses in France and charged by the Commons with exploiting royal power for personal advantage. Henry intervened in May 1450 and exiled Suffolk for five years, though popular hatred towards him was such that he was murdered by mutinous sailors as he left for France. Further popular disturbances erupted and in June 1450 a group of rebels led by Kentishman Jack Cade marched on London calling for the removal of the corrupt ministers responsible for domestic and overseas misgovernment. Cade's rebellion was defeated on 6 July but perhaps their most provocative demand was that Henry should 'take about his noble person his true blood of his royal realm [...] the high and mighty prince the Duke of York, exiled from our sovereign lord's person by the noising of the false traitor the Duke of Suffolk and his affinity' (Tuck 1999: 264). Richard, Duke of York, was one of the most powerful magnates in the kingdom and, as a descendant of Edward III's fourth son, heir to the throne since Henry (until 1453) was childless. In September 1450 he returned from service in Ireland presenting himself as a champion of reform. Henry suffered a severe mental and physical collapse between 1453 and 1455, and York was made Protector. York used the period of temporary elevation to consolidate his position against the rival court faction of Edmund Beaufort, Duke of Somerset, who had occupied Suffolk's place in royal favour. The ducal power struggle reached its inevitable bloody con-clusion in St Albans in May 1455 when royalist forces clashed with the Yorkists, including York's new allies Richard Neville, Earl of Salisbury and his son Richard, Earl of Warwick. Henry was wounded and Somerset slain, though after the fighting York submitted himself to the king and escorted him to Westminster. York, never-theless, demonstrated that he had the might and ability to restore strong government to England.

By 1458, Henry's queen, Margaret of Anjou, emerged as the focal point for royalist – or at least anti-Yorkist – supporters. The first battle of the Wars of the Roses proper took place at Blore Heath, Staffordshire, on 23 September 1459, where Salisbury defeated a large Lancastrian army but left with sorely depleted forces who were caused to flee when confronted by another royalist army at Ludford three weeks later. York, his sons Edward (Earl of March) and Edmund (Earl of Rutland), Salisbury and Warwick managed to escape overseas and for nine months it seemed as if Lancastrian rule had been vindicated. The Yorkists were declared traitors and attainted, and their claim to be acting in England's interests was dismantled in one of the last Lancastrian propaganda tracts, the *Somnium Vigilantis* (Gilson 1911). The Yorkists renewed the offensive in June 1460 when Salisbury, Warwick and March landed in Kent and headed for London; the court, meanwhile, decamped to Coventry. John Scattergood cites a poem that was displayed on the gates of Canterbury welcoming the Yorkist leaders to illustrate how popular support for new political order was articulated (Scattergood 1971: 182–4; Robbins 1959: 207–10). After being welcomed into London on 2 July the Yorkists headed north to Northampton where they defeated the king's army on 10 July. A contemporary poem recounts the battle using an extended hunting conceit that alludes back to *The Master of Game* (*c.*1406–13), a treatise translated by York's father (Robbins 1959: 210–15). As Warwick and March returned south York himself landed and processed to London with all of the pomp and posturing of royalty and once at Westminster it was clear he had come to make himself king. The lords refused to withdraw their allegiance to Henry but agreed to recognise York as Henry's heir, thus disinheriting the king's son, Edward.

Margaret and the remaining Lancastrians refused, however, to accept the agreement and planned their counter-attack. When York and Salisbury faced the Lancastrian army at Wakefield on 30 December the tables were now turned: the Yorkists were outnumbered and the duke and his son, Rutland, were slain. The duke's head was displayed over the city gates of York bearing a paper crown. The Lancastrians achieved another victory at St Albans on 17 March 1461 and recovered the king. The Earl of March, now heir to the throne, meanwhile responded decisively to Wakefield and after defeating the Earl of Pembroke at Mortimer's Cross returned hastily to London where he was warmly received by the citizenry. Claiming that Henry had broken the Westminster agreement and set himself in opposition to the government of the realm, the nineteen-year-old son of York took possession of the crown and kingdom on 4 March as Edward IV. By the end of the month he had assembled another army and delivered a decisive, bloody victory for the Yorkists at Towton on 29 March. Edward was crowned three months later; Henry and Margaret fled to Scotland. Yorkist propaganda now proceeded to establish the kind of providential narrative structure, used thereafter by Shakespeare and others, that cast the Lancastrian usurpation as an injury to England itself and the cause of subsequent misrule, as Edward's 1461 parliamentary declaration of title also made explicit (Pollard 2000: 2–3). The poem 'Edward, Dei Gratia' written following the coronation endorsed Edward's hereditary title, suggesting that 'Out of þe stoke that longe lay dede/ God hathe causede the to sprynge & sprede'. 'A Political Retrospect' (1462) went further and sought to efface the legitimacy of the three Lancastrian Henries' rule, outlining the harm caused to England during their reigns and praising the restoration of order: 'iij kynges have regned by erroure, / The thred put ouȝt & the right brought agayne, / Whos absence hath caused endleȝ langoure' (Robbins 1959: 221–4).

The Lancastrian dynasty was defeated but the crown's struggles with over-mighty subjects continued through the 1460s as tensions grew between Edward and his ally Warwick. Edward's marriage to Elizabeth Woodville in 1464, and the swift rise of her family at court, aroused Warwick's jealousy and was interpreted as a snub to the power behind the king's throne. Aided by Edward's brother George, Duke of Clarence, Warwick shifted allegiance to Margaret and Henry, and in September 1470 landed at Dartmouth with a French-backed army and put Edward to flight with alarming speed. While Edward fled to Burgundy, Henry was restored to the throne, though neither he nor Warwick now garnered popular support. Henry VI's 'readeption' lasted little over six months and Edward returned to England in March 1471, seized Henry and then moved north to meet Warwick's forces at Barnet. On 14 April Edward achieved another great victory and Warwick was killed. Margaret and the remaining Lancastrians meanwhile arrived from France and, at Tewkesbury on 4 May, the armies of York and Lancaster clashed once more; again Edward won the field. Henry's son was killed, Margaret surrendered and the majority of the Yorkists' principal enemies were now defeated. Edward entered London in triumph on 21 May and the same day ordered that the last of the Lancastrian line should be eliminated. Henry was murdered in the Tower of London and subsequently buried at Chertsey Abbey. Many historians have placed much of the blame for the mid-fifteenth-century catastrophes in England and France firmly on Henry VI's personal ineptitude, political weakness and general disinterest in affairs of state (McFarlane 1973: 120–21). But this does not necessarily mean that all of his subjects wished to see him deposed, and indeed a popular cult soon formed about his person casting him as saintly figure who sought reconciliation and social peace (Pollard 2000: 159). Though disapproved of by the king, Henry's cult flourished during Edward IV's reign and was actively promoted by Richard III and Henry VII (Freeman 2005). John Blacman wrote a hagiographic account of Henry in 1483–4 and his image often appeared alongside other celebrated saintly English monarchs as, for example, on the rood screen at St Michael's church, Barton Turf, Norfolk.

The civil war of 1459–71 was never known to contemporaries as the Wars of the Roses; the term only became established after its use in Sir Walter Scott's 1829 novel *Anne of Geierstein*. Although the Yorkists were identified by the badge of the white rose, the Lancastrians only adopted the red rose intermittently, and Shakespeare's scene in *1 Henry VI* of rival parties selecting their emblems in the Temple garden is purely fictional. One should also be wary of automatically accepting Yorkist and Tudor propaganda that emphasised the scale of the horrors of the Wars of the Roses when fashioning their narratives of providentially restored order. The period of active campaigning between 1455 and 1487 (the Battle of Stoke; see below) amounted to around thirteen weeks (Lander 1969: 162). The armies themselves were often hastily mustered and small in size, even at decisive encounters such as St Albans and Wakefield. By far the largest battle was Towton, where contemporaries numbered the combatants at 28,000 (Harriss 2005: 645). England was not in anarchy nor subjected to the kind of pillage and desecration suffered in contemporary France or during the seventeenth-century English civil wars. The uncertain political climate and continued magnate power struggles nevertheless find their way into mid-fifteenth-century literary texts. John Metham in *Amoryus and Cleopes* (1449) wondered whether the 'encreasing of vexation' in England during the 1440s had curtailed the composition of new chivalric romances (Cooper 1999: 695). It is also difficult not to compare the destructive factionalism found in Thomas Malory's *Morte Darthur* (*c*. 1470) with the contemporary political situation, and the author himself highlighted this point for his readers (Malory 1971: 708). The Wars of the Roses also have an undeniable presence in the private correspondence of the Stonor and Paston families.

Richard III and the Tudor Accession

Critics and historians studying either Richard III or Henry VII must negotiate a welter of both demonising representations of the former and eulogising accounts of the latter dating from the very start of the Tudor accession in 1485. Both figures exhibit how the fifteenth century is lengthened, in a fashion, through the longevity of the received view of events leading up to the Battle of Bosworth. Much of Richard's infamy derives from the issue of what happened to the twelve-year-old heir to Edward IV's throne, Edward V, and his brother the Duke of York. Edward IV died on 9 April 1483 leaving the country to reel again in shock at the prospect of renewed instability under another boy-king. A contemporary poem on Edward's passing offered a series of *ubi sunt* laments about his reign but remained ominously silent about what lay ahead (Robbins 1959: 111–13). Rather than making the late king's brother Richard, Duke of Gloucester, Protector, it was decided that Edward V be crowned immediately and the young king was escorted from Ludlow to London. Fearing for their prospects in Edward's court, which was now to be dominated by the Woodvilles (the family of Edward IV's widow), Richard and the Duke of Buckingham intercepted the king en route and escorted him to London themselves. Richard was appointed Protector and, seeking to consolidate control during the minority, imprisoned the Woodvilles. Richard's coup had won him power and removed his opponents but he now went further and on 13 June during a council meeting at the Tower he suddenly had his former ally William Hastings arrested and summarily executed on allegations of treason. Richard then arranged for it to be publicised that Edward V and his brother were illegitimate, and thus ineligible to rule, since Edward IV was already promised to someone else when he married Elizabeth Woodville. There were also earlier charges concerning Edward IV's own bastardy. On 25 June a deputation of London lords and gentlemen petitioned Richard to assume the throne. He duly accepted the following day and was crowned on 6 July. The deposed Edward and his brother had been detained in the Tower for all of this time, though at some point between mid-June and mid-September 1483 they were murdered, almost certainly at Richard's behest. He had surely learned the dangers of leaving potential heirs alive from his father's interrupted reign. Rumours of the boys' deaths circulated quickly and an Italian envoy, Dominic Mancini, wrote about widespread suspicions over their disappearance in his report on Richard's 'occupation' of the throne compiled during 1483 (Pollard 2000: 332).

Richard toured the country on progress after his coronation attempting to demonstrate continuity between Edward IV's stable government and his own regime. But Richard's rapid rise to power again proved to ambitious magnates what might be achieved through decisive action. Acting on rumours of the deaths of the princes in the Tower, Richard's enemies – both diehard Lancastrians and disaffected Yorkists – looked to Henry Tudor, Earl of Richmond, as the most credible alternative contender for the throne. He had spent thirteen years exiled in Brittany after escaping the field at Tewkesbury and had a dual, albeit relatively weak, title as the son of Edmund

Tudor and Margaret Beaufort (great-granddaughter of John of Gaunt), and grandson of Henry V's widow Catherine. In October 1483 Buckingham led an ill-conceived revolt against Richard intended to install Richmond to the throne, though he was defeated within a month and Richmond – who had attempted to land at Poole – returned to Brittany where he was betrothed to Edward IV's daughter Elizabeth on 25 December. Neither Richard nor his enemies saw the failure of Buckingham's revolt as the end to further invasion plans and the king's lineal isolation was compounded in April 1484 when his only son died, to be followed by his wife less than a year later. In November 1484 the French government recognised Richmond's claim to the English throne and promised backing, and from this point Richard prepared for another confrontation.

Richmond landed at Milford Haven on 7 August 1485 with approximately 1000 men. He gathered troops as he marched through Wales and Shropshire and gained muted support from Lord Thomas Stanley and his brother William. Richard moved quickly to meet Richmond in battle and thus prove his right to rule, and the armies finally met near Market Bosworth, Leicestershire, on 22 August. Michael Jones's revisionist study of Bosworth situates the battle on a plain to the north-east of Atherstone, Warwickshire, and also draws attention to how Richard enacted a ritual re-consecration of his authority before battle – effectively a second coronation – demonstrating to his followers his conviction that as England's true king, surrounded by experienced allies, he would dismiss the *arriviste* challenger (Jones 2002: 146–62). Richmond's army, by comparison, was a mixture of nationalities and mainly mercenaries. In the event, professionalism, tactics and politicking won the day over ceremony: many of Richard's supporters hesitated to commit themselves and so when Richard sighted Richmond and charged to meet him in person he was left exposed. Richmond's Swiss-trained pikemen halted the cavalry whilst Stanley, finally siding with Richmond, cut Richard down; he was the last English king to die in battle. Richmond was proclaimed King Henry VII as Richard's body was taken for burial at Leicester.

Work now began on authenticating and consolidating Henry's title. At his first parliament he declared that his right to rule was confirmed by victory in battle and then dated his reign from 21 August so he could attaint Richard and his followers for treason. Henry's marriage to Elizabeth of York on 18 January 1486 provided Tudor propagandists with their most effective image: the reconciliation of the warring Yorkist and Lancastrian factions symbolised by iconographic union of the white and red roses. Henry's Lancastrian lineage (via John of Gaunt) was tenuous but he emphasised his political, moral and onomastic connections with Henry VI (King 1989: 23–31). Repetition of the myth and image of union substantiated its veracity. It appeared in the entry pageant at York in April 1486; in celebratory contemporary verse such as 'The Roses Entwined', which looks ahead to offspring of the union (Robbins 1959: 94–5); and remained a fixture of Tudor propaganda into the sixteenth century, witness the magnificent 1550 title-page of Edward Hall's chronicle. The composite Tudor rose embodied the notion that Henry's accession was a natural, restorative deliverance of the kingdom; this was certainly the view perpetuated by early panegyricists such as Bernard André and Polydore Vergil. Henry also began to negotiate the relative innovation of the Tudors by tracing the royal house's genealogy back through the line of British kings (drawing on Geoffrey of Monmouth's *Historia Regum Britanniae*) to Arthur, Cadwallader and Brutus, the mythical founder of Britain (Anglo 1992: 40–60). Henry bore Cadwallader's red dragon standard at Bosworth to stress the Tudors' Welsh descent whilst the Arthurian provenance informed the choice of name for Henry's eldest son, and was used extensively by subsequent Tudor monarchs (Simpson 2002: 296–300; Summers 1997).

Henry's aggrandisement was complemented by systematic denigration of Richard's character and Tudor chroniclers were quick to portray the late king as a tyrant; Henry's usurpation was thus repackaged as revenge for unholy transgression. John Rous's *Historia regum Anglie* (1486) compared Richard to the Antichrist 'confounded at his moment of greatest pride'. Rous also suggested that Richard's moral monstrosity was reflected physically by contriving that he was 'retained within his mother's womb for two years and emerging with teeth and hair to his shoulders [...] and unequal shoulders, the right higher and the left lower' (Hanham 1975: 120–21, 123). Sir Thomas More elaborated Rous's construction in his *History of King Richard the Third* (1513) and it was this crook-backed figure that entered popular currency through later sixteenth-century chronicle and dramatic sources. Contemporary portraits make no suggestion of deformity (though some were altered later to do so), and nor do extant records of Richard's coronation, where he all but stripped to the waist for anointing (Sutton and Hammond 1983: 221).

Following a by-now familiar pattern, the Tudor usurper soon found his own position assailed. Margaret of Burgundy, sister of Edward IV and Richard III, refused to accept Henry's title. With Burgundian support she promoted the rival cause of Edward, Earl of Warwick, son of her late brother Clarence. Henry held Warwick prisoner but the conspirators had a man named Lambert Simnel imitate his identity to serve as a rallying-point for their allies and he was 'crowned' Edward VI in Ireland. By 1487, the conspirators, now led by the Earl of Lincoln, had gathered an army hoping to emulate Henry's vindication of title through arms but they were summarily defeated at Stoke on 16 June. A further attempt to advance an impostor's cause occurred in 1493 when one Perkin Warbeck assumed the role of Richard, Duke of York, one of the murdered princes in the Tower. He was fêted in Ireland, France and Scotland as an exiled monarch for four years and eventually attempted to use an uprising in Cornwall in 1497 to his advantage. The uprising was defeated within two months; Warbeck confessed he was an impostor and executed in 1499. The somewhat picaresque nature of Warbeck's rise and fall belies the fact that, for over a decade, Henry's regime still seemed susceptible to speculative or implausible opportunistic counter-claims. By the early years of the sixteenth century, however, Henry had consolidated his position greatly: the 1492 treaty of Étaples with France established peace between the kingdoms and enriched royal coffers through agreed payments of £5000 per year (Pollard 2000: 359); he established more centralised administrative, executive and judicial structures; and he negotiated the marriages of his daughter

Margaret to James IV of Scotland and his heir Arthur to the Spanish Infanta Catherine of Aragon. The issue of whether Arthur and Catherine consummated their marriage would haunt Tudor politics long after Arthur's death on 2 April 1502 and that of Henry on 21 April 1509.

Social Structure and Mobility

The structure of medieval society had long been conceived using various different models, the best known being the division into three 'estates': the nobility, the clergy and the commons. This was obviously an idealised configuration that particularly served the interests of the ruling classes since it was accompanied by the implication that one should acknowledge and retain one's place in a structure that was essentially divinely ordained, as writers such as Langland, Gower and Lydgate maintained (Scattergood 1971: 271–4). Even by 1400 the model seemed strained: the ecclesiastical estate had always been a mirror of secular society operating with its own broad hierarchy, and the commons was more a residual grouping for all that fell outside the other two (Rigby 1995: 190–91). One early fifteenth-century poem divided society into five: 'Riche comouns, and wyse clergy; / Marchaundes, squyers, chiualry' (Kail 1904: 11). Many writers offering literary advice for princes proposed alternate models predicating a more reciprocal interdependence between classes based on Aristotelian ideas of the body politic. The king is clearly the head in this model, ruling over, but still part of, the body of society. A verse elaboration of this model in Bodleian Library, MS Digby 102 dating from Henry IV's reign presents the nobility as the shoulders and backbone, merchants as the thighs ('Þat beren þe body quantite'), the legs as craftsmen and feet as ploughmen (Kail 1904: 64–9). George Ashby's poem *The Active Policy of a Prince* (1463), written for Henry VI's son, calls to mind the disastrous mid-century governance of the realm and suggests a more balanced, cautious appeasement of subjects: encourage them to prosper but subdue all rebellion ruthlessly (Ashby 1899: 25–7). Sir John Fortescue's treatise *The Governance of England* (1471) proposed that England was best served by limited rather than absolute monarchy: by a monarch ruling through the laws of the realm exercised through the legislature and executive (Fortescue 1997: 83–90). Henry VI's reign had shown, however, the inherent weakness of a political system reliant to any degree on the person of the king.

Both the estates and body politic models are still essentially hierarchical and offer an unrepresentatively static picture of fifteenth-century society. The Black Death of the mid-fourteenth century had reduced England's inhabitants by nearly a half. It was indiscriminate regarding social status but had particularly affected the young, meaning that the ageing population – around 2.5 million in 1377 – had difficulty replacing itself and may have declined further during the fifteenth century (Harriss 2005: 218). For those left alive, however, there were many opportunities as land became available, the value of labour (and thus wages) increased, and the consequent rise in disposable incomes boosted production of foodstuffs, housing and household items such as textiles (Pollard 2000: 182). There was also a rapid shift between 1380 and 1430 from the manorial control over rural labour based on servile obligation of serfs to their lord to cash-based rent tenancies. Living standards amongst the peasantry rose, as did life expectancy: from 30 years in 1400 to 35 years by 1450 (Harriss 2005: 239). The fifteenth century saw the rise of a peasant 'aristocracy', a yeoman class of those holding land of around sixty acres or more who employed others to work for them. Landholders were still vulnerable to the incessant challenges to tenurial ownership common in medieval land law. The Paston letters bear witness to medieval litigiousness but also represent one of the best examples of social advancement from the yeomanry. The son of Clement Paston, a husbandman holding a watermill and some land in late-fourteeenth-century Norfolk, pursued a highly successful career in law that enabled him to purchase manorial estates and by the 1440s enter the ranks of the local gentry; Clement's great-grandson was knighted for fighting at Stoke in 1487. Sensitivity remained about the family's lowly origins, as when Margaret Paston was harangued in 1448 by another *nouveau riche* landowner who claimed 'the Pastons and all their kin were churls of Gimingham' (Castor 2004: 38–40).

The period saw the rise of a similar yeoman class of craftsmen and traders in towns, in which we might locate Margery Kempe's abortive ventures in brewing and horse-milling. But fifteenth-century urban culture was dominated increasingly by the richer merchant dynasties whose members formed the upper echelons of the craft guilds that came to exert greater regulation over social, commercial and religious aspects of civic life, and who were instrumental in organising the great dramatic cycles in towns such as York and Chester. Greater connections between the mercantile class and county gentry now developed, as one reads of in the correspondence from the 1470s and 1480s of the London-based wool-merchants, the Cely family (Hanham 1986). The fifteenth century saw a transition in English trade from an emphasis on the export of raw materials, particularly wool, to an economy based on finished goods, especially cloth (Pollard 2000: 179–80). Cloth exports rose from 40,000 pieces per year in 1420 to the upper 50,000s in 1437–47; wool exports in the same period fell to below 10,000 sacks annually from 1430 (Harriss 2005: 256). England's export trade inspired the author of a curious poem called *The Libelle of Englyshe Polycye* (1436) – 'libel' meaning treatise – to eulogise native wool and berate foreign merchants' chicanery. The cloth trade was less regulated than the wool trade and taxed far less. It also employed far more people because there are multiple stages in the production process, all of which were usually coordinated by the retailing merchant (Keen 1990: 82). The industry of whole communities was devoted to cloth production in towns such as Lavenham and Castle Combe, and the cloth trade enriched and enlarged cities like Bristol, Norwich and Coventry, as well as London. Wool obviously remained at the heart of cloth production and stimulated a major shift in the fifteenth century from arable to pasture farming. Sheep farming had the attraction of lower costs than tillage, simply requiring the enclosure of land and eviction of tenants. Nottinghamshire merchant John Barton acknowledged the source of his prosperity in lines inscribed over the door of his house: 'I thank God and ever shall / It is the sheep hath payed for all' (Scattergood 1971: 331). Not everyone was so fortunate, however. Rural degeneration through enclosures became widespread and continued into the sixteenth century; witness More's comments in *Utopia* (1516) about sheep devouring humans (More 1992: 12–13).

Commerce was not the only means of social elevation to the gentry during the fifteenth century. By this point the word 'gentilman' denoted a member of a broad group of those below the status of knight, 'the defining criterion for which was probably the exercise of lordship over land and men through the possession of a manor and court' (Harriss 2005: 137). As the Paston letters attest, the law offered excellent opportunities for acquiring land, so much so that William Worcester's *Boke of Noblesse* (1471) complains of how those practised in law now administering local justice are more esteemed than gentlemen who spent thirty or forty years fighting in the wars (Worcester 1972: 76–8). Lawyers invited the perennial accusations of avarice and corruption, and the typical misfortunes that might beset a provincial person coming to London seeking legal redress are evoked wonderfully in the anonymous *London Lickpenny* (*c.* 1410), which anticipates the commonplaces of sixteenth-century coney-catching literature (Robbins 1959: 130–34). Marriage was also a way of gaining land, yet usually only if one first possessed land of one's own. Military service provided a route for advancement across the social scale and a sound basis for long-running noble patronage. Linked to this was the concept of 'bastard feudalism' whereby the nobility rewarded service in their retinue with payment and the issue of liveries, a practice widely abused in the period and frequently restricted by monarchs and censured by writers (Keen 1990: 22–3; Scattergood 1971: 311–16). Estate management and secretarial duties for the nobility and crown offered some hopes for elevation, though as Hoccleve laments in *La Male Regle* (*c.* 1406), this could be a frustrating path.

One finds frequent indications of increasing class consciousness throughout the fifteenth century in measures such as the 1413 Statute of Additions specifying that all legal indictments should give the parties' status or occupation, or the 1429 legislation establishing that only those with forty shillings of freehold land could elect parliamentary shire representatives. Peter Idley's verse *Instructions to his Son* (*c.* 1445–50) lamented that nowadays 'a man shall not know a knave from a knight, for all be alike in clothing and array' (Pollard 2000: 185), sentiments implicit in the 1463 sumptuary law that sought to restrict what one could wear depending on one's income level. Alongside texts offering advice to princes, a number of works such as *The Book of Curtasye* (*c.* 1460) and *Babees Book* (1475) attempted to instruct the nobility and their children in matters of etiquette, discipline and practice. John Russell's *Boke of Nurture* (*c.* 1440–50) provided a detailed verse conspectus of social ranks for servants of the nobility based on his own experience attending Humphrey, Duke of Gloucester. Class consciousness was equally prevalent at the top of the social scale, particularly with fifteenth-century first-generation nobility such as Lord Ralph Cromwell and Sir John Fastolf, both of whom displayed their new status through major building projects at Tattershall and Caister.

English society was also increasingly imagined and represented at a national level. Although some historians maintain that the concept of nationhood is more the product of post-Enlightenment thinking, one nevertheless finds a national consciousness developing during the fifteenth century. Richard II's deposition precipitated a more insular, less cosmopolitan court culture in the early years of the century (Rubin 2005: 185) and events of Henry V's reign further enhanced awareness of a distinct sense of English national identity. At the ecclesiastical Council of Constance in 1417, a statement issued on Henry's authority asserting England's continued recognition alongside other international deputations maintained that it was both a common language and the dominance of that language in a territory that distinguished a nation, an argument then used to justify dominion over Scotland, Wales and Ireland. Ongoing hostilities with France stimulated a more patriotic outlook that manifested itself in many ways, and from 1416 Henry used English in all official proclamations and informal correspondence. Patricia Ingham suggests that the prolonged hostilities with France prompted renewed interest in Arthurian literature, enabling the nobility to sever dynastic ties to the French and claim their own 'insular heritage' (Ingham 2001: 6). One also finds an economic nationalism advanced in the *Libelle of Englyshe Polycye*, centred on the nation's geographical insularity, and encouraging England to rule the waves if it is to prosper (Warner 1926: 1). Perceptions of national identity could be amplified in relation to difference, and there were sizeable foreign merchant communities (predominantly German, Italian and Flemish) in English ports, particularly London. Such perceptions were also intensified through contact with the conquered cultures of Ireland and Wales and policed through statutes proscribing linguistic, social and legal interactions with the subjects of each. Fascination with national differences is, nevertheless, hard to resist and in 1457 John Paston received a letter about the trial in Hereford of some Welsh border gentry that set out names of those involved so he might 'see and laugh at their Welsh names descended of old pedigrees' (Griffiths 2003: 3).

Lollardy

With its roots in the fourteenth century and an afterlife in the sixteenth, the heretical movement known as Lollardy offers another example of a 'long' fifteenth-century concept. Origins of the word 'Lollardy' are contested, and it has etymological roots relating to mumbling and idleness, but it first appears as a derogatory term denoting a specific heretical sect as early as 1382 (Hudson 1988: 2). Many Ricardian poets had criticised perceived abuses in the late medieval Church but it was the theories and writings of the Oxford theologian John Wyclif that formed the basis of the first English heresy. During the late 1370s and early 1380s Wyclif's works systematically interrogated and denounced the limitations, abuses and errors of orthodox theology and Church government. Wyclif began by condemning the institutional Church's ownership of goods, arguing that ecclesiastical property contradicted Christ's teachings that the clergy should live in simplicity and poverty (Justice 1999: 665). He went on to attack more theological principles and denounced the concept of transubstantiation, where the Eucharistic bread and wine actually 'become' the body and blood of Christ. Wyclif also rejected the hearing of confession, the proliferation of images in churches, saints' cults, pilgrimages, in fact any expression of worship predicated upon the established Church's intermediary or interpretative role.

By the time Wyclif died in 1384 his ideas had taken root with the popular laity and at court, and were soon taken up and promoted further by his followers. In 1395 a Lollard manifesto known as the *Twelve Conclusions* was posted on the doors of Westminster Hall, reasserting Wyclif's ideas concerning the Church's temporal excesses. Wyclif had maintained that the only true authority was the Bible itself, and insisted that Scripture and debate on Scripture be accessible to all through vernacular translation. The laity's stake in theological debate was one of the central planks of Lollardy and the movement was hugely instrumental in propagating the development of the English language as the medium for spiritual and intellectual debate. The prologue to the Lollard Bible made clear that one should engage with Scripture firsthand without mediation or exegesis from the clergy; over 250 copies survive, as do nearly 300 Lollard sermons and commentaries in English. These were the product of what amounted to Lollard 'schools' and scriptoria, and evidence for their existence re-appears throughout the fifteenth century and beyond until the eve of the Reformation (Hudson 1988: 174–227). Lollardy also found support amongst the nobility and court. Wyclif himself received patronage and protection from John of Gaunt, who was receptive to Lollard ideas on disendowing the Church. A contemporary chronicler, Henry Knighton, also identified a distinct group of Lollard knights at Richard II's court (who may have posted the *Twelve Conclusions*), several of whom retained their positions into the fifteenth century (Knighton 1995: 294–5).

During Henry IV's reign moves were made to persecute and punish Lollardy in earnest under the aegis of Thomas Arundel, Archbishop of Canterbury. In 1401 Arundel persuaded the new king – whom he had supported in 1399 – to pass the statute *De Heretico Comburendo* authorising the burning of relapsed heretics; in the same year, William Sawtry was the first English Lollard to be burnt. As Strohm argues, the statute allied state power with that of the Church and, in turn, provided the Lancastrians with religious authority for prosecuting secular and political transgression (Strohm 1998: 32–62). Arundel's attempts to eradicate Lollardy intensified in 1409 when he issued the *Constitutions* forbidding the teaching and discussion of Wycliffite matter and the translation of the Bible into English. It also imposed draconian surveillance measures on sermons and literary production by requiring licensing for all preaching and prohibiting the translation of Scripture in any book, pamphlet or treatise without episcopal approval, upon penalty of excommunication. This condemned a potentially vast amount of English religious writing, and Nicholas Watson argues that Arundel's *Constitutions* may have restricted the imaginative range of fifteenth-century vernacular religious literature (Watson 1995). Margery Kempe fell foul of the strictures against public preaching and was questioned by Arundel himself in 1413 (Kempe 2000: 109–12). The Lollards responded to Arundel with a treatise, *The Lantern of Light* (*c.* 1409–15), condemning the *Constitutions* and translating Scripture widely.

In January 1414 a former friend of Henry V, Sir John Oldcastle, instigated an uprising in London, planning to kidnap and kill the king and his brothers. The rebellion was swiftly quelled and those involved executed for treason, though Oldcastle himself was only apprehended and burnt in 1417. The uprising prompted several condemnations in verse. 'Defend Us from All Lollardy' (*c.* 1414–17) censures Oldcastle's actions though it makes little attempt to understand any detail of the Lollards' arguments (Robbins 1959: 152–7). Hoccleve's *Address to Sir John Oldcastle* (1415) tries to pacify the knight by suggesting he 'Clymbe no more in holy writ so hie' but read more appropriate works of chivalric romance (Hoccleve 1892: 14). Strohm questions the level of threat that the Lollards actually presented but the incident provided Henry with an opportunity early in his reign to consolidate his position as a pious, orthodox ruler and an unassailable political power (Strohm 1998: 63–86). Oldcastle's uprising reified for Henry the analogy between heresy and sedition (Aston 1960). Lollardy never had a fixed creed or set of tenets with which all those acknowledging (or accused of) partisanship might be identified, but it served as an expedient catch-all term – comparable to the word 'terror' in twenty-first-century politics – for a broad range of perceived injuries against the Church and state.

After 1414 any remaining support for Lollardy amongst the nobility withered and the movement was driven underground. Evidence of fifteenth-century Lollardy derives largely from trial documents, and there are records of periodic persecutions of local sects in Norwich between 1428 and 1431, in the Thames valley and Chilterns in the 1460s, in Berkshire during the 1480s and 1490s and at Coventry at the turn of the century (Hudson 1988: 446–72). Trial documentation makes frequent reference to female Lollard activity throughout the period and suggests that women were active readers and teachers (Keen 1990: 295). Lollardy also occasioned contemporary textual defences of orthodoxy. Reginald Pecock, bishop of Chichester, attempted to confute the logic of the Lollards' arguments by appealing to logic and reason in a series of English treatises, including the *Repressor of Over Much Blaming of the Clergy* (1455). Unfortunately, Pecock's works became contentious themselves through their reiteration of Lollard arguments and advocacy of vernacular debate; he was charged with heresy in 1457 and forced to recant. Simpson discusses how Nicholas Love's *Mirror of the Blessed Life of Jesus Christ* (*c.* 1410) and John Capgrave's *Life of St Katherine* (*c.* 1445) offered more successful responses to Lollardy by grounding themselves in orthodoxy and eschewing theological controversy (Simpson 2002: 420–29, 477–8). Lollard ideas on theology, disendowment and translation obviously anticipated the central principles of the sixteenth-century English and Continental Reformations, and were conceived by reformist historiographers like John Foxe as proto-Protestantism. Anne Hudson suggests that wider literacy and the advent of the printing press, together with royal endorsement, underpinned the more lasting success of the sixteenth-century Reformations (Hudson 1988: 510–14).

One should be cautious of approaching the fifteenth century teleologically and of detecting antecedents of later concepts and developments at every turn, as with Lollardy and Protestantism. There is a temptation to identify in the long fifteenth century the intellectual foundations of the 'new learning', or 'humanism', that is so often treated as a defining characteristic of the early English Renaissance. With origins in late fourteenth-century Italian thought and studies, humanism placed great emphasis on the potential of individual human beings as works of divine creation and on the application of education, rhetoric and textual study. Educational provision in England did expand during the fifteenth century. There was widespread institution and endowment of local grammar and chantry schools, and in 1441 Henry VI founded Eton College. At university level many new colleges were founded: at Cambridge, King's College in 1441 (conceived in concert with Eton), Queens' College (1448), St Catherine's (1473) and Jesus College (1496); at Oxford, Lincoln College (1429), All Souls College (1438) and Magdalen College (1448). University education nevertheless remained oriented towards the training of clergy throughout the century, although law degrees grew in popularity, as did legal training at the London Inns of Court. The foundation statutes for the new colleges remind us of their fundamentally re-ligious character and foreground their function as defenders of orthodoxy (Lincoln College, Oxford was established specifically to combat Lollardy) and as chantries responsible for praying for the benefactors' souls, like All Souls, Oxford. There were exceptions and in 1439 a London rector, William Bingham, established God's House (later Christ's College, Cambridge) with specific stipulations that lectures should concentrate on Latin language and literature to prepare masters to teach (Simon 1967: 45). William Waynflete propounded similar regulations for Magdalen College, Oxford though it was figures educated at Magdalen during the late fifteenth century, such as John Colet, Richard Fox and Thomas Wolsey, who would have a greater impact on the cultivation of humanist studies in England during the early sixteenth century. Even by the late fifteenth century universities were still conservative in outlook and offered few of the opportunities to engage with, for example, critical and historical study of Scripture in original texts as was practised in contemporary Italian universities (Simon 1967: 52–3).

Humanist scholarship nevertheless had a presence in England during the fifteenth century within noble households and at court. Humphrey, Duke of Gloucester, funded scholars travelling to Italy and amassed his own collection of classical and Italian humanist texts that later formed the basis of the Bodleian library at Oxford. Duke Humphrey was also a great patron during the 1430s and 1440s of Continental humanists such as Tito Livio (biographer of Henry V) and Antonio Beccaria (Weiss 1967; Saygin 2002). John Tiptoft, Earl of Worcester, served and studied in Italy between 1459 and 1461, translated classical texts and likewise left his books to Oxford. After something of a hiatus during Henry VI's majority and the Wars of the Roses, the court became a significant centre of cultural patronage under Edward IV and Henry VII, a pattern that became firmly established under the later Tudors. Henry commissioned scholars like the historian Polydore Vergil and poet Pietro

Carmeliano to ennoble the Tudor title and celebrate its perpetuation. But as Alistair Fox observes, humanist scholars such as More, Erasmus and Colet, who had far more interest in educational change than the visiting Italians, had to wait until Henry VIII's accession in 1509 to gain courtly patronage and influence (Fox 1989: 18–19). The point at which an indigenous humanist tradition begins to establish itself at the Tudor court – and achieves the kind of intellectual critical mass that was earlier found (and proved so inspiring) in fifteenth-century Italy – is a signal moment in English literary and cultural history but also a fitting place at which to conclude an examination of the late medieval period; the long fifteenth century is surely long enough.

References and Further Reading

Anglo, Sydney (1992). *Images of Tudor Kingship*. London: Seaby.

Ashby, George (1899). *Poems*. Ed. Mary Bateson. Early English Text Society, e.s. 76. London: Kegan Paul.

Aston, M. E. (1960). Lollardy and sedition, 1381–1431. *Past and Present*, 17, 1–44.

Castor, Helen (2004). *Blood and Roses: The Paston Family and the Wars of the Roses*. London: Faber.

Chaucer, Geoffrey (1987). *The Riverside Chaucer*. Ed. Larry D. Benson. Oxford: Oxford University Press.

Cooper, Helen (1999). Romance after 1400. In David Wallace (ed.). *The Cambridge History of Medieval English Literature* (pp. 690–719). Cambridge: Cambridge University Press.

Cooper, Helen and Sally Mapstone (eds) (1997). *The Long Fifteenth Century: Essays for Douglas Gray*. Oxford: Clarendon Press.

Du Boulay, F. R. H. (1970). *An Age of Ambition: English Society in the Late Middle Ages*. London: Nelson.

Fortescue, Sir John (1997). *On the Laws and Governance of England*. Ed. Shelley Lockwood. Cambridge: Cambridge University Press.

Fox, Alistair (1989). *Politics and Literature in the Reigns of Henry VII and Henry VIII*. Oxford: Blackwell.

Freeman, Thomas S. (2005). 'Ut verus christi sequester': John Blacman and the cult of Henry VI. In Linda Clark (ed.). *The Fifteenth Century V* (pp. 127–42). Woodbridge: Boydell.

Gilson, J. P. (1911). A defence of the proscription of the Yorkists in 1459. *English Historical Review*, 26, 512–25.

Gower, John (1962). *Major Latin Works*. Trans. Eric W. Stockton. Seattle: University of Washington Press.

Gray, Douglas (ed.) (1988). *The Oxford Book of Late Medieval Verse and Prose*. Oxford: Oxford University Press.

Griffiths, Ralph (2003). Introduction. In R. Griffiths (ed.). *Short Oxford History of the British Isles: The Fourteenth and Fifteenth Centuries* (pp. 1–29). Oxford: Oxford University Press.

Hanham, Alison (1986). *The Celys and Their World: An English Merchant Family of the Fifteenth Century*. Cambridge: Cambridge University Press.

Hanham, Alison (1975). *Richard III and His Early Historians 1483–1535*. Oxford: Clarendon Press.

Harriss, Gerald (2005). *Shaping the Nation: England 1360–1461*. Oxford: Clarendon Press.

Hoccleve, Thomas (1892). *The Minor Poems*. Ed. F. J. Furnivall and I. Gollancz. Early English Text Society, o.s. 61, 73. London: Kegan Paul.

Hudson, Anne (1988). *The Premature Reformation*. Oxford: Clarendon Press.

Ingham, Patricia Clare (2001). *Sovereign Fantasies: Arthurian Romance and the Making of Britain*. Philadelphia: University of Pennsylvania Press.

Jacob, E. F. (1961). *The Fifteenth Century 1399–1485*. London: Oxford University Press.

Jones, Michael (2002). *Bosworth 1485: Psychology of a Battle*. Stroud: Tempus.

Justice, Steven (1999). Lollardy. In David Wallace (ed.). *The Cambridge History of Medieval English Literature* (pp. 662–89). Cambridge: Cambridge University Press.

Kail, J. (ed.) (1904). *Twenty-Six Political and Other Poems from the Oxford MSS Digby 102 and*

Douce 322. Early English Text Society, o.s. 124. London: Kegan Paul.

Keen, Maurice (1990). *English Society in the Later Middle Ages 1348–1500*. London: Penguin.

Kempe, Margery (2000). *The Book of Margery Kempe*. Ed. Barry Windeatt. Cambridge: D. S. Brewer.

King, John N. (1989). *Tudor Royal Iconography: Literature and Art in an Age of Religious Crisis*. Princeton: Princeton University Press.

Knighton, Henry (1995). *Knighton's Chronicle 1337–1396*. Ed. G. H. Martin. Oxford: Clarendon Press.

Lander, J. R. (1969). *Conflict and Stability in Fifteenth-Century England*. London: Hutchinson.

McFarlane, K. B. (1973). *The Nobility of Late Medieval England*. Oxford: Clarendon Press.

Malory, Sir Thomas (1971). *Complete Works*. Ed. Eugène Vinaver. 2nd edn. Oxford: Oxford University Press.

More, Sir Thomas (1992). *Utopia*. Trans. Robert Adams. New York: Norton.

Pollard, A. J. (2000). *Late Medieval England 1399– 1509*. Harlow: Longman.

Rigby, S. H. (1995). *English Society in the Later Medieval Ages: Class, Status and Gender*. Basingstoke: Macmillan.

Robbins, Rossell Hope (ed.) (1959). *Historical Poems of the XIVth and XVth Centuries*. New York: Columbia University Press.

Rubin, Miri (2005). *The Hollow Crown: A History of Britain in the Late Middle Ages*. London: Allen Lane.

Saygin, Susanne (2002). *Humphrey, Duke of Gloucester (1390–1447) and the Italian Humanists*. Leiden: Brill.

Scattergood, V. J. (1971). *Politics and Poetry in the Fifteenth Century*. London: Blandford Press.

Simon, Joan (1967). *Education and Society in Tudor England*. Cambridge: Cambridge University Press.

Simpson, James (2002). *The Oxford English Literary History. Volume 2. 1350–1547: Reform and Cultural Revolution*. Oxford: Oxford University Press.

Strohm, Paul (1998). *England's Empty Throne: Usurpation and the Language of Legitimation 1399–1422*. New Haven: Yale University Press.

Summers, David A. (1997). *Spenser's Arthur: The British Arthurian Tradition and The Faerie Queene*. New York: University Press of America.

Sutton, Anne F. and P. W. Hammond (eds) (1983). *The Coronation of Richard III: The Extant Documents*. Gloucester: Sutton.

Tuck, Anthony (1999). *Crown and Nobility: England 1272–1461*. 2nd edn. Oxford: Blackwell.

Usk, Adam (1997). *The Chronicle of Adam Usk 1377–1421*. Ed. and trans. C. Given-Wilson. Oxford: Clarendon Press.

Wallace, David (ed.) (1999). *The Cambridge History of Medieval English Literature*. Cambridge: Cambridge University Press.

Warner, George (ed.) (1926). *The Libelle of Englyshe Polycye*. Oxford: Clarendon Press.

Watson, Nicholas (1995). Censorship and cultural change in late medieval England: vernacular theology, the Oxford translation debate, and Arundel's Constitutions of 1409. *Speculum*, 70, 822–64.

Weiss, R. (1967). *Humanism in England During the Fifteenth Century*. Oxford: Blackwell.

[Worcester, William.] (1972). *The Boke of Noblesse*. New York: Franklin.

28

Poetic Language in the Fifteenth Century

A. S. G. Edwards

The Preface to the edition of John Gower's *Confessio Amantis* published by Thomas Berthelet in 1532 includes the following comment on the poetry of an earlier age:

> For the wryters of later dayes the whiche beganne to loth and hate these old vulgares whan they themselfe wolde wryte in our englysshe tonge were constrayned to brynge in in their writynges newe termes (as some calle them) whiche they borowed out of Latyne Frenche and other langages whiche caused that they that vnderstode not those langages from whens these newe vulgares are fette coude not perceyue theyr wrytynges. And though our most allowed olde autors dydde otherwyse vse to borowe of other langages eyther bycause of theyr metre or elles for lacke of a feete englysshe worde yet that ought not to be a president to vs to heape them in where as nedeth not and where as we haue all redy wordes approued and receyued of the same effecte and strength. The whiche if any man wante let hym resorte to this worthy olde wryter Iohn Gower that shall as a lanterne gyue hym lyghte to wryte counnyngly and to garnysshe his sentencis in our vulgar tonge.
>
> (Sig. aaii^v)

The passage offers one writer's sense of the state of literary English in the early sixteenth century. Here the past, as represented by Gower, is seen 'as a lanterne' embodied in 'these old vulgares', forms of diction to be preserved against the 'newe termes' and 'newe vulgares' of contemporary linguistic excess 'borowed out of Latyne Frenche and other langages'. The rhetoric incites the reader to look back to an earlier state when literary language was purer and more effective, a state embodied in Gower's poetry composed at the very end of the fourteenth century. What happened to poetic language between that point and 1532 is the subject of this essay.

If 1532 seems an arbitrary point of reference here it is worth recalling that it was the date of publication not only of Gower's *Confessio*, but also, far more significantly, of William Thynne's first edition of the collection he titled *The Workes of Geffray*

Chaucer. This is an edition not just of Chaucer's own poetry and prose but also of other materials, particularly verse, loosely associated with his writings. Later sixteenth-century editions of Chaucer follow Thynne's model and make various further additions both of authentic works and of this wider 'Chaucerian' corpus. His edition canonises in print both Chaucer and a tradition of writings linked to his name. It does so at the same moment that Berthelette's edition of Gower draws attention to the rejection of that tradition. 1532 is pivotal in the reception of medieval literature in general and Chaucer in particular. For henceforth, only Middle English poetry by Chaucer or linked closely to him was to be consistently accessible in print.

1532 constitutes a watershed in the shaping of the subsequent literary history of early English poetry. It can be profitably set against another much earlier date. A little more than a decade after Chaucer's death in 1400, the poet Thomas Hoccleve (*c.* 1387–1426) drew attention to Chaucer's linguistic importance by acclaiming him as 'the firste fyndere of our fair langage' (Blyth 1999, 4978). It was an extraordinary accolade so early in Chaucer's literary afterlife, one that implicitly acknowledged the most remarkable aspect of his poetic achievement: that Chaucer wrote in English at all. In the centuries after the Norman Conquest the English vernacular had enjoyed a subordinate position, beneath Norman French and Latin (languages in which Gower also wrote) in the hierarchies of literary production. The inferior status of English was the cause of intermittent complaint in Middle English verse (see the examples in Boffey and Edwards 2008, 381–2). Only in the last quarter of the fourteenth century is there clear evidence of its emergence as a sophisticated poetic language in the various versions of William Langland's *Piers Plowman*, Gower's *Confessio* and, particularly, Chaucer's poems. His earliest datable poem, *The Book of the Duchess* (*c.* 1368), is made largely out of passages translated from the writings of contemporary French poets, Machaut, Deschamps and Froissart, works with which Chaucer's courtly audience would have been familiar. In presenting such writings in English for such an audience Chaucer seems to be offering simultaneously both a demonstration and a challenge: a demonstration of the literary potential of English and a challenge to an influential audience steeped in French culture to appreciate the equivalent achievement of English poetry.

Chaucer left abundant evidence of his own sense of the complexity of literary English language as an agent of style and meaning. We glimpse it in his awareness or occasional deployment of native literary traditions, as in his reference to and (very rare) use of alliterative verse in *The Canterbury Tales* (in the Prologue to the *Parson's Tale*, X 42–3, and the *Knight's Tale*, I, 2605–16), and the *Legend of Good Women*, (635–47), or his superb parody of tail-rhyme romance in *Sir Thopas*. He also demonstrates his awareness of registers of language, of the consonance of diction and style in his dictum in the *Manciple's Tale*: 'If men shall telle properly a thyng, / The word moot cosyn be to the werkyng' (IX, 208–9). And, most remarkably, he shows an understanding, and a degree of pessimism, about the possibility of literary language as a means of communication in a culture where language was still dialectal, and hence subject to incomprehension as it passed from region to region, as he reveals in his prayer near the end of *Troilus & Criseyde*:

> And for ther is so gret diversite
> In Englissh and in writynge of oure tonge [...]
> That thow be understonde, God I biseche!
>
> (V, 1793–4, 1798)

Chaucer's sense of the hazards of poetic transmission and the survival of his works in a regional manuscript-based culture makes the extent of his influence in the fifteenth century all the more remarkable.

The terms of Hoccleve's praise of Chaucer were to become an historical commonplace. And Hoccleve's own poetry reveals an alert reading of many of Chaucer's works. (He himself may even have known Chaucer personally.) He is clearly aware of the range of Chaucer's oeuvre, and mentions several of his works by name, while his own verse shows an assimilation of Chaucerian diction and idiom. Consider this passage from near the beginning of Hoccleve's longest poem, *The Regiment of Princes* (c. 1411):

Passe over whan this stormy nyght was goon		*gone*
And day gan at my wyndowe in to prye,		
I roos me up, for boote fond I noon	115	*comfort*
In myn unresty bed lenger to lye.		*unrestful*
Into the feeld I dressid me in hye,		*hurried; haste*
And in my wo I herte-deep gan wade,		
As he that was bareyne of thoghtes glade.		*empty*
By that I walkid hadde a certeyn tyme,	120	
Were it an hour I not, or more or lesse,		
A poore old hoor man cam walkynge by me,		*grey*
And seide, 'Good day, sire, and God yow blesse!'		
But I no word, for my seekly distresse		*disabling*
Forbad myn eres usen hir office,	125	*to function*
For which this old man heeld me lewde and nyce,		*uncouth and silly*
Til he took heede to my drery cheere,		*sad expression*
And to my deedly colour pale and wan.		*deathly complexion*
Than thoghte he thus: 'This man that I see heere		
Al wrong is wrestid, by aght I see can.'	130	*anything*
He stirte unto me and seide, 'Sleepstow, man?		*turned*
Awake!' and gan me shake wondir faste,		*very quickly*
And with a sigh I answerde atte laste: (113–33)		

The passage assimilates a number of situations and associated diction from Chaucer. The unhappy, sleepless lover (119) comes from the *Book of the Duchess*, as does his desire for 'boote' (115), which recalls that of the narrator there (38). His movement 'into the feeld' (117) comes from the *Prologue to the Legend of Good Women*. The advent of the 'poore old hoor man' (122) echoes the appearance of such a figure in the *Pardoner's Tale*. His imperative 'Awake!' (132) recalls the similar injunction to the narrators of both *Book of the Duchess* and *The House of Fame*. There are a number of specific Chaucerian phrasal borrowings: 'Passe over' (113) (cf. *Book of the Duchess*, 41); 'lewde and nyce' (126) (cf. *Canon's Yeoman's Tale*, VIII, 925); 'drery cheere' (127) (cf. *House of Fame* 179); 'pale and wan' (128) (cf. *Troilus and Criseyde*, II, 551, IV, 235, V, 1221); the adjective 'unresty' (116) is also from *Troilus and Criseyde* (V, 1355). The texture of Hoccleve's language in this passage suggests not uncritical appropriation but the consequences of extended immersion in Chaucerian style and idiom that carries with it the capacity to adapt this poetic legacy for his own purposes. In this respect he anticipates what later fifteenth-century poets were recurrently to demonstrate: the pervasive sense of Chaucer as a presence and a linguistic and stylistic resource for their own writings. More particularly, his praise of his 'master' sets the terms for subsequent acknowledgements of what Chaucer has accomplished (see Lerer 1993). Evidence of such acknowledgements can be found in the recurrent allusions to Chaucer throughout the fifteenth century (on which see Spurgeon 1925). There is additional evidence of his influence in the various fifteenth-century attempts at continuation and addition to *The Canterbury Tales* (see Bowers 1992), as well as in such genres as the romance and the dream vision. Various romances like *Parthonope of Blois* (see Windeatt 1990) and *Amoryus and Cleopes* (see Page 1999) demonstrate verbal and stylistic indebtedness, as do dream visions like *The Kingis Quair* and The *Flower and the Leaf* (on both of these see Boffey 2003), which are firmly rooted in Chaucerian idiom.

Borrowing from Chaucer in the fifteenth century is a subject that has yet to receive exhaustive study and cannot be properly examined here. To a significant degree the history of literary language in the fifteenth century is the history of the appropriation not just of Chaucer's lexis but its related literary effects and the creation of traditions of poetic assimilation that are, in their most basic form, little more than plagiarism of varying degrees of deftness as in this stanza from the first (unpublished) version of John Hardyng's *Chronicle* from around the middle of the fifteenth century:

> O ye yonge fresshe and lusty Creatures
> In whiche the pride vpgroweth with youre Age
> Take hede of this vnsely Auentures [misfortunes]
> Of this ladise and of alle thaire lynage [ancestry]
> And thynke on God that after his ymage
> Yow made and thynke this world shall pass away
> As sone as done the floures fresshe and gay
> (BL MS Lansdowne 201, fol. 16)

Hardyng is here appropriating one of the most famous instances of Chaucerian high style, from the end of *Troilus and Criseyde*:

> O yonge, fresshe folkes, he or she
> In which that love up groweth with youre age,
> Repeyreth home fro worldly vanyte,   *return*
> And of youre herte up casteth the visage   *lift up*
> To thilke God that after his ymage   *that*
> Yow made, and thynketh al nys but a faire,   *transient*
> This world that passeth soone as floures faire
> > (V, 1835–41)

It is an appropriation that succeeds in reducing Chaucer to banality as it tries to
adapt his moral exhortation to historically specific circumstance, most obviously in
the lines 'Repeyreth home fro worldly vanyte, / And of youre herte up casteth the
visage', which in Hardyng become 'Take hede of this vnsely Auentures / Of this
ladise and of alle thaire lynage', and the loss of the force of Chaucer's final image,
strengthened by syntactical inversion and the use of rime riche: '. . . and thynketh al
nys but a faire, / This world that passeth soone as floures faire', which becomes the
trite 'this world shall pass away / As sone as done the floures fresshe and gay'.

Against this can be set a brief passage in the late fifteenth-century *Lancelot of
the Laik*:

> As I thus lay. Rycht to my spreit was sen   *consciousness*
> A birde, þat was as any lawrare gren,   *that*
> Alicht, and sayth in to hir birdis chere [. . .]
> > (Gray 1912, 81–3)

This again draws on a passage in *Troilus and Criseyde*:

> A nyghtyngale, upon a cedre grene,
> Under the chambre wal ther as she ley,
> Ful loude song ayein the moone shene,   *towards*
> Peraunter on his briddes wise a lay   *by chance*
> Of love . . .
> > (II, 918–22)

Here the passage has been fully internalised by the later poet so that the indebtedness
to Chaucer is not slavish but the consequence of a much more complex assimilation
of his idiom, reflected in the deft redeployment of Chaucerian phraseology. Chaucer's
'nyghtyngale, upon a cedre grene' becomes 'A birde, þat was as any lawrare gren';
whereas Chaucer's bird 'song [. . .] on his briddes wise a lay' the Scottish bird 'sayth
in to hir birdis chere'. Chaucer has been absorbed into poetic technique here so that
the debt to him is still palpable.

The most crucial figure in the early assimilation of Chaucer's poetic legacy is the
poet John Lydgate (*c.* 1370–1499). Lydgate was a monk, who lived for much of his
life at the Benedictine Abbey of Bury St Edmunds in Suffolk. While not all of his

massive verse corpus (it has been estimated to amount to as much as 150,000 lines but the size of his canon has never been properly established) reflects Chaucer's influence, many of his most important poems are self-consciously in his debt. Lydgate's earliest major work, the *Troy Book* (*c.* 1412–20), draws on *Troilus and Criseyde* for its style and language. His *Siege of Thebes* (*c.* 1420) is explicitly a continuation of *The Canterbury Tales*. Both *Troilus* and the *Monk's Tale* lie to various degrees behind his longest poem (over 36,000 lines), *The Fall of Princes* (*c.* 1432–38). And several of his dream visions, notably *The Temple of Glass* and *The Complaint of the Black Knight*, demonstrate a detailed awareness of Chaucer's own contributions to the genre. Lydgate does not seem to have known Chaucer personally, but his assimilation of Chaucerian modes and diction is only partly indicated in his frequent tributes to his 'master'. Lydgate's verse also has an important role in the 'standardisation' of aspects of Chaucer's poetic language, by his frequent copying of lines or passages or of stylistic traits from Chaucer. The range and nature of these appropriations have been well discussed by Derek Pearsall who identifies the ways in which Lydgate turns Chaucerian forms into formulae, stylistic reflexes he reaches for instinctively, to reduce some aspects of Chaucerian rhetoric to stock responses. This tendency can be seen with such forms as exclamatio and anaphora ('Lo here...Lo here...Lo here'), terminal apostrophes ('Go little book'), as well as the borrowing and adaptation of individual lines or larger clusters of lines (see Pearsall 1970: 51–58 and 1990).

Lydgate had an important role in the fifteenth-century appreciation of Chaucer's achievement. Their works often circulated together in manuscript, a fact that emphasises their close literary relationship in the consciousness of posterity. And the wide dissemination of Lydgate's own works in manuscript further extended the range of awareness of Chaucerian language and style. Indeed, in the fifteenth century more manuscripts survive that contain works by Lydgate than there do containing Chaucer's works. And surviving early printed editions of Lydgate's works in the period *c.* 1476–1500 confirm the extent of his popularity.

Hence Lydgate's own thorough assimilation of Chaucerian modes and language often makes it difficult usefully to isolate his own direct stylistic influence from Chaucer's own. Indeed, at times Lydgate's absorption of Chaucer's style becomes a verbal amalgam that fluidly blends his master's voice with his own diction:

O ye fresshe louers, that lyuyn euer in doublenesse	*deceit*
And hurt yourself full oft with your owne knyfe.	
Your wofull ioy ys medlyd ay with byttyrnesse,	*mingled*
Now glad, now sory, now lyte, now pensyfe.	*happy; sad*
Thus with yourself ye fall euer at stryfe,	*in conflict*
Betwene two wawes ay possyd to and fro,	*tossed*
That in contraryosnes ye stryuyn euyr mo.	*conflict*
(MacCracken 1911, I, 314/113–19)	

Here the initial borrowing 'O ye fresshe louers' obviously recalls the start of the apostrophe at the end of *Troilus* to 'O yonge, fresshe folkes' (V, 1835). The following

line adapts from the *Merchant's Tale* the adage that a man may [...] ne hurte hym-
selven with his owene knyf (V, 1839–40). The next three lines appear Lydgate's own
before the final couplet adapts three proximate lines from elsewhere in *Troilus*: '[...]
Thus possed to and fro [...] bitwixen wyndes two' (I, 415, 417–18). The passage
demonstrates the depths of Lydgate's immersion in Chaucer's works and shows his
capacity to draw appositely and flexibly from these sources.

Lydgate's sense of the potentiality of literary language did have other dimensions,
beyond those derived from Chaucer, some of which were demonstrably popular. The
most compelling evidence of this is the following stanza from his *Fall of Princes*:

Deceit deceyueth and shal be deceyued,	
For be deceite who is deceyuable,	*deceitful*
Thouh his deceitis be nat out parceyued,	
To a deceyuour deceit is retournable;	*returned*
Fraude quit with fraude is guerdoun couenable	*fitting reward*
For who with fraude fraudulent is founde,	
To a diffraudere fraude will ay rebounde.	*defrauder*

(Bergen 1924, II, 4432–8)

The wordplay here (eight uses of different forms of 'deceit' in four lines; six of 'fraud'
in three) demonstrates a level of dexterity. Lydgate did not often use such wordplay
but when he did his early readers clearly found it appealing: this series of easily
remembered aphorisms was copied as an independent extract in a dozen manuscripts,
often informally on the flyleaves. The stanza offers a rare demonstration of Lydgate's
own distinctive verbal skill.

Lydgate's assimilation and transmission of Chaucerian style led, however, to another
innovative technique with its own degree of influence. This is his development of
what is now termed the aureate diction, a style that is best defined as 'a way of
"foregrounding" by means of words of Latin origin [...] Aureation is essentially a
matter of register and it is important to notice that, because the words used by
aureate poets are of low statistical frequency, they have less impact' (Gradon 1971:
351). Lydgate first uses the term in his *Troy Book* (1412–20) in a modesty topos,
when he describes his style as 'bareyn [...] of aureat lycour' (Bergen 1906: Prologue,
31), that is, lacking any degree of poetic ornament. More positively, in the *Fall of
Princes*, he has Boccaccio contrast his own style with Petrarch's, 'the rudnesse of my
style / With aureat colors of your fressh langage' (VIII, 81). Elsewhere such style is
described as 'sugred' ('sweetened') by 'aureat licour' (literally 'golden liquid') (*Fall of
Princes*, I, 461), a transferred epithet through which the expensive adornment of
gilded letters (those made from liquid gold leaf) in a manuscript comes to reflect a
style of high value.

The characteristics of this style are both lexical and tonal. Lydgate reserves his
aureate style for occasions of high seriousness, most frequently in religious contexts.
It is employed particularly in devotional poems, as in this example where the

devotional mode is established by Latinate polysyllabic forms ('luminary', 'laudacion', 'Eclypsyd', 'superexcellence'), sometimes supplemented by actual Latin liturgical phrases ('Aue regina celorum'):

Hayle luminary & benigne lanterne,	*light*
Of Ierusalem the holy ordres nyne	
As quene of quenes laudacion eterne	*eternal praise*
They yeue to thee, O excellente virgyne!	*give*
Eclypsyd I am, for to determyne	*in the dark* [*fig.*]
Thy superexcellence of Cantica cantorum,	*song of songs*
The aureat beames do nat in me shyne,	
Aue regina celorum!	*Hail Queen of the heavens*
(MacCracken 1911, 291, 1–7)	

In such contexts the language creates a sonorously reverential tone. Elsewhere Lydgate supplements this polysyllabic, exclamatory mode with sequences of varying alliterative patterns:

O closid gardeyn al void of weedes wicke,	*empty of evil weed*
Cristallyn welle of clennesse cler consigned,	*pure*
Fructifying olyve of foilys faire and thicke,	*leaves*
And redolent cedyr most derworthly ydyned,	*scented*
(MacCracken 1911, 256, 36–42)	

The conjoining of the techniques of 'native' alliteration and Latin derived polysyllabism is oddly effective at a localised level; the alliteration provides a degree of verbal emphasis that saves the passage from the risk of sonorous vacuity.

Aureate diction, with its polysyllabic descriptive weight, was not a style that found frequent imitators in the fifteenth century, though its effect has been discerned in such sixteenth-century poets as Stephen Hawes and Edmund Spenser. The chief manifestation of its influence in the fifteenth century is in the ornate style of the Scots court poet William Dunbar (*c.* 1460–1513?). This is an example from one of his religious poems:

Hale, sterne superne, hale, in eterne	*on high*
In Godis sicht to schyne,	*sight*
Lucerne in derne for to discerne,	*Lamp in darkness by which to see*
Be glory and grace devyne.	
Hodiern, modern, sempitern,	*for today, now and eternity*
Angelicall regyne...	*Queen*
(Bawcutt 1998: 83/1–6)	

Here the rhetorical effect of aureate diction is to create a sonorous and rhythmical tonality, in which the invocation is sustained by alliteration and assonance, partially created through quasi-Latinate forms that become more frequent as the passage develops: 'superne' (1), 'Lucerne' (3), 'Hodiern, modern, sempitern, / Angelicall regyne' (5–6). The tonality creates an effect of plangent resonance appropriate to the devotional mode.

But such a style is not limited in Dunbar's verse to religious poems. It achieves some of its most elaborate effects in the courtly allegorical dream vision *The Golden Targe*, with its ornate opening:

Ryght as the stern of day begouth to schyne,	*star; began*
Quhen gone to bed was Vesper and Lucyne,	*When*
I raise and by a rosere did me rest.	*rose bush*
Wp sprang the goldyn candill matutyne,	*Up; light of morning*
With clere depurit bemes cristallyne,	*pure crystal beams*
Glading the mery foulis in thair nest.	
Or Phebus was in purpur cape reuest	*Before; clothed*
Wp raise the lark, the hevyns menstrale fyne,	
In May in till a morow myrthfullest.	*merriest*

(Bawcutt 1998: 184/1–9)

The advent of day is defined in terms that are quite literally glittering: 'stern', 'goldyn candill matutyne', 'clere depurit bemes cristallyne', supported by the classical allusions to 'Vesper and Lucyne' and 'Phebus' and by associated natural sounds, those of the 'mery foulis' and 'the lark'. Nature becomes artfully decorated, an aspect of the elaborate courtly world in which the poem's action is set.

Such an aureate, polysyllabic style is employed by Dunbar in both the devotional and courtly modes of his verse. It demonstrates his debt to Lydgate. But the range of Dunbar's poetic effects extends in other, wholly original directions as he creates the demotic diction of his 'flytings', satiric attacks on his contemporaries. In these poems we see a new kind of poetry of invective characterised by a rich vein of linguistic inventiveness in which alliteration is an important element:

But fowll iow iowrdane hedit ievellis,	*infidel; rascals with heads like chamber-pots*
Cowkin kenseis and culroun kewellis,	*low ruffians; coarse knaves*
Stuffettis, strekouris and stafische strummellis,	*grooms?; dogs; stubborn beasts*
Wyld haschbaldis, haggarbaldis and hummellis,	*all terms of abuse; obscure*
Druncartis, dysouris, dyowris, drewellis...	*drunkards; gamblers; Bankrupts; drudges*

(Bawcutt 1998: 67/15–19)

And so on. The exact meaning of many of the words here is not readily accessible even to lexicographers. But meanings are not very important in the rhetoric of Dunbar's abuse. Clearly what matters here is the overall tonal effect. Here sound becomes more important than sense; or rather it creates its own sense, together with the irregular rhythms that give Dunbar's complaint its energy through the variations in the patterns of accumulating nouns, both in their numbers and intermittent allocation of adjectives to them, and the links between groups of words created by alliteration. Dunbar constructs a form of poetic discourse that achieves its effects largely at a non-verbal level, a rhetoric of noise.

The poetic language of Dunbar's Scottish near contemporary Robert Henryson (*c.* 1430–*c.* 1505) lacks his exuberant range. It maintains a level of focused moral seriousness that has consequences for both tone and subject. But within this narrower range it achieves powerful effects. This stanza from his later fifteenth-century work *The Testament of Cresseid*, his continuation of Chaucer's *Troilus and Criseyde*, may stand as representative of a number of aspects of his achievement. Here, Cresseid, doomed by the gods to death as a leper, contemplates the consequences of her unfaithfulness to her former lover Troilus:

Thy lufe, thy lawtie, and thy gentilnes	*love; loyalty*
I countit small in my prosperitie,	*little*
So efflated I was in wantones,	*puffed up; pride*
And clam vpon the fickill quheill sa hie.	*climbed; wheel*
All faith and lufe I promissit to the	*thee*
Was in the self fickill and friuolous:	
O fals Cresseid and trew knicht Troilus!	

(Fox 1981: 129/547–53)

Her words serve to emphasise the moral bases of her self-assessment here, primarily through the repetition of the crucial words 'lufe' (547, 551) and 'fickill' (550, 552). 'Thy lufe' is set against the 'lufe I promissit to the.' The 'fickill quheill' of changeable Fortune' becomes particularised in the conduct of 'the self fickill and friuolous' of Cresseid herself. And the poignancy of her appraisal is emphasised by the terms of intimacy it employs, the recurrent first and second person pronouns 'I' (548, 549, 511), 'thy' (547 – three times), 'the' (that is 'thee,' 551), which contrast with the impersonal force of the refrain's condemnation: 'O fals Cresseid and trew knicht Troilus!' (553). This stark summation is itself linked to a pattern of alliteration that develops, starting with the unusual 'efflated' (549) and continuing with 'fickill', 'faith,' 'fickill and friuolous' and 'fals', words that link sound and sense to provide a causality of Criseyde's infidelity. The unobtrusive construction of moral analysis out of such strategies demonstrates the nature of Henryson's art.

Henryson's capacity actually to enact, rather than simply assert, meaning in his verse is one of its distinguishing qualities, as in the opening lines from his fable of 'The Cock and the Fox':

Thocht brutall beistis be irrationall,	
That is to say, wantand discretioun,	*lacking judgement*
ȝyt ilk ane in their kyndis naturall	*Yet each one*
Hes mony diuers inclinatioun:	*Has many different disposition*
The bair busteous, the volff, the wylde lyoun,	*violent bear; wolf*
The fox fenȝeit, craftie and cawtelos,	*deceitful; cunning*
The dog to bark on nicht and keip the hows.	*night*

(Fox 1981: 19/397–403)

The stanza opens with its bald assertion 'beistis be irrationall [...] wantand dis-
cretioun', and proceeds to employ irrationality as a descriptive principle in the
characterization of these creatures. In the line 'The bair busteous, the volff, the wylde
lyoun' (401), the first description reverses natural adjective + noun order, the second
has no adjective and the third follows natural order, while the fox (402) is given three
adjectives. The final line uses verbs, not adjectives to define the dog's qualities: 'to
bark on nicht and keip the hows' (403). The shifts in descriptive mode here also
emphasise the 'diuers inclinatioun' of 'brutall beistis'. The dog's function is positive,
protective and custodial, hence defined actively, in contrast to the attributes of the
earlier creatures. Both in its modal contrast and in its final position in the stanza's
sequence the description gives poetic force to the distinction in qualities that is
asserted here.

Dunbar and Henryson both demonstrate, in different ways, that while the shadow
of Chaucer was clearly a long one in the history of fifteenth-century poetic language
it did not necessarily inhibit the development of originality in the possibilities of
poetic language.

There were, of course, forms of 'native' idiom that continued to find articulation.
The tradition of alliterative poetry most significantly embodied in William Langland's
Piers Plowman had only a limited continuity largely in works that survive in single
manuscripts from the very early fifteenth century (see further Barr 1993). It survives
otherwise as a regional form, confined to the north of England where it was employed
as late as the early sixteenth century, when it was used in the poem *Scotish Feilde*
to celebrate the English victory over the Scots at Flodden Field (see Baird 1982).
There are only scattered examples of alliterative verse elsewhere, as in a passage from
a ballad on the English victory at Agincourt in 1415:

Stedes þer stumbelyd in þat stownde,	*horses; moment*
Þat stode stere stuffed vnder stele;	*brave; padded under armour*
With gronyng grete þei felle to grownde	
Here sydes federed whan þei gone fele.	*wounded*
Owre lord þe kynge he foght ryght wele,	
Scharpliche on hem his spere he spent,	
Many on seke he made þat sele,	*Many one sick; good (man)*
Thorow myght of god omnipotent.	
(Robbins 1959: 75–6/1–8)	

There is variation in the number of alliterating staves from line to line, but a general
appreciation of the potential of alliteration in describing battle scenes and an
appreciation of when to abandon the technique: 'Owre lord þe kynge he foght ryght
wele' (5), 'Thorow myght of god omnipotent' (8). The passage shows the tactical
value of alliteration in the larger rhetorical design of the description, where relatively
prosaic assertion can be juxtaposed against it to give weight to important declarative points.

The most frequent evidence of these continuing native traditions is the lyric, both religious and secular. Often in such verse artistry lies in economy, in the adaptation of formal constraint as an agent of meaning. Such an achievement can be seen in one of the religious carols of James Ryman, a Franciscan monk living in Kent, who wrote towards the end of the fifteenth century. Ryman has left one of the largest surviving bodies of work in this form. The following Nativity carol is a representative example:

Mary so myelde of hert and myende	*mind*
Hath borne a child to save mankyende	
[1]	
Mary so myelde and good of fame,	*reputation*
By vertu of the Holy Ghost	*the power*
Hath borne a chyelde, Jhesus by name,	
To save mankyende, the whiche was lost.	
[2]	
Mary so myelde in hert and myende,	
As Gabriell her behight,	*promised*
Hath borne a chielde to save mankynde,	
The Son of God and Kyng of Myght.	
[3]	
Mary so myelde, that quene of grace,	
Hath borne a chielde (Scripture seith soo)	
To bringe mankyende out of that place	
Where is bothe peyne and endeles woo.	
[4]	
Mary so myelde in worde and thoughte	
Hath borne a chielde, Jhesus soo good	
The whiche ayene mankyende hath bought	
On the roode tree with his hert bloode	
[5]	
Mary so myelde in dede and wille	
Hath borne a chielde that made alle thing,	
To whom al thing obeyeth by skille	*fittingly*
As to theire prince, theire lorde and king	
[6]	
Mary so myelde, so pure and clene,	
Vnto hir chielde, that hath no pere,	
By hir mekenes she is a meane	*intermediary*
That we shalle come to heven quene.	
[7]	
Mary so myelde, moder and may,	*maid*
Hath borne a chielde by hir mekenesse	
That shall bringe vs at domesday	*judgement day*
Fro thraldome, peyn, woo, and distresse.	*slavery*
(Greene 1977, no. 54)	

The emphasis here, reflected in both form and lexis, is on celebratory clarity enacted with artful simplicity. The form involves the reiteration of two fixed elements in each stanza, the phrases 'Mary so myelde' and 'Hath borne a chielde'; their proximity (in the first two stanzas at the beginning of the first and third lines, otherwise in the first and second lines) is reinforced by the shared internal rhyme ('myelde', 'chielde') that directly links mother and child, the central figures of the nativity story. (The only variation from this fixed pattern is in the second line of stanza [6] where 'Hath borne a chielde' is changed to 'Vnto a chielde' possibly a transcriptional error since the stanza's sense is not clear.) These fixed elements are accompanied by variation, as Mary's characterisation is linked to different attributes ('good of fame', etc.) culminating in the final stanza in the acknowledgement of her paradoxical status as 'moder and may' and the eschatological importance of that role. Christ shall 'bringe vs at domesday / Fro thraldome, peyn, woo, and distresse'.

The carol's simple pattern of phrasal repetition is linked to a chronology that moves from Annunciation to Last Judgement. In this sequence smaller patterns of repetition become significant, particularly that of the word 'mankyende' (repeated in each of the first four stanzas and in the burden), one that reminds the poem's auditors that it is they who are the beneficiaries of Christ's miraculous birth and resurrection. Ryman's poem draws, of course, on shared doctrinal assumptions between poet and audience that permit him to substitute allusion for extended exposition and to rely on quite simple strategies of form and language to develop its 'argument'. It represents a style of limited artfulness, one that seeks (relative) expository clarity through its language and structure.

At an extreme from Ryman's lyrics is the courtly lyric sequence of the French poet Charles d'Orléans (1394–1465), written during his captivity in England from 1415–40. These poems are largely translations of his own French poems, in various verse forms. They demonstrate a much more deliberate and developed concern with form and rhetorical structure, as here, in a passage that has no parallel in Charles's French verse:

> For dedy lijf, my lyvy deth y wite;
> For ese of payne, in payne of ese y dye;
> For me so lite, woo lengtith lengthe of woo,   *extends*
> That quyk y dye, and yet as ded lyue y.   *living*
> Thus nygh a fer y fele the fer is ny
> Of thing certeyne that y vncerteyne seche,   *seek*
> Which is the dethe, sith Deth hath my lady.   *since*
> O wofull wrecche! O wrecche, lesse onys thi speche!
>   (Arn 1994: 2082–89)

The crucial rhetorical principle here is chiasmus, the balancing of the same or similar elements in both parts of the line. The construction has the potential to become mechanical but here the poet is able to introduce appropriate balance through forms of phrasal inversion ('dedy lijf [...] lyvy deth;' 'ese of payne [...] payne of ese'), sometimes combined with more extended wordplay ('For lengthe of woo, woo lengtith') and alliteration ('nygh a fer y fele the fer is ny'). The stanza runs the risk of simply becoming mechanically clever; but in the final line it shifts to a direct exclamatory mode that uses simple repetition ('wrecche! O wrecche') to define the situation of the speaker. The deftness of control over the elements of the stanza demonstrates Charles's sureness of touch even when writing in a 'foreign' language.

The forms of the lyric represented by Ryman and Charles d'Orleans clearly demonstrate different potentialities for literary language. They stand not just at an extreme from each other but also from new factors that emerged from early in the fifteenth century that are reflected in other more 'scholarly' kinds of poetic diction. Prominent among these was the sense of verse as a proper form for the translation of Latin classical works, represented in renderings of works by Boethius, Vegetius and Claudian, among others. This interest is apparent shortly after Chaucer's death in John Walton's (fl. 1410) translation of Boethius' *Consolation of Philosophy*, partly into ballade, partly into rhyme royal stanzas. Walton drew on Chaucer's own prose version, but contrived his own often poetically deft rendering that proved popular in its own terms (more than twenty manuscripts survive). This stanza suggests something of the qualities of Walton's diction:

> This plesaunt fortune mennys hertes byndeth
> Wiþ false goodes wich þei haue on honde;
> Bot froward fortune losyth and vnbyndeth   *perverse; loosens*
> And techeþ hem to knowe and vndirstande   *teaches*
> Þat weelfulnesse is freel and variande.   *fickle; changeable*
> Þe firste seest þou fletyng as þe wynde,   *flitting*
> And of itself vnware and vnkunnande,   *unaware and unknown*
> And haþ hireself forleten out of mynde.   *forgotten*
>   (Science, 1927: 121)

The chief characteristic of Walton's style here is clear, the use of doublets: 'losyth and vnbyndeth', 'knowe and vndirstande', 'freel and variande', 'vnware and vnkunnande'. This was to be a recurrent strategy for English translators, both in verse and in prose, as they sought to convey with appropriate exactitude the verbal implications of their source texts. Here it is saved from becoming leadenly mechanical by the simultaneous use of a less obvious technique: the binding together of the stanza's argument by cross-line alliteration. The concern with qualities of 'fortune' is emphasised by a filament of inter-linear alliteration that winds its way through the stanza, linking the concept to qualities associated with it: 'false', 'froward', 'freel', 'flete', 'forleten'. Walton was not a slavish translator. He found ways to enact in his poetic techniques the argument his translation sought to convey.

Other verse translations from the classics in this period were conceived and executed with variable degrees of success. *Knyghthode and Bataile* is a translation into rhyme royal stanzas of Vegetius's *De re militari*, a widely influential prose military manual.

Made in 1458 by a 'person of Caleys' (33), it is a translation that reminds us that verse remained a utilitarian medium throughout the fifteenth century. Such language can be employed for clear technical and instructional purposes, as here to give directions for the use of an incendiary arrow (a 'malliol'):

> A malliol, a bolt of wilde fier
>> A fallary, a shafte is of the same;   *fire arrow*
> Thorgh fel & hide hem shoote: al on fier is;   *through*
>> But shoote hem thorgh into the tymber frame;
> With myghti alblastris go to this game,   *bows*
>> Brymston, rosyn, glewe, oyle incendiary   2495 *rosin*
> With flax doon on this shafte is necessary.
>> (Dyboski and Arend 1935: 2490–96)

The passage has a functional expository clarity: the terminology is defined (2490–91), the instructions are accessible (2495–96) and the directions for use are emphasised by the repetition of the main verb 'shoote' in proximate lines (2492, 2493).

Very rarely the interjection of personal feeling offers some commentary on the linguistic problems of dealing with this sort of translation:

> VIII thousand werreours was a phalange   *phalanx*
>> In dayes olde, and of VI M men
> Was a caterve, but this diagalange
>> Is, as to this, not worth a pulled hen.
>> (Dyboski and Arend 1935: 670–73)

The rare word 'diagalange' ('a superfluous aggregate of terms or details') provides its own commentary on the translator's sense of his undertaking, especially when followed by the lapse into the colloquial 'not worth a pulled hen'. It shows an awareness of register and linguistic irony that points to the difficulty of faithful but readable translation. There are moments when *Knyghthode and Bataile* seems to play with this awareness, as it appears to teeter on the point collapsing under the weight of its own lexis:

> The gentil is smal, rutilaunt, glad-chered,   *reddish*
>> That other horribil, elenge and sloggy,   *wretched*
> Drawinge his wombe abrede, and vgly-hered,
>> To grete the bolk, and tremulent and droggy,   *shaking and sluggish*
> The lymes hery, scabious & ruggy.   *hairy, scabby and shaggy*
>> (Dyboski and Arend 1935: 236–40)

Here the combination of Latinate adjectives ('rutilaunt', 'tremulent', 'scabious') and English ones ('smal', 'sloggy', 'droggy', 'ruggy') and compound forms ('glad-chered', 'vgly-hered') creates multiple possibilities of definition, so various as to offer obfuscation rather than any certain clarity. The passage indicates the difficulty of sustaining expository appropriateness in such a technical work, a problem inhering not just in the constraints of verse form but in the nature of the English language as the translator perceives it.

The translation of parts of Claudian's *De Consulatu Stilichonis* ('On the Consulate of Stilicho'), made in 1445 in Clare, Suffolk, possibly by the Augustinian friar Osbern Bokenham, is unusual in a number of respects. The translation is largely composed in a form of blank verse that has no Middle English precedent, and is set out with the Latin original on facing page to the translation. Its sense of its relationship to its Latin source is reflected in its style:

> Soone venus þan was brouȝte to hous with flyght of culverys fele
> Where mariage the thridde she ioyned togider with knotte of regaly
> Plumyd loves she sett aboute vnto this lusty prynce
> Which fyre him selfe by the maydens mowthe þat sett him was to love
> She this was doughtir vnto themperours high & emperours also sustir
> (Flügel 1905: 390–94)

The attempt to mirror the verse form and syntax of the Latin original in this rendering creates obscurities, not least because Middle English lacks the inflectional resources of Latin which help to clarify relationships between words and phrases. Such phrases as 'mariage the thridde she ioyned togider' (translating 'tercia iungit connubia' literally 'joined in marriage for the third time') and 'She this was doughtir vnto themperours high & emperours also sustir' (translating 'Progenitam augustis augustorum que sororem' literally 'daughter and sister of a noble emperor') display an unhelpful fidelity to both the diction and the word order of the Latin: 'the thridde' needs the added noun 'time' to make its sense clear; the clumsy duplication of 'themperours high & emperours' mirrors the Latin only to obfuscate sense. The uneasy syntax and clumsy language expose the limits of this attempt to give English form (and life) to Claudian's verse.

If such translations look forward to a new sixteenth-century humanism they also indicate the distance that had yet to be travelled. It is in the trajectory of the literary career of John Skelton (*c.* 1460–1529) that the transition from earlier forms of literary language to the establishing of self-consciously innovative forms of diction is most apparent. Skelton's earliest verse is relatively conventional in its use of medieval forms, as in his earliest substantial work, the elegy 'Upon the Dolorous Dethe [...] of the Mooste Honorable Erle of Northumberland' (*c.* 1489) and his dream vision *The Bouge of Courte* (1499), both written in decasyllabic rhyme royal stanzas. In such modes his language looks back to the fifteenth century, as in the opening lines of *The Bouge of Courte*:

> In autumpne, whan the sonne is in Vyrgyne
> By radyante hete enryped hath our corne,

> Whan Luna, full of mutabylyte,
> As emperes the dyademe hath worne
> Of our pole artyke, smylynge halfe in scorne
> At our folye and our unstedfastnesse;
> The tyme whan Mars to werre hym dyd dres...
> (Boffey 2003: 1–7)

There is nothing that, in style or lexis, Lydgate would have found curious: time is defined by astrological allusion ('Vyrgyne', 'Luna', 'Mars') linked to an extended periphrasis that confirms the autumn season.

But by the early sixteenth century Skelton had moved to more flexible shorter lines and an entirely different lexis that he deployed in a range of poems, satiric, comic and bawdy (sometimes all three at the same time). He is most distinctively identified with the form Skeltonics, sequences of short lines linked by shared rhyme, often extending over a number of lines, sometimes with alliteration and assonance, as in this passage from his satire on Cardinal Wolsey, 'Why Come Ye Nat to Courte?':

> For trewly to expresse,
> There hath ben moche excesse: *much*
> With banketyng braynlesse,   *banqueting*
> With ryotynge rechelesse
> With gambaudynge thryftlesse,   *capering*
> With, 'Spende,' and wast witlesse,
> Treatinge of trewse restlesse,
> Pratynge for peace peaslesse.   *chattering*
>   (Scattergood 1983: 280/69–76)

Sometimes in later works these techniques are combined with passages in Latin and in other languages. This is a new style of poetry, although it has some obvious affiliations with Dunbar's 'flyting' style discussed above. It is marked by a breathless energy, in which a colloquial form of address is linked to a kind of polysyllabic accumulation of neologisms and/or nonce coinages that creates its own form of (non)sense, in which the poetry's love of its own discordant noise is paramount, transcending the possibility of any engagement at a more rational level. Perhaps Skelton's verse is perhaps symptomatic of the 'newe termes' and 'newe vulgares' to which Gower's editor alludes so disapprovingly in 1532, representing as it does a radical disjuncture from the language of the medieval past. Understanding the different forms of that past, at least in terms of the language of English poetry in the fifteenth century, does not require a dismissal of the new, of the different poetic registers we begin to experience not just with Skelton's works, but also with the poetry of Thomas Wyatt and Henry Howard a little after him. Conversely, an appreciation of the new no longer needs to mean pouring critical scorn on fifteenth- century verse, as was the case during much of the twentieth century. A more balanced judgement is now possible. I hope that I have succeeded in indicating something of the range and the nature of the century's poetic language.

REFERENCES AND FURTHER READING

Arn, Mary-Jo (ed.) (1994). *Fortunes Stabilnes: Charles of Orleans English Book of Love: A Critical Edition.* Binghamton, NY: Medieval & Renaissance Texts & Studies.

Baird, I. F. (ed.) (1982). *Scotish Feilde and Flodden Feilde: Two Flodden Poems.* New York: Garland.

Barr, Helen (ed.) (1993). *The Piers Plowman Tradition.* London: Dent.

Bawcutt, Priscilla (ed.) (1998). *The Poems of William Dunbar.* 2 vols. Glasgow: Association for Scottish Literary Studies.

Bergen, H. (ed.) (1906, 1908, 1910, 1935). *Lydgate's 'Troy Book'.* 4 vols. Early English Text Society, e.s. 97, 103, 106, 126. London: Kegan Paul, Trench, Trübner & Co.

Bergen, H. (ed.) (1924, 1927). *Lydgate's 'Fall of Princes'.* 4 vols. Early English Text Society, e.s. 121–124. London: Oxford University Press.

Blyth, Charles (ed.) (1999). Thomas Hoccleve. *Regiment of Princes.* Kalamazoo, MI: Medieval Institute Publications.

Boffey, Julia (ed.) (2003). *Fifteenth-Century English Dream Visions: An Anthology.* Oxford: Oxford University Press.

Boffey, Julia and A. S. G. Edwards (2008). Middle English literary writings. In Nigel J. Morgan and Rodney M. Thompson (eds). *The Cambridge History of the Book in Britain.* Cambridge: Cambridge University Press.

Bowers, John M. (1992). *The Canterbury Tales: Fifteenth-Century Continuations and Additions.* Kalamazoo, MI: Medieval Institute Publications.

Dyboski, R. and Arend, Z. M. (eds) (1935). *Knyghthode and Bataile.* Early English Text Society, o.s. 206. London: Oxford University Press.

Flügel, E. (1905). Eine mittelenglische Claudian-Ubersetzung (1445). *Anglia,* 28, 255–99.

Fox, Denton (ed.) (1981). *The Poems of Robert Henryson.* Oxford: Clarendon Press.

Gradon, Pamela (1971). *Form and Style in Early English Literature.* London: Methuen.

Gray, Margaret Muriel (ed.) (1912). *Lancelot of the Laik.* Scottish Text Society, n.s. No. 2. Edinburgh: William Blackwood.

Greene, R. L. (ed.) (1977). *The Early English Carols.* 2nd edn. Oxford: Clarendon Press.

Lerer, Seth (1993). *Chaucer and his Readers.* Princeton, NJ: Princeton University Press.

MacCracken, H. N. (ed.) (1911). *The Minor Poems of John Lydgate.* Part I, Early English Text Society, e.s. 107. London: Oxford University Press.

Page, Stephen F. (ed.) (1999). *Amoryus and Cleopes.* Kalamazoo, MI: Medieval Institute Publications.

Pearsall, Derek (1970). *John Lydgate.* London: Routledge.

Pearsall, Derek (1977). *Old English and Middle English Poetry.* London: Routledge.

Pearsall, Derek (1990). Chaucer and Lydgate. In Ruth Morse and Barry Windeatt (eds). *Chaucer Traditions: Studies in Honour of Derek Brewer* (pp. 39–53). Cambridge: Cambridge University Press.

Robbins, R. H. (ed.) (1959). *Historical Poems of the XIVth and XVth Centuries.* New York: Columbia University Press.

Scattergood, John (ed.) (1983). *John Skelton: The Complete English Poems.* Harmondsworth: Penguin.

Spurgeon, Caroline (1925). *Five Hundred Years of Chaucer Criticism and Allusion.* 3 vols. Cambridge: University Press.

Science, Mark (ed.) (1927). John Walton, *Boethius: 'De consolatione philosophie'.* Early English Text Society, o.s. 170. London: Oxford University Press.

Windeatt, Barry (1990). Chaucer and fifteenth-century romances: 'Parthonope of Blois.' In Ruth Morse and Barry Windeatt (eds). *Chaucer Traditions: Studies in Honour of Derek Brewer* (pp. 62–80). Cambridge: Cambridge University Press.

29

Manuscript and Print: Books, Readers and Writers

Julia Boffey

One of the most illuminating accounts of the late medieval processes of reading and literary composition is sketched in Thomas Hoccleve's *Series*, a collection of verse and prose pieces which begins with a *Complaint* written after Hoccleve's recovery from a period of 'wyld infirmytie' (probably mental instability of some kind; see Burrow 1999). At the heart of the *Series* is a set of interactions between Hoccleve and an anonymous friend who talks with him about what he should and shouldn't write now that he has recovered his creative vigour. Their conversations suggest some of the virtues that readers may find in particular texts – consolation, instruction, diversion, flattery – and hint too at the unfortunate results that can follow from reading the wrong thing; the friend is particularly concerned that Hoccleve's health may suffer if he devotes himself to the translation of a treatise on dying. They discuss the variety of impulses that might generate the composition of a literary work, from obeying the commandment of a noble patron (Hoccleve is reminded that he 'owes' a work to Duke Humphrey of Gloucester) to undertaking a favour for a friend (Hoccleve's interlocutor requests an improving exemplum for his wayward son). They also review the different forms of reception that an author must expect: Hoccleve is conscious that his earlier poems may have offended women, and swayed by the friend's suggestion that he can put things right by turning his hand to something more complimentary. A number of material volumes are invoked in their miniature review of the processes of literary production and reception. First Hoccleve's book of consolation is returned to its owner, who has requested it back; then the friend reads a copy of Hoccleve's *Complaint* and offers a critique. When Hoccleve's source for the pro-feminist exemplum he writes turns out to lack the concluding moralisation, the friend produces his own copy, which rectifies the omission; and finally the friend supplies the source for the tale that rounds off the work.

Authors and Readers

Few Middle English authors are as specific as this about the sociology and material processes of literary production, perhaps precisely because few were as comprehensively qualified as Hoccleve – a practising London scribe and privy seal clerk, as well as a poet – to understand the intricacies of these matters and the anxieties to which they might give rise. The production of medieval manuscript books was a slow and labour-intensive business, and there were no established commercial systems of publishers' advances or royalties (even the so-called *pecia* system by which student textbooks were semi-commercially replicated in medieval Paris by the parcelling out of separate sections for copying would not have rewarded authors in any way). A medieval 'author' would not have been readily able to make a living from literary composition, and like Hoccleve would probably have had some other occupation as well as devoting time to literary endeavour. Patronage was invaluable to authors (as to those in many other roles in the Middle Ages), since it could provide financial and other kinds of support, and sometimes a means of publicising an author's name and thus extending his clientèle.

Writers working in a culture of patronage might execute compositions on commission, and might also be drawn to specific literary forms such as eulogies and petitions. Some numbers of works in these and related forms survive from the fifteenth century, as from the medieval period as a whole, and along with them a scattering of reflections on the anxieties that authors experienced as their patrons vacillated or were slow to pay up (Lucas 1997: 249–84). Sections of John Lydgate's *Fall of Princes* expound feelingly on the vagaries of the support offered by Duke Humphrey of Gloucester, who asked Lydgate to produce a translation of the work in English (Hammond 1927: 149, 174). While it is clear from many medieval works that cultivating the benevolence of readers was an important authorial strategy, the specifics of how readers responded to what they read (or had read to them) are less easy to chart. The relative popularity of particular works can be postulated in an approximate way from the numbers of surviving manuscript copies or early printed editions, but this evidence is complicated by factors like the randomness of material survivals, and the probability that the oral circulation of some kinds of material remained a reality well beyond the fifteenth century. It is clear from references in proverbs that 'rhymes of Robin Hood', for example, were well known in England in the late Middle Ages, but surviving material evidence of the circulation of these stories is comparatively scanty.

More direct evidence of reader response is equally hard to trace. Few individual readers have left remarks about their tastes, or annotated their books with anything more helpful than the occasional underlining or pointing marginal hand. Some sense of particular preferences can be built up from the contents of specific libraries and collections, information about which can be gleaned from documents like inventories or lists of payments, and from signs in books (signatures or coats of arms, for example) which relate surviving volumes to early owners and readers. To piece together these bits of information about the provenance and readership of individual copies of a work can afford valuable opportunities to reconstruct its early readership: learning by these means that women constituted a significant audience for romances or female saints' lives, for instance, can for modern readers illuminate the content and construction of such works.

What non-professional scribes chose to copy into commonplace books or rough-and-ready anthologies for their own use can also tell us a little about contemporary taste, although in assessing this evidence it is important to remember that many irrecoverable factors (especially the availability of exemplars from which to copy) may have determined what the compiler chose to include. Arguments about the medieval reception of certain texts are sometimes based on the quality and nature of the forms in which they survive. That most of the manuscripts of Gower's *Confessio Amantis* and of Lydgate's *Fall of Princes* are well-produced and sometimes pleasingly illustrated books, requiring large amounts of expensive materials and labour, suggests something about the spending power, and thus the likely social status, of the readers who commissioned or bought copies. At the other end of the spectrum, many late Middle English lyrics are found on fly-leaves or squashed into odd spaces in copies of unrelated works, as if transcribed almost as a matter of accident; the fact that they seem not to have circulated in formally produced collections may point to certain conclusions about the nature of their cultural capital.

Manuscripts of Major Verse Texts

The major verse texts of Chaucer, Gower and Langland, composed in the late fourteenth century, seem to have been most actively circulated after 1400, presumably as the copies made for use in the authors' own circles were transmitted further afield after their deaths. The beginning of the fifteenth century in fact saw the start of the significant production of English literary manuscripts: it is hard before that point to locate verse texts which enjoyed wide geographical circulation, or whose transmission involved commercial networks and copies commissioned or speculatively produced for sale (Edwards and Pearsall 1989). The status of Chaucer, Gower and Langland as in some sense London authors, all producing major vernacular works of topical significance, must have been an important factor in the ready multiplication of copies of their works. London was well supplied with the forms of labour necessary for the production of books – parchment-makers, scribes, illuminators, 'stationers' able to commission and co-ordinate work from skilled artisans – and fluid metropolitan conditions of labour seem to have meant that the book trade could also profit from the out-of-hours activities of those (like Hoccleve) whose day-jobs might have been in government offices, or livery halls, or courts. The researches of A. I. Doyle and Malcolm Parkes, especially in connection with a scribe (named 'D' by them, for convenience) who worked on manuscripts of Chaucer and Gower, have effectively demonstrated that the production of English literary manuscripts in London involved the parcelling out of exemplars, and considerable amounts of piece-work among scribes who may have had only an approximate sense of the finished product to which their work contributed (Doyle and Parkes 1978).

The habits of an author like Chaucer, during his own lifetime, probably involved the transmission of rough drafts of composition (possibly on wax tablets) to a scribe who would produce a fair copy. The 'Adam Scriveyn' to whom Chaucer addressed a complaint has been tentatively identified as an Adam Pinkhurst who was a London scrivener, and thus may have taken on other copying work in his own time (Mooney 2006). Pinkhurst's hand has been identified in the famous Ellesmere and Hengwrt manuscripts of *The Canterbury Tales* (San Marino, Huntington Library MS Ellesmere 26 C 9, and Aberystwyth, National Library of Wales MS Peniarth 392D), produced either at the very end of Chaucer's life or after his death. Unlike Gower, who apparently took some pains over the publication of *Confessio Amantis* and his other works, Chaucer seems to have been relatively unconcerned to leave an ordered literary archive, and the transmission of his works during the fifteenth century reflects the results of this. There is, it seems, less homogeneity in the layout and appearance of Chaucer manuscripts than there is in copies of Gower's works; and in the case of *Piers Plowman* manuscripts, where transmission was more regionally diffuse, still less standardisation (Edwards and Pearsall 1989). Fifteenth-century attempts to patch *lacunae* in some of Chaucer's poems include the incorporation of the romance *Gamelyn* into *Canterbury Tales* manuscripts to make good the unfinished *Cook's Tale*, and a variety of expansions of the text of the song which concludes *The Parliament of Fowls* (see Hanna 1996: 185–90).

The simple fact that by the start of the fifteenth century there now existed a number of long, self-consciously 'poetic' texts in English was no doubt of real significance, not just to the processes by which manuscripts were produced (especially in London), but also to English manuscript-owners and readers. The emergence of a body of English poets whose works took material form in large manuscript volumes may well have been influential on would-be authors, as well. Hoccleve's sense of himself as an author, so vividly realised in the content of the works which make up the *Series*, is concretised in the manuscripts of that compilation which he copied for presentation (Durham, University Library MS Cosin V. iii. 9, originally made for Joan Beaufort, Countess of Westmorland, and San Marino, Huntington Library MSS HM 111 and HM 744, originally perhaps one volume: see Burrow 1994: 50–54). Lydgate too wrote works for presentation, and although no surviving manuscripts of his poems are in his own hand, it is possible that he took an active interest in their production, particularly those containing the *Life of St Edmund* (patron saint of Lydgate's Benedictine house in Bury St Edmunds, Suffolk), and the lengthy *Troy Book* and *Fall of Princes*, multiple copies of which were made by one particular scribe (Edwards and Pearsall 1989: 268–69). Some of the manuscripts of Lydgate's long poems also represent the high points of the illustration of Middle English verse texts: *The Fall of Princes* in London, British Library MS Harley 1766, the *Troy Book* in Manchester, John Rylands Library MS English 1 (see Figure 29.1) and *The Life of St Edmund* in London, British Library MS Harley 2278 are examples of well-produced manuscripts with picture-cycles. Although some copies of Gower's *Confessio Amantis* have miniatures, Chaucer manuscripts, in contrast, have only sporadic and partial programmes of illustration (the Canterbury pilgrim portraits in the Ellesmere manuscript, for example, and the *Troilus* frontispiece in the other wise uncompleted cycle of miniatures intended for Cambridge, Corpus Christi College MS 61).

Metropolitan Book Production

The multiplication of copies of all these long English late fourteenth- and early fifteenth-century English poems was one dimension of a general increase in book supply and demand in the fifteenth century, taking place alongside an increase in literacy and a growth in the availability of paper (as an option to replace parchment) as a means of producing books more cheaply. Recoverable evidence about scribal activity and about the role of stationers seems to indicate that, certainly in London, book production became more systematised over the course of the fifteenth century, with the result that the choices open to would-be readers were several (Christianson 1999). Manuscripts could be commissioned within the household, using the labour of readily available clerks; or from a stationer, who would organise copying, and could contract out matters like decoration, illumination and binding; they could be bought ready-made (first- or second-hand), from a stationer or perhaps a mercer; they could be bought directly from an acquaintance, or received through inheritance or bequest; and (a final option open to those sufficiently proficient) they could be made by do-it-yourself methods (Sutton and Visser-Fuchs 1995).

The identification of certain hands in numbers of surviving manuscript copies of Middle English verse texts would seem to indicate that by the fifteenth century there were in London systems for the commercial production of literary man-uscripts (Edwards and Pearsall 1989). The so-called 'hooked –g' scribe, another scribe named Stephen Doddesham, and one more anonymous scribe known as the 'Ham-mond scribe' (after the scholar who first wrote about his work) all produced more than one copy of the same work. Doddesham's hand, for example, has been identified in a total of twenty-seven manuscripts, including three separate copies of Lydgate's *Siege of Thebes*; the Hammond-scribe's hand in fifteen manuscripts, including two copies of Hoccleve's *Regiment of Princes* and two of *The Canterbury Tales* (Mooney 2000). The Hammond-scribe also seems to have had some association with manu-script anthologies produced in London at a slightly earlier point in the fifteenth century by a named scribe, John Shirley (Boffey and Thompson 1989; Connolly 1998). Shirley had a long career as a member of the retinue of Richard Beauchamp,

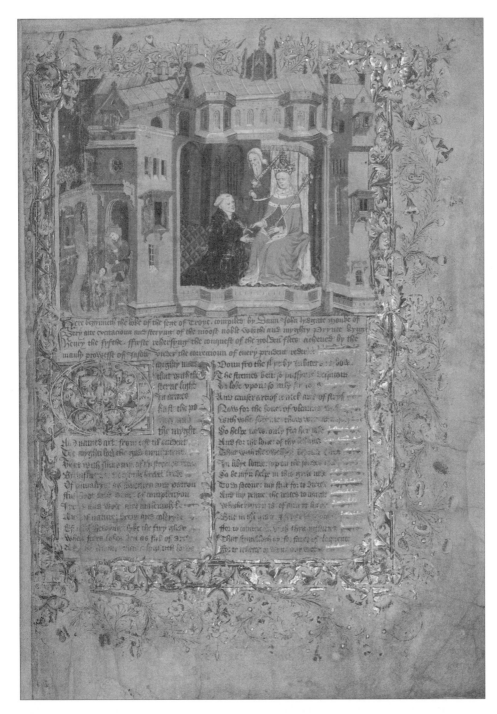

Figure 29.1 Rylands English MS 1, fol. 1r, Lydgate, *Troy Book*, late 1440s. Lydgate presenting his book.
Courtesy of the John Rylands University Library, Manchester.

Earl of Warwick, and he may also have had some direct acquaintance with Lydgate, many of whose works are included in the anthologies he compiled, at a relatively late stage in his long life, for some kind of wider circulation. He supplied a marginal commentary to some of the texts he copied, most memorably to extracts from Lydgate's *Fall of Princes*, comically upbraiding the author for his misogynistic remarks (Connolly 1998: 180).

Shirley's anthologies are developed models of the kind of mixed-content manuscript in which much later Middle English verse – apart from long works like Lydgate's *Fall of Princes*, *Troy Book* and *The Life of Our Lady*, Hoccleve's *Regiment of Princes*, or late copies of earlier compilations like the *South English Legendary* or *The Prick of Conscience* – have survived. Few such collections have anything of the flavour of Shirley's volumes, where prefatory or marginal comments about authors and the circumstances in which their works were composed or delivered create a definable context of some sort. Indeed the reasons behind particular assortments of texts are mostly now obscured, although this has not prevented much speculation about possible thematic links, or audience preferences, which might explain why particular groups of items were brought together. A small number of extant 'twin' manuscripts, in which runs of contents are identically replicated, suggests that some anthologies were produced in standard form, for speculative sale, and/or that those commissioning them based their choice of contents on existing models (Boffey and Thompson 1989: 279–80). In other instances, small runs of material are replicated within the context of different larger wholes, as if certain clusters of texts tended to circulate together; this phenomenon can be observed in some of the manuscripts containing Lydgate's shorter poems.

The construction of a manuscript from a number of 'booklets', or self-contained groups of quires, apparently became during the fifteenth century a relatively common way of making an anthology (Boffey and Thompson 1989; Hanna 1996: 21–34). This model has obvious appeal for the do-it-yourself manuscript-maker, who could simply bring into being or accumulate booklets in a piecemeal way to make a potentially further expandable volume. But it apparently also took hold as a commercial model of production. It is detectable, for example, in the compilation of a number of manuscript anthologies which contain Chaucer's minor poems and the various debate and dream poems (by authors like Clanvowe, Lydgate and Hoccleve) that became associated with them, and in some metropolitan anthologies from the end of the fifteenth century which draw together verse of assorted kinds with prose texts and chronicles (Boffey and Thompson 1989). The propensity of readers to collect unbound individual quires or booklets presumably explains the references that sometimes occur in wills and inventories to manuscripts 'in quaterniis' (in quires). These were sometimes protected in loose vellum wrappers, a cheap form of temporary binding, of which some examples have been preserved. The currency of manuscript booklets was very probably influential on the decision made by some early printers to produce small pamphlets (occasionally in approximations of uniform editions), for serial collection and possible later binding (see below, p. 551).

Non-Metropolitan Manuscripts

The production of manuscripts of later Middle English verse was by no means confined to London. Labour and materials for producing manuscripts may have been somewhat less ready to hand and less systematically organised outside the metropolis, but they certainly existed, and – from the evidence of what can be deduced from the transmission of regionally-composed verse texts – were often quite energetically exploited. Some pockets of manuscript production, and of manuscript acquisition and use, were centred on aristocratic households, such as that of the Gloucestershire Berkeley family, under whose auspices the Augustinian canon John Walton appears *c.* 1410 to have made a verse translation of Boethius's *De Consolatione Philosophiae* for Elizabeth Berkeley, having probably already made a prose translation of Vegetius's *De Re Militari* for her father Sir Thomas (see Hammond 1927: 39–52). Although no autograph or presentation copy of the Boethius translation survives, the fact that it was in the sixteenth century first printed in Tavistock, rather than London (STC 3200), suggests that it may have retained through the fifteenth century its status as a 'local' West Country text, as well as travelling further afield. Other noble families whose households in the regions were involved in the production and use of manuscripts of verse texts include the Percys, the Nevilles, the Beauchamps, and in Scotland the Sinclairs. Smaller concentrations of interest in verse texts can be detected in the reading matter of regional networks of gentry families, like those in Derbyshire implicated in the production and circulation of the (largely verse) anthology now known as the Findern manuscript (Cambridge University Library Ff. 1. 6), or of Alice Chaucer and her circle, charged for a period with the guardianship of the noble French prisoner-poet Charles d'Orléans, whose English poems are extant in BL MS Harley 682. The activities of authors like the Oxfordshire Peter Idley, whose verse *Instructions to his son* survive in nine more or less complete copies, or of John Metham in Norfolk, author of the romance *Amoryus and Cleopes* (surviving only in Princeton University Library MS Garrett 141) may have taken place in similar milieux.

Religious houses – established centres for composition and copying for many centuries – continued to be hospitable to many aspects of literary production, although it is worth noting that an author such as Lydgate, whose official home was the Benedictine house at Bury St Edmunds, and who produced among other vocation-specific works a life of St Edmund for his own house and lives of Saints Alban and Amphabel at the request of the abbot of the Benedictine house at St Albans, was in fact able to work elsewhere (and on the commission of other patrons) for quite significant parts of his verse-writing life. Manuscripts associated with other religious houses include the collected carols of James Ryman, a Franciscan friar from Canterbury (Cambridge, University Library MS Ee. 1. 12, produced in 1492); an anthology of the devotional poems and carols of John Audelay, an Augustinian friar who became chaplain and chantry priest at Haughmond in Shropshire (Oxford, Bodleian Library MS Douce 302); copies of the lives of Saints Norbert and Katharine by John

Capgrave, prior of the house of Augustinian friars at Bishop's Lynn (*St Norbert* surviving in an autograph copy; Lucas 1997: 14, 281–84), and some repertories of both religious and secular lyrics and carols possibly connected with other East Anglian houses (London, British Library MS Sloane 2593; Oxford, Bodleian Library MS Eng. poet. e. 1) .

Manuscripts such as these last-mentioned repertories had obvious functions in the everyday life of a religious institution, while the anthology of Audelay's works, if not performatively functional, may have been conceived as a commemorative archive. Other texts and manuscripts produced within the ambit of religious houses may have played a role in outreach activities in the local community. Some of Capgrave's writings were of this kind, and survive in manuscripts made by the author, or by a scribe working in association with him, William Gybbe of Wisbech (Lucas 1997: 127–65. *The Life of St Katharine* now survives only in copies made further afield in East Anglia, although it too presumably once existed in a Capgrave holograph; Lucas 1997: 14). The *Legendys of Hooly Wummen*, by Osbern Bokenham, an Augustinian friar at Stoke-by-Clare in Suffolk, appear to have circulated originally in booklets among the local families for whose female members they were compiled, and then at a subsequent stage to have been assembled together as reading matter for an East Anglian women's religious house (in London, British Library Arundel 327, copied in Cambridge for a one 'Frere Thomas Burgh', probably for presentation; see Edwards 1994).

The notable (and mostly wool-based) affluence of fifteenth-century East Anglia has made this a particularly rewarding area for the investigation of regional manuscript production, whether in connection with religious houses, or urban centres such as Bury St Edmunds and Norwich, or particular households and family networks. Patterns of local patronage and the work of East Anglian scribes are just two of a number of areas which have been illuminatingly studied (see Beadle 1991). One thing such studies make clear is that authors, texts and scribes could and did travel, often surprising distances. Although John Metham's romance *Amoryus and Cleopes* may not have been widely known outside the locale of its production, other East Anglian works (some of those produced by Lydgate for patrons close to Bury St Edmunds, or Bokenham's *Legend of St Dorothy*, for example) appear in anthologies with no discernible local associations. Many manuscripts came into the hands of East Anglian readers from outside the region, as illustrated by the scope of the large library accumulated at Caister in Norfolk by Sir John Fastolf, a veteran of the Hundred Years' War, who procured volumes in France which included poems by Christine de Pizan and Alain Chartier, and also employed London-based scribes and artists on some of the manuscripts he commissioned. William Ebesham, a Westminster scribe whose hand has been identified in a number of manuscripts, appears to have travelled periodically to Norfolk to complete work on a compilation for John Paston I that survives as London, British Library MS Lansdowne 285 (Beadle 1991: 91n, 98–99). While regional manuscript production was certainly a reality, links between London and the regions were dynamic and numerous.

Manuscripts of Scottish Verse Texts

The less systematic forms of book production observable outside London seem to have been characteristic also of fifteenth-century Scotland, where it is relatively common for a text to survive in only one exemplar, as if confined in circulation to a delimited coterie. An extensive compilation of Scottish saints' lives, similar in scope to the much more widely circulating *South English Legendary*, survives in only one copy (in Cambridge, University Library MS Gg. 2. 6), as do *The Kingis Quair* (in Oxford, Bodleian Library MS Arch. Selden. B. 24) and the romance *Lancelot of the Laik* (in Cambridge, University Library MS Kk. 1. 5). The verse texts that seem to have enjoyed more established kinds of circulation are histories like Barbour's *Bruce* (even this in only two fifteenth-century manuscripts), Wyntoun's *Chronicle of Scotland* (nine more or less complete copies), and in the early sixteenth century Douglas's *Eneydos* translation (five complete early to mid-sixteenth-century manuscripts), the most authoritative copy of which was overseen by the author, and described by its scribe as 'the first correk copy' (Cambridge, Trinity College MS O. 3.12).

More strikingly still, a number of the best-known fifteenth-century Scottish poems are extant only in much later manuscripts or printed editions: among these are Richard Holland's alliterative *The Buke of the Howlat*, Gilbert Haye's *Buke of King Alexander the Conquerour*, the anonymous *Taill of Rauf Coilyear*, and much of the verse of both Henryson and Dunbar (Fox 1977). Even within the corpus of fifteenth-century manuscripts, there are startling discrepancies between dates of composition and dates of copying: the composition of *The Kingis Quair* is usually assigned to the late 1420s or early 1430s, and must – if James I was its author – predate that king's murder in 1437, but the unique copy is one that cannot have been made before 1488, and resides in a manuscript anthology which was itself revised and reshaped over time.

The energies of sixteenth-century Edinburgh manuscript compilers like the notary John Asloan and the antiquarian George Bannatyne preserved a number of texts which had perhaps previously circulated in relatively ephemeral shape: Asloan's manuscript (Edinburgh, National Library of Scotland MS 16500) was copied some time after 1513, Bannatyne's (Edinburgh, National Library of Scotland Adv. 1.1.6) in 1568. It is not hard to see why some of the texts brought together in these collections have not survived in other copies. Many of Dunbar's short poems relating to court life, for example, are sufficiently occasion- or person-specific for their transmission to have been fairly limited to immediate court circles, and the kinds of short devotional poem collected by Asloan and Bannatyne (as by the compiler of London, British Library MS Arundel 285, a striking devotional anthology) may in their early life have circulated orally or in materially vulnerable forms on single leaves or bifolia, or in short pamphlets.

The absence of early copies of Henryson's poems is puzzling, since these are in the main fairly substantial and not obviously occasional works, but it is possible here that the evidence of the pattern of survivals is simply misleading. Extracts from Henryson's *Fables* were jotted into a late fifteenth-century student notebook (the

'Makculloch manuscript', Edinburgh, University Library MS 205), and *Orpheus and Eurydice* and *The Testament of Cresseid* were printed sufficiently early in the sixteenth century to hint at some wider earlier circulation of which the material traces have simply disappeared. *The Traitie of Orpheus* (as it is called in the printed edition) was issued in Edinburgh in 1508 by the pioneer Scottish printers Chepman and Myllar (STC 13166), as part of a series which also included some works by Dunbar; the *Testament* was printed in London in 1532 with works by and associated with Chaucer (STC 5068). In these cases, as with much other late medieval Scottish verse, the relations between manuscript transmission and printed circulation are complex (Fox 1977). It is likely that a number of the texts hand-copied into the Asloan and Bannatyne collections, as also into British Library MS Arundel 285 and other sixteenth-century Scottish manuscripts, derive from printed exemplars – an instance of the actually quite common reversal of the 'script-to-print' model of textual transmission.

Later Middle English Verse in Print

The first printing press in England was established at Westminster in 1476 by William Caxton, a prosperous member of the Mercers' Company, who had taken himself from Flanders to Germany to learn about the new technology in the early 1470s, and tested the English market for printed books by producing some in Bruges, starting probably in 1473/4 with a printed edition of his prose translation of Raoul le Fèvre's compilation of classical narratives *The Recuyell of the Historyes of Troye*. Caxton took pains to point out in the epilogue to this work the significantly different potentialities of the manuscript and the printed book: 'I have practysed and lerned at my grete charge and dispense to ordeyne this said book in prynte after the maner and forme as ye may here see; and [it] is not wreton with penne and ynke as other bokes ben to th'ende that every man may have them attones' (Blake 1973: 100). What he stresses is that a number of readers can have copies at the same time ('every man may have them attones'), without being subjected to the delay inherent in the hand-written replication of texts.

The introduction of printing was important to many dimensions of late medieval life, not least those administrative, legal and ecclesiastical ones that increasingly relied on the production and circulation of documents. In some contexts printing might have been regarded as a new-fangled and dirty business which put scribes and illustrators out of work and generated offensively mass-produced volumes (a practice sentence in a Latin textbook of 1519 states that 'Pryntynge hathe almooste vndone scriueners crafte'; William Horman, *Vulgaria*, STC 13811, sig. Oiir), but it is hard to find significant signs that it was not generally welcomed, and Caxton certainly did his utmost, in the prologues and epilogues to his own productions, to enhance the cultural capital of his own enterprise (see the collection in Blake 1973). Part of this strategy, perhaps, was his early effort to give the poems of Chaucer and of Lydgate a printed existence (Gillespie 2006). Works by both authors are among the very first books printed by Caxton at Westminster. He began with shortish poems – Lydgate's *Churl and Bird*, *Horse, Sheep and Goose*, *The Temple of Glass*; Chaucer's *Parliament of Fowls* and *Anelida and Arcite* (STC 17008, 17018, 17032, 5091, 5090), perhaps sensibly testing the waters before in 1478 releasing his first edition of *The Canterbury Tales* (STC 5082) and building on this in the 1480s with a second edition (STC 5083) and then *Troilus and Criseyde* (STC 5094), *The House of Fame* (STC 5087) and Lydgate's *Life of Our Lady* (STC 17023). Along the way he added another major verse work, Gower's *Confessio Amantis* (STC 12142). Notably absent from his output are alliterative verse, plays, metrical romances, comic verse narratives, carols, or extended collections of lyrics (although he used a small number of these last as 'fillers' with longer items); Hoccleve's poems do not figure either, even though *The Regiment of Princes* especially had a wide fifteenth-century circulation in manuscript. English verse, for Caxton's purposes, appears to have meant texts from a narrowly defined tradition, and texts from the past.

That these works had a hallowed past did not mean that Caxton ignored the chance to make innovations as he printed them. His concern to offer the best available text evidently led him to revise his edition of *The Canterbury Tales* – a proceeding described and justified at some length in the prologue to the second edition (STC 5083; Blake 1973: 61–63) – and he solved the difficulty of printing the seemingly unfinished *House of Fame* by supplying a conclusion of his own (STC 5087; Blake 1973: 102–3). Woodcut illustrations could enhance the visual appeal of a book, and a series of pilgrim portraits, following what seems to have been the most influential model of illustration in the manuscript tradition, was introduced into the second edition of *The Canterbury Tales*. Experimentation with the visual appeal of printed books was to be continued by the successor to Caxton's business, Wynkyn de Worde, who not only took over some of Caxton's texts and the woodcut illustrations that accompanied them, but also introduced ornamented or illustrative title-pages. De Worde's two c. 1500 editions of Lydgate's *Horse, Sheep and Goose*, for example (STC 17020, 17021), have title-page illustrations depicting animals (not the right ones, but at least a gesture to appropriateness); his 1517 edition of *Troilus and Criseyde* (STC 5095), unlike Caxton's earlier one, is illustrated with several woodcut images.

At the very end of the fifteenth century, when it was no doubt clear that printing was here to stay, de Worde took the decision to relocate his business in the city of London. His new premises at the sign of the sun in Fleet Street, while further from the abbey and government contacts which had been useful to Caxton at Westminster, were closer to St Paul's, and to the areas around the cathedral which had traditionally been associated with the book trade. In the city he was also nearer to the premises of other printers like Richard Pynson, who had begun by specialising in the printing of legal texts and was to become King's Printer to Henry VIII, but who like de Worde evidently saw a commercial advantage in expanding the kinds of verse text available in print. Evidence of their periodic collaboration suggests that the relationship between de Worde and Pynson was something other than rivalry; they certainly seem to have had a shared understanding of the potential market – largely ignored by Caxton – for forms of verse writing outside the Chaucerian tradition. Both printed metrical romances like *Guy of Warwick*, *Bevis of Hampton* and *Richard Coeur de Lion*; comic tales like *Jack and his Stepdame*; collections of carols and scurrilous or antifeminist texts; moral plays like *Everyman* and *Hick Scorner*; and single saints' lives in verse. Both also commissioned translations, largely from French, of works known to have had a wide continental circulation: an anonymous translator produced for de Worde an English version of the frequently reprinted *Les quinze joies de mariage* (the *fyftene Ioyes of maryage*, STC 15257.5), while Pynson produced *a lytell treatyse cleped La conusaunce damours* (STC 5631).

Many of these English works, like the Chaucer and Lydgate printed by Caxton, were not new: they had circulated in manuscript copies throughout the fifteenth century, mostly anonymously, and in some cases continued to have a manuscript circulation alongside a print one. There are, however, some grounds for supposing that, for poets who wanted to forge a name for themselves, print was an attractive new medium. Almost all the works of Stephen Hawes and Alexander Barclay survive only in printed editions, from de Worde and Pynson respectively, as if these authors strove for 'publication' of what was, in late medieval terms, a novel kind. But John Skelton's attitude to the recording and transmission of his works is less clear-cut, and perhaps a more accurate reflection of the fluid relationship between the established and the new modes of textual transmission. Although Skelton's writing appeared very early in print with the satirical dream vision *The Bowge of Court* (de Worde, 1499; STC 22597), and several more of his poems were printed in his lifetime, he does not seem to have forged the relationship with an individual printer that Hawes and Barclay did, and a number of his works anyway circulated primarily in manuscript: *A Lawde and Prayse Made for Our Sovereigne Lord the King* from 1509 survives in a unique, probably holograph copy (National Archives E 32–68); *Speke Parrott*, *Collyn Clout* and *Why Come Ye Nat To Courte*, all circulating in manuscript during his lifetime, were not printed until after his death. The *Garlande or Chapelet of Laurell* was printed by Richard Fakes in October 1523 (STC 22610) and survives also in a now fragmentary manuscript copy (London, British Library MS Cotton Vitellius E. x). Its wide-ranging review of the potential causes of authorial anxiety includes some pointed remarks about the material difficulties of finding and keeping literary fame.

Printing Outside London

Skelton's connections with printers and the court, and the strongly metropolitan associations of the early manuscript copies of his works, have meant that he is generally constructed as a London author – with some small concurrent claim, on the grounds of his period of residence in Diss in Norfolk, to be an East Anglian one (see Scattergood 1991). The *Garlande or Chapelet of Laurell*, printed and probably also copied in London, nonetheless situates itself as a work 'studyously dyvysed at Sheryfhotten Castle' – Sheriff Hutton Castle, the Yorkshire home of Thomas Howard, Earl of Surrey and third Duke of Norfolk, whose family members Skelton addresses in some of the inset lyrics – and it serves as a reminder that literary production went on energetically in the regions through the whole of the period that Caxton, de Worde, Pynson and other printers were establishing metropolitan businesses. Barclay's poems, too, although printed in London, were mostly written outside it, in Devon, where he was a chaplain at Ottery St Mary, and later in Ely, where he became a Benedictine monk. The transmission to London of such regionally produced works, and conversely, the dissemination outside London of works printed there, bespeaks the existence of a variety of networks, some perhaps commercial, others connected maybe with household or court circles. Some printing businesses were established outside London: as well as the press at the Benedictine house of Tavistock which produced Walton's Boethius translation (as *the boke of confort*; STC 3200), a press at St Albans, probably operating from the Benedictine abbey, produced Lydgate's *Lyfe of Seint Albon* (STC 17025), *c*.1535; more Lydgate was printed in the 1520s and 1530s, along with *Boccus and Sydracke* (STC 31860), at a press connected with St Augustine's abbey in Canterbury.

'Smal Pamfletes' and Big Books

The 1508 Edinburgh experiment of Chepman and Myllar involved the printing of nine small books, quarto-sized and between 8 and 48 pages long, offering a selection of what were presumably deemed attractive works, among them a romance, a Robin Hood poem, and samples of the works of Dunbar, Henryson and Lydgate. Many of the verse texts issued by de Worde and Pynson (and indeed some of Mychell's Canterbury Lydgate works) were in books of a similar size, as if replicating in printed form the 'booklets' common in late medieval manuscript production. Short printed books of this kind might contain one single text (the satirical *Treatise of a Galaunt*, for example; STC 24240 etc.), or a collection (some 'proverbs' attributed to Lydgate, for instance; STC 17026). With the addition of suitable woodcut ornamentation and title-pages, they could even implicitly be offered as potential parts of a uniform edition, for serial collection and possibly eventual binding together in the kind of composite book that is today called a *Sammelband*. Some surviving examples of these composite volumes contain what were obviously purchases from one supplier; others group together books of the same size from different sources, and even occasionally contain manuscript booklets alongside their printed ones.

Alongside the production of such 'small storyes and pamfletes', as they were described by de Worde's contemporary and colleague Robert Copland (in his preface to *Kynge Appolyn*, STC 708.5), went increasingly elaborate efforts to circumscribe the 'works' of individual authors within a single volume or edition. Some evidence of this can be adduced from fifteenth-century manuscripts such as the Chaucer anthology in Cambridge, University Library MS Gg. 4. 27, the Hoccleve autographs, the poems of Charles d'Orléans in London, British Library MS Harley 682, and the Anglo-Scottish materials assembled around Chaucer's name in Oxford, Bodleian Library MS Arch. Selden. B. 24. In 1526 Pynson took steps towards a collected Chaucer by printing three uniform folio volumes containing *Troilus and Criseyde*, *The Canterbury Tales* and an anthology of the shorter poems (together with some non-Chaucerian verse) called *the boke of fame* (STC 5096, 5086, 5088). Then in 1532 Thomas Godfray produced *The workes of Geffray Chaucer newly printed* (STC 5068), a huge compendium assembled by William Thynne and a group of court associates, with a prologue addressed to King Henry VIII. In the course of the later sixteenth century Skelton's works were to be collected in a similar, if slightly less voluminous, way.

Middle English Verse in the Sixteenth Century

The printing of a collected works of Chaucer is of course some kind of milestone in the history of the transmission of late medieval English verse. But it is important not to see it as the culmination of this history, or indeed to regard the history itself as having a smooth forwards trajectory. Much Middle English verse, from the fifteenth century and indeed earlier, remained in circulation in manuscript in the sixteenth century, and readers' annotations indicate a continuing engagement with it; printed texts took their place alongside this material, and did not necessarily supersede it. Just as manuscripts of Middle English verse served printers as copy-text, so scribes were to go on using printed editions as the source for new hand-written copies of the sort produced in Edinburgh by Asloan and Bannatyne. Fifteenth-century and earlier Middle English poems were to be revived in print in the sixteenth century for (sometimes covert) new polemical purposes. *Piers Plowman*, for example, took on new significance in an age of religious reform, available in existing and newly copied manuscripts and then at last printed, first by Crowley for Richard Grafton in 1550 (STC 19906), and in several further editions. That no trace should survive of the printing of Hoccleve's major works may indicate that his poems indeed fell into oblivion; or it may result from random material losses which preclude any accurate assessment of the longevity of his reputation. Either way, the curious discrepancy of his disappearance underlines just how much our understanding of the material production and reception of Middle English poetry depends on an evidence base that is at best partial. Accounts of late fifteenth- and early sixteenth-century literary history, or of the history of the book during this period, have to accommodate the likelihood that seemingly detectable trends may be no more than unrepresentative blips, and that every survival is to be offset against unfathomable losses. The lengthy account of his own works which Skelton inserts into the *Garlande or Chapelet of Laurell* (lines 1376–1501; Scattergood 1983), with its many references to texts which seem to have completely disappeared, is a potent reminder that reconstructing a literary canon, or a history of literary production, is an approximate art.

REFERENCES AND FURTHER READING

Primary Texts and Sources

Further details of the Middle English verse of this period are to be found in Hammond 1927, with updated information about surviving manuscripts in J. Boffey and A. S. G. Edwards, *A New Index of Middle English Verse* (London: The British Library, 2005), and about printed editions in *A Short Title Catalogue of Books Printed in England, Scotland and Ireland 1475–1640*, first compiled by A. W. Pollard and G. R. Redgrave, 2nd edn begun by W. A. Jackson and F. S. Ferguson, completed by K. F. Pantzer, 3 vols (Oxford: Oxford University Press, 1976–1986), here abbreviated to STC. Digital facsimiles of many of the books listed in STC are available through EEBO (Early English Books Online: http://eebo.chadwyck.com/home). Images from a number of the manuscripts mentioned can be consulted on the websites of the libraries in which they are now held.

Secondary Reading

Beadle, R. (1991). Prolegomena to a literary geography of later medieval Norfolk. In F. Riddy (ed.). *Regionalism in Late Medieval Manuscripts and Texts: Essays Celebrating the Publication of 'A Linguistic Atlas of Late Mediaeval English'*. York Manuscripts Conference: Proceedings Series, 2 (pp. 90–108). Cambridge: D. S. Brewer.

Blake, N. F. (ed.) (1973). *Caxton's Own Prose*. London: André Deutsch.

Boffey, J. and J. J. Thompson (1989). Anthologies and miscellanies: production and choice of texts. In J. Griffiths and D. Pearsall (eds). *Book Production and Publishing in Britain 1375–1475* (pp. 279–315). Cambridge: Cambridge University Press.

Boffey, J. and A. S. G. Edwards (1999). Literary texts. In L. Hellinga and J. Trapp (eds). *The Cambridge History of the Book in Britain. Volume III, 1400–1557* (pp. 555–75). Cambridge: Cambridge University Press.

Burrow, J. A. (1994). *Thomas Hoccleve*. Authors of the Middle Ages 4. Aldershot: Variorum.

Burrow, J. A. (ed.) (1999). *Thomas Hoccleve's Complaint and Dialogue*. Early English Text Society o.s. 313. Oxford: Oxford University Press

Christianson, C. P. (1999). The rise of London's book-trade. In L. Hellinga and J. Trapp (eds). *The Cambridge History of the Book in Britain. Volume III, 1400–1557* (pp. 128–47). Cambridge: Cambridge University Press.

Connolly, M. (1998). *John Shirley: Book Production and the Noble Household in Fifteenth-century England*. Aldershot: Ashgate Publishing.

Doyle, A. I. and M. B. Parkes (1978). The production of copies of the 'Canterbury Tales' and the 'Confessio Amantis' in the early fifteenth century. In M. B. Parkes and A. G. Watson (eds). *Medieval Scribes, Manuscripts and Libraries: Essays Presented to N. R. Ker* (pp. 163–210). London: Scolar Press.

Edwards, A. S. G. and D. Pearsall (1989). The manuscripts of the major English poetic texts. In J. Griffiths and D. Pearsall (eds). *Book Production and Publishing in Britain 1375–1475* (pp. 257–78). Cambridge: Cambridge University Press.

Edwards, A. S. G. (1994). Osbern Bokenham's 'Legendys of Hooly Wummen'. In A. J. Minnis (ed.). *Late-Medieval Religious Texts and their Transmission: Essays in Honour of A. I. Doyle*. York Manuscripts Conferences: Proceedings Series 3 (pp. 157–67). Cambridge: D. S. Brewer.

Edwards, A. S. G. (2000). Fifteenth-century Middle English verse author collections. In A. S. G. Edwards, V. Gillespie and R. Hanna (eds). *The English Medieval Book. Studies in Memory of Jeremy Griffiths* (pp. 101–12). London: British Library.

Edwards, A. S. G. and Pearsall, D. (1989). The manuscripts of the major English poetic texts. In J. Griffiths and D. Pearsall (eds). *Book Production and Publishing in Britain 1375–1475* (pp. 257–78). Cambridge: Cambridge University Press.

Fox, D. (1977). Manuscripts and prints of Scots poetry in the sixteenth century. In A. J. Aitken, M. P. McDiarmid and D. S. Thomson (eds). *Bards & Makars. Scottish Language and Literature: Medieval and Renaissance* (pp. 156–71). Glasgow: University of Glasgow Press.

Gillespie, A. (2006). *Print Culture and the Medieval Author. Chaucer, Lydgate and their Books, 1473–1557*. Oxford: Oxford University Press.

Griffiths, J. and D. Pearsall (eds) (1989). *Book Production and Publishing in Britain 1375–1475*. Cambridge: Cambridge University Press.

Hammond, E. P. (1927). *English Verse between Chaucer and Surrey*. Durham, NC: Duke University Press.

Hanna, R. III (1996). *Pursuing History. Middle English Manuscripts and Their Texts*. Stanford, CA: Stanford University Press.

Hellinga, L. and J. B. Trapp (eds) (1999). *The Cambridge History of the Book in Britain. Volume III, 1400–1557*. Cambridge: Cambridge University Press.

Lerer, S. (1993). *Chaucer and his Readers. Imagining the Author in Late-Medieval England*. Princeton, NJ: Princeton University Press.

Lucas, P. J. (1997). *From Author to Audience: John Capgrave and Medieval Publication*. Dublin: University College Dublin Press.

Mooney, L. R. (2000). Professional scribes? Identifying English scribes who had a hand in more than one manuscript. In D. Pearsall (ed.). *New Directions in Later Medieval Manuscript Studies. Essays from the 1998 Harvard Conerence* (pp. 131–41). York: York Medieval Press.

Mooney, L. R. (2006). Chaucer's scribe. *Speculum*, 81, 97–138.

Scattergood, J. (ed.) (1983). *John Skelton: The Complete English Poems*. Harmondsworth: Penguin.

Scattergood, J. (1991). The London manuscripts of John Skelton's poems. In F. Riddy (ed.). *Regionalism in Late Medieval Manuscripts and Texts. Essays Celebrating the Publication of 'A Linguistic Atlas of Late Mediaeval English'*. York Manuscripts Conference: Proceedings Series, 2 (pp. 171–82). Cambridge: D. S. Brewer.

Sutton, A. and L. Visser-Fuchs (1995). Choosing a book in late fifteenth-century England and Burgundy. In C. Barron and N. Saul (eds). *England and the Low Countries in the Late Middle Ages* (pp. 60–98). Stroud: Alan Sutton.

Poets and Poems

30
Hoccleve and Lydgate

Daniel Wakelin

Symple is my goost and scars my letterure   *spirit, literary skill*
Unto your excellence for to wryte
Myn inward love [...]
(RP: 2073–5) [1]

For rowth of whiche of his wo to endyte   *pity, compose*
My penne I feele qwakyng as I wryte.
[...] I want konnyng his peynes to descryve.   *lack*
(TG: 966–7, 971)

In these lines, the fifteenth-century poets Thomas Hoccleve (*c.* 1367–1426) and John Lydgate (*c.* 1370–1449/50?) deny their own ability to write well. Some readers have taken these and similar confessions as an accurate description of the poetry of these men, and have dismissed it. Yet these lines in fact reveal the rich complexities of their work. First, both writers are clear that poetry is a complex art which needs 'konnyng' or 'letterure', a word which means something like 'knowledge of other literature' or 'of learned matters'. Despite their worry that they lack these things, they achieve them: for example, Lydgate's worry about his shaky hand is a motif slyly borrowed from Chaucer (*Troilus and Criseyde*, IV: 13–14), which thereby cleverly copies the sentimental narration of that story; and his highlighting of the verb 'feele', by delaying it, and laying it next to 'qwakyng' so that it sounds as though both pen and poet quake, shows a rhetorical skill in pathos.[2] Yet, though they are cleverer than they profess to be in style, lines such as these might condemn the poets by their content – especially for readers seeking something personal in art. In the second quotation, Lydgate is reporting with 'rowth' not his own feelings but those of a character in his dream-vision *The Temple of Glass*, which may concern the affairs of Queen Katherine of Valois (Mitchell 2008: 57). And in the first quotation from *The Regiment of Princes*, Hoccleve is writing to 'your excellence' Prince Henry, the future Henry V, so the confession might seem obsequious and the 'love' merely flattery. Hoccleve himself elsewhere condemns the 'poesie' of 'flaterie' (*MR*: 260–64). This poetry might seem like impersonal convention, rhetorical performance or even politicking.

Much of the best-known poetry of Hoccleve and Lydgate is political rather than personal in its subject: advice to princes, such as Hoccleve's *The Regiment of Princes* and Lydgate's *The Fall of Princes*, or responses to the upheavals of the day, such as Hoccleve's attack on the heretic Sir John Oldcastle or Lydgate's attack on the Flemish enemies of the realm (*MP*, II, no. 25). There is much, though, that is fascinating in this rhetorical performance of impersonal, communal verse. This chapter will first focus less on the politics of such poems than on the stylistic and poetic elements of 'public' and apparently impersonal writing. An analysis of the style of the poetry will suggest some complexities in the ideas conveyed and in the 'politics' of who is writing, who implied to be reading, poetry in this style. (Some models for such stylistic analyses appear in one excellent defence of Lydgate's syntax by Hardman 2006.) Then the chapter will consider some genres or modes used by these poets which might seem less political or 'public', namely the many autobiographical moments in Hoccleve's *Complaint* and *Dialogue*, accounts of his recovery from some mental disturbance, and the devotional moments in Lydgate's religious lyrics. But the chapter will suggest that both poets make intimate subjects – individual life, prayer and faith – into public ones in order to strengthen with vivid directness the public address of their verse. For example, although Hoccleve writes of a prince in *The Regiment* (in the opening quotation), he does profess a strikingly personal 'love' for him, and a few lines earlier is 'ful tendre' for him (*RP*: 2021). Similarly, although Lydgate writes of some anonymous lover, he professes to feel 'rowth' for him and, in that nice experiential touch, to 'feele' his own pen quaking; by contrast, when Chaucer uses this motif (*Troilus and Criseyde*, IV: 13–14) he does not mention the physicality of holding the shaky pen nor capture the sense of stepping outside oneself, observing one's own discombobulation – which strengthens this discombobulation. There is some personal feeling here within the writing for or about others.

There is no clear divide between 'public' and more intimate elements in the poetry of Hoccleve or Lydgate or in that of their contemporaries, for instance James I of Scotland, John Audelay or George Ashby. This might represent a slight shift from the public poetry of the fourteenth century, in which, as Anne Middleton (1978: 109) has shown, the speaker appears 'not as the realisation of an individual identity, but as the realisation of the human condition' – for example, the allegorical 'Will' or 'Amans' of Langland or Gower. A generation later, Hoccleve and Lydgate do appeal to the public of readers one-to-one and conjure up a public voice of great immediacy, professed sincerity and directness.

Poets and Politics

In this period before the growth of full-time professional authors, both Hoccleve and Lydgate had to write poetry alongside their 'day jobs', one a secular bureaucrat, the other a monk. Their clerkly occupations perhaps trained them – especially Hoccleve – in the impersonal, rhetorical skill observed so far. Hoccleve worked for nearly forty years as a clerk in the office of the Privy Seal, part of the bureaucracy of government at Westminster. In this milieu, Hoccleve probably knew Chaucer who also worked there: Hoccleve wrote out a document from Henry IV confirming a payment to Chaucer and was among the men who first transcribed and circulated the works of Chaucer and Gower, in the years either side of 1400 (Burrow 1994: 3–8, 10, 17; Mooney 2007: 312). Moreover, Hoccleve tells us in ironic and subtle ways of the inspiration afforded him by Chaucer (for example, *Dial.*, 694–96), while Chaucer's poetry also informed Hoccleve's writing for public purposes: in his most ambitious poem, *The Regiment of Princes*, Hoccleve justifies opining on politics and addressing the prince directly by claiming that Chaucer 'taght' him to write, or tried to, and that Chaucer had written to illuminate 'al this land', as if a national public were implied in his poetry (*RP*: 1865–67, 1958–74, 2077–79, 4978–98).

By contrast, Lydgate probably did not know Chaucer directly, for he spent his early life as a monk at the wealthy monastery of Bury St Edmunds in Suffolk, close to his birthplace, and in further studies at Oxford. His monastic upbringing impinged on his poetic career at times: for example, Lydgate wrote a life of St Edmund, patron-saint of his own monastery, and other poems for ecclesiastical patrons: the abbot of the nearby monastery of St Albans commissioned a verse biography of *St Alban and St Amphibalus* – the first ever commission for English poetry for which there survives a record of direct payment (Pearsall 1997: 12–18, 34–35). Lydgate also wrote poetry for patrons beyond the ecclesiastical hierarchy, at the highest political level: he wrote a verse life of the Virgin Mary and a romance set in Troy for Henry V (ibid.: 18–23); and by the 1420s and 1430s other works for royal and aristocratic patrons, culminating in two works of political advice (discussed below).

Such writing for powerful political figures or for a wider politically engaged 'public' is intriguing because conflict over the crown recurred from the reign of Henry IV through to the reign of Henry VI, and even the military successes in France of Henry V did not make the Lancastrian dynasty secure. (See further the essay by Matthew Woodcock in this volume.) Hoccleve and Lydgate were affected in slight ways by the political ups and downs: for example, Hoccleve survived the deposition of Richard II with no disruption but seems to have been affected by gentle shifts in the fortunes of Prince Henry/Henry V (Mooney 2007: 311, 313). More importantly, both he and Lydgate wrote some shorter poems that serve the interests of Henry V, Henry VI and their allies quite directly. For example, in 1426 Lydgate translated from French a verse pedigree of Henry VI, commissioned by the young king's guardian, the Earl of Warwick (*MP*, II, no. 28: 279–323), in which Lydgate over-insists on the 'trouth' of his 'playn translaciou*n*'; he even declares his purpose in the opening lines as being to 'make folkys their language for to lette'. The word *language* often meant something like gossip or treasonous muttering; *let* meant not only *allow* but *prevent*; thus the poem promises to replace treasonous words with poetry (*MP*, II, no. 28: 2, 261, 264, 277, 285). These pieces of Lancastrian propaganda are shameless in the transparency of their meaning: they are useful works designed to *tell* people what or what not to think, rather than imaginative works designed to let readers think for themselves. Hoccleve and Lydgate did often write poems for the most powerful men of their time and might be forgiven for writing what such powerful, often violent, men wanted people to hear. But recent critics have uncovered more complex politics in such poetry: for example, Maura Nolan (2005) and Claire Sponsler (2008) have described Lydgate's poetry as contributing to the 'public culture' of the 1420s – a more subtle notion than describing his poetry as merely 'political' or 'propagandist'. So in the verse pedigree, for example, the 'playn' language makes the poem more accessible for a 'public' – those 'folkys' who need telling – which is itself an act of political inclusion. And of course, one could read such protests of plainness against the grain. Did Hoccleve and Lydgate write simply what the princes wanted people to hear or did they cultivate public reflection of a more complex sort?

The question is especially pertinent to some poems of the 1410s and early 1420s, written during the early manhood and then the reign of Henry V. These poems are Hoccleve's *The Regiment of Princes* (*c.* 1410–11), Lydgate's *Troy Book* (1412–20) and *The Siege of Thebe*s (undated, but perhaps written around 1422). The poems are longer, more intellectually expansive and therefore less 'playn' in meaning. Lydgate's *Troy Book* and *The Siege of Thebe*s are the best known of his works, for they fit a genre familiar from Chaucer, that of the *roman antique* – chivalric romance set in classical antiquity, such as *Troilus and Criseyde* or *The Knight's Tale*. In fact, *The Siege of Thebes* is confessedly a sequel to *The Canterbury Tales*, presented as a tale told by Lydgate who joins the pilgrims on their journey home (*ST*: 1–176), and its action ends with the scene of the women pleading to Theseus that opens the *Knight's Tale*, which is cited directly (ST: 4501–53). *Troy Book* covers the entire history of the city of Troy and therefore necessarily includes the story of Troilus in its books III and IV (intermittently from *TB*, III: 982, to IV: 3097). Recently some critics have seen some political agenda in Lydgate's poetic work in *Troy Book* of imitating Chaucer. The poem openly praises its dedicatee, Henry V, and it is often suggested that Lydgate's decision to write in an avowedly Chaucerian vein for Henry V glorifies the king with a sort of literary nationalism (Fisher 1990: 1176; Pearsall 1994: 397–98). After all, when he first introduces Criseyde, and begins to retell her story, Lydgate praises Chaucer who 'owre englishe gilt[e]' ('gilded') and 'Gan oure tonge firste to magnifie' (*TB*, III: 4237–43), with 'owre' uniting the poet with the readers. Then Lydgate promises 'hym to magnifie / In my writynge, pleinly, til I dye' (*TB*, III: 4261–62). An echo emerges between Chaucer and Lydgate, both of whom 'magnifie'; and what Lydgate magnifies Chaucer magnifying is the national tongue. Lydgate is impersonal here both in writing for the whole national community and in imitating the work of another poet.

Lydgate promises to praise 'pleinly', but is the poem plain and unifying? It panders sometimes to a simple taste for chivalry and its trappings, especially in books III and IV: these books include numerous long descriptions of knights 'with pompe ful royal' and 'passingly arrayed', turning trained killers into objects of visual delight (*TB*, III: 717–19). Lydgate lingers over the gross violence like Malory's that he evidently thought would appeal to readers, as Hector splits people in two, for example (*TB*, III: 2603–2605). Lydgate's descriptions of battles, in particular, surpass Chaucer's, who, when he describes the Trojan war, is not much concerned with military chivalry. At first glance, *Troy Book* may seem objectionable. Yet the work does not only pander to the chivalric ideology of the fifteenth-century reading public; it also contains lessons about the failures and horrors of chivalry. Sometimes Lydgate flinches from the violence. Thus he doubts whether the wounded Hector could kill a thousand knights: 'ȝif it be so that men may ȝeue feyth' (*TB*, III: 1926–35). And he doubts the morality of his heroes: there are ominous lines where Hector tells Troilus to avoid 'wilfulnes' in battle, identifying something which one might, if dourly moralistic, see to be Troilus's sin in Chaucer's poem (*TB*, III: 172–247). And throughout *Troy Book*, especially in book II, wise counsellors, suffering women or Lydgate himself criticise warfare in long and powerful speeches. They repeatedly warn military heroes to think 'prudently', and prudent reflection is encouraged in the reader by these moments of critique, or by what Lydgate sometimes calls the instructive 'example' of Troy (*TB*, II: 1797–1902; see for example II: 2183–2304, 2900–2984). In these moments – found also in *The Siege of Thebes* – some scholars have detected powerful criticism of the chivalric ideals and military policies of Henry V and his brothers (Simpson 1997; Straker 1999: 146). *Troy Book* and *The Siege of Thebes* serve readers who enjoy the chivalry and Chaucerianism, but also offer critical or moral instruction which might be considered less public (in the sense of less *open*) or of a different public usefulness.

Public Hoccleve

But a narrative poem can convey nationalism, instil the virtues of chivalry or even offer critique only obliquely. If a classical history does refer to contemporary politics – beyond the prologues deferential to patrons – it can do so only allegorically or metaphorically. Consequently, contemporary politics seem more explicitly discussed in a genre that is declaredly political: the 'mirror for princes'. This genre is most moulded by two works of Latin prose: the anonymous *Secreta Secretorum* ('the secret of secrets'), which descends from Arabic sources but purports to be a work sent by Aristotle to Alexander the Great; and Giles of Rome's enormous *De Regimine Principum* ('the guidance of princes'). Amid a general trend to translate these works into English at this time, Lydgate translated parts of *Secreta Secretorum* as *Secrees of Old Philisoffres*, and both treatises were among the sources for Hoccleve's *The Regiment of Princes*, as he tells us (*RP*: 2038–58, 2108–14; Perkins 2001: 87–93). Such works explicitly offer advice to princes or kings, and therefore their politics might be plainer than those of the romances. Thus Hoccleve's *Regiment* has been seen as a work 'unabashedly partisan' to the prince and legitimating his rule (Strohm 1999: 644; Pearsall 1994).

Yet one thing that distinguishes the mirrors for princes of Hoccleve and Lydgate from others is the greater degree of storytelling in them; thus they share more with the classical histories than might be expected. In his *Regiment* Hoccleve intersperses direct advice with numerous short stories, which Latin mirrors for princes tend not to do, and also increases the length or humour of some of the stories (Perkins 2001: 103–14). However, this use of exemplary stories invites some questions about the ways they work. Do they offer models of how Prince Henry *does* behave? Of how he *should and does* behave? Of how he *should but does not yet* behave? Or of how he *never will* behave? How we answer these questions will reflect whether, on close reading, we see this poem as prince-pleasing or boldly counselling. Some stories continue one common element of Middle English poetry: the use of fiction, often in pithy verse, to offer examples or fables that teach lessons in a vivid or humorous form (Scanlon 1994). For example, the witty ripostes of 'Smylynge' Caesar or Antigonus make the virtue of patience – a sort of forgiveness – look cool and assured rather than meek (*RP*: 3522–25, 3539–42). Yet Hoccleve's stories do not always teach messages: for example, the story of John of Canace seems to teach nothing but craftiness (*RP*: 4180–4354).

Wisely, then, Hoccleve does also advise more directly. For example, he tells us how emperors 'in dayes olde' had to choose their tombs when they were first crowned, in order to remind themselves that they were mortal and might leave behind only a reputation. Hoccleve links the story to its lesson with phrases that recur in exemplary poetry, in order to make the lesson plain ('This was doon for to [...]', 'Al this considered [...]', *RP*: 2864, 2868) and then spells out the lesson further:

> Thus, my good Lord, wynneth your peples vois,
> For peples vois is Goddes vois, men seyn.
> And He that for us starf upon the Crois   *died*
> Shal qwyte it yow, I doute it nat certeyn;   *reward you for it*
> Your labour shal nat ydil be ne veyn.
> 'No good dede unrewarded is or qwit,   *repaid*
> Ne evel unpunysshid,' seith Holy Writ.
> (*RP*: 2885–91)

In lines such as these – found throughout Hoccleve's *Regiment*, as well as in George Ashby's *The Active Policy of a Prince* or the interpretative 'envoys' in Lydgate's *The Fall of Princes* – the giving of advice is completely clear, and much more so than in the stories. He keeps insisting how 'playn' the meaning is: 'I doute it nat certeyn', Hoccleve comments, filling the rhyme, protesting too much but also, in essence, emphasising the simplicity of what he says. This seeming lucidity determines Hoccleve's poetic language. For example, he frequently uses the imperative or commanding form of the verb ('wynneth your peples vois')[3] or the only slightly less forceful verb *let* (for example, 'Let vertu thanne therto yow excyte', *RP*: 2915). When the fifteenth-century poet writes thus, he is purposefully direct and impersonal, writing not for himself but for the education of the reader.

Yet how did Hoccleve get away with advising the prince so directly? What these tricks of phrasing do is present plain instruction as public instruction, neither the product of the poet's own mind nor a rebuke of any one prince in particular. To avoid the presumption of a subject instructing a prince, Hoccleve refers frequently to other discourses: he cites by name the sources he is translating (for example *RP*, 3655) and he cites other learned or Christian authorities ('seith Holy Writ'). To support this disclaiming of personal responsibility for what he writes, Hoccleve prepared for his poem a set of marginal notes, which give excerpts from the Latin works whence the authority of the poem came. For example, when he tells Prince Henry to embrace peace not war – this being the Henry who later triumphed at Agincourt and Harfleur – in the margin Hoccleve cites and defers to the words of St Jerome: 'It is written, "Who embraces peace in the hospice of his mind"' – that is, whoever does so, welcomes Christ. The incompleteness of this and some other quotations might perhaps force the reader to draw this conclusion for himself, rather than letting Hoccleve be accused of criticism of the prince ('Scriptum est, / Qui amplectitur pacem in mentis hospitio', *RP*: notes on 5020). Similar quotations from common sources occur in the margins of a few copies of Lydgate's *The Fall of Princes*, in Ashby's *The Active Policy of a Prince* and in several other works of the fifteenth century (Wakelin 2010).

Besides referring to other written sources, Hoccleve further impersonalises his words by referring to common opinion ('men seyn'), or forms lines that sound like common proverbs because of their pithiness and lack of enjambment ('peples vois is Goddes vois, men seyn'). There is also a sense of universal applicability in Hoccleve's references to *justice* and *virtue*, and other abstract concepts about which many have argued, casually, as if we all easily understood what they were. He introduces such words with the declarative verb *is*, asserting confidently what justice or virtue 'is', and with adjectives which give them categorical force such as *no*, *never*, *every*, *all* or *verray* (which means *true*):

> Humilitee verray, as seith Cesarie,   *True humility*
> May nevere be withouten charitee,
> And shee is a vertu moost necessarie;
> Amonges alle vertues that be,
> Shee on hem alle obteeneth dignitee.   *is most dignified of them*
>   (*RP*: 3592–96)

There is also universality in some of Hoccleve's grammar: he is fond of imagining hypothetical scenarios with no precise reference to Prince Henry himself:

> Lawful justice is, as in maneere,
> Al vertu; and who wole han this justice,
> The lawe of Cryst to keepe moot he leere.
>   (*RP*: 2500–2)

Wisely he does not say that Prince Henry needs to learn to keep Christ's law; to say this would rudely imply that the prince was currently failing to keep it. Rather, Hoccleve frequently says that 'who' or *whoever* wants justice needs to learn to follow

Christ's law.[4] He uses the indirect article *a* in a similar way, giving the obligations not of *the* king but of 'a kyng', implying *any* king (*RP*: 2899, 3629). Through its grammar, Hoccleve's public poetry often avoids comment on Prince Henry in particular, or on his (Hoccleve's) own opinion; the style turns the poem not only into timely politicking but also into timeless political philosophy. It is a public poetry with a noble conception of its public. And a wide 'reading public' beyond the immediate persons of the poet and dedicatee – scholars, clergy and gentry as well as royalty – responded to and chose to own and read Hoccleve's verse (Perkins 2001: 168–77).

Public Lydgate

Lydgate's most important mirror for princes offers a different but still generalising and lofty tone. This is the similarly popular poem *The Fall of Princes*, composed not for Prince Henry/Henry V but for his brother, Humfrey Duke of Gloucester, between 1431 and 1438. It is a translation, from an intervening French version, of Boccaccio's *De casibus virorum illustrium* ('On the falls of famous men'). Like *The Regiment of Princes*, *The Fall of Princes* is filled with short stories: each section is a biography of some powerful person who fell from power and in most cases died. Impersonality is the point: fortune strikes all men of rank, and the force of the poem's lugubrious message comes from the accumulation of the multiple stories. Moreover, Lydgate spells out the lessons of the stories in sixty-nine envoys or conclusions, added to his source at his patron's request (Mortimer 2005: 58–61). According to Lydgate, the envoys 'conueied be resoun' the stories told, or rationalised them (*FP*, II: 141–61), thus stressing the universal lesson of each – not least by repeating it in a line of chiming refrain at the end of every stanza of the envoy. Universality and directness are cleverly, if dauntingly, conveyed.

Another feature of *The Fall of Princes* that gives it a lofty and generalising public tone is the use of what Lydgate calls, inventing a word, the 'aureate' style (Ebin 1988: 25–27, 33). This aureate style employs long, polysyllabic and rare words derived from Latin, French or Latin though intervening French, or words formed by adding to English words new endings echoing the endings of Latin or French words (*-age*, *-al*, *-ance*, *-ation*, *-ious*, *-ity*, *-ive*, *-ure*). French and Latin were the languages of aristocracy, international affairs, scholarship and liturgy, and the English words derived from these tongues therefore bring with them the prestige and intellectual reach of these aspects of medieval culture (as Simon Horobin has shown in this volume); they tend to refer to grand and generalising concepts. The aureate style is influenced by the Latin of the Church and is therefore especially common, and used to grand effect, in some of Lydgate's religious lyrics (for example, *MP*, I: nos 48, 50, 53, 54, 58) and in some yet more remarkable lyrics by anonymous poets of the fifteenth century (for example ed. Brown 1939: nos 38, 51). The aureate style might also, however, be influenced to some extent by the growing interest in the study of the classical humanities, known then as the *studia humanitatis*, now as *humanism*, which was supported in England from the 1420s or 1430s by a small clique of men, and notably by Lydgate's patron, Duke Humfrey (Wakelin 2007: 23–31). This new influence would explain why it was not the earlier Chaucer, Gower or Hoccleve, but Lydgate who tuned the aureate style to the highest pitch. It is the prestige and intellectual ambition of classical culture that Lydgate invokes when he adopts the aureate style in the following lines (not the most extremely aureate in the poem) from *The Fall of Princes*:

> So the langage of rethoriciens
> Is a glad obiect to man*n*ys audience,
> W*ith* song mellodious of musiciens,
> Which doth gret cou*n*fort to euery hih p*re*sence.
> Bexau*m*ple as Amphiou*n*, *with* song & elloquence
> Bilte the wallis of Thebes the cite,
> He hadde of rethorik so gret subtilite.

> In his langage ther was so gret plesau*n*ce,
> Fyndyng therbi so inli gret proffit,   *very*
> That al the contre kam to his obeissau*n*ce,   *came to obey him*
> To heere hym speke thei hadde so gret delit;
> The peeple envirou*n* hadde such an appetit   *round about*
> In his persone, in pes & in bataille:
> Heer men may seen what rethorik doth auaille!   *achieves*
> *(FP*, VI: 3487–3500)

The aureate style is created here through the use of words ending in *-age*, *-ail*, *-ance*, *-ence*, *-it*, *-ity* and *-oun*, echoing the inflections on Latin and French. These words are often placed at the end of the line, so that the rhyme alerts us to their recurrence; this elegant sound-patterning of word-endings would occur more naturally in Latin than in English. Besides the aureate style, there are other ingredients typical of Lydgate's grand public poetry. There is the allusion to a classical myth (that of Amphion) typical of mid-fifteenth-century poetry and prose: such allusions appear when writers seek prestige or persuasiveness. The allusions are largely influenced by Chaucer but also by the 'humanist' studies of antiquity (Wakelin 2007: 62–66). Finally, there are the gushy words with which Chaucer likes to modify adjectives (*so*, *such* and *ful*) and the words, which Hoccleve also uses, that universalise the poem in some way (*all*, *every* and *man* or *men*, the latter very frequently used by Lydgate): as he concludes here, 'men may seen' what he writes; this is a poetry of clear and public statements.

   Why does Lydgate write like this? Helpfully, he hints at the reason when, in these lines, he implies the merits of such a style by commenting on the merits of music and of rhetoric. Lydgate is in fact the first person recorded to use the word *rhetorician* in English (*TB*: prol. 57). He tells us of Amphion, who built Thebes by the force of his music alone, an act that Lydgate allegorises as symbolic of the force of musical language – of poetry, with its musically patterned words and line-endings; he also recounts and interprets the 'syngyng' of Amphion thus in *The Siege of Thebes* (*ST*: 194–292). And in his comment on how Amphion's 'langage' made all the country obey him, Lydgate alludes to the power of persuasive or impressive language to bring political power (Simpson 1997: 17). This idea of the force of rhetoric is found in the works of the classical orator and philosopher Cicero, and Lydgate's defence of rhetoric here follows a biography of Cicero, one of the best sections of *The Fall of Princes* (*FP*, VI: 2948–3276). It is an optimistic vision of the power of words: indeed, a few lines earlier Lydgate tells us that the power of using speech is what distinguishes men from beasts, another thought borrowed from Cicero: 'Al erthli beestis be muet of nature, / Sauf onli man' (*FP*, VI: 3375–76). If rhetoric and music have the force in public life to build cities, control people or even determine the nature of humanity, it is quite understandable that Lydgate here and elsewhere uses the aureate style, with its musicality and pompous adjectives and adverbs.

This mixture of aureation, allusion and assertive adjectives and adverbs is typical of Lydgate's poetry, and renders his style definitely 'public' in its sense of intellectual reach and universal importance. Under his huge influence, aureation and pseudo-classical allusion found a receptive public and shaped the grandest poetry and prose of the following century; Lydgate deserves recognition for forging a new style of 'public' poetry. Yet the aureate style differs from the declaredly plain or middling style of fourteenth-century poetry (on which see Middleton 1978: 95–96, 99) or even the style of Hoccleve. It might seem a more private or deliberately obscure and artful language in its neologisms and allusions. It might also, with its bombast (Ebin 1988: 38–48), appeal more to the passions, to the personal stirrings of each individual reader, even to snobbery, rather than to reason. Thus Lydgate's need to cultivate fine language betrays a sense that language might fail in its effects on the public. He does indeed express some doubts about the power of poetry: after all, in *The Fall of Princes* Cicero, whose biography precedes the defence of rhetoric, is executed by foes who cut off the hand which he used 'To write of vertues many [a] famous book', as a warning to future word-weavers (*FP*, VI: 3263–76; see also Simpson 1997: 31–2). The uneasy balance between public address and fear of its failure is one of the most intriguing elements of fifteenth-century poetry. And as the opening quotations above showed, both Lydgate and Hoccleve expressed doubts whether they had the 'konnyng' and the 'letterure' to write for public consumption.

Intimate Hoccleve

As these two poets reflect on their power to write, they also both, of course, refer to their own roles as writers in more personal ways, with inward love, quaking pens and so on. Hoccleve sounds this intimate note more loudly and more often than Lydgate, making it seem a dominant strain in his verse. Given its prominence in Hoccleve's oeuvre, how does such poetry sit alongside his more public poetry? Could it even be thought of as private poetry? In fact Hoccleve's intimate moments do contribute to his public writing; and Lydgate's intimate moments, although briefer and quieter, do so yet more clearly.

Hoccleve's intimate poems have become well known as a form of autobiography, and might be compared with works such as Margery Kempe's *Boke* or William Thorpe's *Testimony*. An autograph copy of these poems survives (see Figure 30.1). Hoccleve's *La Male Regle* is an apology for his 'misrule' in youth (as the French title says); his *Complaint* is a poem of personal lament about the stigma he endures as a result of some period of mental illness six years earlier, probably in 1414 (Burrow 1994: 22); this poem is followed by his *Dialogue*, between the character Hoccleve and a 'frende', whom Hoccleve allows to read the *Complaint* and with whom he then discusses how best to restore his reputation. Some wariness is needed in reading these poems as autobiographical: *La Male Regle* is a confession, a genre recognisable in French and English literature of the preceding centuries, for example in Chaucer's *The Pardoner's Prologue*; Hoccleve's *Complaint* and *Dialogue* also share some of their autobiographical elements with the French poetic genre of the *dit* (Burrow 1997: 43, 46–48). Not everything in these poems is definitely true. But, luckily, being a bureaucrat Hoccleve left a paper-trail from which people have recently verified his poor payments and his absence from work during the months in which he claims to have been ill (Mooney 2007: 301–7). These poems did, it transpires, refer directly to the poet's life – although that does not exhaust their meaning.

Moreover, they are certainly intimate in tone. How is this intimacy evoked in poetry? First, the settings are often the interiors of Hoccleve's private 'chaumbre', which we enter after a knock at the door, or a tavern; and even in public settings, Hoccleve wanders alone in solitude; in 'Westmynstir Halle' or in the streets he sees the anonymous 'prees' of people who shun him – the greater loneliness of being in a crowd (*Dial.*: 1–2; *MR*: 186; *Comp.*: 72–73). Then, being autobiographical to some degree, the poems use the first person pronouns, the *I* and *my* of the narrator, twice as frequently relative to the poems' lengths as *The Regiment* does. We hear too in Hoccleve's *Dialogue* delightful short bursts of intimate, naturalistic speech: snappy phrases, repetitions and interruptions which evoke a halting conversation with somebody for whose sanity one fears, or who is acting in a slightly critical manner. Sometimes this effect is heightened by counterpoint with the rime royal stanza (rhyming *ababbcc*), which does not here create stately echoes and declarations, as it does in *The Fall of Princes*, but instead heightens, by contrast, the cut-and-thrust of speech: the verse-form forces some enjambment and suppleness of utterance (*Dial.*: 12–13, 18–19, 23–25), and often one speaker strikingly answers or conflicts the other by taking over speaking mid-line or by completing a rhyme begun by him (*Dial.*: 34–35, 197–203, 368–69, 617–30, 736–42, 753–54, 778–84). Furthermore, although Hoccleve does sometimes employ clichéd images – life waning like autumn, the world stormy like the sea – at other times he uses striking words that edge towards privatised or inventive metaphors. He employs startling phrases for mental and moral decay: 'Excesse at borde hath leyd his knyf with me' (*MR*: 112). Sometimes the

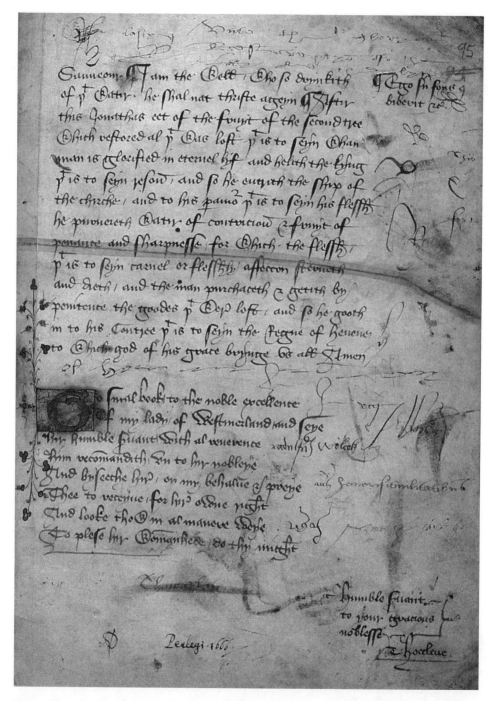

Figure 30.1   Durham University Library, Cosin MS V.iii.9, Thomas Hoccleve, *Complaint, Dialogue,*
etc., autograph copy, written for Joan Beaufort (d.1440). Hoccleve's signature may be found at the
foot of the page on the right-hand side. Durham University Library.

slightest word brings a curious physicality to Hoccleve's descriptions of mental states: for example, he cannot cope with continued living, 'in my skyn to tourne', a phrase that suggests, with its idea of tossing and turning, or of uncomfortable twisting, a discord between interiority and the body (*Comp.*: 303); when he worries what he cannot achieve, he worries about what he cannot 'gripe', as if clinging onto existence (*Comp.*: 265). Sometimes he will take a common metaphor but extend it with inventive excess: he begins with the cliché that fortune has brought him 'cloudy' weather; but then notes that fortune used to be sunny, whereas under the 'dirke shour' of the present he must 'swymme'; 'swymme' evokes a whole flood of unfortunate rain, carrying him away; but then the grief 'swal' and 'bolned' ('swelled'), in a metaphor which recalls the unpleasant sensation of water-retention, until Hoccleve finally 'braste oute' speaking, like a container of liquid splitting (*Comp.*: 23–35). By contrast, abstract words such as *virtue* and *honour*, common in *The Regiment*, seldom appear. These elements of Hoccleve's *Complaint* and *Dialogue* eschew the tone of proverbial or lofty public address – although, with their physical and circumstantial detail, they share a certain directness of reference, or frankness, with it.

Yet although these poems sound intimate in tone, the intimate self presented here is not necessarily unique and is certainly not private. After all, Hoccleve claims that he is writing his *Complaint* and *Dialogue* in order to prove to other people that he is not still mentally disturbed and to win back their company. In his *Dialogue* he shows his *Complaint* to a friend who asks 'Hast þou maad þis compleint forth to goo / Amonge þe peple?', and he answers, 'ʒe, frende, so I mente'. The friend tells him not to reveal things to 'mo folke' (*Dial.*: 18–24). Yet it is 'folke', a public that will respond to him, which Hoccleve seeks. And of course we, the readers, are already communicating with him when we come to these lines. On the one hand, this deliberate exposure of intimacy suggests that Hoccleve – perhaps like most people – understands himself as others see him, as a 'public' presentation of self. His intimate writing has a public purpose. That sense of self linked to the understanding of other people is strengthened when, in his *La Male Regle* and *Complaint*, Hoccleve borrows words to describe himself from other writers (for example *MR*: 249) and even from Scripture:

> As seide is in þe sauter miʒt I sey,   *Psalms*
> 'They þat me sy, fledden awey fro me'.
> Forʒeten I was al oute of mynde awey.
> (*Comp.*: 78–80)

Although intimate, he is not alone, for he finds resemblances of himself in other books (here Psalm 30:12, famously echoed by Wyatt's poem 'They fle from me that sometyme did me seke'). There is an example here, as David Watt has argued, of how habits of *compilatio* or compiling sources, common in medieval Latin and Middle English literature, establish one person's understanding of the world through another's, as recorded in books (Watt 2003: 152). And the compiler himself in turn becomes the subject from which a reader might learn, as Hoccleve's intimate compilation becomes something approaching a public textbook, giving example of God's judgement:

> Almy3ty God, as liketh his goodnesse,
> Visiteþ folke alday, as men may se,   *Afflicts*
> With los of good and bodily sikenesse,
> And amonge othir, he for3at not me.
> (*Comp.*: 36–39)

Hoccleve here becomes a lesson for others; elsewhere he is a 'mirour [...] of riot and excesse' – an image evoking the public genre of the mirror for princes – into which we might look (*MR*: 330). He not only wants to share his work *with* 'folke', but also offers orthodox pieties *about* 'folke' and how they fare 'alday', in vague, universalising terms; and what he says about folk is common knowledge, 'as men may se'. Here Hoccleve's intimate poetry blends with his public poetry.

This blend is common across Hoccleve's poems. For example, *The Regiment of Princes* begins with a long prologue in which Hoccleve describes his sleepless 'smert of thoght', again using a somatic metaphor for the pains of thinking (*RP*: 106); as a remedy he is counselled to write a poem for Prince Henry, both to keep his mind busy and to win financial support (*RP*: 1828–58, 1877–1911). This personal prologue gives Hoccleve the opportunity to clarify his motive and his credentials as a public poet: orthodox Christian, clerk of the Privy Seal, who is familiar with government business and known to the prince, and a student of Chaucer. The universalising advice in *The Regiment* is sometimes introduced with first-person phrases such as 'Thus fynde I writen, as I undirstonde' (*RP*: 2842). Similarly, *La Male Regle* moves smoothly into a request to the Lord Treasurer Furnivall for payment of Hoccleve's wages (*MR*: 417–24), a section that was later excerpted by one reader of the poem to form a more universally applicable religious lyric (Meyer-Lee 2007: 100). Similarly, Hoccleve's *Complaint* and *Dialogue* are not self-standing autobiographies but a prologue to his collection of poems on the vices and virtues of women and on preparing for death. (We now call the *Complaint*, *Dialogue* and these other poems Hoccleve's *Series*, but there was no original title for the whole collection.) Though they present him intimately, the *Complaint* and *Dialogue* present Hoccleve as a literary persona or personality (Burrow 1994: 31). The intimate presentation of Hoccleve gives his public poems, whether they're addressing us with advice or even telling fictional stories, a powerful immediacy, as they seem to come from one carefully realised speaker.

Intimate Lydgate

Hoccleve's intimate tone is easily heard; Lydgate's is less often recognised, for it is much less frequent and more muted. It is there, though. Briefly, but repeatedly and consistently, he gives us circumstantial details of himself: he is from the village of Lidgate in Suffolk, and he blames his 'lak' of literary skill on his rural upbringing

(*FP*, IX: 3431, 3436–42); he is a monk in the nearby monastery in Bury St Edmunds and he gives his 'professioun' as a reason for writing (*ST*: 92–93, 132; *MP*, I, no. 68: 459); he tells us about his patrons in Suffolk, London and elsewhere, and requests money from them. Yet these references, like Hoccleve's to Westminster, are only those which we hear if we listen for what tends to be valued in the 'real world' – references to topography, genealogy, work and money that can be mapped, named or counted. Lydgate is more personal in referring more vaguely to his no less real but much less readily mapped, named and counted experiences as a person. He tells us in his poems of his position not just in Bury St Edmunds but in his bedroom, 'Withinne my closet & my lytel couche, [...] And be my beddes syde' (*MP*, I, no. 68: 89–90; see also *MP*, I, no. 55). Moreover, throughout his shorter religious poems, as throughout Hoccleve's poetry, words bring to mind Lydgate's physical body and its position and gestures of praying or kneeling in these bedrooms or chapels; indeed, Lydgate's *Testament* even has a refrain rhyming on 'kne', gently insisting on his bodily humility; many of his poems profess to be a prayer (*MP*, I, no. 49: 21; *MP*, I, no. 68: 8, 445, 447). He tells us that he wears spectacles (*FP*, IX: 3335) and that his ink blots his book; fourteen times he tells us that his pen is quaking as he writes and eleven times that he is quaking (for example, *TB*, V: 1044–45; *MP*, I, no. 37: 57). In these fleeting but persistent physical references Lydgate comes alive.

But these private lives have a public purpose, just as Hoccleve's do – and even more obviously. Sometimes these moments of self-presentation work as a sort of 'poetic self-aggrandisement', creating a role for the poet (Meyer-Lee 2007: 56, 60–61). Yet these intimate references to his mood and gestures also set the scene for the poem to be delivered. For example, the closet or bedroom is well suited to night-thoughts of mortality or of Christ's horrific death. The greenwood that Lydgate evokes in a deft pastiche of Chaucer's *General Prologue* is the perfect setting for a warning against being tempted away from 'greuous study' by the 'lusty sesoun' (*MP*, I, no. 12: 1–34). Whenever he tells us the feast-day on which he writes in the course of his *Life of Our Lady*, it always fits with typological perfection the event in her life of which he writes. And in what purports to be his last poem, his translation of a mirror for princes called *The Secrees of Old Philisoffres*, Lydgate even manages to die on cue, having just compared the life of man to the four seasons and reached winter and death; Benedict Burgh completed the poem thenceforth (*SOP*: 1296–1491). Lydgate's intimacy, then, is an artful part of his public address as a poet.

Moreover, once the intimate moment becomes part of a poem, it is no longer supposed only to be Lydgate's, but is also the reader's (Pearsall 1970: 255; Pearsall 1997: 11). Lydgate's intimacy is always designed, as Hoccleve's is, to be shared in some way. His 'rowth' in *The Temple of Glass*, as we have seen, made him take up his quaking pen to communicate. Once when, in the dark of the night, he read a contemplative 'meditacioun' he was not prompted to silent thought but 'Took a penne, and wroot in my maneere' with a strange self-consciousness, in the reference to 'my maneere', about his poetic oeuvre (*MP*, I, no. 51: 15, 34). In another poem he speaks of prayer by which 'we remember', using the first person plural *we* to imagine that other people share his piety; and when he offers the poem to the Virgin Mary, he echoes Chaucer's self-referential comments on publication: 'Go, litel bille, pray to this pur virgine' (*MP*, I, no. 54: 57, 72; cf. *Troilus and Criseyde*, V, 1786). The phrasing often creates a tone of invitation to such prayer, through further references to the plural 'we knelyng' (*MP*, I, no. 52: 7), through deictic adjectives such as *this*, which encourage us to imagine ourselves close in space and time and able to see *this*, or through the vocative mode of addressing the reader, or sometimes God, with the singular and familiar *thou* rather than the plural or formal *ye*. Lydgate explains too that he wrote many of his religious poems for some public purpose. Some were to accompany pictures on display, pictures which are referred to with casual immediacy as 'this ffygure' or 'this' virgin weeping which, in the present tense, 'thow sest'. One instructive poem was commissioned by the abbot of Lydgate's monastery, 'At his chirche to hang it on the wal'. There is still personal devotion here, but it is devotion not *unique or private* to Lydgate; rather it is *performed* by Lydgate in order to inspire others to perform too, to pray 'W*ith* contrit herte [...] meekly knelyng dou*n*' before the picture in question (*MP*, I, no. 47: 2, 50–56; *MP*, I, no. 62: 26; *MP*, I, no. 16: 161–68). In fact, excerpts of the poem that professes to be the most autobiographical, Lydgate's *Testament*, ended up painted on the wall of a chapel in Long Melford, Suffolk (Pearsall 1970: 182–83), sharing its intimacy as an instructional aid in a place of worship. Thus this religious poetry resembles the 'affective piety' of many other fifteenth-century religious lyrics – a piety grounded in personal feelings that develop one's connection with God; yet, it is important to understand, this piety which works through personal feelings or 'affects' is not a solitary piety but rather a piety mediated by the Church and shared with others, as Shannon Gayk has shown well (2006: 187, 190, 197, 200). In such writing, intimacy is not a mark of private writing but a guarantee of the fitness of this writing for public circulation: it acts as a badge of honest intention and expression.

It is to enable communication with the wider public that the poems of both Hoccleve and Lydgate recognise the individual, and refer to the poet and reader as intimately and directly as they do to ideas. The intimacy of both poets accords with their directness in evoking proverbial wisdom or in glorifying the princes of their day, the very qualities that make their work so public. Each speaks a language supposedly suffused with immediacy of reference and meaning. One could even argue that Lydgate's development of the aureate style offers, if not a similar plainness of style, then a similar directness of address to a grandly conceived public and its emotions. This blend of public and private elements, and of the proverbial and of the aureate styles, influenced many religious and secular lyricists of the fifteenth century (Lawton 1987) and, under Lydgate's long influence, of the mid-sixteenth century too. Such poetry eschews the deliberate obliquity of much twenty-first-century poetry in English. But there remain many complexities to explore as the poets cultivate this personal frankness and directness. After all, as they openly tell us, to 'wryte' and 'descryve' people, feelings and ideas so *seemingly* directly in fact required 'konnyng' and 'letterure'.

NOTES

1 The list of Primary Sources below gives the abbreviations used in parenthetical references to Hoccleve's and Lydgate's poems.

2 However, one manuscript has 'quaken', which removes the ambiguity (ed. Robinson 1980: fol. 90r).

3 The inflection *-eth* was used when giving orders to more than one person or to somebody who deserved the polite address *ye/you/your*, as a prince would (Mustanoja 1960: 474).

4 *Who* in Middle English is often a generalising relative pronoun meaning *whoever* or *whosoever* (Mustanoja 1960: 192–3). It may also echo Latin constructions with *qui*, such as that of St Jerome quoted above: 'Qui amplectitur pacem [...]'.

REFERENCES AND FURTHER READING

Primary Texts

The abbreviated titles are used in parenthetical references.

Comp.   Hoccleve, Thomas (2001). 'My Compleinte'. In Roger Ellis (ed.). *'My Compleinte' and Other Poems* (pp. 115–130). Exeter: University of Exeter Press.

Dial.   Hoccleve, Thomas (2001). 'A Dialogue'. In Roger Ellis (ed.). *'My Compleinte' and Other Poems* (pp. 131–59). Exeter: University of Exeter Press.

FP   Lydgate, John (1924–1927). *The Fall of Princes*. 4 vols. Ed. Henry Bergen. Early English Text Society, e.s. pp. 121–24. London: Oxford University Press.

MP   Lydgate, John (1911–1934). *Minor Poems*. 2 vols. Ed. Henry Noble MacCracken. Early English Text Society, e.s. 107, o.s. 192. London: Oxford University Press.

MR   Hoccleve, Thomas (2001). 'La Male Regle'. In Roger Ellis (ed.). *'My Compleinte' and Other Poems* (pp. 64–78). Exeter: University of Exeter Press.

RP   Hoccleve, Thomas (1999). *The Regiment of Princes*. Ed. Charles R. Blyth. Kalamazoo, MI: Medieval Institute Publications.

SOP   Lydgate, John, and Burgh, Benedict (1894). *Secrees of Old Philisoffres*. Ed. Robert Steele. Early English Text Society, e.s. 66. London: Kegan Paul, Trench, Trübner.

ST   Lydgate, John (1911–1930). *The Siege of Thebes*. 2 vols. Ed. Axel Erdmann and E. Ekwall. Early English Text Society, e.s. 108, 125.

TB   Lydgate, John (1906–1935). *Troy Book*. 4 vols. Ed. Henry Bergen. Early English Text Society, e.s. 97, 103, 106, 126. London: Kegan Paul, Trench, Trübner.

TG   Lydgate, John (2003). 'The Temple of Glass'. In Julia Boffey (ed.). *Fifteenth-Century English Dream Visions: An Anthology* (pp. 15–89). Oxford: Oxford University Press.

Secondary Reading

Brown, Carleton (ed.) (1939). *Religious Lyrics of the XVth Century*. Oxford: Clarendon Press.

Burrow, John (1994). *Thomas Hoccleve*. Aldershot: Variorum.

Burrow, John (1997). Hoccleve and the Middle French Poets. In Helen Cooper and Sally Mapstone (eds). *The Long Fifteenth Century: Essays for Douglas Gray* (pp. 36–49). Oxford: Clarendon Press.

Ebin, Lois A. (1988). *Illuminator, Makar, Vates: Visions of Poetry in the Fifteenth Century*. Lincoln, NE: University of Nebraska Press.

Fisher, John (1990). A language policy for Lancastrian England. *PMLA*, 107, 1168–1180.

Gayk, Shannon (2006). Images of pity: the regulatory aesthetics of John Lydgate's religious lyrics. *Studies in the Age of Chaucer*, 28, 175–203.

Lawton, David (1987). Dullness and the fifteenth century. *English Literary History*, 54, 761–799.

Meyer-Lee, Robert (2007). *Poets and Power from Chaucer to Wyatt*. Cambridge: Cambridge University Press.

Middleton, Anne (1978). The idea of public poetry in the reign of Richard II. *Speculum*, 53, 94–114.

Mitchell, J. Allan (2008). Queen Katherine and the secret of Lydgate's 'Temple of Glas'. *Medium Ævum*, 77, 54–76.

Mooney, Linne R. (2007). Some new light on Thomas Hoccleve. *Studies in the Age of Chaucer*, 29, 293–340.

Mortimer, Nigel (2005). *John Lydgate's 'Fall of Princes': Narrative Tragedy in its Literary and Political Contexts*. Oxford: Oxford University Press.

Mustanoja, Tauno F. (1960). *A Middle English Syntax: Part I. Parts of Speech*. Helsinki: Société Neophilologique.

Nolan, Maura (2005). *John Lydgate and the Making of Public Culture*. Cambridge: Cambridge University Press.

Pearsall, Derek (1970). *John Lydgate*. London: Routledge and Kegan Paul.

Pearsall, Derek (1994). Hoccleve's 'Regement of Princes': the poetics of royal self-representation. *Speculum*, 69, 386–410.

Pearsall, Derek (1997). *John Lydgate (1371–1449): A Bio-bibliography*. English Literary Studies Monograph Series, 71. Victoria, BC: University of Victoria.

Perkins, Nicholas (2001). *Hoccleve's 'Regiment of Princes': Counsel and Constraint*. Cambridge: D. S. Brewer.

Robinson, Pamela (ed.) (1980). *Manuscript Tanner 346: A Facsimile*. Norman, OK: Pilgrim Books.

Scanlon, Larry (1994). *Narrative, Authority and Power: The Medieval Exemplum and the Chaucerian Tradition*. Cambridge: Cambridge University Press.

Simpson, James (1997). 'Dysemol daies and fatal houres': Lydgate's 'Destruction of Thebes' and Chaucer's 'The Knight's Tale'. In Helen Cooper and Sally Mapstone (eds). *The Long Fifteenth Century: Essays for Douglas Gray* (pp. 15–33). Oxford: Clarendon Press.

Sponsler, Claire (2008). Lydgate and London's public culture. In Lisa H. Cooper and Andrew Denny-Brown (eds). *Lydgate Matters: Poetry and Material Culture in the Fifteenth Century* (pp. 13–33). Basingstoke: Palgrave Macmillan.

Straker, Scott-Morgan (1999). Rivalry and reciprocity in Lydgate's 'Troy Book'. *New Medieval Literatures*, 3, 119–47.

Strohm, Paul (1999). Hoccleve, Lydgate and the Lancastrian court. In David Wallace (ed.). *The Cambridge History of Medieval English Literature* (pp. 640–661). Cambridge: Cambridge University Press.

Wakelin, Daniel (2007). *Humanism, Reading, and English Literature 1430–1530*. Oxford: Oxford University Press.

Wakelin, Daniel (2010). Instructing readers in early poetic manuscripts. *Huntington Library Quarterly*, 73.

Watt, David (2003). 'I this book shal make': Thomas Hoccleve's self-publication and book production. *Leeds Studies in English*, 34, 133–60.

31
Women and Writing

C. Annette Grisé

Fourteenth-century Middle English poetry actively engaged in debates about the representation of gender: employing a wide array of perspectives on female experience, drawing attention to gender inequalities and illustrating the boundaries (sometimes working within, sometimes pushing against them) of female conduct and authority. Interestingly, most of this work was performed through the complex female characters created by male poets. For example, the Wife of Bath, Criseyde, the Pearl Maiden and Lady Bertilak linger in the imagination long after we read the poems written about them. The strong masculine narratorial voices in much of this poetry are at times critical and at times sympathetic in their perceptions of female characters, commenting on current debates and engaging their audiences to (re)consider the multiple representations of contemporary femininity and masculinity.

The stage is set in Chaucer's time, yet it is not until the fifteenth century that we begin to find Middle English poetry with female characters, speakers and narrators unmediated by a male poet-speaker. In this period, as noble and gentry women were acquiring higher levels of literacy and gaining greater access to manuscript culture, there developed two subgenres of poems written in the female voice, neither of which was concerned with naming the poets or marking the author's gender. The first is the anonymously authored narrative poem adopting a female speaker, exemplified by *The Assembly of Ladies* and *The Floure and the Leafe*, two dream-vision poems whose sixteenth-century attributions to Chaucer were rejected by scholars in the eighteenth and nineteenth centuries respectively. The second comprises love lyrics and verse letters written from a female perspective, such as those found in the Findern manuscript (Cambridge University Library MS Ff. 1. 6). They are typically written as articulations of female desire for an absent lover, framed as personal poetry intended for limited circulation. These anonymous long poems and lyrics are not signed or attributed; however, the use of the female voice for the speaker represents a reversal of the usual pattern of love poetry, and critics have argued convincingly for the possibility that women wrote them. By the end of the fifteenth century there is a more conscious acknowledgment of women's contributions to poetry. In the decades leading up to the Reformation scribes and printers make a greater effort to attribute poems to women: Elizabeth Woodville, probably Edward IV's wife, is said to have written 'A Hymn to Venus'; a Hymn to the Virgin is attributed to 'an holy Ankaresse of Maunsffeld' by its scribe; and the verse translation of the prayer 'Gaude virgo, mater Christi' made by Eleanor Percy, Duchess of Buckingham is transcribed by her sister into a Book of Hours.

The proportion of elite women in fifteenth-century England who possessed literacy skills was higher than ever before, and these women actively used these skills by patronising, borrowing and sharing vernacular manuscripts (see, for example, the foundational work by Carol Meale and Felicity Riddy). The greater level of participation of women in Middle English manuscript culture mirrored an increase in female participation in secular poetry, not just as readers and patrons but also as narrators, speakers and authors of poetry. Although Alexandra Barratt's point that literate Englishwomen did not receive training in composing secular poetry is well taken (Barratt 1992), it is possible to argue that with greater exposure to poetry came a sense of familiarity, which in turn bred confidence to participate in writing love poetry. Invited to engage in debates about gender in the poetry they were reading, the female audience moved from being objects in poetry to being subjects and writers.

Scholars (such as Sarah McNamer, Alexandra Barratt, Carl Whithaus and Linne R. Mooney) have argued for the inclusion of anonymous fifteenth-century poems with female speakers in the canon of late-medieval women's writings. Factors influencing their assessments include the use of a female speaker, the treatment of subjects considered personal and domestic (such as romance and courtly love), the authenticity of the representation of female experience, the use of a uniquely feminine voice, the critique of traditional female roles, the use of literary innovation, and the evidence of manuscript provenance and transmission. While none of these factors offers definitive proof (although the evidence for women's involvement in household books like the Findern manuscript is very compelling), it is plausible that, just as male poets adopt a male narrator-speaker, so the use of a female narrator-speaker implies a female poet. At the very least, we see a new interest in female speakers of secular verse.

Late-medieval English poetry often concerned itself with issues of gender: in love, family, household and community. Male speakers and narrators frequently consider the female perspective, looking in on women's conversations or commenting on female characters. Their perceptions vacillate between satiric portrayals in comedy and sympathetic portrayals in tragedy, illustrating both mockery and pathos in the experiences of both male and female characters. For example, while *The Book of the Duchess* and *Pearl* depict male grief at the death of the female beloved (wife or daughter), *The Legend of Good Women* presents examples of the woman's grief at being martyred for love. *Troilus and Criseyde* provides an excellent example of the sympathetic male narrator, while *The Canterbury Tales* is a tour-de-force of the variety of subjectivities under scrutiny at the end of the fourteenth century: gender, as much as estates, religion, spirituality, family and mercantilism (the list could go on), is explored by many speakers in many tales.

In the fifteenth century 'Chaucerian' writers continued the satiric representation of female experience, a prime example of which is found in William Dunbar's *Tretise of the Twa Mariit Wemen and the Wedo*, but they also strove to reveal the pathos of female tragic experience, exemplified in Henryson's *The Testament of Cresseid*. In the same period, poems such as *The Floure and the Leafe* and *The Assembly of Ladies* presented alternatives in their use of female narrators. Such poems reveal a subtle yet pointed critique of male infidelity and inconstancy, presenting an everywoman narrator whose experiences reflect those of the other women in the poems. No grand, tragic female figures dominate; the female speakers in the dream visions, lyrics and verses illustrate the pathos of ordinary female experiences of love, giving voice to female desire and making male absence and female community a necessity.

The dream-vision poems *The Floure and the Leafe* and *The Assembly of Ladies* present tableaux – rich in allegorical detail – of female constancy in love, witnessed by a female narrator who, as convention dictates, writes down the dream in the form of the poem. Both poems begin in natural settings, in gardens that reveal the beauty of the natural world but are controlled by human labour, in arbours and hedges, such as the narrator finds in the maze in *The Assembly*. When the narrator enters into the secluded natural (yet mediated) setting, she begins her figurative journey into the workings of society, notably the world of courtly love and its idealisations of gendered conduct. Allegorical figures populate the meadows and palaces of the poems, revealing a strict code of female loyalty and honour. Men are absent or ornamental, while queens and ladies hold court and offer hospitality. The audience sees courtly love from the female perspective, according to which women are steadfast, faithful and wronged in love. While the ladies act as exemplars for conduct in love, the narrator learns from them about the proper codes of behaviour for romance, chivalry and courtesy, thus instructing the reader through these experiences.

The role of the narrator is crucial to this process of moral instruction. She is witness, participant, student and reporter. Both narrators begin their poems as simple women: not foolish or unintelligent, but unschooled in love, romance and their codes. The *Floure* narrator names herself, 'I simplest of all' (Pearsall 1990: 566–9). Both are inquisitive from the start, one setting out to seek the nightingale in the *Floure*, the other trying to solve the maze in the *Assembly*. Their curiosity makes them very observant, and they report their visions with a certain level of ironic detachment: as the narrator explains in the *Assembly* when she is asked to sum up her personal experiences of love in a motto, 'for my word, I have none, this is trewe' (312). As the poems progress the narrators find themselves being drawn in. In *The Floure and The Leafe* the speaker questions one of the participants, asking for an interpretation of the allegory she has just witnessed. The lady replies and requires the narrator to choose her allegiance to the flower or the leaf before she continues on her way, whereupon the speaker returns home to write her vision down. *The Assembly of Ladies* concludes in a similar fashion with the narrator being drawn in to add her bill of complaint at the tribunal, then returning home to write down her vision for the service of others. These poems illustrate 'women talking about the things of love' to paraphrase Felicity Riddy's influential statement concerning the ways in which female devotional culture developed in late-medieval England through women sharing spiritual writings with each other. The parallel development in the secular love poems with female speakers shows female characters writing and reading of love, talking and walking together, teaching each other about female experiences of love, and cherishing the positive qualities of women's conduct in romance. The concept of the female community speaking of love continued to be relevant throughout the fifteenth century into the early sixteenth century when Caxton highlighted Lady Margaret Beaufort's involvement in the printing of romances (Summit 1995).

The Floure and the Leafe presents the reader with two representations of such conduct in the flower, illustrating inconstancy, carnality, and the fleeting nature of youth and beauty, and the leaf, showing fidelity and the everlasting nature of constancy and true love. The poem presents a debate about courtly love and its precepts through a dream vision granted to the female narrator, who has awoken in the night and sets out to hear the nightingale's song. As she finds a beautiful hidden arbour she hears first a male goldfinch and then a female nightingale sing. The nightingale's song is magnificent, transcending mortal understanding and transporting the narrator into raptures. There quickly appears a 'world' (136) of ladies singing and dancing, and again the narrator is overcome by the sights and sounds of the procession, in which the ladies sing like angels and wear the most sumptuous array, especially jewel-encrusted robes, white surcoats, gold circlets on their heads and green wreaths made from the leaves of different trees and shrubs: 'Some of laurer, and some ful pleasantly / Had chapelets of woodbind, and sadly / Some of Agnus castus were also / Chapelets fresh' (158–61). The most beautiful of all the ladies leads the song and dance, wearing a crown and carrying a branch of Agnus castus, associated with chastity. These ladies begin a mayday-type gathering in a meadow so close to the narrator that she could see 'Who fairest was, who coud best dance or sing, / Or who most womanly was in all thing' (188–9). Then comes a great company of men dressed richly in white with green wreaths on their heads as well. The knights begin to joust and those who win gain crowns of laurel. After the games the knights join the ladies on the meadow, pair off and walk toward a giant laurel tree that could shelter a hundred people, within the shade of which they continue their singing and dancing.

The narrator then spies a 'lusty company' (324) who are walking in the field wearing clothes of green and wreaths of white and red flowers on their heads. They are not described in the same detail as the ladies and lords in white, yet we find out that they are also dressed richly and are dancing and singing like the company dressed in white with the green wreaths. A sweetly singing lady leads her company in song, a lovely pastoral song in praise of the daisy, familiar to those who know Chaucer's paean to the marguerite at the start of the *Legend of Good Women*. But misfortune befalls the lords and ladies of the flower, for first they are caught in the sweltering heat of the sun and then they are caught out in a storm. The fair flowers wilt and are pummelled with hail and rain, while those devoted to the leaf are sheltered from harm by the laurel tree. The Queen of the Leafe shows her grace and courtesy by taking the hand of the Flower Queen and leading her to shelter, offering her hospitality to all of the company of the Flower. The ladies of the leaf take the ladies of the flower by hand, the knights of the leaf taking their lead and bringing the knights of the flower under their protection, making fires to dry clothes, finding herbs to heal wounds and making salads for nourishment. The Lady of the Leaf then invites the Lady of the Flower to sup with her, and the entire companies of the Leaf and Flower set off together, passing by the narrator who is astonished one last time when the nightingale flies to the Queen of the Leaf and the goldfinch to the Queen of the Flower. As the narrator leaves to return home she meets a lady in white and asks her about the meaning of the tableau she has just witnessed. This lady engages in a platonic dialogue with our narrator, calling her 'My faire doughter' (466), and proceeds to explicate the allegory. She declares she is part of the company of the Leaf, whose queen is Diana, goddess of chastity. Those who follow the Leaf live in chastity and demonstrate the particular form of their loyalty through the kind of leaves used in their chaplets: for examples, the laurel symbolises strength in deed, while the wood-bine illustrates steadfastness in love. The knights who follow the Leaf are the very epitome of courtly chivalry, including the Nine Worthies (great heroes of the past), the Knights of the Round Table, the Twelve Peers of France, and those who were dedicated to the Order of the Garter – all are vowed to the laurel, which shows honour to them. The Queen of Flowers is Flora, whose followers 'are such that loved idleness / And not delite of no business / But for to hunt and hauke, and pley in medes, / And many other such idle dedes' (536–9). The lady dismisses the knights of the flower as those who do not persevere 'To seeke honour without feintise and slouth, / Fro wele to better, in all maner thing' (549–50). There is here a criticism of men who do not fulfil the requirements for action and courage in the masculine code of chivalry, while the female counterpart is underplayed. The lady concludes by asking our narrator 'to whome doe ye owe / Your service?' (571–2). The narrator rightly answers that she owes her observance to the Leafe, and her teacher then sets off to meet the rest of the company. The narrator continues on her way home to write down her dream, setting her book free with the conventional blessing and use of the modesty topos.

The Assembly of Ladies also presents an allegory about courtly love told from the female perspective. In this poem, however, there is another layer between the speaker and audience: a knight or squire who initiates the telling of the tale by engaging the narrator in conversation and asking for her story. The narrator replies that while she and her friends were playing in a maze she fell asleep in a beautiful arbour. Along came a well-dressed gentlewoman named Perseveraunce who lives with Loyalty, a lady of great estate, and invites the narrator and her friends to a council of women in seven days. They are given specific instructions to dress in blue, create a motto to wear on a sleeve and bring a bill of complaint; then they will have a turn to make a request of the council. At the time specified, the women set out to Lady Loyalty's estate, which is peopled with allegorical figures in the manner of much late-medieval poetry, most famously *Le Roman de la Rose*. Whereas the quest for and conquest of the Rose involves the Lover gaining entry to her castle through his encounters with satirical portraits of characteristics of courtly love, *The Assembly* follows the tradition of the gentle female portraits found in, for instance, *The Abbey of the Holy Ghost*. The Assembly's narrator encounters positive representations of female conduct in love: for example, Diligence is the guide, Contenaunce is the porter, Largesse the steward and Remembraunce the chamberlain. These portraits consistently note not only how beautiful and well-dressed the ladies are, but also how uniformly gentle, modest and demure their comportment is. Perseveraunce's description of the narrator's guide to Loyalty's council sets the tone for the other depictions:

> And Diligence this gentil womman hight,
> A womman of right famous governaunce
> And wele cherisshed, I sey yow for certeyne;
> Hir felawship shal do yow grete plesaunce,
> Hir porte is suche, hir manere is trewe and playne;
> She with glad chiere wil do hir busy peyne
> To bryng yow there.
>
>   (133–39)

The conduct and dress of the allegorical figures (as well as those of the narrator and her fellowship) are exemplary – there is nothing to be criticised in the looks and behaviour of these ladies. In the palace of Plesaunt Regard, the narrator meets several women who help prepare her as she moves inward to the council room: Perseveraunce the messenger and right-hand woman of Loiaulte, Diligence the guide, Contenaunce the porter, Discrecioun the purveyor, Acqueyntaunce the herbegyer (lodgings officer), Largesse the steward, Bealchiere the marshal of the hall, Remembraunce the chamberlain, Aviseness the secretary. All play a role in preparing the narrator and her friends, helping them to dress in their blue gowns, discuss their mottoes and gather the bills of complaint, and then leading them into the council chambers.

The council chambers are fantastically opulent, with crystal walls and a dazzling throne of gems. That the walls play an allegorical role is undoubted. Upon them are engraved scenes of classic female loyalty and suffering in love: the narrator tells us there are too many to recite, singling out particular martyrs for love, Phyllis, Thisbe and Cleopatra, and those who are betrayed by their lovers, Melusine and Anelida. The walls are too bright – and by extension, the tableaux too poignant – to be viewed directly by this sympathetic audience and have been covered with light gauze to soften them.

To the throne comes the epitome of female courtly behaviour, Lady Loiaulte, announced by Perseveraunce and followed by a noble company (recalling the procession in the *Floure*, for example). The narrator first remarks upon Perseveraunce's comportment again:

Thus as we stoode a doore opened anon;
A gentil womman semely of stature,
Beryng a mace, com out, hir self alone –
Triewly, me thought, a goodely creature.
She spak nothyng to lowde, I yow ensure,
Nor hastily, but bi goodely warnyng:
'Make roome,' quod she, 'my lady is comyng.'

(491–7)

With this the council begins, after the narrator describes Loiaulte's elegant dress and rich ornaments in detail. Following a pronouncement, Loiaulte starts the proceedings and the bills are read in turn by the secretary Avisement, beginning with those that arrived first. The narrator and her company thus go forward in pairs, the ladies taking precedence over the gentlewomen. These bills and mottoes form the core of the final section of the poem. The women present their stories of love lost and betrayed, the mottoes integrated into the telling of the tales. They use generalities to describe their experiences, focusing on the futility and frustration of their fidelity and their devotion to uncaring, unloving, inconstant and unfaithful lovers. It is the articulation of their thwarted desires that is significant here: the poem puts their experiences and feelings into words, both verbal and written, in the bills and on their sleeves, which are then recited by Avisement in the tribunal. The narrator is the last to present her bill, which is even more vague and general than those which came before, but she appears more desperate than the others, beginning with a desire to die to end her suffering, and stating that she cannot suffer it much longer. Yet the tribunal provides her with no succour, for the poem stops short of pronouncing a judgment, instead deferring this until the court of parliament can meet, provide a remedy and supply it to the complainants in writing.

After they leave the palace the narrator wakes up and writes down her dream vision, which she then relates to the listener of the poem. He asks for the name of her book, 'La semble de Dames' (752), of which he approves – thus a form of judgment is supplied for the poem as a whole despite the deferral of judgment at the council. Like Chaucer's dream visions (for instance, *The Parliament of Fowls*), this poem does not close the debate at the end, suggesting closure instead through the dreamer returning to a waking state and writing down the dream. It is therefore the communication of the dream in writing that is the primary objective for this kind of poem, as well as the encouragement of debate among the listeners about the topic at hand: in this case, the loyalty of women in love. The emphasis in this poem is not on the wrongs done by men but rather on the suffering women endure in the name of love: it is women's experiences and emotions that are primary here.

The articulation of female desire is key to both *The Floure and the Leafe* and *The Assembly of Ladies*. In the former desire is figured through song and speech, while in the latter women reveal their emotional longings primarily through written communication. Our attention is first drawn to the theme of the female voice when the narrator notes the recent absence of the nightingale's song: 'I, that couth not yet in no manere / Heare the nightingale of all the yere, / Full busily herkened with hart and with eare / If I her voice perceive coud any where' (39–42). She sets out to recover this lost female voice, achieving success beyond her dreams. The nightingale's song transforms her hidden arbour into a prelapsarian paradise filled with innocent, sensual delights into which the ladies of the Leaf come singing and dancing, with the Queen leading not only their procession but also their song. Flora performs the same role with her company of the Flower, and the poem ends with a female instructor engaging in dialogue with the narrator before the speaker goes to write her account of the event and send it off to be read and heard by others. It is not simply that women speak and sing, but that the sound of female voices is superlative and transcendent. The speaker hears the ladies of the Leaf approaching:

> And as I sat, the birds harkening thus,
> Me thought that I heard voices sodainly,
> The most sweetest and most delicious
> That ever any wight, I trow trewly,
> Heard in their life, for the armony
> And sweet accord was in so good musike
> That the voice to angels most was like.
>
> (127–33)

When the Queen of the Leaf leads the ladies in song, the speaker thinks it was 'the sweetes melody / That ever I heard in my life, soothly' (181–2). These voices are unearthly and heavenly. They have an extraordinary effect on the reader, as the dream vision engages all of the speaker's senses. The most attention is paid to the nightingale at the start of the poem, where she sets the stage for the coming tableau:

> The nightingale with so merry a note
> Answered him that all the wood rong,
> So sodainly that, as it were a sote,
> I stood astonied; so was I with the song
> Thorow ravished, that, till late and long,
> I ne wist in what place I was ne where;
> And ayen, me thought, she song even by mine ere.
>
> (99–105)

The smell of the roses assists in transporting the speaker into full sensory overload in the *hortus conclusus*, where she recalls 'I surely ravished was / Into Paradise' (114–15). The nightingale plays a crucial role in the poem, illustrating the beauty of the female voice. Women astound with their voices, both to entertain and instruct. They offer beauty and wisdom. Women lead and rule; they listen, watch and observe; they dance and sing; they teach and delight.

From the wonders and marvels the speaker beholds she is pulled back by the lady who explicates the vision at the end. She provides historical analogues, she explicates key symbols in the dream, and then relates them back to the speaker's behaviour: what side are you on, she enquires? Asked to reflect on her own moral conduct, the speaker addresses the lady with great respect and deference, listening closely to her answers and assimilating and applying the lecture to herself.

While the *Floure* emphasises women's voices, the *Assembly* prioritises women's stories: not only in speeches to each other, but also in written words – embroidered on sleeves and contained in complaints to be presented to the council – and in pictures – the tableaux of famous, wronged women engraved in the crystal walls in Lady Loyalty's Palace. Female instruction and women helping women are central to this poem. The narrator requires a great deal of guidance, an effective device for initiating the audience into the dream vision, while also establishing the narrator's role as observer and participant in the poem. She communicates often with the allegorical figures she encounters, making 'bold' several times to ask for further information from the courteous women of the palace. Information is exchanged, stories told, bills and mottoes written: speech and writing are crucial to the expression of female experience in this poem. Although the emphasis remains on comportment and conveying the interior state in external representation, this is achieved by having the acts of writing and reading maintain the alliance between the internal and external. Moreover, the fact that women witness and judge (that is, see and hear) the stories is significant. The procession of the narrator and her company into the tribunal sets the scene very effectively, for on the chamber's beryl and crystal walls 'was graven of storyes many oon' (456), exempla of women betrayed by love. Classical examples dominate in the short list provided: Phyllis, Thisbe, Cleopatra, Melusine and Anelida. The brevity of the list is qualified, however, to illustrate the ubiquity of the theme of women as martyrs for love:

> Al these storyes wer graven ther certayne
> And many mo than I reherce yow here –
> It were to long to telle yow al in feere.
> And bicause the wallis shone so bright
> With fyne umple they were al over-spredde
> To that entent folk shuld nat hurt theyr sight,
> And thurgh that the storyes myght be redde.
>
> (449–73)

The brilliance of these translucent, reflective tales can inflict pain upon those who see them. The gauzy covering diminishes the effect, yet does not obscure the exempla from view. The creation of the female experiences in visual representations on the walls provides a further example of female narration that resonates with the other instances of women's stories being told in a female community.

Women are constantly writing (not being written) in this poem: the allegorical figures have their mottoes inscribed on their sleeves, and the fellowship of women invited to the council write mottoes on their sleeves as well as bringing bills of complaint. The structure of the council also implies a reliance on the written word as it makes use of a legal context. The council summons the complainants, listens to the complaints and decides to provide a judgment. They agree to debate the judgment at their parliament, after which they will send Diligence out to the ladies to bring them the date when the council will next convene. The emphasis on writing leads to a recognition of the importance of articulating female experience on the written page – writing on the sleeve further suggests the corporeal reality of female experience, the effects of love and suffering on the body and how such experience affects the identity of women as well as their bodies. It is therefore significant that there is so much listening in the poem: from the sympathetic knight in the frame, to the large body of women involved in the council who pay witness to women's experiences and suffering in love. This poem illustrates the value of female expression to a sympathetic audience who understands a female perspective. Moreover, the topic left unjudged at the end of the poem does not suggest the usual opening up of a debate that we see in other such dream poems; rather it seems to imply that listening to the female perspective is what is required: soliciting this point of view and being sympathetic to women's opinions is key.

The context of sympathy is highlighted in the female communities created in the poems. In *The Floure and the Leafe* the ladies lead the procession onto the field and the knights follow first to joust and then to disport with their lovers. The queens govern both leaf and flower, representing female sovereignty over their own conduct and those of the ladies who follow them. The lady who speaks with the narrator at the end of the poem demonstrates the value of women's counsel as she exhorts the narrator to lead an exemplary life devoted to chastity and loyalty. This poem places female conduct in courtly love within an enhanced frame of duty to the larger community of women and the ideals of female purity and sovereignty. Courtesy is directed by women to women, whereas the knights offer mere amusement to the ladies. *The Assembly of Ladies* takes this point even further, suggesting that male conduct in courtly love instigates suffering and bother while women offer sympathy and support. Indeed, the narrator is in a company of ladies and gentlewomen who identify themselves as a group (signalled by the narrator waiting for her fellowship before joining the council), and the estate is governed by women only, as is the council. When the narrator questions why no men are allowed at Loyalty's estate (probably a satiric comment on men's lack of fidelity), her guide equivocates:

> 'Yit,' quod I, 'ye must telle me this cace,
> If we shal any men unto us calle?'
> 'Nat one,' quod she, 'may come among yow alle.'
>
> 'Nat one?' quod I, 'ey, benedicite!
> What have they don, I pray yow, telle me that.'
> 'Now, be my lif, I trowe but wele,' quod she,
> 'But evere I can beleve ther is somwhat,
> And for to sey yow trowth, more can I nat;
> In questions nothyng may I be to large,
> I medle me no further than is my charge.'
>
> (145–54)

While men are excluded on account of treating women poorly in love, in the palace the ladies find positive valuation in female companionship, counsel and judgment about women's conduct in love. Although what brings the ladies and gentlewomen together is their experiences in love, the poem maintains that it is the shared experiences of the female community that are key. Women comment on and evaluate each other's conduct, offer assistance to each other, and govern the code of female behaviour in the council. Nonetheless, the poem concludes with a symbol of male approbation, for the frame provides a male listener who offers his approval of the narrator's tale at the end of the poem. This may imply, as does the participation of the knights in the *Floure* vision, the necessity of bridging female and male in order to restore social harmony, yet the poem also prioritises the feminine experience and women's relationships.

The dream visions offer a response to female representation and a desire to illustrate the female point of view. The identification with and sympathy for feminine experience in courtly love is key to these poetic representations of female desire and conduct. The poems explore how interior emotions and attitudes inform outward behaviour as well as how outward experiences transform inner emotional states: the poems attempt to delve beyond surface representations, to connect female conduct to emotions and experiences, and then examine the articulation of this connection in song, speech, and writing expressing female desire. The poems thus present a performance of feminine conduct in love, using allegorical representations of characteristics attributed to women which often challenge traditional stereotypes, for example by means of outward manifestations of female loyalty and constancy.

In contrast to the extended depictions of women's conduct in love found in the *Assembly* and the *Floure*, the shorter poems with female speakers written in the fifteenth century shift their focus to become intense expressions of female interiority in love. Both genres concentrate on the articulation of female desire, but in the lyrics and verse letters this is in response to the lover's actions, inactions, or absence. Whereas allegorical dream visions teach, illustrate, empathise and instruct, lyrics project. The nightingale's song in the *Floure* and the mottoes written on sleeves in the *Assembly* resonate with the lyrics' condensed expressions of women's desire, where the external surface detail and narrative are stripped down to bare the inner beauty and emotions of the nightingale. Women wear their hearts on their sleeves figuratively in the lyrics, as we see the transference of passive suffering into active voicing.

It is in fifteenth-century manuscripts that we begin to find examples of Middle English lyrics written in a female voice, some as verse letters to a lover. The best known instance is the Findern manuscript (Cambridge, University Library MS Ff. 1. 6), a collection of poetry used by a community of women in a noble household in Derbyshire in the fifteenth and sixteenth centuries. This manuscript offers a fascinating example of women's involvement in vernacular poetic activity, for not only do we have several lyrics written in women's voices but also there is a number of women's names inscribed in this manuscript, as well as plausible evidence for women transcribing male-authored poetry emphasising female perspectives. Oxford, Bodleian

MS Rawlinson C.813 is similar in some regards to Findern: it includes a number of poems told from a female perspective, in a manuscript written in many hands. Lyrics with female speakers appear in other verse miscellanies, such as Cambridge, Trinity College, MS R.3.19, which includes a thirteen-stanza rhyme royal poem, 'A woman's reply to her lover' (fols 7v–8), in a mid- to late-fifteenth-century manuscript of Middle English poetry. Lynne R. Mooney has examined the connections between the primary scribe of this manuscript and the Hammond scribe, thereby linking the Trinity College MS to the verse materials of John Shirley (Mooney 1997: 10). Mooney has also uncovered a further example of household readers turning writers on the flyleaves of a printed copy of Anthony Woodville's 1477 *Dictes or Sayeingis of the Philosophres* (Caxton, 1477, STC 6826), where there are written by hand three lyrics from a female perspective. More research on individual manuscripts and their contexts (like that done by McNamer, Barratt, Meale, Mooney and Marshall) will undoubtedly add further poems to this body of work.

As with the dream visions, scholars have considered various aspects of the production and reception of these poems and consider it likely that some of them could have been written by women. Critics vary in their response to this possibility: while Julia Boffey (1985) notes that the difficulties in obtaining conclusive evidence cast doubt on female authorship, McNamer, Mooney and Barratt (1992) take a more positive view, arguing in favour of female authorship. Their arguments are persuasive and serve an important function within the study of Middle English verse, opening up discussion of lyric poetic traditions in ways that chime with the *Assembly* and the *Floure*, through the exploration of female narration, voice and subjectivity, as well as women's participation in poetic activities as authors, compilers, scribes and patrons. Whereas the long poems used narrative tableaux to develop their critiques of courtly love and the conduct of lovers (both men and women) from the woman's perspective, these lyrical poems often produced condensed expressions of female desire and frustration, speaking back to male lovers and turning the tables on them. The best examples of this are the rewriting of Chaucer's 'Against Women Unconstant' in the flyleaves of *The Dictes and Sayeingis* to present man as unconstant and 'A woman's reply to her lover', both of which provide the female perspective in a way that Robert Henryson's *Testament of Cresseid* purports to do but cannot within the frame of the Chaucerian male narrator's viewpoint. The ripostes offered in lyrics with female speakers suggest that fifteenth-century verse worked dialectically, that male and female voices spoke to each other about love and lovers. Although this call and response may have already been happening in songs (Plummer 1981; Barratt 1992) we see it preserved here in the fifteenth-century manuscripts that offer a woman's point of view, and present alternatives to traditional assumptions about women: their physiology, psychology, behaviour and experiences.

Critics disagree as to whether the men described in verse lyrics are courtly lovers or husbands (see Hanson-Smith 1979 and McNamer 1991), but I think what is significant is that the lyrics do not situate themselves specifically: even the details given at the conclusion to 'A woman's reply to her lover' (Mooney 1997: 23–5) play with offering clues to the lovers' identity, referring to a 'Royal Ox' and the 'swan' (87–8), while remaining inscrutable to modern scholars. This inscrutability serves the subgenre very well: the poems are not meant to be a comment on specific lovers, or even specific kinds of lovers; rather they are concerned with the effects of love and lovers on their female subjects. Their main subject, then, is the nature of paradox: how the absent lover increases feminine desire; how the lover's inability to meet the needs (social, emotional, romantic, or otherwise) of his beloved creates a space for female speech.

The poems' speakers are intensely affected by the presence or absence of the beloved: presence can bring great joy, while absence causes sorrow. For example, in the Findern manuscript we find this lament:

> My wooful hert, thus clad in payn,
> Wote natt welle what do nor seyn:
>   Longe absens grevyth me so.
>
> For lakke of syght nere am I sleyn,
> All joy myne hert hath in dissedeyn:
>   Comfort fro me is go.
>   (Pearsall 1999: 403, stanzas 1–2)

As in much Middle English love poetry, physical discomfort follows emotional unease: pain and near-death experiences are likened to the sorrow caused by the absence of the beloved. Much is made of contrasts and paradoxes, for example, between joy and sorrow, presence and absence:

> Come home, dere herte, from tarieng –
> Kausith me to wepe, bothe weile and wring,
> Also to lyve evere in distresse
> So gret there may no wight expresse:
> Al my joye ye torne to mournyng.
>   (Pearsall 1999: 404, stanza 1)

The imagery is not original, but the contrast between female stasis and male errancy neatly parallels the discussions of female constancy also found in these poems. For instance, a poem in the Rawlinson manuscript describes a lover's change of heart convincingly:

> Now wyll I sey as I thynke yn my harte
> Of yow, sweteharte, whyche I fynde soo strange,
> As on of them that wyll nott turne nor converte,
> By my assent ye shall begyne the range.
> I was not ware ye cast yow forto change
> But, for all thys, I shall doo my dever
> To love you well, butt trust ye me for ever.
>   (Barratt 1992: 265, stanza 2)

The motif of the lover's turning and conversion is effectively juxtaposed here with the speaker's fidelity and certainty. The poem emphasises her innocence of her lover's change of heart and her inability to consider such behaviour herself: he breaks the rules of their relationship, alienating his lover and challenging her expectations of love. We also find a poem in the Findern manuscript concluding with a declaration of constancy:

> To hym I woll be trywe and playn,
> And evyr his owne in serteyn
>   Tyll deth departe us to.

> My hert shall I never fro hym refrayn:
> I gave hitt hym withowte constrayn,
>   Evyr to contenue so.
>   (Pearsall 1999: 403, stanzas, 6–7)

The lyrics develop a sustained focus on the female affective response to the love object. The trope of loyalty thus remains the central focus of many of the lyrics, extending the differences of comportment between I and him, female and male.

Women in the lyrics are constant, loyal, steadfast and true, whereas male lovers are fickle, changeable and often absent. In 'A woman's reply to her lover' the speaker counsels her lover to be patient: 'Ye must in chyef lerne to be sufferaunt,/ Servyseable, secret, without avaunt' (34–5), arguing that if it is required, 'Spare nat to serve trewly fro yere to yere' (38) (Mooney 1997: 24). Willingness to keep their love secret – away from public gossip – demonstrates discretion. Counselling patience, secrecy and loyalty reverses the traditional expectations of the love lyric: women in love are neither hardhearted nor fickle, and they cannot be rushed or forced to love where their hearts do not belong. Men are urged to be proper lovers, not to think only of themselves but of their lovers' needs and reputations:

> Unto thys poynt wolde your humanyte
> I yow demaunde the thyng of my desyre,
> That were so fer ayenst femynte?
> How coude ye of me suche thyng requyre
> As shuld do nought but tonges set on fyre?
> And eke yef I purveyed for that pleasaunce
> Ye myght well sey I coude of chevesaunce.
>   (15–21)

Cognisant of the consequences of publicising their secret love, the speaker challenges her lover to examine his motives. His requests are placed in a wider context than the satisfaction of individual desire; they can set tongues on fire as fodder for gossipers. Society's need for gossip and the place of the lovers within the community restrains their individual actions, causing a loss for both. Caught between society's expectations and those of her lover, the speaker attempts to instruct her beloved in the ways of true love: the state of unconsummated desire is exacerbated not by the female lover's indifference but by the social restraints on her conduct.

As late-medieval English devotional culture turned inward in the fifteenth century, and a feminised interiority was manifested through the rise in popularity of the Virgin Mary's role in Christ's life and passion, the feminised body of Christ, and the experiences of holy women, so fifteenth-century secular lyric poetry sought expressions of the feminised heart and mind: sincere outpourings of emotion, personalised reflections on experiences of love, convincing alternatives to conventional representations of women. These employ neither the playful satire of fourteenth-century poetry about love nor the sometimes heavy-handed irony of the fifteenth-century Chaucerians, but comprise brief, intense dramas of suffering and joy. In these love lyrics the absence of the male lover forces the speaker to turn inwards to an affective experience of desire. The love poem becomes an expression of the desire for union that cannot be satisfied and a cry for understanding:

> So depe ye be
> Graven, parde
>   Withyn myn hert
> That afore mee
> Ever I yow see
>   In thought covert.
> (Pearsall 1999: 405, stanza 2)

Because her love for him is so intense, the speaker engraves her lover's image within her heart. The physical and emotional overlaps in this image, which causes a doubling of vision: although he is gone, she can still see him in her mind. Moreover, the use of the term 'graven' draws our attention to the parallels between the process of internationalisation and the physical act of creating a visual image.

Then we find that this internalising turns outward in the poems. For example, one of the lyrics in the Rawlinson manuscript ends with the statement 'All my harte I have here wrytton, / To sende yow yn a byll' (Barratt 1992: 264). Recalling the ladies at the assembly, she puts her heart – her emotions, the picture of her love – into words of complaint that in this case are supposed to be shared with the lover but are also shared by the other readers of the manuscript: another community of readers who share the experience and read the words. This process of externalising is seen as purgative and generative, moving the speaker from emotion to action, from feeling to doing, from the emotional response to a literary communication of the response. The goal is to produce a poem that speaks sincerely and feelingly. Thus, the lyrics shy away from excessive ornamentation in favour of clarity, rhythmic regularity and brevity. They recall not the hustle and bustle of the court, but the personal spaces of the country household. They represent whispers and cries from the heart elegantly and sparingly related to the reader.

The attitudes revealed in these poems are not new or original, participating as they do in the contemporary debates about female and male romantic conduct and the biological/social constructions of gender. Nevertheless it is new in the fifteenth century to have female speakers contributing to the debates, rather than having the female perspective filtered through the gaze or voice of a male narrator and speaker. Whether they were written by women or not (we may recall that Carl Whithaus declared this a 'dead issue' in 1999: 37), these female speakers argue for women's passion, suffering and constancy in the face of absent or untrue lovers – a very different picture of women in love than the Wife of Bath and Criseyde, for example, present, and one without the ambiguity of Chaucer's *Legend of Good Women*.

The anonymous poems with female speakers found in collections of secular lyrics are traditional in subject and form, much like the other poetry written by women between the times of Chaucer and Spenser (to evoke the title of Pearsall's excellent anthology). For example, the 'Anchoress's Hymn to the Virgin' (Ashmole 59) is found in a mis-cellany copied by John Shirley in the 1440s, and in the early sixteenth century Queen Elizabeth's 'Hymn to the Virgin' is set in a manuscript context similar to many of the fifteenth-century lyrics (Rawl C.86). Dame Juliana Berners's connection with *The Book of St. Alban's*, especially the treatises on hunting, fishing and hawking, is perhaps a novelty, yet the explicit in the manuscript giving her name to one or more of these texts to her seems more of an association rather than an attribution (Boffey 2004). It appears that associating certain kinds of texts with women (for example, romances and venacular religious literature) was viewed as an asset, and during the fifteenth century as in no previous period we see categories of literature being opened to female participation. The proliferation of voices and perspectives we find in this period is astounding: rich and varied, all probe the limits of poetic endeavour.

The field of women's writings in fifteenth-century Middle English verse is a fas-cinating if complicated one. Much of the scholarly attention has necessarily focused on identifying poetry written in a female voice and arguing for its inclusion in a female-authored verse tradition. This work needs to continue. Other recent work has moved on to the next stage: examining critical issues, offering poetic analysis and considering codicological coherence. This is an exciting time to be studying fifteenth-century women's poetry: there is more to explore as we discover useful vocabularies and concepts for discussion of these works.

References and Further Reading

Barratt, Alexandra (1987). 'The Flower and the Leaf' and 'The Assembly of Ladies': is there a (sexual) difference? *Philological Quarterly*, 66, 1–24.

Barratt, Alexandra (ed.) (1992). *Women's Writing in Middle English*. London: Longman.

Battles, Paul (2003). 'In folly ripe, in reason rotten': The Flower and the Leaf and the 'purgatory of cruel beauties'. *Medium Ævum*, 72, 238–59.

Boffey, J. (2004). Berners, Juliana. *Oxford Dictionary of Biography*. Oxford: Oxford University Press.

Boffey, J. (1985). *Manuscripts of English Courtly Love Lyrics in the Later Middle Ages*. Cambridge: Cambridge University Press.

Chance, Jane (1994). Christine de Pizan as literary mother: women's authority and subjectivity in 'The Floure and the Leafe' and 'Assembly of Ladies.' In Margarete Zimmermann and Dina de Rentiis (eds). *The City of Scholars: New Approaches to Christine de Pizan* (pp. 245–59). Berlin: Walter de Gruyter.

Connelly, Colleen (1994). 'Withoute wordes': the medieval lady dreams in 'The Assembly of Ladies'. *Journal of the Rocky Mountain Medieval and Renaissance Association*, 15, 35–55.

Doyle, K. A. (2006). Thisbe out of context: Chaucer's female readers and the Findern Manuscript ('Legend of Good Women,' 'Legend of Thisbe'). *Chaucer Review*, 40, 231–61.

Forni, Kathleen (1997). The swindling of Chaucerians and the critical fate of 'The Floure and the Leafe'. *Chaucer Review*, 31, 379–400.

Klinck, Anne L. and Ann Marie Rasmussen (eds) (2002). *Medieval Woman's Song: Cross-Cultural Approaches*. Philadelphia: University of Philadelphia Press.

Marshall, Simone Celine (2008). *The Female Voice in 'The Assembly of Ladies': Text and Context in Fifteenth-Century England*. Newcastle: Cambridge Scholars.

McCash, June Hall (2003). Negotiating the text: women patrons and the poetic process. *Romance Philology*, 57, 27–43.

McNamer, Sarah (2003). Lyrics and romances. In Carolyn Dinshaw and David Wallace (eds). *The Cambridge Companion to Medieval Women's Writing* (pp. 195–209). Cambridge: Cambridge University Press.

McNamer, Sarah (1991). Female authors, provincial settings: the re-versing of courtly love in the Findern Manuscript. *Viator*, 22, 303–10.

Meale, Carol M. (2007). Women's voices and roles. In Peter Brown (ed.). *A Companion to Medieval English Literature and Culture, c. 1350–c. 1500* (pp. 74–90). Oxford: Blackwell.

Meale, Carol M. (1993) '... Alle the bokes that I haue of Latyn, Englisch, and Frensch': laywomen and their books in late Medieval England.' In Carol M. Meale (ed.). *Women and Literature in Britain, 1150–1500* (pp. 128–58). Cambridge: Cambridge University Press.

Mooney, Linne R. (1997). 'A Woman's Reply to Her Lover' and four other new courtly love lyrics in Cambridge, Trinity College MS R. 3. 19. *Medium Ævum*, 67, 250–51.

Pearsall, Derek Albert (ed.) (1999). *Chaucer to Spenser: An Anthology of Writings in English, 1375–1575*. Oxford: Wiley-Blackwell.

Pearsall, Derek Albert (ed.) (1990). *The Floure and the Leafe; the Assembly of Ladies; the Isle of Ladies*. Kalamazoo, MI: TEAMS; Medieval Institute Publications, Western Michigan University.

Plummer, John F. (1981). The woman's song in Middle English and its European backgrounds. In John F. Plummer (ed.). *Vox Feminae: Studies in Medieval Woman's Songs* (pp. 135–54). Kalamazoo, MI: Medieval Institute Publications.

Riddy, Felicity (1993). 'Women talking about the things of God': a late medieval sub-culture.' In Carole Meale (ed.). *Women and Literature in Britain 1150–1500* (pp. 104–27). Cambridge: Cambridge University Press.

Snyder Cynthia, Lockard (1993). 'The Floure and the Leafe': an alternative approach. In David Chamberlain (ed.). *New Readings of Late Medieval Love Poems* (pp. 145–171). Lanham, MD: University Press of America.

Summit, Jennifer (1995). William Caxton, Margaret Beaufort and the romance of female patronage. In Lesley Smith and Jane H. M. Taylor (eds). *Women, the Book and the Worldly: Selected Proceedings of the St Hilda's Conference, 1993*. Vol. 2 (pp. 151–65). Cambridge: D. S. Brewer.

Summit, Jennifer (2003). Women and authorship. In Carolyn Dinshaw and David Wallace (eds). *The Cambridge Companion to Medieval Women's Writing* (pp. 91–108). Cambridge: Cambridge University Press.

Whithaus, Carl (1999). 'Wrethen in fere': narrative voice, gender and chastity in 'The Floure and the Leafe'. *Women and Language*, 22, 37–43.

32
Medieval Scottish Poetry

Douglas Gray

The modern Scottish poet Edwin Morgan, in one of his 'Sonnets from Scotland', imagines the words of a thirteenth-century English monk and chronicler, Matthew Paris, on the land:

> North and then north and north again we sailed,
> not that God is in the north or the south
> but that the north is great and strange, a mouth
> of baleen filtering the unknown, veiled
> spoutings and sportings, curtains of white cold.
> I made a map, I made a map of it.
> Here I have bristly Scotland, almost split
> in two, what sea-lochs and rough marches, old
> forts, new courts, when Alexander their king
> is dead will they live in love and peace, get
> bearings, trace mountains, count stars, take capes, straits
> in their stride as well as crop and shop, bring
> luck home? *Pelagus vastissimus et*
> *invium*, their element, my margin, waits.
>
> (Edwin Morgan, 'Matthew Paris', in *Collected Poems*
> [1990]. Reprinted by permission of Carcanet Press Ltd.)

Although he made a map of Scotland we do not know if the St Albans monk ever made the perilous journey to the country. He certainly would have thought of it as a remote, wild and strange place (his map says of the North-West coast that it 'looks only towards a sea where there is nought but the abode of monsters'; it is a 'country marshy and impassable, fit for cattle and shepherds'). Other southern travellers found it so: the Italian humanist Aeneas Silvius Piccolomini, who visited it briefly in the earlier fifteenth century, found it cold and poor, and generally uninviting. How very different from the modern view, derived from Romantic and post-Romantic travellers. The Preface to the old *Blue Guide* begins, 'Scotland is a small country, but its appeal is so manifold that it is difficult to catalogue its attractions'. In fact, medieval Scotland also had many attractions – not least, especially in the fifteenth and early sixteenth centuries, a literature of outstanding imaginative quality.

Unfortunately, for many English readers this early literature is still as remote and strange as the country was thought to be by Matthew Paris. Students of medieval English poetry often know little or nothing about it: it is too often left out on the margin of the better known world of 'Old English' and 'Middle English', rather like the mysterious medieval land. A student needs to embark on a voyage of discovery in order to find its treasures – and they are many. This essay will concentrate on the major late medieval poets, but it must be emphasised that there is much else to be found besides Robert Henryson and William Dunbar.

This intellectual journey is an exciting one. It may not present the physical dangers that a real-life medieval English traveller had to face (in those days, of course, it was for him a separate and 'foreign' kingdom), but it has its obstacles. One obvious one is the problem of 'lost literature'. Any student of Middle English literature will have come on this, but it is especially vexing north of the border. Thus, we have many references to plays and semi-dramatic pieces, but the hostility of Reformers has meant that the texts of the early Scottish drama have not survived. We know that we have lost some poems by our major poets. We know nothing or next to nothing of some of the 'makars' whom Dunbar lists in his famous lament. Quite often we have to read our medieval poets in texts and copies which were made much later. It is very tempting to compare this situation to the Scottish landscape now, dotted with the ruins (often impressive ruins) of old forts and ancient abbeys. But it is important not to paint too gloomy a picture. Henryson's Dunfermline has suffered much – Defoe's early eighteenth-century *Tour through the Whole Island of Great Britain* speaks of the place's 'full perfection of decay' (like other early travellers he had some taste for melancholy ruins) – but it still has the very impressive remains of its abbey and palace, and its great poetic son has given it a memorial more lasting than stone. Another barrier which confronts the modern mental traveller is that of language, but this is not an insuperable one. 'Bristly Scotland' was in fact almost split in two linguistically as well as geographically, a large area in the highlands and the Western Isles speaking Gaelic, a Celtic language, forming a society which had its own social and cultural structures, and another large predominantly lowland area speaking a version of northern Middle English, now often called 'Older Scots'; it is from this area that our poets come. Its characteristic forms (e.g. -*is* in the 3rd plural of verbs ('clerkis sayis' ['scholars say'] as well as in the 3rd singular) and spellings (some a trifle 'bristly', like *quhat* for 'what') can quickly be mastered by anyone who has studied Middle English, and some will not sound strange to one who has listened to modern Scots speech (*auld* 'old', *gude* 'good', *nicht* 'night', etc.). It is certainly no more forbidding than the language of *Sir Gawain and the Green Knight*. The poets can use 'oure Inglisch' with a self-confident skill and virtuosity. In the literary kinds and forms which they use the traveller who has read some Middle English poetry will also find much that is familiar to him, but often handled with a new enthusiasm and emphasis, and sometimes wonderfully transformed. They produce excellent lyrics and satires, and they excel in narrative, in all its medieval forms – romances, tales, fables and chronicles or 'history in verse'. There are dream visions and allegories, and the older English alliterative verse form lives on triumphantly. We catch glimpses of the characteristic scenery alluded to in Morgan's poem (although this is not as central for the poets or as fascinating as it becomes for their successors) – the sea lochs and the rough marches (the borders famed for lairds and reivers and freebooters as well as for tale-tellers and ballad-singers). More often we are given a sense of contemporary life, both ordinary and extraordinary, by a remarkable poetic realism.

Although their independence from English claims was firmly established by Bruce's victory at Bannockburn in 1314, the Scots did not live in love and peace after their king Alexander was dead: Matthew Paris recorded the death (in 1249) of Alexander II, whom he describes as a wise and modest man for most of his life, but who yielded to greed at the end; Morgan thinks rather of his successor Alexander III, whose death in 1286 seems to have been recorded in popular verse, preserved by a fifteenth-century chronicler, Wyntoun:

> qwhen Alexander our kynge was dede,
> That Scotland lede in lauche [*law*] and le [*peace*]
> Away was sons [*abundance*] of ale and brede...
> ...Crist, borne in virgynyté
> Succoure Scotland and ramede [*bring remedy*]
> That stade [*put*] is in perplexité!
>
> (VII, 3621–28)

But although there was internal strife, it seems to have been kept in check, and although there was certainly much injustice and violence, the realm did not fall into chaos.

The Scots did not leave their country in the great numbers that were forced away in later centuries (and so often distinguished themselves in exploration, government and intellectual life), but the travelling Scot had made his appearance – whether as a student, pilgrim, ambassador or soldier, he made notable contributions. And those who remained at home also made contributions, not just to literature, but in different ways to what was clearly a lively intellectual and cultural landscape, notably in education (three of the four oldest Scottish universities were founded in this period) and in philosophy and theology. We begin to see the growing influence of the new humanism.

The poetry of the Older Scots makars makes a spirited beginning in the fourteenth century with *The Bruce* of John Barbour, imaginatively celebrating the victorious campaigns for independence led by that 'gud king' which culminated in Bannockburn. It is a fine poem, combining epic with romance, and presenting the stirring events in a genuinely exciting narrative, heightening no doubt the courage and nobility of the Scots and their king. Before battle is joined at Bannockburn the Scots kneel in prayer, and the English king says 'Yhon folk knelis till [*to*] ask mercy' – but one of his knights remarks, 'Thai ask mercy, bot nocht at yhow: / For thair trespas to God thai cry /...yhon folk will wyn all or de [*die*], /For dout [*fear*] of ded [*death*] thar sall nane fle' (XII, 484–490). Barbour delights in splendid martial scenes – when the English army rides out northwards from Berwick

> Bath hillis and valayis helyt [*covered*] thai,
> As the bataillis that war braid [*broad*]
> Departyt, our the feldis raid [*rode*],
> The sone wes brycht and schynand cler,
> And armouris, that burnysyt wer,
> Sua blomyt with the sonnys beme,
> That all the land wes in a leme [*flame*],
> With baneris richt freschly flawmand [*brightly fluttering*],
> And penselys [*pennants*] to the wyn wavand...
> (XI, 192–200)

But he also records the grimmer side of medieval warfare, as when Kildrummy castle is treacherously set on fire ('the fyre our all the castell spred, / Thar mycht no fors of men it red [*save*]' IV, 131–32). Not surprisingly, 'old forts' figure prominently – there is an exciting account of how Earl Thomas Randolph won Edinburgh castle and another of the siege and capture of Berwick and of its defence against the English in 1318–19. And there are occasional glimpses of the landscape, whenever that is relevant to the narrative – in book X, the Bruce fights with John of Lorn in a pass (the pass of Brander?):

> ...in ane evill place,
> That so strayt and sa narow was,
> That twasum sammyn [*together*] mycht nocht ryde
> In sum place off the hillis sid.
> The nethyr halff was peralous;
> For a schor [*sheer*] crag, hey and hydwous,
> Raucht [*reached*] till the se, doun fra the pas.
> On athyr half [*side*] the montane was
> Sua combrous [*difficult*] hey and stay [*steep*],
> That it wes hard to pas that way,
> Crechinben [*Ben Cruachan*] hecht [*was called*] that montane,
> I trow nocht that in all Bretane,
> Ane heyar hill may fundyn be...
> (X, 17–19)

For all the vigorous scenes of adventure, Barbour's poem is by no means bereft of ideas. He includes a famous passage in praise of freedom (as against 'foul thraldom'). He celebrates and to some extent explores the dominant ideas of heroic poetry – loyalty (as against its loathed opposite, treachery) and honour or 'worschip' in war, which is praiseworthy if followed intelligently (it lies between the extremes of 'fulehardy-ment' and cowardice). His Bruce is the epitome of the heroic, and chivalric, leader who unites fortitude and wisdom. He is nicely differentiated from his foremost sup-porters – the loyal Douglas, and his brother Sir Edward Bruce. Barbour makes use of ancient exempla and contemporary romance (his Bruce comforts his small band of followers by Loch Lomond by reading them the romance of 'worthi Ferambrace'). All this, and a passage on the nature of the good 'captain', suggests strongly that Barbour had given thought to the nature of good prince, a theme that is remarkably prominent in Older Scots writing.

Another significant interest is suggested by the opening lines of Barbour's poem on 'history' and 'story', traditional enough, but with a rather self-conscious interest in the manner of writing – 'Storys to red are delitabill', he says, 'Suppos that [*even though*] thai be nocht bot fabill' / Than suld storys that suthfast [*true*] wer, / And [*if*] thai war said on gud maner, / Have doubill plesance in heryng . . .' (I, 1–5). His most obvious successor in the writing of 'history' (in the rather generous medieval sense of the word) in verse is the poet Hary, the author of *The Wallace*, but we also find later writers who are interested in the question of the truth of fiction, and others who enjoy writing stories which do not pretend to be 'suthfast'. *The Wallace* is an eloquent poem, often as exciting as *The Bruce* but less thoughtful, and much less tolerant of the Saxon enemy. It is also much more brutal: the vengeful episode of the burning of the barns of Ayr (developed from a hint in Barbour) has an almost gleeful gruesomeness – 'till slepand men that walkning [*wakening*] was nocht soft', 'the reik [*smoke*] mellyt with fylth of carioune', etc., but it also has lines of simple power. When Wallace asks a woman if her uncle is dead, she replies:

> 'Out off yon bern,' scho said, 'I saw him born,
> Nakit, laid law on cald erd [*earth*] me beforn,
> His frosty mouth I kissit in that sted;
> Rycht now manlik, now bar, and brocht to ded,
> And with a claith I coverit his licaym [*corpse*].'
> (VII. 277–81)

Other narratives treat quite different material. *The Kingis Quair* – 'the King's little book' – almost certainly by James I of Scotland, is a dream vision in the Chaucerian manner, written in rhyme royal, which recounts the story (no doubt in heightened and fictionalised form) of his love in captivity (James spent nearly 20 years in English captivity, and in 1424, the year of his release, he married Joan Beaufort, the sister of the earl of Somerset). It is an imaginative and thoughtful poem, which in Chau-cerian manner raises and discusses general ideas concerning love, the lover – and the prince – and fortune (see also Barry Windeatt's essay in this volume). It is highly self-conscious, and beautifully constructed and eloquently written. It is probably the best of all the fifteenth-century 'Chaucerian' love-visions. Different again is *The Buke of the Howlat* by Richard Holland (?1448), an alliterative poem in intricate stanzas.

It is written for the wife of Archibald Douglas, and the powerful Douglas family is celebrated in it in the legend of how Sir James Douglas took the heart of the Bruce to the Holy Land and fought the Saracens. These heroic stanzas bring out the best in the poem's style. In this poem the poet does not fall asleep and dream, but walks out alone and finds himself in a beautiful spring landscape, and overhears an owl lamenting his ugly appearance. This is the beginning of a fable-narrative, involving an appeal to the Pope and Emperor, a lively assembly of birds, and Nature's permission for the owl to change its appearance. However, the owl lords it so mightily over the other birds that Nature rescinds her decree and at the end the poet is left alone with him, as he laments like a fallen prince, an implicit warning to the overweening and overmighty.

Later in the fifteenth century another writer brought a touch of genius to the narrative poem. We know little of the life of Robert Henryson (?*c.* 1420–?*c.* 1505): probably a graduate of Glasgow University, and perhaps also, earlier, of some other university; probably a schoolmaster at Dunfermline, a man of some legal knowledge, and possibly a notary public. One of his two major works is a collection of fables, most of them based on the Latin fables of Aesopic tradition sometimes used as school-texts, but some coming from the widespread stories of Reynard the fox. Fables and animal stories were common in the Middle Ages, and were often used by preachers and moralists; they also seem to have enjoyed wide circulation in oral and popular form. They were not just part of formal education, but seem also to have been part of what later became 'children's literature'. And we sometimes find writers recalling them fondly – Thomas More mentions a 'Mother Maud' who used to tell the children stories when she sat by the fire, 'fond childish tales', which include 'How the Ass and the Wolf came on a time to Confession to the Fox', while Wyatt begins one of his satires, 'My mothers maydes when they did sow and spynne, / They sang somtyme a song of the feld mowse', who decided to 'goo seke her townysshe systers howse'. This is an example of what John Locke said of fables – 'stories apt to delight and entertain a child' but which 'may yet afford useful reflections to a grown man' (*Some Thoughts Concerning Education* [1693]), and it illustrates the paradoxical nature of the fable – appealing to both 'high' and 'low' and existing in both 'learned' and 'popular' levels of literature.

Henryson transformed the brief, succinct Aesopic fable of antiquity into a sophisticated verse short story. It was a brief and, in style at least, a simple form: Henryson expanded it discreetly, but in a remarkable way contrived to maintain its brevity (and its memorable pointedness). His first fable (in the order of the sixteenth-century Bassandyne print followed by most modern editors: an order which seems coherent and well-structured, and which may possibly be authorial in origin), 'The Cock and the Jasp', is similar to the ancient fable: it has a single character and a single episode, and gives us a simple 'speaking picture'. There is conflict, but it is an interior one; details of the outside world and questions of character and motivation are suggested, but are not developed. Other fables are more complex in structure, with a number of protagonists (though not very many) and more than one episode. But even here there is much of the original simplicity – a liking for simple oppositions, encounters between two characters, and simple episodes and motifs, which often suddenly reveal the 'soul' of a situation. The narrator's voice is always present, but rarely obtrusive, though it may suggest both an interest and involvement in the story and a detachment from it. His asides are always interesting: in 'The Trial of the Fox' we are given a fine catalogue of the animals, and the poet remarks somewhat startlingly, 'And quhat thay wer, to me as Lowrence leird [*informed*] / I sall reheirs...' (884–85) – a rather witty citation of an eye-witness, who happens to be the fox, the archtrickster of the fable! He always seems close to his animal protagonists – indeed, in 'The Preaching of the Swallow' he sees the action for himself: like the poet of *The Buke of the Howlat* he walks out in springtime, sits down under a hawthorn tree and is surrounded by 'ane ferlie [*marvellous*] flicht', 'ane mekill [*great*] multitude' of small birds (1730, 1733). In the animal fable, as Dr Johnson said, 'beings irrational...are for the purpose of moral instruction feigned to act and speak with human interest and passions'; the more heavy-handed moral instructors were fond of emphasising that wicked and sinful men were like animals in their passions and behaviour. Henryson's technique is lighter in touch, though decidedly incisive. In his creatures the balance of animal and human is an artfully shifting and ambiguous one, which can produce comic moments as well as instruction – the town mouse, irritated by her country sister, 'hevilie scho [*she*] kest [*cast*] hir browis doun', and halff in hething [*scorn*]' says of the country fare that is offered to her that 'this victuall and your royall feist / May weill suffice unto ane rurall beist' (241–45). Henryson has the imagination to enter into the personalities of his animals and to bring us into the heart of the situations and adventures in which they find themselves, from social snobbery in the humble 'hole' of the country mouse to moments of 'epiphany', as when in 'The Wolf and the Wether' the Wether, disguised as a dog, assumes not only the duties of a shepherd's guard dog, but, it seems, its personality as well. He relentlessly pursues a wolf, who at last is so terrified that he throws away the lamb he has stolen, 'for weill he kennit the kenenes [*fierceness*] of the doig' – but this does not satisfy the wether, who announces 'Na...in faith, we part not swa: / It is not the lamb, but the, that I desyre!' and continues the chase (with disastrous results) (2531–55). The handling of the narrative in the *Fables* is masterly. Not surprisingly, Henryson is fond of direct speech and dialogue, and uses it much more extensively than the ancient and medieval Latin fable does. His source for 'The Two Mice' has very little, apart from a final speech by the country mouse: in Henryson's version seven stanzas are completely in dialogue, and seven others contain some direct speech. He will sometimes have a character speak 'in mind' or 'to himself'. Direct speech and dialogue are found in plenty in the animal tales of the Reynard cycle, and it may well be that this influenced Henryson's technique. Certainly the material he took from these stories spectacularly increases the variety of plot and tone in his collection. It encourages the use of a more extended and complex narrative, sequences of vivid scenes and scene-settings. In tone too there is an effect. The Aesopic tradition had made extensive use of traditional animal characteristics – the noble lion, the cunning fox, etc. – but in the figure of Reynard and his many descendants medieval literature had found a trickster par excellence, and writers like Henryson delight in the comic and satiric possibilities of his numerous amoral shifts and ruses. The fable sometimes comes close to the fabliau. Reynard's spirit of disorder, roguery and cynicism brings a new level and a new ambiguity to the moral world of Henryson's fables. In 'The Fox and the Wolf' the fox reads his destiny in the stars, and it is not a promising one; perhaps surprisingly (because his father sent him to school, he suggests), he decides to amend his 'misliving' (because 'deid [*death*] is reward off sin and schamefull end') and find a confessor. And, as it happens, he sees one approaching, a wolf, 'ane worthie doctour in divinitie, / Freir Wolff Waitskaith, in science wonder sle...' (666–67). Henryson warms to the possibilities of satirising friars, but does more than that – in the scene between them he gives us an exchange full of sustained irony and double talk: 'Your bair feit and your russet coull of gray, / Your lene cheik, your paill pietous face, / Schawis to me your perfite halines...' (679–81) says the fox; the wolf, with a laugh, says 'it plesis me that ye ar penitent' (685). The fox does very badly in his confession, revealing his true nature and his cynicism – to the question 'Art thow contrite and sorie in thy spreit / For thy trespas?' he gives an alarmingly truthful reply: 'Na, schir, I can not duid [*do it*]. / Me think that hennis ar sa honie-sweit, / And lambes flesche that new ar lettin bluid; / For to repent my mynd can not concluid [*decide*], / Bot off this thing – that I haif slane sa few' (698–703). As to penance, they decide after some discussion on something fairly light – the fox should refrain from meat except twice a week. They part, and the fox goes off to the water intending to catch fish, but is made comically melancholy by the sight of the water and waves ('better that I had bidden [*stayed*] at hame / Nor [*than*] bene a fischar, in the devillis name' [738–39]). Looking around for food he sees a flock of goats – 'than wes he blyith [*delighted*]' – and steals a little kid, which he takes to the water and immerses twice or thrice, saying (in one of Henryson's most memorable lines), 'Ga doun schir Kid, cum up schir Salmond [*salmon*], agane!', and 'off that new-maid salmond [he] eit anewch [*plenty*]' (753). But his destiny catches up with him – just as he basks in the sun stroking his belly and carelessly remarking that it would make a good target, the goatherd pierces him with an arrow. And yet this splendid anti-hero has the last word: 'Me think na man may speik ane word in play, / Bot nowondayis in ernist it is tane' (770–71). This fable is an excellent example of Henryson's skill in the art of narrative, in the construction of scenes and the control of narrative tempo. It also demonstrates his Chaucerian ease in the treatment of a narrative's significance and of moral matters in general. It was of course traditional for a fable to end with a 'morality' and Henryson often treats this with the verve and elegance that he shows in his narration. In 'The Fox and the Wolf' the moral is straightforward and expected – this 'suddand deith and unprovysit [*unforeseen*] end / Of this fals tod [*fox*]...'/ Exempill [*example*] is exhortand folk to amend' (775–77) – although other significances and suggestions have been evident in the tale. His moralities will, again in traditional manner, concentrate on one of several significances. They are not always as straightforward as that of 'The Fox and the Wolf', or as urbanely warning as that of 'The Two Mice' – 'Blissed be sempill lyfe withoutin dreid; / Blissed be sober feist in quietie [*quietness*].../ Thy awin fyre, freind, thocht [*though*] it be bot ane gleid [*ember*], / It warmis weill, and is worth gold to the' (373–90). Sometimes the moral comes as a surprise, as in the opening fable, where the jasp 'betakinnis perfite [*perfect*] prudence and cunning [*knowledge*]', and the cock 'may till [*to*] ane fule be peir [*equal*]', and is concealed under the veil of allegory (so that a large cheese 'may be callit covetyce [*covetousness*]' [128, 142, 2448]). In the final fable, 'The Paddock and the Mouse', a poor gullible mouse is deceived by a toad into swimming across a river tied to him; the toad intends to drown the mouse, but in the ensuing struggle they are both carried off by a kite and slaughtered. We are given a double morality: first, some general reflections arising from the action of the fable, on the danger of a wicked mind together with fair and subtle words; then we are told to 'this hald in mynd' for 'rycht more' instruction, namely that the toad is man's body, the mouse is man's soul, the water is the world 'ay welterand [*always surging*] / With mony wall [*wave*] of tribulatioun,' and the kite is death 'that cummis suddandlie / As dois ane theif, and cuttis sone the battall [*cuts short the battle*]' (2934–63). Then this extended piece of exposition is itself cut short by a Henrysonian witticism – if anyone should ask you why I conclude so shortly, say that I left the rest to the friars 'to mak a sample [*example*] or similitude'. Like the narratives, the moralities are characteristically concerned with man's life in this unstable world:

> For in this warld thair is na thing lestand;
> Is na man wait [*who knows*] how long his stait will stand,
> His lyfe will lest, nor how that he sall end
> Efter his deith, nor quhidder [*wither*] he sall wend.
>
> (1940–3)

In the *Fables* the grim, treacherous and unforgiving world of Aesop and Reynard merges with that of a late medieval Christian, a rather Augustinian view of the fallen world, and the spiritual struggles of a man on earth in a life that is 'brukill [*fragile*] and ay mortall'. Henryson is especially concerned with man's life in society, and in a distinctively Scottish society, against the background of the lowland landscape often glimpsed in the narratives, where the labourers work in the fields, 'sum makand dyke, and sum the pleuch [*plough*] can wynd [*guided*], / sum sawand seidis fast frome place to place, / The harrowis hoppand in the saweris [*sowers'*] trace [*track*]', where there are burghs and manor-houses, and cadgers (itinerant pedlars), husbandmen and servant girls that sweep the house.

References to life in society come easily, whether in general reflections of an Aesopic and proverbial nature – 'The Wolf and the Wether' warns us that 'riches of array / Will cause pure [*poor*] men presumpteous for to be.../ he was wyse that bad his sone consider: / "Bewar in welth, for hall-benkis [*hall-benches*] ar rycht slider [*slippery*]"' (2595–608) – or in scenes of gross injustice in society, as in 'The Sheep and the Dog', where the sheep 'may present the figure / Of pure [*poor*] commounis, that daylie ar opprest / be tirrane [*tyrannous*] men...' (1258–60). Henryson is a sharp critic of oppression and injustice, whether legal (false coroners who for a bribe will alter documents, and 'scraip out Johne and wryte in Will or Wat', etc.) or ecclesiastical. 'The Lion and the Mouse' has a central position here, and is given a special prominence by being told to the poet by the venerable Aesop himself in a dream. It is concerned with good governance and the duties and obligations of the ruler (the lion is caught in a trap and is rescued by the little mouse to whom he had previously shown mercy). It has been argued that Henryson had some particular moment in Scottish history in mind, but this remains unproven. Yet even if the advice is general it is most emphatically expressed – Aesop prays 'that tressoun of this cuntrie be exyld, / And justice regne, and lordis keip thair fay / Unto thair soverane lord baith nycht and day' (1617–19). These moralities are delivered with the force and eloquence of Henryson's narrative style, his characteristic blend of piety and wit and his delight in the proverbial and less than solemn manner – the ever-present threat of death once finds expression as 'the cat cummis, and to the mous hes ee [*eye*]' (384). The world the *Fables* present is often dark and terrible but it is not totally and bleakly pessimistic. Divine providence is there in the background, although it is often hard for the sufferers to see it. A blend of despair and almost pietistic resignation suffuses the sheep's lament at the end of the 'The Sheep and the Dog':

> 'Seis thow not, lord, this warld overturnit is...
> ...Allace, gude lord, quhy tholis [*sufferest*] thow it so?
> Thow tholis this evin for our grit offence;
> Thow sendis us troubill and plaigis soir,
> As hunger, derth, grit weir, or pestilence;
> Bot few amendis now thair lyfe thairfoir,
> We pure [*poor*] pepill as now may do no moir
> Bot pray to the: sen [*since*] that we are opprest
> Into this eirth, grant us in hevin gude rest.'
>
> (1307–20)

Foresight and prudence are recommended, as are wisdom and self-knowledge. And there are moments of peace and harmony, although we often have a sense of unresolved tensions. Henryson's own attitudes achieve a Chaucerian blend of detachment and sympathy. Readers often catch echoes of Chaucer and of Chaucerian techniques, but Henryson is not overwhelmed by his great predecessor; in 'The Cock and the Fox', for instance, where he is generally following Chaucer's story, he boldly adds a lively little interlude – just when the fox is carrying off the unfortunate Chantecleir and the distraught widow falls in a swoon, his hens fall into a 'disputatioun' concerning his qualities (all of them assuming that he is dead), the first giving what is perhaps an over-rhetorical lament, the second, a merry widow, dwelling rather on his faults and shortcomings, while the third, speaking like an ecclesiastic, declares that it is the hand of God punishing him for his sins; at this the widow revives, and the pursuit of the fox continues. The scene is a miniature example of the imaginative boldness and the control of narrative tempo which must surely make Henryson's collection the outstanding example of the fable form in English.

The careful and self-conscious interest in style and diction which is present through-out the *Fables* are found elsewhere in his poetry, and we occasionally find a more experimental and virtuosic passage which makes us think of Henryson's successor Dunbar. In a short poem, 'Ane Prayer for the Pest', for instance, Henryson briefly makes use of Latinate 'aureate' diction, combined with internal rhymes – 'Superne lucerne [*lantern*], guberne this pestilens, / Preserve and serve that we nocht sterf [*die*] thairin...'; in 'Sum Practysis of Medecyne', a burlesque medical 'recipe' in alliterative stanzas, he combines fantasy and decidedly low matter and diction – '...*Recipe* thre sponfull of the blak spyce, / With ane grit gowpene [*fistfull*] of the gowk [*cuckoo*] fart, / The lug [*ear*] of ane lyoun, the gufe [*?grunt*] of a gryce [*young pig*]...', etc.

Henryson also wrote other narrative poems, each of them distinctive and sometimes experimental. *Robene and Makene* is a witty little poem mostly in dialogue, presenting a rural tale of love, rejection and counter-rejection which leaves the protagonists – Robene, a herdsman whose devotion to his sheep is more impressive than his intel-ligence, and 'mirry' Makene, wiser in the ways of love, still apart – 'Robene murnit and Malkyne lewche [*laughed*]; / Scho sang, he sichit sair [*bitterly*]' – illustrating the proverbial dictum, 'The man that will nocht quhen [*when*] he may / Sall haif [*have*] nocht quhen he wald [*would (have it)*]' (123–24, 91–92). *The Bludy Serk* is a version of a popular religious tale, of Christ the lover-knight who died rescuing his lady (in the allegory, man's soul), and gave her his bloodstained shirt. Here Henryson chooses to write in the simple formulaic style of popular romance. There are echoes of popular romance also in the longer and more ambitious poem *Orpheus and Eurydice* (alongside the surviving formal Scottish verse romances, there are fragments of popular versions, indeed of a *King Orpheus*; we would dearly like to know if the narrative Scottish ballads, recorded mostly in the eighteenth and nineteenth centuries, were also current in this period – titles of songs like 'the tayl of the yong Tamlene' (mid-sixteenth century) suggest strongly that some of these stories were known but do not disclose anything substantial about their form or style. Henryson's *Orpheus* is a long and ambitious poem, in which he retells one of the medieval world's favourite stories. An imaginative expansion of a fine lyric in the *Consolation of Philosophy* of Boethius, it becomes a *conte moralisé* with an expository *moralitas*, which for many modern readers is overlong and sometimes surprising in its allegorical essays. But in general the moral fits the nar-rative well, linking the sorrowful elegiac note that comes into Henryson's voice even as he celebrates the early flame of love between the two, the sorrow at their last parting ('Quhat art thou lufe? How sall I the dyffyne?', 401) and the final prayer to God to give us 'grace to stand / In parfyte lufe', and bringing out the Platonic ideas implicit in Boethius's poem (and in the Middle Ages this myth seems positively to have demanded some exposition of its significances). The narrative itself is a highly imaginative piece of work: Gavin Douglas later referred to it as 'New Orpheus', and one can only speculate what he found 'new' and, presumably, admirable in it. He certainly seems to have admired some of the learning (he mentions the passage on the muses), and perhaps warmed to the easy way that it combines 'sentence' with narrative adventure – the lords of Greece and the duties of rulers, that favourite Scottish topic, for instance. One might also hazard a guess that he might have admired the boldness of style, the way in which a more learned word will sit easily alongside the simplest vernacular expression – 'And quhen he saw this lady solitar, / Barfute with schankis quhytar [*whiter*] than the snawe...' (99–100) – and the way the underworld has a moor with thorns and a 'brig o' dread' like the Lykewake Dirge, and is yet eerie and terrible, far from the light, where every creature 'is ay deyand [*dying*] and nevire more may dee' (316). The poem is always eloquent and splendidly rhetorical, as when Orpheus first laments to his harp: 'O dulfull harpe with many dolly [*doleful*] stryng, /Turne all thi mirth and musik in murnyng...' (134–5), but constantly uses proverbial and wonderfully simple diction – 'Bot [*only*] for a luke my lady is forlore' (412). This fine line is also an excellent example of Henryson's characteristic blend of sympathy and detachment. It is hard not to share Orpheus's sense of disappointment and unfairness at this last blow, even though the narrator has warned us of the instability of life and love. Human love may not have the serene perfection of celestial concord or of the divine love adumbrated in the moralitas, but it is strangely impressive in its heroic and tragic excess.

The Testament of Cresseid is Henryson's best-known poem. It is also his most complex and difficult one. If the *Fables* present through the animal actors a kind of mirror of human life that is reminiscent in some ways of *The Canterbury Tales*, here Chaucer's other great poem is a constant presence. Reading *Troilus and Criseyde* leads the poet to take up 'another book' (whether real or imaginary) and tell the fate of Chaucer's heroine rather than his hero. As always his treatment is bold and original, and the result has been the occasion of a large mass of critical comment and disagreement. It certainly raises some large questions. Is Henryson's attitude to Chaucer's poem sympathetic? Is he severely critical of Cresseid and her behaviour? What are we to make of the figure and function of the narrator? Are we given answers to the questions of fate and freewill and divine justice which the poem seems to raise? Is the poem totally fixed in its ancient pre-Christian setting, or is there an underlying Christian pattern implicit in it – of repentance and perhaps redemption or at least the finding of a new self knowledge?

The following remarks are not primarily intended to increase the already vast body of critical comment on these questions, but simply to offer a few comments on the work as a narrative poem. The reader will be struck by some similarities between it and *Orpheus and Eurydice* but its narrative structure is different, and boldly so. It is announced as a 'tragedy', in the medieval sense of a narrative poem with a disastrous end, 'ane cairfull dyte [*sorrowful poem*]'. The 'I' who begins to write it in line 3 continues as the narrative voice, sometimes simply presenting the tale, sometimes commenting on it in the manner of a tragic chorus, expressing horror and pity ('O cruell Saturne...Hard is thy dome and to [*too*] malitious!' [323–4], etc.). After the opening scene, in an appropriately 'doolie sessoun [*dismal season*]', in which the narrator presents himself as 'ane man of age' concerned with the fading of love and the coldness of age, we are given the successive stages of Creisseid's tragedy in narrative sections punctuated by a series of formal rhetorical laments (the long central one being 'marked off' by a different stanza form), a deliberate mixture of forward-moving narrative action and lyrical and reflective lament.

The action begins with Diomeid's abrupt rejection of Cresseid. Isolated and desolate, she walks up and down in the court, as 'sum men sayis', a promiscuous woman (77). Returning 'destitute of all comfort' to the house of her father Calchas, a priest of Venus; he offers some human comfort – 'douchtir, weip thow not.../ Peraventure all cummis for the best' – but it is bitterly ironic (92–93, 103–4). Her despair leads her into action, but action of a dangerous kind, a 'terrible deed'; she cries out 'angerly' against Venus and Cupid, blaspheming the gods in their own temple (124). Nemesis comes swiftly in a strange dream of the assembly and judgement of the gods. The description of the eerie (and mostly sinister) ancient planetary gods descending from their spheres is one of Henryson's most impressive set pieces – the judgement is delivered by the cruel Saturn, who lays a frosty wand on her head, and banishes her beauty, changing her mirth into melancholy and her 'moisture' and 'heit' into 'cald and dry'; she is to become one of his 'children' and live and die as a beggar and a leper (318). Cresseid's 'passion' begins, marked by a terrifying moment when she looks into a mirror and sees her face deformed, and a wonderful piece of pathetic dramatic irony when a child comes in to tell her super is ready, and innocently passes on her father's remark – 'He hes merwell [*marvels*] sa lang on grouf [*prostrate*] ye ly, / And sayis your beedes [*prayers*] bene to lang sum deill [*are too long*]; The goddis wait [*know*] all your intent full weill' (362–64). As would have been the case in Henryson's Scotland, Cresseid has to leave her father and make another solitary and secret journey to the leper house. Her life as a leper continues until the final scene, a chance meeting with Troilus, also an eerie event, a 'recognition scene' in which neither in fact recognises the other, but which has a powerful emotional and spiritual effect, again emphasised by a human 'gossipy' remark from one of the lepers who has noticed something significant in Troilus' reaction – 'Yone lord hes mair affectioun, / However it be, unto yone lazarous [*leper*] than to us all...' (530–32). The action and the setting owe much to Henryson's essentially 'medieval' humanism, which does not see, as the newer humanism of Petrarch and Erasmus did, a great gulf between the ancient and the contemporary world, but responds more to human similarities, giving the sense of a kind of 'eternal present' in which these ancient figures act out their fates. The very eloquent laments of Cresseid, culminating in a great aria of remorse, with the refrain 'O fals Cresseid and trew knicht Troilus', are flanked by shorter laments and comments from the narrator, Calchas and other 'bystanders', but it is her voice which dominates the poem throughout. The remarkable sense of imaginative unity is also strengthened by echoic imagery and recurrent image patterns – the intense cold at the beginning and the gruesome coldness of Saturn, the leaden colour of Saturn and Cynthia the moon, and the deformed face of the leper Cresseid, for instance, and the less prominent but intermittent flashes of more happy or hopeful things – the 'goldin face' of 'fair Venus, the bewtie of the nicht' at the beginning, the golden chariot of Phebus 'lanterne and lamp of licht', and perhaps even the golden letters on Cresseid's tomb of gray marble. All in all it is a strangely gripping and suggestive poem.

Henryson's younger contemporary, William Dunbar (?*c.* 1460–*c.* 1513) was probably a graduate of the University of St Andrews, and had become a priest by the early sixteenth century, but seems not to have had the benefice or ecclesiastical preferment he wished for. He was a member of the royal court, a 'servitour' rather than a formal 'court poet'; records of payments to him survive from 1501 to 1513. In some ways his work shows the interests and techniques of the poets already mentioned, though in a heightened and sometimes idiosyncratic form; an interest in the possibilities of language becomes in him a dazzling linguistic virtuosity, and a 'display of poetic energy' as Edwin Morgan described it. A self-conscious interest in poetry and poets is found in both serious and comic contexts – from the list of the 'makars' carried off by Death in the famous 'Lament for the Makars' to his own 'writer's block' in 'My heid did yak [*ache*] yester nicht' and the comic appearance of 'Dunbar the mackar' in a dance at court. In other ways, however, Dunbar is very different. He writes on a great range of topics, in many different genres and styles, and although he tells us much about himself, seems to remain elusive or to have a number of 'poetic salves'. He seems to prefer the shorter poem to the extended narrative – although he has some interesting brief examples (in dream visions and satires and, even a (rather coarse) animal fable), and is a master of the vivid and pungent brief scene. His few religious lyrics are among the finest in the whole Middle English corpus; the triumphantly energetic poem of Christ's Resurrection – 'Done is a battell on the dragon blak; / Our campioun [*champion*] Chryst condfoundit hes his force; / The yettis [*gates*] of hell ar brokin with a crak, / The signe triumphant rasit [*raised*] of the croce [*cross*]...' – or the brilliant invocation of the Virgin Mary which blends high 'aureate' diction with the homely Scots vernacular – 'Hale sterne [*star*] superne [*supernal*], hale in eterne, / In Godis sicht to schyne! / Lucerne [*lantern*] in derne [*darkness*] for to discerne [*by which to see*], / Be glory and grace devyne!...' (see also the essay by A. S. G. Edwards in this volume). He can also write an elegant courtly lyric, but his most interesting shorter secular poems are about himself, especially in his serio-comic petitions for preferment; in one of these, 'This Waverand Warldis Wretchidnes', a general lament on the sorry state of the world with the refrain 'Quhilk [*which*] to considder is ane pane', gradually narrows to the state of the church, and then to the distribution of benefices ('Sum men hes sevin and I nocht ane [*one*]'), and to the length of time his is in coming – though this 'breikis my hairt and birstis my brane', he will be humbly content with little ('Greit abbais grayth [*wealth*] I nill [*do not wish*] to gather / Bot ane kirk scant coverit with hadder [*heather*], / For I of lytill wald [*would*] be fane [*glad*]...').

The setting for these shorter poems and satires is not the countryside of Lowland Scotland, but its towns and cities, especially Edinburgh and especially its royal court. A number seem to relate to court occasions; others give glimpses of rivalry and anxieties in this court, or celebrate in a mock-heroic manner some of the characters at court – Thomas Norny, perhaps a fool, James Doig or Dog, a keeper of the queen's wardrobe, and others. Sometimes we look beyond the court. In one clever parody of the Office for the Dead, Dunbar, safe in the comforts of Edinburgh, 'prays' for the less fortunate members of the court removed to Stirling:

> ...We pray to all the sanctis [*saints*] in hevin,
> That ar abuif the sternis sevin,
> Yow to delyver out of your pennance
> That ye may sone play, sing and dance
> And into Edinbirgh mak gud cheir,
> Quhair [*where*] welthe and weilfair is but weir [*without doubt*].

In another, a *flyting* (a comic exchange of abuse) with the poet Kennedy, he imagines his opponent pursued by a crowd down an Edinburgh street:

> Than rynis [*run*] thow down the gait [*street*] with gild [*clamour*] of boyis,
> And all the toun tykis [*curs*] hingand [*hanging*] in thy heilis;
> Of laidis [*boys*] and lownis [*rogues*] thair rysis sic ane noyis

...that the horses run away and the fishwives throw down their baskets and tubs, and attack him. Sometimes Dunbar's satirical scenes have a troublingly nightmarish as well as comic tone – in one an abbot attempting to fly is 'mobbed' by startled birds:

> The air was dirkit [*darkened*] with the fowlis
> That come with yawmeris [*screeches*] and with yowlis [*howls*],
> With skryking [*shrieking*], skrymming [*darting*] and with scowlis [*fierce looks*]
> To tak him in the tyde [*at the time*].

One poem ('In secreit place this hyndir nycht') which presents a comic and bawdy rustic humble wooing scene makes us think momentarily of Henryson's much wittier *Robene and Makyne*; others, however (such as the dream visions *The Golden Targe* or *The Thrissill and the Rois*), are serious and courtly. Dunbar's longest poem, the *Tretis of the Twa Mariit Wemen and the Wedo*, written in long unrhymed alliterative lines, treats the topic of women discussing their husbands which Henryson touched on very briefly in his 'The Cock and the Fox'. It is quite un-Henrysonian in spirit, and is a highly distinctive and original tour de force, in a heady mixture of alliterative formulae and colloquial diction. It consists of a vivacious exchange between the two wives and the widow on the inadequacies of their husbands and the 'wo that is in mariage'. It owes much to the *Wife of Bath's Prologue*, but there is a strong element of burlesque exaggeration; ironies abound, and the 'discussion' is set in the long midsummer night, and seems to be a carnival display of 'misrule'.

My hasty account of the literary treasures to be found in this great and strange land to the north concludes with the briefest mention of a younger contemporary of Dunbar, the poet Gavin Douglas, potentially even more talented and brilliant. It is an accident, but perhaps a significant one, that he completed his translation of Virgil's

Aeneid (the first complete translation into English) in 1513; later that year occurred the great Scottish defeat at Flodden, which certainly marks the end of a chapter in Scottish history. In many ways Douglas seems to sum up the achievements of his predecessors – a boldly experimental dream vision, *The Palice of Honour* (1501), elaborate, ornate and rhetorical, linking narrative and lyric, with startling juxtapositions and changes of register, and an almost violent alternation of high seriousness and grotesque farcical comedy but which still contrives to treat the topic of 'honour' in an interesting way; the brilliant translation of Virgil's epic, which becomes in his version the greatest narrative poem of this period; and a wonderful and self-conscious eloquence. Here more than in his predecessors the Scottish landscape emerges, not only in the famous prologues set in winter and spring, but also in the way Douglas responds to Virgilian scenes and storms. Even more than his predecessors he encourages the English reader to embark on an intellectual journey to the north.

REFERENCES AND FURTHER READING

Bawcutt, P. (1976). *Gavin Douglas*. Edinburgh: Edinburgh University Press.

Bawcutt, P. (1992). *Dunbar the Makar*. Oxford: Oxford University Press.

Bawcutt, P. (ed.) (1998). *The Poems of William Dunbar*. 2 vols. Glasgow: Association for Scottish Literary Studies.

Bawcutt, P. (ed.) (2003). *The Shorter Poems of Gavin Douglas*. 2nd edn. Edinburgh: Scottish Text Society.

Bawcutt, P. and Felicity Riddy (eds) (1987). *Longer Scottish Poems*. Vol. 1. Edinburgh: Scottish Academic Press.

Bawcutt, Priscilla and Janet Hadley Williams (ed.) (2006). *A Companion to Medieval Scottish Poetry*. Cambridge: D. S. Brewer.

Coldwell, David F. C. (ed.) (1957–64). *Virgil's 'Aeneid' Translated into Scottish Verse by Gavin Douglas*. 4 vols. Edinburgh: Scottish Text Society.

Duncan, A. A. M. (ed.) (1997). *The Bruce*. Edinburgh: Canongate Classics.

Fox, Denton (ed.) (1981). *The Poems of Robert Henryson*. Oxford: Oxford University Press.

Gray, D. (1979). *Robert Henryson*. Leiden: E. Brill.

Gray, D. (ed.) (1998). *Selected Poems of Robert Henryson and William Dunbar*. Harmondsworth: Penguin.

Gray, D. (2008). *Later Medieval English Literature*. Oxford: Oxford University Press. [Section IV.]

Kinsley, J. (ed.) (1979). *The Poems of William Dunbar*. Oxford: Oxford University Press.

McDiarmid, M. P. (ed.) (1968–69). *Hary's 'Wallace'*. Edinburgh: Scottish Text Society.

McDiarmid, Matthew P. and James A. C. Stevenson (eds) (1980–85). *Barbours Bruce*. 3 vols. Edinburgh: Scottish Text Society.

Morgan, Edwin (1989). *Sonnets from Scotland*. Glasglow: Mariscat. (Repr. in *Collected Poems*. Manchester: Carcanet, 1990.)

Norton-Smith, John (ed.) (1981). *The Kingis Quair*. 2nd edn. Leiden: Brill.

Tasioulas, J. A. (ed.) (1999). *The Makars: The Poems of Henryson. Dunbar and Douglas*. Canongate Classics 88. Edinburgh: Canongate.

33

Courtiers and Courtly Poetry

Barry Windeatt

> And more paper I thinke to blot
> To the court why I cam not,
> Desyring you above all thynge
> To kepe you from laughynge
> Whan ye fall to redynge
> Of this wanton scrowle...
> (John Skelton 'Why come ye nat to courte?',
>   *c.* 1522; 826–31, in Scattergood 1983)

What is the place of poetry in courts in later medieval England, and what is courtly poetry? In the 'Black Book' of household ordinances that regulated Edward IV's court there are glimpses of the customary pastimes in which long afternoons and evenings might be spent at court:

> Thes esquiers of the houshold of old be acustomed, wynter and somer, in after nonys and in euenynges, to drawe to lordez chambrez within courte, there to kepe honest company aftyr theyre cunyng, in talkyng of cronycles of kinges and of other polycyez, or in pypyng, or harpyng, syngyng, other actez marciablez, to help ocupy the court and acompany straungers, tyll the tym require of departing.
>
> (Myers 1959: 129)

Amidst such harping and singing, it might be surmised, could arise the opportunity for courtly poetry, for song is part of the very rhythm of the courtly year, as in this provision for 1 November:

> MEMORANDUM that the king hath a song before hym in his hall or chambre vppon All Halowen-day at the later graces, by some of thes clerkes and children of chapell, in remembraunce of Cristmasse...but after the song on All Halowen-day is don, the

steward and thesaurer of houshold shall be warned where hit likith the king to kepe his Cristmasse.

(Myers 1959: 136)

And since being at court – and near the fount of honour and patronage – is about getting on in life, the 'Black Book' reflects the educative role implicit in the daily routine of a court, providing for a master of grammar (to instruct in Latin grammar, poetry and rhetoric), and a master of song, who teaches the children of the chapel royal 'as well in the scoole of facet [proper conduct] as in song'. For well-born young men in attendance at court a master is provided:

> to show the scoolez of urbanitie and nourture of Inglond, to lern them to ride clenly and surely, to drawe them also to justes, to lerne hem to were theyre harneys; to haue all curtesy in wordez, dedes, and degrees, dilygently to kepe them in rules of goynges and sittinges, after they be of honour. Moreouer, to teche them sondry langages and othyr lernynges vertuous, to herping, to pype, sing, daunce, and with other honest and temperate behauing and pacience.

(Myers 1959: 127)

Out of such 'langages and othyr lernynges vertuous', in a setting where song and music-making was part of life, derived the context for the arts of courtly speaking and courtly poetry.

And what is courtly poetry? One kind includes satire and mockery of life at courts, of which there is a long medieval tradition in Latin and the vernaculars and which, as Skelton implies, may be no laughing matter. Another kind gives expression to the values of courtly society, and especially to one quintessential courtly preoccupation and pastime: the arts of courtship and the pursuit of love. By the fifteenth century, moreover, the readership of, and fascination with, such a literature of courtliness extends well beyond the court itself into gentry and middle-class audiences, as evidence from manuscript production indicates. Courtly poetry may still be written mostly by those within a court ambience, but also nourishes the fantasies and aspirations of those outside courts and may be imitated by them. These two traditions, of court satire and the poetry of courtship, not infrequently will overlap and draw upon each other, and by the reign of Henry VIII poets such as Skelton (the King's boyhood tutor) and Sir Thomas Wyatt – who until his downfall enjoyed a precariously brilliant career as a courtier – can convey through their writings a vivid impression of early Tudor courtiers and courtly life.

In Skelton's dream poem of the same name (*c*.1498), *The Bowge of Courte* is a ship boarded at Harwich by the dreamer narrator, called Drede. A sea voyage is a traditional emblem of the uncertainties of this-worldly life, and a 'bouge' is court rations, the allowance of food and drink granted by a king or nobleman to members of his household. In leaving behind firm ground and entrusting his fortunes to the *Bowge*, Skelton implies that Drede is now navigating the courtier's life of dependency. The ship's owner is Dame Saunce-Pere (Lady Peerless) and its cargo is 'Favore-to-stonde-in-her-good-grace', but Lady Peerless remains pointedly invisible, enthroned behind a rich fabric screen and attended by two gentlewomen. Of these, Daunger (Disdain) duly puts the dreamer down, whilst Desyre encourages his craving for advancement and profit rather than for affairs of the heart. As the *Bowge* sails off, piloted by Fortune, the nervous dreamer sights seven 'Full subtyll persones' – allegorical figures representing aspects of court life – whose conversations with him, variously unsettling and insinuating, form the rest of the poem and dramatise the nightmarish paranoia of living among courtiers. These seven figures are: 'Favell, full of flatery' (134); 'Suspecte' (136), later named 'Suspycyon' (181); Harvey Hafter (i.e. trickster); together with 'Dysdayne', 'Ryotte', 'Dyssymuler' [Dissimulation] and 'Subtylte' (later called 'Disceyte'). Their conversations with the dreamer are linked by intervals of Drede's observations, in a format like a dreamed morality play, where most declarations prove unreliable. Favell discourses flatteringly to the dreamer ('I can not flater, I muste be playne to the', 164), claiming to have spoken up for Drede 'Whan there were dyverse that sore dyde you manace' (159). In thanking Favell, Drede observes 'he ware on hym a cloke / That lyned was with doubtfull doublenes' (177–8) and creeps up to eaves-drop on Suspecte, who is obsessed with extracting what Favell may have told Drede about him (204–10). Suspecte gives the proverbial advice to see and hear much but say little, and of the court remarks: 'Ye never dwelte in suche an other place, / For here is none that dare well other truste' (201–2). While listening next to the sharper, Harvey Hafter, the dreamer is nervous of being robbed, and then overhears Dysdayne contemptuously denigrating Drede's intelligence to Harvey (who proposes they throw Drede overboard). Dysdayne now comes over to talk, only to open conver-sation menacingly with a disconcerting reference to a supposedly earlier conversation of which the dreamer is unaware ('Remembrest thou what thou sayd yesternyght? / Wylt thou abyde by the wordes agayne?' 323–4). Here, the attribution to Drede of something undisclosed but which he never said represents how court life may be manipulated by false imputation and insinuation. In comparison, the appearance of Ryotte ('His gowne so shorte that it ne cover myghte / His rumpe...' 354–5), and his smutty boasting of sexual licence, is merely an embarrassing interruption by the uncouthly uncourtly side of courtly sexual performativity before Drede notices Dysdayne intercepting Dyssymulacyon ('But there was poyntynge and noddynge with the hede / And many wordes sayde in secrete wyse', 421–2), which only exacerbates Drede's paranoia. Like the other 'subtyll persones' Dyssymulacyon insincerely condemns the very insincerity he patently practises ('I wolde eche man were as playne as I...I hate this faynynge...' 463, 465), undermining Drede with unspecific warnings that he is being maligned, but 'I dare not speke, we be so layde awayte [spied upon], / For all our courte is full of dysceyte' (468–9). With a knife hidden up one sleeve and a golden spoon full of honey up the other (433–7), there are symbolic features in Dyssymulacyon's attire as in the other figures, but it is their talk that is even more emblematic, re-enacting the paranoid anxiety of court life through recurrent insinuations that Drede is disempowered by lacking information known to them. From the seventh figure Disceyte (who looks like a page and a pilferer) Drede receives further insinuation of collusion against him, bafflingly coded against eavesdroppers –

> 'Parde, remembre whan ye were there,
> There I wynked on you – wote ye not where?
> In A *loco*, I mene *juxta* B...'
>
> (515–17)

– and is warned he will be cheated by unspecified third parties ('Who deleth with shrewes hath nede to loke aboute!' 525). Now convinced that he sees 'lewde felawes' approaching, intent on murdering him, Drede is about to jump overboard to escape them when he is jolted awake, and promptly sets about writing down this night-marish vision of court life.

Court life as a hell and a kind of imprisonment also finds echoes in the *Eclogues* (*c*.1514) of Alexander Barclay, where 'the court is in earth an ymage infernall, / Without [outside] fayre paynted, within uggly and vile', while 'sometyme the courtier remayneth halfe the yere / Close within walles muche like a prisonere', only to discover that:

> ...in court moste part doth dwell
> Flatterers and lyers, curriers of fafell   *favour*
> Jugglers and disers, and such a shamefull rable
> Which for a dinner laude men nothing laudable.   *praise*
>   (White 1928: 29; lines 825–28)

Such too is the court implied in Wyatt's *Epistolary Satires*. Here, to one friend he rejoices to 'flee the press of courts' and no longer 'The friendly foe with his double face / Say he is gentle and courteous therewithal' (CXLIX, 3, 65–6), while to another friend at court Wyatt ironically recommends 'whoso can seek to please / Shall purchase friends where truth shall but offend' (CLI, 32–3) (Rebholz 1978). Courtier and diplomat, translator of Petrarch, rumoured lover of Queen Anne Boleyn and author of a handful of immortal lyric poems – Sir Thomas Wyatt is the very epitome of the courtly poet. Yet Wyatt is a courtly poet not least through his deployment of convention, and his enlistment in the game and play that is love at court, through which so much of his courtly poetry looks back to the traditions of late-medieval courtly poetry. Through the chance of war, it is a French prince who is Wyatt's most significant medieval precursor as a courtly poet in English, for Charles d'Orléans is among the most fascinating – and still overlooked – writers in Middle English.

A nephew of Charles VI of France, Charles, Duke of Orléans (1394–1465), was captured at Agincourt in 1415 and, as an important pawn in Anglo-French negotiations, was detained in England until 1440. Charles was mostly lodged as an honoured guest-prisoner – always under surveillance, and with restricted movements and contacts – in the households of various aristocratic host-gaolers. These included, between 1432 and 1436, William de la Pole, Earl (later Duke) of Suffolk, who became a friend, and possibly composed courtly poetry himself, including the 'Fairfax Sequence'. Charles was a prolific and distinguished courtly poet in French, who produced an extensive series of French lyric poems collected together in a manuscript owned and partly copied by the poet (BN MS F.fr. 25458) (Arn: 2008). Moreover, in one English manuscript (BL MS Harley 682) survives a 6531-line sequence of English lyrics, about half of which represent versions of Charles's French ballades and chansons, along with English poems on related themes for which no French equivalents are known. The sequences of corresponding poems in the French and English manuscript collections run broadly in parallel. One of the fascinations of the Harley 682 poems is that they almost certainly represent a poet's self-translation, probably mostly from French to English, although English may have preceded French in some cases. During his twenty-five-year captivity in England Charles is likely to have gained a good knowledge of English, and the Harley 682 collection most probably represents English versions of his French poems made by the poet himself, together with other poems composed only in English. Although the English poems strive to match the equivalent French poems' versification with high metrical accomplishment, some unidiomatic English syntax and phraseology suggest a non-native author, yet one who has moved beyond the French poems in developing his own distinctive courtly lyric style in English. As such, Harley 682 preserves what no poet in English had yet attempted: the largest single-authored sequence of lyrics from the English Middle Ages, for Charles d'Orléans is the only major medieval poet writing lyrics in England who so carefully assembles and arranges his poems (in English as in French).

In 1440 Charles took home with him to France the manuscript containing his French poems, which are organised more by lyric genres than by an implied personal narrative. By contrast, the Harley 682 manuscript of his English poems – which he evidently left behind in England – embodies Charles's attempt to innovate a new form, which builds a culminative unity through the implied narrative of an inner emotional life and progress, however much fictionalised and at whatever remove from 'the duk that folkis calle / Of Orlyaunce' (5) (Arn 1994).[1] There are linking narrative interludes, with intercalated speeches and documents, perhaps inspired by the format of the French *dits amoureux*. Unlike Charles's French manuscript – kept with him and successively augmented by later compositions to become an album of his life's work – the English manuscript preserves a snapshot of Charles's ideas at one particular point, probably in the later 1430s, as to how his prolific output of short courtly poems might be understood as a whole oeuvre articulated through a framing narrative. In the themes, concerns and aesthetic features of such frame devices are significant pointers to the conceptualisation of courtly poetry by Charles and by contemporary courtly poets. The more dynamic but experimental features that differentiate the English sequence from the French can be highlighted by means of the following summary representation of the English sequence's contents (in which elements common to both French and English collections are in bold, and English-only elements are in italics):

[The first quire of the English MS has been lost, probably containing the equivalent of the French sequence's opening 400 lines, an allegorical account of the narrator's introduction to Love.]

Charles receives his letter patent from Cupid (1–55);
Remonstrates at Cupid's retention of his heart as a pledge but, persuaded to pursue his suit to his lady in writing, Charles retreats into an arbour with pen, paper, and Hope (56–202);
First sequence of ballades, the order in English as in French (203–2025);
Four extra English ballades included in response to his lady's death (2026–2109);
Conclusion of ballade sequence, with some re-ordering in English (2110–2514);
One extra English ballade in conclusion, begging for his own death (2515–39).
Dream sequence, with interleaved quasi-legal documents, in which Charles, counselled by Age, petitions to be dispensed from Love's service and retires to the castle of Nonchaloir or No Care; here Charles sets out on providing lovers with his Jubilee (retirement banquet) of songs (2540–3109);
An English-only ballade develops the symbolism of a feast: 'Instede of mete, I fede yow shall with song' (3110–37)
Jubilee sequence of 52 roundels, in English as in French (3138–3900);
Jubilee completed by 51 further English roundels without French equivalents (3901–4318);
Banquet's end marked by a mock grace (4319–88);
In place of washing after grace, Charles, with a play on words, substitutes 'wishing', providing a series of paradigmatic wishes for lovers (4389–4479);
Feast closes with an invitation to dancing (4480–4568), the dances represented by
Three caroles present in both French and English collections (4569–4637);
In retirement from love Charles composes ballades and roundels at the request of lovers; commissioned to 'biwayle Fortunes stabilnes' he composes a seven-stanza complaint on a rocky seashore (4638–4735), then falls asleep;
Dream sequence: he encounters Venus, then Fortune with her wheel, on which he sees a lady apparently identical to his first, dead lady (4736–5183);
On waking, Charles is enlisted by a courtly company playing a game of tag, under cover of which he can declare himself to his new lady, who permits him to write to her (5184–5351);
Second sequence of ballades (5352–6531), of which only 4, and one epistle of complaint, have French equivalents.

Such comparison of Charles's French and English collections immediately establishes the impetus to a more sustained narrative of the self that draws the English poems into a sequence that goes far beyond the less interconnected French, and in which transitions and interconnections are carefully signalled (4486; 5349/51). Especially prominent among those aspects emphasised or only present in the English sequence are: first, an incorporation into the poems' implied story of the ceremonious observance and performance of courtly life as game and play; second, a self-consciousness about the poet's role, a sense of writerliness and textuality about poems that divulge one side of an intimate and secret correspondence with an absent lady; and third, an extended use of dream and visionary encounter. These three features determine the thematic implications of Charles' English sequence and, in the rest of this chapter, will serve to guide and structure our exploration of later medieval courtly poetry more generally, its character and preoccupation.

Much courtly poetry is often judged to amount to no more than gambits in playing the game that was the courtly performance of love: petitions, verse epistles and complaints; verse that might accompany lovers' giftgiving; poems that reflect the love-casuistry, puzzles and *demaundes d'amour* that entertained courtly audiences (so, the Fairfax Sequence: 'If tweyn love oon, this th'apoyntement: / Loke who can best deserve to stande in grace'; MacCracken 1911: 172). In his English poems Charles d'Orléans goes out of his way to inscribe within his texts their context in imaginary courtly occasion, observance and performance, and the effect is to lend vivacity and concreteness. If his jubilee of roundels are to resemble a feast, then in English Charles contextualises this social occasion, adding allusions to the menu, the concluding grace, hand washing and dancing. The poet's entertainment of his audience is likened to feeding them with exquisitely dainty delicacies: these roundels are more like roast quail or skylark than heavier viands 'for folk say "short song is good in ale"' (3118). In the mock grace which in English rounds off the banquet of song ('Were I a clerk, than wold I say yow grace', 4319), Charles warns especially against deceptive use of all those devices, embroidered insignia and other emblems which – along with the symbolism of gems, flowers and rings, the true-love knots and hearts, posies and mottoes – contributed to that semiotics of love within which courtly poetry played its part. That a feast's closing ritual of hand *washing* has been punningly rewritten into a series of courtly *wishings* – chiefly for accomplishment as a lover – is itself emblematic of how outward courtly observance and ceremony serves the aspiration to a perfection in love. And that this English jubilee closes with the poet's invitation to dance to the poems he provides not only reflects the central place of dance in courtly life (and as an opportunity for, and emblem of, love) but also underlines how dance will be a song to be danced to, in which the individual and the group will have their interrelating places. A dance-like pattern of moves also governs the poet's experience of the game of 'Post and Pillar', the climactic part of the English sequence that brings Charles to declare his love to a new lady and initiates a second series of ballades, pointedly less sustained and wholehearted than the first. Here the potent role of play and game in courtly life, and in the love that occurs within its framework, is implicit in the absorption of the courtly company in this game. That such a game symbolises courtly life and love is suggested by the fact that Charles has already recalled to Venus that it was during a playing of this very same game that he declared his love to his first lady too, among various other courtly pastimes as he recollects them (4834–40).

To perform one's role in so elaborate a game as the love depicted in courtly poetry required familiarity with a variety of conventions and forms. Charles is confident that such a 'craft', although difficult for those lacking discernment, is available to be learned by lovers:

> But though this craft wol not be lernyd sone
> And be full hard to suche as wanten brayne,
> Yet fervent love kan cause it to be doon.
>
> (4375–7)

This fiction of love with its rulebooks and guidebooks – to which due deference and application should bring success in love – is variously presented in late-medieval writing, from the literalism of a poem such as 'The Ten Commandments of Love' –

> Secretly behave you in your werkes,
>   In shewing countenance or meving of your eye;
> Though soche behavor to some folke be darke,
>   He that hath loved woll it sone aspie –
>   (Robbins 1952: 166; lines 43–46)

– to the playful ironies of *The Court of Love* (*c.* 1535), which offers a wryly sophisticated retrospect on the forms and conventions of fifteenth-century courtly poetry in English (Skeat 1897). Probably written out of a familiarity with Chaucer renewed by Thynne's edition of the collected works (1532), this is a stylishly poised reprise of the Chaucerian love vision, voiced in a Troilian idiom alive to love's possibilities and aspirations, and furnished with settings and props fondly recycled and rewritten from Chaucer's dream poems. The eighteen-year-old author ('of Cambridge clerk', 913) is viewed by the King of Love as a suspiciously late starter (280–2) but pardoned in return for promised future service to love and directed to the Court of Love, a space landscaped out of Chaucer's *Parliament*. Here the apprentice lover is guided to peruse the twenty statutes governing a male lover's conduct, a lengthy set-piece allowing the poem both to recapitulate and burlesque the conventions of love as something quintessentially and absurdly over-regulated. Many statutes are predictable enough: 'Secretly to kepe / Councell of Love' (309–10); 'Not to be daungerous' (330); 'To be pacient' (344); 'Mete and drink forgete' (484). Others reflect the sparkle of a courtly culture in which novelty and emblematic gift-giving make an impression: the lover is enjoined 'Be jolif, fresh, and fete, with thinges newe' (473) and must spare no expense to send his lady 'Some hert, or ring, or lettre, or device, / Or precious stone' (398–9). Yet other statutes represent the lover's vocation of obedience in more ironic tones: 'Sey as she seith, than shalt thou not be shent, / The crow is whyte; ye, truly, so I rede' (430–1). The fourteenth statute archly enjoins self-delusion about the lover's lady ('And though thow seest a faut right at thyne eye, / Excuse it blyve, and glose it pretily' (419–20). Indeed, this same statute frankly enjoins the lover to live out his erotic fantasies

('And nightly dreme, thow hast thy hertes wyfe / Swetely in armes, straining her as blyfe', 403–4), while the sixteenth statute legislates for an exacting obligation to daily sexual athleticism from every lover:

> The *sixteenth* statut, kepe it if thow may –
> Seven sith at night thy lady for to plese,   *times*
> And seven at midnight, seven at morow-day...
>
>   (435–7)

Having sworn to the statutes, but forbidden to peek into the parallel statutes governing women in love ('Plesaunt thay be, and to their own purpose...' 528), the lover is despatched to pray at Venus's temple, subsequently discovers the tomb where Pity is buried and – the next set-piece of courtly poeticism – presents his bill of petition to his lady. Here he applies the old argument that she should reward his service with pity, which she rejects, deeming him precipitate (963–6). Such an impasse over the bestowal of mercy is resolved through a rehearsal of *Troilus and Criseyde*, for the non-plussed lover falls into a swoon (995ff). Like Criseyde, the lady relents, charging him to obey the rules and observe the statutes, although he pleads for some leeway on that sixteenth statute, to which she blushingly assents. In a moment that crystallises the function of courtly petition, the lover describes his success in terms of achieving a reciprocation of speech from his lady, which evidently symbolises some future sexual concession ('Thus have I won, with wordes grete and small, / Some goodly word of hir that I love best, / And trust she shall yit set myne harte in rest', 1020–2). After an assembly of different birds has sung a mass, the court goes forth to gather blossom for garlands. Courtiers then pelt each other with flowers, until the lover's lady makes her move and hurls at him a true-love knot, a sudden token of her feelings that smites the lover to the heart and hence abruptly ends the poem.

It is the composing of courtly petition as something quintessentially 'gentil' and noble that is highlighted in a much expanded exchange with Cupid that forms the more ambitious prologue to Charles d'Orléans' English sequence of poems. A bourgeois woman of the merchant classes – Cupid observes – may be won over with gifts, but for the nobility all depends on the art of petition, whether pursued in conversation or writing:

> For gentill must be wonne with gentiles,
> Bi goodly speche and curteys countenance...
> For to nobles longith sewte of curteys speche
> As he fynt tyme bi mouth or writyng seche.
>
>   (140–1, 145–6).

The ensuing sequence of ballades is thus represented as the outcome of the poet's determining to take up pen and paper and 'make a bill' to his lady. Introducing his roundels, Charles hopes to prompt grateful lovers to pray for his soul, or to write the lovers' wishes he would once have wished – and this reflects how some courtly poetry is devised for others' use. According to the rubric, Lydgate wrote one ballade 'at the request of a squyer that serued in loves court' (MacCracken 1934: 379) and Skelton's complaint 'Go, pytyous hart' ostensibly was written 'at the instance of a nobyll lady'. When retired from love, Charles can perform the role of a poet of love who is not himself a lover, commissioned by other lovers to write poems expressing those lovers' sorrows, presumably for use in petitioning their ladies ('Wherfore sum thing I trust in this bok is / To fede them on, if hit be well out sought', 3128–9). It is this petitionary impulse that lies near the centre of Charles' poems, as of other courtly poetry, even when as ironically treated as in *The Craft of Lovers* (c.1459) (Kooper 1987) or *La Belle Dame Sans Merci* (c.1450), Sir Richard Roos's quite faithful English version of Alain Chartier's French original (Skeat 1897). In *The Craft* the lady initially distrusts the lover ('Me semes by your langage ye be...som curious gloser deceyvable', 78–9) and wonders 'Why mannes langage wil procure and transvert / The wille of wymmen and vyrgyns innocent?' (124–5). She starts by dismissing his petition ('It is but wynd, flateryng and adulacioun', 38), but despite his admission that 'My name is Triewe Love of Carnal Desiderary, / Of mannys copulacioun the verray exemplary' (88–9), she ends their dialogue by accepting him and his unpersuasive persuasions. By contrast, *La Belle Dame* presents a courtly verbal duel in which the impassioned lover and his icily unmoved lady, speaking alternately in speeches each one stanza long, make their moves in a kind of anti-courtship. Throughout, the pitiless lady withholds the concession of 'mercy' that conventionally yields to male petition and plaint ('Free am I now and free wil I endure', 314), for the lady's clear-eyed disdain for anything men traditionally say by way of wooing makes her immune to the conventional stratagems and rhetoric of courtly petition, which the poem's dialectic subjects to sustained critique. 'Ladies be not so simple', in La Belle Dame's view, as to believe men's 'fayre langage, paynted ful plesauntly / Which ye and mo holde scoles of, dayly', and such ladies have the power to disregard it: 'But sone they can away their hedes wrye / And to fair speche lightly their eres close' (325–32). For La Belle Dame, men's oaths scarcely outlast the moment of utterance (375–6), and she contrasts men's courtly discourse with the cur within ('A currish herte, a mouth that is curteys', 389), before concluding 'Wherfore to ladies what men speke or pray, / It shuld not be bileved in no wyse' (747–8). Particularly incredible to La Belle Dame is any expectation that women might take literally the conventional emotional blackmail that their admirers will die unless their love is reciprocated. Indeed, the second lady of Charles d'Orléans – abruptly informed during their first conversation that he will die unless he gains her grace – retorts drily 'But many suche as ye in wordis dy / That passyng hard ther graffis [graves] ar to spy' (5294–5). Similarly unconvinced, the Dame remarks briskly 'This sicknesse is right esy to endure, / But fewe people it causeth for to dy' (293–4), coolly concluding that, if love indeed hurts so grievously, it limits harm if one person suffers rather than two (299–300). Throughout, La Dame rebuts any imputed responsibility for the lover's suffering feelings ('Though ye be seke, it doth me nothing plese', 311). To the lover's pitiful question – 'Plese it you more to see me dy this hour...Than for to shewe som comfort or socour...?' (721–3) – the Dame only replies bracingly:

'Also, ye shal not dye for my plesaunce, / Nor for your hele I can no surety make' (727–8). To the merciless lady goes the withering final put-down, as she heads off to a dance ('There hurteth you nothing but your conceyt... / Ye noy me sore, in wastyng al this wynde', 791, 795). To her lover goes the pyrrhic moral victory of indeed dying for his unrequited love ('And in himself took so gret hevinesse / That he was deed, within a day or twayne', 811–12), but to end with this shock of the real is exceptional in courtly poetry. More typical is Cupid's inconclusive 'Parlement' that ends the Fairfax Sequence of complaints, letters and 'supplicacion' ('That I wold faynest have, therof I fayle, / And though I playn, yt is to non avayle', p. 167). This allows lovers to rehearse their sorrows but is then adjourned, with an envoy advising lovers to pray to Venus 'Off your matters sych tydynges yow to sende' (p. 174).

   Through the poet's encounters with Venus and Fortune Charles d'Orléans' English sequence of poems is counterpointed by a boldly comic version of those self-revelatory encounters with allegorical figures that recur in much courtly poetry. When 'A lady nakid all thing save hir here' (although around her waist is 'a kercher of plesaunce') comes skimming across the waves as the poet sleeps by the seashore, he fails to recognise Venus at first and offends the goddess's dignity by trying to kiss her. Having realised his blunder, he characterises his present life as a kind of love's anchorite or hermit, given up to contemplation of past courtly pursuits with his now-dead lady, but of this Venus predictably disapproves:

> 'How thenke ye, lo – nys hit contemplatiif?'
> 'No, certis!' 'Whi?' 'Ye do yowre silf confound!'
>   (4864–5)

For Venus there is a clear argument against such reclusiveness: he is a man 'And have of nature als yowre lymys goode, / So ought ye kyndely, thenk me, spend it than' (4870–1). While the goddess is demolishing his objections to resuming a lover's role ('The craft of love is straunge, who to hit goth!' he whines), the dreamer is looking over her shoulder and sees descending in a golden chariot another allegorical figure, lengthily described and bearing in her hand a turning wheel. Courtly comedy of manners ensues when, alerted by the dreamer and having contrived a reason to turn round and look, Venus recognises Dame Fortune but is seized with absurd embarrassment at being discovered unchaperoned with a man and longs for some bushes to hide in. Nonetheless, it is by hanging on to her intimate 'kercher' that Venus helps the lover ascend towards the lady he sees on Fortune's wheel (but he feels himself falling and awakens). This is to be his new lady and the recipient of his second ballade series, and her near-identity with his first, dead lady is the revelatory psychological kernel at the heart of this dream, which holds together the earlier and later parts of Charles's courtly sequence through his encounter with Venus and Fortune.

   It is through such visionary encounters with Venus, Fortune and Minerva that another of the finest fifteenth-century courtly poets, also a prisoner in England, accomplishes a distinctive understanding of love in his own work. *The Kingis Quair* is uniquely preserved in a Scottish anthology of Chaucerian poetry including *Troilus*, some Chaucer dream poems, Lydgate's *Complaint of the Black Knight*, Clanvowe's *Boke of Cupid* and some Scottish poems. The 'King's Book' apparently fictionalises aspects of the personal experience of James I of Scotland (1394–1437), and is usually assumed to have been written by the king himself during his long captivity in England. To escape unrest in Scotland under his father Robert III, James was being sent to safety in France when his ship was captured by the English in 1406. As a significant political pawn, the young Scottish king (he succeeded his father in 1407) remained a captive in England until 1424 when, in a dynastic alliance that was also a love-match, he married Joan Beaufort, a granddaughter of John of Gaunt, and returned to his kingdom.

The individual poetic voice of *The Kingis Quair* succeeds in balancing immediacy of personal feeling and philosophical reflectiveness within a graceful allegory of courtly experience. It is one of the finest accomplishments of courtly poetry in English by Chaucer's successors. Yet however much steeped in Chaucer's poetry, James is original in using Chaucer's poems to think with. For although the sheer stylistic poise and eloquence of *The Kingis Quair* could scarcely have been written without a deep familiarity with Chaucer, James goes far beyond mere imitation in the structure, settings and ethical seriousness of this allegorical re-enactment and interpretation of his life and love at court. On a starlit winter's night 'Quhen as I lay in bed allone waking' (Norton-Smith 1971: 8), the sleepless poet picks up a copy of Boethius's *Consolation of Philosophy*, perusing 'the writing of this noble man / That in himself the full recover wan / Of his infortune…' (32–4), and afterwards brooding on his own fate until, in the sound of the midnight matins bell, the poet thinks he hears himself urged 'Tell on, man, quhat thee befell' (77). Here, reading a book does not lead directly to a dream (as in the *Book of the Duchess* or *Parliament*), but instead to the poet's picking up pen and paper to set down an account of his life, or rather, of two key sequences in it: his capture and imprisonment, and his falling in love with his lady, glimpsed outside in a garden from his prison window. His capture at sea is evoked in a cleverly layered poetic sequence charged with double meaning. This reworks Chaucer's proem to Book II of *Troilus* into a prologue to James's book of his life but simultaneously draws on its imagery of boat and sea-voyage, symbolic both of poetic composition and of this worldly life's insecurity, in order to create a context for recollecting his arrest on the high seas ('Upon the wawis weltering to and fro…. / Of inymyis takin and led away / We weren all, and broght in thair contree', 162–7). Notably, in this designedly abstract self-account, the nationality of his captors goes unmentioned, as too of the gaolers who keep him closely guarded in prison where, as he laments:

> The bird, the best, the fisch eke in the see,
> They lyve in fredome, everich in his kynd,
> And I a man, and lakkith libertee!
>
> (183–5)

Although the scene in which James first sights his lady from his prison tower has its model in Palamon and Arcite's sighting of Emelye in the *Knight's Tale*, the garden in which the lady walks is modelled on Criseyde's in *Troilus*, Book II, while the birds in this garden have evidently just flown in from singing their roundel at the close of Chaucer's *Parliament* ('And sing with us, "Away, winter, away! / Cum, somer, cum, the swete sesoun and sonne!"', 234–5). It is these birds' thankful praise of love that introduces the theme of love, prompting the poet to reflect wonderingly on love's nature ('Hath he upon oure hertis suich maistrye?', 258), after which he glimpses the lady in the garden below and undergoes an ecstatic transformation ('My hert, my will, my nature and my mynd, / Was changit clene ryght in anothir kynd', 314–15). All the conventional motifs of the lover's courtly observance – such as a quasi-religious devotion to his lady – are invested by James with a refreshed eloquence:

> And to that sanct, walking in the schade,   *saint*
> My bedis thus with humble hert entere   *prayers*
> Devotly I said on this manere:
> 'Quhen sall your merci rew upon your man...?'
>   (432–5)

His lyrical account of his lady's beauty serves to underscore his desolation in that beauty's absence when she leaves the garden, still unaware of him and his feelings. It is only now that his dream begins, transporting him to the successive visionary interviews with Venus, Minerva and Fortune that help James attain his poem's distinctive interpretation of love.

'Half sleping and half swoun' with his head resting on the cold stone window-sill, he is aware of a blinding light entering his window. Soon the prisoner can leave his room by the door, unchallenged, only to find himself experiencing a Troilus-like ascent – 'Ascending upward ay fro spere to spere' (526) – towards the realm of Venus. Here he finds himself in a celestial assembly of lovers that merges recollections of Chaucer's *Parliament* with the scenes of plaintiffs from the *House of Fame*. Here too he encounters not the sultry topless Venus from the *Parliament* but a goddess altogether more respectably and less scantily clad ('Fond I Venus upon hir bed, that had / A mantill cast over hir schuldris quhite', 670–1). This is a Venus 'That am your hevin and your paradise' (857), and who represents herself as governing a parallel universe of quasi-religious eternal rewards:

> And for your meryt here perpetualye
> Ressave I sall your saulis, of my grace,
> To lyve with me as goddis in this place...
>   (859–61)

Yet this is also a Venus who, after lecturing him high-mindedly on a lover's duties, dispatches him to the 'court riall' of Minerva, guided by Gude Hope, because he needs the counsel of this goddess of wisdom and prudence. In turn, Minerva urges him to identify virtue with his love, yet is strikingly accommodating towards human desire ('"Desire," quod sche, "I nyl it noght deny, / So thou it ground and set in Cristin wise"', 988–9). Satisfied by the lover's declaration of his very honourable intentions towards his lady, and that 'in vertew thy lufe is set with treuth' (1003), Minerva sends the lover back into the world for a vision of Fortune's wheel and to understand how the extent of Fortune's influence is contingent upon human wisdom or otherwise:

> Fortune is most and strangest evermore
> Quhare leste foreknawing or intelligence
> Is in the man...
> (1038–40)

Bewildered after awakening from his dream of Fortune's wheel, the lover is encouraged when a turtle-dove lands at his window bearing a spray of gillyflowers inscribed in gold with a hopeful text ('lufar, I bring / The newis glad...', 1247–8). After praying for categories of lovers and before sending his poem on its way ('Go, litill tretise...') and commending it to Gower and Chaucer – so blending echoes of both the opening and close of *Troilus* – the poet indicates with courtly circumspection that he came into 'the presence swete and delitable' and that his courtship had its reward:

> Sche hath me tak, hir humble creature.
> And thus befell my blisfull aventure
> In youth, of lufe that now from day to day
> Flourith ay newe...
> (1348–51)

The implication here that the poet looks back from within a continuing, settled love for his lady is characteristic of how *The Kingis Quair* reinterprets the aspirations of courtly love poetry with a distinctive moral seriousness. The dream of Minerva is pivotal, for James implies that desire can indeed be accommodated within responsible relationships and that wisdom can overcome misfortune – and with all the authority of a royal poet who could claim to know this from experience. It is a poem in which the prisoner poet cuts a solitary figure, always alone, for this is courtly poetry in the sense of focussing intently on refined introspection about love. Anticipating that some might object that he has written too much about too little, his candid defence is that our own pleasures and pains command our attention: 'And every wicht his awin swete or sore / Has maist in mynde, I can say you no more', 1273–4). Yet this testimony of a heart is also enlivened throughout by a sprightly wryness and humorous grace, as when the poet longs to swap places with his lady's pet dog, has his ear tweaked eye-wateringly by Dame Fortune, or has to wheedle a work-shy nightingale into singing of love.

After his release, James I was perhaps too preoccupied with kingship to write courtly poetry, although an account of his assassination records how his last evening was spent 'att the playing of the chesse, att the tables, yn redyng of Romans, yn syngyng and pypyng, in harpyng, and in other honest solaces of grete pleasance and disport' (Stevenson 1837: 54). By contrast, after his return to France Charles d'Orléans not only continued to compose poems in French but also commissioned translation of his poems into Latin (Coldiron 2000: Chapter 5). This suggests he saw in the high artistry and intense, if stylised, emotion of his vernacular poems a matter and substance worth preserving in Latin's timeless medium. What Charles had the means and self-regard to commission poses a challenge, in its ambition, to the dismissively trivialising twentieth-century view of fifteenth-century courtly poetry – deriving from anachronistic New Critical prejudices about what constitutes 'life', 'deadness', 'staleness' and so forth in poetry – which it is high time to move beyond. Too long derided for its 'lifeless' conventionality, the language of fifteenth-century poetry is a sophisticated ideolect always open to reinvention, as when Charles d'Orleans takes up its idiom in a passionate speaking voice that can be intimately personal, dramatic and colloquial, as well as witty, stylish and poised, as in some of his arresting opening lines:

> 'What menyst thou, Hope? Dost thou me skoffe and skorne?' (1811)
> (Cf. 'Me mocques vous, joyeux Espoir?' B52)
> 'How is hit? How? Have ye forgoten me? (4613)
> (Cf. 'M'avez vous point mis en oubly?' Carole III)

There is also his gift for catching blurted speech and the wavering progression through indecision to resolution, as when challenged by Venus on whether he recognises Fortune:

> 'O no, Madame!...Whi yes! Bi God, now...now...
> I am...I am right wel on hir bithought...'
> (5101–2)

Throughout the sequence Charles experiments with ballade form, where four occurrences of a refrain, reinterpreted at each repetition, and relinquished in a concluding envoy, accord with the emotional logic through which his poems characteristically develop mood and subject. The outcome distils emotion through a highly crafted rhetorical artifice that, far from a constraint on feeling, is in its very accomplishment precisely the expression of sublimated feeling and its aspirations.

Charles d'Orléans occupied a uniquely fascinating position as a poet working in two overlapping cultures of French and English, writing equivalent poems and setting out to express equivalent sentiments in both languages and in both literary and cultural traditions. Those traditions were hardly equal, of course, for France was the wellspring of medieval courtly culture. Why then was Charles so much more experimental and innovative in English than in his equivalent French work? For he is more inventive in English, both structurally and in his more vigorously concrete, emphatic and conversational idiom. The ballades that present largely one side of an idealised courtship – introverted, rhetoricised, abstract – are newly contextualised in English within a quasi-autobiographical implied narrative enlivened by a comic sense and by startlingly specific recollections of settings and occasions for love in courtly society ('In yonder bayne [bath] so se I hir all naked…/ And here I baste [kissed] hir fayre, round pappis [breasts] white…' 4827–40). Charles sets his ballades (presumably mostly written first in French) within his English sequence as two perspectives on love, probably deriving from different cultural circumstances. If his English poems read like courtly poetry in a process of becoming, Charles's French poems are exquisitely finished and often allegorical in mode. (From the French ballades derives the role played by the poet's heart as almost a separate character and hence a mode of interiority, conveyed through dialogue with fragmented aspects of the self, that is well suited to the divided self of the English sequence.) These different aspects of equivalent poems go beyond differences intrinsic to French and English, offering insights into the two cultures and the differing potential that Charles as a courtly poet saw in each. In French, Charles could work with assurance within a long-established courtly literary tradition in the vernacular (and in French literary history Charles is prized as the greatest poet of the late Middle Ages). By contrast, Charles's English poems, even where close in substance to their French equivalents, are written as if thinking aloud, and under the impress of urgently personal feeling. After news comes of the lady's death the English sequence interpolates three English-only ballades passionately expressing Charles's desolation ('In slepe ben leyd all song, daunce, or disport', 2026). In the French series follows an elegant ballade in which the lover loses at chess with Fortune, but in English Charles interrogates this indignantly in another ballade ('Shulde I me make a lady newe? Fy! Fy!' 2141), and later rounds off his English sequence with an English-only ballade that, in its yearning for death, directs a spotlight on to Charles's experience and feelings.

Along with this more inward and emotional dimension to the English sequence comes an unsettling edginess, particularly in the preoccupation with the interplay between speech and writing, presence and absence. The brief Fairfax sequence occasionally reflects such concerns too, but Charles's English poems witness to a sustained ambivalence about writing (although this notably lapses during the roundels, even if Charles reserves the right to revise these in future [3137]). An early ballade has the refrain 'As bi the mowth I levyr had yow told' and rewrites the French to insist 'That with glad hert I shew here myn entent: / Resceyvith hit as hit is to yow ment', 765–6). When he is in such desolation, or when his readers know the score, several envoys present only in English ask 'What nede I more my papir spende, or enke?' (820; also 1000–1). In one added English envoy dismissing the poem ('O goo, thou derke, fordullid, rude myture [poem]') he insists there is no lying (1407), and in another wishes he had his lady with him, and without any candlelight (1806–8). In such cases a longing for the presence made real by the poem chafes against the sense of absence underlined by the poem's turning into a document through writing and sending. In the French ballade 47 the lady writes to him lovingly the words that form the poem's refrain, but in the equivalent English ballade Charles vividly recollects her presence and body language when uttering those same words at their last meeting ('Tredyng my foot, and that so pratily', 1665). By the time of the second sequence, however, Charles is urging the lady not to regard his pain less 'though I kan bettir playne / Bi writyng then bi mouth' (5404–5), and this fits with his checking at their first meeting whether his second lady can read (5311) and his seeming preference for correspondence rather than meetings, although this too becomes wearisome:

> Now, good swet hert, biholdith this scripture
> And fynde a bettir moyan for us twayne   *arrangement*
> (5600–1)

and he later complains:

> What may I more yow write at wordis fewe?...
> Welcome as oft as tonge kan say on rewe!
> (5836/8)

suggesting that Charles d'Orléans never resolved the ambivalence about writing that characterises his poems in English.

It is tempting to see this writerly self-consciousness in Charles's English sequence – together with the bolder and more informal features of his English poems – as reflecting the less securely established literary tradition of courtly poetry in fifteenth-century England, yet also what might be achieved by a writer who brought into English all Charles's command of courtly subject matter, diction and verse form. Writing in English, but from French tradition, Charles could address courtly topics through his self-translations with an aplomb and a mastery of versification, but also with a brilliant freedom and élan, that reinvent the traditions of courtly poetry in English. In his English exile Charles evidently felt at liberty to experiment in ways that produce a fresher, more individual and sometimes more troubled voice than in his poems in French. Indeed, while Sir Thomas Wyatt wrote some brilliantly achieved and far more famous courtly poems, there is room for argument that, comparing the whole oeuvre of each poet as courtly lyricists, the French prince is the more consistently successful, for Charles d'Orléans is undoubtedly the most accomplished poet in English between Chaucer and Wyatt.

NOTE

1   Some spellings and punctuation have been slightly modernised in this chapter.

References and Further Reading

Arn, Mary-Jo (ed.) (1994). *Fortunes Stabilnes: Charles of Orleans's English Book of Love.* Binghamton, NY: Medieval and Renaissance Texts and Studies.

Arn, Mary-Jo (ed.) (2000). *Charles d'Orléans in England 1415–1440.* Cambridge: D. S. Brewer.

Arn, Mary-Jo (2008). *The Poet's Notebook: The Personal Manuscript of Charles of Orléans (Paris, BnF MS Fr. 25458).* Turnhout: Brepols.

Camargo, Martin (1991). *The Middle English Verse Love Epistle.* Tübingen: M. Niemeyer.

Champion, Pierre (ed.) (1971). *Charles d'Orléans: Poésies.* 2 vols. CFMA, 34 (1923), 56 (1927). Repr. 1971. Paris: Champion.

Coldiron, A. E. B. (2000). *Canon, Period, and the Poetry of Charles of Orleans: Found in Translation.* Ann Arbor: University of Michigan Press.

Green, Richard Firth (1980). *Poets and Princepleasers: Literature and the English Court in the Late Middle Ages.* Toronto: University of Toronto Press.

Kooper, Erik (1987). Slack water poetry: an edition of 'The Craft of Lovers'. *English Studies,* 68, 473–89.

MacCracken, H. N. (1911). An English friend of Charles of Orleans. *PMLA,* 26, 142–80.

MacCracken, H. N. (ed.) (1934). *The Minor Poems of John Lydgate: Part II,* Early English Text Society, o.s. 192. Oxford: Oxford University Press.

Myers, A. R. (ed.) (1959). *The Household of Edward IV: The Black Book and the Ordinance of 1478.* Manchester: Manchester University Press.

Norton-Smith, John (ed.) (1971). *James I of Scotland: The Kingis Quair.* Oxford: Clarendon Press.

Ouy, Gilbert (2008). *La librairie des frères captifs: Les manuscrits de Charles d'Orléans et Jean d'Angoulême.* Turnhout: Brepols.

Pearsall, Derek (2000). The literary milieu of Charles of Orleans and the Duke of Suffolk, and the authorship of the Fairfax Sequence. In Mary-Jo Arn (ed.). *Charles d'Orléans in England 1415–1440* (pp. 145–156). Cambridge: D. S. Brewer.

Rebholz, R. A. (ed.) (1978). *Sir Thomas Wyatt: The Complete English Poems.* Harmondsworth: Penguin.

Robbins, Rossell Hope (ed.) (1952). *Secular Lyrics of the XIVth and XVth Centuries.* Oxford: Clarendon Press.

Scattergood, J. (ed.) (1983). *John Skelton: The Complete English Poems.* Harmondsworth: Penguin.

Skeat, W. W. (ed.) (1897). *Chaucerian and Other Pieces.* Oxford: Clarendon Press.

Spearing, A. C. (2005). *Textual Subjectivity.* Oxford: Oxford University Press.

Stevens, John (1961). *Music and Poetry in the Early Tudor Court.* London: Methuen.

Stevenson, Joseph (ed.) (1837). 'The Dethe of the Kynge of Scotis'. Trans. John Shirley. *The Life and Death of King James the First of Scotland* (pp. 47–67). Edinburgh: Maitland Club.

White, E. B. (ed.) (1928). *Alexander Barclay: The Eclogues.* Early English Text Society, o.s. 175. Oxford: Oxford University Press.

34

Drama: Sacred and Secular

Pamela King

The full extent of the lost entertainment industry of medieval England is still emerging. The Records of Early English Drama project continues to unearth material offering new contexts in which to study the relatively few surviving play scripts. No longer can we fall back on a secure, co-aeval body of 'mystery cycles' and 'morality plays'. In the former category, the only complete true cycles are York's and Chester's — although the manuscript history of the latter is complex — as the pageants in the Towneley manuscript, and the so-called N. Town plays from East Anglia, are now recognised to be compilations.[1] And although there are enough sixteenth-century moral interludes to establish the auspices of a genre, the medieval moralities consist of only the three plays in the Macro manuscript (*The Castle of Perseverance, Mankind* and *Wisdom*), the Anglo-Irish *Pride of Life* and *Everyman*, which is a translation from the Dutch (King 2008: 235–62).

The surviving body of English medieval plays is more securely viewed as a random and eccentric corpus of texts written by unknown authors for ephemeral performance and recorded in a variety of manuscripts. They are not a cross-section of the largely lost dramatic activity of medieval England, nor can they provide us with the centrifugal and centripetal patterns of influence offered by the products of high culture. There is virtually no record of the spoken texts of dramatic entertainments outside the royal entry, regularly enjoyed by courtly society in pre-Tudor England. Moreover the manuscripts in which English medieval plays survive were written for a variety of different reasons, but hardly ever as performance scripts. Many of them are not strictly 'finished', but are imperfect on-going and interrupted attempts at civic control, or at record-keeping, or are the products of early antiquarian exercises in retrospective preservation. All post-date original performance, some by a considerable period. For example, the surviving manuscripts of the Chester Play all date from the late sixteenth and early seventeenth centuries, by which time the Play had ceased to be performed. They include modifications made to the Play to accommodate the Reformation, but we can also be confident that they represent much of what was performed in the streets of Chester in the fifteenth century. Equally we know that Coventry had dramas based on salvation history throughout the fifteenth century, although the two surviving pageants are a rewrite from the 1530s of the Weavers Pageant, and an early nineteenth-century antiquarian copy of the lost pageant of the Shearmen and Taylors.[2] Yet, when all the difficulties presented by the corpus of texts have been taken into account, we can be confident that what survives of medieval English drama is most usefully understood in the context of the long fifteenth century.

All surviving medieval English plays are written in verse, and the search for poetically well-made plays could drive us back to the anthology pieces that reliably stand up against the canon of Ricardian and Lancastrian poetry in yielding satisfyingly rich close readings. Another approach is proposed here in open acknowledgement of the fractured canon of medieval drama, and that is that we look at examples of the textual and modal variety across the range, rather than at the consistency and quality of single scripts, in search of the auspices of this very particular kind of performance poetry.

Most surviving medieval plays in English are persuasive in purpose and devotional in content. Commonly persuasive performance is associated with the 'colours' of rhetoric, and some playwrights do indeed display knowledge of formal rhetorical theory, particularly in Prologues. Predictably, *Everyman*, the English translation of one of the products of a Dutch *rederijkerskamer*, 'chamber of rhetoric', clearly signals in its opening stanzas the formal distinction between 'matter', 'intention' and 'manner of presentation' (Cawley 1956: 205–34):

> *Messenger.*
> I pray you all gyue your audyence,
> And here this mater with reuerence,
> By fygure a morall playe.
> *The Somonynge of Eueryman* called it is,
> That of our lyues and endynge shewes
> How transytory we be all daye.
> This mater is wonders precyous;
> But the entent of it is more gracyous,
> And swete to bere awaye.
> The story sayth: Man, in the begynnynge
> Loke well, and take good heed to the endynge,
> Be you neuer so gay!
>
> (1–12)

The source is not Cicero but Peter Lombard, omnipresent in ecclesiastical libraries in England, who discusses these distinctions in his commentary on the Psalms. It was translated into English by Richard Rolle[3]:

Þe mater of þis boke es Crist and his spouse þat es, haly kirk, or ilke a rightwys mans
saule. Þe entent es to confourme þo þat ere fyled in Adam tille Crist in newness of lyf.
Þe maner of lare es swilke: vmstunt he spekys of Crist in his godhead, vmstunt in his
manhede, vmstunt in þat þat he vses þe voice of his servauntes.

Here is the character called Contemplacio, opening the N. Town *Mary Play* (Meredith
1997)[4]:

> Cryst conserve þis congregacyon
> Fro perellys past, present and future,
> And þe personys here pleand, þat þe pronunciacyon
> Of her sentens to be seyd mote be sad and sure,
> And þat non oblocucyon make þis matere obscure,   *error*
> But it may profite and plese eche persone present,
> From þe gynnynge to þe endynge so to endure
> Þat Cryst and every creature with þe conceyte be content.

> This matere here mad is of þe modyr of mercy;
> How be Joachym and Anne was here concepcyon,
> Sythe offred into þe temple, compiled breffly,
> Than maryed to Joseph, and so, folwing þe salutacyon,
> Metyng with Elyzabeth, and þerwith a conclusion
> In fewe wurdys talkyd þat it xulde nat be tedyous
> To lernyd nyn to lewd, nyn to no man of reson.
> Þis is þe processe; now preserve ʒow, Jhesus.

The figure called Poeta, who opens the Digby *Killing of the Children*, also distinguishes
between 'story', 'entent' and 'process' (Baker et al. 1982: 96–115).[5]

This apparent formality in the mode of telling plays to a tenacious understanding
that medieval drama is 'didactic' in a narrowly scholastic way. It is, however, a mode
almost entirely concentrated in openings, and often the matter of late additions (Rich
2007: 237). In the Middle Ages, rhetoric and poetry were recognised to be modally
distinct. Hermann the German is clear on the subject:

> The purpose of rhetoric is to make the opposing side abandon vice by vanquishing it.
> But the purpose of poetry is to win its listeners to the practice of virtue through praise
> and encouragement.

He adds, '...rhetoric is not an adequate method of proceeding in moral matters'.[6]
Two early witnesses support the understanding that despite its public, performative
and persuasive function, devotional drama owes more to the procedures of poetry
than to the formal rhetoric of either Cicero or the pulpit. The author of the *Tretise
of Miraclis Pleyinge* observes (Walker 2000: 198):

…ofte syþis by siche myraclis pleyinge men and wymmen, seynge þe Passioun of Crist and Hise seyntis ben movyd to compassion and devocion, wepynge bitere teris, þanne þei ben not scornynge of God but worschipyng.

Then, in the early sixteenth century, Nicholas Grimald, in his dedicatory epistle to his Latin play *Christus Redivivus* gives an author's account of the process of writing scriptural history as dramatic dialogue. He reflects on the need to create a sense of immediacy, to match register to character and circumstance, to control metrical arrangement, to avoid padding with bad jokes, to bear in mind that the central character is the originator of language, and therefore not to be too contrived but to make the plain story vividly eloquent by the means available to a writer for the theatre:

> *Primum enim non id me suscipere atque profiteri, ut reuelem atdita mysteria: sed ut nudam ac veram historiam enarrem, & modo quodam Pöetica, hoc est, claro et illustri spectaculo patefaciam.*

> I did not attempt or profess to reveal hidden mysteries, but to tell a plain unadorned tale, and to set it forth in a certain poetical manner, so to speak, that is, by a bright and glorious spectacle.

Grimald goes on to commend 'earnest reflection and unremitting prayer' over 'the Ciceros, Aristotles, and Galens' (Merrill 1969: 106–7).

Just as this drama derives its modes of expression from a repertoire wider than that offered by formal rhetoric, so too its devotional content is theologically eclectic.[7] The combination of faith, plus knowledge of scripture, plus Aristotelian logic – scholastic theology – was on its own admission elite. Evidently aware of this, playwrights, while sporadically showing off their school-room understanding of the nature of holy writ, draw more heavily on the monastic theological tradition to foster lay piety. This is in turn further elaborated to make it powerfully and directly accessible through the procedures of the most fundamentally poetic of medieval theologies, now referred to as 'vernacular theology', with its direct appeals to spirituality. The project was to move the community of believers to penance, hence the works which more profoundly influence the quality of English verse scriptural drama are not those of Aquinas, Lombard and Abelard, but in Latin the *Meditationes Jesu Christi*, Jacobus de Voragine's *Legenda Aurea*, Richard Rolle's *Incendium Amoris* [*The Fire of Love*], and in English such works as *The Charter of the Abbey of the Holy Ghost* and, of course, Nicholas Love's *Mirror of the Blessed Life of Jesus Christ*. In short, the inspiration behind the imaginative construction of most English devotional drama derives not from the schoolroom marriage of classical rhetoric and scholastic theology, but from an understanding of the goals of vernacular theology transmitted to the audience through a variety of poetic discourses whose overall aesthetic goal is to move.

The presenter figure in the Prologue to the Bodley *Burial of Christ* is closer to this understanding of what constitutes a play (Baker et al. 1982: 141–68). From the outset the function of the play is presented as affective:

> A soule that list to singe of loue
>> Of Crist, that com tille vs so lawe,   *who came to us so lowly*
> Rede this treyte, it may hym moue,   *read this treatise*
> And may hym teche lightly with-awe.
>
>> (1–4)

Elsewhere, the business of conveying the story is fully integrated into the dialogue. In the Old Testament sequence in the York Play (Beadle 1982), it is God himself who takes on the explicatory role at the start of each pageant. As the *Mary Play* progresses, Contemplacio, initially a presenter figure, responds directly and emotionally to the action, inhabiting the same time-scheme as the other characters. Thus, on the brink of the Assumption he prays:

> Wolde God þu woldyst breke þin hefne myghtye
> And com down here into erth,
> And levyn ȝerys thre and threttye,   *years*
> Thyn famyt folke with fode to fede;   *famished*
> To staunche þi thryste lete þi side blede,
> For erste wole not be mad redempcyon.
> Cum vesyte vs in þis tyme of need;
> Of þi careful creaturys, Lord, haue compassion!
>> (1068–75)

Anticipating the debate of the four daughters of God which follows, he elides the historical Incarnation of Christ with the perpetual presence of mercy in the world, and in particular the ritual means of its fulfilment through the sacrament of the altar. Contemplacio truly is a liminal figure, at once participant in the drama of the Incarnation and celebrant in its sacramental mirror. The sacraments of the Church, especially the sacrament of penance, are a major focus in fifteenth-century English vernacular theology. At the heart of penance is contrition, and to arrive at true contrition the believer must be moved, preferably to tears. English scriptural plays, responding to the devotional climate in which they flourished, developed their own performance poetics of affect.

Affect is achieved in religious prose by anatomising and offering up for meditation the human sufferings of Christ and the Virgin Mary in a homely register or middle style. Various things happen when this is adapted to the exigencies of drama. Here is the Angel Gabriel urging Mary to submit to the Holy Ghost in the *Mary Play*:

> Mary, come of and haste the,
> And take hede in thyn entent
> Whow þe Holy Gost, blyssyd he be,

Abydyth þin answere and þin assent.
Thorwe wyse werke of dyvinyté
The secunde persone, verament,   *truly*
Is mad man by fraternyté
Withinne þiself in place present.

Ferthermore take hede þis space
Whow all þe blyssyd spyrytys of vertu
Þat are in hefne byffore Goddys face,
And all þe gode levers and trew   *living people*
That arre here in þis erthely place –
Thyn owyn kyndrede þe soothe ho knew –
And þe chosyn sowlys þis tyme of grace
Þat are in helle and byde rescu.

As Adam, Abraham, and Davyd, in fere,   *together*
And many othere of good reputacyon,
Þat þin answere desire to here
And þin assent to þe incarnacyon,
In which þu standyst as persever   *recipient*
Of all mankende savacyon.
Gyff me myn answere now, lady dere,
To all these creaturys comfortacyon.
(1324–47)

Gabriel's expression of urgency and anxiety about Mary's reply follows Nicholas Love's *Mirrour* closely. Love's text is, however, a narrative meditation in the authorial voice on how all creation waited for Mary's reply (Love 2005: 26); it is the playwright's stroke of dramatic genius to turn this into a poignant and personal plea from Gabriel. What the dialogue adds to the source is an enhancement of the suspense of the moment. Its cool middle style turns the Angel Gabriel into a dramatic character, and invites the audience to participate in the momentous responsibility faced by both. It also uses the deixis of the dialogue, that is the way in which what is referred to is 'pointed at', in an extraordinarily dynamic way as a counterpart to the visual arrangement of the scene. The stage direction immediately preceding Gabriel's speech reads:

Here þe aungel makyth a lytyl restynge and Mary beholdyth hym, and þe aungel seyth ...

One imagines Mary, as is iconographically almost invariable, kneeling at her prie-dieu opposite the angel, who is probably on one knee with the lily stretched out towards her. By gesture, and by the repeated use of the second person pronoun, the archangel, draws the eye to the person of the Virgin at the very brink of the Incarnation. Gabriel then opens out the picture from the intimate confines of the chamber to encompass first the Trinity and all the company of heaven, then the good livers and true in the earthly space, including the audience, and finally the prophets and patriarchs waiting below in limbo. The audience is, thereby, affectingly included in the moment at which all the cosmos holds its breath waiting for a particular girl to 'come off and haste', to 'take heed', as imperative verbs issuing from a gorgeous, friendly, but impatient archangel urge her on to make the most momentous decision since Eve took the apple from the serpent. This is, broadly, the way that vernacular theology is, in the right hands, peculiarly well adapted to the stage.

The strategic insertion of meditative moments into narrative dialogue is often used by medieval dramatists as a way of controlling the pace and nature of the emotional impact of the action. The most obvious examples are the speeches spoken from the Cross by the crucified Christ, drawing on a variety of non-gospel sources. The dramatist of the York Pinners' pageant develops his from the Good Friday *Improperia*, drawing direct inspiration from the liturgy (Beadle 1982: 315–23). The later Towneley dramatist's Christ, in a pageant that develops and amalgamates the material of the York Pinners' and Butchers' pageants, is more vocal still (Stevens and Cawley 1994: 294–95; Woolf 1962: 1–16). Using a technique similar to that observed above in the *Mary Play*, the Crucified Christ here speaks out directly to the audience. The pattern of an almost haranguing series of rhetorical questions – *improperia* means 'reproaches' – is followed by the affecting quietude of the declarative statement of the speaker's unique lack of sanctuary. The image is biblical, not the poet's own, but is here exploited poetically for maximum affect, drawing the audience's eye not to the conventional five effusions of blood but to the iconic gesture of the head resting on the shoulder, a tiny movement of immense pathos:

> My folk, what haue I done to the,
> > That thou all thus shall tormente me?
> > > Thy syn by I full sore.
> What haue I greuyd the? answere me,
> > That thou thus nalys me to a tre,
> > > And all for thyn erroure;
> > > > Where shall thou seke socoure?
> > > > This mys how shall thou amende?   *fault*
> > > > When that thou thy saveoure
> > > > Dryfes to this dyshonoure,   *compels*
> > > > And nalys thrugh feete and hende!
> All creatoures that kynde may kest,   *accord with nature*
> Beestys, byrdys, all haue thay rest,
> > When thay ar wo begon;
> Bot godys son, that shuld, be best,
> Hase not where apon his hede to rest,
> Bot on his shuder bone.
>
> > > (244–260)

In the York Butchers' more complex pageant of the Death of Christ (Beadle 1982: 323–33), the dramatist uses dialogue to move the narrative from one moment to the next, then freezes the action whenever it resolves into an iconic image, accompanying the chosen moment of stasis with an affecting lyric, such as when the Virgin delivers her conventional complaint at the base of the cross, and when Longeus speaks a hymn of praise for Christ's restoration of his sight:

> O maker vnmade, full of myght,
>   O Jesu so jentill and jente
> þat sodenly has sente me my sight,
>   Lorde, louyng to þe be it lente.   *praising*
>   On rode arte þou ragged and rente,
>   Mankind for to mende of his mys.   *make amends for his sin*
>   Full spitously spilte is and spente   *spitefully killed*
>   Thi bloode, lorde, to bringe vs to blis
>   Full free.
>   A, mercy my socoure,
>   Mercy, my treasoure,
>   Mercy, my sauioure,
>   þi mercy be markid in me.
>   (300–12)

In this way, lyric tropes accompany iconic visual images to create meditative nodes for reflection.

The York Winedrawers' *Christ's Appearance to Mary Magdalene* is a comparatively simple two-hander in which Mary Magdalene encounters Christ as the gardener after the Resurrection (Beadle 1982: 356–59). Yet this whole pageant is shot through with expressions of emotional state with a more complex trajectory. Mary insistently refers to her distress in her first speech. This is held in the foreground while the dialogue also works proleptically, so that the audience is led to anticipate the fulfilment of her wishes to be reunited with Christ. She acts as an inciter of emotion throughout the sequence, although the audience's comfort anticipates hers as they immediately identify her interlocutor.[8] Christ then draws further attention to her emotional state and keeps it continuously in the foreground. He does not himself express explicitly any emotions, but his look-but-don't-touch body, its wounds displayed, is the fetishised object of the scene, offering both the comfort of looking at it and the possibility of renewed pity for which the Magdalene has served as the warm-up act. Between them they then offer a compressed retrospective narrative of the Crucifixion, culminating in her renewed expressions of distress:

> Of bale howe schulde I blynne?   *woe; make an end*
> To se þis ferly foode   *wondrous person*
> Þus ruffully dight,   *pitifully put to death*
> Rugged and rente on a roode,
> Þis is a rewfull sight...
>   (107–11)

Christ then reveals that she must soon relinquish his physical presence for good, so there is no apparent narrative justification for Mary's sudden emotional reversal:

> Alle for joie me likes to synge,
> Myne herte is gladder þanne þe glee,
> And all for joie of þy risyng
> Þat suffered dede vpponne a tree.
>
> (123–26)

She has, however, been through an emotionally cathartic process which releases her to dwell on the Resurrection. The pageant thus ends by completing the emotional cycle of distress, comfort and joy, which may be seen as analogising confession, contrition and satisfaction.

What we are observing here is a contrapuntal relationship between the shape described by the narrative of the scene and that described by the development of its affective rise and fall. The sustained monologue of lament by Mary at the base of the Cross in the Bodley *Burial of Christ* (Furnivall 1967: 171–200), effectively a vernacular *planctus Mariae* – the liturgical trope which imitates the Virgin Mary's lament at the base of the Cross – works in a similar way. In these examples the audience is first brought into emotional proximity with remote biblical characters, then put through a cathartic experience. The chief tools in this process are not those of dramatic realism but of performance poetry.

Geoffrey of Vinsauf in his *Poetria Nova*, found three 'languages' that should be used in reciting: 'first, that of the mouth; next that of the speaker's countenance, and, third, that of gesture' (Vinsauf 1971, 105–6). His view of oral delivery is highly stylised, matching tone of voice and pace to subject matter. He then takes as his example how to replicate anger:

> If you represent the person of this angry man, what, as a speaker, will you do? Imitate true rages. Yet be not yourself enraged; behave partially like the character, but not inwardly. Let your behaviour be the same in every detail but not to such an extent; and suggest wrath becomingly.

Modern analyses of how emotion is represented in performance poetry are interestingly close to Geoffrey's. In performance, the choice has to be made of whether or not to add direct emotional expression – gasps, sobs, sighs – or to trust to the particular arrangement of the spoken text. In life emotional cognition does not share the same temporal dynamic as thought and speech: at moments of great emotion incoherent expletives precede articulation. What affective poetry does is to unify the time-scales of emotion and concept in its own verbal music (Oliver 1989: 168):

> ...the poet can make the speed of thought and the speed of imagined emotion coincide, since conceptions share the same time-scale. He distances the real emotion and uses it rather as a painter uses paint; whereas the aesthetic emotional tension may be high.

Moreover,

> Intonation cannot mime its reaction to imaginary emotion without copying the
> necessary relation it has to real emotions: the coding is already there in the usage
> of language...our delicacy in perceiving the emotional effect of intonational patterns
> is even more fine in poetry than in ordinary speech, owing to the more evident
> patterning.

Aesthetic success with affect is dependent on the authenticity of the intonation
pattern, and in dramatic actions the success of a scene depends on its visual and
aural reception working in concert.

Affect is not achieved only by concealed artifice or by the middle style favoured
by prose writers such as Love; it can in this drama also be the product of high
style and grand artifice. Taking an example once more from the *Mary Play*, at the
culmination of the Virgin's visit to Elizabeth, the two women recite together the
Magnificat, Mary in Latin, Elizabeth interpolating an English verse translation. In
the macaronic text, the English expounds the Latin, but that is not the primary effect.
Rather, metrical and aural patterning dominate, and give the verse a sinuousness
reminiscent of antiphonal chant, moving forward recursively to the conclusion.
Here the fulfilment of a stylised pattern provides the audience with a sense of
completion.

Liturgy's handling of scriptural history stands in particular relation to poetry,
for it does not work according to the procedures of narrative telling, but has
a recursive and thematic construction following the patterning of the hours of
worship (King 2006: 56). This thematic recurrence is not simply aesthetic, but
characterises Augustinian figural views of history. In liturgical performance this
is replicated in the antiphonal use of voices, as lesson, response and versicle move
to and fro between events and their outcomes, dwelling on selected verses from
the gospel text of the day. The pattern is interspersed with psalmody which is
wholly lyrical in mode, and other familiar non-narrative materials of which
the *Magnificat* is one, along with the *Te Deum, Nunc dimittis* and the hymns of For-
tunatus (King 2006: 146). The memorable climaxes of liturgical telling are not
concerned with narrative agency but with vocalisation as part of the devout sensuality
of sound, gesture and incense. Playwrights steeped in the procedures of worship
knew how to exploit the momentous and dwelt-on moment by combining iconic
sight with sound.

We know from the visual arts how stylised and demonstrative action may
have resolved itself into familiar images, but we have paid less attention to sound.
In performance poetry, rhythm gives a sense of movement by combining prosody
and intonation. Anticipating modern musicology, John of Garland recognised
how rhythmic patterning generates emotional impact. The seventh book of his
twelfth-century *Parisiana Poetria*, 'Incipit ars rithmica' (Garland 1974: 136–223),
relates rhythm in poetry to music. The English fifteenth-century dramatists were

demonstrably also aware that the poetics of affect depend not only on simple accessibility, but on the emotional impact afforded by the memory and memorability of the church's special discourse, and on its concomitant highly stylised aural arrangement.

In passus XII of the B-text of *Piers Plowman*, Will mounts a defence of the supremacy of poetry over the didactic discourses of the Church, distinguishing between 'kind wit' and 'clergy', the former being a superior way of arriving at truth. The argument is uncannily similar to what Samuel Taylor Coleridge was later to describe in his theory of poetry as the 'ideal of compression... a commingling of thought and feeling which defies and overrides the sequential operation of the reasoning faculties'. Coleridge observed that there is 'something in the human mind which makes it know... that in all finite quantity there is infinite, in all measure of time an eternal' concluding (Poston 1986: 163, 121):

> The symbolic language of poetry is thus by its nature sacramental, for it connects finite and infinite consubstantiality...

Poetry, expressed in these terms, takes on the special properties of a metadiscourse enacting the operation of the Word. Understood in this way, the moments of highly stylised poetry not only allude to sacred text, but call to its service particular intonational patterns matched to moments of iconic stillness of visual image. This produces a peculiar compression and heightening that supplies an emotional range beyond that of prose. It is capable not only of generating sorrow, contrition and comfort, but also of leading the audience at strategic moments into wonder and awe unrelated to the scale of the theatrical production.

It is particularly important to deploy all these tools at the moment of opening a large performance which has to capture the attention of a street audience at a festive event, and this is exactly the strategy of the author of the York Play's first speech, as God opens the Barkers' Fall of the Angels (Beadle 1982: 49–53). Attracted by the resonant Latin of the first line, the attentive audience member holds and savours the whole stanza in the immediate memory, uniting past and future in the present moment – in the manner that the ear receives a symphonic theme in music:

> *God*
> *Ego sum Alpha et nouissimus.*
> I am gracyus and grete, God withoutyn begynnyng,
> I am maker vnmade, all mighte es in me;
> I am lyfe and way vnto welth-wynnyng,
> I am formaste and fyrste, als I byd sall it be.
> My blyssyng o ble sall be blendyng,   *countenance; dazzling*
> And heldand, fro harme to be hydande,   *pouring forth; hiding*
> My body in blys ay abydande,   *remaining*
> Vnendande, withoutyn any endyng.

(I, 1–9)

This is the expression of the word by the Word, the *logos*, in preparation for the ultimate speech-act, the act of Creation.

Dramatic writing is not simply a matter of big speeches, however; in all drama, narrative is dispersed amongst a series of different voices. Each speaking voice emanates from a particular material body, but the goal need not be one of verisimilitude of person, any more than staging aims always to reproduce particularities of real space in real time. Vernacular theology offered the authors of scriptural drama a range of creative opportunities which achieved three things: first it evaded doctrinal issues by not engaging in scholastic argument; second it realised the potential of the direct aural effect of spoken text, of the musicality of metre and the familiar yet luminous quality of liturgical Latin to move its audience in ways that owe more to chant than to semantics; and third its meditative dwelling on images in the mind's eye translated itself perfectly into a deictic style that allowed for the intersection of the verbal and the visual. All of these are the tools of a very specialised form of performance poetry.

There is, however, another type of dramatic writing in many of the plays that exploits the self-conscious textuality on which we have focused so far to anatomise the ungodly by foregrounding different forms of dis-orderly language. The York Coopers' Satanas (Beadle 1982: 64–69) gives the audience rather redundant warning that they are about to hear lies. Lying, like disguising, is second nature to the forces of evil In the York pageant of the Resurrection (Beadle 1982: 344–55), the newly awoken soldiers who were supposed to have been guarding Christ's tomb conclude their lively exchange of frantic questions with the resolve:

> *II Miles*   Vs muste make lies, for þat is need,
> Oureselue to saue.
>
> (320–21)

Language is a particularly morally charged sign-system in this drama. Taking its cue from the theology which understands the deity to be an embodiment of the *logos*, it consistently exploits its own metatextual potential to collapse sign and signified together. Moreover this takes place against the background of an Augustinian tradition which cast verbal perversion as deviant. A strong catechetical tradition anatomised sins of speech, while at the same time imposing strict ordering principles on the systematised utterances through which individuals affirmed their faith and orthodoxy. The catechetical tradition is in turn reflected in the drama, when, for example, the Chester apostles at Pentecost recite the Creed (Lumiansky and Mills 1986: I, 378–95), the N. Town Mary and Elizabeth, as we have seen, say the *Magnificat*, and the sheep are divided from the goats in all Last Judgement pageants according to the duly rehearsed Works of Corporal Mercy. We see the influence of this tradition of systematised statements of faith, which reduces poetry by its repetitive formulaic structure to its mnemonic function, reflected in Anima's affirmation of her faith in *Wisdom*, where the form as much as the content signals her soundness (Eccles 1969: 114–52):

> Soveren Lord, I am bounde to Thee
> Wan I was noughte Þou made me thus gloryus;
> Wan I perysshede thorow synne Þou savyde me;
> Wen I was in grett perell Þou kept me, Cristus;
> Wen I erryde Þou reducyde me, Jhesus;   *led me back*
> Wen I was ignorant Þou tawt me truthe;
> Wen I synnyde Þou correcte me thus;
> Wen I was hewy Þou comfortede me by ruthe...   *pity*
>   (309–16)

Books like *The Lay Folks' Catechism*, and *The Stanzaic Life of Christ*, influential in particular on the Chester play, offer much of the catechetical agenda in vernacular verse, which is memorable and accessible. In the hands of a good dramatist, such material can provide a punctuating and arresting moment, but one of the challenges of the stage is that disproportionate language, that is the language of evil, presents so many opportunities for more engaging dialogue.

Audiences are by turns seduced, warned and cajoled into an understanding that the word is the deed, as these dramatists demonstrate the correct and perverted uses of language, a barometer of moral condition. There are good speakers, like Mercy in *Mankind*, who deliver their messages in the Latinate discourse of the Church, in orderly whole lines of metrical regularity, often in whole stanzas (Eccles 1969: 153–84). But then there are also bad speakers, like the scions of Herod's court in the York *Christ before Herod* who speak French (Beadle 1982: 270–82), false Latin, and some notable nonsense:

> I faute in my reuerant in otill moy,
> I am of fauour, loo, fairer be ferre.
> Kyte oute yugilment. Vta! Oy! Oy!
> Be any witte þat Y watte it will waxe were.
>   (239–42)

Here orderly stanzas degenerate into stichomythic dialogue and broken syntax in which everyone seems to be rudely interrupting everyone else. The message that there is no authoritative voice needs no overt statement. The elaborate alliterative stanza of this and the other trial pageants in the York play lends itself particularly to chaotic dialogue, as much as to the pomping speeches of a succession of tyrants whose mouths are as over-full of words as their heads are full of their own deluded self-importance.

In the post-Wyclifite period the use of the vernacular in matters associated with Holy Writ had become politically charged. The language of poetry is a disguise, a mask, which sometimes slips to reveal the unruliness of the tongue and to warn the audience that the power of the word, which can lead them into greater spiritual enlightenment, or move them to pious tears, can also bring about a fall. In discussing why the Holy Spirit took the form of tongues of flame at Pentecost, the author of the *Golden Legend* warns that the tongue is the member of the body that is hardest to control, yet most useful when well-controlled, so most needful of the direct intervention of the Holy Spirit (Voragine 1993: I: 304–05).

'Bad' or subversive language is given a particular focus in two medieval English plays: in *Mankind* and in the Towneley *Judicium* (Stevens and Cawley 1994: 401–25), the devil in charge of punishments associated with the unruly tongue, Titivillus/Tutivillus, is cast as a dramatic character. He has a long and complicated history, derived from his association with the two types of verbal sin: saying too little and saying too much. Specifically, although the Church valorised silence in a number of contexts, it deplored the lazy priest who omitted words or syllables from the divine office, so that Titivillus in one of his incarnations collected them up in his sack. This sack-carrying devil described by Jacques de Vitry in the early thirteenth century is, as Michael Clanchy remarks, concerned with oral rather than literal skills in the clergy, and is vividly depicted in *The Myroure of Oure Ladye* (Clanchy 1993: 183–88). Related to him, and also appearing in the thirteenth century, is, however, the recording demon, concerned with writing down the superfluous words of those who gossiped in church.

In verse sermon exempla, references to Tutivillus are characteristically macaronic, beginning in Latin before descending into English epithets for those who bungle the delivery of divine office. One such verse in MS Lansdowne 765, a treatise on music, deplores the ruination of the ancient music of the Psalms by slothful priests (Jennings 1977: 18–19):

> Destestacio contra perverse psallentes
> Qui psalmos resecant, qui verba rescisa volutant,
> Non magis illi ferent quam si male lingue tacerant,
> Hi sunt psalmos corrumpunt nequitur almos:
> Quos sacra scriptura dampnat, reprobant quo que jura;
> Ionglers cum Jappers, Nappers, Galpers, quoque Drawers,
> Momlers, Fforskippers, Over(r)enners, sic Overhippers.
> Fragmina verborum TUTIVILLUS colligit horum.

I condemn perverted singers of the Psalms, who shorten them and tumble about the excised words. They say no more than if their evil tongues had been silent (?), those who corrupt sweet Psalms wretchedly. Those whom sacred scripture condemns, they also reject the laws, such as Jongleurs, Japers, Nappers, Gulpers, as well as Drawers, Mumblers, Foreskippers, Overrunners, and Overhippers. It is fragments of these words that Tutivillus collect.

What is interesting for our purposes is again the cross-over between music and language: it is the violation of the sound of divine office that is condemned. The syllables that Titivillus collected were the result of syncope, or the omission of unstressed syllables, as the slovenly priest did not understand his Latin grammar so simply slurred over or omitted the unstressed inflectional endings. True syncopation is not mimicked in

any of our dramas, but evil characters do tend to speak in short lines with a predominance of accentuated syllables.

Consider Lucifer in *Wisdom*. *Wisdom* is written predominantly in an eight-line stanza,
with lines of nine or ten syllables rhyming ababbcbc, whose pivotal fourth and fifth lines
convey to the ear a sense of the progress of reasoned symmetrical argument which contributes to the tone of this most genteel of dramas. How much more striking is it then,
when Lucifer bursts in upon the scene and delivers four stanzas in short regular lines of
one spondaic foot followed by an iamb, each line beginning and ending with a stressed
syllable, and rhyming with an equally emphatic aaabaaab – the devil is angry:

> Owt, harrow, I rore!
> For envy I lore.
> My place to restore
> God hath made a man.
> All cum þey not thore,
> Woode and þey wore.   *mad*
> I xall tempte hem so sorre,
> For I am he þat syn begane...
>   (325–56)

In this play, metrical change is managed closely to reflect moral degeneration in a
way that presages John Skelton's *Magnificence*, where 'Skeltonics', the author's signature
verse form, is used to chart the fall of the protagonist into folly (Skelton 1980).

Recognition of the mirroring of moral degeneracy by linguistic collapse in *Mankind*
has become a commonplace in criticism (Neuss 1973; Ashley 1975). The verbal crimes
associated with Titivillus are both evidenced in the play. Notably the audience is seduced
into idleness of tongue by their participation in the obscene audience song with its
blasphemous refrain, 'Hoylyke, holyke, holyke! Holyke, holyke holyke!' (344). The
play's use of 'dog' Latin is also well known: in 'Corn seruit bredibus, chaffe horsibus,
straw fyrybusque' (57), Mischief's addition of the final grammatically exact 'que'
gives the line an additional twist of insolence. Two lines further on, the ending 'et
reliqua' ('and the rest') explicitly parodies lazy priests: the words are part of the rubric
after the incipit of biblical readings in the Breviary, indicating that the rest should
be read. Mankind's own language disintegrates as he falls into sin, to ragged expletives:
'A tapster, a tapster! Stow statt stow!' (730). Although in this play, 'no word, whether
Latin or English, is incorruptible', individual characters, and their audience, are free
to resist the degeneration of language, and 'while the surface play of words enacts
subversive manoeuvres, the structure of the action recuperates the authority of the
sacred Word' (Dillon 1998: 65–66). Within the logic of the play's overarching structure
this is indisputable, as Mercy ends directly addressing the audience:

> Mankend ys wrechyd, he hath sufficyent prowe.   *advantage*
> Therefore God grant ȝow all *per suam misericordiam*   *through his mercy*

Þat ye may be pleyferys with þe angellys abowe
And hawe to ȝour porcyon *vitam eetrnam*. Amen!   *share; eternal life*

(912–15)

Yet in terms of muscular discourse, supported by striking theatrical devices, in delivery and reception, the devil does indeed have all the best tunes. Titivillus, coming 'with my leggys wnder me' (454), possibly on stilts, and evidently with a huge devil-mask, his 'hede þat is of grett omnipotens' (461), sets up an immediate rapport with the audience, by enlisting them as co-conspirators in his plot to make Mankind 'schyte lesynges':

Not a worde, I charge yow, peyn of forty pens.	*on pain of (a fine)*
A praty game xall be scheude yow or ȝe go hens.	*shown; before*
ȝe may here hym snore, he ys sade aslepe.	
Qwyst! pesse! Þe Deull ys dede! I xall go ronde in hys ere.	*whisper*
Alasse, Mankind, alasse! Mercy stown a mere!	*has stolen*
He ys runn away fro hys master, þer wot no man where;	*knows*
Moreover, he stale both a hors and a nete.	*ox*

(590–96)

In the Towneley *Judicium*, Tutivillus has a much broader role, setting deficiencies in religious observation in the broader context of what amounts to general fecklessness, such as the wearing of fashionable clothing by the 'witles' (344) while their children starve. Those who chatter in church and fail to pay attention are gathered up with a list of others whose chief failing seems to be a grievously short attention span and the desire to get rich quick and make a flashy show. Though he describes himself as 'master Lollar', this Tutivillus is no linguistic slouch, thanks to the poetic virtuosity of his creator:[9]

Here a roll of ragman	*investigation*
Of the rownde tabill,	
Of breffes in my bag, man,	*writs*
Of synnes dampnabill;	
Vnnethes may I wag, man,	*scarcely; stir*
For-wery in youre stabill	
Whils I set my stag, man...	*unruly horse*

(326–32)

Women are, according to this Tutivillus, peculiarly prone to the sins which he specialises in recording:

And Nell with her nyfyls	*fripperies*
Of crisp and of sylke,	
Tent well youre twyfyls,	*ruffles*
Youre nek abowte as mylke;	
With youre bendys and youre bridyls	*sashes; braids*

Of Sathan, the whilke
Sir Sathanas idylls   *makes worthless*
You for tha ilke,   *those same*
This Gill knaue   *Jill-knave*
It is open behynde,
Before is it pynde;
Bewar of the west wynde,
Youre smok lest it wafe.

(469–81)

The decision of the latest editors of the Towneley Plays to present the 'Wakefield' pageants in thirteen line stanzas points up the comparability in sheer verbal dexterity, of Tutivillus' attacks on sinners, with poems such as John Skelton's 'The Tunnyng of Eleanor Rummyng', or William Dunbar's 'Ane Dance in the Quenis Chalmer'. All share the property of injecting energy and movement into subjects which are essentially grotesque descriptive snapshots. Manipulation of the same verse form is deployed to a variety of purposes in the famous *Secunda Pastorum* (Stevens and Cawley 1994: 126–57). Here the stanza is used for burlesque action, as when the shepherds discover that Mac's 'heir' is their lost lamb:

Tercius Pastor.
Gyf me lefe hym to kys
And lyft vp the clowtt.
What the dewill is this?
He has a long snowte.

(842–45)

But equally, in the opening speeches of the shepherds, it can evoke the lyric of popular complaint, and, in the voice of the Virgin Mary, it can be turned into the poetry of high ceremonial seriousness as she sends her visitors on their way.

One suspects that one attraction to the modern reader of *Secunda Pastorum*, apart from the evident quality of the writing, is the fact that its sub-plot offers a piece of secular invention in the midst of so many Bible stories. England has few surviving secular dramatic texts from the Middle Ages; little to rival the farces which survive from the Low Countries and France. The Records of Early English Drama project may have revealed a landscape rich in theatre, but without texts we can say little about the poetic qualities of the numerous lost plays. The scraps of Robin Hood plays that survive contain dialogue made up of formulaic prompts to action and nothing of the reflective or lyrical (Knight and Ohlgren 1997). The literary secular drama of late medieval England belonged to the milieux reflected in the *Records of Early English Drama* electronic databases of aristocratic patrons and hired performers, a growing catalogue of long-lost and anonymous entertainments.[10] What these statistical accumulations do demonstrate is the close affinity, even the interchangeability, between minstrelsy and playing in socially refined circles which retained or hosted troupes of entertainers. And if liturgical chant lent its peculiar lyricism to scriptural drama, we can surmise that secular balladry and romance crossed over into the plays with which the well-to-do layman was entertained. The poem known as 'The Nut Brown Maid', for example, attributed to the fifteenth century and preserved in the commonplace book of affluent early sixteenth-century London grocer Richard Arnold, the so-called *Customs of London*, demonstrates the performability by two voices of a text which would more usually be categorised as a tail-rhyme romance rather than play, and how the boundary between plays and other genres of writing is very permeable in a culture of mixed oral entertainment.[11]

The few secular plays from court circles which survive, however, display a literary taste far removed from popular balladry. Henry Medwall had wide experience of a number of dramatic traditions from his London city upbringing and his years as a student at Cambridge (Medwall 1980). His two extant plays, *Fulgens and Lucres* and *Nature*, are richly mixed entertainments encompassing low-life topical repartee, mock jousts, dancing and singing – but their poetry belongs to a very particular milieu and influence which brings us back full circle to classical rhetoric via humanist dialogue and the procedures of legal pleading:

> Who taught the cok hys watche howres to observe
> And syng of corage with shrill throte on hye?
> Who taught the pellycan her tender hart to carve
> For she nolde suffer her byrdys to dye?
> Who taught the nyghtyngall to recorde besyly
> Her strange entunys in silence of the nyght?
> Certes I, Nature, and none other wyght.
>
> (43–49)

This is the character Nature in Medwall's play of the same name providing advice to Man, and the humanist argument, about the need to find a temperate mean between the extremes of reason and sensuality in the long voyage through this world, will develop as the lengthy speech progresses. The fact that it is delivered in rime royale contributes rhetorical colouring, but also perfectly imposes a reasoned control on delivery that matches the message. As Medwall's editor has observed, the gravitas of a character is marked by speeches in complete stanzas, often, as here, with a single thought being sustained throughout. Delivery, that is speaking, is all the action in the early scenes of this play. Later, by contrast, different stanza forms characterise the rapid dialogue of the vices.

The same formula is applied in *Fulgens and Lucres*, where Gaius, the suitor of worth as opposed to birth, wins the day and the girl by delivering a speech of seventeen rime royal stanzas. The play is marked out as a coterie piece written for connoisseurs of rhetorical technique, the polar opposite of dramas which have to use their dialogue to capture the attention of a street audience. Yet *Fulgens and Lucres* taken as a whole is also a supremely sophisticated piece of theatrical writing:

A: Tusshe, here is no man that settyth a blank
     By thy consell or konneth the thank –
          Speke therof no more!
     They know that remedy better than thow.
     But what shall we twayne do now?
          I care most therfore –

     Me thinketh that matter wolde be wist.
B: Mary, we may go hens whan we lyst –   *choose*
          No man saith us nay.
A: Why than, is the play all do?   *over*
B: Ye, by my feyth, and we were ons go   *if we were to go*
          It were do streght wey.   *it would end straight away*
                    (866–77)

With these characters A and B, who emerge from the audience and have the last word, Medwall shows that, in addition to the high style of the main plot, he can write verse dialogue that exhibits a different kind of artifice from all the examples examined above, and one set to win the approbation of our own times. Henry Medwall's poetry here so closely imitates natural speech rhythms that '...a man shall not lightly / Know a player from a nother man' (55–56).

Notes

1   For background to the disputed provenance of the pageants in the Towneley manuscript, see Palmer (2002). For the status of the N. Town plays, see Meredith (1997). For the difficulties presented by the surviving forms of the Chester Play, see Mills (1992: esp. xvii).

2   For the textual history of the Chester and Coventry Plays see the introductions to their recent editions, respectively Mills (1992) and King and Davidson (2000).

3   Minnis (1988: 191), quoting Allen (1931: 7).

4   It is now commonly understood that British Library MS Cotton Vespasian D VIII, the so-called N. Town Plays, is a compilation of East Anglian provenance, incorporating a number of formerly free-standing dramas, including a play about the early life of the Virgin Mary, a Passion play and a play of the Assumption of the Virgin, all built into a scriptural cycle which covers similar material to the York and Chester plays.

5   Oxford, Bodleian Library MS Digby 133, is a compilation of plays on biblical subjects dating from the early sixteenth century. The original circumstances of their production are obscure, but there is evidence that they were written for annual performance, *The Killing of the Children* at Candlemas, and possibly associated with Chelmsford in Essex. See further Coldewey (1993: 253–73, 256).

6   Quoted in A. J. Minnis and A. B. Scott, with the assistance of Wallace (1988: 311–12).

7   I am grateful for access to Carolyn Muessig's forthcoming article 'Communities of discourse: religious authority and the role of holy women in the Later Middle Ages', which focuses on inclusive definitions of medieval theology.

8   On how such characters serve in the performance circumstances of processional production to incite emotion in the crowd see Twycross (1981).

9   For the continuing vigorous debate about the status, provenance and authorship of the pageants in the Towneley manuscript see notably Palmer (2002).

10 *Patrons and Performers Web Site*, http://link.library.utoronto.ca/reed. Records of Early English Drama: Patrons and Performances 2003–2008.

11 From Richard Arnold, *Customs of London* (London, 1502?), and published in modernised spelling in Arthur Quiller-Couch (1919).

REFERENCES AND FURTHER READING

Allen, H. E. (1931). *The English Writings of Richard Rolle*. Oxford: Clarendon Press.

Arnold, Richard (1502?). *Customs of London*. London. (Pub. in modernised spelling in Arthur Quiller-Couch (ed.) (1919). *The Oxford Book of English Verse*. Oxford: Clarendon Press. No. 25. http://www.bartleby.com/101/25.html.)

Ashley, Kathleen (1975). Titivillus and the battle of words in 'Mankind'. *Annuale Medievale*, 16, 128–150.

Baker, Donald C., John L. Murphy, and Louis B. Hall Jr (eds) (1982). *The Late Medieval Religious Plays of Bodleian MSS Digby 133 and e Musaeo 160*. Early English Text Society, o.s. 283. Oxford: Oxford University Press.

Beadle, Richard (ed.) (1982). *The York Plays*. London: Edward Arnold.

Cawley, A. C. (ed.) (1956). *Everyman and Medieval Miracle Plays*. London: Dent.

Clanchy, Michael (1993). *From Memory to Written Record: England 1066–1307*. 2nd edn. Oxford: Blackwell.

Coldewey, John D. (ed.) (1993) *Early English Drama: An Anthology*. London: Routledge.

Dillon, Janette (1998). *Language and Stage in Medieval and Renaissance England*. Cambridge: Cambridge University Press.

Eccles, Mark (ed.) (1969). *The Macro Plays*, Early English Text Society, o.s. 262. Oxford: Oxford University Press.

Furnivall, F. J. (ed.) (1967). *The Digby Plays*. Oxford: Oxford University Press. (First pub. Early English Text Society, e.s. 70, London: K. Paul, Trench and Trubner, 1896.)

Garland, John of (1974). *The Parisiana Poetria of John of Garland*. Ed. Traugott Lawler. New Haven and London: Yale University Press.

Jennings, Margaret (1977). Tutivillus: the literary career of the recording demon. *Studies in Philology*, 74(5), 1–95.

King, Pamela M. (2006). *The York Mystery Cycle and the Worship of the City*. Cambridge: D. S. Brewer.

King, Pamela M. (2008). Morality plays. In Richard Beadle and Alan Fletcher (eds). *The Cambridge Companion to Medieval English Theatre* (pp. 235–62). 2nd edn. Cambridge: Cambridge University Press.

King, Pamela M. and Clifford Davidson (eds) (2000). *The Coventry Plays*. Kalamazoo, MI: Medieval Institute Publications.

Knight, Stephen and Thomas Ohlgren (eds) (1997). *Robin Hood and Other Outlaw Tales*. Kalamazoo, MI: TEAMS Medieval Texts.

Love, Nicholas (2005). *The Mirror of the Blessed Life of Jesus Christ: a Full Critical Edition*. Ed. Michael J. Sargent. Exeter: Exeter University Press.

Lumiansky, R. M. and David Mills (eds) (1986). *The Chester Mystery Cycle*. 2 vols. Early English Text Society, s.s. 3 and s.s. 9. Oxford: Oxford University Press.

Medwall, Henry (1980). *The Plays of Henry Medwall*. Ed. Alan R. Nelson. 2 vols. Cambridge: D. S. Brewer.

Meredith, Peter (ed.) (1997). *The Mary Play from the N. Town Manuscript*. Revised 2nd edn. Exeter: University of Exeter Press. (First pub. London: Longman, 1987.)

Merrill, L. R. (1969). *The Life and Poems of Nicholas Grimald*. Hamden, CT: Archon Books. (First pub. Newhaven, CT: Yale University Press, 1925.)

Mills, David (ed.) (1992). *The Chester Mystery Cycle*. East Lansing, MI: Colleagues Press.

Minnis, Alistair (1988). *Medieval Theory of Authorship*. Aldershot: Scolar Press.

Minnis, A. J. and A.B. Scott, with the assistance of David Wallace (1988). *Medieval Literary Theory and Criticism c. 1100–1375: The Commentary Tradition*. Oxford: Clarendon Press.

Neuss, Paula (1973). Active and idle language: dramatic images in 'Mankind'. In Neville Denny (ed.). *Medieval Drama* (pp. 41–68). Stratford on Avon Studies 16. London: Edward Arnold.

Oliver, Douglas (1989). *Poetry and Narrative in Performance*. London: Macmillan.

Palmer, Barbara D. (2002). Recycling 'The Wakefield Cycle': the records, *Research Opportunities in Renaissance Drama*, 41: 88–130.

Poston, Lawrence (1986). Poetry as pure act: a Coleridgean ideal in early Victorian England. *Modern Philology*, 84(2), 162–84.

Rich, K. Janet (2007). The role of the presenter in medieval drama. In David N. Klausner and Karen Sawyer Marsalek (eds). *'Bring furth the pagents': Essays in Early English Drama presented to Alexandra F. Johnston* (pp. 230–69). Toronto: University of Toronto Press.

Skelton, John (1980). *Magnificence*. Ed. Paula Neuss. Manchester: Manchester University Press.

Stevens, Martin and Cawley, A. C. (eds) (1994). *The Towneley Play*. 2 vols, Early English Text Society, s.s. 13 and 14. Oxford: Oxford University Press.

Twycross, Meg (1981). 'Playing the Resurrection'. In P. L. Heyworth (ed.). *Medieval Studies for J.A.W. Bennett, aetatis suae LXX* (pp. 273–96). Oxford: Clarendon Press.

Vinsauf, Geoffrey de (1971). *Poetria Nova*. In J. J. Murphy, *Three Medieval Rhetorical Arts*. Berkeley: University of California Press.

Voragine, Jacobus de (1993). *The Golden Legend: Readings on the Saints*. Trans. William Granger Ryan. 2 vols. Princeton, NJ: Princeton University Press.

Walker, Greg (ed.) (2000). *Medieval Drama an Anthology*. Oxford: Blackwell.

Woolf, Rosemary (1962). The theme of Christ the lover knight in medieval English literature. *RES*, 13, 1–16.

Epilogue: Afterlives of Medieval English Poetry

Corinne Saunders

As this volume has shown, rewriting and adaptation are intrinsic to the medieval poetic tradition. Late in the Anglo-Saxon period, an anonymous poet employed the tropes of Germanic legend to shape a powerful memorial of the defeat of the English by the Vikings in 991. 'The Battle of Maldon', like Tennyson's 'The Charge of the Light Brigade', creates out of loss and death a celebration of heroic deeds, and to achieve this, relies on the ideals and poetic conventions of the Anglo-Saxon past. Few rewritings engage so explicitly with contemporary situations, but it is the intersection of past and present that consistently shapes poetic tradition – as is powerfully evident in the rewritings of the Arthurian legend both within and beyond the medieval period. The first essays in this volume emphasise the balance between conservatism and innovation, the inherited and the original. This is true of not only Old English but also Middle English poetry, and more than ever is a distinguishing feature of fifteenth-century writing. The poets of the medieval period were scattered and often unknown to each other; their audiences and readers were only partially conversant with developing literary traditions. Yet for all this, there is a strong sense of poetic heritage, of writing within established genres, of adapting familiar conventions, and of shaping new matter from 'olde bokes'. Such reworking would be sustained with a certain ebb and flow across the Renaissance but would fade in the early modern period, to be reinvigorated in the eighteenth century and to flourish with peculiar vigour from the Romantic period onwards. The imaginative appeal of the medieval, far from abating, seems to be growing, and the poetry of the Middle Ages, remarkably, remains a living tradition. This epilogue surveys just some highlights of that tradition in the centuries that followed the late medieval period.

There was, of course, no absolute boundary between the Middle Ages and the Renaissance, though such extraordinary cultural shifts occurred in the fifteenth and sixteenth centuries as to transform both language and literature dramatically – from the establishment of the printing press, to the rediscovery of Greek texts, to the religious upheaval of the Reformation. Reading interests began to change as a result of new intellectual emphases. Chaucer remained a focal point, partly because his writing lent itself to so many different interpretations. Fifteenth- and sixteenth-century readers praised Chaucer for courtliness, eloquence, rhetoric and learning, but also for a variety of religious views, first orthodox, then Protestant, and even (John Foxe) as a Wycliffite. Chaucer was viewed from early on as the 'father of English poetry'. For Caxton, he was the 'laureate poete', who 'by his labour enbelys-shyd, ornated and made fair our Englisshe' (Proem, 1484).[1] His writing seemed to look forward to an English Renaissance: George Puttenham placed Chaucer 'as the most renowned of them all' for his translation, wit and metre in the 'first age' of English poetry, followed by a second 'company of courtly makers', Wyatt and Surrey (*The Art of English Poesy* I, 1589). From Caxton's edition onwards, there was an interest in printing Chaucer's entire *Works* (evinced in the editions of Richard Pynson [1492, 1526], Wynkyn de Worde [1498], William Thynne [1532, 1542, 1545], John Stowe [1561] and Thomas Speght [1598, 1602, 1687], so that his poetry was widely available in a way that no other early poetry was. Langland, at least as popular in his time as Chaucer, suffered a different fate (see Bowers 2007). His language was more difficult; his explicitly moral subject more rooted in a distinct and distant political and religious culture. Caxton was not interested in printing this non-courtly work. *Piers Plowman* was, however, printed (anonymously) in 1550 as *The Vision of Pierce Plowman*, by the polemical Protestant writer Robert Crowley, who modernised the text and annotated it to emphasise its critique of the Church and defence of the weak. *Pierce Plowman* was taken up by the Reformers for its anti-clericalism, and was twice reprinted; the poem was read by Spenser and Marlowe, and possibly Shakespeare.

In sixteenth-century writing, the ancient genres were maintained and many echoes of the medieval, Chaucerian and otherwise, can be heard. But there are also striking differences. The lyrics of Wyatt and Surrey, for instance, look back to familiar courtly conventions but deploy these within newly charged political and cultural contexts. Romance flourished in the Renaissance, its circulation much increased by printing, and its appeal to women evident in new female-authored romances. Verse romances such as *Sir Bevis of Hampton* enjoyed a long print life, but by the sixteenth century, romance had become predominantly a prose narrative tradition in which it is easy to see the origins of the modern novel. The single most influential medieval work after Chaucer's *Canterbury Tales* was a prose romance, Malory's *Morte Darthur*. The most radical developments were in secular drama, though even here there are continuities. Tudor dramas are obvious successors to mora-lity plays, and it is possible to see links between moral dramas such as Marlowe's *Dr Faustus*, and earlier treatments of the devil's pursuit of the human soul. The chronicle tradition also played a crucial role both in pageant and in drama. It was most of all the self-fashioning of sixteenth-century poets, their presentation of themselves as Renaissance writers, that long drew scholars to de-emphasise continuities between medieval and Renaissance. Sixteenth-century culture was characterised by looking forward into a 'brave new world', and so medieval writing, despite its formative influence, began to be placed as archaic, conventional, representative of ideals to be questioned and challenged. In this context, Shakespeare and Spenser stand out for their creative engagement with medieval poetry.

Few of Shakespeare's plays directly use medieval poetic sources, though his English history plays and some of his tragedies are indebted to medieval chronicle. The genre of romance, however, was crucial to his drama, first, in the comedies, which repeatedly employ the conventions of love-sickness, separation and testing of lovers, marriage as a return to order, and the otherworld, whether this is the forest of Arden, a wood near Athens, or Illyria. *As You Like It* deliberately evokes the idea of the greenwood, inhabited by Robin Hood and his merry men – but as is typical of the comedies, conventions are problematised: Shakespeare also emphasises the winter and rough weather of natural fact. *A Midsummer Night's Dream*, and more directly *The Two Noble Kinsmen*, reshape elements of the *Knight's Tale*. Whereas Chaucer's text addresses destiny and tragedy, however, in *A Midsummer Night's Dream* the questions and confusions are light-hearted, rooted in sophisticated undercutting of convention and a mixture of modes – romance and broad comedy; classical and English; then and now. By contrast, *King Lear* (based on an anonymous play) exploits the tensions developed by Laȝamon: founded on the expectations of romance, its shock results in part from their failure. This is also true of the play that most obviously engages with Chaucer, *Troilus and Cressida*, which opposes romance, chivalry and idealism (the Trojans) with realism, wit and cynicism (the Greeks). Shakespeare's late plays are also conspicuously mixed in mode, with their interweaving of comedy and tragedy, and their use of masque and music. They are rooted in the great conventions of romance, in particular the patterns of loss and return, separation and reunion, exile and return, birth, death and regeneration, and the motifs of journeying, time, family, nobility, miracle and magic. Their dramatic tension, however, is often situated in clashes of tone, and in the under-cutting of romance patterns through comedy, grotesque, tragedy and most of all realism. Only *Pericles* employs medieval poetic sources directly. Here, 'ancient Gower' has become the voice of the past, his explicit medievalism marking the archaic quality of the story, his voice that of the Chorus commenting on its moral lessons. The play combines the power of wonder manifested in quasi-magical family reunions with the seedy realism of sex as commodity.

The poet who most notably adopted the now elite form of verse romance, Edmund Spenser, consciously problematised its conventions. *The Faerie Queene* offers a series of representations of Queen Elizabeth that corresponds to a series of romance ideals. The extraordinary craft and artifice of the *Faerie Queene*, however, renders it unlike any medieval romance, though its language and conventions so conspicuously draw on works such as *Bevis of Hampton*. Spenser explicitly emulates Chaucer's 'heroick' language, and places him as 'Dan Chaucer, well of English undefyled' (IV.ii.32), master of moral tales, lovers' complaints, and high romances (views reiterated in *The Shepheardes Calender* and *Colin Clout*). The quest of Redcrosse echoes the dragon-slaying of Bevis, but the pattern of romance has become a Protestant allegory: the knight-hero's enemies are versions of the Roman church, his lady represents the true faith, and his quest is for

Holiness. In some ways, Spenser's colourful, visionary allegory most resembles *Piers Plowman* (also a source for *The Shepheardes Calender*, which partly uses alliterative form). The conflict and debate of *Piers Plowman* are more negatively manifest in the *Faerie Queene*: the central hero, Arthur, never achieves his vision; the romance of Faerie land proves impossible to sustain. The text remains incomplete, straying ever further from the proposed coherence of Spenser's plan.

The afterlife of Old English was very different, as a result of the dramatic changes in English language and culture in the course of the post-Conquest period. Although Old English texts were preserved and studied in monastic libraries, they were not generally known: Chaucer did not read *Beowulf*. Only a vague sense of England's Anglo-Saxon heritage endured, preserved in romance and chronicle. Sixteenth-century concepts of nationhood renewed interest in Anglo-Saxon England: the anthology of moral tales, *A Mirror for Magistrates*, descended from Lydgate's *Fall of Princes*, included in its later editions a series of Anglo-Saxon subjects – St Edmund, Abbess Ebba, Æthelraed the Unready, Edward the Confessor. Old English continued to be of interest to antiquarians and scholars, among whom John Leland (*c.* 1503–52) was particularly remarkable, a humanist scholar and priest with a visionary notion of the past focused on Alfred and Arthur, who was commissioned (*c.* 1533) to examine in detail the treasures of monastic libraries, with a view to establishing a royal library for Henry VIII. His notes offer precious clues to the lost works of the Middle Ages. His eventual insanity may have been partly rooted in his distress at the wanton destruction of manuscripts accompanying the Dissolution of the Monasteries, as well as by his ambitious plan to write a fifty-book history of the nation and its antiquities.

Though Leland's work was taken up by a series of notable scholars, their interest was not in poetry but in religious history, particularly the possibility that the Anglo-Saxon Church was more independent from Rome than its successor, and could thus be seen as heralding the true English Church. Leland's contemporary, John Bale (1495–1563), a former Carmelite priest, used Bede's history to develop a version of English history focussing on English struggles against Rome; Bale also wrote and staged numerous polemical plays that employed the medieval mystery and morality traditions to satirise Catholicism. His scholarly interests were wide-ranging, and his catalogue of manuscripts celebrated Chaucer as equal among the English to Dante and Petrarch in Italy. The Archbishop of Canterbury, Matthew Parker (1504–75), was a moving force among such scholars. His ideological interest in the Anglo-Saxon Church was accompanied by a desire to preserve historical evidence, and his extraordinary collection of manuscripts was bequeathed to his former college, Corpus Christi, Cambridge. After Parker's death, his work was taken up by the Elizabethan Society of Antiquaries (founded in 1586), and particularly by the politician Robert Cotton (1571–1631), who built up a remarkable library of manuscripts relating to early English history, including Old English texts. Cotton's historical knowledge shaped his perspectives on British law, constitution and government, but when he fell out of favour the Society was dissolved and the Library closed. Its holdings had, however, provided the resources for two great English historians, William Camden (1551–1623), who endowed the first chair of Civil History at Oxford, and Henry Spelman (1563/4–1641), who established a Cambridge lectureship for 'Antiquitates Britannicae et Saxonicae', which was to include the study of Old English.

The shifts in religion and learning, but also in language, that marked the sixteenth century, meant that by the seventeenth century, both Old and Middle English had become the voices of the past. Some Anglo-Saxon texts had been published in the sixteenth century, but they comprised prose religious, historical and legal works. The only poem to have been printed was Alfred's metrical preface to his translation of Gregory's *Pastoral Care*, in an edition of the deeds and life of Alfred (1574). Antiquarian interests, however, gradually began to extend to Old English poetry and its techniques. The first holder of Spelman's lectureship, Abraham Wheelock (*c.* 1595–1653), translated a Hebrew poem into Old English, but used rhyming couplets rather than alliteration. A Dutchman, Francis Junius (1591–1677), librarian of the earl of Arundel and a philologist trained in Germanic languages, transcribed many manuscripts, pointing his work to show poetic metre; he also acquired and edited the 'Cædmon' manuscript, containing the Old English poem 'Genesis'. Junius' transcriptions were crucial in preserving the texts destroyed or damaged in the Cotton Library fire of 1731.

Middle English poetry had become largely inaccessible with the exception of Chaucer, whose works had been printed and reprinted right across the sixteenth century. As the seventeenth century progressed, even Chaucer's popularity waned, and apart from a reprint of Speght's edition in 1687, no new edition was published after 1602. Chaucer's language had become less familiar and new learning had replaced that of the Middle Ages: 'age has rusted what the poet writ, / Worn out his language and obscur'd his wit', wrote Addison in 1694. It was Dryden who reinvigorated Chaucer by, in his *Fables Ancient and Modern* (1700), translating the *Knight's Tale*, the *Nun's Priest's Tale* and the *Wife of Bath's Tale*. Dryden's Preface pays particular tribute to Chaucer's realism:

> He must have been a man of a most wonderful comprehensive nature, because, as it has been truly observed of him, he has taken into the compass of his *Canterbury Tales* the various manners and humours (as we now call them) of the whole English nation, in his age. Not a single character has escaped him....

> ...there is such a variety of game springing up before me, that I am distracted in my choice, and know not which to follow. 'Tis sufficient to say according to the proverb, that here is God's plenty. (Burrow 1969: 66–67)

Yet even while Dryden celebrated Chaucer as the father of English poetry, he also argued that Chaucer's imperfect metre required modernisation. Pope took a similar view in his free translation of the *Merchant's Tale* (1709). This renewal of interest led to a new edition by John Urry (1721), but there was also unease about Chaucer's profanity: while some early translations revelled in the bawdiness of *The Canterbury Tales*, others offered bowdlerised versions.

Very little else was known of medieval literature before *c.* 1760. The fourteenth-century account of the travels of John Mandeville, with its fantastic journeys, monsters and marvels, remained popular reading matter, and copies of Caxton's print of the *Morte Darthur* were occasionally still available, but even Malory's work was not reprinted between 1634 and 1816. Prose versions of *Bevis of Hampton* and *Guy of Warwick* retained a certain popularity, and such works were turned into broadside ballads (cheaply printed popular lyrics on single large sheets, sold on the street) and 'chapbooks' – cheap, highly abbreviated, simple prose adventure stories, sold by itinerant 'chapmen' and read especially by children. For more sophisticated readers, the Middle Ages was most defined by its treatment in the epic poems of Ariosto, Tasso and especially Spenser – as a period of 'chivalry and knight errantry' (Johnston 1964: 5). The engagement of eighteenth-century intellectual circles with the subjects of national history and primitive societies, however, fuelled scholarly interest in early ballads. James Macpherson's proto-medieval poetry, attributed to 'Ossian' (a supposed primitive Gaelic bard, based on the Old Irish legendary figure Oisin, son of Finn), was read as a haunting evocation of ancient Celtic society (*Fragments of Ancient Poetry Collected in the Highlands of Scotland and Translated from the Gaelic or Erse Language*, 1760). Thomas Chatterton's series of supposed fifteenth-century poems (1764 onwards), attributed to 'Thomas Rowley', used a Spenserian stanza and archaic word forms, and treated Arthurian subject matter. It was argued that the romance genre represented a crucial stage in the development both of primitive society and of fiction, and *The Faerie Queene* was seen as exemplifying this Gothic past. Thomas Warton's influential *Observations on the Faerie Queene* (1754, rev. 1762) presented Spenser's poem as rooted in medieval romance, while Bishop Richard Hurd's *Letters on Chivalry and Romance* (1762) argued for chivalry, knight errantry and magic as the stuff of poetry – though he knew little about actual texts. Warton was also a serious scholar, who found the Harley Lyrics, published *The Kingis Quair*, and revisited the romances once seen as children's fare; he also rediscovered (though he did not admire) *Piers Plowman*. His *History of English Poetry* included details, summaries and extracts, particularly from the romances he studied, which he identified as the keys to the medieval world, a special site of the 'civilising quality of the imagination'.

Gradually, scholars began to rediscover the medieval works that lay behind the chapbooks, using the British Museum, opened in 1759, and newly published catalogues. Most influential was Thomas Percy's *Reliques of Ancient English Poetry* (1765), which was partly based on the Percy Folio (*c.* 1640), a manuscript containing very late versions of ballads and romances, which Percy, in something of the manner of a medieval scribe, adapted and modernised. Thomas Tyrwhitt's monumental five-volume edition of Chaucer (1775) reflected a newly scholarly approach: Tyrwhitt revised the order of the tales, identified some tales as spurious, and defended Chaucer's metre. A second generation of scholars began to produce editions, in particular of ballads and romances, including collections such as George Ellis's three-volume *Specimens of the Early English Poets* (1790), Joseph Ritson's *Ancient English Metrical Romances* (1802) and Henry Weber's three-volume *Metrical Romances* (1810) – though there were striking omissions: *Sir*

Gawain and the Green Knight was not discovered until 1831. In 1804, Sir Walter Scott published the first scholarly edition of a medieval romance, *Sir Tristrem*, and with Robert Southey urged the reprinting of Malory's *Morte Darthur*, of which two editions appeared in 1816. Learned societies such as the Roxburghe Club (1812) and the Bannatyne Club (1822) were founded to print medieval works. Such enthusiasm for early language, literature and culture included a new interest in Anglo-Saxon history. Percy's *Northern Antiquities* (1770), which translated a French study of the Scandinavians, corrected the confusion that Gauls and Germans, or Britons and Saxons, were the same people – and hence effected an interest in the specifically Anglo-Saxon as well as the Celtic. Sharon Turner's three-volume *History of the Anglo-Saxons from the Earliest Period to the Norman Conquest* (1799–1805), drawing on Anglo-Saxon and Latin sources to present a vision of Alfred as ideal king, and incorporating (often inaccurate) summaries, paraphrases and quotations, enjoyed such popularity that it was published in seven editions (7th, 1852).

Romances were chiefly known in abbreviated ballad form, and through collections like those of Ritson and Ellis, gradually supplemented by new editions. But romance's 'enchanted ground', peopled by knights and ladies, damsels in distress and faeries, and coloured by the ideals and manners of chivalry and feudalism, represented powerful cultural capital. Medievalism had a serious political basis: in opposition to all that the French Revolution had destroyed, chivalry and courtesy were seen by Edmund Burke as fundamental ideals, the preservation of which could contribute to political stability. Chaucer's writing was read as conveying universal human truths. William Blake's single longest piece of critical writing is his discussion of the Canterbury Pilgrims in the context of his own painting of the subject (*A Descriptive Catalogue*, 1809). Blake explores the significance of the characters as representing

> the characters which compose all ages and nations: as one age falls, another rises, different to mortal sight, but to immortals only the same; for we see the same characters repeated again and again, in animals, vegetables, minerals, and in men; nothing new occurs in identical existence; Accident ever varies, Substance can never suffer change nor decay.

Blake places Chaucer as 'the great poetical observer of men, who in every age is born to record and eternize its acts'.

Scott's imaginative writing was deeply informed by his medieval scholarship and by the notion of the romance genre as a vehicle for the communication of enduring human and social values. His 'Essay on Romance' (1824) defines romance as 'a fictitious narrative in prose or verse; the interest of which turns upon marvellous and uncommon incidents': the power of the genre is situated in its fluidity (Robertson in Saunders 2004: 293). Scott's romances may be read as 'fables of changes accommodated and differences contained and reconciled within the mutual obligations of idealised traditional societies' (Alexander 2007: 30). Scott's *Lay of the Last Minstrel* (1805), which he composed after editing *Sir Tristrem*, weaves together elements of Percy's ballads and other medieval sources, including the *Knight's Tale*, to create a six-canto poem in which a minstrel recounts tales of wizards, monks and lovers within feuding Border families. *Ivanhoe* (1819), set in the period of conflict between Normans and Saxons, uses Chaucer's figures of the Yeoman and Monk, as well as drawing on the *Knight's Tale* for the epigraphs. It was works such as these, in verse and prose, that conveyed the medieval world and its ideals to a wider readership.

The medieval revival was a powerful influence on other Romantic poets, although ideas of romances as for children also lingered. Coleridge was damning about the unsuitability of such subject matter for serious writing: 'as to Arthur, you could not by any means make a poem on him national to Englishmen. What have *we* to do with him?' (*Table Talk*, 4 Sept. 1833); similarly Wordsworth had dismissed as possible subject matter for an epic poem, 'Some old / Romantic tale by Milton left unsung' or 'dire enchantments' (*The Prelude*, 1805, 179–80), or 'the dragon's wing, the magic ring' (*Peter Bell*, 1819, Prologue, 136). Wordsworth and Coleridge saw romances as crucial, however, in shaping the child's imaginative faculty, which would in turn stimulate the passions and shape understanding; they aimed to re-create this effect in *Lyrical Ballads* (1798). Coleridge was to direct his endeavours 'to persons and characters supernatural, or at least romantic' (*Biographia Literaria* 1817, xiv). *Kubla Khan* (1816) uses the conventions of medieval romance (the 'woman wailing for her demon lover') and the idea of enchantment to evoke a surreal world that inspires poetry, but is fragmented, glimpsed only in dreams. In Keats's *Ode to a Nightingale* (1820), the music of the bird's song, reminiscent of 'faery lands forlorn', similarly opens onto imaginary otherworlds. *The Eve of St Agnes*, in the same collection, weaves in words an opulently coloured medieval tapestry, employing a Spenserian stanza form to achieve the effect of an ancient tale, while at the same time romance is re-fracted through a contemporary lens to depict almost tangible sensuality and passion. The prominent role played in the Romantic imagination by the enchantresses of medieval romance is evident in Coleridge's *Christabel* (1816), his most explicitly medieval work (experimenting with a ballad form recalling Old English metre), and in Keats's *La Belle Dame Sans Merci* and *Lamia* (also 1820). The enchantress's fatal lure is associated with sexuality and death, but also desire and poetic vision.

By the 1830s the new interest in the medieval world was reflected in religion, politics and social thought, literature, architecture, painting and the decorative arts. The first recorded use of the term 'medieval' occurs in an antiquarian's letter in *The Gentleman's Magazine* in 1827; 'medievalism' is recorded in 1849. Each age invented a version of the medieval that suited its own needs. The early Victorian period emphasised both the Catholicism and the communitarianism of the Middle Ages. The Oxford Movement looked to the medieval to assert the Catholic foundation of the Church of England, and to shape a new form of High Church Anglicanism that emphasised the vitality of liturgy and ceremony. The emphasis in Scott's writing on humane ideals of social community was sustained in an interest in the medieval as showing a mode of pre-industrial and pre-capitalist social and economic organisation, reflected in the fiction and social commentary of Carlyle, Morris and Ruskin. This emphasis underpinned too the anti-utilitarian and anti-industrial ideals and art of the Pre-Raphaelite Brotherhood.

Similar social ideals were evident in Tennyson's *Idylls of the King*, dedicated in an epilogue to the memory of Prince Albert (1869) as well as to Tennyson's friend Arthur Hallam, and perhaps the single most influential poem of the medieval revival. Though the *Idylls* was inspired not by medieval poetry but by the *Morte Darthur*, Malory's book opened onto a long tradition of Arthurian poetry and in many ways he was seen as a proto-poet. Tennyson's *The Lady of Shallott* (1832, revised 1842), with its related subject matter, tapestry of images recalling those in medieval manuscripts, and opposition of art and reality, had laid the ground for the *Idylls*. For Tennyson the power of the Arthurian story was rooted in its portrayal of ideal, pre-destined Christian rule; but his vision of a lost world is memorable for much else, from the image in the first *Idyll* ('The Coming of Arthur') of the babe snatched by Merlin from the fiery waves, whose destiny is endorsed by the 'subtler magic' of the Lady of the Lake, 'mystic, wonderful', to, in the final *Idyll* ('The Passing of Arthur'), the magnificent portrayal of 'that last weird battle in the west', the image of the keening, black-hooded queens who bear Arthur to Avalon, and the rhyme Sir Bedivere hears, 'From the great deep to the great deep he goes'. Arthur's active embodiment of Christian virtue is a version of the muscular Christianity characteristic of the Victorian religious sensibility, and is threatened by the rarefied, celestial world of the Grail and by the forces of sexual desire and adultery to which Merlin, the artist-poet, succumbs. Morris's *The Defence of Guinevere* (1858) engages too with the fatal threat of female beauty. Morris was most strongly influenced by Norse legend, but also wrote a series of verse romances in *The Earthly Paradise* (1868–70), which recalls the structure of *The Canterbury Tales*, differently memorialised in the Kelmscott Chaucer (1896) designed by Morris and Burne-Jones.

The shift in the course of the nineteenth century away from the fantastic towards a more serious, historicised notion of the medieval was reflected in scholarly initiatives. The new philology, particularly the work of Sir William Jones on correspondences between Indo-European languages, opened up Germanic languages for serious study. A comparable scholarly trend in Scandinavia led the Icelandic scholar and National Archivist of Denmark, Grímur Jónson Thorkelin, to Britain to seek evidence of the relationships between Germanic languages, and hence to transcribe the *Beowulf* manuscript, which was published in 1815 with a Latin translation, and translated into Danish in 1820. English scholarship developed slowly, however, until Benjamin Thorpe and John Mitchell Kemble founded the Philological Society of London (1842), which established plans for a New English Dictionary, later to become the Oxford English Dictionary, and began the systematic editing and publication of texts; it was eventually replaced by the Early English Text Society (1864). In 1867, the Rawlinson-Bosworth Chair in Old English at Oxford was established. The legendary heroes and epic battles of the newly discovered Anglo-Saxon poetry evidently appealed to Victorian society, and various scholars and poets tried their hands at modern renditions. Nineteenth-century translations of *Beowulf* included versions by Longfellow and by Morris; Tennyson translated *The Battle of Brunanburh* into verse (1880). It is often argued that Gerard Manley Hopkins (who is unlikely to have been able to read Old English) found in the alliterative form and scansion of Anglo-Saxon poetry the model for 'sprung rhythm', though Hopkins himself uses this term in relation to 'the old English verse seen in *Pierce Ploughman*' (manuscript 'Author's Preface'). Hopkins' poetry seems to have a peculiar affinity with the verbally creative quality of Anglo-Saxon, but such influence as there is on his style comes from the later alliterative, not the Old English tradition.

In the early twentieth century, the writing of G. K. Chesterton echoed many of the ideals of Ruskin, Morris and the Arts and Crafts movement, but from a Roman Catholic perspective. As well as a polemical defence of Orthodoxy, Chesterton wrote a verse romance treating Alfred's defence of Wessex, the *Ballad of the White Horse* (1911), while his critical study of Chaucer emphasised the poet's humanism. In about the same period, Yeats took medievalism in a rather different direction, his aesthetic catalysed by the great myths of earlier civilisations, including that of Tristan and Isolde, as well as by early Irish legend. The enormous cultural upheavals of this period, and the advent of modernism, might be expected to have signalled the end of medievalism. T. S. Eliot condemned what he saw as the naïve archaism of Chesterton's *Ballad of the White Horse* as representative of the 'forces of death' (Alexander 2007: 212). Yet the great modernist poets, particularly Pound, were considerably more influenced by the medieval than is often supposed, an influence different in kind, now that Old and Middle English poetry had become readily available in print, and were subjects of serious study.

Engagement with Old English was just one aspect of Pound's attempt to create a new poetry from diverse sources, principally Chinese, but also classical and medieval European. His translation of *The Seafarer* (1912) confronts the reader with the alien nature of the poem's language and metric, and its particular experience of desolation. Though an isolated experiment in translation, it nevertheless filtered into Pound's original work in a major way: he used a free version of Old English alliterative metre to set the tone of his *Cantos*. A crucial work of modernism, the *Cantos* begins with Odysseus making the dead speak: a Homeric episode, filtered through a Renaissance (Latin) translation, is rendered in a quasi-medieval alliterative style. This beginning is an end: though Pound's great poetic exemplars are often medieval – Dante, Cavalcanti, the troubadours, *El Cid*, Villon; the poets discussed in his *The Spirit of Romance* (1910) – they are mostly not English. But at the climax of a Pisan Canto 'libretto' (81), on the musical element that Pound saw as crucial to poetry, he produces Chaucer – the opening of the great lyric, 'Your eyen two wol sleye me sodenly': 'And for 180 years almost nothing'. It is a judgement congruent with his lavish praise of Chaucer among the 'exhibits' of *ABC of Reading* (1934): Chaucer is 'the greatest poet of his day...more compendious than Dante...the father of "litterae humaniores" for Europe'. The best of Old and Middle English, in different ways, is a resource for the modern poet.

Pound's writing may be placed in the context of new anthropological ideas, memorably treated in Frazer's *The Golden Bough* (2 vols, 1890; 3rd edn, in 12 vols, 1906–15), challenging the separation of primitive and civilised, and a new richness and energy discovered in other and early cultures. Jessie Weston's *From Ritual to Romance* (1920) placed the story of the Fisher King as an ancient, pagan fertility myth, providing the grounds for later imaginative literature. Such ideas inspired modernist works, most famously T. S. Eliot's *The Waste Land* (1922), in which remnants of art and culture become fragments to shore against the protagonist's ruin and perhaps against the ruin of his civilisation. Yet the poem also begins with a reference to *The Canterbury Tales*, 'April is the cruellest month', and references to Dante and perhaps to Malory (the most probable source of the poem's title) are aspects of a more general emphasis on continuity of tradition. While the opening of *Little Gidding* (1942) – 'Midwinter spring is its own season / Sempiternal though sodden towards sundown' – recalls the first lines of *Piers Plowman*, both in its metre and its reference to the seasons as they echo the liturgical year, the crucial medieval poet in Eliot's later work is Dante. The English medieval writer most prominent in *Four Quartets* is Julian of Norwich, from whom Eliot learned not a style but a religious vision.

David Jones, Eliot's near-contemporary, takes as inspiration for his allusive verse and prose narrative of the First World War, *In Parenthesis* (1937), the medieval ideal of chivalry embodied in the image of Christ jousting in Jerusalem in *Piers Plowman*. W. H. Auden's poetry too takes up many of the preoccupations of the modernists, particularly Pound. Auden was most influenced by Old Norse poetry, myth and legend, the poetic fruit of which was (with the scholar Paul Taylor) a collection of translations form the *Edda* (1969) and experiments throughout his work with syllabic metres. But Auden was introduced to what he called 'the "barbaric" poetry of the North' (*A Certain World*, 1970) through Old English as an undergraduate at Oxford, where his teachers included Tolkien and the translator of Chaucer, Nevill Coghill. Auden's early *Paid on Both Sides*, on the subject of a Germanic family feud, took its title from *Beowulf*, and imitated Old English alliterative verse in its rhythmical prose. Later works, including *The Orators* (1932) and *The Age of Anxiety* (1948), make intermittent use of the alliterative line of Old English poetry, one aspect of Auden's life-long experimentation with the forms of verse. As with Pound (Canto 81), free imitation of Old English offered a way 'to break the pentameter' – or at least, for the less iconoclastic Auden, to extend the stylistic repertoire of a distinctively modern verse. Auden's near-contemporary Edwin Morgan, by contrast, in his translation of *Beowulf* (1952) engaged with the rich and strange vocabulary of Old English, as well as with the ways that its heroism and homosocial society resonated with the experience of the servicemen in the Second World War. Morgan saw Old English alliterative tradition as sustained longest in the north, and medieval Scots poetry as inheriting that tradition. His later writing, which includes further translations of Old English, also draws on Middle English and medieval Scots poetry, especially that of Dunbar.

Twentieth-century popular medievalism perhaps owes most to one of the greatest of medieval scholars, J. R. R. Tolkien. Tolkien not only produced the definitive edition of *Sir Gawain and the Green Knight* (1925), but also engaged over many years in translating the poem, its archaic, richly detailed style recalled in his prose fictions, which contain a range of proto-medieval poetry and song. Tolkien weaves together Old Norse and much other Old and Middle English material to create *The Hobbit* (1937) and *The Lord of the Rings* trilogy (1954–55). The Shire presents an idealised version of Alfred's Wessex, while successive locations recall both epic sites of battle and the demonic and enchanted otherworlds of romance. These fictions depend upon the great structures of epic and romance – quest, test, adventure, honour, prowess and the battle between good and evil. It is not coincidental that another great medievalist, Tolkien's contemporary C. S. Lewis, also turned to the genre of romance for his allegorical science fiction, beginning with *That Hideous Strength* (1945), and for his *The Chronicles of Narnia* series (1950–56), which in the guise of magical adventure and fantasy reworks the conventions of religious allegory.

The enduring nature of modern engagement with medieval poetry is particularly evident in Seamus Heaney's writing, which includes translations of *Beowulf* (1999) and Henryson's *Testament of Cresseid* (2004). These works are part of a wider project of translation, from classical, Eastern European, Irish and Scots Gaelic works. Heaney's *Sweeney Redivivus* sequence draws on *Sweeney Astray* (1983), his earlier translation of a medieval Irish poem, *Buile Suibhne*, while his *Station Island* sequence (1984) adapts Dante's *Commedia*. His use of both Old English and the medieval Scots vernacular signals a more general interest in language that challenges the familiar, in the inventive richness of the alien, and the possibilities it offers to the modern poet. The stories and traditions of the past can both mirror and oppose the politics of the present – the feuds in *Beowulf*, the woman as outcast in the *Testament*. While the interests of the modernists and their successors was primarily in technique, especially rhythm, Heaney's is predominantly in vocabulary – the richness of Old English kennings, the 'word hoard'. Geoffrey Hill, by contrast, draws on the vocabulary and structures of liturgical chant in his *Mercian Hymns*, a series of prose poems inspired by the Anglian 'hymns', glosses on the Psalms and Canticles, published in Sweet's *Anglo-Saxon Reader* (1876). Like Morgan's poetry, the poems of Heaney and Hill are deeply engaged with the intersection of past and present, with continuities as well as change.

Sir Gawain and the Green Knight has played a particularly prominent role in modern poetry. A remarkable number of writers, several of whom acknowledge their debt to Pound, have tried their hands at modernisation. Ted Hughes' *Wodwo* (1967) plays on the green man legend, and Hughes also translated sections of *Sir Gawain*. In the last ten years, poets from Britain, America and Australia have translated *Sir Gawain*. Keith Harrison (1998) aimed to preserve 'a strong ghost of the alliterative texture'; Bernard O'Donoghue (2006) celebrates the English 'sprung rhythm' that appealed so strongly to Hopkins, Auden and Heaney; W. S. Merwin (2003) admires the 'spirit of romance'; and Simon Armitage (2007) writes of the need for a poetic response that both retains the alliterative art of the original and translates its spirit. These works point once again to the creative power of medieval poetry as reaching far beyond its historical status, stimulating experimentation and new directions in writing more than ever before.

Medieval poetry has repeatedly found its way into the other arts, and continues to do so. Pound tried his hand at writing an opera about Villon. George Dyson composed an oratorio, *The Canterbury Pilgrims* (1931). Once the texts of medieval lyrics became more readily available in modern editions composers began to set them to music. Britten's engagement with the lyrics was the most notable, yielding four separate collections. The extraordinary dramatic and visual potential of *Sir Gawain* led Harrison Birtwhistle to create his opera *Gawain!* (1991) employing ballet and mime, and using a verse libretto by David Harsent that places the enchantress Morgan le Fay at the centre of the narrative. Film-makers have repeatedly been drawn to medieval subject matter, from King Arthur to Robin Hood. The art films of Pasolini include, as well as a version of the *Decameron*, a film of *The Canterbury Tales* (*I Racconti di Canterbury*, 1972) that revels in and heightens the sexuality of Chaucer's bawdy tales. Animated film versions have been made of both *Sir Gawain and the Green Knight* (dir. Tim Fernée, 2002) and *The Canterbury Tales* (dir. Jonathon Myerson, 1998), while a series loosely based on *The Canterbury Tales* has recently been made for television. The films of *The Lord of the Rings* (dir. Peter Jackson, 2001–3) have enjoyed phenomenal success, while the film of *Beowulf* (dir. Robert Zemeckis, 2007) – with whatever distortions – indicates that Old English legend has firmly entered the sphere of popular knowledge. The new technology is not limited to scholarly databases and digital editions but has produced all kinds of 'medieval' computer games that use the broad conventions of epic and romance. The ability of medieval poetry to inspire such a diverse range of high art and popular culture could not more clearly signal its enduring, vibrant quality in the twenty-first century.

NOTES

1   The critical views of and allusions to Chaucer cited in this essay may be found in J. A. Burrow's (1969) anthology of early Chaucer criticism. See also Spurgeon (1960) and Brewer (1978).

REFERENCES AND FURTHER READING

Alexander, Michael (2007). *Medievalism: The Middle Ages in Modern England.* New Haven: Yale University Press.

Ashton, J. (1882). *Chapbooks of the Eighteenth Century.* London: Chatto and Windus. (Repr. London: Skoob Books, 1990.)

Bowers, John (2007). *Chaucer and Langland: The Antagonistic Tradition.* Notre Dame, IN: University of Notre Dame Press.

Brewer, Derek (1978). *Geoffrey Chaucer: The Critical Heritage.* London: Routledge.

Burrow, J. A. (ed.) (1969). *Geoffrey Chaucer: A Critical Anthology.* Penguin Critical Anthologies. Harmondsworth: Penguin Books.

Cooper, Helen (2004). *The English Romance in Time: Transforming Motifs from Geoffrey of Monmouth to the Death of Shakespeare.* Oxford: Oxford University Press.

Ellis, Steve (2005). *Chaucer: An Oxford Guide.* Oxford: Oxford University Press. [See Part IV, 'Afterlife', pp. 479–591.]

Fulton, Helen (ed.) (2009). *A Companion to Arthurian Literature.* Blackwell Companions to Literature and Culture. Oxford: Blackwell.

Hamilton, A. C. (1990). *The Spenser Encyclopedia.* Toronto: University of Toronto Press.

Johnston, Arthur (1964). *Enchanted Ground: The Study of Medieval Romance in the Eighteenth Century.* London: Athlone Press.

Jones, Chris (2006). *Strange Likeness: The Use of Old English in Twentieth-Century Poetry.* Oxford: Oxford University Press.

Kelen, Sarah A. (2007). *Langland's Early Modern Identities.* The New Middle Ages. Houndmills: Palgrave Macmillan.

Kucich, Greg (1991). *Keats, Shelley and Romantic Spenserianism.* University Park: Pennsylvania State University Press.

Lerer, Seth (1999). Old English and its afterlife. In David Wallace (ed.). *The Cambridge History of Medieval English Literature* (pp. 7–34). Cambridge: Cambridge University Press.

Lewis, C. S. (1936). *The Allegory of Love: A Study in Medieval Tradition.* Oxford: Clarendon Press.

McCarthy, Conor (2008). *Seamus Heaney and Medieval Poetry.* Cambridge: D. S. Brewer.

Mitchell, Jerome (1987). *Scott, Chaucer, and Medieval Romance: A Study in Sir Walter Scott's Indebtedness to the Literature of the Middle Ages.* Lexington: University of Kentucky Press.

Parker, Patricia A. (1979). *Inescapable Romance: Studies in the Poetics of a Mode.* Princeton, NJ: Princeton University Press. [Covers romance from the Renaissance to the Romantic period.]

Perry, Curtis and John Watkins (eds) (2009). *Shakespeare and the Middle Ages.* Oxford: Oxford University Press.

Pettet, E. C. (1949). *Shakespeare and the Romance Tradition.* London: Staples Press.

Pound, Ezra (1952). *The Spirit of Romance.* Revised edn. London: Peter Owen. (First pub. 1910.)

Saunders, Corinne (ed.) (2001). *Chaucer.* Blackwell Guides to Criticism. Oxford: Blackwell.

Saunders, Corinne (ed.) (2004). *A Companion to Romance: From Classical to Contemporary.* Blackwell Companions to Literature and Culture. Oxford: Blackwell.

Scattergood, John (2000). *The Lost Tradition: Essays on Middle English Alliterative Poetry.* Dublin: Four Courts.

Simpson, Roger (1990). *Camelot Regained.* Cambridge: D. S. Brewer. [On Tennyson and Victorian romance.]

Spurgeon, Caroline (1960). *Five Hundred Years of Chaucer Criticism and Allusion, 1357–1900.* 3 vols. 2nd edn. New York: Russell and Russell. (First pub. 1914–22.)

Taylor, Beverly and Elisabeth Brewer (1983). *The Return of King Arthur: British and American Arthurian Literature since 1800.* Arthurian Studies 9. Cambridge: D. S. Brewer; Totowa, NJ: Barnes and Noble.

Treharne, Elaine and Phillip Pulsiano (2001). *A Companion to Anglo-Saxon Literature.* Blackwell Companions to Literature and Culture. Oxford: Blackwell. [See Part V, 'Debates and Issues', pp. 401–510, on Anglo-Saxon studies from the post-Conquest period to the present.]

Trigg, Stephanie (2002). *Congenial Souls: Reading Chaucer from Medieval to Postmodern.* Medieval Cultures 30. Minneapolis: University of Minnesota Press.

Index